Contemporary Authors®

NEW REVISION SERIES

Contemporary Authors®

A Bio-Bibliographical Guide to
Current Writers in Fiction, General Nonfiction,
Poetry, Journalism, Drama, Motion Pictures,
Television, and Other Fields

NEW REVISION SERIES *volume* 133

THOMSON
★
GALE

Detroit • New York • San Francisco • San Diego • New Haven, Conn. • Waterville, Maine • London • Munich

THOMSON

GALE

Contemporary Authors, New Revision Series, Vol. 133

Project Editor
Tracey L. Matthews

Editorial
Katy Balcer, Sara Constantakis, Michelle Kazensky, Julie Keppen, Lisa Kumar, Mary Ruby, Lemma Shomali, Maikue Vang

Permissions
Denise Buckley, Bill Sampson, Sheila Spencer

Imaging and Multimedia
Leslie Light, Michael Logusz

Composition and Electronic Capture
Carolyn Roney

Manufacturing
Drew Kalasky

LIBRARY OF CONGRESS CATALOG CARD NUMBER 81-640179

ISBN 0-7876-6725-0
ISSN 0275-7176

Printed in the United States of America
10 9 8 7 6 5 4 3 2 1

Contents

Indexing note: All *Contemporary Authors* entries are indexed in the *Contemporary Authors* cumulative index, which is published separately and distributed twice a year.

As always, the most recent Contemporary Authors cumulative index continues to be the user's guide to the location of an individual author's listing.

Preface

Contemporary Authors (*CA*) provides information on approximately 115,000 writers in a wide range of media, including:

- Current writers of fiction, nonfiction, poetry, and drama whose works have been issued by commercial publishers, risk publishers, or university presses (authors whose books have been published only by known vanity or author-subsidized firms are ordinarily not included)

- Prominent print and broadcast journalists, editors, photojournalists, syndicated cartoonists, graphic novelists, screenwriters, television scriptwriters, and other media people

- Notable international authors

- Literary greats of the early twentieth century whose works are popular in today's high school and college curriculums and continue to elicit critical attention

A *CA* listing entails no charge or obligation. Authors are included on the basis of the above criteria and their interest to *CA* users. Sources of potential listees include trade periodicals, publishers' catalogs, librarians, and other users.

How to Get the Most out of *CA*: Use the Index

The key to locating an author's most recent entry is the *CA* cumulative index, which is published separately and distributed twice a year. It provides access to *all* entries in *CA* and *Contemporary Authors New Revision Series* (*CANR*). Always consult the latest index to find an author's most recent entry.

For the convenience of users, the *CA* cumulative index also includes references to all entries in these Thomson Gale literary series: *Authors and Artists for Young Adults, Authors in the News, Bestsellers, Black Literature Criticism, Black Literature Criticism Supplement, Black Writers, Children's Literature Review, Concise Dictionary of American Literary Biography, Concise Dictionary of British Literary Biography, Contemporary Authors Autobiography Series, Contemporary Authors Bibliographical Series, Contemporary Dramatists, Contemporary Literary Criticism, Contemporary Novelists, Contemporary Poets, Contemporary Popular Writers, Contemporary Southern Writers, Contemporary Women Poets, Dictionary of Literary Biography, Dictionary of Literary Biography Documentary Series, Dictionary of Literary Biography Yearbook, DISCovering Authors, DISCovering Authors: British, DISCovering Authors: Canadian, DISCovering Authors: Modules* (including modules for Dramatists, Most-Studied Authors, Multicultural Authors, Novelists, Poets, and Popular/Genre Authors), *DISCovering Authors 3.0, Drama Criticism, Drama for Students, Feminist Writers, Hispanic Literature Criticism, Hispanic Writers, Junior DISCovering Authors, Major Authors and Illustrators for Children and Young Adults, Major 20th-Century Writers, Native North American Literature, Novels for Students, Poetry Criticism, Poetry for Students, Short Stories for Students, Short Story Criticism, Something about the Author, Something about the Author Autobiography Series, St. James Guide to Children's Writers, St. James Guide to Crime & Mystery Writers, St. James Guide to Fantasy Writers, St. James Guide to Horror, Ghost & Gothic Writers, St. James Guide to Science Fiction Writers, St. James Guide to Young Adult Writers, Twentieth-Century Literary Criticism, 20th Century Romance and Historical Writers, World Literature Criticism,* and *Yesterday's Authors of Books for Children.*

A Sample Index Entry:

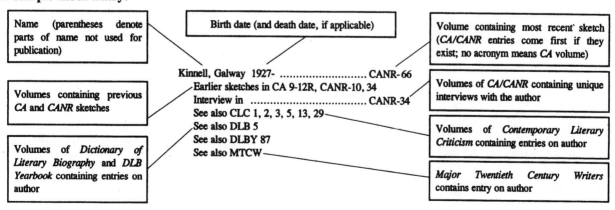

How Are Entries Compiled?

The editors make every effort to secure new information directly from the authors; listees' responses to our questionnaires and query letters provide most of the information featured in *CA*. For deceased writers, or those who fail to reply to requests for data, we consult other reliable biographical sources, such as those indexed in Thomson Gale's *Biography and Genealogy Master Index,* and bibliographical sources, including *National Union Catalog, LC MARC,* and *British National Bibliography.* Further details come from published interviews, feature stories, and book reviews, as well as information supplied by the authors' publishers and agents.

An asterisk (*) at the end of a sketch indicates that the listing has been compiled from secondary sources believed to be reliable but has not been personally verified for this edition by the author sketched.

What Kinds of Information Does An Entry Provide?

Sketches in *CA* contain the following biographical and bibliographical information:

- **Entry heading:** the most complete form of author's name, plus any pseudonyms or name variations used for writing

- **Personal information:** author's date and place of birth, family data, ethnicity, educational background, political and religious affiliations, and hobbies and leisure interests

- **Addresses:** author's home, office, or agent's addresses, plus e-mail and fax numbers, as available

- **Career summary:** name of employer, position, and dates held for each career post; resume of other vocational achievements; military service

- **Membership information:** professional, civic, and other association memberships and any official posts held

- **Awards and honors:** military and civic citations, major prizes and nominations, fellowships, grants, and honorary degrees

- **Writings:** a comprehensive, chronological list of titles, publishers, dates of original publication and revised editions, and production information for plays, television scripts, and screenplays

- **Adaptations:** a list of films, plays, and other media which have been adapted from the author's work

- **Work in progress:** current or planned projects, with dates of completion and/or publication, and expected publisher, when known

- **Sidelights:** a biographical portrait of the author's development; information about the critical reception of the author's works; revealing comments, often by the author, on personal interests, aspirations, motivations, and thoughts on writing

- **Interview:** a one-on-one discussion with authors conducted especially for *CA*, offering insight into authors' thoughts about their craft

- **Autobiographical essay:** an original essay written by noted authors for *CA*, a forum in which writers may present themselves, on their own terms, to their audience

- **Photographs:** portraits and personal photographs of notable authors

- **Biographical and critical sources:** a list of books and periodicals in which additional information on an author's life and/or writings appears

- **Obituary Notices** in *CA* provide date and place of birth as well as death information about authors whose full-length sketches appeared in the series before their deaths. The entries also summarize the authors' careers and writings and list other sources of biographical and death information.

Related Titles in the *CA* Series

Contemporary Authors Autobiography Series complements *CA* original and revised volumes with specially commissioned autobiographical essays by important current authors, illustrated with personal photographs they provide. Common topics include their motivations for writing, the people and experiences that shaped their careers, the rewards they derive from their work, and their impressions of the current literary scene.

Contemporary Authors Bibliographical Series surveys writings by and about important American authors since World War II. Each volume concentrates on a specific genre and features approximately ten writers; entries list works written by and about the author and contain a bibliographical essay discussing the merits and deficiencies of major critical and scholarly studies in detail.

Available in Electronic Formats

GaleNet. *CA* is available on a subscription basis through GaleNet, an online information resource that features an easy-to-use end-user interface, powerful search capabilities, and ease of access through the World-Wide Web. For more information, call 1-800-877-GALE.

Licensing. *CA* is available for licensing. The complete database is provided in a fielded format and is deliverable on such media as disk, CD-ROM, or tape. For more information, contact Thomson Gale's Business Development Group at 1-800-877-GALE, or visit us on our website at www.galegroup.com/bizdev.

Suggestions Are Welcome

The editors welcome comments and suggestions from users on any aspect of the *CA* series. If readers would like to recommend authors for inclusion in future volumes of the series, they are cordially invited to write the Editors at *Contemporary Authors*, Thomson Gale, 27500 Drake Rd., Farmington Hills, MI 48331-3535; or call at 1-248-699-4253; or fax at 1-248-699-8054.

Contemporary Authors Product Advisory Board

The editors of *Contemporary Authors* are dedicated to maintaining a high standard of excellence by publishing comprehensive, accurate, and highly readable entries on a wide array of writers. In addition to the quality of the content, the editors take pride in the graphic design of the series, which is intended to be orderly yet inviting, allowing readers to utilize the pages of *CA* easily and with efficiency. Despite the longevity of the *CA* print series, and the success of its format, we are mindful that the vitality of a literary reference product is dependent on its ability to serve its users over time. As literature, and attitudes about literature, constantly evolve, so do the reference needs of students, teachers, scholars, journalists, researchers, and book club members. To be certain that we continue to keep pace with the expectations of our customers, the editors of *CA* listen carefully to their comments regarding the value, utility, and quality of the series. Librarians, who have firsthand knowledge of the needs of library users, are a valuable resource for us. The *Contemporary Authors* Product Advisory Board, made up of school, public, and academic librarians, is a forum to promote focused feedback about *CA* on a regular basis. The seven-member advisory board includes the following individuals, whom the editors wish to thank for sharing their expertise:

- **Anne M. Christensen,** Librarian II, Phoenix Public Library, Phoenix, Arizona.

- **Barbara C. Chumard,** Reference/Adult Services Librarian, Middletown Thrall Library, Middletown, New York.

- **Eva M. Davis,** Youth Department Manager, Ann Arbor District Library, Ann Arbor, Michigan.

- **Adam Janowski, Jr.,** Library Media Specialist, Naples High School Library Media Center, Naples, Florida.

- **Robert Reginald,** Head of Technical Services and Collection Development, California State University, San Bernadino, California.

- **Stephen Weiner,** Director, Maynard Public Library, Maynard, Massachusetts.

International Advisory Board

Well-represented among the 115,000 author entries published in *Contemporary Authors* are sketches on notable writers from many non-English-speaking countries. The primary criteria for inclusion of such authors has traditionally been the publication of at least one title in English, either as an original work or as a translation. However, the editors of *Contemporary Authors* came to observe that many important international writers were being overlooked due to a strict adherence to our inclusion criteria. In addition, writers who were publishing in languages other than English were not being covered in the traditional sources we used for identifying new listees. Intent on increasing our coverage of international authors, including those who write only in their native language and have not been translated into English, the editors enlisted the aid of a board of advisors, each of whom is an expert on the literature of a particular country or region. Among the countries we focused attention on are Mexico, Puerto Rico, Spain, Italy, France, Germany, Luxembourg, Belgium, the Netherlands, Norway, Sweden, Denmark, Finland, Taiwan, Singapore, Malaysia, Thailand, South Africa, Israel, and Japan, as well as England, Scotland, Wales, Ireland, Australia, and New Zealand. The sixteen-member advisory board includes the following individuals, whom the editors wish to thank for sharing their expertise:

- **Lowell A. Bangerter,** Professor of German, University of Wyoming, Laramie, Wyoming.

- **Nancy E. Berg,** Associate Professor of Hebrew and Comparative Literature, Washington University, St. Louis, Missouri.

- **Frances Devlin-Glass,** Associate Professor, School of Literary and Communication Studies, Deakin University, Burwood, Victoria, Australia.

- **David William Foster,** Regent's Professor of Spanish, Interdisciplinary Humanities, and Women's Studies, Arizona State University, Tempe, Arizona.

- **Hosea Hirata,** Director of the Japanese Program, Associate Professor of Japanese, Tufts University, Medford, Massachusetts.

- **Jack Kolbert,** Professor Emeritus of French Literature, Susquehanna University, Selinsgrove, Pennsylvania.

- **Mark Libin,** Professor, University of Manitoba, Winnipeg, Manitoba, Canada.

- **C. S. Lim,** Professor, University of Malaya, Kuala Lumpur, Malaysia.

- **Eloy E. Merino,** Assistant Professor of Spanish, Northern Illinois University, DeKalb, Illinois.

- **Linda M. Rodríguez Guglielmoni,** Associate Professor, University of Puerto Rico—Mayagüez, Puerto Rico.

- **Sven Hakon Rossel,** Professor and Chair of Scandinavian Studies, University of Vienna, Vienna, Austria.

- **Steven R. Serafin,** Director, Writing Center, Hunter College of the City University of New York, New York City.

- **David Smyth,** Lecturer in Thai, School of Oriental and African Studies, University of London, England.

- **Ismail S. Talib,** Senior Lecturer, Department of English Language and Literature, National University of Singapore, Singapore.

- **Dionisio Viscarri,** Assistant Professor, Ohio State University, Columbus, Ohio.

- **Mark Williams,** Associate Professor, English Department, University of Canterbury, Christchurch, New Zealand.

CA Numbering System and Volume Update Chart

Occasionally questions arise about the *CA* numbering system and which volumes, if any, can be discarded. Despite numbers like "29-32R," "97-100" and "225," the entire *CA* print series consists of only 286 physical volumes with the publication of *CA* Volume 226. The following charts note changes in the numbering system and cover design, and indicate which volumes are essential for the most complete, up-to-date coverage.

CA First Revision	• 1-4R through 41-44R (11 books) *Cover:* Brown with black and gold trim. There will be no further First Revision volumes because revised entries are now being handled exclusively through the more efficient *New Revision Series* mentioned below.
CA Original Volumes	• 45-48 through 97-100 (14 books) *Cover:* Brown with black and gold trim. 101 through 226 (126 books) *Cover:* Blue and black with orange bands. The same as previous *CA* original volumes but with a new, simplified numbering system and new cover design.
CA Permanent Series	• *CAP*-1 and *CAP*-2 (2 books) *Cover:* Brown with red and gold trim. There will be no further Permanent Series volumes because revised entries are now being handled exclusively through the more efficient *New Revision Series* mentioned below.
CA New Revision Series	• CANR-1 through CANR-133 (133 books) *Cover:* Blue and black with green bands. Includes only sketches requiring significant changes; **sketches are taken from any previously published CA, CAP, or CANR volume.**

If You Have:	You May Discard:
CA First Revision Volumes 1-4R through 41-44R and *CA Permanent Series* Volumes 1 and 2	*CA* Original Volumes 1, 2, 3, 4 and Volumes 5-6 through 41-44
CA Original Volumes 45-48 through 97-100 and 101 through 226	**NONE:** These volumes will not be superseded by corresponding revised volumes. Individual entries from these and all other volumes appearing in the left column of this chart may be revised and included in the various volumes of the *New Revision Series*.
CA New Revision Series Volumes *CANR*-1 through *CANR*-133	**NONE:** The *New Revision Series* does not replace any single volume of *CA*. Instead, volumes of *CANR* include entries from many previous *CA* series volumes. All *New Revision Series* volumes must be retained for full coverage.

A Sampling of Authors and Media People Featured in This Volume

Maya Angelou

Angelou, the acclaimed writer of *I Know Why the Caged Bird Sings,* is also notable as a civil rights activist and educator. Critics praise her ability to write beautiful prose and commend her for providing an amazing example of the human potential to rise above defeat. In 2004 Angelou published *I Know Why the Caged Bird Sings: The Collected Autobiographies of Maya Angelou,* an essay collection titled *Hallelujah! The Welcome Table,* and a collection of children's books: *Angelina of Italy, Izak of Lapland, Renie Marie of France,* and *Mikale of Hawaii.*

Margaret Atwood

Atwood is a preeminent literary figure in her native Canada and has been honored worldwide for her distinctive poetry, like *The Circle Game,* and novels like *The Handmaid's Tale.* A serious writer who has earned best-seller status and popularity with critics and readers alike, Atwood holds up a mirror to society in a manner that is complex and passionate. Her most recent publications include the novel *Oryx and Crake* and the children's book *Rude Ramsay and the Roaring Radishes.*

J. G. Ballard

Ballard, the author of the best-seller *Empire of the Sun,* is a British writer who uses the framework of science fiction to explore the realm of the mind. Known for his richly metaphoric prose and his emphasis on psychological and technological themes, Ballard has dazzled readers with his dark and hypnotic stories and earned awards like the James Tait Black Memorial Prize. *Millennium People,* published in 2003, is Ballard's most recent novel.

E. L. Doctorow

Doctorow, a novelist and playwright, is the award-winning author of *Welcome to Hard Times* and *Ragtime,* both of which became major motion pictures. Known for his serious philosophical probings, the subtlety and variety of his prose style, and his presentation of multidimensional characters, Doctorow specializes in building many of his stories around actual persons and events in American history. In 2004, he published his latest collection of short stories, *Sweet Land Stories.*

John Grisham

Grisham, a publishing phenomenon and former lawyer, is the author of seventeen back-to-back bestsellers, many of which have been turned into blockbuster movies, like *The Firm, The Pelican Brief,* and *The Client.* Though some critics find his legal thrillers formulaic and his characters at times wooden, all credit him as a first-rate storyteller, confirmed by the hundred of millions of his books sold worldwide. Grisham's latest novel is *The Last Juror,* published in 2004.

Anne Rice

Rice is the popular author of "The Vampire Chronicles" series, as well as mainstream fiction under the pseudonym Anne Rampling and sadomasochistic fantasies as A. N. Roquelaure. According to critics, Rice's unusual and sympathetic treatment of vampires gives her "Vampire Chronicles" their particular appeal and helped to create a legion of devoted fans. Rice has alerted her fans that the series may come to an end with her latest novel, *Blood Canticle,* published in 2003.

Salman Rushdie

Rushdie is the Indian-born British author who came to international prominence when Islamic fundamentalists put a price on his head after the publication of his novel *Satanic Verses.* Winner of the Booker McConnell Prize and the Whitbread Prize, among many others, Rushdie is known for a body of work that experiments in language while exploring the world of the post-colonial multiethnic emigrant. His most recent publication is *Step across This Line: Collected Nonfiction, 1992-2002,* published in 2003.

John Updike

Updike, a best-selling author and winner of almost every American literary award, is recognized by critics and readers as one of the great American novelists of his generation. Known for portraying the anxieties and frustrations of contemporary middle-American life, Updike is praised for his brilliant command of the langue and the subtlety of his observations in books like *Rabbit, Run* and its three sequels. Updike expanded his canon in 2004 with *The Early Stories: 1953-1975* and the novel *Villages.*

Acknowledgments

Grateful acknowledgment is made to those publishers, photographers, and artists whose work appear with these authors' essays. Following is a list of the copyright holders who have granted us permission to reproduce material in this volume of *CA*. Every effort has been made to trace copyright, but if omissions have been made, please let us know.

Photographs/Art

Sherman Alexie: Alexie, photograph by Jim Cooper. AP/Wide World Photos. Reproduced by permission.

Julia Alvarez: Alvarez, photograph by Jerry Bauer. Copywright © by Jerry Bauer. Reproduced by permission.

Maya Angelou: Angelou, photograph. Copywright © George Shepard/Zuma/Corbis.

Piers Anthony: Anthony, photograph. Reproduced by permission.

J. G. Ballard: Ballard, photograph. Copywright © Bettman/Corbis.

Amiri Baraka: Baraka, photograph by Mike Derer. Copyright © AP/Wide World Photos.

Clive Barker: Barker, photograph. Sebastian Artz/Getty Images. Reproduced by permission.

Charles Baxter: Baxter, photograph by Janet Hostetter. Copyright © AP/Wide World Photos.

Harold Bloom: Bloom, photograph. Copyright © by Getty Images.

André Brink: Brink, photograph. Copyright © Fougere Eric/Corbis.

William F. Buckley, Jr.: Buckley, photograph. Copyright © Getty Images.

A. S. Byatt: Byatt, photograph. Copyright © Bassouls Sophie/Corbis Sygma.

Orson Scott Card: Card, photograph by Sophie Bassouls. Copyright © Bassouls Sophie/Corbis.

Mary Higgins Clark: Clark, photograph. Copyright © Getty Images.

J. M. Coetzee: Coetzee, photograph by Rob Hutchinson. Copyright © AP/Wide World Photos.

Mahmoud Darwish: Darwish, photograph by Jacqueline Larma. Copyright © AP/Wide World Photos.

Jacques Derrida: Derrida, photograph by James Leynse. Copyright © James Leynse/Corbis Saba.

Anita Desai: Desai, photograph by Penny Tweedie. Copyright © by Tweedie/Corbis.

James Ellroy: Ellroy, photograph. Copyright © Pacha/Corbis.

Michael Frayn: Frayn, photograph by Brad Rickerby. Copyright © Reuters NewMedia Inc./Corbis.

Louise Glück: Glück, photograph by Sigrid Estrada. Copyright © AP/Wide World Photos.

A

ALBOROUGH, Jez 1959-

PERSONAL: Born November 13, 1959, in Kingston-upon-Thames, Surrey, England; son of John Warmen (an accountant) and Cecily (a librarian; maiden name, Gathercole) Alborough; married Rikke Buhl (a therapist), July 18, 1987. *Education:* Norwich School of Art, degree in graphic design, 1981. *Religion:* "I am religious but have no religion."

ADDRESSES: Home—24-26 Nottingham House, Shorts Gardens, London WC2H 9AX, England.

CAREER: Writer and illustrator.

AWARDS, HONORS: Runner-up, Mother Goose Award, 1985, for *Bare Bear;* Graphics for Children Prize (with others), Bologna Children's Book Fair, 1987, for *The Great Games Book;* highly commended book citation, Kate Greenaway Medal, British Library Association, 2002, for *Fix-It Duck.*

WRITINGS:

FOR CHILDREN; SELF-ILLUSTRATED

Bare Bear, Knopf (New York, NY), 1984.
Running Bear, Knopf (New York, NY), 1985.
Willoughby Wallaby, Walker Books (London, England), 1986.
The Grass Is Greener, A. & C. Black (London, England), 1987, published as *The Grass Is Always Greener,* Dial (New York, NY), 1987.
Esther's Trunk, Walker Books (London, England), 1988.
The Tale of Hillary Hiccup, Macmillan (London, England), 1988.
Cupboard Bear, Walker Books (London, England), 1989.
Beaky, Houghton (Boston, MA), 1990, reprinted as *Hello, Beaky,* Walker Books (London, England), 1998.
Archibald, Macmillan (London, England), 1991.
Shake before Opening (poems), Hutchinson (London, England), 1991.
Where's My Teddy?, Candlewick Press (Cambridge, MA), 1992.
Cuddly Dudley, Candlewick Press (Cambridge, MA), 1993.
Washing Line, Walker Books (London, England), 1993, published as *Clothesline,* Candlewick Press (Cambridge, MA), 1993.
Hide and Seek, Walker Books (London, England), 1993, Candlewick Press (Cambridge, MA), 1994.
It's the Bear! (sequel to *Where's My Teddy?*), Candlewick Press (Cambridge, MA), 1994.
There's Something at the Letter Box, Walker Books (London, England), 1994, published as *There's Something at the Mail Slot,* Candlewick Press (Cambridge, MA), 1995.
Can You Jump Like a Kangaroo?, Candlewick Press (Cambridge, MA), 1996.
Can You Peck Like a Hen?, Candlewick Press (Cambridge, MA), 1996.

Ice Cream Bear, Candlewick Press (Cambridge, MA), 1997, Walker Books (London, England), 1999.

Watch Out! Big Bro's Coming, Candlewick Press (Cambridge, MA), 1997.

My Friend Bear (sequel to *It's the Bear!*), Candlewick Press (Cambridge, MA), 1998.

Balloon, Collins (London, England), 1998.

Whose Socks Are Those?, Candlewick Press (Cambridge, MA), 1999.

Hug, Walker Books (London, England), Candlewick Press (Cambridge, MA), 2000.

The Latest Craze, Walker Books (London, England), 2002.

Some Dogs Do, Candlewick Press (Cambridge, MA), 2003.

"DUCK" SERIES; SELF-ILLUSTRATED

Duck in the Truck, Collins (London, England), 1999, HarperCollins (New York, NY), 2000.

Fix-It Duck, Collins (London, England), 2001, Harper-Collins (New York, NY), 2002.

Captain Duck, Collins (London, England), 2002, Har-perCollins (New York, NY), 2003.

"FEATHERBY HOUSE FABLES" SERIES; SELF-ILLUSTRATED

The Candle's Story, Gollancz (London, England), 1988.

The Clock's Story, Gollancz (London, England), 1988.

The Umbrella's Story, Gollancz (London, England), 1988.

The Mirror's Story, Gollancz (London, England), 1988.

ILLUSTRATOR

Peter Eldin, compiler, *Dotty Definitions,* Piccolo (London, England), 1984.

Pat Thomson, *Can You Hear Me, Grandad?,* Delacorte (New York, NY), 1986.

Oscar Wilde, *The Canterville Ghost,* Oxford University Press (Oxford, England), 1987.

Dick King-Smith, *Martin's Mice,* Gollancz (London, England), 1988, Knopf (New York, NY), 1989.

Contributing illustrator to *The Great Games Book,* A. & C. Black (London, England), 1985.

OTHER

Also author of *Wordoodles* (poems), *Aurum,* and of unpublished book, *Mabel at the Table.*

ADAPTATIONS: Where's My Teddy?, It's the Bear, and *My Friend Bear* have been adapted into a cartoon named *Eddy and the Bear* by Collingwood O'Hare Entertainment, Ltd., in 2001.

SIDELIGHTS: Jez Alborough's picture books for young children feature rhyming texts and exaggerated drawings of animal characters in humorous scenarios that teach simple lessons to preschoolers. Alborough usually includes silly or ridiculous incidents in his picture books, and critics note that his cartoon-like drawings emphasize the humorous intent of his words, with his use of color, in particular, garnering applause. While Alborough's plots are sometimes faulted as overly conventional, critics invariably find his illustrations apt, vibrant, and appealing to children.

Alborough has published several books with bears as the central character. His first book, *Bare Bear,* follows a polar bear home, where he strips down to his pink skin after removing sunglasses, boots, and finally his fur coat. The story is told in simple, two-line rhymes, and to convey the arctic setting the artist relies on cool blues, whites, and dark shadows that many reviewers found fitting. A *Publishers Weekly* critic praised the work for its "peculiar slapstick brand of humor that little kids adore." In *Running Bear,* a sequel to *Bare Bear,* Polar Bear decides to lose weight by jogging but slips into the ocean instead and comes home with a cold. Although Janet E. Fricker of *School Library Journal* found some of Alborough's exaggerated illustrations unpleasant and felt that children unfamiliar with *Bare Bear* would find this story confusing, she allowed that "*Running Bear* is colorfully illustrated and sometimes humorous."

Where's My Teddy? is another of the author's self-illustrated picture books to feature a bear. An "irresistible bedtime story," according to *Publishers Weekly, Where's My Teddy?* tells the story of Eddy, a little boy who ventures into some dark and scary woods to search for his lost teddy bear. While he finds a giant-sized teddy bear that a real bear has lost and mistakes it for his own grown large, a bear finds Eddy's teddy bear and thinks his own toy has shrunk. The two meet, realize their mistakes, exchange teddy bears, and the book ends with each tucked into his own bed with his own stuffed toy. Martha Topol of *School Library Journal* praised Alborough's rhyming text, adding that "[readers'] fear of the unknown and the ensuing visual absurdity will keep them riveted." A *Kirkus Reviews* critic focused on the effectiveness of Alborough's illustrations: "The striking, expressive watercolors are just right for this satisfying, nicely symmetrical tale."

The Grass Is Greener, published in the United States as *The Grass Is Always Greener,* features sheep in a story based on the old adage, "The grass is always greener on the other side." Thomas, the lead sheep, decides that the grass on top of the hill in the next pasture must be fresher than that in his own field, and convinces all the other sheep to go there, except Lincoln Lamb, who cannot be bothered to stop playing. Once the sheep get to the hill, they decide that a beautiful green pasture in the distance must have even better grass, but when they get there, they see Lincoln and realize it is the pasture where they started. While noting that *The Grass Is Always Greener* is not a particularly original portrayal of the old saw, John Philbrook of *School Library Journal* praised Alborough's illustrations: "Color is nicely used . . . vivid greens and lighter pastels make the countryside come alive."

Alborough's *Beaky* explores the theme of identity for preschoolers. In this picture book, a bird's egg falls from a tree and Beaky is hatched, but in the absence of others like him on the forest floor, he does not know who he is. A passing frog helps him until a beautiful song draws Beaky into a tree where he discovers a large version of himself—a bird of paradise. A *Publishers Weekly* critic commented: "It is an uplifting moment when Beaky discovers his true identity and soars above the treetops."

Cuddly Dudley employs Alborough's signature wordplay to tell the story of a penguin who is so cute that his family always wants to hug and kiss him. Dudley finally runs away in an attempt to get some peace but encounters a man who feels the same way about him, so he returns home. Reviewers enjoyed Alborough's action-packed illustrations more than the somewhat conventional story. Christine A. Moesch of *School Library Journal* thought "the images of lots of snuggly penguins might appeal to children."

Alborough has also earned praise for his entertaining rhymes. In *Archibald,* the author and illustrator tells of a man inordinately proud of his red hair. However, the

man loses it one day and is teased by the friends whom he had earlier slighted. *Junior Bookshelf* reviewer R. Baines found this "a lively and enjoyable read" that is "enlivened by being told in rhyming couplets." Alborough's book of poems, *Shake before Opening,* covers such topics of interest to youngsters as body parts, animals, school, and other subjects with humor, rhymes, and sketchy drawings. Alborough "uses rhyme expertly," according to a critic for *Junior Bookshelf,* who concluded: "If you need a lift, a grin on your lips, then this jumpy, hoppity book will do the business."

Hug is perhaps the easiest book to read that Alborough has written. The entire story is told with just three different words—"hug," "Bobo," and "Mummy"—but "like a wordless book, the story unfolds through a series of expressive pictures rather than language," explained a *Publishers Weekly* contributor. A tiny chimp named Bobo wanders the jungle forlornly. "HUG," he says as he sees parents and children of various species hugging each other. The pair of elephants tries to help, but Bobo only gets sadder. Then his mother appears to give him a hug of his own, and all is well. "Alborough's simplicity results in another gem," concluded *School Library Journal* reviewer Gay Lynn Van Vleck.

Alborough began a new series in 2000 with the publication of *Duck in the Truck.* In this and subsequent tales, Alborough again makes good use of rhyme and of his signature cartoon style. Throughout the series, the hapless Duck drags his long-suffering barnyard friends Goat, Sheep, and Frog through various adventures. In *Duck in the Truck,* Duck crashes his truck, and the others have to help push him out of the mud. *Fix-It Duck* finds Duck destroying Sheep's home as he tries to fix a leak that is not really a leak: Duck's bath is just overflowing. Then, in *Captain Duck,* Duck accidentally sails off in Goat's boat, dragging Frog along behind. "The animals burst out of the boisterous, colorful pictures," wrote Bina Williams about *Captain Duck* in *School Library Journal,* while a *Publishers Weekly* reviewer praised *Duck in the Truck*'s "infectious, hard-hitting beat with more than a few rhythmic surprises."

Alborough once commented: "I write to awaken and realize the child in myself, and hopefully to do so in those who read my books. To me, 'the child' is that part of oneself which is still innocent, heartful, mindless, and unaffected by upbringing and the conditioning of society. When I see some people read my books, I can see the child shining through, and I am happy."

BIOGRAPHICAL AND CRITICAL SOURCES:

BOOKS

Alborough, Jez, *Hug,* Walker Books (London, England), Candlewick Press (Cambridge, MA), 2000.

PERIODICALS

Booklist, October 1, 1992, Deborah Abbott, review of *Where's My Teddy?,* p. 333; September 1, 1997, Julie Corsaro, review of *Watch Out! Big Bro's Coming!,* p. 131; January 1, 1999, Carolyn Phelan, review of *My Friend Bear,* p. 883; December 15, 1999, Carolyn Phelan, review of *Duck in the Truck,* p. 788; April 1, 2002, Ellen Mandel, review of *Fix-It Duck,* p. 1331.

Christian Science Monitor, November 6, 1992, Heather Vogel Frederick, review of *Where's My Teddy?,* p. 11.

Horn Book, January-February, 1989, Ethel R. Twichell, review of *Martin's Mice,* pp. 71-72.

Junior Bookshelf, December, 1987, p. 267; August, 1990, p. 164; October, 1991, R. Baines, review of *Archibald,* p. 200; December, 1991, review of *Shake before Opening,* p. 247; April, 1993, p. 56.

Kirkus Reviews, November 1, 1987, p. 1569; July 1, 1992, review of *Where's My Teddy?,* p. 845; March 1, 2002, review of *Fix-It Duck,* p. 328.

Publishers Weekly, August 17, 1984, review of *Bare Bear,* p. 59; December 9, 1988, review of *Martin's Mice,* p. 65; July 27, 1990, review of *Beaky,* p. 231; July 6, 1992, review of *Where's My Teddy?,* p. 54; April 12, 1993, review of *Cuddly Dudley,* p. 61; November 21, 1994, review of *It's the Bear!,* p. 76; November 16, 1998, review of *My Friend Bear,* p. 73; January 10, 2000, review of *Duck in the Truck,* p. 66; November 20, 2000, review of *Hug,* p. 67; January 22, 2001, review of *My Friend Bear,* p. 326; December 3, 2001, review of *Hug,* pp. 62-63; March 18, 2002, review of *Fix-It Duck,* pp. 105-106; April 8, 2002, review of *Duck in the Truck,* p. 230; May 5, 2003, review of *Captain Duck,* p. 224.

School Librarian, May, 1990, p. 58; February, 1993, p. 14; May, 1995, p. 57.

School Library Journal, January 1, 1985, review of *Bare Bear,* p. 62; October, 1986, Janet E. Fricker, review of *Running Bear,* p. 154; November, 1987, John Philbrook, review of *The Grass Is Always Greener,* pp. 85-86; January, 1989, Anne Connor, review of *Martin's Mice,* p. 78; October, 1990, Heide Piehler, review of *Beaky,* p. 84; August, 1992, Martha Topol, review of *Where's My Teddy?,* p. 132; April, 1993, Christine A. Moesch, review of *Cuddly Dudley,* p. 90; February, 1995, Rosanne Cerny, review of *It's the Bear!,* p. 72; January, 1997, review of *Martin's Mice,* p. 37; August, 1997, Sally R. Dow, review of *Watch Out! Big Bro's Coming!,* p. 128; December, 1998, Kit Vaughan, review of *My Friend Bear,* p. 75; December, 2000, Gay Lynn Van Vleck, review of *Hug,* p. 94; May, 2002, Laurie von Mehren, review of *Fix-It Duck,* p. 104; July, 2003, Bina Williams, review of *Captain Duck,* p. 86; December, 2003, Mary Elam, review of *Some Dogs Do,* p. 102.

Times Educational Supplement, September 16, 1988, p. 32; March 30, 1990, p. B10; June 8, 1990, William Feaver, review of *Beaky,* p. B14; March 29, 1991, p. 23; October 26, 2001, review of *Fix-It Duck,* p. 22; December 21, 2001, interview with Alborough, p. 28.

Times Literary Supplement, September 30, 1988, Linda Taylor, review of *Martin's Mice,* p. 1081.

ONLINE

Book Trusted Online, http://www.booktrusted.com/ (November 3, 2003), "Jez Alborough."

World Book Day Web Site, http://www.worldbookday festival.com/ (November 3, 2003), interview with Alborough.*

*   *   *

ALEXIE, Sherman (Joseph, Jr.) 1966-

PERSONAL: Born October 7, 1966, in Spokane, WA; son of Sherman Joseph and Lillian Agnes (Cox) Alexie. *Education:* Attended Gonzaga University, 1985-87; Washington State University, B.A., 1991.

ADDRESSES: Home—P.O. Box 376, Wellpinit, WA 99040. *Agent*—Hanging Loose Press, 231 Wyckoff St., Brooklyn, NY 11217.

Sherman Alexie

CAREER: Writer, c. 1992—; song writer and music composer; director of films, including *The Business of Fancydancing,* 2003.

AWARDS, HONORS: Poetry fellow, Washington State Arts Commission, 1991; National Endowment for the Arts grant, 1992; Slipstream chapbook contest winner, 1992, for *I Would Steal Horses;* American Book Award, 1996, for *Reservation Blues;* three-time World Heavyweight Championship Poetry Bout winner; nominated for Independent Spirit Award for best first screenplay, c. 1998, Outstanding Achievement in Writing award, First Americans in the Arts, 1999, and Florida Film Critics Circle Award, all for *Smoke Signals;* Outstanding Screenwriting Award, OUTFEST, 2003, for *The Business of Fancydancing;* Los Angeles Times Book Prize for fiction finalist, 2003, for *Ten Little Indians.*

WRITINGS:

The Business of Fancydancing (poems), Hanging Loose Press (Brooklyn, NY), 1992.
I Would Steal Horses (poems), Slipstream, 1992.

First Indian on the Moon (poems), Hanging Loose Press (Brooklyn, NY), 1993.
The Lone Ranger and Tonto Fistfight in Heaven (short stories), Atlantic Monthly Press (New York, NY), 1993.
Old Shirts and New Skins (poems), UCLA American Indian Studies Center (Los Angeles, CA), 1993.
Water Flowing Home (poems), Limberlost Press (Boise, ID), 1994.
Seven Mourning Songs for the Cedar Flute I Have Yet to Learn to Play (poems), Whitman College Press, 1994.
Reservation Blues (novel), Grove/Atlantic (New York, NY), 1994, published as *Coyote Spring,* Atlantic (New York, NY), 1995.
(With Jim Boyd) *Reservation Blues: The Soundtrack* (recording), Thunderwolf Productions, 1995.
The Indian Fighter (radio script), National Public Radio, 1995.
Because My Father Was the Only Indian Who Saw Jimi Hendrix Play the Star-spangled Banner at Woodstock (radio script), aired on *This American Life,* National Public Radio, 1996.
Indian Killer, Atlantic Monthly Press (New York, NY), 1996.
The Summer of Black Widows, Hanging Loose Press (Brooklyn, NY), 1996.
The Man Who Loves Salmon (poems), Limberlost Press (Boise, ID), 1998.
Smoke Signals: Introduction, Screenplay, and Notes, Miramax (New York, NY), 1998.
One Stick Song (poems), Hanging Loose Press (Brooklyn, NY), 2000.
The Toughest Indian in the World (stories), Atlantic Monthly Press (New York, NY), 2000.
(Author of introduction) Gwendolyn Cates and Richard W. West, *Indian Country,* Grove/Atlantic (New York, NY), 2001.
(Editor) *Scribner's Best of the Fiction Workshops,* Simon & Schuster (New York, NY), 2002.
(Author of foreword, with Robert Hershon) *The CLMP Directory of Literary Magazines and Presses,* Manic D Press, 2002.
(Author of introduction) Percival Everett, *Watershed,* Beacon Press (Boston, MA), 2003.
The Business of Fancydancing (screenplay), Hanging Loose Press (Brooklyn, NY), 2003.
(With others) *The Business of Fancydancing: Music from the Movie* (soundtrack), 2003.
Ten Little Indians: Stories, Grove Press (New York, NY), 2003.

Contributing editor, *Contentville,* 2000—. Contributor to periodicals, including *New York Times Magazine, Ploughshares, Left Bank, Seattle Weekly,* and *New York Times;* contributor to poetry anthologies, including *Voices of the City,* Hanging Loose Press, 2003; contributor to recordings, including *Talking Rain: Spoken Word and Music from the Pacific Northwest,* 1995, *Honor: A Benefit for the Honor the Earth Campaign,* 1996, *Jack Hammer Lobotomy,* 1991, and *Roadkill-basa,* 1994.

WORK IN PROGRESS: Tattoo Tears, a collection of short stories; *House Fire,* a novel.

SIDELIGHTS: Drawing heavily upon his experiences as a native Spokane/Coeur d'Alene tribal member who grew up and still lives on the Spokane Indian Reservation in Wellpinit, Washington, writer, performer, and filmmaker Sherman Alexie has garnered high praise for his poems and short stories of contemporary Native American reservation life, among them *The Business of Fancydancing,* a poetry collection Alexie has since adapted into a film. Alexie, who performs many of his poems at poetry slams, festivals, and other venues, has received praise for the energy and emotion he brings to his work.

When Alexie was a child, his mother supported the family by working at the Wellpinit Trading Post and selling her hand-sewn quilts, while his alcoholic father was absent from the home much of the time. Alexie spent most of his childhood reading every book in the Wellpinit school library, and in the eighth grade he decided to attend Reardan High School, located thirty-two miles outside the reservation. His achievements in high school secured his admission to Spokane's Jesuit Gonzaga University in 1985, where pressure to succeed led him to begin abusing alcohol. Alexie transferred to Washington State University in 1987 to be with his high-school girlfriend, and it was there that he began writing poetry and short fiction. In 1990 Alexie's works were published in *Hanging Loose* magazine, and this success gave him the will and incentive to quit drinking, which he did that same year.

In his short-story and poetry collections, Alexie delineates the despair, poverty, and alcoholism that often pervade the lives of Native Americans living on reservations. He has been lauded for writings that evoke sadness and indignation yet leave readers with a

sense of respect and compassion for characters who are in seemingly hopeless situations. Involved with crime, alcohol, or drugs, Alexie's protagonists struggle to survive the constant battering of their minds, bodies, and spirits by white American society and by their own self-hatred and sense of powerlessness. As Alexie asserted in *The Lone Ranger and Tonto Fistfight in Heaven*: Native Americans "have a way of surviving. But it's almost like Indians can easily survive the big stuff. Mass murder, loss of language and land rights. It's the small things that hurt the most. The white waitress who wouldn't take an order, Tonto, the Washington Redskins." While he depicts the lives of Native Americans who attempt to escape their situation through alcohol and other forms of self-abuse, Alexie also finds a mental, emotional, and spiritual outlet in his writing, which he refers to as "fancydancing."

A key characteristic of Alexie's writing is his irony, surfacing in dark humor buoyed by his exquisite sense of timing. His poetry collections *The Business of Fancydancing, First Indian on the Moon,* and *Old Shirts and New Skins* reveal this irony by exposing the "fraudulent illusions that tempt us all in America today," noted Andrea-Bess Baxter in *Western American Literature.* Alexie, commented Baxter, has a "talent for frequently turning history upside down" by placing historical characters such as Crazy Horse and Christopher Columbus in modern contexts with ironic twists. For example, in one instance Crazy Horse comes to life in the Smithsonian but is misidentified as an anonymous Hopi male; in another Columbus is cast as a real estate agent. Carl L. Bankston III, reviewing Alexie's oeuvre for the *Bloomsbury Review,* wrote that the author "combines a gift for startling associations and a fluid ease of literary style with an intimate familiarity with the quotidian facts of modern reservation life. As a result, his poems are simultaneously documentaries of tribal existence and revelations of the spirit and inner significance of that existence."

Commenting on *The Business of Fancydancing,* Alexie's first published poetry collection, Leslie Ullman in *Kenyon Review* wrote that the author "weaves a curiously soft-blended tapestry of humor, humility, pride and metaphysical provocation out of the hard realities . . . : the tin-shack lives, the alcohol dreams, the bad luck and burlesque disasters, and the self-destructive courage of his characters." Noted Bankston in his review of *The Business of Fancydancing,* "The most impressive quality of Alexie's writing is his ability to let poetry appear unexpectedly from . . . themes of everyday life in an unadorned, conversational idiom. There is no straining after effect."

Alexie introduces several characters in his poetry that resurface later in his short-story collection *Tonto and the Lone Ranger Fistfight in Heaven* and his novel *Reservation Blues*. These include Big Mom, mystical matriarch and "the best fry bread cook" on the reservation; Thomas Builds-the-Fire, a young storyteller; and Thomas's friends Victor Joseph and Junior Polatkin. In *Reservation Blues* the young friends, now in their thirties, come into possession of legendary blues musician Robert Johnson's magical guitar, which provides Victor with a measure of unnatural talent and the boys with something to do: form a rock band. Their trials and tribulations bring together Native and Anglo worlds in a resounding crash, as Verlyn Klinkenborg notes in the *Los Angeles Times Book Review*. Klinkenborg found that Alexie writes effectively for "a divided audience, Native American and Anglo. He is willing to risk didacticism whenever he stops to explain the particulars of the Spokane, and, more broadly, the Native American experience to his readers. But Alexie never sounds didactic. His timing is too good for that. *Reservation Blues* never misses a beat, never sounds a false note." Abigail Davis in *Bloomsbury Review* declared that "this first novel by Sherman Alexie comes as close to helping a non-Native American understand the modern Indian experience as any attempt in current literature. The reader closes the book feeling troubled, hurt, hopeful, profoundly thoughtful, and somehow exhausted, as if the quest of the characters had been a personal experience." Frederick Busch in the *New York Times Book Review,* however, saw Alexie's work as falling short in the novel form. "Though there is wonderful humor and profound sorrow in this novel, and brilliant renditions of each, there is not enough structure to carry the dreams and tales that Mr. Alexie needs to portray and that we need to read. . . . But the talent is real, and it is very large, and I will gratefully read whatever he writes, in whatever form."

In an interview with John and Carl Bellante for the *Bloomsbury Review,* Alexie commented on his progression from poems to short stories to novels as occurring "pretty naturally because . . . my poems are stories. It felt natural for me to evolve to a larger form. Not to say it wasn't difficult for me at first, though. . . . I had this thing about going beyond one page, typewritten. I'd get to the bottom of a page and freak out, because I wouldn't know what to do next. But the stories kept getting bigger and bigger. . . . They began to demand more space than a poem could provide."

Comparing Alexie's novels to his short stories, Ken Foster suggested in the *San Francisco Chronicle* that the author's longer works have "an odd, aggressive, middlebrow sensibility to them." Conversely, according to Foster, the 2000 short-story collection *The Toughest Indian in the World* "blessedly lacks" such qualities. The nine stories in the collection retrace Alexie's familiar territory of Native-white conflict while sustaining "a consistently dark comic tone," in Foster's opinion. The author "doesn't feel the need to instruct his readers in the details of contemporary American Indian culture, and why should he? The lives he portrays are so finely detailed . . . that even the most culturally sheltered reader is transported."

The title story in *The Toughest Indian in the World* finds its narrator, a Native journalist who feels all-too-assimilated in the white world, deciding to reconnect with his heritage by seducing a young Native fighter. At the end of the story, "the narrator is no more gay than he was at the start," noted Foster, "and yet the attraction between these two men, on this particular night, seems apt and true." In "Dear John Wayne" a young Navajo woman engages in a brief affair with the cowboy star during the 1950s filming of John Ford's epic western *The Searchers.* Interracial themes also figure in "South by Southwest," about a white drifter who takes a down-and-out Indian with him on a "nonviolent killing spree" across the West. What *Denver Post* contributor Ron Franscell found impressive in these two entries is the way Alexie "puts himself inside the heads and hearts of non-Indians. The result is tender, touching and erotic." *The Toughest Indian in the World* "proves once again that [Alexie is] the real deal: a master stylist, a born storyteller as well as a writer of inspired formal innovations and experiments," declared Emily White in a *Seattle Weekly* review.

While Alexie has been the recipient of numerous awards and grants, White commented that the author "nevertheless manifests a palpable hostility toward whiteness; it's clear that the idea of the great melting pot he is paid by publishers and grant committees actually makes his blood boil." Indeed, being a mass-market author is not in Alexie's plans either: "Good art doesn't come out of assimilation—it comes out of tribalism," he was quoted as saying in the *Denver Post.*

Alexie broke further barriers when he helped create the first all-Indian movie. *Smoke Signals,* for which he wrote the screenplay based on his short stories, was produced, directed, and acted by Native American talent. The plot follows a young man living an aimless life in Idaho. Victor Joseph, who has lost contact with his Native roots, embarks on a journey to "discover his past and accept his present," as *Los Angeles Magazine* writer James Greenberg put it. The finished film took top honors at the Sundance Film Festival; on the occasion of its 1998 wide release, Alexie told a *Time* interviewer that he hoped *Smoke Signals* would open doors for Indian filmmakers. He pointed to African-American director Spike Lee as a role model: "Spike didn't necessarily get films made as much as he inspired filmmakers to believe in themselves. That's what's going to happen here. These 13-year-old Indian kids who've been going crazy with their camcorders will finally see the possibilities."

BIOGRAPHICAL AND CRITICAL SOURCES:

PERIODICALS

Bloomsbury Review, September, 1992; May-June, 1993, p. 5; May-June, 1994; July-August, 1995.
Chicago Tribune, September 27, 1993.
Denver Post, May 21, 2000, Ron Franscell, "Alexie's Tribal Perspective Universal in Its Appeal."
Kenyon Review, summer, 1993, p. 182.
Kirkus Reviews, August 1, 1996.
Kliatt, May, 1994, p. 23.
Library Journal, November 15, 1993; October 15, 1994, p. 72; August, 1996, p. 109.
Los Angeles, July, 1998, review of *Smoke Signals,* p. 107.
Los Angeles Times Book Review, June 18, 1995.
New Yorker, May 10, 1993.
New York Times Book Review, October 11, 1992; October 17, 1993; July 16, 1995, p. 9; May 21, 2000, Joanna Scott, "American Revolutions."
New York Times Magazine, October 4, 1992; January 18, 1998, p. 16.
Prairie Schooner, spring, 1996, p. 70.
Publishers Weekly, July 29, 1996, p. 70; April 17, 2000, review of *The Toughest Indian in the World,* p. 52.
San Francisco Chronicle, May 21, 2000, Ken Foster, review of *The Toughest Indian in the World.*
School Library Journal, July, 1993, p. 112.
Seattle Weekly, May 11-17, 2000, Emily White, review of *The Toughest Indian in the World.*
Time, June 29, 1998, review of *Smoke Signals* and interview, p. 69.
Western American Literature, fall, 1994, p. 277.
World Literature Today, spring, 1994.

ONLINE

Sherman Alexie Web site, http://www.shermanalexie.com/ (April 7, 2004).*

* * *

ALVAREZ, Julia 1950-

PERSONAL: Born March 27, 1950, in New York, NY; married Bill Eichner (a physician and farmer), June 3, 1989. *Education:* Attended Connecticut College, 1967-69; Middlebury College, B.A. (summa cum laude), 1971; Syracuse University, M.F.A., 1975; attended Bread Loaf School of English, 1979-80.

ADDRESSES: Agent—Susan Bergholz Literary Services, 17 West 10th St., No. 5B, New York, NY 10011-8769.

CAREER: Writer and educator. Poet-in-the-Schools in KY, DE, and NC, 1975-78; Phillips Andover Academy, Andover, MA, instructor in English, 1979-81; University of Vermont, Burlington, visiting assistant professor of creative writing, 1981-83; George Washington University, Washington, DC, Jenny McKean Moore Visiting Writer, 1984-85; University of Illinois at Urbana, assistant professor of English, 1986-88; Middlebury College, Middlebury, VT, associate professor, 1988-1996, professor of English, 1996-98, writer-in-residence, 1998—. Owner of Café Alta Gracia, an organic coffee farm in the Dominican Republic.

MEMBER: PEN (National Members Council, 1997-1999), Sigma Tau Delta (honorary member).

AWARDS, HONORS: Benjamin T. Marshall Poetry Prize, Connecticut College, 1968 and 1969; prize from Academy of American Poetry, 1974; creative writing fellowship, Syracuse University, 1974-75; Kenan grant, Phillips Andover Academy, 1980; poetry award, La Reina Press, 1982; exhibition grant, Vermont Arts Council, 1984-85; Robert Frost Poetry fellowship, Bread Loaf Writers' Conference, 1986; Third Woman Press Award, first prize in narrative, 1986; award for younger writers, General Electric Foundation, 1986; National Endowment for the Arts grant, 1987-88; syndicated fiction prize, PEN, for "Snow"; grant from Ingram Merrill Foundation, 1990; Josephine Miles Award, PEN Oakland, 1991, notable book designation, American Library Association, 1992, and "Twenty-one Classics for the Twenty-first Century" designation, New York Librarians, all for *How the García Girls Lost Their Accents*; notable book designation, 1994, American Library Association; National Book Critics Circle Award finalist, 1995; Best Books for Young Adults designation, 1995, American Library Association, all for *In the Time of the Butterflies*; Jessica Nobel-Maxwell Poetry Prize, 1995, American Poetry Review; Doctor of Humane Letters, City University of New York, John Jay College, 1996; Alumni Achievement Award, 1996, Middlebury College; Dominican Republic Annual Book Fair, 1997, dedicated to Alvarez's body of work; selected "Woman of the Year," *Latina Magazine,* 2000; Sor Juana Award, 2002; Hispanic Heritage Award, Hispanic Heritage Awards Foundation, 2002; Américas Award for Children's and Young Adult Literature, Consortium of Latin American Studies Programs, 2002, and Pura Belpré Award, American Library Association, 2004, both for *Before We Were Free.*

WRITINGS:

NOVELS

How the García Girls Lost Their Accents, Algonquin Books (Chapel Hill, NC), 1991.
In the Time of the Butterflies, Algonquin Books (Chapel Hill, NC), 1994.
¡Yo!, Algonquin Books (Chapel Hill, NC), 1997.
In the Name of Salomé, Algonquin Books (Chapel Hill, NC), 2000.

POETRY

(Editor) *Old Age Ain't for Sissies,* Crane Creek Press (Sanford, NC), 1979.

The Housekeeping Book, illustrations by Carol Mac-Donald and Rene Schall, Burlington (Burlington, VT), 1984.
Homecoming, Grove Press (New York, NY), 1984, revised edition, Plume (New York, NY), 1996.
The Other Side/El Otro Lado, Dutton (New York, NY), 1995.
Seven Trees, Kat Ran Press (North Andover, MA), 1998.
The Woman I Kept to Myself, Algonquin Books (Chapel Hill, NC), 2004.

OTHER

Something to Declare (essays), Algonquin Books (Chapel Hill, NC), 1998.
The Secret Footprints (picture book), illustrations by Fabian Negrin, Knopf (New York, NY), 2000.
How Tía Lola Came to Stay (juvenile), Knopf (New York, NY), 2001.
A Cafecito Story, Chelsea Green Publishers (White River Junction, VT), 2001, bilingual edition published as *A Cafecito Story/El cuento del cafecito,* Chelsea Green Publishers (White River Junction, VT), 2002.
Before We Were Free (young adult), Knopf (New York, NY), 2002.

Contributor to anthologies, including *The One You Call Sister: New Women's Fiction,* edited by Paula Martinac, Cleis Press (Pittsburgh, PA), 1989; *The Best American Poetry 1991,* edited by David Lehman, Scribner's (New York, NY), 1991; *Poems for a Small Planet: Contemporary American Nature Poetry,* edited by Robert Pack and Jay Parini, Middlebury College Press (Middlebury, VT), 1993; *Mondo Barbie,* edited by Lucinda Ebersole and Richard Peabody, St. Martin's Press (New York, NY), 1993; *Growing up Female: Short Stories by Women Writers from the American Mosaic,* edited by Susan Cahill, Penguin (New York, NY), 1993; *A Formal Feeling Comes: Poems in Form by Contemporary Women,* edited by Annie Finch, Story Line Press, 1994; and *New Writing from the Caribbean,* Macmillan (New York, NY), 1994.

Contributor of fiction to periodicals, including *Caribbean Writer, Commonwoman, Greensboro Review, High Plains Literary Review, Green Mountain Review, New Mexico Humanities Review, Story,* and *Syracuse*

Magazine. Contributor of poetry to periodicals, including *Barataria Review, Burlington Review, Caribbean Writer, Florilegia, George Washington Review, Green Mountain Review, Helicon Nine, Jar, Kentucky Poetry Review, Kenyon Review, Latinos in the U.S. Review, Poetry, Poetry Miscellany, Wind,* and *Womanspirit.* Contributor of translations to *Barataria Review, Bitter Oleander, Pan American Review, Pulse: The Lamar Review,* and *Tower.* Editor of *Special Reports/Ecology,* 1971.

ADAPTATIONS: In the Time of the Butterflies was adapted as a television movie starring Salma Hayek for Showtime in 2001.

WORK IN PROGRESS: Finding Miracles, a young adult novel, for Knopf; *A Gift of Thanks: The Legend of Altagracia,* a picture book, expected 2005.

SIDELIGHTS: Julia Alvarez, who was born in New York City but raised until the age of ten in the Dominican Republic, is a distinguished novelist and poet. Alvarez was forced to flee with her family from the Dominican Republic in 1960 after the discovery of her father's involvement in a plot to overthrow dictator Rafael Trujillo. Since that time she has lived in the United States, but has retained ties to the Dominican Republic and visits the nation frequently. Much of her fiction and poetry can be viewed as semi-autobiographical, dealing both with the immigrant experience and bicultural identity. *Seattle Times* reporter Irene Wanner described Alvarez as "a lyrical writer with passions for individuals, particularly women, who affect history. Her chosen but difficult genre is intensely rewarding."

Alvarez's first book-length work of fiction, *How the García Girls Lost Their Accents,* is often referred to as a novel. Actually, it consists of fifteen interrelated stories detailing the experiences of four sisters and their family both before and after their exile from the Dominican Republic, and their subsequent life in New York City. The book begins with a series of episodes in which the sisters are already Americanized: sex and drugs and mental breakdowns all figure into life as the girls live it in the late 1960s and early 1970s. The book's central portion concerns the difficult periods of adjustment experienced by the García sisters while growing up as immigrants in vast, fast-paced New York City. It closes with a collection of tales recalling

the way of life experienced by the sisters while youngsters, both in the Dominican Republic and as newcomers to the United States. Donna Rifkind, writing in the *New York Times Book Review,* noted that the volume's reverse chronology constitutes "a shrewd idea," and she declared that Alvarez has "beautifully captured the threshold experiences of the new immigrant, where the past is not yet a memory and the future remains an anxious dream." At the same time, Rifkind felt that the depiction of the four sisters' experiences in the United States is less successful and that "Alvarez has not yet quite found a voice." Stephen Henighan in the Toronto *Globe and Mail* characterized *How the García Girls Lost Their Accents* as a "humane, gracefully written novel."

In her second novel, *In the Time of the Butterflies,* Alvarez recalls a grim incident in Dominican history: the untimely deaths in 1960 of three sisters—the Mirabals—who had denounced Rafael Trujillo's dictatorship. Alvarez chooses to portray these events from a subjective fictional perspective rather than as historical biography. According to Roberto Gonzalez Echevarria, writing in the *New York Times Book Review,* "by dealing with real historical figures in this novel, Ms. Alvarez has been much more ambitious than she was in her first, as if she needed to have her American self learn what it was really like in her native land." *In the Time of the Butterflies* is constructed in four sections, one for each of the dead sisters and one for their surviving sibling. It is through the surviving sister that the reader obtains background on the others; she recalls their love affairs and marriages as well as the activist actions that led to their deaths. *Nation* reviewer Ilan Stavans stated that, although Alvarez's subject matter is not unique, "her pen lends it an authenticity and sense of urgency seldom found elsewhere." Stavans went on to deem *In the Time of the Butterflies* "enchanting" and added that the book serves as "a wonderful examination of how it feels to be a survivor." *Progressive* contributor Elizabeth Martinez felt that Alvarez "moves [her] characters forward in the shadow of impending doom, yet never victimizes, never negates human complexity." Although Elsa Walsh noted in the *Washington Post Book World* that *In the Time of the Butterflies* is not without flaws—Trujillo is depicted only as a caricature—she praised the novel as "at once personal and political, both sweet and sweeping in scale."

In Alvarez's third novel, *¡Yo!,* the author returns to the four sisters portrayed in *How the García Girls Lost*

Their Accents. The title of the book is a triple-entendre. "Yo" is Spanish for "I"; it is a call for attention, and it is also the nickname of the book's central character, Yolanda García. Like Alvarez herself, Yolanda has become a successful novelist who bases much of her fiction on her own life experiences. However, it is not Yolanda who tells the story in *¡Yo!*, but rather the people who have known her. Each of the sixteen chapters in the novel presents the voice of a different character, including Yolanda's sisters, her parents, a former professor, her husband, a lover, and even an obsessed fan. A *Publishers Weekly* reviewer found *¡Yo!* to be a "splendid sequel" to *How the García Girls Lost Their Accents,* and observed that "Alvarez's command of Latino voices has always been impeccable, but here she is equally adept at conveying the personalities of a geographically diverse group of Americans."

In the Name of Salomé is in many ways Alvarez's most ambitious work of fiction. Based on the historical figures Salomé Ureña and her daughter, Camila, the novel explores the lives of two women dedicated to revolutionary causes and the bond between them that exists despite the mother's early death. Salomé is a Dominican political poet of national stature; Camila is a college professor at Vassar whose ties to the Caribbean are enhanced by her attempts to put her mother's papers in order. The story spans a century, alternating between Salomé's first-person recollections and Camila's third-person, reverse chronological narrative. "It's this long view, this hundred-year reach, that makes *In the Name of Salomé* original and illuminating," maintained Suzanne Ruta in the *New York Times Book Review.* Ruta added that the book, despite its anecdotal nature, "delivers a strong sense of who these people were." In a *Creative Loafing Online* review, Amy Rogers wrote: "*In the Name of Salomé* takes readers on an epic journey from pre-Revolutionary Cuba to the world of academia, from the mid-19th century to the late 20th, and from the political and moral sensibilities that once limited modern women to those that now liberate them. . . . A family saga that imagines the lives of real-life Dominican poet Salomé Ureña and her daughter, Camila Henriquez Ureña, it is a work both dense and deeply layered with intertwining stories." *Christian Science Monitor* contributor Kendra Nordin concluded: "This novel gives the impression of sitting at the feet of an old woman recounting her long life in jumbled order, but with emphasis on important moments, passionate impressions, wisdom learned and shared."

Alvarez's poetry has also received considerable critical attention. *Homecoming* combines a series of poems about the everyday chores of housekeeping with forty-one autobiographical sonnets. "This vivid and engaging collection proves [Alvarez] to be a talented poet," noted Christine Stenstrom in *Library Journal.* Another collection of poetry, *The Other Side/El Otro Lado,* is titled after its centerpiece, a twenty-one-canto poem about Alvarez's residency at a Dominican artists' colony and her experiences with the people she meets in a nearby fishing village. Sandra M. Gilbert, writing in *Poetry,* stated: "A novelist as well as a poet, Alvarez produces memoristic narratives in a range of sometimes quite complex forms along with prose poems, love poems, and elegiac lyrics."

In *The Woman I Kept to Myself,* Alvarez "writes candidly of epic concerns and everyday realities in this unfailingly lucid collection of autobiographical poems," according to Donna Seaman in *Booklist.* Discussing the work on her home page, Alvarez stated, "For me, poetry is that cutting edge of the self, the part which moves out into experience ahead of every other part of the self. It's a way of saying what can't be put into words, our deepest and most secret and yet most universal feelings."

In 2000 Alvarez produced her first work for young readers, a picture book titled *The Secret Footprints.* She followed that with the middle-grade reader *How Tía Lola Came to Stay,* about a young Dominican boy who experiences culture shock when his family moves from New York City to Vermont. In *School Library Journal,* Maria Otero-Boisvert remarked, "Alvarez does an excellent job of capturing the social unease of the child of immigrants who is unsure of where he belongs." *Before We Were Free,* a young adult novel, focuses on the life of Anita, a twelve-year-old girl in the Dominican Republic under the Trujillo regime. When Anita's father is arrested for plotting to overthrow the dictator, the girl and her mother are forced into hiding. According to Lauren Adams in *Horn Book,* *Before We Were Free,* is "a realistic and compelling account of a girl growing up too quickly while coming to terms with the cost of freedom." For the work, Alvarez received the 2004 Pura Belpré Award.

In her review of *In the Time of the Butterflies,* Walsh declared that the versatile Alvarez has joined "a growing list of ethnic writers breaking into mainstream American literature, but as with the best and most authentic side of diversity, her voice is a universal one." Insisting that "the experience of enduring the disorientations of learning a new culture" informs all of Alvarez's work, *New York Times Book Review* correspondent Christina Cho commended the author for a "graceful fusion of lush imagery and poetic economy."

Alvarez once commented: "I think of myself at ten years old, newly arrived in this country, feeling out of place, feeling that I would never belong in this world of United States of Americans who were so different from me. Back home in the Dominican Republic, I had been an active, lively child, a bad student full of fun with plentiful friends. In New York City I was suddenly thrown back on myself. I looked around the schoolyard at unfriendly faces. A few of the boys called me a name. I didn't know what it meant, but I knew it couldn't be anything good from the ugly looks on their faces.

"And then, magic happened in my life. I didn't even recognize it as magic until years later: it looked like schoolwork, a writing assignment. An English teacher asked us to write little stories about ourselves. I began to put into words some of what my life had been like in the Dominican Republic. Stories about my gang of cousins and the smell of mangoes and the iridescent, vibrating green of hummingbirds. Since it was my own little world I was making with words, I could put what I wanted in it. I could make things up. If I needed more yellow in that mango, I could put it in. Set amapola blooming in January. Make the sun shine on a cloudy day. If I needed to make a cousin taller, I could make her grow two inches with an adjective so she could reach that ripe yellow mango on the tree. The boys in the schoolyard with ugly looks on their faces were not allowed into this world. I could save what I didn't want to lose—memories and smells and sounds, things too precious to put anywhere else.

"I found myself turning more and more to writing as the one place where I felt I belonged and could make sense of myself, my life, all that was happening to me. I realized that I had lost the island we had come from, but with the words and encouragement of my teacher, I had discovered an even better world: the one words can create in a story or poem. 'Language is the only homeland,' the exiled Polish poet, Czeslaw Milosz, has said. And that was where I landed when we left the Dominican Republic, not in the United States but in the English language."

BIOGRAPHICAL AND CRITICAL SOURCES:

BOOKS

Contemporary Literary Criticism, Volume 93, Gale (Detroit, MI), 1996.

Dictionary of Hispanic Biography, Gale (Detroit, MI), 1996.

Dictionary of Literary Biography, Volume 282: *New Formalist Poets,* Gale (Detroit, MI), 2003.

Encyclopedia of World Biography, 2nd edition, Gale (Detroit, MI), 1998.

Notable Hispanic American Women, 2nd edition, Gale (Detroit, MI), 1998.

Novels for Students, Gale (Detroit, MI), Volume 5, 1999, Volume 9, 2000.

Sirias, Silvio, *Julia Alvarez: A Critical Companion,* Greenwood (Westport, CT), 2001.

PERIODICALS

Americas, March, 1995, Barbara Mujica, review of *In the Time of the Butterflies,* p. 60; January, 2001, Ben Jacques, "Julia Alvarez: Real Flights of Imagination," p. 22, and Barbara Mujica, review of *In the Name of Salomé,* p. 60.

Americas Review, Ibis Gomez-Vega, review of *¡Yo!,* pp. 242-245.

Antioch Review, summer, 1991, review of *How the García Girls Lost Their Accents,* pp. 474-475.

Atlanta Journal-Constitution, March 23, 2003, Teresa K. Weaver, "Books: Writer Alvarez's 'Rays of Light' Sometimes Irritate the Powerful," p. C1.

Belles Lettres, spring, 1995, Janet Jones Hampton, review of *In the Time of the Butterflies,* pp. 6-7.

Bilingual Review, January-April, 2001, Ricardo Castells, "The Silence of Exile in *How the García Girls Lost Their Accents,*" pp. 34-42.

Black Issues Book Review, March, 2001, Milca Esdaille, "Same Trip, Different Ships," p. 40.

Bloomsbury Review, March, 1992, pp. 9-10.

Booklist, July, 1994, Brad Hooper, review of *In the Time of the Butterflies,* p. 1892; September 15, 1996, Brad Hooper, review of *¡Yo!,* p. 180; August, 1998, Donna Seaman, review of *Something to Declare,* p. 1952; March 15, 2000, Veronica Scrol, review of *In the Name of Salomé,* p. 1292; August, 2000, Connie Fletcher, review of *The Secret Footprints,* p. 2143, and Isabel Schon, reviews of *In* *the Time of the Butterflies* and *¡Yo!,* p. 2154; February 15, 2001, Hazel Rochman, review of *How Tía Lola Came to Stay,* p. 1138; August, 2002, Hazel Rochman, review of *Before We Were Free,* p. 1945; March 1, 2004, Donna Seaman, review of *The Woman I Kept to Myself,* p. 1126.

bookWOMEN, October-November, 2002, "Beyond Words."

Boston Globe, June 28, 2000, Vanessa E. Jones, "Writing Her Book of High Grace."

Callaloo, summer, 2000, William Luis, review of "A Search for Identity in Julia Alvarez's *How the García Girls Lost Their Accents,*" p. 839.

Christian Science Monitor, October 17, 1994, Katherine A. Powers, review of *In the Time of the Butterflies,* p. 13; October 29, 1998, Kendra Nordin, review of *Something to Declare,* p. B7; July 6, 2000, Kendra Nordin, "Recalling the Dreams of a Caribbean Past."

Commonweal, April 10, 1992, review of *How the García Girls Lost Their Accents,* pp. 23-25.

E, May-June, 2002, Starre Vartan, review of *A Cafecito Story,* p. 60.

Entertainment Weekly, August 14, 1992, review of *How the García Girls Lost Their Accents,* p. 56.

Globe and Mail (Toronto), August 31, 1991, p. C6.

Hispanic, June, 1991, David D. Medina, review of *How the García Girls Lost Their Accents,* p. 55; December, 1994, Mary Bats Estrada, review of *In the Time of the Butterflies,* p. 82; March, 1997, Monica Hsu, review of *¡Yo!,* pp. 68-69.

Horn Book, September-October, 2002, Lauren Adams, review of *Before We Were Free,* pp. 563-565.

Intertexts, spring, 1999, Ibis Gomez-Vega, "Hating the Self in the 'Other' or How Yolanda Learns to See Her Own Kind in Julia Alvarez's *How the García Girls Lost Their Accents,*" pp. 85-98.

Journal of Adolescent and Adult Literacy, March, 2003, Susan Carlile, review of *How Tía Lola Came to Stay,* p. 528.

Kirkus Reviews, June 15, 2002, review of *Before We Were Free,* p. 876.

Knight-Ridder/Tribune News Service, August 9, 2000, Mary Ann Horne, review of *In the Name of Salomé,* p. K3161.

Lambda Book Report, October, 2000, Karen Helfrich, "Living in the Shadows," p. 28.

Latin American Literature and Arts Review, Volume 54, 1997, Heather Rosaria-Sievert, "Conversation with Julia Alvarez," pp. 31-37.

Library Journal, May 1, 1991, Ann H. Fisher, review of *How the García Girls Lost Their Accents,*

p. 102; April 1, 1996, Christine Stenstrom, review of *Homecoming: New and Selected Poems,* p. 84; October 1, 1996, Janet Ingraham, review of *¡Yo!,* p. 124; August, 1998, Nancy Shires, review of *Something to Declare,* p. 88; July, 1999, review of *¡Yo!,* p. 76; May 1, 2000, Eleanor J. Bader, review of *In the Name of Salomé,* p. 151; September 1, 2000, "Noah's Ark Choices," p. 168; February 15, 2004, Diane Scharper, review of *The Woman I Kept to Myself,* pp. 129-130.

Los Angeles Times, January 20, 1997, p. E3; March 23, 1997, Maria Elena Fernandez, "Two Sides of an American Identity," p. E1.

Los Angeles Times Book Review, February 26, 1995, p. 8.

Melus, spring, 1998, Julie Barak, "'Turning and Turning in the Widening Gyre': A Second Coming into Language in Julia Alvarez's *How the García Girls Lost Their Accents,*" p. 159; winter, 2002, Charlotte Rich, "Talking Back to El Jefe: Genre, Polyphony, and Dialogic Resistance in Julia Alvarez's *In the Time of Butterflies,*" pp. 165-184; winter, 2003, Catherine E. Wall, "Bilingualism and Identity in Julia Alvarez's Poem 'Bilingual Siesta', " pp. 125-144.

Mosaic, June, 2003, Kelli Lyon Johnson, "Both sides of the Massacre: Collective Memory and Narrative on Hispaniola," pp. 75-91.

Ms., September-October, 1994, Ava Roth, review of *In the Time of the Butterflies,* pp. 79-80; March-April, 1997, Julie Phillips, review of *¡Yo!,* p. 82; August-September, 2000, Dylan Siegler, review of *In the Name of Salomé,* p. 85.

Nation, December 30, 1991, pp. 863-864; November 7, 1994, Ilan Stavans, review of *In the Time of the Butterflies,* pp. 552-556.

New England Review & Breadloaf Quarterly, winter, 1986, pp. 231-232.

Newsweek, April 20, 1992, Susan Miller, review of *How the García Girls Lost Their Accents,* p. 78; October 17, 1994, Susan Miller, review of *In the Time of the Butterflies,* pp. 77-78.

New York Times Book Review, October 6, 1991, Donna Rifkind, review of *How the García Girls Lost Their Accents,* p. 14; December 18, 1994, Roberto Gonzalez Echevarria, review of *In the Time of the Butterflies,* p. 28; July 15, 1995, Philip Gambone, review of *The Other Side/El Otro Lado,* p. 20; February 9, 1997, Abby Frucht, review of *¡Yo!,* p. 19; September 20, 1998, Christina Cho, review of *Something to Declare;* July 16, 2000, Suzanne Ruta, "Daughters of Revolution," p. 24; December

2, 2001, Linnea Lannon, review of *How Tía Lola Came to Stay,* p. 83.

New York Times Magazine, March 23, 1997, pp. 67-68.

People Weekly, January 20, 1997, Clare McHugh, review of *¡Yo!,* p. 33; September 21, 1998, Laura Jamison, review of *Something to Declare,* p. 49.

Poetry, August, 1996, p. 285.

Postscript, Volume 16, 1999, Richard Vela, "Daughter of Invention: The Poetry of Julia Alvarez," pp. 33-42.

Prairie Schooner, summer, 2000, Maria Garcia Tabor, "The Truth according to Your Characters," pp. 151-156.

Progressive, July, 1995, p. 39.

Publishers Weekly, April 5, 1991, Sybil Steinberg, review of *How the García Girls Lost Their Accents,* p. 133; July 11, 1994, review of *In the Time of the Butterflies,* p. 62; April 24, 1995, p. 65; March 18, 1996, review of *Homecoming,* p. 67; October 14, 1996, review of *¡Yo!,* p. 62; December 16, 1996, Jonathan Bing, "Julia Alvarez: Books That Cross Borders," p. 38; May 15, 2000, review of *In the Name of Salomé,* p. 86. April 5, 1991; July 11, 1994; April 24, 1995; March 18, 1996; October 14, 1996; December 16, 1996; July 13, 1998, review of *Something to Declare,* p. 67; September 21, 1998; May 15, 2000; August 14, 2000, review of *The Secret Footprints,* p. 354; February 26, 2001, review of *How Tía Lola Came to Stay,* p. 87; July 22, 2002, review of *Before We Were Free,* p. 180; March 22, 2004, review of *The Woman I Kept to Myself,* p. 82.

Quill and Quire, May, 2000, review of *In the Name of Salomé,* p. 23.

San Francisco Chronicle, February 5, 1997, Patricia Holt, "Reality Continues in Fiction in *Yo,*" p. E1.

School Library Journal, September 1, 1991, Pam Spencer, review of *How the García Girls Lost Their Accents,* p. 292; April, 1997, Dottie Kraft, review of *¡Yo!,* p. 166; April, 1999, Francisca Goldsmith, review of *Something to Declare,* p. 162; September, 2000, Barbara Scotto, review of *The Secret Footprints,* p. 213; April, 2002, Maria Otero-Boisvert, review of *How Tía Lola Came to Stay,* p. S63; August, 2002, Kathleen Isaacs, review of *Before We Were Free,* p. 182.

Seattle Times, July 23, 2000, Irene Wanner, review of *In the Name of Salomé.*

Sojourners, May, 2001, Jim Wallis, review of *In the Name of Salomé,* p. 53.

Tribune Books (Chicago, IL), January 26, 1997, section 14, p. 2.

USA Today Magazine, March, 1999, Steven G. Kellman, review of *Something to Declare,* p. 80.

Washington Post Book World, November 27, 1994, Elsa Walsh, "Arms and the Women," p. 7; January 19, 1997, p. 9; June 11, 2000, Joanne Omang, "Revolutionary Fervor," p. X03.

Women's Review of Books, July, 1991, p. 39; May, 1995, Ruth Behar, review of *In the Time of the Butterflies,* pp. 6-7; November, 1998, Rosellen Brown, review of *Something to Declare,* pp. 7-8; September, 2002, Judith Grossman, "La musa de la patria," p. 5.

Women's Studies, February, 2000, Shara McCallum, "Reclaiming Julia Alvarez: *In the Time of the Butterflies,*" pp. 93-117.

World & I, December, 2000, Linda Simon, "Poetry and Patria: In Her Fourth Novel, Alvarez Explores Personal and Political Exigencies in the Lives of Two Passionate Women," pp. 232-236; November, 2002, Linda Simon, "Mixed Breed—A Profile of Julia Alvarez."

World Literature Today, summer, 1992, review of *How the García Girls Lost Their Accents,* p. 516; autumn, 1995, Kay Pritchett, review of *In the Time of the Butterflies,* p. 789; autumn, 1997, Cynthia Tompkins, review of *¡Yo!,* p. 785; winter, 2001, Fernardo Valerio-Holguin, review of *In the Name of Salomé,* p. 113.

ONLINE

Café Alta Gracia Web site, http://www.cafealtagracia.com/ (April 20, 2004).

Creative Loafing Online, http://web.cin.com/ (July 26, 2001), Amy Rogers, "Magical History."

Frontera Magazine, http://www.fronteramag.com/issue5/ (July 26, 2001), Marny Requa, "The Politics of Fiction."

Julia Alvarez Home Page, http://www.alvarezjulia.com (April 10, 2004).

Middlebury College Online, http://www.middlebury.edu/ (April 10, 2004), "Julia Alvarez.*"

*   *   *

ANGELOU, Maya 1928-

PERSONAL: Surname is pronounced "Ahn-ge-low"; born Marguerite Annie Johnson, April 4, 1928, in St. Louis, MO; daughter of Bailey (a doorman and naval dietician) and Vivian (a registered nurse, professional

Maya Angelou

gambler, and a rooming house and bar owner; maiden name, Baxter) Johnson; married Tosh Angelos, 1950 (divorced); married Paul Du Feu, December, 1973 (divorced, 1981); children: Guy. *Education:* Attended public schools in Arkansas and California; studied music privately, dance with Martha Graham, Pearl Primus, and Ann Halprin, and drama with Frank Silvera and Gene Frankel; studied cinematography in Sweden.

ADDRESSES: Home—Winston-Salem, NC. *Agent*—c/o Dave La Camera, Lordly and Dame, Inc., 51 Church Street, Boston, MA 02116.

CAREER: Author, poet, scriptwriter, playwright, performer, actress, and composer. *Arab Observer* (English-language newsweekly), Cairo, Egypt, associate editor, 1961-62; University of Ghana, Institute of African Studies, Legon-Accra, Ghana, assistant administrator of School of Music and Drama, 1963-66; freelance writer for *Ghanaian Times* and Ghanaian Broadcasting Corporation, 1963-65; *African Review,* Accra, feature editor, 1964-66. Lecturer at University of California, Los Angeles, 1966; writer-in-residence

at University of Kansas, 1970; distinguished visiting professor at Wake Forest University, Wichita State University, and California State University, Sacramento, 1974; Reynolds Professor of American Studies at Wake Forest University, 1981—; visiting professor, universities in the United States; lecturer at various locations in the United States. Southern Christian Leadership Conference, northern coordinator, 1959-60; appointed member of American Revolution Bicentennial Council by President Gerald R. Ford, 1975-76; member of the Presidential Commission for International Women's Year, 1978-79; Board of Governors, University of North Carolina, Maya Angelou Institute for the Improvement of Child & Family Education at Winston-Salem State University, Winston-Salem, NC, 1998. Writer of poems for Hallmark greeting cards and gifts, 2002—.

Appeared in *Porgy and Bess* on twenty-two nation tour sponsored by the U.S. Department of State, 1954-55; appeared in Off-Broadway plays, *Calypso Heatwave,* 1957, and Jean Genet's *The Blacks,* 1960; produced and performed in *Cabaret for Freedom,* Off-Broadway, 1960; appeared in *Mother Courage* at University of Ghana, 1964; appeared in *Medea* in Hollywood, 1966; television narrator, interviewer, and host for African American specials and theater series, 1972—; made Broadway debut in *Look Away,* 1973; directed film, *All Day Long,* 1974; appeared in television miniseries *Roots,* 1977; directed play, *And Still I Rise,* Oakland, CA, 1976; directed play, *Moon on a Rainbow Shawl,* by Errol John, London, 1988; appeared as Aunt June in film, *Poetic Justice,* 1993; appeared as Lelia Mae in television film, *There Are No Children Here,* 1993; appeared in advertising for the United Negro College Fund, 1994; appeared as Anna in film, *How to Make an American Quilt,* 1995; narrator of the film *The Journey of the August King,* 1995; narrator of the video *Elmo Saves Christmas,* 1996; appeared in the film *Down in the Delta,* 1998; appeared in film *The Amen Corner* and television series *Down in the Delta,* both 1999; appeared as Conjure Woman in the television special *The Runaway,* 2000; appeared as herself in various television specials.

MEMBER: American Film Institute (member of board of trustees, 1975—), Directors Guild of America, Equity, American Federation of Television and Radio Artists, Women's Prison Association (member of advisory board), National Commission on the Observance of International Women's Year, Harlem Writer's Guild,

Horatio Alger Association of Distinguished Americans, W. E. B. DuBois Foundation, National Society of Collegiate Scholars, National Society for the Prevention of Cruelty to Children.

AWARDS, HONORS: National Book Award nomination, 1970, for *I Know Why the Caged Bird Sings;* Yale University fellow, 1970; Pulitzer Prize nomination, 1972, for *Just Give Me a Cool Drink of Water 'fore I Diiie;* Tony Award nomination, 1973, for performance in *Look Away;* Rockefeller Foundation scholar in Italy, 1975; named Woman of the Year in Communications, *Ladies' Home Journal,* 1976; Emmy Award nomination, 1977, for performance in *Roots;* appointed first Reynolds Professor of American Studies at Wake Forest University, 1981; Matrix Award in the field of books, Women in Communication, Inc., 1983; North Carolina Award in Literature, 1987; Langston Hughes Award, City College of New York, 1991; Horatio Alger Award, 1992; Inaugural poet for President Bill Clinton, 1993; Grammy, Best Spoken Word Album, 1994, for recording of "On the Pulse of Morning"; etiquette award, National League of Junior Cotillions, 1993; Medal of Distinction, University of Hawaii Board of Regents, 1994; President's Award, Collegiate of Language Association for Outstanding Achievements, 1996; Southern Christian Leadership Conference of Los Angeles and Martin Luther King, Jr., Legacy Association National Award, 1996; named to the New York Black 100 list, Schomburg Center and The Black New Yorkers, 1996; distinguished merit citation, National Conference of Christians and Jews, 1997; Homecoming Award, Oklahoma Center for Poets and Writers, 1997; North Carolina Woman of the Year Award, North Carolina Black Publishers Association, 1997; Presidential & Lecture Series Award, University of North Florida, 1997; Cultural Keeper Awards, Black Caucus of the American Library Association, 1997; Humanitarian Contribution Award, Boston, MA, 1997; Alston/Jones International Civil and Human Rights Award, 1998; Christopher Award, New York, NY, 1998; American Airlines Audience, Gold Plaque Choice Award, Chicago International Film Festival, 1998, for *Down in the Delta;* Sheila Award, Tubman African American Museum, 1999; Lifetime Achievement Award for Literature, 1999; named one of the 100 best writers of the twentieth century, *Writer's Digest,* 1999; National Medal of Arts, 2000; Grammy award, 2002, for recording of *A Song Flung Up to Heaven;* recipient of over fifty honorary degrees from colleges and universities.

WRITINGS:

AUTOBIOGRAPHY

I Know Why the Caged Bird Sings, Random House (New York, NY), 1970, reprinted, 2002.
Gather Together in My Name, Random House (New York, NY), 1974, reprinted, 1990.
Singin' and Swingin' and Gettin' Merry like Christmas, Random House (New York, NY), 1976.
The Heart of a Woman, Random House (New York, NY), 1981.
All God's Children Need Traveling Shoes, Random House (New York, NY), 1986.
A Song Flung up to Heaven, Random House (New York, NY), 2002.
I Know Why the Caged Bird Sings: The Collected Autobiographies of Maya Angelou (omnibus edition of all six autobiographies), Modern Library (New York, NY), 2004.

POETRY

Just Give Me a Cool Drink of Water 'fore I Diiie, Random House (New York, NY), 1971.
Oh Pray My Wings Are Gonna Fit Me Well, Random House (New York, NY), 1975.
And Still I Rise, Random House (New York, NY), 1978, new version published as *Still I Rise,* illustrated by Diego Rivera, edited by Linda Sunshine, Random House (New York, NY), 2001.
Shaker, Why Don't You Sing?, Random House (New York, NY), 1983.
Poems, four volumes, Bantam (New York, NY), 1986.
Now Sheba Sings the Song (illustrated poem), illustrations by Tom Feelings, Dutton (New York, NY), 1987.
I Shall Not Be Moved, Random House (New York, NY), 1990.
On the Pulse of Morning, Random House (New York, NY), 1993.
The Complete Collected Poems of Maya Angelou, Random House (New York, NY), 1994.
A Brave and Startling Truth, Random House (New York, NY), 1995.
Phenomenal Woman: Four Poems Celebrating Women, Random House (New York, NY), 1995, new edition published as *Phenomenal Woman,* paintings by Paul Gaugin, edited by Linda Sunshine, Random House (New York, NY), 2000.

Also author of *The Poetry of Maya Angelou,* 1969. Contributor of poems in *The Language They Speak Is Things to Eat: Poems by Fifteen Contemporary North Carolina Poets* and to *Mary Higgins Clark, Mother,* Pocket Books (New York, NY), 1996.

ESSAYS

Lessons in Living, Random House (New York, NY), 1993.

Wouldn't Take Nothing for My Journey Now, Random House (New York, NY), 1993.

Even the Stars Look Lonesome, Random House (New York, NY), 1997.

Hallelujah! The Welcome Table, Random House (New York, NY), 2004.

CHILDREN'S PICTURE BOOKS

Mrs. Flowers: A Moment of Friendship (selection from *I Know Why the Caged Bird Sings*) illustrated by Etienne Delessert, Redpath Press (Minneapolis, MN), 1986.

Life Doesn't Frighten Me (poem), edited by Sara Jane Boyers, illustrated by Jean-Michel Basquiat, Stewart, Tabori & Chang (New York, NY), 1993.

(With others) *Soul Looks Back in Wonder,* illustrated by Tom Feelings, Dial (New York, NY), 1993.

My Painted House, My Friendly Chicken, and Me, photographs by Margaret Courtney-Clarke, Crown (New York, NY), 1994.

Kofi and His Magic, photographs by Margaret Courtney-Clarke, Crown (New York, NY), 1996.

Angelina of Italy, illustrated by Lizzy Rockwell, Random House (New York, NY), 2004.

Izak of Lapland, illustrated by Lizzy Rockwell, Random House (New York, NY), 2004.

Renie Marie of France, illustrated by Lizzy Rockwell, Random House (New York, NY), 2004.

Mikale of Hawaii, illustrated by Lizzy Rockwell, Random House (New York, NY), 2004.

PLAYS

(With Godfrey Cambridge) *Cabaret for Freedom* (musical revue), produced at Village Gate Theatre, New York, 1960.

The Least of These (two-act drama), produced in Los Angeles, 1966.

(Adapter) *Sophocles, Ajax* (two-act drama), produced at Mark Taper Forum, Los Angeles, 1974.

(And director) *And Still I Rise* (one-act musical), produced in Oakland, CA, 1976.

(Author of poems for screenplay) *Poetic Justice* (screenplay), Columbia Pictures, 1993.

(Author of lyrics, with Alistair Beaton) *King,* book by Lonne Elder, III, music by Richard Blackford, London, 1990.

Also author of the play *Gettin' up Stayed on My Mind,* 1967, a drama, *The Best of These,* a two-act drama, *The Clawing Within,* 1966, a two-act musical, *Adjoa Amissah,* 1967, and a one-act play, *Theatrical Vignette,* 1983.

FILM AND TELEVISION SCRIPTS

Georgia, Georgia (screenplay), Independent-Cinerama, 1972.

(And director) *All Day Long* (screenplay), American Film Institute, 1974.

(Writer of script and musical score) *I Know Why the Caged Bird Sings,* CBS, 1979.

Sister, Sister (television drama), National Broadcasting Co., Inc. (NBC-TV), 1982.

(Writer of poetry) *John Singleton, Poetic Justice* (motion picture), Columbia Pictures, 1993.

Composer of songs, including two songs for movie *For Love of Ivy,* and composer of musical scores for both her screenplays. Author of *Black, Blues, Black,* a series of ten one-hour programs, broadcast by National Educational Television (NET-TV), 1968. Also author of *Assignment America,* a series of six one-half-hour programs, 1975, and of *The Legacy* and *The Inheritors,* two television specials, 1976. Other documentaries include *Trying to Make It Home* (Byline series), 1988, and *Maya Angelou's America: A Journey of the Heart* (also host). Public Broadcasting Service Productions include *Who Cares about Kids, Kindred Spirits, Maya Angelou: Rainbow in the Clouds,* and *To the Contrary.* Writer for television series *Brewster Place,* Harpo Productions.

RECORDINGS

Miss Calypso (audio recording of songs), Liberty Records, 1957.

The Poetry of Maya Angelou (audio recording), GWP Records, 1969.

An Evening with Maya Angelou (audio cassette), Pacific Tape Library, 1975.

I Know Why the Caged Bird Sings (audio cassette with filmstrip and teacher's guide), Center for Literary Review, 1978, abridged version, Random House (New York, NY), 1986.

Women in Business (audio cassette), University of Wisconsin, 1981.

Making Magic in the World (audio cassette), New Dimensions, 1988.

On the Pulse of Morning (audio production), Ingram, 1993.

Wouldn't Take Nothing for My Journey Now (audio production), Ingram, 1993.

Phenomenal Woman (audio production), Ingram, 1995.

Been Found, 1996.

OTHER

Conversations with Maya Angelou, edited by Jeffrey M. Elliot, Virago Press (London, England), 1989.

Maya Angelou (four-volume boxed set), Ingram (London, England), 1995.

(With Mary Ellen Mark) *Mary Ellen Mark: American Odyssey,* Aperture (New York, NY), 1998.

Contributor to books, including *Poetic Justice: Filmmaking South Central Style,* Delta, 1993; *Bearing Witness: Contemporary Works by African American Women Artists,* Rizzoli International Publications, 1996; *The Journey Back: A Survivor's Guide to Leukemia,* Rainbow's End Company, 1996; *The Challenge of Creative Leadership,* Shephard-Walwyn, 1998; and *Amistad: "Give Us Free": A Celebration of the Film by Stephen Spielberg,* Newmarket Press, 1998.

Author of forewords to *African Canvas: The Art of African Women,* by Margaret Courtney-Clarke, Rizzoli (New York, NY), 1991; *Dust Tracks on the Road: An Autobiography,* by Zora Neale Hurston, HarperCollins (New York, NY), 1991; *Caribbean & African Cooking,* by Rosamund Grant, Interlink (Northampton, MA), 1993; *Double Stitch: Black Women Write about Mothers & Daughters,* HarperCollins, 1993; *African Americans: A Portrait,* by Richard A. Long, Crescent Books (New York, NY), 1993; and *Essence: Twenty-five Years Celebrating Black Women,* edited by Patricia M. Hinds, Harry N. Abrams (New York, NY), 1995; author of introduction to *Not without Laughter,* by Langston Hughes, Scribner (New York, NY), 1995;

author of preface to *Mending the World: Stories of Family by Contemporary Black Writers,* edited by Rosemarie Robotham, BasicCivitas Books (New York, NY), 2003.

Author, with Charlie Reilly and Amiri Bakara, *Conversations with Amiri Bakara.* Short stories are included in anthologies, including *Harlem* and *Ten Times Black.* Contributor of articles, short stories, and poems to national periodicals, including *Harper's, Ebony, Essence, Mademoiselle, Redbook, Ladies' Home Journal, Black Scholar, Architectural Digest, New Perspectives Quarterly, Savvy Woman,* and *Ms.* Magazine.

ADAPTATIONS: I Know Why the Caged Bird Sings was adapted as a television movie by Columbia Broadcasting System, Inc. (CBS-TV), 1979; *And Still I Rise* was adapted as a television special by Public Broadcasting Service (PBS-TV), 1985; *I Know Why the Caged Bird Sings* was produced for audio cassette and compact disk, Ingram, 1996.

SIDELIGHTS: As a young black woman growing up in the South, and later in wartime San Francisco, Maya Angelou faced racism from whites and poor treatment from many men. She found that, in this position, few things in life came easily to her. But instead of letting forces beyond her control overcome her, Angelou began to forge art from her early experiences and to change the world as she'd once known it. She became a singer, dancer, actress, composer, and Hollywood's first female black director. She became a writer, editor, essayist, playwright, poet, and screenwriter. She became known, as Annie Gottlieb wrote in the *New York Times Book Review,* as a person who "writes like a song, and like the truth. The wisdom, rue and humor of her storytelling are borne on a lilting rhythm completely her own."

Angelou also became a civil rights activist—she worked at one time for Dr. Martin Luther King and once staged a protest at the United Nations—as well as an educator. By 1975, wrote Carol E. Neubauer in *Southern Women Writers: The New Generation,* "Angelou had become recognized not only as a spokesperson for blacks and women, but also for all people who are committed to raising the moral standards of living in the United States." She did so by writing about herself, by fighting for civil and women's rights, and by providing an amazing example of the human potential to rise above defeat. Angelou explained this herself in an interview with George Plimpton in the *Paris Review:* "In all my work, in the movies I write, the lyrics, the poetry, the prose, the essays, I am saying that we may encounter many defeats—maybe it's imperative that we encounter the defeats—but we are much stronger than we appear to be, and maybe much better than we allow ourselves to be."

Angelou was born in St. Louis, Missouri, and lived her early years in Long Beach, California. As she related in *I Know Why the Caged Bird Sings,* the first book of her six-volume memoirs, she was just three years old when her parents divorced. Her father sent Angelou and her four-year-old brother alone by train to the home of his mother in Stamps, Arkansas. In Stamps, a segregated town, "Momma" (as Angelou and her brother Bailey called their grandmother) took care of the children and ran a lunch business and a store. The children were expected to stay clean and sinless, and to do well in school. Although she followed the example of her independent and strong-willed grandmother, and was a healthy child, Angelou felt ugly and unloved. When her mother, who lived in St. Louis, requested a visit from the children, Angelou was shocked by her mother's paler complexion, and by the red lipstick her grandmother would have thought scandalous. Angelou was almost as overwhelmed by her mother's wildness and determination as she was by her beauty.

Life in St. Louis was different from that in Stamps; Angelou was unprepared for the rushing noises of city life and the Saturday night parties. Then, when she was just seven-and-a-half years old, something terrible happened. In one of the most evocative (and controversial) moments in *I Know Why the Caged Bird Sings,* Angelou described how she was first lovingly cuddled, then raped by her mother's boyfriend. When the man was murdered by her uncles for his crime, Angelou felt responsible, and she stopped talking. She and her brother were sent back to Stamps. Angelou remained mute for five years, but she developed a love for language and the spoken word. She read and memorized books, including the works of black authors and poets Langston Hughes, W. E. B. Du Bois, and Paul Lawrence Dunbar. Even though she and Bailey were discouraged from reading the works of white writers at home, Angelou read and fell in love with the works of William Shakespeare, Charles Dickens, and Edgar Allan Poe. When Angelou was twelve and a half, Mrs.

Flowers, an educated black woman, finally got her to speak again. Mrs. Flowers, as Angelou recalled in *Mrs. Flowers: A Moment of Friendship,* emphasized the importance of the spoken word, explained the nature of and importance of education, and instilled in her a love of poetry. Angelou graduated at the top of her eighth-grade class.

When race relations made Stamps a dangerous place for Angelou and her brother, "Momma" took the children to San Francisco, where Angelou's mother was working as a professional gambler. World War II was raging, and while San Franciscans prepared for air raids that never came, Angelou prepared for the rest of her life by attending George Washington High School and by taking lessons in dance and drama on a scholarship at the California Labor School. When Angelou, just seventeen, graduated from high school and gave birth to a son, she began to work as well. She worked as the first female and black street car conductor in San Francisco. As she explained in *Singin' and Swingin' and Gettin' Merry like Christmas,* she also "worked as a shake dancer in night clubs, fry cook in hamburger joints, dinner cook in a Creole restaurant and once had a job in a mechanic's shop, taking the paint off cars with my hands." For a time, Angelou also managed a couple of prostitutes.

Angelou married a white ex-sailor, Tosh Angelos, in 1950. The pair did not have much in common, and Angelou began to take note of the reaction of people—especially African Americans—to their union. After they separated, Angelou continued her study of dance in New York City. She returned to San Francisco and sang in the Purple Onion cabaret. There, Angelou garnered the attention of talent scouts. From 1954 to 1955, she was a member of the cast of a touring production of *Porgy and Bess;* she visited twenty-two countries before leaving the tour to return to her son. During the late 1950s, Angelou sang in West Coast and Hawaiian nightclubs. After some time living in a houseboat commune in Sausalito, California, she returned to New York.

In New York, Angelou continued her stage career with an appearance in an Off-Broadway show, *Calypso Heatwave.* Then, with the encouragement of writer John Killens, she joined the Harlem Writers Guild and met James Baldwin and other important writers. It was during this time that Angelou had the opportunity to hear Dr. Martin Luther King speak. Inspired by his message, she decided to become a part of the struggle for civil rights. So, with comedian Godfrey Cambridge, she wrote, produced, directed, and starred in *Cabaret for Freedom* in 1960, a benefit for Dr. King's Southern Christian Leadership Conference (SCLC). Given the organizational abilities she demonstrated as she worked for the benefit, she was offered a position as the northern coordinator for Dr. King's SCLC. She appeared in Jean Genet's play, *The Blacks,* which won an Obie Award, in 1960.

Angelou began to live with Vusumzi Make, a South African freedom fighter; with Angelou's son Guy, they relocated to Cairo, Egypt. There, Angelou found work as an associate editor at the *Arab Observer.* As she recalled in *The Heart of a Woman,* she learned a great deal about writing there, but Vusumzi could not tolerate the fact that she was working. After her relationship with him ended, Angelou went on to Ghana, in West Africa, in 1962. She later worked at the University of Ghana's School of Music and Drama as an assistant administrator. She worked as a freelance writer and was a feature editor at *African Review.* As she related in *All God's Children Need Traveling Shoes,* Angelou also played the title role in *Mother Courage* during this time.

Angelou returned to the United States in the mid-1960s and found a position as a lecturer at the University of California in Los Angeles in 1966. She also played a part in the play *Medea* in Hollywood. In this period, she was encouraged by author James Baldwin and Random House publishers to write an autobiography. Initially, Angelou declined offers, and went to California for the production of a series of ten one-hour programs that she'd written, "Black, Blues, Black," which were broadcast in 1968. But eventually Angelou changed her mind and wrote *I Know Why the Caged Bird Sings.* The book, which chronicles Angelou's childhood and ends with the birth of her son Guy, bears what Selwyn R. Cudjoe in *Black Women Writers* calls a burden: "to demonstrate the manner in which the Black female is violated . . . in her tender years and to demonstrate the 'unnecessary insult' of Southern girlhood in her movement to adolescence." *I Know Why the Caged Bird Sings* won immediate success and a nomination for a National Book Award.

Although Angelou did not write *I Know Why the Caged Bird Sings* with the intention of writing other autobiographies, she eventually wrote five more, which

may be read with the first as a series. Most critics have judged the subsequent autobiographies in light of the first, and *I Know Why the Caged Bird Sings* remains the most highly praised. *Gather Together in My Name* begins when Angelou is seventeen and a new mother; it describes a destructive love affair, Angelou's work as a prostitute, her rejection of drug addiction, and the kidnapping of her son. *Gather Together in My Name* was not as well received by critics as *I Know Why the Caged Bird Sings.* As Mary Jane Lupton reported in *Black American Literature Forum,* in this 1974 autobiography, "the tight structure" of *I Know Why the Caged Bird Sings* "appeared to crumble; childhood experiences were replaced by episodes which a number of critics consider disjointed or bizarre." Lupton thought, however, that there is an important reason why Angelou's later works are not as tight as the first, and why they consist of episodes: these "so-called 'fragments' are reflections of the kind of chaos found in actual living. In altering the narrative structure, Angelou shifts the emphasis from herself as an isolated consciousness to herself as a black woman participating in diverse experiences among a diverse class of peoples."

Singin' and Swingin' and Gettin' Merry like Christmas is Angelou's account of her tour in Europe and Africa with *Porgy and Bess.* Much of the work concerns Angelou's separation from her son during that time. In *The Heart of a Woman,* Angelou describes her acting and writing career in New York and her work for the civil rights movement. She recalls visits with great activists Dr. Martin Luther King, Jr., and Malcolm X, and the legendary singer Billie Holiday. She also tells of her move to Africa, and her experiences when her son was injured in a serious car accident; the book ends with Guy's move into a college dormitory at the University of Ghana. "Angelou's message is one blending chorus: Black people and Black women do not just endure, they triumph with a will of collective consciousness that Western experience cannot extinguish," wrote Sondra O'Neale in *Black Women Writers.* *All God's Children Need Traveling Shoes* once again explores Guy's accident; it moves on from there to recount Angelou's travels in West Africa and her decision to return, without her son, to America.

It took Angelou fifteen years to write the final volume of her autobiography, *A Song Flung up to Heaven,* after *All God's Children Need Traveling Shoes* was published. The book covers four years, from the time

Angelou returned from Ghana in 1964 through the moment when she sat down at her mother's table and began to write *I Know Why the Caged Bird Sings* in 1968. Angelou hesitated so long to start the book and took so long to finish it, she told *Knight Ridder/ Tribune News Service* interviewer Sherryl Connelly, because so many painful things happened to her, and to the entire African-American community, in those four years. "I didn't know how to write it," she said. "I didn't see how the assassination of Malcolm [X], the Watts riot, the breakup of a love affair, then [the assassination of Dr.] Martin [Luther] King [Jr.], how I could get all that loose with something uplifting in it." Malcolm X's and King's assassinations were particularly painful for Angelou because in both cases the men were killed shortly after Angelou had agreed to work for them; it was, in fact, the offer of a job with Malcolm X that brought Angelou back from Africa. *A Song Flung up to Heaven* deals forthrightly with these events, and "the poignant beauty of Angelou's writing enhances rather than masks the candor with which she addresses the racial crisis through which America was passing," Wayne A. Holst wrote in *Christian Century*. But as Angelou intended, "not everything in [*A Song Flung up to Heaven*] is bleak," Cassandra Spratling commented in a review for *Knight Ridder/Tribune News Service*. "Tales of parties with writers and other friends; her bond with a woman with whom her Ghanian manfriend cheated; and descriptions of her closeness with the late writer James Baldwin lighten the story."

Angelou's poetry has often been lauded more for its content—praising black beauty, the strength of women, and the human spirit; criticizing the Vietnam War; demanding social justice for all—than for its poetic virtue. Yet *Just Give Me a Cool Drink of Water 'fore I Diiie,* which was published in 1971, was nominated for a Pulitzer Prize in 1972. This volume contains thirty-eight poems, some of which were published in *The Poetry of Maya Angelou*. According to Carol Neubauer in *Southern Women Writers,* "the first twenty poems describe the whole gamut of love, from the first moment of passionate discovery to the first suspicion of painful loss." In the other poems, "Angelou turns her attention to the lives of black people in America from the time of slavery to the rebellious 1960s. Her themes deal broadly with the painful anguish suffered by blacks forced into submission, with guilt over accepting too much, and with protest and basic survival."

As Angelou wrote her autobiographies and poems, she continued her career in film and television. She was the first black woman to get a screenplay (*Georgia, Georgia*) produced in 1972. She was honored with a nomination for an Emmy award for her performance in *Roots* in 1977. In 1979, Angelou helped adapt her book, *I Know Why the Caged Bird Sings,* for a television movie of the same name. Angelou wrote the poetry for the 1993 film *Poetic Justice* and played the role of Aunt June. She also played Lelia Mae in the 1993 television film *There Are No Children Here* and appeared as Anna in the feature film *How to Make an American Quilt* in 1995. Also in 1995, Angelou's poetry helped to commemorate the fiftieth anniversary of the United Nations. She had elevated herself to what Richard Grenier in *National Review* called a "dizzying height of achievement." As a title from an article by Freda Garmaise in *Gentleman's Quarterly* proclaimed, "Maya-ness" was "next to godliness."

One of the most important sources of Angelou's fame in the early 1990s was President Bill Clinton's invitation to write and read the first inaugural poem in decades. Americans all across the country watched the six-foot-tall, elegantly dressed woman as she read her poem for the new president on January 20, 1993. "On the Pulse of Morning" begins "A Rock, a River, a Tree" and calls for peace, racial and religious harmony, and social justice for people of different origins, incomes, genders, and sexual orientations. It recalls the civil rights movement and Dr. Martin Luther King, Jr.'s famous "I have a dream" speech as it urges America to "Give birth again/To the Dream" of equality. Angelou challenged the new administration and all Americans to work together for progress: "Here, on the pulse of this new day,/You may have the grace to look up and out/And into your sister's eyes, and into/Your brother's face, your country/And say simply/Very simply/With hope—Good morning."

While some viewed President Clinton's selection of Angelou as a tribute to the poet and her lifelong contribution to civil rights and the arts, Angelou had her own ideas. She told Catherine S. Manegold in an interview for the *New York Times:* "In all my work, what I try to say is that as human beings we are more alike than we are unalike." She added, "It may be that Mr. Clinton asked me to write the inaugural poem because he understood that I am the kind of person who really does bring people together."

During the early 1990s, Angelou wrote more poetry and several books for children. *Now Sheba Sings the Song* is just one poem inspired by the work of artist

Tom Feelings; the lines or phrases are isolated on each page with eighty-four of Tom Feelings' sepia-toned and black-and-white drawings of black women. *I Shall Not Be Moved* is a collection that takes its title from a line in one of the book's poems. *Phenomenal Woman,* a collection of four poems, takes its title from a poem which originally appeared in *Cosmopolitan* magazine in 1978; the narrator of the poem describes the physical and spiritual characteristics and qualities that make her attractive.

Angelou dedicated *Wouldn't Take Nothing for My Journey Now,* a collection of twenty-four short essays, to Oprah Winfrey, the television talk-show host who celebrated Angelou's sixty-fifth birthday with a grand party. The essays in this book contain declarations, complaints, memories, opinions, and advice on subjects ranging from faith to jealousy. Genevieve Stuttaford, writing in *Publishers Weekly,* described the essays as "quietly inspirational pieces." Anne Whitehouse of the *New York Times Book Review* observed that the book would "appeal to readers in search of clear messages with easily digested meanings." Yet not all critics appreciated this collection. Richard Grenier of *National Review* concluded that the book "is of a remarkably coherent tone, being from first page to last of a truly awesome emptiness."

Although Angelou's autobiographies are written, in part, for young people, they are beyond the comprehension of most young children. But with the publication of *Mrs. Flowers: A Moment of Friendship,* children can access one of the stories that Angelou tells in *I Know Why the Caged Bird Sings.* Another book for children, *Life Doesn't Frighten Me,* consists of one poem. Each line or phrase is accompanied by the dynamic, abstract, colorful paintings of the late artist Jean-Michel Basquiat. The poem lists scary things that the narrator should be afraid of, and Basquiat's art illustrates those terrors vividly, but, with the refrain of "They don't frighten me at all," "fear is answered with dancing energy and daring imagination and laughter," Hazel Rochman explained in *Booklist.* "Pairing Angelou's reassuring poem with Basquiat's unsettling, childlike images was a stroke of genius," wrote *Artforum International* contributor Dan Cameron.

In *My Painted House, My Friendly Chicken, and Me,* with photographs by Margaret Courtney-Clarke, a young African girl introduces herself and discusses her life. She tells about her friend, a pet chicken to whom she tells all of her best secrets. She displays her beautiful home, and explains how her mother has carefully painted it. The girl also explains how, although she must go to school wearing uniforms her father has purchased in town, she loves to wear her traditional beads and clothing. She expresses a wish that she and the reader can be friends despite the physical and cultural distance that separates them.

Kofi and His Magic is a second picture book by Angelou and Courtney-Clark which allows young readers to get to know an African child, another culture, and another worldview. Through Angelou's text and Courtney-Clarke's colorful photographs, a West African boy named Kofi shows off his beautiful earth-toned home and tells of his life. Kofi's town, Bonwire, is famous for its Kente cloth production. He explains how, even though he is still quite young, he is a trained weaver of Kente cloth. Then, Kofi takes readers on a journey to visit other nearby towns and people, and finally, to see the ocean (which he initially thinks is a big lake). At the end of the book, after Kofi returns to Bonwire, he reveals why he calls himself a magician. Kofi's magic involves allowing the reader to imagine that she or he can visit Kofi and become his friend: the reader must only close her eyes and open her mind for the magic to work.

As Angelou has been busy furthering her career, critics and scholars have attempted to keep up with her, and to interpret her continuing work. While many critics have pointed out that the message in Angelou's prose is universal, Mary Jane Lupton has called attention to the theme of motherhood in Angelou's work. In five volumes of autobiography, Angelou "moves forward: from being a child, to being a mother; to leaving the child; to having the child, in the fifth volume, achieve his independence." In her interview with George Plimpton in the *Paris Review,* Angelou agreed with him that the love of her child was a "prevailing theme" in her autobiographical work.

Some critics have argued that Angelou's poetry is inferior to her prose. Unlike her autobiographical work, Angelou's poetry has not received much of what William Sylvester of *Contemporary Poets* would call "serious critical attention." In Sylvester's opinion, however, Angelou's poetry is "sassy." When "we hear her poetry, we listen to ourselves." In addition, as Lynn Z. Bloom pointed out in *Dictionary of Literary Biography,* "Angelou's poetry becomes far more interesting when she dramatizes it in her characteristically dynamic stage performances." Colorfully dressed, Angelou usually recites her poems before spellbound crowds.

Angelou takes her writing very seriously. She told Plimpton, "Once I got into it I realized I was following a tradition established by Frederick Douglass—the slave narrative—speaking in the first-person singular talking about the first-person plural, always saying I meaning 'we.' And what a responsibility. Trying to work with that form, the autobiographical mode, to change it, to make it bigger, richer, finer, and more inclusive in the twentieth century has been a great challenge for me."

While many critics have described Angelou's ability to write beautiful prose as a natural talent, Angelou has emphasized that she must work very hard to write the way she does. As she has explained to Plimpton and others, very early each morning she goes to a sparse hotel room to concentrate, to lie on the bed and write. She spends the morning on first draft work, and goes home in the afternoon to shower, cook a beautiful meal, and share it with friends. Later that night, she looks at what she's written, and begins to cut words and make revisions. Critics who suggest writing is easy for her, Angelou explained to Plimpton, "are the ones I want to grab by the throat and wrestle to the floor because it takes me forever to get it [a book] to sing. I work at the language."

BIOGRAPHICAL AND CRITICAL SOURCES:

BOOKS

Angelou, Maya, *Gather Together in My Name,* Random House (New York, NY), 1974.

Angelou, Maya, *Singin' and Swingin' and Gettin' Merry like Christmas,* Random House (New York, NY), 1976.

Angelou, Maya, *The Heart of a Woman,* Random House (New York, NY), 1981.

Angelou, Maya, *All God's Children Need Traveling Shoes,* Random House (New York, NY), 1986.

Angelou, Maya, *I Know Why the Caged Bird Sings,* Bantam (New York, NY), 1993.

Angelou, Maya, *Lessons in Living,* Random House (New York, NY), 1993.

Angelou, Maya, *Even the Stars Look Lonesome,* Random House (New York, NY), 1997.

Angelou, Maya, *A Song Flung up to Heaven,* Random House (New York, NY), 2002.

Bloom, Harold, editor, *Maya Angelou's I Know Why the Caged Bird Sings,* Chelsea House Publishers (New York, NY), 1995.

Braxton, Joanne M., editor, *Maya Angelou's I Know Why the Caged Bird Sings: A Casebook,* Oxford University Press (New York, NY), 1999.

Concise Dictionary of American Literary Biography Supplement: Modern Writers, 1900-1998, Gale (Detroit, MI), 1998.

Contemporary Black Biography, Volume 15, Gale (Detroit, MI), 1997.

Contemporary Heroes and Heroines, Book 1, Gale (Detroit, MI), 1990.

Contemporary Poets, seventh edition, St. James Press (Detroit, MI), 2001.

Contemporary Popular Writers, St. James Press (Detroit, MI), 1997.

Contemporary Southern Writers, St. James Press (Detroit, MI), 1999.

Contemporary Women Poets, St. James Press (Detroit, MI), 1998.

Dictionary of Literary Biography, Volume 38: *Afro-American Writers after 1955: Dramatists and Prose Writers,* Gale (Detroit, MI), 1985.

Encyclopedia of World Biography, second edition, seventeen volumes, Gale (Detroit, MI), 1998.

Evans, Mari, editor, *Black Women Writers (1950-1980): A Critical Evaluation,* Anchor Press-Doubleday (New York, NY), 1984.

Inge, Tonette Bond, editor, *Southern Women Writers: The New Generation,* University of Alabama Press (Tuscaloosa, AL), 1990.

King, Sarah E., *Maya Angelou: Greeting the Morning,* Millbrook Press (Brookfield, CT), 1994.

Kirkpatrick, Patricia, compiler, *Maya Angelou,* Creative Education (Mankato, MN), 2003.

Lisandrelli, Elaine Slivinski, *Maya Angelou: More than a Poet,* Enslow Publishers (Berkeley Heights, NJ), 1996.

Literature and Its Times: Profiles of 300 Notable Literary Works and the Historical Events That Influenced Them, Volume 4: *World War II to the Affluent Fifties (1940s-1950s),* Gale (Detroit, MI), 1997.

Newsmakers 1993, Issue 4, Gale (Detroit, MI), 1993.

Notable Black American Women, Book 1, Gale (Detroit, MI), 1992.

Poetry Criticism, Volume 32, Gale (Detroit, MI), 2001.

St. James Encyclopedia of Popular Culture, five volumes, St. James Press (Detroit, MI), 2000.

St. James Guide to Young Adult Writers, second edition, St. James Press (Detroit, MI), 1999.

Spain, Valerie, *Meet Maya Angelou,* Random House (New York, NY), 1994.

Women Filmmakers and Their Films, St. James Press (Detroit, MI), 1998.

Writers for Young Adults, three volumes, Scribner's (New York, NY), 1997.

PERIODICALS

Artforum International, December, 1993, Dan Cameron, review of *Life Doesn't Frighten Me,* p. 74.

Black American Literature Forum, summer, 1990, Mary Jane Lupton, "Singing the Black Mother: Maya Angelou and Autobiographical Continuity," pp. 257-276.

Black Issues Book Review, March, 2001, Maitefa Angaza, "Maya: A Precious Prism," p. 30; March-April, 2002, Elsie B. Washington, review of *A Song Flung up to Heaven,* pp. 56-57.

Book, March-April, 2002, Beth Kephart, review of *A Song Flung up to Heaven,* p. 72.

Booklist, January 1, 1994, Hazel Rochman, review of *Life Doesn't Frighten Me,* pp. 829-830; October 1, 1994, Hazel Rochman, review of *My Painted House, My Friendly Chicken, and Me,* p. 329; August, 1997, Donna Seaman, review of *Even the Stars Look Lonesome,* p. 1842; January 1, 2002, Gillian Engberg, review of *A Song Flung up to Heaven,* p. 774.

Christian Century, June 19, 2002, Wayne A. Holst, review of *A Song Flung up to Heaven,* pp. 35-36.

Ebony, February, 1999, review of *Down in the Delta,* p. 96.

Essence, December, 1992, Marcia Ann Gillespie, interview with Angelou, pp. 48-52; August, 1998, Lisa Funderberg, interview with Angelou and Congresswoman Eleanor Holmes Norton, pp. 70-76.

Five Owls, September, 1995, p. 2.

Gentlemen's Quarterly, July, 1995, Freda Garmaise, "Maya-ness Is Next to Godlinesss," p. 33.

Herizons, winter, 2003, Heather Marie, review of *A Song Flung Up to Heaven,* pp. 40-41.

Jet, December 21, 1998, review of *Down in the Delta,* p. 58.

Kirkus Reviews, January 1, 2002, review of *A Song Flung up to Heaven,* p. 25.

Kliatt, July, 2002, Janet Julian, review of *Even the Stars Look Lonesome,* p. 58.

Knight Ridder/Tribune News Service, November 5, 1997, Fon Louise Gordon, review of *Even the Stars Look Lonesome,* p. 1105K5928; March 14, 2002, Leigh Dyer, "Shrugging off Criticism, Angelou Relishes Getting Her Words before So Many," p. K0392; April 3, 2002, Cassandra Spratling, "Maya Angelou, Still Rising: Turbulent Times Mark the Celebrated Author's Latest Memoir," p. K7652; April 10, 2002, Sherryl Connelly, "Maya Angelou, a Life Well Chronicled," p. K2443; April 30, 2002, Lamar Wilson, review of *A Song Flung up to Heaven,* p. K4586.

Library Journal, October 1, 1995, p. 102; September 15, 1997, Ann Burns, review of *Even the Stars Look Lonesome,* p. 74; March 15, 2002, Amy Strong, review of *A Song Flung up to Heaven,* pp. 79-80.

Mother Jones, May-June, 1995, Ken Kelley, interview with Angelou, pp. 22-25.

National Post, July 20, 2002, Marcie Good, "Inspiration for Hire: Hallmark Has Hired Poet Maya Angelou," p. SP1.

National Review, November 29, 1993, Richard Grenier, review of *Wouldn't Take Nothing for My Journey Now,* p. 76.

New Republic, May 20, 2002, John McWhorter, review of *A Song Flung up to Heaven,* p. 35.

New York Times, January 20, 1993, Catherine S. Manegold, "A Wordsmith at Her Inaugural Anvil," pp. C1, C8.

New York Times Book Review, June 16, 1974, Annie Gottlieb, review of *Gather Together in My Name;* December 19, 1993, Anne Whitehouse, review of *Wouldn't Take Nothing for My Journey Now,* p. 18; June 5, 1994, p. 48.

Paris Review, fall, 1990, Maya Angelou, and George Plimpton, "The Art of Fiction CXIX: Maya Angelou," pp. 145-167.

People, January 11, 1999, review of *Down in the Delta,* p. 35.

Poetry, August, 1976, Sandra M. Gilbert, review of *Oh Pray My Wings Are Gonna Fit Me Well.*

Publishers Weekly, September 20, 1993, review of *Life Doesn't Frighten Me,* p. 71; September 27, 1993, Genevieve Stuttaford, review of *Wouldn't Take Nothing for My Journey Now,* pp. 53-54; September 12, 1994, review of *My Painted House, My Friendly Chicken, and Me,* p. 91; August 4, 1997, review of *Even the Stars Look Lonesome,* pp. 54-55.

School Library Journal, October, 1987, Joseph Harper, review of *Now Sheba Sings the Song,* p. 146; May, 1995, p. 57; July, 2002, Karen Sokol, review of *A Song Flung up to Heaven,* p. 144.

Smithsonian, April, 2003, Lucinda Moore, interview with Angelou, p. 96.

Southern Literary Journal, fall, 1998, Marion M. Tangum, "Hurston's and Angelou's Visual Art: The Distancing Vision and the Beckoning Gaze," p. 80.

Variety, September 21, 1998, Joe Leydon, review of *Down in the Delta,* p. 110.

ONLINE

Official Maya Angelou Web site, http://www.maya angelou.com (April 24, 2004).*

*   *   *

ANTHONY, Piers 1934-
(Robert Piers, a joint pseudonym)

PERSONAL: Born Piers Anthony Dillingham Jacob, August 6, 1934, in Oxford, England; immigrated to United States, 1940, naturalized U.S. citizen, 1958; son of Alfred Bennis and Norma (Sherlock) Jacob; married Carol Marble, June 23, 1956; children: Penelope Carolyn, Cheryl. *Education:* Goddard College, B.A., 1956; University of South Florida, teaching certificate, 1964. *Politics:* Independent. *Hobbies and other interests:* Tree farming, archery.

ADDRESSES: Home—Inverness, FL. *Office*—c/o Author Mail, Tor Books, 175 Fifth Ave., New York, NY 10010. *E-mail*—PiersAnthony@hipiers.com.

CAREER: Novelist. Electronic Communications, Inc., St. Petersburg, FL, technical writer, 1959-62; freelance writer, 1962-63, 1966—; Admiral Farragut Academy, St. Petersburg, teacher of English, 1965-66. *Military service:* U.S. Army, 1957-59.

MEMBER: Authors Guild, Authors League of America, National Writers Union.

AWARDS, HONORS: Science fiction award, Pyramid Books/*Magazine of Fantasy and Science Fiction*/Kent Productions, 1967, for *Sos the Rope;* British Fantasy Award, 1977, for *A Spell for Chameleon.*

Piers Anthony

WRITINGS:

SCIENCE FICTION

Chthon, Ballantine (New York, NY), 1967.

(With Robert E. Margroff) *The Ring,* Ace Books (New York, NY), 1968.

Macroscope, Avon (New York, NY), 1969.

(With Robert E. Margroff) *The E.S.P. Worm,* Paperback Library (New York, NY), 1970.

Prostho Plus, Berkley Publishing (New York, NY), 1973.

Race against Time, Hawthorne (New York, NY), 1973.

Rings of Ice, Avon (New York, NY), 1974.

Triple Detente, DAW Books (New York, NY), 1974.

Phthor (sequel to *Chthon*), Berkley Publishing (New York, NY), 1975.

(With Robert Coulson) *But What of Earth?,* Laser (Toronto, Ontario, Canada), 1976, corrected edition, Tor Books (New York, NY), 1989.

(With Frances T. Hall) *The Pretender,* Borgo Press (San Bernadino, CA), 1979.

Mute, Avon (New York, NY), 1981.

Ghost, Tor Books (New York, NY), 1986.
Shade of the Tree, Tor Books (New York, NY), 1986.
(Editor with Barry Malzberg, Martin Greenberg, and Charles G. Waugh) *Uncollected Stars* (short stories), Avon (New York, NY), 1986.
Total Recall, Morrow (New York, NY), 1989.
Balook, illustrated by Patrick Woodroffe, Underwood-Miller (Novato, CA), 1990.
Hard Sell, Tafford (Houston, TX), 1990.
(With Roberto Fuentes) *Dead Morn,* Tafford (Houston, TX), 1990.
MerCycle, illustrated by Ron Lindahn, Tafford (Houston, TX), 1991.
(With Philip José Farmer) *Caterpillar's Question,* Ace Books (New York, NY), 1992.
Killobyte, Putnam (New York, NY), 1993.
The Willing Spirit, Tor Books (New York, NY), 1996.
Volk Internet 1996, Xlibris (Philadelphia, PA), 1997.
(With Clifford Pickover) *Spider Legs,* Tor Books (New York, NY), 1998.
(With J. R. Goolsby and Alan Riggs) *Quest for the Fallen Star,* Tor Books (New York, NY), 1998.
(With Julie Brady) *Dream a Little Dream,* Tor Books (New York, NY), 1999.
(With Jo An Taeusch) *The Secret of Spring,* Tor Books (New York, NY), 2000.
(With Ron Leming) *The Gutbucket Quest,* Tor Books (New York, NY), 2000.
Realty Check, Xlibris (Philadelphia, PA), 2000.

"OMNIVORE" SERIES; NOVELS

Omnivore, Ballantine (New York, NY), 1968, reprinted, Mundania Press (Cincinnati, OH), 2004.
Orn, Avon (New York, NY), 1971.
Ox, Avon (New York, NY), 1976.

"BATTLE CIRCLE" SERIES; NOVELS

Sos the Rope, Pyramid (New York, NY), 1968.
Var the Stick, Faber (London, England), 1972.
Neq the Sword, Corgi (London, England), 1975.
Battle Circle (contains *Sos the Rope, Var the Stick,* and *Neq the Sword*), Avon (New York, NY), 1978.

"CLUSTER" SERIES; NOVELS

Cluster, Avon (New York, NY), 1977, published as *Vicinity Cluster,* Panther (London, England), 1979.
Chaining the Lady, Avon (New York, NY), 1978.

Kirlian Quest, Avon (New York, NY), 1978.
Thousandstar, Avon (New York, NY), 1980.
Viscous Circle, Avon (New York, NY), 1982.

"TAROT" TRILOGY

God of Tarot, Jove (New York, NY), 1979.
Vision of Tarot, Berkley Publishing (New York, NY), 1980.
Faith of Tarot, Berkley Publishing (New York, NY), 1980.
Tarot (contains *God of Tarot, Vision of Tarot,* and *Faith of Tarot*), Ace Books (New York, NY), 1988.

"BIO OF A SPACE TYRANT" SERIES; NOVELS

Refugee, Avon (New York, NY), 1983.
Mercenary, Avon (New York, NY), 1984.
Politician, Avon (New York, NY), 1985.
Executive, Avon (New York, NY), 1985.
Statesman, Avon (New York, NY), 1986.

FANTASY NOVELS

Hasan, Borgo Press (San Bernardino, CA), 1977.
(With Robert Kornwise) *Through the Ice,* illustrated by D. Horne, Underwood-Miller (Novato, CA), 1989.
(With Mercedes Lackey) *If I Pay Thee Not in Gold,* Baen (New York, NY), 1993.

"MAGIC OF XANTH" SERIES; FANTASY NOVELS

A Spell for Chameleon, Del Rey (New York, NY), 1977.
The Source of Magic, Del Rey (New York, NY), 1979.
Castle Roogna, Del Rey (New York, NY), 1979.
The Magic of Xanth (contains *A Spell for Chameleon, The Source of Magic,* and *Castle Roogna*), Doubleday (New York, NY), 1981, published as *Piers Anthony: Three Complete Xanth Novels,* Wings Books (New York, NY), 1994.
Centaur Aisle, Del Rey (New York, NY), 1982.
Ogre, Ogre, Del Rey (New York, NY), 1982.
Night Mare, Del Rey (New York, NY), 1983.
Dragon on a Pedestal, Del Rey (New York, NY), 1983.

Crewel Lye: A Caustic Yarn, Del Rey (New York, NY), 1985.

Golem in the Gears, Del Rey (New York, NY), 1986.

Vale of the Vole, Avon (New York, NY), 1987.

Heaven Cent, Avon (New York, NY), 1988.

Man from Mundania, Avon (New York, NY), 1989.

(With Jody Lynn Nye) *Piers Anthony's Visual Guide to Xanth,* illustrated by Todd Cameron Hamilton and James Clouse, Avon (New York, NY), 1989.

Isle of View, Morrow (New York, NY), 1990.

Question Quest, Morrow (New York, NY), 1991.

The Color of Her Panties, Avon (New York, NY), 1992.

Demons Don't Dream, Tor Books (New York, NY), 1993.

Harpy Thyme, Tor Books (New York, NY), 1994.

Geis of the Gargoyle, Tor Books (New York, NY), 1995.

Roc and a Hard Place, Tor Books (New York, NY), 1995.

Yon Ill Wind, Tor Books (New York, NY), 1996.

Faun and Games, Tor Books (New York, NY), 1997.

Zombie Lover, Tor Books (New York, NY), 1998.

Xone of Contention, Tor Books (New York, NY), 1999.

The Dastard, Tor Books (New York, NY), 2000.

Swell Foop, Tor Books (New York, NY), 2001.

Up in a Heaval, Tor Books (New York, NY), 2001.

Cube Route, Tor Books (New York, NY), 2003.

Currant Events, Tor Books (New York, NY), 2004.

"INCARNATIONS OF IMMORTALITY" SERIES; FANTASY NOVELS

On a Pale Horse, Del Rey (New York, NY), 1983.

Bearing an Hourglass, Del Rey (New York, NY), 1984.

With a Tangled Skein, Del Rey (New York, NY), 1985.

Wielding a Red Sword, Del Rey (New York, NY), 1986.

Being a Green Mother, Del Rey (New York, NY), 1987.

For Love of Evil, Morrow (New York, NY), 1988.

And Eternity, Morrow (New York, NY), 1990.

"DRAGON'S GOLD" SERIES; FANTASY NOVELS

(With Robert E. Margroff) *Dragon's Gold,* Tor Books (New York, NY), 1987.

(With Robert E. Margroff) *Serpent's Silver,* Tor Books (New York, NY), 1988.

(With Robert E. Margroff) *Chimaera's Copper,* Tor Books (New York, NY), 1990.

(With Robert E. Margroff) *Orc's Opal,* Tor Books (New York, NY), 1990.

(With Robert E. Margroff) *Mouvar's Magic,* Tor Books (New York, NY), 1992.

(With Robert E. Margroff) *Three Complete Novels* (contains *Dragon's Gold, Serpent's Silver,* and *Chimaera's Copper*), Wings Books (New York, NY), 1993.

"APPRENTICE ADEPT" SERIES; SCIENCE-FICTION/FANTASY NOVELS

Split Infinity, Del Rey (New York, NY), 1980.

Blue Adept, Del Rey (New York, NY), 1981.

Juxtaposition, Del Rey (New York, NY), 1982.

Double Exposure (contains *Split Infinity, Blue Adept,* and *Juxtaposition*), Doubleday (New York, NY), 1982.

Out of Phaze, Ace Books (New York, NY), 1987.

Robot Adept, Ace Books (New York, NY), 1988.

Unicorn Point, Ace Books (New York, NY), 1989.

Phaze Doubt, Ace Books (New York, NY), 1990.

"MODE" SERIES; SCIENCE FICTION/FANTASY NOVELS

Virtual Mode, Putnam (New York, NY), 1991.

Fractal Mode, Putnam (New York, NY), 1992.

Chaos Mode, Putnam (New York, NY), 1993.

DoOon Mode, Tor Books (New York, NY), 2001.

"CHROMAGIC" SERIES; NOVELS

Key to Havoc, Mundania Press (Cincinnati, OH), 2003.

Key to Chroma, Mundania Press (Cincinnati, OH), 2003.

Key to Destiny, Mundania Press (Cincinnati, OH), 2004.

"JASON STRIKER" SERIES; MARTIAL ARTS NOVELS

(With Roberto Fuentes) *Kiai!,* Berkley Publishing (New York, NY), 1974.

(With Roberto Fuentes) *Mistress of Death,* Berkley Publishing (New York, NY), 1974.

(With Roberto Fuentes) *The Bamboo Bloodbath,* Berkley Publishing (New York, NY), 1974.
(With Roberto Fuentes) *Ninja's Revenge,* Berkley Publishing (New York, NY), 1975.
(With Roberto Fuentes) *Amazon Slaughter,* Berkley Publishing (New York, NY), 1976.

"GEODYSSEY" SERIES; HISTORICAL SCIENCE FICTION

Isle of Woman, Tor Books (New York, NY), 1993.
Shame of Man, Tor Books (New York, NY), 1994.
Hope of Earth, Tor Books (New York, NY), 1997.
Muse of Art, Tor Books (New York, NY), 1999.

OTHER

Steppe (science fiction/history), Millington (London, England), 1976, Tor Books (New York, NY), 1985.
Anthonology (short stories), Tor Books (New York, NY), 1985.
Bio of an Ogre: The Autobiography of Piers Anthony to Age Fifty, Ace Books (New York, NY), 1988.
Pornucopia (erotic fantasy), Tafford (Houston, TX), 1989.
Firefly (novel), Morrow (New York, NY), 1990.
Tatham Mound (historical fiction), Morrow (New York, NY), 1991.
Alien Plot (short stories), Tor Books (New York, NY), 1992.
Letters to Jenny (nonfiction), Tor Books (New York, NY), 1993.
(Editor with Richard Gilliam) *Tales from the Great Turtle,* Tor Books (New York, NY), 1994.
How Precious Was That While: An Autobiography, Tor Books (New York, NY), 2001.
The Magic Fart (erotica), Mundania Books (Cincinnati, OH), 2003.

Also author of novel *The Unstilled World.* Contributor to *Science against Man,* edited by Anthony Cheetham, Avon (New York, NY), 1970; *Nova One: An Anthology of Original Science Fiction,* edited by Harry Harrison, Delacorte Press (New York, NY), 1970; *Again, Dangerous Visions,* edited by Harlan Ellison, Doubleday (New York, NY), 1972; *Generation,* edited by David Gerrold, Dell (New York, NY), 1972; and *The Berkley Showcase,* edited by Victoria Schochet and John Silbersack, Berkley Publishing (New York, NY), 1981. Also contributor, with Robert E. Margroff under joint pseudonym Robert Piers, of a short story to *Adam Bedside Reader.* Contributor of short stories to periodicals, including *Analog, Fantastic, Worlds of If, Worlds of Tomorrow, Amazing, Magazine of Fantasy and Science Fiction, SF Age, Vegetarian Times, Twilight Zone, Books and Bookmen, Writer, Gauntlet, Chic, Far Point, Starburst, Vertex,* and *Pandora.*

ADAPTATIONS: Macroscope, A Spell for Chameleon, The Source of Magic, Castle Roogna, Through the Ice, Chaos Mode, Virtual Mode, and *Fractal Mode* have been adapted to audio cassette.

WORK IN PROGRESS: Pet Peeve, a novel in the "Magic of Xanth" series, to be published by Tor Books, 2005; other novels in the "Magic of Xanth" series; *Climate of Change,* a novel in the "Geodyssey" series.

SIDELIGHTS: Prolific author Piers Anthony is widely known in the science-fiction and fantasy genres for his many popular series—including the ongoing "Magic of Xanth" novels—and his various novels and collections; he has published more than one hundred books since 1967. "I am an SF writer today," he told Cliff Biggers in a *Science Fiction* interview, "because without SF and writing I would be nothing at all today."

Within a childhood affected by illness and isolation, Anthony escaped by immersing himself in books. "From the time I was 13, I had been hooked on science fiction," Anthony recalled in an interview with the *Science Fiction Radio Show (SFRS)* published in *The Sound of Wonder.* "It's what I did for entertainment. It was a whole different world, multiple worlds, each one of them better than the one I knew. And so when I thought about writing [science fiction], I thought I could be original because I had read everything in the field."

Among the traumatic events of Anthony's youth were his family's moves to Spain when he was five and to the United States the following year, the loss of his cousin to cancer at age fifteen, and his parents' divorce when he was eighteen. As members of the Quaker faith, his parents were involved with the British Friends Service Committee during the Spanish Civil War, and Anthony spent the first years of his life in

England under the care of his grandparents and a nanny. When he and his sister joined his parents after the war, they "seemed like acquaintances rather than close kin," the author recounted in an essay for *Something about the Author Autobiography Series* (*SAAS*). The family soon moved to the United States, where Anthony found it difficult to fit in. He often had to deal with bullies at school, and this compounded the alienation he suffered because of his parents' divorce. "The dominant emotion of my later childhood was fear," he recalled in his essay. "Fear of bigger kids at school, of a monster in the forest, and fear of the corpse. Fear, really, of life. I hated being alone, but others neither understood nor cared, so I was alone a lot. That is, often physically, and almost always emotionally. Today when I get a letter from a reader who feels almost utterly alone, I understand, because I remember."

In addition, the young Anthony had difficulty at school. "Everyone in my immediate family was academically gifted except me," he explained in *SAAS*. "I was the dunce who made up for it all, pulling the average down." It wasn't until he was an adult that he discovered his academic problems had been due to some type of learning disability. "In my day things like learning disabilities or dyslexia didn't exist, just stupid or careless children," he wrote. Nevertheless, encouraged by his parents, who read and told stories to him, Anthony became a regular reader. "I think that nightly reading, and the daytime storytelling when we worked together outside, was the most important influence on my eventual choice of career. I knew that books contained fascinating adventures, and those stories took me away from my dreary real life," he recalled.

Anthony began to write at age twenty, deciding in college to make writing his career. He told Holly Atkins of the *St. Petersburg Times,* "I did not know I wanted to be a writer until I needed to decide on my college major. I thought about it overnight and realized that writing was it. From that point my ambition never changed, though for several years I had to take mundane jobs to support my family. Finally my wife went to work, so that I could stay home and write full time; that's when I started selling stories, and later novels. Now I write all the time that is available." After eight years of submitting stories to magazines, Anthony sold his first piece, "Possible to Rue," to *Fantastic* in 1962. In the next several years he worked

variously as a freelance writer and English teacher, but finally decided to devote all of his time to writing. His first published novel, *Chthon,* came out in 1967. It received numerous award nominations and caught the attention of both critics and readers in the science fiction genre.

The novel traces the escape efforts of Aton Five, a man imprisoned on the planet Chthon and forced to work in its garnet mines. A *Publishers Weekly* reviewer commented that Anthony has combined language, myth, suspense, and symbolism to create "a bursting package, almost too much for one book, but literate, original and entertaining." Those elements—and Anthony's liberal use of them—would become his trademark. In a detailed analysis of *Chthon* and its sequel, *Phthor,* in his study *Piers Anthony,* Michael R. Collings noted Anthony's many references to mythological symbols. Literary references are present as well, exemplified by the resemblance of the prison caverns of Chthon to Dante's depiction of Hell in *The Inferno.* To *Books and Bookmen* contributor Leo Harris, in *Chthon,* "Anthony has created a whole new world, a dream universe which you find yourself living in and, after a while, understanding. Very poetic and tough and allegorical it all is, and it will rapidly have thee in thrall." While *Chthon* focuses on Aton's life, *Phthor* follows Aton's son, Arlo, who symbolizes Thor of Norse mythology. "The mythologies embedded in *Chthon* and *Phthor* go far beyond mere ornamentation or surface symbolism," Collings related. "They define the thematic content of the novels. Initially, there is a clear demarcation between myth and reality. Yet early in *Chthon* Anthony throws that clear demarcation into question."

Anthony won a prize in a contest jointly sponsored by Pyramid Books, Kent Productions, and the *Magazine of Fantasy and Science Fiction* for *Sos the Rope,* the first entry in the "Battle Circle" series, which is Anthony's first trilogy. *Sos the Rope* is based on a chapter of his 1956 B.A. thesis novel titled "The Unstilled World." The titles of *Sos the Rope* and the other installments in the series are characters' names; the trilogy's warriors are named after their weapons. The first novel explores the efforts of a group of radiation survivors led by Sos as they attempt to rebuild their society after the Blast. Yet the resulting Empire soon becomes a malevolent force and Sos sets out to destroy it. The novel speaks against the dangers of centralized civilization and overpopulation: millions of shrews, like the Biblical plague of locusts, invade the area and consume every living creature within their reach. Eventually the horde destroys itself with its enormity and its wholesale pillaging. The shrews' rampage and ultimate demise serve as a metaphor for humanity's overcrowding and abuse of the environment. Humankind, like the shrews, will be decimated when it outgrows the Earth's ability to sustain it. In *Var the Stick* and *Neq the Sword,* the "Battle Circle" story is completed. Collings observed similarities to the epic works of Homer, Virgil, and John Milton in "Battle Circle," which "investigates the viability of three fundamental forms of epic: the Achilean epic of martial prowess; the Odyssean epic of wandering; and the Virgillian/Miltonic epic of self-sacrifice and restoration."

The "Omnivore" trilogy provided a forum for Anthony to further his exploration of the dangers humankind continues to inflict upon itself, and introduced his support of vegetarianism. "Like 'Battle Circle,' *Chthon,* and *Phthor,*" Collings observed, "'Omnivore' deals with control—specifically, with controlling the most dangerous omnivore of all, man." Three interplanetary explorers, the herbivorous Veg, carnivorous Cal, and omnivorous Aquilon, play out Anthony's views. The three journey to the planet Nacre, reporting back to investigator Subble and subsequently revealing to readers their adventures and clues to the secret threatening to destroy Earth. In the sequel, *Orn,* the three explorers venture to the planet Paleo, which resembles the Earth of sixty-five million years past, and encounter Orn, a creature whose racial memory endows it with the knowledge of its ancestors and enables it to survive the changes bombarding its planet. In *Ox,* the final volume of the trilogy, Veg, Cal, and Aquilon gradually uncover the existence of a sentient supercomputer while exploring alternative worlds. As with Anthony's other books, reviewers noted that the "Omnivore" volumes contain substantial discussions of technical and scientific issues. A *Publishers Weekly* reviewer described *Ox* as "a book for readers willing to put a lot of concentration into reading it."

The similarly challenging *Macroscope,* described by Collings as "one of Anthony's most ambitious and complex novels," seeks to place humanity in its proper context within the galaxy. The book enhanced Anthony's reputation but, due to a publisher's error, was not submitted for consideration for the important Nebula Award and lost one crucial source of publicity. Nevertheless, *Macroscope* was a milestone in Anthony's career. In a *Luna Monthly* review, Samuel Mines observed, "*Macroscope* recaptures the tremen-

dous glamour and excitement of science fiction, pounding the reader into submission with the sheer weight of its ideas which seem to pour out in an inexhaustible flood."

Beginning with the "Cluster" series, Anthony began expanding beyond trilogies. "Cluster" became a series of five novels, while "Magic of Xanth" has grown to about thirty titles and been supplemented by the companion book *Piers Anthony's Visual Guide to Xanth.* "Magic of Xanth" and the "Apprentice Adept" series, which had seven entries published between 1980 and 1990, were originally planned as trilogies. In the case of the "Xanth" books, Anthony attributes his decision to continue the series to reader response. "We did a third [Xanth novel], and said, 'Let's wrap it up as a trilogy and not do any more,'" Anthony remarked to *SFRS.* "Then the readers started demanding more, and more, and more, and finally both the publisher and the author were convinced. It's hard to say 'No' when the readers are begging for more."

A Spell for Chameleon, the first of the "Xanth" books, marked Anthony's branching-out from science fiction into fantasy. Although one early work, *Hasan,* was fantasy, it was *Chameleon,* his second fantasy novel, that established Anthony in the genre. The switch to fantasy came as a result of Anthony's much-publicized split with his first publisher, Ballantine Books. The author told *SFRS,* Ballantine "was sending me statements-of-account that were simply not true. I sent a letter demanding a correct statement and correct payments. Rather than do that, they blacklisted me for six years." Anthony moved to Avon Books; six years later, with a new administration at Ballantine, he found himself invited back and wanted to give Ballantine another chance. His contract at Avon, however, prohibited him from writing science fiction for another publisher, so he decided to try fantasy. Anthony knew and liked the fantasy editor at Ballantine, Lester del Rey; Ballantine's Del Rey imprint went on to publish the first nine "Xanth" novels as well as the early "Apprentice Adept" and "Incarnations of Immortality" entries. Anthony differentiates between his science fiction and fantasy works in their content as well as their popularity. "For the challenge and sheer joy of getting in and tackling a difficult problem and surmounting it, science fiction is better," Anthony explained to *SFRS.* "But if I need money, fantasy is better." He later added, "I talk about writing fantasy in the sense of doing it for the money, but I also enjoy it. If I didn't enjoy it, I wouldn't do it for the money."

The "Xanth" series was still continuing over two decades after its first book appeared. The novels in the series are generally less complex and easier to read than Anthony's earlier works, and they appeal to younger readers as well as adults. *A Spell for Chameleon,* a 1978 Hugo Award nominee, introduces Bink, who tackles another recurring topic in Anthony's novels: maturity and control. The first "Xanth" installment chronicles Bink's growing-up; his son, Dor, and subsequent generations of the family feature in later books. The land of Xanth closely resembles Anthony's long-time home state of Florida in size and shape, and its place names are often wittily twisted versions of Floridian ones. In Xanth, everyone and everything—even a rock or tree—has a magical talent, except Bink. *Chameleon* follows Bink on his quest to discover his talent or face exile to the boring, powerless land of Mundania. In the process, Bink gains not only knowledge of his talent but emotional maturity as well. Bink sets out on another adventure in *The Source of Magic,* in which he is assigned to discover the source of all magic in Xanth. In *Castle Roogna,* Bink's son Dor travels 800 years back in time to rescue his nurse's boyfriend. Throughout each book, Bink and Dor encounter innumerable illusions and feats of magic. "Anthony apparently decided to invest his magical land of Xanth with every fantastical conception ever invented," a reviewer for *Isaac Asimov's Science Fiction Magazine* remarked. "It has quests, enchanted castles, riddles, unicorns, griffins, mermaids, giants (not to mention invisible giants), zombies, ghosts, elves, magicians, man-eating trees, enchantresses, and a host of inventions from Anthony's own fertile mind."

"The Magic of Xanth" continues with *Centaur Aisle, Ogre, Ogre,* and *Night Mare,* the next "trilogy" of "Xanth" books. The first of these finds Dor filling in for Xanth's King Trent while he and Queen Iris take a trip to Mundania, a good experience for Dor since he will one day become king. When the king and queen fail to return, Dor sets out on another adventure. Anthony once again explores the process of maturing, as Dor leads a search party through Xanth and into Mundania, and falls in love with Princess Irene. In *Ogre, Ogre* the half-human, half-ogre Smash must protect the half-human, half-nymph Tandy. A stupid, insensitive creature at the beginning of the tale, Smash gradually acquires more human traits until he finally realizes that he is in love with Tandy.

Other entries in the series further develop Anthony's portrait of the fantastic land of Xanth, with storylines including the rescue of the kingdom by a creature responsible for delivering bad dreams (*Night Mare*), the adventures of three-year-old Princess Ivy, lost and wandering in the forest with newfound friends Hugo and the Gap Dragon (*Dragon on a Pedestal*), the diminutive Golem's quest to rescue a lost baby dragon and prove himself worthy of attention (*Golem in the Gears*), Prince Dolph's protest against the Adult Conspiracy that keeps children ignorant of adult matters (*Heaven Cent*), Princess Ivy's trip to Mundania in search of Good Magician Humfrey (*Man from Mundania*), and the search of Gloha, Xanth's only half-harpy/half-goblin, for advice from Magician Trent to further a quest for her true love (*Harpy Thyme*). In the opinion of *Fantasy Review* contributor Richard Mathews, the "Xanth" series "ranks with the best of American and classic fantasy literature."

Anthony's use of puns and other language tricks is a hallmark of the "Xanth" novels. "In Xanth," Collings noted, Anthony "incorporates much of this interest in language in furthering the plot and in establishing the essence of his fantasy universe. In Xanth, language is literal, especially what in Mundania would be called metaphors." As a result, the critic continued, "breadfruit bears loaves of bread; shoetrees bear shoes in varying sizes and styles; nickelpedes are like centipedes, only five times larger and more vicious; and sunflowers are flowers whose blossoms are tiny suns blazing at the top of the stalk—a potent weapon if an enemy looks directly at them." In a *Voice of Youth Advocates* review of *Ogre, Ogre,* Peggy Murray observed that the "sophomoric humor and bad puns" in Anthony's stories "have tremendous appeal with YA fantasy readers." In fact, Anthony's readers sent him some of the puns used in *Harpy Thyme. Sarasota Herald Tribune* writer Cindy Cannon commented of Anthony's "Xanth" wordplay, "Where else will you hit an imp ass, eat pun-kin pies, see a river bank lien or meet a character named Ann Arky?" She summed up the series by saying, "I can't think of a better place to meet up with centaurs, merfolk, zombies, ghosts, magically-talented humans and assorted half-breeds of every shape and kind than in one of Piers Anthony's many Xanth novels."

Cluster, the first novel in the series of the same name, was published in the same year as the first "Xanth" book. Intergalactic travel and adventure are the subjects of the "Cluster" books, in which Anthony introduces the concept of Kirlian transfer, a type of out-of-body travel that requires much less energy than the outmoded "mattermission." The Kirlian transfer and other innovations are fundamental to the outcomes of the First and Second Wars of Energy, described in the first two "Cluster" volumes, and to the battle of an intergalactic force against the space amoeba in *Kirlian Quest.* "More than anything, the Cluster series is an exercise in enjoyment" for Anthony, Collings remarked. The author apparently relishes the opportunity to create bizarre beings and situations unlike any the reader has experienced.

The original "Cluster" trilogy led to *Tarot,* published in three volumes as *God of Tarot, Vision of Tarot,* and *Faith of Tarot.* In fact, Anthony originally wrote *Tarot* as the ending to *Kirlian Quest* and intended that the two be published as one volume. Anthony emphasized in his interview with *SFRS* that *Tarot* is not a trilogy, but "a quarter-million-word novel." The novel was published not only in three parts, but in two different years. "It bothered me because I feel that this is the major novel of my career," Anthony remarked in *SFRS.* "Split into three parts and published in two years—it washed me out totally. I had no chance to make a run for any awards or anything like that. It was simply gone." He resents referrals to the book as a trilogy because this term implies that each volume is a full novel, when in fact each is one-third of a novel. Brother Paul, a character introduced in the "Cluster" trilogy and featured in *But What of Earth?,* is the central figure in *Tarot,* in which Anthony attempts to develop a definition of God. Collings acknowledged that the "brutality, horror, and disgust" present in the book, while expressed in many other Anthony novels, are combined in *Tarot* with religious references, a controversial strategy that offended some readers. *Tarot* "is certainly not for the squeamish, nor is it altogether for those who enjoyed the first installment of Tarot civilization in the Cluster novels. Anthony himself admits this," Collings noted.

Anthony returned to pure fantasy in the "Incarnations of Immortality" series, which begins with *On a Pale Horse* and is set in "a world very much like ours, except that magic has been systematized and is as influential as science," a *Publishers Weekly* reviewer related. The abstract concepts of Time, War, Nature, Fate, and Death are all real people—the Incarnations—and all are involved in the battle of Satan against God. Diana Pharaoh Francis, a contributor to *Contemporary Popular Writers,* observed that *On a Pale Horse* "may

be the best of Anthony's fantasy novels. . . . The characterization and dramatization are superbly handled and engage the reader. Besides clever social commentary, it provides a good read." In *Bearing an Hourglass,* a grief-stricken man agrees to take on the role of Chronos, the Incarnation of Time, and soon finds himself locked in a battle with Satan. *Booklist* reviewer Roland Green commented that "even people who may disagree with [Anthony's] ideas will recognize" that the religious and ethical aspects of the series are "intelligently rendered." Subsequent volumes feature the Incarnations of Fate (*With a Tangled Skein*), War (*Wielding a Red Sword*), Nature (*Being a Green Mother*), Evil (*For Love of Evil*), and finally, Good (*And Eternity*). "This grand finale showcases Anthony's multiple strengths" including his humor, characterizations, and themes, a *Library Journal* reviewer concluded.

Virtual Mode is a novel "to which teens relate well," Anthony remarked. Published in 1991, *Virtual Mode* introduces the "Mode" series, in which characters traverse the universe through the use of "skew paths" anchored by other people. As the anchors change, the paths and destinies of the travelers are affected and new stories are presented. In *Virtual Mode,* Darius of Hlahtar ventures to Earth to bring the girl he loves, the suicidal Colene, back to his universe. Together Darius and Colene discover that they must build a skew path to complete the journey. *Publishers Weekly* writer Sybil Steinberg described Colene as "a clearly defined character, virtues, flaws and all" who is "brought fully to life in this skillful, enjoyable book."

Another work with appeal to teen readers is *MerCycle,* Anthony's story about five people recruited to pedal bicycles under the waters of the Gulf of Mexico on a secret mission to save the Earth from collision with a meteor. The novel was originally written in 1971 but then shelved after Anthony was unable to find a publisher for it. After he was established as a bestselling author, Anthony returned to the manuscript and revised it extensively. The story deals heavily with themes of human nature and survival: the bicyclists experience being "out of phase" and "phased in" to other Earth life, are kept unaware of their mission, and meet up with Chinese mermaids. "The result," reported a *New York Times Book Review* critic, "is an engaging tall tale, spun out of the most unpromising raw material." Also of interest to youths is *Tatham Mound.* The story of fifteen-year-old Throat Shot, a sixteenth-century native of the land that would eventually become the state of Florida, *Tatham Mound* is based on an actual Indian burial mound discovered in north Florida and features historically accurate reconstructions of Spanish explorer Hernando de Soto's march across the region and his battles with the Indian tribes of the area. A *Library Journal* reviewer found *Tatham Mound* a "heartfelt tribute to a lost culture" and a "labor of both love and talent."

Likewise based on history, but spanning eight million years, are the works in the "Geodyssey" series. *Isle of Woman* is made up of a series of vignettes that center on two prehistoric families who are reborn into succeeding centuries up to twenty-first-century America. *Library Journal* contributor Jackie Cassada called *Isle of Woman* Anthony's "most ambitious project to date." *Shame of Man* explores evolution one generation at a time, beginning with families of gorillas and chimpanzees on through the species of homo sapiens that has evolved by 2050 A.D. Called "speculative fiction" by *Voice of Youth Advocates* reviewer Kim Carter, *Shame of Man* encompasses more than twenty-five years of Anthony's research in "history, archaeology, anthropology, and human nature," as well as showcasing some of the author's personal theories on these subjects.

Virtual Mode, Tatham Mound, and *Shame of Man* exemplify Anthony's desire to produce works of lasting value along with those written simply for entertainment. While he wants readers to enjoy his work, the author hopes also to provoke contemplation of the serious issues he presents. "I'd like to think I'm on Earth for some purpose other than just to feed my face," Anthony remarked to *SFRS.* "I want to do something and try to leave the universe a better place than it was when I came into it."

In *How Precious Was That While,* a sequel to his earlier volume of autobiography, *Bio of an Ogre,* Anthony "tacitly and emphatically acknowledges that his readers mean more to him than critics, publishers or editors," according to a *Publishers Weekly* reviewer. He is devoted to his many readers, and often spends two days a week answering their letters. The book also contains many of Anthony's strong opinions, including his continuing distrust and dislike of Dallas, Texas, because President John F. Kennedy was assassinated there. Anthony also takes on publishing executives with whom he has had disagreements over the years. *Booklist*'s Roland Green called the autobiography "a frank, eye-opening memoir."

Evaluating Anthony's career in the *St. James Guide to Fantasy Writers,* Andy Sawyer drew attention to the author's loyalty to his fans, remarking that Anthony's "large body of fantasy is viewed (together with his growing propensity for 'series' novels) as a surrender to commercial pressures and fashionable trends. To some extent this may be so, although this judgment would neglect the part played by Anthony's own writings in creating the market for a particular form of fantasy. In fact, he has created a fiercely loyal readership (whom he frequently addresses directly in lengthy afterwords to his novels) and much of this loyalty is due to his provision of a type of escapism which embodies an easily grasped symbolism." Writing in *Twentieth-Century Young Adult Writers,* Lesa Dill concluded: "While entertaining his readers with his inventive word play, numerous literary allusions, apt symbolism, humorous satire, and wild adventures, Anthony effectively conveys his personal convictions about man's responsibilities in and to the universe."

BIOGRAPHICAL AND CRITICAL SOURCES:

BOOKS

Collings, Michael R., *Piers Anthony,* Starmont House (Mercer Island, WA), 1983.
Contemporary Literary Criticism, Volume 35, Gale (Detroit, MI), 1985, pp. 34-41.
Contemporary Popular Writers, St. James Press (Detroit, MI), 1997.
Lane, Daryl, William Vernon, and David Carson, *The Sound of Wonder: Interviews from "The Science Fiction Radio Show,"* Volume 2, Oryx (Phoenix, AZ), 1985.
St. James Guide to Fantasy Writers, St. James Press (Detroit, MI), 1996.
St. James Guide to Science Fiction Writers, 4th edition, St. James Press (Detroit, MI), 1996.
Something about the Author Autobiography Series, Volume 22, Gale (Detroit, MI), 1996.
Twentieth-Century Young Adult Writers, St. James Press (Detroit, MI), 1994.

PERIODICALS

Analog, January, 1989, p. 182; August, 1992, pp. 165-166.
Booklist, July, 1984, p. 1497; May 1, 1999, Patricia Monaghan, review of *Muse of Art,* p. 1582; October 15, 1999, Roland Green, review of *Xone*

of Contention, p. 424; April 15, 2000, Ray Olson, review of *The Gutbucket Quest,* p. 1527; October 15, 2000, Roland Green, review of *The Dastard,* p. 426; March 1, 2001, Roland Green, review of *DoOon Mode,* p. 1232; September 1, 2001, Roland Green, review of *How Precious Was That While,* p. 42; October 1, 2001, Roland Green, review of *Swell Foop,* p. 304.

Books and Bookmen, April, 1970, pp. 26-27.

Computimes (Malaysia), May 3, 2001, "An Old Sci-Fi Book with Foresight."

Fantasy and Science Fiction, August, 1986, pp. 37-40.

Fantasy Review, March, 1984, pp. 24-25.

Horn Book, October 6, 1989, p. 84.

Isaac Asimov's Science Fiction Magazine, September, 1979, p. 18.

Kirkus Reviews, August 15, 1993, p. 1034; August 1, 2001, review of *Swell Foop,* p. 1075.

Kliatt, November, 1992, p. 13.

Library Journal, December, 1989, p. 176; August, 1991, p. 150; September 15, 1993, p. 108; October 15, 1998, p. 104; January, 1999, p. 166; October 15, 1999, Jackie Cassada, review of *Xone of Contention,* p. 111; May 15, 2000, Jackie Cassada, review of *The Gutbucket Quest,* p. 129; October 15, 2000, Jackie Cassada, review of *The Dastard,* p. 108; April 15, 2001, Jackie Cassada, review of *DoOon Mode,* p. 137; November 15, 2002, Jackie Cassada, review of *Up in a Heaval,* p. 106.

Luna Monthly, September, 1970, p. 22.

New York Times Book Review, April 20, 1986, p. 27; September 13, 1992, p. 28.

Publishers Weekly, June 5, 1967, p. 180; July 26, 1976, p. 78; September 2, 1983, p. 72; July 25, 1986, p. 174; August 29, 1986, p. 388; May 29, 1987, p. 73; February 10, 1989, p. 58; August 11, 1989, p. 444; August 25, 1989, p. 58; April 20, 1990, p. 61; May 11, 1990, p. 251; August 10, 1990, p. 431; December 21, 1990, p. 57; January 4, 1991, p. 61; October 18, 1991, p. 55; July 20, 1992, p. 237; November 29, 1993, pp. 57-58; September 5, 1994, p. 96; September 21, 1998, p. 79; December 14, 1998, p. 61; April 26, 1999, p. 61; September 27, 1999, review of *Xone of Contention,* p. 78; March 6, 2000, review of *The Secret of Spring,* p. 88; May 1, 2000, review of *The Gutbucket Quest,* p. 55; October 2, 2000, review of *The Dastard,* p. 64; March 5, 2001, review of *DoOon Mode,* p. 66; July 23, 2001, review of *How Precious Was That While,* p. 59; August 27, 2001, review of *Swell Foop,* p. 59; November 4, 2002, review of *Up in a Heaval,* p. 67.

St. Petersburg Times (St. Petersburg, FL), July 13, 2001, p. P5; March 11, 2002, Holly Atkins, "Fantasy Flourishes in Florida Forests," p. D4.

Sarasota Herald Tribune, November 26, 2000, p. E4; July 23, 2001, p. 59.

Science Fiction, November, 1977, p. 60.

Voice of Youth Advocates, April, 1983, p. 44; December, 1992, p. 290; August, 1994, p. 152; February, 1995, p. 343.

Writer, August, 1989, pp. 11-13, 35.

Writer's Digest, January, 1991, p. 32.

ONLINE

Piers Anthony's Web site, http://www.hipiers.com (April 25, 2004).*

* * *

ATWOOD, Margaret (Eleanor) 1939-

PERSONAL: Born November 18, 1939, in Ottawa Ontario, Canada; daughter of Carl Edmund (an entomologist) and Margaret Dorothy (Killam) Atwood; married Graeme Gibson (a writer); children: Jess (daughter). *Education:* University of Toronto, B.A., 1961; Radcliffe College, A.M., 1962; Harvard University, graduate study, 1962-63 and 1965-67. *Politics:* "William Morrisite." *Religion:* "Immanent Transcendentalist."

ADDRESSES: Home—Toronto, Ontario, Canada. *Agent*—c/o Random House, 299 Park Ave., New York, NY, 10171-0002.

CAREER: Writer. University of British Columbia, Vancouver, Canada, lecturer in English literature, 1964-65; Sir George Williams University, Montreal, Quebec, Canada, lecturer in English literature, 1967-68; York University, Toronto, Ontario, Canada, assistant professor of English literature, 1971-72; House of Anansi Press, Toronto, editor and member of board of directors, 1971-73; University of Toronto, writer-in-residence, 1972-73; University of Alabama, Tuscaloosa, writer-in-residence, 1985; New York University, New York, NY, Berg Visiting Professor of English, 1986; Macquarie University, North Ryde, Australia, writer-in-residence, 1987. Worked variously as camp counselor and waitress.

Margaret Atwood

MEMBER: PEN International, Amnesty International, Writers' Union of Canada (vice chair, 1980-81), Royal Society of Canada (fellow), Canadian Civil Liberties Association (member of board, 1973-75), Canadian Centre, American Academy of Arts and Sciences (honorary member), Anglophone (president, 1984-85).

AWARDS, HONORS: E. J. Pratt Medal, 1961, for *Double Persephone;* President's Medal, University of Western Ontario, 1965; YWCA Women of Distinction Award, 1966 and 1988; Governor General's Award, 1966, for *The Circle Game,* and 1986, for *The Handmaid's Tale;* first prize in Canadian Centennial Commission Poetry Competition, 1967; Union Prize for poetry, 1969; Bess Hoskins Prize for poetry, 1969 and 1974; City of Toronto Book Award, Canadian Booksellers' Association Award, and Periodical Distributors of Canada Short Fiction Award, all 1977, all for *Dancing Girls and Other Stories;* St. Lawrence Award for fiction, 1978; Radcliffe Medal, 1980; *Life before Man* selected a notable book of 1980, American Library Association; Molson Award, 1981; Guggenheim fellowship, 1981; named Companion of the Order of Canada, 1981; International Writer's Prize,

Welsh Arts Council, 1982; Book of the Year Award, Periodical Distributors of Canada/Foundation for the Advancement of Canadian Letters, 1983, for *Bluebeard's Egg and Other Stories;* Ida Nudel Humanitarian Award, 1986; named Woman of the Year, *Ms.* magazine, 1986; Toronto Arts Award for writing and editing, 1986; *Los Angeles Times* Book Award, 1986, and Arthur C. Clarke Award for Best Science Fiction, and Commonwealth Literature Prize, both 1987, all for *The Handmaid's Tale;* Canadian Council for the Advancement and Support of Education silver medal, 1987; Humanist of the Year award, 1987; Royal Society of Canada fellow, 1987; named *Chatelaine* magazine's Woman of the Year; City of Toronto Book Award, Coles Book of the Year Award, Canadian Booksellers' Association Author of the Year Award, Book of the Year Award, Foundation for Advancement of Canadian Letters citation, Periodical Marketers of Canada Award, and Torgi Talking Book Award, all 1989, all for *Cat's Eye;* Harvard University Centennial Medal, 1990; Order of Ontario, 1990; Trillium Award for Excellence in Ontario Writing, and Periodical Marketers of Canada Book of the Year Award, both 1992, both for *Wilderness Tips and Other Stories;* Commemorative Medal for 125th Anniversary of Canadian Confederation; Trillium Award, Canadian Authors' Association Novel of the Year Award, Commonwealth Writers' Prize for Canadian and Caribbean Region, and *Sunday Times* Award for Literary Excellence, all 1994, and Swedish Humour Association's International Humourous Writer Award, 1995, all for *The Robber Bride;* Chevalier dans l'Ordre des Arts et des Lettres (France), 1994; named best local author, *NOW* magazine readers' poll, 1995 and 1996; Trillium Award, 1995, for *Morning in the Burned House;* Norwegian Order of Literary Merit, 1996; Booker Prize shortlist, and Giller Prize, both 1996, both for *Alias Grace;* International IMPAC Dublin Literary Award shortlist, Dublin City Library, 1998; Booker Prize, 2000, International IMPAC Dublin Literary Award nomination, and Dashiell Hammett Prize, International Association of Crime Writers (North American branch), 2001, all for *The Blind Assassin;* Booker prize shortlist and Governor General's literary award nominee, both 2003, both for *Oryx and Crake;* recipient of numerous honorary degrees, including Trent University, 1973, Concordia University, 1980, Smith College, 1982, University of Toronto, 1983, Mount Holyoke College, 1985, University of Waterloo, 1985, University of Guelph, 1985, Victoria College, 1987, University of Montreal, 1991, University of Leeds, 1994, Queen's University, 1974, Oxford University, 1998, and Cambridge University, 2001.

WRITINGS:

POETRY

Double Persephone, Hawkshead Press (Ontario, Canada), 1961.

The Circle Game, Cranbrook Academy of Art (Bloomfield Hills, MI), 1964, revised edition, House of Anansi Press (Toronto, Ontario, Canada), 1978.

Kaleidoscopes Baroque: A Poem, Cranbrook Academy of Art (Bloomfield Hills, MI), 1965.

Talismans for Children, Cranbrook Academy of Art (Bloomfield Hills, MI), 1965.

Speeches for Doctor Frankenstein, Cranbrook Academy of Art (Bloomfield Hills, MI), 1966.

The Animals in That Country, Little, Brown (Boston, MA), 1968.

The Journals of Susanna Moodie, Oxford University Press (Toronto, Ontario, Canada), 1970.

Procedures for Underground, Little, Brown (Boston, MA), 1970.

Power Politics, House of Anansi Press (Toronto, Ontario, Canada), 1971, Harper (New York, NY), 1973.

You Are Happy, Harper & Row (New York, NY), 1974.

Selected Poems, 1965-1975, Oxford University Press (Toronto, Ontario, Canada), 1976, Simon & Schuster (New York, NY), 1978.

Marsh Hawk, Dreadnaught Press (Toronto, Ontario, Canada), 1977.

Two-headed Poems, Oxford University Press, 1978, Simon & Schuster (New York, NY), 1981.

Notes Toward a Poem That Can Never Be Written, Salamander Press (Toronto, Ontario, Canada), 1981.

True Stories, Oxford University Press (Toronto, Ontario, Canada), 1981, Simon & Schuster (New York, NY), 1982.

Snake Poems, Salamander Press (Toronto, Ontario, Canada), 1983.

Interlunar, Oxford University Press (Toronto, Ontario, Canada), 1984.

Selected Poems II: Poems Selected and New, 1976-1986, Oxford University Press (Toronto, Ontario, Canada), 1986.

Morning in the Burned House, Houghton Mifflin (Boston, MA), 1995.

Eating Fire: Selected Poetry, 1965-1995, Virago Press (London, England), 1998.

Also author of *Expeditions,* 1966, and *What Was in the Garden,* 1969.

NOVELS

The Edible Woman, McClelland & Stewart (Toronto, Ontario, Canada), 1969, Little, Brown (Boston, MA), 1970, reprinted, Anchor Press (New York, NY), 1998.

Surfacing, McClelland & Stewart (Toronto, Ontario, Canada), 1972, Simon & Schuster (New York, NY), 1973, reprinted, Anchor Press (New York, NY), 1998.

Lady Oracle, Simon & Schuster (New York, NY), 1976, reprinted, Anchor Press (New York, NY), 1998.

Life before Man, Simon & Schuster (New York, NY), 1979, reprinted, Anchor Press (New York, NY), 1998.

Bodily Harm, McClelland & Stewart (Toronto, Ontario, Canada), 1981, Simon & Schuster (New York, NY), 1982, reprinted, Anchor Press (New York, NY), 1998.

Encounters with the Element Man, William B. Ewert (Concord, NH), 1982.

Unearthing Suite, Grand Union Press (Toronto, Ontario, Canada), 1983.

The Handmaid's Tale, McClelland & Stewart (Toronto, Ontario, Canada), 1985, Houghton Mifflin (Boston, MA), 1986.

Cat's Eye, McClelland & Stewart (Toronto, Ontario, Canada), 1988, Doubleday (Garden City, NY), 1989.

The Robber Bride, Doubleday (New York, NY), 1993.

Alias Grace, Doubleday (New York, NY), 1996.

The Blind Assassin, Random House (New York, NY), 2000.

Oryx and Crake, Nan A. Talese (New York, NY), 2003.

STORY COLLECTIONS

Dancing Girls and Other Stories, McClelland & Stewart (Toronto, Ontario, Canada), 1977, Simon & Schuster (New York, NY), 1982, reprinted, Anchor Press (New York, NY), 1998.

Bluebeard's Egg and Other Stories, McClelland & Stewart (Toronto, Ontario, Canada), 1983, Anchor Doubleday (New York, NY), 1998.

Murder in the Dark: Short Fictions and Prose Poems, Coach House Press (Toronto, Ontario, Canada), 1983.

Wilderness Tips and Other Stories, Doubleday (New York, NY), 1991.

Good Bones, Coach House Press (Toronto, Ontario, Canada), 1992, published as *Good Bones and Simple Murders,* Doubleday (New York, NY), 1994.

A Quiet Game: And Other Early Works, edited and annotated by Kathy Chung and Sherrill Grace, Juvenilia Press (Edmonton, Alberta, Canada), 1997.

OTHER

The Trumpets of Summer (radio play), Canadian Broadcasting Corporation (CBC-Radio), 1964.

Survival: A Thematic Guide to Canadian Literature, House of Anansi Press (Toronto, Ontario, Canada), 1972.

The Servant Girl (teleplay), CBC-TV, 1974.

Days of the Rebels, 1815-1840, Natural Science Library, 1976.

The Poetry and Voice of Margaret Atwood (recording), Caedmon (New York, NY), 1977.

Up in the Tree (juvenile), McClelland & Stewart (Toronto, Ontario, Canada), 1978.

(Author of introduction) Catherine M. Young, *To See Our World,* GLC Publishers, 1979, Morrow (New York, NY), 1980.

(With Joyce Barkhouse) *Anna's Pet* (juvenile), James Lorimer, 1980.

Snowbird (teleplay), CBC-TV, 1981.

Second Words: Selected Critical Prose, House of Anansi Press (Toronto, Ontario, Canada), 1982.

(Editor) *The New Oxford Book of Canadian Verse in English,* Oxford University Press (Toronto, Ontario, Canada), 1982.

(Editor with Robert Weaver) *The Oxford Book of Canadian Short Stories in English,* Oxford University Press (Toronto, Ontario, Canada), 1986.

(With Peter Pearson) *Heaven on Earth* (teleplay), CBC-TV, 1986.

(Editor) *The Canlit Foodbook,* Totem Books (New York, NY), 1987.

(Editor with Shannon Ravenal) *The Best American Short Stories, 1989,* Houghton Mifflin (Boston, MA), 1989.

For the Birds, illustrated by John Bianchi, Firefly Books (Richmond Hill, Ontario, Canada), 1991.

(Editor with Barry Callaghan and author of introduction) *The Poetry of Gwendolyn MacEwen,* Exile Editions (Toronto, Ontario, Canada), Volume 1: *The Early Years,* 1993, Volume 2: *The Later Years,* 1994.

Princess Prunella and the Purple Peanut (juvenile), illustrated by Maryann Kovalski, Workman (New York, NY), 1995.

Strange Things: The Malevolent North in Canadian Literature (lectures), Oxford University Press (Toronto, Ontario, Canada), 1996.

Some Things about Flying, Women's Press (London, England), 1997.

(With Victor-Levy Beaulieu) *Two Solicitudes: Conversations* (interviews), translated by Phyllis Aronoff and Howard Scott, McClelland & Stewart (Toronto, Ontario, Canada), 1998.

(Author of introduction) *Women Writers at Work: The "Paris Review" Interviews,* edited by George Plimpton, Random House (New York, NY), 1998.

Negotiating with the Dead (nonfiction), Cambridge University Press (New York, NY), 2002.

Rude Ramsay and the Roaring Radishes (juvenile), Key Porter Books (Toronto, Ontario, Canada), 2003.

Contributor to anthologies, including *Five Modern Canadian Poets,* 1970, *The Canadian Imagination: Dimensions of a Literary Culture,* Harvard University Press, 1977, and *Women on Women,* 1978. Contributor to periodicals, including *Atlantic, Poetry, New Yorker, Harper's, New York Times Book Review, Saturday Night, Tamarack Review,* and *Canadian Forum.*

ADAPTATIONS: Reflections: Progressive Insanities of a Pioneer, a six-minute visual interpretation of Atwood's poem by the same name, was produced by Cinematics Canada, 1972 and by Universal as *Poem as Imagery: Progressive Insanities of a Pioneer,* 1974. *The Journals of Susanna Moodie* was adapted as a screenplay, Tranby, 1972; *Surfacing* was adapted for film, Pan-Canadian, 1979; *The Handmaid's Tale* was filmed by Cinecom Entertainment Group, 1989, and was adapted as an opera by Danish composer Poul Ruders, for the Royal Danish Opera Company. *The Atwood Stories,* adaptations of Atwood's fiction, appeared as six half-hour episodes on W Network. *Alias Grace* was being adapted for film by Working Title Films. Union Pictures planned to produce a four-part miniseries based on *The Blind Assassin.* Many of Atwoods books are available as sound recordings.

SIDELIGHTS: As a poet, novelist, story writer, and essayist, Margaret Atwood holds a unique position in contemporary Canadian literature. Her books have received critical acclaim in the United States, Europe, and her native Canada, and she has been the recipient of numerous literary awards. Ann Marie Lipinski, writing in the *Chicago Tribune*, described Atwood as "one of the leading literary luminaries, a national heroine of the arts, the *rara avis* of Canadian letters." Atwood's critical popularity is matched by her popularity with readers. She is a frequent guest on Canadian television and radio, her books are bestsellers, and "people follow her on the streets and in stores," as Judy Klemesrud reported in the *New York Times*. Atwood, Roy MacGregor of *Maclean's* explained, "is to Canadian literature as Gordon Lightfoot is to Canadian music, more institution than individual." Atwood's popularity with both critics and the reading public has surprised her. "It's an accident that I'm a successful writer," she told MacGregor. "I think I'm kind of an odd phenomenon in that I'm a serious writer and I never expected to become a popular one, and I never did anything in order to become a popular one."

Atwood first came to public attention as a poet in the 1960s with her collections *Double Persephone*, winner of the E. J. Pratt Medal, and *The Circle Game*, winner of a Governor General's award. These two books marked out the terrain her subsequent poetry has explored. *Double Persephone* concerns "the contrast between the flux of life or nature and the fixity of man's artificial creations," as Linda Hutcheon explained in the *Dictionary of Literary Biography*. *The Circle Game* takes this opposition further, setting such human constructs as games, literature, and love against the instability of nature. Human constructs are presented as both traps and shelters; the fluidity of nature as both dangerous and liberating. Sherrill Grace, writing in *Violent Duality: A Study of Margaret Atwood*, identified the central tension in all of Atwood's work as "the pull towards art on one hand and towards life on the other." This tension is expressed in a series of "violent dualities," as Grace termed it. Atwood "is constantly aware of opposites—self/other, subject/object, male/female, nature/man—and of the need to accept and work within them," Grace explained. "To create, Atwood chooses violent dualities, and her art re-works, probes, and dramatizes the ability to see double."

Linda W. Wagner, writing in *The Art of Margaret Atwood: Essays in Criticism*, asserted that in Atwood's poetry "duality [is] presented as separation." This separation leads her characters to be isolated from one another and from the natural world, resulting in their inability to communicate, to break free of exploitative social relationships, or to understand their place in the natural order. "In her early poetry," Gloria Onley wrote in the *West Coast Review*, Atwood "is acutely aware of the problem of alienation, the need for real human communication and the establishment of genuine human community—real as opposed to mechanical or manipulative; genuine as opposed to the counterfeit community of the body politic." Speaking of *The Circle Game*, Wagner wrote that "the personae of those poems never did make contact, never did anything but lament the human condition. . . . Relationships in these poems are sterile if not destructive."

Atwood's sense of desolation, especially evident in her early poems, and her use of frequently violent images, moved Helen Vendler of the *New York Times Book Review* to claim that Atwood has a "sense of life as mostly wounds given and received." About *The Circle Game* and *Procedures for Underground*, Peter Stevens noted in *Canadian Literature* that both collections contain "images of drowning, buried life, still life, dreams, journeys and returns." In a review of *True Stories* for *Canadian Forum*, Chaviva Hosek stated that the poems "range over such topics as murder, genocide, rape, dismemberment, instruments of torture, forms of torture, genital mutilation, abortion, and forcible hysterectomy," although Robert Sward of *Quill and Quire* explained that many reviewers of the book have exaggerated the violence and given "the false impression that all thirty-eight poems . . . are about torture." Yet, Scott Lauder of *Canadian Forum* spoke of "the painful world we have come to expect from Atwood."

Suffering is common for the female characters in Atwood's poems, although they are never passive victims. In her later works, her characters take active measures to improve their situations. Atwood's poems, *West Coast Review* contributor Onley maintained, concern "modern woman's anguish at finding herself isolated and exploited (although also exploiting) by the imposition of a sex role power structure." Atwood explained to Klemesrud in the *New York Times* that her suffering characters come from real life: "My women suffer because most of the women I talk to seem to have suffered." By the early 1970s, this stance had made Atwood into "a cult author to faithful feminist readers," as *Chicago Tribune* reviewer Lipinski commented. Atwood's popularity in the feminist community was unsought. "I began as a profoundly apolitical writer," she told Lindsy Van Gelder of *Ms.,* "but then I began to do what all novelists and some poets do: I began to describe the world around me."

Atwood's 1995 book of poetry, *Morning in the Burned House,* "reflects a period in Atwood's life when time seems to be running out," observed John Bemrose in *Maclean's.* Noting that many of the poems address grief and loss, particularly in relationship to her father's death and a realization of her own mortality, Bemrose added that the book "moves even more deeply into survival territory." Bemrose further suggested that in this book, Atwood allows the readers greater latitude in interpretation than in her earlier verse: "Atwood uses grief . . . to break away from that airless poetry and into a new freedom."

Atwood's feminist concerns also emerge clearly in her novels, particularly in *The Edible Woman, Surfacing, Life before Man, Bodily Harm,* and *The Handmaid's Tale.* These novels feature female characters who are, as Klemesrud reported, "intelligent, self-absorbed modern women searching for identity. . . . [They] hunt, split logs, make campfires and become successful in their careers, while men often cook and take care of their households." Like her poems, however, Atwood's novels "are populated by pained and confused people whose lives hold a mirror to both the front page fears—cancer, divorce, violence—and those that persist quietly, naggingly—solitude, loneliness, desperation," Lipinski wrote.

The Edible Woman tells the story of Marian McAlpin, a young woman engaged to be married, who rebels against her upcoming nuptials. Her fiancé seems too stable, too ordinary, and the role of wife too fixed and limiting. Her rejection of marriage is accompanied by her body's rejection of food; she cannot tolerate even a spare vegetarian diet. Eventually Marian bakes a sponge cake in the shape of a woman and feeds it to her fiancé because, she explains, "You've been trying to assimilate me." After the engagement is broken off, she is able to eat some of the cake herself.

Reaction to *The Edible Woman* was divided, with some reviewers pointing to the flaws commonly found in first novels. John Stedmond of *Canadian Forum,* for example, believed that "the characters, though cleverly sketched, do not quite jell, and the narrative techniques

creak a little." Linda Rogers in *Canadian Literature* found that "one of the reasons *The Edible Woman* fails as a novel is the awkwardness of the dialogue." But other critics noted Atwood's at least partial success. Tom Marshall, writing in his *Harsh and Lovely Land: The Major Canadian Poets and the Making of a Canadian Tradition,* called *The Edible Woman* "a largely successful comic novel, even if the mechanics are sometimes a little clumsy, the satirical accounts of consumerism a little drawn out." Millicent Bell in the *New York Times Book Review* termed it "a work of feminist black humor" and claimed that Atwood's "comic distortion veers at times into surreal meaningfulness." And Hutcheon described *The Edible Woman* as "very much a social novel about the possibilities for personal female identity in a capitalistic consumer society."

In *Life before Man* Atwood dissects the relationships between three characters: Elizabeth, a married woman who mourns the recent suicide of her lover; Elizabeth's husband, Nate, who is unable to choose between his wife and his lover; and Lesje, Nate's lover, who works with Elizabeth at a museum of natural history. All three characters are isolated from one another and unable to experience their own emotions. The fossils and dinosaur bones on display at the museum are compared throughout the novel with the sterility of the characters' lives. As Laurie Stone noted in the *Village Voice, Life before Man* "is full of variations on the theme of extinction."

Although *Life before Man* is what Rosellen Brown of *Saturday Review* called an "anatomy of melancholy," MacGregor pointed out in *Maclean's* a tempering humor in the novel as well. *Life before Man,* MacGregor wrote, "is not so much a story as it is the discarded negatives of a family album, the thoughts so dark they defy any flash short of Atwood's remarkable, and often very funny, insight." Comparing the novel's characters to museum pieces and commenting on the analytical examination to which Atwood subjects them, Peter S. Prescott wrote in *Newsweek* that, "with chilly compassion and an even colder wit, Atwood exposes the interior lives of her specimens." Writing in the *New York Times Book Review,* Marilyn French made clear that in *Life before Man,* Atwood "combines several talents—powerful introspection, honesty, satire and a taut, limpid style—to create a splendid, fully integrated work." The novel's title, French believed, relates to the characters' isolation from themselves, their history, and from one another. They have not yet achieved truly human stature. "This novel suggests," French wrote, "that we are still living life before man, before the human—as we like to define it—has evolved." Prescott raised the same point. The novel's characters, he wrote, "do not communicate; each, in the presence of another, is locked into his own thoughts and feelings. Is such isolation and indeterminacy what Atwood means when she calls her story 'Life before Man'?" This concern is also found in Atwood's previous novels, French argued, all of which depict "the search for identity . . . a search for a better way to be—for a way of life that both satisfies the passionate, needy self and yet is decent, humane and natural."

Atwood further explores this idea in *Bodily Harm.* In this novel, Rennie Wilford is a Toronto journalist who specializes in light, trivial pieces for magazines. She is, Anne Tyler explained in the *Detroit News,* "a cataloguer of current fads and fancies." Isabel Raphael of the London *Times* called Rennie someone who "deals only in surfaces; her journalism is of the most trivial and transitory kind, her relationship with a live-in lover limited to sex, and most of her friends 'really just contacts.'" Following a partial mastectomy, which causes her lover to abandon her, Rennie begins to feel dissatisfied with her life. She takes on an assignment to the Caribbean island of St. Antoine in an effort to get away from things for a while. Her planned magazine story, focusing on the island's beaches, tennis courts, and restaurants, is distinctly facile in comparison to the political violence she finds on St. Antoine. When Rennie is arrested and jailed, the experience brings her to a self-realization about her life. "Death," Nancy Ramsey remarked in the *San Francisco Review of Books,* "rather than the modern sense of ennui, threatens Rennie and the people around her, and ultimately gives her life a meaning she hadn't known before."

Frank Davey asserted in the *Canadian Forum* that *Bodily Harm* follows the same pattern set in Atwood's earlier novels: "Alienation from natural order . . . followed by descent into a more primitive but healing reality . . . and finally some reestablishment of order." Although Davey was "troubled" by the similarities between the novels, he concluded that "these reservations aside, *Bodily Harm* was still a pleasure to read." Other critics had few such reservations about the book. Anatole Broyard in the *New York Times,* for example, claimed that "the only way to describe my response to

[*Bodily Harm*] is to say that it knocked me out. Atwood seems to be able to do just about everything: people, places, problems, a perfect ear, an exactly right voice and she tosses off terrific scenes with a casualness that leaves you utterly unprepared for the way these scenes seize you." Tyler called Atwood "an uncommonly skillful and perceptive writer," and went on to state that, because of its subject matter, *Bodily Harm* "is not always easy to read. There are times when it's downright unpleasant, but it's also intelligent, provocative, and in the end—against all expectations—uplifting."

In *The Handmaid's Tale* Atwood turns to speculative fiction, creating the dystopia of Gilead, a future America in which fundamentalist Christians have killed the president and members of Congress and imposed their own dictatorial rule. In this future world, polluted by toxic chemicals and nuclear radiation, few women can bear children; the birthrate has dropped alarmingly. Those women who can bear children are forced to become Handmaids, the official breeders for society. All other women have been reduced to chattel under a repressive religious hierarchy run by men.

The Handmaid's Tale is a radical departure from Atwood's previous novels. Her strong feminism was evident in earlier books, but *The Handmaid's Tale* is dominated by the theme. As Barbara Holliday wrote in the *Detroit Free Press,* Atwood "has been concerned in her fiction with the painful psychic warfare between men and women. In *The Handmaid's Tale* . . . she casts subtlety aside, exposing woman's primal fear of being used and helpless." Atwood's creation of an imaginary world is also new. As Mary Battiata noted in the *Washington Post, The Handmaid's Tale* is the first of Atwood's novels "not set in a worried corner of contemporary Canada."

Atwood was moved to write her story only after images and scenes from the book had been appearing to her for three years. She admitted to Mervyn Rothstein of the *New York Times,* "I delayed writing it . . . because I felt it was too crazy." But she eventually became convinced that her vision of Gilead was not far from reality. Some of the anti-female measures she had imagined for the novel actually exist. "There is a sect now, a Catholic charismatic spinoff sect, which calls the women handmaids," Atwood told Rothstein. "A law in Canada," Battiata reported, "[requires] a woman to have her husband's permission before obtaining an abortion." And Atwood, speaking to Battiata, pointed to repressive laws in the totalitarian state of Romania as well: "No abortion, no birth control, and compulsory pregnancy testing, once a month." *The Handmaid's Tale,* Elaine Kendall explained in the *Los Angeles Times Book Review,* depicts "a future firmly based upon actuality, beginning with events that have already taken place and extending them a bit beyond the inevitable conclusions. *The Handmaid's Tale* does not depend upon hypothetical scenarios, omens, or straws in the wind, but upon documented occurrences and public pronouncements; all matters of record." Stephen McCabe of the *Humanist* called the novel "a chilling vision of the future extrapolated from the present."

Yet, several critics voiced a disbelief in the basic assumptions of *The Handmaid's Tale.* Mary McCarthy, in her review for the *New York Times Book Review,* complained that "I just can't see the intolerance of the far right . . . as leading to a super-biblical puritanism." And although acknowledging that "the author has carefully drawn her projections from current trends," McCarthy asserted that "perhaps that is the trouble: the projections are too neatly penciled in. The details . . . all raise their hands announcing themselves present. At the same time, the Republic of Gilead itself, whatever in it that is not a projection, is insufficiently imagined." Richard Grenier of *Insight* observed that the Fundamentalist-run Gilead does not seem Christian: "There seems to be no Father, no Son, no Holy Ghost, no apparent belief in redemption, resurrection, eternal life. No one in this excruciatingly hierarchized new clerical state . . . appears to believe in God." Grenier also found it improbable that "while the United States has hurtled off into this morbid, feminist nightmare, the rest of the democratic world has been blissfully unaffected." Writing in the Toronto *Globe and Mail,* William French stated that Atwood's "reach exceeds her grasp" in *The Handmaid's Tale,* "and in the end we're not clear what we're being warned against." Atwood seems to warn of the dangers of religious fanaticism, of the effects of pollution on the birthrate, and of a possible backlash to militant feminist demands. The novel, French stated, "is in fact a cautionary tale about *all* these things . . . but in her scenario, they interact in an implausible way."

Despite what he saw as a flaw, French saw *The Handmaid's Tale* as being "in the honorable tradition of *Brave New World* and other warnings of dystopia.

It's imaginative, even audacious, and conveys a chilling sense of fear and menace." Prescott compared the novel to other dystopian books. It belongs, he wrote, "to that breed of visionary fiction in which a metaphor is extended to elaborate a warning. . . . Wells, Huxley and Orwell popularized the tradition with books like *The Time Machine, Brave New World* and *1984*—yet Atwood is a better novelist than they." Christopher Lehmann-Haupt identified *The Handmaid's Tale* as a book that goes far beyond its feminist concerns. Writing in the *New York Times,* the critic explained that the novel "is a political tract deploring nuclear energy, environmental waste, and anti-feminist attitudes. But it [is] so much more than that—a taut thriller, a psychological study, a play on words." Van Gelder saw the novel in a similar light: "[It] ultimately succeeds on multiple levels: as a page-turning thriller, as a powerful political statement, and as an exquisite piece of writing."

In *The Robber Bride,* Atwood again explores women's issues and feminist concerns, this time concentrating on women's relationships with each other—both positive and negative. Inspired by the Brothers Grimm's fairy tale "The Robber Bridegroom," the novel chronicles the relationships of college friends Tony, Charis, and Roz with their backstabbing classmate Zenia. Now middle-aged women, the women's paths and life choices have diverged, yet Tony, Charis, and Roz have remained friends. Throughout their adulthood, however, Zenia's manipulations have nearly destroyed their lives and cost them husbands and careers. Lorrie Moore, writing in the *New York Times Book Review,* called *The Robber Bride* "Atwood's funniest and most companionable book in years," adding that its author "retains her gift for observing, in poetry, the minutiae specific to the physical and emotional lives of her characters." About Zenia, Moore commented, "charming and gorgeous, Zenia is a misogynist's grotesque: relentlessly seductive, brutal, pathologically dishonest," postulating that "perhaps Ms. Atwood intended Zenia, by the end, to be a symbol of all that is inexplicably evil: war, disease, global catastrophe." Judith Timson commented in *Maclean's* that *The Robber Bride* "has as its central theme an idea that feminism was supposed to have shoved under the rug: there are female predators out there, and they will get your man if you are not careful."

Atwood maintained that she had a feminist motivation in creating Zenia. The femme fatale all but disappeared from fiction in the 1950s due to that decade's sanitized ideal of domesticity; and in the late 1960s came the women's movement, which in its early years encouraged the creation of only positive female characters, Atwood asserted in interviews. "I think we're now through with all that, and we can put the full cast of characters back on the stage," she told Lauri Miller in an interview in the *San Francisco Review of Books.* "Because to say that women can't be malicious and intentionally bad is to say that they're congenitally incapable of that, which is really very limiting." Atwood also commented that "there are a lot of women you have to say are feminists who are getting a big kick out of this book," according to interviewer Sarah Lyall in the *New York Times.* "People read the book with all the wars done by men, and they say, 'So, you're saying that women are crueler than men,'" the novelist added. "In other words, that's normal behavior by men, so we don't notice it. Similarly, we say that Zenia behaves badly, and therefore women are worse than men, but that ignores the helpfulness of the other three women to each other, which of course gives them a power of their own."

Francine Prose, reviewing *The Robber Bride* for the *Washington Post Book World,* recommended the book "to those well-intentioned misguided feminists or benighted sexists who would have us believe that the female of the species is 'naturally' nicer or more nurturing than the male." Prose found the book "smart and entertaining" but not always convincing in its blend of exaggerated and realistic elements. *New York Times* critic Michiko Kakutani also thought Atwood has not achieved the proper balance in this regard: "Her characters remain exiles from both the earthbound realm of realism and the airier attitudes of allegory, and as a result, their story does not illuminate or entertain: it grates."

Alias Grace represents Atwood's first venture into historical fiction, but the book has much in common with her other works in its contemplation of "the shifting notions of women's moral nature" and "the exercise of power between men and women," wrote *Maclean's* contributor Diane Turbide. Based on a true story Atwood had explored previously in a television script titled *The Servant Girl, Alias Grace* centers on Grace Marks, a servant who was found guilty of murdering her employer and his mistress in northern Canada in 1843. Some people doubt Grace's guilt, however, and she serves out her sentence of life in prison, claiming not to remember the murders. Eventu-

ally, reformers begin to agitate for clemency for Grace. In a quest for evidence to support their position, they assign a young doctor, versed in the new science of psychiatry, to evaluate her soundness of mind. Over many meetings, Grace tells the doctor the harrowing story of her life—a life marked by extreme hardship. Much about Grace, though, remains puzzling; she is haunted by flashbacks of the supposedly forgotten murders and by the presence of a friend who had died from a mishandled abortion. The doctor, Simon Jordan, does not know what to believe in Grace's tales.

Several reviewers found Grace a complicated and compelling character. "Sometimes she is prim, naive, sometimes sardonic; sometimes sardonic because observant; sometimes observant because naive," commented Hilary Mantel in the *New York Review of Books. Los Angeles Times Book Review* critic Richard Eder lauded Atwood for making Grace "utterly present and unfathomable" and called her story "pure enchantment." Eder continued, "We are as anxious as Jordan to know what [Grace] is, yet bit by bit it seems to matter less. What matters is that she becomes more and more distinct and unforgettable." Turbide added that Grace is more than an intriguing character: she is also "the lens through which Victorian hypocrisies are mercilessly exposed."

Mantel also remarked upon the novel's portrait of Victorian life. "We learn as much about Grace's daily routine . . . as if Atwood had written a manual of antique housewifery, and yet the information neither intrudes nor slows the action," she observed. Atwood's use of period detail goes beyond mere background, Mantel asserted: "Other authors describe clothes; Atwood feels the clothes on her characters' backs." Prose, however, writing in the *New York Times Book Review,* thought the historical trivia excessive. "The book provides, in snippets, a crash course in Victorian culture. . . . Rather than enhancing the novel's verisimilitude, these mini-lessons underline the distance between reader and subject," she contended. Prose added that "Some readers may feel that the novel only intermittently succeeds in transcending the burden of history, research and abstraction. . . . Others will admire the liveliness with which Ms. Atwood toys with both our expectations and the conventions of the Victorian thriller."

"Dying octogenarian Iris Chasen's narration of the past carefully unravels a haunting story of tragedy, corruption, and cruel manipulation," summarized Beth

E. Andersen in a *Library Journal* review of Atwood's *The Blind Assassin.* The novel, which earned its author the Booker Prize, involves multiple story lines. It is Iris's memoir, retracing her past with the wealthy and conniving industrialist Richard Griffen and the death of her sister Laura, her husband, and her daughter. Iris "reveals at long last the wrenching truth about herself and Laura amid hilariously acerbic commentary on the inanities of contemporary life," wrote Donna Seaman in *Booklist.* Interspersed with these narrative threads are sections devoted to Laura's novel, *The Blind Assassin,* published after her death. Seaman called the work a "spellbinding novel of avarice, love, and revenge." Andersen noted that some readers may guess how the story will pan out before the conclusion, but argued that "nothing will dampen the pleasure of getting there." Michiko Kakutani in the *New York Times* called *The Blind Assassin* an "absorbing new novel" that "showcases Ms. Atwood's narrative powers and her ardent love of the Gothic." Kakutani also noted that Atwood writes with "uncommon authority and ease."

Atwood has remained a noted writer of short stories as well as novels. *Wilderness Tips and Other Stories,* published in 1991, is a collection of ten "neatly constructed, present-tense narratives," reported Merle Rubin in the *Christian Science Monitor.* While finding Atwood's writing style drab and unappealing, Rubin nevertheless praised the author for her "ability to evoke the passing of entire decades . . . all within the brief compass of a short story." The tales in Atwood's 1992 collection, *Good Bones*—published in 1994 as *Good Bones and Simple Murders*—"occupy that vague, peculiar country between poetry and prose," stated John Bemrose in *Maclean's.* Describing Atwood as "storyteller, poet, fabulist and social commentator rolled into one," Bemrose claimed that "the strongest pieces in *Good Bones* combine a light touch with a hypnotic seriousness of purpose." In the *New York Times Book Review,* Jennifer Howard labeled *Good Bones and Simple Murders* a "sprightly, whimsically feminist collection of miniatures and musings, assembled from two volumes published in Canada in 1983 and 1992." A *Publishers Weekly* reviewer, who characterized the entries as "postmodern fairy tales, caustic fables, inspired parodies, witty monologues," declared each piece to be "clever and sharply honed."

Survival: A Thematic Guide to Canadian Literature is Atwood's most direct presentation of her strong support of Canadian nationalism. In this work, she dis-cerns a uniquely Canadian literature, distinct from its American and British counterparts, and discusses the dominant themes to be found in it. Canadian literature, she argues, is primarily concerned with victims and with the victim's ability to survive. Atwood, Onley explained, "perceives a strong sado-masochistic patterning in Canadian literature as a whole. She believes that there is a national fictional tendency to participate, usually at some level as Victim, in a Victor/Victim basic pattern." But "despite its stress on victimization," Hutcheon wrote, "this study is not a revelation of, or a reveling in, [masochism]." What Atwood argues, Onley asserted, is that "every country or culture has a single unifying and informing symbol at its core: for America, the Frontier; for England, the Island; for Canada, Survival."

Several critics find that Atwood's own work exemplifies this primary theme of Canadian literature. Her examination of destructive gender roles and her nationalistic concern over the subordinate role Canada plays to the United States are variations on the victor/victim theme. As Marge Piercy explained in the *American Poetry Review,* Atwood believes a writer must consciously work within his or her nation's literary tradition. The author argues in *Survival,* Piercy wrote, "that discovery of a writer's tradition may be of use, in that it makes available a conscious choice of how to deal with that body of themes. She suggested that exploring a given tradition consciously can lead to writing in new and more interesting ways." Because Atwood's own work closely parallels the themes she sees as common to the Canadian literary tradition, *Survival* "has served as the context in which critics have subsequently discussed [Atwood's] works," Hutcheon stated.

Although she has been labeled a Canadian nationalist, a feminist, and even a gothic writer, Atwood incorporates and transcends these categories. Writing in *Saturday Night* of Atwood's several perceived roles as a writer, Linda Sandler concluded that "Atwood is all things to all people . . . a nationalist . . . a feminist or a psychologist or a comedian . . . a maker and breaker of myths . . . a gothic writer. She's all these things, but finally she's unaccountably Other. Her writing has the discipline of a social purpose but it remains elusive, complex, passionate. It has all the intensity of an act of exorcism." Atwood's work finally succeeds because it speaks of universal concerns. Piercy wrote, "Atwood is a large and remarkable writer. Her concerns are nowhere petty. Her novels and poems move and engage me deeply, can matter to people who read them."

BIOGRAPHICAL AND CRITICAL SOURCES:

BOOKS

Beran, Carol L., *Living over the Abyss: Margaret Atwood's Life before Man,* ECW Press (Toronto, Ontario, Canada), 1993.

Bloom, Harold, editor, *Margaret Atwood,* Chelsea House (Philadelphia, PA), 2000.

Bouson, J. Brooks, *Brutal Choreographies: Oppositional Strategies and Narrative Design in the Novels of Margaret Atwood,* University of Massachusetts Press (Amherst, MA), 1993.

Contemporary Literary Criticism, Gale (Detroit, MI), Volume 2, 1974, Volume 3, 1975, Volume 4, 1975, Volume 8, 1978, Volume 13, 1980, Volume 15, 1980, Volume 25, 1983, Volume 44, 1987.

Cooke, John, *The Influence of Painting on Five Canadian Writers: Alice Munro, Hugh Hood, Timothy Findley, Margaret Atwood, and Michael Ondaatje,* Edwin Mellen (Lewiston, NY), 1996.

Cooke, Nathalie, *Margaret Atwood: A Biography,* ECW Press (Toronto, Ontario, Canada), 1998.

Davidson, Arnold E., *Seeing in the Dark: Margaret Atwood's Cat's Eye,* ECW Press (Toronto, Ontario, Canada), 1997.

Davidson, Arnold E., and Cathy N. Davidson, editors, *The Art of Margaret Atwood: Essays in Criticism,* House of Anansi Press (Toronto, Ontario, Canada), 1981.

Dictionary of Literary Biography, Volume 53: *Canadian Writers since 1960,* Gale (Detroit, MI), 1986.

Gibson, Graeme, *Eleven Canadian Novelists,* House of Anansi Press (Toronto, Ontario, Canada), 1973.

Grace, Sherrill, *Violent Duality: A Study of Margaret Atwood,* Véhicule Press (Montreal, Quebec, Canada), 1980.

Grace, Sherrill, and Lorraine Weir, editors, *Margaret Atwood: Language, Text, and System,* University of British Columbia Press (Vancouver, British Columbia, Canada), 1983.

Hengen, Shannon, *Margaret Atwood's Power: Mirrors, Reflections, and Images in Select Fiction and Poetry,* Second Story Press (Toronto, Ontario, Canada), 1993.

Howells, Coral Ann, *Margaret Atwood,* St. Martin's Press (New York City), 1996.

Irvine, Lorna, *Collecting Clues: Margaret Atwood's Bodily Harm,* ECW Press (Toronto, Ontario, Canada), 1993.

Lecker, Robert, and Jack David, editors, *The Annotated Bibliography of Canada's Major Authors,* ECW Press (Toronto, Ontario, Canada), 1980.

Marshall, Tom, *Harsh and Lovely Land: The Major Canadian Poets and the Making of a Canadian Tradition,* University of British Columbia Press (Vancouver, British Columbia, Canada), 1978.

McCombs, Judith, and Carole L. Palmer, *Margaret Atwood: A Reference Guide,* G. K. Hall (Boston, MA), 1991.

Michael, Magali Cornier, *Feminism and the Postmodern Impulse: Post-World War II Fiction,* State University of New York Press (Albany, NY), 1996.

Nicholson, Colin, editor, *Margaret Atwood: Writing and Subjectivity: New Critical Essays,* St. Martin's Press (New York, NY), 1994.

Nischik, Reingard M., editor, *Margaret Atwood: Works and Impact,* Camden House (Rochester, NY), 2000.

Rao, Eleanora, *Strategies for Identity: The Fiction of Margaret Atwood,* P. Lang (New York, NY), 1993.

Sandler, Linda, editor, *Margaret Atwood: A Symposium,* University of British Columbia (Vancouver, British Columbia, Canada), 1977.

Stein, Karen F., *Margaret Atwood Revisited,* Twayne (New York, NY), 1999.

Sullivan, Rosemary, *The Red Shoes: Margaret Atwood Starting Out,* HarperFlamingo Canada (Toronto, Ontario, Canada), 1998.

Thompson, Lee Briscoe, *Scarlet Letters: Margaret Atwood's The Handmaid's Tale,* ECW Press (Toronto, Ontario, Canada), 1997.

Twigg, Alan, *For Openers: Conversations with Twenty-four Canadian Writers,* Harbour Publishing (Madeira Park, British Columbia, Canada), 1981.

Woodcock, George, *The Canadian Novel in the Twentieth Century,* McClelland & Stewart (Toronto, Ontario, Canada), 1975.

PERIODICALS

American Poetry Review, November-December, 1973; March-April, 1977; September-October, 1979.

Atlantic, April, 1973.

Book Forum, Volume 4, number 1, 1978.

Booklist, June 1, 2000, Donna Seaman, review of *The Blind Assassin,* p. 1796.

Books in Canada, January, 1979; June-July, 1980: March, 1981.

Canadian Forum, February, 1970; January, 1973; November-December, 1974; December-January, 1977-78; June-July, 1981; December-January, 1981-82.

Canadian Literature, autumn, 1971; spring, 1972; winter, 1973; spring, 1974; spring, 1977.

Chicago Tribune, January 27, 1980; February 3, 1980; May 16, 1982; March 19, 1989.

Christian Science Monitor, June 12, 1977; December 27, 1991, p. 14; November 19, 1993, p. 19.

Commonweal, July 9, 1973.

Communique, May, 1975.

Detroit Free Press, January 26, 1986.

Detroit News, April 4, 1982.

Essays on Canadian Writing, spring, 1977.

Globe and Mail (Toronto, Ontario, Canada), July 7, 1984; October 5, 1985; October 19, 1985; February 15, 1986; November 15, 1986; November 29, 1986; November 14, 1987.

Hudson Review, autumn, 1973; spring, 1975.

Humanist, September-October, 1986.

Insight, March 24, 1986.

Journal of Canadian Fiction, Volume 1, number 4, 1972.

Library Journal, August 9, 2000, Beth E. Andersen, review of *The Blind Assassin.*

Los Angeles Times, March 2, 1982; April 22, 1982; May 9, 1986; January 12, 1987.

Los Angeles Times Book Review, October 17, 1982; February 9, 1986; December 23, 1987; November 14, 1993, pp. 3, 11; December 15, 1996, p. 2.

Maclean's, January 15, 1979; October 15, 1979; March 30, 1981; October 5, 1992; October 4, 1993; February 6, 1995; September 23, 1996, pp. 42-45; October 14, 1996, p. 11; July 1, 1999, Atwood, "Survival, Then and Now," p. 54.

Malahat Review, January, 1977.

Manna, number 2, 1972.

Meanjin, Volume 37, number 2, 1978.

Modern Fiction Studies, autumn, 1976.

Ms., January, 1987.

New Leader, September 3, 1973.

New Orleans Review, Volume 5, number 3, 1977.

Newsweek, February 18, 1980; February 17, 1986.

New Yorker, September 18, 2000, John Updike, review of *The Blind Assassin,* p. 142.

New York Review of Books, December 19, 1996, Hilary Mantel, "Murder and Memory."

New York Times, December 23, 1976; January 10, 1980; February 8, 1980; March 6, 1982; March 28, 1982; September 15, 1982; January 27, 1986;

February 17, 1986; November 5, 1986; October 26, 1993, p. C20; November 23, 1993, pp. C13, C16; September 3, 2000, Thomas Mallon, review of *The Blind Assassin;* September 8, 2000, Michiko Kakutani, review of *The Blind Assassin.*

New York Times Book Review, October 18, 1970; March 4, 1973; April 6, 1975; September 26, 1976; May 21, 1978; February 3, 1980; October 11, 1981; February 9, 1986; October 31, 1993, pp. 1, 22; December 11, 1994; April 28, 1996, p. 22; December 29, 1996, p. 6.

Observer (London, England), June 13, 1982.

Ontario Review, spring-summer, 1975.

Open Letter, summer, 1973.

Parnassus, spring-summer, 1974.

People Weekly, May 19, 1980.

Poetry, March, 1970; July, 1972; May, 1982.

Publishers Weekly, August 23, 1976; October 3, 1994; August 28, 1995, pp. 107-108; October 7, 1996, p. 58; April 13, 1998, p. 65; July 24, 2000, review of *The Blind Assassin,* p. 67; July 24, 2000, "*PW* Talks to Margaret Atwood," p. 68.

Quill and Quire, April, 1981; September, 1984.

Room of One's Own, summer, 1975.

San Francisco Review of Books, January, 1982; summer, 1982; February-March, 1994, pp. 30-34.

Saturday Night, May, 1971; July-August, 1976; September, 1976; May 1981; July-August, 1998, Rosemary Sullivan, "The Writer-Bride," p. 56.

Saturday Review, September 18, 1976; February 2, 1980.

Saturday Review of the Arts, April, 1973.

Shenandoah, Volume 37, number 2, 1987.

Studies in Canadian Literature, summer, 1977.

Time, October 11, 1976.

Times (London, England), March 13, 1986; June 4, 1987; June 10, 1987.

Times Literary Supplement, March 21, 1986; June 12, 1987.

Tribune Books (Chicago, IL), January 26, 1986; November 21, 1993, p. 1.

University of Toronto Quarterly, summer, 1978.

Village Voice, January 7, 1980.

Vogue, January, 1986.

Washington Post, April 6, 1986.

Washington Post Book World, September 26, 1976; December 3, 1978; January 27, 1980; March 14, 1982; February 2, 1986; November 7, 1993, p. 1.

Waves, autumn, 1975.

West Coast Review, January, 1973.

ONLINE

Atwood Society Web site, http://www.cariboo.bc.ca/ atwood/ (March 30, 2004).*

B

BALLARD, J(ames) G(raham) 1930-

PERSONAL: Born November 15, 1930, in Shanghai, China; son of James (a chemist and business executive) and Edna (Johnstone) Ballard; married Helen Mary Matthews, 1953 (died 1964); children: James, Fay, Beatrice. *Education:* Studied medicine at King's College, Cambridge, 1949-51.

ADDRESSES: Home—36 Old Charlton Rd., Shepperton, Middlesex, TW17 8AT, England. *Agent*—Margaret Hanbury, 27 Walcot Sq., London SE11 44B, England.

CAREER: Novelist and author of short fiction. Institute for Research in Art and Technology, trustee. *Military service:* Royal Air Force, 1954-57; became pilot.

AWARDS, HONORS: Guardian Fiction Prize, and nomination for Booker Prize, both 1984, and James Tait Black Memorial Prize, 1985, all for *Empire of the Sun;* European Science Fiction Society Award for short story writer, 1984.

WRITINGS:

NOVELS

The Wind from Nowhere (also see below), Berkley Publishing (New York, NY), 1962.
The Drowned World (also see below), Berkley Publishing (New York, NY), 1962.
The Burning World, Berkley Publishing (New York, NY), 1964, revised as *The Drought,* J. Cape (London, England), 1965.

J. G. Ballard

The Drowned World [and] *The Wind from Nowhere,* Doubleday (New York, NY), 1965.
The Crystal World, Farrar, Straus & Giroux (New York, NY), 1966.
Crash, J. Cape (London, England), 1972, Farrar, Straus & Giroux (New York, NY), 1973, reprinted, 2000.
Concrete Island, Farrar, Straus & Giroux (New York, NY), 1974.

46

High-rise, J. Cape (London, England), 1975, Holt (New York, NY), 1977.

The Unlimited Dream Company, Holt (New York, NY), 1979.

Hello America, J. Cape (London, England), 1981.

Empire of the Sun, Simon & Schuster (New York, NY), 1984.

The Day of Creation, Gollancz (London, England), 1987, Farrar, Straus & Giroux (New York, NY), 1988, reprinted, Picador USA (New York, NY), 2001.

Running Wild, Hutchinson (London, England), 1989.

The Kindness of Women, Farrar, Straus & Giroux (New York, NY), 1991.

Rushing to Paradise, Picador USA (New York, NY), 1995.

Cocaine Nights, Counterpoint (Washington, DC), 1996.

Super-Cannes, Flamingo (London, England), 2000, Picador USA (New York, NY), 2001.

Millennium People, Flamingo (London, England), 2003.

STORY COLLECTIONS

The Voices of Time and Other Stories, Berkley Publishing (New York, NY), 1962.

Billenium and Other Stories, Berkley Publishing (New York, NY), 1962.

The Four-dimensional Nightmare, Gollancz (London, England), 1963, revised edition, 1974, published as *The Voices of Time*, Phoenix (London, England), 1998.

Passport to Eternity and Other Stories, Berkley Publishing (New York, NY), 1963.

Terminal Beach, Berkley Publishing (New York, NY), 1964, revised edition published as *The Terminal Beach*, Gollancz, 1964.

The Impossible Man and Other Stories, Berkley Publishing (New York, NY), 1966.

The Disaster Area, J. Cape (London, England), 1967.

By Day Fantastic Birds Flew through the Petrified Forests, Esographics for Firebird Visions, 1967.

The Day of Forever, Panther Books, 1967, revised edition, 1971.

The Overloaded Man, Panther Books, 1968.

The Atrocity Exhibition, J. Cape (London, England), 1970, published as *Love and Napalm: Export U.S. A.*, Grove Press (New York, NY), 1972.

Vermilion Sands, Berkley Publishing (New York, NY), 1971.

Chronopolis and Other Stories, Putnam (New York, NY), 1971.

Low-flying Aircraft and Other Stories, J. Cape (London, England), 1976.

The Best of J. G. Ballard, Futura Publications, 1977, revised edition published as *The Best Short Stories of J. G. Ballard*, Holt (New York, NY), 1978.

The Venus Hunters, Granada, 1980.

Myths of the Near Future, J. Cape (London, England), 1982.

Memories of the Space Age, Arkham House (Sauk City, WI), 1988.

War Fever, Farrar, Straus & Giroux (New York, NY), 1990.

The Complete Short Stories, Flamingo (London, England), 2001.

OTHER

(Editor, with others) *Best Science Fiction from "New Worlds,"* Medallion, 1968.

The Assassination Weapon (play; produced in London, England), 1969.

(Author of introduction) *Salvador Dali*, Ballantine (New York, NY), 1974.

(Author of introduction) Brian Ash, editor, *The Visual Encyclopaedia of Science Fiction*, Pan Books, 1977.

A User's Guide to the Millennium: Essays and Reviews, Picador (New York, NY), 1996.

Contributor to *The Inner Landscape*, Allison & Busby, 1969; and *Re/Search: J. G. Ballard*, edited by V. Vale and Andre Juno, Re/Search Publishing, 1984. Also contributor to publications, including *New Worlds, Ambit, Guardian, Transatlantic Review, Triquarterly, Playboy, Encounter*, and *Evergreen Review*.

ADAPTATIONS: Empire of the Sun was adapted as a film by Tom Stoppard and Menno Meyjes (uncredited), produced and directed by Steven Spielberg, Warner Bros., 1987; *Crash* was adapted as a film, written and directed by David Cronenberg, starring Holly Hunter and James Spader, Fine Line, 1996; "Low-flying Aircraft" was adapted by Swedish director Solveig Nordlund into a Portuguese-language film; *Running Wild* and *Super-Cannes* have both been optioned for film.

SIDELIGHTS: J. G. Ballard uses the language and symbols of science fiction to "explore the collective unconscious, the externalized psyche, which is plainly visible around us and which belongs to us all," as David Pringle stated in his study *Earth Is the Alien Planet: J. G. Ballard's Four-dimensional Nightmare.* Ballard's obsessive characters, searching "for a reality beyond 'normal' life," as Douglas Winter described it in the *Washington Post Book World,* attempt to manifest their private visions in landscapes that reflect their own mental states. Whether he uses post-holocaust or electronic media landscapes, what characterizes this surreal fusion of environment and the unconscious, Ballard wrote in an essay for *New Worlds,* "is its redemptive and therapeutic power. To move through these landscapes is a journey of return to one's innermost being."

This idea is echoed by Joseph Lanz who, in *Re/Search: J. G. Ballard,* also pointed out the neurotic nature of Ballard's characters. Ballard's science fiction, Lanz wrote, "replaces the intergalactic journey with excursions into the convoluted psyche. In Ballard's realm, neurosis is an ultracivilized version of primitive ritual where object and subject meld into an alchemical union. The outside world is just a projection of private fetishes." Pringle claimed that Ballard's characters "are driven by obsessions" and often choose "to strand themselves in some bizarre terrain which reflects their states of mind." Ballard addressed this question in an interview with Douglas Reed in *Books and Bookmen.* "My psychological landscapes," he explained, "are the sort that might be perceived by people during major mental crises—not literally, of course, but they represent similar disturbed states of mind." Speaking with Thomas Frick for *Paris Review,* Ballard further explained his intentions: "I quite consciously rely on my obsessions in all my work. . . . I deliberately set up an obsessional state of mind."

This obsessional quality is reflected in Ballard's recurring use of a few powerful symbols—symbols that have become so closely associated with his work that some critics label them "Ballardian." Sand dunes, abandoned buildings, crashed automobiles, low-flying airplanes, drained swimming pools, and beaches are found in story after story. They are used, Charles Platt wrote in *Dream Makers: The Uncommon People Who Write Science Fiction,* "as signposts, keys to the meaning of technology, the structure of the unconscious, and the promise of the Future." Noting the repetitive

use of these symbols, Galen Strawson observed in the *Times Literary Supplement* that "sometimes it seems as if Ballard's oeuvre is just the systematic extrapolation . . . of an initial fixed set of possibilities, obsessions, and palmary symbols."

Ballard's richly metaphoric prose and his emphasis on psychological and technological themes make him a unique and important figure on the contemporary literary scene. Malcolm Bradbury, writing in the *New York Times Book Review,* stressed the psychological insights in Ballard's work. Ballard is, Bradbury believed, "an explorer of the displacements produced in modern consciousness by the blank ecology of stark architecture, bare high-rises, dead super-highways, and featureless technology." In similar terms, Emma Tennant wrote in the *New Statesman* that "Ballard's talent . . . is to show us what we refuse to see—the extraordinary mixture of old ideas and modern architecture, the self-contradictory expectation of 'human' responses in a landscape constructed to submerge all traces of identity—and to prove that it is only by knowing ourselves that we can understand the technology we have created."

Ballard began his writing career in the 1950s, selling his short stories to science-fiction magazines in his native England and in the United States. Encouraged by E. J. Carnell, the editor of *New Worlds,* to follow his own inclinations, Ballard soon adopted a distinctive style and choice of subject matter. "By the late 1950s," Robert Silverberg wrote in *Galactic Dreamers: Science Fiction as Visionary Literature,* Ballard "was dazzling and perplexing science-fiction readers with his dark and hypnotic stories and novels, typified by intelligent though passive characters in the grips of inexplicable cosmic catastrophes."

The catastrophes and ruined landscapes of Ballard's fiction find their roots in his childhood, which was spent in Shanghai during World War II. The son of a British businessman, Ballard was a child when the war began and the Japanese conquered the city. After several months of separation from his parents, during which he wandered the city alone, he was reunited with his family in a prisoner-of-war camp. The startling inversions brought about by the war and occupation, the empty or ruined buildings, the sudden evacuations, and the societal instability are all echoed in his fiction. He told Platt that the abandoned buildings and drained swimming pools found in his fiction are based on Shanghai's luxury hotels, which were closed for the duration of the war. Ballard told Platt about going to visit a friend whose building had been evacuated during the night: "I remember going there and suddenly finding that the building was totally empty, and wandering around all those empty flats with the furniture still in place, total silence, just the odd window swinging in the wind." "Conventional life," he added, "places its own glaze over everything, a sort of varnish through which the reality is muffled. In Shanghai, what had been a conventional world for me was exposed as no more than a stage set whose cast could disappear overnight; so I saw the fragility of everything, the transience of everything, but also, in a way, the *reality* of everything."

In 1984's *Empire of the Sun* Ballard deals directly with his childhood experiences. "Perhaps," he mused to Frick, "I've always been trying to return to the Shanghai landscape, to some sort of truth that I glimpsed there." The semi-autobiographical novel of a young boy on his own in war-torn Shanghai, *Empire of the Sun* received high praise from reviewers, and made the British best-seller lists. Reviewing the novel for *Newsweek*, David Lehman and Donna Foote placed the book "on anyone's short list of outstanding novels inspired by the second world war . . . [It] combines the exactness of an autobiographical testament with the hallucinatory atmosphere of twilight-zone fiction." Although *Empire of the Sun* is more realistic than Ballard's other writings, John Gross in the *New York Times* was reluctant to describe it as a "conventional novel . . . because many of the scenes in it are so lurid and bizarre, so very nearly out of this world. Among other things, they help to explain why in his work up till now Mr. Ballard should have been repeatedly drawn to apocalyptic themes." Lehman and Foote wrote, "It's ironic that *Empire of the Sun* . . . has earned him accolades denied to his earlier 'disaster novels,' since it has more in common with them than immediately meets the eye. Like its predecessors, the book explores the zone of 'inner space' that Ballard sees as 'the true domain of science-fiction.'" Winter saw *Empire of the Sun* as something new for Ballard, "a union of apparent irreconcilables—autobiography, naturalistic storytelling, and surrealism. Ballard has not only transcended science fiction, he has pushed at the limits of fiction itself, producing a dream of his own life that is both self-critique and story, an entertainment that enriches our understanding of the fact and fantasy in all our lives."

The Kindness of Women, a sequel to *Empire of the Sun*, traces four decades of the author's life and times,

beginning with his medical studies in the 1950s to the death of his wife in a freak accident and his relationships with the various women for whom the book is named. "The main thrust of Ballard's writing," wrote Nick Kimberley in *New Statesman & Society*, "is to weld us, his characters, to what we are not—the world we live in."

In his first four novels, Ballard depicts global catastrophes that destroy modern civilization: high winds in *The Wind from Nowhere*, melting ice caps in *The Drowned World*, drought in *The Burning World*, and a spreading, cancerous mutation in *The Crystal World*. These catastrophes alter the perceptions of Ballard's protagonists who, feeling a kinship with the destruction around them, respond by embracing it. Ballard's heroes, wrote Platt, are "solitary figures, courting the apocalypse and ultimately seduced by it. To them, a private, mystical union with a ruined world [is] more attractive than the pretense of a 'normal' lifestyle among organized bands of survivors."

Although some critics viewed these early novels as pessimistic because of their seemingly passive and self-destructive characters, Ballard disagrees. "I haven't got any sort of 'deathwish,'" he told Reed. "This aspect of my work parallels the self-destructive but curiously consistent logic of people enduring severe mental illness. There is a unique set of laws governing their actions, laws as constant as those controlling sane behavior but based on different criteria." Speaking to Platt on the same topic, Ballard claimed his work is not pessimistic. "It's a fiction of psychological fulfillment," he clarified. "The hero of *The Drowned World*, who goes south toward the sun and self-oblivion, is choosing a sensible course of action that will result in absolute psychological fulfillment for himself. . . . All my fiction describes the merging of the self in the ultimate metaphor, the ultimate image, and that's psychologically fulfilling." Graeme Revell, writing in *Re/Search: J. G. Ballard*, saw these books as "'transformation' rather than 'disaster' stories, involving not a material solution, but one of psychic fulfillment for the hero. . . . The hero is the only one who pursues a meaningful course of action—instead of escaping or trying to adapt to the material environment, he stays and comes to terms with the changes taking place within it and, by implication, within himself."

Ballard's early novels, particularly *The Drowned World* and *The Crystal World*, "helped make his name as a topographer of post-cataclysmic landscape," according to a reviewer for the *Times Literary Supplement*. This reputation changed in the late 1960s when Ballard became a leading spokesman for "New Wave" science fiction, a genre introducing experimental literary techniques and more sophisticated subject matter. In his fiction Ballard now began to explore the media landscape through a nonlinear writing style, entering his most experimental period. Many of his stories from this period are found in *The Atrocity Exhibition*. In this collection of related stories, Ballard explained to Reed, he writes of "a doctor who's had a mental breakdown. He has been shocked and numbed by events like the deaths of the Kennedys and Marilyn Monroe. To make sense of the modern world he wants to immerse himself in its most destructive elements. He creates a series of psycho-dramas that produce grim paradoxes." As a critic for the *Times Literary Supplement* saw it, *The Atrocity Exhibition* "presents extreme examples of the private psyche being invaded by public events." In a preface to the U.S. edition of the book, William S. Burroughs called it "profound and disquieting. . . . The nonsexual roots of sexuality are explored with a surgeon's precision."

Because of objections to some of the book's content—in particular, the stories "Why I Want to Fuck Ronald Reagan" and "The Assassination of John Fitzgerald Kennedy Considered as a Downhill Motor Race," as well as certain unflattering references to consumer activist Ralph Nader—two U.S. publishers accepted and then rejected the book before Grove Press released it in 1972. Called by Joseph W. Palmer of *Library Journal* an "ugly, nauseating, brilliant, and profound" book, *The Atrocity Exhibition* might well be considered "a long poem on metaphysical themes," Jerome Tarshis claimed in the *Evergreen Review*. "That is the difficult part; the horrifying part is that this philosophical investigation is conducted in terms of violent death and perverse sexuality." This opinion was echoed by Paul Theroux in the *New York Times Book Review*. *The Atrocity Exhibition*, Theroux wrote, "is a kind of toying with horror, a stylish anatomy of outrage. . . . It is not [Ballard's] choice of subject, but his celebration of it, that is monstrous."

The sex and violence of *The Atrocity Exhibition* are also found in three other Ballard novels—*Crash, Concrete Island,* and *High-rise*—each of which presents an urban disaster and deals with the perverse violence of modern society. *Crash,* an attempt to discover the

"true significance of the automobile crash," as one character states, tells the story of crash victim James Ballard and photographer Vaughan, a man obsessed with the idea of dying in an auto crash with Elizabeth Taylor, the two of them receiving identical wounds to their genitalia. It is, wrote a *Times Literary Supplement* critic, "a fetishist's book. . . . Ballard's endless reiteration of crashes—of the famous, on acid, with dummies, on film—begins to seem like a frantic litany, grotesque mantras in a private meditation." John Fletcher of the *Dictionary of Literary Biography* called *Crash* "an unsentimental scrutiny of the dehumanized eroticism and the brutality [Ballard] . . . feels are inseparable from the new technologies."

Critical reaction to *Crash* was sometimes harsh. D. Keith Mano wrote in the *New York Times Book Review* that the novel is "the most repulsive book I've yet to come across. . . . Ballard choreographs a crazed, morbid roundelay of dismemberment and sexual perversion. *Crash* is well written: credit given where due. But I could not, in conscience, recommend it." A critic for the *Times Literary Supplement* believed that with *The Atrocity Exhibition* and *Crash,* Ballard has "produced a compendium of twentieth-century pathological imagery which earned him the disparaging reputation of being the intellectual of avant-garde science-fiction." Revell observed that *The Atrocity Exhibition* and *Crash* seemed to many critics to be "some kind of perverse aberration in the career of their author. . . . These new works developed previously latent ideas to a malignancy which burst out of the confines of science-fiction. The fiction seemed to have become real, too real, and there were dangerous questions: moral, existential, even political."

The idea for *Crash* originated in a scene from *The Atrocity Exhibition*. One of the psycho-dramas staged by Ballard's protagonist in that book is an art exhibit consisting of crashed cars. Before beginning *Crash,* Ballard also staged an exhibit of crashed cars at the New Arts Laboratory in London. "I had an opening party at the gallery," *Studio International* quoted Ballard as saying. "I'd never seen 100 people get drunk so quickly. Now, this had something to do with the cars on display. I also had a topless girl interviewing people on closed circuit TV, so that people could see themselves being interviewed around the crashed cars by this topless girl. This was clearly too much. I was the only sober person there. Wine was poured over the crashed cars, glasses were broken, the topless girl was nearly raped. . . . It was not so much an exhibition of sculpture as almost of experimental psychology using the medium of the fine art show. People were unnerved, you see. There was enormous hostility." Ironically, two weeks after completing *Crash,* Ballard was involved in a serious car accident in which his car rolled over and into the oncoming traffic lane. "This is," Ballard told James Goddard of *Cypher,* "an extreme case of nature imitating art."

Concrete Island again concerns a car crash. In this novel Robert Maitland has an accident on the freeway and is stranded on an isolated strip of land between the interweaving lanes of an interchange. Because of his injuries, Maitland cannot climb the embankment to get out. After a time he finds survival more important than escape and comes to accept his situation. Martin Levin in the *New York Times Book Review* noted that "Ballard plays two themes in this compact little book. The external theme is the Robinson Crusoe gambit. . . . The internal theme is the search-for-self motif." *Concrete Island,* wrote a *Times Literary Supplement* reviewer, "is a most intelligent and interesting book" in which Ballard "reveals undertones of savagery and desolation beneath a metaphor of apparent neutrality. . . . [Ballard is] our foremost iconographer of landscape."

Ballard's novel *High-rise* is set in a forty-story apartment block, the residents of which revert to tribal savagery after a power failure, transforming their building into a re-creation of man's prehistoric past. The apartments are ruled, Fletcher explained, "by the brutally simple law of the jungle: to survive one must prey on others and keep out of the way of those who would prey upon oneself." In a review for *Listener,* Neil Hepburn found the novel "well stocked with bizarre and imaginative strokes . . . but requiring such an effort for the suspension of disbelief as to become tiresome." Mel Watkins saw little merit in *High-rise,* claiming in his *New York Times Book Review* appraisal that it "exploits both technology and human emotion in a compulsively vulgar manner." According to Pringle, however, *High-rise* "makes the point that the high-rise building is not so much a machine for living in as a brutal playground full of essentially solitary children. It is a concrete den which encourages every anti-social impulse in its inhabitants rather than serving as a physical framework for a genuine social structure."

In the novel *Rushing to Paradise* Ballard reexamines the dark side of human nature. His main character—obsessive doctor Barbara Rafferty—becomes an ecological crusader and founder of an albatross sanctuary after losing her right to practice medicine. But the opportunistic doctor's intentions are far from selfless: she seeks to establish a utopian colony of women who will bear female children after being impregnated by disposable males. As a London *Observer* reviewer put it, "*Rushing to Paradise* is full of passive witnesses who will not admit the significance of the dramas unfolding in front of their eyes. This is a violent novel, but it also possesses an eerie calm, a glassy formality of texture which is as frightening as it is beautiful."

The violent underpinnings of seemingly placid communities is the focus of the novels *Cocaine Nights* and *Super-Cannes.* In *Cocaine Nights* Ballard posits a dystopian society deadened by leisure. Scores of retirement communities line the Costa del Sol in Spain, full of early-retired people with no purpose or will left in their lives. When his brother is charged with firebombing a house and killing five people in the sleepy town of Estrella de Mar, travel writer Charles Prentice goes down to investigate. In a story that is more of a detective novel than Ballard's previous disaster novels, Prentice uncovers a wide-ranging plot, masterminded by local tennis pro Bobby Crawford, to energize and mobilize the lazy retirees by introducing random violence into their lives.

Rex Roberts of *Insight on the News* called *Cocaine Nights* "one of the author's most accessible novels," even though its theme is the typically Ballardian one of "palpable evil lurking beneath [a] placid surface, a hidden world of drugs, illicit sex and violence." While Roberts claimed that "Ballard seems more moralist than nihilist," a reviewer for *Publishers Weekly* called *Cocaine Nights* "fairly mild," although he credited Ballard for painting a "bleak picture of trouble in paradise [that] has the ring of truth." A. O. Scott, writing in the *New York Times Book Review,* maintained that the book contains "a curious blend of deadpan detachment and almost comical self-consciousness." He quoted Bobby Crawford's explanation of why Estrella de Mar has more culture than the surrounding towns on the Costa del Sol: "Crime and creativity go together, and always have done. The greater the sense of crime, the greater the civic awareness and richer the civilization. Nothing else binds a community together." In the end, Smith said, Ballard overreaches with this idea: "Just as explaining a joke kills the humor, so does theorizing transgression blunt the thrill."

Super-Cannes also explores the sinister forces that wage violence on a supposedly utopian society. The setting is the high-tech office mecca of Eden-Olympia, a new development outside the French city of Cannes. Paul Sinclair, an airplane pilot who suffered injuries in a plane crash, moves to the soulless office park with his new wife, Jane, a doctor he met while convalescing. The former occupant of their house in Eden-Olympia was Dr. Greenwood, a seemingly benevolent figure who died after gunning down ten people and then shooting himself. He was also Jane's former lover. While Jane works long hours in Eden-Olympia's medical building, Paul obsesses about Greenwood and the reason for his killing spree. His investigations lead him to Wilder Penrose, Eden-Olympia's resident psychiatrist, who "believes that Eden-Olympia is a model for a future where leisure has been replaced by work and indulgence in premeditated violence is the surest way for members of the corporate elite to stay sane," according to a critic in the *Economist.* Paul uncovers a diabolical plot that indicates Penrose manipulated Greenwood into abusing the orphans in his care, and that Greenwood's murder spree was an attempt to rid Eden-Olympia of Penrose and other high-ranking administrators who had succumbed to his ideas.

John Gray, reviewing *Super-Cannes* for the *New Statesman,* commented that the book "presents a clairvoyantly lucid vision of what the future will be like." Gray wrote that if the novel "has a lesson, it is that the hyper-capitalism that is emerging in Europe cannot function without manufacturing psychopathology. It needs to satisfy repressed needs for intimacy and excitement, and it will not shrink from trying to apply to that task the same efficiency that has worked so well in the rest of the economy." "Ballard quickly and effectively makes the point that corporatism has crushed our souls," observed Barbara Hoffert in *Library Journal,* adding that the novel's "final pages" are "persuasive and gripping."

"*Cocaine Nights* and *Super-Cannes* rely on an idea central to Ballard's fiction: that forbidden activity can provide extreme liberation," wrote Sam Gilpin in *London Review of Books.* Furthermore, Gilpin continued, "in both novels there is a manipulative figure who orchestrates the vice and justifies it intellectually." Speaking of *Super-Cannes,* Helen Brown wrote in *Books Online* that "the novel asks us if we can be programmed to meet the abstract targets of the multinationals without compromising our humanity. Can we

protest against it without resorting to even greater violence and madness?"

Introducing *Millennium People* to readers as a "wonderfully warped new novel," an *Economist* contributor detailed the novel's plot: deranged pediatrician Richard Gould has inflamed the Volvo-driving, yuppie upscale masses to commit acts of gratuitous violence as a way of combating social unrest. When his wife dies in a senseless accident, psychologist David Markham is converted to Gould's mantra and, as the level of violence accelerates, ultimately helps firebomb England's National Film Theatre, joined in this act of violence by several well-dressed residents of an upscale gated community. "With its allusions to the 11 September attacks on the World Trade Center," the novel will hold meaning for some readers, maintained *Spectator* critic Steve King; however, "others will no doubt be appalled by its characters' insistence on the life-affirming delights of terrorism, though it's hard to say how seriously Ballard wants us to take all this." As the author himself explained to *Bookseller* interviewer Benedicte Page, "I am interested in whether there is something in the air we breathe that encourages a very small minority of people to carry out violent acts of terrorism, I won't say as a cry for help, but as an act of last resort—an act of desperation." Noting references to the writing of Joseph Conrad, *New Statesman* critic John Gray argued that *Millennium People* is "a mesmerising novel" that "could be read as a Conradian fable of loss and dereliction set on the banks of the Thames." Noting that the novel "dissects the perverse psychology that links terrorists with their innocent victims," Gray added: "This is news from the near future, another despatch from one of the supreme chroniclers of our time."

BIOGRAPHICAL AND CRITICAL SOURCES:

BOOKS

Aldiss, Brian, and Harry Harrison, editors, *SF Horizons,* two volumes, Arno Press, 1975.

Burns, Alan, and Charles Sugnet, editors, *The Imagination on Trial: British and American Writers Discuss Their Working Methods,* Allison & Busby, 1981.

Clareson, Thomas D., editor, *SF: The Other Side of Realism—Essays on Modern Fantasy and Science-fiction,* Bowling Green University (Louisville, KY), 1971.

Clareson, Thomas D., editor, *Voices for the Future: Essays on Major Science-fiction Writers,* Bowling Green University (Louisville, KY), Volume I, 1976, Volume II, 1979.

Contemporary Fiction in America and England, 1950-1970, Gale (Detroit, MI), 1976.

Contemporary Literary Criticism, Gale (Detroit, MI), Volume 3, 1975, Volume 6, 1976, Volume 14, 1980, Volume 36, 1986.

Dictionary of Literary Biography, Volume 14: *British Novelists since 1960,* two volumes, Gale (Detroit, MI), 1983.

Goddard, James, and David Pringle, editors, *J. G. Ballard: The First Twenty Years,* Bran's Head Books, 1976.

James, Langdon, editor, *The New Science-Fiction,* Hutchinson, 1969.

Neilson, Keith, editor, *Survey of Science-Fiction Literature,* Salem Press, 1979.

Platt, Charles, *Dream Makers: The Uncommon People Who Write Science Fiction,* Berkley Publishing (New York, NY), 1980.

Pringle, David, *Earth Is the Alien Planet: J. G. Ballard's Four-dimensional Nightmare,* Borgo Press (San Bernardino, CA), 1979.

Pringle, David, *J. G. Ballard: A Primary and Secondary Bibliography,* G. K. Hall (Boston, MA), 1984.

Rose, Mark, *Alien Encounters: Anatomy of Science Fiction,* Harvard University Press (Cambridge, MA), 1981.

Ross, Lois, and Stephen Ross, *The Shattered Ring: Science Fiction and the Quest for Meaning,* John Knox Press, 1970.

Short Story Criticism, Volume 1, Gale (Detroit, MI), 1988.

Silverberg, Robert, editor, *The Mirror of Infinity,* Harper (New York, NY), 1970.

Silverberg, Robert, editor, *Galactic Dreamers: Science Fiction as Visionary Literature,* Random House (New York, NY), 1977.

Vale, V., and Andrea Juno, editors, *Re/Search: J. G. Ballard,* Re/Search Publishing (San Francisco, CA), 1984.

PERIODICALS

Booklist, May 1, 1998, review of *Cocaine Nights,* p. 1500.

Books and Bookmen, April, 1971; March, 1977.

Bookseller, June 20, 2003, Benedicte Page, review of *Millennium People,* p. 27.

Chicago Tribune, December 11, 1987.

Cypher, October, 1973.

Economist (U.S.), October 14, 2000, review of *Super-Cannes,* p. 106; October 4, 2003, review of *Millennium People,* p. 92.

Evergreen Review, spring, 1973.

Foundation, November, 1975, Volume 9, "Some Words about *Crash!*" pp. 44-54; February, 1982.

Globe and Mail (Toronto, Ontario, Canada), November 7, 1987.

Guardian, September 11, 1970; September 13, 2000, Stephen Moss, "Mad about Ballard."

Hudson Review, winter, 1973-74.

Independent, November 10, 2001, Gareth Evans, "A Crash Course in the Future," p. 10.

Insight on the News, September 21, 1998, Rex Roberts, review of *Cocaine Nights,* p. 36.

Kirkus Reviews, March 15, 1996, p. 413; March 1, 1998, review of *Cocaine Nights,* p. 282.

Library Journal, July, 1970; June 15, 1996, p. 64; October 15, 2000, Barbara Hoffert, review of *Super-Cannes,* p. 105.

Listener, December 11, 1975, Neil Hepburn, review of *High-Rise.*

London Review of Books, February 2, 1989; November 16, 2000, Sam Gilpin, "Vaguely on the Run," p. 22.

Los Angeles Times, October 20, 1988.

Los Angeles Times Book Review, October 20, 1985; May 1, 1988; October 27, 1991, p. 3; May 19, 1996, p. 11.

Magazine Litteraire, April, 1974.

Magazine of Fantasy and Science-fiction, September, 1976.

New Review, May, 1974.

New Statesman, May 10, 1974; November 15, 1975; December 20, 1999, Martin Amis, review of *High-Rise,* p. 126; September 11, 2000, John Gray, review of *Super-Cannes,* p. 53; November 19, 2001, Sebastian Shakespeare, review of *The Complete Short Stories,* p. 55; September 8, 2003, John Gray, review of *Millennium People,* p. 50.

New Statesman & Society, September 27, 1991, Nick Kimberley, "The Sage of Shepperton," p. 52.

Newsweek, January 28, 1985, David Lehman and Donna Foote, review of *Empire of the Sun.*

New Worlds, November, 1959; May, 1962; July, 1966; October, 1966.

New York Review of Books, January 25, 1979.

New York Times, May 11, 1977; October 13, 1984, John Gross, "A Survivor's Narrative," p. 18; April

5, 1988, John Gross, "Fable of Man as a River-borne Creator-Destroyer," p. C17.

New York Times Book Review, September 23, 1973; December 1, 1974; December 9, 1979; November 11, 1984, John Calvin Batchelor, "A Boy Saved by the Bomb," p. 11; May 15, 1988; October 16, 1988, Gregory Benford, "Buicks and Madmen," p. 22; December 17, 1989; November 10, 1991, David R. Slavitt, "The Monster He Became," p. 22; November 5, 1995, p. 26; May 26, 1996, p. 14; July 12, 1998, A. O. Scott, "Pinter on the Beach," p. 16; March 7, 1999, review of *War Fever* and *The Day of Creation,* p. 28; November 25, 2001, Geoff Nicholson, review of *Super-Cannes,* p. 29.

Observer (London, England), September 4, 1994, p. 16.

Paris Review, winter, 1984, Thomas Frick, interview with Ballard, pp. 133-160.

Penthouse, September, 1970; April, 1979.

Publishers Weekly, March 11, 1988; July 25, 1991; February 26, 1996, p. 90; April 13, 1998, review of *Cocaine Nights,* p. 54; September 3, 2001, review of *Super-Cannes,* p. 58.

Rolling Stone, November 19, 1987.

Science-Fiction Studies, July, 1976, Charles Nicol, "J. G. Ballard and the Limits of Mainstream SF," pp. 150-157.

Search and Destroy, number 10, 1978.

Spectator, September 17, 1994, p. 38; September 13, 2003, Steve King, review of *Millennium People,* p. 60.

Studio International, October, 1971.

Thrust, winter, 1980.

Time, November 13, 1989.

Times (London, England), September 20, 1984; September 10, 1987; November 3, 1988; November 8, 1990; November 8, 2001, Giles Whittell, "Terrorism, the British Psyche, and the M25" (interview), p. S5.

Times Literary Supplement, July 9, 1970; November 30, 1973; April 26, 1974; December 5, 1975; November 30, 1979; June 12, 1981; September 14, 1984; September 11, 1987; January 13, 1989; November 23, 1990; March 17, 1995, p. 22; April 12, 1996, p. 32; January 2, 1998, review of *The Voices of Time,* p. 20; December 13, 2001, Christopher Taylor, review of *The Complete Short Stories,* p. 20; September 7, 2003, Bharat Tandon, review of *Millennium People,* pp. 6-7.

Transatlantic Review, spring, 1971.

Tribune Books (Chicago, IL), April 10, 1988; December 22, 1991, p. 5; June 4, 1995, p. 3.

Vector, January, 1980.

Washington Post, February 21, 1989.

Washington Post Book World, November 25, 1979; October 28, 1984; July 26, 1987; April 17, 1988; June 12, 1988; May 21, 1995, p. 2; August 2, 1998, review of *Cocaine Nights,* p. 5; February 27, 1999, review of *War Fever* and *The Day of Creation,* p. 6.

Writer, June, 1973.

ONLINE

Books Online, http://www.booksonline.co.uk/ (September 10, 2000), Helen Brown, "Sex as a Means of Sedation."

Fine Line Features Web site, http://www.flf.com/ (January 30, 2002), interview with Ballard.

J. G. Ballard Web site, http://www.jgballard.com (March 14, 2001).

Spike Online, http://www.spikemagazine.com/ (August 31, 2001), David B. Livingstone, "Prophet with Honor"; (August 31, 2001) Chris Hall, "Flight and Imagination" (interview with Ballard).

OTHER

The Unlimited Dream Company (film), Royal College of Art School of Films, 1983.*

*   *   *

BARAKA, Amiri 1934-
(LeRoi Jones; Fundi, a joint pseudonym)

PERSONAL: Born Everett LeRoi Jones, October 7, 1934, in Newark, NJ; name changed to Imamu ("spiritual leader") Ameer ("blessed") Baraka ("prince"); later modified to Amiri Baraka; son of Coyette Leroy (a postal worker and elevator operator) and Anna Lois (Russ) Jones; married Hettie Roberta Cohen, October 13, 1958 (divorced, August, 1965); married Sylvia Robinson (Bibi Amina Baraka), 1966; children: (first marriage) Kellie Elisabeth, Lisa Victoria Chapman; (second marriage) Obalaji Malik Ali, Ras Jua Al Aziz, Shani Isis, Amiri Seku, Ahi Mwenge.

Amiri Baraka

Education: Attended Rutgers University, 1951-52; Howard University, B.A., 1954; Columbia University, M.A. (philosophy); New School for Social Research, M.A. (German literature).

ADDRESSES: Office—Department of Africana Studies, State University of New York, Long Island, NY 11794-4340. *Agent*—Joan Brandt, Sterling Lord Literistic, 660 Madison Ave., New York, NY 10021.

CAREER: State University of New York at Stony Brook, assistant professor, 1980-83, associate professor, 1983-85, professor of African studies, 1985—. Instructor, New School for Social Research (now New School University), New York, NY, 1962-64; visiting professor, University of Buffalo, summer, 1964, Columbia University, fall, 1964, and 1966-67, San Francisco State University, 1967, Yale University, 1977-78, George Washington University, 1978-79, and Rutgers University, 1988. Founded *Yugen* magazine and Totem Press, 1958; co-editor and founder of *Floating Bar* magazine, 1961-63; editor of *Black Nation*. Founder and director, Black Arts Repertory Theatre/School, 1964-66; director of Spirit House (black com-

munity theater; also known as Heckalu Community Center), 1965-75, and head of advisory group at Treat Elementary School, both in Newark; Kimako Blues People (community arts space), co-director. Founder, Congress of African People, 1970-76. Member, Political Prisoners Relief Fund, and African Liberation Day Commission. Candidate, Newark community council, 1968. National Black Political Assembly, former secretary general and co-governor; National Black United Front, member; Congress of African People, co-founder and chair; League of Revolutionary Struggle, member. *Military service:* U.S. Air Force, 1954-57; weather-gunner; stationed for two and a half years in Puerto Rico with intervening trips to Europe, Africa, and the Middle East.

MEMBER: All-African Games, Pan African Federation, Black Academy of Arts and Letters, Black Writers' Union, United Brothers (Newark), Newark Writers Collective.

AWARDS, HONORS: Longview Best Essay of the Year award, 1961, for "Cuba Libre"; John Whitney Foundation fellowship for poetry and fiction, 1962; *Village Voice* Best American Off-Broadway Play ("Obie") award, 1964, for *Dutchman;* Guggenheim fellowship, 1965-66; Yoruba Academy fellow, 1965; second prize, International Art Festival (Dakar), 1966, for *The Slave;* National Endowment for the Arts grant, 1966; D.H.L. from Malcolm X College, 1972; Rockefeller Foundation fellow (drama), 1981; Poetry Award, National Endowment for the Arts, 1981; New Jersey Council for the Arts award, 1982; American Book Award, Before Columbus Foundation, 1984, for *Confirmation: An Anthology of African-American Women;* Drama Award, 1985; PEN-Faulkner Award, 1989; Langston Hughes Medal, 1989, for outstanding contribution to literature; Ferroni award (Italy), and Foreign Poet Award, 1993; Playwright's Award, Winston-Salem Black Drama Festival, 1997; appointed poet laureate of State of New Jersey (position abolished, 2003).

WRITINGS:

PLAYS

(Under name LeRoi Jones) *A Good Girl Is Hard to Find,* produced in Montclair, NJ, 1958.
(Under name LeRoi Jones) *Dante* (one act; excerpted from novel *The System of Dante's Hell;* also see below), produced in New York, NY, 1961, produced as *The Eighth Ditch,* 1964.

(Under name LeRoi Jones) *Dutchman,* (also see below; produced Off-Broadway, 1964; produced in London, 1967), Faber & Faber (London, England), 1967.

(Under name LeRoi Jones) *The Baptism: A Comedy in One Act* (also see below; produced Off-Broadway, 1964, produced in London, 1970-71), Sterling Lord, 1966.

(Under name LeRoi Jones) *The Toilet* (also see below; produced with *The Slave: A Fable* Off-Broadway, 1964), Sterling Lord, 1964.

Dutchman [and] The Slave: A Fable, Morrow (New York, NY), 1964.

(Under name LeRoi Jones) *J-E-L-L-O* (one act comedy; also see below; produced in New York, NY, by Black Arts Repertory Theatre, 1965), Third World Press, 1970.

(Under name LeRoi Jones) *Experimental Death Unit #1* (one act; also see below), produced Off-Broadway, 1965.

(Under name LeRoi Jones) *The Death of Malcolm X* (one act; produced in Newark, NJ, 1965), published in *New Plays from the Black Theatre,* edited by Ed Bullins, Bantam (New York, NY), 1969.

(Under name LeRoi Jones) *A Black Mass* (also see below), produced in Newark, NJ, 1966.

Slave Ship (also see below; produced as *Slave Ship: A Historical Pageant* at Spirit House, 1967; produced in New York, NY, 1969), Jihad, 1967.

Madheart: Morality Drama (one act; also see below), produced at San Francisco State College, 1967.

Arm Yourself, or Harm Yourself, A One-Act Play (also see below; produced at Spirit House, 1967), Jihad, 1967.

Great Goodness of Life (A Coon Show) (one act; also see below), produced at Spirit House, 1967; produced Off-Broadway at Tambellini's Gate Theater, 1969.

The Baptism [and] The Toilet, Grove (New York, NY), 1967.

Home on the Range (one act comedy; also see below), produced at Spirit House, 1968; produced in New York, NY, 1968.

Junkies Are Full of SHHH . . . , produced at Spirit House, 1968; produced with *Bloodrites* (also see below), Off-Broadway, 1970.

Board of Education (children's play), produced at Spirit House, 1968.

Resurrection in Life (one-act pantomime), produced as *Insurrection* in Harlem, NY, 1969.

Four Black Revolutionary Plays: All Praises to the Black Man (contains *Experimental Death Unit #1,*

A Black Mass, Great Goodness of Life (A Coon Show), and *Madheart*), Bobbs-Merrill (New York, NY), 1969.

Black Dada Nihilism (one act), produced Off-Broadway, 1971.

A Recent Killing (three acts), produced Off-Broadway, 1973.

Columbia the Gem of the Ocean, produced in Washington, DC, 1973.

The New Ark's A-Moverin, produced in Newark, NJ, 1974.

The Sidnee Poet Heroical, in Twenty-nine Scenes (one act comedy; also see below; produced Off-Broadway, 1975), Reed & Cannon, 1979.

S-1: A Play with Music (also see below), produced in New York, NY, 1976.

(With Frank Chin and Leslie Siko) *America More or Less* (musical), produced in San Francisco, CA, 1976.

The Motion of History (four-act; also see below), produced in New York, NY, 1977.

The Motion of History and Other Plays (contains *Slave Ship* and *S-1*), Morrow (New York, NY), 1978.

What Was the Relationship of the Lone Ranger to the Means of Production? (one-act; also see below; produced in New York, NY, 1979), Anti-Imperialist Cultural Union, 1978.

Dim Cracker Party Convention, produced in New York, NY, 1980.

Boy and Tarzan Appear in a Clearing, produced Off-Broadway, 1981.

Money: Jazz Opera, produced Off-Broadway, 1982.

Song: A One-Act Play about the Relationship of Art to Real Life, produced in Jamaica, NY, 1983.

General Hag's Skeezag, 1992.

Also author of plays *Police,* published in *Drama Review,* summer, 1968; *Rockgroup,* published in *Cricket,* December, 1969; *Black Power Chant,* published in *Drama Review,* December, 1972; *The Coronation of the Black Queen,* published in *Black Scholar,* June, 1970; *Vomit and the Jungle Bunnies, Revolt of the Moonflowers,* 1969, *Primitive World,* 1991, *Jackpot Melting,* 1996, *Election Machine Warehouse,* 1996, *Meeting Lillie,* 1997, *Biko,* 1997, and *Black Renaissance in Harlem,* 1998.

Plays included in anthologies, including Woodie King and Ron Milner, editors, *Black Drama Anthology* (includes *Bloodrites* and *Junkies Are Full of SHHH . . .*),

New American Library, 1971; and Rochelle Owens, editor, *Spontaneous Combustion: Eight New American Plays* (includes *Ba-Ra-Ka*), Winter House, 1972.

SCREENPLAYS

Dutchman, Gene Persson Enterprises, Ltd., 1967.
Black Spring, Jihad Productions, 1968.
A Fable (based on *The Slave: A Fable*), MFR Productions, 1971.
Supercoon, Gene Persson Enterprises, Ltd., 1971.

POETRY

April 13 (broadside), Penny Poems (New Haven, CT), 1959.
Spring and So Forth (broadside), Penny Poems (New Haven, CT), 1960.
Preface to a Twenty Volume Suicide Note, Totem/Corinth, 1961.
The Disguise (broadside), [New Haven, CT], 1961.
The Dead Lecturer (also see below), Grove (New York, NY), 1964.
Black Art (also see below), Jihad, 1966.
Black Magic (also see below), Morrow (New York, NY), 1967.
A Poem for Black Hearts, Broadside Press, 1967.
Black Magic: Sabotage; Target Study; Black Art; Collected Poetry, 1961-1967, Bobbs-Merrill (New York, NY), 1969.
It's Nation Time, Third World Press, 1970.
Spirit Reach, Jihad, 1972.
Afrikan Revolution, Jihad, 1973.
Hard Facts: Excerpts, People's War, 1975, 2nd edition, Revolutionary Communist League, 1975.
Spring Song, Baraka, 1979.
AM/TRAK, Phoenix Bookshop, 1979.
Selected Poetry of Amiri Baraka/LeRoi Jones (includes Poetry for the Advanced), Morrow (New York, NY), 1979.
In the Tradition: For Black Arthur Blythe, Jihad, 1980.
Reggae or Not!, Contact Two, 1982.
LeRoi Jones—Amiri, Thunder's Mouth Press, 1991.
Transbluency: The Selected Poems of Amiri Baraka/LeRoi Jones (1961-1995), Marsilio, 1995.
Funk Lore: New Poems, 1984-1995, Sun & Moon Press, 1996.
Beginnings and Other Poems, House of Nehesi (Fredericksburg, VA), 2003.

ESSAYS

Cuba Libre, Fair Play for Cuba Committee (New York, NY), 1961.
Blues People: Negro Music in White America, Morrow (New York, NY), 1963, reprinted, Greenwood Press (Westport, CT), 1980, published as *Negro Music in White America,* MacGibbon & Kee (London, England), 1965.
Home: Social Essays (contains "Cuba Libre," "The Myth of a 'Negro Literature,'" "Expressive Language," "The Legacy of Malcolm X, and the Coming of the Black Nation," and "State/meant"), Morrow (New York, NY), 1966, Ecco Press (Hopewell, NJ), 1998.
Black Music, Morrow (New York, NY), 1968.
Raise, Race, Rays, Raze: Essays since 1965, Random House (New York, NY), 1971.
Strategy and Tactics of a Pan-African Nationalist Party, Jihad, 1971.
Kawaida Studies: The New Nationalism, Third World Press, 1972.
Crisis in Boston!, Vita Wa Watu People's War, 1974.
Daggers and Javelins: Essays, 1974-1979, Morrow (New York, NY), 1984.
(With wife, Amina Baraka) *The Music: Reflections on Jazz and Blues,* Morrow (New York, NY), 1987.
Jesse Jackson and Black People, 1996.
The Essence of Reparation, House of Nehesi (Fredericksburg, VA), 2003.

Contributor of essays to *Lorraine Hansberry, A Raisin in the Sun;* and *The Sign in Sidney Brustein's Window,* Vintage Books (New York, NY), 1995.

EDITOR

January 1st 1959: Fidel Castro, Totem, 1959.
Four Young Lady Poets, Corinth, 1962.
(And author of introduction) *The Moderns: An Anthology of New Writing in America,* 1963, published as *The Moderns: New Fiction in America,* 1964.
(And co-author) *In-formation,* Totem, 1965.
Gilbert Sorrentino, *Black & White,* Corinth, 1965.
Edward Dorn, *Hands Up!,* Corinth, 1965.
(And contributor) *Afro-American Festival of the Arts Magazine,* Jihad, 1966, published as *Anthology of Our Black Selves,* 1969.

(With Larry Neal and A. B. Spellman) *The Cricket: Black Music in Evolution*, Jihad, 1968, published as *Trippin': A Need for Change*, New Ark, 1969.

(And contributor, with Larry Neal) *Black Fire: An Anthology of Afro-American Writing*, Morrow (New York, NY), 1968.

A Black Value System, Jihad, 1970.

(With Billy Abernathy under pseudonym Fundi) *In Our Terribleness (Some Elements of Meaning in Black Style)*, Bobbs-Merrill (New York, NY), 1970.

(And author of introduction) *African Congress: A Documentary of the First Modern Pan-African Congress*, Morrow (New York, NY), 1972.

(With Diane Di Prima) *The Floating Bear, A Newsletter, No.1-37, 1961-1969*, McGilvery, 1974.

(With Amina Baraka) *Confirmation: An Anthology of African-American Women*, Morrow (New York, NY), 1983.

OTHER

The System of Dante's Hell (novel; includes the play *Dante*), Grove (New York, NY), 1965.

(Author of introduction) David Henderson, *Felix of the Silent Forest*, Poets Press, 1967.

Striptease, Parallax, 1967.

Tales (short stories), Grove (New York, NY), 1967.

(Author of preface) *Black Boogaloo (Notes on Black Liberation)*, Journal of Black Poetry Press, 1969.

Focus on Amiri Baraka: Playwright LeRoi Jones Analyzes the 1st National Black Political Convention (sound recording), Center for Cassette Studies, 1973.

Three Books by Imamu Amiri Baraka (LeRoi Jones), (contains *The System of Dante's Hell, Tales*, and *The Dead Lecturer*), Grove (New York, NY), 1975.

Selected Plays and Prose of Amiri Baraka/LeRoi Jones, Morrow (New York, NY), 1979.

The Autobiography of LeRoi Jones/Amiri Baraka, Freundlich, 1984, Lawrence Hill Books (Chicago, IL), 1997.

(Author of introduction) Martin Espada, *Rebellion Is the Circle of a Lover's Hand*, Curbstone Press, 1990.

(Author of introduction) *Eliot Katz, Space, and Other Poems*, Northern Lights, 1990.

The LeRoi Jones/Amiri Baraka Reader, Thunder's Mouth Press, 1991.

Thornton Dial: Images of the Tiger, Harry N. Abrams (New York, NY), 1993.

Jesse Jackson and Black People, Third World Press, 1994.

Shy's Wise, Y's: The Griot's Tale, Third World Press, 1994.

(With Charlie Reilly) *Conversations with Amiri Baraka* (also see below), University Press of Mississippi (Jackson, MS), 1994.

Eulogies, Marsilio Publishers (New York, NY), 1996.

The Fiction of LeRoi Jones/Amiri Baraka, foreword by Greg Tate, Lawrence Hill, 2000.

Works represented in anthologies, including *A Broadside Treasury, For Malcolm, The New Black Poetry, Nommo*, and *The Trembling Lamb*. Contributor to *Black Men in Their Own Words*, 2002; contributor to periodicals, including *Evergreen Review, Poetry, Downbeat, Metronome, Nation, Negro Digest*, and *Saturday Review*. Editor with Diane Di Prima, *The Floating Bear*, 1961-63.

Baraka's works have been translated into Japanese, Norwegian, Italian, German, French, and Spanish.

SIDELIGHTS: Amiri Baraka, who published under his birth name LeRoi Jones until 1967, is known for his strident social criticism and an incendiary style that has made it difficult for some audiences and critics to respond with objectivity to his works. Baraka's art stems from his African-American heritage. Throughout his career his method in poetry, drama, fiction, and essays has been confrontational, calculated to shock and awaken audiences to the political concerns of black Americans during the second half of the twentieth century. Baraka's own political stance has changed several times, thus dividing his oeuvre into periods; a member of the avant garde during the 1950s, Baraka became a black nationalist, and more recently a Marxist with socialist ideals. In the wake of the September 11, 2001, bombings of the World Trade Center, Baraka was accused of adding anti-Semite to his political outlook when in his poem "Somebody Blew up America" he suggested that New York's Jews had been warned in advance not to enter the doomed buildings on that fateful day; public outcry became so great that the State of New Jersey took action to abolish the position of poet laureate Baraka then held. Baraka, for his part, threatened legal action.

Throughout his career Baraka has stirred controversy, some praising him for speaking out against oppression and others arguing that he fosters hate. Critical opinion has been sharply divided between those who feel, with *Dissent* contributor Stanley Kaufman, that Baraka's race and political moment have created his celebrity, and those who feel that Baraka stands among the most important writers of the twentieth century. In *American Book Review,* Arnold Rampersad counted Baraka with Phyllis Wheatley, Frederick Douglass, Paul Laurence Dunbar, Langston Hughes, Zora Neale Hurston, Richard Wright, and Ralph Ellison "as one of the eight figures . . . who have significantly affected the course of African-American literary culture."

Baraka did not always identify with radical politics, nor did he always channel his writing into use as their tool. He was born in Newark, New Jersey, and enjoyed a middle-class education. During the 1950s he attended Rutgers University and Howard University. Then he spent three years in the U.S. Air Force, where he was stationed for most of that time in Puerto Rico. When he returned to New York City, he attended Columbia University and the New School for Social Research. Baraka lived in Greenwich Village's lower east side where he made friends with Beat poets Allen Ginsberg, Frank O'Hara, and Gilbert Sorrentino. The white avant garde—primarily Ginsberg, O'Hara, and leader of the Black Mountain poets Charles Olson—and Baraka believed that writing poetry is a process of discovery rather than an exercise in fulfilling traditional expectations of what poems should be. Baraka, like the projectivist poets, believed that a poem's form should follow the shape determined by the poet's own breath and intensity of feeling. In 1958 Baraka founded *Yugen* magazine and Totem Press, important forums for new verse. His first play, *A Good Girl Is Hard to Find,* was produced at Sterington House in Montclair, New Jersey, that same year.

Preface to a Twenty Volume Suicide Note, Baraka's first published collection of poems, appeared in 1961. M. L. Rosenthal wrote in *The New Poets: American and British Poetry since World War II* that these poems show Baraka's "natural gift for quick, vivid imagery and spontaneous humor." The reviewer also praised the "sardonic or sensuous or slangily knowledgeable passages" that fill the early poems. While the cadence of blues and many allusions to black culture are found in the poems, the subject of blackness does not predominate. Throughout, rather, the poet shows his integrated, Bohemian social roots. For example, the poem "Notes for a Speech" states, "African blues / does not know me . . . Does / not feel / what I am,"

and the book's last line is "You are / as any other sad man here / american."

With the rise of the civil rights movement Baraka's works took on a more militant tone, and he began a reluctant separation from his Bohemian beginnings. His trip to Castro's Cuba in July of 1959 marked an important turning point in his life. His view of his role as a writer, the purpose of art, and the degree to which ethnic awareness deserved to be his subject changed dramatically. In Cuba he met writers and artists from third world countries whose political concerns included the fight against poverty, famine, and oppressive governments. They felt he was merely being self-indulgent, "cultivating his soul" in poetry while there were social problems to solve in America. In *Home: Social Essays,* Baraka explains how he tried to defend himself against these accusations, and was further challenged by Jaime Shelley, a Mexican poet, who had said, "'In that ugliness you live in, you want to cultivate your soul? Well, we've got millions of starving people to feed, and that moves me enough to make poems out of.'" Soon Baraka began to identify with third world writers and to write poems and plays with strong ethnic and political messages.

Dutchman, a play of entrapment in which a white woman and a middle-class black man both express their murderous hatred on a subway, was first performed Off-Broadway in 1964. The one-act play makes many references to sex and violence and ends in the black man's murder. While other dramatists of the time were using the techniques of naturalism, Baraka used symbolism and other experimental techniques to enhance the play's emotional impact. Lula, the white woman, represents the white state, and Clay, the black man in the play, represents ethnic identity and non-white manhood. Lula kills Clay after taunting him with sexual invitations and insults such as "You ain't no nigger, you're just a dirty white man. Get up, Clay. Dance with me, Clay." The play established Baraka's reputation as a playwright and has been often anthologized and performed. Considered by many to be the best play of the year, it won the *Village Voice* Obie Award in 1964. Later, Anthony Harvey adapted it for a film made in Britain, and in the 1990s it was revived for several productions in New York City. Darryl Pinckney commented in the *New York Times Book Review* that *Dutchman* survived the test of time better than other protest plays of the 1960s due to its economic use of vivid language, its surprise ending, and its quick pacing.

The plays and poems following *Dutchman* expressed Baraka's increasing disappointment with white America and his growing need to separate from it. He wrote in *Cuba Libre* that the Beat generation had become a counterculture of drop-outs who did not generate very meaningful politics. Baraka felt there had to be a more effective alternative to disengagement from the political, legal, and moral morass the country had become. In *The Dead Lecturer* Baraka explored the alternatives, finding no room for compromise: if he identified with an ethnic cause, he would find hope of meaningful action and change; but if he remained in his comfortable assimilated position, writing "quiet" poems, he would remain "a dead lecturer." Critics observed that as Baraka's poems became more politically intense, they left behind some of the flawless technique of the earlier poems. *Nation* review contributor Richard Howard wrote: "These are the agonized poems of a man writing to save his skin, or at least to settle in it, and so urgent is their purpose that not one of them can trouble to be perfect."

To make a clean break with the Beat influence, Baraka turned to writing fiction in the mid-1960s, penning *The System of Dante's Hell*, a novel, and *Tales*, a collection of short stories. The novel echoes the themes and structures found in his earlier poems and plays. The stories, like the poems in *Black Magic*, also published in 1967, are "'fugitive narratives' that describe the harried flight of an intensely self-conscious Afro-American artist/intellectual from neo-slavery of blinding, neutralizing whiteness, where the area of struggle is basically within the mind," Robert Elliot Fox wrote in *Conscientious Sorcerers: The Black Postmodernist Fiction of LeRoi Jones/Baraka, Ishmael Reed, and Samuel R. Delany.* The role of violent action in achieving political change is more prominent in these stories. Unlike Shakespeare's Hamlet, who deliberates at length before taking violent action, Baraka sought to stand with "the straight ahead people, who think when that's called for, who don't when they don't have to," as he explained in *Tales.* The role of music in black life is seen more often in these books, also. In the story "Screamers," the screams from a jazz saxophone galvanize the people into a powerful uprising.

Baraka's classic history *Blues People: Negro Music in White America,* published in 1963, traces black music from slavery to contemporary jazz. The blues, a staple of black American music, grew out of the encounter between African and American cultures in the South

to become an art form uniquely connected to both the African past and the American soil. Finding indigenous black art forms was important to Baraka at this time, as he was searching for a more authentic ethnic voice for his own poetry. From this important study Baraka became known as an articulate jazz critic and a perceptive observer of social change. As Clyde Taylor stated in *Amiri Baraka: The Kaleidoscopic Torch,* "The connection he nailed down between the many faces of black music, the sociological sets that nurtured them, and their symbolic evolutions through socio-economic changes, in *Blues People,* is his most durable conception, as well as probably the one most indispensable thing said about black music."

Baraka will also be long remembered for his other important studies, *Black Music,* which expresses black nationalist ideals, and *The Music: Reflections on Jazz and Blues,* which expresses his Marxist views. In *Black Music* John Coltrane emerges as the patron saint of the black arts movement after replacing "weak Western forms" of music with more fluid forms learned from a global vision of black culture. Though some critics have maintained that Baraka's essay writing is not all of the same quality, Lloyd W. Brown commented in *Amiri Baraka* that Baraka's essays on music are flawless: "As historian, musicological analyst, or as a journalist covering a particular performance Baraka always commands attention because of his obvious knowledge of the subject and because of a style that is engaging and persuasive even when the sentiments are questionable and controversial."

After Black Muslim leader Malcolm X was killed in 1965, Baraka moved to Harlem and became a black nationalist. He founded the Black Arts Repertory Theatre/School in Harlem and published the collection *Black Magic.* Poems in *Black Magic* chronicle Baraka's divorce from white culture and values and also display his mastery of poetic techniques. As Taylor observed, "There are enough brilliant poems of such variety in *Black Magic* and *In Our Terribleness* to establish the unique identity and claim for respect of several poets. But it is beside the point that Baraka is probably the finest poet, black or white, writing in this country these days." There was no doubt that Baraka's political concerns superseded his just claims to literary excellence, and the challenge to critics was to respond to the political content of the works. Some critics who felt the best art must be apolitical, dismissed Baraka's newer work as "a loss to literature."

Kenneth Rexroth wrote in *With Eye and Ear* that Baraka "has succumbed to the temptation to become a professional Race Man of the most irresponsible sort. . . . His loss to literature is more serious than any literary casualty of the Second War." In 1966 Bakara moved back to Newark, New Jersey, and a year later changed his name to the Bantuized Muslim appellation Imamu ("spiritual leader," later dropped) Ameer (later Amiri, "blessed") Baraka ("prince").

A new aesthetic for black art was being developed in Harlem and Baraka was its primary theorist. Black American artists should follow "black," not "white" standards of beauty and value, he maintained, and should stop looking to white culture for validation. The black artist's role, he wrote in *Home: Social Essays,* is to "aid in the destruction of America as he knows it." Foremost in this endeavor was the imperative to portray society and its ills faithfully so that the portrayal would move people to take necessary corrective action.

By the early 1970s Baraka was recognized as an influential African American writer. Randall noted in *Black World* that younger black poets Nikki Giovanni and Don L. Lee (later Haki R. Madhubuti) were "learning from LeRoi Jones, a man versed in German philosophy, conscious of literary tradition . . . who uses the structure of Dante's *Divine Comedy* in his *System of Dante's Hell* and the punctuation, spelling and line divisions of sophisticated contemporary poets." More importantly, Arnold Rampersad wrote in the *American Book Review,* "More than any other black poet . . . he taught younger black poets of the generation past how to respond poetically to their lived experience, rather than to depend as artists on embalmed reputations and outmoded rhetorical strategies derived from a culture often substantially different from their own."

After coming to see black nationalism as a destructive form of racism, Baraka denounced it in 1974 and became a third world socialist. Hatred of non-whites, he declared in the *New York Times,* "is sickness or criminality, in fact, a form of fascism." Beginning in 1974 he produced a number of Marxist poetry collections and plays, his newly adopted political goal the formation of socialist communities and a socialist state. *Daggers and Javelins* and the other books produced during this period lack the emotional power of the works from the black nationalist period, contended many critics. However, some reviewers agreed with

his new politics, exiled Filipino leftist intellectual E. San Juan praising Baraka's work of the late 1970s. San Juan wrote in *Amiri Baraka: The Kaleidoscopic Torch* that Baraka's 1978 play *What Was the Relationship of the Lone Ranger to the Means of Production?* was "the most significant theatrical achievement of 1978 in the Western hemisphere." Joe Weixlmann responded in the same book to the tendency to categorize the radical Baraka instead of analyze him: "At the very least, dismissing someone with a label does not make for very satisfactory scholarship. Initially, Baraka's reputation as a writer and thinker derived from a recognition of the talents with which he is so obviously endowed. The subsequent assaults on that reputation have, too frequently, derived from concerns which should be extrinsic to informed criticism."

In more recent years, recognition of Baraka's impact on late twentieth-century American culture has resulted in the publication of several anthologies of his literary oeuvre. *The LeRoi Jones/Amiri Baraka Reader* presents a thorough overview of the writer's development, covering the period from 1957 to 1983. The volume presents Baraka's work from four different periods and emphasizes lesser-known works rather than the author's most-famous writings. Although criticizing the anthology for offering little in the way of original poetry, *Sulfur* reviewer Andrew Schelling termed the collection "a sweeping account of Baraka's development." A *Choice* contributor also praised the volume, calling it "a landmark volume in African American literature." *Transbluency: The Selected Poems of Amiri Baraka/LeRoi Jones (1961-1995),* published in 1995, was hailed by Daniel L. Guillory in *Library Journal* as "critically important." And Donna Seaman, writing in *Booklist,* commended the "lyric boldness of this passionate collection."

Baraka's legacy as a major poet of the second half of the twentieth century remains matched by his importance as a cultural and political leader. His influence on younger writers was significant and widespread, and as a leader of the Black Arts movement of the 1960s Baraka did much to define and support black literature's mission into the next century. His experimental fiction of the 1960s is yet considered some of the most significant contribution to black fiction since that of Jean Toomer, who wrote during the Harlem Renaissance of the 1920s. Writers from other ethnic groups have credited Baraka with opening "tightly guarded doors" in the white publishing establishment, noted Murice Kenney in *Amiri Baraka: The Kaleido-scopic Torch,* adding: "We'd all still be waiting the invitation from the *New Yorker* without him. He taught us how to claim it and take it."

BIOGRAPHICAL AND CRITICAL SOURCES:

BOOKS

Allen, Donald M., and Warren Tallman, editors, *Poetics of the New American Poetry,* Grove (New York, NY), 1973.

Anadolu-Okur, Nilgun, *Contemporary African American Theater: Afrocentricity in the Works of Larry Neal, Amiri Baraka, and Charles Fuller,* Garland (New York, NY), 1997.

Baraka, Amiri, *Tales,* Grove (New York, NY), 1967.

Baraka, Amiri, *Black Magic: Sabotage; Target Study; Black Art; Collected Poetry, 1961-1967,* Bobbs-Merrill (New York, NY), 1969.

Baraka, Amiri, *The Autobiography of LeRoi Jones/ Amiri Baraka,* Freundlich Books, 1984.

Baraka, Amiri, and Charlie Reilly, *Conversations with Amiri Baraka,* University Press of Mississippi (Jackson, MS), 1994.

Baraka, Amiri, and Larry Neal, editors, *Black Fire: An Anthology of Afro-American Writing,* Morrow (New York, NY), 1968.

Benston, Kimberly A., editor, *Baraka: The Renegade and the Mask,* Yale University Press (New Haven, CT), 1976.

Benston, Kimberly A., editor, *Imamu Amiri Baraka (LeRoi Jones): A Collection of Critical Essays,* Prentice-Hall, 1978.

Bigsby, C. W. E., *Confrontation and Commitment: A Study of Contemporary American Drama, 1959-1966,* University of Missouri Press, 1968.

Bigsby, C. W. E., *The Second Black Renaissance: Essays in Black Literature,* Greenwood Press (Westport, CT), 1980.

Bigsby, C. W. E., editor, *The Black American Writer, Volume II: Poetry and Drama,* Everett/Edwards, 1970, Penguin (Harmondsworth, England), 1971.

Birnebaum, William M., *Something for Everybody Is Not Enough,* Random House (New York, NY), 1972.

Black Literature Criticism, Gale (Detroit, MI), 1991.

Brown, Lloyd W., *Amiri Baraka,* Twayne (New York, NY), 1980.

Concise Dictionary of American Literary Biography, Volume 1: The New Consciousness, Gale (Detroit, MI), 1987.

Contemporary Literary Criticism, Gale (Detroit, MI), Volume 1, 1973, Volume 2, 1974, Volume 3, 1975, Volume 5, 1976, Volume 10, 1979, Volume 14, 1980, Volume 33, 1985.

Cook, Bruce, *The Beat Generation,* Scribner (New York, NY), 1971.

Dace, Letitia, *LeRoi Jones (Imamu Amiri Baraka): A Checklist of Works by and about Him,* Nether Press, 1971.

Debusscher, Gilbert, and Henry I. Schvey, editors, *New Essays on American Drama,* Rodopi, 1989.

Dictionary of Literary Biography, Gale (Detroit, MI), Volume 5: *American Poets since World War II,* 1980, Volume 7: *Twentieth-Century American Dramatists,* 1981, Volume 16: *The Beats; Literary Bohemians in Postwar America,* 1983, Volume 38: *Afro-American Writers after 1955: Dramatists and Prose Writers,* 1985.

Dukore, Bernard F., *Drama and Revolution,* Holt (New York, NY), 1971.

Elam, Harry Justin, *Taking It to the Streets: The Social Protest Theater of Luis Valdez and Amiri Baraka,* University of Michigan Press (Ann Arbor, MI), 1997.

Ellison, Ralph, *Shadow and Act,* New American Library (New York, NY), 1966.

Emanuel, James A., and Theodore L. Gross, editors, *Dark Symphony: Negro Literature in America,* Free Press (New York, NY), 1968.

Fox, Robert Elliot, *Conscientious Sorcerers: The Black Postmodernist Fiction of LeRoi Jones/Baraka, Ishmael Reed, and Samuel R. Delany,* Greenwood Press (Westport, CT), 1987.

Frost, David, *The Americans,* Stein & Day, 1970.

Gayle, Addison, *The Way of the New World: The Black Novel in America,* Anchor/Doubleday (New York, NY), 1975.

Gayle, Addison, editor, *Black Expression: Essays by and about Black Americans in the Creative Arts,* Weybright & Talley, 1969.

Gwynne, James B., editor, *Amiri Baraka: The Kaleidoscopic Torch,* Steppingstones Press, 1985.

Harris, William J., *The Poetry and Poetics of Amiri Baraka: The Jazz Aesthetic,* University of Missouri Press, 1985.

Haskins, James, *Black Theater in America,* Crowell (New York, NY), 1982.

Henderson, Stephen E., *Understanding the New Black Poetry: Black Speech, and Black Music as Poetic References,* Morrow (New York, NY), 1973.

Hill, Herbert, *Soon, One Morning,* Knopf (New York, NY), 1963.

Hill, Herbert, editor, *Anger, and Beyond: The Negro Writer in the United States,* Harper (New York, NY), 1966.

Hudson, Theodore, *From LeRoi Jones to Amiri Baraka: The Literary Works,* Duke University Press, 1973.

Inge, M. Thomas, Maurice Duke, and Jackson R. Bryer, editors, *Black American Writers: Bibliographic Essays; Richard Wright, Ralph Ellison, James Baldwin, and Amiri Baraka,* St. Martin's Press (New York, NY), 1978.

Jones, LeRoi, *Blues People: Negro Music in White America,* Morrow (New York, NY), 1963.

Jones, LeRoi, *The Dead Lecturer,* Grove (New York, NY), 1964.

Jones, LeRoi, *Home: Social Essays,* Morrow (New York, NY), 1966.

Keil, Charles, *Urban Blues,* University of Chicago Press (Chicago, IL), 1966.

King, Woodie, and Ron Milner, editors, *Black Drama Anthology,* New American Library (New York, NY), 1971.

Knight, Arthur, and Kit Knight, editors, *The Beat Vision,* Paragon House, 1987.

Kofsky, Frank, *Black Nationalism and the Revolution in Music,* Pathfinder, 1970.

Lacey, Henry C., *To Raise, Destroy, and Create: The Poetry, Drama, and Fiction of Imamu Amiri Baraka (LeRoi Jones),* Whitson Publishing Company, 1981.

Lewis, Allan, *American Plays and Playwrights,* Crown (New York, NY), 1965.

Littlejohn, David, *Black on White: A Critical Survey of Writing by American Negroes,* Viking (New York, NY), 1966.

O'Brien, John, *Interviews with Black Writers,* Liveright (New York, NY), 1973.

Olaniyan, Tejumola, *Scars of Conquest/Masks of Resistance: The Invention of Cultural Identities in African, African-American, and Caribbean Drama,* Oxford University Press (New York, NY), 1995.

Ossman, David, *The Sullen Art: Interviews with Modern American Poets,* Corinth, 1963.

Rexroth, Kenneth, *With Eye and Ear,* Herder & Herder, 1970.

Rosenthal, M. L., *The New Poets: American and British Poetry since World War II,* Oxford University Press (New York, NY), 1967.

Sollors, Werner, *Amiri Baraka/LeRoi Jones: The Quest for a "Populist Modernism,"* Columbia University Press (New York, NY), 1978.

Stepanchev, Stephen, *American Poetry since 1945,* Harper (New York, NY), 1965.

Weales, Gerald, *The Jumping-off Place: American Drama in the 1960s,* Macmillan (New York, NY), 1969.

Whitlow, Roger, *Black American Literature: A Critical History,* Nelson Hall (New York, NY), 1973.

Williams, Sherley Anne, *Give Birth to Brightness: A Thematic Study in Neo-Black Literature,* Dial (New York, NY), 1972.

PERIODICALS

African-American Review, summer-fall, 2003, special Baraka issue.

American Book Review, February, 1980; May-June, 1985.

Atlantic, January, 1966; May, 1966.

Avant Garde, September, 1968.

Black American Literature Forum, spring, 1980; spring, 1981; fall, 1982; spring, 1983; winter, 1985.

Black Issues Book Review, Robert Fleming, "Trouble Man," p. 22.

Black World, April, 1971; December, 1971; November, 1974; July, 1975.

Booklist, January 1, 1994, p. 799; February 15, 1994, p. 1052; October 15, 1995, p. 380.

Book Week, December 24, 1967.

Book World, October 28, 1979.

Boundary 2, number 6, 1978.

Callaloo, summer, 2003, Matthew Rebhorn, "Flying Dutchman: Maosochism, Minstrelsy, and the Gender Politics of Amiri Baraka's 'Dutchman', " p. 796.

Chicago Defender, January 11, 1965.

Chicago Tribune, October 4, 1968.

Commentary, February, 1965.

Contemporary Literature, Volume 12, 1971; winter, 2001, Michael Magee, "Tribes of New York," p. 694.

Detroit Free Press, January 31, 1965.

Detroit News, January 15, 1984; August 12, 1984.

Dissent, spring, 1965.

Ebony, August, 1967; August, 1969; February, 1971.

Educational Theatre Journal, March, 1968; March, 1970; March, 1976.

Esquire, June, 1966.

Essence, September, 1970; May, 1984; September, 1984; May, 1985.

Jazz Review, June, 1959.

Journal of Black Poetry, fall, 1968; spring, 1969; summer, 1969; fall, 1969.

Library Journal, January, 1994, p. 112; November, 1995, pp. 78-79.

Los Angeles Free Press, Volume 5, number 18, May 3, 1968.

Los Angeles Times, April 20, 1990.

Los Angeles Times Book Review, May 15, 1983; March 29, 1987.

Nation, October 14, 1961; November 14, 1961; March 13, 1964; April 13, 1964; January 4, 1965; March 15, 1965; January 22, 1968; February 2, 1970; November 18, 2002, Art Winslow, "Prosody in Motion," p. 11.

Negro American Literature Forum, March, 1966; winter, 1973.

Negro Digest, December, 1963; February, 1964; Volume 13, number 19, August, 1964; March, 1965; April, 1965; March, 1966; April, 1966; June, 1966; April, 1967; April, 1968; January, 1969; April, 1969.

Newsweek, March 13, 1964; April 13, 1964; November 22, 1965; May 2, 1966; March 6, 1967; December 4, 1967; December 1, 1969; February 19, 1973.

New York, November 5, 1979.

New Yorker, April 4, 1964; December 26, 1964; March 4, 1967; December 30, 1972; October 14, 2002, Nick Paumgarten, "Goodbye, Paramus."

New York Herald Tribune, March 25, 1964; April 2, 1964; December 13, 1964; October 27, 1965.

New York Post, March 16, 1964; March 24, 1964; January 15, 1965; March 18, 1965.

New York Review of Books, May 22, 1964; January 20, 1966; July 2, 1970; October 17, 1974; June 11, 1984; June 14, 1984.

New York Times, April 28, 1966; May 8, 1966; August 10, 1966; September 14, 1966; October 5, 1966; January 20, 1967; February 28, 1967; July 15, 1967; January 5, 1968; January 6, 1968; January 9, 1968; January 10, 1968; February 7, 1968; April 14, 1968; August 16, 1968; November 27, 1968; December 24, 1968; August 26, 1969; November 23, 1969; February 6, 1970; May 11, 1972; June 11, 1972; November 11, 1972; November 14, 1972; November 23, 1972; December 5, 1972; December 27, 1974; December 29, 1974; November 19, 1979; October 15, 1981; January 23, 1984; February 9, 1991.

New York Times Book Review, January 31, 1965; November 28, 1965; May 8, 1966; February 4, 1968; March 17, 1968; February 14, 1971; June 6, 1971;

June 27, 1971; December 5, 1971; March 12, 1972; December 16, 1979; March 11, 1984; July 5, 1987; December 20, 1987.

New York Times Magazine, February 5, 1984.

Salmagundi, spring-summer, 1973.

Saturday Review, April 20, 1963; January 11, 1964; January 9, 1965; December 11, 1965; December 9, 1967; October 2, 1971; July 12, 1975.

Skeptical Inquirer, January-February, 2003, Kevin Christopher, "Baraka Buys Bunk," p. 8.

Studies in Black Literature, spring, 1970; Volume 1, number 2, 1970; Volume 3, number 2, 1972; Volume 3, number 3, 1972; Volume 4, number 1, 1973.

Sulfur, spring, 1992.

Sunday News (New York, NY), January 21, 1973.

Time, December 25, 1964; November 19, 1965; May 6, 1966; January 12, 1968; April 26, 1968; June 28, 1968; June 28, 1971.

Times Literary Supplement, November 25, 1965; September 1, 1966; September 11, 1969; October 9, 1969; August 2, 1991.

Tribune Books (Chicago, IL), March 29, 1987.

Village Voice, December 17, 1964; May 6, 1965; May 19, 1965; August 30, 1976; August 1, 1977; December 17-23, 1980; October 2, 1984.

Washington Post, August 15, 1968; September 12, 1968; November 27, 1968; December 5, 1980; January 23, 1981; June 29, 1987.

Washington Post Book World, December 24, 1967; May 22, 1983.

ONLINE

Academy of American Poets Web site, http://www.poets.org/ (July 19, 2001), "Amiri Baraka.*"

*   *   *

BARKER, Clive 1952-

PERSONAL: Born 1952, in Liverpool, England; son of Len (dock worker) and Joan (nurse) Barker; children: Nicole. *Education:* Received degree from University of Liverpool.

ADDRESSES: Home—Los Angeles, CA. *Office*—Stealth Press, 128 East Grant St., 4th Fl., Lancaster, PA 17602-2854.

Clive Barker

CAREER: Illustrator, painter, actor, playwright, screen-writer, and author. Founder of Dog Company (theatre group) and Seraphim Productions (producer of Barker's novels, films, plays, CD-ROMs, comic books, and paintings). Director of short films, including *Salome,* 1973, and *The Forbidden,* 1978; director of feature-length films, including *Hellraiser,* 1987, *Night-breed,* 1990, *Lord of Illusions,* 1995, and *Tortured Souls,* 2004. Executive producer of films, including *Hellbound: Hellraiser II,* 1989, *Hellraiser III: Hell on Earth,* 1992, *Candyman,* 1992, *Candyman II: Farewell to the Flesh,* 1995, and *Gods and Monsters,* 1998. *Exhibitions:* Barker's paintings and drawings have appeared at Bess Cutler Gallery, New York, NY, 1993; South Coast Plaza branch, Laguna Art Museum, Costa Mesa, CA, 1995; and Pacific Design Center, West Hollywood, CA, 2002.

AWARDS, HONORS: Two British Fantasy awards from British Fantasy Society; World Fantasy Award for best anthology/collection from World Fantasy Convention, 1985, for *Clive Barker's Books of Blood.*

WRITINGS:

SHORT FICTION

Clive Barker's Books of Blood, Volume One (contains "The Book of Blood," "In the Hills, the Cities," "The Midnight Meat Train," "Pig Blood Blues," "Sex, Death, and Starshine," and "The Yattering and Jack"), introduction by Ramsey Campbell, Sphere (London, England), 1984, Berkley (New York, NY), 1986.

Clive Barker's Books of Blood, Volume Two (contains "Dread," "Hell's Event," "Jaqueline Ess: Her Will and Testament," "New Murders in the Rue Morgue," and "The Skins of the Fathers"), Sphere (London, England), 1984, Berkley (New York, NY), 1986.

Clive Barker's Books of Blood, Volume Three (contains "Confessions of a [Pornographer's] Shroud," "Human Remains," "Rawhead Rex," "Scape-Goats," and "Son of Celluloid"), Sphere (London, England), 1984, Berkley (New York, NY), 1986.

Books of Blood, Volumes 1-3, Weidenfeld & Nicolson (London, England), 1985, published in one volume, Scream/Press (Santa Cruz, CA), 1985.

Clive Barker's Books of Blood, Volume Four (contains "The Age of Desire," "The Body Politic," "Down, Satan!," "The Inhuman Condition," and "Revela-tions"), Sphere (London, England), 1985, published as *The Inhuman Condition: Tales of Terror,* Poseidon (New York, NY), 1986.

Clive Barker's Books of Blood, Volume Five (contains "Babel's Children," "The Forbidden," "In the Flesh," and "The Madonna"), Sphere (London, England), 1985, published as *In The Flesh: Tales of Terror,* Poseidon (New York, NY), 1986.

Clive Barker's Books of Blood, Volume Six (includes "How Spoilers Breed," "The Last Illusion," "The Life of Death," "On Jerusalem Street," and "Twi-light at the Towers"), Sphere (London, England), 1985.

Books of Blood, Volumes 4-6, Weidenfeld & Nicolson (London, England), 1986.

The Hellbound Heart (novella), published in *Night Vi-sions 3,* edited by George R. R. Martin, Dark Har-vest (Arlington Heights, IL), 1986, published sepa-rately, Simon & Schuster (New York, NY), 1988.

Cabal (includes novella "Cabal," and stories "How Spoilers Breed," "The Last Illusion," "The Life of Death," and "Twilight at the Towers"), Poseidon (New York, NY), 1988.

London, Volume One: Bloodline, Fantaco (Albany, NY), 1993.

Saint Sinner, Marvel Comics (New York, NY), 1993-1994.

Clive Barker's A-Z of Horror, compiled by Stephen Jones, HarperPrism (New York, NY), 1997.

Books of Blood (contains volumes 1-6), Stealth Press (Lancaster, PA), 2001.

Tapping the Vein, Checker Book Co. (Centerville, OH), 2002.

NOVELS

The Damnation Game, Weidenfeld & Nicolson (London, England), 1985, Putnam (New York, NY), 1987.

Weaveworld, Poseidon (New York, NY), 1987, illustrated by the author, Collins (London, England), 1987.

The Great and Secret Show: The First Book of the Art, Harper (New York, NY), 1989.

Imajica, HarperCollins (New York, NY), 1991, published in two volumes as *Imajica I: The Fifth Dominion* and *Imajica II: The Reconciliation,* Harper (New York, NY), 1995, published in one volume with new illustrations, 2002.

The Thief of Always: A Fable, illustrated by Clive Barber, HarperCollins (New York, NY), 1992.

Everville: The Second Book of the Art (sequel to *The Great and Secret Show*), HarperCollins (New York, NY), 1994.

Sacrament, HarperCollins (New York, NY), 1996.

Galilee, HarperCollins (New York, NY), 1998.

Coldheart Canyon: A Hollywood Ghost Story, HarperCollins (New York, NY), 2001.

"ABARAT QUARTET"; FOR CHILDREN; SELF-ILLUSTRATED

Abarat, HarperCollins (New York, NY), 2002.

Days of Magic, Nights of War, Joanna Cotler Books (New York, NY), 2004.

SCREENPLAYS

(With James Caplin) *Underworld,* Limehouse Pictures, 1985.

Rawhead Rex (adapted from his short story of the same title), Empire, 1986.

(And director) *Hellraiser* (adapted from his novella *The Hellbound Heart*), New World, 1987.

(And director) *Nightbreed* (adapted from his novella *Cabal*), Twentieth Century-Fox, 1990.

(And director and producer) *Lord of Illusions* (adapted from his short story "The Last Illusion"), United Artists, 1995.

(With Bernard Rose) *The Thief of Always* (adapted from his novel of the same title), Universal Pictures, 1998.

(And producer) *Saint Sinner,* Sci Fi Channel, 2002.

OTHER

(Author of introduction) Ramsey Campbell, *Scared Stiff: Tales of Sex and Death,* Scream/Press (Santa Cruz, CA), 1987.

(Author of introduction) *Night Visions Four* (anthology), Dark Harvest (Arlington Heights, IL), 1987.

(Author of introduction) *Taboo,* edited by Stephen R. Bissette, SpiderBaby Grafix and Publications (Wilmington, VT), 1988.

Theatre Games, Heinemann (London, England), 1988.

(Illustrator) Fred Burke, *Clive Barker: Illustrator,* edited by Steve Niles, Arcane/Eclipse (Forestville, CA), 1990.

Clive Barker's Nightbreed: The Making of the Film, Fontana (London, England), 1990.

(Author of introduction) *H. R. Giger's Necronomicon,* Morpheus International (Beverly Hills, CA), 1991.

(Author of introduction) Stephen King, *Salem's Lot* ("Stephen King Collectors Editions"), New American Library/Dutton (New York, NY), 1991.

Clive Barker's Shadows in Eden (autobiography), edited by Stephen Jones, Underwood-Miller (San Francisco, CA), 1991.

Pandemonium: The World of Clive Barker (autobiography), Eclipse (Forestville, CA), 1991.

(Illustrator) Fred Burke, *Illustrator II: The Art of Clive Barker,* edited by Amacker Bullwinkle, Eclipse (Forestville, CA), 1993.

Incarnations: Three Plays, HarperPrism (New York, NY), 1995.

Forms of Heaven: Three Plays, HarperPrism (New York, NY), 1996.

(Author of introduction) *Dark Dreamers,* photographs by Beth Gwinn, commentary by Stanley Wiater, Cemetery Dance (Abingdon, MD), 2001.

(Editor, with others) *Clive Barker's Hellraiser: Collected Best II,* Checker (Centerville, NY), 2003.

Author of plays, including *Frankenstein in Love, The History of the Devil, Subtle Bodies,* and *The Secret Life of Cartoons.* Work represented in anthologies, including *Cutting Edge* and *I Shudder at Your Touch: Twenty-two Tales of Sex and Horror.* Has written stories for comic books, including *Razorline* for Marvel Comics. Also co-creator, with Todd McFarlane, of *Tortured Souls,* a serial novella combined with action figures, and film, produced by Universal. Contributor to periodicals, including *American Film* and *Omni.*

ADAPTATIONS: Barker's short story "The Forbidden" was adapted as the film *Candyman* in 1992; the short stories "In the Hills, the Cities" and "Son of Celluloid" were adapted for the Organic Theater in 1994. Film rights to Barker's "Arabat Quartet" novel series were purchased by the Walt Disney Company. A television series is being adapted from *Lord of Illusions.*

WORK IN PROGRESS: Further novels in the "Arabat Quartet"; book three in the "Book of the Art" trilogy; a sequel to *Galilee.*

SIDELIGHTS: "Renaissance man" is a tag often associated with Clive Barker, and for good reason. Since exploding into the publishing scene in the mid-1980s with six volumes of horror short stories known as the "Books of Blood," Barker steadily expanded his reach to the point where he became the driving force behind a creative empire. He has written short stories, novellas, novels, plays, and screenplays. He has directed, produced, and acted in films and plays. His drawings and paintings have appeared in books, comic books, art galleries, and museums. Others have adapted his work for the stage, the screen, for comic books, and for audiobooks. Still others have been inspired by his worlds and characters to create new films and comic books, carrying his creations even farther.

Due to the success of the six volumes of his "Books of Blood" series in both Great Britain and the United States, Barker has been hailed for his combination of unprecedented ugliness and literary touch. "I have seen the future of the horror genre, and his name is Clive Barker," Stephen King was quoted as saying in *Publishers Weekly* following the publication of one of the first books in the series. "What Barker does makes the rest of us look like we've been asleep for 10 years." Fellow Briton Ramsey Campbell offered a similar view as quoted in *Books and Bookmen,* term-

ing Barker "the first true voice of the next generation of horror writers." Barker continues to make publishing history with his "Abarat Quartet," targeted for young adults as a competitor to J. K. Rowling's "Harry Potter" books and bankrolled to the tune of $8 million by the Walt Disney Studio for film, multimedia, and theme park rights.

Journalists who meet Barker observe that despite his nightmarish imagination, he seems very well adjusted: smiling, personable, and boyishly enthusiastic. In fact, Barker did not always intend to write horrific short stories. Born in Liverpool, England, in 1952, not far from the Penny Lane made famous by those other famous Liverpudlians, the Beatles, Barker came of age in an England still struggling to find its place in the postwar world. His father was a dock worker and his mother worked as a nurse. He developed a taste for the macabre and for fantastic literature as a youth, enjoying the works of authors Herman Melville, Ray Bradbury, C. S. Lewis, and Kenneth Grahame, among others. Speaking with Mikal Gilmore in *Rolling Stone,* Barker recalled, "I never read much material that didn't have some element of the extraordinary or the fantastic in it. Of course my parents were not really in sympathy with the surreal. I suppose that made it into a vice, which wasn't altogether a bad thing." Art also captured his attention as a youth. Increasingly he came to think of himself as an imaginer. "The whole point is to make your imagination work in the most potent way possible," Barker told S. C. Ringgenberg in an interview for *Comics Journal.* "Pretty early in my life I realized that I could do that and enjoy doing that, that it gave me, I suppose, a sense of power to do it. It was recognized by my parents, although not necessarily liked by them."

Barker's parents would have liked him to focus more on academics than fantasy. As the author told Ringgenberg, although his parents valued creativity, "they [came] from a generation where art was thought of as being practically indulgent, and in their hearts they probably still do." After studying English and philosophy at college in Liverpool, Barker moved to London, where he worked in the theater, did illustrations, and sometimes lived on welfare. As he told Ringgenberg, "Right from [the] start I was unemployed—*gainfully* unemployed, in the sense that I was writing plays and painting pictures." The theatre-going public soon saw the curtain go up on such Barker-penned fantasy plays as *The History of the Devil* and *Frankenstein in Love.*

"The pieces were . . . very often surreal," Barker told Ringgenberg, "very often dark, and, I like to think, stimulating and a little controversial, which never hurts. By the age of 30 it was pretty apparent I wasn't going to make any money from this stuff." At this point, he decided to concentrate on the short fiction he had begun writing, but which only friends had seen.

After reading *Dark Forces,* a 1980 anthology edited by Stephen King's agent, Kirby McCauley, Barker perceived an audience for a new, more audacious kind of horror writing, and he quickly penned the first three volumes in the "Books of Blood" series. Initially Barker's fiction was only published in England, but his work caused such a stir among fantasy fans in North America that U.S. publishers soon produced their own editions. "I was completely unprepared for the fact that these things would find such favor," Barker told Ringgenberg. "I always thought that the work that I did was too off the beaten track really to find wide popular appeal. I remain astonished by that." Barker's "Books of Blood" series ultimately stretched to six volumes published between 1984 and 1986, firmly establishing him on both sides of the Atlantic as a major force in the new wave of horror writers.

Barker's stories, reviewers warn, are relentlessly graphic. Many consider such lack of restraint to be his trademark and his chief innovation. The author "never averts his gaze, no matter how gruesome the scene," explained Beth Levine in *Publishers Weekly.* "He follows every story through to its logical end, never flinching from detail. The result is mesmerizing, disturbing and elating, all at once." The story "In the Hills, the Cities" depicts an ancient quarrel between a pair of Yugoslavian towns: the townspeople abjure their individuality and form themselves into two lumbering giants who do battle. The title character of "Rawhead Rex," a flesh-eating monster, lingers indulgently over his evening meal, a freshly killed child, and especially enjoys the kidneys. As Mikal Gilmore wrote in *Rolling Stone,* "Barker's willingness to enter the sensibilities of his characters—to make their terrible desires comprehensible, even sympathetic—raises questions about both his work and modern horror in general. Namely, does it merely appeal to the meanness of the modern spirit?"

Barker and his admirers would respond that tales of terror can be valid as works of art and as social commentary. "I feel that horror literature is touching

upon the big issues time and time again," the author told *Omni:* "death and life after death, sex after death, insanity, loneliness, anxiety. Horror writers are addressing the deepest concerns of the human condition." In remarks quoted in *Publishers Weekly* he rejected the common view of horror fiction as a defender of social and cultural norms, in which the monster is an outsider who is reassuringly destroyed. "I don't believe that's true of the world," he said. "We can't destroy the monster because the monster is us." Yet, as he explained to Richard Harrington of the *Washington Post,* these social and cultural norms try to block this realization. "We're attracted and repulsed, but our culture doesn't allow us to say, 'I like these guys; they are a part of me.' We define our humanity because we are not monsters—and that's a lie, a complete lie." The role of the horror writer, in Barker's view, is to expose this lie.

As Michael Morrison suggested in *Fantasy Review,* Barker's stories become a strongly worded commentary on human nature. In "Jaqueline Ess: Her Will and Testament," an embittered, suicidal woman discovers that psychokinetic powers can liberate her from the tyranny of men but not from her own hatred of life. In "The Skins of the Fathers," the monsters who approach a small town to reclaim their half-human child seem less repugnant than the cold, tough Americans who oppose them. Writers such as Barker, said Kim Newman in *New Statesman,* "raise the possibility that horror fiction is the most apt form for dealing with the subject of life in the late 20th century."

While he relishes horror stories, Barker has not confined himself to a single genre. By broadening his approach to handling the themes of his work, he has proven that for him there is more than gore. He told *Books and Bookmen* that he believes his work belongs to a broader category—"imaginative fiction"—which is a valid part of the larger literary tradition. "Mainstream" writers, Barker contended, readily use the techniques of imaginative fiction, though they may not admit it. Along with these techniques, Barker's works also show a deep interest in and respect for the power of the human imagination. As he told Robert W. Welkos in the *Los Angeles Times,* "Something that profoundly touches the imagination carries more weight in your present mental geography than things that actually happen to you." This power of imagination is a key element of Barker's novels.

Barker's first novel, *The Damnation Game,* "a tour-de-force of gruesome supernatural horror" in the words of Chris Morgan of *Fantasy Review,* made the *New York Times* best-seller list within a week of its publication in 1987. The story is one of betrayal and vengeance involving two mythic figures, the Thief and the Cardplayer. Just after World War II in war-torn Warsaw, Poland, the Thief betrays the Cardplayer. Forty years later the Thief has become Joseph Whitehead, the wealthy head of a London drug company. The centuries-old Cardplayer, also known as Mamoulian, tracks down his nemesis and looks to exact revenge on Whitehead as payment for his betrayal.

As in his short stories, in *The Damnation Game* Barker combines unflinching horror with a literary sensibility. Morgan noted that "the most startling features of his work are the fact that he allows no depth of nastiness, cruelty or perversion to go unplumbed and the beautifully figurative and allusive nature of his prose style." Colin Greenland drew a similar conclusion, commenting in *British Book News* that "Barker is generous with the gore and grue . . . , but he is also a highly literate fantasist, and makes powerful use of the subtleties and ambiguities inherent in the situation." Barker also draws on his experience in a variety of creative forms. "The author's experience with short stories, and also with stage and film plays," noted Greenland, "shows strongly in his organization of the action by tableaux." This is not always used to the best effect, suggested Greenland. "At times he is apt to load more emotional or symbolic weight onto a scene than its position in the plot will easily bear, but he never loses his grip on the reader's nerve-ends."

Some reviewers found that Barker's first novel lacked the depth required of true literature. In his review of *Damnation Game,* *New York Times Book Review* contributor Alan Caruba found that Barker's "unremitting devotion to the most sickening imagery" overwhelms any deeper meaning the story might have. The critic added, "The absence of meaning in all this is the flaw that runs through what might have been an allegory of evil, an extended commentary on the various addictions that entrap people." Laurence Coven conceded in the *Washington Post Book World* that Barker's "overkill deprives us of a sense of anticipation, and . . . suspense." Yet, he also observed, "Time after time Barker makes us shudder in revulsion. In pure descriptive power there is no one writing horror fiction now who can match him. And to his credit, Barker does not write in a social vacuum. His terrors arise, at least in part, from a profound sadness and misery he perceives in the human condition."

In his 1987 novel *Weaveworld,* Barker pushes his writing even farther beyond the bounds of horror toward the fantasy genre, to what the author himself calls "the fantastique." "The fantastique," he explained to Richard Harrington in the *Washington Post,* "at its heart is a genre, or a collection of genres, which grow because of the ambiguities, because they're not about fixed moral codes; they're about shifting moral codes." *Weaveworld* is still punctuated by Barker's characteristically graphic writing, but, as Colin Greenland related in the *Times Literary Supplement,* the book "is almost classically a romance, a heraldic adventure in which figures possessed by principles, of love or greed or despair, pursue one another headlong with spells or pistols through a vague locality full of numinous things." *Weaveworld* is the story of a magic carpet, but one unlike those of the Arabian Nights which transport people from one place to another. This magic carpet contains within its weave a mystical realm created by the last of a race of magicians as a means to escape from sinister intruders, both mortal and supernatural.

In creating his story of this magical-carpet world and its contact with our own world, Barker follows the example of the weaver, bringing together many different threads to create a complex, intertwined whole. He also projects the dreamy, imaginative state of anyone who, in contemplating the complex design of a well-made rug, gets lost in its weave. As Phil Normand put it in the *Bloomsbury Review, Weaveworld* "is a tapestry of themes and characters. Beyond the chase-and-capture plot," he added, "we are called to rejoice in the strength of dream. This is a book of fantasy *about* fantasy, the struggle for man's dominion over the ungovernable casts of the imagination. It is about finding a place as close as breath where all things have a special purpose and meaning." Reviewer John Calvin Batchelor recognized the fantasy elements of Barker's novel, but found that the author's fantasy resonates into contemporary times. "Barker reveals his prodigious talent for erecting make-believe worlds in the midst of [British Prime Minster Margaret] Thatcher's tumbledown kingdom of Windsorian privilege and secretly policed ghettos," Batchelor wrote in the *New York Times Book Review.* "Reaching into its degraded and strangely fertile streets, he creates a fantastic romance of magic and promise that is at once popular fiction and utopian conjuring."

The Great and Secret Show and *Everville* are the first two installments in Barker's "Book of the Art" trilogy. The Art is a magical power that gives those who wield it control in our world and the dimensions beyond. As with his other novels, Barker finds dramatic tension and a spotlighted canvas on which to compose his thematic concerns in bringing together the mundane and the supernatural. In *The Great and Secret Show,* Randolf Jaffe—a postman in the dead-letter office at the Omaha post office—discovers the existence of a secret dream-sea that lies beyond the world as we know it. On further investigation, he learns of the Art and sets out to master it. In the course of his quest, Jaffe enlists the help of scientist Richard Fletcher, but the partnership eventually devolves into a rivalry over who will be the first to possess the Art. Ken Tucker, in a *New York Times Book Review* piece, called *The Great and Secret Show* "a cross between 'Gravity's Rainbow' and J. R. R. Tolkien's 'Lord of the Rings,' allusive and mythic, complex and entertaining."

While Tucker recognized that Barker set high goals for the novel, the reviewer found that the author had come up short. "From 'The Great and Secret Show,' it is clear that Mr. Barker's intention is to force the horror genre to encompass a kind of dread, and existential despair, that it hasn't noticeably evinced until now," Tucker commented. "This is a tall order, one that this novel, which is skillful and funny but ultimately overwrought, doesn't quite accomplish." *Washington Post* reviewer David Foster Wallace also noted Barker's execution. He contended, "Barker demands that the reader take him seriously but declines to do the artistic work necessary to make his story believable or even coherent."

For reviewer Barry Schechter, however, *The Great and Secret Show* is worthy of praise, both for its author's craft and its thematic concerns. In a *Chicago Tribune* piece, Schechter observed that Barker "proves himself an expert tactician, smoothly deploying over 40 characters and any number of careening, converging plots. He renders it all in a precise, ironic, measured style that avoids both campy humor and pretentious solemnity." He added, "A Britisher, Barker seems fascinated by the contrast between the American Dream and the atrophying American imagination: Even his self-created gods are hemmed in by lack of imagination and the trashy Hollywood images cluttering their minds." In conclusion, Schechter commented, "At a time of literary minimalism, read-my-lips political discourse and a moribund pop culture, 'The Great and Secret Show' is a maelstrom of fresh air."

Everville: The Second Book of the Art begins in 1848 with a party of pioneers setting out from Missouri to travel the Oregon Trail to the Northwest Territory. These pioneers face all of the hardships that have made their historical counterparts part of American legend. Yet, this is the work of Clive Barker: An otherworldly beast enters the mix and helps the party to found a new town on a border, not between territories, but between our world and the dream-sea introduced in *The Great and Secret Show.* The clock then moves forward to present-day Oregon, where a rift is opening between the two worlds and with consequences that threaten to be disastrous. The story that results, according to Elizabeth Hand in the *Washington Post Book World,* is "less a classic struggle between Good and Evil than it is a race to see who will put his (or her, or its) finger in the dike, and who will help the walls come tumbling down and loose the awful" creatures from the other world upon us.

As with many sequels, *Everville* faces the challenge of connecting with its predecessor and yet still having enough of its own elements to stand alone. Hand found that the novel's fast-paced action and the many characters and themes made it dependent on its previous volume. "Barker's strength is not really in his plotting," she observed. "*Everville* rolls along like an out-of-control juggernaut, and a reader who hasn't been primed by reading *The Great and Secret Show* should prepare to hang on for dear life or risk being crushed." Yet, in the opinion of Bruce Allen in the *New York Times Book Review,* this effort on the part of readers is well rewarded. "Readers who'll hang on for the wild ride throughout this exhilarating trilogy-in-progress may be surprised by the depths and heights thus encountered," he suggested. "Barker is much more than a genre writer, and his extravagantly unconventional inventions are ingenious refractions of our common quest to experience and understand the mysterious world around us and the mysteries within ourselves."

In novels such as *Imajica, Sacrament,* and *Galilee,* as well as in the children's horror story *The Thief of Always,* Barker continues to explore his vision of the fantastique that arises where the real and imagined collide, and how this vision sheds light on the human condition. A failed murder inspired by jealousy becomes entwined with a failed attempt to unite our world with a supernatural otherworld in *Imajica.* This 1991 dark fantasy is "rich in plot twists, byzantine intrigues and hidden secrets," noted Stefan Dziemianowicz in the *Washington Post Book World.* "*Imajica* is a Chinese puzzle box constructed on a universal scale. Not only has Barker imagined a commonplace world in which wonders lurk beneath the most banal surfaces, he has also taken the issues of our time— AIDS, the intransigence of sexual and racial politics, censorship, political repression, class struggle—and turned them into the stuff of myth."

Sacrament is the tale of Will Rabjohns, a wildlife photographer who is attacked and left for dead by a polar bear in northern Canada. In a coma, Rabjohns relives pivotal moments from his childhood. After he returns to consciousness and recovers, he travels to San Francisco and his native England to reconcile some personal metaphysical issues. A contributor to *Kirkus Reviews* characterized the novel variously as "suspenseful, intellectually exciting, wildly melodramatic, turgid, and bombastic." The reviewer added, "Barker's novel is charged—in its complex development and surprising resolution—with very real, very human emotion. A weirdly absorbing and entertaining tale that offers more disturbing delights from one of our most inventive and risk-taking writers."

Barker's novel *Galilee* is a saga that pits two families in a centuries-old struggle. A reviewer for *Publishers Weekly* reported that "the novel's scale is smaller than that of previous Barker efforts—missing are the titanic battles of form vs. chaos, good vs. evil, the riot of wonders and terrors. But it's less cluttered, too, despite abundant inspiration and invention." A *Kirkus Reviews* writer termed *Galilee* "a black comedy of miscegenation and its discontents that has to be a sendup of both the Harlequin romance and the American Southern Gothic novel."

In 2001 Barker released his first novel in three years, *Coldheart Canyon,* a Hollywood Babylon fantasy-chiller. The story follows movie star Todd Pickett, a character who "bears the strongest resemblance to Tom Cruise that is legally possible," as *New York Times* reviewer Janet Maslin remarked. Sadly for Todd, his sex appeal is fading as he ages, so on the advice of a studio head, he opts for plastic surgery. Of course, complications ensue: "Barker wouldn't have a story if the chemical peel didn't go horribly awry," Maslin noted. Seeking to hide his deformities, Todd takes refuge in an old Los Angeles mansion that was once the site of wild parties and is now haunted by the ghosts of Hollywood past. Todd encounters the house's mistress, Katya Lupi, who must be at least one hundred years old yet appears as youthful and nubile as

she did in her days as a silent-screen vamp. As Katya turns her seductive powers toward Todd, the book reveals the mansion as a netherworld that features sadistic sex between all manner of creatures, both real and imagined.

Coldheart Canyon runs an epic-length 600 pages, surprising even its author, who revealed to *Clive Barker Revelations* online interviewers Phil and Sarah Stokes that the original concept "was really going to be a very simple book about a rather narcissistic actor in Hollywood who encounters some ghosts . . . and as I got into it I realised these ghosts are sort of really interesting, and I want to write about them because they represent old Hollywood and here I have a chance not only to talk about new Hollywood but also to talk about old Hollywood and to contrast their methodologies."

Barker's depiction of Tinseltown scandal and gothic horror caught the eye of reviewers, including Maslin, who said *Coldheart Canyon* "unfolds with genuine momentum, the vigorous style of a fully engaged storyteller." *USA Today* contributor Robert Allen Papinchak likewise enjoyed the book, saying that "lush, musky prose and crisp, staccato dialogue propel the ghost story as assuredly as the perfumed breezes of the Santa Ana winds that open and close this endlessly entertaining novel."

In 2001 Barker also announced that he was beginning work on a novel series suitable for younger readers, the series to be called the "Abarat Quartet." Film rights to the still-unwritten books were promptly bought by family-friendly Walt Disney Company. Barker voiced high expectations for this series; as he told Phil and Sarah Stokes, "Abarat" "is bigger than we thought it was going to be. . . . Originally I thought it was going to be a sort of Narnia size, now it turns out to be more sort of a Harry Potter size!" Working from a plethora of self-painted illustrations of the characters—a technique the author often employs—Barker toyed with the idea of the fictional place called Abarat for many years. "It began with a painting," noted Jeff Jensen in *Entertainment Weekly*. "A portrait of a cranky old man in a canary suit, six squished hats stacked atop his head." For Barker, this portrait began his journey into the world of Abarat. For seven years Barker continued to paint the characters forming in his imagination, pictures that are both "whimsical and weird," according to Jensen, "Cirque du Soleil meets circus freak show." According to Jensen, the resulting first novel of the quartet is a "blend of *Alice in Wonderland* and *The Lion, the Witch, and the Wardrobe.*"

Indeed, Barker has long wanted to concoct a children's epic that would be a tip of the hat to C. S. Lewis and his "Chronicles of Narnia," but his publishers initially resisted the idea. Finally he got his chance at such a large-scale children's book, in the self-illustrated *Abarat* fashioning a tale of Candy Quackenbush, a heroine partly modeled after Barker's adopted daughter, Nicole. Candy is fed up with her quiet life in Chickentown, Minnesota, and longs for adventures. Cutting class one day and walking in the fields near town, she gets her wish. Diving into a mysterious sea that suddenly appears, she is transported to the magical world of Abarat with its twenty-five islands, one for every hour of the day, plus an extra one called Time outside of Time. As she travels from island to island in the bizarre archipelago, Candy is thrust into a battle for power between Christopher Carrion, the Lord of Midnight, and his arch-rival, Rojo Pixler of Commexo City. Slowly Candy begins to understand that her journey to Abarat is not merely some incredible accident, but actually her destiny. Included in the first "Abarat" novel are over one hundred of Barker's "quirky, grotesque, and campy" illustrations, as *Booklist*'s Sally Estes described the artwork.

Abarat presents a "beautiful and frightening world," according to Alison Ching in *School Library Journal,* who prophesied that the quartet "is sure to be a rollicking, epic ride." Estes had praise for the novel, calling it a "multilayered adventure story" reminiscent of "Oz, Wonderland, and Narnia . . . [as well as] Aldous Huxley's *Brave New World.*" A critic for *Kirkus Reviews* similarly found *Abarat* "an intriguing creation deserving of comparison to Oz." However, the same reviewer found a "peculiar lifelessness to all this imaginative fecundity." A contributor for *Publishers Weekly* also felt that Barker's "imagination runs wild as he conjures up striking imagery." For this critic, the novel is "unwieldy," but also full of "thrills and chills." The second installment of the quartet, *Days of Magic, Nights of War,* continues Candy's adventures as Carrion and Pixler's efforts to launch all-out war against each other help the young heroine learn her purpose in Barker's amazing fantasy world.

In addition to his printed works, Barker has continued to display a broad range of artistic talents. Most visible to the public eye have been the movies for which Barker has served as screenwriter, director, or executive producer. Barker's *Hellraiser* and *Candyman* have attracted a cult following and have taken on a life of their own. With his 1995 *Lord of Illusions* he brought his own short story, "The Last Illusion," to the screen. In 1999 he broke into a more serious mode by producing the critically acclaimed *Gods and Monsters,* which examines the complex personal life of aging homosexual film director James Whale, who made the 1930s horror classic *Frankenstein.*

In his movies, his writings, and his other creations, Barker has been credited with pushing the horror genre to new levels of gory violence. Yet, as he expanded his creative powers and as his audience has grown, he has been able to compose a broader understanding of horror. Barker suggested to Mikal Gilmore in *Rolling Stone* that an interest in horror can be natural and healthy. "Within the circle of your skull you have an immense imaginative freedom," he told Gilmore. "For Christ's sake, use it to understand your response to death . . . eroticism . . . all the things that come to haunt you and attract you and repulse you in your dreams. Because as soon as you relinquish control and lay your head down on the pillow, those things are going to come anyway." Reflecting the opinion of many critics, *Guardian* contributor China Mieville noted: "Barker is one of the few writers who has altered an entire field: more than anyone since [H. P.] Lovecraft, he has changed the shape, the corporeality of horror."

BIOGRAPHICAL AND CRITICAL SOURCES:

BOOKS

Badley, Linda, *Writing Horror and the Body: The Fiction of Stephen King, Clive Barker, and Anne Rice,* Greenwood Press (Westport, CT), 1996.
Barbieri, Suzanne J., *Clive Barker: Mythmaker for the Millennium,* British Fantasy Society (Stockport, Lancashire, England), 1994.
Bestsellers '90, issue 3, Gale (Detroit, MI), 1990.
Contemporary Literary Criticism, Volume 52, Gale (Detroit, MI), 1989.
Hoppenstand, Gary, editor, *Clive Barker's Short Stories: Imagination as Metaphor in the Books of Blood and Other Works,* McFarland (Jefferson, NC), 1994.
Jones, Stephen, editor, *Clive Barker's Shadows in Eden* (bibliography), Underwood-Miller (Lancaster, PA), 1991.

McCauley, Kirby, editor, *Dark Forces: New Stories of Suspense and Supernatural Horror,* Bantam (New York, NY), 1980.

St. James Encyclopedia of Popular Culture, St. James Press (Detroit, MI), 2000.

St. James Guide to Horror, Ghost, and Gothic Writers, St. James Press (Detroit, MI), 1998.

PERIODICALS

Advocate, September 28, 1999, review of *The Essential Clive Barker,* p. 98.

American Theatre, May-June, 1993, p. 6.

Billboard, July 21, 2001, Christa Titus, "Unlikely Couple Weaving Musical Magic into Barker's Art," p. 78.

Bloomsbury Review, September-October, 1987, Phil Normand, review of *Weaveworld,* p. 21.

Booklist, October 15, 1992, p. 379; February 1, 1994, p. 989; September 15, 1994, p. 83; June 1, 1996, p. 1628; November 15, 1999, review of *The Essential Clive Barker,* p. 608; August, 2001, Ray Olson, review of *Coldheart Canyon,* p. 2049; September 1, 2002, Sally Estes, review of *Abarat,* p. 120; June 1, 2003, Ray Olson, review of *Clive Barker's Hellraiser: Collected Best II,* p. 1724.

Books and Bookmen, July, 1985; September, 1987.

Bookwatch, April, 1999, review of *The History of the Devil* (audio version), p. 10.

British Book News, December, 1985, Colin Greenland, review of *The Damnation Game,* p. 742.

Chicago Tribune, September 15, 1987; February 5, 1990, section 5, p. 3; February 19, 1990, section 5, p. 3; December 29, 1992, section 5, p. 3; May 23, 1993, section 13, p. 22; August 25, 1995, p. 7H.

Comics Journal, September, 1994, S. C. Ringgenberg, "A Man for All Seasons: Clive Barker Interview."

Detroit Free Press, December 23, 1988.

Entertainment Weekly, September 25, 1992, p. 43; September 15, 1995, p. 87; October 4, 2002, Jeff Jensen, review of *Abarat,* p. 21.

Fantasy Review, February, 1985; June, 1985, p. 15; August, 1985; September, 1985, p. 16; October, 1986, p. 19; April, 1987, Chris Morgan, review of *The Damnation Game,* p. 32.

Guardian, October 17, 1986; October 19, 2002, China Mieville, review of *Abarat.*

Journal of Popular Culture, winter, 1993, p. 35.

Kirkus Reviews, August 1, 1987, p. 1085; May 15, 1996, review of *Sacrament;* May 11, 1998, review of *Galilee;* October 15, 1999, review of *The Essential Clive Barker,* p. 1603; August 1, 2001, review of *Coldheart Canyon,* p. 1043; September 1, 2002, review of *Abarat,* p. 1303.

Kliatt, November, 2002, Michele Winship, review of *Abarat,* p. 6.

Library Journal, January, 1990, p. 145; December, 1991; February, 1993; July, 1996, p. 152; November 1, 1999, review of *The Essential Clive Barker,* p. 80; August, 2001, Nancy McNicol, review of *Coldheart Canyon,* p. 156; February 1, 2002, Michael Rogers, review of *Books of Blood,* p. 138.

Locus, December, 1992, p. 17; January, 1993, p. 19; November, 1994, p. 17.

Los Angeles Magazine, October, 2002, "Buzz Cuts," p. 26.

Los Angeles Times, February 19, 1990, p. F4; October 11, 1992, p. CAL3; August 22, 1995, p. F1; August 25, 1995, p. F10.

Los Angeles Times Book Review, August 10, 1986; June 14, 1987; October 11, 1992, p. 3.

Magazine of Fantasy and Science Fiction, August, 1987; May, 1990, p. 44; April, 1993, p. 26; July, 1999, review of *Galilee,* p. 37.

New Statesman, July 18, 1986, p. 29; October 5, 1990, p. 30; December 7, 1990, p. 34; March 22, 1996, p. 38.

New Theater Quarterly, February, 1990, p. 5.

New York, May 26, 1986.

New York Times, September 20, 1987; February 17, 1990, p. A19; August 25, 1995, p. C6; October 25, 2001, Janet Maslin, "Sex with Dead Film Stars Means Breakfast for One"; February 1, 2002, Michael Rogers, review of *Books of Blood,* p. 138.

New York Times Book Review, September 21, 1986, p. 26; February 15, 1987, p. 20; June 21, 1987, p. 22; November 22, 1987, p. 32; December 18, 1988; February 11, 1990, Ken Tucker, review of *The Great and Secret Show,* p. 11; November 20, 1994, Bruce Allen, review of *Everville,* p. 18.

Notes on Contemporary Literature, November, 1994, p. 7.

Observer (London, England), December 27, 1987, p. 17; December 17, 1989, p. 46; February 14, 1993, p. 59.

Omni, October, 1986.

Orlando Business Journal, August 24, 2001, Alan Byrd, "Clive Barker and Disney: Now There's an E-Ticket Ride," p. 3.

People, June 15, 1987; September 18, 1995, p. 27; November 5 2001, Bernard Welt, review of *Coldheart Canyon,* p. 51.

Publishers Weekly, December 13, 1985; July 4, 1986; December 22, 1989, p. 44; September 28, 1992; September 12, 1994, p. 78; May 27, 1996, p. 63; July 1, 1996, p. 30; May 11, 1998, p. 49; April 12, 1999, review of *The History of the Devil* (audio version), p. 32; October 11, 1999, review of *The Essential Clive Barker,* p. 57; March 26, 2001, review of *Dark Dreamers,* p. 68; July 23, 2001, review of *Coldheart Canyon,* p. 55; February 4, 2002, review of *The Thief of Always,* p. 78; February 11, 2002, review of *Books of Blood,* p. 167; June 24, 2002, review of *Abarat,* p. 58; August 11, 2003, review of *Clive Barker's Hellraiser: Collected Best II,* p. 259.

Rolling Stone, February 11, 1988.

School Library Journal, October, 2002, Alison Ching, review of *Abarat,* pp. 154-155.

Time, March 19, 1990, p. 84.

Times (London, England), October 17, 1986.

Times Literary Supplement, February 12, 1988, Colin Greenland, review of *Weaveworld,* p. 172.

Tribune Books (Chicago, IL), September 14, 1986; April 26, 1987.

USA Today, August 25, 1995, p. D12.

USA Weekend, October 9-11, 1987; January 26, 1990, p. 8; June 24, 1994, p. 4.

Variety, August 21, 1995, p. 67.

Video, April, 1988.

Village Voice, December 2, 1986, p. 63.

Washington Post, September 30, 1987; November 17, 1988; February 19, 1990, David Foster Wallace, review of *The Great and Secret Show,* p. D3; September 11, 1992, p. B1.

Washington Post Book World, August 24, 1986, p. 6; June 28, 1987, p. 10; September 27, 1987; October 27, 1991, p. 8; February 28, 1993, p. 6; December 18, 1994, Elizabeth Hand, review of *Everville,* p. 5.

ONLINE

Clive Barker Official Web site, http://www.clivebarker. com (June 4, 2003).

Clive Barker Revelations, http://www.clivebarker.dial. pipex.com/ (April 7, 2004), Phil Stokes and Sarah Stokes, "Open Roads. . . . What Price Wonderland?"

January Magazine, http://www.januarymagazine.com/ (June 4, 2003), Linda Richards, "Clive Barker Biography."

USA Today, http://wwww.usatoday.com/ (October 26, 2001), Robert Allen Papinchak, "Clive Barker Fills 'Canyon' with Secrets, Dead Souls."*

*   *   *

BAXTER, Charles (Morley) 1947-

PERSONAL: Born May 13, 1947, in Minneapolis, MN; son of John Thomas and Mary Barber (Eaton) Baxter; married Martha Ann Hauser (a teacher), July 12, 1976; children: Daniel John. *Education:* Macalester College, B.A., 1969; State University of New York at Buffalo, Ph.D., 1974.

ADDRESSES: Home—Minneapolis, MN. *Office*— Department of English, University of Minnesota, 210G Lind Hall, 207 Church St. SE, Minneapolis, MN 55455. *E-mail*—baxte029@umn.edu.

CAREER: High school teacher in Pinconning, MI, 1969-70; Wayne State University, Detroit, MI, assistant professor, 1974-79, associate professor, 1979-85, professor of English, 1985-89; Warren Wilson College, faculty member, beginning 1986; University of Michigan, Ann Arbor, visiting faculty member, 1987, professor of English, 1989-99, adjunct professor of creative writing, 1999-2003; University of Minnesota, Minneapolis, Edelstein-Keller Senior Fellow in Creative Writing, 2003—.

AWARDS, HONORS: Faculty research fellowship, Wayne State University, 1980-81; Lawrence Foundation Award, 1982, and Associated Writing Programs Award Series in Short Fiction, 1984, both for *Harmony of the World;* National Endowment for the Arts fellowship, 1983, Michigan Council for the Arts fellowship, 1984; Faculty Recognition Award, Wayne State University, 1985 and 1987; Guggenheim fellowship, 1985-86; Michigan Council of the Arts grant, 1986; Arts Foundation of Michigan Award, 1991; Lawrence Foundation Award, 1991; *Reader's Digest* Foundation fellowship, 1992; Michigan Author of the Year Award, Michigan Foundation, 1994; *Harvard Review* Award and O. Henry Prize, both 1995; Award in Literature, American Academy of Arts and Letters, 1997; finalist, National Book Award in Fiction, 2000, for *The Feast of Love.*

Charles Baxter

WRITINGS:

Chameleon (poetry), illustrated by Mary E. Miner, New Rivers Press (New York, NY), 1970.

The South Dakota Guidebook, New Rivers Press (New York, NY), 1974.

Harmony of the World (short stories), University of Missouri Press (Columbia, MO), 1984.

Through the Safety Net (short stories), Viking (New York, NY), 1985.

First Light (novel), Viking (New York, NY), 1987.

Imaginary Paintings and Other Poems, Paris Review Editions (Latham, NY), 1990.

A Relative Stranger (short stories), Norton (New York, NY), 1990.

Shadow Play (novel), Norton (New York, NY), 1993.

Believers (short stories and novella), Pantheon (New York, NY), 1997.

Burning down the House: Essays on Fiction, Graywolf Press (St. Paul, MN), 1997.

(Editor) *The Business of Memory: The Art of Remembering in an Age of Forgetting,* Graywolf Press (St. Paul, MN), 1999.

The Feast of Love (novel), Pantheon (New York, NY), 2000.

(Editor, with Peter Turchi) *Bringing the Devil to His Knees: The Craft of Fiction and the Writing Life,* University of Michigan Press (Ann Arbor, MI), 2001.

Saul and Patsy (novel), Pantheon (New York, NY), 2003.

(Editor, with Edward Hirsch and Michael Collier) *A William Maxwell Portrait: Memories and Appreciations,* Norton (New York, NY), 2004.

Poems have been featured in numerous anthologies, including *The Fifth Annual Best Science Fiction,* edited by Harry Harrison and Brian Aldiss, Putnam (New York, NY), 1972; *Toward Winter,* edited by Robert Bonazzi, New Rivers Press (New York, NY), 1972; *The Pushcart Prize Anthology XVI,* Pushcart Press (Wainscott, NY), 1991; and *Best American Short Stories,* 1982, 1986, 1987, 1989, and 1991. Contributor to periodicals, including *Minnesota Review, Kayak, Prairie Schooner, Antioch Review, Michigan Quarterly Review, Georgia Review, New England Review, Centennial Review, New York Times,* and *Journal of Modern Literature.* Associate editor, *Minnesota Review,* 1967-69, and *Criticism;* editor of *Audit/Poetry,* 1973-74.

Baxter's works have been translated into Japanese, Swedish, German, Russian, Romanian, French, Spanish, Catalan, Italian, Portugese, and Chinese.

SIDELIGHTS: Charles Baxter initially caught critics' attention with his poetry and criticism, but it is the graceful prose and human understanding of his short stories and novels that have gained him entry into the pantheon of leading American writers of the twentieth century. In the words of Chuck Wachtel in *Nation,* "Baxter is a remarkable storyteller" who, in each new book, "has offered his readers an increasingly significant, humane and populous reflection, one in which we keep finding things we have sensed the presence of but have not before seen." Another *Nation* critic, Theodore Solotaroff, noted that Baxter "has the special gift of capturing the shadow of genuine significance as it flits across the face of the ordinary." Baxter's sharply drawn, unique characters—one of his hallmarks—elicited praise from Jonathan Yardley in the *Washington Post Book World:* "Unlike so many other young American writers . . . Baxter cares about his people, recognizes the validity and dignity of their lives, grants them humor and individuality."

Born in Minnesota and a longtime resident of Michigan, Baxter has created a fictional world that embraces the Midwest. As a reviewer for *Ploughshares* explained, the author portrays "in luminous, precise language, solid Midwestern citizens, many of whom reside in the fictional town of Five Oaks, Michigan, whose orderly lives are disrupted, frequently by an accident or incident or a stranger." The reviewer added: "The limits of geography tend to elicit introspection, and when even a small calamity befalls Baxter's characters, they brood over surprisingly large issues of morality and theodicy, grappling with good and evil and the mysteriousness of existence."

Baxter's first volume of short stories, *Harmony of the World,* includes the award-winning title story as well as several others. "Harmony of the World," originally published in the *Michigan Quarterly Review,* is about a young pianist who decides to become a newspaper critic after one of his performances elicits a particularly scathing review from a music teacher. His affair with a somewhat untalented singer and the events that bring both of their lives to a crisis are the means through which Baxter explores "the ache of yearning for perfection, in love and art, a perfection human beings can never attain, however close they come to apprehending it," to quote Laurence Goldstein in the *Ann Arbor News.* Goldstein praised Baxter for the "imaginative sympathy and marvelous craft" of his short stories, a view shared by Peter Ross of the *Detroit News:* "There are no weak spots in *Harmony of the World,* no falterings of craft or insight. Baxter's influences are many and subtle, but his voice is his own and firmly in control. . . . *Harmony of the World* is a serious collection by a serious writer; it deserves as much attention, study and praise as anything being written today."

Baxter's second collection of short stories, *Through the Safety Net,* was published just one year after *Harmony of the World* and was received with great enthusiasm by critics. "It's a nice surprise that a second collection is so speedily upon us and that it improves on the first," wrote Ron Hansen in the *New York Times Book Review. Through the Safety Net* is an exploration of the inevitable perils of everyday life. Baxter's characters—among them an unsuccessful graduate student, a five-year-old boy trying to understand his grandmother's death, and a spurned lover who becomes obsessed with the object of his desire—spend their energies trying to escape pain and loss, but inevitably

fail. In the title story, Diana visits a psychic only to be told that she is headed for a great calamity. "What kind? The Book of Job kind," the psychic tells her. "I saw your whole life, your house, car, that swimming pool you put in last summer, the career, your child, and the whole future just start to radiate with this ugly black flame from the inside, poof, and then I saw you falling, like at the circus, down from the trapeze. Whoops, and down, and then down through the safety net. Through the ground." In another narrative, a psychopath, lamenting his lack of fame, remarks: "If you are not famous in America, you are considered a mistake. They suspend you in negative air and give you bad jobs working in basements pushing mops from eight at night until four in the morning."

Yardley characterized the people in Baxter's stories as individuals without purpose, "amiably retreating from life's challenges . . . though the forms of their retreats and the motives for them vary." A *Publishers Weekly* reviewer found the stories "flawed by a fondness for excessive detail, implausible turns and mere trickiness," but conceded that they contained "bright flashes of unmistakable talent." Baxter's careful attention to detail was praised by a *New York Times* critic: "An extraordinarily limber writer, Mr. Baxter makes his characters' fears palpable to the reader by slowly drawing us into their day-to-day routine and making us see things through their eyes." The stories in *Through the Safety Net,* concluded Hansen, are "intelligent, original, gracefully written, always moving, frequently funny and—that rarest of compliments—wise."

When Baxter's first novel, *First Light,* was published in 1987, it immediately garnered praise for its unique structure. Prefaced by a quote from Danish philosopher Sören Kierkegaard—"Life can only be understood backwards, but it must be lived forwards"—the novel presents events in reverse chronological order. Thus, each chapter is a step further back into the past of the characters. At the outset of *First Light,* Hugh Welch and his sister Dorsey are uneasy adults reunited for a Fourth of July celebration. Their strained, distant relationship is clearly a source of anguish to them both. As the novel progresses, Hugh and Dorsey become younger and younger, and the many layers of their life-long bond are slowly uncovered. "We see their youth and childhoods revealed, like rapidly turning pages in a snapshot album," observed Michiko Kakutani in the *New York Times.* By the time the novel ends, Hugh is a young child being introduced to his newborn baby sister. "In reading of these events," Kakutani wrote, "we see why Dorsey and Hugh each made the choices they did, how their childhood dreams were translated into adult decisions." The combination of Baxter's unique narrative structure and fine characterization results in "a remarkably supple novel that gleams with the smoky chiaroscuro of familial love recalled through time," concluded Kakutani.

Although *First Light* was Baxter's first published novel, it was not his first attempt at the novel form. His first three novels, he remarked in the *New York Times,* are "apprentice" efforts he would never consider publishing. "I did take a brief episode out of one of them but, for the most part, I can't stand to look at them now, so I wouldn't want anyone else to." Describing the structure of *First Light,* he commented: "The technique resembles those little Russian dolls that fit into each other—you open them up and they keep getting smaller and smaller. What I am trying to say is that grownups don't stop being the people they were many years before, in childhood."

Baxter's 1990 collection of short stories, *A Relative Stranger,* features characters "constantly having odd encounters with strangers that disrupt their quiet, humdrum lives and send them skidding in unexpected new directions," Kakutani stated in a *New York Times* review. In one story, a man's attempt to help an insane, homeless man sparks the jealousy of his wife and son. In another, a woman who is secretly in love with her husband's best friend develops an irrational fear of burglars. Describing the couple's suburban home as one of many "little rectangular temples of light," the friend scoffs at the wife's fear. "Nothing here but families and fireplaces and Duraflame logs and children of God," he tells the husband. "Not the sort of place," he continues, "where a married woman ought to be worried about prowlers."

Recommending *A Relative Stranger* in *Nation,* Theodore Solotaroff commented: "Baxter is well on his way to becoming the next master of the short story." *A Relative Stranger* was also praised by Kakutani: "All the stories in this collection attest to Mr. Baxter's ability to orchestrate the details of mundane day-to-day reality into surprising patterns of grace and revelation, his gentle but persuasive knack for finding and describing the fleeting moments that indelibly define a life. . . . We finish the book with the satisfaction of

having been immersed in a beautifully rendered and fully imagined world."

Baxter's 1993 novel, *Shadow Play,* revolves around Wyatt Palmer, a man whose chaotic childhood has left him unable to deal with emotions. Instead, he focuses on maintaining a neatly ordered life with his understanding wife and two children. Wyatt's job as an assistant city manager leads him to cross paths with a former high school classmate interested in starting a chemical company in their economically depressed hometown. The former classmate, Jerry Schwartzwalder, asks Wyatt to bend the rules in order to help him launch his new company. In exchange for his cooperation, Jerry offers Wyatt's unstable foster brother, Cyril, a job at the plant. When Cyril shows signs of a fatal disease caused by exposure to toxins, Wyatt becomes enraged and vows to take revenge. According to *New York Times Book Review* contributor Lorrie Moore, *Shadow Play* is reminiscent of "The Lottery," by Shirley Jackson. Like Jackson's story, Baxter's novel "takes large themes of good and evil and primitive deal making, and situates them in municipal terms and local ritual. He is interested in those shadowy corners of civilization in which barbarity manages to nestle and thrive. The America of this book has become a kind of hell." Or, as Winston Groom, the author of *Forrest Gump,* put it in the *Los Angeles Times Book Review,* "Baxter has created a scenario in which alienation and anxiety are the norm, a kind of dubious universe where people are neither good nor evil but instead are driven by 20th-century pragmatism into a twilight zone of utter practicality."

In unfolding Wyatt's story of conflict in small-town America, Baxter brings to bear many of his talents as a storyteller. "To convey this sense of abandonment and emptiness without losing the reader is not easy," observed R. Z. Sheppard in *Time.* "*Shadow Play* could have turned into another clever existential dead end. But Baxter fills the void with a hundred human touches, a style as intimate as chamber music, and a hero who rouses himself to reject the banality that hoohah happens." A *Publishers Weekly* critic also drew a musical analogy to describe Baxter's command of style. The story of how Wyatt deals with his emotional handicaps is told in "language so carefully honed it sings." The reviewer continued that the author's "metaphors and apercus are striking and luminous, and several scenes—notably Wyatt and Cyril's final bonding—are unforgettable." Baxter's achievement, in the opinion of Lorrie Moore, is that "he has steadily taken beautiful and precise language and gone into the ordinary and secret places of people—their moral and emotional quandaries, their typically American circumstances, their burning intelligence, their negotiations with what is tapped, stunted, violent, sustaining, decent or miraculous in their lives."

Jane Smiley, writing in Chicago's *Tribune Books,* conceded the eloquence of Baxter's writing and the wisdom of his observations, but she found "Wyatt himself is something of a cipher, a blank at the center whose moral odyssey is less than compelling. . . . The very vividness" of the fictional characters' "eccentricities finally limits the broader appeal of their situation." Moore drew a different conclusion. She maintained that "one of Mr. Baxter's great strengths as a writer has always been his ability to capture the stranded inner lives of the Middle West's repressed eccentrics. And here, in his second novel, he is full throttle." For a contributor to the *Yale Review,* the situations represented in *Shadow Play* achieve broad appeal because they demonstrate that Baxter "has a feeling for nuance, for what's being said and not said, for the complexities of social class and social privilege, for the resonance of personal history, for how much we are the authors—and the products—of our experience." The reviewer continued: "He's not only generous to his characters, but compassionate, endlessly patient, and tolerant of their human frailties and flaws." Richard Locke concluded in the *Wall Street Journal,* "After a decade of so much play-it-safe fiction of photorealistic gloom, it's a pleasure to encounter a novel in the great tradition of American moral realism touched by shards of gnostic faith and glints of transcendental light."

While some reviewers hailed *Shadow Play* as the book that would thrust Baxter into the national literary limelight, Baxter himself refused to set such high expectations. "When *First Light* came out, I was full of the American Dream," he recalled in the *Detroit News.* "I thought the birds of money were going to land in a huge flock on the roof, and I'd be proclaimed from housetop to housetop. It was foolish, and that's what young writers are. . . . I'm trying not to get my hopes up. I worked on [*Shadow Play*] so long, I just want it to do well. I just want people to like it and to find it interesting and find it has some meaning to their lives."

Baxter published another collection of short stories, with a novella, in 1997. A *Publishers Weekly* reviewer described *Believers* as "ambitious and accomplished," adding that "the shorter works here tackle slippery themes and subjects—fleeting moments of truth; the ambiguities of daily life and the defenses through which ordinary men and women attempt to clarify them." These stories are "Michigan stories," commented Frederick Busch in the *Los Angeles Times Book Review.* "They occur in the lives of those with intelligence, leisure in which to use it, walls behind which they may retreat and time enough for contemplation." "The book's self-scrutinizers," Busch added, "those who believe and those who cannot . . . are the middle class in the middle of the nation." Like Baxter's readers, they often experience "failures of will, of nerve, of ethics, of feeling," Busch suggested. "But . . . they are like us in that their souls do not only sink: They strive to climb."

Believers "will remind us that [Baxter] is an exemplary writer because he works in persuasive solidities, in what is actual," concluded Busch. Chuck Wachtel offered greater praise in his *Nation* review. "Rarely . . . have I been stopped by what I read and moved so deeply as I was in the novella and stories that make up *Believers.* Baxter, a master craftsman, knows that craft is more than something to be good at."

Baxter's National Book Award-nominated *The Feast of Love* begins with a character—named Charles Baxter—whose chronic insomnia leads him to a deserted park bench in Ann Arbor, Michigan. It is there that the fictional Baxter encounters a neighbor named Bradley who offers his own life story of two marriages—and two divorces—as grist for a new novel. After initial resistance, Baxter delves into Bradley's past and present, where each of his former wives, as well as his coworkers, help to enlarge the emerging group portrait. "*The Feast of Love* is as precise, as empathetic, as luminous as any of Baxter's past work," declared Jacqueline Carey in the *New York Times Book Review.* "It is also rich, juicy, laugh-out-loud funny and completely engrossing." A *Publishers Weekly* critic felt that Baxter's particular gift in the novel "is to catch the exact pitch of a dozen voices in an astutely observed group of contemporary men and women." Carey also noted the old-fashioned sense of community underlying the work. "In *The Feast of Love,* Charles Baxter shows us the hard-won generosity of spirit that day-to-day dealings with other human beings require," she stated. "He builds a community right on the page before us, using a glittering eye, a silvery tongue—and just a little moonlight."

Similar to *The Feast of Love, Saul and Patsy* focuses on married life in the Midwest, in this case on a newlywed couple who settle in a small town and find themselves moth-balled in their comfortable, middle-class neighborhood. At least Saul, the Jewish, former city-dwelling husband, feels stifled, "shipwrecked in the plainspoken, poker-faced Midwest," explained *Atlantic* contributor James Marcus, although the critic was quick to add that the novel is also "a valentine to the Midwest, whose terrain the author describes with almost luminarist ardor." Calling Baxter "a master of the distributed plot, the deceptively looping situation that discloses its tensions gradually," *Book* critic Sven Birkerts praised the novel's depiction of the "inevitably mine-studded marital terrain" traversed by his transplanted couple as they negotiate the role of outsider. Praising Baxter's characters, which include a troubled, obsessive teen, and a plot that rises to a tense and tragic denouement, *Booklist* reviewer Donna Seaman dubbed Baxter's protagonists "magnetic, his humor incisive, his decipherment of the human psyche felicitous, and his command of the storyteller's magic absolute."

In addition to authoring fiction, Baxter has also served as editor of anthologies which focus on various aspects of the writing process. *The Business of Memory: The Art of Remembering in an Age of Forgetting,* for instance, explores the art of memoir and the process by which artists of all sorts recover and interpret memories. In *Library Journal,* Julia Burch wrote of the work: "These are self-conscious and beautifully written essays that deftly explore the act of memoir-making and the art of storytelling." A *Publishers Weekly* correspondent likewise found the essays "often engaging and occasionally quite inspired."

In both his short stories and novels, Baxter's exploration of his characters' inner desires and outward realities has struck a chord in critics and readers alike. "If there is a consistent theme in Baxter's work, it is the difficulty people have in accommodating themselves to a world that is complex, mysterious, and demanding, that offers rewards that glitter all the more brightly because so few attain them," Yardley summarized in the *Washington Post Book World.* "Whether he's writing about an overly self-conscious intellectual or an inarticulate street person," concluded Kakutani, "Mr. Baxter is able to map out their emotions persuasively and delineate the shape of their spiritual confusion." Praising the fluid beauty of the author's style, John

Saari wrote in the *Antioch Review:* "Many writers today feel no depth of compassion for their characters. Baxter, in contrast, is adept at portraying his characters as human beings, even when some of them are not the best examples."

A self-described insomniac, Baxter also admitted in *Ploughshares* that he likes a routine and will sometimes fixate on even the slightest intrusions or variations from his schedule. Noting that he is "conscious of pattern-making" in his day-to-day life, the author added: "I think if you are somewhat compulsive or habitual in your ordinary life, it gives you some latitude to be wild in your creative work."

BIOGRAPHICAL AND CRITICAL SOURCES:

BOOKS

Baxter, Charles, *Through the Safety Net,* Viking (New York, NY), 1985.

Baxter, Charles, *A Relative Stranger,* Norton (New York, NY), 1990.

Contemporary Literary Criticism, Gale (Detroit, MI), Volume 45, 1987, Volume 78, 1993.

Contemporary Popular Writers, St. James Press (Detroit, MI), 1997.

Dictionary of Literary Biography, Volume 130: *American Short-Story Writers since World War II,* Gale (Detroit, MI), 1993.

PERIODICALS

Ann Arbor News, May 16, 1982.

Antioch Review, fall, 1985, p. 498; summer, 1993, p. 465.

Atlantic, September, 2003, James Marcus, review of *Saul and Patsy,* p. 152.

Book, September-October, 2003, Sven Birkerts, review of *Saul and Patsy,* p. 74.

Booklist, April 15, 2000, Grace Fill, review of *The Feast of Love,* p. 1522; August, 2003, Donna Seaman, review of *Saul and Patsy,* p. 1924.

Detroit Free Press, December 23, 1992.

Detroit News, May 20, 1984; December 28, 1992, p. 1D.

Entertainment Weekly, September 12, 2003, Thom Geier, review of *Saul and Patsy,* p. 156.

Hudson Review, spring, 1991, p. 133.

Kirkus Reviews, July 1, 2003, review of *Saul and Patsy,* p. 869.

Library Journal, April 15, 1990, p. 96; December, 1992, p. 184; September 15, 1993, p. 136; May 1, 1999, Julia Burch, review of *The Business of Memory: The Art of Remembering in an Age of Forgetting,* p. 76; September 1, 2003, David W. Henderson, review of *Saul and Patsy,* p. 204.

Los Angeles Times Book Review, July 6, 1986, p. 10; December 6, 1987, p. 3; September 29, 1991; March 21, 1993, p. 5; March 30, 1997, p. 10.

Nation, December 30, 1991, p. 862; April 7, 1997, p. 33.

New England Review, summer, 1992, p. 234.

New York Times, June 26, 1985; August 24, 1987; September 7, 1987; September 4, 1990; September 29, 1991.

New York Times Book Review, August 25, 1985, p. 1; October 4, 1987, p. 18; October 23, 1988, p. 60; October 21, 1990, p. 18; February 14, 1993, p. 7; May 7, 2000, Jacqueline Carey, "The Ex Files."

People, February 1, 1993, p. 22; February 24, 1997, p. 65.

Ploughshares, fall, 1999, Don Lee, "About Charles Baxter: A Profile."

Publishers Weekly, May 24, 1985; October 19, 1992, p. 57; December 7, 1992, p. 45; February 24, 1997, p. 65; March 29, 1999, review of *The Business of Memory: The Art of Remembering in an Age of Forgetting,* p. 76; March 6, 2000, review of *The Feast of Love,* p. 79; July 28, 2003, review of *Saul and Patsy,* p. 76.

Southern Review, April, 1991, p. 465.

Time, September 7, 1987, p. 81; September 14, 1987; January 25, 1993, p. 70.

Tribune Books (Chicago, IL), January 17, 1993, p. 4.

Wall Street Journal, February 5, 1993, p. A9.

Washington Post Book World, July 10, 1985; January 17, 1993, p. 3.

Yale Review, July, 1993, p. 122.

*   *   *

BERESFORD, Anne 1929-

PERSONAL: Born September 10, 1929, in Redhill, Surrey, England; daughter of Richmond (a film representative) and Margaret (a musician; maiden name, Kent) Beresford; married Michael Hamburger (a poet), 1951 (divorced, 1970; remarried 1974); children: Mary

Anne, Richard, Claire. *Education:* Attended Central School of Speech Training and Dramatic Art, 1944-46. *Politics:* Socialist.

ADDRESSES: Home—Marsh Acres, Middleton, Saxmundham, Suffolk IP17 3NH, England.

CAREER: Writer. British Broadcasting Corp., London, England, broadcaster, 1960-70; high school drama teacher in Wimbledon, England, 1969-73; Arts Educational School, London, drama teacher, 1973-76. Cockpit Theatre, London, teacher for Poetry Workshop, 1970-72; teacher of drama and elocution in London. Actress, 1948-70.

MEMBER: Poetry Society of Great Britain, Inner London Education Authority.

WRITINGS:

POETRY

Walking without Moving, edited by Edward Lucie-Smith, Turret (London, England), 1967.

The Lair, Rapp & Whiting (London, England), 1968.

The Courtship, Unicorn Bookshop (Brighton, England), 1972.

Footsteps on Snow, Agenda Editions (London, England), 1972.

Modern Fairy Tale, Sceptre Press (Knotting, Bedfordshire, England), 1972.

The Curving Shore, Agenda Editions (London, England), 1975.

Unholy Giving, Sceptre Press (Knotting, Bedfordshire, England), 1978.

Songs a Thracian Taught Me, M. Boyars (London, England), 1980.

The Sele of the Morning, Agenda Editions (London, England), 1988.

Snapshots from an Album 1884-1895, Katabasis (London, England), 1992.

Charm with Stones, Claudia Gehrke (Tübingen, Germany), 1993.

Landscape with Figures, Agenda Editions (London, England), 1994.

Duet for Three Voices and Coda, Dedalus Press (London, England), 1997.

Selected Poems, Agenda Editions (London, England), 1997.

No Place for Cowards, Katabasis (London, England), 1998.

Hearing Things, Katabasis (London, England), 2002.

OTHER

(Translator) Vera Lungu, *Alexandros: Selected Poems,* Agenda Editions (London, England), 1975.

Author of radio plays, including (with husband, Michael Hamburger) *Struck by Apollo,* 1965, and *The Villa,* 1968.

SIDELIGHTS: Anne Beresford began taking herself seriously as a writer in 1961, she once told *CA,* when, at the age of thirty-three, she "sent some poems to Christopher Middleton and he wrote back telling me to go on writing. Since everyone in my family is a musician, it seemed more natural for me to choose the stage or music for a career rather than writing. But poetry was one of the things that made life worth living. It has always been so, and will always be so—for me at any rate." Since that time, Beresford has published several collections of her verse.

Beresford's oeuvre has been characterized by critics as subtle, and she has been referred to more than once as a mystic poet. In the *Dictionary of Literary Biography,* essayist William Cookson noted of Beresford's work that its "quiet subtlety . . . stems from her attempts to define moments and states of mind, those aspects of consciousness and daily life which are most difficult to describe in words." Citing such works as "The Duke's Book of Hours," a 1975 poem sequence from *The Curving Shore,* Cookson also cited the presence of such foundational elements as legend, fairy tale, and myth in Beresford's works. While admitting that her subtlety sometimes borders on fragility and a lack of power, the reviewer added that "this weakness is at times offset by a clarity and simplicity of imagery which evoke much."

When asked by *CA,* Beresford labeled the influences upon her work as "varied," adding that "it's hard to say whether the poets I admire have influenced my writing." Her advice to young writers: "read everything and anything, and to study those poets you most admire."

"One of my favorite pastimes is walking in the country near where we live," Beresford continued. "Some of my images certainly come from the countryside. And others come from my odd, and at times, macabre, imagination."

BIOGRAPHICAL AND CRITICAL SOURCES:

BOOKS

Contemporary Women Poets, St. James Press (Detroit, MI), 1997.

Dictionary of Literary Biography, Volume 40: *Poets of Great Britain and Ireland since 1960,* Gale (Detroit, MI), 1985.

PERIODICALS

Library Journal, January 15, 1981, p. 151.

Publishers Weekly, January 9, 1991, p. 70.

Queen's Quarterly, September, 1971.

Times Literary Supplement, October 13, 1972; July 9, 1976; April 10, 1981, p. 416.

*   *   *

BLIGHT, Rose
   See GREER, Germaine

*   *   *

BLISS, Frederick
   See CARD, Orson Scott

*   *   *

BLOOM, Harold 1930-

PERSONAL: Born July 11, 1930, in New York, NY; son of William (a garment factory worker) and Paula (Lev) Bloom; married Jeanne Gould, May 8, 1958; children: Daniel Jacob, David Moses. *Education:* Cornell University, B.A., 1951; Yale University, Ph.D., 1955. *Religion:* Jewish.

Harold Bloom

ADDRESSES: Home—179 Linden St., New Haven, CT 06511. *Office*—Whitney Humanities Center, Yale University, 53 Wall St., New Haven, CT 06520-8298.

CAREER: Yale University, New Haven, CT, instructor, 1955-60, assistant professor, 1960-63, associate professor, 1963-65, professor of English, 1965-74, DeVane Professor of Humanities, 1974-77, professor of humanities, 1977—, Sterling Professor of Humanities, 1983—. Visiting Professor at Hebrew University, Jerusalem, 1959, Breadloaf Summer School, 1965-66, and Cornell University, Society for Humanities, 1968-69. New School for Social Research, visiting professor, 1982-84; Harvard University, Charles Eliot Norton Professor of Poetry, 1987-88; New York University, Berg Visiting Professor of English, 1998-2004.

MEMBER: American Academy of Arts and Letters, American Philosophical Society.

AWARDS, HONORS: Fullbright fellowship, 1955; John Addison Porter Prize, Yale University, 1956, for *Shelley's Mythmaking;* Guggenheim fellowship, 1962-

63; Newton Arvin Award, 1967; Melville Cane Award, Poetry Society of America, 1971, for *Yeats;* National Book Awards juror, 1973; Zabel Prize, American Institute of Arts and Letters, 1982; MacArthur Prize fellowship, 1985; Christian Guass Award, 1988, for *Ruin the Sacred Truths; Boston Book Review* Rea Nonfiction Prize, 1995, for *The Western Canon: The Books and School of the Ages;* National Book Award finalist, nonfiction, National Book Critics Circle Award finalist, criticism, *New York Times* Notable Book of the Year, one of *Publishers Weekly* Best Books of the Year, and *Booklist* Editor's Choice, all 1998, all for *Shakespeare: The Invention of the Human;* D.H.L., 14th Catalonia International Prize, 2002, Alfonso Reyes Prize of Mexico, 2003. D.H.L., Boston College, 1973, Yeshiva University, 1975, University of Bologna, 1997, St. Michael's College, 1998, University of Rome, 1999, University of Massachusetts at Dartmouth, 2002.

WRITINGS:

NONFICTION

Shelley's Mythmaking, Yale University Press (New Haven, CT), 1959.

The Visionary Company: A Reading of English Romantic Poetry, Doubleday (New York, NY), 1961, revised edition, Cornell University Press (Cornell, NY), 1971.

Blake's Apocalypse, Doubleday (New York, NY), 1963.

(Author of commentary) David V. Erdman, editor, *The Poetry and Prose of William Blake,* Doubleday (New York, NY), 1965, revised edition published as *The Complete Poetry and Prose of William Blake,* 1982.

Yeats, Oxford University Press (New York, NY), 1970.

(Compiler) *Romanticism and Consciousness: Essays in Criticism,* Norton (New York, NY), 1970.

The Ringers in the Tower: Studies in Romantic Tradition, University of Chicago Press (Chicago, IL), 1971.

The Anxiety of Influence: A Theory of Poetry, Oxford University Press (New York, NY), 1973, with new preface, 2001.

A Map of Misreading, Oxford University Press, 1975, with new preface, 2003.

Kabbalah and Criticism, Seabury Press, 1975.

Poetry and Repression: Revisionism from Blake to Stevens, Yale University Press (New Haven, CT), 1976.

Figures of Capable Imagination, Seabury Press, 1976.

Wallace Stevens: The Poems of Our Climate, Cornell University Press, 1977.

The Flight to Lucifer: A Gnostic Fantasy, Farrar, Straus (New York, NY), 1979.

(With J. Hillis Miller, Paul de Man, and Jacques Derrida) *Deconstruction and Criticism,* Seabury Press, 1979.

Agon: Towards a Theory of Revisionism, Oxford University Press (New York, NY), 1982.

The Breaking of the Vessels, University of Chicago Press (Chicago, IL), 1982.

The Strong Light of the Canonical: Kafka, Freud, and Scholem as Revisionists of Jewish Culture and Thought, privately printed, 1987.

Poetics of Influence, Schwab, 1989.

Ruin the Sacred Truths: Poetry and Belief from the Bible to the Present, Harvard University Press (Cambridge, MA), 1989.

(Interpreter) *The Book of J,* translated by David Rosenberg, Grove & Weidenfeld (London, England), 1990.

The American Religion: The Emergence of the Post-Christian Nation, Simon & Schuster (New York, NY), 1992.

(Interpreter) *The Gospel of Thomas: The Hidden Sayings of Jesus,* translated, with introduction, critical edition of the Coptic text, and notes by Marvin Meyer, HarperSanFrancisco (San Francisco, CA), 1992.

(Compiler with Paul Kane) Ralph Waldo Emerson, *Collected Poems and Translations,* Library of America (New York, NY), 1994.

The Western Canon: The Books and School of the Ages, Harcourt (New York, NY), 1994.

Omens of Millennium: The Gnosis of Angels, Dreams, and Resurrection, Riverhead (New York, NY), 1996.

Shakespeare: The Invention of the Human, Riverhead (New York, NY), 1998.

How to Read and Why, Simon & Schuster (New York, NY), 2000.

Genius: A Mosaic of One Hundred Exemplary Creative Minds, Warner Books (New York, NY), 2002.

Hamlet: Poem Unlimited, Riverhead (New York, NY), 2003.

Where Shall Wisdom Be Found?, Riverhead (New York, NY), 2004.

Eudora Welty, Chelsea House (Philadelphia, PA), 2004.

Italian Renaissance, Chelsea House (Philadelphia, PA), 2004.

Hamlet: Poem Unlimited, Riverhead (New York, NY), 2003.

EDITOR

English Romantic Poetry, An Anthology, Doubleday (New York, NY), 1961, two-volume revised edition, Anchor (New York, NY), 1963.

(With John Hollander) *The Wind and the Rain,* Doubleday (New York, NY), 1961.

(With Frederick W. Hilles) *From Sensibility to Romanticism: Essays Presented to Frederick A. Pottle,* Oxford University Press, 1965.

Percy Bysshe Shelley, *Selected Poetry,* New American Library (New York, NY), 1966.

Walter Horatio Pater, *Marius the Epicurean: His Sensations and Ideas,* New American Library (New York, NY), 1970.

Samuel Taylor Coleridge, *Selected Poetry,* New American Library (New York, NY), 1972.

The Romantic Tradition in American Literature, 33 volumes, Arno, 1972.

(With Lionel Trilling) *Romantic Prose and Poetry,* Oxford University Press, 1973.

(With Lionel Trilling) *Victorian Prose and Poetry,* Oxford University Press, 1973.

(With Frank Kermode, Hollander, and others) *Oxford Anthology of English Literature,* two volumes, Oxford University Press, 1973.

(With Adrienne Munich) *Robert Browning: A Collection of Critical Essays,* Prentice-Hall, 1979.

(With David Lehman) *The Best of the Best American Poetry, 1988-1997,* Scribner (New York, NY), 1998.

The Best Poems of the English Language: From Chaucer through Robert Frost, HarperCollins (New York, NY), 2004.

Selected Poems/Walt Whitman, Library of America, (New York, NY), 2003.

STUDY GUIDES; EDITOR AND AUTHOR OF INTRODUCTION

The Literary Criticism of John Ruskin, Anchor (New York, NY), 1965.

Selected Writings of Walter Pater, New American Library (New York, NY), 1974.

Hamlet, Chelsea House (New York, NY), 1990.

Caddy Compson, Chelsea House (Philadelphia, PA), 1990.

Cleopatra, Chelsea House (Philadelphia, PA), 1990.

French Poetry: The Renaissance through 1915, Chelsea House (Philadelphia, PA), 1990.

Edwardian and Georgian Fiction, 1880 to 1914, Chelsea House (Philadelphia, PA), 1990.

French Prose and Criticism, 1790 to World War II, Chelsea House (Philadelphia, PA), 1990.

French Prose and Criticism through 1789, Chelsea House (Philadelphia, PA), 1990.

Holden Caulfield, Chelsea House (Philadelphia, PA), 1990.

Huck Finn, Chelsea House (Philadelphia, PA), 1990.

Clarissa Dalloway, Chelsea House (Philadelphia, PA), 1990.

Modern Latin American Fiction, Chelsea House (Philadelphia, PA), 1990.

Bigger Thomas, Chelsea House (Philadelphia, PA), 1990.

Toni Morrison, Chelsea House (Philadelphia, PA), 1990.

Sophocles, Chelsea House (Philadelphia, PA), 1990.

Shylock, Chelsea House (Philadelphia, PA), 1991.

Odysseus/Ulysses, Chelsea House (Philadelphia, PA), 1991.

Ahab, Chelsea House (Philadelphia, PA), 1991.

Antonia, Chelsea House (Philadelphia, PA), 1991.

Brett Ashley, Chelsea House (Philadelphia, PA), 1991.

Macbeth, Chelsea House (Philadelphia, PA), 1991.

Willy Loman, Chelsea House (Philadelphia, PA), 1991.

Gatsby, Chelsea House (Philadelphia, PA), 1991.

Joan of Arc, Chelsea House (Philadelphia, PA), 1992.

Falstaff, Chelsea House (Philadelphia, PA), 1992.

David Copperfield, Chelsea House (Philadelphia, PA), 1992.

Iago, Chelsea House (Philadelphia, PA), 1992.

Caliban, Chelsea House (Philadelphia, PA), 1992.

Marlow, Chelsea House (Philadelphia, PA), 1992.

Isabel Archer, Chelsea House (Philadelphia, PA), 1992.

King Lear, Chelsea House (Philadelphia, PA), 1992.

Rosalind, Chelsea House (Philadelphia, PA), 1992.

Heathcliff, Chelsea House (Philadelphia, PA), 1993.

Lolita, Chelsea House (Philadelphia, PA), 1993.

Classic Science-Fiction Writers, Chelsea House (Philadelphia, PA), 1994.

Science-Fiction Writers of the Golden Age, Chelsea House (Philadelphia, PA), 1994.

Modern Fantasy Writers, Chelsea House (Philadelphia, PA), 1994.

Modern Mystery Writers, Chelsea House (Philadelphia, PA), 1994.

Classic Fantasy Writers, Chelsea House (Philadelphia, PA), 1994.

Julius Caesar, Chelsea House (Philadelphia, PA), 1994.

Black American Prose Writers of the Harlem Renaissance, Chelsea House (Philadelphia, PA), 1994.

Black American Prose Writers: Before the Harlem Renaissance, Chelsea House (Philadelphia, PA), 1994.

Black American Poets and Dramatists: Before the Harlem Renaissance, Chelsea House (Philadelphia, PA), 1994.

Contemporary Horror Writers, Chelsea House (Philadelphia, PA), 1994.

Major Modern Black American Writers, Chelsea House (Philadelphia, PA), 1994.

Contemporary Black American Fiction Writers, Chelsea House (Philadelphia, PA), 1994.

Classic Horror Writers, Chelsea House (Philadelphia, PA), 1994.

Modern Horror Writers, Chelsea House (Philadelphia, PA), 1994.

Modern Black American Poets and Dramatist, Chelsea House (Philadelphia, PA), 1994.

Emma Bovary, Chelsea House (Philadelphia, PA), 1994.

Contemporary Black American Poets and Dramatists, Chelsea House (Philadelphia, PA), 1994.

Major Black American Writers through the Harlem Renaissance, Chelsea House (Philadelphia, PA), 1994.

Black American Women Fiction Writers, Chelsea House (Philadelphia, PA), 1994.

Modern Black American Fiction Writers, Chelsea House (Philadelphia, PA), 1995.

Classic Mystery Writers, Chelsea House (Philadelphia, PA), 1995.

Classic Crime and Suspense Writers, Chelsea House (Philadelphia, PA), 1995.

Robinson Crusoe, Chelsea House (Philadelphia, PA), 1995.

Black American Poets and Dramatists of the Harlem Renaissance, Chelsea House (Philadelphia, PA), 1995.

Modern Crime and Suspense Writers, Chelsea House (Philadelphia, PA), 1995.

Beowulf, Chelsea House (Philadelphia, PA), 1996.

Dante's "Divine Comedy: The Inferno," Chelsea House (Philadelphia, PA), 1996.

Emily Bronte's "Wuthering Heights," Chelsea House (Philadelphia, PA), 1996.

Charles Dickens' "Great Expectations," Chelsea House (Philadelphia, PA), 1996.

Harper Lee's "To Kill a Mockingbird," Chelsea House (Philadelphia, PA), 1996.

Arthur Miller's "The Crucible," Chelsea House (Philadelphia, PA), 1996.

Mark Twain's "Adventures of Huckleberry Finn," Chelsea House (Philadelphia, PA), 1996.

F. Scott Fitzgerald's "The Great Gatsby," Chelsea House (Philadelphia, PA), 1996.

Joseph Conrad's "Heart of Darkness" and "The Secret Sharer," Chelsea House (Philadelphia, PA), 1996.

George Orwell's "Nineteen Eighty-four," Chelsea House (Philadelphia, PA), 1996.

Homer's "The Odyssey," Chelsea House (Philadelphia, PA), 1996.

John Milton's "Paradise Lost," Chelsea House (Philadelphia, PA), 1996.

Sophocles' Oedipus Plays: "Oedipus the King," "Oedipus at Colonus," and "Antigone," Chelsea House (Philadelphia, PA), 1996.

John Steinbeck's "The Grapes of Wrath," Chelsea House (Philadelphia, PA), 1996.

Charles Dickens' "A Tale of Two Cities," Chelsea House (Philadelphia, PA), 1996.

Alex Haley and Malcolm X's "The Autobiography of Malcolm X," Chelsea House (Philadelphia, PA), 1996.

Nathaniel Hawthorne's "The Scarlet Letter," Chelsea House (Philadelphia, PA), 1996.

Harriet Beecher Stowe's "Uncle Tom's Cabin," Chelsea House (Philadelphia, PA), 1996.

William Shakespeare's "Othello," Chelsea House (Philadelphia, PA), 1996.

George Orwell's "Animal Farm," Chelsea House (Philadelphia, PA), 1996.

William Shakespeare's "A Midsummer Night's Dream," Chelsea House (Philadelphia, PA), 1996.

George Eliot's "Silas Marner," Chelsea House (Philadelphia, PA), 1996.

William Shakespeare's "Romeo and Juliet," Chelsea House (Philadelphia, PA), 1996.

Charlotte Bronte's "Jane Eyre," Chelsea House (Philadelphia, PA), 1996.

Herman Melville's "Billy Budd," "Benito Cereno," and "Bartleby the Scrivener," Chelsea House (Philadelphia, PA), 1996.

Maya Angelou's "I Know Why the Caged Bird Sings," Chelsea House (Philadelphia, PA), 1996.

Black American Women Poets and Dramatists, Chelsea House (Philadelphia, PA), 1996.

Fyodor Dostoevsky's "Crime and Punishment," Chelsea House (Philadelphia, PA), 1996.

Homer's "Iliad," Chelsea House (Philadelphia, PA), 1996.

Ernest Hemingway's "The Sun Also Rises," Chelsea House (Philadelphia, PA), 1996.

Ralph Ellison's "Invisible Man," Chelsea House (Philadelphia, PA), 1996.

Ernest Hemingway's "The Old Man and the Sea," Chelsea House (Philadelphia, PA), 1996.

Richard Wright's "Native Son," Chelsea House (Philadelphia, PA), 1996.

Thomas Hardy's "Tess of the D'Urbervilles," Chelsea House (Philadelphia, PA), 1996.

Aldous Huxley's "Brave New World," Chelsea House (Philadelphia, PA), 1996.

Mary Shelley's "Frankenstein," Chelsea House (Philadelphia, PA), 1996.

Jane Austen's "Pride and Prejudice," Chelsea House (Philadelphia, PA), 1996.

Jonathan Swift's "Gulliver's Travels," Chelsea House (Philadelphia, PA), 1996.

Vergil's "Aeneid," Chelsea House (Philadelphia, PA), 1996.

Herman Melville's "Moby Dick," Chelsea House (Philadelphia, PA), 1996.

Arthur Miller's "The Crucible," Chelsea House (Philadelphia, PA), 1996.

Stephen Crane's "The Red Badge of Courage," Chelsea House (Philadelphia, PA), 1996.

William Shakespeare's "Henry IV, Part 1," Chelsea House (Philadelphia, PA), 1996.

Ernest Hemingway's "A Farewell to Arms," Chelsea House (Philadelphia, PA), 1996.

William Golding's "Lord of the Flies," Chelsea House (Philadelphia, PA), 1996.

John Steinbeck's "Of Mice and Men," Chelsea House (Philadelphia, PA), 1996.

J. D. Salinger's "The Catcher in the Rye," Chelsea House (Philadelphia, PA), 1996.

Caribbean Women Writers, Chelsea House (Philadelphia, PA), 1997.

American Women Fiction Writers, Chelsea House (Philadelphia, PA), 1997.

Asian American Women Writers, Chelsea House (Philadelphia, PA), 1997.

British Women Fiction Writers, 1900-1960, Chelsea House (Philadelphia, PA), 1997.

Lesbian and Bisexual Fiction Writers, Chelsea House (Philadelphia, PA), 1997.

Ben Johnson, Chelsea House (Philadelphia, PA), 2001.

Don Quixote, Chelsea House (Philadelphia, PA), 2001.

D. H. Lawrence, Chelsea House (Philadelphia, PA), 2001.

Edgar Allan Poe, Chelsea House (Philadelphia, PA), 2001.

Elie Wiesel's "Night," Chelsea House (Philadelphia, PA), 2001.

Erich Maria Remarque's "All Quiet on the Western Front," Chelsea House (Philadelphia, PA), 2001.

Henry James, Chelsea House (Philadelphia, PA), 2001.

Homer, Chelsea House (Philadelphia, PA), 2001.

Italio Calvino, Chelsea House (Philadelphia, PA), 2001.

Jack London, Chelsea House (Philadelphia, PA), 2001.

Jean Paul Sartre, Chelsea House (Philadelphia, PA), 2001.

John Irving, Chelsea House (Philadelphia, PA), 2001.

John Keats, Chelsea House (Philadelphia, PA), 2001.

John Updike, Chelsea House (Philadelphia, PA), 2001.

Anton Chekov, Chelsea House (Philadelphia, PA), 2001.

Joseph Conrad, Chelsea House (Philadelphia, PA), 2001.

Katherine Anne Porter, Chelsea House (Philadelphia, PA), 2001.

Kurt Vonnegaut's "Slaughterhouse Five," Chelsea House (Philadelphia, PA), 2001.

Maya Angelou, Chelsea House (Philadelphia, PA), 2001.

Nathaniel Hawthorne, Chelsea House (Philadelphia, PA), 2001.

Percy Bysshe Shelley, Chelsea House (Philadelphia, PA), 2001.

Ray Bradbury, Chelsea House (Philadelphia, PA), 2001.

Ray Bradbury's "Fahrenheit 451," Chelsea House (Philadelphia, PA), 2001.

Robert Browning, Chelsea House (Philadelphia, PA), 2001.

Samuel T. Coleridge, Chelsea House (Philadelphia, PA), 2001.

Shirley Jackson, Chelsea House (Philadelphia, PA), 2001.

Stephen Crane, Chelsea House (Philadelphia, PA), 2001.

Sylvia Plath, Chelsea House (Philadelphia, PA), 2001.

Tom Wolfe, Chelsea House (Philadelphia, PA), 2001.

W. E. B. Dubois, Chelsea House (Philadelphia, PA), 2001.

William B. Yeats, Chelsea House (Philadelphia, PA), 2001.

Margaret Atwood's "The Handmaid's Tale," Chelsea House (Philadelphia, PA), 2001.

Chinua Achebe's "Things Fall Apart," Chelsea House (Philadelphia, PA), 2002.

Christopher Marlowe, Chelsea House (Philadelphia, PA), 2002.

Cormac McCarthy, Chelsea House (Philadelphia, PA), 2002.

E. L. Doctorow, Chelsea House (Philadelphia, PA), 2002.

Edith Wharton, Chelsea House (Philadelphia, PA), 2002.

Elizabeth Barrett Browning, Chelsea House (Philadelphia, PA), 2002.

Elizabeth Bishop, Chelsea House (Philadelphia, PA), 2002.

H. D., Chelsea House (Philadelphia, PA), 2002.

James Joyce, Chelsea House (Philadelphia, PA), 2002.

Leo Tolstoy, Chelsea House (Philadelphia, PA), 2002.

Moliére, Chelsea House (Philadelphia, PA), 2002.

Neil Simon, Chelsea House (Philadelphia, PA), 2002.

Octavio Paz, Chelsea House (Philadelphia, PA), 2002.

Oscar Wilde, Chelsea House (Philadelphia, PA), 2002.

Poets of World War I: Wilfred Owen and Issac Rosenberg, Chelsea House (Philadelphia, PA), 2002.

Raymond Carver, Chelsea House (Philadelphia, PA), 2002.

Robert Frost, Chelsea House (Philadelphia, PA), 2002.

Stendhal, Chelsea House (Philadelphia, PA), 2002.

Ken Kesey's "One Flew over the Cuckoo's Nest," Chelsea House (Philadelphia, PA), 2002.

Kurt Vonnegut's "Cat's Cradle," Chelsea House (Philadelphia, PA), 2002.

Tennessee William's "Cat on a Hot Tin Roof," Chelsea House (Philadelphia, PA), 2002.

Thomas Mann, Chelsea House (Philadelphia, PA), 2002.

Upton Sinclair's "The Jungle," Chelsea House (Philadelphia, PA), 2002.

Virginia Woolf, Chelsea House (Philadelphia, PA), 2002.

William Styron's "Sophie's Choice," Chelsea House (Philadelphia, PA), 2002.

Albert Camus's "The Stranger," Chelsea House (Philadelphia, PA), 2002.

Amy Tan's "The Joy Luck Club," Chelsea House (Philadelphia, PA), 2002.

African-American Poets, 2 volumes, Chelsea House (Philadelphia, PA), 2003.

American Renaissance, Chelsea House (Philadelphia, PA), 2003.

Bram Stoker's "Dracula," Chelsea House (Philadelphia, PA), 2003.

Cormac McCarthy's "All the Pretty Horses," Chelsea House (Philadelphia, PA), 2003.

Dante Alighieri, Chelsea House (Philadelphia, PA), 2003.

David Guterson's "Snow Falling on Cedars," Chelsea House (Philadelphia, PA), 2003.

Derek Walcott, Chelsea House (Philadelphia, PA), 2003.

Don Delillo, Chelsea House (Philadelphia, PA), 2003.

Don Delillo's "White Noise," Chelsea House (Philadelphia, PA), 2003.

Doris Lessing, Chelsea House (Philadelphia, PA), 2003.

E. E. Cummings, Chelsea House (Philadelphia, PA), 2003.

The Eighteenth-Century English Novel, Chelsea House (Philadelphia, PA), 2003.

Eugene Ionesco, Chelsea House (Philadelphia, PA), 2003.

Euripides, Chelsea House (Philadelphia, PA), 2003.

Franz Kafka, Chelsea House (Philadelphia, PA), 2003.

Gabriel García Márquez's "One Hundred Years of Solitude: Essays," Chelsea House (Philadelphia, PA), 2003.

George Eliot, Chelsea House (Philadelphia, PA), 2003.

Gwendolyn Brooks, Chelsea House (Philadelphia, PA), 2003.

Hart Crane, Chelsea House (Philadelphia, PA), 2003.

Herman Melville, Chelsea House (Philadelphia, PA), 2003.

Hermann Hesse, Chelsea House (Philadelphia, PA), 2003.

Honoré de Balzac, Chelsea House (Philadelphia, PA), 2003.

The House on Mango Street, Chelsea House (Philadelphia, PA), 2003.

Huck Finn, Chelsea House (Philadelphia, PA), 2003.

Isabel Allende, Chelsea House (Philadelphia, PA), 2003.

Johann Wolfgang von Goethe, Chelsea House (Philadelphia, PA), 2003.

John Cheever, Chelsea House (Philadelphia, PA), 2003.

Leo Tolstoy, Chelsea House (Philadelphia, PA), 2003.

Marianne Moore, Chelsea House (Philadelphia, PA), 2003.

Mark Strand, Chelsea House (Philadelphia, PA), 2003.

Milan Kundera, Chelsea House (Philadelphia, PA), 2003.

Norman Mailer, Chelsea House (Philadelphia, PA), 2003.

A Passage to India, Chelsea House (Philadelphia, PA), 2003.

Philip Roth, Chelsea House (Philadelphia, PA), 2003.

Poets of World War I: Rupert Brooke & Siegfried Sassoon, Chelsea House (Philadelphia, PA), 2003.

Ralph Ellison, Chelsea House (Philadelphia, PA), 2003.

Salman Rushdie, Chelsea House (Philadelphia, PA), 2003.

Sam Shepard, Chelsea House (Philadelphia, PA), 2003.

Seamus Heady, Chelsea House (Philadelphia, PA), 2003.

Sherwood Anderson, Chelsea House (Philadelphia, PA), 2003.

Sir John Falstaff, Chelsea House (Philadelphia, PA), 2003.

T. S. Eliot, Chelsea House (Philadelphia, PA), 2003.

The Tale of Genji, Chelsea House (Philadelphia, PA), 2003.

Thomas Pynchon, Chelsea House (Philadelphia, PA), 2003.

Aeschylus, Chelsea House (Philadelphia, PA), 2003.

Agatha Christie, Chelsea House (Philadelphia, PA), 2003.

American and Canadian Women Poets, 1300 to Present, Chelsea House (Philadelphia, PA), 2003.

American Women Poets, 1650-1950, Chelsea House (Philadelphia, PA), 2003.

Aristophanes, Chelsea House (Philadelphia, PA), 2003.

August Wilson, Chelsea House (Philadelphia, PA), 2003.

Bertolt Brecht, Chelsea House (Philadelphia, PA), 2003.

American Naturalism, Chelsea House (Philadelphia, PA), 2004.

Arthur Koestler's "Darkness at Noon," Chelsea House (Philadelphia, PA), 2004.

E. L. Doctorow's "Ragtime," Chelsea House (Philadelphia, PA), 2004.

Edward Fitzgerald's "The Rubaiyat of Omar Khayyam," Chelsea House (Philadelphia, PA), 2004.

Elizabethan Drama, Chelsea House (Philadelphia, PA), 2004.

English Romantic Poets, Chelsea House (Philadelphia, PA), 2004.

Greek Drama, Chelsea House (Philadelphia, PA), 2004.

Jack Kerouac's "On the Road," Chelsea House (Philadelphia, PA), 2004.

James Joyce's "Ulysses," Chelsea House (Philadelphia, PA), 2004.

Jane Austen's "Persuasion," Chelsea House (Philadelphia, PA), 2004.

Literature of the Holocaust, Chelsea House (Philadelphia, PA), 2004.

David Mamet, Chelsea House (Philadelphia, PA), 2004.

Alan Tate, Chelsea House (Philadelphia, PA), 2004.

Philip Roth's "Portnoy's Complaint," Chelsea House (Philadelphia, PA), 2004.

William Shakespeare's "As You Like It," Chelsea House (Philadelphia, PA), 2004.

Elizabeth Bennet, Chelsea House (Philadelphia, PA), 2004.

Emile Zola, Chelsea House (Philadelphia, PA), 2004.

George F. Babbitt, Chelsea House (Philadelphia, PA), 2004.

Guy de Maupassant, Chelsea House (Philadelphia, PA), 2004.

Hester Prynne, Chelsea House (Philadelphia, PA), 2004.

Issac Babel, Chelsea House (Philadelphia, PA), 2004.

John Ashbery, Chelsea House (Philadelphia, PA), 2004.

Julio Cortazar, Chelsea House (Philadelphia, PA), 2004.

King Arthur, Chelsea House (Philadelphia, PA), 2004.

Leopold Bloom, Chelsea House (Philadelphia, PA), 2004.

Nick Adams, Chelsea House (Philadelphia, PA), 2004.

William Gaddis, Chelsea House (Philadelphia, PA), 2004.

Nikolai Gogol, Chelsea House (Philadelphia, PA), 2004.

Paul Auster, Chelsea House (Philadelphia, PA), 2004.

Raskolnikov and Svidrigailov, Chelsea House (Philadelphia, PA), 2004.

Rudyard Kipling, Chelsea House (Philadelphia, PA), 2004.

W. S. Merwin, Chelsea House (Philadelphia, PA), 2004.

William Gaddis, Chelsea House (Philadelphia, PA), 2004.

STUDY GUIDES; EDITOR AND AUTHOR OF INTRODUCTION; JUVENILE

Stories and Poems for Extremely Intelligent Children of All Ages, Chelsea House (Philadelphia, PA), 2001.

F. Scott Fitzgerald, Chelsea House (Philadelphia, PA), 2001.

Joseph Conrad, Chelsea House (Philadelphia, PA), 2001.

William Shakespeare, Chelsea House (Philadelphia, PA), 2002.

William Faulkner, Chelsea House (Philadelphia, PA), 2002.

Maya Angelou, Chelsea House (Philadelphia, PA), 2002.

Langston Hughes, Chelsea House (Philadelphia, PA), 2002.

Jorge Luis Borges, Chelsea House (Philadelphia, PA), 2002.

Jane Austen, Chelsea House (Philadelphia, PA), 2002.

Stephen Crane, Chelsea House (Philadelphia, PA), 2002.

Robert Frost, Chelsea House (Philadelphia, PA), 2002.

Stephen King, Chelsea House (Philadelphia, PA), 2003.

Walt Whitman, Chelsea House (Philadelphia, PA), 2003.

William Blake, Chelsea House (Philadelphia, PA), 2003.

William Wordsworth, Chelsea House (Philadelphia, PA), 2003.

Zora Neale Hurston, Chelsea House (Philadelphia, PA), 2003.

A. E. Housman, Chelsea House (Philadelphia, PA), 2003.

Albert Camus, Chelsea House (Philadelphia, PA), 2003.

Aldous Huxley, Chelsea House (Philadelphia, PA), 2003.

Arthur Miller, Chelsea House (Philadelphia, PA), 2003.

Charles Dickens, Chelsea House (Philadelphia, PA), 2003.

Emily Dickinson, Chelsea House (Philadelphia, PA), 2003.

Ernest Hemingway, Chelsea House (Philadelphia, PA), 2003.

Geoffrey Chaucer, Chelsea House (Philadelphia, PA), 2003.

Henry David Thoreau, Chelsea House (Philadelphia, PA), 2003.

James Joyce, Chelsea House (Philadelphia, PA), 2003.

John Milton, Chelsea House (Philadelphia, PA), 2003.

John Steinbeck, Chelsea House (Philadelphia, PA), 2003.

Joseph Conrad, Chelsea House (Philadelphia, PA), 2003.

Marcel Proust, Chelsea House (Philadelphia, PA), 2003.

Mark Twain, Chelsea House (Philadelphia, PA), 2003.

Nathaniel Hawthorne, Chelsea House (Philadelphia, PA), 2003.

Tennessee Williams, Chelsea House (Philadelphia, PA), 2003.

The Brontë Sisters, Chelsea House (Philadelphia, PA), 2003.

Lord Byron, Chelsea House (Philadelphia, PA), 2004.

Also author of *Freud: Transference and Authority,* 1988.

WORK IN PROGRESS: A book on the traditions of Jesus and Yahweh.

SIDELIGHTS: Sterling Professor of Humanities at Yale University, Harold Bloom "is arguably the best-known literary critic in America, probably the most controversial and undoubtedly as idiosyncratic as they come—a description with which he would not quarrel," according to *Newsweek* writer David Lehman. Describing the influence of the past upon poetry as a relationship of conflict, Bloom's writings have consistently contradicted mainstream trends in literary theory.

Bloom sees poetry as an agonistic—that is, competitive—response to previous poetry. In the *New York Times Book Review,* Edward Said commented, "it is the essence of Bloom's vision that every poem is the result by which another, earlier poem is deliberately misread, and hence re-written." Such a vision sets each poem in a hostile relationship with others: "No text can be complete," Said noted, "because on the one hand it is an attempt to struggle free of earlier texts impinging on it and, on the other, it is preparing itself to savage texts not yet written by authors not yet born."

When Bloom declared his theory of poetic creation in *The Anxiety of Influence* and its companion work, *A Map of Misreading,* he built his discussion on the model of Oedipal conflict asserted by Sigmund Freud, the founder of modern psychoanalysis. Freud stated that each infant views its father as a rival for its mother's attention, and wishes to take its father's place. Bloom's adaptation of Freud recasts the infant, father, and mother in the roles of belated poet, precursor poet, and Muse of poetic inspiration, respectively. Bloom also states that, like the Freudian concept of "repression" of motives from consciousness and behavior, literary influence is sometimes notable by

omission. In a *Diacritics* interview with Robert Moynihan, Bloom acknowledged conventional methods of tracing the presence of similarities between poems, but then asserted the importance of looking at what is not in a particular poem: "I think this is a much more interesting and vital area in which interpoetic relationships tend to cluster. That is, what is it which is missing or all but present in a poem, what is suggested or evaded? That is usually, I think, a much better path, or hidden path, hidden channel, for what is taking place between two poems. . . . To a considerable extent, I try to study those hidden pressures."

Also in the *Diacritics* interview, Bloom proposed an alternative to the tradition of Eliot and Matthew Arnold—who anticipated some of Eliot's views—in academia, stating, "It's quite clearly the tradition that moves from [John] Ruskin through [Walter] Pater and [Oscar] Wilde that interests me and which I would certainly want to set up more as a model for the professorial or academic criticism of poetry than the Arnoldian, Eliotic line." Consistent with his critical preference, Bloom has edited an edition of Pater's *Marius the Epicurean: His Sensations and Ideas,* and he has also edited and written introductions for *Selected Writings of Walter Pater* and *The Literary Criticism of John Ruskin.*

Bloom links the Ruskin/Pater/Wilde tradition of criticism with the ancient Greco-Roman philosophies of Stoicism and Epicureanism when he told Moynihan that "there is an element of Stoic and indeed explicitly Epicurean mode of interpretation that does get into Pater very strongly, and before him does exist implicitly in Ruskin, and I would suppose that Ruskin, Pater, Wilde, and in this country, [Ralph Waldo] Emerson, who was a kind of intuitive Gnostic, are the major influences on my work." Bloom further contended that as an alternative to the mainstream of literary criticism descended from Plato and Aristotle, "Stoic and Epicurean models in terms of philosophy, and Gnostic and Kabbalistic models in terms of religion, which themselves owe a good deal I think to Stoic doctrines, are of more interest."

In addition to borrowing from Freud, Gnosticism, and the Kabbalah, Bloom invents vocabulary, structures, and interstructural relations that may challenge the general reader. *The Anxiety of Influence* asserts six "revisionary ratios," methods of misreading to which Bloom attaches specialized Greek names. In *Contem-*

porary Literature, Paul de Man asserted that "the main interest of *The Anxiety of Influence,* is not the literal theory of influence it contains but the structural interplay between the six types of misreading, the six 'intricate evasions' that govern the relationships between texts." "*A Map of Misreading,*" noted Michael Wood in an article for the *New York Review of Books,* "adds six rhetorical tropes, six psychic defenses, six sets of imagery, and three movements of creation to Bloom's original six ratios of revision." Observing the use of invented and Kabbalistic terminology throughout Bloom's theoretical works, Helen Regueiro Elam in the *Dictionary of Literary Biography* stated, "Readers may feel hopelessly bewildered by this proliferation of terms, but for Bloom they constitute a basic vocabulary which, despite constant revisions and refinements, retains its parallels from text to text."

Several reviewers charge that Bloom's literary theory is excessively reductive. "In *The Breaking of the Vessels* [Bloom] says that his kind of reading 'does not know a poem as being apart from the agon it enacts,'" noted Denis Donoghue in the *Times Literary Supplement.* The critic then asked, "if a reading doesn't know a poem as being apart from the agon it enacts, what prevents the reading from reducing the poem to that agon?" Writing for the *New York Times Book Review,* Christopher Ricks noted repetition in the arguments appearing in *The Anxiety of Influence, A Map of Misreading, Kabbalah and Criticism,* and *Poetry and Repression,* then declared, "Bloom had an idea; now the idea has him. . . . He now has nothing left to do but to say the same things about new contests and with more decibels." However, in a *New Republic* review of *Agon: Towards a Theory of Revisionism,* Helen Vendler wrote, "Any collection of essays and addresses composed in the span of a few years by a single powerful mind will tend to return to the same questions, and to urge (even covertly) the same views."

Some critics have complained of a tendency toward assertion rather than exposition in Bloom's works. Discussing statements of influence between particular poems in *A Map of Misreading, Yale Review* critic Jonathan Culler said, "If Bloom were to consider how he knows these things, tell us the story of his formidable poetic perceptions, he would produce a far more valuable and instructive book." "Bloom hasn't validated his values, he has merely urged them," wrote Donoghue in his *Times Literary Supplement* article.

Bloom engages in his own theological revisionism in *The Book of J,* which presents the text of David

Rosenberg's new translation of the "J" strand of the Bible—"J" for "Jehovah," an incorrect transliteration of "Yahweh," the "J"-text author's name for God—and Bloom's interpretation of the text. "The earliest known texts of the Hebrew Bible were not religious writings at all but a sublime work of literature, a comic masterpiece of ironic power," said Richard Bernstein in summary of Bloom's thesis in the *New York Times Book Review.* Bernstein further reported that Bloom suggests the "J" author was a court woman writing immediately after the reign of Solomon. *Chicago Tribune* critic Joseph Coates noted Bloom asserts that later segments of the Pentateuch, the first five books of the bible, traditionally ascribed to Moses, were revisions written "by priests and redactors who over a period of 600 years inflicted later forms of patriarchal Judaism on the work of a secular, and often quite bawdy, author." In his conclusion, Coates suggested that *The Book of J* is "restoring to Western literature a major author at the very beginning of the canon." According to Bloom, the grouping of texts into a canon is an extension of the agonistic action of literary criticism. Elam commented, "Canonization expresses the critic's own will-to-power over texts and is the most extreme form of literary revisionism."

Omens of Millennium is a more personal book on a similar subject in which Bloom discusses contemporary spirituality and his own admitted Gnosticist beliefs. "While presenting an informative history of ideas and provocative cultural critique," according to Mark Taylor in the *New York Times Book Review,* "*Omens of Millennium* is, above all else, a spiritual autobiography." As *Los Angeles Times Book Review* critic Jonathan Kirsch wrote, "The whole point of Bloom's book is that the offerings of the so-called New Age—'an endless saturnalia of ill-defined longings,' as he defines it—are shallow and silly when compared to what the ancients knew." Bloom offers the teachings of the Gnostic tradition as an alternative to millenarian spiritual malaise, accompanied by glancing examples from his own life. Commenting on Bloom's disclosure of his struggle with depression in his thirties, Kirsch noted that Bloom "is apparently too courtly, too cerebral and perhaps too shy to engage in much baring of the soul." Instead, as *Washington Post Book World* critic Marina Warner noted, Bloom invokes the wisdom of ancient Zoroastrianism, early Christian Gnosticism, medieval Sufism, and Kabbalism "in order to create an antidote to the New Age." Praising the "trenchancy, verve and learning" of the book, Warner wrote that, "*Omens of Millennium* is born of despair, but it focuses throughout on possibility, with a true teacher's refusal to give up the job of stimulating and informing, no matter how restless the class or desolate the wasteland of the schoolyard outside."

In *The Western Canon,* Bloom focuses his attention on select writings of twenty-six authors, including Dante, Chaucer, Shakespeare, Jane Austen, Charles Dickens, Marcel Proust, Virginia Woolf, and Samuel Beckett, whom he contends are among the most significant figures of the Western literary tradition. Concerned over the current underappreciation of serious reading and literary study among students and educators, Bloom laments, as quoted by Norman Fruman in the *New York Times Book Review,* "we are destroying all intellectual and esthetic standards in the humanities and social sciences, in the name of social justice." Fruman praised Bloom's effort as "a heroically brave, formidably learned and often unbearably sad response to the present state of the humanities," particularly Bloom's vehement opposition to "the School of Resentment" in which he corrals "Feminists, Marxists, Lacanians, New Historicists, Deconstructionists, Semioticians." Bloom is "supremely confident of his own esthetic judgment," according to Fruman, "he takes little notice of the vagaries of individual taste or the pressure of cultural or national loyalties." Commenting on the tone of "sorrowful resignation" that permeates the book, Michael Dirda wrote in *Washington Post Book World,* "Such mournful authority is irresistible, and it is this unswerving defense of reading, of 'hard' reading, that transmutes *The Western Canon* into a work of power and plangency."

"*Shakespeare: The Invention of the Human* is, simply, the book of a lifetime, the culmination of a career," wrote Frank McConnell in *Commonweal.* The book contains Bloom's views on Shakespeare's plays, which loosely argues the theory that Shakespeare invented the human personality. In this "series of brilliant, persuasive, highly idiosyncratic readings," according to a reviewer for *Publishers Weekly,* Bloom presents the reader with, wrote Hugh Kenner in *National Review,* "a theme that each visit amplifies and deepens but cannot wholly clarify." To Bloom the most important Shakespearean characters are Falstaff and Hamlet. McConnell wrote: "Falstaff is . . . the very archetype of life in the moment, of consciousness as perpetual, minute-by-minute celebration of itself, and all it sees, for all the ill it sees . . . Hamlet is . . . transcendence,

aware to the point of pain of the world's complexity, and wanting nothing so much as to evade it all for the absoluteness of one's being." Delivering his case against the politicizing of college departments of English, Bloom "cheerfully calls himself a 'wicked old aesthete'" related Donald Lyons in *Commentary,* as he dismisses feminist, revisionist, and structuralist theories imposed on Shakespeare's works. Michiko Kakutani in *New York Times* noted, "Indeed, this volume is best read as an old-fashioned humanistic commentary on Shakespeare's plays that gives us a renewed appreciation of the playwright's staggering achievement." McConnell wrote, "In a world where academic criticism is ever more aridly formalist and/or politically correct, ever less connected to the needs of human readers, this book is exhilaratingly old-fashioned, arguing . . . that we read poetry to save, or find, our lives." James Shapiro for the *New York Times Book Review* felt the work "marred by a compulsion to denigrate" Shakespeare's contemporaries, but admits that "the most exhilarating observations—and the best chapters are littered with them—have the quality of aphorisms." A critic for the *Economist* wrote that "what is most heartening about his book is the sheer joy, awe, and wonder that the plays still inspire in him after a lifetime of studying and teaching them."

How to Read and Why is Bloom's attempt to communicate to readers the best way to read. The book is broken into sections on short stories, poems, novels, and plays. Colin Walters in the *Washington Times* described the work as "a roundup of favorite reading treats accumulated over sixty years." "This book is a testament to Bloom's view that reading is above all a pleasurably therapeutic event," concluded a critic for *Publishers Weekly,* while Henry Carrigan in *Library Journal* described the book as an "apologia for the art of reading well."

Bloom's love of literature and wish to tell everyone about it has also extended to children. He has written a series of study guides for grade school children and up. These books cover authors such as F. Scott Fitzgerald, Ernest Hemingway, Langston Hughes, and many, many more. Each volume in the series includes Bloom's essay "The Work in the Writer" and a different introduction written for each volume. Bloom also includes a brief biography of the author, discussion of the author's accomplishments, and as noted by Susan D. Yutzey in *Book Report,* "an original critical essay that puts the author's works into cultural and historical perspective."

Despite a large output of criticisms for young adult readers, Bloom has not forgotten the sophisticated adult reader. In his 2002 book *Genius: A Mosaic of One Hundred Exemplary Creative Minds* he discusses his choice for the one hundred most influential writers in world history. Ranging from Homer to Ralph Ellison, Bloom's choices—among them William Shakespeare, John Milton, Miguel Cervantes, and Leo Tolstoy—would not surprise those who have followed the educator's career or literary predilections. However, as noted by Jonathan Rose writing in the *Europe Intelligence Wire, Genius* includes "some provocative surprises." Rose went on to add, "You will wake up when he introduces you to Machade de Assis (a Brazilian zany in the tradition of Laurence Sterne) and Ea de Queriroz (a Portuguese satirist who 'united Voltaire and Robert Louis Stevenson in a single body')." Bloom begins his book by discussing genius and outlining how he has grouped the writers included, which is according to the ten divine attributes in the ancient Jewish text the Kabbalah. Each of the subsequent chapters focuses on one writer. As noted by an *M2 Best Books* contributor, "There are 814 pages present in this book and each one is crammed to the brim with analysis, observations and opinions on each."

Writing in *Book,* Penelope Mesic found *Genius* to "have a lack of focus [that] contributes to a more serious deficiency: the absence of a point to be made." Mesic found the groupings based on the Kabbalah to "reflect not an underlying truth about these authors' works but rather Bloom's past scholarship and predilections." *Booklist* contributor Donna Seaman believed that the groupings worked, noting, "This makes for some wonderfully fresh and provocative juxtapositions, and for an elevating concentration on how each writer extends the path toward wisdom." Writing in *Library Journal,* Shana C. Fair commented, "Although the book is a delight to read, its real value lies in the author's ability to provoke the reader into thinking about literature, genius, and related topics."

Bloom's assertion that literary activity is a struggle against past and future literary actions has, throughout his career, provided a controversial and provocative alternative to the widely followed traditional schools of criticism. "Since the publication of [*The Anxiety of Influence*], it has been impossible to discuss theories of influence and tradition without reference to Bloom," wrote Elam. In the *New York Times,* Anatole Broyard concluded, "Bloom may be right, and if he's not, he is

one of the most brilliantly wrong critics writing today." Bloom has, in fact, become an outcast among many of his colleagues due to his idiosyncratic and independent approach, explained Larissa Macfarquhar in the *New Yorker.* For Bloom's part, he does not see himself in the role of literary curmudgeon: he explained that while he still believes "Shakespeare is still the best of all writers. . . . I also enormously admire such current authors as Philip Roth, Don DeLillo, Thomas Pynchon, and Cormac McCarthy among novelists, John Ashbery the poet, and Tony Kushner the dramatist."

BIOGRAPHICAL AND CRITICAL SOURCES:

BOOKS

Allen, Graham, *Harold Bloom: Poetics of Conflict,* Harvester Wheatsheaf (New York, NY), 1994.
Contemporary Literary Criticism, Volume 24, Gale (Detroit, MI), 1983.
De Bolla, Peter, *Harold Bloom: Toward Historical Rhetorics,* Routledge (New York, NY), 1988.
Dictionary of Literary Biography, Volume 67: *Modern American Critics since 1955,* Gale (Detroit, MI), 1988.
Eliot, T. S., *Selected Essays,* Harcourt (New York, NY), 1964.
Fite, David, *Harold Bloom: The Rhetoric of Romantic Vision,* University of Massachusetts Press (Amherst, MA), 1985.
Lentricchia, Frank, *After the New Criticism,* University of Chicago Press (Chicago, IL), 1974.
Mileur, Jean-Pierre, *Literary Revisionism and the Burden of Modernity,* University of California Press, 1985.
Moynihan, Robert, *A Recent Imagining: Interviews with Harold Bloom, Geoffrey Hartman, J. Hillis Miller, Paul De Man,* Archon, 1986.
Saurberg, Lars Ole, *Versions of the Past—Visions of the Future: The Canonical in the Criticism of T. S. Eliot, F. R. Leavis, Northrop Frye, and Harold Bloom,* St. Martin's Press (New York, NY), 1997.
Scherr, Barry J., *D. H. Lawrence's Response to Plato: A Bloomian Interpretation,* P. Lang (New York, NY), 1995.

PERIODICALS

Book, November-December, 2002, Penelope Mesic, review of *Genius: A Mosaic of One Hundred Exemplary Creative Minds,* p. 79.

Booklist, September 1, 2002, Donna Seaman, review of *Genius,* p. 2.

Book Report, May-June, 2002, Theresa Micelson, "Bloom's Major Novelists," p. 67; September-October 2002, Susan D. Yutzey, "Bloom's Bio Critiques," p. 70.

Chicago Tribune, November 1, 1990.

Commentary, April, 1999, Donald Lyons, review of *Shakespeare: The Invention of the Human,* p. 53.

Commonweal, Frank McConnell, review of *Shakespeare: The Invention of the Human,* p. 20.

Contemporary Literature, summer, 1974.

Diacritics, fall, 1983.

Economist, February 6, 1999, "Good Will Shakespeare," p. 89.

Europe Intelligence Wire, October 26, 2002, Jonathan Rose, review of *Genius.*

Library Journal, October 1, 1998, Neal Wyatt, review of *Shakespeare: The Invention of the Human,* p. 84; May 1, 2000, Henry Carrigan, review of *How to Read and Why,* p. 111; September 15, 2002, Shana C. Fair, review of *Genius,* p. 62.

Los Angeles Times Book Review, December 15, 1996, p. 6.

M2 Best Books, April 16, 2003, review of *Genius.*

Modern Philology, February, 1973.

National Review, Hugh Kenner, review of *Shakespeare: The Invention of the Human,* p. 51.

New Criterion, December, 1998, Paul Dean, review of *Shakespeare: The Invention of the Human,* p. 77.

New Republic, May 19, 1979; February 17, 1982.

New Statesman, March 12, 1999, Terence Hawkes, review of *Shakespeare: The Invention of the Human,* p. 45.

Newsweek, August 18, 1986; May 18, 1992, p. 69.

New Yorker, September 30, 2002, Larissa Macfarquhar, "The Prophet of Decline."

New York Review of Books, April 17, 1975; February 19, 1976.

New York Times, January 2, 1982; October 24, 1990; October 17, 1994, Christopher Lehmann-Haupt, review of *The Western Canon,* p. B2; October 27, 1998, Michiko Kakutani, "*Shakespeare:* The Vast Shakespearean Drama, with All People as Players," p. E1.

New York Times Book Review, March 14, 1973; April 13, 1975; December 21, 1975; March 14, 1976; June 12, 1977; May 13, 1979; November 25, 1979; January 31, 1982; May 10, 1992, p. 7; October 9, 1994, Norma Fruman, review of *The Western Canon,* p. 9; September 8, 1996, p. 11; November 1, 1998, James Shapiro, "Soul of the Age," p. 8.

New York Times Magazine, September 25, 1994, Adam Begley, "Colossus among Critics," p. 32.

Publishers Weekly, September 14, 1998, review of *Shakespeare: The Invention of the Human,* p. 56; May 8, 2000, review of *How to Read and Why,* p. 212.

Time, Jodie Morse, review of *Shakespeare: The Invention of the Human,* p. 122.

Times Literary Supplement, June 20, 1980; July 30, 1982; April 19, 1991.

Washington Post Book World, June 22, 1975; May 17, 1992, p. 4; September 25, 1994, p. 1; September 15, 1996, p. 11.

Washington Times, June 18, 2000, Colin Walters, "When the Book's the Thing," p. 6; April 6, 2003, David Veington, review of *Hamlet: Poem Unlimited,* p. B08.

Yale Review, October, 1975.

ONLINE

Atlantic Unbound, http://www.theatlantic.com/ (July 16, 2003), Jennie Rothenberg, interview with Bloom.

*   *   *

BORGES, Jorge Luis 1899-1986
(F. Bustos, pseudonym; H. Bustos Domecq, B. Lynch Davis, B. Suarez Lynch, joint pseudonyms)

PERSONAL: Born August 24, 1899, in Buenos Aires, Argentina; died of liver cancer, June 14, 1986, in Geneva, Switzerland; buried in Plainpalais, Geneva, Switzerland; son of Jorge Guillermo Borges (a lawyer, teacher, and writer) and Leonor Acevedo Suarez (a translator); married Elsa Astete Millan, September 21, 1967 (divorced, 1970); married Maria Kodama, April 26, 1986. *Education:* Attended College Calvin, Geneva, Switzerland, 1914-18; also studied in Cambridge, England, and Buenos Aires, Argentina.

CAREER: Writer. Miguel Cane branch library, Buenos Aires, Argentina, municipal librarian, 1937-46; teacher of English literature at several private institutions and lecturer in Argentina and Uruguay, 1946-55; National Library, Buenos Aires, director, 1955-73; University of Buenos Aires, Buenos Aires, Argentina, professor of English and U.S. literature, beginning in 1956. Visiting professor or guest lecturer at numerous universities in the United States and throughout the world, including University of Texas, 1961-62, University of Oklahoma, 1969, University of New Hampshire, 1972, and Dickinson College, 1983; Charles Eliot Norton Professor of Poetry, Harvard University, 1967-68.

MEMBER: Argentine Academy of Letters, Argentine Writers Society (president, 1950-53), Modern Language Association of America (honorary fellow, 1961-86), American Association of Teachers of Spanish and Portuguese (honorary fellow, 1965-86).

AWARDS, HONORS: Buenos Aires Municipal Literary Prize, 1928, for *El Idioma de los argentinos;* Gran Premio de Honor, Argentine Writers Society, 1945, for *Ficciones, 1935-1944;* Gran Premio Nacional de la Literatura (Argentina), 1957, for *El Aleph;* Premio de Honor and Prix Formentor, International Congress of Publishers (shared with Samuel Beckett), 1961; Commandeur de l'Ordre des Arts et des Lettres (France), 1962; Fondo de les Artes, 1963; Ingram Merrill Foundation Award, 1966; Matarazzo Sobrinho Inter-American Literary Prize, Bienal Foundation, 1970; nominated for Neustadt International Prize for Literature, *World Literature Today* and University of Oklahoma, 1970, 1984, and 1986; Jerusalem Prize, 1971; Alfonso Reyes Prize (Mexico), 1973; Gran Cruz del Orden al Merito Bernardo O'Higgins, Government of Chile, 1976; Gold Medal, French Academy, Order of Merit, Federal Republic of Germany, and Icelandic Falcon Cross, all 1979; Miguel de Cervantes Award (Spain) and Balzan Prize (Italy), both 1980; Ollin Yoliztli Prize (Mexico), 1981; T. S. Eliot Award for Creative Writing, Ingersoll Foundation and Rockford Institute, 1983; Gold Medal of Menendez Pelayo University (Spain), La Gran Cruz de la Orden Alfonso X, el Sabio (Spain), and Legion d'Honneur (France), all 1983; Knight of the British Empire; National Book Critics Circle Award for Criticism, 1999, for *Selected Non-Fictions.* Recipient of honorary degrees from numerous colleges and universities, including University of Cuyo (Argentina), 1956, University of the Andes (Colombia), 1963, Oxford University, 1970, University of Jerusalem, 1971, Columbia University, 1971, and Michigan State University, 1972.

WRITINGS:

POETRY

Fervor de Buenos Aires (title means "Passion for Buenos Aires"), Serantes (Buenos Aires, Argentina), 1923, revised edition, Emecé (Buenos Aires, Argentina), 1969.

Luna de enfrente (title means "Moon across the Way"), Proa (Buenos Aires, Argentina), 1925.

Cuaderno San Martín (title means "San Martin Copybook"), Proa (Buenos Aires, Argentina), 1929.

Poemas, 1923-1943, Losada, 1943, 3rd enlarged edition published as *Obra poética, 1923-1964,* 1964, translation published as *Selected Poems, 1923-1967* (bilingual edition; also includes prose), edited, with an introduction and notes, by Norman Thomas di Giovanni, Delacorte (New York, NY), 1972, enlarged Spanish-language edition published as *Obra poética 1923-1976,* Emecé (Buenos Aires, Argentina), 1977.

Nueve poemas, El Mangrullo (Buenos Aires, Argentina), 1955.

Límites, Francisco A. Colombo (Buenos Aires, Argentina), 1958.

Seis poemas escandinavos (title means "Six Scandinavian Poems"), privately printed, 1966.

Siete poemas (title means "Seven Poems"), privately printed, 1967.

El Otro, el mismo (title means "The Other, the Same"), Emecé (Buenos Aires, Argentina), 1969.

Elogio de la sombra, Emecé (Buenos Aires, Argentina), 1969, translation by Norman Thomas di Giovanni published as *In Praise of Darkness* (bilingual edition), Dutton (New York, NY), 1974.

El Oro de los tigres (also see below; title means "The Gold of Tigers"), Emecé (Buenos Aires, Argentina), 1972.

Siete poemas sajones/Seven Saxon Poems, Plain Wrapper Press (Austin, TX), 1974.

La Rosa profunda (also see below; title means "The Unending Rose"), Emecé (Buenos Aires, Argentina), 1975.

La Moneda de hierro (title means "The Iron Coin"), Emecé (Buenos Aires, Argentina), 1976.

Historia de la noche (title means "History of Night"), Emecé (Buenos Aires, Argentina), 1977.

The Gold of Tigers: Selected Later Poems (contains translations of *El Oro de los tigres* and *La Rosa profunda*), translation by Alastair Reid, Dutton (New York, NY), 1977.

La Cifra, Emecé (Buenos Aires, Argentina), 1981.

Also author of *Los Conjurados* (title means "The Conspirators"), Alianza (Madrid, Spain), 1985.

Inquisiciones (title means "Inquisitions"), Proa (Buenos Aires, Argentina), 1925.

El Tamano de mi esperanza (title means "The Measure of My Hope"), Proa (Buenos Aires, Argentina), 1926.

El Idioma de los argentinos (title means "The Language of the Argentines"), M. Gleizer (Buenos Aires, Argentina), 1928, 3rd edition (includes three essays by Borges and three by Jose Edmundo Clemente), Emecé (Buenos Aires, Argentina), 1968.

Figari, privately printed, 1930.

Las Kennigar, Francisco A. Colombo (Buenos Aires, Argentina), 1933.

Historia de la eternidad (title means "History of Eternity"), Viau & Zona (Buenos Aires, Argentina), 1936, revised edition published as *Obras completas,* Volume 1, Emecé (Buenos Aires, Argentina), 1953.

Nueva refutacion del tiempo (title means "New Refutation of Time"), Oportet & Haereses (Buenos Aires, Argentina), 1947.

Aspectos de la literatura gauchesca, Número (Montevideo, Uruguay), 1950.

El Lenguaje de Buenos Aires, Emecé (Buenos Aires, Argentina), 1963.

(With Delia Ingenieros) *Antiguas literaturas germanicas,* Fondo de Cultura Economica (Mexico City, Mexico), 1951, revised edition with Maria Esther Vazquez published as *Literaturas germanicas medievales,* Falbo, 1966.

Otras inquisiciones, Sur (Buenos Aires, Argentina), 1952, published as *Obras completas,* Volume 8, Emecé (Buenos Aires, Argentina), 1960, translation by Ruth L. C. Simms published as *Other Inquisitions, 1937-1952,* University of Texas Press (Austin, TX), 1964.

(With Margarita Guerrero) *El "Martín Fierro,"* Columba (Buenos Aires, Argentina), 1953.

(With Bettina Edelberg) *Leopoldo Lugones,* Troquel (Buenos Aires, Argentina), 1955.

(With Margarita Guerrero) *Manual de zoologia fantastica,* Fondo de Cultura Economica (Mexico City, Mexico), 1957, translation published as *The Imaginary Zoo,* University of California Press (Berkeley, CA), 1969, revised Spanish edition published as *El Libro de los seres imaginarios,* Kier (Buenos Aires, Argentina), 1967, translation and revision by Norman Thomas di Giovanni and Borges pub-

lished as *The Book of Imaginary Beings,* Dutton (New York, NY), 1969.

La Poesia gauchesca (title means "Gaucho Poetry"), Centro de Estudios Brasileiros, 1960.

(With Maria Esther Vazquez) *Introducción a la literatura inglesa,* Columba (Buenos Aires, Argentina), 1965, translation by L. Clark Keating and Robert O. Evans published as *An Introduction to English Literature,* University Press of Kentucky (Lexington, KY), 1974.

(With Esther Zemborain de Torres) *Introducción a la literatura norteamericana,* Columba (Buenos Aires, Argentina), 1967, translation by L. Clark Keating and Robert O. Evans published as *An Introduction to American Literature,* University of Kentucky Press (Lexington, KY), 1971.

(With Alicia Jurado) *Qué es el budismo?* (title means "What Is Buddhism?"), Columba (Buenos Aires, Argentina), 1976.

Nuevos ensayos dantescos (title means "New Dante Essays"), Espasa-Calpe (Madrid, Spain), 1982.

The Library of Babel, translation by Andrew Hurley, David R. Godine (Boston, MA), 2000.

Prólogos de "La Biblioteca de Babel," Alianza (Madrid, Spain), 2001.

Museo: Textos inéditos, Emecé (Buenos Aires, Argentina), 2002.

SHORT STORIES

Historia universal de la infamia, Tor (Buenos Aires, Argentina), 1935, revised edition published as *Obras completas,* Volume 3, Emecé (Buenos Aires, Argentina), 1964, translation by Norman Thomas di Giovanni published as *A Universal History of Infamy,* Dutton (New York, NY), 1972.

El Jardin de senderos que se bifurcan (also see below; title means *Garden of the Forking Paths*), Sur (Buenos Aires, Argentina), 1941.

(With Adolfo Bioy Casares, under joint pseudonym H. Bustos Domecq) *Seis problemas para Isidro Parodi,* Sur (Buenos Aires, Argentina), 1942, translation by Norman Thomas di Giovanni published under authors' real names as *Six Problems for Don Isidro Parodi,* Dutton (New York, NY), 1983.

Ficciones, 1935-1944 (includes *El Jardin de senderos que se bifurcan*), Sur (Buenos Aires, Argentina), 1944, revised edition published as *Obras completas,* Volume 5, Emecé (Buenos Aires, Argentina), 1956, translation by Anthony Kerrigan and others published as *Ficciones,* edited and with an introduction by Kerrigan, Grove Press (New York, NY), 1962, new edition with English introduction and notes by Gordon Brotherson and Peter Hulme, Harrap (London, England), 1976.

(With Adolfo Bioy Casares, under joint pseudonym H. Bustos Domecq) *Dos fantasias memorables,* Oportet & Haereses (Buenos Aires, Argentina), 1946, reprinted under authors' real names with notes and bibliography by Horacio Jorge Becco, Edicom (Buenos Aires, Argentina), 1971.

El Aleph, Losada (Buenos Aires, Argentina), 1949, revised edition, 1952, published as *Obras completas,* Volume 7, Emecé (Buenos Aires, Argentina), 1956, translation and revision by Norman Thomas di Giovanni in collaboration with Borges published as *The Aleph and Other Stories, 1933-1969,* Dutton (New York, NY), 1970.

(With Luisa Mercedes Levinson) *La Hermana de Eloísa* (title means "Eloisa's Sister"), Ene (Buenos Aires, Argentina), 1955.

(With Adolfo Bioy Casares) *Crónicas de Bustos Domecq,* Losada (Buenos Aires, Argentina), 1967, translation by Norman Thomas di Giovanni published as *Chronicles of Bustos Domecq,* Dutton (New York, NY), 1976.

El Informe de Brodie, Emecé (Buenos Aires, Argentina), 1970, translation by Norman Thomas di Giovanni in collaboration with Borges published as *Dr. Brodie's Report,* Dutton (New York, NY), 1971.

El Matrero, Edicom (Buenos Aires, Argentina), 1970.

El Congreso, El Archibrazo (Buenos Aires, Argentina), 1971, translation by Norman Thomas di Giovanni in collaboration with Borges published as *The Congress* (also see below), Enitharmon Press (London, England), 1974, translation by Alberto Manguel published as *The Congress of the World,* F. M. Ricci (Milan, Italy), 1981.

El Libro de arena, Emecé (Buenos Aires, Argentina), 1975, translation by Norman Thomas di Giovanni published with *The Congress* as *The Book of Sand,* Dutton (New York, NY), 1977.

(With Adolfo Bioy Casares) *Nuevos cuentos de Bustos Domecq,* Librería de la Ciudad (Buenos Aires, Argentina), 1977.

Rosa y azul (contains *La Rosa de Paracelso* and *Tigres azules*), Sedmay (Madrid, Spain), 1977.

Veinticinco agosto 1983 y otros cuentos de Jorges Luis Borges (includes interview with Borges), Siruela (Madrid, Spain), 1983.

OMNIBUS VOLUMES

La Muerte y la brujula (stories; title means "Death and the Compass"), Emecé (Buenos Aires, Argentina), 1951.

Obras completas, ten volumes, Emecé (Buenos Aires, Argentina), 1953-67, published in one volume, 1974.

Cuentos (title means "Stories"), Monticello College Press, 1958.

Antologia personal (prose and poetry), Sur (Buenos Aires, Argentina), 1961, translation published as *A Personal Anthology,* edited and with foreword by Anthony Kerrigan, Grove Press (New York, NY), 1967.

Labyrinths: Selected Stories and Other Writings, edited by Donald A. Yates and James E. Irby, New Directions Press (New York, NY), 1962, augmented edition, 1964.

Nueva antologia personal, Emecé (Buenos Aires, Argentina), 1968.

Prólogos, con un prólogo de prólogos, Torres Aguero (Buenos Aires, Argentina), 1975.

(With others) *Obras completas en colaboracion* (title means "Complete Works in Collaboration"), Emecé (Buenos Aires, Argentina), 1979.

Narraciones (stories), edited by Marcos Ricardo Bamatan, Catedra, 1980.

Prose completa, two volumes, Bruguera (Barcelona, Spain), 1980.

Antología poética (1923-1977), Alianza (Madrid, Spain), 1981.

Borges: A Reader (prose and poetry), edited by Emir Rodriguez Monegal and Alastair Reid, Dutton (New York, NY), 1981.

Ficcionario: Una Antologia de sus textos, edited by Rodriguez Monegal, Fondo de Cultura Economica (Mexico City, Mexico), 1985.

Textos cautivos: Ensayos y resenas en "El Hogar" (1936-1939) (title means "Captured Texts: Essays and Reviews in 'El Hogar'"), edited by Rodriguez Monegal and Enrique Sacerio-Gari, Tusquets (Barcelona, Spain), 1986.

El Aleph borgiano, edited by Juan Gustavo Cobo Borda and Martha Kovasics de Cubides, Biblioteca Luis-Angel Arango (Bogota, Colombia), 1987.

Biblioteca personal: Prologos, Alianza (Madrid, Spain), 1988.

Obras completas, 1975-1985, Emecé (Buenos Aires, Argentina), 1989.

Collected Fictions, edited and translated by Andrew Hurley, Viking Press (New York, NY), 1998.

Selected Poems, edited by Alexander Coleman, Viking Press (New York, NY), 1999.

Selected Non-Fictions, edited and translated by Eliot Weinberger, Esther Allen, and Suzanne Jill Levine, Viking Press (New York, NY), 1999.

Jorge Luis Borges, Nextext (Evanston, IL), 2001.

OTHER

(Author of afterword) Ildefonso Pereda Valdes, *Antologia de la moderna poesia uruguaya,* El Ateneo (Buenos Aires, Argentina), 1927.

Evaristo Carriego (biography), M. Gleizer (Buenos Aires, Argentina), 1930, revised edition published as *Obras completas,* Volume 4, Emecé (Buenos Aires, Argentina), 1955, translation by Norman Thomas di Giovanni published as *Evaristo Carriego: A Book about Old-Time Buenos Aires,* Dutton (New York, NY), 1984.

Discusión, Gleizer (Buenos Aires, Argentina), 1932, revised edition, Emecé (Buenos Aires, Argentina), 1976.

(Translator) Virginia Woolf, *Orlando,* Sur (Buenos Aires, Argentina), 1937.

(Editor, with Pedro Henriquez Urena) *Antologia clasica de la literatura argentina* (title means "Anthology of Argentine Literature"), Kapelusz (Buenos Aires, Argentina), 1937.

(Translator and author of prologue) Franz Kafka, *La Metamorfosis,* [Buenos Aires, Argentina], 1938.

(Editor, with Adolfo Bioy Casares and Silvina Ocampo) *Antologia de la literatura fantastica* (title means "Anthology of Fantastic Literature"), with foreword by Bioy Casares, Sudamericana, 1940, enlarged edition with postscript by Bioy Casares, 1965, translation of revised version published as *The Book of Fantasy,* with introduction by Ursula K. Le Guin, Viking (New York, NY), 1988.

(Author of prologue) Adolfo Bioy Casares, *La Invencion de Morel,* Losada, 1940, translation by Ruth L. C. Simms published as *The Invention of Morel and Other Stories,* University of Texas Press (Austin, TX), 1964.

(Editor, with Adolfo Bioy Casares and Silvina Ocampo and author of prologue) *Antologia poetica argentina* (title means "Anthology of Argentine Poetry"), Sudamericana (Buenos Aires, Argentina), 1941.

(Translator) Henri Michaux, *Un Barbaro en Asia,* Sur (Buenos Aires, Argentina), 1941.

(Compiler and translator, with Adolfo Bioy Casares) *Los Mejores cuentos policiales* (title means "The Best Detective Stories"), Emecé (Buenos Aires, Argentina), 1943.

(Translator and author of prologue) Herman Melville, *Bartleby, el escribiente,* Emecé (Buenos Aires, Argentina), 1943.

(Editor, with Silvina Bullrich) *El Compadrito: Su destino, sus barrios, su mûsica* (title means "The Buenos Aires Hoodlum: His Destiny, His Neighborhoods, His Music"), Emecé (Buenos Aires, Argentina), 1945, 2nd edition, Fabril, 1968.

(With Adolfo Bioy Casares, under joint pseudonym B. Suarez Lynch) *Un Modelo para la muerte* (novel; title means "A Model for Death"), Oportet & Haereses (Buenos Aires, Argentina), 1946.

(Editor with Bioy Casares) Francesco de Quevedo, *Prosa y verso,* Emecé (Buenos Aires, Argentina), 1948.

(Compiler and translator, with Adolfo Bioy Casares) *Los Mejores cuentos policiales: Segunda serie,* Emecé (Buenos Aires, Argentina), 1951.

(Editor and translator, with Adolfo Bioy Casares) *Cuentos breves y extraordinarios: Antologia,* Raigal (Buenos Aires, Argentina), 1955, revised and enlarged edition, Losada, 1973, translation by Anthony Kerrigan published as *Extraordinary Tales,* Souvenir Press (New York, NY), 1973.

(With Adolfo Bioy Casares) *Los Orilleros* [and] *El Paraiso de los creyentes* (screenplays; titles mean "The Hoodlums" and "The Believers' Paradise"; *Los Orilleros* produced by Argentine director Ricardo Luna, 1975), Losada (Buenos Aires, Argentina), 1955.

(Editor and author of prologue, notes, and glossary, with Adolfo Bioy Casares) *Poesia gauchesca* (title means "Gaucho Poetry"), two volumes, Fondo de Cultura Economica (Mexico City, Mexico), 1955.

(Translator) William Faulkner, *Las Palmeras salvajes,* Sudamericana (Buenos Aires, Argentina), 1956.

(Editor, with Adolfo Bioy Casares) *Libro del cielo y del infierno* (anthology; title means "Book of Heaven and Hell"), Sur (Buenos Aires, Argentina), 1960.

El Hacedor (prose and poetry; Volume 9 of *Obras completas;* title means "The Maker"), Emecé, 1960, translation by Mildred Boyer and Harold Morland published as *Dreamtigers,* University of Texas Press (Austin, TX), 1964.

(Editor and author of prologue) *Macedonio Fernandez,* Culturales Argentinas, Ministerio de Educacion y Justicia, 1961.

Para las seis cuerdas: Milongas (song lyrics; title means "For the Six Strings: Milongas"), Emecé (Buenos Aires, Argentina), 1965.

Dialogo con Borges, edited by Victoria Ocampo, Sur (Buenos Aires, Argentina), 1969.

(Translator, editor, and author of prologue) Walt Whitman, *Hojas de hierba,* Juarez (Buenos Aires, Argentina), 1969.

(Compiler and author of prologue) Evaristo Carriego, *Versos,* Universitaria de Buenos Aires (Buenos Aires, Argentina), 1972.

Borges on Writing (lectures), edited by Norman Thomas di Giovanni, Daniel Halpern, and Frank MacShane, Dutton (New York, NY), 1973.

(With Adolfo Bioy Casares and Hugo Santiago) *Les Autres: Escenario original* (screenplay; produced in France and directed by Santiago, 1974), C. Bourgois (Paris, France), 1974.

(Author of prologue) Carlos Zubillaga, *Carlos Gardel,* Jucar (Madrid, Spain), 1976.

Cosmogonias, Librería de la Ciudad (Buenos Aires, Argentina), 1976.

Libro de suenos (transcripts of Borges's and others' dreams; title means "Book of Dreams"), Torres Aguero, 1976.

(Author of prologue) Santiago Dabove, *La Muerte y su traje,* Calicanto, 1976.

Borges-Imagenes, memorias, dialogos, edited by Vazquez, Monte Avila, 1977.

Adrogue (prose and poetry), privately printed, 1977.

Borges para millones, Corregidor (Buenos Aires, Argentina), 1978.

Poesía juvenile de Jorge Luis Borges, edited by Carlos Meneses, José Olañeta (Barcelona, Spain), 1978.

(Editor, with Maria Kodoma) *Breve antología anglosajona,* Emecé (Buenos Aires, Argentina), 1979.

Borges oral (lectures), edited by Martin Mueller, Emecé (Buenos Aires, Argentina), 1979.

Siete noches (lectures), Fondo de Cultura Economica (Mexico City, Mexico), 1980, translation by Eliot Weinberger published as *Seven Nights,* New Directions Press (New York, NY), 1984.

(Compiler) Paul Groussac, *Jorge Luis Borges selecciona lo mejor,* Fraterna (Buenos Aires, Argentina), 1981.

(Compiler and author of prologue) Francisco de Quevedo, *Antologia poetica,* Alianza (Madrid, Spain), 1982.

(Compiler and author of introduction) Leopoldo Lugones, *Antologia poetica,* Alianza (Madrid, Spain), 1982.

Milongas, Dos Amigos (Buenos Aires, Argentina), 1983.

(Compiler and author of prologue) Pedro Antonio de Alarcon, *El Amigo de la muerte,* Siruela (Madrid, Spain), 1984.

(With Maria Kodama) *Atlas* (prose and poetry), Sudamericana (Buenos Aires, Argentina), 1984, translation by Anthony Kerrigan published as *Atlas,* Dutton (New York, NY), 1985.

En voz de Borges (interviews), Offset, 1986.

Libro de dialogos (interviews), edited by Osvaldo Ferrari, Sudamericana (Buenos Aires, Argentina), 1986, published as *Dialogos ultimos,* 1987.

A/Z, Siruela (Madrid, Spain), 1988.

Borges en la Escuela Freudiana de Buenos Aires, Agalma (Buenos Aires, Argentina), 1993.

(Editor, with James F. Lawrence), *Testimony to the Invisible: Essays on Swedenborg,* Chrysalis Books (West Chester, PA), 1995.

Borges en Revista multicolor: Obras, resenas y traducciones ineditas de Jorge Luis Borges: Diario Critica, Revista multicolor de los sabados, 1933-1934, edited by Irma Zangara, Atlantida (Buenos Aires, Argentina), 1995.

Borges: Textos recobrados, 1919-1929, edited by Irma Zangara, Emecé (Buenos Aires, Argentina), 1997.

Borges professor: Curso de literature inglesa en la Universidad de Buenos Aires, edited by Martín Arias and Martín Hadis, Emecé (Buenos Aires, Argentina), 2000.

This Craft of Verse, edited by Calin-Andrei Mihailescu, Harvard University Press (Cambridge, MA), 2000.

Borges en "El Hogar," 1935-1958, Emecé (Buenos Aires, Argentina), 2000.

(With Alvaro Miranda) *Conversaciones, versaciones,* Ediciones del Mirador (Montevideo, Uruguay), 2001.

(With others) *Cuentos de hijos y padres: Estampas de familia,* Editorial Páginas de Espuma (Madrid, Spain), 2001.

Destino y obra de Camoens, Comunidades Portuguesas (Buenos Aires, Argentina), 2001.

(With others) *Cuentos históricos: De la piedra al átomo,* Páginas de Espuma (Madrid, Spain), 2003.

El Círculo secreto: Prólogos y notas, Emecé (Buenos Aires, Argentina), 2003.

Editor, with Adolfo Bioy Casares, of series of detective novels, "The Seventh Circle," for Emecé, 1943-56. Contributor, under pseudonym F. Bustos, to *Critica,* 1933. Contributor, with Bioy Casares, under joint pseudonym B. Lynch Davis, to *Los Anales de Buenos Aires,* 1946-48. Founding editor of *Prisma* (mural magazine), 1921; founding editor of *Proa* (Buenos Aires literary revue), 1921 and, with Ricardo Guiraldes and Pablo Rojas Paz, 1924-26; literary editor of weekly arts supplement of *Critica,* beginning 1933; editor of biweekly "Foreign Books and Authors" section of *El Hogar* (magazine), 1936-39; coeditor, with Bioy Casares, of *Destiempo* (literary magazine), 1936; editor of *Los Anales de Buenos Aires* (literary journal), 1946-48.

ADAPTATIONS: "Emma Zunz," a short story, was made into the movie *Dias de odio (Days of Wrath)* by Argentine director Leopoldo Torre Nilsson, 1954, a French television movie directed by Alain Magrou, 1969, and a film called *Splits* by U.S. director Leonard Katz, 1978; "Hombre de la esquina rosada," a short story, was made into an Argentine movie of the same title directed by Rene Mugica, 1961; Bernardo Bertolucci based his *La Strategia de la ragna (The Spider's Stratagem),* a movie made for Italian television, on Borges's short story, "El Tema del traidor y del heroe," 1970; Hector Olivera, in collaboration with Juan Carlos Onetti, adapted Borges's story "El Muerto" for the Argentine movie of the same name, 1975; Borges's short story "La Intrusa" was made into a Brazilian film directed by Carlos Hugo Christensen, 1978; three of the stories in *Six Problems for Don Isidro Parodi* were dramatized for radio broadcast by the British Broadcasting Corporation.

SIDELIGHTS: Argentine author Jorge Luis Borges exerted a strong influence on the direction of literary fiction through his genre-bending metafictions, essays, and poetry. Borges was a founder, and principal practitioner, of postmodernist literature, a movement in which literature distances itself from life situations in favor of reflection on the creative process and critical self-examination. Widely read and profoundly erudite, Borges was a polymath who could discourse on the great literature of Europe and America and who assisted his translators as they brought his work into different languages. He was influenced by the work of such fantasists as Edgar Allan Poe and Franz Kafka, but his own fiction "combines literary and extraliterary genres in order to create a dynamic, electric genre," to quote Alberto Julián Pérez in the *Dictionary of Literary Biography.* Pérez also noted that Borges's work "constitutes, through his extreme linguistic conscience and a formal synthesis capable of representing the

most varied ideas, an instance of supreme development in and renovation of narrative techniques. With his exemplary literary advances and the reflective sharpness of his metaliterature, he has effectively influenced the destiny of literature."

In his preface to *Labyrinths: Selected Stories and Other Writings,* French author André Maurois called Borges "a great writer." Maurois wrote that Borges "composed only little essays or short narratives. Yet they suffice for us to call him great because of their wonderful intelligence, their wealth of invention, and their tight, almost mathematical style. Argentine by birth and temperament, but nurtured on universal literature, Borges [had] no spiritual homeland."

Borges was nearly unknown in most of the world until 1961 when, in his early sixties, he was awarded the Prix Formentor, the International Publishers Prize, an honor he shared with Irish playwright Samuel Beckett. Prior to winning the award, according to Gene H. Bell-Villada in *Borges and His Fiction: A Guide to His Mind and Art,* "Borges had been writing in relative obscurity in Buenos Aires, his fiction and poetry read by his compatriots, who were slow in perceiving his worth or even knowing him." The award made Borges internationally famous: a collection of his short stories, *Ficciones,* was simultaneously published in six different countries, and he was invited by the University of Texas to come to the United States to lecture, the first of many international lecture tours.

Borges's international appeal was partly a result of his enormous erudition, which becomes immediately apparent in the multitude of literary allusions from cultures around the globe that are contained in his writing. "The work of Jorge Luis Borges," Anthony Kerrigan wrote in his introduction to the English translation of *Ficciones,* "is a species of international literary metaphor. He knowledgeably makes a transfer of inherited meanings from Spanish and English, French and German, and sums up a series of analogies, of confrontations, of appositions in other nations' literatures. His Argentinians act out Parisian dramas, his Central European Jews are wise in the ways of the Amazon, his Babylonians are fluent in the paradigms of Babel." In the *National Review,* Peter Witonski commented: "Borges's grasp of world literature is one of the fundamental elements of his art."

The familiarity with world literature evident in Borges's work was initiated at an early age, nurtured by a love of reading. His paternal grandmother was

English and, since she lived with the Borgeses, English and Spanish were both spoken in the family home. Jorge Guillermo Borges, Borges's father, had a large library of English and Spanish books, and his son, whose frail constitution made it impossible to participate in more strenuous activities, spent many hours reading. "If I were asked to name the chief event in my life, I should say my father's library," Borges stated, in "An Autobiographical Essay," which originally appeared in the *New Yorker* and was later included in *The Aleph and Other Stories, 1933-1969.*

Under his grandmother's tutelage, Borges learned to read English before he could read Spanish. Among the first English-language books he read were works by Mark Twain, Edgar Allan Poe, Henry Wadsworth Longfellow, Robert Louis Stevenson, and H. G. Wells. In Borges's autobiographical essay, he recalled reading even the great Spanish masterpiece, Cervantes's *Don Quixote,* in English before reading it in Spanish. Borges's father encouraged writing as well as reading: Borges wrote his first story at age seven and, at nine, saw his own Spanish translation of Oscar Wilde's "The Happy Prince" published in a Buenos Aires newspaper. "From the time I was a boy," Borges noted, "it was tacitly understood that I had to fulfill the literary destiny that circumstances had denied my father. This was something that was taken for granted. . . . I was expected to be a writer."

Borges indeed became a writer, one with a unique style. Critics were forced to coin a new word— Borgesian—to capture the magical world invented by the Argentine author. Jaime Alazraki noted in *Jorge Luis Borges:* "As with Joyce, Kafka, or Faulkner, the name of Borges has become an accepted concept; his creations have generated a dimension that we designate 'Borgesian.'" In the *Atlantic,* Keith Botsford declared: "Borges is . . . an international phenomenon . . . a man of letters whose mode of writing and turn of mind are so distinctively his, yet so much a revealed part of our world, that 'Borgesian' has become as commonplace a neologism as the adjectives 'Sartrean' or 'Kafkaesque.'"

Once his work became known in the United States, Borges inspired many young writers there. "The impact of Borges on the United States writing scene may be almost as great as was his earlier influence on Latin America," commented Bell-Villada. "The Argentine reawakened for us the possibilities of farfetched fancy,

of formal exploration, of parody, intellectuality, and wit." Bell-Villada specifically noted echoes of Borges in works by Robert Coover, Donald Barthelme, and John Gardner. Another American novelist, John Barth, confessed Borges's influence in his own fiction. Bell-Villada concluded that Borges's work paved the way "for numerous literary trends on both American continents, determining the shape of much fiction to come. By rejecting realism and naturalism, he . . . opened up to our Northern writers a virgin field, led them to a wealth of new subjects and procedures."

The foundation of Borges's literary future was laid in 1914 when the Borges family took an ill-timed trip to Europe. The outbreak of World War I stranded them temporarily in Switzerland, where Borges studied French and Latin in school, taught himself German, and began reading the works of German philosophers and expressionist poets. He also encountered the poetry of Walt Whitman in German translation and soon began writing poetry imitative of Whitman's style. "For some time," Emir Rodriguez Monegal wrote in *Borges: A Reader,* "the young man believed Whitman was poetry itself."

After the war the Borges family settled in Spain for a few years. During this extended stay, Borges published reviews, articles, and poetry and became associated with a group of avant-garde poets called Ultraists (named after the magazine, *Ultra,* to which they contributed). Upon Borges's return to Argentina in 1921, he introduced the tenets of the movement—a belief, for example, in the supremacy of the metaphor—to the Argentine literary scene. His first collection of poems, *Fervor de Buenos Aires,* was written under the spell of this new poetic movement. Although in his autobiographical essay he expressed regret for his "early Ultraist excesses," and in later editions of *Fervor de Buenos Aires* eliminated more than a dozen poems from the text and considerably altered many of the remaining poems, Borges still saw some value in the work. In his autobiographical essay he noted, "I think I have never strayed beyond that book. I feel that all my subsequent writing has only developed themes first taken up there; I feel that all during my lifetime I have been rewriting that one book."

One poem from the volume, "El Truco" (named after a card game), seems to testify to the truth of Borges's statement. In the piece he introduced two themes that appear over and over again in his later writing: circular time and the idea that all people are but one person. "The permutations of the cards," Rodriguez Monegal observed in *Jorge Luis Borges: A Literary Biography,* "although innumerable in limited human experience, are not infinite: given enough time, they will come back again and again. Thus the cardplayers not only are repeating hands that have already come up in the past. In a sense, they are repeating the former players as well: they are the former players."

Although better known for his prose, Borges began his writing career as a poet and was known primarily for his poetry in Latin America particularly. In addition to writing his own original poetry, he translated important foreign poets for an Argentinian audience. He also authored numerous essays and gave whole series of lectures on poetry and various poets from Dante to Whitman. Observing that Borges "is one of the major Latin American poets of the twentieth century," Daniel Balderston in the *Dictionary of Literary Biography* added that in Latin America, Borges's poetry "has had a wide impact: many verses have been used as titles for novels and other works, many poems have been set to music, and his variety of poetic voices have been important to many younger poets."

Illusion is an important part of Borges's fictional world. In *Borges: The Labyrinth Maker,* Ana Maria Barrenechea called it "his resplendent world of shadows." But illusion is present in his manner of writing as well as in the fictional world he describes. In *World Literature Today,* William Riggan quoted Icelandic author Sigurdur Magnusson's thoughts on this aspect of Borges's work. "With the possible exception of Kafka," Magnusson stated, "no other writer that I know manages, with such relentless logic, to turn language upon itself to reverse himself time after time with a sentence or a paragraph, and effortlessly, so it seems, come upon surprising yet inevitable conclusions."

Borges expertly blended the traditional boundaries between fact and fiction and between essay and short story, and was similarly adept at obliterating the border between other genres as well. In a tribute to Borges that appeared in the *New Yorker* after the author's death in 1986, Mexican poet and essayist Octavio Paz wrote: "He cultivated three genres: the essay, the poem, and the short story. The division is arbitrary. His essays read like stories, his stories are poems; and his poems make us think, as though they were essays."

In *Review,* Ambrose Gordon, Jr. similarly noted, "His essays are like poems in their almost musical development of themes, his stories are remarkably like his essays, and his poems are often little stories." Borges's "Conjectural Poem," for example, is much like a short story in its account of the death of one of his ancestors, Francisco Narciso de Laprida. Another poem, "The Golem," is a short narrative relating how Rabbi Low of Prague created an artificial man.

To deal with the problem of actually determining to which genre a prose piece by Borges might belong, Martin S. Stabb proposed in *Jorge Luis Borges,* his book-length study of the author, that the usual manner of grouping all of Borges's short fiction as short stories was invalid. Stabb instead divided the Argentinian's prose fiction into three categories which took into account Borges's tendency to blur genres: "'essayistic' fiction," "difficult-to-classify 'intermediate' fiction," and those pieces deemed "conventional short stories." Other reviewers saw a comparable division in Borges's fiction but chose to emphasize the chronological development of his work, noting that his first stories grew out of his essays, his "middle period" stories were more realistic, while his later stories were marked by a return to fantastic themes.

"Funes the Memorious," listed in Richard Burgin's *Conversations with Jorge Luis Borges* as one of Borges's favorite stories, is about Ireneo Funes, a young man who cannot forget anything. His memory is so keen that he is surprised by how different he looks each time he sees himself in a mirror because, unlike the rest of us, he can see the subtle changes that have taken place in his body since the last time he saw his reflection. The story is filled with characteristic Borgesian detail. Funes's memory, for instance, becomes excessive as a result of an accidental fall from a horse. In Borges an accident is a reminder that people are unable to order existence because the world has a hidden order of its own. Alazraki saw this Borgesian theme as "the tragic contrast between a man who believes himself to be the master and maker of his fate and a text or divine plan in which his fortune has already been written." The deliberately vague quality of the adjectives Borges typically uses in his sparse descriptive passages is also apparent: Funes's features are never clearly distinguished because he lives in a darkened room; he was thrown from his horse on a dark "rainy afternoon"; and the horse itself is described as "blue-gray"—neither one color nor the other. "This dominant chiaroscuro imagery," commented Bell-Villada, "is further reinforced by Funes's name, a word strongly suggestive of certain Spanish words variously meaning 'funereal,' 'ill-fated,' and 'dark.'" The ambiguity of Borges's descriptions lends a subtle, otherworldly air to this and other examples of his fiction.

In "Partial Magic in the *Quixote*" (also translated as "Partial Enchantments of the *Quixote*") Borges describes several occasions in world literature when a character reads about himself or sees himself in a play, including episodes from Shakespeare's plays, an epic poem of India, Miguel de Cervantes's *Don Quixote,* and *The One Thousand and One Nights.* "Why does it disquiet us to know," Borges asked in the essay, "that Don Quixote is a reader of the *Quixote,* and Hamlet is a spectator of *Hamlet?* I believe I have found the answer: those inversions suggest that if the characters in a story can be readers or spectators, then we, their readers, can be fictitious."

That analysis was Borges's own interpretation of what John Barth referred to in the *Atlantic* as "one of Borges's cardinal themes." Barrenechea explained Borges's technique, noting: "To readers and spectators who consider themselves real beings, these works suggest their possible existence as imaginary entities. In that context lies the key to Borges's work. Relentlessly pursued by a world that is too real and at the same time lacking meaning, he tries to free himself from its obsessions by creating a world of such coherent phantasmagorias that the reader doubts the very reality on which he leans." Pérez put it this way: "In his fiction Borges repeatedly utilizes two approaches that constitute his most permanent contributions to contemporary literature: the creation of stories whose principal objective is to deal with critical, literary, or aesthetic problems; and the development of plots that communicate elaborate and complex ideas that are transformed into the main thematic base of the story, provoking the action and relegating the characters—who appear as passive subjects in this inhuman, nightmarish world—to a secondary plane."

For example, in one of Borges's variations on "the work within a work," Jaromir Hladik, the protagonist of Borges's story "The Secret Miracle," appears in a footnote to another of Borges' stories, "Three Versions of Judas." The note refers the reader to the "Vindication of Eternity," a work said to be written by Hladik. In this instance, Borges used a fictional work written by one of his fictitious characters to lend an air of erudition to another fictional work about the works of another fictitious author.

These intrusions of reality on the fictional world are characteristic of Borges's work. He also uses a device, which he calls "the contamination of reality by dream," that produces the same effect of uneasiness in the reader as "the work within the work," but through directly opposite means. Two examples of stories using this technique are "Tlon, Uqbar, Orbis Tertius" and "The Circular Ruins." The first, which Stabb included in his "difficult-to-classify 'intermediate' fiction," is one of Borges's most discussed works. It tells the story, according to Barrenechea, "of an attempt of a group of men to create a world of their own until, by the sheer weight of concentration, the fantastic creation acquires consistency and some of its objects—a compass, a metallic cone—which are composed of strange matter begin to appear on earth." By the end of the story, the world as we know it is slowly turning into the invented world of Tlon. Stabb called the work "difficult-to-classify" because, he commented, "the excruciating amount of documentary detail (half real, half fictitious) . . . make[s] the piece seem more like an essay." There are, in addition, footnotes and a postscript to the story as well as an appearance by Borges himself and references to several other well-known Latin-American literary figures, including Borges's friend Bioy Casares.

"The Circular Ruins," which Stabb considered a "conventional short story," describes a very unconventional situation. (The story is conventional, however, in that there are no footnotes or real people intruding on the fictive nature of the piece.) In the story a man decides to dream about a son until the son becomes real. Later, after the man accomplishes his goal, much to his astonishment, he discovers that he in turn is being dreamt by someone else. "The Circular Ruins" includes several themes seen throughout Borges's work, including the vain attempt to establish order in a chaotic universe, the infinite regression, the symbol of the labyrinth, and the idea of all people being one.

The futility of any attempt to order the universe, seen in "Funes the Memorious" and in "The Circular Ruins," is also found in "The Library of Babel" where, according to Alazraki, "Borges presents the world as a library of chaotic books which its librarians cannot read but which they interpret incessantly." The library was one of Borges's favorite images, often repeated in his fiction, reflecting the time he spent working as a librarian himself. In another work, Borges uses the image of a chessboard to elaborate the same theme. In his poem "Chess," he speaks of the king, bishop, and queen, who "seek out and begin their armed campaign." But, just as the dreamer dreams a man and causes him to act in a certain way, the campaign is actually being planned by someone other than the members of royalty. "They do not know it is the player's hand," the poem continues, "that dominates and guides their destiny." In the last stanza of the poem Borges uses the same images to suggest the infinite regression: "God moves the player, he in turn, the piece. / But what god beyond God begins the round / of dust and time and sleep and agonies?" Another poem, "The Golem," which tells the story of an artificial man created by a rabbi in Prague, ends in a similar fashion: "At the hour of anguish and vague light, / He would rest his eyes on his Golem. / Who can tell us what God felt, / As he gazed on His rabbi in Prague?" Just as there is a dreamer dreaming a man, and beyond that a dreamer dreaming the dreamer who dreamt the man, then, too, there must be another dreamer beyond that in an infinite succession of dreamers.

The title of the story, "The Circular Ruins," suggests a labyrinth. In another story, "The Babylon Lottery," Stabb explained that "an ironically detached narrator depicts life as a labyrinth through which man wanders under the absurd illusion of having understood a chaotic, meaningless world." Labyrinths or references to labyrinths are found in nearly all of Borges's fiction. The labyrinthine form is often present in his poems, too, especially in Borges's early poetry filled with remembrances of wandering the labyrinth-like streets of old Buenos Aires.

In "The Circular Ruins," Borges returns to another favorite theme: circular time. This theme embraces another device mentioned by Borges as typical of fantastic literature: time travel. Borges's characters, however, do not travel through time in machines; their travel is more on a metaphysical, mythical level. Circular time—a concept also favored by Nietzsche, one of the German philosophers Borges discovered as a boy—is apparent in many of Borges's stories, including "Three Versions of Judas," "The Garden of the Forking Paths," "Tlon, Uqbar, Orbis Tertius," "The Library of Babel," and "The Immortal." It is also found in another of Borges's favorite stories, "Death

and the Compass," in which the reader encounters not only a labyrinth but a double as well. Stabb offered the story as a good example of Borges's "conventional short stories."

"Death and the Compass" is a detective story. Erik Lonnrot, the story's detective, commits the fatal error of believing there is an order in the universe that he can understand. When Marcel Yarmolinsky is murdered, Lonnrot refuses to believe it was just an accident; he looks for clues to the murderer's identity in Yarmolinsky's library. Red Scharlach, whose brother Lonnrot had sent to jail, reads about the detective's efforts to solve the murder in the local newspaper and contrives a plot to ambush him. The plan works because Lonnrot, overlooking numerous clues, blindly follows the false trail Scharlach leaves for him.

The final sentences—in which Lonnrot is murdered—change the whole meaning of the narrative, illustrate many of Borges's favorite themes, and crystalize Borges's thinking on the problem of time. Lonnrot says to Scharlach: "'I know of one Greek labyrinth which is a single straight line. Along that line so many philosophers have lost themselves that a mere detective might well do so, too. Scharlach, when in some other incarnation you hunt me, pretend to commit (or do commit) a crime at A, then a second crime at B. . . . then a third crime at C. . . . Wait for me afterwards at D. . . . Kill me at D as you now are going to kill me at Triste-le-Roy.' 'The next time I kill you,' said Scharlach, 'I promise you that labyrinth, consisting of a single line which is invisible and unceasing.' He moved back a few steps. Then, very carefully, he fired."

"Death and the Compass" is in many ways a typical detective story, but this last paragraph takes the story far beyond that popular genre. Lonnrot and Scharlach are doubles (Borges gives us a clue in their names: rot means red and scharlach means scarlet in German) caught in an infinite cycle of pursuing and being pursued. "Their antithetical natures, or inverted mirror images," George R. McMurray observed in his study *Jorge Luis Borges,* "are demonstrated by their roles as detective/criminal and pursuer/pursued, roles that become ironically reversed." Rodriguez Monegal concluded: "The concept of the eternal return . . . adds an extra dimension to the story. It changes Scharlach and Lonnrot into characters in a myth: Abel and Cain endlessly performing the killing."

Doubles, which Bell-Villada defined as "any blurring or any seeming multiplication of character identity," are found in many of Borges's works, including "The Waiting," "The Theologians," "The South," "The Shape of the Sword," "Three Versions of Judas," and "Story of the Warrior and the Captive." Borges's explanation of "The Theologians" (included in his collection, *The Aleph and Other Stories, 1933-1969*) reveals how a typical Borgesian plot involving doubles works. "In 'The Theologians' you have two enemies," Borges told Richard Burgin in an interview, "and one of them sends the other to the stake. And then they find out somehow they're the same man." In an essay in *Studies in Short Fiction,* Robert Magliola noticed that "almost every story in *Dr. Brodie's Report* is about two people fixed in some sort of dramatic opposition to each other." In two pieces, "Borges and I" (also translated as "Borges and Myself") and "The Other," Borges appears as a character along with his double. In the former, Borges, the retiring Argentine librarian, contemplates Borges, the world-famous writer. It concludes with one of Borges's most-analyzed sentences: "Which of us is writing this page, I don't know."

Some critics saw Borges's use of the double as an attempt to deal with the duality in his own personality: the struggle between his native Argentine roots and the strong European influence on his writing. They also pointed out what seemed to be an attempt by the author to reconcile through his fiction the reality of his sedentary life as an almost-blind scholar with the longed-for adventurous life of his dreams, like those of his famous ancestors who actively participated in Argentina's wars for independence. Bell-Villada pointed out that this tendency is especially evident in "The South," a largely autobiographical story about a library worker who, like Borges, "is painfully aware of the discordant strains in his ancestry."

The idea that all humans are one, which Anderson-Imbert observed calls for the "obliteration of the I," is perhaps Borges's biggest step toward a literature devoid of realism. In this theme we see, according to Ronald Christ in *The Narrow Act: Borges' Art of Illusion,* "the direction in Borges's stories away from individual psychology toward a universal mythology." This explains why so few of Borges's characters show any psychological development; instead of being interested in his characters as individuals, Borges typically uses them only to further his philosophical beliefs.

All of the characteristics of Borges's work, including the blending of genres and the confusion of the real

and the fictive, seem to come together in one of his most quoted passages, the final paragraph of his essay "A New Refutation of Time." While in *Borges: A Reader* Rodriguez Monegal called the essay Borges's "most elaborate attempt to organize a personal system of metaphysics in which he denies time, space, and the individual 'I,'" Alazraki noted that it contains a summation of Borges's belief in "the heroic and tragic condition of man as dream and dreamer."

"Our destiny," wrote Borges in the essay, "is not horrible because of its unreality; it is horrible because it is irreversible and ironbound. Time is the substance I am made of. Time is a river that carries me away, but I am the river; it is a tiger that mangles me, but I am the tiger; it is a fire that consumes me, but I am the fire. The world, alas, is real; I, alas, am Borges."

Since his death from liver cancer in 1986, Borges's reputation has only grown in esteem. In honor of the centenary of his birth, Viking Press issued a trilogy of his translated works, beginning with *Collected Fictions,* in 1998. The set became the first major summation of Borges's work in English, and *Review of Contemporary Fiction* writer Irving Malin called the volume's debut "the most significant literary event of 1998." The collection includes "The Circular Ruins," "Tlon, Uqbar, Orbis Tertius," and the prose poem "Everything and Nothing," along with some of the Argentine writer's lesser-known works. "I admire the enduring chill of Borges," concluded Malin. "Despite his calm, understated style, he manages to make us unsure of our place in the world, of the value of language."

The second volume from Viking was *Selected Poems,* with Borges's original Spanish verse alongside English renditions from a number of translators. *Nation* critic Jay Parini commended editor Alexander Coleman's selections of poems from different periods of Borges's life, praised some of the English translations, and described Borges's work as timeless. "Borges stands alone, a planet unto himself, resisting categorization," Parini noted, adding, "Although literary fashions come and go, he is always there, endlessly rereadable by those who admire him, awaiting rediscovery by new generations of readers."

Selected Non-Fictions, the third in the commemorative trilogy, brings together various topical articles from Borges. These include prologues for the books of others, including Virginia Woolf, and political opinion pieces, such as his excoriating condemnation of Nazi Germany as well as to the tacit support it received from some among the Argentine middle classes. Borges also writes about the dubbing of foreign films and the celebrated Dionne quintuplets, born in Canada in the 1930s. "One reads these," noted Richard Bernstein in the *New York Times,* "with amazement at their author's impetuous curiosity and penetrating intelligence." *Review of Contemporary Fiction* critic Ben Donnelly, like other critics, felt that all three volumes complemented each other, as Borges's own shifts between genres did: "The best essays here expose even grander paradoxes and erudite connections than in his stories," Donnelly noted.

In 2000, Harvard University Press issued *This Craft of Verse,* a series of lectures delivered by Borges at Harvard University in the late 1960s. They languished in an archive for some thirty years until the volume's editor, Calin-Andrei Mihailescu, found the tapes and transcribed them. Micaela Kramer, reviewing the work for the *New York Times,* commented that its pages show "Borges's ultimate gift" and, as she noted, "his unwavering belief in the world of dreams and ideas, the sense that life is 'made of poetry.'" In his essay on Borges, Pérez observed that the author "created his own type of post-avant-garde literature—which shows the process of critical self-examination that reveals the moment in which literature becomes a reflection of itself, distanced from life—in order to reveal the formal and intellectual density involved in writing."

BIOGRAPHICAL AND CRITICAL SOURCES:

BOOKS

Alazraki, Jaime, *Critical Essays on Jorge Luis Borges,* G. K. Hall (Boston, MA), 1987.

Alazraki, Jaime, *Jorge Luis Borges,* Columbia University Press (New York, NY), 1971.

Balderston, Daniel, *The Literary Universe of Jorge Luis Borges: An Index to References and Allusions to Persons, Titles, and Places in His Writings,* Greenwood Press (Westport, CT), 1986.

Balderston, Daniel, *Out of Context: Historical References and the Representation of Reality in Borges,* Duke University Press (Durham, NC), 1993.

Barnstone, Willis, *Borges at Eighty: Conversations,* Indiana University Press (Bloomington, IN), 1982.

Barrenechea, Ana Maria, *Borges: The Labyrinth Maker,* translated by Robert Lima, New York University Press (New York, NY), 1965.

Bell-Villada, Gene H., *Borges and His Fiction: A Guide to His Mind and Art,* University of North Carolina Press (Chapel Hill, NC), 1981.

Burgin, Richard, *Conversations with Jorge Luis Borges,* Holt (New York, NY), 1969.

Christ, Ronald J., *The Narrow Act: Borges' Art of Illusion,* New York University Press (New York, NY), 1969.

Contemporary Literary Criticism, Gale (Detroit, MI), Volume 1, 1973, Volume 2, 1974, Volume 3, 1975, Volume 4, 1975, Volume 6, 1976, Volume 8, 1978, Volume 9, 1978, Volume 10, 1979, Volume 13, 1980, Volume 19, 1981, Volume 44, 1987, Volume 48, 1988.

Cortínez, Carlos, editor, *Borges the Poet,* University of Arkansas Press (Fayetteville, AR), 1986.

Cottom, Daniel, *Ravishing Tradition: Cultural Forces and Literary History,* Cornell University Press (Ithaca, NY), 1996.

Dictionary of Literary Biography, Gale (Detroit, MI), Volume 113: *Modern Latin-American Fiction Writers, First Series,* 1992, pp. 67-81; Volume 238: *Modern Spanish American Poets, First Series,* 2001, pp. 41-58.

Dictionary of Literary Biography: Yearbook, 1986, Gale (Detroit, MI), 1987.

Di Giovanni, Norman Thomas, editor, *In Memory of Borges,* Constable (London, England), 1988.

Di Giovanni, Norman Thomas, editor, *The Borges Tradition,* Constable (London, England), 1995.

Friedman, Mary L., *The Emperor's Kites: A Morphology of Borges' Tales,* Duke University Press (Durham, NC), 1987.

Hernandez Martin, Jorge, *Readers and Labyrinths: Detective Fiction in Borges, Bustos Domecqu, and Eco,* Garland Publishers (New York, NY), 1995.

Irwin, John T., *The Mystery to a Solution: Poe, Borges, and the Analytic Detective Story,* Johns Hopkins University Press (Baltimore, MD), 1994.

Kinzie, Mary, *Prose for Borges,* Northwestern University Press (Evanston, IL), 1974.

Maier, Linda S., *Borges and the European Avant-Garde,* P. Lang (New York, NY), 1996.

McMurray, George R., *Jorge Luis Borges,* Ungar (New York, NY), 1980.

Molloy, Sylvia, and Oscar Montero, *Signs of Borges,* Duke University Press (Durham, NC), 1994.

Rodriguez Monegal, Emir, *Jorge Luis Borges: A Literary Biography,* Dutton (New York, NY), 1978.

Stabb, Martin S., *Borges Revisited,* Twayne (Boston, MA), 1991.

Stabb, Martin S., *Jorge Luis Borges,* Twayne (Boston, MA), 1970.

Sturrock, John, *Paper Tigers: The Ideal Fictions of Jorge Luis Borges,* Clarendon Press (Oxford, England), 1977.

Woodall, James, *Borges: A Life,* Basic Books (New York, NY), 1997.

PERIODICALS

Americas, January, 2000, Barbara Mujica, review of *Selected Non-Fictions,* p. 60; April, 2000, Barbara Mujica, review of *Collected Fictions,* p. 63.

Atlantic Monthly, January, 1967; August, 1967; February, 1972; April, 1981.

Booklist, April 1, 1999, Donna Seaman, review of *Selected Poems,* p. 1379; August, 1999, Brad Hooper, review of *Selected Non-Fictions,* p. 2010; August, 2000, Ray Olson, review of *This Craft of Verse,* p. 2097.

Commentary, July, 1999, Marc Berley, review of *Collected Fictions* and *Selected Poems,* p. 89.

Cross Currents, summer, 1999, "Editor's Choice," p. 260.

Detroit News, June 15, 1986; June 22, 1986.

Library Journal, August, 2000, Jack Shreve, review of *This Craft of Verse,* p. 102.

Los Angeles Times, June 15, 1986.

Nation, December 29, 1969; August 3, 1970; March 1, 1971; February 21, 1972; October 16, 1972; February 21, 1976; June 28, 1986; May 31, 1999, Jay Parini, "Borges in Another Metier," p. 25.

National Review, March 2, 1973.

New Criterion, November, 1999, Eric Ormsby, "Jorge Luis Borges and the Plural I," p. 14; January, 2001, Alexander Coleman, review of *This Craft of Verse,* p. 79.

New Republic, November 3, 1986.

New Yorker, July 7, 1986.

New York Review of Books, August 14, 1986.

New York Times, June 15, 1986; October 6, 1999, Richard Bernstein, "So Close, Borges' Worlds of Reality and Invention"; October 15, 2000, Micaela Kramer, review of *This Craft of Verse.*

Publishers Weekly, July 4, 1986; March 29, 1999, review of *Selected Poems,* p. 97; July 12, 1999, review of *Selected Non-Fictions,* p. 80.

Review, spring, 1972; spring, 1975; winter, 1976; January-April, 1981; September-December, 1981.

Review of Contemporary Fiction, spring, 1999, Irving Malin, review of *Contemporary Fictions,* p. 175; spring, 2000, Ben Donnelly, review of *Selected Non-Fictions,* p. 192; spring, 2001, Thomas Hove, review of *This Craft of Verse,* p. 209.

Studies in Short Fiction, spring, 1974; winter, 1978.

Time, June 23, 1986.

USA Today, June 16, 1986.

Washington Post, June 15, 1986.

World Literature Today, autumn, 1977; winter, 1984.

Yale Review, October, 1969; autumn, 1974.*

* * *

BOWLER, Tim 1953-

PERSONAL: Born November 14, 1953, in Leigh-on-Sea, Essex, England; married; wife is a teacher. *Education:* Attended East Anglia University. *Hobbies and other interests:* Squash, rugby, swimming, sailing, basketball, soccer, yoga, reading, listening to music.

ADDRESSES: Home—Devon, England. *Agent*—Caroline Walsh, David Higham Associates Ltd., 5-8 Lower John St., Golden Square, London W1F 9HA, England. *E-mail*—tim@timbowler.co.uk.

CAREER: Worked in the forestry and the timber trade; spent seven years as a teacher of foreign languages and of English as a second language, ending as head of modern languages at a school in Newton Abbot, Devon, England; full-time freelancer, translator, and writer, 1990—.

AWARDS, HONORS: Books for the Teen Age selection, New York Public Library, 1995, for *Midget;* Carnegie Medal, British Library Association, 1997, and Angus Book Award, 1999, both for *River Boy;* Angus Book Award, and Children's Book of the Year Award, Lancashire County Library, both 2000, both for *Shadows;* South Lanarkshire Book Award, 2002, for *Storm Catchers.*

WRITINGS:

Midget, Oxford University Press (Oxford, England), 1994, Margaret K. McElderry (New York, NY), 1995.

Dragon's Rock, Oxford University Press (Oxford, England), 1995.

River Boy, Oxford University Press (Oxford, England), 1997, Margaret K. McElderry (New York, NY), 2002.

Shadows, Oxford University Press (Oxford, England), 1999.

Storm Catchers, Oxford University Press (Oxford, England), 2001, Margaret K. McElderry (New York, NY), 2003.

Starseeker, Oxford University Press (Oxford, England), 2002, published as *Firmament,* Margaret K. McElderry (New York, NY), 2004.

Two short stories, originally written as birthday presents for his wife, have been published by Egmont Books (London, England) in the collections *Straight from the Heart* and *Family Tree.*

ADAPTATIONS: Film rights have been sold for *Midget, River Boy,* and *Storm Catchers.*

WORK IN PROGRESS: A novel.

SIDELIGHTS: Tim Bowler started writing at the age of five, but it did not become his career for many years. He worked in forestry and then as a language teacher for nearly twenty years, doing his writing between 3 a.m. and 7 a.m. before he left for work. He started his first novel, *Midget,* when he was twenty-five, writing in this fashion; it was not published until he was over forty years old. Even though Bowler now writes full-time, he still prefers to write early in the morning while drinking a thermos of maté tea he makes the night before. "My workroom is a converted bedroom overlooking the churchyard with trees and flowers and rolling hills beyond," he commented on his Web site, continuing, "All my books have been written to the sound of birdsong."

Midget is a psychological thriller that "might have been a Twilight Zone episode," commented a *Publishers Weekly* contributor. *Horn Book* reviewer Nancy Vasilakis praised *Midget,* saying, "The tightly scripted plot with its steadily building tension will keep readers spellbound to the end." *Midget* is a tiny fifteen-year-old boy, physically and emotionally warped by the abuse he suffers at the hands of his outwardly devoted older brother, Seb. The story is set in Bowler's native Leigh-on-Sea, a fishing village in southeastern England, and the ocean features prominently in the tale. Midget's one escape is the marina, where he takes great pleasure in watching Old Joseph work on fixing up an old, wooden sailboat. Midget wants to sail this boat, a fact which is apparently known to Joseph, who leaves the boat to Midget in his will. Around this time, Midget has discovered his ability to influence events with his mind, a skill which he uses to do minor harm to his therapist and to win a sailboat race against his brother. Seb, furious at his defeat, tries to carry out his oft-repeated threat to kill Midget, so Midget uses his new powers to cripple Seb. He thinks about killing him, but stops at the last minute. Then he walks out into the sea and disappears. "He acts the way he does because he realizes that the power he has acquired— after being so long in the power of another—has not fulfilled him or released him from his pain, but has actually corrupted him and made things worse," Bowler noted on his Web site.

On his Web site, Bowler discussed his experiences writing *Midget:* "The level of violence isn't something you choose as a writer. At least I don't. When I'm writing a story, the characters and scenes and places start to form pictures, and then the momentum builds up and it's as though you find the direction the story wants to go. . . . It's the writing itself for me that unlocks the story. Writing *Midget* scared the pants off me when the violent stuff started coming out. I started to wonder what was wrong with me and it took ten drafts to work the thing out."

Bowler is also the author of *River Boy,* the winner of a Carnegie Medal. It is a story about "the embodiment of hope, the circle of life, and an artist's spiritual quest," in the words of *School Library Journal* critic Alison Follos. Jess's grandfather is dying. He convinces Jess's parents to take him back to his boyhood home, along the banks of a river flowing through the countryside, so he can finish his painting, "River Boy," before he dies. While he works on this painting, fifteen-year-old Jess, a competitive swimmer, explores the river. There she meets the "river boy," a mysterious, otherworldly character with some connection to her grandfather. The river boy wants to swim from the source of the river to its mouth at the ocean, and he wants Jess to accompany him.

Several critics praised Bowler's writing style in *River Boy.* "There's poetry in the simple, elemental words and the space between them," Hazel Rochman commented in a review for *Booklist,* while Follos praised Bowler's "lyrical metaphors and fluid writing style."

Additionally, Bowler "succeeds in conveying the strong bond between Jess and her grandfather," noted a *Publishers Weekly* contributor.

Shadows, Bowler's next book after *River Boy,* is the story of a young man named Jamie who is pushed by his obsessive and abusive father to become a champion squash player. His relationship with his father begins to change when Jamie finds a pregnant teen named Abby hiding in his shed as she flees from a very bad situation. "The story zips along," commented *Observer* reviewer Caroline Boucher, who also thought that this book was "much tighter, grittier, and, I think, better," than *River Boy.* In a review for *School Librarian,* Michael Lockwood noted that *Shadows,* with its faced-paced narrative and dramatic tension, was "very different from *River Boy* in style, but just as successful in its own terms."

Like *Shadows, Storm Catchers* also features a flawed father and a young woman in danger. Ella, the thirteen-year-old middle child, is kidnapped from her family's seaside home one stormy night while her parents are out. Her fifteen-year-old brother Fin is guilt-wracked; three-year-old Sam begins seeing the ghost of another girl. The point of view alternates between Fin, Ella, and Sam, as they slowly learn about their family's dark secret and the motive of the young kidnapper. "It's the fast, realistic action and dialogue and the stormy coastal setting that drive this story," *Booklist*'s Rochman thought. But as Connie Tyrrell Burns noted in *School Library Journal,* "The complex themes of guilt and betrayal enhance the suspense."

Bowler commented on his Web site: "Some people think there must be a set of rules for writing, but the truth is there aren't any. It's more like tickling trout, holding your hand out and trying to coax the ideas to swim into your grasp; or being a potter, throwing the rough clay of your thoughts down and letting the story twist out under the palms of your hands; or being a sorcerer, stirring the cauldron of your imagination and watching the vapour of the story rise. Writing is all these things and many more. It's something you never bottom, never crack, never stop learning about. And that's why I love it."

BIOGRAPHICAL AND CRITICAL SOURCES:

PERIODICALS

Booklist, May 1, 2000, Hazel Rochman, review of *River Boy,* p. 1660; September 1, 2003, Hazel Rochman, review of *Storm Catchers,* p. 112.

Book Report, November-December, 1995, Jo Rae Peiffer, review of *Midget,* p. 31.
Books for Keeps, November, 1995, Val Randall, review of *Dragon's Rock,* p. 13; July, 2000, Lesley de Meza, review of *Shadows,* p. 6.
Horn Book, March-April, 1996, Nancy Vasilakis, review of *Midget,* pp. 203-204.
Independent (London, England), July 16, 1998, Anne Treneman, "You Can Cry Me a River," p. S10.
Junior Bookshelf, August, 1995, review of *Dragon's Rock,* p. 142.
Kirkus Reviews, September 15, 1999, review of *Midget,* p. 1347; May 15, 2003, review of *Storm Catchers,* p. 746.
Magpies, March, 2002, Rayma Turton, review of *Storm Catchers,* p. 41.
Observer (London, England), February 14, 1999, Caroline Boucher, review of *Shadows,* p. 15; October 27, 2002, Nicci Gerrard, review of *Starseeker,* p. 18.
Publishers Weekly, September 25, 1995, review of *Midget,* p. 57; July 10, 2000, review of *River Boy,* p. 64; June 2, 2003, review of *Storm Catchers,* p. 53.
School Librarian, summer, 1999, Michael Lockwood, review of *Shadows,* p. 98.
School Library Journal, October, 1995, Kelly Diller, review of *Midget,* p. 152; October, 1999, Brian E. Wilson, review of *River Boy,* p. 88; August, 2000, Alison Follos, review of *River Boy,* p. 177; May, 2003, Connie Tyrrell Burns, review of *Storm Catchers,* p. 144.
Spectator, July 18, 1998, Jane Gardam, review of *River Boy,* pp. 36-37.
Times Educational Supplement, September 23, 1994, Geoff Fox, review of *Midget,* p. A19; May 12, 1995, David Buckley, review of *Dragon's Rock,* p. 16; July 17, 1998, Geraldine Brennan, "Journey Man," p. A12; February 12, 1999, Geraldine Brennan, review of *Shadows,* p. 27; September 27, 2002, Linda Newbery, review of *Starseeker,* p. 12.

ONLINE

Oxford University Press, http://www.oup.co.uk/ (November 6, 2001), "Oxford Children's Authors: Tim Bowler."
Read In!, http://www.readin.org/ (November 6, 2001), "Tim Bowler @ The Read In!"
Tim Bowler Home Page, http://www.timbowler.co.uk (November 6, 2001).

BRINK, André (Philippus) 1935-

PERSONAL: Born May 29, 1935, in Vrede, Orange Free State, South Africa; son of Daniel (a magistrate) and Aletta (a teacher; maiden name, Wolmarans) Brink; married Estelle Naudé, October 3, 1951 (divorced); married Salomi Louw, November 28, 1965 (divorced); married Alta Miller (a potter), July 17, 1970 (divorced); married Marésa de Beer, November 16, 1990; children: (first marriage) Anton; (second marriage) Gustav; (third marriage) Danie, Sonja. *Education:* Potchefstroom University, B.A., 1955, M.A. (Afrikaans), 1958, M.A. (Afrikaans and Dutch), 1959; postgraduate study at Sorbonne, University of Paris, 1959-61.

ADDRESSES: Home—6 Banksia Rd., Rosebank, Cape Town 7700, South Africa. *Office*—Department of English, University of Cape Town, Rondebosch 7700, South Africa. *Agent*—Ruth Liepman, Maienburgweg 23, Zurich, Switzerland.

CAREER: Author. Rhodes University, Grahamstown, South Africa, lecturer, 1963-73, senior lecturer, 1974-75, associate professor, 1976-79, professor of Afrikaans and Dutch literature, 1980-90; University of Cape Town, Cape Town, South Africa, professor of English, 1991—. Director of theatrical productions.

MEMBER: South African PEN, Afrikaans Writers' Guild (president, 1978-80).

AWARDS, HONORS: Reina Prinsen Geerligs prize, 1964; Central News Agency award for Afrikaans literature, 1965, for *Olé,* and for English literature, 1979, for *Rumours of Rain,* 1983, for *A Chain of Voices;* prize for prose translation from South African Academy, 1970, for *Alice se Avonture in Wonderland,* and 1982; D.Litt., Rhodes University, 1975, Witwatersrand University, 1985, and University of the Orange Free State, 1997; Central News Agency award for English literature, 1978, for *Rumours of Rain;* Martin Luther King, Jr., Memorial Prize and Prix Médicis Étranger, both 1980, both for *A Dry White Season;* named chevalier de Legion d' Honneur and officier de l'Ordre des Arts et des Lettres, promoted to commandeur, 1992; Premio Mondello, 1997, for *Imaginings of Sand;* honorary doctorate, Rhodes University, 2001.

WRITINGS:

FICTION

Die meul teen die hang, Tafelberg (Cape Town, South Africa), 1958.

André Brink

Die gebondenes, Afrikaanse Pers (Johannesburg, South Africa), 1959.

Die eindelose weë, Tafelberg (Cape Town, South Africa), 1960.

Lobola vir die lewe (title means "Dowry for Life"), Human & Rousseau (Cape Town, South Africa), 1962

Die Ambassadeur, Human & Rousseau (Cape Town, South Africa), 1963, translated by Brink as *File on a Diplomat,* Longmans, Green (London, England), 1965, revised translation published as *The Ambassador,* Faber (New York, NY), 1985.

Orgie, John Malherbe (Cape Town, South Africa), 1965.

(With others) *Rooi,* Malherbe (Cape Town, South Africa), 1965.

Miskien nooit: 'n Somerspel, Human & Rousseau (Cape Town, South Africa), 1967.

A Portrait of Woman as a Young Girl, Buren (Cape Town, South Africa), 1973.

Oom Kootjie Emmer (short stories), Buren (Cape Town, South Africa), 1973.

Kennis van die aand (novel), Buren (Cape Town, South Africa), 1973, translated by Brink as *Look-*

ing on Darkness, W. H. Allen (London, England), 1974, Morrow (New York, NY), 1975.

Die Geskiedenis van oom Kootjie Emmer van Witgratworteldraai, Buren (Cape Town, South Africa), 1973.

'n Oomblik in die wind, Taurus, 1975, translated as *An Instant in the Wind,* W. H. Allen (London, England), 1976, Morrow (New York, NY), 1977.

Gerugte van Reen (novel), Human & Rousseau (Cape Town, South Africa), 1978, translated as *Rumours of Rain,* Morrow (New York, NY), 1978, published as *Rumors of Rain,* Penguin (New York, NY), 1984,

'n Droe wit seisoen, Taurus, 1979, translated as *A Dry White Season,* W. H. Allen (London, England), 1979, Morrow (New York, NY), 1980.

'n Emmertjie wyn: 'n versameling dopstories, Saayman & Weber (Cape Town, South Africa), 1981.

Houd-den-bek (title means "Shut Your Trap"), Taurus, 1982, translated as *A Chain of Voices,* Morrow (New York, NY), 1982.

Oom Kootjie Emmer en die nuwe bedeling: 'n stinkstorie, Taurus (Johannesburg, South Africa), 1983.

Die Muur van die pes, Human & Rousseau (Cape Town, South Africa), 1984, translated as *The Wall of the Plague,* Summit (New York, NY), 1984.

Loopdoppies: Nog dopstories, Saayman & Weber (Cape Town, South Africa), 1984.

States of Emergency, Penguin, 1988, Summit (New York, NY), 1989.

Die Eerste lewe van Adamastor, Saayman & Weber (Cape Town, South Africa), 1988, translated as *Cape of Storms: The First Life of Adamastor: A Story* (novel), Simon & Schuster (New York, NY), 1993, published as *The First Life of Adamastor,* Secker & Warburg (London, England), 1993.

Mal en ander stories: 'n omnibus van humor, three volumes, Saayman & Weber (Cape Town, South Africa), 1990.

Die kreef raak gewoond daaraan, Human & Rousseau (Cape Town, South Africa), 1991.

An Act of Terror, Secker & Warburg (London, England), 1991, Summit (New York, NY), 1992.

Inteendeel, Human & Rousseau (Cape Town, South Africa), 1993.

On the Contrary: A Novel: Being the Life of a Famous Rebel, Soldier, Traveler, Explorer, Reader, Builder, Scribe, Latinist, Lover, and Liar, Little, Brown (Boston, MA), 1993.

Sandkastele, Human & Rousseau (Cape Town, South Africa), 1995, translated as *Imaginings of Sand,* Harcourt (New York, NY), 1996.

Duiwelskloof, Human & Rousseau (Cape Town, South Africa), 1998, translated as *Devil's Valley,* Harcourt (New York, NY), 1999.

Donkermaan, Human & Rousseau (Cape Town, South Africa), 2000, translated as *The Rights of Desire,* Secker & Warburg (London, England), 2000, Harcourt (New York, NY), 2001.

The Other Side of Silence, Harcourt (Orlando, FL), 2002.

DRAMA

Die band om ons harte (title means "The Bond around Our Hearts"), Afrikaanse Pers (Johannesburg, South Africa), 1959.

Caesar (first produced at Stellenbosch, Cape Province, 1965), Nasionale Boekhandel (Capetown, South Africa), 1961.

(With others) *Die beskermengel en ander eenbedrywe* (title means "The Guardian Angel and Other One-Act Plays"), Tafelberg (Cape Town, South Africa), 1962.

Bagasie: Triptiek vir die toneel (contains *Die koffer, Die trommel,* and *Die tas;* first produced in Pretoria, South Africa, 1965), Tafelberg (Cape Town, South Africa), 1964.

Elders mooiweer en warm (three-act play; title means "Elsewhere Fine and Warm"; first produced in Bloemfontein, South Africa, 1970), John Malherbe, 1965.

Die Rebelle: Betoogstuk in nege episodes (title means "The Rebels"), Human & Rousseau (Cape Town, South Africa), 1970.

Die verhoor: Verhoogstuk in drie bedrywe (first produced in Pretoria, South Africa, 1975), Human & Rousseau (Cape Town, South Africa), 1970.

Kinkels innie kabel: 'n verhoogstuk in elf episodes (adaptation of Shakespeare's *Much Ado about Nothing;* title means "Knots in the Cable"), Buren (Cape Town, South Africa), 1971.

Afrikaners is plesierig (two one-act plays; title means "Afrikaners Make Merry"), Buren (Cape Town, South Africa), 1973.

Bobaas van die Boendoe (adaptation of Synge's *Playboy of the Western World;* first produced in Bloemfontein, South Africa, 1974), Human & Rousseau (Cape Town, South Africa), 1974.

Pavane (three-act play; first produced in Cape Town, 1974), Human & Rousseau (Cape Town, South Africa), 1974.

Die hamer van die hekse (title means "The Hammer and the Witches"), Tafelberg (Cape Town, South Africa), 1976.

Toiings op die langpad (title means "Toiings on the Long Road"), Van Schaik (Pretoria, South Africa), 1979.

Die Jogger, Human & Rousseau (Cape Town, South Africa), 1997.

FOR CHILDREN

Die bende (title means "The Gang"), Afrikaanse Pers (Johannesburg, South Africa), 1961.

Platsak (title means "Broke"), Afrikaanse Pers (Johannesburg, South Africa), 1962.

Die verhaal van Julius Caesar (title means "The Story of Julius Caesar"), Human & Rousseau (Cape Town, South Africa), 1963.

LITERARY HISTORY AND CRITICISM

Orde en chaos: 'n studie oor Germanicus en die tragedies van Shakespeare, Nasionale Boekhandel (Cape Town, South Africa), 1962.

Aspekte van die nuwe prosa (title means "Aspects of the New Fiction"), Academica (Pretoria, South Africa), 1967, revised edition, 1975.

Die Poësie van Breyten Breytenbach, Academica (Pretoria, South Africa), 1971.

Inleiding tot die Afrikaanse letterkunde, onder Redaksie van E. Lindenberg, Academica (Pretoria, South Africa), 1973.

Aspekte van die nuwe Drama (title means "Aspects of the New Drama"), Academica (Pretoria, South Africa), 1974.

Voorlopige Rapport: Beskouings oor die Afrikaanse Literatuur van Sewentig (title means "Preliminary Report: Views on Afrikaans Literature in the 1970s"), Human & Rousseau (Cape Town, South Africa), 1976.

Tweede voorlopige Rapport: Nog beskouings oor die Afrikaanse Literature van sewentig (title means "Second Preliminary Report"), Human & Rousseau (Cape Town, South Africa), 1980.

Why Literature?/Waarom literatuur? (essays), Rhodes University (Grahamstown, South Africa), 1980.

(With others) *Perspektief en profiel: 'n geskiedinis van die Afrikaanse letterkunde,* Perskor, 1982.

Literatuur in die strydperk (essays; title means "Literature in the Arena"), Human & Rousseau (Cape Town, South Africa), 1985.

Vertelkunde: 'n inleiding tot die lees van verhalende tekste, Academica (Pretoria, South Africa), 1987.

The Novel: Language and Narrative from Cervantes to Calvino, New York University Press (New York, NY), 1998.

TRANSLATOR

Pierre Boulle, *Die Brug oor die rivier Kwaï,* Tafelberg (Cape Town, South Africa), 1962.

André Dhôtel, *Reisigers na die Groot Land,* Tafelberg (Cape Town, South Africa), 1962.

Joseph Kessel, *Die Wonderhande,* HAUM (Cape Town, South Africa), 1962.

L. N. Lavolle, *Nuno, die Visserseun,* HAUM (Cape Town, South Africa), 1962.

Léonce Bourliaguet, *Verhale uit Limousin,* Human & Rousseau (Cape Town, South Africa), 1963.

Léonce Bourliaguet, *Die slapende Berg,* Human & Rousseau (Cape Town, South Africa), 1963.

Leonard Cottrell, *Land van die Farao's,* Malherbe (Cape Town, South Africa), 1963.

Michel Rouzé, *Die Bos van Kokelunde,* Malherbe (Cape Town, South Africa), 1963.

Marguerite Duras, *Moderato Cantabile,* HAUM (Cape Town, South Africa), 1963.

Paul-Jacques Bonzon, *Die Goue kruis,* Malherbe (Cape Town, South Africa), 1963.

Leonard Cottrell, *Land van die Twee Riviere,* Malherbe (Cape Town, South Africa), 1964.

C. M. Turnbull, *Volke van Afrika,* Malherbe (Cape Town, South Africa), 1964.

Lewis Carroll, *Alice se Avonture in Wonderland,* Human & Rousseau (Cape Town, South Africa), 1965.

Die mooiste verhale uit die Arabiese Nagte, Human & Rousseau (Cape Town, South Africa), 1966.

James Reeves, *Die Avonture van Don Quixote,* HAUM (Cape Town, South Africa), 1966.

Elyesa Bazna, *Ek was Cicero,* Afrikaanse Pers (Johannesburg, South Africa), 1966.

Jean de Brunhoff, *Koning Babar,* Human & Rousseau (Cape Town, South Africa), 1966.

Colette, *Die Swerfling,* Afrikaanse Pers (Johannesburg, South Africa), 1966.

Miguel Cervantes, *Die vindingryke ridder, Don Quijote de la Mancha,* Human & Rousseau (Cape Town, South Africa), 1966.

Simenon, *Speuder Maigret, Maigret en sy Dooie, Maigret en die Lang Derm,* and *Maigret en die Spook,* four volumes, Afrikaanse Pers (Johannesburg, South Africa), 1966-69.

Charles Perrault, *Die mooiste Sprokies van Moeder Gans,* Human & Rousseau (Cape Town, South Africa), 1967.

Ester Wier, *Die Eenspaaier,* Human & Rousseau (Cape Town, South Africa), 1967.

Graham Greene, *Die Eendstert,* Human & Rousseau (Cape Town, South Africa), 1967.

P. L. Travers, *Mary Poppins in Kersieboomlaan,* Malherbe (Cape Town, South Africa), 1967.

C. S. Lewis, *Die Leeu, die Heks en die Hangkas,* Human & Rousseau (Cape Town, South Africa), 1967.

(With others) *Die groot Boek oor ons Dieremaats,* Human & Rousseau (Cape Town, South Africa), 1968.

(With others) *Koning Arthur en sy Ridders van die Ronde Tafel,* Human & Rousseau (Cape Town, South Africa), 1968.

Lucy Boston, *Die Kinders van Groenkop,* Human & Rousseau (Cape Town, South Africa), 1968.

Lewis Carroll, *Alice deur die Spieël,* Human & Rousseau (Cape Town, South Africa), 1968.

Ian Serraillier, *Die Botsende rotse, Die Horing van Ivoor,* and *Die Kop van de Gorgoon,* four volumes, HAUM (Cape Town, South Africa), 1968.

Dhan Gopal Mukerji, *Bontnek,* HAUM (Cape Town, South Africa), 1968.

Henry James, *Die Draai van die Skroef,* Afrikaanse Pers (Johannesburg, South Africa), 1968.

Oscar Wilde, *Die Gelukkige Prins en ander Sprokies,* Human & Rousseau (Cape Town, South Africa), 1969.

William Shakespeare, *Richard III,* Human & Rousseau (Cape Town, South Africa), 1969.

Charles Perrault, *Die Gestewelde kat,* Human & Rousseau (Cape Town, South Africa), 1969.

Pearl S. Buck, *Die groot Golf,* Human & Rousseau (Cape Town, South Africa), 1969.

Hans Christian Andersen, *Die Nagtegaal,* HAUM (Cape Town, South Africa), 1969.

Albert Camus, *Die Terroriste,* Dramatiese Artistieke en Letterkundige Organisasie (Johannesburg, South Africa), 1970.

Michel de Ghelderode, *Eskoriaal,* Dramatiese Artistieke en Letterkundige Organisasie (Johannesburg, South Africa), 1971.

Nada Curcija-Prodanovic, *Ballerina,* Malherbe (Cape Town, South Africa), 1972.

Anton Chekhov, *Die Seemeeu,* Human & Rousseau (Cape Town, South Africa), 1972.

Synge, *Die Bobaas van die Boendoe,* Human & Rousseau (Cape Town, South Africa), 1973.

Richard Bach, *Jonathan Livingston Seemeeu,* Malherbe (Cape Town, South Africa), 1973.

Henrik Ibsen, *Hedda Gabler,* Human & Rousseau (Cape Town, South Africa), 1974.

Kenneth Grahame, *Die Wind in die Wilgers,* Human & Rousseau (Cape Town, South Africa), 1974.

William Shakespeare, *Die Tragedie van Romeo en Juliet,* Human & Rousseau (Cape Town, South Africa), 1975.

Claude Desailly, *Die Tierbrigade,* Tafelberg (Cape Town, South Africa), 1978.

Claude Desailly, *Nuwe Avontuur van die Tierbrigade,* Tafelberg (Cape Town, South Africa), 1979.

Oscar Wilde, *Die Nagtegaal en die Roos,* Human & Rousseau (Cape Town, South Africa), 1980.

Kenneth Grahame, *Rot op Reis,* Human & Rousseau (Cape Town, South Africa), 1981.

Elizabeth Janet Gray, *Adam van die Pad,* Human & Rousseau (Cape Town, South Africa), 1981.

Charles Perrault, *Klein Duimpie,* Human & Rousseau (Cape Town, South Africa), 1983.

OTHER

Pot-pourri: Sketse uit Parys (travelogue; title means "Pot-pourrie: Sketches from Paris"), Human & Rousseau (Cape Town, South Africa), 1962.

Sèmpre diritto: Italiaanse reisjoernaal (travelogue; title means "Always Straight Ahead: Italian Travel Journal"), Afrikaanse Pers (Johannesburg, South Africa), 1963.

Olé: Reisboek oor Spanje (travelogue; title means "Olé: A Travel Book on Spain"), Human & Rousseau (Cape Town, South Africa), 1966.

Midi: Op reis deur Suld-Frankyrk (travelogue; title means "Midi: Traveling through the South of France"), Human & Rousseau (Cape Town, South Africa), 1969.

Parys-Parys: Return, Human & Rousseau (Cape Town, South Africa), 1969.

Fado: 'n reis deur Noord-Portugal (travelogue; title means "Fado: A Journey through Northern Portugal"), Human & Rousseau (Cape Town, South Africa), 1970.

Portret van di vrou as 'n meisie (title means "Portrait of Woman as a Young Girl"), Buren (Cape Town, South Africa), 1973.

Brandewyn in Suid-Afrika, Buren (Cape Town, South Africa), 1974, translated by Siegfried Stander as *Brandy in South Africa,* 1974.

Dessertwyn in Suid-Afrika, Buren (Cape Town, South Africa), 1974, translated as *Dessert Wine in South Africa,* 1974.

(With others) *Ik ben er geweest: Gesprekken in Zuid-Afrika* (title means "I've Been There: Conversations in South Africa"), Kok (Kampen, South Africa), 1974.

Die Wyn van bowe (title means "The Wine from up There"), Buren (Cape Town, South Africa), 1974.

Die Klap van die meul (title means "A Stroke from the Mill"), Buren (Cape Town, South Africa), 1974.

Jan Rabie se 21, Academica (Cape Town, South Africa), 1977.

(Editor) *Oggendlied: 'n bundel vir Uys Krige op sy verjaardag 4 Februarie 1977,* Human & Rousseau (Cape Town, South Africa), 1977.

(Editor) Top Naeff, *Klein Avontuur,* Academica (Pretoria, South Africa), 1979.

Heildronk uit Wynboer Saamgestel deur AB ter viering van die Blad se 50ste bestaansjaar, Tafelberg (Cape Town, South Africa), 1981.

Die Fees van die Malles: 'n keur uit die humor, Saayman & Weber (Cape Town, South Africa), 1981.

Mapmakers: Writing in a State of Siege (essays), Faber (New York, NY), 1983, revised edition published as *Writing in a State of Siege: Essays on Politics and Literature,* Summit (New York, NY), 1983.

(Editor with J. M. Coetzee) *A Land Apart: A South African Reader,* Faber (London, England), 1986, Viking (New York, NY), 1987.

Latynse reise: 'n keur uit die reisbeskrywings van André P. Brink, Human & Rousseau (Cape Town, South Africa), 1990.

The Essence of the Grape, Saayman & Weber (Cape Town, South Africa), 1993.

(Compiler) *SA, 27 April 1994: An Author's Diary,* Queillerie (Pretoria, South Africa), 1994.

(Compiler) *27 April: One Year Later/Een Jaar later,* Queillerie (Pretoria, South Africa), 1995.

Reinventing a Continent: Writing and Politics in South Africa (essays), Secker & Warburg (London, England), 1996, revised edition, preface by Nelson Mandela, Zoland Books (New York, NY), 1998.

Destabilising Shakespeare, Shakespeare Society of Southern Africa (Grahamstown, South Africa), 1996.

(Compiler) *Groot Verseboek 2000,* Tafelberg (Cape Town, South Africa), 2000.

Jan Vermeiren: A Flemish Artist in South Africa, Lanoo (Tielt, South Africa), 2000.

Author of scenarios for South African films and television series, including *The Settlers.* Contributor to books on Afrikaans literature and to periodicals, including *World Literature Today, Asahi Journal,* and *Theatre Quarterly.* Editor of *Sestiger* magazine, 1963-65; editor of *Standpunte,* 1986-87; editor of weekly book page in *Rapport.*

Brink's manuscripts are housed at the University of the Orange Free State, Bloemfontein, and the National English Literary Museum, Grahamstown, South Africa.

ADAPTATIONS: A Dry White Season was adapted for film by Euzhan Palcy and Colin Welland, directed by Palcy, Metro-Goldwyn-Mayer, 1989.

SIDELIGHTS: As an Afrikaner, novelist, playwright, essayist, and educator André Brink is "a rarity in anti-apartheid literature," Scott Kraft stated in the *Los Angeles Times.* A product of his country's exclusionary white culture, Brink repudiated its policies of apartheid during his studies in Paris in 1960 but was drawn back to the land of his birth to witness and record its turmoil and injustice. Earning both international recognition and governmental censure for his work in the years that followed, "Brink is one of the leading voices in the literary chorus of dissent, and for two decades his tales of black hope and white repression have shamed the nation," remarked Curt Suplee in the *Washington Post.*

Brink writes in both English and Afrikaans, the latter a language derived from that spoken by South Africa's seventeenth- and eighteenth-century Dutch, French, and German settlers. In an interview with *Contemporary Authors, (CA)* Brink once noted: "There is a certain virility, a certain earthy, youthful quality about Afrikaans because it is such a young language, and because, although derived from an old European language like Dutch, it has found completely new roots in Africa and become totally Africanized in the process. . . . One can do almost anything with it. If you haven't got a word for something you want to express, you simply make a word or pluck a word from another language and shape it to fit into yours. Working in this young and very vital language is quite exhilarating, which creates a very special sense of adventure for authors working in it. And if one works in both languages, there is the wonderful experience of approaching the same subject, the same territory, through two totally different media. One is the more or less rigorous English language, the world language, and although one can still do a hell of a lot of new things in it, so much of it has already become standardized: it's almost as if one looks at the African experience through European eyes when one writes English. Through the Afrikaans language, it is a totally different, a more 'immediate,' experience. It's a language that can take much more emotionalism, for instance, whereas English tends toward understatement, Afrikaans is more overt, more externalized, more extroverted in its approach."

Brink translated his 1963 novel *Die Ambassadeur* from Afrikaans into English. Published in England as *File on a Diplomat,* and in the United States as *The Ambassador,* the novel relates a story about a French ambassador to South Africa and his third secretary who become involved with the same young, promiscuous female and are drawn into the wild nightlife of Paris until jealousy destroys them both, reported Savkar Altinel in a *Times Literary Supplement* essay. Fred Pfeil suggested in a *Nation* review that the novel "sets forth Brink's vision of sexual-existential liberation with nary a nod toward any political considerations." Altinel called the novel "an elegantly tidy creation which, with its trinity of somewhat stylized central characters and its economically evoked setting, seems very much the unified product of a powerful initial vision." In a London *Times* review of the revised version of the novel in 1985, Henry Stanhope wrote that, despite "something ever so slightly dated about it," *The Ambassador* "remains a good book, intelligent in its exploration of human behaviour under emotional and political stress."

"In 1968 I left South Africa to settle in Paris with the exiled poet Breyten Breytenbach," Brink once explained to *CA,* "but the nature of the student revolt of that year forced me to reassess my situation as a writer and prompted my return to South Africa in order to accept full responsibility for whatever I wrote, believing that, in a closed society, the writer has a specific social and moral role to fill. This resulted in a more committed form of writing exploring the South African political situation and notably my revulsion of apartheid. My first novel to emerge from this experience was *Kennis van die aand,* which became the first Afrikaans book to be banned by the South African censors. This encouraged me to turn seriously to writing in English in order not to be silenced in my own

language. Under the title *Looking on Darkness,* it became an international success, with translations into a dozen languages, including Finnish, Turkish, Japanese, Czechoslovakian, and Russian."

In Brink's *Looking on Darkness,* protagonist Joseph Malan murders his white lover, Jessica Thomson, in a mutual pact and then sits in jail, awaiting execution. Calling the 1973 novel "ambitious and disturbing," Jane Larkin Crain concluded in the *Saturday Review* that "a passionately human vision rules here, informed by an imagination that is attuned at once to complex and important abstractions and to the rhythms and the texture of everyday experience." Noting that the "novel is structured in the form of a confessional," Martin Tucker added in *Commonweal* that its style "is compelling: it is a work that throbs with personal intensity." Because of the novel's explicit treatment of sex, racism, persecution, and the torture of political prisoners in South African jails, C. J. Driver suggested in the *Times Literary Supplement* that it is not difficult to understand why it was banned; however, Driver concluded that "within its context this is a brave and important novel and in any terms a fine one."

Publication of *Looking on Darkness* in Europe coincided with the Soweto riots of 1976, and the novel became something of a handbook on the South African situation. Regarding racism generally, Brink once told *CA:* "America seems to be slowly working its way through racism; whereas in South Africa it is entrenched in the whole system and framework of laws on which society has had its base. It is not just a matter of sentiment, of personal resentment, of tradition and custom, but these negative aspects of society are so firmly rooted in the framework of laws that it is very, very difficult to eradicate. *Looking on Darkness* elicited much comment because it is one of the first Afrikaans novels to confront openly the apartheid system. This account of an illicit love between a 'Cape Coloured' man and a white woman evoked, on the one hand, one of the fiercest polemics in the history of that country's literature and contributed, on the other, to a groundswell of new awareness among white Afrikaners of the common humanity of all people regardless of color. In numerous letters from readers I was told that for the first time in my life I now realize that 'they' feel and think and react just like 'us.'"

"In *An Instant in the Wind,*" Brink once explained to *CA,* "I used essentially the same relationship—a black man and a white woman—but placed it in the midst of the eighteenth century in an attempt to probe the origins of the racial tensions of today. An episode from Australian history in which a shipwrecked woman and a convict return to civilization on foot is here transposed to the Cape Colony with so much verisimilitude that many readers have tried to look up the documentation in the Cape Archives." In the *Spectator,* Nick Totten described the plot further: "A civilised woman, her husband dead, is lost in the wilderness . . . rescued by an escaped black prisoner . . . with whom she experiences for the first time fulfilled sexual love, but whom she betrays after the long trek back to civilisation." Calling it "a frank confrontation with miscegenation in a contemporary South African setting," Robert L. Berner commented in *World Literature Today:* "What Brink has produced is a historical novel with an almost documentary degree of verisimilitude. . . . But more than for its interest as evidence of Brink's artistic development, it is the recognition of the relationship of sex to politics that makes *An Instant in the Wind* a remarkable work of South African literature." R. A. Sokolov suggested in the *New York Times Book Review* that "it is important for political reasons that Brink should be published, but doubtful on the evidence of this book that he will be read for his art as a writer." Richard Cima contended in *Library Journal* that "the subject is important and the novelistic achievement impressive."

"*Rumours of Rain,* set on the eve of the Soweto riots, is placed on a much larger stage," Brink once remarked to *CA* about his 1978 novel. "The apartheid mind is demonstrated in the account given by a wealthy businessman of the one weekend in which his whole familiar world collapsed through the conviction of his best friend for terrorism, the revolt of his son, the loss of his mistress, and the sale of his family's farm. In spite of his efforts to rigorously separate all the elements of his life, he becomes the victim of his own paradoxes and faces an apocalypse." The novel is about Martin Mynhardt, a mining entrepreneur, whose "only principles are money and safety," observed Phoebe-Lou Adams in the *Atlantic,* "and for them he betrays friend, colleague, brother, mother, wife, and mistress, and will eventually betray his son." According to C. G. Blewitt in *Best Sellers,* "Much insight is shed on the life of the Afrikaner, his judicial system and the horrors of apartheid." Similarly, Daphne Merkin commented in *New Republic* that "Brink has taken a large, ideologically-charged premise and proceeds to render it in intimate terms without . . . sacrificing any of its hard-edged 'political' implications." Moreover,

Merkin believed that the book "is an ambitious resonant novel that depicts a volatile situation with remarkable control and lack of sentimentality."

"In comparison with the complex structures" of *Rumours of Rain,* Brink once commented to *CA* that his *A Dry White Season* "has a deceptively simple plot: a black man dies while being detained by the security police. In all good faith his white friend tries to find out what really happened, and as a result the whole infernal machinery of the State is turned against him." According to June Goodwin in the *Christian Science Monitor,* "Few novels will speak to the Afrikaner—or to foreigners who want to understand the Afrikaner—as well as this one." *A Dry White Season* is about Afrikaner Ben Du Toit, who helps a black school janitor investigate the questionable circumstances surrounding the death of his son at the hands of the police. Mel Watkins, in a *New York Times Book Review* essay, found that the novel "demonstrates André Brink's continuing refinement of his fictional technique, without sacrificing any of the poignancy that his previous books have led us to expect."

"Brink's writing is built on conviction," remarked Dinah Birch in the London *Times.* "His characters move in a world of absolutes: goodness and truth war with cruelty and greed, and the reader is never left in any doubt as to which is which." Although not considering Brink "a 'great' writer," Eric Redman pointed out in the *Washington Post Book World* that "he's an urgent, political one and an Afrikaner other Afrikaners can't ignore." Moreover, noting that "big books have sparked change throughout South Africa's recent history," Redman observed that "this much is certain: the era of the trivial South African novel is dead, and courage killed it." Remarking to *CA* that the novel was begun "almost a year before the death in detention of black-consciousness leader Steve Biko in 1976," Brink added: "In fact, the death of Biko came as such a shock to me that for a long time I couldn't go back to writing. I believe that however outraged or disturbed one may be, a state of inner serenity must be obtained before anything meaningful can emerge in writing."

Brink went on to add that in 1982's *A Chain of Voices* he worked to "extend and expand my field of vision. Using as a point of departure a slave revolt in the Cape Colony in 1825, I used a series of thirty different narrators to explore the relationships created by a society shaped by the forces of oppression and suffering. The 'separateness' of the voices haunted me; masters and slaves, all tied by the same chains, are totally unable to communicate because their humanity and their individuality are denied by the system they live by. I tried to broaden and deepen the enquiry by relating the voices, in four successive sections, to the elements of earth, water, wind, and fire."

Many critics consider *A Chain of Voices* to be Brink's best work to date. Suplee labeled it "an incendiary success abroad and a galling phenomenon at home." According to Julian Moynahan in the *New York Times Book Review,* "Like all good historical novels, [it] is as much about the present as the past. . . . Brink searches the bad old times for a key to understanding bad times in South Africa today, and what he sees in the historical record is always conditioned by his awareness of the South African racial crisis now." However, while Jane Kramer suggested in the *New York Review of Books* that "Brink may have an honorable imagination," she believed that "he has written a potboiler of oppression" in which the "voices" of the novel "end up more caricature than character." On the other hand, Moynahan compared the device of telling a story from multiple viewpoints to the novels of William Faulkner in which he "counts the moral cost of white racism, both before and after Emancipation, in terms of the tragic spoliation of all relationships, not merely those between white oppressors and their non-white or partially white victims."

In *States of Emergency* Brink tells a story within a story. A writer's attempt to compose an apolitical love story is marred by the reality of racism, violence, and death. When the narrator receives an impressive but unpublishable manuscript from Jane Ferguson, a young writer who subsequently commits suicide by setting herself on fire, he abandons the historical novel he has been writing about South Africa and begins to compose a love story based on Ferguson's manuscript. The novel he writes is centered around a professor of literary theory and a student with whom he has an affair. According to a *Publishers Weekly* contributor, Brink "demonstrates that neither love nor art offers an escape; even the imagination is determined by political realities." Finding intensity between "reality and the author's idea of just what reality best suits his characters," Alfred Rushton commented in the Toronto *Globe and Mail* that the reader becomes aware that "no writer owns his or her characters, just as the state doesn't own people no matter what method is used to justify the attempt."

Not all critics responded positively to *States of Emergency.* For example, *Los Angeles Times* book critic Richard Eder suggested that "it is one thing for contemporary theory to come in afterward and argue that the fiction we have read tells us not about real characters but only about how its text was created. It is another for this reductivism to be applied in the moment of creation. It is literary contraception; nothing emerges alive." However, calling the novel "complicated and forceful" as well as "richly developed," Michael Wood maintained in the London *Observer* that Brink "does depict, with great compassion and authority, the 'weight and madness of the violence' surrounding individuals." And Rushton concluded that the novelist "also successfully challenges those people, writers and artists included, who persist in believing reason will somehow prevail over passion."

In *An Act of Terror* Brink portrays the political tension in South Africa in 1988, a particularly brutal period of police repression. The narrative centers on Thomas Landman, a member of a guerrilla group of blacks and whites who are planning to assassinate the president. When the plan fails, Landman seeks to escape from the police, and revisits the scenes of his past life. Reviewers found much to praise in the work. Adam Hochschild wrote in the *Los Angeles Times Book Review,* "the meal that Brink cooks up is an intricate, fast-moving story that succeeds in keeping us at the table for more than 600 pages of this 834-page behemoth of a book." *Nation* contributor Jenefer Shute similarly praised the novel's ambition, asserting that *An Act of Terror* "soars in its aspiration, its revised creation myth for a race 'conceived and born in lies,' its hope for a history that might open out instead of shutting down." Several critics, however, judge that the novel's lengthy, oratorical conclusion, in which Landman chronicles his family's presence in South Africa from the first Dutch settlers in the seventeenth century to the present day, compromises the work as a whole. Hochschild maintained that "Brink's skill as a storyteller collapses" in this "interminable" chronicle. Similarly, Randolph Vigne, commenting in the *San Francisco Review of Books,* characterized the conclusion as "a heavy dose of cheap magazine fiction."

Brink returned to historical fiction in his next two novels, *Cape of Storms: The First Life of Adamastor* and *On the Contrary.* In the first of these works, Brink draws on Greek mythology and Renaissance European literature to shape an allegorical commentary on the colonial history of southern Africa. The novel is narrated by T'kama, a Khoi who witnesses the arrival of the first Europeans and inadvertently precipitates an attack on his people by frightening a white woman who has come ashore to bathe. Despite the humorous style of the novel, Brink told Laurel Graeber in the *New York Times Book Review* that "under the humor there's a deep and serious concern with the origins of racial animosities in South Africa and everywhere." In reviewing the novel for that same publication, Mario Vargas Llosa echoed this concern, asserting that "however much we enjoy reading the book, André Brink's beautiful mythological re-creation leaves us anguished over what appear to be its predictions regarding a society where, after a bloody past of injustice and institutionalized racism, different races and cultures are finally preparing to try co-existence under conditions of equality."

In *On the Contrary* Brink again concentrates on the racial tensions of early South Africa by telling the story of the historical figure Estienne Barbier, who immigrated from France to South Africa in the eighteenth century and who was executed by the Dutch East India Company for his role in fomenting rebellion in the Cape in 1739. The novel is presented as a single letter—comprising over three hundred sections interweaving fact and fantasy—that is written to a slave-girl on the eve of the protagonist's execution. Critics gave the work a mixed reception. *New York Times Book Review* contributor Peter S. Prescott, for example, maintained that while the novel is "ambitious and imaginative," it nevertheless suffers from a "serious confusion of styles" and a lack of humor and wit. Boyd Tomkin, writing in the *Observer,* noted that "though he conjures up the sun-dried veldt, Brink's prose gorges on a lush glut of ideas. It leaves its readers as drunk as its hero, addled but inspired."

Brink returns to contemporary political concerns with his 1996 novel *Imaginings of Sand.* This work concentrates on the experiences of Kristien, a disaffected Afrikaner who living in self-imposed exile in England returns to her native land to care for her dying grandmother during the elections that ultimately bring an end to the apartheid system. Critics were divided in their assessment of Brink's handling of female characters in this work. *Spectator* reviewer Barbara Trapido asserted that the main character, "who is offered to the reader as the spirit of defiance, a left-hander, a 'witch,' never really rises above drag act and disappoints with

her ordinariness." Amanda Hopkinson maintained in the *New Statesman,* however, that "Brink raises even familiar feminist issues in intelligent ways." Similarly, the quality of the writing itself elicited conflicting responses. Hopkinson found Brink's style "varied and highly accomplished," while *New York Times* reviewer Richard Bernstein characterized *Imaginings of Sand* as "a ramshackle, muddled work always threatening to blow apart by virtue of its very extravagance." *Washington Times* contributor Martin Rubin described the work as Brink's "finest achievement yet. . . . More substantial than Nadine Gordimer's recent novels and more authentically rooted in myth than J. M. Coetzee's work." Alan Cheuse offered similar praise in his review for the *Chicago Tribune,* contending that "Brink presents his kinsmen in the patterns and rhythms of myth and legend, sometimes employing the techniques of magical realism, thus making his novel seem thoroughly African in texture and effect."

Devil's Valley concerns a group of Afrikaner settlers who have been isolated from the rest of the world for some 150 years. Their remote valley is difficult and dangerous for outsiders to visit, while those who leave the valley and talk too much tend to die mysteriously. When crime reporter Flip Lochner finds his way to Devil's Valley, the insular community begins to fall apart. According to Lorna Sage, reviewing the book for the *New York Times, Devil's Valley* "stages a ritual resurrection and reburial of the Afrikaner past."

Translated as *The Rights of Desire, Donkermaan* is a novel about a May-December romance. Ruben Olivier is an aging former librarian who lost his job to a black man after South Africa's white government fell from power. He has retreated into his home, listening to classical music, reading books, and contemplating his life, which includes the loss of his wife in an accident. Olivier's children, who have moved out of the country, urge him to leave, too. Barring that, they ask him to take on a boarder so that there is someone else in the house with him. Ruben takes their advice and brings a young woman named Tessa Butler into his home. Tessa, who seems to be in some sort of trouble and is in need of a place to stay, is a rather radical figure in Ruben's life. She smokes dope, is promiscuous, and even flirts with Ruben. The two form a bond that is linked in interesting conversations—not just sexual tensions—and Tessa's unique perspective on life forces Ruben to reexamine his past, including his political beliefs, and realize that he is not the man he has convinced himself he is. Into this tale, Brink also throws in Ruben's maid, Margrieta Daniels, whose keen sensibilities prevent Ruben from getting away with anything, even in his own house, and Antje of Bengal, the ghost of a woman who was a slave and accomplice to murder, who was executed for her crime.

While calling *The Rights of Desire* "probably the most intimate one Brink has ever written," Ludo Stynen commented in *World Literature Today* that the author "makes it very clear that writing without politics is impossible as far as he is concerned." The politics of living in South Africa seep into the story inevitably. Stynen added, "Reminiscences and fragments of other texts, historical facts and fiction, the mystery element, and the in fact predictably unpredictable woman make the work an unmistakable Brink novel. It is a well-told story and a valuable contribution to the social debate." Other reviewers, commenting on *The Rights of Desire,* did not rank it with Brink's best efforts. Edward B. St. John, for example, commented in *Library Journal* that "this novel is essentially an old-fashioned and somewhat predictable May-December romance." A *Publishers Weekly* reviewer similarly felt the novel "isn't Brink's best effort"; however, the critic went on to praise Brink as "a consummately professional storyteller, and the voice of his narrator, with its subtle wit and vulnerability, is a welcome one."

In the 2002 novel *The Other Side of Silence* Brink pens an indictment of colonialism and sexism in German South-West Africa, which is modern-day Nambia. Set in the early 1900s, the novel tells the story of Hanna X, an orphan whose ultimate life journey is one of degradation and violence. The first part of the novel focuses on Hanna's life in Germany and the humiliation she suffers working as a domestic in family households, where the husbands typically make sexual advances towards her. Hanna ends up immigrating to South-West Africa as part of a German government-sponsored movement promoting emigration by single women to provide brides for male farmers and traders living in the colony. Hanna's journey is not one to safety, however. She is attacked and mutilated, and her tongue cut out, by a sadistic German officer named Bohlke. Hanna ends up at a terrifying outpost known as the Frauenstein, where unwanted and abused women are kept. For the remainder of the book, Brink details Hanna's escape and trail of revenge as she forms a small vigilante group that murders German soldiers as they hunt for Bohlke.

Writing in the *Washington Times,* Judith Chettle found Brink's characters in *The Other Side of Silence* some-

what stereotypical: "The white men, with rare exceptions, are sexually obsessed brutes, the Africans noble, and the women, especially the heroine Hanna X, helpless victims." Chettle went on to note, "But though the settings are vividly evoked, and the story often compelling, it is too message-driven to completely satisfy." A *Publishers Weekly* contributor also found Hanna to be, at times, a "one-dimensional character" because of the relentless violence depicted. Nevertheless, the reviewer noted that "the imagery from this haunting novel will stay with readers as will the frightening allure of all-consuming hatred." Brendan Driscoll, writing in *Booklist,* maintained that *The Other Side of Silence* "proves provocative by evoking these themes [—violence, memory, and apartheid—] within the unconventional setting of German colonialism." In a review for *Library Journal,* Lawrence Rungren commented, "Brutal in its action while poetic in its language, this is an unflinching portrayal of the savagery just beneath civilization's skin."

Reinventing a Continent: Writing and Politics in South Africa is a collection of Brink's essays concerning apartheid, the Afrikaners who settled his homeland, and the grim chaos of South Africa's struggling democratic government. Throughout the book, Brink focuses on the role of the writer in political matters and asks what role those writers who opposed apartheid for so long can now play in a black-run society. "Brink chronicles," Vanessa Bush noted in *Booklist,* "a 15-year period in the political and social transformation of South Africa." According to a reviewer for *Publishers Weekly,* the novelist presents readers with "a thoughtful and human response to injustice."

Brink turns his attention to the crafting of literature in his nonfiction work *The Novel: Language and Narrative from Cervantes to Calvino,* a survey of fifteen classic novels. While his own novels have been marked by their strong political preoccupations, Brink argues that the genre is really about a play with language. He backs up his argument with examples from such works as *Don Quixote* and Italo Calvino's *If on a Winter Night a Traveller.* Writing in the *New York Times,* Peter Brooks found that "Brink is an alert, enthusiastic and engaging reader, who reports his reading experiences with wit and fluency." Thomas L. Cooksey concluded in *Library Journal* that Brink's text is "marked by clarity, insight, and comprehension."

"Since my tastes in literature are catholic," Brink once remarked to *CA,* "I have never been a disciple of any one school. The most abiding influence on my work, however, has been Albert Camus, notably in his view of man in a state of incessant revolt against the conditions imposed upon him, and reacting creatively to the challenge of meaninglessness. In much of my work this is linked to an element of mysticism derived from the Spanish writers of the seventeenth century. The other most abiding influence on my writing is the study of history. All my work is pervaded with a sense of 'roots,' whether in the collective history of peoples or in the private history of an individual." Brink added, "However close my work is to the realities of South Africa today, the political situation remains a starting point only for my attempts to explore the more abiding themes of human loneliness and man's efforts to reach out and touch someone else. My stated conviction is that literature should never descend to the level of politics; it is rather a matter of elevating and refining politics so as to be worthy of literature."

BIOGRAPHICAL AND CRITICAL SOURCES:

BOOKS

Contemporary Literary Criticism, Gale (Detroit, MI), Volume 18, 1981, Volume 36, 1986.

Jolly, Rosemary Jane, *Colonization, Violence, and Narration in White South African Writing: André Brink, Breyten Breytenbach, and J. M. Coetzee,* Ohio University Press (Athens, OH), 1995.

PERIODICALS

Atlantic, October, 1978.

Best Sellers, February, 1979.

Booklist, July, 1998, Vanessa Bush, review of *Reinventing a Continent: Writing and Politics in South Africa,* p. 1852; March 15, 1999, review of *Devil's Valley,* p. 1288; May 15, 2003, Brendan Driscoll, review of *The Other Side of Silence,* p. 1637.

Bookwatch, October, 1998, review of *Reinventing a Continent,* p. 9.

Canadian Forum, December, 1983.

Chicago Tribune, September 5, 1995; October 16, 1996; November 24, 1996.

Choice, November, 1998, review of *The Novel,* p. 515.

Christian Science Monitor, March 10, 1980; July 21, 1982; April 10, 1985; June 4, 1986.

Commonweal, September 12, 1975; July 13, 1984.

English Journal, January, 1998, Patricia Faith Goldblatt, review of *Imaginings of Sand,* p. 111.

Globe and Mail (Toronto, Ontario, Canada), August 20, 1988.

Kirkus Reviews, March 15, 1989; March 1, 1998, review of *The Novel,* p. 310; July 1, 1998, review of *Reinventing a Continent,* p. 940; January 15, 1999, review of *Devil's Valley,* p. 81; January 15, 2001, review of *The Rights of Desire,* p. 69.

Library Journal, August, 1975; February 15, 1977; April 1, 1985; April 15, 1998, Thomas L. Cooksey, review of *The Novel,* p. 78; February 15, 1999, review of *Devil's Valley,* p. 181; January 1, 2001, Edward B. St. John, review of *The Rights of Desire,* p. 151; March 1, 2003, Lawrence Rungren, review of *The Other Side of Silence,* p. 116.

Listener, October 8, 1987.

London Magazine, June, 1979.

London Review of Books, August 4, 1988.

Los Angeles Times, August 19, 1987; May 18, 1989; September 29, 1989; October 7, 1989; October 15, 1989; April 17, 1990; January 26, 1992; August 29, 1993.

Los Angeles Times Book Review, March 21, 1999, review of *Devil's Valley,* p. 2.

Maclean's, May 10, 1982.

Nation, June 21, 1986; April 6, 1992, p. 455.

New Leader, January 14-28, 1985.

New Republic, October 21, 1978; April 30, 1984.

New Statesman, November 17, 1978; October 5, 1979; July 8, 1983; September 28, 1984; December 6, 1985; August 29, 1986; August 27, 1993, p. 37; February 23, 1996, p. 45.

Newsweek, December 2, 1974.

New Yorker, August 25, 1975.

New York Review of Books, December 2, 1982; April 25, 1985.

New York Times, February 2, 1984; March 6, 1984; September 17, 1989; September 20, 1989; September 25, 1989; December 11, 1996; August 2, 1998, Peter Brooks, "What Flaubert Knew."

New York Times Book Review, February 27, 1977; March 23, 1980; June 13, 1982; March 17, 1985; June 29, 1986; January 12, 1992, p. 6; July 25, 1993, p. 1; August 14, 1994, p. 94; August 2, 1998, review of *The Novel,* p. 20; March 21, 1999, Lorna Sage, "Escape from Paradise," p. 8.

Observer (London, England), May 15, 1988; August 29, 1993; August 16, 1998, review of *Devil's Valley,* p. 15.

Publishers Weekly, March 10, 1989; June 22, 1998, review of *Reinventing a Continent,* p. 74; January 18, 1999, review of *Devil's Valley,* p. 326; March 5, 2001, review of *The Rights of Desire,* p. 60; April 7, 2003, review of *The Other Side of Silence,* p. 42.

Reference and Research Book News, November, 1998, review of *The Novel,* p. 198; February, 1999, review of *Reinventing a Continent,* p. 35.

San Francisco Review of Books, January, 1992.

Saturday Review, August 23, 1975.

Shakespeare Quarterly, summer, 1998, review of *Destabilising Shakespeare,* p. 235.

Spectator, September 18, 1976; October 6, 1984; February 17, 1996.

Studies in the Novel, spring, 2002, Isidore Diala, "History and the Inscriptions of Torture as Purgatorial Fire in André Brink's Fiction," p. 60; winter, 2002, Isidore Diala, "The Political Limits of (Western) Humanism in André Brink's Early Fiction," p. 422.

Times (London, England), May 6, 1982; November 14, 1985; March 3, 1990.

Times Literary Supplement, November 15, 1974; September 17, 1976; October 20, 1978; May 14, 1982; September 16, 1983; October 5, 1984; January 10, 1986; February 26, 1993; September 3, 1993; February 9, 1996; October 2, 1998, review of *The Novel,* p. 32.

UNESCO Courier, September, 1993, p. 4.

Voice Literary Supplement, November, 1987.

Washington Post, May 28, 1982; July 13, 1989; September 22, 1989; September 26, 1989.

Washington Post Book World, January 20, 1980; February 17, 1985; July 13, 1989; March 15, 1992.

Washington Times, November 24, 1996; June 22, 2003, Judith Chettle, review of *The Other Side of Silence,* p. B08.

World Literature Today, autumn, 1977; summer, 1984; winter, 1985; summer, 1986; spring, 1989; summer, 1998, Sheila Roberts, review of *Die Jogger,* p. 674; autumn, 1998, review of *The Novel,* p. 908; spring, 1999, review of *Reinventing a Continent,* p. 381; spring, 2001, Barend J. Toerien, review of *Groot verseboek 2000,* p. 311; summer-autumn, 2001, Ursula A. Barnett, review of *The Rights of Desire,* p. 106, and Ludo Stynen, review of *Donkermaan,* p. 123.*

*   *   *

BUCKLEY, William F(rank) Jr. 1925-

PERSONAL: Born November 24, 1925, in New York, NY; son of William Frank (a lawyer and oilman) and Aloise (Steiner) Buckley; married Patricia Austin Taylor, July 6, 1950; children: Christopher Taylor. *Education:* Attended University of Mexico, 1943-44; Yale

William F. Buckley

University, B.A. (with honors), 1950. *Politics:* Republican. *Religion:* Roman Catholic.

ADDRESSES: Office—National Review, Inc., 215 Lexington Ave., New York, NY 10016-6023.

CAREER: Yale University, New Haven, CT, instructor in Spanish, 1947-51; affiliated with Central Intelligence Agency (C.I.A.) in Mexico, 1951-52; *American Mercury* (magazine), New York, NY, associate editor, 1952; freelance writer and editor, 1952-55; *National Review* (magazine), New York, NY, founder, president, and editor-in-chief, 1955-90, editor-at-large, 1990—; syndicated columnist, 1962—; host of *Firing Line* (weekly television program), 1966-99. Conservative Party candidate for mayor of New York City, 1965; member of Advisory Commission on Information, U.S. Information Agency, 1969-72; public member of U.S. delegation to United Nations, 1973. Lecturer, New School for Social Research (now New School University), 1967-68; Froman Distinguished Professor, Russell Sage College, 1973. Chair of the board, Starr Broadcasting Group, Inc., 1969-78. *Military service:* U.S. Army, 1944-46; became second lieutenant.

MEMBER: Council on Foreign Relations, Century Club, Mont Pelerin Society, New York Yacht Club.

AWARDS, HONORS: Freedom Award, Order of Lafayette, 1966; George Sokolsky Award, American Jewish League against Communism, 1966; Best Columnist of the Year Award, 1967; University of Southern California Distinguished Achievement Award in Journalism, 1968; Liberty Bell Award, New Haven County Bar Association, 1969; Emmy Award, National Academy of Television Arts and Sciences, 1969, for *Firing Line;* Man of the Decade Award, Young Americans for Freedom, 1970; Cleveland Amory Award, *TV Guide,* 1974, for best interviewer/interviewee on television; fellow, Sigma Delta Chi, 1976; Bellarmine Medal, 1977; Americanism Award, Young Republican National Federation, 1979; Carmel Award, American Friends of Haifa University, 1980, for journalism excellence; American Book Award for Best Mystery (paperback), 1980, for *Stained Glass;* New York University Creative Leadership Award, 1981; Lincoln Literary Award, Union League, 1985; Shelby Cullom Davis Award, 1986; Lowell Thomas Travel Journalism Award, 1989; Julius Award for Outstanding Public Service, University of Southern California School of Public Administration, 1990; Presidential Medal of Freedom, 1991; Gold Medal Award, National Institute of Social Sciences, 1992. Honorary degrees: L.H.D. from Seton Hall University, 1966, Niagara University, 1967, Mount Saint Mary's College, 1969, University of South Carolina, 1985, Converse College, 1988, and University of South Florida, 1992, Adelphi University, 1995, Yale University, 2000; LL.D. from St. Peter's College, 1969, Syracuse University, 1969, Ursinus College, 1969, Lehigh University, 1970, Lafayette College, 1972, St. Anselm's College, 1973, St. Bonaventure University, 1974, University of Notre Dame, 1978, New York Law School, 1981, and Colby College, 1985; D.Sc.O. from Curry College, 1970; Litt.D. from St. Vincent College, 1971, Fairleigh Dickinson University, 1973, Alfred University, 1974, College of William and Mary, 1981, William Jewell College, 1982, Albertus Magnus College, 1987, College of St. Thomas, 1987, Bowling Green State University, 1987, Coe College, 1989, Saint John's University (Minnesota), 1989, and Grove City College (Pennsylvania), 1991.

WRITINGS:

NONFICTION

God and Man at Yale: The Superstitions of "Academic Freedom," Regnery (Washington, DC), 1951.

(With L. Brent Bozell) *McCarthy and His Enemies: The Record and Its Meaning,* Regnery (Washington, DC), 1954.

Up from Liberalism, Obolensky, 1959.

Rumbles Left and Right: A Book about Troublesome People and Ideas, Putnam (New York, NY), 1963.

The Unmaking of a Mayor, Viking (New York, NY), 1966.

The Jeweler's Eye: A Book of Irresistible Political Reflections, Putnam (New York, NY), 1968.

(Author of introduction) Edgar Smith, *Brief against Death,* Knopf (New York, NY), 1968.

(Author of introduction) *Will Mrs. Major Go to Hell?: The Collected Work of Aloise Buckley Heath,* Arlington House (New York, NY), 1969.

David Franke, compiler, *Quotations from Chairman Bill: The Best of William F. Buckley Jr.,* Arlington House, 1970.

The Governor Listeth: A Book of Inspired Political Revelations, Putnam (New York, NY), 1970.

Cruising Speed: A Documentary, Putnam (New York, NY), 1971.

Inveighing We Will Go, Putnam (New York, NY), 1972.

Four Reforms: A Guide for the Seventies, Putnam (New York, NY), 1973.

United Nations Journal: A Delegate's Odyssey, Putnam (New York, NY), 1974.

Execution Eve and Other Contemporary Ballads, Putnam (New York, NY), 1975.

Airborne: A Sentimental Journey, Macmillan (New York, NY), 1976.

A Hymnal: The Controversial Arts, Putnam (New York, NY), 1978.

Atlantic High: A Celebration, Doubleday (New York, NY), 1982.

Overdrive: A Personal Documentary, Doubleday (New York, NY), 1983.

Right Reason, Doubleday (New York, NY), 1985.

Racing through Paradise: A Pacific Passage, Random House (New York, NY), 1987.

On the Firing Line: The Public Life of Our Public Figures, Random House (New York, NY), 1989.

Gratitude: Reflections on What We Owe to Our Country, Random House (New York, NY), 1990.

Windfall: End of the Affair, Random House (New York, NY), 1992.

In Search of Anti-Semitism, Continuum (New York, NY), 1992.

Happy Days Were Here Again, Random House (New York, NY), 1993.

Buckley: The Right Word, edited by Samuel S. Vaughan, Random House (New York, NY), 1996.

Nearer, My God: An Autobiography of Faith, Doubleday (New York, NY), 1997.

(Author of foreword) Ernest W. Lefever, *The Irony of Virtue: Ethics and American Power,* Westview Press (New York, NY), 1998.

(Author of introduction) Lee Edwards and William E. Simon, *The Power of Ideas: The Heritage Foundation at Twenty-five Years,* Jameson Books, 1998.

Let Us Talk of Many Things: The Collected Speeches of William F. Buckley Jr., Forum (Roseville, CA), 2000.

The Fall of the Berlin Wall, John Wiley (Hoboken, NJ), 2004.

Miles Gone By: A Literary Autobiography, Regnery (Washington, DC), 2004.

FICTION

The Temptation of Wilfred Malachey (juvenile), Workman Publishing (New York, NY), 1985.

Brothers No More (novel), Doubleday (New York, NY), 1995.

The Redhunter: A Novel Based on the Life of Senator Joe McCarthy, Little, Brown (Boston, MA), 1999.

Spytime: The Undoing of James Jesus Angleton, Harcourt (New York, NY), 2000.

Elvis in the Morning, Harcourt (New York, NY), 2001.

Nuremberg: The Reckoning, Harcourt (New York, NY), 2002.

Getting it Right (novel), Regnery (Washington, DC), 2003.

NOVELS; "BLACKFORD OAKES" SERIES

Saving the Queen, Doubleday (New York, NY), 1976.

Stained Glass (also see below), Doubleday (New York, NY), 1978.

Who's on First, Doubleday (New York, NY), 1980.

Marco Polo, If You Can, Doubleday (New York, NY), 1982.

The Story of Henri Tod, Doubleday (New York, NY), 1984.

See You Later, Alligator, Doubleday (New York, NY), 1985.

High Jinx, Doubleday, 1986.

Mongoose, RIP (also see below), Random House (New York, NY), 1988.

Tucker's Last Stand, Random House (New York, NY), 1990.

A Very Private Plot, Morrow (New York, NY), 1994.

The Blackford Oakes Reader, Andrews & McMeel (Kansas City, MO), 1994.

OTHER

(Editor with others) *The Committee and Its Critics: A Calm Review of the House Committee on Un-American Activities,* Putnam (New York, NY), 1962.

(Editor) *Odyssey of a Friend: Whittaker Chambers' Letters to William F. Buckley Jr., 1954-1961,* Putnam (New York, NY), 1970.

(Editor) *Did You Ever See a Dream Walking?: American Conservative Thought in the Twentieth Century,* Bobbs-Merrill (New York, NY), 1970, revised edition published as *Keeping the Tablets: Modern American Conservative Thought,* Perennial Library (New York, NY), 1988.

(Editor) *The Lexicon: A Cornucopia of Wonderful Words for the Inquisitive Word Lover,* Harcourt (New York, NY), 1998.

Contributor to books, including *Racing at Sea,* Van Nostrand (New York, NY), 1959; George B. DeHuzar, editor, *The Intellectuals: A Conservative Portrait,* Free Press (New York, NY), 1960; F. S. Meyer, editor, *What Is Conservatism?,* Holt (New York, NY), 1964; *Dialogues in Americanism,* Regnery (Washington, DC), 1964; Edward D. Davis, editor, *The Beatles Book,* Cowles, 1968; S. Endleman, editor, *Violence in the Streets,* Quadrangle (New York, NY), 1968; R. Campbell, editor, *Spectrum of Catholic Attitudes,* Bruce Publishing, 1969; *Great Ideas Today Annual, 1970,* Encyclopaedia Britannica (Chicago, IL), 1970; Fritz Machlup, editor, *Essays on Hayek,* New York University Press (New York, NY), 1976; and *Stained Glass* (play; based on Buckley's novel; produced in Louisville, KY, 1989), S. French (New York, NY), 1989.

Author of syndicated column "On the Right," 1962—. Contributor to *Esquire, Saturday Review, Harper's, Atlantic, Playboy, New Yorker, New York Times Magazine,* and other publications.

Beinecke Library at Yale University houses Buckley's correspondence since 1951 and material concerning the *National Review.*

SIDELIGHTS: William F. Buckley, Jr., is one of the most recognized and articulate spokesmen for American political conservatives. As host of his television program *Firing Line,* in the pages of *National Review,* the magazine he founded, and through the books and syndicated columns he writes, Buckley has argued throughout his career for individual liberty, the free market, and the traditional moral values of Western culture. His eloquence, wit, and appealing personal style have made him palatable even to many of his political opponents. "The Buckley substance," a writer for *Time* reported, "is forgiven for the Buckley style."

Buckley's writings are considered instrumental to the phenomenal growth of the U.S. conservative movement in the second half of the twentieth century. In the 1950s, when Buckley first appeared on the scene, conservatism was a peripheral presence on the national political spectrum. But in 1980 conservative voters elected Ronald Reagan, a longtime reader of Buckley's *National Review,* as president of the United States. "When the tide of intellectual and political history seemed headed inexorably leftward," Morton Kondracke wrote in the *New York Times Book Review,* "Mr. Buckley had the temerity to uphold the cause of Toryism. He and his magazine nurtured the movement . . . and gave it a rallying point and sounding board as it gradually gained the strength and respectability to win the Presidency. Conservatism is not far from the dominant intellectual force in the country today, but neither is liberalism. There is now a balance between the movements, a permanent contest, and Mr. Buckley deserves credit for helping make it so."

Buckley first came to public attention in 1951 when he published *God and Man at Yale: The Superstitions of "Academic Freedom,"* an attack against his alma mater, Yale University. The book accuses Yale of fostering values—such as atheism and collectivism—which are an anathema to the school's supporters. Further, Buckley claims that Yale stifles the political freedom of its more conservative students. Those students who spoke out against the liberal views of their professors were often ostracized. The book's charges stemmed from Buckley's own experiences while attending Yale, where his views on individualism, the free market, and communism found little support among liberal academics.

God and Man at Yale raised a storm of controversy as Yale faculty members denounced the charges made against them. Some reviewers joined in the

denunciation. McGeorge Bundy, writing in the *Atlantic Monthly,* called the book "dishonest in its use of facts, false in its theory, and a discredit to its author." Peter Viereck agreed with Buckley that "more conservatism and traditional morality" were needed at universities and wrote in the *New York Times* that "this important, symptomatic, and widely held book is a necessary counterbalance. However, its Old Guard antithesis to the outworn Marxist thesis is not the liberty security synthesis the future cries for."

His position as a right-wing spokesman was vastly strengthened in 1955 when Buckley founded *National Review,* a magazine of conservative opinion. In a statement of purpose published in the magazine's first issue, Buckley stated: "The profound crisis of our era is, in essence, the conflict between the Social Engineers, who seek to adjust mankind to conform with scientific utopias, and the disciples of Truth, who defend the organic moral order." At the time of the magazine's founding, Richard Brookhiser recalled in *National Review*'s thirtieth anniversary issue that "the forces of conservatism in American thinking were insignificant."

With the growth of the conservative movement, *National Review* eventually boasted a circulation of over 100,000, including some highly influential readers. Former president Ronald Reagan, for example, declared *National Review* his favorite magazine. Speaking at the magazine's thirtieth anniversary celebration in 1985—a celebration attended by such notables as Charlton Heston, Tom Selleck, Jack Kemp, and Tom Wolfe—Reagan remarked: "If any of you doubt the impact of *National Review*'s verve and attractiveness, take a look around you this evening. The man standing before you now was a Democrat when he picked up his first issue in a plain brown wrapper; and even now, as an occupant of public housing, he awaits as anxiously as ever his biweekly edition—without the wrapper."

Buckley presents a fictionalized account of the founding of the *National Review* in his 2003 novel *Getting It Right.* Following the rise of author Ayn Rand and her Objectivism philosophy as it caught fire with many mid-century intellectuals, Buckley also weaves the radical John Birch Society and that organization's response to the Communist scare into a novel that a *First Things* contributor dubbed "fascinating and informative." Noting the novel's strongly factual basis—Buckley footnotes his fiction—*Library Journal* contributor Barbara Conaty recommended *Getting It Right* for followers of Buckley's novels, adding that the author's "writing is so polished that he could turn the Yellow Pages into a spy novel or the federal budget into a sparkling memoir."

In addition to his writing and editing for *National Review,* Buckley has also contributed a syndicated column, "On the Right," to 250 newspapers two times weekly, as well as articles of opinion for various national magazines. Many of these columns and articles have been published in book-length collections. These shorter pieces display Buckley's talent for political satire. John P. Roche of the *New York Times Book Review,* critiquing Buckley's articles collected in *Execution Eve and Other Contemporary Ballads,* claimed that "no commentator has a surer eye for the contradictions, the hypocrisies, the pretensions of liberal and radical pontiffs . . . even when you wince, reading Buckley is fun."

Happy Days Were Here Again, Buckley's 1993 collection, is a comprehensive primer of his ideas. It contains more than 120 articles and addresses written between 1985 and 1993. John Grimond commented in the *New York Times Book Review* that Buckley is "eloquent" on the subjects of anti-communism, conservatism, sailing, and illegitimacy. Yet, Grimond continued: "It is a pity his range is not wider. A columnist needs to be able to say something interesting on many more issues than these if he is to delight his readers as much as himself. . . . Especially among the articles in which he is supposedly appreciating others, the self-serving references to himself occur with tedious frequency. The strongest single quality to emerge from this book is not percipience or wit; it is vanity."

Buckley again showed his willingness to confront flaws in the conservative ranks with his book *In Search of Anti-Semitism.* It grew out of a special issue of *National Review*—December 30, 1991—in which he explored the subject of anti-Semitism in depth. Furthermore, he criticized two friends and conservative brethren, Joseph Sobran and Pat Buchanan, for anti-Semitic attitudes and remarks. The book is comprised of Buckley's original article, comment from readers, and additional comment from Buckley. "Leave it to William Buckley to see right to the heart of a complex issue," declared Jacob Neusner in *National Review.* "Instead of assuming that 'we all know' what anti-Semitism is, he takes up the burden of sorting matters out. This he does with wit, insight, common sense—and unfeigned affection for the Jews and appreciation of what the State of Israel stands for. . . . In sorting matters out with the obvious affection and respect for the Jews and Judaism that this book shows, Buckley should win from those most affected . . . the trust that is needed so that people can stop choosing up sides and start sorting out their conflicts—and resolving them." *New York Times Book Review* contributor Nathan Glazer also praised the book as "fascinating reading: some of our most skillful, subtle and elegant conservative analysts of political trends can be read here, often in private correspondence with Mr. Buckley. He evokes very good letters—in part because he is such a good writer and letter-writer himself."

In other books, Buckley turns from politics to his personal life. *Cruising Speed: A Documentary* is a diary-like account of a typical Buckley week. *Overdrive: A Personal Documentary* follows a similar format. Because of the many activities in which he is typically engaged, and the social opportunities afforded by his political connections and inherited wealth, Buckley's life makes fascinating reading. And he unabashedly shares it with his readers, moving some reviewers to criticize him. Nora Ephron, writing in the *New York Times Book Review,* called *Overdrive* "an astonishing glimpse of a life of privilege in America today." She complained that "it never seems to cross [Buckley's] mind that any of his remarks might be in poor taste, or his charm finite." And yet Carolyn See of the *Los Angeles Times* believed that while the portrait Buckley may desire to paint of himself in *Overdrive* "is a social butterfly, a gadabout, a mindless snob (or so he would have us believe). . . . Buckley shows us a brittle, acerbic, duty-bound, silly, 'conservative' semi-fudd, with a heart as vast and varicolored and wonderful to watch as a 1930s jukebox."

In 1997 Buckley continued in the autobiographical mode with *Nearer, My God: An Autobiography of Faith.* The book represents a return to the subject that occupied the author in his first publication, 1951's *God and Man at Yale:* the role of religion in American public life. The first chapters are narratives of Buckley's Catholic boyhood, but later chapters turn to a more argumentative mode, asserting that multiculturalism has replaced spirituality, and defending the concept of sin as useful for instilling a sense of social responsibility which Buckley believes U.S. society lacks. The book was received with ideologically polarized reviews. *Houston Chronicle* religion writer Richard Vara called *Nearer, My God* "engaging reading," praising it for the "vigorous questioning and debate that courses throughout." In the *New York Times Book Review* Christopher Lehmann-Haupt wrote, "what best invites the reader's belief is the joy with which Buckley goes about his business in this 'Autobiography of Faith,'" but said that "the problem, at least for the nonbelieving reader, is that where almost every logical contradiction arises, we are asked simply to accept what we can't understand."

When not writing about politics or sailing, Buckley has also found time to pen a series of bestselling espionage novels featuring C.I.A. agent Blackford Oakes. The "arch and politically sophisticated" novel series, as Derrick Murdoch described it in the Toronto *Globe and Mail,* is set in the cold-war years of the 1950s and 1960s and takes readers behind the scenes of the major political crises of the time. In doing so, the novels provide Buckley with the opportunity to dramatize some of his ideas concerning East-West relations. As Lehmann-Haupt remarked in the *New York Times,* "not only can Buckley execute the international thriller as well as nearly anyone working in the genre . . . he threatens to turn this form of fiction into effective propaganda for his ideas."

Saving the Queen, the first of the "Blackford Oakes" novels, is based in part on Buckley's own experiences in the C.I.A. "The training received by Blackford Oakes is, in exact detail, the training I received," the author explained. "In that sense, it's autobiographical." Oakes, a thinly disguised version of his creator, also shares Buckley's school years at an English public school and at Yale University. The story concerns a leak of classified information at the highest levels of the British government. Oakes is sent to locate the source of the leak, and his investigation uncovers a treasonous cousin in the royal family. Robin W. Winks of the *New Republic* found *Saving the Queen* to be "replete with ambiguity, irony, suspense—all those qualities we associate with [Eric] Ambler, [Graham] Greene, [and John] le Carre." Amnon Kabatchnik of the *Armchair Detective* called *Saving the Queen* "an entertaining yarn, graced with a literate style, keen knowledge and a twinkling sense of humor [that] injected a touch of sophistication and a flavor of sly irony to the genre of political intrigue."

Stained Glass is set in post-World War II Germany and revolves around the efforts of both East and West to prevent the reunification of Germany under the popular Count Axel Wintergrin. Both sides fear that a united Germany would be a military threat to the peace of Europe. Oakes penetrates Wintergrin's political organization disguised as an engineer hired to restore a local church. His restoring of broken church windows contrasts ironically with his efforts to keep Germany divided. "This novel is a work of history," Winks maintained, "for it parallels those options that might well have been open to the West [in the 1950s]. . . . *Stained Glass* is closer to the bone than le Carre has ever cut." Jane Larkin Crain in the *Saturday Review* called Buckley's novel a "first-rate spy story and . . . a disturbing lesson in the unsavory realities of international politics." *Stained Glass* earned its author an American Book Award in 1980.

In building his novels around actual events, Buckley is obliged to include historical figures in his cast of characters. Speaking of *See You Later, Alligator,* Murdoch believed that "the telling personal [details] are helping to make the Blackford Oakes series unique in spy fiction." In his review of *The Story of Henri Tod,* Anatole Broyard claimed in the *New York Times* that "the best part" of the novel is Buckley's "portrait of former President John F. Kennedy. His rendering of Nikita Khrushchev is quite good too, and this tempts me to suggest that Mr. Buckley seems most at home when he projects himself into the minds of heads of state." Similarly, Elaine Kendall in the *Los Angeles Times Book Review* speculated that Buckley may be evolving into "a psychic historian who can project himself into the most convoluted political minds."

A Very Private Plot, Buckley's tenth offering in the "Blackford Oakes" series, takes his hero to the end of the cold war. Commenting on the author's development as a novelist, D. Keith Mano wrote in *National Review,* "He is a better fiction writer now by leagues than he was in 1976, when *Saving the Queen* took off. New directness and clarity jumpstart his prose. He has command of several voices and can modulate each. And, structurally, his later volumes . . . have had an arrow-shaped ease and purpose." Furthermore, in Mano's opinion, "no one, Right or Left, has chronicled the Cold War period with more imagination or authority." Robin W. Winks mused in *Washington Post Book World:* "One wonders what Buckley would write, and what Oakes would do, were they to begin a 10-book trek now through the intricacies of intelligence in a post-Cold War world of enormously dangerous and very dirty small wars."

Buckley's novel *Brothers No More* finds its author departing from his "Blackford Oakes" series. Described as "an epic saga of doomed Yalies" by Joe Queenan in the *New York Times Book Review,* the novel turns on the changing fortunes of two men who share a foxhole during World War II. One becomes a corrupt businessman, the other a tenacious reporter. Years after their initial encounter, their paths cross again in a strange twist of fate. In Queenan's opinion, the novel's plot is flimsy and contrived, the book "best thought of as patrician trash." He went on to say that Buckley's fine writing actually sabotages the novel: "For trash to work, the writing has to be genuinely trashy, as in Jackie Collins, Danielle Steel, Judith Krantz. For trash to work, the writing has to be positively awful." Queenan speculated that Buckley intended *Brothers No More* to be a genuinely serious book, but that it falls far short of that ambition. A *Publishers Weekly* reviewer rated the book as enjoyable, but concluded that "this is just a potboiler, deftly stirred but no match for Buckley's best."

Buckley cowrote *McCarthy and His Enemies: The Record and Its Meaning* with L. Brent Bozell in 1954 in support of the Wisconsin senator who, after the conviction of spy Alger Hiss in 1950, led hearings to uncover suspected communists in the United States. He revisits this subject in his 1999 novel *The Redhunter: A Novel Based on the Life of Senator Joe McCarthy.* Caspar W. Weinberger, reviewing the novel in *Forbes,* called *The Redhunter* "one of the year's best books, full of tension, excitement, suspense, and realism." The protagonist is Harry Bontecou, a history professor and McCarthy supporter whose life parallels that of the young Buckley. Terry Teachout wrote in *National Review* that *The Redhunter* "tells us much of what he [Buckley] knows about the anti-Communist movement, and does so in a way that is likely to engage the attention of a great many readers who might not otherwise question the received wisdom regarding Joe McCarthy." *Fortune* reviewer Sam Tanenhaus called the novel "an arresting hybrid of fact and invention" and "a penetrating account of McCarthy's intellectual laziness and lack of discipline, which were heightened by his dependence on both the vodka bottle and the advice of Roy Cohn, his sinister young aide." A *Publishers Weekly* reviewer opined that "what's missing from this account is the suffering of those whose lives were torn apart by unsubstantiated allegations," while *Booklist* reviewer Mary Carroll added: "one can only hope readers will understand that Buckley . . . is telling only one side of this very complicated story."

Like the books in Buckley's "Blackford Oakes" series, *Spytime: The Undoing of James Jesus Angleton* is a fictional account of the life of a Yale graduate who served as a spy for the United States in Italy during World War II, then returned to head the counterintelligence operation of the C.I.A. for twenty years. A *Publishers Weekly* reviewer called Buckley's perspective on Angleton's life "perceptive," but added that *Spytime* "suffers from glaring gaps in the master spy's biography." David Pitt wrote in *Booklist* that "readers familiar with Buckley's politics will find much to enjoy here . . . but those looking for a fully formed novel may be a tad disappointed." "This novel successfully explores the enigmatic life of a Cold Warrior," praised Barbara Conaty in *Library Journal.*

Let Us Talk of Many Things, published in 2000, contains about one third of the speeches Buckley delivered during the last half of the twentieth century. *Booklist* reviewer Ray Olson noted that "scattered throughout are delicious anecdotes, piquant quotations, and much evidence of a keen moral sensibility." "From his earliest efforts in the 1950s to the very last page, Buckley's speeches are alive with wit, conviction, and a lucid, fluent grace few of his contemporaries can match," added Aram Bakshian, Jr., in *National Review.* "And they are as much of a delight on the printed page as from the podium. Patinated rather than rusted, they have stood the severest test of all for public utterances—the test of time."

As columnist, television host, novelist, and magazine editor, Buckley became "one of the most articulate, provocative, and entertaining spokesmen for American conservatism" in the twentieth century, according to Gene M. Moore in his *Dictionary of Literary Biography Yearbook* essay. For his role in the development of the modern conservative movement that fueled the careers of commentators such as George Will and Rush Limbaugh, Buckley "is a man who richly deserves praise," Kondracke argued. "He is generous, erudite, witty and courageous, and he has performed a service to the whole nation, even to those who disagree with him." Writing in the *Los Angeles Times Book Review,* John Haase called Buckley "witty, erudite, multifaceted, perhaps one of the few great exponents of the English language. He is politically contentious, a 'farceur,' I suspect, but we are willing to forgive all, because mostly Buckley is fun." Summing up Buckley's role in the nation's political life, Moore found that his "flickering tongue and flashing wit have challenged a generation to remember the old truths while searching for the new, to abhor hypocrisy and to value logic, and to join in the worldwide struggle for human rights and human freedom."

BIOGRAPHICAL AND CRITICAL SOURCES:

BOOKS

Cain, Edward R., *They'd Rather Be Right: Youth and the Conservative Movement,* Macmillan (New York, NY), 1963.

Contemporary Literary Criticism, Gale (Detroit, MI), Volume 7, 1977, Volume 18, 1981, Volume 37, 1986.

Dictionary of Literary Biography Yearbook: 1980, Gale (Detroit, MI), 1981.

Forster, Arnold, and B. R. Epstein, *Danger on the Right,* Random House (New York, NY), 1964.

Judis, John, *William F. Buckley, Jr.: Patron Saint of the Conservatives,* Simon & Schuster (New York, NY), 1988.

Markmann, Charles L., *The Buckleys: A Family Examined,* Morrow (New York, NY), 1973.

PERIODICALS

America, January 31, 1998, Thomas M. King, review of *Nearer, My God: An Autobiography of Faith,* p. 32.

American Book Review, June 16, 1993.

American Spectator, August, 1997, pp. 70-71.

Armchair Detective, June, 1976.

Atlantic Monthly, November, 1951; May, 1954; July, 1968.

Booklist, July, 1995, p. 1835; November 15, 1996, p. 547; September 1, 1997, Ray Olson, review of *Nearer, My God,* p. 4; March 15, 1999, Mary Carroll, review of *The Redhunter: A Novel Based on the Life of Senator Joe McCarthy,* p. 1259; April 15, 2000, David Pitt, review of *Spytime: The Undoing of James Jesus Angleton,* p. 1498; May 1, 2000, Ray Olson, review of *Let Us Talk of Many Things,* p. 1639; February 1, 2003, Mary Carroll, review of *Getting It Right,* p. 955.

Boston Globe, January 25, 1988, p. 28; August 20, 1988, p. 25; February 19, 1991, p. 30; September 7, 1991, p. 21.

Chicago Tribune, November 8, 1959; January 10, 1988, p. B2; June 22, 1989, p. 1; October 26, 1990, p. 3; January 3, 1992, p. 5; March 20, 1994, p. 2; June 23, 1995, p. 3.

Christian Century, July 3, 1968; November 19, 1997, D. G. Hart, review of *Nearer, My God,* pp. 1091-1094.

Christianity Today, November 17, 1997, John Wilson, review of *Nearer, My God,* p. 59.

Christian Science Monitor, August 29, 1968; August 16, 1978; December 20, 1980; February 24, 1984; June 30, 1988, p. 29; July 18, 1988, p. 21; November 29, 1990, p. 19.

Commentary, April, 1974; November, 1983; February, 1992.

Commonweal, February 15, 1952; May 3, 1963; December 23, 1966; March 1, 1974; March 13, 1998, Neil Coughlan, review of *Nearer, My God,* p. 15.

Esquire, January, 1961; November, 1966; January, 1968; August, 1969; September, 1969; February, 1972; July, 1976.

First Things, May, 2003, review of *Getting It Right,* p. 74.

Forbes, October 10, 1994, pp. 60-69; August 9, 1999, p. 41.

Fortune, June 7, 1999, Sam Tanenhaus, "W. F. Buckley's Auto-Revisionism," p. 48.

Globe and Mail (Toronto, Ontario, Canada), February 18, 1984; April 13, 1985.

Harper's, March, 1967; November, 1971; October, 1983.

Houston Chronicle, January 9, 1998.

Kirkus Reviews, November 1, 1996, review of *Buckley: The Right Word;* August 1, 1997, review of *Nearer, My God;* January 15, 2003, review of *Getting It Right,* p. 103.

Library Journal, September 15, 1997, Richard S. Watts, review of *Nearer, My God,* p. 79; November 1, 1998, Lisa J. Cihlar, review of *The Lexicon: A Cornucopia of Wonderful Words for the Inquisitive Word Lover,* p. 80; June 15, 1999, Barbara Conaty, review of *The Redhunter,* p. 105; May 1, 2000, Barbara Conaty, review of *Spytime,* p. 152; February 1, 2003, Barbara Conaty, review of *Getting It Right,* p. 114.

Life, September 17, 1965.

Los Angeles Times, August 11, 1983; January 17, 1988, p. B10; July 1, 1988, p. VI25; July 14, 1988, p. V1; May 7, 1989, p. B1; November 11, 1990, p. E1; November 25, 1990, p. M4; July 6, 1991, p. F1; July 1, 1994, p. F34; November 17, 1995, p. B6; June 2, 1996, p. A13.

Los Angeles Times Book Review, February 7, 1982; September 12, 1982; January 22, 1984; April 7, 1985; March 23, 1986.

Nation, October 2, 1972; April 26, 1980; January 25, 1993, pp. 92-96, 98-99.

National Catholic Reporter, January 24, 1992; November 7, 1997, review of *Nearer, My God,* p. 27.

National Review, May 7, 1963; November 15, 1966; July 30, 1968; September 13, 1974; October 24, 1975; December 5, 1975; February 20, 1976; May 13, 1977; June 9, 1978; November 24, 1978; April 4, 1980; January 22, 1982; October 15, 1982; September 2, 1983; February 24, 1984; December 31, 1985; July 31, 1987, pp. 44-6; January 6, 1992; May 11, 1992; December 28, 1992, pp. 40-2; October 4, 1993, pp. 55-7; February 21, 1994, pp. 58-60; October 23, 1995, p. 57; June 5, 2000, Aram Bakshian, Jr., "Music for Our Ears"; June 14, 1999, Terry Teachout, "McCarthy and His Friends," p. 47; March 10, 2003, Austin Bramwell, review of *Getting It Right;* March 24, 2003, "Objectivist Sex—And Politics" (interview).

New American, March 10, 2003, William Norman Greig, review of *Getting It Right,* p. 25.

New Republic, October 19, 1959; June 10, 1978; February 10, 1992.

Newsweek, October 17, 1966; March 25, 1968; August 2, 1971; September 30, 1974; January 5, 1976; February 19, 1979.

New Yorker, August 8, 1970; August 21, 1971; August 28, 1971; October 12, 1992, pp. 114-18.

New York Review of Books, July 18, 1974; October 13, 1983.

New York Times, November 4, 1951; April 4, 1954; October 6, 1971; April 5, 1978; February 6, 1980; February 25, 1981; December 28, 1981; August 18, 1983; December 21, 1983; February 4, 1985; March 27, 1986; January 24, 1988, p. 11; May 15, 1988, p. 12; August 16, 1988, p. B1; March 31, 1989, p. B2; May 28, 1989, p. 7; October 1, 1989, p. 27; October 13, 1988, p. B2; May 4, 1989, p. C24; October 12, 1990, p. B2; October 15, 1990, p. C16; September 6, 1991, p. B2; January 22, 1992, p. C20; July 13, 1992, p. C13; October 25, 1992, p. 14; July 7, 1993, p. C18; January 5, 1994, p. B2; September 3, 1995, p. 37; January 2, 1996, pp. 12-13; October 2, 1997, p. B7; December 19, 1997, p. B26.

New York Times Book Review, March 25, 1962; April 28, 1963; October 30, 1966; September 15, 1968; August 2, 1970; September 26, 1971; October 8, 1972; January 13, 1974; September 28, 1975; December 26, 1976; January 11, 1978; May 14, 1978; November 19, 1978; February 17, 1980; March 30, 1980; January 24, 1982; March 7, 1982; September 5, 1982; August 7, 1983; February 5, 1984; March 3, 1985, pp. 12, 13; January 5, 1986, p. 14; February 9, 1986; April 6, 1986; May 31, 1987, p. 34; January 24, 1988, p. 11; May 15, 1988, p. 12; May 28, 1989, pp. 7, 8; October 28, 1990, pp. 1, 39; February 17, 1991, p. 15; September 27, 1992, pp. 3, 24; October 3, 1993, p. 14; February 6, 1994, p. 14; September 10, 1995, p. 16; September 28, 1997, p. 16.

New York Times Magazine, September 5, 1965.

Publishers Weekly, August 26, 1974; February 24, 1989, p. 211; August 7, 1995, p. 441; September 29, 1997, review of *Nearer, My God,* p. 84; April 26, 1999, p. 50; July 5, 1999, review of *The Redhunter* (audio), p. 34; May 22, 2000, review of *Spytime,* p. 70.

San Francisco Review of Books, November-December, 1993, p. 28.

Saturday Review, April 3, 1954; October 10, 1959; April 27, 1963; August 8, 1970; May 13, 1978; January, 1982.

Time, October 31, 1960; November 4, 1966; November 3, 1967; August 2, 1971; November 18, 1974; January 5, 1976; December 6, 1976; June 19, 1978; February 19, 1979; February 25, 1980; January 18, 1982; October 25, 1982; December 9, 1985; February 4, 1986; March 31, 1986; June 15, 1987; November 10, 1997, John Elson, review of *Nearer, My God,* p. 111; June 7, 1999, Lance Morrow, "Alger 'Ales' and Joe: Was McCarthy on the Right Track?," p. 66.

Times Literary Supplement, March 12, 1976; July 27, 1984.

Vanity Fair, September, 1993.

Village Voice, February 21, 1974; December 8, 1975.

Wall Street Journal, November 15, 1966; January 31, 1967; February 11, 1994, p. A11; April 29, 1994, p. A14; December 23, 1997, p. A12.

Washington Post, February 12, 1980; October 6, 1990, p. C1; September 7, 1991, p. G1; December 12, 1991, p. B1; December 17, 1991, p. A21; June 29, 1992, pp. B1, B5.

Washington Post Book World, June 30, 1968; January 23, 1972; February 12, 1980; January 10, 1982; September 4, 1983; March 24, 1985; March 9, 1986; May 24, 1987; April 30, 1989, p. 4; October 28, 1990, p. 1; January 22, 1991, p. B3; June 29, 1992, p. B1; January 25, 1994, p. C2; August 7, 1994, p. 4.*

BUSTOS, F(rancisco)
    See BORGES, Jorge Luis

*   *   *

BUSTOS DOMECQ, H(onorio)
    See BORGES, Jorge Luis

*   *   *

BYATT, A(ntonia) S(usan Drabble) 1936-

PERSONAL: Born August 24, 1936, in Sheffield, England; daughter of John Frederick (a judge) and Kathleen Marie (Bloor) Drabble; married Ian Charles Rayner Byatt (an economist), July 4, 1959 (divorced, 1969); married Peter John Duffy, 1969; children: (first marriage) Antonia, Charles; (second marriage) Isabel, Miranda. *Education:* Newnham College, Cambridge, B.A. (first class honors), 1957; graduate study at Bryn Mawr College, 1957-58, and Somerville College, Oxford, 1958-59.

ADDRESSES: Home—37 Rusholme Rd., London SW15 3LF, England.

CAREER: University of London, London, England, staff member in extramural department, 1962-71; Central School of Art and Design, London, part-time lecturer in department of liberal studies, 1965-69; University College, London, lecturer, 1972-81, senior lecturer in English, 1981-83, admissions tutor in English, 1980-83, fellow, beginning 1984; writer, 1983—. Associate of Newnham College, Cambridge, 1977-82; British Council Lecturer in Spain, 1978, India, 1981, and in Germany, Australia, Hong Kong, China, and Korea; George Eliot Centenary Lecturer, 1980. Member of panel of judges for Booker Prize, 1973, Hawthornden Prize, and David Higham Memorial Prize; member of British Broadcasting Corp. (BBC) Social Effects of Television advisory group, 1974-77; member of Communications and Cultural Studies Board, Council for National Academic Awards, 1978; member of Kingman Committee on the Teaching of English, 1987-88; member of British Council of Literature advisory panel, 1990-98, and board, 1993-98.

MEMBER: British Society of Authors (member of committee of management, 1984-88; chair of committee, 1986-88), PEN.

A. S. Byatt

AWARDS, HONORS: English-speaking Union fellowship, 1957-58; fellow of Royal Society of Literature, 1983; Silver Pen Award for *Still Life;* Booker Prize, 1990, *Irish Times*-Aer Lingus International Fiction Prize, 1990, and Best Book in Commonwealth Prize, 1991, all for *Possession;* Commander of the Order of the British Empire, 1990, Dame Commander, 1999; honorary fellow, Newham College, Cambridge, 1999, London Institute, 2000. D.Litt. from University of Bradford, 1987, University of Durham, 1991, University of Nottingham, 1992, University of Liverpool, 1993, University of Portsmouth, 1994, University of London, 1995, Cambridge University, 1999, and Sheffield University, 2000; D.Univ. from University of York, 1991.

WRITINGS:

FICTION

The Shadow of the Sun, Harcourt (London, England), 1964.
The Game, Chatto & Windus, 1967 (London, England), Scribner (New York, NY), 1968.

The Virgin in the Garden (first novel in tetralogy), Chatto & Windus (London, England), 1978, Knopf (New York, NY), 1979.

Still Life (second novel in tetralogy), Chatto & Windus (London, England), 1985, Scribner (New York, NY), 1987.

Sugar and Other Stories, Scribner (New York, NY), 1987.

Possession: A Romance, Random House (New York, NY), 1990.

Angels and Insects: Two Novellas, (contains "Morpho Eugenia" and "The Conjugial Angel"), Chatto & Windus (London, England), 1992.

The Matisse Stories, Chatto & Windus (London, England), 1993, Random House (New York, NY), 1995.

The Djinn in the Nightingale's Eye: Five Fairy Tales, Chatto & Windus (London, England), 1994.

Babel Tower (third novel in tetralogy), Random House (New York, NY), 1996.

Elementals: Stories of Fire and Ice, Chatto & Windus (London, England), 1998, Random House (New York, NY), 1999.

The Biographer's Tale, Chatto & Windus (London, England), 2000, Knopf (New York, NY), 2001.

A Whistling Woman (fourth novel in tetralogy), Knopf (New York, NY), 2002.

Little Black Book of Stories, Knopf (New York, NY), 2004.

OTHER

Degrees of Freedom: The Novels of Iris Murdoch, Barnes & Noble (New York, NY), 1965, published as *Degrees of Freedom: The Early Novels of Iris Murdoch,* Vintage (London, England), 1994.

Wordsworth and Coleridge in Their Time, Nelson (London, England), 1970, Crane, Russak (New York, NY), 1973, published as *Unruly Times: Wordsworth and Coleridge in Their Time,* Hogarth (London, England), 1989.

Iris Murdoch, Longman (London, England), 1976.

(Editor and author of introduction) George Eliot, *The Mill on the Floss,* Penguin (Middlesex, England), 1979.

(Editor) George Eliot, *Selected Essays, Poems and Other Writings,* Penguin (Middlesex, England), 1989.

(Editor) Robert Browning, *Dramatic Monologues,* Folio Society (London, England), 1990.

Passions of the Mind, Chatto & Windus (London, England), 1991.

(Editor with Alan Hollinghurst) *New Writing 4,* Vintage (London, England), 1995.

(With Ignes Sodre) *Imagining Characters: Conversations about Women Writers: Jane Austen, Charlotte Brontë, George Eliot, Willa Cather, Iris Murdoch, and Toni Morrison,* Chatto & Windus (London, England), 1995, Vintage (New York, NY), 1997.

(Editor with others) *New Writing 6,* Vintage (London, England), 1997.

(Editor) *The Oxford Book of English Short Stories,* Oxford University Press (New York, NY), 1998.

On Histories and Stories, Chatto & Windus (London, England), 2000, Harvard University Press (Cambridge, MA), 2001.

Portraits in Fiction, Chatto & Windus (London, England), 2001.

Contributor to books, including Isobel Armstrong, editor, *The Major Victorian Poets Reconsidered,* Routledge (London, England), 1969; Malcolm Bradbury, editor, *The Contemporary English Novel,* Edward Arnold (London, England), 1979; and *Patrick Heron,* Tate Gallery Publications (London, England), 1998. Author of prefaces to books, including Elizabeth Bowen, *The House in Paris,* Penguin, 1976; Grace Paley, *Enormous Changes at the Last Minute,* Virago, 1979; Paley, *The Little Disturbances of Man,* Virago, 1980; Willa Cather, *My Antonia* and *A Lost Lady,* Virago, 1980, and *My Mortal Enemy, Shadow on the Rock, Death Comes to the Archbishop, O Pioneers!* and *Lucy Grayheart;* and George Eliot, *Middlemarch,* Oxford University Press, 1999. Also author of radio documentary on Leo Tolstoy, 1978, and of dramatized portraits of George Eliot and Samuel Taylor Coleridge for National Portrait Gallery. Contributor of reviews to London *Times, New Statesman, Encounter, New Review,* and *American Studies.* Member of editorial board, *Encyclopaedia,* Longman-Penguin, 1989.

ADAPTATIONS: "Morpho Eugenia" was adapted to film as *Angels and Insects; Possession* was adapted for a film by director Neil LaBute, David Henry Hwang, and Laura Jones, starring Gwyneth Paltrow and Aaron Eckhart, USA Films, 2002.

SIDELIGHTS: A. S. Byatt is a widely experienced critic, novelist, editor, and lecturer who "offers in her work an intellectual kaleidoscope of our contemporary world," according to Caryn McTighe Musil in the *Dictionary of Literary Biography*. Musil added: "Her novels, like her life, are dominated by an absorbing, discriminating mind which finds intellectual passions as vibrant and consuming as emotional ones." A celebrated polymath—whose fiction delves into science, the visual arts, Victorian history and sensibilities, and the postmodern concept of writing about writing—the London-based Byatt has attracted a reading audience on both sides of the Atlantic. In *Publishers Weekly* John F. Baker called Byatt "somewhat of a pillar in the English intellectual establishment . . . whose mind is so compendious that deciding what to leave out of her books is more of a problem than an author's usual frantic search for ideas."

Byatt was relatively unknown as a fiction writer until 1990, the year in which she published her bestseller—and Booker Prize-winning novel—*Possession.* Since then she has been in demand not only as a writer, but also as a lecturer and a judge of others' works. Her own fiction seeks to disprove that writing about the academy must necessarily be fraught with intellectual legerdemain. "All through Byatt's writing life, she has reflected on the way we earthly beings dream of spirit," Michael Levenson observed in the *New Republic.* "She is a Realist, a post-Christian, a sometime academic living in skeptical times. . . . For Byatt these are simply the latest natural conditions for our spirit-hunger. It's no use whining. Her point is not to confirm religious truth, but to enlarge the religious sense, which locates value not in the infinite but in the yearning for the infinite, not in God but in the search for God." As Donna Seaman put it in *Booklist,* Byatt is simultaneously "a dazzling storyteller and a keen observer of the power and significance of her medium. . . . She revels, to her readers' considerable delight, in the infinite potential of the storyteller's art."

Byatt grew up in a scholarly family. Her father was a judge, and her sister, Margaret Drabble, also pursued writing. Byatt attended both Cambridge and Oxford, where she studied art and literature, all the while writing fiction as well. Her career progressed relatively slowly—but considering that she raised four children while teaching, she in fact made commendable strides. Byatt has been a full-time writer since 1983, but still pursues scholarly work in the form of literary criticism, edited volumes, and the writing of introductions for new editions of classic fiction. To quote Hilma Wolitzer in the *New York Times Book Review,* Byatt

"has always been concerned with the ways in which art and literature inform and transform our lives."

Byatt's first novel, *The Shadow of the Sun,* reflects the author's own struggle to combine the role of critic with that of novelist on the one hand, and the role of mother with that of visionary on the other, according to Musil. The critic wrote that *The Game,* "a piece of technical virtuosity, is also a taut novel that explores with a courage and determined honesty greater than [D. H.] Lawrence's the deepest levels of antagonism that come with intimacy. Widely reviewed, especially in Great Britain, *The Game* established Byatt's reputation as an important contemporary novelist."

Byatt's novel *The Virgin in the Garden* was described by *Times Literary Supplement* reviewer Michael Irwin as a "careful, complex novel." The book's action is set in 1953, the year of the coronation of Queen Elizabeth II, and Irwin reported that "its theme is growing up, coming of age, tasting knowledge." The book "is a highly intellectual operation," pointed out Iris Murdoch in *New Statesman.* "The characters do a great deal of thinking, and have extremely interesting thoughts which are developed at length." "The novel's central symbol," Musil related, "is Queen Elizabeth I, a monarch Byatt sees as surviving because she used her mind and thought things out, unlike her rival, Mary, Queen of Scots, who was 'very female and got it wrong.'" In Musil's opinion, the work initiated "the middle phase" of Byatt's writing career. "Much denser" than her previous novels "and dependent on her readers' erudition, [*The Virgin in the Garden*] achieves a style that suits Byatt. It blends her acquisitive, intellectual bent with her imaginative compulsion to tell stories." *The Virgin in the Garden* is the first in a series of novels featuring the character Frederica Potter, who, like Byatt, has grown up in the north of England, attended Cambridge, and has become a respected—if beleaguered—academician.

With *Babel Tower* and *A Whistling Woman* Byatt completes a fictional quartet that began with *The Virgin in the Garden* and continued with *Still Life. Babel Tower* finds Frederica Potter trying to overcome a soured marriage and make it on her own as a single mother in the tumult of 1960s London. The novel, which continues Byatt's sweeping portrayal of post-World War II England, also serves, in the words of *New York Times Book Review* critic Ann Hulbert, as a "portrait of the reader as a young woman," wherein Byatt questions the value of literature in modern culture. *Time* magazine reviewer Paul Gray deemed Byatt's subject "certainly worthy but perhaps not sufficiently vivid to propel readers through a long, long literary haul." Hulbert assessed this third novel as "bolder" than Byatt's earlier installments in the series. She wrote that in *Babel Tower,* Byatt's "usual impressive command of slippery ideas and the solidest of details . . . mix and move with new energy, even abandon." In his *Maclean's* review, John Bemrose suggested that "what propels *Babel Tower* into a whole new orbit of achievement is Byatt's fresh and keenly intelligent interpretation of the Sixties—an era many would argue has been documented to death." Bemrose styled the work "a brilliant novel of ideas . . . about the courage required to cope with change."

Noting Byatt's characteristic use of embedded narrative threads within her fiction, *World Literature Today* contributor Mary Kaiser commented that in *A Whistling Woman* "there is also a skein of symbolic threads in this intricate narrative tapestry, in which birds and women are linked as singers, spiritual vehicles, and embodiments of beauty." In this fourth novel in the series, Potter—now a thirty-something single mother and working as a teacher—has found a loyal and growing readership for her fiction. As Potter's acclaim and celebrity grows as a result of the publication of her novel *Laminations,* so too do the successes of her creative friends, often at the cost of romantic love. Potter's decision to shift from teaching to hosting a talk show puts her into the center of 1960s culture and the battle between the status quo and a liberation of social and cultural views, a counterpoint being the destructive influence of charismatic cult leader Joshua Ramsden. Potter represents the prototypical feminist of the period: according to a *Publishers Weekly* contributor, a woman who is "literate, shrewd and knowing, a character who could only be the product of centuries of Enlightenment." Ramsden, in contrast, is "dark, ecstatic," a man "whose psychotic episodes begin to bleed into his essential charismatic goodness," according to the critic. Praising Byatt as "Astute and omnipotent," *Booklist* contributor Donna Seaman described the novel's subject as "nothing less than Western civilization and its endless redefining of faith and fact, good and evil, art and science."

The 1990 publication of *Possession* finally brought Byatt into the mainstream in both English and American letters. *Possession* tells the story of Roland Michell

and Maud Bailey, two contemporary literary scholars whose paths cross during their research. Roland is an expert on the famous Victorian poet Randolph Henry Ash, while Maud's interest is Christabel LaMotte, an obscure poet of the same period. Roland and Maud discover evidence that the two Victorians were linked in a passionate relationship; their joint investigation into the lives of the two writers leads to a love affair of their own. Byatt has been widely acclaimed for her skillful handling of this complex story. In a *Spectator* review, Anita Brookner called *Possession* "capacious, ambitious . . . marvelous," and noted that it is "teeming with more ideas than a year's worth of ordinary novels." Danny Karlin declared in the *London Review of Books* that Byatt's romance is "spectacular both in its shortcomings and its successes; it has vaulting literary ambitions and is unafraid to crash."

Much of the plot of *Possession* is conveyed through poetry and correspondence attributed to Ash and LaMotte, and many reviewers marveled at Byatt's sure touch in creating authentic voices for her fictional Victorians. *New York Times Book Review* contributor Jay Parini commented: "The most dazzling aspect of *Possession* is Ms. Byatt's canny invention of letters, poems and diaries from the nineteenth century. She quotes whole vast poems by Ash and LaMotte, several of which . . . are highly plausible versions of [Robert] Browning and [Christina] Rossetti and are beautiful poems on their own." Parini was also enthusiastic about the manner in which the love story of Ash and LaMotte serves as "ironic counterpoint" to the modern affair between Maud and Roland. Parini concluded: "*Possession* is a tour de force that opens every narrative device of English fiction to inspection without, for a moment, ceasing to delight." The literary world's high regard for the novel is reflected in the fact that Byatt won both the prestigious Booker Prize and the *Irish Times*-Aer Lingus International Fiction Prize for *Possession* in 1990.

Critical praise for Byatt's work continued when *Angels and Insects* was published in 1992. This volume contains two novellas set in the Victorian era. The first, "Morpho Eugenia," concerns a biologist who becomes part of a wealthy household with an ugly secret. The second, "The Conjugial Angel," revolves around the Victorian fascination with spiritualism. Marilyn Butler, a reviewer for *Times Literary Supplement,* called *Angels and Insects* "more fully assured and satisfying than *Possession*" and rated it Byatt's "best work to date." *Belles Lettres* contributor Tess Lewis asserted that "Byatt brings vividly to life the divided Victorian soul—split between faith in the intellect and instinct, free will and determinism, and rationalism and spiritualism. . . . The sheer beauty of many scenes as well as Byatt's luxurious, evocative language remain with the reader long after the clever plots and intriguing, but occasionally too lengthy, intellectual constructs have faded. Byatt's writing is masterful."

Byatt's novel *The Biographer's Tale* is the story of Phineas G. Nanson, a graduate student who, tired of postmodern abstractions, turns to biography in an attempt to deal with solid facts. He begins to read a biography of Elmer Bole, a nineteenth-century scholar, and is intrigued; he resolves to write a biography of the biographer. Byatt includes much of what Phineas reads, mimicking the dry voice of the biographer and providing information on the customs of Lapland, discussions of anthropometric measuring equipment, and descriptions of entomology. Through the course of his studies, Phineas is hired at a travel agency and becomes involved with two women, echoing the life of Elmer Bole, who was married to two women. The biography Phineas himself writes becomes something of an autobiography, and his search to find facts reveals itself as a search to find himself.

"Through clever, lively prose, Byatt . . . moves the action along briskly, treating the reader to numerous witty observations on contemporary academic and social mores along the way," wrote Starr E. Smith in the *Library Journal.* Many reviewers, however, were disappointed with the inclusions of the factual texts. As Jean Blish Siers noted in the *Knight Ridder/Tribune,* "That Phineas should dive into these artifacts is only right. That readers should be forced to read the manuscripts in their entirety is uncalled for." But Lynne Sharon Schwartz, in a review of *The Biographer's Tale* for the *New Leader* praised Byatt's handling of the shifts in narration, writing: "Like a genie rising from a bottle, the novel swirls out of these notes . . . demanding half a dozen voices that Byatt does expertly." A *Publishers Weekly* reviewer concluded, "The book is an erudite joke carried off with verve and humor" and "will appeal to discriminating readers ready for intellectual stimulation."

In Byatt's more recent short fiction, such as the works collected in *The Matisse Stories,* the author adopts a more concrete style. These stories all make some ref-

erence to French impressionist painter Henri Matisse. "The lasting impression the reader has of Antonia Byatt's three stories in this collection is of an extravagance of color, a riot of color, venous-blue and fuchsia-red and crimson and orange henna and copper," David Plante related in the *Los Angeles Times Book Review.* "Byatt's fiction . . . is essentially informed by an intelligent, even a scholarly mind, pitched more to interpretation rather than fact in itself, to 'ideas' rather than 'things.' But it is as though in 'The Matisse Stories' Byatt were trying to break out onto another level, that of making art." London *Observer* writer Helen Dunmore voiced a similar opinion: "These stories show us Byatt still advancing in her technique and range. Like Matisse she is excited by the way a vase of flowers, a white book or a human being stands in the stream of everyday light, and like Matisse she knows how to set down her observations."

In *The Djinn in the Nightingale's Eye* Byatt presents a collection of contemporary and self-reflexive fairy tales, two of the stories having appeared earlier, woven into the plot of *Possession.* The title story, which is the longest of the five, dramatizes literary theories of the fairy tale through the story of a middle-aged narratologist who encounters a djinn, or genie, with the power to grant her the traditional three wishes. Because she is a scholar of fairy tales, she knows all of the pitfalls, and so her wishes are anything but traditional. "The conversations between the genie and the scholar are beyond all praise," wrote Nancy Willard in the *New York Times Book Review,* "and the description of their lovemaking is a gem of exuberant metaphor and linguistic constraint." *Baltimore Sun* writer Susan Reimer claimed that "the scent of sandalwood and myrrh that rose from the pages of this book caused me to wish for my own wishes."

Elementals: Stories of Fire and Ice includes both realistic and fantastic tales which illustrate the deep connections between literature and life. In one of the pieces, a grieving widow begins to confront her personal tragedy during conversations about folktales with a new friend. In another, a princess who must constantly be freezing cold overcomes supernatural odds to marry a glass-blower in the desert. A *Publishers Weekly* reviewer deemed the work a "virtuosic and beguiling collection" that reveals "an unfettered imagination, an intense lyricism combined with distilled and crystalline prose, and an astute grasp of the contradictory impulses of human nature." In *Booklist* Veronica

Scrol likewise noted that *Elementals* "showcases Byatt's ability to get to the heart of the human condition," while *New York Times Book Review* critic Wolitzer concluded that the tales are "fired by a fierce intelligence and related in shimmering prose." The five tales included in *Little Black Book of Stories* continue the motifs of *Elementals,* creating a collection wherein "the writing is dauntingly precise and realistic, even as it points to something unnatural and bizarre," according to *Spectator* contributor Stephen Abell: "'always aiming,' as Byatt herself has characterised 'good' modern prose, 'at an impossible exactness which it knows it will never achieve.'"

Byatt once commented: "Perhaps the most important thing to say about my books is that they try to be about the life of the mind as well as of society and the relations between people. I admire—am excited by— intellectual curiosity of any kind (scientific, linguistic, psychological) and also by literature as a complicated, huge, interrelating pattern. I also like recording small observed facts and feelings. I see writing and thinking as a passionate activity, like any other."

BIOGRAPHICAL AND CRITICAL SOURCES:

BOOKS

Contemporary Literary Criticism, Gale (Detroit, MI), Volume 19, 1981, Volume 65, 1991.

Dictionary of Literary Biography, Volume 14: *British Novelists since 1960,* Gale (Detroit, MI), 1983.

Kelly, Kathleen Coyne, *A. S. Byatt,* Twayne (New York, NY), 1996.

PERIODICALS

Atlantic, January, 2001, Stephen Amidon, review of *The Biographer's Tale,* p. 84.

Baltimore Sun, January 6, 1998.

Belles Lettres, fall, 1993, pp. 28-29.

Book, January-February, 2003, Penelope Mesic, review of *A Whistling Woman,* p. 69.

Booklist, April, 1996, p. 100; September 1, 1997, Donna Seaman, review of *The Djinn in the Nightingale's Eye,* p. 6; March 1, 1999, Veronica Scrol, review of *Elementals: Stories of Fire and Ice,* p. 1103; January 1, 2000, Karen Harris, review

of *Possession,* p. 948; November 15, 2000, Donna Seaman, review of *The Biographer's Tale,* p. 587; November 15, 2002, Donna Seaman, review of *A Whistling Woman,* p. 547.

Books and Bookmen, January 4, 1979.

Chicago Tribune, June 13, 1993, sec. 14, p. 3.

Chicago Tribune Book World, January 12, 1986.

Christian Science Monitor, March 31, 1992, p. 13; May 25, 1993, p. 13; April 20, 1995, p. 12; September 25, 1997, p. B8.

Economist, June 15, 1996, p. 3.

Encounter, July, 1968.

English Journal, March, 1995, p. 92.

Kirkus Reviews, November 1, 2002, review of *A Whistling Woman,* p. 1548; March 15, 2004, review of *Little Black Book of Stories,* p. 237.

Knight Ridder/Tribune, February 21, 2001, p. K6940.

Lancet, November 7, 1998, Gail Davey, "Still Life and the Rounding of Consciousness," p. 1544.

Library Journal, May 1, 1999, Ann H. Fisher, review of *Elementals,* p. 114; June 1, 2000, Nancy R. Ives, review of *Elementals,* p. 230; December, 2000, Starr E. Smith, review of *The Biographer's Tale,* p. 186; January, 2003, Edward Cone, review of *A Whistling Woman,* p. 151.

London Review of Books, March 8, 1990, pp. 17-18.

Los Angeles Times, November 18, 1985.

Los Angeles Times Book Review, October 28, 1990, pp. 2, 13; June 13, 1993, p. 8; April 23, 1995.

Maclean's, July 1, 1996, John Bemrose, review of *Babel Tower,* p. 59.

Ms., June, 1979.

New Criterion, February, 1991, pp. 77-80.

New Leader, April 23, 1979; January, 2001, Lynne Sharon Schwartz, "Not by Facts Alone," p. 26.

New Republic, January 7-14, 1991, pp. 47-49; August 2, 1993, Michael Levenson, review of *Angels and Insects: Two Novellas,* p. 41.

New Statesman, November 3, 1978; May 3, 1996, p. 40; June 12, 2000, Miranda Seymour, "History Lesson," p. 53.

New Statesman & Society, March 16, 1990, p. 38.

New York Review of Books, June 6, 1996, J. M. Coetzee, review of *Babel Tower,* p. 17; June 10, 1999, Gabriele Annan, review of *Elementals,* p. 28.

New York Times, October 25, 1990, Christopher Lehmann-Haupt, "When There Was Such a Thing as Romantic Love"; July 9, 1996, p. C11; January 23, 2001, Michiko Kakutani, "A Bumbling Literary Sleuth Ends up Clueless," p. B9.

New York Times Book Review, July 26, 1964; March 17, 1968; April 1, 1979; November 24, 1985; July

19, 1987; October 21, 1990, pp. 9, 11; June 27, 1993, p. 14; April 30, 1995, p. 9; June 9, 1996, p. 7; September 14, 1997, p. 27; November 9, 1997, Nancy Willard, "Dreams of Jinni," p. 38; May 10, 1999, Hilma Wolitzer, "Secret Sorrow: Fantasy and Parable."

New York Times Magazine, May 26, 1991, Mira Stout, "What Possessed A. S. Byatt?: A British Novelist's Breakthrough Surprises Everyone but the British Novelist," p. 12.

Observer (London, England), March 11, 1990, p. 68; January 2, 1994, p. 17.

People, April 1, 1991, Michelle Green, "After Years in Her Sister's Shadow, Sibling Rival A. S. Byatt Makes Her Best-selling Mark with *Possession,*" p. 87; April 17, 1995, p. 32.

Publishers Weekly, May 20, 1996, John F. Baker, "A. S. Byatt: Passions of the Mind," p. 235; March 29, 1999, review of *Elementals,* p. 89; November 6, 2000, review of *The Biographer's Tale,* p. 70; November 11, 2002, review of *A Whistling Woman,* p. 41.

Spectator, March 3, 1990, p. 35; January 15, 1994, p. 28; November 29, 2003, Stephen Abell, "Making It a Just so Story," p. 58.

Time, May 20, 1996, p. 76.

Times (London, England), June 6, 1981; April 9, 1987; March 1, 1990.

Times Literary Supplement, January 2, 1964; January 19, 1967; November 3, 1978; June 28, 1985; March 2, 1990, pp. 213-214; October 16, 1992, p. 22.

Vogue, November, 1990, pp. 274, 276.

Wall Street Journal, May 6, 1996, pp. A11-A12.

Washington Post, March 16, 1979; November 22, 1985.

Washington Post Book World, March 29, 1992, p. 11; May 2, 1993, pp. 1, 10.

World Literature Today, October-December, 2003, Mary Kaiser, review of *A Whistling Woman,* p. 93.

Writer, May, 1997, Lewis Burke Frumkes, "A Conversation with A. S. Byatt," p. 15.

Yale Review, October, 1993, Walter Kendrick, review of *Angels and Insects: Two Novellas,* pp. 135-137.

ONLINE

A. S. Byatt: An Overview, http://landow.stg.brown.edu/post/uk/ (March 6, 2001).

A. S. Byatt Home Page, http://www.asbyatt.com (April 10, 2004).

OTHER

Scribbling (television documentary), BBC-2, 2003.*

C

CARD, Orson Scott 1951-
(Frederick Bliss, Brian Green, P. Q. Gump, Dinah Kirkham, Byron Walley)

PERSONAL: Born August 24, 1951, in Richland, WA; son of Willard Richards (a teacher) and Peggy Jane (a secretary and administrator; maiden name, Park) Card; married Kristine Allen, May 17, 1977; children: Michael Geoffrey, Emily Janice, Charles Benjamin (deceased), Zina Margaret, Erin Louisa (deceased). *Education:* Brigham Young University, B.A. (with distinction), 1975; University of Utah, M.A., 1981. *Politics:* Moderate Democrat. *Religion:* Church of Jesus Christ of Latter-Day Saints (Mormon). *Hobbies and other interests:* Computer games.

ADDRESSES: Agent—Barbara Bova Literary Agency, 3951 Gulf Shore Blvd. North #PH1B, Naples, FL 34103-3639.

CAREER: Mormon missionary in Brazil, 1971-73; operated repertory theater in Provo, UT, 1974-75; Brigham Young University Press, Provo, editor, 1974-76; *Ensign,* Salt Lake City, UT, assistant editor, 1976-78; freelance writer and editor, 1978—; Compute! Books, Greensboro, NC, senior editor, 1983; Lucasfilm Games, game design consultant, 1989-92. Instructor at Brigham Young University, University of Utah, University of Notre Dame, Appalachian State University, Clarion West Writers' Workshop, Cape Cod Writer's Workshop, and Antioch Writers' Workshop. Has served as local Democratic precinct election judge and Utah State Democratic Convention delegate.

AWARDS, HONORS: John W. Campbell Award for best new writer of 1977, World Science Fiction Con-

Orson Scott Card

vention, 1978; Hugo Award nominations, World Science Fiction Convention, 1978, 1979, 1980, for short stories, 1986, for novelette *Hatrack River,* and 1988, for *Seventh Son;* Nebula Award nominations, Science Fiction Writers of America, 1979, and 1980, for short stories; Utah State Institute of Fine Arts prize, 1980, for epic poem "Prentice Alvin and the No-Good Plow"; Hamilton-Brackett Award, 1981, for *Songmas-*

ter; Nebula Award, 1985, and Hugo Award and Hamilton-Brackett Award, both 1986, all for *Ender's Game;* Nebula Award, 1986, and Hugo Award and Locus Award, both 1987, all for *Speaker for the Dead;* World Fantasy Award, 1987, for *Hatrack River;* Hugo Award, and Locus Award nomination, both 1988, both for novella "Eye for Eye"; Locus Award, World Fantasy Award nomination, and Mythopoeic Society Fantasy Award, all 1988, all for *Seventh Son;* Locus Award, 1989, for *Red Prophet;* Hugo Award for nonfiction, 1991, for *How to Write Science Fiction and Fantasy;* Israel's Geffen Award for Best Science Fiction book, 1999, for *Pastwatch: The Redemption of Christopher Columbus;* Grand Prix de L'Imaginaire, 2000, for *Heartfire.*

WRITINGS:

SCIENCE FICTION AND FANTASY

Capitol (short stories), Ace (New York, NY), 1978.
Hot Sleep: The Worthing Chronicle, Baronet, 1978.
A Planet Called Treason, St. Martin's Press (New York, NY), 1979, revised edition, Dell (New York, NY), 1980, published as *Treason,* St. Martin's Press (New York, NY), 1988.
Songmaster, Dial (New York, NY), 1980, reprinted, Orb (New York, NY), 2002.
Unaccompanied Sonata and Other Stories, Dial (New York, NY), 1980.
(Editor) *Dragons of Darkness,* Ace (New York, NY), 1981.
Hart's Hope, Berkley (New York, NY), 1983, reprinted, Orb (New York, NY), 2003.
(Editor) *Dragons of Light,* Ace (New York, NY), 1983.
The Worthing Chronicle, Ace (New York, NY), 1983.
(With others) *Free Lancers,* Baen (New York, NY), 1987.
Wyrms, Arbor House (New York, NY), 1987, reprinted, Orb (New York, NY), 2003.
Folk of the Fringe (short stories), Phantasia Press (Huntington Woods, MI), 1989.
The Abyss (novelization of screenplay by James Cameron), Pocket Books (New York, NY), 1989.
Eye for Eye (bound with *The Tunesmith* by Lloyd Biggle, Jr.), Tor (New York, NY), 1990.
Maps in a Mirror: The Short Fiction of Orson Scott Card (includes stories originally published under pseudonym Byron Walley), Tor (New York, NY), 1990.
Worthing Saga, Tor (New York, NY), 1990.

(Editor) *Future on Fire,* Tor (New York, NY), 1991.
The Changed Man, Tor (New York, NY), 1992.
Cruel Miracles, Tor (New York, NY), 1992.
Flux, Tor (New York, NY), 1992.
Monkey Sonatas, Tor (New York, NY), 1993.
(With Kathryn H. Kidd) *Lovelock* (first novel in "Mayflower" trilogy), Tor (New York, NY), 1994.
(Editor) *Future on Ice* (companion volume to *Future on Fire*), Tor (New York, NY), 1998.
Magic Mirror, illustrated by Nathan Pinnock, Gibbs Smith Publisher (Salt Lake City, UT), 1999.
(Editor) *Masterpieces: The Best Science Fiction of the Century,* Ace Books (New York, NY), 2001.
(Editor, with Keith Olexa) *Empire of Dreams and Miracles: The Phobos Science Fiction Anthology,* foreword by Lawrence Krauss, Phobos Books (New York, NY), 2002.
(Editor with Keith Olexa) *Hitting the Skids in Pixeltown: The Phobos Science Fiction Anthology,* Phobos Books (New York, NY), 2003, Volume 2 also with Christian O'Toole, 2003.
(With Doug Chiang) *Robota: Reign of Machines,* Chronicle Books (San Francisco, CA), 2003.

Also author of novelette *Hatrack River,* 1986. Contributor to *The Bradbury Chronicles: Stories in Honor of Ray Bradbury,* edited by William F. Nolan and Martin H. Greenberg, New American Library (New York, NY), 1991. Contributor to numerous anthologies.

"ENDER" SERIES; SCIENCE FICTION

Ender's Game (also see below), Tor (New York, NY), 1985.
Speaker for the Dead (also see below), Tor (New York, NY), 1986.
Ender's Game [and] *Speaker for the Dead,* Tor (New York, NY), 1987.
Xenocide, Tor (New York, NY), 1991.
Children of the Mind, Tor (New York, NY), 1996.
First Meetings: In the Enderverse (includes "Ender's Game," "The Polish Boy," and "Teacher's Pest"), Tor (New York, NY), 2003.

"HEGEMON" SERIES; SCIENCE FICTION

Ender's Shadow, Tor (New York, NY), 1999.
Shadow of the Hegemon, Tor (New York, NY), 2001.
Shadow Puppets, Tor (New York, NY), 2002.
The Shadow Saga, Orbit (New York, NY), 2003.

"TALES OF ALVIN MAKER" SERIES

Seventh Son, St. Martin's Press (New York, NY), 1987.
Red Prophet, Tor (New York, NY), 1988.
Prentice Alvin, Tor (New York, NY), 1989.
Alvin Journeyman, Tor (New York, NY), 1995.
Heartfire, Tor (New York, NY), 1998.
The Crystal City, Tor (New York, NY), 2003.

"HOMECOMING" SERIES

The Memory of Earth (also see below), Tor (New York, NY), 1992.
The Call of the Earth (also see below), Tor (New York, NY), 1993.
The Ships of Earth (also see below), Tor (New York, NY), 1993.
Earthfall, Tor (New York, NY), 1994.
Homecoming: Harmony (contains *The Memory of Earth, The Call of Earth,* and *The Ships of Earth*), Science Fiction Book Club, 1994.
Earthborn, Tor (New York, NY), 1995.

PLAYS

(And director) *Tell Me That You Love Me, Junie Moon* (adaptation of novel by Marjorie Kellogg), produced in Provo, UT, 1969.
The Apostate, produced in Provo, UT, 1970.
In Flight, produced in Provo, UT, 1970.
Across Five Summers, produced in Provo, UT, 1971.
Of Gideon, produced in Provo, UT, 1971.
Stone Tables, produced in Provo, UT, 1973.
A Christmas Carol (adapted from the story by Charles Dickens), produced in Provo, UT, 1974.
Father, Mother, Mother, and Mom (produced in Provo, UT, 1974), published in *Sunstone,* 1978.
Liberty Jail, produced in Provo, UT, 1975.
Fresh Courage Take, produced in Salt Lake City, UT, 1978.
Elders and Sisters (adaptation of novel by Gladys Farmer), produced in American Fork, UT, 1979.
Barefoot to Zion (book and lyrics), music composed by Arlen L. Card, produced in North Salt Lake City, UT, 1997.

Also author, under pseudonym Brian Green, of *Rag Mission,* published in *Ensign,* July, 1977. Author of *Wings* (fragment), produced in 1982.

OTHER

Listen, Mom and Dad, Bookcraft (Salt Lake City, UT), 1978.
Saintspeak: The Mormon Dictionary, Signature Books (Midvale, UT), 1981.
Ainge, Signature Books (Midvale, UT), 1982.
A Woman of Destiny (historical novel), Berkley (New York, NY), 1983, published as *Saints,* Tor (New York, NY), 1988.
Compute's Guide to IBM PCjr Sound and Graphics, Compute (Greensboro, NC), 1984.
Cardography, Hypatia Press, 1987.
Characters and Viewpoint, Writer's Digest (Cincinnati, OH), 1988.
(Author of introduction) Susan D. Smallwood, *You're a Rock, Sister Lewis,* Hatrack River Publications, 1989.
How to Write Science Fiction and Fantasy, Writer's Digest (Cincinnati, OH), 1990.
Lost Boys, HarperCollins (New York, NY), 1992.
(Editor, with David C. Dollahite), *Turning Hearts: Short Stories on Family Life,* Bookcraft (Salt Lake City, UT), 1994.
Treasure Box (novel), HarperCollins (New York, NY), 1996.
Pastwatch: The Redemption of Christopher Columbus, Tor (New York, NY), 1996.
Stone Tables (novel), Deseret Book Co. (Salt Lake City, UT), 1997.
Homebody (novel), HarperCollins (New York, NY), 1998.
Enchantment, Del Rey (New York, NY), 1999.
Sarah (first novel of "Women of Genesis" series), Shadow Mountain (Salt Lake City, UT), 2000.
Rebekah (second novel of "Women of Genesis" series), Shadow Mountain (Salt Lake City, UT), 2001.
An Open Book (poetry collection), Subterranean Press/ Hatrack River Publications (Burton, MI), 2003.
Rachel and Leah (third novel of "Women of Genesis" series), Shadow Mountain (Salt Lake City, UT), 2004.

Also author of audio plays for Living Scriptures; coauthor of animated videotapes. Contributor of regular review columns, including "You Got No Friends in This World," *Science Fiction Review,* 1979-86, "Books to Look For," *Fantasy and Science Fiction,* 1987-94, and "Gameplay," *Compute!,* 1988-89; contributor of columns and editorials to Web sites *Hauvoo* and *Or-*

nery American. Contributor of articles and reviews to periodicals, including *Washington Post Book World, Science Fiction Review, Destinies,* and *The Rhinoceros Times* (Greensboro, NC). Author of works under pseudonyms Frederick Bliss and P. Q. Gump.

Card's manuscripts are housed at Brigham Young University. His books have been translated into Catalan, Danish, Dutch, Finnish, French, German, Hebrew, Italian, Japanese, Polish, Portuguese, Romanian, Russian, Slovakian, Spanish, and Swedish.

ADAPTATIONS: Xenocide was adapted as an audiobook read by Mark Rolston, Audio Renaissance, 1991; *Seventh Son* was adapted as an audiobook, read by Card, Literate Ear, Inc., 1991; *Maps in a Mirror* was adapted as an audiobook, Dove Audio (Los Angeles, CA), 1999; audiobook productions of most of Card's novels have been acquired by Blackstone Audiobooks (Ashland, OR). Card's short stories "Clap Hands and Sing," "Lifeloop," and "Sepulcher of Songs" were adapted for the stage as *Posing as People* by Scott Brick, Aaron Johnston, and Emily Janice Card respectively, produced 2004.

WORK IN PROGRESS: Rasputin, in the "Mayflower" trilogy; *Magic Street,* a contemporary fantasy novel.

SIDELIGHTS: Orson Scott Card is the award-winning author of over sixty books of science fiction, fantasy, history, and ghost stories. With the creation of Andrew "Ender" Wiggin, the young genius of *Ender's Game,* Card launched an award-winning career as a science fiction and fantasy writer. Since his debut in the field in 1977, when the short story "Ender's Game" appeared in *Analog* magazine, Card went on to become the first writer to win the genre's top awards, the Nebula and the Hugo, for consecutive novels in a continuing series. These two novels—*Ender's Game* and *Speaker for the Dead*—have been described by *Fantasy Review* contributor Michael R. Collings as "allegorical disquisitions on humanity, morality, salvation, and redemption"—evaluations that many critics have applied to Card's other works as well. Such thematic concerns, in part influenced by Card's devout Mormonism, are what critics feel set him apart from other writers in the science-fiction field. Beyond the "Ender" series, Card's other projects include creating the American fantasy series "Tales of Alvin Maker," a retelling of ancient scripture in the "Homecoming"

series, contemporary novels with occult and ghost themes such as *Lost Boys, Treasure Box,* and *Homebody,* and a series with a religious theme, "Women of Genesis," begun with the novels *Sarah* and *Rebekah.*

In many of his works Card focuses on the moral development of young protagonists whose abilities to act maturely and decisively while in challenging situations often determine the future of their communities. Card, a devout Mormon, is intrigued by the role of the individual in society, and credits his solid religious background with instilling in him both a strong sense of community and an affinity for storytelling. "I don't want to write about individuals in isolation," he told Graceanne A. DeCandido and Keith R. A. DeCandido in *Publishers Weekly.* "What I want to write about is people who are committed members of the community and therefore have a network of relationships that define who they are. I think if you're going to write about people, you have to write about storytelling." In his works Card is deeply concerned with his own unresolved moral and philosophical questions as well, and maintains that science fiction affords him the benefit of exploring these issues against a futuristic and imaginative backdrop. "In some of the best SF, you move into a universe where all moral bets are off, where you have a group of aliens, or humans in an alien setting, who live by different rules because some key aspect of life that we take for granted as human beings has been changed radically. . . . After a while we can see ourselves through their eyes and see how bizarre we are. Then you come back and you question everything."

Though a profoundly moral writer, Card dismisses standard black-and-white versions of good and evil. As he told Laura Ciporen of *Publishers Weekly,* such representations are "so boring." Card further explained, "When a character comes upon a case of right and wrong and chooses to do wrong, that shows you he's the kind of jerk who'd do that. My characters wrestle with real moral dilemmas where all the choices have steep prices. If they make the selfish choice, then I show the consequences. I'm not trying to teach that lesson, though it underlies everything I write."

Card was born in 1951, in Richland, Washington, the son of a teacher father and an administrator mother. Card moved often in his youth, growing up in California, Arizona, and finally Utah. As a teenager, both the theater and science fiction captured Card's attention.

At only sixteen, he entered Brigham Young University and three years later saw his first play, *Tell Me That You Love Me, Junie Moon,* produced in Provo, Utah. Ten plays and adaptations followed through the seventies, mostly with scriptural or historical themes, but Card's education and writing were put on hold for several years in the early 1970s when Card served as a missionary in Brazil. Returning to Provo, Card founded a theater company and earned his B.A., with honors, in 1975. Thereafter he became an editor at *Ensign* magazine, the official publication of the Church of Jesus Christ of Latter-Day Saints, and also worked for the Brigham Young University Press. There was, however, little money in writing plays. "I was supporting myself on the pathetic wages paid to an editor at a university press—and BYU's wages were even more pathetic than usual," he told the DeCandidos. "I knew there was no hope of paying off my debts through my salary, so I made a serious effort to write fiction as a career."

"All the time that I was a playwright," Card once said, "these science fictional ideas that never showed up in my plays were dancing around in the back of my mind." The genre, he felt, offered him the most expedient way of getting published, since the field thrives on up-and-coming talent and fresh ideas. He also admitted that he chose science fiction because, as he noted, "I knew the genre. While it was never even half my reading, I had read enough to be aware of the possibilities within it. It allowed the possibility of the kind of high drama that I'd been doing with religious plays for the Mormon market. . . . In order to write the kind of intense romantic drama that I wanted to write, I needed the possibilities that science fiction and fantasy offered."

Hoping to break into the field, Card sent "The Tinker," one of his first short stories, to Ben Bova, then editor of the leading science-fiction magazine *Analog.* Bova in turn rejected the work, though he did not crush the aspirations of its author. "Apparently he [Bova] saw some reason to hope that I might have some talent," Card explained to the DeCandidos. "His rejection letter urged me to submit a real science fiction story, because he liked the way I wrote." The real story became "Ender's Game," which, upon its publication, garnered Card the World Science Fiction Convention's John W. Campbell Award for best new writer.

Though Card was thrilled with his sudden success, he later admitted to a *Publishers Weekly* interviewer that

he was "not so stupid as to quit my job." He retained his position as editor for *Ensign* and in 1978 began composing audio plays for Living Scriptures. He also continued honing his writing skills and released his first book, *Capitol,* during that same year. A collection of short stories, the work follows the fall of the planet Capitol and revolves in part around the drug somec, which induces a state of suspended animation in its user and allows him to live for several thousand years. At least one reviewer remarked upon Card's literary skill in *Capitol.* The collection "demonstrates a fine talent for storytelling and characterization," decided a critic for *Publishers Weekly.* Card's 1980 novel *Songmaster* generated praise as well. The lyrical tale, set in a futuristic galactic society that reveres those who sing, focuses on Ansset, a "Songbird" who is summoned to serve the emperor. The work encompasses "personal growth and exploration melded into a tale of interplanetary politics and court intrigue," asserted Richard A. Lupoff in *Washington Post Book World.* "*Songmaster* is a first-class job." Some of Card's other early works, however, including *Hot Sleep* and *A Planet Called Treason,* encountered critical censure for employing standard science fiction elements and for containing what some reviewers considered gratuitous violence. George R. R. Martin in the *Washington Post Book World* especially criticized Card's 1981 work, *Unaccompanied Sonata and Other Stories,* which he found filled "with death, pain, mutilation, dismemberment, all described in graphic detail." The volume includes such unfortunate characters as a malformed infant who is drowned in a toilet and whose body is sliced to pieces, and a woman whose breasts are chopped off and eaten. Apart from these negative evaluations, the general critical consensus of Card's early works was that they display imagination, intelligence, literary aptitude, and promise. "Card is a young, talented, and ambitious writer," conceded Martin.

In 1985 Card released *Ender's Game.* This novel began as a short story, which Card once described as "still the most popular and the most reprinted of my stories, and I still have people tell me that they like it better than the novel. . . . When I started working on the novel that became *Speaker for the Dead,* a breakthrough for me in that story was realizing that the main character should be Ender Wiggin. That made it a kind of sequel, although its plot had nothing to do with the original plot; it was just using a character. . . . I told the publisher, Tom Doherty, that I needed to do a novel version of 'Ender's Game' just to set up *Speaker for the Dead.* That's the only reason 'Ender's Game' ever became a novel."

Ender's Game concerns the training of Ender Wiggin, a six-year-old genius who is the Earth's only hope for victory over invading "bugger" aliens. While this plot appears to be standard science-fiction fare, *New York Times Book Review* critic Gerald Jonas observed that "Card has shaped this unpromising material into an affecting novel full of surprises that seem inevitable once they are explained." The difference, asserted Jonas and other critics, is in the character of Ender Wiggin, who remains sympathetic despite his acts of violence. A *Kirkus Reviews* contributor, for example, while noting the plot's inherent weakness, admitted that "the long passages focusing on Ender are nearly always enthralling," and concluded that *Ender's Game* "is altogether a much more solid, mature, and persuasive effort" than the author's previous work. Writing in *Analog,* Tom Easton noted that *Ender's Game* "succeeds because of its stress on the value of empathy," and *Washington Post Book World* reviewer Janrae Frank concluded that "Card is a writer of compassion."

Following the success of *Ender's Game,* its sequel, *Speaker for the Dead,* was hailed as "the most powerful work Card has produced" by Michael R. Collings in *Fantasy Review.* "*Speaker* not only completes *Ender's Game* but transcends it. . . . Read in conjunction with *Ender's Game, Speaker* demonstrates Card's mastery of character, plot, style, theme, and development." Ender Wiggin, now working as a "Speaker for the Dead," travels the galaxy to interpret the lives of the deceased for their families and neighbors; as he travels, he also searches for a home for the eggs of the lone surviving "hive queen" of the race he destroyed as a child. "Like *Game, Speaker* deals with issues of evil and empathy, though not in so polarized a way," observed Tom Easton in his *Analog* review. Some critics found an extra element of complexity in the "Ender" books; *Washington Post Book World* contributor Janrae Frank, for example, saw "quasi-religious images and themes" in the conclusions of both novels.

With the publication of 1991's *Xenocide,* Card's reputation as an unflinching explorer of both moral and intellectual issues was firmly established. In this novel, Card picks up the story of Ender as he works feverishly with his adopted Lusitanian family to neutralize a deadly virus. Many critics venture that with *Xeno-*

cide, Card relies more on the scientific ruminations of a multitude of contemplative characters rather than on a plot. "The real action is philosophical: long, passionate debates about ends and means among people who are fully aware that they may be deciding the fate of an entire species, entire worlds," observed Gerald Jonas in the *New York Times Book Review.*

In 1996 Card published *Children of the Mind,* the final volume of the "Ender" series. In this novel, Ender is already moving off the stage, playing a relatively minor part in the hectic attempt to avoid destruction of the planet Lusitania by the Starways Congress. Characters who take a more active role in this episode are Peter and Young Valentine, who are copies of Ender's brother and sister, and both products of Ender's mind. Also instrumental in Ender's current bid to save his adopted planet is Jane, a rather irascible Artificial Intelligence who has the uncanny knack of transcending the light-speed barrier. Together these three must roam the galaxy to find a new home for the three races of Lusitania that may all too soon become refugees. Meanwhile, they also try and convince politicians to halt the Starways Congress from destroying the planet. "Card's prose is powerful here," commented a reviewer for *Publishers Weekly,* "as is his consideration of mystical and quasi-religious themes." The same writer went on to wonder whether this book, "billed as the final Ender novel," would in fact be the last the reader hears of Ender or his world. "[T]his story leaves enough mysteries unexplored to justify another entry."

When Card once again approached that same world it was not from Ender's point of view, but from the perspective of a young orphan named Bean. In the first book in the four-part "Hegemon" series, 1999 *Ender's Shadow,* he again enters his parallel universe. *Library Journal's* Jackie Cassada noted that "Card returns to the world of his award-winning *Ender's Game* to tell the story of a child's desperate struggle for recognition and self-worth." The superhuman child in question, Bean, is taken from the streets of Rotterdam and sent to the Battle School to learn to fight the insect-like Buggers. Bean wins selection to the Battle School by his understanding of personal motivation—a skill that kept him alive in the mean streets when he was a starving child. At Battle School he learns how to command fleets for the war with the alien Buggers. When he comes into contact with Ender, Bean wants to understand what makes this larger-than-life figure tick. "Thus Bean's story is twofold," wrote a *Publishers*

Weekly contributor, "he learns to be a soldier, and to be human." Through Bean the reader learns about the formation of Ender's Dragon army and also about the last of Ender's games. "Everyone will be struck by the power of Card's children," concluded the same reviewer, "always more and less than human, perfect yet struggling, tragic yet hopeful, wondrous and strange." Cassada felt that Card's "superb storytelling and his genuine insight into the moral dilemmas that lead good people to commit questionable actions" blend together to make the novel a "priority purchase."

Questioned by Laura Ciporen in *Publishers Weekly* about his child protagonists, Card observed that, for children, life is very real. "They don't think of themselves as cute or sweet. I translate their thoughts from the language available to children into the language available to adults." For Card, children are every bit as complex as adults, and in fact their thoughts and fears—because they have fewer such to compare with—can be even more real than those of adults. Card's ability to portray young protagonists sympathetically yet not condescendingly is part of what makes him a popular writer for adults and juveniles alike.

The "Hegemon" series continues with *Shadow of the Hegemon* and *Shadow Puppets*. With the wars over and Ender off to colonize a new world, the children of the Battle School become increasingly important to those nations wishing to gobble up their neighbors, and Peter Wiggin rises to the position of hegemon, ruler of the Earth government. In *Shadow of the Hegemon*, Bean is second best of the Battle School children and aide to Wiggin; he is wooed for his powers by Wiggin's nemesis, Achilles, an unbalanced genius who wishes to conquer Earth. In *Shadow Puppet* Bean is forced to confront his mortality—his body grows too quickly, dooming him to an early death—and with his young wife Petra pregnant, he seeks an antidote against a similar fate for his unborn children. "The complexity and serious treatment of the book's young protagonists will attract many sophisticated YA readers," observed a writer for *Publishers Weekly* in a review of *Shadow of the Hegemon*, the reviewer further commenting that Card's "impeccable prose, fast pacing and political intrigue will appeal to adult fans of spy novels, thrillers and science fiction." *Library Journal* reviewer Jackie Cassada dubbed the same novel a "gripping story of children caught up in world-shaking events," while in *Booklist* Sally Estes praised *Shadow Puppets*

for Card's ability to maintain "the action, danger, and intrigue levels" of the previous series installments.

Card's storytelling techniques are further displayed in the "Tales of Alvin Maker" series. "This series began as an epic poem I was writing during graduate study at the University of Utah," Card once commented, "when I was heavily influenced by Spenser and playing games with allegory. That epic poem won a prize from the Utah State Institute of Fine Arts, but I realized that there is very little future for an epic poem in terms of reaching an audience and telling a story to real people, so I converted it and expanded it and, I think, deepened and enriched it into something much longer and larger." The series includes the novels *Seventh Son*, *Red Prophet*, *Prentice Alvin*, and *The Crystal City*.

The first novel in the "Tales of Alvin Maker" series, *Seventh Son*, "begins what may be a significant recasting in fantasy terms of the tall tale in America," wrote *Washington Post Book World* reviewer John Clute. Set in a pioneer America where the British Restoration never happened, where the Crown colonies exist alongside the states of Appalachia and New Sweden, and where folk magic is readily believed and practiced, *Seventh Son* follows the childhood of Alvin Miller, who has enormous magical potential because he is the seventh son of a seventh son. While *Fantasy Review* contributor Martha Soukup admitted that "this could easily have been another dull tale of the chosen child groomed to be the defender from evil," she asserted that Card's use of folk magic and vernacular language, along with strongly realized characters, creates in *Seventh Son* "more to care about here than an abstract magical battle."

"Because we know it is a dream of an America we do not deserve to remember, Orson Scott Card's luminous alternate history of the early 19th century continues to chill as it soothes," Clute explained in a review of *Red Prophet*, the second volume of Alvin's story. The novel traces Alvin's kidnaping by renegade Reds employed by "White Murderer" William Henry Harrison, who wishes to precipitate a massacre of the Shaw-Nee tribe. Alvin is rescued by the Red warrior Ta-Kumsaw, however, and learns of Native American ways even as he attempts to prevent the conflict caused by his supposed capture and murder. While "*Red Prophet* seems initially less ambitious" than its predecessor, covering a period of only one year, a *West Coast Review of*

Books contributor commented that, "In that year, Card creates episodes and images that stun with the power of their emotions." Sue Martin, however, believed that the setting was not enough to overcome the plot, which she described in the *Los Angeles Times Book Review* as "yet another tale of Dark versus Light." She conceded, however, that while Alvin "seems almost Christlike" in his ability to heal and bring people together, the allegory is drawn "without the proselytizing." *Booklist* writer Sally Estes summarized, "Harsher, bleaker, and more mystical than *Seventh Son*," Card's second volume displays his strong historical background, "keen understanding of religious experience, and, most of all, his mastery of the art of storytelling."

In *Prentice Alvin* and *Alvin Journeyman* Card explores Alvin's life during and following his apprenticeship. In the second volume Alvin's bad but similarly talented brother, Calvin, leaves for Europe, hoping to learn the arts of manipulation and domination from Napoleon Bonaparte. Alvin himself is forced to leave Vigor Church after being accused of improprieties by a girl dreaming of his passion. He returns to Hatrack River, his birthplace and the location of his apprenticeship, but has to defend himself in court. Written with the input of Card's fans via online forums, the story could have descended into mediocrity, as Martin Morse Wooster noted in the *Washington Post Book World.* However, Wooster declared, "Card appears to have resisted the encroachments of his admirers because *Alvin Journeyman* is a well-written, engaging entertainment."

Heartfire and *The Crystal City* continue the Alvin Maker adventures. *Heartfire* sees Alvin traveling to New England during Puritan times with historical friends such as John James Audubon, seeking to put an end to anti-witch laws. Meantime Alvin's wife, Peggy, who has the ability to see into the hearts of others, tries to put an end to slavery in the South and to stop Alvin's more malevolent brother, Calvin, from destroying her husband. In *The Crystal City* Alvin's ability to channel Native American and African magic works to his advantage as he works to heal the frontier's ills and create a peaceful utopia he calls the Crystal City. "Card's antebellum settings, dialogue and historical figures seem authentic and thoroughly researched," according to a writer for *Publishers Weekly,* who noted however that in *Heartfire* Card "is as occasionally windy and preachy as ever." Jackie Cassada, reviewing the novel in *Library Journal,*

concluded that the fifth installment to the "Tales of Alvin Maker" series "exhibits the same homespun charm of its predecessors." Noting that *The Crystal City* "still enchants," a *Publishers Weekly* contributor commented that "a large part of the appeal" of the sixth "Alvin Maker" installment "lies in the book's homegrown characters using their powers for ordinary purposes."

In 1992 Card introduced his "Homecoming" series with *The Memory of Earth,* a novel many critics found to be a mixture of philosophy, futuristic technology, and biblical lore. *Memory* opens on the planet Harmony, where for forty million years humans have been controlled by Oversoul, a powerful, global computer programmed to prevent humanity from destroying itself through needless wars. David E. Jones, in Chicago's *Tribune Books,* argued that "what Card gives us [in *The Memory of Earth*] is an interaction between supreme intelligence and human mental capability that is at once an intellectual exercise, a Biblical parable and a thoroughly enjoyable piece of storytelling."

Card joined forces with a newer science fiction voice, Kathryn H. Kidd, for the publication of *Lovelock* in 1994. The title shares its name with the central character, a genetically enhanced monkey, who is trained to record the activities of important persons for posterity. Realizing his own servitude and the indifferent neglect of his masters, *Lovelock* plots his escape. The work was welcomed by several critics as a solid blending of two talents. "Masterful," commented Maureen F. McHugh in the *Washington Post Book World,* who found the character of Lovelock to be, "Clearly as nasty and clever as a genetically enhanced capuchin monkey could be expected to be." McHugh continued, "None of Card's previous tellings has possessed the satirical bite we see here, which makes for a welcome change."

Card concludes his "Homecoming" series with the fourth and fifth novels, *Earthfall* and *Earthborn.* In *Earthfall,* the wandering humans return from Harmony to Earth to continue the species when it appears Harmony is about to self destruct. They meet two new species who have evolved in the absence of humans and must make peace with them. "As in other Card novels, plotting is intricate, characters are multifaceted, and strange creatures co-exist with humans," observed Pam Carlson in *Voice of Youth Advocates. Earthborn* focuses on the three groups from *Earthfall* who are speaking a common language but who differ in their habitat. The sky people are able to fly as angels; the earth people or diggers are treated as slaves; the returned humans from Harmony are known as the middle people. As Gerald Jonas noted in the *New York Times Book Review,* "As in all Mr. Card's novels, the characters spend . . . time talking about what they are going to do and why they are going to do it." The critic continued, "these long philosophical discussions crackle with tension." While several reviewers appreciated the "Homecoming" series, the concluding volume received mixed reviews.

Though firmly established as a successful author of science fiction, Card has not limited himself to that genre, publishing throughout his career numerous works of nonfiction, drama, and, most notably, historical fiction. In *A Woman of Destiny* (later published as *Saints*), for example, he returns to the subject of the life of Joseph Smith, first touched upon in *Seventh Son. A Woman of Destiny* offers an account of the lives of Smith, the founder of Mormonism, and Dinah Kirkham, a (fictional) English woman who is converted to Mormonism and becomes Smith's polygamous wife. When Smith is murdered in 1844, Kirkham escapes with a group of fellow Mormons to Utah, where she becomes a staunch leader as well as one of the wives of Brigham Young, Smith's successor as president of the Mormon Church. *Los Angeles Times Book Review* critic Kristiana Gregory pronounced *Saints* an "engrossing epic," stressing that Card "is a powerful storyteller."

Card's *Treasure Box* is billed as a mainstream novel, yet it contains elements of the supernatural. Quentin Fears loses his beloved older sister Lizzy as a young boy. However, he continues to confide in her following her death. A millionaire, following his sellout of his computer firm, he meets his true love, Madeleine, at a party and marries her. But there are gaps in her background, and when he finally meets his in-laws at a spooky mansion in upstate New York, events unravel following Madeleine's insistence that Quentin open a box supposedly containing her inheritance. 1998's *Homebody* is another mainstream supernatural fantasy, combining elements of spirituality, the occult, and psychological insight in a haunted house tale. *Homebody* tells the story of Don Lark who, grieving the death of his two-year-old daughter, sets out to renovate the Bellamy House, a grand old Victorian mansion in a terrible state of disrepair. His three elderly neighbors warn him about the house's dark powers, but he goes

forward with his project and becomes attached to a squatter who lives there. She is the occult key to the violent history of the house as a brothel and speakeasy. A writer for *Kirkus Reviews* assessed the novel as "solid but undistinguished work, not high in either tension or in depth." A *Publishers Weekly* reviewer found more to like, saying that the novel has "great potential that shines through its superfluous detail," and describing it as "a powerful tale of healing and redemption that skillfully balances supernatural horrors with spiritual uplift."

Card turns from the realms of the haunted to those of fairy tales with *Enchantment,* a blending of the story of Sleeping Beauty with Russian mythology. Ten-year-old Ivan is both frightened by and attracted to a lovely woman frozen in time in the midst of a Russian forest. A decade later and now an up-and-coming track star, Ivan returns to the forest to set this bewitched woman free. Drawn back into the ninth-century world of his princess, Ivan discovers that his modern-day talents do not stand him in good stead in his desperate battle to defeat the mythical witch Baba Yaga and claim his princess. Ivan takes Princess Katerina back to the modern world for a time, and the pair learns each other's powers before returning to battle the witch. A *Publishers Weekly* reviewer felt that Card's "new look at a classic tale is clever . . . [due to] adding attractive whimsical twists and cultural confluences to a familiar story."

In *Stone Tables* Card returns to biblical themes, telling the story of Moses and retelling Exodus in a novel "that exhibits the same profound and compassionate understanding of human nature that marks his best sf and fantasy efforts," according to a contributor to *Publishers Weekly.* Card puts the focus here on the difficult relationship between Moses and his siblings. With *Sarah* Card inaugurated a new series, "Women of Genesis." In Card's retelling, Sarah is to become a priestess of Asherah until she meets a man named Abram, a mystic and desert wanderer. Sarah realizes that her destiny is tied up with Abram's and she waits eight years for his return, only to have many more years of a childless marriage test her belief in Abram's God. "Card adds depth, understanding, and human frailty to the woman who became known as Sarah," wrote Melanie C. Duncan in a *Library Journal* review. Duncan felt the novel "will attract secular readers as well." A reviewer for *Publishers Weekly* maintained that Card's rendering of Sarah as "a wise and virtuous figure who struggles to have the unflinching faith of Abraham," and his portrait of Biblical life and times, creates a "playfully speculative novel" that "succeeds in bringing Sarah's oft-overlooked character into vivid relief."

In a critique of the author's 1990 story collection, *Maps in a Mirror: The Short Fiction of Orson Scott Card, Analog* reviewer Easton characterized Card as "an intensely thoughtful, self-conscious, religious, and community-oriented writer." In spite of such critical acclaim and the numerous awards his writing has earned, Card seems to prefer a simpler description of himself; as he told the DeCandidos, "I'm Kristine's husband, Geoffrey and Emily and Charlie's dad, I'm a Mormon, and I'm a science fiction writer, in that order." Replying to a query by Ciporen of *Publishers Weekly* as to why he writes mainly science fiction, Card replied: "The truth is, SF is the most powerful genre available right now. Mainstream literature is so stultifyingly rigid. I don't just want to talk to people who believed everything their English teacher told them. I want to reach people who read books for the sheer pleasure of it, because those are the people who are open to having their lives changed by what they read."

BIOGRAPHICAL AND CRITICAL SOURCES:

BOOKS

Collings, Michael R., *Storyteller: Official Guide to the Works of Orson Scott Card,* Overlook Connection Press (Woodstock, CA), 2001.

Collings, Michael R., and Boden Clarke, *The Work of Orson Scott Card: An Annotated Bibliography and Guide,* Borgo Press (San Bernardino, CA), 1995.

Contemporary Literary Criticism, Gale (Detroit, MI), Volume 44, 1987, Volume 47, 1988, Volume 50, 1988.

Contemporary Popular Writers, St. James Press (Detroit, MI), 1997.

Tyson, Edith S., *Orson Scott Card: Writer of the Terrible Choice,* Scarecrow Press (Lanham, MD), 2003.

PERIODICALS

Analog, July, 1983, p. 103; July, 1985, Tom Easton, review of *Ender's Game,* p. 180; June, 1986, Tom Easton, review of *Speaker for the Dead,* p. 183;

mid-December, 1987; September, 1988, p. 179; August, 1989, p. 175; January, 1990, p. 305; March, 1991, p. 184; mid-December, 1991; January, 1996, Tom Easton, review of *Pastwatch,* p. 277; June, 1996, p. 145; February, 2003, Tom Easton, review of *Shadow Puppets,* p. 136.

Booklist, December 15, 1985, p. 594; December 15, 1987, Sally Estes, review of *Red Prophet;* December 1, 1995, p. 586; June 1 & 15, 1996, Roland Green, review of *Pastwatch,* p. 1629; July, 2002, Sally Estes, review of *Shadow Puppets,* p. 1796.

Economist, September 5, 1987, p. 92.

Fantasy Review, April, 1986, Michael R. Collings, "Adventure and Allegory," p. 20; June, 1987, Martha Soukup, review of *Seventh Son;* July/August, 1987.

Kirkus Reviews, December 1, 1980, p. 1542; November 1, 1984, p. 1021; May 1, 1994, p. 594; June 15, 1995, p. 864; June 15, 1996, p. 839; February 2, 1998, review of *Homebody;* June 15, 2002, review of *Shadow Puppets,* p. 846.

Kliatt, April, 1991, p. 15.

Library Journal, February 15, 1989, p. 179; November 15, 1990; September 1, 1991; October 15, 1991; January, 1994, p. 172; June 15, 1994, p. 99; May 15, 1995, p. 99; December, 1995, p. 163; July, 1996, p. 154; April 15, 1998, Jackie Cassada, review of *Stone Tablets,* p. 111; August, 1998, Jackie Cassada, review of *Heartfire,* p. 140; September 14, 1999, Jackie Cassada, review of *Ender's Shadow,* p. 115; November 1, 2000, Melanie C. Duncan, review of *Sarah,* p. 60; December, 2000, Jackie Cassada, review of *Shadow of the Hegemon,* p. 196; September 15, 2003, Jackie Cassada, review of *First Meetings,* p. 96.

Locus, April, 1991, p. 15; February, 1992, pp. 17, 57; May, 1994, p. 48; February, 1995, p. 17.

Los Angeles Times Book Review, September 28, 1980; March 6, 1983; July 22, 1984, Kristiana Gregory, review of *A Woman of Destiny,* p. 8; February 3, 1985; August 9, 1987; February 14, 1988, Sue Martin, "Battling the Natives along the Mississippi"; July 20, 1990.

Magazine of Fantasy and Science Fiction, January, 1980, p. 35.

New York Times Book Review, June 16, 1985, Gerald Jonas, review of *Ender's Game,* p. 18; October 18, 1987, p. 36; September 1, 1991, Gerald Jonas, review of *Xenocide,* p. 13; March 15, 1992; May 8, 1994, p. 25; July 9, 1995, Gerald Jonas, review of *Earthborn,* p. 18.

Publishers Weekly, December 4, 1978, review of *Capitol,* p. 62; January 2, 1981, p. 49; January 24,

1986, p. 64; December 25, 1987, p. 65; September 16, 1988; May 19, 1989, p. 72; August 17, 1990, p. 55; November 30, 1990, interview with Card, pp. 54-55; June 14, 1991, p. 48; June 20, 1994, p. 97; January 30, 1995, p. 89; April 10, 1995, p. 58; August 7, 1995, p. 445; January 22, 1996, review of *Pastwatch,* pp. 61-62; June 24, 1996, review of *Children of the Mind,* pp. 45, 49; August 12, 1996, p. 20; February 2, 1998, review of *Homebody,* p. 79; June 29, 1998, review of *Heartfire,* p. 40; September 28, 1998, p. 77; March 8, 1999, review of *Enchantment,* p. 52; July 5, 1999, review of *Ender's Shadow,* p. 63; November 1, 1999, p. 48; September 11, 2000, review of *Sarah,* p. 71; November 20, 2000, Laura Ciporen, "PW Talks with Orson Scott Card," p. 51, and review of *Shadow of the Hegemon,* p. 50; July 15, 2002, review of *Shadow Puppets,* p. 59; October 27, 2003, review of *The Crystal City,* p. 48.

School Library Journal, January, 1991, p. 123; November, 1991; June, 2001, Jan Tarasovic, review of *Shadow of the Hegemon,* p. 183; January, 2004, Mara Alpert, review of *First Meetings,* p. 124.

Science Fiction and Fantasy Book Review, April, 1979, p. 27; December, 1979, p. 155; June, 1983, p. 21.

Science Fiction Review, August, 1979; February, 1986, p. 14.

SF Chronicle, June, 1988, p. 50.

Tribune Books (Chicago, IL), March 1, 1990; March 1, 1992, David E. Jones, "Trapped in a Serial Universe."

Voice of Youth Advocates, October, 1992, p. 236; August, 1995, Pam Carlson, review of *Earthfall* and *Earthborn,* p. 167.

Washington Post Book World, August 24, 1980, Richard A. Lupoff, "Beasts, Songbirds, and Wizards," p. 6; January 25, 1981, George R. R. Martin, "Scanning the Stars of the Short Story," pp. 9, 11; March 27, 1983; February 23, 1986, Janrae Frank, "War of the Worlds," p. 10; August 30, 1987, John Clute, review of *Seventh Son;* February 28, 1988, John Clute, review of *Red Prophet;* March 19, 1992; September 25, 1994, Maureen F. McHugh, review of *Lovelock,* p. 14; September 24, 1995, Martin Morse Wooster, review of *Alvin Journeyman.*

West Coast Review of Books, March, 1984; July, 1986; no. 2, 1987; no. 4, 1988, review of *Red Prophet.*

Wilson Library Bulletin, February, 1994, p. 70.

Writer's Digest, October, 1986, p. 26; November, 1986, p. 37; December, 1986, p. 32; May, 1989, p. 31.*

ONLINE

Fantastic Fiction http://www.fantasticfiction.co.uk/ (September 16, 2003).

Hatrack River (Orson Card Official Web site), http://www.hatrack.com/ (February 9, 2001).

Nauvoo Web site, http://www.nauvoo.com/ (June 28, 2004), Card's Latter-Day Saints site.

Ornery American, http://www.ornery.org/ (June 28, 2004).

*   *   *

CLARK, Mary Higgins 1929(?)-

PERSONAL: Born December 24, 1929 (some sources say 1931), in New York, NY; daughter of Luke Joseph (a restaurant owner) and Nora C. (a buyer; maiden name, Durkin) Higgins; married Warren F. Clark (an airline executive), December 26, 1949 (died September 26, 1964); married Raymond Charles Ploetz (an attorney), August 8, 1978 (marriage annulled); married John J. Conheeney (in business), November 30, 1996; children: Marilyn, Warren, David, Carol, Patricia. *Education:* Attended Villa Maria Academy, Ward Secretarial School, and New York University; Fordham University, B.A. (summa cum laude), 1979. *Politics:* Republican. *Religion:* Roman Catholic. *Hobbies and other interests:* Traveling, skiing, tennis, playing piano.

ADDRESSES: Home—Saddle River, NJ; and 210 Central Park South, New York, NY 10019. *Agent*—Eugene H. Winick, McIntosh & Otis, Inc., 475 Fifth Ave., New York, NY 10017.

CAREER: Writer. Remington Rand, New York, NY, advertising assistant, 1946; Pan American Airlines, flight attendant, 1949-50; Robert G. Jennings, radio scriptwriter and producer, 1965-70; Aerial Communications, New York, NY, vice president, partner, creative director, and producer of radio programming, 1970-80; David J. Clark Enterprises, New York, NY, chair of board and creative director, 1980—. Chair, International Crime Writers Congress, 1988.

MEMBER: Mystery Writers of America (president, 1987; member of board of directors), Authors Guild, Authors League of America, American Academy of

Mary Higgins Clark

Arts and Sciences, American Society of Journalists and Authors, American Irish Historical Society (member of executive council).

AWARDS, HONORS: New Jersey Author Award, 1969, for *Aspire to the Heavens,* 1977, for *Where Are the Children?* and 1978, for *A Stranger Is Watching;* Grand Prix de Litterature Policiere (France), 1980; Women of Achievement Award, Federation of Women's Clubs in New Jersey; Irish Woman of the Year Award, Irish-American Heritage and Cultural Week Committee of the Board of Education of the City of New York; Gold Medal of Honor Award, American-Irish Historical Society; Spirit of Achievement Award, Albert Einstein College of Medicine of Yeshiva University; Gold Medal in Education, National Arts Club; Horatio Alger Award, 1997; thirteen honorary doctorates, including Villanova University, 1983, Rider College, 1986, Stonehill College and Marymount Manhattan College, 1992, Chestnut Hill, Manhattan College, and St. Peter's College, 1993; named Dame of the Order of St. Gregory the Great, Dame of Malta, and Dame of the Holy Sepulcher of Jerusalem.

WRITINGS:

Aspire to the Heavens: A Biography of George Washington, Meredith Press (New York, NY), 1969.
Where Are the Children? (also see below), Simon & Schuster (New York, NY), 1975.
A Stranger Is Watching (also see below), Simon & Schuster (New York, NY), 1978.
The Cradle Will Fall (also see below), Simon & Schuster (New York, NY), 1980.
A Cry in the Night, Simon & Schuster (New York, NY), 1982.
Stillwatch, Simon & Schuster (New York, NY), 1984.
(With Thomas Chastain and others) *Murder in Manhattan,* Morrow (New York, NY), 1986.
Weep No More, My Lady, Simon & Schuster (New York, NY), 1987.
(Editor) *Murder on the Aisle: The 1987 Mystery Writers of America Anthology,* Simon & Schuster (New York, NY), 1987.
While My Pretty One Sleeps (also see below), Simon & Schuster (New York, NY), 1989.
The Anastasia Syndrome and Other Stories, Simon & Schuster (New York, NY), 1989.
Loves Music, Loves to Dance (also see below), Simon & Schuster (New York, NY), 1991.
All around the Town (also see below) Simon & Schuster (New York, NY), 1992.
Missing in Manhattan: The Adams Round Table, Longmeadow Press (Stamford, CT), 1992.
Mists from Beyond: Twenty-two Ghost Stories and Tales from the Other Side, New American Library/Dutton (New York, NY), 1993.
I'll Be Seeing You, Simon & Schuster (New York, NY), 1993.
Remember Me, Simon & Schuster (New York, NY), 1994.
The Lottery Winner: Alvirah and Willy Stories, Simon & Schuster (New York, NY), 1994.
Silent Night: A Novel, Simon & Schuster (New York, NY), 1995.
Mary Higgins Clark: Three Complete Novels (includes *A Stranger Is Watching, The Cradle Will Fall,* and *Where Are the Children?*), Wings Books (New York, NY), 1995.
Let Me Call You Sweetheart, Simon & Schuster (New York, NY), 1995.
Moonlight Becomes You: A Novel, Simon & Schuster (New York, NY), 1996.
Mary Higgins Clark, Three New York Times Bestsellers (includes *While My Pretty One Sleeps, Loves*

Music, Loves to Dance, and *All around the Town*)
Wings Books (New York, NY), 1996.

My Gal Sunday, Simon & Schuster (New York, NY),
1996.

Pretend You Don't See Her, Simon & Schuster (New
York, NY), 1997.

(Editor) *The Plot Thickens,* Pocket Books (New York,
NY), 1997.

All through the Night, Simon & Schuster (New York,
NY), 1998.

You Belong to Me, Simon & Schuster (New York, NY),
1998.

We'll Meet Again, Simon & Schuster (New York, NY),
1999.

Before I Say Goodbye, Simon & Schuster (New York,
NY), 2000.

(With daughter, Carol Higgins Clark) *Deck the Halls,*
Simon & Schuster (New York, NY), 2000.

On the Street Where You Live, Simon & Schuster (New
York, NY), 2001.

(With daughter, Carol Higgins Clark) *He Sees You
When You're Sleeping,* Simon & Schuster (New
York, NY), 2001.

Kitchen Privileges (memoir), Simon & Schuster (New
York, NY), 2002.

Daddy's Little Girl, Simon & Schuster (New York,
NY), 2002.

Mount Vernon Love Story, Simon & Schuster (New
York, NY), 2002.

The Second Time Around, Simon & Schuster (New
York, NY), 2003.

Nighttime Is My Time, Thorndike Press (Waterville,
ME), 2004.

Contributor to books, including *The Best "Saturday
Evening Post" Stories,* 1962; *I, Witness,* Times Books
(New York, NY), 1978; and *The International Association of Crime Writers Presents Bad Behavior,* Harcourt
Brace (San Diego, CA), 1995. Author of syndicated
radio dramas. Writer, with John Rutter, of the television story *Haven't We Met Before?* in 2002. Contributor of stories to periodicals, including *Saturday
Evening Post, Redbook, McCall's,* and *Family Circle.*

ADAPTATIONS: A Stranger Is Watching was filmed
by Metro-Goldwyn-Mayer in 1982; *The Cradle Will
Fall* was shown on CBS-TV as a "Movie of the Week"
in 1984; *A Cry in the Night* was filmed by Rosten
Productions in 1985; *Where Are the Children?* was
filmed by Columbia in 1986; *Stillwatch* was broadcast
on CBS-TV in 1987; Ellipse, a French production

company, produced *Weep No More My Lady, A Cry in
the Night* (starring Clark's daughter Carol), and two
stories from *The Anastasia Syndrome.* Many of Clark's
books have been adapted as sound recordings. Filmed
adaptations of *Lucky Day, Loves Music, Loves to
Dance, You Belong to Me, All around the Town, Pretend You Don't See Her,* and *Haven't We Met Before?*
were released as *Mary Higgins Clark Mystery Movie
Collection,* Lion's Gate Home Productions, 2004.

Simon & Schuster planned to rerelease all of Clark's
works in e-book format.

SIDELIGHTS: "You can set your bestseller clock each
spring for a new Mary Higgins Clark winner," observed *Publishers Weekly* contributor Dick Donahue in
2001. The prolific mystery author began her writing
career as a newly widowed mother of five and has
instilled her passion for suspense stories in her children, including daughter Carol, also a best-selling
novelist. Clark's stories have proven so popular that
her publisher, Simon & Schuster, signed her to a then-
record-breaking $11.4 million contract in 1989 to pro-
duce four novels and a short story collection and in
1992 to a $35 million contract for five novels and a
memoir. By 2000, Clark had over fifty million titles in
print and enjoyed bestseller status around the world.

Clark had always intended to become a writer. "When
I was fifteen I was picking out clothes that I would
wear when I became a successful writer," she told
Powells.com interviewer Dave Welch. "I was sure I'd
make it." For the first nine years of her first marriage,
Clark wrote short stories. "The first one was rejected
for six years," she confided to Welch. "Then it sold
for $100." Confronted with the daunting task of sup-
porting five young children after the early death of her
husband, Clark turned to suspense novels. Her first,
Where Are the Children?, became a bestseller in 1975,
earning more than $100,000 in paperback royalties.
She followed that with another thriller, *A Stranger Is
Watching,* which earned more than $1 million in paper-
back rights and was filmed by Metro-Goldwyn-Mayer
in 1982. For Clark, this meant financial security. Her
writing earnings "changed my life in the nicest way,"
she told Bina Bernard in *People.* "It took all the chok-
ing sensation out of paying for the kids' schools."

The key to Clark's popularity, according to several
critics, is her technique. Jean M. White of the *Washington Post* maintained that Clark "is a master storyteller

who builds her taut suspense in a limited time frame," noting that *Where Are the Children?* takes place in one day and *A Stranger Is Watching* in three. Carolyn Banks, moreover, pointed out in the *Washington Post* that there is a kind of "Mary Higgins Clark formula" that readers both expect and enjoy: "There are no ambiguities in any Clark book. We know whom and what to root for, and we do. Similarly, we boo and hiss or gasp when the author wants us to. Clark is a master manipulator." Although Clark wants to provide her readers with entertainment and romance, she once commented: "I feel a good suspense novel can and should hold a mirror up to society and make a social comment."

Clark's style is to write about "terror lurking beneath the surface of everyday life," observed White. She "writes about ordinary people suddenly caught up in frightening situations as they ride a bus or vacuum the living room," such as the characters in *Loves Music, Loves to Dance,* who encounter a murderer when they agree to participate in an experiment involving newspaper personal ads. Other stories play on readers' fears of unfamiliar or undesirable situations. For example, Clark explores mental illness in *Loves Music, Loves to Dance,* in which the killer's behavior is caused by a personality disorder, and in *All around the Town,* in which the main character is afflicted with a multiple personality disorder attributed to severe sexual abuse in her childhood. In *I'll Be Seeing You* Clark's characters find themselves victimized by villains more knowledgeable than they in the issues of genetic manipulation and in-vitro fertilization. Many of the events and details of Clark's stories come from the lives of her friends and family, news events, and even her own experiences. Clark told *New York Times* interviewer Shirley Horner that the burglary the heroine interrupts in *Stillwatch* was based on break-ins Clark herself had endured. "Everything that a writer experiences goes up in the mental attic," she told Horner.

In Clark's more recent novels, nice people vanquish the powers of darkness with great flair. In *Moonlight Becomes You,* Maggie Holloway, a young photographer and amateur sculptor, visits her deceased stepmother's home in Newport, Rhode Island, in order to investigate the woman's mysterious death. Maggie's search leads her to a nursing home plagued by a series of sudden deaths, and she begins to suspect that she, too, is being targeted by the killer who does not want her to expose his diabolical plot. A reviewer for *Booklist*

acknowledged that, "though this is not her finest book, Clark's popularity will surely put *Moonlight* on the lists."

In her short-story collection *My Gal Sunday,* Clark introduces a new detective team. Henry Parker Britland, IV, is a former U.S. president enjoying an early retirement, and his wife, Sandra—nicknamed "Sunday"—has just been elected to Congress and appointed the darling of the media. Henry and Sunday specialize in solving crimes that occur among their friends in political society. In one story, when Henry's former secretary of state is indicted for the murder of his mistress, Henry and Sunday determine he is willing to take the fall for a crime of passion he did not commit.

In *Pretend You Don't See Her* Clark takes on the federal witness protection program. While working as a real estate agent in Manhattan, Lacey Farrell witnesses a client's murder and is given a new name and a new identity by the government. However, merely changing her name does not protect her from the web of danger and deceit that surrounds the crime. As new clues emerge, Lacey realizes that a link exists between her family and the murder. In the meantime, romance enters her life and leads her to embark on a perilous journey to reclaim her old identity. A *Booklist* reviewer found the story "briskly paced," though with few surprises. Kimberly Marlowe noted in the *New York Times Book Review* that in her fifteenth novel, Clark covers "a lot of ground . . . life, death threats and the perfect date."

By the late 1990s some critics began to suggest that Clark's writing was growing rather stale. In a review of *You Belong to Me* a *Publishers Weekly* contributor commented that the book gives fans "the page-flipping perils they expect without challenging them . . . one whit." However, Clark's popularity remained as strong as ever among her fans. *We'll Meet Again,* in which a greedy head of a Connecticut H.M.O. is murdered, shot straight to the top of bestseller lists after just one week. *New York Times Book Review* contributor Marilyn Stasio appreciated "the diabolical plot that Clark prepares so carefully and executes with such relish," while *Booklist* reviewer Jenny McLarin deemed *We'll Meet Again* "first-rate entertainment." *Before I Say Goodbye,* also an immediate top-seller, was hailed as one of Clark's "page-turning best" by *Booklist* contributor Kristine Huntley. And *On the Street Where You Live,* Clark's third novel in a row to capture the number-one slot in its first week, intrigued critics with its premise: that a serial killer from a century past might be stalking young women in a present-day New Jersey resort town. "Clark's prose ambles as usual," commented a reviewer for *Publishers Weekly,* "but it takes readers where they want to go—deep into an old-fashioned tale of a damsel in delicious distress."

When reviewing *The Second Time Around* for *Booklist,* Mary Frances Wilkens commented: "Clark isn't the subtlest crime writer, but she knows how to spin an intriguing tale." A *Publishers Weekly* reviewer echoed that sentiment: "There's something special about Clark's thrillers, and it's not just the gentleness with which the bestselling writer approaches her often lurid subject matter . . . Special above all is the compassion she extends to her characters—heroines, villains and supporting cast alike."

Writing has become a family affair for the Clarks. Daughter Carol Higgins Clark's first novel, *Decked,* appeared on the paperback bestseller list at the same time as her mother's *I'll Be Seeing You* was departing the hardcover list after seventeen weeks. Reacting to critics who suggest that Clark may have contributed to her daughter's books, Sarah Booth Conroy noted in the *Washington Post* that Clark "writes deadly serious novels about the sort of chilling fears that come to women in the middle of the night" while her daughter "spoons in a bit of bawdy, a soupçon of slapstick." Carol Higgins Clark has, however, exerted some influence on her mother's writing: she is responsible for restoring to readers two of Clark's most popular characters, Alvirah, a cleaning woman who wins the lottery, and Alvirah's husband, Willy. When they first appeared in a short story, Alvirah was poisoned and Clark planned to finish her off, until Carol convinced her mother to allow Alvirah to recover. The two have since become recurring characters and are featured in *The Lottery Winner: Alvirah and Willy Stories,* published in 1994.

Mother and daughter took their literary bond to a further level with *Deck the Halls,* a mystery novel they co-wrote that featured both Alvirah and Carol Higgins Clark's popular sleuth, Regan Reilly.

BIOGRAPHICAL AND CRITICAL SOURCES:

BOOKS

Bestsellers '89, number 4, Gale (Detroit, MI), 1989.
Newsmakers 2000, Gale (Detroit, MI), 2000.
St. James Guide to Young Adult Writers, second edition, St. James Press (Detroit, MI), 1999.

PERIODICALS

Best Sellers, December, 1984.
Booklist, October 15, 1994, p. 371; April 15, 1996; April, 1998, Mary Frances Wilkens, review of *You Belong to Me,* p. 1277; September 15, 1998, Kathleen Hughes, review of *All Through the Night,* p. 172; April 15, 1999, Jenny McLarin, review of *We'll Meet Again,* p. 1468; April 15, 2000, Kristine Huntley, review of *Before I Say Goodbye,* p. 1500; November 1, 2000, Stephanie Zvirin, review of *Deck the Halls,* p. 492; April 15, 2001, Kristine Huntley, review of *On the Street Where You Live,* p. 1508; May 1, 2003, Mary Frances Wilkens, review of *The Second Time Around,* p. 1538.
Chicago Tribune, September 20, 1987; July 31, 1989.
Cosmopolitan, May, 1989.
English Journal, December, 1979, p. 80.
Good Housekeeping, November, 1996, pp. 23-24.
Kirkus Review, November 1, 2000, review of *Deck the Halls,* p. 1519.
Newsweek, June 30, 1980.
New Yorker, August 4, 1980; June 27, 1994, p. 91.
New York Times, January 22, 1982; December 6, 1989; May 18, 1997.
New York Times Book Review, May 14, 1978; November 14, 1982; May 2, 1993, p. 22; December 15, 1996; May 5, 1996; April 19, 1998, Marilyn Stasio, review of *You Belong to Me,* p. 30; June 29, 1997; May 23, 1999, Marilyn Stasio, review of *We'll Meet Again;* April 16, 2000, Marilyn Stasio, review of *Before I Say Goodbye,* p. 32.
Observer (London, England), May 7, 1978, p. 34.
People, March 6, 1978; May 9, 1994, p. 35; December 16, 1996, pp. 54-56.
Progressive, May, 1978, p. 45.
Publishers Weekly, May 19, 1989; October 14, 1996, pp. 28-29; March 30, 1998, review of *You Belong to Me,* p. 70; September 14, 1998, review of *All through the Night,* p. 52; October 30, 2000, review of *Deck the Halls,* p. 47; April 2, 2001, review of *On the Street Where You Live,* p. 41; April 30, 2001, "Clark's Spark Marks," p. 20; April 7, 2003, review of *Second Time Around,* p. 47.
Tribune Books (Chicago, IL), June 8, 1980.
Wall Street Journal, May 29, 1996, p. A16; December 7, 1998, Tom Nolan, review of *All through the Night,* p. A28; December 11, 2000, Tom Nolan, review of *Deck the Halls,* p. A38.
Washington Post, May 19, 1980; July 17, 1980; October 18, 1982; August 10, 1987.

Powells.com, http://www.powells.com/ (January 12, 2001), "Mary Higgins Clark Reveals."

Writers Write, http://www.writerswrite.com/ (January 12, 2001), "A Conversation with Mary Higgins Clark."*

*   *   *

COETZEE, J(ohn) M(axwell) 1940-

PERSONAL: Born February 9, 1940, in Cape Town, South Africa; son of an attorney (father) and a schoolteacher (mother); married, 1963 (divorced, 1980); children: Nicholas, Gisela. *Education:* University of Cape Town, B.A., 1960, M.A., 1963; University of Texas, Austin, Ph.D., 1969.

ADDRESSES: Home—P.O. Box 92, Rondebosch, Cape Province 7700, South Africa. *Agent*—Peter Lampack, 551 Fifth Ave., New York, NY 10017.

CAREER: International Business Machines (IBM), London, England, applications programmer, 1962-63; International Computers, Bracknell, Berkshire, England, systems programmer, 1964-65; State University of New York at Buffalo, NY, assistant professor, 1968-71, Butler Professor of English, 1984, 1986; University of Cape Town, Cape Town, South Africa, lecturer in English, 1972-82, professor of general literature, 1983—. Johns Hopkins University, Hinkley Professor of English, 1986, 1989; Harvard University, visiting professor of English, 1991.

MEMBER: International Comparative Literature Association, Modern Language Association of America.

AWARDS, HONORS: CNA Literary Award, 1977, for *In the Heart of the Country;* CNA Literary Award, James Tait Black Memorial Prize, and Geoffrey Faber Award, all 1980, all for *Waiting for the Barbarians;* CNA Literary Award, Booker-McConnell Prize, and Prix Femina Etranger, all 1984, all for *The Life and Times of Michael K;* D. Litt., University of Strathclyde, Glasgow, 1985; Jerusalem Prize for the Freedom of the Individual in Society, 1987; Sunday Express Book

J. M. Coetzee

of the Year Prize, 1990, for *Age of Iron;* Premio Modello, 1994, and *Irish Times* International Fiction Prize, 1995, for *The Master of Petersburg;* Booker Prize, National Book League and Commonwealth Writer's Prize: Best Novel, for *Disgrace;* Life Fellow, University of Cape Town; Nobel Prize in Literature, 2003.

WRITINGS:

NOVELS

Dusklands (contains two novellas, *The Vietnam Project* and *The Narrative of Jacobus Coetzee*), Ravan Press (Johannesburg, South Africa), 1974, Penguin Books (New York, NY), 1985.

From the Heart of the Country, Harper (New York, NY), 1977, published as *In the Heart of the Country,* Secker & Warburg (London, England), 1977.

Waiting for the Barbarians, Secker & Warburg (London, England), 1980, Penguin Books (New York, NY), 1982.

The Life and Times of Michael K., Secker & Warburg (London, England), 1983, Viking (New York, NY), 1984.

Foe, Viking (New York, NY), 1987.

Age of Iron, Random House (New York, NY), 1990.

The Master of Petersburg, Viking (New York, NY), 1994.

(With others) *The Lives of Animals,* edited with an introduction by Amy Gutmann, Princeton University Press (Princeton, NJ), 1999.

Disgrace, Viking (New York, NY), 1999.

Elizabeth Costello, Viking (New York, NY), 2003.

OTHER

(Translator) Marcellus Emants, *A Posthumous Confession,* Twayne (Boston, MA), 1976.

(Translator) Wilma Stockenstroem, *The Expedition to the Baobab Tree,* Faber (London, England), 1983.

(Editor, with Andre Brink) *A Land Apart: A Contemporary South African Reader,* Viking (New York, NY), 1987.

White Writing: On the Culture of Letters in South Africa (essays), Yale University Press (New Haven, CT), 1988.

Doubling the Point: Essays and Interviews, edited by David Attwell, Harvard University Press (Cambridge, MA), 1992.

(With Graham Swift, John Lanchester, and Ian Jack) *Food: The Vital Stuff,* Penguin (New York, NY), 1995.

Giving Offense: Essays on Censorship, University of Chicago Press (Chicago, IL), 1996.

Boyhood: Scenes from Provincial Life, Viking (New York, NY), 1997.

(With Bill Reichblum) *What Is Realism?,* Bennington College (Bennington, VT), 1997.

(With Dan Cameron and Carolyn Christov-Bakargiev) *William Kentridge,* Phaidon (London, England), 1999.

Stranger Shores: Literary Essays, 1986-1999, Viking (New York, NY), 2001.

The Humanities in Africa/Die Geisteswissenschaften in Afrika, Carl Friedrich von Siemens Stiftung (Munich, Germany), 2001.

Youth: Scenes from Provincial Life II, Viking (New York, NY), 2002.

(Editor) *Landscape with Rowers: Poetry from the Netherlands,* Princeton University Press (Princeton, NJ), 2003.

Contributor of introduction, *The Confusions of Young Törless,* by Robert Musil, Penguin (New York, NY), 2001. Contributor of reviews to periodicals, including *New York Review of Books.*

ADAPTATIONS: An adaptation of *In the Heart of the Country* was filmed as *Dust,* by ICA (England), 1986.

SIDELIGHTS: J. M. Coetzee, recipient of the 2003 Nobel Prize in Literature, explores the implications of oppressive societies on the lives of their inhabitants, often using his native South Africa as a backdrop. As a South African, however, Coetzee is "too intelligent a novelist to cater for moralistic voyeurs," Peter Lewis declared in *Times Literary Supplement.* "This does not mean that he avoids the social and political crises edging his country towards catastrophe. But he chooses not to handle such themes in the direct, realistic way that writers of older generations, such as Alan Paton, preferred to employ. Instead, Coetzee has developed a symbolic and even allegorical mode of fiction—not to escape the living nightmare of South Africa but to define the psychopathological underlying the sociological, and in doing so to locate the archetypal in the particular."

Though many of his stories are set in South Africa, Coetzee's lessons are relevant to all countries, as *Books Abroad*'s Ursula A. Barnett wrote of *Dusklands,* which contains the novellas *The Vietnam Project* and *The Narrative of Jacobus Coetzee.* "By publishing the two stories side by side," Barnett remarked, "Coetzee has deliberately given a wider horizon to his South African subject. Left on its own, *The Narrative of Jacobus Coetzee* would immediately have suggested yet another tale of African black-white confrontation to the reader." Although each is a complete story, "their nature and design are such that the book can and should be read as a single work," Roger Owen commented in *Times Literary Supplement. Dusklands* "is a kind of diptych, carefully hinged and aligned, and of a texture so glassy and mirror-like that each story throws light on the other." Together the tales present two very different outcomes in confrontations between the individual and society.

The Vietnam Project introduces Eugene Dawn, employed to help the Americans win the Vietnam War through psychological warfare. The assignment eventually costs Dawn his sanity. The title character of *The Narrative of Jacobus Coetzee,* a fictionalized ancestor of the author, is an explorer and conqueror in the 1760s who destroys an entire South African tribe over his perception that the people have humiliated him through their indifference and lack of fear. H. M. Tiffin, writing in *Contemporary Novelists,* found that the novellas in *Dusklands* are "juxtaposed to offer a scarifying account of the fear and paranoia of imperialists and aggressors and the horrifying ways in which dominant regimes, 'empires,' commit violence against 'the other' through repression, torture, and genocide."

Coetzee's second novel, *In the Heart of the Country,* also explores racial conflict and mental deterioration. A spinster daughter, Magda, tells the story in diary form, recalling the consequences of her father's seduction of his African workman's wife. Both jealous of and repulsed by the relationship, Magda murders her father, then begins her own affair with the workman. The integrity of Magda's story eventually proves questionable. "The reader soon realizes that these are the untrustworthy ravings of a hysterical, demented individual consumed by loneliness and her love/hate relationship with her patriarchal father," Barend J. Toerien reported in *World Literature Today.* Magda's "thoughts range widely, merging reality with fantasy, composing and recomposing domestic dramas for herself to act in and, eventually introducing voices . . . to speak to her from the skies," Sheila Roberts noted in *World Literature Written in English.* "She imagines that the voices accuse her, among other things, of transforming her uneventful life into a fiction." *World Literature Today*'s Charles R. Larson found *In the Heart of the Country* "a perplexing novel, to be sure, but also a fascinating novelistic exercise in the use of cinematic techniques in prose fiction," describing the book as reminiscent of an overlapping "series of stills extracted from a motion picture."

Coetzee followed *In the Heart of the Country* with *Waiting for the Barbarians,* in which he, "with laconic brilliance, articulates one of the basic problems of our time—how to *understand* . . . [the] mentality behind the brutality and injustice," Anthony Burgess wrote in *New York.* In the novel, a magistrate attempting to protect the peaceful nomadic people of his district is imprisoned and tortured by the army that arrives at the frontier town to destroy the "barbarians" on behalf of the Empire. The horror of what he has seen and experienced affects the magistrate in inalterable ways, bringing changes in his personality that he cannot understand. Doris Grumbach, writing in the *Los Angeles Times Book Review,* found *Waiting for the Barbarians* a book with "universal reference," an allegory which can be applied to innumerable historical and contemporary situations. "Very soon it is apparent that

the story, terrifying and unforgettable, is about injustice and barbarism inflicted everywhere by 'civilized' people upon those it invades, occupies, governs." "The intelligence Coetzee brings us in *Waiting for the Barbarians* comes straight from Scripture and Dostoevsky," Webster Schott asserted in the *Washington Post Book World.* "We possess the devil. We are all barbarians."

Foe, a retelling of Daniel Defoe's *Robinson Crusoe,* marked a transitional stage for Coetzee, according to Maureen Nicholson in *West Coast Review.* Nicholson found many areas in which *Foe* differs from Coetzee's previous work. "Coetzee initially appeared to me to have all but abandoned his usual concerns and literary techniques" in *Foe,* Nicholson commented. "I was mistaken. More importantly, though, I was worried about why he has chosen *now* to write this kind of book; I found his shift of focus and technique ominous. Could he no longer sustain the courage he had demonstrated [in *Waiting for the Barbarians* and *The Life and Times of Michael K.*], turning instead to a radically interiorized narrative?" Nicholson concluded, "Perhaps *Foe* is best viewed as a pause for recapitulation and evaluation, transitional in Coetzee's development as a writer." Ashton Nichols, however, writing in *Southern Humanities Review,* found that Coetzee had not strayed far from his usual topics. "Like all of Coetzee's earlier works, *Foe* retains a strong sense of its specifically South African origins, a sociopolitical subtext that runs along just below the surface of the narrative," Nichols remarked. The reviewer emphasized Coetzee's role as "an archeologist of the imagination, an excavator of language who testifies to the powers and weaknesses of the words he discovers," a role Coetzee has performed in each of his novels, including *Foe.* Central to this idea are the mute Friday, whose tongue was cut out by slavers, and Susan Barton, the castaway who struggles to communicate with him. Daniel Foe, the author who endeavors to tell Barton's story, is also affected by Friday's speechlessness. Both Barton and Foe recognize their duty to provide a means by which Friday can relate the story of his escape from the fate of his fellow slaves who drowned, still shackled, when their ship sank; but both also question their right to speak for him. "The author, whether Foe or Coetzee, . . . wonders if he has any right to speak for the one person whose story most needs to be told," Nichols noted. "Friday is . . . the tongueless voice of millions."

In *Age of Iron* Coetzee addresses the crisis of South Africa in direct, rather than allegorical, form. The story of Mrs. Curren, a retired professor dying of cancer and attempting to deal with the realities of apartheid in Cape Town, *Age of Iron* is "an unrelenting yet gorgeously written parable of modern South Africa, . . . a story filled with foreboding and violence about a land where even the ability of children to love is too great a luxury," Michael Dorris wrote in Chicago *Tribune Books.* As her disease and the chaos of her homeland progress, Mrs. Curren feels the effects her society has had on its black members; her realization that "now my eyes are open and I can never close them again" forms the basis for her growing rage against the system. After her housekeeper's son and his friend are murdered in her home, Mrs. Curren runs away and hides beneath an overpass, leaving her vulnerable to attack by a gang. She is rescued by Vercueil, a street person she has gradually allowed into her house and her life, who returns her to her home and tends to her needs as the cancer continues its destruction. The book takes the form of a letter from Mrs. Curren to her daughter, living in the United States because she cannot tolerate apartheid. "Dying is traditionally a process of withdrawal from the world," Sean French commented in *New Statesman and Society.* "Coetzee tellingly reverses this and it is in her last weeks that [Mrs. Curren] first truly goes out in the baffling society she has lived in." As her life ends, Mrs. Curren's urgency to correct the wrongs she never before questioned intensifies. "In this chronicle of an aged white woman coming to understand, and of the unavoidable claims of her country's black youth, Mr. Coetzee has created a superbly realized novel whose truths cut to the bone," Lawrence Thornton wrote in the *New York Times Book Review.*

In Coetzee's next novel, *The Master of Petersburg,* the central character is the Russian novelist Fyodor Dostoevsky, but the plot is only loosely based on his real life. In Coetzee's story, the novelist goes to St. Petersburg upon the death of his stepson, Pavel. He is devastated by grief for the young man, and begins an inquiry into his death. He discovers that Pavel was involved with a group of nihilists and was probably murdered either by their leader or by the police. During the course of his anguished investigation, Dostoevsky's creative processes are exposed; Coetzee shows him beginning work on his novel *The Possessed.*

In real life, Dostoevsky did have a stepson named Pavel; but he was a foppish idler, a constant source of annoyance and embarrassment to the writer. The

younger man outlived his stepfather by some twenty years, and as Dostoevsky died, he would not allow Pavel near his deathbed. Some reviewers were untroubled by Coetzee's manipulation of the facts. "This is not, after all, a book about the real Dostoevsky; his name, and some facts connected to it, form a mask behind which Coetzee enacts a drama of parenthood, politics and authorship," Harriett Gilbert explained in *New Statesman and Society.* She went on to praise Coetzee's depiction of "the barbed-wire coils of grief and anger, of guilt, of sexual rivalry and envy, that Fyodor Mikhailovich negotiates as he enters Pavel's hidden life. From the moment he presses his face to the lad's white suit to inhale his smell, to when he sits down, picks up his pen and commits a paternal novelist's betrayal, his pain is depicted with such harsh clarity that pity is burnt away. If the novel begins uncertainly, it ends with scorching self-confidence."

Coetzee's nonfiction works include *White Writing: On the Culture of Letters in South Africa, Doubling the Point: Essays and Interviews,* and *Giving Offense: Essays on Censorship.* In *White Writing,* the author "collects his critical reflections on the mixed fortunes of 'white writing' in South Africa, 'a body of writing [not] different in nature from black writing,' but 'generated by the concerns of people no longer European, yet not African,'" Shaun Irlam observed in *MLN.* The seven essays included in the book discuss writings from the late seventeenth century to the present, through which Coetzee examines the foundations of modern South African writers' attitudes. Irlam described the strength of *White Writing* as its ability "to interrogate succinctly and lucidly the presuppositions inhabiting the language with which 'white writers' have addressed and presumed to ventriloquize Africa." In *Doubling the Point: Essays and Interviews,* a collection of critical essays on Samuel Beckett, Franz Kafka, D. H. Lawrence, Nadine Gordimer, and others, Coetzee presents a "literary autobiography," according to Ann Irvine in a *Library Journal* review. Discussions of issues including censorship and popular culture and interviews with the author preceding each section round out the collection.

Giving Offense: Essays on Censorship was Coetzee's first collection of essays in nearly ten years, since *White Writing* appeared. The essays collected in *Giving Offense* were written over a period of about six years. Here Coetzee—a writer quite familiar with the varying forms of censorship and the writer's response to them—attempts to complicate what he calls "the two tired images of the writer under censorship: the moral giant under attack from hordes of moral pygmies and the helpless innocent persecuted by a mighty state apparatus." Coetzee discusses three tyrannical regimes: Nazism, Communism, and apartheid; and, drawing upon his training as an academic scholar as well as his experiences as a fiction writer, argues that the censor and the writer have often been "brother-enemies, mirror images one of the other" in their struggle to claim the truth of their position.

In *Boyhood: Scenes from Provincial Life,* Coetzee experiments with autobiography, a surprising turn for a writer, as Caryl Phillips noted in the *New Republic,* "whose literary output has successfully resisted an autobiographical reading." *Boyhood,* written in the third person, "reads more like a novella than a true autobiography. Coetzee develops his character, a young boy on the verge of adolescence, through a richly detailed interior monolog," wrote Denise S. Sticha in *Library Journal.* He recounts his life growing up in Worcester, South Africa, where he moved with his family from Cape Town after his father's latest business failure. There, he observes the contradictions of apartheid and the subtle distinctions of class and ethnicity with a precociously writerly eye. Rand Richards Cooper, writing for the *New York Times Book Review,* stated that "Coetzee's themes lie where the political, the spiritual, the psychological and the physical converge: the nightmare of bureaucratic violence; or forlorn estrangement from the land; a Shakespearean anxiety about nature put out of its order; and the insistent neediness of the body." Coetzee, an Afrikaner whose parents chose to speak English, finds himself between worlds, neither properly Afrikaner nor English. Throughout his boyhood, he encounters the stupid brutalities inflicted by arbitrary divisions between white and black, Native and Coloured, Afrikaner and English. Phillips speculated that "as a boy Coetzee feels compelled to learn how to negotiate the falsehoods that white South Africa offers up to those who wish to belong. In short, he develops the mentality of the writer. He fills his world with doubt, he rejects authority in all its forms—political, social, personal—and he cultivates the ability to resign himself to the overwhelming insecurity of the heart."

Youth: Scenes from Provincial Life II begins six years after *Boyhood* ends. According to *New Yorker* critic John Updike, the sequel "lacks the bucolic bright spots

and familial furies of *Boyhood* but has an overriding, suspenseful issue: when and how will our hero find his vocation, evident to us readers if not yet to him, as a world-class novelist?" Coetzee's narrator leaves South Africa to pursue his education in London, where, despite his desire to write poetry, he finds work as a computer programmer and drifts through a series of affairs. As Hazel Rochman noted in *Booklist,* "this wry, honest, edgy memoir is the portrait of the young artist as a failure." "Coetzee's delicate self-mockery threatens to become condescending," Updike remarked, "and *Youth*'s repeated rhetorical questions verge on burlesque." But Updike also observed that "the suspense attached to this stalled life is real, at least for any reader who has himself sought to find his or her voice and material amid the crosscurrents of late modernism. Coetzee, with his unusual intelligence and deliberation, confronted problems many a writer, more ebulliently full of himself, rushes past without seeing." As Penelope Mesic noted in *Book,* the narrator's growing awareness of the world's complexity is at the heart of the work: "He stands like a man on the edge of a great abyss, amid obscurity, fear, self-doubt and confusion. To discard what he has been told and act in accordance with his own true emotional responses to the world—to women, to cricket, to books, to political injustice—is something he is just learning to do. In that growing sense of authenticity lies the power that will carry him forward, to the passionately honest novels, including *The Life and Times of Michael K.* and *Disgrace,* that he will eventually write."

The Lives of Animals is a unique effort by Coetzee, incorporating his own lectures on animal rights with the fictional story of Elizabeth Costello, a novelist obsessed by the horrors of human cruelty to animals. In this "wonderfully inventive and inconclusive book," as Stephen H. Webb described it in *Christian Century,* Coetzee poses questions about the morality of vegetarianism and the guilt of those who use animal products. But his arguments are not simplistic: he wonders, for example, if vegetarians are really trying to save animals, or only trying to put themselves in a morally superior position to other humans. The character of Elizabeth Costello is revealed as deeply flawed, and the author's ambiguity about her "forces us to think," added Webb. Are her lectures "academic hyperbole and prophetic provocation? Are we meant to feel sorry for her or, angered by her poor reception, to stand up and defend her and her cause?" Following the novella, there are responses to Costello's arguments from four real-life scholars who have written about animals: Barbara Smuts, Peter Singer, Marjorie Garber, and Wendy Doniger. The sum of the book, wrote Marlene Chamberlain in *Booklist,* is valuable "for Coetzee fans and others interested in the links between philosophy, reason, and the rights of nonhumans."

Disgrace, Coetzee's next novel, is a strong statement on the political climate in post-apartheid South Africa. The main character, David Lurie, is an English professor at University of Cape Town. He sees himself as an aging, but still handsome, Lothario. He has seduced many young women in his day, but an affair with one of his students finally proves his undoing. Charged with sexual harassment, he leaves his post in disgrace, seeking refuge at the small farm owned by his daughter, Lucy. Lucy and David are anything but alike. While his world is refined and highly intellectualized, Lucy works at hard physical labor in simple surroundings. David has allowed his sexual desires to lead him, while Lucy is living a life of voluntary celibacy. While David was in an elitist position, Lucy works alongside her black neighbors. David's notions of orderliness are overturned when three men come to the farm, set him afire, and rape Lucy. Father and daughter survive the ordeal, only to learn that Lucy has become pregnant. Eventually, in order to protect herself and her simple way of life, she consents to become the third wife in her neighbor's polygamous family, even though he may have arranged the attack on her in order to gain control of her property.

The complex story of *Disgrace* drew praise from critics. "The novel's many literary allusions are remarkably cohesive on the subject of spiritual alienation: Lucifer, Cain, the tragedy of birth in Wordsworth—there is a full and even fulsome repertoire of soullessness," remarked Sarah Ruden in *Christian Century.* "The same theme can be found in many modernist and postmodernist writers, but Coetzee cancels the usual pretentious and self-pitying overtones." *Antioch Review* contributor John Kennedy noted, "In its honest and relentless probing of character and motive . . . this novel secures Coetzee's place among today's major novelists. . . . The impulses and crimes of passion, the inadequacies of justice, and the rare possibilities for redemption are played out on many levels in this brilliantly crafted book." The author's deft handling of the ambiguities of his story was also praised by Rebecca Saunders, who in *Review of Contemporary Fiction* warned that *Disgrace* is "not for

the ethically faint of heart." Saunders felt Coetzee has "strewn nettles in the bed of the comfortable social conscience," and his book is written in the style "we have come to expect" from him, "at once taciturn and blurting out the unspeakable."

Insight into the workings of Coetzee's mind is afforded through *Stranger Shores: Literary Essays, 1986-1999,* which collects twenty-six essays of literary criticism by the author, focusing on authors such as Franz Kafka, Salman Rushdie, Nadine Gordimer, and Jorge Luis Borges. "These are not puff pieces," warned James Shapiro in *New York Times Book Review.* In his criticism, "Coetzee wields a sharp scalpel, carefully exposing the stylistic flaws, theoretical shortcuts and, on occasion, bad faith of writers he otherwise admires." An *Economist* contributor found the tone of the book "dry tending to arid," and Alberto Manguel in *Spectator* suggested that the collection lacked a needed "touch of passion." Yet Shapiro thought that *Stranger Shores* is a fine model of "blunt, elegant and unflinching criticism at a time when novelists tend to go rather easy when reviewing their colleagues." Finally, Shapiro concluded, *Stranger Shores* is valuable for the "light it casts on a stage in the intellectual journey of one of the most cerebral and consequential writers of our day."

The 2003 work *Elizabeth Costello* "blurs the bounds of fiction and nonfiction while furthering the author's exploration of urgent moral and aesthetic questions," according to a critic in *Publishers Weekly.* In *Elizabeth Costello,* the title character, an aging Australian writer best known for a feminist novel she wrote in the 1960s, delivers a series of formal talks addressing issues such as animal rights and the nature of evil. A contributor in *Kirkus Reviews* noted that "Coetzee has here reimagined in semifictional form several of his recent nonfiction essays and lectures" and called the work "a disappointing hybrid that cannot, except by the loosest possible definition, be called fiction." *New Statesman* contributor Roy Robins believed that the work "has neither the gravity and compulsion of Coetzee's best fiction, nor the precision and intensity of his finest critical writing," Keir Graff offered a different opinion in *Booklist,* stating, "Coetzee may be exploding the genre, but *Elizabeth Costello* has real novelistic force."

In 2003 Coetzee was awarded the Nobel Prize in Literature. In announcing its selection, the Swedish Academy stated in *Africa News Service,* "J. M.

Coetzee's novels are characterised by their well-crafted composition, pregnant dialogue, and analytical brilliance. But at the same time he is a scrupulous doubter, ruthless in his criticism of the cruel rationalism and cosmetic morality of western civilisation." Per Wästberg, a member of the Swedish Academy, observed, "Coetzee sees through the obscene poses and false pomp of history, lending voice to the silenced and the despised. Restrained but stubborn, he defends the ethical value of poetry, literature and imagination."

In addition to his writing, Coetzee has produced translations of works in Dutch, German, French, and Afrikaans, served as editor for others' work, and taught at the University of Cape Town. "He's a rare phenomenon, a writer-scholar," Ian Glenn, a colleague of Coetzee's, told the *Washington Post*'s Allister Sparks. "Even if he hadn't had a career as a novelist he would have had a very considerable one as an academic." Coetzee told Sparks that he finds writing burdensome. "I don't like writing so I have to push myself," he said. "It's bad if I write but it's worse if I don't." Coetzee hesitates to discuss his works in progress, and views his opinion of his published works as no more important than that of anyone else. "The writer is simply another reader when it is a matter of discussing the books he has already written," he told Sparks. "They don't belong to him anymore and he has nothing privileged to say about them—while the book he is engaged in writing is far too private and important a matter to be talked about."

BIOGRAPHICAL AND CRITICAL SOURCES:

BOOKS

Attwell, David, *J. M. Coetzee: South Africa and the Politics of Writing,* University of California Press (Berkeley, CA), 1993.

Coetzee, J. M., *Giving Offense: Essays on Censorship,* University of Chicago Press (Chicago, IL), 1996.

Contemporary Literary Criticism, Gale (Detroit, MI), Volume 66, 1991, Volume 117, 1997.

Contemporary Novelists, 7th edition, St. James Press (Detroit, MI), 2001.

Dictionary of Literary Biography, Volume 225: *South African Writers,* Gale (Detroit, MI), 2000.

Durrant, Sam, *Postcolonial Narrative and the Work of Mourning: J. M. Coetzee, Wilson Harris, and Toni Morrison,* State University of New York Press (Albany, NY), 2004.

Encyclopedia of World Biography, 2nd edition, Gale (Detroit, MI), 1998.

Gallagher, Susan V., *A Story of South Africa: J. M. Coetzee's Fiction in Context,* Harvard University Press (Cambridge, MA), 1991.

Goddard, Kevin, *J. M. Coetzee: A Bibliography,* National English Literary Museum (Grahamstown, South Africa), 1990.

Head, Dominic, *J. M. Coetzee,* Cambridge University Press (New York, NY), 1998.

Huggan, Graham, and Stephen Watson, editors, *Critical Perspectives on J. M. Coetzee,* introduction by Nadine Gordimer, St. Martin's Press (New York, NY), 1996.

Jolly, Rosemary Jane, *Colonization, Violence, and Narration in White South African Writing: Andre Brink, Breyten Breytenbach, and J. M. Coetzee,* Ohio University Press (Athens, OH), 1996.

Kossew, Sue, *Pen and Power: A Post-Colonial Reading of J. M. Coetzee and Andre Brink,* Rodopi (Atlanta, GA), 1996.

Kossew, Sue, editor, *Critical Essays on J. M. Coetzee,* G. K. Hall (Boston, MA), 1998.

Moses, Michael Valdez, editor, *The Writings of J. M. Coetzee,* Duke University Press (Durham, NC), 1994.

Penner, Dick, *Countries of the Mind: The Fiction of J. M. Coetzee,* Greenwood Press (New York, NY), 1989.

PERIODICALS

African Business, November, 1999, Stephen Williams, review of *Disgrace,* p. 42.

Africa News Service, October 3, 2003, "Coetzee Celebrates Nobel, in Private"; October 6, 2003, "Coetzee Swells South Africa's Nobel Haul"; December 22, 2003, "The Nobel Prize in Literature 2003—Presentation to J. M. Coetzee."

Africa Today, number 3, 1980.

America, September 25, 1982.

Antioch Review, summer, 2000, John Kennedy, review of *Disgrace,* p. 375.

Ariel, April, 1985, pp. 47-56; July, 1986, pp. 3-21; October, 1988, pp. 55-72.

Atlantic, March, 2000, Phoebe-Lou Adams, review of *Disgrace,* p. 116.

Book, July-August, 2002, "Confessions of a Computer Programmer," pp. 70-71.

Booklist, November 1, 1994, p. 477; April 1, 1996, p. 1328; August, 1997, p. 1869; March 15, 1999, Marlene Chamberlain, review of *The Lives of Ani-*

mals, p. 1262; November 15, 1999, Hazel Rochman, review of *Disgrace,* p. 579; March 15, 2001, review of *Disgrace,* p. 1362; August, 2001, Donna Seaman, review of *Stranger Shores: Literary Essays, 1986-1999,* p. 2075; June 1, 2002, Hazel Rochman, review of *Youth: Scenes from a Provincial Life II,* p. 1666; September 15, 2003, Keir Graff, review of *Elizabeth Costello,* p. 180; February 1, 2004, Ray Olson, review of *Landscape with Rowers: Poetry from the Netherlands,* p. 943.

Books Abroad, spring, 1976.

Books and Culture, March, 1997, p. 30.

Books in Canada, August/September, 1982.

Boston Globe, November 20, 1994, p. B16.

British Book News, April, 1981.

Charlotte Observer, December 29, 1999, Lawrence Toppman, review of *Disgrace.*

Chicago Tribune Book World, April 25, 1982; January 22, 1984, section 14, p. 27; November 27, 1994, p. 3.

Choice, November, 1999, S. H. Webb, review of *The Lives of Animals,* p. 552.

Christian Century, May 19, 1999, Stephen H. Webb, review of *The Lives of Animals,* p. 569; August 16, 2000, Sarah Ruden, review of *Disgrace,* p. 840.

Christian Science Monitor, December 12, 1983; May 18, 1988, pp. 503-505; November 10, 1999, Ron Charles, "A Morality Tale with No Easy Answers," p. 20; November 18, 1999, review of *Disgrace,* p. 12.

Commentary, March, 2000, Carol Iannone, review of *Disgrace,* p. 62.

Contemporary Literature, summer, 1988, pp. 277-285; fall, 1992, pp. 419-431.

Contrast, September, 1982, Peter Knox-Shaw, "Dusklands: A Metaphysics of Violence."

Critical Survey, May, 1999, Sue Kossew, "Resistance, Complicity, and Post-Colonial Politics," pp. 18-30, Myrtle Hooper, "'Sweets for My Daughter,'" pp. 31-44, and Derek Attridge, "J. M. Coetzee's *Boyhood,* Confession, and Truth," pp. 77-93.

Critique: Studies in Modern Fiction, winter, 1986, pp. 67-77; spring, 1989, pp. 143-154; spring, 2001, review of *Foe,* p. 309.

Economist (U.S.), June 18, 1988, "Oh, but Our Land Is Beautiful," p. 96; December 4, 1999, review of *Disgrace,* p. S4; September 15, 2001, review of *Stranger Shores,* p. 93; March 16, 2002, review of *Youth.*

Encounter, October, 1977; January, 1984.

English Journal, March, 1994, p. 97.

Entertainment Weekly, October 17, 2003, Rebecca Ascher-Walsh, review of *Elizabeth Costello,* p. 85.

Globe and Mail (Toronto, Ontario, Canada), August 30, 1986; October 2, 1999, review of *Disgrace,* p. D18; November 27, 1999, review of *Disgrace,* p. D49.

Harper's, June, 1999, review of *The Master of Petersburg,* p. 76.

Hudson Review, summer, 2000, Thomas Filbin, review of *Disgrace,* p. 333; Harold Fromm, review of *The Lives of Animals,* p. 336.

Journal of Commonwealth Literature, spring, 1996, Mike Marais, "Places of Pigs," p. 83.

Journal of Southern African Studies, October, 1982, Paul Rich, "Tradition and Revolt in South African Fiction."

Kirkus Reviews, February 15, 1999, review of *The Lives of Animals,* p. 264; May 1, 2002, review of *Youth,* p. 631; September 1, 2003, review of *Elizabeth Costello,* pp. 1087-1088.

Library Journal, June 1, 1992, p. 124; September 1, 1994, p. 213; March 15, 1996, p. 70; September 1, 1997, p. 181; December, 1999, Marc A. Kloszewski, review of *Disgrace,* p. 182; July, 2001, Gene Shaw, review of *Stranger Shores,* p. 89; May 15, 2002, Henry L. Carrigan, Jr., review of *Youth: Scenes from a Provincial Life II,* p. 97; October 1, 2003, Barbara Love, review of *Elizabeth Costello,* p. 114; October 15, 2003, Louis McKee, review of *Landscape with Rowers,* pp. 72-73.

Listener, August 18, 1977.

London Review of Books, September 13, 1990, pp. 17-18; October 14, 1999, reviews of *The Lives of Animals* and *Disgrace,* p. 12.

Los Angeles Times, October 3, 2003, Ann M. Simmons, "South African Wins Nobel Prize in Literature."

Los Angeles Times Book Review, May 23, 1982, p. 4; January 15, 1984; February 22, 1987; November 20, 1994, p. 3; December 12, 1999, review of *Disgrace,* p. 2.

Maclean's, January 30, 1984, p. 49.

MLN, December, 1988, pp. 1147-1150; December 17, 1990, pp. 777-780.

Nation, March 28, 1987, pp. 402-405; March 6, 2000, Joseph McElroy, review of *Disgrace,* p. 30.

Natural History, June, 1999, Steven N. Austad, review of *The Lives of Animals,* p. 18.

New Leader, December 13, 1999, Brooke Allen, review of *Disgrace,* p. 27; November-December, 2003, Rosellen Brown, "Countering the Obscene," pp. 35-37.

New Republic, December 19, 1983; February 6, 1995, pp. 170-172; October 16, 1995, p. 53; November 18, 1996, p. 30; February 9, 1998, p. 37; December 20, 1999, review of *Disgrace,* p. 42.

New Statesman, October 18, 1999, Douglas McCabe, review of *Disgrace,* p. 57; October 25, 1999, Jason Cowley, "The Ideal Chronicler of the New South Africa, He Deserves to Make Literary History as a Double Booker Winner," p. 18; November 29, 1999, review of *Disgrace,* pp. 79-80; April 22, 2002, Pankaj Mishra, "The Enigma of Arrival," pp. 50-51; September 15, 2003, Roy Robins, "Alter Ego," pp. 50-51; October 13, 2003, Jason Cowley, "Despite a Booker Nomination and a Nobel Prize, These Writers, Unheard in Their Own Land, Feel Oppressed by Emptiness," pp. 22-24.

New Statesman and Society, September 21, 1990, p. 40; February 25, 1994, p. 41; November 21, 1997, p. 50.

Newsweek, May 31, 1982; January 2, 1984; February 23, 1987; November 15, 1999, review of *Disgrace,* p. 90.

Newsweek International, November 8, 1999, "South Africa's Prize Winner," p. 72.

New York, April 26, 1982, pp. 88, 90.

New Yorker, July 12, 1982; July 5, 1999, review of *The Lives of Animals,* p. 80; November 15, 1999, review of *Disgrace,* p. 110; July 15, 2002, John Updike, "The Story of Himself."

New York Review of Books, December 2, 1982; February 2, 1984; November 8, 1990, pp. 8-10; November 17, 1994, p. 35; June 29, 2000, Ian Hacking, review of *The Lives of Animals,* p. 20; January 20, 2000, John Banville, review of *Disgrace,* p. 23; December 5, 2002, Ian Buruma, "Portraits of the Artists," pp. 52-53.

New York Times, December 6, 1983, p. C22; February 11, 1987; April 11, 1987; November 18, 1994, p. C35; October 7, 1997, p. B7; October 26, 1999, Sarah Lyall, "South African Writer Wins Top British Prize for Second Time," p. A4; November 11, 1999, Christopher Lehmann-Haupt, "Caught in Shifting Values (and Plot)," p. B10; November 14, 1999, Rachel L. Swarns, "After Apartheid, White Anxiety," p. WK1; October 3, 2003, Alan Riding, Coetzee, "Writer of Apartheid, as Bleak Mirror, wins Nobel," p. A1, and Michiko Kakutani, "Chronicling Life Perched on a Volcano's Edge as Change Erupts," p. A6; October 21, 2003, Janet Maslin, "The Mockery Can Still Sting with a Target in the Mirror," p. E7.

New York Times Book Review, April 18, 1982; December 11, 1983, pp. 1, 26; February 22, 1987; September 23, 1990, p. 7; November 20, 1994, p. 9; September 22, 1996, p. 33; November 2, 1997, p. 7; November 28, 1999, review of *Disgrace,* p. 7; December 5, 1999, review of *Disgrace,* p. 8; September 16, 2001, James Shapiro, review of *Stranger Shores,* p. 29; July 7, 2002, William Deresiewicz, "Third-Person Singular," p. 6; July 14, 2002, "Youth (and Bear in Mind)," p. 22.

Novel, fall, 2000, Derek Attridge, review of *Disgrace,* p. 98.

Observer (London, England), July 18, 1999, review of *Disgrace,* p. 13.

Publishers Weekly, September 5, 1994, p. 88; January 22, 1996, p. 52; July 28, 1997, p. 59; February 8, 1999, review of *The Lives of Animals,* p. 193; November 1, 1999, Jean Richardson, "Coetzee Wins the Booker Again," p. 15; November 22, 1999, review of *Disgrace,* p. 42; September 22, 2003, review of *Elizabeth Costello,* pp. 80-81.

Quadrant, December, 1999, Paul Monk, review of *Disgrace,* p. 80.

Quarterly Review of Biology, June, 2001, David Fraser, review of *The Lives of Animals,* p. 215; May 6, 2002, review of *Youth,* p. 44.

Research in African Literatures, fall, 1984, Paul Rich, "Apartheid and the Decline of the Civilization Idea"; fall, 1986, pp. 370-392; winter, 1994, Chiara Briganti, "A Bored Spinster with a Locked Diary," pp. 33-49; summer, 2003, Sue Kossew, "The Politics of Shame and Redemption in J. M. Coetzee's *Disgrace,*" pp. 155-162.

Review of Contemporary Fiction, summer, 2000, Rebecca Saunders, review of *Disgrace,* p. 167; spring, 2002, E. Kim Stone, review of *Stranger Shores,* p. 151.

Salmagundi, spring-summer, 1997, Joanna Scott, "Voice and Trajectory," pp. 82-102, and Regina Janes, "'Writing without Authority,'" pp. 103-121.

Sewanee Review, winter, 1990, pp. 152-159; April, 1995, p. R48; fall, 2000, Merritt Moseley, review of *Disgrace,* p. 648; summer, 2001, John Reese Moore, review of *The Lives of Animals,* p. 462.

South Atlantic Quarterly, winter, 1994, pp. 1-9, 33-58, 83-110.

Southern Humanities Review, fall, 1987, pp. 384-386.

Speak, May-June, 1978, Stephen Watson, "Speaking: J. M. Coetzee."

Spectator, December 13, 1980; September 20, 1986; April 3, 1999, Antony Rouse, review of *The Lives of Animals,* p. 41; July 10, 1999, Katie Grant, review of *Disgrace,* p. 34; November 20, 1999, review of *Disgrace,* p. 47; September 22, 2001, Alberto Manguel, review of *Stranger Shores: Essays 1986-1999,* p. 46; April 20, 2002, Hilary Mantel, "Craving Fire and Ardour," p. 39; September 13, 2003, Anita Brookner, *A Brave Stance to Take,* p. 63.

Sun-Sentinel, December 22, 1999, Chauncey Mabe, review of *Disgrace.*

Time, March 23, 1987; November 28, 1994, pp. 89-90; November 29, 1999, review of *Disgrace,* p. 82; October 13, 2003, Rian Malan, "Only the Big Questions," p. 80.

Time International, November 15, 1999, Elizabeth Gleick, review of *Disgrace,* p. 96; September 15, 2003, Michael Fitzgerald, "Talking about Writing," p. 65.

Times (London, England), September 29, 1983; September 11, 1986; May 28, 1988.

Times Literary Supplement, July 22, 1977; November 7, 1980, p. 1270; January 14, 1983; September 30, 1983; September 23, 1988, p. 1043; September 28, 1990, p. 1037; March 4, 1994, p. 19; April 16, 1999, Maren Meinhardt, review of *The Lives of Animals,* p. 25; June 25, 1999, Ranti Williams, review of *Disgrace,* p. 23; May 19, 2000, Peter D. McDonald, "Not Undesirable," p. 14; October 5, 2001, Michael Gorra, review of *Stranger Shores,* p. 23; April 26, 2002, Peter Porter, "Bedsit Blues," p. 22; September 5, 2003, Oliver Herford, "Tears for Dead Fish," pp. 5-6.

Tribune Books (Chicago, IL), February 15, 1987, pp. 3, 11; September 16, 1990, p. 3.

Tri-Quarterly, spring-summer, 1987, pp. 454-464.

U.S News and World Report, October 13, 2003, Lisa Stein, "A Novel Nobel," p. 13.

Village Voice, March 20, 1984.

Voice Literary Supplement, April, 1982.

Wall Street Journal, November 3, 1994, p. A16; October 26, 1999, Paul Levy, "Eyes on the Booker Prize," p. A24; November 26, 1999, Philip Connors, review of *Disgrace,* p. W8; July 5, 2002, Merle Rubin, review of *Youth,* p. W7.

Washington Post, October 29, 1983.

Washington Post Book World, May 2, 1982, pp. 1-2, 12; December 11, 1983; March 8, 1987; September 23, 1990, pp. 1, 10; November 27, 1994, p. 6.

West Coast Review, spring, 1987, pp. 52-58.

Whole Earth Review, summer, 1999, review of *The Lives of Animals,* p. 13.

World Literature Today, spring, 1978, pp. 245-247; summer, 1978, p. 510; autumn, 1981; autumn, 1988, pp. 718-719; winter, 1990, pp. 54-57; winter, 1995, p. 207; winter, 1996, "An Interview with J. M. Coetzee," pp. 107-110; autumn, 1996, p. 1038; winter, 2000, review of *Disgrace,* p. 228; spring, 2002, J. Roger Kurtz, review of *Stranger Shores,* p. 249; January-April, 2004, Kristjana Gunnars, "A Writer's Writer," pp. 11-13, Tony Morphet, "Reading Coetzee in South Africa," pp. 14-16, Richard A. Barney, "Between Swift and Kafka," pp. 17-23, Michael Fitzgerald, "Serendipity," pp. 24-25, and Charles Sarvan, "Disgrace?: A Path to Grace," pp. 26-29.

World Literature Written in English, spring, 1980, pp. 19-36; spring, 1986, pp. 34-45; autumn, 1987, pp. 153-161, 174-184, 207-215.

World Press Review, July, 1985, Bernard Genies, *Lifting Coetzee's Veil,* pp. 59-60.

ONLINE

David Higham Associates, http://www.davidhigham.co.uk/ (April 10, 2004), "J. M. Coetzee."

J. M. Coetzee Web site, http://www.tiac.net/users/jgm (April 8, 2002).

Nobel e-Museum, http://www.nobel.se/ (April 10, 2004), "John Maxwell Coetzee."

University of Chicago Chronicle, http://chronicle.uchicago.edu/ (April 8, 2002), Arthur Fournier, "J. M. Coetzee Honored with Booker Prize, Top British Fiction Award."*

D

DARWISH, Mahmoud 1942(?)-

PERSONAL: Name also transliterated as Mahmoud Darweesh and Mahmud Darwish; born March 13, 1942 (one source says 1941), in Birwa, Palestine (now Israel); refugee in Lebanon, 1948-49; son of a farmer and laborer; married Rana Kabbani (marriage ended). *Education:* Attended Arab secondary schools in Galilee, and school in Moscow. *Politics:* Palestinian nationalist.

ADDRESSES: Agent—Riad el-Rayyes Books, 56 Knightsbridge, London SW1X 7NJ, England.

CAREER: Al-Ittihad ("Unity") daily newspaper and *al-Jadid* weekly newspaper, Haifa, Israel, journalist and editor, until c. late 1960s; *Al-Ahram* daily newspaper, Cairo, Egypt, journalist, 1971-72; Center for Palestinian Studies, editor of *Shu'un Filastiniyya* ("Palestinian Issues") magazine, Beirut, Lebanon, 1972-82; *Al-Karmal* magazine, editor, beginning 1981. Formerly active in Israeli Communist party; active in Palestinian politics.

MEMBER: Palestine Liberation Organization (member of executive committee, 1987-93).

AWARDS, HONORS: Lotus Prize, Union of Afro-Asian Writers, 1969; Mediterranean Prize, 1980; Lenin Peace Prize, 1983; Knight of Arts and Belles Lettres medal (France), 1997; Lannan Foundation Award for Cultural Freedom, 2001; Sultan bin Ali al Owais Cultural Award for cultural and scientific achievement, 2004.

Mahmoud Darwish

WRITINGS:

Asafir bila ajnihah (title means "Sparrows without Wings"), 1960.

Awraq al-zaytun (title means "Olive Branches"), 1964, Dar al-'Awdah (Beirut, Lebanon), 1969.

Ashiq min Filastin (title means "A Lover from Palestine"), 1966.

Akhir al-layl (title means "The End of Night"), Dar al-'Awdah (Beirut, Lebanon), 1967.

Asafir bila anjinah al-diwan al-awwal, Dar al-'Awdah (Beirut, Lebanon), 1969.

Habibati tanhadu min nawmiha, Dar al-'Awdah (Beirut, Lebanon), 1969.

Yawmiyat jurh Filastini, Dar al-'Awdah (Beirut, Lebanon), 1969.

Ma'a Mamhoud Darwish fi diwanih, Abd al-Rahman, 1969.

A Letter from Exile (selected poems), League of Arab States Mission (New Delhi, India), 1970.

Diwan (selected poems), 1970.

Kitabah ala daw' bunduqiyah, Dar al-'Awdah (Beirut, Lebanon), 1970.

Al-asafir tamut fi al-Jalil (title means "The Sparrows Die in Galilee"), 1970.

Habibati tanhad min nawmiha (title means "My Beloved Wakes Up"), 1971.

Matar na'im fi kharif ba'id, Matba'ah wa-Awfsat al-Hakim (Nasiriyah, Iraq), 1971.

Shay' 'an al-watan (autobiography; title means "Something about Home"), 1971.

Uhibbuki aw la uhibbuk (title means "Love You, Love You Not"), Manshourat Dar al-Adab (Beirut, Lebanon), 1972.

The Palestinian Chalk Circle, Arab Women's Information Committee (Beirut, Lebanon), 1972.

Yawmiyat al-huzn al-'adi (autobiography; title means "Diaries of Ordinary Grief"), Markaz al-Abhath (Beirut, Lebanon), 1973.

Selected Poems, translated by Ian Wedde and Fawwaz Tuqan, Carcanet Press (Manchester, England), 1973.

Wada'an ayyatuha al-harb, wada'an ayyaha al-salam (title means "Farewell War, Farewell Peace"), 1974, Manshurat al-Aswar (Acre, Israel), 1985.

Muhawalah raqm sab'ah (title means "The Seventh Attempt"), 1974.

Splinters of Bone, edited and translated by B. M. Bennani, introduction by Joseph Langland, Greenfield Review Press (Greenfield Center, NY), 1974, bilingual edition translated by Rana Kabbani published as *Ahmad al-Za'tar,* illustrated by Kalam Boullata, calligraphy by Elias Nico, Manshourat afaq (Beirut, Lebanon), 1977.

Tilk suratuha wa-hadha intihar al-'ashiq (title means "That Is Her Picture and This Is Her Lover's Suicide"), Markaz al-Abhath (Beirut, Lebanon), 1975.

A'ras (title means "Weddings"), Dar al-'Awdah (Beirut, Lebanon), 1977.

Diwan Mahmoud Darwish (selected poems), Dar al-'Awdah (Beirut, Lebanon), 1977.

The Music of Human Flesh, edited and translated by Denys Johnson-Davies, Three Continents Press (Washington, DC), 1980.

Madih al-zill al-'ali, Dar al-'Awdah (Beirut, Lebanon), 1983.

(Contributor) *Victims of a Map: A Bilingual Translation of Arabic Poetry,* translated by Abdullah al-Udhari, Al-Saqi Books (London, England), 1984.

Hisar li-mada'ih al-bahr (title means "Ban on Panegyrics to the Sea"), Manshourat al-Aswar (Acre, Israel), 1984.

Mukhtarat al-shi'riyah, foreword by Tawfiq Bakkar, illustrated by Rashid al-Qurayshi, Dar al-Janub lil-Nashr (Tunis, Tunisia), 1985.

Sand and Other Poems, edited and translated by Rana Kabbani, KPI (New York, NY), 1986.

Hiya ughniyah, hiya ughniyah (title means "It Is a Song, It Is a Song"), Dar al-Kalimah lil-Nashr (Beirut, Lebanon), 1986.

Ward aqall (poems; title means "Lesser Roses"), Dar Tubqal (al-Dar al-Bayda, Morocco), 1986.

Zakirah lil-nisyan (title means "A Memory of Oblivion"), Al Mu'assasah al-'Arabiyyah lil-Dirasat wa-al-Nashr (Beirut, Lebanon), 1987.

Fi intizar al-barabirah, Wikalat Abou Arafeh (Haifa, Israel), 1987.

Fi wasf halatina: maqalat mukhtarah, 1975-1985, Dar al-Aswar (Acre, Israel), 1987.

(With others) *Palestine mon pays: l'affaire du poème,* introduction by Simone Bitton, Minuit (Paris, France), 1988.

Dhakirah lil-nisyan: al-zaman, Bayrout, al-makan, ab 1982, Manshourat al-Yasar (Haifa, Israel), 1987, published as *Memory for Forgetfulness: August, Beirut, 1982,* translated and with an introduction by Ibrahim Muhawi, University of California Press (Berkeley, CA), 1995.

Ma'sat al-Nirjis wa-malhat al-fiddah (title means "The Tragedy of Narcissus and the Comedy of Silver"), Riad el-Rayyes (London, England), 1989.

Ara ma urid (title means "I See What I Want"), 1990.

(With Samih al-Qasim) *Al-Rasa'il* (correspondence), Dar Tubqal lil-Nashr (al-Dar al-Bayda, Morocco), 1990.

Abirouna fi kalam 'abir: maqalat mukhtarah, Dar Toubqal (al-Dar al-Bayda, Morocco), 1991.

Ara ma urid: shi'r, Mu'assasat al-Aswar (Acre, Israel), 1991.

Ihda 'ashar kawkaba (title means "Eleven Planets"), 1992.

Ahada 'ashara kawkaban, Dar Darwish (Beirut, Lebanon), 1992.

Ara ma urid, Dar al-Jadid (Beirut, Lebanon), 1993.

Psalms: Poems, translated and with an introduction by Ben Bennani, Three Continents Press (Colorado Springs, CO), 1994.

Falastin, Falastin (poems), Sang-i M-il Pabl-ikeshanz (Lahore, Pakistan), 1994.

Mahmoud Darwish, edited by Sabri Hafiz, illustrated by Ammar Salman, Dar al-Fata al-Arabi (Cairo, Egypt), 1994.

Li-Madha Tarakta al-Hisan Wahidan (title means "Why Have You Left the Horse Alone"), Riy-ad al-Rayyis lil-Kutub wa-al-Nashr (London, England), 1995.

Meno Rose, Cafoscarina (Venice, Italy), 1997.

(With Rene Backmann) *Then Palestine,* illustrated by Larry Towell, Aperture (New York, NY), 1998.

Sarir el Ghariba (love poems; title means "Bed of the Stranger"), 1998.

Jidariyat Mahmoud Darweesh: Qasidah KRutibat 'am 1999 (poems), Riy-ad al-Rayyis lil-Kutub wa-al-Nashr (Beirut, Lebanon), 2000.

The Adam of Two Edens, edited by Munir Akash and Daniel Moore, Syracuse University Press (Syracuse, NY), 2000.

Halat hisar (title means "State of Siege"), Riyad al-Rayyis lil-Kutub wa-al-Nashr (Beirut, Lebanon), 2002.

Rilit al-shi'r wa-al-hayah, edited by Dib Ali Hasan, Dar al-Manarah lil-Tiba'ah wal-al-Nashr (Beirut, Lebanon), 2002.

Unfortunately, It Was Paradise (selected poems), translated and edited by Munir Akash and Carolyn Forché, with Sinan Antoon and Amira El-Zein, University of California Press (Berkeley, CA), 2003.

La ta'Tadhir 'amma fa'alt, Riyad al-Rayyis lil-Kutub wa-al-Nashr (Beirut, Lebanon), 2004.

Author of *Bayrout, Filastin, al-shi'r,* c. 1980s. Contributor to *Palestinian Leaders Discuss the New Challenges for the Resistance,* Palestine Research Center (Beirut, Lebanon), 1974; *Israéliens, Palestiniens: Photographies, poèmes calligraphiés,* Edifra (Paris, France), 1994; and *Le voyage en Palestine de la délégation du Parlement international des écrevains en réponse à,* 2002; and to poetry collections.

Darwish's works have been translated into French, Spanish, German, Hebrew, and numerous other languages.

SIDELIGHTS: Hailed as one of the leading Palestinian poets of the twentieth century, Mahmoud Darwish was born in Palestine before the founding of the Israeli state. His family fled Israel's war of independence in 1948 and spent a year as refugees in Lebanon, before returning to Israel. Their original village had been destroyed and replaced by a Jewish settlement, so the family settled in a new village nearby, in Galilee. Darwish's formerly wealthy father was forced to work in a quarry to support the large family. These experiences influenced Darwish greatly and helped to mold his poetic imagination and voice. "Cut off from the rest of the Arab world, second-class citizens in a Jewish state, by law required to carry an identity card at all times, the Arabs in Israel had to work at maintaining their Palestinian identity," explained Inea Bushnaq in *Parnassus.* This predicament is addressed in "Identity Card," one of Darwish's best-known poems.

Darwish's first poem, written at age fourteen, is a lament on the inequities existing between Arab and Jewish children. After Darwish read this poem aloud at school, the local military authority told him to stop writing poetry and threatened that his father would lose his job otherwise. "From this early age, Darwish realised that poetry is action and relished the impact of his simple, innocent words on the mighty establishment," declared Sabry Hafez in *Contemporary World Writers.* His first poetry collection, *Asafir bila ajnihah* ("Sparrows without Wings"), was published when he was nineteen years old. In the 1960s he wrote and saw publication of three additional collections of poems; his second, *Awraq al-zaytun* ("Olive Branches"), secured his place as the leading poet of the Palestinian resistance movement. Darwish was jailed after the publication of each collection and subjected to long terms of house arrest between his imprisonments. His diary, *Yawmiyat al-huzn al-'adi* ("Diaries of Ordinary Grief"), paints the poet during this period of nighttime house arrests as a figure of light and the authorities as figures of darkness.

Darwish also worked as a journalist in Haifa, Israel, and was active in the Israeli Communist party until he left Israel in 1971 to complete his education in Moscow. Over the years he lived in numerous capital cities of the world before returning to Palestine in 1996. Since then he has lived in Ramallah, the city where the Palestinian Liberation Organization (PLO) is headquartered. He set up an office in the Sakakini Centre, the home of a not-for-profit group dedicated to advancing Palestinian culture, and continued his work editing a long-running Arabic-language literary review, *Al-Karmal.* As he has been for much of his life, Darwish remains active in Palestinian national politics, but he sees a disconnect between his literary and political activities. "I don't think there is any role for poetry [in a Palestinian state]. Poems can't establish a state," Darwish told a *Newsweek International* interviewer in 2000. "But they can establish a metaphorical homeland in the minds of the people. I think my poems have built some houses in this landscape."

Although critics group Darwish's poetry into three phases, much of it deals with the loss of Palestine and requires readers to have some knowledge of Palestinian history. The first phase includes the first six poetry collections produced before Darwish left Israel. This poetry is "overtly political," Hafez wrote, "charged with the power to evoke tremendous resistance, which enabled it to capture and even inflame the imagination of its readers throughout the Arab world." Simple, direct, declamatory, and defiant, these poems' political purpose was to fortify Palestinians' determination to resist Israeli attempts to uproot them from their ancestral land. Influenced by Pablo Neruda, Federico García Lorca, and Karl Marx, these works were typified by their "lyrical iconography of simple Palestinian objects" and "celebrated the simple fact of being Palestinian in an atmosphere hostile to everything Palestinian," noted Hafez. Characterized by a sense of injury and loss, these first poems are also tempered by the poet's belief in the Palestinian cause and hope for its eventual success.

Darwish spent two years under house arrest in Israel in the late 1960s, and when he was released he went into exile. He studied in Moscow for a year, then settled in what was at that time the capital of the Arabic cultural world—Beirut, Lebanon. Darwish's second phase, corresponds to the decade he spent living in Beirut, from 1972 until 1982. His earlier poems had focused on the purer emotions of grief at what Palestinians had lost and optimism that it would soon be regained, but his poems from this period, characterized as refined and tense, instead detail the poet's struggle to remember the old faces and physical characteristics of his homeland. Poems spanning the first twenty-five years of Darwish's work and reflecting these first two periods are collected in *The Music of Human Flesh,* translated and published in 1980.

Darwish and the rest of the PLO were forced out of Beirut by the Israeli invasion of Lebanon in 1982. He wrote movingly of the destruction of Beirut in the book *Dhakirah lil-nisyan: al-zaman, Bayrout, al-makan, ab 1982,* later published in English as *Memory for Forgetfulness: August, Beirut, 1982.* Darwish's third, post-Beirut phase is marked by several long, narrative poems that chastise the Arab regimes and describe the failure of Arab politics in the aftermath of the Israeli siege of Lebanon in 1982. "Darwish's poetry has become more pensive and sophisticated," stated Hafez, "for he thinks of himself as a maker of symbols rather than a receiver of symbols made by external reality." Several of Darwish's works from this period were collected in *Victims of a Map: A Bilingual Translation of Arabic Poetry* in 1984.

In 1988 Darwish caught world attention and caused a furor when a poem he wrote during the first Intifada (Palestinian uprising) questioned the idea that Palestinians and Jews could live together peacefully and seemed to demand that the Jews leave Israel. (Darwish has said that he only meant that Israel should withdraw from the West Bank and Gaza Strip.) This poem, "Passing Between Passing Words," has become a classic. It has been debated twice in the Knesset, the Israeli parliament, once when it was first published in Hebrew and once in 2000, when Education Minister Yossi Sarid suggested that this and other of Darwish's poems should be studied by Israeli high school students. While Prime Minister Ehud Barak vetoed the suggestion to make the poems mandatory, they have since been offered as part of an elective class.

More of Darwish's poetry became available to English-speaking readers with the publication of two collections, *The Adam of Two Edens* and *Unfortunately, It Was Paradise.* The former work, published near the beginning of the second Intifada, "could not have appeared at a more crucial time" for the Palestinian cause, maintained *Arab Studies Quarterly* contributor Moustafa Bayoumi. These new poems reveal Darwish's continued progression away from traditional forms of poetry and concrete imagery into more abstract works, "yet somehow [his poetry] remains intimate and revelatory," Bayoumi commented.

Bushnaq commended Darwish's ability, throughout his career, to convey the anger, passion, and suffering that stemmed from the poet's love for his lost homeland, reflected in the poet's treatment of Palestine as his female, human lover in some of the poems. What Bushnaq expressed in a summary of the work of Palestinian poets overall can be applied to Darwish in particular: "It is as though the Palestinian poet, in the bleakness of his political situation, has become kin to the ancient poet of the desert—his poetry the only fixed indication that his people exist." Bayoumi wrote similarly in his review: "The unremitting and introspective 'I' of Darwish's poetry reverberates in poem after poem. . . . Darwish's 'I' is never settled or satisfied, but nervously proclaims itself in order not to disappear or be forgotten."

BIOGRAPHICAL AND CRITICAL SOURCES:

BOOKS

Contemporary World Writers, St. James Press (Detroit, MI), 1993.

PERIODICALS

Arab Studies Quarterly, winter, 2002, Moustafa Bayoumi, review of *The Adam of Two Edens,* pp. 95-97.
Asia Africa Intelligence Wire, January 5, 2004, Bassam Za'za', "Darwish and Adonis Win Owais Award for Cultural Achievement."
Books & Culture, September-October, 2003, review of *Unfortunately, It Was Paradise,* pp. 8-9.
Choice, April, 1975, p. 230; June, 1985, p. 1502.
Christian Science Monitor, April 5, 1988, George D. Moffett III, "Israeli Left Finds Words, like Stones, Can Hurt," p. 1.
Grand Street, winter, 1994, Edward W. Said, "On Mahmoud Darwish," pp. 112-115.
Index on Censorship, May-June, 2000, Mouna Naim and Judith Vidal-Hall, profile of Darwish, pp. 154-160.
Journal of Palestine Studies, spring, 2001, Norbert Scholz, review of *Then Palestine,* p. 118; winter, 2002, Sinan Antoon, "Mahmud Darwish's Allegorical Critique of Oslo," pp. 66-77; spring, 2002, interview with Darwish, pp. 67-78.
Library Journal, November 1, 1974, p. 2853.
Los Angeles Times, March 7, 2000, Tracy Wilkinson, "Israelis Irate at Thought of Palestinian Poet in Schools," p. A1.
Middle East Journal, autumn, 1984, pp. 786-787, spring, 1987, Fouzi el Asmar, review of *Sand and Other Poems,* pp. 306-307.

Nation, September 17, 1990, p. 280; April 10, 2000, Ammiel Alcalay, "Israel's Five-Poem Word," p. 29.
New Republic, April 25, 1988, Leon Wieseltier, "A Poem Makes News," p. 15.
New Statesman, March 8, 1974, p. 333; June 17, 2002, John Pilger, interview with Darwish, pp. 13-14.
Newsweek International, March 20, 2000, interview with Darwish, p. 62.
New York Times, April 5, 1988, "Palestinian's Poem Unnerves Israelis," p. A8; May 10, 1996, "Suitcase No Longer His Homeland, a Poet Returns," p. A4; March 7, 2000, Susan Sachs, "Poetry of Arab Pain: Are Israeli Students Ready?," p. A4; December 22, 2001, Adam Shatz, "A Poet's Palestine as a Metaphor: The Loss of Eden, the Sorrows of Exile and Dispossession," pp. A17, A19.
Parnassus, Volume 14, number 2, 1988, pp. 150-188.
Progressive, May, 2002, Nathalie Handal, "Mahmoud Darwish: Palestine's Poet of Exile," pp. 24-26.
Publishers Weekly, March 26, 2001, review of *The Adam of Two Edens,* p. 86; November 25, 2002, review of *Unfortunately, It Was Paradise,* p. 59.
Tikkun, May-June, 2003, review of *Unfortunately, It Was Paradise,* p. 96.
Times Educational Supplement, January 25, 1985, p. 34.
Times Literary Supplement, January 11, 1974, p. 28.
World Literature Today, winter, 1978, p. 169; summer, 1985, p. 482.

ONLINE

Khalil Sakakini Cultural Centre Web site, http://www.sakakini.org/ (April 20, 2004), "Mahmoud Darwish."
Pegasos, http://www.kirjasto.sci.fi/ (April 23, 2004), "Mahmoud Darwish (1942—)."*

*   *   *

DAVIS, B. Lynch
See BORGES, Jorge Luis

*   *   *

DeLILLO, Don 1936-

PERSONAL: Born November 20, 1936, in New York, NY; married. *Education:* Fordham University, graduated, 1958.

ADDRESSES: Agent—Lois Wallace, Wallace Literary Agency, 177 East 70th St., New York, NY 10021.

CAREER: Writer. Worked as an advertising copywriter in early 1960s.

MEMBER: American Academy of Arts and Letters, PEN.

AWARDS, HONORS: Guggenheim fellowship, 1979; American Academy of Arts and Letters Award in Literature, 1984; National Book Award in fiction, and National Book Critics Circle Award nomination, both 1985, both for *White Noise; Irish Times* International Fiction Prize, National Book Award nomination, and National Book Critics Circle Award nomination, all 1989, all for *Libra;* PEN/Faulkner Award, 1992, and Pulitzer Prize nomination, both for *Mao II;* National Book Award nomination, and National Book Critics Circle Award nomination, both 1997, Pulitzer Prize nomination, and William Dean Howells Medal, American Academy of Arts and Letters, 2000, all for *Underworld;* Jerusalem Prize, 2000.

WRITINGS:

NOVELS

Americana, Houghton (Boston, MA), 1971.
End Zone, Houghton (Boston, MA), 1972.
Great Jones Street, Houghton (Boston, MA), 1973.
Ratner's Star, Knopf (New York, NY), 1976.
Players, Knopf (New York, NY), 1977.
Running Dog, Knopf (New York, NY), 1978.
The Names, Knopf (New York, NY), 1982.
White Noise, Viking (New York, NY), 1985.
Libra, Viking (New York, NY), 1988.
Mao II, Viking (New York, NY), 1991.
Underworld, Scribner (New York, NY), 1997, prologue published separately as *Pafko at the Wall,* 2001.
The Body Artist, Scribner (New York, NY), 2001.
Cosmopolis, Scribner (New York, NY), 2003.

OTHER

The Day Room (play; produced at American Repertory Theatre, Cambridge, MA, 1986), Knopf (New York, NY), 1987.
Valparaiso (play; produced at American Repertory Theatre, Cambridge, MA, 1999), Scribner (New York, NY), 1999.

Also author of play *The Engineer of Moonlight,* published in *Cornell Review,* winter, 1979; author of one-minute plays *The Rapture of the Athlete Assumed into Heaven,* published in *Quarterly,* 1990, and *The Mystery at the Middle of Ordinary Life,* published in *Zoetrope,* winter, 2000. Work included in anthologies *Stories from Epoch,* edited by Baxter Hathaway, Cornell University Press, 1966; *The Secret Life of Our Times,* edited by Gordon Lish, Doubleday, 1973; *Cutting Edges,* edited by Jack Hicks, Holt, 1973; *On the Job,* edited by William O'Rourke, Random House, 1977; and *Great Esquire Fiction,* edited by L. Rust Hills, Viking, 1983. Contributor of essay to *Novel History: Historians and Novelists Confront America's Past (and Each Other),* edited by Mark C. Carnes, Simon & Schuster, 2001; contributor of essays and short stories to periodicals, including *Dimensions, New Yorker, New York Times Magazine, Conjunctions, Harper's, Grand Street, Paris Review, Esquire, Granta, Sports Illustrated, Kenyon Review,* and *Rolling Stone.*

ADAPTATIONS: DeLillo's novels have been adapted as audiobooks.

SIDELIGHTS: With each of his novels Don DeLillo has enhanced his literary reputation and gained a wider audience for his carefully crafted prose. He first attracted critical attention in the early 1970s when he published two ambitious and elusive novels about games: *End Zone,* an existential comedy that parlays football into a metaphor for thermonuclear war, and *Ratner's Star,* a surrealistic science fiction that is structurally akin to the mathematical formulas it employs. The verbal precision, dazzling intelligence, and sharp wit of these books made DeLillo a critical favorite, "but without bestseller sales figures or a dependable cult following, he has become something of a reviewer's writer," according to R. Z. Sheppard in *Time.*

DeLillo's 1985 novel *White Noise* received front-page *New York Times Book Review* coverage and garnered the National Book Award in fiction that year. His name became even more widely known after *Underworld* achieved bestsellerdom in several countries, including the United States. "In fact," wrote Chicago *Tribune Books* contributor John W. Aldridge, on the heels of *White Noise,* "DeLillo has won the right not only to be ranked with [Thomas] Pynchon and [William] Gaddis but recognized as having surpassed them in brilliance, versatility, and breadth of imagination. DeLillo shares with them, but in a degree greater than theirs, that rarest of creative gifts, the ability to identify and describe, as if from the perspective of another galaxy, the exact look and feel of contemporary reality." DeLillo's novel *Libra,* is an account of the life of Lee Harvey Oswald, John F. Kennedy's assassin. A stunning success—*Libra* was nominated for the National Book Award and won the newly inaugurated International Fiction Prize from the *Irish Times*—Walter Clemons in *Newsweek* dubbed the work "overwhelming."

DeLillo's obsession with language links him to other members of literature's school. "Like his contemporaries, William Gass, Robert Coover, and John Barth, he may be termed a 'metafictionist,'" wrote Michael Oriard in *Critique.* "Like these writers, he is strongly aware of the nature of language and makes language itself, and the process of using language, his themes." In his *Contemporary Literature* interview with Thomas LeClair, DeLillo suggested that after writing *End Zone,* he realized "that language was a subject as well as an instrument in my work." Later, he elaborated: "What writing means to me is trying to make interesting, clear, beautiful language. Working at sentences and rhythms is probably the most satisfying thing I do as a writer. I think after a while a writer can begin to know himself through his language. He sees someone or something reflected back at him from these constructions. Over the years it's possible for a writer to shape himself as a human being through the language he uses. I think written language, fiction, goes that deep."

While DeLillo's sentiments may have intimidated some readers, they have attracted enthusiastic critics. Rising to his challenge of commitment, reviewers have offered thoughtful interpretations of his complex work, recognizing recurring themes which darken and turn more ominous as the work evolves. "From *Americana* to *End Zone* to *Great Jones Street* to *Ratner's Star* DeLillo traces a single search for the source of life's meaning," explained Oriard. "By the end of *Ratner's Star,* the quest has been literally turned inside out, the path from chaos to knowledge becomes a Moebius strip that brings the seeker back to chaos."

The quest in DeLillo's first novel, *Americana,* involves a disillusioned television executive's search for a national identity. Abandoning his job, producer David

Bell embarks on a cross-country odyssey to "nail down the gas-driven, motel-housed American soul," *Village Voice* contributor Albert Mobilio explained. Even in this early work, DeLillo's obsession with language dominates the narrative: his first-person narrator describes his quest as a "literary venture," using images that compare the western landscape to linguistic patterns on a page. "For years I had been held fast by the great unwinding mystery of this deep sink of land, the thick paragraphs and imposing photos, the gallop of panting adjectives, prairie truth and the clean kills of eagles," says Bell. *Americana,* like most first novels, was not widely reviewed, but it did attract favorable notice from some established New York critics, who expressed enthusiasm for DeLillo's remarkable verbal gifts. "It is a familiar story by now, flawed in the telling," noted *New York Times* contributor Christopher Lehmann-Haupt in a representative review. "But the language soars and dips, and it imparts a great deal." *New York Times Book Review* contributor Thomas R. Edwards deemed it "a savagely funny portrait of middle-class anomie in a bad time," but also noted that the book is "too long and visibly ambitious, and too much like too many other recent novels, to seem as good as it should have."

Edwards found DeLillo's second novel—in which the quest for meaning is transferred from the American roadside to the sports arena—a more successful venture. "In *End Zone,*" wrote Edwards, "DeLillo finds in college football a more original and efficient vehicle for his sense of things now." This episodic, largely plotless novel focuses on the final attempt college athlete Gary Harkness makes to prove himself as a football player in a small west Texas school. Gary, who spends his free time playing war games, is attracted to carefully structured systems of ordered violence that afford opportunities for complete control. Edwards speculates that "Gary's involvement with [football] is a version of his horrified fascination with the vocabulary, theory and technology of modern war." Out on the playing field, Gary wins all but one of his football games, but "it's a season of losses all the same," Edwards concludes, for not only do minor characters suffer setbacks and tragedies but Gary "ends up in the infirmary with a mysterious brain-fever being fed through plastic tubes."

Gary's hunger strike has been interpreted as a final existential attempt to exert control. "He's paring things down. He is struggling, trying to face something he felt had to be faced," DeLillo told LeClair. Thus the "end zone" of this novel becomes a symbolic setting that represents "not only the goal of the running back in a football game, but the human condition at the outer extremity of existence, a place where the world is on the verge of disintegration, and the characters teeter between genius and madness," Oriard believes. "In this region of end zones that DeLillo describes, characters struggle for order and meaning as their world moves inexorably towards chaos. DeLillo's men and women fight the natural law of entropy, while human violence hastens its inevitable consequences."

The next American milieu DeLillo tackles is the world of rock stars and the drug culture in the novel *Great Jones Street.* Walter Clemons's assessment of the novel as an "in-between book" is representative of critical opinion, and while critics realized DeLillo was extending himself as a writer, they were not completely satisfied with the result. "The rock stars, drug dealers and hangers-on that populate *Great Jones Street* are so totally freaked out, so slickly devoted to destruction and evil, so obsessed with manipulating and acquiring that they're beyond redemption," wrote *New York Times Book Review* contributor Sara Blackburn, who deemed the work "more of a sour, admirably written lecture than a novel, a book that is always puffing to keep up with the power and intensity of its subject."

DeLillo turned to the genre of science fiction for his fourth book, *Ratner's Star,* a pivotal work about a fourteen-year-old mathematical genius and Nobel laureate, Billy Twillig. "There is no easy way to describe *Ratner's Star,* a cheerfully apocalyptic novel," wrote Amanda Heller in the *Atlantic.* "Imagine *Alice in Wonderland* set at the Princeton Institute for Advanced Studies." A reviewer for the *New Yorker* found it "a whimsical, surrealistic excursion into the modern scientific mind." *New York Times Book Review* contributor George Stade described it as "not only interesting, but funny (in a nervous kind of way). From it comes an unambiguous signal that DeLillo has arrived, bearing many gifts. He is smart, observant, fluent, a brilliant mimic and an ingenious architect."

Modeled after Lewis Carroll's *Alice in Wonderland, Ratner's Star* is comprised of two sections, "Adventures" and "Reflections," that mimic the structural divisions of Carroll's book. "The comic, episodic discontinuous style of the book's first half is reflected in reverse in its symmetrically opposite second part,"

explained G. M. Knoll in *America.* He continued, "All that has been asserted or hypothesized about the signals from Ratner's Star is here denied. Billy's assignment is now to assist in the development of a language to answer the star's message rather than decipher the meaning of the signals." DeLillo's goal in this venture, according to *Time*'s Paul Gray, "is to show how the codification of phenomena as practiced by scientists leads to absurdity and madness." In his interview with LeClair, however, DeLillo says that his primary intention was "to produce a book that would be naked structure. The structure would be the book."

Ratner's Star marked a turning point in DeLillo's fiction, according to critics who noted a shift in the pacing and tone of the novelist's subsequent books. "Since *Ratner's Star,* the apogee or nadir of his mirrorgame experiments, DeLillo has opened his fiction to the possibilities of more extroverted action," observed *New Republic* contributor Robert Towers. "The speeded-up pace in both *Players* and *Running Dog* seems to me all to the good." Accompanying this accelerated narrative, however, is a noticeable change in the kinds of people DeLillo is writing about. Hardened by exposure to modern society, cynical in their views of life, these characters "are not sustained by the illusion that answers to cosmic questions can be found," Oriard believed. Nor are their self-serving quests particularly admirable, according to *Dictionary of Literary Biography* contributor Frank Day, who maintained that readers may have a hard time sympathizing with protagonists whose lives are "parables of betrayal and degeneration. The frail, confused youths of the early novels are here displaced by characters influenced by popular espionage fiction."

In *Players* DeLillo employs a prologue—a sophisticated bit of pure fiction in which the characters are temporarily suspended outside the apparatus of the story—to introduce his themes. Before the narrative starts, DeLillo collects his as-yet-unnamed protagonists on an empty airplane, seating them in the lounge to watch a grisly film. "The Movie," as this prelude is called, depicts an unsuspecting band of Sunday golfers being attacked and murdered by marauding hippies who splatter the scenic green landscape with blood. Without earphones the passengers can not hear the dialogue, so the pianist improvises silent-movie music to accompany the scene. "The passengers laugh, cheer, clap," noted *New York Times Book Review* contributor Diane Johnson. "It is the terrorists whom they applaud." When the movie ends, the lights come up and the passengers, now identified as protagonists Lyle and Pammy Wynant and friends, step off the plane and into the story—a tale of terrorists, murder, and wasted lives.

A hip New York couple, Pammy and Lyle are bored to distraction by each other and their jobs. Pammy works as a promotional writer at the Grief Management Council, an organization that "served the community in its efforts to understand and assimilate grief," while Lyle is a stockbroker on Wall Street who spends his free time parked in front of the TV set, flipping channels, not in hopes of finding a good program, but because "he simply enjoyed jerking the dial into fresh image burns."

Pammy moves out, heading off to Maine with a pair of homosexual lovers, one of whom will become her lover and commit suicide, but she will ultimately return home. Lyle takes up with a mindless secretary who is linked to a terrorist group responsible for murdering a man on the stock exchange floor. Intrigued by the glamour of revolutionary violence, Lyle joins forces with the terrorists, but also covers himself by informing on their activities to law enforcement agencies. "The end," noted John Updike in the *New Yorker,* "finds him in a motel in Canada, having double-crossed everybody but on excellent terms, it seems, with himself." Both he and Pammy have become players in the game.

Noting that DeLillo is that rare kind of novelist who looks "grandly at the whole state of things," Johnson postulated that, "since Freud, we've been used to the way novelists normally present a character: looks normal, is secretly strange and individual. In the first of many inversions of appearance and reality that structure the book, Pammy and Lyle look interesting and seem to do interesting things, but do not interest themselves. The richness is only superficial. . . . Pammy and Lyle have no history; they are without pasts, were never children, come from nowhere. They worry that they have become too complex to experience things directly and acutely, but the opposite is true. They are being reduced by contemporary reality to numb simplicity, lassitude."

DeLillo followed *Players* with two psychological thrillers, *Running Dog* and *The Names,* the latter of which was praised for its improved characterization.

But it was with *White Noise* that DeLillo most impressed critics with his rendition of fully realized characters in a minimalist prose style. Noting that with each book DeLillo has become increasingly elliptical, *Village Voice* contributor Albert Mobilio observed that "the distillation is matched by a more subtle and convincing treatment of his characters' inner lives. This broadened emotional vocabulary charges *White Noise* with a resonance and credibility that makes it difficult to ignore. Critics who have argued that his work is too clever and overly intellectual should take notice: DeLillo's dark vision is now hard-earned. It strikes at both heart and head."

A novel about technology and death, *White Noise* unfolds as the first-person narrative of Jack Gladney, chair of the department of Hitler studies at a small liberal arts school, College-on-the-Hill. Gladney lives with his fourth wife Babette—an ample, disheveled woman who teaches an adult education class in posture and reads to the blind—and their four children from previous marriages: Wilder, Steffie, Denise, and Heinrich. Life seems full for the Gladneys, but early on Jack confesses that he and Babette are obsessed with a troubling question: "Who will die first?" Even as they debate it, small signs of trouble begin to surface: the children are evacuated from grade school because of an unidentified toxin in the atmosphere, and Babette's memory is impaired, a side effect of a prescribed medication. One winter day a major chemical spill jeopardizes the whole city. Everyone is forced to evacuate and, on his way to the shelter Jack stops to get gas, inadvertently exposing himself to the "airborne toxic event." Informed that "anything that puts you in contact with actual emissions means we have a situation," Jack becomes convinced he is dying. (As proof, his computerized health profile spews out "bracketed numbers with pulsing stars.") When Jack discovers Babette's medication—which she has committed adultery to obtain—is an experimental substance said to combat fear of death, he vows to find more of the substance for himself. His quest to obtain the illicit drug at any cost forms the closing chapters of the novel.

Newsweek contributor Walter Clemons wrote that *White Noise* should win DeLillo "wide recognition, till now only flickeringly granted as one of the best American novelists. Comic and touching, ingenious and weird, *White Noise* looks, at first, reassuringly like an example of a familiar genre, the campus novel." But,

Clemons went on to say, the novel "tunes us in on frequencies we haven't heard in other accounts of how we live now. Occult supermarket tabloids are joined with TV disaster footage as household staples providing nourishment and febrile attractions. Fleeting appearances or phone calls from the Gladneys' previous spouses give us the start of surprise we experience when we learn that couples we know have a previous family we haven't heard about." Also commenting on DeLillo's depiction of domestic scenes, Jay McInerney wrote in the *New Republic* that the novelist's "portrait of this postnuclear family is one of the simpler pleasures of this novel." Bert Testa hypothesized in the Toronto *Globe and Mail* that "*White Noise* plays off the familiar and the disturbing without ever tipping into the merely grotesque. When DeLillo constantly returns to Jack's quotidian family life, he means his readers to enter a firmly drawn circle that not even a little toxic apocalypse can break."

"The world of *Libra* is not the modern or technological world that characters in my other novels try to confront," DeLillo explained to *New York Times* reviewer Herbert Mitgang of his 1988 novel. In *Libra* the author mixes fact with fiction in a discussion of the events that led to the assassination of President John F. Kennedy on November 22, 1963, in Dallas, Texas. He dispels the accepted truth that Kennedy was shot by a lone gunman, Lee Harvey Oswald, by uncovering information supporting a conspiracy theory acknowledged by some historians. DeLillo spent three years researching and writing about Oswald's life, tracing the assassin's career as a Marxist in the U.S. military and his consequent defection to the USSR and return to the United States. DeLillo surmises that a coterie of underworld and U.S. government figures—enemies of Kennedy—recruited Oswald as a scapegoat for an assassination attempt that should have been botched.

"At what point exactly does fact drift over into fiction?" Anne Tyler asked in her *New York Times Book Review* critique of *Libra*. "The book is so seamlessly written that perhaps not even those people who own . . . copies of the Warren report could say for certain." Richard Eder in the *Los Angeles Times Book Review* agreed, noting that in the novel "DeLillo disassembles his plots with the finest of jigsaw cuts, scrambles their order and has us reassemble them. As the assorted characters go about their missions, we discern them more by intuition than by perception.

The chronology goes back and forth, disorienting us. We do not so much follow what is going on as infiltrate it." Robert Dunn observed in *Mother Jones* that in his study of the president's assassin DeLillo "has found a story beyond imagination, one whose significance is indisputable and ongoing . . . and he carefully hews to known facts and approaches all events with respect, even awe. By giving Oswald and the forces he represents full body, DeLillo has written his best novel."

Mao II, further solidified DeLillo's place in the leading ranks of contemporary American novelists. The winner of the 1992 PEN/Faulkner Award for fiction, the novel revolves around a reclusive novelist, Bill Gray, whose first two works made him famous but who has labored for more than twenty years to produce his third novel. Completely hidden from public view on his rural New York estate, Gray has human contact only with his secretary and helper, Scott, and a young woman, Karen, who is coping with the dissolution of her marriage. In typical DeLillo fashion, Karen's was not a standard marriage: the novel's opening scene shows her wedding her husband along with six thousand other couples in a ceremony staged by the Reverend Sun Myung Moon at Yankee Stadium. Convinced that Gray's long-awaited novel will be a failure, Scott urges him not to publish it, arguing that his cult-like celebrity will increase if the novel never appears in print. Gray, however, tiring of his isolation, does something more momentous than publishing his novel: he allows himself to be photographed by Brita, a Swedish photographer.

In *Underworld* DeLillo paints an encyclopedic portrait of late-twentieth-century American life through the story of accused murderer Nick Shay, as Shay's path collides with great moments of history, including the 1951 ball game in which the Giants won the pennant. Michiko Kakutani reviewed *Underworld* admiringly in the *New York Times,* calling it a "remarkable" tale of "the effluvia of modern life, all the detritus of our daily and political lives" that has been "turned into a dazzling, phosphorescent work of art." Like most of DeLillo's novels, time is not a straight trajectory in *Underworld,* and a current of conspiracy, paranoia, and terrorism weaves through the story. This technique brings the alienated protagonist in close contact with events that define his century, including the political suspense of the cold war. In a review for the *New York Times,* Martin Amis claimed that *Underworld* "may or may not be a great novel," but added: "there is no doubt that . . . DeLillo is a great novelist." Noting that nuclear war is the central theme of the book, Amis added that *Underworld*'s "main actors are psychological 'downwinders,' victims of the fallout from all the blasts—blasts actual and imagined."

Coming on the heels of the impressive *Underworld, The Body Artist* reinforced the belief held by many critics that DeLillo is not a writer to traverse the same path more than once. *The Body Artists* opens to the breakfast-table rambling of married couple Lauren and Rey; only later in the book do readers learn that Rey has committed suicide that same day. The rest of the novel focuses on Lauren, a performance artist who creates different characters by transforming her physical self. Grieving over Rey, she withdraws and becomes housebound, then begins to hear noises. Finally she discovers a strange, diminutive man, Mr. Tucker, who has the strange ability to repeat back to her the last rambling conversations between Lauren and her husband. Who Mr. Tucker is—a real, perhaps mentally disturbed person or a figment of Lauren's overwrought imaginings—is purposefully never made clear, DeLillo's central purpose to cause readers to reflect on "the fragility of identity, the nature of time, the way the words we employ in the face of death have become . . . worn to the point of transparency," according to *Newsweek* contributor Malcolm Jones. "Like all DeLillo's fiction," added a *Publishers Weekly* contributor, *The Body Artist* "offers a vision of contemporary life that expresses itself most clearly in how the story is told." While an *Economist* critic found the novel as "slight as a blade of grass," Donna Seaman praised the challenging work in *Booklist,* noting that "Each sentence is like a formula that must be solved, and each paragraph adds up to unexpected disclosures regarding our sense of time, existence, identity, and connection."

More compressed in time than *The Body Artist, Cosmopolis* takes place for the most part inside a stretch limousine belonging to wealthy, twenty-something, and less-than-likeable financier Eric Packer. Packer's trip across town to the barber is thwarted by traffic snarls into an all-day excursion, forcing the mildly paranoid Packer to turn to his in-car computer to track his financial wheelings and dealings, teleconference with clients and lackeys, and make brief excursions from the limo to eat, shop, take in the sights of midtown Manhattan, and even commit murder. While the movement of Packer's limo is "glacial," according to an *Economist* reviewer, *Cosmopolis,* "with Mr. DeLillo at the wheel, zooms along, blowing up great billowing clouds of rhetorical dust. . . . full of wordy ruminations on the relationship between technology and capitalism."

Critics responded with characteristic vigor to *Cosmopolis,* although the novel, DeLillo's thirteenth, was not treated with overwhelming kindness. "There is no real plot," bemoaned *Spectator* contributor Peter Dempsey, "there are no fully rounded characters nor any character development, and though the novel ends dramatically, there is no sense of a conventionally satisfying conclusion." Noting that such expectations on the part of many critics are intentionally unmet by DeLillo, Dempsey described *Cosmopolis* as "a meditation on various kinds of speculation, most importantly financial and philosophical," that, as a work of fiction, "is redeemed by its beguiling structure and the cool intensity of its compelling descriptions of New York City." "Where did DeLillo lose me exactly?," Richard Lacayo queried in *Time.* "It may have been the scene in which Packer gets a digital rectal exam in his parked limousine while he chats with . . . his chief of finance. I like surrealism too, but sometimes I wish they would keep it in France." In contrast, *Review of Contemporary Fiction* critic Robert L. McLaughlin stayed the course, writing that the author "has captured the essence of a particular American moment," and ranked the novel as "a beautiful and brilliant book." "One senses that DeLillo continues to challenge himself," added Kyle Minor in *Antioch Review,* ". . . and the result is a mature work of fiction, greatly satisfying."

BIOGRAPHICAL AND CRITICAL SOURCES:

BOOKS

Civello, Paul, *American Literary Naturalism and Its Twentieth-Century Transformations: Frank Norris, Ernest Hemingway, Don DeLillo,* University of Georgia Press (Athens, GA), 1994.

Contemporary Literary Criticism, Gale (Detroit, MI), Volume 8, 1978, Volume 10, 1979, Volume 13, 1980, Volume 27, 1984, Volume 39, 1986, Volume 54, 1989, Volume 76, 1993.

DeLillo, Don, *Americana,* Houghton (Boston, MA), 1971.

Dictionary of Literary Biography, Volume 6: *American Novelists since World War II, Second Series,* Gale (Detroit, MI), 1980.

Hantke, Steffen, *Conspiracy and Paranoia in Contemporary American Fiction: The Works of Don DeLillo and Joseph McElroy,* P. Lang (New York, NY), 1994.

LeClair, Tom, *In the Loop: Don DeLillo and the Systems Novel,* University of Illinois Press, 1988.

Lentricchia, Frank, *Introducing Don DeLillo,* Duke University Press, 1991.

Lentricchia, Frank, editor, *New Essays on White Noise,* Cambridge University Press (New York, NY), 1991.

Osteen, Mark, *American Magic and Dread: Don DeLillo's Dialogue with Culture,* University of Pennsylvania Press, 2000.

Ruppersburg, Hugh M., and Tim Engles, editors, *Critical Essays on Don DeLillo,* G. K. Hall (New York, NY), 2000.

PERIODICALS

America, August 7, 1976; July 6-13, 1985.

Antioch Review, spring, 1972; winter, 1983; summer, 2003, Kyle Minor, review of *Cosmopolis,* p. 581.

Atlantic, August, 1976; February, 1985.

Booklist, November 1, 1993, p. 499; October 1, 2000, Donna Seaman, review of *The Body Artist,* p. 292; December 1, 2002, Donna Seaman, review of *Cosmopolis,* p. 628.

Choice, April, 1988, p. 1242.

Christian Century, May 2, 2001, Gordon Houser, review of *The Body Artist,* p. 27.

Commonweal, August 9, 1991, pp. 490-491.

Contemporary Literature, winter, 1982, Tom LeClair, "An Interview with Don DeLillo," pp. 19-31

Critique, Volume XX, number 1, 1978.

Detroit News, February 24, 1985.

Economist (U.S.), February 17, 2001, review of *The Body Artist,* p. 8; April 19, 2003, review of *Cosmopolis.*

Entertainment Weekly, April 11, 2003, Chris Nashawaty, "Prophet Statement" (interview), p. 48; April 18, 2003, Ken Tucker, review of *Cosmopolis,* p. 72.

Esquire, February, 2000, Sven Birkerts, review of *The Body Artist,* p. 38.

Financial Post, November 1, 1997, Allan Hepburn, review of *Underworld,* p. 28.

Globe and Mail (Toronto, Ontario, Canada), March 9, 1985; August 27, 1988.

Harper's, September, 1977; December, 1982; June, 1999, Jonathan Dee, review of *Libra,* p. 76.

Hudson Review, summer, 1999, Richard Hornby, review of *Valparaiso,* p. 287.

Journal of Men's Studies, fall, 1999, p. 73.

Journal of Modern Literature, spring, 1996, p. 453.

Kirkus Reviews, January 1, 2003, review of *Cosmopolis,* p. 8.

Library Journal, January, 1988, p. 96; January 1, 2001, Mirela Roncevic, review of *The Body Artist,* p. 152l; December, 2002, Edward B. St. John, review of *Cosmopolis,* p. 176.

Los Angeles Times, July 29, 1984; August 12, 1988; October 8, 1997, David L. Ulin, "Merging Myth and Mystery," p. E1; December 14, 1997, Richard Eder, review of *Underworld,* p. 11.

Los Angeles Times Book Review, November 7, 1982; January 13, 1985; July 31, 1988; June 9, 1991, p. 3.

Maclean's, November 13, 1978, pp. 62, 64; August 29, 1988.

Modern Fiction Studies, summer, 1994, p. 229.

Mother Jones, September, 1988.

Nation, September 17, 1977; October 18, 1980; December 11, 1982; February 2, 1985; September 19, 1988.

National Review, October 28, 1977.

New Republic, October 7, 1978; November 22, 1982; February 4, 1985.

New Statesman, February 2, 1979, p. 158.

Newsweek, June 7, 1976; August 29, 1977; October 25, 1982; January 21, 1985; August 15, 1988; January 15, 2001, Malcolm Jones, review of *The Body Artist,* p. 61.

New Yorker, July 12, 1976; March 27, 1978; September 18, 1978; April 4, 1983; September 15, 1997, David Remnick, "Exile on Main Street," pp. 42-48.

New York Review of Books, June 29, 1972; December 16, 1982; March 14, 1985; June 9, 1991, pp. 7, 49; June 27, 1991, pp. 17-18; February 22, 2001, John Leonard, review of *The Body Artist,* p. 14.

New York Times, May 6, 1971; March 22, 1972; April 16, 1973; May 27, 1976; August 11, 1977; September 16, 1980; October 12, 1982; January 7, 1985; December 20, 1987; December 21, 1987; July 19, 1988; May 18, 1989; September 24, 1989; September 16, 1997, Michiko Kakutani, review of *Underworld,* p. E1; October 5, 1997, p. E2; September 10, 1998, David Firestone, "Reticent Novelist Talks Baseball, Not Books," p. B2; February 24, 1999, Peter Marks, "Ticket Mix-up Brings Fifteen Minutes of Fame," p. E1.

New York Times Book Review, May 30, 1971; April 9, 1972; April 22, 1973; June 20, 1976; September 4, 1977; November 12, 1978; October 10, 1982, Robert R. Harris, "A Talk with Don DeLillo," p. 23; January 13, 1985, Caryn James, "I Never Set out to Write an Apocalyptic Novel," p. 31; May 28, 1991, p. C15; October 5, 1997, Martin Amis, review of *Underworld,* p. 12; December 7, 1997, review of *Underworld,* p. 95; July 24, 1998, Kim Heron, "Haunted by His Book," p. 23.

New York Times Magazine, May 19, 1991, Vince Passaro, "Dangerous Don DeLillo," pp. 36-38, 76-77.

Partisan Review, number 3, 1979.

Publishers Weekly, August 19, 1988; November 20, 2000, review of *The Body Artist,* p. 43; December 9, 2002, review of *Cosmopolis,* p. 58.

Review of Contemporary Fiction, spring, 2001, David Seed, review of *The Body Artist,* p. 189; summer, 2003, Robert L. McLaughlin, review of *Cosmopolis,* p. 120.

Saturday Review, September 3, 1977; September 16, 1978.

Spectator, September 7, 1991, pp. 34-35; June 7, 2003, Peter Dempsey, review of *Cosmopolis,* p. 38.

Time, June 7, 1976; November 8, 1982; January 21, 1985; August 1, 1988; June 10, 1991, p. 68; April 21, 2003, Richard Lacayo, review of *Cosmopolis,* p. 74.

Times (London, England), January 23, 1986.

Times Literary Supplement, September 14, 1973; December 9, 1983; January 17, 1986.

Tribune Books (Chicago, IL), November 7, 1982; January 13, 1985; July 31, 1988; June 23, 1991, pp. 1, 4.

USA Today, January 11, 1985.

Vanity Fair, September, 1997, David Kamp, "DeLillo's Home Run," pp. 202-204.

Variety, March 1, 1999, Markland Taylor, review of *Valparaiso,* p. 93.

Village Voice, April 30, 1985; June 18, 1991, p. 65.

Voice Literary Supplement, December, 1981; November, 1982; October, 1988.

Wall Street Journal, June 13, 1991, review of *Mao II,* p. A14; September 26, 1997, James Bowman, review of *Underworld,* p. A20.

Washington Post, August 24, 1988; May 11, 1989; May 14, 1992, "Don DeLillo's Gloomy Muse," p. C1; November 11, 1997, David Streitfeild, "Don DeLillo's Hidden Truths," p. D1.

Washington Post Book World, April 16, 1972; April 15, 1973; June 13, 1976; August 21, 1977; October 15, 1978; October 10, 1982; January 13, 1985; July 31, 1988; May 26, 1991, pp. 1-2.

World and I, October, 2001, Linda Simon, "Voice from a Silent Landscape," p. 253.

World Literature Today, winter, 1992.

Yale Review, April, 1995, p. 107.

* * *

DERRIDA, Jacques 1930-

PERSONAL: Born July 15, 1930, in El Biar, Algeria; son of Aime and Georgette (Safar) Derrida. *Education:* Attended École Normale Superieure, 1952-56; University of Paris, Sorbonne, Licence es Lettres, 1953, Licence de Philosophie, 1953, Diplome d'Etudes Superieures, 1954; received Certificat d'Ethnologie, 1954, Agregation de Philosophie, 1956, Doctorat en Philosophie, 1967, Doctorat d'Etat es Lettres, 1980; graduate study at Harvard University, 1956-57.

ADDRESSES: Home—Paris, France. *Office*—École des Hautes Etudes en Sciences Sociales, 54 bis Raspail, 75006 Paris, France. *Agent*—c/o Author Mail, University of Chicago Press, 5801 South Ellis Ave., Chicago, IL 60637.

CAREER: Philosopher and educator. Lycée du Mans, professor, 1959-60; University of Paris, Sorbonne, Paris, France, professor of philosophy, 1960-64; École Normale Superieure, Paris, professor of philosophy, 1964-84; École des Hautes Etudes en Sciences Sociales, Paris, director, 1984—. College International de Philosophie, member of planning board, 1982-83, director, 1983-84, member of administrative council, 1986. Visiting professor and lecturer at numerous universities in Europe and the United States, including Johns Hopkins University, Yale University, University of California—Irvine, Cornell University, and City University of New York.

MEMBER: Institut des Textes et Manuscrits Modernes (member of steering committee, 1983-86), Groupe de Recherches sur l'Enseignement Philosophique (president), Association Jan Hus (vice president), Fondation Culturelle Contre l'Apartheid, American Academy of

DERRIDA

Jacques Derrida

Arts and Sciences (foreign honorary member), Modern Language Association of America (honorary member), Academy for the Humanities and Sciences (honorary member).

AWARDS, HONORS: Prix Cavailles, Societe des Amis de Jean Cavailles, 1964, for translation into French of Edmund Husserl's *Origin of Geometry;* named to Liste d'Aptitude a l'Enseignement Superieur, 1968; named chevalier, 1968, officier, 1980, of Palmes Academiques; named Commandeur des Arts et des Lettres, 1983; Prix Nietzsche, Association Internationale de Philosophie, 1988; named Chevalier, Legion d'Honneur (France), 1995. Honorary doctorates from Columbia University, 1980, University of Louvain, 1983, and University of Essex, 1987.

WRITINGS:

(Translator and author of introduction) Edmund Husserl, *L'origine de la geometrie,* Presses Universitaires de France (Paris, France), 1962, translation by John P. Leavy published as *Edmund Husserl's "Origin of Geometry": An Introduction,* Nicolas-Hays (York Beach, ME), 1977.

La voix et le phenomene: introduction au probleme du signe dans la phenomenologie de Husserl, Presses Universitaires de France (Paris, France), 1967, translation by David B. Allison published as *Speech and Phenomena and Other Essays on Husserl's Theory of Signs,* Northwestern University Press (Evanston, IL), 1973.

L'ecriture et la difference, Seuil (Paris, France), 1967, translation by Alan Bass published as *Writing and Difference,* University of Chicago Press (Chicago, IL), 1978.

De la grammatologie, Minuit (Paris, France), 1967, translation by Gayatri Chakravorty Spivak published as *Of Grammatology,* Johns Hopkins University Press (Baltimore, MD), 1976.

La dissemination, Seuil (Paris, France), 1972, translation by Barbara Johnson published as *Dissemination,* University of Chicago Press (Chicago, IL), 1981.

Marges de la philosophie, Minuit (Paris, France), 1972, translation by Alan Bass published as *Margins of Philosophy,* University of Chicago Press (Chicago, IL), 1982.

Positions: entretiens avec Henri Ronse, Julia Kristeva, Jean-Louis Houdebine, Guy Scarpetta (interviews), Minuit (Paris, France), 1972, translation by Alan Bass published as *Positions,* University of Chicago Press (Chicago, IL), 1981.

L'archeologie du frivole (first published as introduction to Etienne de Condillac, *L'essai sur l'origine des connaissances humaines,* Galilée, 1973), Denoël (Paris, France), 1976, translation by John P. Leavey, Jr., published as *The Archaeology of the Frivolous: Reading Condillac,* Duquesne University Press (Atlantic Highlands, NJ), 1980.

Glas, Galilée (Paris, France), 1974, translation by John P. Leavey, Jr., and Richard Rand published as *Glas,* University of Nebraska Press (Lincoln, NE), 1986.

Eperons: les styles de Nietzsche, Flammarion (Paris, France), 1976, translation by Barbara Harlow published as *Spurs: Nietzsche's Styles,* University of Chicago Press (Chicago, IL), 1979.

Limited Inc: abc, Johns Hopkins University Press (Baltimore, MD), 1977.

La vérité en peinture (title means "Truth in Painting"), Flammarion (Paris, France), 1978.

La carte postale: de Socrate a Freud et au-dela, Flammarion (Paris, France), 1980, translation by Alan Bass published as *The Post Card: From Socrates to Freud and Beyond,* University of Chicago Press (Chicago, IL), 1987.

L'oreille de l'autre: otobiographies, transferts, traductions; textes et debats, VLB (Montreal, Quebec, Canada), 1982, translation by Peggy Kamuf published as *The Ear of the Other: Otobiography, Transference, Translation,* Schocken (New York, NY), 1985.

D'un ton apocalyptique adopte naguere en philosophie, Galilée (Paris, France), 1983.

Feu la cendre/Cio'che resta del fuoco, Sansoni (Florence, Italy), 1984, published as *Feu la cendre,* Des Femmes, 1987.

Signeponge/Signsponge (French and English text; English translation by Richard Rand), Columbia University Press (New York, NY), 1984, revised, Seuil (Paris, France), 1988.

Otobiographies: l'enseignement de Nietzsche et la politique du nom propre, Galilée (Paris, France), 1984.

Droit de regards, Minuit (Paris, France), 1985.

La faculté de juger, Minuit (Paris, France), 1985.

Parages, Galilée (Paris, France), 1986.

De l'esprit: Heidegger et la question, Galilée (Paris, France), 1987, translation by Geoffrey Bennington and Rachel Bowlby published as *Of Spirit: Heidegger and the Question,* University of Chicago Press (Chicago, IL), 1989.

Psyche: inventions de l'autre, Galilée (Paris, France), 1987.

Memoires: pour Paul de Man, Galilée (Paris, France), 1988, translation by Cecile Lindsay, Jonathan Culler, and Eduardo Cadava published as *Memoires: Lectures for Paul de Man,* Columbia University Press (New York, NY), 1989.

Le probleme de la genese dans la philosophie de Husserl, Presses Universitaires de France (Paris, France), 1990.

De droit a la philosophie, Galilée (Paris, France), 1990.

Memoires de' aveugle, l'autoportrait et autres ruins, Reunion des musees nationaux, 1990, translation by Pascale Ann Brault and Michael Nass published as *Memoirs of the Blind, the Self-Portrait and Other Ruins,* University of Chicago Press (Chicago, IL), 1993.

Donner le temps, 1, Fausse monnai, Galilée (Paris, France), 1991, translation by Peggy Kamuf published as *Given Time, 1: Counterfeit Money,* University of Chicago Press (Chicago, IL), 1992.

L'autre cap; suivre de la democratie ajournaee, Minuit (Paris, France), 1991, translation by Pascale-Anne Brault and Michael Naas published as *The Other Heading: Reflections of Today's Europe,* Indiana University Press (Bloomington, IN), 1992.

A Derrida Reader: Between the Blinds, edited by Peggy Kamuf, Columbia University Press (New York, NY), 1991.

Cinders, translation by Ned Lukacher, University of Nebraska Press (Lincoln, NE), 1991.

(With Geoffrey Derrida) *Jacques Derrida,* Seuil (Paris, France), 1991.

Prejuges, Passagen, 1992.

Acts of Literature, edited by Derek Attridge, Routledge (London, England), 1992.

Donner la mort, Seuil (Paris, France), 1992, translation by David Wells published as *The Gift of Death,* University of Chicago Press (Chicago, IL), 1995.

Passions, Galilée (Paris, France), 1993.

Khora, Galilée (Paris, France), 1993.

Apories: mourir-s'attendre aux "limites de la vérite," Galilée (Paris, France), 1993, translation by Thomas Dutoit published as *Aporias: Dying-Awaiting (One Another at) the "Limits of Truth,"* Stanford University Press (Stanford, CA), 1993.

Spectres de Marx: l'état de la dette, le travail du deuil et la nouvelle internationale, Galilée (Paris, France), 1993, translation by Peggy Kamuf published as *Spectres of Marx, State of the Debt, the Work of Mourning, and the New International,* Routledge (London, England), 1994.

Force de loi; le "fondement mystique de l'autorité," Galilée (Paris, France), 1994.

Politiques de l'amitié, Galilée (Paris, France), 1994, translation by George Collins published as *The Politics of Friendship,* Verso (London, England), 1997.

On the Name, edited by Thomas Dutoit, translated by David Wood and others, Stanford University Press (Stanford, CA), 1995.

Mal d'archive, une impression freudienne, Galilée (Paris, France), 1995, translation by Eric Predowitz published as *Archive Fever: A Freudian Impression,* University of Chicago Press (Chicago, IL), 1996.

Deconstruction and Philosophy: The Texts of Jacques Derrida, translation by David Wells, University of Chicago Press (Chicago, IL), 1995.

(With others) *Deconstruction and Pragmatism,* Routledge (London, England), 1996.

Résistances, de la psychanalyse, Galilée (Paris, France), 1996, published as *Resistances of Psychoanalysis,* Stanford University Press (Stanford, CA), 1998.

La monolinguisme de l'autre, ou La prothèse d'origine, Galilée (Paris, France), 1996, translation by Patrick Mensa published as *Monolingualism of the Other; or, The Prosthesis of Origin,* Stanford University Press (Stanford, CA), 1998.

Passions de la littaerature: avec Jacques Derrida, Galilée (Paris, France), 1996.

(With Bernard Stiegler) *Echographies de la télévision,* Galilée (Paris, France), 1996.

(With Peter Eisenman) *Chora L Works,* Monacelli Press, 1997.

Deconstruction in a Nutshell: A Conversation with Jacques Derrida, edited by John D. Caputo, Fordham University Press (Bronx, NY), 1997.

(With Paule Thevenin) *Secret Art of Antonin Artaud,* translation by Mary Ann Caws, MIT Press (Cambridge, MA), 1997.

Cosmopolites de tous les pays, encore un effort, Galilée (Paris, France), 1997, translated as *On Cosmopolitanism and Forgiveness,* Routledge (New York, NY), 2001.

Adieu à Emmanuel Lévines, Galilée (Paris, France), 1997, translation by Pascale-Anne Brault and Michael Naas published as *Adieu to Emmanuel Levinas,* Stanford University Press (Stanford, CA), 1999.

De l'hospitalité/Anne Duformantelle invite Jacques Derrida à répondre, Calmann Levy (Paris, France), 1997, translation by Rachel Bowlby published as *Of Hospitality: Anne Dufourmantelle Invites Jacques Derrida to Respond,* Stanford University Press (Stanford, CA), 2000.

Sur parole: instantanés philosophiques, Aube (Tour d'Aigues, France), 1999.

Le toucher, Jean-Luc Nancy/Jacques Derrida: accompagné de travaux de lecture de Simon Hantai, Galilée (Paris, France), 1999.

(With Catherine Malabou) *Jacques Derrida: La contre-allée,* Quinzaine litteraire-Louis Vuitton (Paris, France), 1999.

Du droit à la philosophie, Galilée (Paris, France), 2000, portions translated by Jan Plug as *Who's Afraid of Philosophy? Right to Philosophy,* Volume 1, Stanford University Press (Stanford, CA), 2003.

Demeure: Fiction and Testimony (published with *The Instant of My Death* by Maurice Blanchot), translated by Elizabeth Rottenberg, Stanford University Press (Stanford, CA), 2000.

(With Safaa Fathy) *Tourner les mots: Au bord d'un film,* Galilée (Paris, France), 2000.

Etats d'âme de la psychanalyse: l'impossible au-delà d'une souveraine cruauté, Galilée (Paris, France), 2000.

The Work of Mourning, edited by Pascale-Anne Brault and Michael Naas, University of Chicago Press (Chicago, IL), 2001.

L'univerité sans condition, Galilée (Paris, France), 2001.

Papier machine: le ruban de machine à écrire et autres résponses, Galilée (Paris, France), 2001.

(With Elisabeth Roudinesco) *De qui demain—dialogue,* Galilée (Paris, France), 2001, translation by Jeff Fort published as *For What Tomorrow: A Dialogue,* Stanford University Press (Stanford, CA), 2004.

Derrida Downunder, edited by Laurence Simmons and Heather Worth, Dunmore Press (Palmerston North, New Zealand), 2001.

Negotiations: Interventions and Interviews, 1971-2001, edited and translated by Elizabeth Rottenberg, Stanford University Press (Stanford, CA), 2002.

Fichus: discours de Francfort, Galilée (Paris, France), 2002.

Des humanités et de la discipline philosophique, [Paris, France], translated and edited by Peter Pericles Trifonas as *Ethics, Institutions, and the Right to Philosophy,* Rowman & Littlefield (Lanham, MD), 2002.

Artaud le Moma: interjections d'appel, Galilée (Paris, France), 2002.

Acts of Religion, edited by Gil Anidjar, Routledge (New York, NY), 2002.

Without Alibi (collected essays), translated and edited by Peggy Kamuf, Stanford University Press (Stanford, CA), 2002.

(With Giovanna Borradori and Jürgen Habermas) *Philosophy in a Time of Terror: Dialogues with Jürgen Habermas and Jacques Derrida,* University of Chicago Press (Chicago, IL), 2003.

Voyous: deux essais sur la raison, Galilée (Paris, France), 2003.

The Problem of Genesis in Husserl's Philosophy, translated by Marian Hobson, University of Chicago Press (Chicago, IL), 2003.

Also author of *Moscou aller-retour,* Aube.

Contributor to books, including *Tableau de la litterature francaise,* Gallimard (Paris, France), 1974; *Mimesis,* Flammarion (Paris, France), 1976; *Politiques de la philosophie,* Grasset (Paris, France), 1976; *Qui a peur de la philosophie?,* Flammarion (Paris, France), 1977; *Les États Generaux de la philosophie,* Flammarion (Paris, France), 1979; *Deconstruction and Criticism,*

Seabury Press (New York, NY), 1979; *Philosophy in France Today,* Cambridge University Press (Cambridge, England), 1983; Joseph H. Smith and William Kerrigan, editors, *Taking Chances: Derrida, Psychoanalysis, and Literature,* Johns Hopkins University Press (Baltimore, MD), 1984; *Text und Interpretation,* Fink, 1984; *Post-structuralist Joyce,* Cambridge University Press (Cambridge, England), 1984; *La faculté de juger,* Minuit (Paris, France), 1985; *Qu'est-ce que Dieu?,* [Brussels], 1985; *Difference in Translation,* Cornell University Press (Ithaca, NY), 1985; *Genese de Babel, Joyce et la creation,* Editions du CNRS (Paris, France), 1985; *Paul Celan,* Galilée (Paris, France), 1986; *La grève des philosophes: école et philosophie,* Osiris, 1986, published as *Raising the Tone of Philosophy,* edited by Peter Fenves, Johns Hopkins University Press (Baltimore, MD), 1993; *La case vide,* Achitectural Association (London, England), 1986; *Pour Nelson Mandela,* Gallimard (Paris, France), 1986; *Romeo et Juliette,* Papiers, 1986; and *Questioning Judaism* (interviews), Stanford University Press (Stanford, CA), 2004.

Codirector of collection *Philosophie en effet.* Member of editorial boards of *Critique, Structuralist Review, Contemporary Studies in Philosophy and the Human Sciences,* and *Revue senegalaise de philosophie.* Associated with *Tel Quel* during 1960s and 1970s.

SIDELIGHTS: Algerian-born French philosopher Jacques Derrida is the leading light of the post-structuralist intellectual movement that significantly influenced philosophy, the social sciences, and literary criticism during the late twentieth century. By means of a "strategy of deconstruction," Derrida and other post-structuralists have sought to reveal the play of multiple meanings in cultural products and expose the tacit metaphysical assumptions they believe exist beneath much of contemporary social thought. The deconstructionist project ignited intense controversy among intellectuals in Europe and the United States, with detractors dismissing it as a particularly insidious form of nihilism, while its advocates argued that deconstructive practice allows the possibility of creating new values amid what they view as cynicism and spiritual emptiness of postmodern society.

Derrida first outlined his seminal ideas in a lengthy introduction to his 1962 French translation of German philosopher Edmund Husserl's *Origin of Geometry.*

The strategy of deconstruction is rigorously delineated in Derrida's difficult masterwork, *Of Grammatology,* but the philosopher explained some of his basic concepts in more accessible terms in a 1972 collection of interviews titled *Positions.* Derrida's thought builds on a variety of so-called subversive literature, including the writings of German philosophers Friedrich Nietzsche and Martin Heidegger, who both sought to overturn established values and depart from the traditional approach to the study of metaphysics; the political, social, and cultural insights of political economist Karl Marx and psychoanalyst Sigmund Freud, who postulated underlying contradictory phenomena beneath the surface of everyday social life; and the linguistic analysis of the Swiss linguist Ferdinand de Saussure, who posited that language functions in a self-referential manner and has no "natural" relation to external reality. Many of Derrida's texts are subtle analyses of the writings of these thinkers and the literature of the modern structuralist movement, another strong influence on the philosopher. While accepting the structuralist notion, derived from Saussure, that cultural phenomena are best understood as self-referential systems of signs, Derrida denies the existence of a common intellectual structure capable of unifying the diverse cultural structures.

In the *New York Times Magazine,* Colin Campbell explained "Post-structuralism" as "a term that lumps together various French and other thinkers who write as though they want to overthrow oppressive philosophic structures by subverting language. Deconstruction was invented by Jacques Derrida . . . and Derrida is still the movement's leading theoretician." Campbell added: "In 1966, Derrida delivered his first lectures in the United States. The movement has been upsetting people and texts since."

Derrida's insistence on the inadequacy of language to render a complete and unambiguous representation of reality forms the basis for his deconstructivist strategy of reading texts. As Campbell stated: "To 'deconstruct' a text is pretty much what it sounds like—to pick the thing carefully apart, exposing what deconstructors see as the central fact and tragic little secret of Western philosophy—namely, the circular tendency of language to refer to itself. Because the 'language' of a text refers mainly to other 'languages' and texts—and not to some hard, extratexual reality—the text tends to have several possible meanings, which usually undermine one another. In fact, the 'meaning' of a piece of writing—it doesn't matter whether it's a poem or a novel or a philosophic treatise—is indeterminate."

In reading, Derrida studies texts for the multiple meanings that underlie and subvert the surface meaning of every piece of writing. To do this, he scrutinizes seemingly marginal textual elements such as idiosyncrasies of vocabulary and style, and subverts what appear to be simple words and phrases with a battery of puns, allusions, and neologisms. He illuminates in particular the continual play of differences in language, a phenomenon he calls "differance." As he wrote in *Positions,* differance prevents any simple element of language from being "*present* in and of itself, referring only to itself." Rather, every element contains differences and spaces within itself and *traces* of other elements that interweave to transform one text into another. There is, in Derrida's famous phrase, "nothing outside the text," that is, no clear and simple meaning represented by words, but only the play of differance and the multiplication of meanings in the deconstructive project. Although a deconstructive reading is never definitive, it is also not arbitrary, and the textual transformations can be followed systematically and even subjected to a structural analysis. Derrida's own deconstructive analyses of philosophical and literary texts include *Margins of Philosophy, Dissemination,* and *Spurs: Nietzsche's Styles.* "Derrida, in a typically bold and outrageous way, has gone so far as to say that writing is more basic than speaking, that speaking is only a form of writing," Campbell related. "But there's more. Because all writing is said to be metaphorical, working by tropes and figures, it follows that trained deconstructors should be able to interpret texts of all sorts, not just 'literature.'"

Given his devotion to textual analysis, Derrida has strongly influenced literary criticism, particularly in France and in the United States. J. Hillis Miller and the late Paul de Man of Yale University are among the best-known American deconstructivists, but younger scholars have also adopted the method. Derrida himself, meanwhile, has attempted to deconstruct the distinction between criticism and creative writing in books such as *Glas* and *The Post Card. Glas* is considered one of the most unusual books ever printed; its pages are divided into two columns, one being a philosophical, psychological, and biographical portrait of the German philosopher G. W. F. Hegel, and the other a critical analysis of the writings of French playwright Jean Genet. The columns are, in turn, fractured within

themselves into sub-columns and boxes. Both texts begin and end in mid-sentence and appear at first to be completely independent from each other—indeed, they can be read that way. The reader can also create his or her own text by uncovering the textual traces that link the two columns and illuminate their differences. In fact, there is a virtually infinite number of ways to read and interpret *Glas,* which stoutly resists any total understanding.

"The disorderly philosophical conduct of this work is so magnificent that it defies linear exposition," Geoffrey H. Hartman remarked of *Glas* in his *Saving the Text: Literature/Derrida/Philosophy.* "Not since *Finnegans Wake* has there been such a deliberate and curious work: less original . . . and mosaic than the *Wake,* even flushed and overreaching, but as intriguingly, wearyingly allusive." *New York Times Book Review* contributor John Sturrock noted that *Glas* "is so made as to impose a certain vagrancy on the eyes and attention of whoever reads it and to break us of our nasty linear habits."

Derrida's strategy of deconstruction had implications far beyond literary criticism in the postmodern age, in the opinion of some moral philosophers. At a time when both religion and secular humanist ideologies had failed for many people, the post-structuralist celebration of difference offered an escape from alienated individualism. The metaphysical search is nostalgic and totalizing—seeking origin and end—while the deconstructive project recognizes no permanence and subverts all hierarchies. Dismissed by some readers and critics as nihilistic, this radical insistence on difference, incompleteness, and ephemerality impressed others as a positive grounding for social tolerance, mutual respect, and open discourse as the world entered the twenty-first century.

Within the fields of philosophy, political philosophy, and literary criticism, Derrida's impact has been felt most strongly. "Derrida is a philosopher from whom many of us have learned what we judge to be important and seductive truths about the nature of language," Sturrock declared, "and it would be good to go on learning from him." Also in the *New York Times Book Review,* Perry Meisel observed: "In fact, literary study in America has never been in better shape. Enriched by a variety of European methodologies since the early 1970s, it has grown into a vast, synthetic enterprise characterized by powerful continuities rather than by disjunctions. Feminism, deconstruction, 'reader-response,' 'New Historicism,' 'postcolonialism'—all share similar ends and similar ways of getting there in a momentous collaboration."

BIOGRAPHICAL AND CRITICAL SOURCES:

BOOKS

Behler, Ernst, *Confrontations: Derrida/Heidegger/Nietzsche,* Stanford University Press (Stanford, CA), 1991.

Caputo, John D., *The Prayers and Tears of Jacques Derrida: Religion without Religion,* Indiana University Press (Bloomington, IN), 1997.

Collins, Jeff, *Introducing Derrida,* Totem Books, 1997.

Contemporary Literary Criticism, Volume 24, Gale (Detroit, MI), 1983.

Derrida, Jacques, *Positions: entretiens avec Henri Ronse, Julia Kristeva, Jean-Louis Houdebine, Guy Scarpetta* (interviews), Minuit (Paris, France), 1972, translation by Alan Bass published as *Positions,* University of Chicago Press (Chicago, IL), 1981.

Garver, Newton, *Derrida and Wittgenstein,* Temple University Press (Philadelphia, PA), 1994.

Gasche, Rodolphe, *The Train of the Mirror: Derrida and the Philosophy of Difference,* Harvard University Press (Cambridge, MA), 1986.

Hartman, Geoffrey H., *Saving the Text: Literature/Derrida/Philosophy,* Johns Hopkins University Press (Baltimore, MD), 1981.

Harvey, Irene E., *Derrida and the Economy of Difference,* Indiana University Press (Bloomington, IN), 1986.

Llewelyn, John, *Derrida on the Threshold of Sense,* Macmillan (New York, NY), 1986.

Lucy, Niall, *Debating Derrida,* Melbourne University Press, 1995.

Magliola, Robert R., *Derrida on the Mend,* Purdue University Press (West Lafayette, IN), 1984.

Megill, Allan, *Prophets of Extremity,* University of California Press (Berkeley, CA), 1985.

Norris, Christopher, *Derrida,* Harvard University Press (Cambridge, MA), 1987.

Staten, Henry, *Wittgenstein and Derrida,* University of Nebraska Press (Lincoln, NE), 1984.

Sturrock, John, editor, *Structuralism and Since: From Levi-Strauss to Derrida,* Oxford University Press (Oxford, England), 1979.

PERIODICALS

Australian Journal of Political Science, July, 2002, Paul Patton, review of *On Cosmopolitanism and Forgiveness,* p. 383.

Choice, June, 2002, S. Barnett, review of *A Taste for the Secret,* p. 1782; September, 2002, R. Puligandia, review of *Acts of Religion,* p. 118.

Contemporary Literature, spring, 1979.

Contemporary Review, June, 2002, review of *On Cosmopolitanism and Forgiveness,* p. 381.

Critical Inquiry, summer, 1978.

Criticism, summer, 1979; winter, 1993.

Ethics, July, 2003, Samir J. Daddad, review of *Who's Afraid of Philosophy?,* p. 923.

International Philosophical Quarterly, September, 2003, David Michael Levin, "Cinders, Traces, Shadows on the Page: The Holocaust in Derrida's Writing," p. 269.

Journal of Ethnic and Migration Studies, March, 2003, Alastair Bonnett, review of *On Cosmopolitanism and Forgiveness,* p. 399.

Journal of the American Academy of Religion, September, 2002, Elliot R. Wolfson, "Assaulting the Border: Kabbalistic Traces in the Margins of Derrida," p. 475.

Modern Theology, April, 2002, James K. A. Smith, "A Principle of Incarnation in Derrida's 'Jungenschriften'," p. 217.

New Literary History, autumn, 1978.

New Republic, April 16, 1977.

New York Review of Books, March 3, 1977; January 14, 1993; June 25, 1998, Mark Lilla, "The Politics of Jacques Derrida," pp. 36-41.

New York Times Book Review, February 1, 1987; September 13, 1987, John Sturrock, "The Book Is Dead, Long Live the Book!" p. 3; May 28, 2000, Perry Meisel, "Let a Hundred Isms Blossom."

New York Times Magazine, February 9, 1986, Colin Campbell, "The Tyranny of the Yale Critics," p. 20.

Partisan Review, number 2, 1976; number 2, 1981.

Research in African Literatures, winter, 2002, p. 124.

Theological Studies, December, 2002, Silvia Benso, review of *A Taste for the Secret,* p. 894.

Time, November 25, 2002, Joel Stein, "Life with the Father of Deconstructionism" (interview), p. 104.

Times Literary Supplement, February 15, 1968; September 30, 1983; December 5, 1986.

Virginia Quarterly Review, winter, 1992.

OTHER

Dick, Kirby, and Amy Ziering Kofman, *Derrida* (documentary film), 2002.*

*   *   *

DESAI, Anita 1937-

PERSONAL: Born June 24, 1937, in Mussoorie, India; daughter of D. N. (an engineer) and Toni Mazumdar; married Ashvin Desai (an executive), December 13, 1958; came to United States, 1987; children: Rahul, Tani, Arjun, Kiran. *Education:* Delhi University, B.A. (with honors), 1957.

ADDRESSES: Home—Cambridge, MA. *Office*—The Program in Writing and Humanistic Studies, Massachusetts Institute of Technology, Cambridge, MA 02139.

CAREER: Writer and educator. Smith College, Northampton, MA, Elizabeth Drew Professor of English, 1987-88; Mount Holyoke College, South Hadley, MA, Purington Professor of English, 1988-93; Massachusetts Institute of Technology, Cambridge, MA, professor of writing, 1993—. Girton College, Cambridge, Helen Cam visiting fellow, 1986-87, honorary fellow, 1988; Clare Hall, Cambridge, Ashby fellow, 1989, honorary fellow, 1991.

MEMBER: Royal Society of Literature (fellow), American Academy of Arts and Letters (honorary fellow).

AWARDS, HONORS: Winifred Holtby Prize, Royal Society of Literature, 1978, for *Fire on the Mountain;* Sahitya Academy award, 1979; Booker Prize shortlist, 1980, for *Clear Light of Day,* 1984, for *In Custody,* and 1999, for *Feasting, Fasting; Guardian* Prize for Children's Fiction, 1983, for *The Village by the Sea; Hadassah* Prize, 1989, for *Baumgartner's Bombay;* Padma Sri, 1990; Literary Lion Award, New York Public Library, 1993; Neil Gunn fellowship, Scottish Arts Council, 1994; Moravia Award (Rome, Italy), 1999; Benson Medal, Royal Society of Literature, 2003.

WRITINGS:

NOVELS

Cry, the Peacock, P. Owen (London, England), 1963.
Voices in the City, P. Owen (London, England), 1965.

Anita Desai

Bye-Bye, Blackbird, Hind Pocket Books (Delhi, India), 1968.
Where Shall We Go This Summer?, Vikas Publishing House (New Dehli, India), 1975.
Fire on the Mountain, Harper & Row (New York, NY), 1977.
Clear Light of Day, Harper & Row (New York, NY), 1980.
In Custody, Heinemann (London, England), 1984, Harper & Row (New York, NY), 1985.
Baumgartner's Bombay, Alfred A. Knopf (New York, NY), 1989.
Journey to Ithaca, Alfred A. Knopf (New York, NY), 1995.
Fasting, Feasting, Chatto & Windus (London, England), 1999, Houghton Mifflin (Boston, MA), 2000.
The Zigzag Way, Houghton Mifflin (Boston, MA), 2004.

JUVENILE

The Peacock Garden, India Book House (Jaipur, India), 1974.

Cat on a Houseboat, Orient Longmans (Calcutta, India), 1976.

The Village by the Sea, Heinemann (London, England), 1982.

OTHER

Games at Twilight and Other Stories, Heinemann (London, England), 1978, Harper & Row (New York, NY), 1980.

(Author of introduction) Lady Mary Wortley Montagu, *Turkish Embassy Letters,* edited by Malcolm Jack, University of Georgia Press (Athens, GA), 1993.

Diamond Dust and Other Stories, Houghton Mifflin (Boston, MA), 2000.

(Author of introduction) E. M. Forster, *Arctic Summer,* Hesperus Press (London, England), 2003.

(Author of introduction) D. H. Lawrence, *Daughters of the Vicar,* Hesperus Press (London, England), 2004.

Contributor of short stories to periodicals, including *Thought, Envoy, Writers Workshop, Quest, Indian Literature, Illustrated Weekly of India, Femina, Harper's Bazaar,* and *Granta.*

ADAPTATIONS: *The Village by the Sea* was filmed by the British Broadcasting Corporation (BBC), 1992; *In Custody* was filmed by Merchant Ivory Productions, 1993.

SIDELIGHTS: Anita Desai focuses her novels upon the personal struggles of her Indian characters to cope with the problems of contemporary life. In this way, she manages to portray the cultural and social changes that her native country has undergone since the departure of the British. One of Desai's major themes is the relationships between family members, especially the emotional tribulations of women whose independence is suppressed by Indian society. Her first novel, *Cry, the Peacock,* concerns a woman who finds it impossible to assert her individuality; the theme of the despairing woman is also explored in Desai's *Where Shall We Go This Summer?* Other novels explore life in urban India (*Voices in the City*), the clash between Eastern and Western cultures (*Bye-Bye, Blackbird*), and the differences between the generations (*Fire on the Mountain*). Desai was shortlisted for Britain's pres-

tigious Booker Prize three times: in 1980, for *Clear Light of Day;* in 1984, for *In Custody;* and in 1999, for *Fasting, Feasting.*

Exile—physical as well as psychological—is also a prominent theme in Desai's writings. In *Baumgartner's Bombay,* Desai (whose father was Indian and mother was German) details the life of Hugo Baumgartner, a German Jew who flees Nazi Germany for India, where he "gradually drifts down through Indian society to settle, like sediment, somewhere near the bottom," wrote Rosemary Dinnage in the *New York Review of Books.* She added: "Baumgartner is a more thoroughly displaced person than Anglicized Indians, and more solitary, for Desai's Indian characters are still tied to family and community, however irksomely. She has drawn on her dual nationality to write on a subject new, I think, to English fiction—the experience of Jewish refugees in India." Pearl K. Bell made a similar statement. "Baumgartner is the loneliest, saddest, most severely dislocated of Desai's fictional creatures," Bell noted in the *New Republic.* However, he "is also a representative man, the German Jew to whom things happen, powerless to resist the evil wind that swept him like a vagrant weed from Berlin to India." Jean Sudrann, writing in the *Yale Review,* praised Desai's narrative skill "in making us feel the cumulative force of Hugo's alienation." At a reading at Northeastern University transcribed on *Northeastern University Brudnick Center on Violence and Conflict* Web site, the novelist said of her protagonist: "You remarked about his being so passive a character. Yes, I did mean him to be an entirely passive character. For the whole idea was to show how history sweeps people up and, like a juggernaut, often crushes them under its wheels. I wanted to write about such a person."

Desai's descriptive powers have been acclaimed by several critics. In the *New Leader,* Betty Falkenberg called *Baumgartner's Bombay* "a mathematical problem set and solved in exquisite prose." Bell observed that "there is a Dickensian rush and tumble to her portrayals of the bazaars, the crowded streets, the packed houses of an Indian metropolis." In general, Desai's "novels are quite short, but they convey a sharply detailed sense of the tangled complexities of Indian society, and an intimate view of the tug and pull of Indian family life."

While noting Desai's mixed German-Indian ancestry, *Spectator* contributor Caroline Moore commended the author for the authentic Indian flavor of her works.

"Westerners visiting India find themselves reeling under the outsider's sense of 'culture shock,' which is compounded more of shock than culture," the critic wrote. "To Anita Desai, of course, the culture is second nature. Yet that intimacy never becomes mere familiarity: her achievement is to keep the shock of genuine freshness, the eyes of the perpetual outsider." This particular engagement with India is evident in many of Desai's novels, as A. G. Mojtabai noted in the *New York Times Book Review*. "Desai is a writer of Bengali-German descent, who stands in a complicated but advantageous relation to India," said the reviewer. "Insiders rarely notice this much; outsiders cannot have this ease of reference." Mojtabai found that Desai is able to delineate characters, settings, and feelings intricately, yet economically, without extraneous detail or excessively populated scenes: "This author has no need of crowds. Properly observed, a roomful of people is crowd enough, and in the right hands—as Anita Desai so amply illustrates—*world* enough."

The complexities of outsiders facing Indian culture form the basis of Desai's 1995 novel *Journey to Ithaca*. The story revolves around an ex-hippie European couple who travel to India for quite different reasons—the husband to find enlightenment, the wife to enjoy a foreign experience. As the husband, Matteo, becomes involved with a spiritual guru known as the Mother, wife Sophie goes on a quest of her own: to find the guru's roots in an effort either to debunk or to understand her. Calling the work "a kind of love triangle set against the madness of extreme spiritual searching," *New York Times* reviewer Richard Bernstein said of *Journey to Ithaca* that "Desai writes with intelligence and power. She has a remarkable eye for substance, the things that give life its texture. Nothing escapes her power of observation, not the thickness of the drapes that blot out the light in a bourgeois Parisian home, or the enamel bowl in the office of an Indian doctor." Moore, in the *Spectator,* though commenting that the main characters are drawn rather sketchily, commended the book as "superbly powerful . . . emotionally and intellectually haunting, teasing and tugging our minds even through its imperfections."

Gabriele Annan, writing in the *Times Literary Supplement,* found other flaws in *Journey to Ithaca*. "This is a curiously inept book for a novelist of Desai's experience," Annan wrote. "The narrative is full of gaps and improbabilities, as well as clichés," and "the dialogue is stagey and unconvincing." *Wall Street Journal* contributor Brooke Allen, while admiring Desai's style of writing, also found much of the story unbelievable. Spiritually inclined readers may find the action plausible, but "others will remain incredulous," Allen asserted.

Fasting, Feasting, Desai's third novel to be shortlisted for the Booker Prize, "tells the apparently spare story of one Indian family and the varying fates of its two daughters and single son; it is only on the novel's final, quiet page that Desai's intricate structure becomes clear and the complexity of her emotional insight makes itself felt," explained Sylvia Brownrigg in *Salon.com*. Uma, the oldest daughter, is charged with the care of her demanding parents, while her sister, Aruna, is unhappily married but has escaped the responsibilities that hinder her older sister. Arun, the brother, is the focus of the second half of the novel. He is smothered by his parents' expectations of his life, and he eventually finds his way to Boston where he attends school, staying with an American family, the Pattons, during a break between semesters. "Arriving in the United States, Arun had exulted in his new-found anonymity: 'no past, no family . . . no country.' But he has not escaped family after all, just stumbled into a plastic representation of it," commented J. M. Coetzee in the *New York Review of Books*. The Pattons, with their excesses, counter the values of the Indian household. "Arun himself, as he picks his way through a minefield of puzzling American customs, becomes a more sympathetic character, and his final act in the novel suggests both how far he has come and how much he has lost," explained a critic for *Publishers Weekly.*

Critics were overwhelmingly positive in their assessment of the novel. "*Fasting, Feasting* is a novel not of plot but of comparison," wrote Brownrigg. "In beautifully detailed prose Desai draws the foods and textures of an Indian small town and of an American suburb. In both, she suggests, family life is a complex mixture of generosity and meanness, license and restriction." Donna Seaman, writing in *Booklist,* commented: "Desai has been compared to Jane Austen, and, indeed, she is a deceptively gracious storyteller, writing like an embroiderer concealing a sword as she creates family microcosms that embody all the delusions and cruelties of society-at-large." Though Coetzee faulted Desai's America as feeling "as if it comes out of books," he lauded her writing, particularly her portraits of India. "Desai's strength as a writer has always been her eye for detail and her ear for the exact word . . . her gift for telling metaphor, and above all her feel for sun and sky, heat and dust, for the elemental reality of central India."

Desai is frequently praised by critics for her ability to capture the local color of her country and the ways in which Eastern and Western cultures have blended together there, and for developing this skill further with each successive novel. A large part of this skill is due to her use of imagery, one of the most important devices in her novels. Because of this emphasis on imagery, she is referred to by reviewers such as *World Literature Today* contributor Madhusudan Prasad as an "imagist-novelist" whose use of imagery is "a remarkable quality of her craft that she has carefully maintained" in her mature novels. Employing this imagery to suggest rather than overtly explain her themes, Desai's stories sometimes appear deceptively simple; but, as Anthony Thwaite pointed out in the *New Republic,* "she is such a consummate artist that she [is able to suggest], beyond the confines of the plot and the machinations of her characters, the immensities that lie beyond them—the immensities of India." In the London *Observer,* Salman Rushdie described Desai's fiction as being "illuminated by the author's perceptiveness, delicacy of language and sharp wit."

BIOGRAPHICAL AND CRITICAL SOURCES:

BOOKS

Afzal-Khan, Fawzia, *Cultural Imperialism and the Indo-English Novel: Genre and Ideology in R. K. Narayan, Anita Desai, Kamala Markandaya, and Salman Rushdie,* Pennsylvania State University Press (University Park, PA), 1993.
Bellioppa, Meena, *The Fiction of Anita Desai,* Writers Workshop, 1971.
Choudhury, Bidulata, *Women and Society in the Novels of Anita Desai,* Creative Books (New Delhi, India), 1995.
Contemporary Literary Criticism, Gale (Detroit, MI), Volume 19, 1981, Volume 37, 1986.
Contemporary Novelists, 6th edition, St. James Press (Detroit, MI), 1996.
Feminist Writers, St. James Press (Detroit, MI), 1996.
Khanna, Shashi, *Human Relationships in Anita Desai's Novels,* Sarup & Sons (New Delhi, India), 1995.

Parker, Michael, and Roger Starkey, editors, *Postcolonial Literature: Achebe, Ngugi, Desai, Walcott,* St. Martin's Press (New York, NY), 1995.
Pathania, Usha, *Human Bonds and Bondages: The Fiction of Anita Desai and Kamala Markandaya,* Kanishka Publishers (New Delhi, India), 1992.
St. James Guide to Children's Writers, 5th edition, St. James Press (Detroit, MI), 1999.
Sharma, Kajali, *Symbolism in Anita Desai's Novels,* Abhinav Publications (New Delhi, India), 1991.
Singh, Sunaina, *The Novels of Margaret Atwood and Anita Desai: A Comparative Study in Feminist Perspectives,* Creative Books, 1994.
Sivanna, Indira, *Anita Desai as an Artist: A Study in Image and Symbol,* Creative Books, 1994.
Solanki, Mrinalini, *Anita Desai's Fiction: Patterns of Survival Strategies,* Kanishka Publishers (New Delhi, India), 1992.

PERIODICALS

Belles Lettres, summer, 1989, p. 4.
Booklist, December 15, 1999, Donna Seaman, review of *Fasting, Feasting,* p. 739.
Boston Globe, August 15, 1995, p. 26.
Chicago Tribune, September 1, 1985.
Globe and Mail (Toronto, Ontario, Canada), August 20, 1988.
Kirkus Reviews, June 15, 1995, p. 799.
Lancet, January 12, 2002, Robin Gerster, "Geographies of the Imagination (Diamond Dust and Other Stories)," p. 178.
Library Journal, February 1, 2000, Dianna Moeller, review of *Fasting, Feasting,* p. 115; June 1, 2000, Faye A. Chadwell, review of *Diamond Dust,* p. 206.
Los Angeles Times, July 31, 1980.
Los Angeles Times Book Review, March 3, 1985; April 9, 1989.
New Leader, May 1, 1989, Betty Falkenberg, review of *Baumgartner's Bombay.*
New Republic, March 18, 1985; April 3, 1989; April 6, 1992, p. 36; August 15, 1994, p. 43.
New York Review of Books, June 1, 1989; December 6, 1990, p. 53; January 16, 1992, p. 42; March 3, 1994, p. 41; May 23, 1996, p. 6; May 25, 2000, J. M. Coetzee, review of *Fasting, Feasting,* pp. 33-35.
New York Times, November 24, 1980; February 22, 1985; March 14, 1989; August 30, 1995, p. B2.

New York Times Book Review, November 20, 1977; June 22, 1980; November 23, 1980; March 3, 1985, p. 7; April 9, 1989, p. 3; January 27, 1991, p. 23; September 17, 1995, p. 12.

Observer (London, England), October 7, 1984, p. 22.

Publishers Weekly, December 6, 1999, review of *Fasting, Feasting,* p. 55.

Spectator, June 3, 1995, pp. 41-42.

Time, July 1, 1985; August 21, 1995, p. 67.

Times (London, England), September 4, 1980.

Times Higher Education Supplement, April 7, 1995, pp. 16-17.

Times Literary Supplement, September 5, 1980; September 7, 1984; October 19, 1984; July 15-21, 1988, p. 787; June 2, 1995, p. 501.

Tribune Books (Chicago, IL), August 23, 1981; March 5, 1989.

Wall Street Journal, August 24, 1995, p. A14.

Washington Post Book World, January 11, 1981, p. 3; October 7, 1984; March 31, 1985; February 26, 1989.

World Literature Today, summer, 1984, pp. 363-369; winter, 1997, p. 221.

Yale Review, spring, 1990, p. 414.

ONLINE

Northeastern University Brudnick Center on Violence and Conflict Web Site, http://www.violence.neu.edu/ (April 18-20, 2001) "Third World Views of the Holocaust."

Salon.com, http://www.salon.com/ (February 17, 2000), Sylvia Brownrigg, review of *Fasting, Feasting.*

*   *   *

DOCTOROW, E(dgar) L(aurence) 1931-

PERSONAL: Born January 6, 1931, in New York, NY; son of David R. (a music store proprietor) and Rose (a pianist; maiden name, Levine) Doctorow; married Helen Esther Setzer (a writer), August 20, 1954; children: Jenny, Caroline, Richard. *Education:* Kenyon College, A.B. (with honors), 1952; Columbia University, graduate study, 1952-53.

ADDRESSES: Home—New Rochelle, NY. *Office*—Department of English, New York University, 19 University Pl., New York, NY, 10003. *Agent*—Amanda Urban, I.C.M., 40 West 57th St., New York, NY 10019.

E. L. Doctorow

CAREER: New American Library, New York, NY, senior editor, 1959-64; Dial Press, New York, NY, editor-in-chief, 1964-69, vice president and publisher, 1968-69; University of California—Irvine, writer-in-residence, 1969-70; Sarah Lawrence College, Bronxville, NY, member of faculty, 1971-78; New York University, New York, NY, Glucksman Professor of English and American Letters, 1982—. Script reader, Columbia Pictures Industries, Inc., 1956-58; creative writing fellow, Yale School of Drama, 1974-75; visiting professor, University of Utah, 1975; visiting senior fellow, Princeton University, 1980-81. *Military service:* U.S. Army, Signal Corps, 1953-55.

MEMBER: American Academy and Institute of Arts and Letters, Authors Guild, PEN, Writers Guild of America, Century Association.

AWARDS, HONORS: Guggenheim fellowship, 1973; Creative Artists Service fellow, 1973-74; National Book Critics Circle Award and American Academy of Arts and Letters award, 1976, both for *Ragtime;* L.H. D., Kenyon College, 1976; Litt.D., Hobart and William Smith Colleges, 1979; National Book Critics

Circle Award, 1982, for *Loon Lake,* and 1989, for *Billy Bathgate;* National Book Award, 1986, for *World's Fair;* L.H.D., Brandeis University, 1989; Edith Wharton Citation of Merit for Fiction, and New York State Author, both 1989-91; PEN/Faulkner Award, and William Dean Howells Medal, American Academy of Arts and Letters, both 1990, both for *Billy Bathgate;* National Humanities Medal, 1998.

WRITINGS:

NOVELS

Welcome to Hard Times, Simon & Schuster (New York, NY), 1960, published as *Bad Man from Bodie,* Deutsch (London, England), 1961.
Big as Life, Simon & Schuster (New York, NY), 1966.
The Book of Daniel, Random House (New York, NY), 1971.
Ragtime, Random House (New York, NY), 1975.
Loon Lake, Random House (New York, NY), 1980.
World's Fair, Random House (New York, NY), 1985.
Billy Bathgate, Random House (New York, NY), 1989.
Three Complete Novels, Wings (New York, NY), 1994.
The Waterworks, Random House (New York, NY), 1994.
City of God, Random House (New York, NY), 2000.

OTHER

Drinks before Dinner (play; first produced off-Broadway at Public Theater, 1978), Random House (New York, NY), 1979.
(Author of text) *American Anthem,* photographs by Jean-Claude Suares, Stewart, Tabori & Chang (New York, NY), 1982.
Daniel (screenplay; based on author's *The Book of Daniel;* also see below), Paramount, 1983.
Lives of the Poets: Six Stories and a Novella, Random House (New York, NY), 1984.
(Author of text) Eric Fischl, *Scenes and Sequences: Fifty-eight Monotypes* (limited edition), Peter Blum (New York, NY), 1989.
Reading and Interview (sound recording), American Audio Prose Library (Columbia, MO), 1991.
The People's Text: A Citizen Reads the Constitution (limited edition), with wood engravings by Barry Moser, Nouveau Press (Jackson, MS), 1992.

Jack London, Hemingway, and the Constitution: Selected Essays, 1977-1992, Random House (New York, NY), 1993.
(Editor, with Katrina Kenison) *The Best American Short Stories 2000,* Houghton Mifflin (Boston, MA), 2000.
(Author of text) *Lamentation 9/11,* photographs by David Finn, Ruder-Fin Press (New York, NY), 2002.
Reporting the Universe (essays), Harvard University Press (Cambridge, MA), 2003.
Three Screenplays (includes *Daniel, Ragtime,* and *Loon Lake*), introduction, commentaries, and interviews by Paul Levine, Johns Hopkins University Press (Baltimore, MD), 2003.
Sweet Land Stories (short stories), Random House (New York, NY), 2004.

ADAPTATIONS: In 1967 Metro-Goldwyn-Mayer produced a movie version of *Welcome to Hard Times,* written and directed by Burt Kennedy and starring Henry Fonda. Doctorow was involved, for a time, with the film version of *Ragtime,* released in 1981 and directed by Milos Forman from a screenplay by Michael Weller; it starred James Cagney in his last screen performance. *Ragtime* was adapted as a musical, with book by Terrence McNally and music and lyrics by Stephen Flahery and Lynn Ahrens, and produced on Broadway in 1998. A film of *Billy Bathgate,* written by Tom Stoppard, directed by Robert Benton, and starring Dustin Hoffman, Nicole Kidman, and Bruce Willis, was released by Touchstone in 1991.

SIDELIGHTS: E. L. Doctorow is a highly regarded novelist and playwright known for his serious philosophical probings, the subtlety and variety of his prose style, and his unusual use of historical figures in fictional works, among them Julius and Ethel Rosenberg in *The Book of Daniel,* Emma Goldman, Harry Houdini, J. P. Morgan, and others in *Ragtime,* and Dutch Schultz in *Billy Bathgate.* Novelist Anne Tyler called Doctorow "a sort of human time machine" in an assessment of the latter novel for the *New York Times Book Review. Times Literary Supplement* critic Stephen Fender, meanwhile, observed that "The project of Doctorow's fiction has been to deconstruct crucial episodes in American political history and to rebuild them out of . . . his own speculative imagination," and *Listener* commentator Andrew Clifford remarked that "Doctorow's trademark of using historical fact to brew up brilliantly imaginative fiction has helped him stake a claim to be the present-day Great American Novelist." His work as a teacher and editor and his nonfiction essays on social and political issues have further contributed to Doctorow's reputation as one of the most important literary figures of the late twentieth century.

Doctorow's father, a lover of literature, named his son after Edgar Allan Poe. Young Edgar quickly developed a passion for words as well; he was in third grade when he decided to make writing his career, he once told an interviewer. He wrote plays while serving in the U.S. Army, and when he left the service he got a job as a script reader for Columbia Pictures, an assignment that led to his first novel, *Welcome to Hard Times.* In an interview for the *Miami Herald,* he told Jonathan Yardley that he "was accursed to read things that were submitted to this company and write synopses of them. . . . I had to suffer one lousy Western after another, and it occurred to me that I could lie about the West in a much more interesting way than any of these people were lying. I wrote a short story, and it subsequently became the first chapter of that novel."

The resulting book, unlike many Westerns, is concerned with serious issues. As Wirt Williams noted in the *New York Times Book Review,* the novel addresses "one of the favorite problems of philosophers: the relationship of man and evil. . . . Perhaps the primary theme of the novel is that evil can only be resisted psychically: when the rational controls that order man's existence slacken, destruction comes. [Joseph] Conrad said it best in *Heart of Darkness,* but Mr. Doctorow has said it impressively. His book is taut and dramatic, exciting and successfully symbolic." Similarly, Kevin Stan, writing in the *New Republic,* remarked that *Welcome to Hard Times* "is a superb piece of fiction: lean and mean, and thematically significant. . . . [Doctorow] takes the thin, somewhat sordid and incipiently depressing materials of the Great Plains experience and fashions them into a myth of good and evil. . . . He does it marvelously, with economy and with great narrative power."

After writing a Western of sorts, Doctorow turned to another form not usually heralded by critics: science fiction. In *Big as Life* two naked human giants materialize in New York harbor. The novel examines the ways in which its characters deal with a seemingly impending catastrophe. Like *Hard Times, Big as Life*

won substantial critical approval. A *Choice* reviewer, for example, commented that "Doctorow's deadpan manner . . . turns from satire to tenderness and human concern. A performance closer to James Purdy than to [George] Orwell or [Aldous] Huxley, but in a minor key." In spite of praise from critics, however, *Big as Life,* like *Welcome to Hard Times,* was not a significant commercial success.

The Book of Daniel, Doctorow's third book, uses yet another traditional form: the historical novel. It is a fictional account based on the relationship between Julius and Ethel Rosenberg and their children. The Rosenbergs were Communists who were convicted of and executed for conspiracy to commit treason. Many feel that they were victims of the sometimes hysterical anticommunist fever of the 1950s. As with *Welcome to Hard Times* and *Big as Life,* Doctorow modified the traditional form to suit his purposes. The work is not an examination of the guilt or innocence of the Rosenbergs but, as David Emblidge observed in *Southwest Review,* a look at the central character Daniel's psychology, his attempts to deal with the trauma he suffered from his parents' death. Thus many critics considered the book, unlike typical historical novels, to be largely independent of historical fact. In *Partisan Review,* Jane Richmond wrote that "if Julius and Ethel Rosenberg had never existed, the book would be just as good as it is." In like manner, Stanley Kauffmann, in the *New Republic,* remarked, "I haven't looked up the facts of the Rosenberg case; it would be offensive to the quality of this novel to check it against those facts."

Kauffmann joined several other critics in deeming *The Book of Daniel* a novel of high quality indeed. Kauffmann termed it "the political novel of our age, the best American work of its kind that I know since Lionel Trilling's *The Middle of the Journey.*" P. S. Prescott in *Newsweek* added that *The Book of Daniel* is "a purgative book, angry and more deeply felt than all but a few contemporary American novels, a novel about defeat, impotent rage, the passing of the burden of suffering through generations. . . . There is no question here of our suspending disbelief, but rather how when we have finished, we may regain stability." And Richmond called it "a brilliant achievement and the best contemporary novel I've read since reading Frederick Exley's *A Fan's Notes.* . . . It is a book of infinite detail and tender attention to the edges of life as well as to its dead center."

In *Ragtime* Doctorow delves further into historical territory. The novel interweaves the lives of an upper-middle-class white family, a poor European immigrant family, and the family of a black ragtime musician together with historical figures such as Morgan, Houdini, Goldman, Henry Ford, and Evelyn Nesbit. Doctorow shows famous people involved in unusual, sometimes ludicrous, situations. In the *Washington Post Book World,* Raymond Sokolov noted that "Doctorow turns history into myth and myth into history. . . . [He] continually teases our suspicion of literary artifice with apparently true historical description. . . . On the one hand, the 'fact' tugs one toward taking the episode as history. On the other, the doubt that lingers makes one want to take the narrative as an invention." Sokolov argued that Doctorow "teases" the reader in order to make him try "to sort out what the author is doing. That is, we find ourselves paying Doctorow the most important tribute. We watch to see what he is doing."

Newsweek's Walter Clemons also found himself teased by *Ragtime*'s historical episodes: "The very fact that the book stirs one to parlor-game research is amusing evidence that Doctorow has already won the game: I found myself looking up details because I wanted them to be true." George Stade, in the *New York Times Book Review,* expressed an opinion similar to Sokolov's. "In this excellent novel," Stade wrote, "silhouettes and rags not only make fiction out of history but also reveal the fictions out of which history is made. It incorporates the fictions and realities of the era of ragtime while it rags our fictions about it. It is an anti-nostalgic novel that incorporates our nostalgia about its subject."

Ragtime also is a deeply political story, and some reviewers, especially those writing for conservative publications, looked less than favorably on its political viewpoint, considering it far-left and simplistic. Hilton Kramer of *Commentary,* for instance, thought that "the villains in *Ragtime,* drawn with all the subtlety of a William Gropper cartoon, are all representatives of money, the middle class, and white ethnic prejudice. . . . *Ragtime* is a political romance. . . . The major fictional characters . . . are all ideological inventions, designed to serve the purposes of a political fable." Similarly, Jeffrey Hart, writing in the *National Review,* made the case that Doctorow judges his revolutionary and minority characters much less harshly than the middle-and upper-class figures, which results in "what can be called left-wing pastoral," a form of sentimentality.

In *Loon Lake* Doctorow continues to experiment with prose style and to evoke yet another period in American history: the Great Depression. The novel's plot revolves around the various relationships between an industrial tycoon, his famous aviatrix wife, gangsters and their entourage, an alcoholic poet, and Joe, a young drifter who stumbles onto the tycoon's opulent residence in the Adirondack Mountains of New York State. The novel works on several levels with "concentrically expanding ripples of implication," according to Robert Towers in the *New York Times Book Review.* For the most part, however, it is Doctorow's portrait of the American dream versus the American reality that forms the novel's core. As Christopher Lehmann-Haupt of the *New York Times* explained, *Loon Lake* "is a complex and haunting meditation on modern American history."

Time contributor Paul Gray believed that "Doctorow is . . . playing a variation on an old theme: The American dream, set to the music of an American nightmare, the Depression." Lehmann-Haupt saw a similar correlation and elaborated, "This novel could easily have been subtitled *An American Tragedy Revisited.* . . . *Loon Lake* contains [several] parallels to, as well as ironic comments on, the themes of [Theodore] Dreiser's story. . . . Had Dreiser lived to witness the disruptions of post-World War II American society—and had he possessed Mr. Doctorow's narrative dexterity—he might have written something like *Loon Lake.*"

Doctorow's narrative style generated much critical comment. "The written surface of *Loon Lake* is ruffled and choppy," Gray remarked. "Swatches of poetry are jumbled together with passages of computerese and snippets of mysteriously disembodied conversation. Narration switches suddenly from first to third person, or vice versa, and it is not always clear just who is telling what." A reviewer for the *Chicago Tribune* found such "stylistic tricks" annoyingly distracting. "We balk at the frequent overwriting, and the clumsy run-on sentences," he observed. "We can see that Doctorow is trying to convey rootlessness and social unrest through an insouciant free play of language and syntax . . . the problem is that these eccentricities draw disproportionate attention to themselves, away from the characters and their concerns."

Doctorow's play *Drinks before Dinner* seems to have been created through an analogous act of exploration. In the *Nation,* Doctorow stated that the play "originated not in an idea or a character or a story but in a sense of heightened language, a way of talking. It was not until I had the sound of it in my ear that I thought about saying something. The language preceded the intention. . . . The process of making something up is best experienced as fortuitous, unplanned, exploratory. You write to find out what it is you're writing." In composing *Drinks before Dinner,* Doctorow worked from sound to words to characters. Does this "flawed" method of composition show a "defective understanding of what theater is supposed to do?" he wondered. His answer: "I suspect so. Especially if we are talking of the American theater, in which the presentation of the psychologized ego is so central as to be an article of faith. And that is the point. The idea of character as we normally celebrate it on the American stage is what this play seems to question."

When the play was produced, *Village Voice* critic Michael Feingold observed that in *Drinks before Dinner,* Doctorow "has tried to do something incomparably more ambitious than any new American play has done in years—he has tried to put the whole case against civilization in a nutshell." Feingold, however, found the ambition thwarted by a "schizoid" plot and "flat, prosy, and empty" writing. "I salute his desire to say something gigantic," Feingold concluded, "how I wish he had found a way to say it fully, genuinely, and dramatically." Richard Eder of the *New York Times* responded more positively: "Doctorow's turns of thought can be odd, witty and occasionally quite remarkable. His theme—that the world is blindly destroying itself and not worrying about it—is hardly original, but certainly worth saying. And he finds thoughtful and striking ways of saying it." Eder added, "and Mr. Doctorow's [ideas] are sharp enough to supplement intellectual suspense when the dramatic suspense bogs down."

Doctorow's novels *World's Fair* and *Billy Bathgate* are set in 1930s New York, and both received much critical acclaim. *World's Fair* relates a boy's experiences in New York City, growing up in a loving, if somewhat financially stressed, Jewish family during the Great Depression, and ends with his visit to the 1939 World's Fair. Numerous reviewers considered it autobiographical—the young protagonist and narrator has Doctorow's first name, Edgar; his parents, like Doctorow's, are named Rose and David; David runs a music store, as Doctorow's father did. Doctorow confirmed that the novel had autobiographical origins. *World's Fair* "is really a story about memory," he told

Herbert Mitgang in an interview for the *New York Times.* "I started writing it before I knew what I was doing. The title came to me one-third of the way through the book."

"'World's Fair' is E. L. Doctorow's portrait of the artist as a young child," commented Richard Eder in the *Los Angeles Times Book Review.* "The author's alter-ego, Edgar Altschuler, grows into an awareness that the world stretches far beyond the protective confines of a Bronx Jewish household." While "the subject of growing up is not so much a literary theme as a literary subspecies," Eder continued, Doctorow's "implacable intelligence" makes this novel stand out among the ranks of coming-of-age stories, "not necessarily in front, but unmistakably by itself." Doctorow, he remarked, "has renewed an old theme in his quite individual way." Edmund White, reviewing for the *Nation,* also found *World's Fair* distinctive. "In so many autobiographical novels the writer is tempted to gift himself with nearly perfect recall and to turn his early experiences into signs of his own later genius," White observed. "Doctorow avoids these temptations and sticks close to memory, its gaps and haziness as well as its pockets of poetic lucidity. He never divines in his Jewish middle-class Bronx childhood of the 1930s the extraordinary eloquence and wisdom he was later to win for himself." The novel, White added, "never becomes just an excursion down memory lane," with Edgar's recollections instead "constructing the anthropology of twentieth-century America." The critic concluded, "Doctorow finds feelings that are deep in the settings of a more innocent past. His past purrs and hisses and is capable of scratching deep enough to draw blood."

Billy Bathgate has the same setting as *World's Fair,* but where that book, as Anne Tyler put it in the *New York Times Book Review,* was a "lingering, affectionate, deeply textured evocation of the Bronx in the 30s . . . with a memoir's loose, easygoing story line, this new book has a plot as tightly constructed as that of 'Huckleberry Finn.' It is Mr. Doctorow's shapeliest piece of work: a richly detailed report of a fifteen-year-old boy's journey from childhood to adulthood, with plenty of cliff-hanging adventure along the way." Indeed, although *World's Fair* received the American Book Award, some critics laud *Billy Bathgate* as an even greater achievement. The story of teenager Billy Behan's initiation into the world of organized crime under the mentorship of Dutch Schultz is a "grand entertainment that is also a triumphant work of art," according to Pete Hamill, writing in the *Washington Post Book World.* Certain reviewers especially appreciated Doctorow's ability to avoid cliched characters. "Even the various gangsters are multidimensional," Tyler remarked. The completion of *Billy Bathgate* was also a milestone for its author. While discussing the novel in the *Washington Post,* Doctorow revealed that he felt he had been "liberated by it to a certain extent. . . . Certain themes and preoccupations, that leitmotif that I've been working with for several years. I think now I can write anything. The possibilities are limitless. I've somehow been set free by this book."

In *The Waterworks,* Doctorow imaginatively revisits old New York of the 1870s, an era of widespread corruption in a city which enjoyed great prosperity because of profiteering during the U.S. Civil War. In this novel, Doctorow's protagonist is a journalist named McIlvaine, who investigates reports that a wealthy man, believed deceased, has been spotted in public on at least two occasions in the city. To his horror, McIlvaine discovers several such specimens of the living dead as well as their reanimator—a rogue scientist named Wrede Sartorius who is either a madman or a genius ahead of his time. Sartorius is capable of bringing to life the recently deceased, using "fluids" obtained from anonymous street urchins held captive in his lair. Major scenes are set at the municipal waterworks, the holding reservoir into which flows Manhattan's water supply from upstate. In this novel, explained Luc Sante in the *New York Review of Books,* the waterworks facility "is identified with the machinery of civilization, a matter of considerable ambiguity. It is both the locus of possibly nefarious deeds and a marvel of engineering no less impressive today than it was then. Within its precincts Sartorius carries out his experiments, which are futuristic and quaint, morally questionable and straightforwardly inquisitive." Paul Gray, reviewing for *Time,* found *The Waterworks* "an entertaining and sometimes truly haunting story," while *Spectator* critic John Whitworth called it "a marvelous book," a novel "of the prelapsarian state, a late nineteenth-century novel, something out of Conrad and James, out of Stevenson and Wells and Conan Doyle."

The story of Doctorow's *City of God* "is at first difficult to discern," noted a *Publishers Weekly* reviewer, "because the abruptly changing voices are not identified. But the episodic selections prove to be passages in a notebook" kept by Doctorow's protagonist,

a writer named Everett. *Time*'s Gray commented that after thirty pages, the reader "will get the hang of things." In the story, Everett is looking for something to write about and finds an idea that interests him: an incident involving a brass cross that was stolen from an Episcopal church tended by a faith-doubting Thomas Pemberton. The cross turns up on the roof of the Synagogue for Evolutionary Judaism. Pemberton is murdered after a trip to eastern Europe, and Everett eventually becomes attracted to Pemberton's widow. The plot does not come across so straightforwardly, however. *City of God,* explained *New York Times Book Review* critic A. O. Scott, "features shifting narrative points of view and loose ends scattered like snippets of telephone wire, as well as extended passages of philosophical speculation, theological rumination and blankish verse." Among the topics Doctorow explores, observed Mark Harris in *Entertainment Weekly,* are "the origins of the known universe and of life on earth, the fathomless horror of the Holocaust, the place of Jewish and Christian worship and of religious faith in general at the dawn of a new millennium, jazz, desire, movies, war, writing . . . in other words, one of our senior literary lions has decided to grapple with cosmic questions."

"Through all its convolutions," noted John Bemrose in *Maclean's,* "*City of God* creates a gripping sense of the moral and spiritual dilemmas faced by humans at the turn of the millennium." *Nation* contributor Melvin Bukiet called the novel Doctorow's "most vital—and most difficult—work yet. . . . Without linear plot or unified voice, *City of God* is tessellated, a mosaic touching on love and loneliness, faith and physics. It glints and glimmers, reflecting off rather than building upon itself, and adding up to a sum greater than its multifarious parts." Francine Prose, reviewing for *People,* wrote that "*City of God* puts great faith in the intelligence and patience of its readers." Prose felt that readers who "rise to the challenge" will find the novel rewarding. Writing in *Library Journal,* Mirela Roncevic termed the novel "courageous" and, praising Doctorow for sensitivity and perceptiveness, described the work as "essential reading." Gray concluded in *Time* that "the true miracle of *City of God* is the way its disparate parts fuse into a consistently enthralling and suspenseful whole. In such novels as *Ragtime* (1975) and *Billy Bathgate* (1989), Doctorow mixed historical and fictional figures in ways that magically challenged ordinary notions of what is real. His new novel repeats this process, with even more intriguing and unsettling consequences."

Doctorow's subsequent publications include collections of screenplays, essays, and short stories. *Three*

Screenplays features the screenplay for *Daniel*—for which Doctorow did see his script used—as well as his unproduced adaptations of *Ragtime* and *Loon Lake*. When *Ragtime* was being prepared for film by director Robert Altman, Doctorow worked for a time on the screenplay, but he left the project after Milos Forman replaced Altman, as Forman and Doctorow disagreed on several aspects of the production. In the preface to *Three Screenplays,* Doctorow reveals that he dislikes writing film scripts: the screenplays, he says, "were motivated only by my desire to protect my work from oversimplification, bowdlerization, and general mauling by other hands."

The essay compilation *Reporting the Universe* and the short-fiction collection *Sweet Land Stories* find Doctorow in literary forms he apparently enjoys more than screenwriting. The pieces in *Reporting the Universe,* originally a series of lectures delivered by Doctorow at Harvard University, deal with some of the subjects that have informed his fiction: his boyhood, American social and political culture, spirituality, freedom of expression. Doctorow's arguments "are brilliantly reasoned and beautifully expressed," related Amanda Heller in the *Boston Globe.* Both this collection and *Sweet Land Stories* show the author "burrowing hard toward the Big Questions," commented Art Winslow in Chicago's *Tribune Books,* adding: "When he examines the role of the writer in society in 'Reporting the Universe,' one can turn to 'Sweet Land Stories' and see how those ideas play out in his fiction." Doctorow's characters in the short stories include murderers, a self-anointed prophet, an abandoned child, and people who abandon or abduct children. "One of Doctorow's great strengths," Winslow remarked, "is in presenting the aberrant mind and antisocial act as relatively rational, under the circumstances. . . . The characters speak to us engagingly from the Dark Fields of Doctorow's Republic." In *Sweet Land Stories,* Doctorow is "boring like a laser into the failures of the American dream," a *Publishers Weekly* reviewer observed, while *Library Journal* contributor Barbara Hoffert reported that "Doctorow takes a simple story and creates a universe," and the collection as a whole "reminds one of the distinction between merely good and truly great authors."

BIOGRAPHICAL AND CRITICAL SOURCES:

BOOKS

Bloom, Harold, editor, *E. L. Doctorow,* Chelsea House Publishers (Philadelphia, PA), 2002.

Concise Dictionary of American Literary Biography: Broadening Views, 1968-1988, Gale (Detroit, MI), 1989.

Contemporary Literary Criticism, Gale (Detroit, MI), Volume 6, 1976, Volume 11, 1979, Volume 15, 1980, Volume 18, 1981, Volume 37, 1986, Volume 44, 1987, Volume 65, 1991.

Contemporary Novelists, 7th edition, St. James Press (Detroit, MI), 2001.

Dictionary of Literary Biography, Gale (Detroit, MI), Volume 2: *American Novelists since World War II,* 1978, Volume 28: *Twentieth-Century American-Jewish Fiction Writers,* 1984.

Dictionary of Literary Biography Yearbook: 1980, Gale (Detroit, MI), 1981.

Doctorow, E. L., *Three Screenplays,* Johns Hopkins University Press (Baltimore, MD), 2003.

Encyclopedia of World Literature in the Twentieth Century, St. James Press (Detroit, MI), 1999.

Johnson, Diane, *Terrorists and Novelists,* Knopf (New York, NY), 1982.

Levine, Paul, *E. L. Doctorow,* Methuen (New York, NY), 1985.

Morris, Christopher, *Models of Misrepresentation: On the Fiction of E. L. Doctorow,* University Press of Mississippi (Jackson, MS), 1991.

Morris, Christopher, *Conversations with E. L. Doctorow,* University Press of Mississippi (Jackson, MS), 1999.

Parks, John, *E. L. Doctorow,* Continuum (New York, NY), 1991.

Tokarczyk, Michelle, and E. L. Doctorow, *E. L. Doctorow: An Annotated Bibliography,* Garland (New York, NY), 1988.

Trenner, Richard, editor, *E. L. Doctorow: Essays and Conversations,* Ontario Review Press (Princeton, NJ), 1983.

Williams, John, *Fiction as False Document: The Reception of E. L. Doctorow in the Postmodern Age,* Camden House (Columbia, SC), 1996.

PERIODICALS

American Literary History, summer, 1992.
American Studies, spring, 1992.
Atlanta Journal and Constitution, February 8, 1998.
Atlantic, September, 1980.
Booklist, October 1, 1994, p. 238; January 1, 2000, Bonnie Smothers, review of *City of God,* p. 833.
Boston Globe, June 22, 2003, Amanda Heller, review of *Reporting the Universe,* p. D7.
Chicago Tribune, September 28, 1980.
Chronicle of Higher Education, May 30, 2003, Jennifer Ruark, "Professor Seeks to Make Film about

Lawyer Who Defended Racist Murderers; Scholarly Press Publishes Screenplays of Three Novels by Doctorow," p. 16.

Commentary, October, 1975; March, 1986.

Detroit Free Press, February 19, 1989.

Detroit News, November 10, 1985.

Drama, January, 1980.

Entertainment Weekly, June 17, 1994, p. 46; February 25, 2000, Mark Harris, review of *City of God,* p. 73.

Globe and Mail (Toronto, Ontario, Canada), March 11, 1989.

Hudson Review, summer, 1986.

Library Journal, March 1, 2000, Mirela Roncevic, review of *City of God,* p. 123; March 1, 2004, Barbara Hoffert, review of *Sweet Land Stories,* p. 110.

Listener, September 14, 1989, Andrew Clifford, "True-ish Crime Stories," p. 29.

London Magazine, February, 1986.

Los Angeles Times Book Review, November 24, 1985, Richard Eder, review of *World's Fair,* p. 3; March 5, 1989, Richard Eder, "Siege Perilous in the Court of Dutch Schultz," p. 3.

Maclean's, July 25, 1994, p. 54; April 17, 2000, John Bemrose, review of *City of God,* p. 56.

Manchester Guardian, February 23, 1986.

Miami Herald, December 21, 1975, Jonathan Yardley, "E. L. Doctorow: Mr. 'Ragtime,'" pp. 88-89.

Midwest Quarterly, autumn, 1983.

Nation, June 2, 1979; September 27, 1980; November 17, 1984; November 30, 1985, Edmund White, review of *World's Fair;* April 3, 1989; June 6, 1994; March 13, 2000, Melvin Bukiet, review of *City of God,* p. 23.

National Review, August 15, 1975; March 14, 1986.

New Leader, December 16-30, 1985.

New Republic, June 5, 1971; July 5, 1975; September 6, 1975; September 20, 1980; December 3, 1984; July 18, 1994, p. 44; March 6, 2000, Robert Alter, review of *City of God,* p. 27.

New Statesman, June 17, 1994, p. 40.

Newsweek, June 7, 1971; July 14, 1975; November 4, 1985; February 21, 2000, Peter Plagens, review of *City of God,* p. 58.

New York, September 29, 1980; November 25, 1985.

New Yorker, December 9, 1985; June 27, 1994, p. 41.

New York Herald Tribune, January 22, 1961.

New York Review of Books, August 7, 1975; December 19, 1985; June 23, 1994, p. 12.

New York Times, August 4, 1978; November 24, 1978; September 12, 1980; March 1, 1981, Tom Buckley, "The Forman Formula," section 6, p. 28; November

ber 6, 1984; October 31, 1985; November 11, 1985, Herbert Mitgang, "Doctorow Revisits the 'World's Fair' of His Novel," p. C13; February 9, 1989; July 8, 1994.

New York Times Book Review, September 25, 1960; July 4, 1971; July 6, 1975; September 28, 1980; December 6, 1984; November 10, 1985; February 26, 1989, Anne Tyler, "An American Boy in Gangland," p. 1; June 19, 1994, p. 1; March 5, 2000, A. O. Scott, review of *City of God,* p. 7.

Partisan Review, fall, 1972.

People, March 20, 1989; July 4, 1994, p. 28; March 13, 2000, Francine Prose, review of *City of God,* p. 55.

Progressive, March, 1986.

Publishers Weekly, June 30, 1975; June 27, 1994, p. 51; January 24, 2000, review of *City of God,* p. 292; August 28, 2000, review of *The Best American Short Stories 2000,* p. 53; March 22, 2004, review of *Sweet Land Stories,* p. 59.

Saturday Review, July 17, 1971; July 26, 1975; September, 1980.

South Atlantic Quarterly, winter, 1982.

Southwest Review, autumn, 1977.

Spectator, May 28, 1994, p. 33.

Time, July 14, 1975; September 22, 1980; December 18, 1985; June 20, 1994, p. 66; February 14, 2000, Paul Gray, review of *City of God,* p. 82.

Times Literary Supplement, February 14, 1986; May 27, 1994, Stephen Fender, "The Novelist as Liar," p. 20.

Tribune Books (Chicago, IL), April 25, 2004, Art Winslow, "Illuminating Stories," p. 2.

Village Voice, July 7, 1975; August 4, 1975; December 4, 1978; November 26, 1985.

Wall Street Journal, February 7, 1986.

Washington Post, March 9, 1998.

Washington Post Book World, July 13, 1975; September 28, 1980; November 11, 1984; November 17, 1985; February 19, 1989.*

*   *   *

DOMECQ, H(onorio) Bustos
See BORGES, Jorge Luis

*   *   *

DUKE, Raoul
See THOMPSON, Hunter S(tockton)

E-F

ELLROY, James 1948-

PERSONAL: Born March 4, 1948, Los Angeles, CA; son of Geneva (a nurse; maiden name, Hilliker) Ellroy; married Mary Doherty, 1988 (marriage ended); married Helen Knode (a journalist and author).

ADDRESSES: Home—New Canaan, CT. *Agent*—Nat Sobel, Sobel, Weber Associates, Inc., 146 East 19th St., New York, NY 10003.

CAREER: Writer. Worked at a variety of jobs, including as a golf caddy in California and New York, 1977-84. *Military service:* U.S. Army, 1965.

AWARDS, HONORS: Edgar Award nomination, Mystery Writers of America, 1982, for *Clandestine;* Prix Mystere Award, 1990, for *The Big Nowhere.*

WRITINGS:

"L.A. QUARTET" CRIME NOVELS

The Black Dahlia, Mysterious Press (New York, NY), 1987.
The Big Nowhere, Mysterious Press (New York, NY), 1988.
L.A. Confidential, Mysterious Press (New York, NY), 1990.
White Jazz, Knopf (New York, NY), 1992.

NOVELS

Brown's Requiem, Avon (New York, NY), 1981.
Clandestine, Avon (New York, NY), 1982.

James Ellroy

Blood on the Moon (also see below), Mysterious Press (New York, NY), 1984.
Because the Night (also see below), Mysterious Press (New York, NY), 1984.
Killer on the Road, Avon (New York, NY), 1986.
Suicide Hill (also see below), Mysterious Press (New York, NY), 1986.
Silent Terror, introduction by Jonathan Kellerman, Avon (New York, NY), 1986.

Hollywood Nocturnes, Otto Penzler Books (New York, NY), 1994.

American Tabloid, Knopf (New York, NY), 1995.

L.A. Noir, (contains *Blood on the Moon, Because the Night,* and *Suicide Hill*), Mysterious Press (New York, NY), 1998.

The Cold Six Thousand, Knopf (New York, NY), 2001.

Destination: Morgue!: L.A. Tales, Knopf (New York, NY), 2004.

Police Gazette, Knopf (New York, NY), forthcoming.

OTHER

(Author of introduction) Jim Thompson, *Heed the Thunder,* Armchair Detective Library (New York, NY), 1991.

My Dark Places: An L.A. Crime Memoir, Knopf (New York, NY), 1996.

Crimewave: Reportage and Fiction from the Underside of L.A., Random House (New York, NY), 1999.

(Author of afterword) Bill O'Reilly, *The No-Spin Zone: Confrontations with the Powerful and Famous in America,* Broadway Books (New York, NY), 2001.

(Editor, with Otto Penzler) *The Best American Mystery Stories, 2002,* American Library Association (New York, NY), 2002.

Author of the story "Dark Blue." Author's personal archives, including handwritten manuscripts and correspondence with editors, are housed at the University of South Carolina's Thomas Cooper Library.

ADAPTATIONS: Blood on the Moon was filmed as *Cop,* Atlantic, 1988. *L.A. Confidential* was filmed in 1997 by New Regency, directed by Curtis Hanson and starring Kevin Spacey, Russell Crowe, Danny DeVito, and Kim Basinger. *L.A. Noir* is available as an audiobook, Books on Tape, 1998. Robert Greenwald directed *James Ellroy's Los Angeles* as a mini-series containing characters from Ellroy's novels, as well as a film version of *My Dark Places;* the 2003 United Artists film *Dark Blue* was adapted from Ellroy's story by David Ayer, directed by Ron Shelton; *The Black Dahlia* was adapted for a film directed by Brian DePalma; a film version of *White Jazz* was in production.

WORK IN PROGRESS: A script for a film about Hollywood lawyer Sidney Korshak titled *The Man Who Kept Secrets.*

SIDELIGHTS: James Ellroy is a prominent crime novelist who has won acclaim for his vivid portraits of Los Angeles, California's seamier aspects. Ellroy himself spent many years on the Los Angeles streets. After an arduous childhood—his parents divorced when he was four, his mother was murdered six years later, and his father died seven years after that—Ellroy took to the streets. Having already been expelled from both high school for excessive truancy and the military for faking a nervous breakdown, he turned to crime, committing petty burglaries to fund his increasing alcohol dependency. From 1965 to 1977 Ellroy was arrested for such crimes as drunkenness, shoplifting, and trespassing on approximately thirty occasions. Twelve times he was convicted and was imprisoned for eight months.

In 1977 Ellroy's life changed radically after he was hospitalized with double pneumonia. Profoundly shaken by his brush with death, he entered an Alcoholics Anonymous program and then managed, through a friend, to obtain employment as a caddy at posh Hollywood golf courses. By this time Ellroy was already determined to pursue a literary career. Before he had been hospitalized, he had spent many hours in public libraries, where he drank discreetly while poring through twentieth-century American literature. He also read the more than two hundred crime novels he had stolen from various markets and bookstores, and it was the crime genre that eventually enticed him into commencing his own literary career.

In 1979, while continuing with his job as a caddy, Ellroy began writing his first book. The result, after more than ten months of steady writing in longhand, was *Brown's Requiem,* the story of a private investigator who uncovers a deadly band of extortionists roaming the streets of Los Angeles.

Brown's Requiem won Ellroy immediate acceptance from an agent who in turn quickly managed to place the manuscript with a publisher. Ellroy's actual earnings from the novel, though, were not enough to support him, and so he remained a golf caddy while he produced a second novel, *Clandestine.* This novel, in which a former police officer tracks down his ex-lover's killer, received a nomination for the crime genre's prestigious Edgar Award from the Mystery Writers of America.

Ellroy followed *Clandestine* with *Blood on the Moon,* the story of two brilliant men—a somewhat unstable police detective, Lloyd Hopkins, and a psychopathic murderer—who clash in Los Angeles. In 1984, the year that this novel appeared in print, Ellroy finally managed to leave his caddying job and devote himself fully to writing. Among the next few novels he published were *Because the Night, Killer on the Road,* and *Suicide Hill,* the last in which Lloyd Hopkins, the temperamental protagonist of the earlier *Blood on the Moon,* opposes a vicious bank robber.

In 1987 Ellroy produced *The Black Dahlia,* the first volume in his "L.A. Quartet" series. *The Black Dahlia* is based on the actual 1947 unsolved murder of prostitute Elizabeth Short, whose severed body was found on a Los Angeles street. The murder bears similarities to that of Ellroy's own mother. Like the Black Dahlia case, the murder of Ellroy's mother was never solved, but in Ellroy's novel he proposes a possible solution to the Black Dahlia mystery. "Ellroy's novel is true to the facts as they are known," wrote David Haldane in the *Los Angeles Times.* "But it provides a fictional solution to the crime consistent with those facts." Haldane added that in tracing the Black Dahlia case Ellroy "conducts an uncompromising tour of the obscene, violent, gritty, obsessive, darkly sexual world" that existed within Los Angeles during the 1940s, "complete with names and places."

Ellroy continued to chart the Los Angeles underworld in *The Big Nowhere,* in which two criminal investigations converge with shocking results. The novel takes place during the McCarthy era of the 1950s, when fear of the communist threat in the United States was widespread. In one investigation, a deputy sheriff probes a rash of killings in the homosexual community. The other case involves a city investigator's efforts to further his career by exposing a band of alleged communists circulating within the film industry. The two cases become one when the ambitious investigator employs the deputy as a decoy to lure an influential leftist known as the Red Queen. This collaborative operation leads to unexpected discoveries.

The Big Nowhere won Ellroy substantial recognition as a proficient writer. According to London *Times* writer Peter Guttridge, it established its author as one "among that handful of crime writers whose work is regarded as literature." Among the novel's enthusiasts was Bruce Cook, who proclaimed in the *Washington Post Book World* that Ellroy has produced "a first-rate crime novel, a violent picture in blood-red and grays, set against a fascinating period background."

Ellroy realized further acclaim with *L.A. Confidential,* in which three police officers cross paths while conducting their affairs in 1950s Los Angeles. The protagonists here are wildly different: Bud White is a brutish, excessively violent law enforcer; Trashcan Vincennes is a corrupt narcotics investigator; and Ed Exley is a rigid, politically ambitious sergeant. The three men come together while probing a bizarre incident in which several coffee shop patrons were gunned down. The ensuing plot, reported Kevin Moore in Chicago's *Tribune Books,* "plays itself out with all the impact—and excess—of a shotgun blast." *People* reviewer Lorenzo Carcaterra judged that *L.A. Confidential* is "violently unsettling" and "ugly yet engrossing." *White Jazz,* the concluding volume in the "L.A. Quartet," appeared in 1992.

After completing his four-book series, Ellroy decided upon a change in course. "I think," he told Guttridge in the London *Times,* "it's time I moved beyond Los Angeles." Ellroy added, however, that he planned to continue to pursue what he called his "one goal—to be the greatest crime writer of all time."

Move beyond Los Angeles he did in his next novel, *American Tabloid,* an ambitious, tightly plotted narrative of national and international conspiracy and crime in the 1960s that culminates with the great "unsolved" American crime: the Kennedy assassination. Two FBI agents and a CIA operative make up the three central characters through which Ellroy spins this complex, disturbing, and visceral tale of American history "from the bottom up," in the words of a *Booklist* critic. *American Tabloid,* rife with Ellroy's signature staccato language and over-the-top violence, sold well and invited positive reviews and colorful critical descriptions. A contributor to *Booklist* characterized the novel as being about the "most potent drug of all"—power. "It's as if Ellroy injects us with a mainline pop of the undiluted power that surges through the veins of his obsessed characters," the critic added. In *Time,* Paul Gray called *American Tabloid* "American history as well as Hellzapoppin, a long slapstick routine careening around a manic premise: What if the fabled American innocence is all shuck and jive?" Gray went on to praise the novel as "a big, boisterous, rude and shameless reminder of why reading can be so engrossing and so much fun."

With his next project, 1996's "crime memoir" *My Dark Places,* Ellroy returns not only to Los Angeles, but also to his own unresolved past. With his early novel

The Black Dahlia, Ellroy had attempted to put to rest questions about his mother's death, but here he sets out to solve his mother's murder himself. He enlists the help of a retired Los Angeles police officer and starts retracing the evidence of the almost thirty-year-old crime. Ellroy reports the facts of the investigation in great detail, using a style similar to that of his crime novels, a decision critics found only partially successful. A writer for *Kirkus Reviews* described the language as "a punchy but monotonous rhythm that's as relentless as a jackhammer," while Bruce Jay Friedman in the *New York Times Review* compared it to something that "might've been fired out of a riveting gun." Ellroy never finds the murderer, but he does speculate on the impact of his mother's death on his character and career and learns more about her life. Although a *Kirkus Reviews* critic warned that "Those expecting an autobiographical expose of the writer's psychological clockwork will feel stonewalled by macho reserve," Friedman found the psychological dimension satisfying. "All in all, a rough and strenuously involving book," he commented in his review of *My Dark Places.* "Early on, Mr. Ellroy makes a promise to his dead mother that seems maudlin at first: 'I want to give you breath.' But he's done just that and—on occasion—taken ours away."

After *My Dark Places,* Elroy publically stated that he was no longer interested in the genre. "I'm not writing crime fiction anymore," he told Jeff Guinn for the *Knight Ridder/Tribune News Service.* "I've moved on with what I wanted to do. I wanted to write fiction about history, to have rewritten history to my own specifications." Despite disappointing crime fans, he kept true to his word; his 2001 novel, *The Cold Six Thousand,* is a follow-up to *American Tabloid* and the second in the projected "Underworld U.S.A." trilogy about politics and racism in America during the 1960s and 1970s. *The Cold Six Thousand* covers the years 1963 through 1968 and includes such historical figures as Howard Hughes, J. Edgar Hoover, Martin Luther King, Jr., and Robert Kennedy. Probing the dark side of America, Ellroy tells of Hoover's hatred of King, a Central Intelligence Agency that smuggles dope, and the mess of the Vietnam War. The story focuses primarily on a Las Vegas police officer named Wayne Tedrow, Jr., who inadvertently becomes involved in the cover up of President John F. Kennedy's assassination. Through the course of the novel Tedrow becomes involved in various unsavory organizations, including the Mafia and the Ku Klux Klan, as Ellroy offers his vision of an America that is anything but innocent.

Although Tedrow is the novel's "hero," by the end he has become a corrupted, ruthless, and vengeful killer who plays a role in the assassination of King. Commenting on the book during an interview with Dorman T. Shindler for *Writer,* Ellroy noted: "The *Cold Six Thousand* is a story about violent men in a violent time doing terrible, violent things. This is the epic of bad white men doing bad things in the name of authority. This is the humanity of bad white men."

Reviewing *The Cold Six Thousand* for the *Knight Ridder/Tribune News Service,* Fred Grimm wondered if perhaps "Ellroy was outdone this time by wider ambition." The novel's look at the assassinations of John and Bobby Kennedy and of King "offers only another variation of theories explored by 10,000 wild-eyed paranoids," the critic added. A *Publishers Weekly* contributor, however, praised the novel as "a career performance," and went on to note that, "With Ellroy's ice-pick declarative prose . . . plus his heart-trembling, brain-searing subject matter, readers will feel kneed, stomped upon and then kicked-right up into the maw of hard truth." Thomas Auger, writing in the *Library Journal,* called the book "readable yet complex in its character development and critical examination of U.S. public policy." Paul Gray wrote in *Time* that *The Cold Six Thousand* is an "exceedingly nasty piece of work," and went on to note: "Yet it is often funny . . . and traces an unexpectedly moral arc through all its mayhem. Pick it up if you dare; put it down if you can."

BIOGRAPHICAL AND CRITICAL SOURCES:

BOOKS

Twentieth-Century Crime and Mystery Writers, 3rd edition, St. James Press (Detroit, MI), 1991, pp. 347-348.

PERIODICALS

Armchair Detective, spring, 1987, p. 206; winter, 1991, p. 31.
Booklist, January 15, 1995.
Christian Science Monitor, October 2, 1987, p. B5.
Interview, December, 1996, p. 70.
Kirkus Reviews, September 15, 1996.

Knight Ridder/Tribune News Service, May 30, 2001, Fred Grimm, review of *The Cold Six Thousand,* p. K7849; June 13, 2001, Jeff Guinn, "Political History, as Told by James Ellroy," p. K5306.

Library Journal, April 15, 2001, Thomas Auger, review of *The Cold Six Thousand,* p. 131.

Los Angeles Times, October 4, 1987; May 27, 1990.

Los Angeles Times Book Review, June 3, 1984, p. 18; September 13, 1987, p. 16; October 9, 1988, p. 12; July 8, 1990, p. 8.

Nation, December 2, 1996, p. 25.

New Statesman, June 19, 1987, p. 31; January 22, 1988, p. 33.

New York Times, November 3, 2003, Virginia Heffernan, "A Writer, Hard-boiled and Shaped by Murder," p. E8.

New York Times Book Review, July 22, 1984, p. 32; July 6, 1986, p. 21; November 8, 1987, p. 62; October 9, 1988, p. 41; September 3, 1989, p. 20; July 15, 1990, p. 26; June 30, 1991, p. 32; November 24, 1996.

Observer, May 13, 1984, p. 23.

People, December 14, 1987; July 2, 1990; November 25, 1996, p. 93.

Publishers Weekly, June 15, 1990, pp. 53-54; May 21, 2001, review of *The Cold Six Thousand,* p. 83.

Spectator, July 21, 1984, p. 29.

Time, April 10, 1995, p. 74; November 25, 1996, p. 115; May 21, 2003, Paul Gray, review of *The Cold Six Thousand,* p. 90.

Times (London, England), November 10, 1990.

Tribune Books (Chicago, IL), September 3, 1989, p. 5; June 10, 1990, p. 1.

Washington Post Book World, October 23, 1988, p. 10.

West Coast Review of Books, January, 1983, p. 43; September, 1983, p. 20; September, 1986, p. 27.

Writer, September, 2001, Dorman T. Shindler, "Fierce Ambition," interview with Ellroy, p. 28.

ONLINE

Salon.com, http://www.salon.com/ (December 9, 1996), interview with Ellroy.*

*   *   *

FRAYN, Michael 1933-

PERSONAL: Born September 8, 1933, in London, England; son of Thomas Allen (a manufacturer's representative) and Violet Alice (Lawson) Frayn; married Gillian Palmer (a psychotherapist), February 18, 1960

Michael Frayn

(divorced, 1989); married Claire Tomalin (an author), June 5, 1996; children: (first marriage) three daughters. *Education:* Emmanuel College, Cambridge, B.A., 1957.

ADDRESSES: Agent—Green & Heaton, 37a Goldhawk Rd., London W12 8QQ, England.

CAREER: Novelist and playwright. *Guardian,* Manchester, England, general-assignment reporter, 1957-59, "Miscellany" columnist, 1959-62; *Observer,* London, England, columnist, 1962-68. *Military service:* British Army, 1952-54.

MEMBER: Royal Society of Literature.

AWARDS, HONORS: Somerset Maugham Award, 1966, for *The Tin Men;* Hawthornden Prize, 1967, for *The Russian Interpreter;* National Press Club Award for distinguished reporting, International Publishing Corporation, 1970, for *Observer* articles on Cuba; Best Comedy of the Year awards, London *Evening Stan-*

dard, 1975, for *Alphabetical Order,* and 1982, for *Noises Off;* Society of West End Theatre Award for best comedy of the year, 1976, for *Donkeys' Years,* and 1982, for *Noises Off;* Best Play of the Year award, *Evening Standard,* Society of West End Theatre Award for best play of the year, and Laurence Olivier Award for best play, all 1984, and *Plays and Players* Award for best new play, and New York Drama Critics' Circle Award for best new foreign play, both 1986, all for *Benefactors;* Antoinette Perry ("Tony") Award nomination for best play, 1984, for *Noises Off;* International Emmy Award, 1989, for *First and Last;* Emmy Award, 1990; *Sunday Express* Book of the Year Award, 1991, for *A Landing on the Sun; Evening Standard* Award for best play, Critics Circle Award for best play, and South Bank Show Award, all 1998, Moliè Award (Paris, France), and Tony Award for best play, 2000, all for *Copenhagen;* Booker Prize shortlist, 1999, for *Headlong;* honorary doctorate, Cambridge University, 2001; Whitbread Novel of the Year Award, 2002, and Twenty-first Century Award for best foreign novel (China), both for *Spies; Evening Standard* Award for best play, Critic's Circle Award for best play, and South Bank Show Award, all 2003, all for *Democracy;* New York Public Library for the Performing Arts tribute, 2003; S. T. Dupont Award for Lifetime Achievement in Literature, PEN English Centre, 2003.

WRITINGS:

The Day of the Dog (columns; originally published in *Guardian*), illustrations by Timothy Birdsall, Collins (London, England), 1962, Doubleday (New York, NY), 1963.

The Book of Fub (columns; originally published in *Guardian*), Collins (London, England), 1963, published as *Never Put off to Gomorrah,* Pantheon (New York, NY), 1964.

On the Outskirts, Collins (London, England), 1964.

At Bay in Gear Street (columns; originally published in *Observer*), Fontana (Huntington, NY), 1967.

Constructions (philosophy), Wildwood House (London, England), 1974.

The Original Michael Frayn, Salamander Press (Edinburgh, Scotland), 1983.

Speak after the Beep (ollected columns), Methuen (London, England), 1995.

The Additional Michael Frayn, Methuen (London, England), 2000.

NOVELS

The Tin Men, Collins (London, England), 1965, Little, Brown (Boston, MA), 1966.

The Russian Interpreter, Viking (New York, NY), 1966.

Towards the End of the Morning, Collins (London, England), 1967, reprinted, Harvill (London, England), 1987, published as *Against Entropy,* Viking (New York, NY), 1967.

A Very Private Life, Viking (New York, NY), 1968.

Sweet Dreams, Collins (London, England), 1973, Viking (New York, NY), 1974.

The Trick of It, Viking (London, England), 1989, Viking (New York, NY), 1990.

A Landing on the Sun, Viking (London, England), 1991, Viking (New York, NY), 1992.

Now You Know, Viking (London, England), 1992, Viking (New York, NY), 1993.

Headlong, Metropolitan Books (New York, NY), 1999.

(With David Burke) *Celia's Secret: An Investigation* (based on the play *Copenhagen*), Faber (London, England), 2000, published as *The Copenhagen Papers,* Metropolitan Books (New York, NY), 2001.

Spies, Metropolitan Books (New York, NY), 2002.

STAGE PLAYS

(With John Edwards) *Zounds!* (musical comedy), produced in Cambridge, England, 1957.

The Two of Us: Four One-Act Plays for Two Players (contains *Black and Silver, The New Quixote, Mr. Foot,* and *Chinamen;* first produced in London's West End, 1970), Fontana (London, England), 1970.

The Sandboy (first produced in London, England, 1971), Fontana (London, England), 1971.

Alphabetical Order (first produced in London's West End, 1975), published with *Donkeys' Years,* Methuen (London, England), 1977.

Donkeys' Years (first produced in London's West End, 1976; produced off-off Broadway, 1987; also see below), S. French (New York, NY), 1977.

Clouds (also see below; first produced in London, England, 1976), S. French (New York, NY), 1977.

Alphabetical Order [and] *Donkeys' Years,* Methuen (London, England), 1977.

Balmoral (also see below; first produced in Guildford, Surrey, England, 1978, revised version produced as *Liberty Hall* in London, England, 1980, produced under original title in London, 1987), Methuen (London, England), 1977, revised, 1987.

Make and Break (also see below; first produced in Hammersmith, England, then in London's West

End, 1980; produced at John F. Kennedy Center for the Performing Arts, 1982), Methuen (London, England), 1980.

Noises Off (three-act; also see below; first produced in Hammersmith, England, then London's West End, 1982, produced in New York, NY, 1983; revival produced on London's West End, 2000, then Broadway, 2001), S. French (New York, NY), 1982, revised version, Doubleday (New York, NY), 2002.

Benefactors (also see below; two-act; first produced in London's West End, 1984; produced on Broadway, 1985), Methuen (London, England), 1984.

(Translator from the French) Jean Anouilh, *Number One* (first produced in London, England, 1984), S. French (New York, NY), 1985.

Plays: One (contains *Alphabetical Order, Donkeys' Years, Clouds, Make and Break,* and *Noises Off*), Methuen (London, England), 1985.

Look Look (first produced as *Spettattori* in Rome, Italy, 1989; produced as *Look Look* in London, England, 1990), Methuen (London, England), 1990, first act published as *Audience,* S. French (New York, NY), 1991.

Listen to This (short plays), Methuen (London, England), 1990.

Plays: Two (contains *Benefactors, Balmoral,* and *Wild Honey*), Methuen (London, England), 1992.

Here (first produced at Donmar Warehouse, 1993), Methuen (London, England), 1993.

(Translator from the French) Jacques Offenbach, *La belle Vivette* (opera), first produced at Rome Coliseum, 1995.

Now You Know (first produced in London, England, 1995), Methuen (London, England), 1995.

Alarms and Excursions, first produced in Guilford, England, 1998.

Copenhagen (first produced in Cottesloe, England, 1998, produced in London's West End, 1999; produced in New York, NY), Methuen Drama (London, England), 1998.

Plays: Three, Methuen Drama (London, England), 2000.

Democracy, first produced in London's West End, 2003.

TRANSLATOR FROM THE RUSSIAN; AND ADAPTER

(And author of introduction) Anton Chekhov, *The Cherry Orchard* (four-act; first produced in London's West End, 1978), Methuen (London, England), 1978.

(And author of introduction) Leo Tolstoy, *The Fruits of Enlightenment* (four-act; first produced in London's West End, 1979), Methuen (London, England), 1979.

(And author of introduction) Anton Chekhov, *Three Sisters* (four-act; produced in Manchester, England, 1985), Methuen (London, England), 1983.

Anton Chekhov, *Wild Honey: The Untitled Play* (also known as *Platonov;* also see above; produced in London's West End, 1984; produced in New York, NY, 1986), Methuen (London, England), 1984.

(And author of introduction) Anton Chekhov, *The Seagull* (produced in London's West End, 1986), Methuen (London, England), 1986.

Trifonov, *Exchange* (produced at Guildhall School of Drama, 1986, then on BBC Radio 3), Methuen (London, England), 1990.

Anton Chekhov, *Uncle Vanya* (produced in London, England, 1988), Methuen (London, England), 1987.

Anton Chekhov, *Chekhov: Plays* (includes *The Seagull, Uncle Vanya, Three Sisters,* and *The Cherry Orchard*), Methuen (London, England), 1988.

(And adaptor) Anton Chekhov, *The Sneeze* (short stories and sketches; produced in London's West End, 1988), Methuen (London, England), 1989.

TELEVISION WORK

What the Papers Say (documentary series), Granada TV, 1962-66.

(With John Bird) *Second City Reports* (series), Granada TV, 1964.

Jamie, on a Flying Visit (teleplay; also see below), British Broadcasting Corp. (BBC-TV), 1968.

(And presenter) *One Pair of Eyes* (documentary film), BBC-TV, 1968.

Birthday (teleplay; also see below), BBC-TV, 1969.

(With John Bird and Eleanor Bron) *Beyond a Joke* (series), BBC-TV, 1972.

(And presenter) *Laurence Sterne Lived Here* (documentary film), BBC-TV, 1973.

Making Faces (six-part comedy miniseries), BBC-TV, 1975.

(And presenter) *Imagine a City Called Berlin* (documentary film), BBC-TV, 1975.

(And presenter) *Vienna: The Mask of Gold* (documentary film), BBC-TV, 1977.

Alphabetical Order (adapted from Frayn's stage play), Granada TV, 1978.

(And presenter) *Three Streets in the Country* (documentary film), BBC-TV, 1979.

Donkeys' Years (adapted from Frayn's stage play), ATV, 1980.

(And presenter) *The Long Straight,* BBC-TV, 1980.

(And presenter) *Jerusalem* (documentary film), BBC-TV, 1984.

Make and Break (adapted from Frayn's stage play), BBC-TV, 1987.

Benefactors (adapted from Frayn's stage play), BBC-TV, 1989.

First and Last (movie; broadcast on BBC-TV, 1989), Methuen, 1989.

Jamie, on a Flying Machine [and] *Birthday* (teleplays), Methuen (London, England), 1990.

(And presenter) *Magic Lantern: Prague* (documentary film), BBC-TV, 1993.

A Landing on the Sun (movie; adapted from Frayn's novel), BBC-TV, 1994.

(And presenter) *Budapest: Written in Water* (documentary film), BBC-TV, 1996.

Copenhagen (movie; adapted from Frayn's stage play), BBC-TV, 2002.

OTHER

(Editor) John Bingham Morton, *The Best of Beachcomber,* Heinemann (London, England), 1963.

(Editor, with Bamber Gascoigne) *Timothy: The Drawings and Cartoons of Timothy Birdsall,* M. Joseph (London, England), 1964.

(With others) *Great Railway Journeys of the World* (based on film broadcast by BBC-TV; contains Frayn's segment on Australia), BBC (London, England), 1981, Dutton (New York, NY), 1982.

Clockwise (screenplay; produced by Universal, 1986), Methuen (London, England), 1986.

Noises Off (screenplay; adapted from Frayn's stage play), Touchstone, 1992.

Remember Me? (screenplay), Channel Four Films, 1997.

Contributor to Michael Sissons and Philip French, *Age of Austerity,* Hodder & Stoughton (London, England), 1963.

SIDELIGHTS: Though best known in the United States as the author of the hit stage farce *Noises Off* and the multi-award-winning play *Copenhagen,* British playwright Michael Frayn has actually produced a wide variety of writings during his long career. Frayn's beginnings as a columnist and critic for two newspapers—the Manchester *Guardian* and the London *Observer*—led to a number of published collections, while his novels, including *Headlong, The Russian Interpreter,* and *Spies,* have garnered praise for both their humor and their insights into the complications of modern times. Among his plays, Frayn's translations of Anton Chekhov's classics draw particular attention. In 1986 the writer ventured into cinema with the produced screenplay *Clockwise,* and has also written for television.

A native Londoner, "Frayn believes his sense of humor began to develop during his years at Kingston Grammar School where, to the delight of his classmates, he practiced the 'techniques of mockery' on his teachers," reported Mark Fritz in the *Dictionary of Literary Biography.* As an adult, he quickly established himself as a keen social satirist on two newspapers, the *Guardian* and *Observer.* For the former, as Frayn saw it, his task in his "Miscellany" column "was to write cool, witty interviews with significant film directors passing through, but there were never enough film directors so he started making up humorous paragraphs to fill," according to Terry Coleman in the *Guardian.* Malcolm Page explained in the *Dictionary of Literary Biography* that Frayn "invented for the column the Don't Know Party and such characters as the trendy Bishop of [Twicester] . . . ; Rollo Swavely, a public relations consultant; and the ambitious suburban couple" Christopher and Lavinia Crumble.

Comparing Frayn's "wit, sophistication, and imagination" to "that of American humorist S. J. Perelman," Fritz declared that Frayn's "satire is sharper." That sense of satire, along with an emerging seriousness, carried the author to his first novel, *The Tin Men.* The story, a satire about the suitability of computers to take over the burden of human dullness, won the Somerset Maugham Award for fiction in 1966.

After *The Tin Men* Frayn produced *The Russian Interpreter,* "a spy story which deals more with the deceit between individuals than between nations," according to Fritz. The action resolves around an English research student studying in Moscow who becomes embroiled in a series of swiftly paced intrigues involving a mysterious businessman, stolen books, and a Russian girl and eventually is incarcerated in a Russian prison. Page characterized the book, which was awarded the Hawthornden Prize, as one of Frayn's more conventional novels, as opposed to his fantasies and satires.

Frayn's novel *A Very Private Life,* written in the future tense, "explains how life has grown more private, first through physical privacy, then through the development of drugs to cope with anger and uncertainty," wrote Page. To *Spectator* reviewer Maurice Capitanchik, "Frayn, in his parable of the horrific future, does not escape the impress which [George] Orwell and [Aldous] Huxley have made upon the genre, nor does he really go beyond the area of authoritarian oppression so brilliantly illumined by [Franz] Kafka, but he does something else both valuable and unique: he shows that his 'Brave New World' is really our cowardly old world, if we did but, shudderingly, know it, in a prose which is often beautiful and, almost, poetry."

In the novel *Sweet Dreams* a young architect dies and goes to a distinctly familiar sort of English heaven, "a terribly decent place, really, where one's pleasantest dreams come true and one's most honest longings are fulfilled," as *Washington Post Book World* critic L. J. Davis described it. Caught in a permanent fantasy world, Howard, the architect, "immediately joins the small, intimate, and brilliantly unorthodox architectural firm he'd always yearned for," Davis continued. After redesigning the Matterhorn, engaging in a dramatic love affair, and realizing other superlative encounters, Frayn's protagonist "sells out to the movies, purges himself with a spell of rustic simplicity, rallies the best minds of his generation by means of letters to *The Times,* meets God . . . and eventually winds up, crinkle-eyed and aging, as prime minister. It is all rather poignant," noted Davis. Page found *Sweet Dreams* to be a "shrewd, sardonic and deceptively charming tale" that Frayn relates with "wit and flourish."

After *Sweet Dreams,* Frayn abandoned the novel form for a decade and a half in order to establish his reputation both as an original playwright and a translator of Chekhov's plays. He returned to the novel in 1989 with *The Trick of It,* in which a young lecturer in literature becomes personally involved with a slightly older, celebrated author on whom he is an expert. During his involvement with the woman, which includes marriage, the man hopes to unravel the secret to her creative success, attempts to influence her writing, and tries unsuccessfully to become a creative writer

himself. Told entirely through letters, the novel was described by Page as "a highly original work . . . linked more closely with a real world than [Frayn's] fantasies." George Craig in the *Times Literary Supplement* called *The Trick of It* "an intensely discomfiting novel, precisely because the elements of farce, social comedy and adventure remain present throughout as potential directions, even as darker and more destructive elements proliferate."

Civil servants are leading characters in Frayn's novels *A Landing on the Sun* and *Now You Know.* In the former, civil servant Brian Jessel is assigned to investigate the supposedly accidental death of colleague Stephen Summerchild fifteen years earlier. Jessel uncovers that Summerchild was overseeing government research into happiness by Elizabeth Serafin, an Oxford philosophy don, and that the two had set up a hidden garret for meetings. "*A Landing on the Sun* tells the wacky and exhilarating story of how Summerchild and Serafin got up into the garret, what they did there and what became of them," explained Richard Eder in the *Los Angeles Times Book Review.* "On that level, it is loony comedy with a mournful ending. Intermittently, it is a lovely satirical speculation on the ways of bureaucracies and academics, on the uses of order and disorder, and the deepest opposite twists in men and women." Page found *A Landing on the Sun* "less ingenious" than *Sweet Dreams,* "although it cleverly unfolds as narrative and explores significant ideas."

In *Now You Know,* a novel-related, play-like work, told through a series of dramatic monologues, Hilary Wood quits her job at the Home Office after meeting Terry Little, who heads OPEN, an organization demanding truth from the government. When she leaves, Hilary illegally takes a file about a police fatality case, the details of which OPEN wants made known. Yet, despite all the talk of openness, secrecy abounds. *Now You Know* is "ingenious, witty, thoughtful and smart. . . . It is also a provocative meditation on the pitfalls of letting it all—most particularly, the truth—hang out," Jonathan Yardley noted in the *Washington Post Book World.* Calling *Now You Know* a book about "truth and when lying may be justified," Yardley added that Frayn's more recent novels "have in common wit, elegance, page-turning storytelling, and a playful treatment of serious themes."

Short-listed for the Booker Prize, the novel *Headlong* is a fascinating mix of comedy, art history, and human desire. Art historian Martin Clay discovers a painting, a lost masterpiece, in a run-down country estate while on vacation in England for a week. Believing Flemish master Pieter Bruegel may have created the painting, Clay is determined to deceive the unsuspecting owner in an effort to claim the painting for himself and sell it for millions of dollars. Complications abound and the young art historian soon discovers that some things are not worth risking everything for. "Clay's five days that shook the world become, in the hands of Frayn, a small jewel of comic shine," according to Terri Natale of the *New Statesman.*

Set in World War II, Frayn's novel *Spies* chronicles the story of two British boys who suspect their neighbors of Nazi espionage and begin following them. The friends—Keith and Steven—live in a quiet little neighborhood until they convince themselves that it is really a network of underground passages and secret laboratories for German infiltrators. "Frayn perfectly captures the dynamics of childhood friendships," stated a *Booklist* critic, while a *Publishers Weekly* reviewer added that Frayn's "enigmatic melodrama will keep readers' attention firmly in hand." Interestingly, *Spies,* which won Frayn the 2002 Whitbread Award for best novel, found its author going head to head against his wife, biographer Claire Tomalin, whose Whitbread Award-winning biography *Samuel Pepys: The Unequalled Self* ultimately won out against *Spies* as the Whitbread Book of the Year.

From his beginnings as a journalist and novelist, Frayn's dramatic work started with television plays, and advanced to satiric and humorous work for the stage. *Contemporary Dramatists* essayist Christopher Innes viewed the playwright's work in terms of "a return to traditional comic values," in response to the didactic "political drama that was sweeping the English stage at the beginning of the 1970s." Discussing the thematic content of Frayn's plays as a whole, Innes stated: "Frayn deals with society in terms of organizations—the news media, a manufacturing industry, the commercial theatre—which intrinsically threaten the survival of humanity. Deadening order is always subverted, however unintentionally; and the life force triumphs, though at the expense of what the individuals concerned are striving for." Frayn, himself, described the overriding theme of his dramatic work as "the way in which we impose our ideas on the world around us."

Among Frayn's stage plays, *Alphabetical Order* and *Donkeys' Years* earned plaudits, profits, and some mea-

sure of reputation for their author. In *Alphabetical Order,* the happy disarray of a newspaper's research department—the "morgue"—is changed forever when a hyper-efficient young woman joins the staff. "By the second act she has transformed [the morgue] into a model of order and efficiency. But somehow the humanness is gone," noted Fritz. "The young woman then proceeds to reorganize the personal lives of the other characters as well. She is not a total villain, however. In a way, the newspaper staff needs her: without a strong-willed person to manipulate them, weak-willed people often stagnate. At the heart of the play is the question: which is better, order or chaos?" Innes pointed out that the play is satirizing "the illusory nature of what our news-fixated culture considers important."

The successful *Donkeys' Years* focuses upon a group of university graduates reunited twenty years later, only to revert to their adolescent roles and conflicts. Voted the best comedy of 1972 by London's Society of West End Theatre, the play was praised by Stephen Holden in the *New York Times* as a "well-made farce that roundly twits English propriety."

Frayn's early theatrical background included a sojourn with the Cambridge Footlights revue during his college days and a walk-on in a production of Nikolai Gogol's *The Inspector General,* the latter a disaster that prefigured the backstage slapstick of his most popular play, *Noises Off.* "I pulled instead of pushed at the door, it jammed in the frame, and there was no other way off," the writer told Benedict Nightingale for a *New York Times Magazine* profile. "So I waited for what seemed like many, many hours while stagehands fought with crowbars on the other side and the audience started to slow-handclap. I've never been on the stage since."

Although many renowned comedies and dramas have used the play-within-a-play format in the past—it is a device that predates Shakespeare—perhaps no self-referential play has been so widely received in this generation as *Noises Off,* a no-holds-barred slapstick farce. Using the kind of manic entrances and mistaken identities reminiscent of French master Georges Feydeau, *Noises Off* invites the audience to witness the turmoil behind a touring company of has-beens and never-weres as they attempt to perform a typically English sex farce called "Nothing On." Referring to the production as "a show that gave ineptitude a good name," *Insight* writer Sheryl Flatow indicated that *Noises Off* was criticized by some as nothing more than a relentless, if effective, laugh-getting machine. The charge of being too funny, however, is not the sort of criticism that repels audiences, and *Noises Off* enjoyed a long run on the West End and Broadway. Describing the play in *Plays: One*, Frayn stated: "The fear that haunts [the cast] is that the unlearned and unrehearsed—the great dark chaos behind the set, inside the heart and brain—will seep back on to the stage. . . . Their performance will break down, and they will be left in front of us naked and ashamed."

"The fun begins even before the curtain goes up," Frank Rich reported in his *New York Times* review of Frayn's comedy. "In the Playbill, we find a program-within-the-program. . . . Among other things, we learn that the author of 'Nothing On' is a former 'unsuccessful gents hosiery wholesaler' whose previous farce 'Socks before Marriage' ran for nine years." When the curtain does rise, Rich continued, "it reveals a hideous set . . . that could well serve all those sex farces . . . that do run for nine years." As the story opens, the "Nothing On" cast and crew are blundering through their final rehearsal; importantly, everyone establishes his onstage and offstage identities. Remarked Rich: "As the run-through is mostly devoted to setting up what follows, it's also the only sporadically mirthless stretch of Mr. Frayn's play: We're asked to study every ridiculous line and awful performance in 'Nothing On' to appreciate the varied replays yet to come. Still, the lags are justified by the payoff: Having painstakingly built his house of cards in Act I, the author brings it crashing down with exponentially accelerating hilarity in Acts II and III."

While the backstage romances simmer, the troupe systematically skewers whatever appeal the cheesy "Nothing On" should have provided. Even the props get involved: by Act II, a plate of sardines is as important an element to the play as any of the actors. By this time, "Frayn's true inspiration strikes," wrote *Washington Post* reviewer David Richards. "The company is a month into its tour and the set has been turned around, so that we are viewing 'Nothing On' from backstage. The innocent little romances in Act I have turned lethal and, while the actors are still vaguely mindful of their cues, they are more mindful of wreaking vengeance upon one another. . . . An ax is wielded murderously, a skirt is torn off, toes are stomped on, shoelaces are tied together, bone-crunching tumbles are taken, bou-

quets are shredded, a cactus is sat upon and, of course, the ingenue's damned [contact] lens pops out again!"

Noises Off established Frayn as a farceur on the order of Feydeau and Ben Travers. To that end, the author told *Los Angeles Times* reporter Barbara Isenberg that farce is serious business. Its most important element, he explained, is "the losing of power for coherent thought under the pressure of events. What characters in farce do traditionally is try to recover some disaster that occurred, by a course of behavior that is so ill-judged that it makes it worse. In traditional farce, people are caught in a compromising situation, try to explain it with a lie and, when they get caught, have then to explain both the original situation *and* the lie. And, when they're caught in that lie, they have to have another one." The play was revised for a revival debuting at London's National Theatre in the fall of 2000 and from there quickly moved across the Atlantic to Broadway.

Frayn's first produced screenplay, *Clockwise,* closely resembles *Noises Off* in its wild construction. Like the play, the film takes a simple premise and lets circumstances run amok. In *Clockwise* protagonist Brian Stimpson (played by Monty Python star John Cleese), a small-town headmaster who is obsessed with punctuality, wins Headmaster of the Year honors and must travel by train to a distant city to deliver his acceptance speech. Inevitably, Brian catches the wrong train, and the thought that he may arrive late drives him to desperate means. By the film's end, he has stolen a car, invaded a monastery, robbed a man of his suit, and set two squadrons of police on his trail. "It isn't the film's idea of taking a prim, controlled character and letting him become increasingly unhinged that makes *Clockwise* so enjoyable; it's the expertise with which Mr. Frayn's screenplay sets the wheels in motion and keeps them going," wrote Janet Maslin in the *New York Times*. Noting that *Clockwise* is "far from perfect—it has long sleepy stretches and some pretty obvious farce situations," *Washington Post* critic Paul Attanasio nonetheless added that, "at its best, here is a comedy unusual in its layered complexity, in the way Frayn has worked everything out. 'Gonna take a bit o' sortin' out, this one,' says one of the pursuing bobbies. The joke, of course, is in the understatement. And rarely has the 'sortin' out' been so much fun."

Departing from farce, Frayn also wrote the stage work *Benefactors,* an acerbic look at a 1960s couple wrestling with their ideals as they try to cope with their troubled neighbors, a couple caught in a failing marriage. Comparing *Benfactors* with *Noises Off,* Frank Rich wrote in the *New York Times:* "It's hard to fathom that these two works were written by the same man. Like *Noises Off, Benefactors* is ingeniously constructed and has been directed with split-second precision . . . but there all similarities end. Mr. Frayn's new play is a bleak, icy, microcosmic exploration of such serious matters as the nature of good and evil, the price of political and psychological change and the relationship of individuals to the social state. Though *Benefactors* evokes Chekhov, *Othello* and *The Master Builder* along its way, it is an original, not to mention demanding, achievement that is well beyond the ambitions of most contemporary dramatists." Likewise, Mel Gussow of the same newspaper found strong ties between Chekhov and Frayn: "Thematically . . . the work remains [close] to Chekhov; through a closely observed, often comic family situation we see the self-defeating aspects of misguided social action."

Also dark in focus, Frayn's *Democracy* features a fractured Cold-War Germany and West German Chancellor Willy Brandt's fall from power. While focusing on Brandt and Günter Guillaume, the communist who caused Brant's downfall, *Democracy* also has a subtext: "the complexity of human beings" and the idea that each individual "contains all the lives that he or she might once have been or could be again," in the words of *Hollywood Reporter*'s Ray Bennett.

Frayn's Tony Award-winning play *Copenhagen* focuses on a meeting during World War II between Nobel Prize-winning nuclear physicists Niels Bohr and Werner Heisenberg. Before the war, their work together had revolutionized atomic physics, and their meeting—which has been heavily debated over the years—has been the subject of much speculation. Both men gave opposing accounts of their meeting following the war, and the real purpose of the encounter remained a mystery. Frayn's play is inspired, in part, by the book *Heisenberg's War: The Secret History of the German Bomb,* which focuses on Heisenberg's efforts to discourage the Nazi atomic bomb program. Moral ambiguities are one of the primary themes Frayn addresses in his play, and as the playwright told a *Guardian* contributor: "whatever was said at the meeting, and whatever Heisenberg's intentions, there is something profoundly characteristic of the difficulties in human relationships, and profoundly painful, in that picture of the two ageing men."

While Frayn has gone on to produce such popular comic works as *Democracy,* his work during the twentieth century is viewed as particularly influential. "Although one cannot say that Michael Frayn's plays revolutionized the British stage during [the late twentieth century], they certainly helped to enliven it," concluded Fritz. Like many of his contemporaries, in his early work he "experimented with dramatic structures borrowed from film and television—perhaps an attempt to find new methods of expression," and went on to produce "a string of lively, witty comedies with some serious philosophical questions lurking beneath the surfaces." Discussing Frayn's overall impact on modern theatre, Innes grouped Frayn with playwrights Trevor Griffiths, Peter Barnes, and Tom Stoppard as creators "of the most inventive contemporary comedy" of their generation.

BIOGRAPHICAL AND CRITICAL SOURCES:

BOOKS

Contemporary Dramatists, 5th edition, St. James Press (Detroit, MI), 1993.
Contemporary Literary Criticism, Gale (Detroit, MI), Volume 3, 1975, Volume 7, 1977, Volume 31, 1985, Volume 47, 1988.
Contemporary Novelists, 6th edition, St. James Press (Detroit, MI), 1996.
Dictionary of Literary Biography, Gale (Detroit, MI), Volume 13: *British Dramatists since World War II,* 1982, Volume 14: *British Novelists since 1960,* 1983.
Page, Malcolm, *File on Frayn,* Methuen Drama (London, England), 1994.

PERIODICALS

American Theatre, October, 2001, Celia Wren, review of *The Copenhagen Papers,* p. 121.
Art in America, July, 2000, Paula Harper, review of *Headlong,* p. 35.
Atlanta Journal-Constitution, April 7, 2002, Steve Murray, review of *Spies,* p. H4.
Back Stage, April 21, 2000, David A. Rosenberg, review of *Copenhagen,* p. 64.
Back Stage West, January 17, 2002, Kristina Mannion, review of *Copenhagen,* p. 16.

Booklist, July, 1999, Brad Hooper, review of *Headlong,* p. 1893; March 15, 2001, Whitney Scott, review of *Headlong,* p. 1412; April 1, 2001, Jack Helbig, review of *The Copenhagen Papers,* p. 1442; February 15, 2002, Joanne Wilkinson, review of *Spies,* p. 991.

Boston Herald, April 19, 2002, Rosemary Herbert, review of *Spies,* p. 35.

Chicago Tribune, November, 1988.

Commonweal, June 16, 2000, Celia Wren, review of *Copenhagen,* p. 17.

Dallas Morning News, May 15, 2002, Jerome Weeks, "A Success on Stages and Pages" (interview with Frayn).

Drama, summer, 1975; July, 1980.

Entertainment Weekly, September 3, 1999, review of *Headlong,* p. 65; December 24, 1999, review of *Headlong,* p. 2145.

Fortune, April 16, 2001, review of *Copenhagen,* p. 460.

Globe and Mail (Toronto, Ontario, Canada), October 30, 1999, review of *Headlong,* p. D19.

Guardian (London, England), October 1, 1968; March 11, 1975; February 9, 2002, Peter Bradshaw, review of *Spies,* p. 10; March 23, 2002, review of *Copenhagen,* p. A1.

Hollywood Reporter, November 27, 2002, Jay Reiner, review of *Copenhagen,* p. 20; October 7, 2003, Ray Bennett, review of *Democracy,* p. 24.

Horizon, January-February, 1986.

Hudson Review, summer, 2000, Abraham Pais, review of *Copenhagen,* p. 182, and Thomas Filbin, review of *Headlong,* p. 330.

Insight, February 3, 1986.

Kirkus Reviews, November 15, 1991, p. 1421; July 15, 1999, review of *Headlong,* p. 1071; March 1, 2001, review of *The Copenhagen Papers,* p. 311; February 1, 2002, review of *Spies,* p. 122.

Library Journal, June 15, 1999, Edward B. St. John, review of *Headlong,* p. 106; April 1, 2001, Mingming Shen Kuo, review of *The Copenhagen Papers,* p. 101; August, 2002, Elizabeth Stifter, review of *Noises Off,* p. 94.

Listener, January 21, 1965; January 15, 1966; March 20, 1975.

London Review of Books, October 8, 1992, p. 13; October 14, 1999, review of *Headlong,* p. 22.

Los Angeles Times, October 30, 1984; February 3, 1985; February 12, 1985; October 10, 1986; July 20, 1987; January 7, 2002, Daryl H. Miller, review of *Copenhagen,* p. F10.

Los Angeles Times Book Review, February 16, 1992, p. 3; September 5, 1999, review of *Headlong,* p. 11.

Massachusetts Review, summer, 2001, Robert L. King, review of *Copenhagen,* p. 165.

New Statesman, October 4, 1968; November 1, 1974; January 26, 1996, p. 32; September 13, 1999, Terri Natale, review of *Headlong,* p. 55; November 29, 1999, review of *Headlong,* p. 82; February 4, 2002, Hugo Barnacle, review of *Spies,* p. 57; January 5, 2004, John Gordon Morrison, review of "The Last Laugh: Why the Art of Farce Is an Extremely Serious Business," p. 32.

Newsweek, February 18, 1974; January 20, 1986.

New Yorker, September 20, 1999, review of *Headlong,* p. 128; April 1, 2002, John Updike, review of *Spies,* p. 94.

New York Review of Books, May 14, 1992, p. 41; December 2, 1999, review of *Headlong,* p. 23.

New York Times, September 11, 1970; June 13, 1971; June 3, 1979; December 12, 1983; July 23, 1984; January 28, 1985; December 23, 1985; January 5, 1986; March 19, 1986; September 4, 1986; October 10, 1986; December 14, 1986; December 19, 1986; March 12, 1987; August 24, 1999, review of *Headlong,* p. E8; October 25, 1999, Sarah Lyall, "Enter Farce and Eruditon," p. B1; March 21, 2000, James Glanz, William J. Broad, review of *Copenhagen,* p. D1; April 12, 2000, Ben Brantley, review of *Copenhagen,* p. B1; May 14, 2000, Rick Marin, review of *Copenhagen,* p. WK2; June 13, 2001, Richard Bernstein, review of *Copenhagen,* p. B9; February 9, 2002, James Glanz, review of *Copenhagen,* p. A15; April 9, 2002, Michiko Kakutani, review of *Spies,* p. B7; April 14, 2002, Jennifer Schuessler, review of *Spies,* p. B7.

New York Times Book Review, September 15, 1968; March 18, 1990; February 16, 1992; January 17, 1993, p. 1; August 29, 1999, review of *Headlong,* p. 7; December 5, 1999, review of *Headlong,* p. 8; January 5, 2003, Scott Veale, review of *Spies,* p. 16.

New York Times Magazine, December 8, 1985.

Observer (London, England), June 11, 1967; July 18, 1976; April 27, 1980; April 4, 1984; August 22, 1999, review of *Headlong,* p. 11; October 3, 1999, review of *The Original Michael Frayn,* p. 16.

Opera News, August, 1996, p. 49.

Plays and Players, September, 1970; March, 1980; December, 1984.

Publishers Weekly, December 6, 1991; November 23, 1992; July 5, 1999, review of *Headlong,* p. 54;

May 7, 2001, review of *The Copenhagen Papers*, p. 234; February 4, 2002, review of *Spies*, p. 48.

St. Louis Post-Dispatch, April 7, 2000, Calvin Wilson, review of *Copenhagen*, p. F3.

San Francisco Chronicle, January 14, 2001, David Perlman, review of *Copenhagen*, p. D1.

Saturday Review, January 15, 1966.

Science, April 14, 2000, David Voss, review of *Copenhagen*, p. 278.

Sewanee Review, fall, 2000, Merritt Moseley, review of *Headlong*, p. 648.

Spectator, November 23, 1962; October 4, 1968; August 29, 1992, p. 28; December 10, 1983; August 7, 1999, Anita Brookner, review of *Headlong*, p. 34; July 24, 2000, Robert Winder, review of *Celia's Secret: An Investigation*, p. 54; January 26, 2002, Jane Gardam, review of *Spies*, p. 53.

Sunday Times (London, England), January 27, 1980.

Time, September 27, 1968; July 12, 1982; January 5, 1987.

Times (London, England), February 25, 1982; February 15, 1983; April 6, 1984; March 14, 1986; November 10, 1986.

Times Literary Supplement, February 1, 1980; March 5, 1982; September 22-28, 1989; August 20, 1999, Hal Jensen, review of *Headlong*, p. 19; September 1, 2000, Maggie Gee, review of *Celia's Secret*, p. 34; February 1, 2002, Jonathan Keats, review of *Spies*, p. 22.

Wall Street Journal, April 12, 2000, Amy Gamerman, review of *Copenhagen*, p. A24.

Washington Post, October 16, 1983; October 27, 1983; December 24, 1985; October 25, 1986.

Washington Post Book World, January 10, 1974; January 31, 1993, p. 3; September 5, 1999, review of *Headlong*, p. 15.

ONLINE

Bomb Online, http://www.bombsite.com/ (May 28, 2002), Marcy Kahan, interview with Frayn.

London Review of Books Online, http://www.lrb.co.uk/ (May 28, 2002), Michael Wood, review of *Headlong*.

Washington Post Online, http://www.washingtonpost.com/ (May 28, 2002), Michael Dirda, review of *Headlong*.

World Socialist Web site, http://www.wsws.org/ (May 28, 2002), Trevor Johnson, review of *Copenhagen*.

*   *   *

FUNDI
See BARAKA, Amiri

G

GLÜCK, Louise (Elisabeth) 1943-

PERSONAL: Surname is pronounced "Glick"; born April 22, 1943, in New York, NY; daughter of Daniel (an executive) and Beatrice (Grosby) Glück; married Charles Hertz, Jr., 1967 (divorced); married John Dranow (a writer and vice president of the New England Culinary Institute), 1977 (divorced); children: Noah Benjamin. *Education:* Attended Sarah Lawrence College, 1962, and Columbia University, 1963-66, 1967-68.

ADDRESSES: Home—Cambridge, MA. *Office*—Williams College, English Department, Williamstown, MA 01267. *E-mail*—Louise.E.Gluck@williams.edu.

CAREER: Poet. Fine Arts Work Center, Provincetown, MA, visiting teacher, 1970; Goddard College, Plainfield, VT, artist-in-residence, 1971-72, member of faculty, 1973-74; poet-in-residence, University of North Carolina, Greensboro, NC, spring, 1973, and Writer's Community, 1979; visiting professor, University of Iowa, Iowa City, IA, 1976-77, Columbia University, New York, NY, 1979, and University of California—Davis, Davis, CA, 1983; Goddard College, member of faculty and member of board of M.F.A. Writing Program, 1976-80; University of Cincinnati, Cincinnati, OH, Ellison Professor of Poetry, spring, 1978; Warren Wilson College, Swannanoa, NC, member of faculty and member of board of M.F.A. Program for Writers, 1980-84; University of California—Berkeley, Berkeley, CA, Holloway Lecturer, 1982; Williams College, Williamstown, MA, Scott Professor of Poetry, 1983, senior lecturer in English, 1984-2004; Yale University, New Haven, CT, Rosenkranz Writer-in-Residence,

Louise Glück

2004—. Regents Professor, University of California—Los Angeles, Los Angeles, CA, 1985-87; Phi Beta Kappa Poet, Harvard University, 1990; Fanny Hurst Professor, Brandeis University, 1996. Special consultant, Library of Congress, Washington, DC, 1999. Poetry panelist or poetry reader at conferences and foundations, including Mrs. Giles Whiting Foundation and PEN Southwest Conference; judge of numerous poetry contests, including Yale Series of Younger Poets, 2003-07.

MEMBER: American Academy of Arts and Letters, Academy of American Poets (chancellor, 1999), PEN (member of board, 1988—).

AWARDS, HONORS: Academy of American Poets Prize, Columbia University, 1966; Rockefeller Foundation fellowship, 1967; National Endowment for the Arts grants, 1969, 1979, fellowship 1988-89; Eunice Tietjens Memorial Prize, *Poetry* magazine, 1971; Guggenheim fellowship, 1975, 1987-88; Vermont Council for the Arts individual artist grant, 1978-79; Award in Literature, American Academy and Institute of Arts and Letters, 1981; National Book Critics Circle Award for poetry, *Boston Globe* Literary Press Award, and Melville Cane Award, Poetry Society of America, 1985, all for *The Triumph of Achilles*; Sara Teasdale Memorial Prize, Wellesley College, 1986; Bobbitt National Prize (with Mark Strand), 1990, for *Ararat*; Pulitzer Prize, and William Carlos Williams Award, Poetry Society of America, 1993, both for *The Wild Iris*; Martha Albrand Award for nonfiction, PEN, 1994, for *Proofs and Theories: Essays on Poetry*; Special Consultant in Poetry, Library of Congress, 1999-2000; M.I.T. Anniversary Medal, 2000; Bingham Poetry Prize, *Boston Book Review*, and best poetry book, *New Yorker* Awards, both 2000, both for *Vita Nova*; Böllingen Prize, Yale University, 2001; National Book Critics Circle Award nomination, 2002, for *The Seven Ages*; U.S. Poet Laureate Consultant in Poetry, Library of Congress, 2003-04; D.Litt. from Williams College, Skidmore College, and Middlebury College.

WRITINGS:

Firstborn, New American Library (New York, NY), 1968.
The House on Marshland, Ecco Press (New York, NY), 1975.
The Garden, Antaeus (New York, NY), 1976.
Descending Figure, Ecco Press (New York, NY), 1980.
The Triumph of Achilles, Ecco Press (New York, NY), 1985.
Ararat, Ecco Press (New York, NY), 1990.
The Wild Iris, Ecco Press (New York, NY), 1992.
(Editor, with David Lehman) *The Best American Poetry 1993,* Collier (New York, NY), 1993.
Proofs and Theories: Essays on Poetry, Ecco Press (New York, NY), 1994.
The First Four Books of Poems, Ecco Press (New York, NY), 1995.

Meadowlands, Ecco Press (New York, NY), 1996.
Vita Nova, Ecco Press (New York, NY), 1999.
The Poet and the Poem from the Library of Congress— Favorite Poets. Louise Glück (sound recording), includes interview by Grace Cabalieri, Library of Congress (Washington, DC), 1999.
The Seven Ages, Ecco Press (New York, NY), 2001.
October (chapbook), Sarabande Books (Louisville, KY), 2004.

Author of introduction to *The Clerk's Tale* by Spencer Reece, Mariner Books (Boston, MA), 2004. Work represented in numerous anthologies, including *The New Yorker Book of Poems,* Viking (New York, NY), 1970; *New Voices in American Poetry,* Winthrop Publishing (Cambridge, MA), 1973; and *The American Poetry Anthology,* Avon (New York, NY), 1975. Contributor to sound recordings from the Library of Congress (Washington, DC), including *Poetry and the American Eagle,* 2000, and *Poetry in America,* 2000. Contributor to various periodicals, including *Antaeus, New Yorker, New Republic, Poetry, Salmagundi,* and *American Poetry Review.*

SIDELIGHTS: Considered by many critics to be one of America's most talented contemporary poets, Louise Glück creates verse that has been described as technically precise, sensitive, insightful, and gripping. In her work, Glück freely shares her most intimate thoughts on such commonly shared human experiences as love, family, relationships, and death. "Glück demands a reader's attention and commands his respect," stated R. D. Spector in the *Saturday Review.* "Glück's poetry is intimate, familial, and what Edwin Muir has called the fable, the archetypal," added *Contemporary Women Poets* contributor James K. Robinson. Within her work can be discerned the influences of poets Stanley Kunitz, with whom Glück studied while attending Columbia University in the mid-1960s, and the early work of Robert Lowell; shadows cast by the confessional poets Sylvia Plath and Anne Sexton also haunt her earliest poetry.

From her first book of poetry, *Firstborn,* through her more mature work, Glück has become internationally recognized as a skilled yet perceptive author who pulls the reader into her poetry and shares the poetic experience equally with her audience. Helen Hennessey Vendler commented in her *New Republic* review of Glück's second book, *The House on Marshland,* that

"Glück's cryptic narratives invite our participation: we must, according to the case, fill out the story, substitute ourselves for the fictive personages, invent a scenario from which the speaker can utter her lines, decode the import, 'solve' the allegory. Or such is our first impulse. Later, I think . . . we read the poem, instead, as a truth complete within its own terms, reflecting some one of the innumerable configurations into which experience falls."

Looking over Glück's early body of work, Dave Smith appraised her ability in a review of *Descending Figure* in the *American Poetry Review:* "There are poets senior to Louise Glück who have done some better work and there are poets of her generation who have done more work. But who is writing consistently better with each book? Who is writing consistently so well at her age? Perhaps it is only my own hunger that wants her to write more, that hopes for the breakthrough poems I do not think she has yet given us. She has the chance as few ever do to become a major poet and no one can talk about contemporary American poetry without speaking of Louise Glück's accomplishment."

For admirers of Glück's work, the poetry in books such as *Firstborn, The House on Marshland, The Garden, Descending Figure, The Triumph of Achilles, Ararat,* and the Pulitzer Prize-winning *The Wild Iris* take readers on an inner journey by exploring their deepest, most intimate feelings. "Glück has a gift for getting the reader to imagine with her, drawing on the power of her audience to be amazed," observed Anna Wooten in the *American Poetry Review,* adding, "She engages a 'spectator' in a way that few other poets can do." Stephen Dobyns maintained in the *New York Times Book Review* that "no American poet writes better than Louise Glück, perhaps none can lead us so deeply into our own nature."

One reason reviewers cite for Glück's seemingly unfailing ability to capture her reader's attention is her expertise at creating poetry that many people can understand, relate to, and experience intensely and completely. Her poetic voice is unique and her language is deceptively straightforward. In a review of Glück's *The Triumph of Achilles,* Wendy Lesser noted in the *Washington Post Book World:* "'Direct' is the operative word here: Glück's language is staunchly straightforward, remarkably close to the diction of ordinary speech. Yet her careful selection for rhythm and repetition, and the specificity of even her idiomati-

cally vague phrases, give her poems a weight that is far from colloquial." Lesser went on to remark that "the strength of that voice derives in large part from its self-centeredness—literally, for the words in Glück's poems seem to come directly from the center of herself."

Because Glück writes so effectively about disappointment, rejection, loss, and isolation, reviewers frequently refer to her poetry as "bleak" or "dark." For example, Deno Trakas observed in the *Dictionary of Literary Biography* that "Glück's poetry has few themes and few moods. Whether she is writing autobiographically or assuming a persona, at the center of every poem is an 'I' who is isolated from family, or bitter from rejected love, or disappointed with what life has to offer. Her world is bleak; however, it is depicted with a lyrical grace, and her poems are attractive if disturbing. . . . Glück's poetry, despite flaws, is remarkable for its consistently high quality." Addressing the subdued character of her verse, *Nation's* Don Bogen felt that Glück's "basic concerns" were "betrayal, mortality, love and the sense of loss that accompanies it . . . She is at heart the poet of a fallen world. . . . Glück's work to define that mortal part shows dignity and sober compassion." Bogen elaborated further: "Fierce yet coolly intelligent, Glück's poem disturbs not because it is idiosyncratic but because it defines something we feel yet rarely acknowledge; it strips off a veil. Glück has never been content to stop at the surfaces of things. Among the well-mannered forms, nostalgia and blurred resolutions of today's verse, the relentless clarity of her work stands out."

Readers and reviewers have also marveled at Glück's custom of creating poetry with a dreamlike quality that at the same time deals with the realities of passionate and emotional subjects. Holly Prado declared in a *Los Angeles Times Book Review* critique of *The Triumph of Achilles* that Glück's poetry works "because she has an unmistakable voice that resonates and brings into our contemporary world the old notion that poetry and the visionary are intertwined." Prado continued to reflect: "The tone of her work is eerie, philosophical, questioning. Her poems aren't simply mystical ramblings. Far from it. They're sternly well-crafted pieces. But they carry the voice of a poet who sees, within herself, beyond the ordinary and is able to offer powerful insights, insights not to be quickly interpreted."

"Glück's ear never fails her; she manages to be conversational and lyrical at the same time, a considerable achievement when so much contemporary poetry is lamentably prosaic," asserted Wooten in the *American Poetry Review.* "Her range is personal and mythical, and the particular genius of the volume rests in its fusion of both approaches, rescuing the poems from either narrow self-glorification or pedantic myopia." This mythical voice, echoing the emotional quandaries of the twentieth century, can be quickly identified in *Meadowlands,* through the voices of Odysseus and Penelope. Describing the collection as "a kind of high-low rhetorical experiment in marriage studies," *New York Times Book Review* critic Deborah Garrison added that, through the "suburban banter" between the ancient wanderer and his wife, *Meadowlands* "captures the way that a marriage itself has a tone, a set of shared vocal grooves inseparable from the particular personalities involved and the partial truces they've made along the way." Commenting on the link between Glück's work and the narrative of Homer, Leslie Ullman added in *Poetry* that the dynamic of *Meadowlands* is "played out through poems that speak through or about principle characters in *The Odyssey,* and it is echoed in poems that do not attempt to disguise their origins in Glück's own experience."

Vita Nova earned Glück the prestigious 50,000 dollar Böllingen Prize from Yale University. In an interview with Brian Phillips of the *Harvard Advocate,* Glück stated: "This book was written very, very rapidly. . . . Once it started, I thought, this is a roll, and if it means you're not going to sleep, okay, you're not going to sleep. I wrote poems in airplanes and hotel rooms and elevators, and as a houseguest in California, and it just didn't matter where I was, it didn't matter who was with me." Phillips observed: "Something . . . that struck me about *Vita Nova* as a title was the irony of its historical reference. Obviously, in the late middle ages in Italy the phrase 'vita nuova' was used by Dante and others to indicate a new commitment of a romantic ideal of love. But you [Glück] seem to sort of update that phrase to mean life after the disintegration of the romantic relationship."

Reviewing *Vita Nova* for *Publishers Weekly,* a critic remarked: "Glück's psychic wounds will impress new readers, but it is Glück's austere, demanding craft that makes much of this . . . collection equal the best of her previous work—bitter, stark, careful, guiltily inward. . . . It is astonishing in its self knowledge,

and above all, memorable." Offering a similar interpretation from a far more critical perspective was William Logan of *New Criterion* who declared: "Reading Louise Glück's new poems is like eavesdropping on a psychiatrist and a particularly agony-ridden . . . shape shifting analysand. . . . The discomfort in *Vita Nova* is not lessened by the suspicion that the psychiatrist may also be the patient, that all roles may be one role to this quietly hand-wringing playactor. . . . It's hard to convey the oppressive weight of these doomed, sacrificial poems." Although the ostensible subject matter of the collection is the examination of the aftermath of a broken marriage, *Vita Nova* is a book suffused with symbols drawn from both personal dreams and classic mythological archetypes. "The poems in this . . . collection allude repeatedly to Greek and Roman myths of the underworld as well as the Inferno," observed Bill Christophersen of *Poetry,* while James Longenbach, writing in *Southwest Review,* noted: "Vita Nova is built around not one but two mythic backbones—the stories of both Dido and Aeneas and of Orpheus and Eurydice." Tom Clark of the *San Francisco Chronicle* observed that "Glück examines her dream material with unsparing honesty. . . . and inscribes it with a quiet, at times painful, candor, willing to suspend judgment and entertain stubborn unclarities to find the epiphanies she obsessively seeks." Clark characterized *Vita Nova* as "a brave and risky book, daring to explore those obscure places by the flickering light of dreams." Taking a different slant on the collection from that of some other reviewers, Longenbach found the central theme of *Vita Nova* to be the poet's desire for change, and Glück's ultimate resolution to involve an embracing of recurrence rather than transcendence. "Having recognized that real freedom exists within repetition rather than in the postulation of some timeless place beyond it," Longenbach concluded, "Glück now seems content to work within the terms of her art. . . . The result is a book suggesting that Glück's poetry has many more lives to live."

Echoing Longenbach's assertion in a review of Glück's next collection, *The Seven Ages,* for the *New York Times Book Review,* Melanie Rehak stated: "It's a book in which repetition functions as incantation, forming a hazy magic that's alternately frightening and beautiful." *The Seven Ages* contains forty-four poems whose subject matter ranges throughout the author's life, from her earliest memories to the contemplation of death. A writer for *Kirkus Reviews* remarked on how the author uses "common childhood images" as a way "to resurrect intense feelings that accompany awakening to the sensual promises of life, and she desperately explores these resonant images, searching for a path that might reconcile her to the inevitability of death." While Rehak acclaimed "every poem in *The Seven Ages* [as] a weighty, incandescent marvel," a *Publishers Weekly* reviewer remarked: "Considering age and aging, summer and fall, 'stasis' and constant loss, Glück's new poems often forsake the light touch of her last few books for the grim wisdom she sought in the 1980s."

According to Longenbach: "The works of poet Louise Glück focus on the changeability of self and the definition of identity. She compares the actions of her poem's characters with their feelings, giving them credibility through colloquial diction. Glück uses extreme situations to augment character complexities and heighten the emotions involved in their search."

In 2003 Glück was named the twelfth Poet Laureate Consultant in Poetry by the Library of Congress. On making the appointment, James H. Billington stated, "Louise Glück will bring to the Library of Congress a strong, vivid, deep poetic voice, accomplished in a series of book-length poetic cycles. Her prize-winning poetry and her great interest in young poets will enliven the Poet Laureate's office during the next year." Glück, an intensely private individual, was quoted in *USA Today* as saying that her first undertaking as Poet Laureate will be "to get over being surprised." Then she hopes to promote young poets and poetry contests.

BIOGRAPHICAL AND CRITICAL SOURCES:

BOOKS

American Writers, Supplement 5, Charles Scribner's Sons (New York, NY), 2000.

Contemporary Literary Criticism, Gale (Detroit, MI), Volume 7, 1977, Volume 22, 1982, Volume 44, 1987.

Contemporary Poets, 7th edition, St. James Press (Detroit, MI), 2000.

Contemporary Women Poets, St. James Press (Detroit, MI), 1997.

Dictionary of Literary Biography, Volume 5: *American Poets since World War II,* Gale (Detroit, MI), 1980.

Dodd, Elizabeth Caroline, *The Veiled Mirror and the Woman Poet: H. D., Louise Bogan, Elizabeth Bishop, and Louise Glück,* University of Missouri Press (Columbia, MO), 1992.

Poetry Criticism, Volume 16, Gale (Detroit, MI), 1996.

Poetry for Students, Gale (Detroit, MI), Volume 5, 1999, Volume 15, 2002.

Trawick, Leonard M., editor, *World, Self, Poem: Essays on Contemporary Poetry from the "Jubilation of Poets,"* Kent State University Press (Kent, OH), 1990.

Upton, Lee, *The Muse of Abandonment: Origin, Identity, Mastery in Five American Poets,* Bucknell University Press (Lewisburg, PA), 1998.

Vendler, Helen, *Part of Nature, Part of Us: Modern American Poets,* Harvard University Press (Cambridge, MA), 1980.

Vendler, Helen, *The Music of What Happens: Poems, Poets, Critics,* Harvard University Press (Cambridge, MA), 1988.

PERIODICALS

America, April 25, 1998, Edward J. Ingebretsen, review of *Meadowlands,* pp. 27-28.

American Poetry Review, July-August, 1975, pp. 5-6; January-February, 1982, pp. 36-46; September-October, 1982, pp. 37-46; November-December, 1986, pp. 33-36; July-August, 1990, Marianne Boruch, review of *Ararat,* pp. 17-19; January-February, 1993, Carol Muske, review of *The Wild Iris,* pp. 52-54; January-February, 1997, Allen Hoey, "Between Truth and Meaning," pp. 37-46; July-August, 2003, Tony Hoagland, "Three Tenors," pp. 37-42.

Antioch Review, spring, 1993, Daniel McGuiness, review of *The Wild Iris,* pp. 311-312; winter, 1997, Daniel McGuiness, review of *Meadowlands,* pp. 118-119.

Belles Lettres, November-December, 1986, pp. 6, 14; spring, 1991, p. 38.

Booklist, February 1, 1999, Donna Seaman and Jack Helbig, review of *Vita Nova,* p. 959; March 15, 2001, Donna Seaman, review of *The Seven Ages,* p. 1346.

Chicago Review, winter, 1997, Maureen McLane, review of *Meadowlands,* pp. 120-122; summer-fall, 1999, Steven Monte, "Louise Gluck," p. 180.

Christianity and Literature, autumn, 2002, William V. Davis, "'Talked to by Silence,'" pp. 47-57.

Classical and Modern Literature, spring, 2002, Sheila Murnaghan and Deborah H. Roberts, "Penelope's Song," pp. 1-32.

Contemporary Literature, spring, 1990, Diane S. Bonds, "Entering Language in Louise Gluck's *The House on the Marshland,*" pp. 58-75; summer, 2001, Ann Keniston, "'The Fluidity of Damaged Form,'" pp. 294-324.

Georgia Review, winter, 1985, pp. 849-863; spring, 1993, Judith Kitchen, review of *The Wild Iris,* pp. 145-159; summer, 2002, Judith Kitchen, "Thinking about Love," pp. 594-608.

Hudson Review, spring, 1993, David Mason, review of *Ararat* and *The Wild Iris,* pp. 223-231; autumn, 2001, Bruce Bawer, "Borne Ceaselessly into the Past," pp. 513-520.

Kenyon Review, winter, 1993, David Baker, review of *The Wild Iris,* pp. 184-192; winter, 2001, Linda Gregerson, "The Sower against Gardens," p. 115, and Brian Henry, review of *Vita Nova,* p. 166; spring, 2003, Willard Spiegelman, "Repetition and Singularity," pp. 149-168.

Kirkus Reviews, April 1, 2001, review of *The Seven Ages,* p. 468.

Landfall, May, 2001, Emma Neale, "Touchpapers," pp. 143-142.

Library Journal, September 15, 1985, p. 84; April 1, 1990; July, 1990, p. 17; May 15, 1992, Fred Muratori, review of *The Wild Iris,* p. 96; September, 1994, Tim Gavin, review of *Proofs and Theories: Essays on Poetry,* p. 71; March 15, 1996, Frank Allen, review of *Meadowlands,* p. 74; March 1, 1999, Ellen Kaufman, review of *Vita Nova,* p. 88; April 15, 2001, Barbara Hoffert, review of *The Seven Ages,* p. 98.

Literary Imagination, fall, 2003, Isaac Cates, "Louise Glück: Interstices and Silences," pp. 462-77.

Literary Review, spring, 1996, Reamy Jansen, review of *Proofs and Theories,* pp. 441-443.

Los Angeles Times Book Review, February 23, 1986, p. 10.

Mid-American Review, Volume 14, number 2, 1994.

Naples Daily News (Naples, FL), October 20, 2003, Justin Pope, "Media-Shy Poet Laureate Won't Follow in Predecessors' Footsteps."

Nation, January 18, 1986, pp. 53-54; April 15, 1991, p. 490; April 29, 1996, p. 28.

New Criterion, June, 1999, William Logan, "Vanity Fair," p. 60; June, 2001, William Logan, "Folk Tales," p. 68.

New England Review, fall, 1991, Bruce Bnod, review of *Ararat,* pp. 216-223; fall, 1993, Henry Hart,

review of *The Wild Iris,* pp. 192-206; fall, 2001, Ira Sadoff, "Louise Gluck and the Last Stage of Romanticism," pp. 81-92.

New Letters, spring, 1987, pp. 3-4.

New Republic, June 17, 1978, pp. 34-37; May 24, 1993, Helen Hennessey Vendler, review of *The Wild Iris,* pp. 35-38.

New Yorker, May 13, 1996, Vijay Seshadri, review of *Meadowlands,* pp. 93-94.

New York Review of Books, October 23, 1986, p. 47.

New York Times, August 29, 2003, Elizabeth Olson, "Chronicler of Private Moments Is Named Poet Laureate," p. A14; November 4, 2003, Andrew Johnston, "Poet Laureate: Louise Gluck and the Public Face of a Private Artist," p. A24.

New York Times Book Review, April 6, 1975, pp. 37-38; October 12, 1980, p. 14; December 22, 1985, pp. 22-23; September 2, 1990, p. 5; August 4, 1996; May 13, 2001, Melanie Rehak, "Her Art Imitates Her Life. You Got That?"

North American Review, July-August, 1994, Annie Finch, review of *The Wild Iris,* pp. 40-42.

Parnassus, spring-summer, 1981.

People Weekly, May 5, 1997, review of *Meadowlands,* p. 40.

PN Review, Volume 25, number 3, Steve Burt, "The Dark Garage with the Garbage," pp. 31-35.

Poetry, April, 1986, pp. 42-44; November, 1990, Steven Cramer, "Four True Voices of Feeling," pp. 96-114; May, 1993; March, 1997, p. 339; December, 2000, Bill Christophersen, review of *Vita Nova,* p. 217; December, 2001, David Wojahn, review of *The Seven Ages,* p. 165.

Prairie Schooner, summer, 2000, Richard Jackson, review of *Vita Nova,* p. 190.

Publishers Weekly, February 16, 1990, p. 63; May 11, 1992, p. 58; July 4, 1994, review of *Proofs and Theories,* p. 49; March 18, 1996, review of *Meadowlands,* p. 66; December 21, 1998, review of *Vita Nova,* p. 62; March 12, 2001, review of *The Seven Ages,* p. 84.

Salmagundi, winter, 1977; spring-summer, 1991, Calvin Bedient, review of *Ararat,* pp. 212-230; fall, 1999, Terence Diggory, "Louise Gluck's Lyric Journey," pp. 303-318.

San Francisco Chronicle, April 4, 1999, Tom Clark, "Poet Finds Dreams Leave Traces in the Waking World," p. 3.

Saturday Review, March 15, 1969, p. 33.

Sewanee Review, winter, 1976.

South Carolina Review, fall, 2000, John Perryman, "Washing Homer's Feat," pp. 176-184.

Southwest Review, spring, 1999, James Longenbach, "Nine Lives," p. 184.

Times Literary Supplement, May 16, 1997, Stephen Burt, review of *The Wild Iris,* p. 25; July 30, 1999, Oliver Reynolds, "You Will Suffer," p. 23; May 25, 2001, Josephine Balmer, review of *Vita Nova,* p. 26.

USA Today, August 29, 2003, "Pulitzer Prize-winner Glück Named Poet Laureate."

Village Voice, September 8, 2003, Joshua Clover, "Time on Her Side."

Virginia Quarterly Review, summer, 1998, Brian Henry, "The Odyssey Revisited," pp. 571-577.

Washington Post Book World, February 2, 1986, p. 11.

Women's Review of Books, May, 1993, Elisabeth Frost, review of *The Wild Iris,* pp. 24-25; November, 1996, Elisabeth Frost, review of *Meadowlands,* pp. 24-25.

Women's Studies, Volume 17, number 3, 1990.

World Literature Today, autumn, 1993, Rochelle Owens, review of *The Wild Iris,* p. 827; winter, 1997, Susan Smith Nash, review of *Meadowlands,* pp. 156-157.

Yale Review, October, 1992, Phoebe Pettingell, review of *The Wild Iris,* pp. 114-115; October, 1996, James Longenbach, review of *Meadowlands,* pp. 158-174.

ONLINE

Academy of American Poets Web Site, http://www.poets.org/ (April 20, 2004), "Louise Glück."

Harvard Advocate, http://www.hcs.harvard.edu/~advocate/ (summer, 1999), Brian Phillips, "A Conversation with Louise Glück."

Library of Congress Web Site, http://www.loc.gov/poetry/ (April 22, 2004), "About the New Poet Laureate, Louise Glück."

Louise Glück: Image and Emotion, http://www.artstomp.com/gluck (April 22, 2004).

Modern American Poetry Web Site, http://www.english.uiuc.edu/maps/ (April 20, 2004), "Louise Glück."*

*   *   *

GRASS, Günter (Wilhelm) 1927-

PERSONAL: Born October 16, 1927, in the Free City of Danzig (Gdansk), (later incorporated into Poland); married Anna Schwarz, 1954 (marriage ended); married Utte Grunert, 1979; children: (first marriage)

Günter Grass

Franz, Raoul, Laura, Bruno. *Education:* Attended Künstakademie (Düsseldorf, Germany); attended Berlin Academy of Fine Arts, 1953-55. *Politics:* Social Democrat. *Religion:* Roman Catholic.

ADDRESSES: Home—Glockengiesserstrasse 21, Lübeck 23552, Germany. *Office*—Niedstrasse 13, Berlin-Grunewald 41, Germany.

CAREER: Novelist, poet, playwright, graphic artist, and sculptor. Former farm laborer in the Rhineland; worked in potash mine near Hildesheim, Germany; black marketeer; apprentice stonecutter during late 1940s, chiseling tombstones for firms in Düsseldorf, Germany; worked as a drummer and washboard accompanist with a jazz band. Speech writer for Willy Brandt during his candidacy for the election of Bundeskanzler, West Germany. Lecturer at Harvard University, Yale University, Smith College, Kenyon College, and at Goethe House and Poetry Center of YM and YWCA, New York, NY, c. 1960s; writer-in-residence at Columbia University, 1966. *Exhibitions:* Drawings, lithographs, and sculptures have been exhibited in the show "Too Far Afield: Graphics, 1970-

2000," Jan van der Donk Gallery, New York, NY, 2001. *Military service:* German Army, drafted during World War II; aide with German Luftwaffe; prisoner of war in Marienbad, Czechoslovakia, 1945-46.

MEMBER: American Academy of Arts and Sciences, Berliner Akademie der Künste (president, 1983-86), Deutscher PEN, Zentrum der Bundesrepublik, Verband Deutscher Schriftsteller, Gruppe 47.

AWARDS, HONORS: Lyrikpreis, Süddeutscher Rundfunk, 1955; prize from Gruppe 47, 1958; Bremen Literary Award, 1959; literary prize from Association of German Critics, 1960; *Die Blechtrommel (The Tin Drum)* selected by a French jury as the best foreign-language book of 1962; a plaster bust of Grass was placed in the Regensburger Ruhmestempel Walhalla, 1963; Georg Büchner Prize, 1965; Fontane prize (West Germany), 1968; Theodor Heuss Preis, 1969; *Local Anaesthetic* selected among ten best books of 1970 by *Time;* Carl von Ossiersky Medal, 1977; Premio Internazionale Mondello, Palermo, 1977; International Literature Award, 1978; *The Flounder* selected among best books of fiction by *Time,* 1979; Alexander-Majokowski Medal, 1979; awarded distinguished service medal, Federal Republic of Germany (declined), 1980; Antonio Feltrinelli award, 1982; Leonhard Frank ring, 1988; Karel Capek prize (Czech Republic), 1994; Nobel Prize for literature, Swedish Academy, 1999. Honorary doctorates from Harvard University and Kenyon College.

WRITINGS:

Die Vorzüge der Windhühner (poems, prose, and drawings; title means "The Advantages of Windfowl"; also see below), Luchterhand (Darmstadt, Germany), 1956, 3rd edition, 1967.

(Author of text; with Herman Wilson) *O Susanna: Ein Jazzbilderbuch: Blues, Balladen, Spirituals, Jazz,* illustrated by Horst Geldmacher, Kiepenheuer & Witsch, 1959.

Die Blechtrommel (novel; also see below), Luchterhand (Darmstadt, Germany), 1959, illustrated by Heinrich Richter, 1968, with an afterword by Hans Mayer, 1984, translation by Ralph Manheim published as *The Tin Drum,* Vintage (New York, NY), 1962, reprinted, Knopf (New York, NY), 1993.

Gleisdreieck (poems and drawings; title means "Rail Triangle"), Luchterhand (Darmstadt, Germany), 1960.

Katz und Maus (novella; also see below), Luchterhand (Neuwied am Rhine, Germany), 1961, edited by Edgar Lohner, Blaisdell (Waltham, MA), 1969, with English introduction and notes, edited by H. F. Brookes and C. E. Fraenkel, Heinemann Educational (London, England), 1971, translation by Ralph Manheim published as *Cat and Mouse,* Harcourt (New York, NY), 1963, reprinted, Harcourt (San Diego, CA), 1991.

Hundejahre (novel; also see below), Luchterhand (Neuwied am Rhine, Germany), 1963, translation by Ralph Manheim published as *Dog Years,* Harcourt (New York, NY), 1965, reprinted, Harcourt (San Diego, CA), 1989.

Die Ballerina (essay), Friedenauer Presse (Berlin, Germany), 1963.

Rede über das Selbstverständliche (speech), Luchterhand (Berlin, Germany), 1965.

(Illustrator) Ingeborg Buchmann, *Ein Ortfür Zufaelle,* Wagenbach (Berlin, Germany), 1965.

Dich singe ich, Demokratie, Luchterhand (Berlin, Germany), 1965.

Fünf Wahlreden (speeches; contains "Was ist des Deutschen Vaterland?," "Loblied auf Willy," "Es steht zur Wahl," "Ich klage an," and "Des Kaisers neue Kleider"), Nuewied (Berlin, Germany), 1965.

Selected Poems (in German and English; includes poems from *Die Vorzüge der Windhühner* and *Gleisdreieck;* also see below), translated by Michael Hamburger and Christopher Middleton, Harcourt (New York, NY), 1966, published as *Poems of Günter Grass,* Penguin (Harmondsworth, England), 1969.

Ausgefragt (poems and drawings; title means "Questioned") Luchterhand (Darmstadt, Germany), 1967.

Der Fall Axel C. Springer am Beispiel Arnold Zweig: Eine Rede, ihr Anlass, und die Folgen, Voltaire (Berlin, Germany), 1967.

Die Vorzüuge der Windhühner, Luchterhand (Berlin, Germany), 1967.

New Poems (includes poems from *Ausgefragt;* also see below), translation by Michael Hamburger, Harcourt (New York, NY), 1968.

Günter Grass, edited by Theodor Wieser, Luchterhand (Berlin, Germany), 1968.

Über meinen Lehrer Döblin, und andere Vorträge, Literarische Colloquium Berlin (Berlin, Germany), 1968.

Über das Selbstverständliche: Reden, Aufsätze, offene Briefe, Kommentare (title means "On the Self-Evident"; also see below), Luchterhand (Berlin,

Germany), 1968, revised and supplemented edition published as *Über das Selbstverständliche: Politische Schriften,* Deutscher Taschenbuch (Munich, Germany), 1969.

(With Pavel Kokout) *Briefe über die Grenze: Versuch eines Ost-West-Dialogs von Günter Grass und Pavel Kohout* (letters), C. Wegner (Hamburg, Germany), 1968.

Über meinen Lehrer Döblin und andere Vorträge (title means "About My Teacher Döblin and Other Lectures"), Literarisches Collequium (Berlin, Germany), 1968.

Günter Grass: Ausgewählte Texte, Abbildungen, Faksimiles, Bio-Bibliographie, edited by Theodor Wieser, Luchterhand (Darmstadt, Germany), 1968, also published as *Porträt und Poesie,* 1968.

(With Kurt Ziesel) *Kunst oder Pornographie?: Der Prozess Grass gegen Ziesel,* J. F. Lehmann (Munich, Germany), 1969.

Speak Out: Speeches, Open Letters, Commentaries (includes selections from *Über das Selbstverständliche: Reden, Aufsätze, offene Briefe, Kommentare*), translation by Ralph Manheim, introduction by Michael Harrington, Harcourt (New York, NY), 1969.

Örtlich betäubt (novel), Luchterhand (Neuwied, Germany), 1969, translation by Ralph Manheim published as *Local Anaesthetic,* Harcourt (New York, NY), 1970, reprinted Harcourt (San Diego, CA), 1989.

Die Schweinekopfsülze, illustrated by Horst Janssen, Merlin Verlag (Hamburg, Germany), 1969.

Poems of Günter Grass, translated by Michael Hamburger and Christopher Middleton, with an introduction by Hamburger, Penguin (Harmondsworth, England), 1969.

Originalgraphik (poem with illustrations), limited edition, Argelander, 1970.

Gesammelte Gedichte (title means "Collected Poems"; also see below), introduction by Heinrich Vormweg, Luchterhand (Neuwied, Germany), 1971.

Dokumente zur politischen Wirkung, edited by Heinz Ludwig Arnold and Franz Josef Goertz, Richard Boorherg, 1971.

Aus dem Tagebuch einer Schnecke, Luchterhand (Darmstadt, Germany), 1972, translation by Ralph Manheim published as *From the Diary of a Snail,* Harcourt (New York, NY), 1973.

Mariazühren Hommageamarie Inmarypraise, photographs by Maria Rama, Bruckmann (Munich, Germany), 1973, bilingual edition with translation by Christopher Middleton published as *Inmarypraise,* Harcourt (New York, NY), 1973.

Der Schriftsteller als Bürger: Eine Siebenjahresbilanz, Dr. Karl Renner Institute (Vienna, Germany), 1973.

Liebe geprüft (poems), [Bremen], 1974.

Günter Grass: Radierungen 1972-1974, Die Galerie (Berlin, Germany), 1974.

Der Bürger und seine Stimme (speeches, essays, and commentary; title means "The Citizen and His Voice"), Luchterhand (Darmstadt, Germany), 1974.

Günter Grass Materialienbuch, edited by Rolf Geissler, Luchterhand (Darmstadt, Germany), 1976.

Der Butt (novel), Luchterhand (Darmstadt, Germany), 1977, translation by Ralph Manheim published as *Flounder,* Harcourt (New York, NY), 1978.

In the Egg and Other Poems (contains poems from *Selected Poems* and *New Poems*), translated by Michael Hamburger and Christopher Middleton, Harcourt (New York, NY), 1977.

Über meinen Lehrer Alfred Döblin, issued with *Döblin's Die drei Sprünge des Wang-lun,* Walter (Olten, Czech Republic), 1977.

Denkzettel: Politische Reden und Aufsätze (title means "Note for Thought"), Luchterhand (Darmstadt, Germany), 1978.

Das Treffen in Telgte, Luchterhand (Darmstadt, Germany), 1979, with a preface by Stephan Hermlin, Reclam (Leipzig, Germany), 1984, translation by Ralph Manheim published as *The Meeting at Telgte,* with an afterword by Leonard Forster, Harcourt (New York, NY), 1981.

Werkverzeichnis der Radierungen (catalogue), Galerie Andre A. Dreher (Berlin, Germany), 1979.

(With Volker Schlöndorff) *Die Blechtrommel als Film,* Zweitausendeins (Frankfurt am Main, Germany), 1979.

Aufsätze zur Literatur, 1957-1979 (title means "Essays on Literature, 1957-1979"), Luchterhand (Darmstadt, Germany), 1980.

Danziger Trilogie (title means "Danzig Trilogy"; contains *Die Blechtrommel, Katz und Maus,* and *Hundejahre*), Luchterhand (Darmstadt, Germany), 1980, translation by Ralph Manheim published as *The Danzig Trilogy,* Harcourt (San Diego, CA), 1987.

Kopfgeburten; oder Die Deutschen sterben aus, Luchterhand (Darmstadt, Germany), 1980, translation by Ralph Manheim published as *Headbirths; or, The Germans Are Dying Out,* Harcourt (New York, NY), 1982.

Radierungen und Texte 1972-1982, edited by Anselm Dreher, text selection and afterword by Sigrid Mayer, Luchterhand (Darmstadt, Germany), 1984.

Zeichnen und Schreiben: Das bildnerische Werk des Schriftstellers Günter Grass, Luchterhand (Darmstadt, Germany), 1982, translation published as *Graphics and Writing,* edited by Anselm Dreher, Harcourt (San Diego, CA), 1983.

Zeichnungen und Texte 1954-1977, edited by Anselm Dreher, text selection and afterword by Sigrid Mayer, Luchterhand (Darmstadt, Germany), 1982.

Günter Grass: Katalog zur Ausstellung im Winter 82/83 der Galerie Schürer, CH-Regensberg: Ausstellung über das zeichnerische, grafische und plastische Werk, Die Galerie (Regensberg, Germany), 1982.

Kinderlied (poems and etchings; originally published in *Gesammelte Gedichte*), Lord John, 1982.

Zeichnungen und Texte, 1954-1977, Luchterhand (Darmstadt, Germany), 1982, translation by Michael Hamburger and Walter Arndt published as *Drawings and Words, 1954-1977,* edited by Anselm Dreher, text selection and afterword by Sigrid Mayer, Harcourt (San Diego, CA), 1983.

Ach, Butt!: Dein Märchen geht böse aus, Luchterhand (Darmstadt, Germany), 1983.

Radierungen und Texte, 1972-1982, Luchterhand (Darmstadt, Germany), 1984, translation by Michael Hamburger and others published as *Etchings and Words, 1972-1982,* edited by Anselm Dreher, text selection and afterword by Sigrid Mayer, Harcourt (San Diego, CA), 1985.

Widerstand lernen: Politische Gegenreden, 1980-1983 (title means "Learning Resistance: Political Countertalk"), Luchterhand (Darmstadt, Germany), 1984.

On Writing and Politics: 1967-1983 (essays), translated by Ralph Manheim, introduction by Salman Rushdie, Harcourt (San Diego, CA), 1985.

Geschenkt Freiheit: Rede zum 8. Mai 1945, Akademie der Künste (Berlin, Germany), 1985.

Werk und Wirkung, edited by Rudolf Wolff, Bouvier (Bonn, Germany), 1985.

(With Heinrich Vormweg) *Günter Grass: Mit Selbstzeugnissen und Bilddokumenten,* Rowohlt (Reinbek bei Hamburg, Germany), 1986.

In Kupfer, auf Stein: Das grafische Werk, edited by G. Fritze Margull, Steidl (Göttingen, Germany), 1986, new edition, 1994.

Die Rättin, Luchterhand (Darmstadt, Germany), 1986, translation by Ralph Manheim published as *The Rat,* Harcourt (San Diego, CA), 1987.

(With Werner Timm) *Günter Grass: Graphik und Plastik,* Museum Ostdeutsche Galerie (Regensburg, Germany), 1987.

Werkausgabe, ten volumes, edited by Volker Neuhaus, Luchterhand (Darmstadt, Germany), 1987.

Ausstellung anlässlich des 60: Geburtstages von Günter Grass, edited by Jens Christian Jensen, Kunsthalle zu Kiel (Kiel, Germany), 1987.

Günter Grass: Radierungen, Lithographien, Zeichnungen, Plastiken, Gedichte, Kunstamt Berlin-Tempelhof (Berlin, Germany), 1987.

Günter Grass: Mit Sophie in die Pilze gegangen, Steidl (Göttingen, Germany), 1987.

Die Gedichte 1955-1986 (poems), afterword by Volker Neuhaus, Luchterhand (Darmstadt, Germany), 1988.

Calcutta: Zeichnungen, Künsthalle Bremen (Bremen, Germany), 1988.

Zunge Zeigen, Luchterhand (Darmstadt, Germany), 1988, translation by John E. Woods published as *Show Your Tongue,* Harcourt (San Diego, CA), 1989.

Skizzenbuch, Steidl (Göttingen, Germany), 1989.

Meine grüne Wiese: Geschichten und Zeichnungen, Manesse (Zurich, Switzerland), 1989.

Meine grüne Wiese: Kurzprosa, Manesse (Zurich, Switzerland), 1989.

Deutscher Lastenausgleich: Wider das dumpfe Einheitsgebot; Reden und Gespräche, Texte zur Zeit, Luchterhand (Frankfurt am Main, Germany), 1990, translation by Krishna Winston with A. S. Wensinger published as *Two States—One Nation?,* Harcourt (San Diego, CA), 1990.

Günter Grass: Begleitheft zur Ausstellung der Stadt- und Universitätsbibliothek Frankfurt am Main, 13. Februar bis 30. März 1990, Die Bibliothek (Frankfurt am Main, Germany), 1990.

Ein Schnäppchen namens DDR: Letzte Reden vorm Glockengeläut, Luchterhand (Frankfurt am Main, Germany), 1990.

Schreiben nach Auschwitz, Luchterhand (Frankfurt am Main, Germany), 1990.

(And illustrator) *Totes Holz,* Steidl (Göttingen, Germany), 1990.

(With Rudolf Augstein) *Deutschland, einig Vaterland?: ein Streitgespräch,* Steidl (Göttingen, Germany), 1990.

Nachdenken über Deutschland, edited by Dietmar Keller, introductory essays by Christoph Hein and others, Der Nation (Berlin, Germany), 1990-91.

Vier Jahrzehnte: Ein Werkstattbericht, edited by G. Fritze Margull, Steidl (Göttingen, Germany), 1991, updated edition published as *Fünf Jahrzehnte: ein Werkstattbericht,* Ettag, 2001.

Rede vom Verlust: Über den Niedergang der politischen Kultur in geeinten Deutschland (speech), Steidl (Göttingen, Germany), 1992.

Unkenrufe (title means "Toad Croaks"), Steidl (Göttingen, Germany), 1992, translation by Ralph Manheim published as *The Call of the Toad*, Harcourt (New York, NY), 1992.

(With Regine Hildebrandt) *Schaden begrenzen, oder auf die Füsse treten: Ein Gespräch*, edited by Friedrich Dieckmann and others, Volk & Welt (Berlin, Germany), 1993.

Novemberland: 13 Sonette, Steidl (Göttingen, Germany), 1993, translation by Michael Hamburger published as *Novemberland: Selected Poems, 1956-1993*, Harcourt (New York, NY), 1996.

Cat and Mouse and Other Writings, edited by A. Leslie Willson, foreword by John Irving, Continuum (New York, NY), 1994.

Ein Weites Feld, Steidl (Göttingen, Germany), 1995, translation by Krishna Winston published as *Too Far Afield*, Harcourt (New York, NY), 2000.

(With Kenzaburo Oe) *Gestern, vor 50 Jahren: Ein Deutsch-Japanischer Briefwechsel* (correspondence), Steidl (Göttingen, Germany), 1995, translation by John Barrett published as *Just Yesterday, Fifty Years Ago: A Critical Dialogue on the Anniversary of the End of the Second World War*, Alyscamps Press (Paris, France), 1999.

Die Deutschen und Ihre Dichter, edited by Daniela Hermes, Deutscher Taschenbuch (Munich, Germany), 1995.

Der Schriftsteller als Zeitgenosse, edited by Daniela Hermes, Deustcher Taschesbuch (Munich, Germany), 1996.

Aesthetik Des Engagements, P. Lang (New York, NY), 1996.

Fundsachen für Nichtleser, Steidl (Göttingen, Germany), 1997.

Rede über den Standort (speech), Steidl (Göttingen, Germany), 1997.

Ohne die Feder zu wechseln: Zeichnungen, Druckgraphiken, Aquarelle, Skulpturen, edited by Peter Joch and Annette Lagler, Steidl (Göttingen, Germany), 1997.

Aus einem fotografischen und politischen Tabebuch: Berlin jenseits der Mauer = Da un diario fotografico e politico: Berlino oltre il muro, photographs by Rean Mazzone, ILA Palma (Palermo, Italy), 1997.

(With Reinhard Höppner and Hans-Jochen Tschiche) *Rotgrüne Reder*, Steidl (Göttingen, Germany), 1998.

(With Harro Zimmerman) *Vom Abentauer der Aufklaerung*, Steidl (Göttingen, Germany), 1999.

Für-und Widerworte, Steidl (Göttingen, Germany), 1999.

Auf einem anderen Blatt: Zeichnungen, Steidl (Göttingen, Germany), 1999.

Mein Jahrhundert, Steidl (Göttingen, Germany), 1999, translation by Michael Henry Heim published as *My Century*, Harcourt (New York, NY), 1999.

Wort und Bild: Tübinger Poetik Vorlesung & Materialien, edited by Jürgen Wertheimer, with Ute Allmendinger, Konkursbuchverlag (Tübingen, Germany), 1999.

Fortsetzung folgt—: Literature und Geschichte, Steidl (Göttingen, Germany), 1999.

(With Michael Martens) *Ich werde die Wunde offen halten: ein Gespräch zur Person und über die Ziet*, H. Boldt (Winsen, Germany), 1999.

(With Harro Zimmermann) *Vom Abenteuer der Auflkärung* (interviews) Steidl (Göttingen, Germany), 1999.

(Editor) *Gemischte Klasse: Prosa, Lyrik, Szenen & Essays*, Swiridoff (Kunzelsau, Germany), 2000.

Ohne Stimme: Reder zugunsten des Volkes der Roma und Sinti, Steidl (Göttingen, Germany), 2000.

Günter Grass: Mit Wasserfarben: Aquarelle, Steidl (Göttingen, Germany), 2001.

(With Daniela Dahn) *In einem reichen Land: Zeugnisse alltäglichen Leidens an der Gessellschaft*, edited by Johano Strasser, Steidl (Göttingen, Germany), 2002.

Im Krebsgang, Steidl (Göttingen, Germany), 2002, translation by Krishna Wilson published as *Crabwalk*, Harcourt (Orlando, FL), 2002.

Günter Grass: Gebrannte Erde, photographs by Dirk Reinartz, Steidl (Göttingen, Germany), 2002.

(With Helen Wolff) *Briefe 1959-1994* (correspondence), edited by Daniela Hermes, translated from the English by Eva Maria Hermes, Steidl (Göttingen, Germany), 2003.

Letzte Tänze, Steidl (Göttingen, Germany), 2003.

PLAYS

Die bösen Köche: Ein Drama in fünf Akten (first produced in West Berlin, Germany, 1961; translation by A. Leslie Willson produced as *The Wicked Cooks* on Broadway, 1967), Luchterhand (Darmstadt, Germany), 1982.

Hochwasser: Ein Stück in zwei Akten (two acts; also see below), Suhrkamp (Frankfurt am Main, Germany), 1963, 4th edition, 1968.

Onkel, Onkel (four acts; title means "Mister, Mister"; also see below), Wagenbach (Berlin, Germany), 1965.

Die Plebejer proben den Aufstand: Ein deutsches Trauerspiel (also see below; first produced in West Berlin, Germany, 1966), Luchterhand (Berlin, Germany), 1966, translation by Ralph Manheim published as *The Plebeians Rehearse the Uprising: A German Tragedy* (produced in Cambridge, MA, at the Harvard Dramatic Club, 1967), with an introduction by Grass, Harcourt (New York, NY), 1966.

The World of Günter Grass, adapted by Dennis Rosa, produced off-Broadway at Pocket Theatre, April 26, 1966.

Hochwasser [and] *Noch zehn Minuten bis Buffalo* (title of second play means "Only Ten Minutes to Buffalo"; also see below), edited by A. Leslie Wilson, Appleton (New York, NY), 1967.

Four Plays (includes *The Flood* [produced in New York, NY, 1986], *Onkel, Onkel* [title means "Mister, Mister"], *Only Ten Minutes to Buffalo,* and *The Wicked Cooks*), with an introduction by Martin Esslin, Harcourt (New York, NY), 1967.

Davor: Ein Stuck in dreizehn Szenen (also see below; first produced in West Berlin at Schiller Theatre, February 16, 1969, translation by Wilson and Ralph Manheim produced as *Uptight* in Washington, DC, 1972), edited by Victor Lange and Frances Lange, Harcourt (New York, NY), 1973, translation by A. Leslie Wilson and Ralph Manheim published as *Max: A Play,* Harcourt (New York, NY), 1972.

Theaterspiele (includes *Hochwasser, Onkel, Onkel, Die Plebejer proben den Aufstand,* and *Davor;* first produced in West Berlin, Germany, 1970), Luchterhand (Neuwied, Germany), 1970.

(With Aribert Reimann) *Die Vogelscheuchen* (ballet in three acts), Ars Viva (Mainz, Germany), 1977.

Other plays include *Beritten hin und zurück* (title means "Rocking Back and Forth"), *Goldmaeulchen,* 1964, and *Zweiunddreizig Zaehne.*

OTHER

Also collaborator with Jean-Claude Carriere, Volker Schlondorff, and Franz Seitz on screenplay for film adaptation of *Katz und Maus,* Modern Art Film, 1967. Author of material for catalogues to accompany his artwork. Work represented in anthologies, including

Deutsche Literatur seit 1945 in Einzeldarstellunger, edited by Dietrich Weber, Kröner, 1968, and *Danzig 1939: Treasures of a Destroyed Community,* edited by Sheila Schwartz, Wayne State University Press (Detroit, MI), 1980. Contributor to *Der Traum der Vernunft: vom Elend der Aufklärung: eine Veranstaltungsreihe der Akademie der Künste, Berlin,* Luchterhand (Darmstadt, Germany), 1985; *Alptraum und Hoffnung: zwei Reden vor dem Club of Rome,* Steidl (Göttingen, Germany), 1989; and *Die Zukunft der Erinnerung,* edited by Martin Wälde, Steidl (Göttingen, Germany), 2001. A recording of selected readings by the author, *Örtlich betaeubt,* has been produced by Deutsche Grammophon Gesellschaft, 1971. Editor, with Heinrich Boell and Carola Stern, of *L-80.* Author of foreword, *Seventeenth Century German Prose,* Hans J. von Grimmelshausen, Continuum (New York, NY), 1992; Contributor of an "Essay on Loss" to *The Future of German Democracy,* edited by Robert Gerald Livingston and Volkmar Sander, Continuum (New York, NY), 1993.

ADAPTATIONS: Die Blechtrommel (The Tin Drum) was adapted for film, New World Pictures, 1980.

SIDELIGHTS: Through his poems, plays, essays, and especially his novels, Nobel Prize-winning author Günter Grass became the conscience of post-World War II Germany. His first published novel, *Die Blechtrommel*—translated into English as *The Tin Drum*—was one of the first works of recognized merit to come out of Germany after 1945, and it has continued to remain a classic. In this book, and in the rest of his writings, Grass attempts to come to terms with Germany's collective guilt regarding World War II and the Holocaust and to figure out where the country should go in the future.

Grass was born in the Free City of Danzig in the period between the World Wars. The city, with its strategic position at the mouth of the Vistula River, changed hands often in European wars. It was historically German and had a mostly German population, but at the time Grass was born it was a free city, under the protection of the League of Nations and closely tied to Poland. The Nazi Party, growing in strength throughout Grass's childhood, dreamed of restoring the German empire and wanted to return the city to German control. The party was popular among the Germans of Danzig, and Grass himself joined the Hitler Youth as a child.

In 1944, at age fifteen, Grass was drafted into the German military. He was wounded, later found himself in an American prisoner-of-war camp, and at one point was forced to see what remained of Dachau, a notorious concentration camp. He was discharged in 1946, still only eighteen years old. His home was gone—the German population of Danzig had fled or been driven out, and the city became Gdansk, Poland. Grass eventually found his parents and sister, who were trying to scratch out a living as refugees in West Germany. Bitter and unhappy, Grass tried to return to school, dropped out, became a tombstone carver, and finally entered the Düsseldorf Academy of Art to study painting and sculpture. He also started to write.

Grass transferred to the Berlin Academy of Art in 1953 and married in 1954. The next year his wife, Anna, sent some of his poems in to a contest sponsored by a radio station, and he won third prize. This brought him to the attention of Group 47, an informal writing workshop that also counted as members now-famous authors Heinrich Böll, Uwe Johnson, and Martin Walser. Grass first attended a meeting of this group in 1955, at the invitation of its founder, Hans Werner Richter. His verse was well received by the members of Group 47, and the following year Grass published his first volume, a slim book of drawings and poetry titled *Die Vorzüge der Windhühner* (*The Advantages of Windfowl*). While this collection of apparently surrealistic poems and fine-lined drawings of oversized insects was hardly noticed at the time—an English translation of certain of its poems was first published in *Selected Poems* in 1965—it contains the seed of much of his future work. Grass's specific kind of creative imagination has been identified as the graphic and plastic arts combined with lyric inspiration. As Kurt Lothar Tank explained in *Günter Grass:* "One thinks of Paul Klee when one takes . . . lines in this volume of poetry and, instead of actually reading them, visualizes them. One feels with tender fervor the gaiety, light as a dream with which the poet nourishes the windfowl of his own invention that lend wings to his creative act."

In 1958 Grass won the coveted prize of Group 47 for a reading from his manuscript *Die Blechtrommel* (*The Tin Drum*), published the following year. This book, which tells the story of the Nazi rise to power in Danzig from the perspective of a gifted but crazed three year old, transformed the author into a controversial international celebrity. Grass commented on the inspi-

ration for and evolution of the book, which he wrote while living with his wife in a basement apartment in Paris, in a 1973 radio lecture, reprinted in *Günter Grass Materialienbuch*. He said that while he was traveling in France in 1952 and constantly occupied with drawing and writing, he conceived a poem whose protagonist is a "Saint on a Column" and who, from this "elevated perspective," could describe life in the village. But, later, tiny Oskar Matzerath, the tin-drummer, became the exact reverse of a pillar-dweller. By staying closer to the earth than normal, the protagonist of *The Tin Drum* acquires a unique point of view. Presumably it took not merely an adventurer in imagination but also a student of sculpture and drawing to discover this unusual perspective.

The viewpoint of a precocious three year old allowed Grass an honest insider's approach to the problem with which all the writers of Group 47 were struggling: the task of coming to terms with the overwhelming experience of World War II, with what had led up to it and with what had followed in its wake as "economic miracle." In January of 1963, shortly before *The Tin Drum* was published in the United States, a writer for *Time* pronounced Grass's work the "most spectacular example" of recent German literature "trying to probe beneath the surface prosperity to the uneasy past." The reviewer called Grass, whose *Tin Drum* was winning prizes and stirring anger all over Europe, "probably the most inventive talent to be heard from anywhere since the war" and described his central character, Oskar, as "the gaudiest gimmick in his literary bag of tricks. . . . For Oskar is that wildly distorted mirror which, held up to a wildly deformed reality, gives back a recognizable likeness." Two decades later, while reviewing Grass's latest volume, John Irving wrote in *Saturday Review:* "In the more than twenty years since its publication, *Die Blechtrommel* . . . has not been surpassed; it is the greatest novel by a living author."

In Germany, reaction to Grass's bestselling novel ranged from critical endorsement to moral outrage. Characteristic of the honors and scandals surrounding the book was the literature prize of Bremen, voted by the jury but withheld by the city senate on moral grounds. Similar charges against Grass's writings took the form of law suits in 1962, were repeated with political overtones on the occasion of the Büchner Prize in 1965, and continued as confrontations with the Springer Press and others.

The formidable task of coming to grips with his country's past, however, is not something Grass could accomplish in one novel, no matter how incisive. By 1963, when *The Tin Drum* appeared in the United States, he had published a second volume of poetry and drawings, *Gleisdreieck* (*Rail Triangle*); a novella, *Katz und Maus* (translated as *Cat and Mouse*); and another novel of epic dimensions, *Hundejahre* (translated as *Dog Years*). The drawings and poems of *Gleisdreieck*, which are translated in *Selected Poems* and in *In the Egg and Other Poems*, make up a volume of more imposing format than Grass's first poetry collection and clearly show his development from a playful style obsessed with detail to a bolder, more encompassing form of expression.

Together with *The Tin Drum, Cat and Mouse* and *Dog Years* form what is called the "Danzig Trilogy," and deal respectively with the pre-war, inter-war, and post-war periods in that city. In the novella *Cat and Mouse,* the central focus and, with it, a sense of guilt are diverted from the first-person narrator, Pilenz, to Mahlke, his high school friend. Mahlke's protruding adam's apple causes his relentless pursuit of the Iron Cross—never referred to by name—with which he intends to cover up his "mouse." But in the end the narrator, who has set up the cat-and-mouse game, can no longer fathom the depth of his friend's fatal complex nor his own role in it.

The years from the prewar to the postwar era are presented in *Dog Years* through the perspective of three different narrators, a team directed by Amsel—alias Brauxel—who makes scarecrows in man's image. The seemingly solid childhood friendship of Amsel and Matem evolves into the love-hate relationship between Jew and non-Jew under the impact of Nazi ideology. When the former friends from the region of the Vistula finally meet again in the West, the ominous führer dog who followed Matem on his odyssey is left behind in Brauxel's subterranean world of scarecrows. While *Dog Years*, like *The Tin Drum*, again accounts for the past through the eyes of an artist, the artist is no longer a demonic tin-drummer in the guise of a child but the ingenious maker of a world of objects reflecting the break between the creations of nature and those of men. Referring to Amsel's "keen sense of reality in all its innumerable forms," John Reddick wrote in *The Danzig Trilogy of Günter Grass*: "Any serious reader of Grass's work will need little prompting to recognize that Grass is in fact describing his own, as well as his persona's art."

In 1961, well into his *Tin Drum* fame, Grass revealed at a meeting of theater experts in Hamburg that, departing from his early poetry, he had written four long plays and two one-act plays during "the relatively short time, from 1954 to 1957." Not all of the plays to which he referred had been staged or published at that time; some, like *Onkel, Onkel* (*Mister, Mister*), appeared later in revised editions. Grass's earliest plays, *Beritten hin und zurück* (*Rocking Back and Forth*) and *Noch zehn Minuten bis Buffalo* (*Only Ten Minutes to Buffalo*), have a clearly programmatic character. They stage diverse attitudes about approaches to drama or poetry. As presentations of Grass's "poetics," they belong in the same category as his important early essays "Die Ballerina" ("The Ballet Dancer") of 1956 and "Der Inhalt als Widerstand" ("Content as Resistance") of 1957.

Die bösen Köche (*The Wicked Cooks*), written in 1956 in Paris and initially performed in 1961 in Berlin, was, in 1967, Grass's first play to be staged in the United States. In 1961 Martin Esslin had included discussion of Grass's early dramatic works in *The Theatre of the Absurd*. But in 1966 Peter Spycher argued in a *Germanisch-Romanische Monatsschrift* article that, at least in the case of *The Wicked Cooks*, the criteria of absurdist theater do not apply. In the play a team of five restaurant cooks find their reputations threatened by the popular "Gray Soup" cooked on occasion by a guest referred to as "the Count." The play revolves around the intrigues of the cooks to obtain the Count's soup recipe. They even try to trade him a nurse, the girlfriend of one of them, in return for the secret. Unfortunately for the cooks, the Count and the nurse fall in love, and when the cooks invade their idyllic existence, the Count shoots both the woman and himself. Spycher justifiably sees the play as an "allegorical parable" or "anti-tale," for the Count assures the cooks that "it is not a recipe, it's an experience, a living knowledge, continuous change."

Grass's initial limited success as a playwright took on the dimensions of a scandal with the 1966 production in West Berlin of *Die Plebejer proben den Aufstand: Ein deutsches Trauerspiel* (*The Plebeians Rehearse the Uprising*), subtitled *A German Tragedy*. The play is loosely based on the 1953 revolt in East Berlin, in which workers in that sector of the city protested the failure of the Communist authorities to deliver on their promises of better conditions. To many members of the audience, Grass's character "The Boss" was interpreted to be Bertolt Brecht, a Communist East German playwright, and they did not find Grass's perspective on Brecht flattering. As Andrzej Wirth explained in *A Günter Grass Symposium,* "The Boss [of the play] was a Versager [failure], a Hamletic victim of his own theorems. . . . And the Berlin audience interpreted the play as a challenge to Brecht's image, as a case of Günter Grass versus Bertolt Brecht." However, as Wirth continued, "the American premiere of *The Plebeians Rehearse the Uprising* (1967) in the Harvard Dramatic Club presented an interesting alternative." Due to the English translation and certain changes in the staging, "the play succeeded in exposing a more universal theme—the dilemma of the artist: the aesthetic man versus the man of action, ideal versus reality."

Throughout the 1960s Grass become more overtly involved in politics, supporting, campaigning for, and even writing speeches for Willy Brandt, a Social Democrat and the mayor of West Berlin. Grass's third volume of poetry and drawings, *Ausgefragt,* reflects the political controversies of the decade. One cycle of poems in this volume is titled "Indignation, Annoyance, Rage" and is inspired by the protest songs of the early 1960s. Intoning the "powerlessness" of the guitar protesters, Grass points to the futility of their ritualistic peace marches. However, student protests gained momentum after 1966 and became a force to be reckoned with. Thus Grass's hope of engaging the protesters in constructive election activity was crushed by the demands of the new, increasingly radical Left.

Within the literary developments of the 1960s, Grass's *New Poems,* which range in subject matter from the private to the public sphere, and from aesthetics to politics, have been described by Heinrich Vormweg—in the introduction to Grass's *Gesammelte Gedichte (Collected Poems)*—as reality training. The perception of individual and social reality has been exceptional in German literature, and as Vormweg pointed out, Grass, in his poems, ignores the most obvious change in the literature of the late 1950s and 1960s. The current objective of literature, as reflected for example in "concrete poetry," was to expose language itself as an unreliable medium, inadequate for identifying things and situations as they are. Grass, however, evinces a fundamental trust in language and its ability to communicate reality. In *New Poems* he attempts to make perfectly visible the inescapable contradictions and conflicts of everyday life, including his own.

Grass's political essays of this period are collected in the volume *Über das Selbstverständliche* (translated as *On the Self-Evident*). The title comes from his acceptance speech for the prestigious Büchner Prize in 1965; in that year the Social Democrats had lost the elections, and Grass was dubbed a bad loser by critics of his speech. Another collection of his speeches, open letters, and commentaries from the 1960s is translated in the volume *Speak Out!,* which also contains Grass's 1966 address—"On Writers as Court Jesters and on Non-Existent Courts"—at the meeting of Group 47 in Princeton, New Jersey. While Grass's references to some of his literary colleagues and himself were rigorously criticized in Germany, the last statement of his Princeton speech became renowned: "A poem knows no compromise, but men live by compromise. The individual who can stand up under this contradiction and act is a fool and will change the world." Three more volumes of political essays and commentaries—*Der Bürger und seine Stimme (The Citizen and His Voice)*, *Denkzettel (Note for Thought)* and *Widerstand lernen: Politische Gegenreden (Learning Resistance: Political Countertalk)*—demonstrate that Grass has remained politically outspoken through the 1970s and beyond.

In 1969, six years after *Dog Years,* Grass published another novel, *Örtlich betäubt* (translated as *Local Anaesthetic*). For the first time he left the Danzig origins of his earlier prose works, concentrating instead on his new home town, the Berlin of the 1960s, and on the student protests against the Vietnam War. Starusch, a high school teacher, while undergoing extensive dental treatment, is confronted with the plan of his favorite student, Scherbaum, to set fire to his dog on Kurfürstendamm. By this act the seventeen year old hopes to awaken the populace to the realities of the war. Yet in the end the dog is not burned, and the student is about to undergo a dental treatment similar to his teacher's.

The reception of this novel in Germany was predictably negative. War protest reduced to the level of a dachshund was conceived as belittlement of the real problems at hand. In the United States, however, *Local Anaesthetic* earned Grass some enthusiastic reviews and a *Time* cover story. The caption read, "Novelist between the Generations: A Man Who Can Speak to the Young." Perhaps the only problem with this hopeful statement was that "the young" did not listen, nor did they read the book; they preferred Hermann

Hesse's *Siddhartha.* However, the *Time* essayist provided a lucid interpretation of *Local Anaesthetic,* while other reviewers of the book found it difficult to make the switch from the generous epic panorama of the "Danzig Trilogy" to the contemporary outrages of the 1960s.

From the Diary of a Snail contains some of Grass's most openly autobiographical statements. It is also a diary recording his experience during Brandt's election campaign of 1969. Most important, however, this book marks a change of emphasis from politics to the more private occupation with the visual arts. Grass writes in the *Diary:* "It's true: I am not a believer; but when I draw, I become devout. . . . But I draw less and less. It doesn't get quiet enough any more. I look out to see what the clamor is; actually it's me that's clamoring and somewhere else." In the context of this self-portrait in the *Diary,* readers also find revealing remarks about Grass's inspiration and technique as graphic artist: "I draw what's left over. . . . A rich, that is, broken line, one that splits, stutters in places, here passes over in silence, there thickly proclaims. Many lines. Also bordered spots. But sometimes niggardly in disbursing outlines."

The image of the snail indicates Grass's withdrawal into an increasingly meditative phase. Although he adopted the snail as his political emblem—"the snail is progress"—his entire field of vision is affected by it. The snail replaces one of the eyeballs in two self-portraits, etchings in copper produced in 1972. Moreover, the English version of the *Diary* contains a reproduction of fifteenth-century artist Albrecht Dürer's engraving "Melancolia I." The "Variations on Albrecht Dürer's Engraving" are summarized in a speech celebrating Dürer's five hundredth birthday in 1971 and appended to the *Diary.* The personifications of both "Melancholy" and her twin sister, "Utopia," are supplemented by a narrative on "Doubt," whose story provides an excursion into the past—a report to the children about the fate of the Jewish community of Danzig during the war. With the exception of this narrative thread, the *Diary* dispenses almost entirely with plot; yet the importance of this book in defining Grass's concerns and motivations has gradually become clear to critics of his work.

Around 1974 Grass again began work on a major novel. At first he referred to it as a "Cookbook." Already in *The Diary of a Snail* he had toyed with plans

of writing "a narrative cookbook: about ninety-nine dishes, about guests, about man as an animal who can cook." At a later stage, the working title for the new novel was modified: "The (female) cook in me." At a still later stage the book was said to be a variation on the Grimms' tale of "The Fisherman and His Wife." When after numerous public readings, including one in New York, the work was published in August 1977, it was titled *Der Butt* (translated as *The Flounder*) and comprised 699 pages of prose laced with forty-six poems.

The Flounder is structured around the nine months of a pregnancy and "nine or eleven" female cooks, each representing a major phase in prehistory and history from the neolithic to the present. The talking flounder functions as an archetypal male element, the tempter, who gradually destroys the mythic golden age of the matriarch. He is duly sentenced and punished by a group of feminists but will resume his destructive influence as future advisor and assistant to womankind instead of mankind. Clearly, the novel is purporting to correct some misconceptions about the roles of women in history and in the present. But the strength of this epic account lies not in its feminist argument but rather, as is usual with Grass, in its historical panorama. The setting for the mythical and historical events, all told by an ever-present first-person narrator, is once again the Baltic shore around the mouth of the Vistula. The representation of major cultural phases and personages, through individual female characters who provide life and nourishment, accounts for much of the fascination the work exerts. In the context of historical settings and figures, many of the images Grass had etched in copper—the fishheads, the mushrooms, and the portraits of women—became dynamic agents of the narrative.

A majority of reviewers, including *New Yorker* contributor John Updike, felt that the richness of the "stew" demands too much digestion. They objected to its length, its preoccupation with food and cooking, with sex and scatology. For some readers, Grass's cooks did not come across as real characters. Nigel Dennis in the *New York Review of Books* labeled *The Flounder* "a very bad novel." Morris Dickstein, on the other hand, concluded in the *New York Times* that "Grass's cooks save him for they give body to his politics. . . . The cooks bring together Grass the novelist and Grass the socialist." With regard to the issue of feminism, *The Flounder* was labeled by Richard

Howard in his *New Leader* review as both "an anti-feminist tract" and "a feminist tract." In a more thorough study of *The Flounder* within the context of Grass's overall work, Michael Hollington speculated in *Günter Grass: The Writer in a Pluralistic Society* "that critical reaction to the book in English-speaking countries was short-sighted" and "that as the novel is digested its distinction will gradually be recognized."

In 1979 Grass published *Das Treffen in Telgte* (translated as *The Meeting at Telgte*). This relatively short narrative is dedicated to Hans Werner Richter, founder of Group 47, in honor of his seventieth birthday. *The Meeting at Telgte,* like *The Flounder,* employs historical material, but because of its compact action, provides more suspenseful reading. Set in 1647, the novel portrays some twenty historical German writers who undertake a fictitious journey to Westphalia because they wish to contribute their share to the peace negotiations that ended the devastating Thirty Years' War. Although the situation parallels that of the writers of Group 47 after World War II, the story is not a *roman à clef.* Still, several of the seventeenth-century writers in Grass's "meeting" have twentieth-century counterparts in Group 47. For example, the mischievous Gelnhausen, who becomes the author of the *Simplicissimus* epic, reflects certain traits of Grass himself, and Simon Dach functions as a seventeenth-century image of Richter. The iconography on the dust jacket, a human hand with a quill rising above a sea of rubble, may represent as wishful a dream for the modern age as it was for the seventeenth century. But its execution in *The Meeting at Telgte* produces a masterpiece, as *German Quarterly* contributor Richard Schade contended, by means of the thistle and writer's hand imagery.

Described alternately as science fiction and fable, Grass's novel *Die Rättin* (*The Rat*) opens with a Christmas scene in which the protagonist—Grass himself—asks for and receives a rat as his present. As the rat observes Grass at work, the author becomes increasingly distracted until, eventually, the rat begins to tell a dream-like, prophetic tale about the extinction of the human race as a result of atomic war, followed by the survival of a race of rats. "This is not a book about what *may* happen; it is a novel, built on our profound need for fable, about what *has* happened to western civilization," Eugene Kennedy declared in Chicago's *Tribune Books.* Also offering praise for the novel, Richard Locke commented in the *Washington Post Book World:* "*The Rat* asks to be read as a kind of modern

Book of Revelation, with Grass the St. John of our time, the delirious prophet of Apocalypse, a nuclear Big Bang that will end human life and leave the earth populated with rats feasting on radioactive human garbage."

Unlike *The Rat,* Grass's novel *Unkenrufe* (*The Call of the Toad*) received mixed reviews. *The Call of the Toad* depicts a couple who sell cemetery plots located in the Polish city of Gdansk to Germans who wish to be buried in what was once their homeland. While the business is successful, the couple becomes plagued by escalating greed and tyranny: "[what they] had envisioned as a peace-promoting, free-will enterprise becomes a symbol of German greed and tyranny in the wake of reunification," thought Donna Rikfind of *Washington Post Book World.* Many reviewers faulted the novel for its stylistic flatness, often commenting that Grass's characters lack depth and interest, despite the interesting intellectual premise of the book.

In the heady year of 1990, when the Berlin Wall had fallen and the world was discussing the potential reunification of East and West Germany, Grass published a collection of speeches and essays arguing against this path. Throughout *Deutscher Lastenausgleich: Wider das dumpfe Einheitsgebot; Reden und Gespräche, Texte zur Zeit*—translated as *Two States—One Nation?*—Grass points to the atrocities of the Holocaust as evidence of the potentially destructive force of a powerful Germany motivated by national self-interest and fear: "German unity has so often proved a threat to our neighbors that we cannot expect them to put up with it anymore," he declared. While a reviewer for the *Los Angeles Times Book Review* found the collection "challenging and disturbing," J. P. Stern in the London *Observer* rejected Grass's arguments as "gripes and sour grapes," and without foundation in terms of the contemporary social reality in Germany. Germans also generally rejected his arguments, and German reunification occurred on October 3, 1990.

Grass returned to the subject of reunification in his 1995 novel *Ein Weites Feld* (*Too Far Afield*), which also generated controversy and skeptical reviews. The novel draws upon the historical figure Theodore Fontane, a nineteenth-century writer who was skeptical of Germany's original unification in 1871. "As always, Grass is interested in how the past inundates the lives of ordinary people as they try desperately to swim with or against history's treacherous tides," noted *New*

York Times Book Review critic James J. Sheehan. *Spectator* reviewer Christian Caryl objected to the novel's approach to the satirizing contemporary politics in Germany "in the harsh light of history," noting that "the construction [of *Ein Weites Feld*] takes absolute precedence over the life of the characters. . . . Never before has [Grass] allowed his self-image as the Great German Writer to weigh so heavily on his style."

The subject of German unification is also a focus of the essays and speeches collected in *On Writing and Politics: 1967-1983.* "Grass, as these speeches show, remains stubbornly loyal to his own vision of Europe, to a 'third force' notion of a continent which must liberate itself from Soviet and American hegemony and from the burden of their armaments," observed Neal Ascherson in the *London Review of Books.* Grass also addresses larger political questions concerning the nature of political power on a global scale and the implications for the future of a world characterized by what Jon Cook in *New Statesman* called "a pretense of democracy," in which "everything is done in the name of the popular will, but in reality crucial areas of decision-making are withheld from the difficult, democratic process of negotiating consent."

Originally published in 1993 as *Novemberland: 13 Sonette, Novemberland: Selected Poems 1956-1993,* a bilingual volume of Grass's poems, was published in 1996. The fifty-four poems cover the tumultuous period of German history from World War II to the beginning of German reunification. An *America* critic noted that "Grass's style is allegorical, or perhaps fable-esque; readers familiar and comfortable with a direct access to the poet in a 'confessional' mode may not always know what to do with these poems." Grass's personal connection with the material is not always clear, according to the reviewer, as the style is surrealistic and works against such direct connections. For example, some poems include a lamentation over the ruins of Berlin, two bitten apples that recall Paradise, and a prophetic glove at the beach.

My Century, which came out in 1999, is an historical novel that consists of one hundred brief vignettes—one for each year of the twentieth century—each told in the first person. The narrators are a diverse lot, ranging from former Nazis to ordinary working-class people. "The sheer variety of Grass's inventions is impressive," observed *New York Times Book Review* contributor Peter Gay, who nonetheless felt that the

book is "a collection of fragments that fail to cohere." A *Publishers Weekly* critic had a different view, finding that this "cacaphony . . . is finally resolved into a complex, multipart harmony." Gay did compliment the individual tales: "Not that the episodes are badly told. Grass's old power of engaging the reader is still there. But the selection of witnesses seems arbitrary." Some critics thought that Grass refers too indirectly to the World War II era, including the Nazi Holocaust; the narrators for this period are a group of war correspondents meeting many years later. "Grass, always before able to face horror and disaster, seems at this late date to be losing his nerve," Gay remarked. *Booklist* contributor Frank Caso, however, found the device of the correspondents looking back to be "most effective."

In his 2002 novel *Im Krebsgang (Crabwalk),* Grass returns to Danzig to tell the story of a forgotten tragedy. In January of 1945, as Soviet troops were advancing on the eastern borders of Germany, tens of thousands of refugees crammed onto ships headed for safety further west. One such ship, the *Wilhelm Gustloff,* was torpedoed by a Russian submarine and sank on January 30, 1945. Because no one knows exactly how many people were on board, the total death toll remains uncertain, but estimates run as high as 10,000—mostly women and children. In Grass's tale, one such woman was Tulla, a pregnant teenage refugee who gives birth to a son, Paul, the night the ship sinks.

A grown-up, fifty-something Paul narrates the tale. Through three generations of his family, Grass weaves together numerous threads from the past and present of Germany, and "the dexterity with which Grass handles them makes this his most powerful book since *The Tin Drum,*" contended *Knight Ridder/Tribune News Service* contributor Michael Upchurch. Speaking about the sufferings of Germans who were ethnically cleansed from the country's former eastern lands was—and for many still is—taboo, because it has been generally accepted that as the instigators of World War II, the German people deserve little sympathy. However Tulla, despite having become a loyal East German communist, still wants the story of the *Wilhelm Gustloff* to be preserved. She pleads with Paul, a journalist, to write about it, but he refuses. Paul, who fled to West Germany and adopted left-wing politics, wants nothing to do with his mother's Nazi past. But Paul's teenage son Konny is another story. He inhabits the fever-swamps of Neo-Nazi Web sites and chat rooms and wants not only the ship *Wilhelm Gustloff* to be recognized, but also the man—a Nazi who was assassinated by a Jewish student named David Frankfurter. Using the handle "Wilhelm," Konny argues with a "David" online. "Their real-life meeting provides the grim climax of a narrative that views fascist hate-mongering, Stalinist lies, capitalist corruption, and the eternal failures of parents with the same angry disdain," wrote a *Kirkus Reviews* contributor. To *Financial Times* reviewer Giles Macdonough, the purpose of the tale is "clearly didactic: too little openness about the past breeds Konnys, who are too often left alone, intentionally uninformed, to fester in their resentment." But Upchurch took a different lesson from the book: "Remembrance, Grass suggests, can end up being repetition."

In 1999 Grass was awarded the Nobel Prize in literature by the Swedish Academy for his body of work, beginning with *The Tin Drum* and continuing through *My Century*. The Swedish Academy commented in its press release that when *The Tin Drum* was published, "it was as if German literature had been granted a new beginning after decades of linguistic and moral destruction." The Academy went on to say that "Grass recreated the lost world from which his creativity sprang, Danzig, his home town, as he remembered it from the years of his infancy before the catastrophe of war. . . . He is a fabulist and a scholarly lecturer, recorder of voices and presumptuous monologist, pasticheur and at the same time creator of an ironic idiom that he alone commands."

BIOGRAPHICAL AND CRITICAL SOURCES:

BOOKS

Brandes, Ute Thoss, *Günter Grass,* Edition Colloquium (Berlin, Germany), 1998.
Contemporary Literary Criticism, Gale (Detroit, MI), Volume 1, 1973, Volume 2, 1974, Volume 4, 1975, Volume 6, 1976, Volume 11, 1979, Volume 15, 1980, Volume 22, 1982, Volume 32, 1985, Volume 49, 1988, Volume 88, 1995.
Dictionary of Literary Biography, Gale (Detroit, MI), Volume 75: *Contemporary German Fiction Writers, Second Series,* 1988, Volume 124: *Twentieth-Century German Dramatists, 1919-1992,* 1992.
Diller, Edward, *A Mythic Journey: Günter Grass's "Tin Drum,"* University Press of Kentucky (Lexington, KY), 1974.

Enright, D. J., *Man Is an Onion: Reviews and Essays,* Open Court (LaSalle, IL), 1972.
Esslin, Martin, *Reflections: Essays on Modern Theatre,* Doubleday (New York, NY), 1960.
Esslin, Martin, *The Theatre of the Absurd,* Doubleday (New York, NY), 1961.
Grass, Günter, *Gesammelte Gedichte* (title means "Collected Poems"), introduction by Heinrich Vormweg, Luchterhand (Neuwied, Germany), 1971.
Grass, Günter, *Aus dem Tagebuch einer Schnecke,* Luchterhand (Darmstadt, Germany), 1972, translation by Ralph Manheim published as *From the Diary of a Snail,* Harcourt (New York, NY), 1973.
Hollington, Michael, *Günter Grass: The Writer in a Pluralistic Society,* Marion Boyars (New York, NY), 1980.
International Dictionary of Theatre, Volume 2: *Playwrights,* St. James Press (Detroit, MI), 1993.
Leonard, Irene, *Günter Grass,* Oliver & Boyd, 1974.
Mason, Ann L., *The Skeptical Muse: A Study of Günter Grass' Conception of the Artist,* Herbert Lang, 1974.
Mayer, Hans, *Steppenwolf and Everyman,* translated by Jack D. Zipes, Crowell (New York, NY), 1971.
Mews, Siegfried, editor, *Günter Grass's "The Flounder" in Critical Perspective,* AMS Press (New York, NY), 1983.
Miles, Keith, *Günter Grass,* Barnes & Noble (New York, NY), 1975.
Neuhaus, Volker, *Günter Grass,* Metzler, 1979.
Newsmakers 2000, issue 2, Gale (Detroit, MI), 2000.
O'Neill, Patrick, *Günter Grass: A Bibliography, 1955-1975,* University of Toronto Press (Toronto, Ontario, Canada), 1976.
O'Neill, Patrick, *Günter Grass Revisited,* Twayne (New York, NY), 1999.
Panichas, George, editor, *The Politics of Twentieth-Century Novelists,* Hawthorn (New York, NY), 1971.
Preece, Julian, *Günter Grass: His Life and Work,* St. Martin's Press (New York, NY), 2000.
Reddick, John, *The Danzig Trilogy of Günter Grass,* Harcourt (San Diego, CA), 1974.
Steiner, George, *Language and Silence,* Atheneum (New York, NY), 1967.
Tank, Kurt Lothar, *Günter Grass,* 5th edition, Colloquium, 1965, translation by John Conway published as *Günter Grass,* Ungar (New York, NY), 1969.
Thomas, Noel, *The Narrative Works of Günter Grass,* John Benjamins (Philadelphia, PA), 1982.
Willson, A. Leslie, editor, *A Günter Grass Symposium,* University of Texas Press (Austin, TX), 1971.

PERIODICALS

America, October 26, 1996, review of *Novemberland: Selected Poems 1956-1993,* p. 26.

Atlantic, June, 1981, Phoebe-Lou Adams, review of *The Meeting at Telgte,* pp. 101-102; April, 1982, Phoebe-Lou Adams, review of *Headbirths; or, The Germans Are Dying Out,* p. 110; June, 1989, Phoebe-Lou Adams, review of *Show Your Tongue,* p. 96; November, 1992, Phoebe-Lou Adams, review of *The Call of the Toad,* p. 162; February, 2000, Phoebe-Lou Adams, review of *My Century,* p. 105.

Book, March-April, 2003, Sean McCann, review of *Crabwalk,* p. 74.

Booklist, September 15, 1992, Stuart Whitwell, review of *The Call of the Toad,* p. 100; November 15, 1999, Frank Caso, review of *My Century,* p. 579; July, 2000, Brian Kenney, review of *Too Far Afield,* p. 1973; February 15, 2003, Frank Caso, review of *Crabwalk,* pp. 1047-1048.

Books Abroad, spring, 1972.

Chicago Review, winter, 1978.

Chicago Tribune, October 29, 1978; June 27, 1980.

Commonweal, May 8, 1970; July 16, 1982, David H. Richter, review of *Headbirths,* pp. 409-410; February 9, 1990, Abigail McCarthy, "'Einig Vaterland!,'" pp. 72-73.

Contemporary European History, May, 2003, Robert G. Moeller, "Sinking Ships, the Lost Heimat and Broken Taboos: Günter Grass and the Politics of Memory in Contemporary Germany."

Contemporary Literature, summer, 1973; winter, 1976; winter, 1993, Reiko Tachibana, "Günter Grass's *The Tin Drum* and Oe Kenzaburo's *My Tears:* A Study in Convergence," pp. 740-766.

Critique, number 3, 1978; spring, 1989, Wayne P. Lindquist, "The Materniads: Grass's Paradoxical Conclusion to the 'Danzig Trilogy,'" pp. 179-192.

Detroit Free Press, October 1, 1999, p. 10A.

Detroit News, May 9, 1982.

Diacritics, number 3, 1973.

Dimension, summer, 1970.

Economist (U.S.), August 2, 1986, review of *Die Rättin,* p. SB13; November 28, 1992, review of *The Call of the Toad,* p. 104; September 2, 1995, "Grass and the Drum of Discord," p. 43; October 18, 1997, review of *Fundsachen für Nichtleser,* pp. S14-S15; October 25, 1997, "Günter Grass, Ever Unmown," p. 57; October 16, 1999, "What the World Is Reading," p. 15; February 16, 2002, review of *Im Krebsgang.*

Encounter, April, 1964; November, 1970.

Entertainment Weekly, October 23, 1992, L. S. Klepp, review of *The Call of the Toad,* pp. 56-57.

Europe, July-August, 1993, Christine Bednarz, "Writer's Corner: Günter Grass," pp. 44-45; March, 2000, Claire Bose, "The Grass Century," p. 25.

Europe Intelligence Wire, May 17, 2003, review of *Crabwalk.*

Financial Times, August 26, 1995, Wolfgang Munchau, "Fiery Reviews Scorch Grass," p. 7; October 1, 1999, Christopher Brown-Humes and Jan Dalley, "Günter Grass Wins Nobel Literature Prize," p. 4; February 16, 2002, Frederick Studemann, review of *Im Krebsgang,* p. 4; April 26, 2003, Frederick Studemann, review of *Crabwalk,* p. 43; November 1, 2003, Giles Macdonough, review of *Crabwalk,* p. 26.

Foreign Policy, March-April, 2003, Robert Gerald Livingston, review of *Im Krebsgang,* pp. 80-82.

Germanic Review, fall, 1993, Lawrence O. Frye, "Günter Grass, *Katz und Maus,* and Gastro-Narratology," pp. 176-184.

Germanisch-Romanische Monatsschrift, number 47, 1966.

German Quarterly, number 54, 1981; number 55, 1982; winter, 1997, Monika Shafi, "Gazing at India: Representations of Alterity in Travelogues by Ingeborg Drewitz, Günter Grass, and Hubert Fichte," pp. 39-56.

Harper's, December, 1978.

Hindu, October 17, 1999, Ravi Vyas, "Reality at Grass Level."

Journal of European Studies, September, 1979; March, 1989, Carl Tighe, "*The Tin Drum* in Poland," pp. 3-20.

Kirkus Reviews, January 1, 2003, review of *Crabwalk,* pp. 11-12.

Kliatt, January, 2002, Bernard D. Cooperman, review of *The Tin Drum* (audiobook), p. 48; November, 2003, Hugh Flick, Jr., review of *Crabwalk* (audiobook), p. 46.

Knight Ridder/Tribune News Service, November 22, 2000, Carlin Romano, review of *Too Far Afield,* p. K3110; January 10, 2001, Jay Goldin, review of *Too Far Afield,* p. K5668; April 30, 2003, Michael Upchurch, review of *Crabwalk,* p. K1370.

Library Journal, March 15, 1981, Gari R. Muller, review of *The Meeting at Telgte,* p. 689; March 15, 1982, review of *Headbirths,* p. 650; July, 1987, Paul E. Hutchison, review of *The Rat,* p. 94; September 15, 1990, Marcia L. Sprules, review of

Two States—One Nation?: Against the Unenlight-ened Clamor for German Reunification, p. 90; September 15, 1992, Michael T. O'Pecko, review of *The Call of the Toad,* p. 94; May 15, 1996, Michael T. O'Pecko, review of *Novemberland,* p. 65; January, 2000, Eric Bryant, review of *My Century,* p. 159; September 15, 2000, Mirela Roncevic, review of *Too Far Afield,* p. 112; January, 2003, Edward Cone, review of *Crabwalk,* p. 154.

Literary Review, summer, 1974.

London Magazine, October, 1978.

London Review of Books, February 5-18, 1981; May 6-19, 1982; October 17, 1985, p. 6; October 17, 1996, p. 3.

Los Angeles Times, May 22, 1981; April 18, 1982; May 20, 1983, "Has Our Writing Lost Its Politics?," p. 3; March 4, 1984, Charles Solomon, review of *Günter Grass: Drawings and Words 1954-1977,* p. 6; June 16, 1985, Salman Rushdie, "A Political Author Migrates from Certainty to Doubt," p. 2; July 21, 1985, Art Seidenbaum, review of *On Writing and Politics, 1967-1983,* p. 2; August 13, 1989; November 29, 1992; September 18, 1995, William Pfaff, "Günter Grass's New Novel Unleashes the PC Censors," p. B5; September 22, 1995, Mary Williams, "The Plot Sickens, German Critics Say," p. A5; October 1, 1999, Carol J. Williams, "Germany Hails Grass's 'Overdue' Literature Nobel," p. A1; March 28, 2002, Carol J. Williams, review of *Im Krebsgang,* p. E-1; April 13, 2003, Thomas McGonigle, review of *Crabwalk,* p. R-4.

Los Angeles Times Book Review, November 17, 1991, p. 14.

Michigan Quarterly Review, winter, 1975.

Midwest Quarterly, autumn, 2001, Ronald Charles Epstein, review of *Too Far Afield,* pp. 113-114.

Modern Fiction Studies, spring, 1971; summer, 1986, p. 334.

Modern Language Review, October, 1995, Julian Preece, "Sexual-Textual Politics: The Transparency of the Male Narrative in *Der Butt* by Günter Grass," pp. 955-966; April, 2001, K. F. Hilliard, "Showing, Telling and Believing: Günter Grass's *Katz und Maus* and narratology," p. 420.

Nation, December 23, 1978; April 24, 1982, Richard Gilman, review of *Headbirths,* pp. 502-504; December 24, 1990, John Leonard, review of *Two States—One Nation?* and overview of Grass's work, pp. 810-816; November 16, 1992, Irmgard Elsner Hunt, review of *The Call of the Toad,* pp. 580-584; July 3, 2000, Pierre Bourdieu, interview with Grass, p. 25; March 31, 2003, Hugh Eakin, review of *Crabwalk,* p. 31.

National Interest, summer, 2000, Jacob Heilbrunn, "Germany's Illiberal Fictions," p. 88.

National Review, October 25, 1999, David Pryce-Jones, "The Failure of Günter Grass: Another Nobel Bomb," p. 30; December 6, 1999, James Gardner, review of *My Century,* p. 67.

New Leader, October 29, 1973; December 4, 1978; December 13, 1999, Rosellen Brown, review of *My Century,* p. 29; March-April, 2003, Benjamin Taylor, review of *Crabwalk,* pp. 24-25.

New Republic, June 20, 1970; April 14, 1982, Joel Agee, review of *Headbirths,* pp. 30-32; August 12, 1985, Timothy Garton Ash, review of *On Writing and Politics,* pp. 31-33; July 13, 1987, Jasoslav Anders, review of *The Rat,* pp. 29-32; January 31, 2000, Ian Buruma, review of *My Century,* p. 31; August 11, 2003, Ruth Franklin, review of *Crabwalk,* p. 30.

New Review, May, 1974.

New Statesman, June 7, 1974; June 26, 1981, Salman Rushdie, review of *The Meeting at Telgte,* p. 21; April 23, 1982, Mike Poole, review of *Headbirths,* p. 27; September 20, 1985, p. 27; June 26, 1987, Michelene Wandor, review of *The Rat,* p. 26; March 19, 1999, Lavinia Greenlaw, review of *Selected Poems: 1956-1993,* pp. 48-49; December 4, 2000, William Cook, review of *Too Far Afield,* p. 55; April 7, 2003, Sarah Schaeffer, review of *Crabwalk,* p. 54.

New Statesman & Society, June 22, 1990, Aafke Steenhuis, interview with Grass, pp. 35-38; October 9, 1992, Martin Chalmers, review of *The Call of the Toad,* p. 37.

Newsweek International, March 11, 2002, Andrew Nagorski and Stefan Theil, review of *Crabwalk,* p. 51.

New York, November 16, 1992, Rhoda Koenig, review of *The Call of the Toad,* p. 78.

New Yorker, April 25, 1970; October 15, 1973; November 27, 1978; August 3, 1981, John Updike, review of *The Meeting at Telgte,* pp. 90-93; June 14, 1982, John Updike, review of *Headbirths,* pp. 129-131; February 6, 1984, review of *Günter Grass: Drawings and Words, 1954-1977,* pp. 128-129; October 19, 1992, Ian Buruma, "Günter's Ghosts: Postcard from Berlin," pp. 45-46; April 21, 2003, John Updike, review of *Crabwalk,* p. 185.

New York Review of Books, November 23, 1978; June 11, 1981, Stephen Spender, review of *The Meeting at Telgte,* pp. 35-38; March 18, 1982, D. J. Enright, review of *Headbirths,* p. 46; July 5, 1987; September 24, 1987, D. J. Enright, review of *The Rat,* pp. 45-46; May 21, 1989; September 30, 1990; November 1, 1992; November 19, 1992, Gabriel Annan, review of *The Call of the Toad,* p. 19; November 30, 2000, Gabriele Annan, review of *Too Far Afield,* pp. 39-41.

New York Times, April 15, 1977; November 9, 1978; November 25, 1978; May 31, 1979; January 26, 1980, John Vincour, "In Any Language, Grass Chooses His Words with Care," p. 2; April 6, 1980, John Vincour, review of *The Tin Drum,* p. D1; April 11, 1980, Vincent Canby, review of *The Tin Drum,* p. C6; April 30, 1981, John Leonard, review of *The Meeting at Telgte,* pp. 19, C21; February 26, 1982, Christopher Lehmann-Haupt, review of *Headbirths,* pp. 21, C22; March 6, 1983, John Russell, "Günter Grass as a Printmaker, Poet, Storyteller, and Fabulist," p. H29; March 8, 1983, Herbert Mitgang, "Author Activism a Topic at German Book Fair," pp. 19, C11; April 18, 1983, "Seven Authors Assail U.S. over Nicaragua Policy," p. 7; June 17, 1985, Christopher Lehmann-Haupt, review of *On Writing and Politics,* pp. 17, C17; January 15, 1986, Edwin McDowell, "Grass Challenges Bellow on U.S. at PEN Meeting," pp. 19, C15; January 19, 1986, "Eavesdropping at a Writers' Conference," p. E6; February 5, 1986, James M. Markham, "The Cold War of Letters Raging in Günter Grass," pp. 19, C21; June 2, 1986, Walter Goodman, review of *Flood,* pp. 21, C14; June 29, 1987, Christopher Lehmann-Haupt, review of *The Rat,* pp. 19, C18; October 3, 1990, Herbert Mitgang, review of *Two States—One Nation?,* pp. B2, C17; February 19, 1991, "Günter Grass Wants Kohl Out," p. A4; November 18, 1992, Herbert Mitgang, review of *The Call of the Toad,* pp. B2, C25; December 29, 1992, Esther B. Fein, "Günter Grass Finds Politics Inescapable," pp. B1, C11; October 1, 1999, Roger Cohen, "Günter Grass Gets Nobel Prize in Literature," p. A13; October 3, 1999, Roger Cohen, "A Nobel for Günter Grass," p. WK2, and James Atlas, "Polemical Prize," p. WK17; January 5, 2000, Richard Bernstein, review of *My Century,* pp. B10, E10; December 14, 2000, Alan Riding, review of *Too Far Afield,* pp. B1, E1; January 26, 2001, Ken Johnson, review of "Too Far Afield: Graphics, 1970-2000," pp. B35, E37; April 8, 2003, Alan Riding, interview with Grass, p. E1; April 24, 2003, Richard Eder, review of *Crabwalk,* p. E8.

New York Times Book Review, August 14, 1966; March 29, 1970; September 30, 1973; November 12,

1978; November 23, 1978; May 17, 1981, Theodore Ziokowski, review of *The Meeting at Telgate,* pp. 7-8; March 14, 1982, review of *Headbirths,* pp. 11-13; May 16, 1982, review of *The Meeting at Telgte,* p. 39; December 5, 1982, review of *Headbirths,* p. 40; February 27, 1983; March 27, 1983; February 19, 1984, Ronald Radosh, review of *Trouble in Our Backyard: Central America and the United States in the Eighties,* pp. 5-6; June 23, 1985, James Markham, review of *On Writing and Politics,* p. 17; July 5, 1987, Janette Turner Hospital, review of *The Rat,* p. 6; May 21, 1989, review of *Show Your Tongue,* p. 12; September 30, 1990, Ralf Dahrendorf, review of *Two States—One Nation?,* p. 9; November 1, 1992, John Bayley, review of *The Call of the Toad,* p. 1; October 22, 1995, Stephen Kinzer, "Günter Grass: Germany's Last Heretic," p. 47; December 19, 1999, Peter Gay, review of *My Century,* p. 9; November 5, 2000, James J. Sheehan, review of *Too Far Afield,* p. 20; January 6, 2002, Scott Veale, review of *Too Far Afield,* p. 20; April 27, 2003, Jeremy Adler, review of *Crabwalk,* p. 12; May 4, 2003, review of *Crabwalk,* p. 26.

New York Times Magazine, April 29, 1984, John Vincour, "Europe's Intellectuals and American Power," pp. 60-69.

Observer (London, England), July 16, 1989, p. 43; October 14, 1990, p. 64.

Publishers Weekly, January 22, 1982, Barbara A. Bannon, review of *Headbirths,* p. 60; March 27, 1982, review of *The Meeting at Telgte,* pp. 42-43; May 3, 1985, review of *On Writing and Politics,* p. 59; May 22, 1987, Sybil Steinberg, review of *The Rat,* p. 64; April 21, 1989, Penny Kaganoff, review of *Show Your Tongue,* pp. 85-86; June 16, 1989, Sybil Steinberg, interview with Grass, pp. 54-55; September 7, 1990, Genevieve Stuttaford, review of *Two States—One Nation?,* p. 70; August 10, 1992, review of *The Call of the Toad,* p. 50; October 4, 1999, "Germany's Grass Wins 1999 Nobel," p. 10; November 15, 1999, review of *My Century,* p. 57; November 6, 2000, review of *Too Far Afield,* p. 72; March 3, 2003, review of *Crabwalk,* p. 51.

Review of Contemporary Fiction, spring, 2001, Richard J. Murphy, review of *Too Far Afield,* p. 192.

San Francisco Review of Books, July-August, 1981.

Saturday Review, May 20, 1972; November 11, 1978; May, 1981, Donald Newlove, review of *The Meeting at Telgte,* p. 71; March, 1982, John Irving, review of *Headbirths,* pp. 57-60.

Scala, number 6, 1981; number 1, 1982.

Spectator, May 18, 1974; January 27, 1996, Christian Caryl, review of *Ein weites Feld,* p. 28; October 17, 1992, Michael Hulse, review of *The Call of the Toad,* p. 6; October 9, 1999, Stephen Schwartz, "Ignoble Nobel," p. 18; January 1, 2000, Robert Macfarlane, review of *My Century,* pp. 26-27; March 29, 2003, Andrew Gimson, review of *Crabwalk,* pp. 49-50.

Statesman (India), January 28, 2001, review of *Show Your Tongue* and profile of Grass.

Time, January 4, 1963; April 13, 1978; April 28, 1980; May 18, 1981, Paul Gray, review of *The Meeting at Telgte,* p. 87; January 27, 1986; July 20, 1987, Paul Gray, review of *The Rat,* p. 73; October 11, 1999, "Milestones," p. 31; April 28, 2003, Michael Elliott, review of *Crabwalk,* p. 70.

Times (London, England), June 22, 1981; April 22, 1982; September 19, 1985; June 21, 1995, Robert Boyes, "Is the Writer a Traitor?," p. 37.

Times Educational Supplement, December 4, 1992, Brian Morton, review of *The Call of the Toad,* p. S10.

Times Literary Supplement, October 13, 1978; September 26, 1980; June 26, 1981; April 23, 1982; June 15, 1990, Peter Graves, review of *Deutscher Lastenausgleich: Wider das dumpfe Einheitsgebot: Reden und Gespräche, Texte zur Zeit* p. 631; June 19, 1992, "High Priests or Nut-Cases?," p. 14; October 9, 1992, Philip Brady, review of *Call of the Toad* and *Vier Jahrzehnte: Ein Werkstattbericht,* p. 24; October 13, 1995, Anne McElvoy, review of *Ein wFeld,* p. 26; August 20, 1999, Chris Greenhalgh, review of *Selected Poems: 1956-1993,* p. 21; October 8, 1999, Rudiger Gorner, review of *Mein Jahrundert,* p. 10; December 24, 1999, Hugh MacPherson, review of *My Century,* p. 20; December 8, 2000, Hugh MacPherson, review of *Too Far Afield,* p. 22; April 4, 2003, Jonathan Fasman, review of *Crabwalk,* p. 22.

Tribune Books (Chicago, IL), May 10, 1981; March 21, 1982; May 21, 1989; November 15, 1992.

Village Voice, October 25, 1973.

Virginia Quarterly Review, spring, 1975; winter, 1988, review of *The Rat,* p. 20.

Washington Post, March 2, 1972; April 10, 1982; February 15, 1993, David Streitfeld, review of *The Call of the Toad,* p. C1; September 26, 1995, Rick Atkinson, "Roar of the Literary Lion: His Book Mauled, Günter Grass Goes on the Attack," p. E1; October 1, 1999, Marc Fisher and Linton Weeks, "Günter Grass Wins Nobel for Literature," p. A01; December 17, 2000, Dennis Drabelle, review of *Too Far Afield,* p. T14.

Washington Post Book World, September 23, 1973; November 5, 1978; August 9, 1981; August 11, 1985, review of *On Writing and Politics,* p. 9; July 12, 1987, p. 5; November 8, 1992, p. 6.

World Literature Today, spring, 1981; autumn, 1981; winter, 1986, p. 194; summer, 1989, Ulf Zimmermann, review of *Zunge zeigen,* p. 477; spring, 1991, Patricia Pollock Brodsky, review of *Totes Holz,* pp. 299-300; autumn, 1991, Wes Blomster, review of *Ein Schnappchen namens DDR: Letzte Reden vorm Glockengelaut,* pp. 703-704; spring, 1993, Patricia Pollock Brodsky, review of *Unkenrufe,* p. 366; summer, 1994, Irmgard Elsner Hunt, review of *Novemberland: 13 Sonette* and *Rede vom Verlust: Uber den Niedergang der politischen Kultur im geeinten Deutschland,* pp. 559-560; summer, 1995, Irmgard Elsner Hunt, review of *In Kupfer, auf ein Stein: Das Grafische Werk,* pp. 578-579; spring, 1996, Christian Grawe, review of *Ein weites Feld,* pp. 387-388; winter, 2000, Theodore Ziolkowski, "Günter Grass's Century," p. 19; April-June, 2003, Irmgard Hunt, review of *Im Krebsgang,* pp. 128-129.

ONLINE

Nobel Prize Internet Archive, http://nobelprizes.com/ (October 1, 1999).*

*   *   *

GREEN, Brian
See CARD, Orson Scott

*   *   *

GREER, Germaine 1939-
(Rose Blight)

PERSONAL: Born January 29, 1939, near Melbourne, Australia; daughter of Eric Reginald (a newspaper advertising manager) and Margaret May Mary (Lanfrancan) Greer; married Paul de Feu (a journalist), 1968 (divorced, 1973). *Education:* University of Melbourne, B.A., 1959; University of Sydney, M.A., 1961; Newnham College, Cambridge, Ph.D., 1967. *Politics:* Anarchist. *Religion:* Atheist.

ADDRESSES: Home—Essex, England. *Agent*—Gillon Aitken Associates Ltd., 18-21 Cavaye Place, London SW10 9PT, England

CAREER: Sydney University, Sydney, Australia, senior tutor, 1963-64; also taught at a girls' school in Australia in the 1960s; University of Warwick, Coventry, England, lecturer in English, 1967-73; *Sunday Times,* London, England, columnist, 1971-73; American Program Bureau, lecturer, 1973-78; University of Tulsa, Tulsa, OK, visiting professor, graduate faculty of modern letters, 1979, and professor of modern letters, 1980-83; founder and director of Tulsa Centre for the Study of Women's Literature, 1979-82; director of Stump Cross Books, 1988—; special lecturer and unofficial fellow, Newnham College, Cambridge, 1989-98; University of Warwick, professor of English and comparative studies, 1998—. Writer. Has been an actress on a television comedy show in Manchester, England.

AWARDS, HONORS: Australian Junior Government scholarship, 1952; Diocesan scholarship, 1956; Senior Government scholarship, 1956; Teacher's College scholarship, 1956; Newnham College Commonwealth Scholar, 1964; J. R. Ackerly Prize, Internationazionale Mondello, 1989, for *Daddy, We Hardly Knew You;* honorary degree from University of Griffith, 1996.

WRITINGS:

The Female Eunuch, MacGibbon & Kee (London, England), 1970, McGraw-Hill (New York, NY), 1971, new edition, Farrar, Straus & Giroux (New York, NY), 2001.

The Obstacle Race: The Fortunes of Women Painters and Their Work, Farrar, Straus & Giroux (New York, NY), 1979, reprinted, Tauris Parke (New York, NY), 2001.

Sex and Destiny: The Politics of Human Fertility, Harper & Row (New York, NY), 1984.

Shakespeare (literary criticism), Oxford University Press (Oxford, England), 1986, new edition published as *Shakespeare: A Very Short Introduction,* Oxford University Press (New York, NY), 2002.

The Madwoman's Underclothes: Essays and Occasional Writings, Picador (New York, NY), 1986.

(Editor, with Jeslyn Medoff, Melinda Sansone, and Susan Hastings) *Kissing the Rod: An Anthology of Seventeenth-Century Women's Verse,* Farrar, Straus & Giroux (New York, NY), 1989.

(Editor and author of introduction and notes) Aphra Behn, *The Uncollected Verse of Aphra Behn,* Stump Cross Books (Stump Cross, Essex, England), 1989.

Daddy, We Hardly Knew You, Viking Penguin (New York, NY), 1989.

The Change: Women, Aging, and the Menopause, Hamish Hamilton (London, England), 1991.

Slip-Shod Sibyls: Recognition, Rejection, and the Woman Poet, Viking (New York, NY), 1995.

The Whole Woman, Alfred A. Knopf (New York, NY), 1999.

The Beautiful Boy, Rizzoli International (New York, NY), 2003, published as *The Boy,* Thames & Hudson (London, England), 2003.

Contributor to *River Journeys,* Hippocrene Books, c. 1985. Contributor to periodicals, including *Esquire, Listener, Oz, Spectator,* and, under pseudonym Rose Blight, *Private Eye.* Coadvisory editor for *The Cambridge Guide to Women's Writing in English,* Cambridge University Press (Cambridge, England), 1999. Cofounder of *Suck.*

SIDELIGHTS: Germaine Greer is a leading feminist, speaker, author, and literary critic, whose bold pronouncements in such works as *The Female Eunuch* and *The Whole Woman* have occasioned a great deal of spirited debate and controversy. Greer's writings, which also include *The Obstacle Race: The Fortunes of Women Painters and Their Work, Sex and Destiny: The Politics of Human Fertility,* a literary study titled *Shakespeare,* and the essay collections *The Madwoman's Underclothes* and *The Beautiful Boy,* have earned her serious consideration from mainstream, academic, and feminist critics. Praise for her work has typically been offered for her scholarly insight—especially notable in *Shakespeare* and her study of great but unrecognized women artists, *The Obstacle Race*—and the criticism has often been for her refusal to routinely espouse whatever literary or feminist ideas are most popular at a given time. In an interview conducted with Greer on the Web site *Enough Rope,* Andrew Denton declared that the author has "affected the lives of millions with her powerful views on how we should live." Belinda Luscombe in *Time International* called Greer "the ultimate Trojan Horse, gorgeous and witty, built to penetrate the seemingly unassailable fortress of patriarchy and let the rest of us foot soldiers in." Luscombe went on to laud Greer as "a joy to read, an eloquent maniac."

Greer became famous in America and abroad upon the publication of *The Female Eunuch.* Such celebrity was consistent with her roles as a television performer and as a self-avowed London "groupie" (her enthusiasm for jazz and popular music had brought her into contact with musicians and other members of Britain's underground culture). Some critics seized upon her slick and frankly sexual image as counterproductive to the feminist cause she espoused, but others welcomed her manifesto as "a rallying cry for sexual liberation," to quote a *Time* reviewer. While *The Female Eunuch* climbed the best-seller charts in both the United States and England, and *Vogue* magazine hailed her as "a super heroine," some members of the women's liberation movement questioned Greer's authority. While a *Newsweek* writer described her as "a dazzling combination of erudition, eccentricity and eroticism," some feminist writers wondered whether an indisputably attractive Shakespearean scholar could speak with understanding about the plight of women in general.

The proof lies in the book sales. *The Female Eunuch,* still in print, was ultimately translated into twelve languages. During a United States promotional tour in the spring of 1971, Greer furthered her message on television and radio talk shows, in *Life* magazine, and in a well-publicized debate with Norman Mailer, a novelist and self-confirmed "male chauvinist." The publicity generated enormous interest in the book, drawing readers from all walks of life.

Greer's basic argument, as explained in the introduction to *The Female Eunuch,* is that women's "sexuality is both denied and misrepresented by being identified as passivity." She explains that women, urged from childhood to live up to an "Eternal Feminine" stereotype, are valued for characteristics associated with the castrate—"timidity, plumpness, languor, delicacy and preciosity"—hence the book's title. From the viewpoint of this primary assumption, Greer examines not only the problems of women's sexuality, but their psychological development, their relationships with men, their social position, and their cultural history. What most struck early critics of the book was that she considered "the castration of our true female personality . . . not the fault of men, but our own, and history's." Thus the *Newsweek* writer considered Greer's work "women's liberation's most realistic and least anti-male manifesto." Christopher Lehmann-Haupt, writing in the *New York Times,* called it "a book that combines the best of masculinity *and* femininity."

Greer followed up the success of *The Female Eunuch* with her account of human social institutions called *Sex and Destiny: The Politics of Human Fertility.* In sharp contrast to the optimism in her first book, the author depicts sexual freedom as a step backward rather than forward in society. On the whole, Greer informs the reader that the modern world is decidedly opposed to reproduction. She writes, "Historically human societies have been pro-child; modern society is unique in that it is profoundly hostile to children." Greer objects to contemporary attitudes toward sex and children, asserting that they are treated as commodities. "In Miss Greer's current view," wrote Carol Iannone in *Commentary,* "the West is now oversexed, subfertile, and hopelessly materialistic."

Greer's collection of essays *The Madwoman's Underclothes: Essays and Occasional Writings* covers such subjects as fertility, fashion, and sex roles. The author comes across as feisty as she did in her first book by challenging the status quo with her confrontational stance on feminism. Her essays range in topic from the legalization of marijuana, to pornography, to the death of rock star Jimi Hendrix. The book is divided into three parts, and the essays encompass the years 1968 to 1985. They serve as an ideal starting ground to those unfamiliar with her work. *New York Times Book Review* critic Linda Blandford said of the book that the author's "strengths and weaknesses, successes and failures are all here; they are the human stumblings of feminism itself, wanting it all while wanting none of it."

In 1989 Greer published a more personal book than her previous volumes, *Daddy, We Hardly Knew You,* which records her painstaking investigations into the life and personality of her father, Reginald "Reg" Greer, after his death in 1983. Greer's "quest" to reconstruct her father's lineage leads to an international tour through the landscape and archives of Britain, Australia, South Africa, India, Tuscany, Malta, and finally Tasmania, where she discovers her father's humble upbringing as a foster child whose lifelong reticence was intended to bury his illegitimate origin. According to Jill Johnston in the *New York Times Book Review,* the story of Reg Greer "is a very sad story, which his daughter glosses with her rage and transcends with her vast knowledge of all sorts of things." The paucity of information produced by her frustrating research is supplemented by expansive digressions that portray the land and people encountered on her travels, including an entire chapter entitled "Sidetrack" that documents various physical and historical aspects of the Australian continent. Nancy Mairs described the book in the *Los Angeles Times Book Review* as "part childhood reminiscence, part travelogue, part genealogy, part history, part social commentary." As the author can no longer view her father as a "hero" or "prince in disguise," Johnston concluded, "In the end Germaine Greer can't reconcile her father's lack of love with her understanding of the fear that made him lie to conceal his lowly origins."

Greer produced a forceful indictment of modern youth culture with *The Change: Women, Aging, and the Menopause,* renaming the later female life stage "climacteria" and invoking the term "anophobia" to describe the irrational fear and hostility directed toward older women. As Joan Frank observed in the *San Francisco Review of Books,* Greer identifies menopause as "a real and crucial transition in a woman's life for which no—repeat, *no*—reliable information, clear role models, rites of passage, historic or cultural sanctions exist as they do for comparable transitions: birth, the onset of menarche, marriage, childbirth, and death." Gleaning evidence from diverse and unlikely sources such as "historical accounts, memoirs, correspondence from the court of Louis XIV, old medical textbooks, anthropology tracts, novels, and poems both familiar and obscure," as Natalie Augier noted in the *New York Times Book Review,* Greer "talks with unvarnished candor about the invisibility of the middle-aged woman in our own culture, the unfairness of a system that lionizes the silver-haired male while scorning his female counterpart as beyond use, pathetic, desiccated, desexualized, a crone." Katha Pollitt remarked in a *New Yorker* review that Greer's version of postmenopausal life is "so charming, so seductively rendered—especially when it's contrasted with the situation of the wistful wives, desperate party girls, and breast-implanted exercise addicts which for her constitutes the only alternative—that the reader may find herself barely able to wait."

In *Slip-Shod Sibyls: Recognition, Rejection, and the Woman Poet,* Greer challenges the validity of feminist revisionism and the status of celebrated female poets in the Western canon, including Sappho, Aphra Behn, Christina Rossetti, and Elizabeth Barrett Browning. As Carol Rumens said in a *Times Literary Supplement* review, "Though Greer admits we should carry on reclaiming women's work, she believes that 'to insist

on equal representation or positive discrimination so that She-poetry appears on syllabuses in our schools and universities is to continue the system of false accounting that produced the double standard in the first place.'" Camille Paglia noted in the *Observer Review* that "the absence of premodern female poets from the curriculum," in Greer's view, "is not entirely due to sexism but rather to a lack of quality." Citing the life and work of Sylvia Plath and Anne Sexton, Greer similarly dismisses contemporary female poetry for its futile, and often fatal, narcissism. According to Greer, as Margaret Anne Doody summarized in the *London Review of Books:* "The twentieth century merely adds to the heap of sickly, self-regarding and self-destructive female poets. Lacking education, training in the Great Tradition, certainty about voice or subject-matter—and in the absence of any sense of how the culture of publicity and publication can work—woman writers of poetry over three centuries have exhibited themselves delving into their emotions. Poetry with them constantly becomes a morbid exercise." Furthermore, Greer contends that women poets were often responsible for their own artistic shortcomings. Fleur Adcock wrote in a *New Statesman & Society* review that Greer suggests such female writers "took bad advice; they fell for flattery; they wrote fast and without revising sufficiently; and they failed to understand 'what was involved in making a poem.'" Praising *Slip-Shod Sibyls* and Greer's significant contribution to feminist criticism, Paglia concluded: "When the history of modern women is written, Germaine Greer will be seen as one who, like Jane Austen, permanently redefined female intellect."

Thirty years after the publication of the groundbreaking *The Female Eunuch,* Greer followed up her arguments with a sequel, *The Whole Woman.* The book is not short on controversy, as Greer urges women to quit struggling for equality with men and instead focus on liberation. In her refusal to accept male-dominated institutions, Greer postulates that the use of birth control is simply a ploy by males to restrict women from having children and being mothers. *The Whole Woman* is a more optimistic—and more libertarian—book than its predecessor. To Greer, women must break away from the weight of cultural conditioning in order to take control of their lives. In a review for the *Los Angeles Times,* Suse Linfield wrote that Greer's view "is neither pessimistic nor triumphal; *The Whole Woman* seeks not to depress women (a clearly redundant task) but to alert them to how and why things are still so bad." A *Time* reviewer called the work "provocative, brilliantly engaging and maddeningly contradictory" and praised Greer for taking "issues on which most progressive women thought they had positions and sets a standard all her own."

Greer's *The Beautiful Boy* muses on the moment in a young man's life when he is no longer a child but just barely a man. Greer sees this fleeting moment as transcendentally inspiring to artists and, if women are frank, sexually exciting as well. She uses historical texts and works of visual art to delve into the changing meanings attached to male beauty in various eras. One point of the work is that women of all ages should feel free to appreciate the beauty of the young male. According to Nadine Dalton Speidel in *Library Journal*, Greer's aim is to encourage both men and women to "have the freedom to see and be seen as sexual beings and more."

Greer remains decidedly liberationist in her views and suggests that her writings need not be seen as blueprints for lifestyle change. "I don't want to tell people to do anything," she said in *Time*. "I have put down what makes my heart ache, and either it will be helpful to people, or it won't." As many critics see it, Greer's personal heartaches echo the sensibilities of a multitude of women at the turn of the twenty-first century.

BIOGRAPHICAL AND CRITICAL SOURCES:

BOOKS

Contemporary Literary Criticism, Volume 131, Gale (Detroit, MI), 2000.
Feminist Writers, St. James Press (Detroit, MI), 1996.
Todd, Janet, editor, *Women Writers Talking*, Holmes & Meier (New York, NY), 1983.
Wallace, Christine, *Germaine Greer: Untamed Shrew*, Faber & Faber (New York, NY), 1998.

PERIODICALS

Alberta Report, August 16, 1999, Celeste McGovern, review of *The Whole Woman*, p. 37.
Atlantic, February, 1990, Phoebe-Lou Adams, review of *Daddy, We Hardly Knew You*, p. 108.

Australian Book Review, May, 1999, review of *The Whole Woman*, pp. 4-5.
Booklist, April 1, 1999, Mary Carroll, review of *The Whole Woman*, p. 1363; December 15, 2003, Ray Olson, review of *The Beautiful Boy*, p. 718.
Book World, May 23, 1999, review of *The Whole Woman*, p. 8.
Chicago Tribune Books, January 11, 1990, p. 6.
Choice, June, 2000, P. Palmer, review of *The Cambridge Guide to Women's Writing in English*, p. 1782.
Commentary, August, 1984, Carol Iannone, review of *Sex and Destiny: The Politics of Human Fertility*, p. 71; September, 1999, Samuel McCracken, "Blast from the Past," p. 65.
Community Care, June 10, 1999, review of *The Whole Woman*, p. 32.
Detroit News, May 9, 1971.
Economist, April 22, 1989, review of *Daddy, We Hardly Knew You*, p. 84; March 13, 1999, review of *The Whole Woman*, p. 4.
First Things: A Monthly Journal of Religion and Public Life, October, 1999, Midge Decter, "Liberating Germaine Greer," p. 21.
Globe and Mail (Toronto, Ontario, Canada), February 25, 1984; October 17, 1987; April 29, 1989; August 5, 1989; May 1, 1999, review of *The Whole Woman*, p. D11.
Guardian (London, England), March 2, 1999, Joan Smith, "Women v. Real Women," p. T6.
Human Life Review, fall, 1999, Faith Abbott McFadden, review of *The Whole Woman*, p. 62.
Independent (London, England), March 3, 1999, "So, Germaine, Since Animals Now Have Rights, How about Men?," p. S1.
Kirkus Reviews, April 15, 1999, review of *The Whole Woman*, p. 599.
JAMA: Journal of the American Medical Association, February 2, 1994, Mona M. Shangold, review of *The Change: Women, Aging and the Menopause*, p. 404.
Journal of Popular Culture, fall, 2002, Roger Neustadter, "Oh Dad Poor Dad," p. 384.
Lancet, December 23, 1995, John Bignall, review of *Slip-shod Sybils: Recognition, Rejection, and the Woman Poet*, p. 1691.
Law Society Journal, August, 2001, Sandra Berns, review of *The Cambridge Guide to Women's Writing in English*, p. 94.
Library Journal, May 15, 1999, Barbara Ann Hutcheson, review of *The Whole Woman*, p. 113;

December, 2003, Nadine Dalton Speidel, review of *The Beautiful Boy,* p. 108.

Life, May 7, 1971.

Listener, October 22, 1970.

London Review of Books, December 14, 1995, p. 14-15; July 15, 1999, review of *The Whole Woman,* p. 7.

Los Angeles Times, March 7, 1984; November 26, 1987; April 5, 1999, Marjorie Miller, "Think You've Come a Long Way, Baby? Think Again, Author Says," p. E1; June 3, 1999, Suse Linfield, "Compelling, If Sloppy, Feminist Manifesto," p. E3.

Los Angeles Times Book Review, September 6, 1987; April 8, 1990, Nancy Mairs, "Germaine Greer As Dogged Daughter," p. 8.

Maclean's, May 24, 1999, Patricia Chisholm, "Greer's Call to Arms," p. 53.

Nation, June 7, 1971, Claudia Dreifus, review of *The Female Eunuch,* p. 728; May 26, 1984, Linda Gordon, review of *Sex and Destiny,* p. 645; December 5, 1987, Carol Sternhell, review of *Madwoman's Underclothes: Essays and Occasional Writings,* p. 690.

National Review, July 13, 1984, Maggie Gallagher, review of *Sex and Destiny,* p. 42; January 18, 1993, Maggie Gallagher, review of *The Change,* p. 49.

Natural Health, March-April, 1993, review of *The Change,* p. 127.

New Leader, March 17, 1971, Anne Richardson Roiphe, review of *The Female Eunuch,* p. 8.

New Republic, May 21, 1984, Barbara Ehrenreich, review of *Sex and Destiny,* p. 32; March 26, 1990, Hermione Lee, "Mother Country," p. 33; January 31, 1994, p. 29; May 31, 1999, Margaret Talbot, "The Female Misogynist," p. 34.

New Statesman, November 21, 1986, Sara Maitland, review of *Madwoman's Underclothes,* p. 29; February 26, 1999, Melanie McDonagh, review of *The Whole Woman,* p. 12; March 12, 1999, Charlotte Raven, review of *The Whole Woman,* p. 48; December 17, 2001, Melanie McDonagh, "Germaine Greer," p. 71.

New Statesman & Society, October 11, 1991, Sara Maitland, "Hagiography," p. 23; October 6, 1995, Fleur Adcock, "Killed with Kindness," p. 37.

Newsweek, March 22, 1971; November 16, 1992, p. 79.

New York, October 12, 1992, Rhoda Koenig, "Cronehood Is Powerful," p. 74.

New Yorker, April 16, 1990, p. 116; November 2, 1992, Katha Pollitt, "The Romantic Climacteric," p. 106.

New York Review of Books, May 31, 1984, Peter Singer, review of *Sex and Destiny,* p. 15.

New York Times, April 20, 1971; November 1, 1979; March 5, 1984; April 23, 1984; May 18, 1999, Michiko Kakutani, "The Female Condition, Re-explored Thirty Years Later," p. B9.

New York Times Book Review, October 11, 1987, Linda Blandford, review of *Madwoman's Underclothes,* p. 14; January 28, 1990, Jill Johnston, review of *Daddy, We Hardly Knew You;* October 11, 1992, Natalie Augier, "The Transit of Woman," p. 32; May 9, 1999, Camille Paglia, "Back to the Barricades," p. 19.

Observer (London, England), October 11, 1970; February 14, 1999, interview with Germaine Greer, p. 27; February 14, 1999, Bella Bathurst, "Do Not Go Genitally into That Good Night," p. 27; March 7, 1999, review of *The Whole Woman,* p. 11.

Observer Review, October 8, 1995, p. 14.

People, May 21, 1984, Deirdre Donahue, review of *Sex and Destiny,* p. 18; May 15, 2000, "Fit to Be Tied: An Obsessed Young Woman Leaves Feminist Writer Germaine Greer Bound and Distressed but Unscathed," p. 78.

Psychology Today, April, 1988, Pamela Black, review of *Madwoman's Underclothes,* p. 79.

Publishers Weekly, May 25, 1984; December 1, 1989, p. 42; August 24, 1992, review of *The Change,* p. 66; March 22, 1999, review of *The Whole Woman,* p. 76.

San Francisco Review of Books, January, 1992, Joan Frank, review of *The Change,* p. 6.

Spectator, March 6, 1999, review of *The Whole Woman,* p. 36.

Sunday Times (London, England), February 28, 1999, Fay Weldon, "Women Are Slaves, but No Longer of Men," p. 19.

Time, April 16, 1984; February 5, 1990, Martha Duffy, review of *Daddy, We Hardly Knew You,* p. 68; October 26, 1992, Barbara Ehrenreich, review of *The Change,* p. 80; May 10, 1999, "The Force Is with Her," p. 88.

Time International, October 25, 1999, Belinda Luscombe, "Germaine Greer: With Verbal Brilliance, Rock 'n' Roll Swagger and a Talent for Outrage, She Became Feminism's First Superstar," p. 76.

Times (London, England), March 20, 1986; October 23, 1986; March 20, 1989; March 25, 1989.

Times Literary Supplement, June 17, 1988; March 17, 1989; October 13, 1995, p. 29; March 19, 1999, Ferdinand Mount, "Still Strapped in the Cuirass," p. 6.

Washington Post, November 22, 1979; January 24,
    1990; June 12, 1999, Jennifer Frey, "Germaine
    Greer's Trouble with Men," pp. C1, C5.
Washington Post Book World, May 23, 1999, Elizabeth
    Ward, "The Trouble with Women," p. 8.
Washington Times, June 28, 1999, Ann Geracimos,
    "Still a Defiant, Feminist Contrarian," p. 8.
Woman's Journal, March, 1999, review of *The Whole
    Woman,* p. 19.
Women's Review of Books, January, 1993.
World Press Review, May, 1999, Kara J. Peterson,
    review of *The Whole Woman,* p. 37.

ONLINE

Enough Rope with Andrew Denton, http://www.abc.
    net.au/enoughrope/stories/ (August 24, 2004),
    "Germaine Greer: Enough Rope, Episode 27,
    Transcript."
Naplesnews.com, http://www.naplesnews.com/ (May
    31, 2002).
New York Times on the Web, http://www.nytimes.com/
    (May 31, 2002), Camille Paglia, biography of Ger-
    maine Greer.
Salon.com, http://www.salon.com/ (May 31, 2002),
    Laura Miller, "Brilliant Careers."*

John Grisham

*   *   *

GRISHAM, John 1955-

PERSONAL: Born February 8, 1955, in Jonesboro,
AR; son of a construction worker and a homemaker;
married Renee Jones; children: Ty, Shea (daughter).
Education: Mississippi State University, B.S., University of Mississippi, J.D. *Religion:* Baptist.

ADDRESSES: Home—Charlottesville, VA. *Agent*—Jay
Garon-Brooke Associates, Inc., 101 West 55th St.,
Suite 5K, New York, NY 10019.

CAREER: Writer and lawyer. Admitted to the Bar of
the State of Mississippi, 1981; lawyer in private practice in Southaven, MS, 1981-90. Served in Mississippi
House of Representatives, 1984-90.

AWARDS, HONORS: Inducted into Academy of
Achievement, 1993.

WRITINGS:

NOVELS

A Time to Kill, Wynwood Press (New York, NY),
    1989.
The Firm, Doubleday (New York, NY), 1991.
The Pelican Brief, Doubleday (New York, NY), 1992.
The Client, Doubleday (New York, NY), 1993.
John Grisham (collection), Dell (New York, NY),
    1993.
The Chamber, Doubleday (New York, NY), 1994.
The Rainmaker, Doubleday (New York, NY), 1995.
The Runaway Jury, Doubleday (New York, NY), 1996.
The Partner, Doubleday (New York, NY), 1997.
The Street Lawyer, Doubleday (New York, NY), 1998.
The Testament, Doubleday (New York, NY), 1999.
The Brethren, Doubleday (New York, NY), 2000.
A Painted House, Doubleday (New York, NY), 2001.
Skipping Christmas, Doubleday (New York, NY),
    2001.
The Summons, Doubleday (New York, NY), 2002.
The King of Torts, Doubleday (New York, NY), 2003.

The Bleachers, Doubleday (New York, NY), 2003.
The Last Juror, Doubleday (New York, NY), 2004.

Also author of screenplays *The Gingerbread Man* (under pseudonym Al Hayes), and *Mickey.*

ADAPTATIONS: The Firm was adapted as a film, directed by Sydney Pollack and starring Tom Cruise, Gene Hackman, and Jeanne Tripplehorn, Paramount, 1993; *The Pelican Brief* was adapted as a film, directed by Alan J. Pakula and starring Julia Roberts and Denzel Washington, 1994; *The Client* was adapted as a film, directed by Joel Schumacher and starring Susan Sarandon and Tommy Lee Jones, 1994; *The Chamber* was adapted as a film, directed by James Foley and starring Chris O'Donnell and Gene Hackman, 1996; *A Time to Kill* was adapted as a film, directed by Schumacher and starring Matthew McConaughey and Sandra Bullock, 1996; *The Rainmaker* was adapted as a film, directed by Francis Ford Coppola and starring Matt Damon and Claire Danes, 1997; *Runaway Jury* was adapted as a film, directed by Gary Fleder and starring Hackman and Dustin Hoffman, 2003; *Skipping Christmas* was adapted as a film, starring Tim Allen and Jamie Lee Curtis, Columbia, 2004.

SIDELIGHTS: The author of seventeen back-to-back bestsellers, many of which have been turned into blockbuster movies, John Grisham can count his revenues and copies sold of his legal thrillers in the hundreds of millions. With his works translated into more than thirty languages, Grisham was one of the major success stories in publishing during the 1990s. As Malcolm Jones noted in *Newsweek,* Grisham was "the best-selling author" of the decade with his formula of "David and Goliath go to court," and the success of his books has helped to make legal thrillers one of the most popular genres among U.S. readers. Jones further commented, "As part of an elite handful of megaselling authors that includes Stephen King, Danielle Steele, Michael Crichton and Tom Clancy, Grisham has literally taken bookselling to places it's never been before—not just to airport kiosks but to price clubs and . . . online bookselling." Grisham's bestsellerdom even extends to countries with a legal system completely different than that in the United States. "He sells to everyone," Jones continued, "from teens to senior citizens, from lawyers in Biloxi to housewives in Hong Kong."

When Grisham began writing his first novel, he never dreamed he would become one of America's best-selling novelists. Yet the appeal of his legal thrillers such as *The Firm, The Pelican Brief, The Client, The Rainmaker,* and *The Summons,* among others, has been so great that initial hardcover print runs number in the hundreds of thousands and the reading public regularly buys millions of copies. The one-time lawyer now enjoys a celebrity status that few writers will ever know. "We think of ourselves as regular people, I swear we do," Grisham was quoted as saying of himself and his family by Keli Pryor in *Entertainment Weekly.* "But then someone will drive 200 miles and show up on my front porch with books for me to sign. Or an old friend will stop by and want to drink coffee for an hour. It drives me crazy." As he told Jones, "I'm a famous writer in a country where nobody reads."

As a youth, Grisham had no dreams of becoming a writer, although he did like to read. Born in Jonesboro, Arkansas, in 1955, he was the son of a construction-worker father and a homemaker mother. His father traveled extensively in his job, and the Grisham family moved many times. Each time the family took up residence in a new town, Grisham would immediately go to the public library to get a library card. "I was never a bookworm," he maintained in an interview for *Bookreporter.com.* "I remember reading Dr. Seuss, the 'Hardy Boys,' *Emil and the Detectives,* Chip Hilton, and lots of Mark Twain and Dickens." Another constant for Grisham was his love of baseball, something he has retained in adulthood. One way he and his brothers gauged the quality of each new hometown was by inspecting its little-league ballpark.

In 1967 the family moved to a permanent home in Southaven, Mississippi, where Grisham enjoyed greater success in high school athletics than he did in English composition, a subject in which he earned a D grade. After graduation, he enrolled at Northwest Junior College in Senatobia, Mississippi, where he remained for a year, playing baseball for the school team. Transferring to Delta State University in Cleveland, Mississippi, he continued with his baseball career until he realized that he was not going to make it to the big leagues. Transferring to Mississippi State University, Grisham studied accounting with the ambition of eventually becoming a tax attorney. By the time he earned his law degree from the University of Mississippi, however, his interest had shifted to criminal law, and he returned to Southaven to establish a practice in that field.

Although his law practice was successful, Grisham grew restless in his new career. He switched to the more lucrative field of civil law and won many cases, but the sense of personal dissatisfaction remained. Hoping to somehow make a difference in the world, he entered politics with the aim of reforming his state's educational system. Running as a Democrat, he won a post in the state legislature; four years later, he was reelected. After a total of seven years in public office, Grisham became convinced that he would never be able to cut through the red tape of government bureaucracy in his effort to improve Mississippi's educational system, and he resigned his post in 1990.

While working in the legislature, Grisham continued to run his law office. His first book, *A Time to Kill,* was inspired by a scene he saw one day in court when a preadolescent girl testified against her rapist. "I felt everything in those moments," Grisham recalled to Pryor. "Revulsion, total love for that child, hate for that defendant. Everyone in that courtroom wanted a gun to shoot him." Unable to get the story out of his mind, be began to wonder what would happen if the girl's father had killed his daughter's assailant. Grisham disclosed to an interviewer with *People,* "I became obsessed wondering what it would be like if the girl's father killed that rapist and was put on trial. I had to write it down." Soon he had the core of a book dealing with a black father who shoots the white man who raped his daughter. "I never felt such emotion and human drama in my life," he said in the interview.

Writing his first novel, let alone publishing it, was no easy task for Grisham. "Because I have this problem of starting projects and not completing them, my goal for this book was simply to finish it," he revealed to *Publishers Weekly* interviewer Michelle Bearden. "Then I started thinking that it would be nice to have a novel sitting on my desk, something I could point to and say, 'Yeah, I wrote that.' But it didn't consume me. I had way too much going on to make it a top priority. If it happened, it happened." Working sixty- to seventy-hour weeks between his law practice and political duties, Grisham rose at five in the morning to write an hour a day on his first novel, thinking of the activity as a hobby rather than a serious effort at publication.

Finishing the manuscript in 1987, Grisham next had to look for an agent. He was turned down by several before finally receiving a positive response from Jay Garon. Agent and author encountered a similarly difficult time trying to find a publisher; 5,000 copies of

the book were finally published by Wynwood Press, and Grisham received a check for 15,000 dollars. He purchased 1,000 copies of the book himself, peddling them at garden-club meetings and libraries and giving many of them away to family and friends. Ironically, *A Time to Kill* is now rated by some commentators as the finest of Grisham's novels. Furthermore, according to Pryor, "Those first editions are now worth 3,900 dollars each," and after being republished, "the novel Grisham . . . couldn't give away has 8.6 million copies in print and has spent eighty weeks on the bestseller lists."

Despite the limited initial success of *A Time to Kill,* Grisham was not discouraged from trying his hand at another novel. The second time around, he decided to follow guidelines set forth in a *Writer's Digest* article for plotting a suspense novel. The result was *The Firm,* the story of a corrupt Memphis-based law firm established by organized crime for purposes of shielding and falsifying crime-family earnings. Recruited to the practice is Mitchell McDeere, a promising Harvard law school graduate who is overwhelmed by the company's apparent extravagance. When his criminal bosses discover that McDeere has been indulging his curiosity, he becomes an instant target of both the firm and the authorities monitoring the firm's activities. When he runs afoul of the ostensible good guys, McDeere finds himself in seemingly endless danger.

Grisham was not as motivated when writing *The Firm* as he had been when composing *A Time to Kill,* but with his wife's encouragement he finished the book. Before he even began trying to sell the manuscript, he learned that someone had acquired a bootlegged copy of it and was willing to give him 600,000 dollars to turn it into a movie script. Within two weeks, Doubleday, one of the many publishers that had previously rejected *A Time to Kill,* offered Grisham a contract.

Upon *The Firm*'s publication, several reviewers argued that Grisham had not attained a high art form, although it was generally conceded that he had put together a compelling thriller. *Los Angeles Times Book Review* critic Charles Champlin wrote that the "character penetration is not deep, but the accelerating tempo of paranoia-driven events is wonderful." Chicago *Tribune Books* reviewer Bill Brashler offered similar praise, proclaiming that *The Firm* reads "like a whirlwind." The novel was listed on the *New York Times* bestseller list for nearly a year and sold approximately ten times as many copies as its predecessor. By the time the film version was released, there were more than seven million copies of *The Firm* in print. This amazing success gave Grisham the means he needed to build his dream house, quit his law practice, and devote himself entirely to writing.

In a mere one hundred days, Grisham wrote another legal thriller, *The Pelican Brief,* which introduces readers to brilliant, beautiful female law student Darby Shaw. When two U.S. Supreme Court justices are murdered, Shaw postulates a theory as to why the crimes were committed. Just telling people about her idea makes her gravely vulnerable to the corrupt law firm responsible for the killings.

In reviewing the book, some critics complained that Grisham follows the premise of *The Firm* too closely, with John Skow writing in his review for *Time* that *The Pelican Brief* "is as close to its predecessor as you can get without running *The Firm* through the office copier." However, Grisham also received praise for creating another exciting story. Frank J. Prial, writing in the *New York Times Book Review,* observed that, despite some flaws in *The Pelican Brief,* Grisham "has an ear for dialogue and is a skillful craftsman." The book enjoyed success comparable to *The Firm,* selling millions of copies.

In just six months, Grisham put together yet another bestseller titled *The Client.* This legal thriller focuses on a young boy who, after learning a sinister secret, turns to a motherly lawyer for protection from both the mob and the FBI. Like *The Firm* and *The Pelican Brief,* the book drew lukewarm reviews but became a bestseller and a major motion picture. During the spring of 1993, after *The Client* came out and *A Time to Kill* was republished, Grisham was in the rare and enviable position of having a book at the top of the hardcover bestseller list and books in the first, second, and third spots on the paperback bestseller list as well.

Grisham acknowledged to an *Entertainment Weekly* interviewer that his second, third, and fourth books are formula-driven. He described his recipe for a bestseller in the following way: "You throw an innocent person in there and get 'em caught up in a conspiracy and you get 'em out." He also admitted to rushing through the writing of *The Pelican Brief* and *The Client,* resulting in "some damage" to the books' quality. Yet he

also complained that the critical community treats popular writers harshly. "I've sold too many books to get good reviews anymore," he told Pryor. "There's a lot of jealousy, because [reviewers] think they can write a good novel or a best-seller and get frustrated when they can't. As a group, I've learned to despise them."

With his fifth novel, Grisham departs from his proven formula and proceeds at a more leisurely pace. Not only did he take a full nine months to write *The Chamber,* a book in which the "good guys" and "bad guys" are not as clearly defined as in his previous efforts, but the book itself, at almost 500 pages, takes time to unravel its story line. The novel is a detailed study of a family's history, an examination of the relationship between lawyer and client, and a description of life on death row. *The Chamber* is "a curiously rich milieu for a Grisham novel," according to *Entertainment Weekly* critic Mark Harris, "and it allows the author to do some of his best writing since [*A Time to Kill.*]" Skow credited Grisham with producing a thought-provoking treatise on the death penalty, and noted in *Time* that *The Chamber* "has the pace and characters of a thriller, but little else to suggest that it was written by the glib and cheeky author of Grisham's legal entertainments. . . . Grisham may not change opinions with this sane, civil book, and he may not even be trying to. What he does ask, very plainly, is an important question: Is this what you want?" A reviewer for the London *Sunday Times* stated that "Grisham may do without poetry, wit and style, and offer only the simplest characterisation. The young liberal lawyer may be colourless and the spooky old prisoner one-dimensional; but there is no doubt that this ex-lawyer knows how to tell a story." While *The Chamber* was less obviously commercial than his previous three books, Grisham had little trouble selling the movie rights for a record fee.

The Rainmaker features a young lawyer, Rudy Baylor, recently graduated from law school, who finds himself desperate for a job when the small firm he had planned to work for is bought out by a large, prestigious Memphis firm that has no use for him. After going to work for Bruiser Stone, a shady lawyer with underworld clients, Baylor finds himself averting an FBI raid on Stone's firm while also trying to pursue a lawsuit brought by a terminally ill leukemia patient against an insurance company that has refused to pay for her treatment. While some reviewers again directed harsh criticism at Grisham for his "pedestrian prose" and "ridiculously implausible" plot—in the words of *New York Times* critic Michiko Kakutani—others praised the novel. Garry Abrams, for instance, writing in the *Los Angeles Times Book Review,* commended the author's "complex plotting," noting: "In his loping, plain prose, Grisham handles all his themes with admirable dexterity and clarity."

Grisham also garnered warm critical comments for *The Runaway Jury,* a novel that details the ability of a few individuals to manipulate a jury in the direction that will bring them the greatest financial reward. Writing in the *New York Times,* Christopher Lehmann-Haupt remarked that Grisham's "prose continues to be clunky, the dialogue merely adequate and the characters as unsubtle as pushpins." But the critic also felt that "the plot's eventual outcome is far more entertainingly unpredictable" than Grisham's previous novels, and he declared that Grisham "for once . . . is telling a story of genuine significance."

Grisham continued his streak of phenomenally popular novels with *The Partner,* about a law-firm partner who fakes his own death and absconds with ninety million dollars. Discussing his less-than-virtuous protagonist, Grisham told Mel Gussow of the *New York Times,* "I wanted to show that with money you can really manipulate the system. You can buy your way out of trouble." *Philadelphia Inquirer* reviewer Robert Drake called *The Partner* "a fine book, wholly satisfying, and a superb example of a masterful storyteller's prowess captured at its peak."

With *Street Lawyer* Grisham once again presents a young lawyer on the fast track who has a life-altering experience. The fast pace and moral stance of the novel attracted a chorus of praise. Reviewing the book in *Entertainment Weekly,* Tom De Haven noted that "success hasn't spoiled John Grisham. Instead of churning out rote legal thrillers, his court reporting keeps getting better." De Haven further noted that Grisham, while lacking the "literary genius" of John Steinbeck, "does share with him the conscience of a social critic and the soul of a preacher." *People* reviewer Cynthia Sanz similarly reported that Grisham "has forsaken some of his usual suspense and fireworks in favor of an unabashedly heart-tugging portrait of homelessness." However, Sanz further noted that the author does not sacrifice his "zippy pacing" to do so. Praise not only appeared in the popular press: "In

a powerful story," wrote Jacalyn N. Kolk in the *Florida Bar Journal,* "John Grisham tells it like it is on both sides of the street." Kolk felt that this "entertaining" novel "may stir some of us [lawyers] to pay more attention to the world around us."

The Testament provides another departure from the usual Grisham formula. As a reviewer for *Publishers Weekly* noted, "Grisham confounds expectations by sweeping readers into adventure in the Brazilian wetlands and, more urgently, into a man's search for spiritual renewal." Grisham has firsthand experience of Brazil, having traveled there often and once even helping to build houses there for the poor. His novel eschews the legal wrangling and courtroom suspense his readers have come to expect. Instead, in this tale he proves he "can spin an adventure yarn every bit as well as he can craft a legal thriller," according to *Newsweek* reviewer Jones. A reviewer for *Publishers Weekly* felt that while the storytelling is not "subtle," Grisham's use of the suspense novel format to "explore questions of being and faith puts him squarely in the footsteps of Dickens and Graham Greene." The same reviewer concluded that *The Testament* is "sincere, exciting, and tinged with wonder." Speaking with Jones, Grisham remarked, "The point I was trying to make . . . was that if you spend your life pursuing money and power, you're going to have a pretty sad life."

Lawyers and judges of a much different ilk populate Grisham's eleventh novel, *The Brethren.* Noting that Grisham veers away from his usual David-and-Goliath scenario, a reviewer for *Publishers Weekly* still felt that "all will be captivated by this clever thriller that presents as crisp a cast as he's yet devised, and as grippingly sardonic yet bitingly moral a scenario as he's ever imagined." Writing in *Entertainment Weekly,* De Haven also commented on the novel's cast of ne'er do wells, noting that "if you can get past [Grisham's] creepy misanthropy, he's written a terrifically entertaining story."

With *A Painted House,* initially serialized in *The Oxford American*—a small literary magazine Grisham co-owns—the author does the unpredictable: he presents readers with a book with no lawyers. "It's a highly fictionalized childhood memoir of a month in the life of a seven-year-old kid, who is basically me," Grisham explained to *Entertainment Weekly*'s Benjamin Svetkey. *Book* contributor Liz Seymour called the novel "genre-busting," and "the unsentimental story of a single harvest season in the Arkansas Delta as seen through the eyes of the seven-year-old son and grandson of cotton farmers." Though the tale may be without lawyers, it is not without conflict and incident, including trouble between the migrant workers young Luke Chandler's family brings in for the cotton harvest and a tornado that threatens to destroy the Chandler livelihood. A reviewer for *Publishers Weekly* noted that Grisham's "writing has evolved with nearly every book," and though the "mechanics" might still be visible in *A Painted House,* there are "characters that no reader will forget, prose as clean and strong as any Grisham has yet laid down and a drop-dead evocation of a time and place that mark this novel as a classic slice of Americana."

Some critics differed with these opinions, however. Writing in *Booklist,* Stephanie Zvirin called into question the merits of Grisham's coming-of-age novel: "The measured, descriptive prose is readable . . . and there are some truly tender moments, but this is surface without substance, simply an inadequate effort in a genre that has exploded with quality over the last several years." As usual with a Grisham novel, however, there was a divergence among critical voices. What Zvirin found "inadequate," *Entertainment Weekly* contributor Bruce Fretts described as a "gem of an autobiographical novel." Fretts further commented, "Never let it be said this man doesn't know how to spin a good yarn." In *Time,* Jess Cagle criticized the book's slow pace but concluded that Grisham's "compassion for his characters is infectious, and the book is finally rewarding—a Sunday sermon from a Friday-night storyteller."

With *The Summons,* Grisham returns to his lawyer roots, to thrillers, and also to Ford County, Mississippi, which was the setting for *A Time to Kill.* Reviewing the book in *Entertainment Weekly,* Svetkey found *The Summons* "not all that tough to put down," and with "few shocking surprises." Nonetheless, shortly after publication, *The Summons* topped the list of hardcover best sellers, selling well over 100,000 copies in its first week of publication alone.

Grisham's next three books—*The King of Torts, The Bleachers,* and *The Last Juror*—all attained best-seller status despite mixed reviews. Of the first, a reviewer for the *Yale Law Journal* commented that, while Grisham's approach is "badly hobbled . . . by a cliche-driven plot . . . [and] failure to support his argument with substantive, realistic criticisms," the author's talent for powerful storytelling and a simple thesis "may yet move millions of casual readers to support serious reform of American tort law." Jennifer Reese of *Entertainment Weekly* was highly critical of *The Bleachers,* describing the story as "a sloppy gridiron mess, a thin and flimsy meditation on football and the dubious role it can play in the lives of young men." "Never a terrific stylist," Reese continued, "Grisham doesn't show any flair for character here." A *Publishers Weekly* reviewer called *The Bleachers* a "slight but likable novel," stating: "Many readers will come away having enjoyed the time spent, but wishing there had been a more sympathetic lead character, more originality, more pages, more story and more depth."

The Last Juror became Grisham's seventeenth book and seventeenth best-seller. Despite its popularity among readers, Rosemary Herbert of the *Boston Herald* warned: "If you expect to be on the edge of your seat while reading John Grisham's latest, think again. The experience is bound to be more like sitting in a jury box. Occasionally, the presentation you'll witness will be riveting. Then again, you've got to listen to a good deal of background material." The story is set in Canton, Mississippi, in the 1970s, and follows aftermath of the rape and murder of a widow that is witnessed by her two young children. Herbert called Grisham "the consummate legal eagle who knows how to pull heartstrings even when the suspense is not thrill-a-minute." Praising *The Last Juror* as Grisham's "best book in years," Sean Daly noted in *People* that the novel quickly bounded to best-seller status.

In little more than a decade, Grisham realized greater success than most writers enjoy in a lifetime. Despite such success, the former lawyer and politician remained realistic about his limitations and maintained that a time might come when he would walk away from writing just as he previously abandoned both law and politics. In his interview with Bearden of *Publishers Weekly,* he compared writers to athletes and concluded: "There's nothing sadder than a sports figure who continues to play past his prime." However, well into his second decade as a novelist, Grisham seemed far from that point. Book ideas "drop in from all directions," he told Svetkey in *Entertainment Weekly.* "Some gestate for years and some happen in a split second. They'll rattle around in my head for a while, and I'll catch myself mentally piecing it together. How do I suck the reader in, how do I maintain the narrative tension, how do I build up to some kind of exciting end? . . . Some of those will work, some won't."

BIOGRAPHICAL AND CRITICAL SOURCES:

BOOKS

Contemporary Literary Criticism, Volume 84, Gale (Detroit, MI), 1995, pp. 189-201.

PERIODICALS

Asia Africa Intelligence Wire, March 15, 2004, Ruel S. De Vera, review of *The Last Juror.*

Book, January, 2001, Liz Seymour, "Grisham Gets Serious," pp. 34-36.

Booklist, February 1, 1993, p. 954; September 15, 2000, p. 259; February 1, 2001, Stephanie Zvirin, review of *A Painted House,* p. 1020.

Boston Herald, March 2, 2004, Rosemary Herbert, review of *The Last Juror,* p. 40.

Christianity Today, October 3, 1994, p. 14; August 9, 1999, p. 70.

Christian Science Monitor, March 5, 1993, p. 10.

Detroit News, May 25, 1994, p. 3D.

Entertainment Weekly, April 1, 1994, Keli Pryor, interview with Grisham, pp. 15-20; June 3, 1994, Mark Harris, "Southern Discomfort," p. 48; July 15, 1994, p. 54; July 29, 1994, p. 23; February 13, 1998, Tom De Haven, review of *The Street Lawyer,* pp. 64-65; February 4, 2000, Tom De Haven, "Law of Desire," p 63; February 11, 2000, Benjamin Svetkey, "Making His Case" (interview), pp. 63-64; February 9, 2001, Bruce Fretts, "Above the Law," pp. 68-69; February 15, 2002, Benjamin Svetkey, "Trial and Errors," pp. 60-61; September 12, 2003, Jennifer Reese, review of *The Bleachers* p. 155.

Florida Bar Journal, June, 1998, Jacalyn N. Kolk, review of *The Street Lawyer,* p. 115.

Forbes, August 30, 1993, p. 24; January 8, 2001, p. 218.

Globe & Mail (Toronto, Ontario, Canada), March 30, 1991, p. C6.

Kirkus Reviews, February 1, 2001.

Library Journal, August, 2000, p. 179; March 1, 2001, p. 131; September 1, 2001, p. 258; December, 2001, Samantha J. Gust, review of *Skipping Christmas,* pp. 170-171.

Los Angeles Times, December 25, 2001, p. E4; February 26, 2002, p. E3.

Los Angeles Times Book Review, March 10, 1991, Charles Champlin, "Criminal Pursuits," p. 7; April 5, 1992, p. 6; April 4, 1993, p. 6; May 14, 1995, Garry Abrams, review of *The Rainmaker,* p. 8.

National Review, April 6, 1998, pp. 51-52.

New Republic, August 2, 1993, p. 32; March 14, 1994, p. 32; August 22, 1994, p. 35.

Newsday, March 7, 1993.

New Statesman, June 9, 1995, p. 35.

Newsweek, February 25, 1991, p. 63; March 16, 1992, p. 72; March 15, 1993, pp. 79-81; December 20, 1993, p. 121; February 19, 1999, Malcolm Jones, "Grisham's Gospel," p. 65.

New York, August 1, 1994, pp. 52-53.

New Yorker, August 1, 1994, p. 16.

New York Times, March 5, 1993, p. C29; July 29, 1994, p. B10; April 19, 1995, Michiko Kakutani, review of *The Rainmaker,* pp. B1, B9; April 28, 1995, p. C33; May 23, 1996, Christopher Lehmann-Haupt, review of *The Runaway Jury,* p. C20; March 31, 1997, Mel Gussow, review of *The Partner,* p. B1; February 4, 2002, p. B1; February 5, 2002, p. B7.

New York Times Book Review, March 24, 1991, p. 37; March 15, 1992, Frank J. Prial, "Too Liberal to Live," p. 9; October 18, 1992, p. 33; March 7, 1993, p. 18; December 23, 2001, p. 17; February 24, 2002, p. 13.

People, April 8, 1991, pp. 36-37; March 16, 1992, pp. 43-44; March 15, 1993, pp. 27-28; June 27, 1994, p. 24; August 1, 1994, p. 16; March 2, 1998, Cynthia Sanz, review of *The Street Lawyer,* p. 37; February 12, 2001, p. 41; February 18, 2002, p. 41; February 23, 2004, Sean Daly, review of *The Last Juror,* p. 45.

Philadelphia Inquirer, March 23, 1997, Robert Drake, review of *The Partner.*

Publishers Weekly, February 22, 1993, Michelle Bearden, "*PW* Interviews: John Grisham," pp. 70-71; May 30, 1994, p. 37; May 6, 1996, p. 71; February 10, 1997; February 1, 1999, review of *The Testament,* p. 78; January 10, 2000, p. 18; January 31, 2000, review of *The Brethren,* p. 84; January 22, 2001, review of *A Painted House,* p. 302; October 29, 2001, p. 20; November 5, 2001, review of *Skipping Christmas,* p. 43; February 18, 2002, p. 22; August 18, 2003, review of *The Bleachers,* p. 56.

Southern Living, August, 1991, p. 58.

Sunday Times (London, England), June 12, 1994, review of *The Chamber,* p. 1.

Time, March 9, 1992, John Skow, "Legal Eagle," p. 70; March 8, 1993, p. 73; June 20, 1994, John Skow, review of *The Chamber,* p. 67; August 1, 1994; February 26, 2001, Jess Cagle, review of *A Painted House,* p. 72.

Tribune Books (Chicago, IL), February 24, 1991, Bill Brashler, review of *The Firm,* p. 6; September 8, 1991, p. 10; February 23, 1992, p. 4; February 28, 1993, p. 7.

Voice Literary Supplement, July-August, 1991, p. 7.

Wall Street Journal, March 12, 1993, p. A6.

Washington Post, January 29, 2002, p. C3.

Yale Law Journal, June, 2003, review of *The King of Torts,* p. 2600.

ONLINE

Bookreporter.com, http://www.bookreporter.com/ (April 8, 2004), "Author Profile: John Grisham."

John Grisham Web Site, http://www.jgrisham.com (April 8, 2004).

University of Mississippi Web Site, http://www.olemiss. edu/ (April 8, 2004), "John Grisham."*

*   *   *

GUMP, P. Q.
See CARD, Orson Scott

*   *   *

GUPPY, Stephen (Anthony) 1951-

PERSONAL: Born February 10, 1951, in Nanaimo, British Columbia, Canada; son of Anthony W. and Mavis R. (Turner) Guppy; married Nelinda Kazenbroot, 1986; children: Sebastian Rhys, Isabel Jane. *Ethnicity:* "Canadian." *Education:* University of Victoria, B.A., 1971, teaching certificate, 1982, M.A., 1988. *Hobbies and other interests:* Guitar, "playing with my kids."

ADDRESSES: Home—2184 Michigan Way, Nanaimo, British Columbia V9R 6S1, Canada. *Office*—Department of Creative Writing and Journalism, Malaspina University College, 900 Fifth St., Nanaimo, British Columbia V9R 5S5, Canada. *E-mail*—guppy@mala. bc.ca.

CAREER: School District #69, Qualicum, British Columbia, Canada, teacher, 1982-85; Malaspina University College, Nanaimo, British Columbia, instructor in English and creative writing, 1986—. Also worked for publishing companies early in career.

AWARDS, HONORS: Second Prize, Scottish International Open Poetry Competition, 1997; shortlisted for Dorothy Livesay Award for Poetry, British Columbia Book Prizes, 2002.

WRITINGS:

Ghostcatcher (poetry), Oolichan (Lantzville, British Columbia, Canada), 1979.

(Editor, with Ron Smith) *Rainshadow: Stories from Vancouver Island,* Oolichan/Sono Nis (Victoria, British Columbia, Canada), 1982.

Another Sad Day at the Edge of the Empire (short stories; includes title story, "The Catch," "A Rural Tale," "Icthus," and "The Tale of the Ratcatcher's Daughter"), Oolichan (Lantzville, British Columbia, Canada), 1985.

Blind Date with the Angel: The Diane Arbus Poems, Ekstasis Editions (Victoria, British Columbia, Canada), 1998.

Understanding Heaven (poetry), Wolsak & Wynn (Toronto, Ontario, Canada), 2002.

Contributor to anthologies, including *Best Canadian Short Stories,* 1995; *The Journey Prize Anthology,* McClelland & Stewart (Toronto, Ontario, Canada), 1998; *Prentice-Hall Guide for Student Writers;* and *Islands West.*

SIDELIGHTS: Stephen Guppy once told *CA:* "Much of my fiction and poetry has been concerned with the landscape, history, and people of Vancouver Island." This includes the anthology *Rainshadow: Stories from Vancouver Island.* The stories that Guppy includes in his first fiction collection, *Another Sad Day at the Edge of the Empire,* also concern life on Vancouver Island.

According to a critic in the Toronto *Globe and Mail,* *Another Sad Day* is characteristic of fiction from Vancouver Island-based authors; its stories portray their island setting as "an eerie place where people disappear into thin air or turn into birds, where magic and the supernatural are routine occurrences." Stories in *Another Sad Day* include the title tale, which features an alcoholic doctor who goes to the office every day in spite of the fact that he has no patients. He goes to meet his mistress. This illicit relationship is not the most sensational thing about the piece, however. Rather, it is the fact that the tide in the area continues to go out, but never comes back in. Eventually, the ocean can no longer be seen on the horizon, and the phenomenon is blamed by the local government upon the Japanese. The *Globe and Mail* reviewer labeled "Another Sad Day" Guppy's "most comic" contribution to the volume.

The same critic felt that "Guppy's views of religion appear most directly in 'A Rural Tale.'" The story is allegorical, and tells of the ways in which a farmer suffers when his brother is declared the messiah of a strange religious sect. The two men were both raised by a strict fundamentalist father, who at one time caused the destruction of the family farm because it was too prosperous to find favor in the eyes of God. In a somewhat similar vein, the story "Icthus" follows a teacher from Nanaimo, British Columbia—Guppy's

own hometown—as he attempts to research the history of an area religious figure who claimed to be able to walk on water. The project ends badly.

Religion also plays a role in "The Tale of the Ratcatcher's Daughter," which centers on an alcoholic minister with the surname of Death who is forced from his calling and his lovely daughter, who bears the strange moniker "Pearly Death." Because he is barred from the ministry, Death tries his hand at catching rats in a local coal mine for a fee. "The meaning is elusive," noted the *Globe and Mail* reviewer. "It's better just to be led into the pit of Hell without asking why."

BIOGRAPHICAL AND CRITICAL SOURCES:

PERIODICALS

ARC, winter, 2002, review of *Understanding Heaven,* pp. 90-91.
Canadian Literature, autumn, 2000, Karen Mulhallen, review of *Blind Date with the Angel: The Diane Arbus Poems,* p. 175.
Globe and Mail (Toronto, Ontario, Canada), July 6, 1985, review of *Another Sad Day at the Edge of the Empire.*

H

HALL, Donald (Andrew, Jr.) 1928-

PERSONAL: Born September 20, 1928, in New Haven, CT; son of Donald Andrew (a businessman) and Lucy (Wells) Hall; married Kirby Thompson, September 13, 1952 (divorced, 1969); married Jane Kenyon (a poet), April 17, 1972 (died, April 22, 1995); children: (first marriage) Andrew, Philippa. *Education:* Harvard University, B.A., 1951; Oxford University, B. Litt., 1953; attended Stanford University, 1953-54.

ADDRESSES: Home—Eagle Pond Farm, Danbury, NH 03230. *Agent*—Gerald McCauley Agency, Inc., Box 844, Katonah, NY 10536.

CAREER: Harvard University, Cambridge, MA, junior fellow in Society of Fellows, 1954-57; University of Michigan, Ann Arbor, 1957-75, began as assistant professor, became professor of English; full-time freelance writer, 1975—. Bennington College graduate Writing Seminars, poet-in-residence, 1993—. Broadcaster on British Broadcasting Corporation radio programs, 1959-80; host of *Poets Talking* (television interview series), 1974-75; has given poetry readings at colleges, universities, schools, and community centers.

MEMBER: PEN, American Academy and Institute of Arts and Letters.

AWARDS, HONORS: Newdigate Prize, Oxford University, 1952, for poem "Exile"; Lamont Poetry Prize, Academy of American Poets, 1955, for *Exiles and Marriages;* Edna St. Vincent Millay Award, Poetry Society of America, 1956; Guggenheim fellowship,

Donald Hall

1963-64, 1972-73; *New York Times* Notable Children's Books citation, 1979, for *Ox-Cart Man;* Sarah Josepha Hale Award, 1983, for writings about New England; *Horn Book* Honor List, 1986, for *The Oxford Book of Children's Verse in America;* Lenore Marshall Prize, 1987, for *The Happy Man;* National Book Critics Circle Award for poetry, and *Los Angeles Times* Book Prize in poetry, both 1989, both for *The One Day;* named poet Laureate of New Hampshire, 1984-89, 1995—; Associated Writing Programs Poetry Publication Award named in Hall's honor.

WRITINGS:

FOR CHILDREN

Andrew the Lion Farmer, illustrated by Jane Miller, F. Watts (New York, NY), 1959, illustrated by Ann Reason, Methuen (London, England), 1961.

Riddle Rat, illustrated by Mort Gerberg, Warne (London, England), 1977.

Ox-Cart Man, illustrated by Barbara Cooney, Viking (New York, NY), 1979.

The Man Who Lived Alone, illustrated by Mary Azarian, Godine (New York, NY), 1984.

(Editor) *The Oxford Book of Children's Verse in America,* Oxford University Press, 1985.

The Farm Summer 1942, illustrated by Barry Moser, Dial (New York, NY), 1994.

I Am the Dog, I Am the Cat, illustrated by Barry Moser, Dial (New York, NY), 1994.

Lucy's Christmas, illustrated by Michael McCurdy, Harcourt Brace (New York, NY), 1994.

Lucy's Summer, illustrated by Michael McCurdy, Harcourt Brace (New York, NY), 1995.

When Willard Met Babe Ruth, illustrated by Barry Moser, Harcourt Brace (New York, NY), 1996.

Old Home Day, illustrated by Emily Arnold McCully, Harcourt Brace, (New York, NY) 1996.

The Milkman's Boy, illustrated by Greg Shed, Walker (New York, NY), 1997.

POETRY

Fantasy Poets No. 4, Fantasy Press, 1952.

Exile, Fantasy Press, 1952.

To the Loud Wind and Other Poems, Pegasus, 1955.

Exiles and Marriages, Viking (New York, NY), 1955.

The Dark Houses, Viking (New York, NY), 1958.

A Roof of Tiger Lilies, Viking (New York, NY), 1964.

The Alligator Bride: Poems, New and Selected, Harper (New York, NY), 1969.

The Yellow Room: Love Poems, Harper (New York, NY), 1971.

The Gentleman's Alphabet Book (limericks), illustrated by Harvey Kornberg, Dutton (New York, NY), 1972.

The Town of Hill, Godine (New York, NY), 1975.

A Blue Wing Tilts at the Edge of the Sea: Selected Poems, 1964-1974, Secker & Warburg (London, England), 1975.

Kicking the Leaves, Harper (New York, NY), 1978.

The Toy Bone, BOA Editions, 1979.

Brief Lives: Seven Epigrams, William B. Ewart, 1983.

The Twelve Seasons, Deerfield Press, 1983.

Great Day in the Cow's House, illustrated with photographs by T. S. Bronson, Ives Street Press, 1984.

The Happy Man, Random House (New York, NY), 1986.

The One Day, Ticknor & Fields, 1988.

Old and New Poems, Ticknor & Fields, 1990.

The Museum of Clear Ideas, Ticknor & Fields, 1993.

The Old Life, Houghton Mifflin (Boston, MA), 1996.

Without, Houghton Mifflin (Boston, MA), 1998.

The Purpose of a Chair, Brooding Heron Press (Waldron Island, WA), 2000.

The Painted Bed, Houghton Mifflin (Boston, MA), 2002.

Contributor of poetry to numerous periodicals, including the *New Yorker, New Republic, New Criterion, Kenyon Review, Iowa Review, Georgia Review, Ohio Review, Gettysburg Review, Nation,* and *Atlantic.*

PROSE

String Too Short to Be Saved: Recollections of Summers on a New England Farm (autobiography), illustrated by Mimi Korach, Viking (New York, NY), 1961, expanded edition, Godine (New York, NY), 1979.

Henry Moore: The Life and Work of a Great Sculptor, Harper (New York, NY), 1966.

As the Eye Moves: A Sculpture by Henry Moore, illustrated with photographs by David Finn, Abrams (New York, NY), 1970.

Marianne Moore: The Cage and the Animal, Pegasus, 1970.

The Pleasures of Poetry, Harper (New York, NY), 1971.

Writing Well, Little, Brown (Boston, MA), 1974, 9th edition (with Sven Birkerts), HarperCollins (New York, NY), 1997.

(With others) *Playing Around: The Million-Dollar Infield Goes to Florida,* Little, Brown (Boston, MA), 1974.

(With Dock Ellis) *Dock Ellis in the Country of Baseball,* Coward (New York, NY), 1976.

Goatfoot Milktongue Twinbird: Interviews, Essays, and Notes on Poetry, 1970-76, University of Michigan Press (Ann Arbor, MI), 1978.

Remembering Poets: Reminiscences and Opinions—Dylan Thomas, Robert Frost, T. S. Eliot, Ezra Pound, Harper (New York, NY), 1978, revised edition published as *Their Ancient Glittering Eyes, Remembering Poets and More Poets,* Ticknor & Fields, 1992.

To Keep Moving: Essays, 1959-1969, Hobart & William Smith Colleges Press, 1980.

To Read Literature, Holt (New York, NY), 1980.

The Weather for Poetry: Essays, Reviews, and Notes on Poetry, 1977-1981, University of Michigan Press (Ann Arbor, MI), 1982.

Fathers Playing Catch with Sons: Essays on Sport (Mostly Baseball), North Point Press, 1985.

Seasons at Eagle Pond, illustrated by Thomas W. Nason, Ticknor & Fields, 1987.

Poetry and Ambition, University of Michigan Press (Ann Arbor, MI), 1988.

Here at Eagle Pond, illustrated by Thomas W. Nason, Ticknor & Fields, 1990.

Life Work, Beacon Press (Boston, MA), 1993.

Death to the Death of Poetry: Essays, Reviews, Notes, Interviews, University of Michigan Press (Ann Arbor, MI), 1994.

Principle Products of Portugal: Prose Pieces, Beacon Press (Boston, MA), 1995.

Willow Temple: New and Selected Stories, Houghton Mifflin (Boston, MA), 2003.

Breakfast Served Any Time All Day: Essays on Poetry New and Selected, University of Michigan Press (Ann Arbor, MI), 2003.

Contributor of short stories and articles to numerous periodicals, including the *New Yorker, Esquire, Atlantic, Playboy, Transatlantic Review,* and *American Scholar.* Author of afterword to Jane Kenyon's *Otherwise: New and Selected Poems.*

PLAYS

An Evening's Frost, first produced in Ann Arbor, MI; produced Off-Broadway, 1965.

Bread and Roses, produced in Ann Arbor, MI, 1975.

Ragged Mountain Elegies (produced in Peterborough, NH, 1983), revised version published as *The Bone Ring* (produced in New York, NY, 1986), Story Line, 1987.

EDITOR

The Harvard Advocate Anthology, Twayne (New York, NY), 1950.

(With Robert Pack and Louis Simpson) *The New Poets of England and America,* Meridian Books, 1957.

Whittier, Dell (New York, NY), 1961.

Contemporary American Poetry, Penguin (London England), 1962, Penguin (Baltimore, MD), 1963.

(With Robert Pack) *New Poets of England and America: Second Selection,* Meridian Books, 1962.

A Poetry Sampler, F. Watts (New York, NY), 1962.

(With Stephen Spender) *The Concise Encyclopedia of English and American Poets and Poetry,* Hawthorn, 1963.

(With Warren Taylor) *Poetry in English,* Macmillan (New York, NY), 1963.

A Choice of Whitman's Verse, Faber & Faber (London, England), 1968.

Man and Boy, F. Watts (New York, NY), 1968.

The Modern Stylists, Free Press (New York, NY), 1968.

American Poetry: An Introductory Anthology, Faber & Faber (London, England), 1969.

(With D. L. Emblem) *A Writer's Reader,* Little, Brown (Boston, MA), 1969, 9th edition, Longman (New York, NY), 2002.

The Pleasures of Poetry, Harper (New York, NY), 1971.

The Oxford Book of American Literary Anecdotes, Oxford University Press (Oxford, England), 1981.

To Read Literature: Fiction, Poetry, Drama, Holt (New York, NY), 1981, 3rd edition, Harcourt (New York, NY), 1992.

Claims for Poetry, University of Michigan Press (Ann Arbor, MI), 1982.

To Read Poetry, Holt (New York, NY), 1982, revised edition published as *To Read a Poem,* Harcourt (New York, NY), 1992.

The Contemporary Essay, St. Martin's Press (New York, NY), 1984, 3rd edition, 1995.

To Read Fiction, Holt (New York, NY), 1987.

(With Pat Corrington Wykes) *Anecdotes of Modern Art: From Rousseau to Warhol,* Oxford University Press (New York, NY), 1990.

Andrew Marvell, *The Essential Marvell,* Ecco Press (New York, NY), 1991.

Edwin Arlington Robinson, *The Essential Robinson,* Ecco Press (New York, NY), 1993.

Oxford Illustrated Book of American Children's Poems, Oxford University Press (New York, NY), 1999.

Former poetry editor, *Paris Review.* Former member of editorial board, Wesleyan University Press poetry series; editor, University of Michigan "Poets on Poetry" series.

SIDELIGHTS: Considered one of the major American poets of his generation, Donald Hall's works explore a longing for the more bucolic past and reflect the poet's abiding reverence for nature. Although Hall gained an early success with his 1955 poetry collection *Exiles and Marriages,* his more recent poetry has generally been regarded as the best of his career. Often compared favorably with such writers as James Dickey, Robert Bly, and James Wright, Hall uses simple, direct language to evoke surrealistic imagery. In addition to his poetry, Hall has built a respected body of prose work that includes essays, short fiction, plays, and children's books. Hall, who lives on the New Hampshire farm he visited in summers as a boy, is also noted for the anthologies he has edited and is a popular teacher, speaker, and reader of his own poems.

Born in 1928, Hall grew up in Hamden, Connecticut, a child of the Great Depression of the 1930s, though not greatly affected by it. The Hall household was marked by a volatile father and a mother who was "steadier, maybe with more access to depths because there was less continual surface," as Hall explained in an essay for *Contemporary Authors Autobiography Series (CAAS)*. "To her I owe my fires, to my father my tears. I owe them both for their reading." By age twelve, Hall had discovered the poet and short story writer Edgar Allan Poe: "I read Poe and my life changed," he remarked in *CAAS*. Another strong influence in Hall's early years was his maternal great-grandfather's farm in New Hampshire, where he spent many summers. The pull of nature became a compulsion in him so strong that decades later he bought that same farm and settled there as a full-time writer and poet.

Hall attended Philips Exeter Academy and despite early frustrations had his first poem published at age sixteen. He was a participant at the prestigious Bread Loaf Writer's Conference that same year. From Exeter, Hall went to Harvard University, where he attended class alongside other poets-in-training, among them Adrienne Rich, Robert Bly, Frank O'Hara, and John Ashbery; he also studied for a year with Archibald MacLeish. In his time at Oxford University, Hall became one of the few Americans to win the coveted Newdigate contest for his poem "Exile."

Returning to the United States, Hall spent three years at Harvard and there assembled *Exiles and Marriages,* a collection crafted in a tightly structured style on which Hall imposes rigid rhyme and meter. In 1957 he took a position as assistant professor of English at the University of Michigan, where he remained until 1975. During those years he wrote volumes of poetry and essays, but Hall had always contemplated returning to the rural paradise that he had found as a youth in New Hampshire. Finally he was in a position to make this a reality, and when his grandmother, who owned Eagle Pond Farm, passed away, he bought the farm, left teaching, and moved there with his second wife, poet Jane Kenyon. With one child in college at the time and another having not yet started, the move to New Hampshire was a risky one. Giving up the relative

security of a tenured position at Michigan was a difficult decision, "but I did not hesitate, I did not doubt," Hall recalled in *CAAS*. "I panicked but I did not doubt." The collections *Kicking the Leaves* and *The Happy Man* reflect Hall's happiness at his return to the family farm, a place rich with memories and links to his past. Many of the poems explore and celebrate the continuity between generations, as the narrative voice in his poetry often reminisces about the past and anticipates the future.

Old and New Poems contains several traditional poems from earlier collections, as well as more innovative verses not previously published. Hall's well-known poem "Baseball," included in *The Museum of Clear Ideas,* is the poet's ode to the great American pastime and is structured around the sequence of a baseball game, with nine stanzas with nine lines each. Written following the 1995 death of his second wife to cancer, *Without* reflects on the changes Kenyon's death made to his life. *The Painted Bed* finds Hall in another phase of the grieving process, the poems included showcasing the poet's "distinctive musical mark" and "exhibiting the terrible suffering of the bereaved with dignity and beauty," according to *Book* contributor Stephen Whited.

Reviewers have continued to praise Hall as the poet continues to challenge both himself and his readers while retaining a sense of tradition and the commonplace. Acclaim has been heaped, in particular, on the award-winning *The One Day,* with *Ploughshares* contributor Liam Rector dubbing it "an eloquent consummation of Modernism." *The One Day* consists of a single poem of 110 stanzas, divided into three sections. Each section presents a unique elderly narrative voice reflecting, in blank verse, upon the meaning of life while looking back on the past. In two of the three sections Hall alternates between male and female narrators.

In addition to his accomplishments as a poet, Hall is respected as an academic who, through writing, teaching, and lecturing, has made significant contributions to the study and craft of writing. As Rector explained, Hall "has lived deeply within the New England ethos of plain living and high thinking, and he has done so with a sense of humor and eros." In *Remembering Poets: Reminiscences and Opinions—Dylan Thomas, Robert Frost, T. S. Eliot, Ezra Pound,* a 1978 work that was expanded as *Their Ancient Glittering Eyes: Remembering Poets and More Poets,* Hall recounts his relationship with fellow poets such as T. S. Eliot, Ezra Pound, Dylan Thomas, and Robert Frost. His books on the craft of writing include *Writing Well*—in its ninth edition by 1997—and *Death to the Death of Poetry. Life Work* is Hall's memoir of the writing life and his tenure at Eagle Pond Farm, while his children's book *Ox-Cart Man* is one among several works that have established him in the field of children's literature. A fable on the cyclical nature of life, *Ox-Cart Man* expresses for readers "the sense that work defines us all, connects us with our world, and we are all rewarded . . . in measure of our effort," according to Kristi L. Thomas in *School Library Journal.*

Hall continues to live and work on his New Hampshire farm, a site which serves as both his abode and an inspiration for much of his work. Following his second wife's death in the spring of 1995, Hall appeared at several tributes to Kenyon's work and composed an afterword to a posthumous collection of her poetry, *Otherwise: New and Selected Poems.*

BIOGRAPHICAL AND CRITICAL SOURCES:

BOOKS

Children's Books and Their Creators, edited by Anita Silvey, Houghton Mifflin (Boston, MA), 1995.

Contemporary Authors Autobiography Series, Volume 7, Gale (Detroit, MI), 1988, pp. 55-67.

Contemporary Literary Criticism, Gale (Detroit, MI), Volume 13, 1980, Volume 37, 1986, Volume 59, 1989.

Dictionary of Literary Biography, Volume 5: American Poets since World War II, Gale (Detroit, MI), 1980.

Hall, Donald, *Riddle Rat,* Warne (London, England), 1977.

Hall, Donald, *The Man Who Lived Alone,* Godine (New York, NY), 1984.

Hall, Donald, *I Am the Dog, I Am the Cat,* Dial (New York, NY), 1994.

PERIODICALS

Book, May-June, 2002, Stephen Whited, review of *The Painted Bed,* p. 85.

Booklist, July 15, 1977, p. 1728; June 1, 1994, p. 1816; August, 1994, p. 2051; September 15, 1994, p. 132; March 15, 1996, Bill Ott, review of *When Willard Met Babe Ruth,* p. 1262; September 1, 1996, p. 724; March 15, 2000, Gillian Engberg, review of *The Oxford Illustrated Book of American Children's Poems,* p. 1380; March 1, 2002, Ray

Olson, review of *The Painted Bed,* p. 1079; April 15, 2003, Ellen Loughran, review of *Willow Temple: New and Selected Stories,* p. 1448.

Bulletin of the Center for Children's Books, February, 1980, Zena Sutherland, review of *Ox-Cart Man,* p. 110; March, 1985, pp. 126-127; July, 1994, Deborah Stevenson, review of *The Farm Summer 1942,* p. 358; October, 1994, Roger Sutton, review of *Lucy's Christmas,* pp. 48-49; December, 1994, Roger Sutton, review of *I Am the Dog, I Am the Cat,* p. 129; June, 1996, p. 336; October, 1996, p. 61.

Emergency Librarian, March, 1995, p. 44; January, 1996, p. 55.

Horn Book, February, 1982, Mary M. Burns, review of *Ox-Cart Man,* pp. 44-45; July-August, 1994, Nancy Vasilakis, review of *The Farm Summer 1942,* p. 441; September-October, 1994, Ann A. Flowers, review of *I Am the Dog, I Am the Cat,* p. 577; November-December, 1994, Elizabeth S. Watson, review of *Lucy's Christmas,* p. 711; May, 1995, pp. 324-325; November, 1996, pp. 724-725.

Junior Bookshelf, December, 1980, review of *Ox-Cart Man,* pp. 283-284.

Kirkus Reviews, August 15, 1994, review of *I Am the Dog, I Am the Cat,* p. 1129; October 15, 1994, review of *Lucy's Christmas,* pp. 1420-1421; November 1, 1984, review of *The Man Who Lived Alone,* p. 88; March 1, 1996, review of *When Willard Met Babe Ruth,* pp. 374-375; July 15, 1996, review of *Old Home Day,* p. 1048; July 15, 1997, p. 1111; March 15, 2003, review of *Willow Temple,* p. 416.

Library Journal, April 15, 2003, review of *Willow Temple,* p. 128.

Los Angeles Times Book Review, August 4, 1996, p. 11.

New York Times Book Review, January 13, 1985, Thomas Powers, review of *The Man Who Lived Alone,* p. 26.

Ploughshares, fall, 2001, Liam Rector, "About Donald Hall," p. 270.

Poetry, December, 2003, review of *Breakfast Served Any Time All Day,* p. 177.

Publishers Weekly, June 13, 1977, review of *Riddle Rat,* p. 108; April 11, 1994, review of *The Farm Summer 1942,* p. 65; review of *Lucy's Summer,* April 10, 1995, p. 62; August 12, 1996, review of *Old Home Day,* p. 82; July 14, 1997, review of *The Milkman's Boy,* p. 83; February 25, 2002, review of *The Painted Bed,* p. 56; March 31, 2003, review of *Willow Temple,* p. 39.

Quill and Quire, May, 1995, review of *Lucy's Summer,* p. 51.

School Library Journal, September, 1977, p. 108; October, 1979, Kristi L. Thomas, review of *Ox-Cart Man,* p. 140; February, 1985, Anna Biagioni Hart, review of *The Man Who Lived Alone,* p. 64; September, 1994, p. 101; May, 1996, p. 113; October, 1996, p. 96; January, 2000, Margaret Bush, review of *The Oxford Illustrated Book of American Children's Poems,* p. 121.

Sewanee Review, winter, 2000, review of *Without,* p. 6.*

* * *

HANDKE, Peter 1942-

PERSONAL: Born December 6, 1942, in Griffen, Carinthia, Austria; son of Bruno (stepfather; an army sergeant) and Maria (Siutz) Handke; married Libgart Schwarz, 1966 (separated, 1972); children: Amina. *Education:* Attended a Jesuit seminary, and University of Graz, 1961-65.

ADDRESSES: Home—53 rue Cecille-Dinant, F-92140 Clamart, France. *Agent*—c/o Author Mail, Suhrkamp Verlag, Postfach 101945, 6001 9 Frankfurt am Main, Germany; c/o Kurt Bernheim, 792 Columbus Ave., New York, NY 10025.

CAREER: Dramatist, novelist, poet, essayist, and screenwriter, 1966—.

AWARDS, HONORS: Gerhart Hauptmann Prize, 1967; Schiller Prize, 1972; Büchner Prize, 1973 (returned, 1999); Kafka Prize, 1979 (refused); Salzburg Literature Prize, 1986.

WRITINGS:

NOVELS

Die Hornissen (title means "The Hornets"), Suhrkamp (Frankfurt, Germany), 1966.

Der Hausierer (title means "The Peddler"), Suhrkamp (Frankfurt, Germany), 1967.

Peter Handke

Die Angst des Tormanns beim Elfmeter (also see below), Suhrkamp (Frankfurt, Germany), 1970, translated by Michael Roloff as *The Goalie's Anxiety at the Penalty Kick,* Farrar, Straus & Giroux (New York, NY), 1972.

Der kurze Brief zum langen Abschied, Suhrkamp (Frankfurt, Germany), 1972, translated by Ralph Manheim as *Short Letter, Long Farewell,* Farrar, Straus & Giroux (New York, NY), 1974.

Die Stunde der wahren Empfindung, Suhrkamp (Frankfurt, Germany), 1975, translated by Ralph Manheim as *A Moment of True Feeling,* Farrar, Straus & Giroux (New York, NY), 1977.

Die linkshändige Frau (also see below), Suhrkamp (Frankfurt, Germany), 1976, translated as *The Left-Handed Woman,* Farrar, Straus & Giroux (New York, NY), 1978.

Three by Peter Handke (contains *A Sorrow beyond Dreams, Short Letter, Long Farewell,* and *The Goalie's Anxiety at the Penalty Kick,*) Avon (New York, NY), 1977.

Langsame Heimkehr (novella), Suhrkamp (Frankfurt, Germany), 1979, translated by Ralph Manheim as "The Long Way Around," in *Slow Homecoming,* Farrar, Straus & Giroux (New York, NY), 1983.

Die Lehre der Sainte-Victoire (novella), Suhrkamp (Frankfurt, Germany), 1980, translated by Ralph Manheim as "The Lesson of Mont Sainte-Victoire," in *Slow Homecoming,* Farrar, Straus & Giroux (New York, NY), 1983.

Kindergeschichte (novella), Suhrkamp (Frankfurt, Germany), 1981, translated by Ralph Manheim as "Children's Stories" in *Slow Homecoming,* Farrar, Straus & Giroux (New York, NY), 1983.

Slow Homecoming, Farrar, Straus & Giroux (New York, NY), 1983.

Across (novella), translated by Ralph Manheim, Farrar, Straus & Giroux (New York, NY), 1986.

Die Wiederholung, Suhrkamp (Frankfurt, Germany), 1986, translated by Ralph Manheim as *Repetition,* Farrar, Straus & Giroux (New York, NY), 1988.

Nachmittag eines Schriftstellers, Suhrkamp (Frankfurt, Germany), 1987, translated by Ralph Manheim as *The Afternoon of a Writer,* Farrar, Straus & Giroux (New York, NY), 1989.

Die Abwesenheit: ein Marchen, Suhrkamp (Frankfurt, Germany), 1987, translated as *Absence,* Farrar, Straus & Giroux (New York, NY), 1990.

Das Spiel vom Fragen; oder, Die Reise zum Sonoren, Suhrkamp (Frankfurt, Germany), 1989, translated as *Voyage to the Sonorous Land; or, The Art of Asking and The Hour We Knew Nothing of Each Other,* Yale University Press (New Haven, CT), 1996.

Langsam im Schatten, Suhrkamp (Frankfurt, Germany), 1992.

Mein Jahr in der Niemandsbucht: Ein Marchen aus den neuen Zeiten, Suhrkamp (Frankfurt, Germany), 1994, translated by Krishna Winston as *My Year in the No-Man's-Bay,* Farrar, Straus & Giroux (New York, NY), 1998.

In einer dunklen Nacht ging ich aus meinem stillen Haus, Suhrkamp (Frankfurt, Germany), 1997, translated by Krishna Winston as *On a Dark Night I Left My Silent House,* Farrar, Straus & Giroux (New York, NY), 2000.

Der Bildverlust, oder, Durch die Sierra de Gredos, Suhrkamp (Frankfurt, Germany), 2002.

PLAYS

Publikumsbeschimpfung (produced in Frankfurt, 1966), published in *Publikumsbeschimpfung und andere Sprechstücke* (see below), translated by Michael Roloff as *Offending the Audience* in *Kaspar and Other Plays,* Farrar, Straus & Giroux (New York, NY), 1969.

Selbstbezichtigung (produced in Öberhausen, Germany, 1966), published in *Publikumsbeschimpfung und andere Sprechstücke* (see below), translated by Michael Roloff as *Self-Accusation* in *Kaspar and Other Plays,* Farrar, Straus & Giroux (New York, NY), 1969.

Publikumsbeschimpfung und andere Sprechstücke, Suhrkamp (Frankfurt, Germany), 1966, translated by Michael Roloff as *Kaspar and Other Plays,* Farrar, Straus & Giroux, 1969, published as *Offending the Audience,* Methuen (London, England), 1971.

Weissagung (produced in Öberhausen, Germany, 1966), published in *Publikumsbeschimpfung und andere Sprechstücke,* translated by Michael Roloff as *Prophecy* in *The Ride across Lake Constance and Other Plays,* Farrar, Straus & Giroux (New York, NY), 1976.

Hilferufe (produced in Stockholm, Sweden, 1967), published in *Deutsches Theater der Gegenwart 2,* 1967, translated by Michael Roloff as *Calling for Help* in *The Ride across Lake Constance and Other Plays,* Farrar, Straus & Giroux (New York, NY), 1976.

Kaspar (produced in Frankfurt, Germany, 1968), Suhrkamp (Frankfurt, Germany), 1968, translated by Michael Roloff (produced in New York, NY, 1973), published in *Kaspar and Other Plays* (Farrar, Strauss & Giroux (New York, NY), 1969, published separately, Methuen (London, England), 1972.

Das Mundel will Vormund sein (produced in Frankfurt, Germany, 1969), published in *Peter Handke,* Suhrkamp (Frankfurt, Germany), 1969, translated by Michael Roloff as *My Foot My Tutor* in *The Ride across Lake Constance and Other Plays* (Farrar, Straus & Giroux (New York, NY), 1976.

Quodlibet (produced in Basle, Switzerland, 1970), published in *Theater Heute,* March, 1970, translated by Michael Roloff in *The Ride across Lake Constance and Other Plays,* Farrar, Straus & Giroux (New York, NY), 1976.

Wind und Meer: 4 Hörspiele (title means "Wind and Sea: Four Radio Plays"), Suhrkamp (Frankfurt, Germany), 1970.

Chronik der laufenden Ereignisse (film scenario; title means "Chronicle of Current Events"), Suhrkamp (Frankfurt, Germany), 1971.

Der Ritt über den Bodensee (produced in Berlin, Germany, 1971), Suhrkamp (Frankfurt, Germany), 1971, translated by Michael Roloff as *The Ride across Lake Constance* (produced in New York,

NY, 1972), published in *The Contemporary German Drama,* Equinox Books (New York, NY), 1972, published separately, Methuen (London, England), 1973.

Die Unvernünftigen sterben aus (produced in Zürich, Switzerland, 1974), Suhrkamp (Frankfurt, Germany), 1973, translated by Michael Roloff and Karl Weber as *They Are Dying Out,* Methuen (London, England), 1975.

The Ride across Lake Constance and Other Plays, Farrar, Straus & Giroux (New York, NY), 1976.

Das ende des Flanierens, Davidpresse, 1976.

(And director) *The Left-Handed Woman* (screenplay; adaptation of Handke's novel), 1978.

Über die Dörfer: Dramatisches (dramatic poem; produced in Salzburg, Austria, 1982), music by Walter Zimmermann, Suhrkamp (Frankfurt, Germany), 1981.

Die Geschichte des Bleistifts, Residenz Verlag (Salzburg, Austria), 1982.

Der Chinese des Schmerzes, Suhrkamp (Frankfurt, Germany), 1983.

Phantasien der Wiederholung, Suhrkamp (Frankfurt, Germany), 1983.

Aber ich lebe nur von den Zwischenreaumen, Ammann, 1987.

(With Wim Wenders) *Der Himmel über Berlin: ein Filmbuch* (screenplay), Suhrkamp (Frankfurt, Germany), 1987, translated as *Wings of Desire,* Orion, 1988.

Die Theaterstucke, Suhrkamp (Frankfurt, Germany), 1992.

Die Stunde da wir nichts voneinander wussten: Ein Schauspiel, Suhrkamp (Frankfurt, Germany), 1992.

Walk about the Village: A Dramatic Poem, Ariadne Press (Riverside, CA), 1996.

Zurüstungen für die Unsterblichkeit: ein Königsdrama, Suhrkamp (Frankfurt, Germany), 1997.

Die Fahrt im Einbaum; oder, Das Stück zum Fiolm vom Kreig (title means "Journey in a Canoe; or, The Play about the Film of the War"; produced in Vienna, Austria, 1999), translated by Scott Abbott, 2001.

Undertagblues: ein Stationendrama, Suhrkamp (Frankfurt, Germany), 2003.

POETRY

Die Innenwelt der Aussenwelt der Innenwelt, Suhrkamp (Frankfurt, Germany), 1969, portions translated by Michael Roloff as *The Innerworld of the Outerworld of the Innerworld,* Seabury Press (New York, NY), 1974.

Als das Wünschen noch geholfen hat, Suhrkamp (Frankfurt, Germany), 1974, translated by Michael Roloff as *Nonsense and Happiness,* Urizen Books (New York, NY), 1976.

Noch einmal für Thukydides, Residenz (Salzburg, Austria), 1990, translated by Tess Lewis as *Once Again for Thucydides,* New Directions (New York, NY), 1999.

OTHER

Begrüssung des Aufsichtsrats (experimental prose pieces; title means "Welcoming the Board of Directors"; also see below), Residenz (Salzburg, Austria), 1967.

(Compiler) *Der gewöhnliche Schrecken* (title means "The Ordinary Terror"), Residenz (Salzburg, Austria), 1969.

Peter Handke: Prosa, Gedichte, Theaterstücke, Hörspiel, Aufsätze (collected works) Suhrkamp (Frankfurt, Germany), 1969.

Deutsche Gedichte (title means "German Poems"), Euphorion-Verlag, 1969.

Ich bin ein Bewohner des Elfenbeinturms (essays; title means "I Live in an Ivory Tower"), Suhrkamp (Frankfurt, Germany), 1972.

Wunschloses Unglück (biography), Residenz Verlag, 1972, translated by Ralph Manheim as *A Sorrow beyond Dreams,* Farrar, Straus & Giroux (New York, NY), 1975, 3rd edition, with notes by Julie Wigmore, St. Martin's Press (New York, NY), 1993, introduction by Jeffrey Eugenides, New York Review of Books (New York, NY), 2002.

Stücke, Suhrkamp (Frankfurt, Germany), 1972.

Stücke 2, Suhrkamp (Frankfurt, Germany), 1973.

(Author of text) *Wiener Läden,* photographs by Didi Petrikat, Hanser (Munich, Germany), 1974.

Falsche Bewegung (film scenario; title means "False Move"), Suhrkamp (Frankfurt, Germany), 1975.

Das Gewicht der Welt: ein Journal, Residenz Verlag, 1977, translated by Ralph Manheim as *The Weight of the World,* Farrar, Straus & Giroux (New York, NY), 1984.

Gedicht an die Dauer, Suhrkamp (Frankfurt, Germany), 1986.

(Author of text) *Walter Pichler: Skupturen, Zeichnugne, Modelle* (exhibition catalogue), Die Galerie (Frankfurt am Main, Germany), 1987.

Versuch über die Mudigkeit (essay), Suhrkamp (Frankfurt, Germany), 1989, published in *The Jukebox, and Other Essays on Storytelling,* Farrar, Straus & Giroux (New York, NY), 1994.

Wiederholung (fairy tales), Collier (New York, NY), 1989.

Versuch über die Jukebox (essay), Suhrkamp (Frankfurt, Germany), 1990, translated in *The Jukebox, and Other Essays on Storytelling,* Farrar, Straus & Giroux (New York, NY), 1994.

Versuch über den gegluckten Tag (essay), Suhrkamp (Frankfurt, Germany), 1991, translated in *The Jukebox, and Other Essays on Storytelling,* Farrar, Straus & Giroux (New York, NY), 1994.

Abschied des Träumers vom Neunten Land (essay; title means "The Dreamer's Farewell from the Ninth Land"), Suhrkamp (Frankfurt, Germany), 1992.

Noch einmal vom Neuten Land, Gespräch mit Jöze Horvat, Wieser, 1993.

André Müller im Gespräch mit Peter Handke, Bibliothek der Provinz, 1993.

The Jukebox, and Other Essays on Storytelling, Farrar, Straus & Giroux (New York, NY), 1994.

Eine Winterliche Reise zu den Flüssen Donau, Save, Morawa, und Drina; oder, Gerechtingkeit für Serbien (essay; originally published in *Süddeutsche Zeitung,* January, 1996), Suhrkamp (Frankfurt, Germany), 1996, translated by Scott Abbott as *A Journey to the Rivers: Justice for Serbia,* Viking (New York, NY), 1997.

Sömmerlicher Nachtrag zu einer Winterlichte Reise (essay; title means "A Summer's Addendum to a Winter's Voyage"), Suhrkamp (Franfurt, Germany), 1996.

Am Felsfenster Morgens: und andere Ortszeiten 1982-1987, Residenz (Salzburg, Austria), 1998.

(With Lisl Ponger) *Ein Wortland: eine Reisse durch Kärnten, Slowenien, Friaul, Istrien und Dalmatien* (travel writing), Wiser (Klagenfurt), 1998.

Lucie im Wald mit den Dingsda: eine Geschichte, Suhrkamp (Frankfurt, Germany), 1999.

Unter Tränen fragend: nachträgliche Aufzeichnungen von zwei Jugoslawien-Durchquerungen im Krieg, März und April 1999 (title means "Notes after the Fact on Two Trips through Yugoslavia during the War, March and April 1999"), Suhrkamp (Frankfurt, Germany), 2000.

(With Dimitri Analis) *Milos Sobaic,* Différence (Paris, France), 2002.

Contributor to periodicals and newspapers, including *Süddeutsche Zeitung.*

ADAPTATIONS: A Sorrow beyond Dreams was dramatized as a monologue by Daniel Freudenberger, and staged at the Marymount Manhattan Theatre, 1977.

SIDELIGHTS: Described by *New York Times Book Review* contributor Lee Siegel as "a cross between Holden Caulfield and Bertolt Brecht," Austrian-born writer Peter Handke rose to prominence as a major figure in postmodern German literature during the 1970s and 1980s. A prolific writer of novels, plays, screenplays, poems, travel writing, and political reportage, Handke is highly respected as a stylistic innovator and as a chronicler of psychological alienation.

Nicholas Hern, in *Peter Handke: Theatre and Anti-Theatre,* joined other critics in suggesting that Handke's legal training may have been an important influence on his prose style. Hern pointed out that the majority of Handke's "plays and novels consist of a series of affirmative propositions each contained within one sentence. . . . The effect . . . is not unlike the series of clauses in a contract or will or statute-book, shorn of linking conjunctions. It is as if a state of affairs or a particular situation were being defined and constantly redefined until the final total definition permits of no mite of ambiguity." Handke's prose has reminded other readers of the propositions making up Ludwig Wittgenstein's *Tractatus Logico-Philosophicus;* the inquiries into language characteristic of both Wittgenstein and the French structuralists touch on themes that are central to Handke's work. Discussing his more strictly literary masters, Handke once said that American novelist William Faulkner remains the most important of all writers to him.

Handke's remarkable style was first displayed in the experimental prose pieces he wrote and published in magazines while still a university student, as well as in *Die Hornissen,* which reminded many reviewers of the French "new novel" of that era. *Die Hornissen,* which appeared in the spring of 1966, was generally well received, but its success was not what made Handke suddenly appear on the international literary scene. In April, 1966, he participated in the twenty-eighth convention of Group 47, an association of German writers that met in Princeton, New Jersey. On the last day of the conference Handke, then aged twenty-four, began what came to be called "Handke-Publicity." In his book, *Group 47,* Siegfried Mandel wrote:

"Shaking his Beatle-mane, Handke . . . railed against what he had been listening to: impotent narrative; empty stretches of descriptive (instead of analytical) writing pleasing to the ears of the older critics; monotonous verbal litanies, regional and nature idyllicism, which lacked spirit and creativeness. The audience warmed up to the invective with cheers, and later even those whose work had been called idiotic, tasteless, and childish came over to congratulate the Group 47 debutant and to patch things up in brotherly fashion."

Handke's first play was a major hit when it was produced during a week of experimental new drama in Frankfurt. In *Publikumsbeschimpfung—Offending the Audience*—all the comfortable assumptions of bourgeois theater are called into question and the audience is systematically mocked and insulted. The play continued to remain popular with German theatregoers, as did Handke's other early "*sprechstücke*"—plays which in various ways investigate the role of language in defining the individual's social identity.

The power of language is also the theme of *Kaspar*, Handke's first full-length play, which focuses on 1828 Nuremberg and the actual case of a sixteen-year-old boy who had apparently been confined all his life in a closet, and who was discovered physically full-grown but with the intellect of an infant. Kaspar Hauser's story intrigued a number of writers, and in Handke's play he is indoctrinated with conventional moral precepts in the process of being taught to speak. As Nicholas Hern put it, "the play is an abstract demonstration of the way an individual's individuality is stripped from him by society, specifically by limiting the expressive power of the language it teaches him." In Germany *Kaspar* was voted play of the year, and was regarded by many critics as one of the country's most important postwar dramas.

Handke has continued to write plays, for stage as well as for radio, television, and the screen. Discussing Handke's second full-length play, *The Ride across Lake Constance,* most critics thought the play dealt with the problems of communication, though in a baroque and bewildering fashion. Handke's approach fascinated reviewers, several of whom could make no sense of it at all. Hern wrote that in this play, "Handke has moved from a Wittgensteinian distrust of language to a Foucaultian distrust of what our society calls reason. His play is by no means surrealist in externals

only: it parallels the surrealists' cardinal desire—the liberation of men's minds from the constraints of reason. Thus Handke continues to demonstrate that the consistently *anti*-theatrical stance which he has maintained throughout his dramatic writing can none the less lend concrete theatrical expression to abstract, philosophical ideas, thereby generating a new and valid form of theatre."

Meanwhile, Handke established a second reputation as one of the most important German novelists of his generation. His first success in this form was *The Goalie's Anxiety at the Penalty Kick,* which reflects the same preoccupations as do his plays. The partly autobiographical *Short Letter, Long Farewell,* about a young Austrian writer's haphazard journey across the United States to a dangerous meeting with his estranged wife, had a mixed but generally favorable reception. And there was little but praise for *A Sorrow beyond Dreams,* Handke's profoundly sensitive account of his mother's life, which ended in suicide. In the *New York Review of Books,* Michael Wood wrote that "Handke's objective tone is a defense against the potential flood of his feelings, of course, but it is also a act of piety, an expression of respect: this woman's bleak life is not to be made into 'literature.' . . . Handke's mother is important not because she is an especially vivid case but because she is not, because she is one of many."

In *The Afternoon of a Writer,* Handke explores a professional writer's feelings of alienation and anxiety. The protagonist of the work makes no deep connections with other people, choosing instead to withdraw into his writing. His greatest fear is that he will lose his gift of language and imagination—a loss that would leave him completely alienated from the world. Ursula Hegi found *The Afternoon of a Writer* "fascinating," and commented in the *Los Angeles Times Book Review* that "Handke's new novel poses interesting questions about the balance between the nature of solitude and the nature of writing." Anthony Vivis of the *Times Literary Supplement,* however, faulted the extreme minimalism of the work and implied an autobiographical connection between its protagonist and Handke; the novelist, Vivis asserted, "appears to fear the threat, rather than confront the challenge, of his creativity."

Handke's novel *Absence* also subverts the expectations of plot and character development that are met with more traditional novels. The book portrays the walking journey of four characters who are identified simply as "old man," "young woman," "gambler," and "soldier." Writing in the *New York Times Book Review,* Elizabeth Tallent commented: "The soldier is defined by his absence, the young woman by her narcissism, the old man by his profound detachment, the gambler by his inability to love. Yet none of them determines the direction of the tale, whose shape is, instead, that of a quest—one conjured from aimlessness." Also praising the novel, Michael Hofmann observed in the *Times Literary Supplement* that "The book is counter-psychological, magical, perception-led."

My Year in the No-Man's-Bay, a sequel to *The Afternoon of a Writer,* presents a protagonist named Gregor Keuschnig—called Gregor K., in what *New York Times Book Review* contributor Lee Siegel identified as a "jab at Kafka"—who is recalling the year of his artistic and spiritual transformation in a nondescript suburb of Paris. Yet Gregor is unable to focus on this particular year; each time he attempts it, he is distracted into telling other stories. "By the time he arrives at the novel's last section," wrote Siegel, "you realize that Gregor has collapsed all time together." Siegel found this structural device "breathtaking," but noted that the result is disappointing. "Rejecting character, plot and psychology as mere fictions," the critic commented, Handke "relies on an ostentatious thematic framework that winds up being more implausible than any old-fashioned novelistic trick."

Handke uses the motif of the journey as a structuring device in *On a Dark Night I Left My Silent House.* In this novel, a middle-aged pharmacist from a small village near Salzburg is beaten by strangers he encounters on a wooded path. Unable to speak after the attack, he joins a pair of drifters on a long, indirect drive across Europe. The group eventually ends up in Spain, after which the pharmacist slowly hikes back to his village. When he arrives, he discovers that some things seem the same and others seem different. Keith Miller observed in a review for the *Times Literary Supplement* that this journey suggests several things, including medieval knightly quests, the attraction of Southern Europe to Germanic romantic thinkers, and even an allegory of contemporary Europe in the age of economic union. Noting that the book has the feel of a dream, Miller observed that "if the novel beguiles or engages, it is through its language rather than the usual questions of what happens to whom." *New York Times Book Review* contributor Kai Maristed also noted the intense interior focus of the book, concluding that "It

is Peter Handke's loving gaze, honed by time and discipline, that shows readers the way out again into the world's prolific and astonishing strangeness." Claiming that Handke's pharmacist can be seen as "a kind of fictional blank slate for the writing of theory," *New York Times* reviewer Richard Bernstein found *On a Dark Night I Left My Silent House* filled with "disparate images . . . [that] all suggest the rich randomness of thought," and added that, though the novel's lack of plot is a weakness, "as an assemblage, these images have the capacity to haunt."

With *The Jukebox and Other Essays on Storytelling,* Handke presents "Essay on Tiredness," "Essay on the Jukebox," and "Essay on the Successful Day." As in Handke's fiction, the psyche of the writer and the seemingly mundane aspects of experience—such as boredom and tiredness—are of central interest. "Essay on the Jukebox," for example, says very little about jukeboxes and instead explores the creative processes of a writer who is preparing to write about jukeboxes. Sven Birkerts commented in the *New York Times Book Review* that, "Shuttling between fiction and essay, [Handke] is making what feels like a new form, a kind of associative philosophical meditation that both maps and manifests the movements of the mind." Critics emphasized Handke's rambling, digressive, idiosyncratic writing style, praising his dry humor and experimentalism, although some also noted that readers may find the work tedious.

Although his philosophical stance on a number of European matters has been considered controversial, Handke's refusal to use his plays and novels as vehicles for political propaganda was much criticized by German socialists. For Handke's part, he has maintained that literature and political commitment are incompatible: "It would be repugnant to me to twist my criticism of a social order into a story or to aestheticize it into a poem," he writes in one of his essays. "I find that the most atrocious mendacity: to manipulate one's commitment into a poem or to make literature out of it, instead of just saying it loud."

The novelist's caveat against mixing politics and writing does not extend to Handke's nonfiction works, and he is unabashedly political in his books of travel and reportage about the former Yugoslavia. In *A Journey to the Rivers: Justice for Serbia,* he expresses regret over the dissolution of the Yugoslav federation into separate countries and emphasizes the shared past of

the various ethnic groups in the region. At the same
time, he argues that the Western media portrayed Serbs
in an unfair light during the late twentieth-century war
in Bosnia. Most journalists, he writes, "confuse their
role . . . with that of judge, or even demagogue,
and . . . are just as nasty as the dogs of war on the
battlefield," emphasizing "the sale of naked, randy,
market-oriented facts, or bogus facts." This position,
which some took to imply support for the regime of
dictator Slobodan Milosovic, earned Handke some ill
will within the European community, especially from
those who supported the NATO bombing during the
conflict. Reviewers, too, raised questions about
Handke's position. In the *Time Literary Supplement,*
Edward Timms acknowledged the impact of *A Journey
to the Rivers,* yet commented that "it cannot be said
that the book is entirely convincing. . . . [Handke]
tends toward polemical generalization, while his coun-
terbalancing narrative of his encounters in Serbia has
an impressionistic subjectivity which at times verges
on the sentimental."

For other critics, however, the book's subjectivity was
seen as a plus. As Bernd Reinhardt explained in a
World Socialist Web site article, "For Handke, the truth
about the war is not one-dimensional," and he is intent
on correcting what he considers to be serious media
distortions. Indeed, though Handke has commented
about keeping political content out of artistic works,
he made the Bosnia War the subject of his play *Journey in a Canoe.* While noting the play's theme, Reinhardt pointed out that it contains "no trace of pro-
Serbian sentiment."

Commenting on Handke's changing role from outspoken experimentalist to a more inward-looking, metaphysical approach, *World Literature Today* contributor
Erich Wolfgang Skwara explained that the author's
unwillingness to go along with social trends in favor
of examining "what existence should and must be in
order to allow for dignity" has caused his work to be
rejected by many critics in Germany. Because of his
outsider status, Handke's more recent works have "suffered unfair rejection and criticism—clearly not aimed
at the always poetic and convincing texts but meant as
a sort of 'revenge' against a poet who refuses to play
along with established opinions."

BIOGRAPHICAL AND CRITICAL SOURCES:

BOOKS

Contemporary Literary Criticism, Gale (Detroit, MI),
    Volume 5, 1976, Volume 8, 1978, Volume 10,
    1979, Volume 15, 1980, Volume 38, 1986.

DeMeritt, Linda C., *New Subjectivity and Prose Forms
    of Alienation: Peter Handke and Botho Strauss,* P.
    Lang (New York, NY), 1987.
Dictionary of Literary Biography, Volume 124:
    *Twentieth-Century German Dramatists, 1919-
    1992,* Gale (Detroit, MI), 1992.
Firda, Richard Arthur, *Peter Handke,* Twayne (New
    York, NY), 1993.
Hern, Nicholas, *Peter Handke: Theatre and Anti-
    Theatre,* Wolff, 1971.
Klinkowitz, Jerome, *Peter Handke and the Postmodern
    Transformation: The Goalie's Journey Home,* Uni-
    versity of Missouri Press, 1983.
Linstead, Michael, *Outer World and Inner World: So-
    cialisation and Emancipation in the Works of Peter
    Handke, 1964-1981,* P. Lang (New York, NY),
    1988.
Mandel, Siegfried, *Group 47,* Southern Illinois Univer-
    sity Press, 1973.
Perrarm, Garvin, *Peter Handke, The Dynamics of the
    Poetics and the Early Narrative Prose,* P. Lang
    (New York, NY), 1992.
Ran-Moseley, Faye, *The Tragicomic Passion: A His-
    tory and Analysis of Tragicomedy and Tragicomic
    Characterization in Drama, Film, and Literature,*
    P. Lang (New York, NY), 1994.
Rischbieter, Henning, *Peter Handke,* Friedrich, 1972.
Schlueter, June, *The Plays and Novels of Peter Handke,*
    University of Pittsburgh Press (Pittsburgh, PA),
    1981.

PERIODICALS

America, April 3, 1999, Robert E. Hosmer, Jr., review
    of *Once Again for Thucydides,* p. 23.
Booklist, January 1-15, 1997, p. 806; October 1, 2000,
    review of *On a Dark Night I Left My Silent House,*
    p. 322.
Chicago Tribune, December 1, 1989; December 15,
    1989.
Drama Review, fall, 1970.
Economist, October 18, 1997, p. 14.
Kirkus Reviews, June 1, 1994, p. 753; November 1,
    1996, p. 1581; November 1, 2000, review of *On a
    Dark Night I Left My Silent House,* p. 1517.
Library Journal, July, 1994, p. 93; January 1, 1997,
    p. 124; December, 2002, Ali Houissa, review of *A
    Sorrow beyond Dreams,* p. 127.
Los Angeles Times, May 22, 1985; June 25, 1986;
    May 20, 1988.

Los Angeles Times Book Review, July 16, 1989, p. 3.

Modern Drama, spring, 1995, p. 143; July, 1996, pp. 39-40; winter, 1996, p. 680.

Nation, December 4, 1989; January 12, 1997, p. 12.

New Leader, October 2, 1989.

New Republic, February 28, 1970; September 28, 1974; May 23, 1988.

New Statesman, August 5, 1988; July 13, 1990, p. 36; July 19, 1991, p. 38.

Newsweek, July 3, 1978.

New Yorker, December 25, 1989.

New York Review of Books, May 1, 1975; June 23, 1977; September 21, 2000, J. S. Marcus, reviews of *My Year in the No-Man's Bay, Repetition,* and *A Sorrow beyond Dreams,* pp. 80-81.

New York Times, January 30, 1977; March 22, 1971; June 17, 1978; January 25, 1980; April 2, 1980; July 12, 1984; June 25, 1986; April 29, 1988; August 28, 1989; September 3, 1989, p. 17; September 7, 1994, p. C17; March 18, 1996, p. A7; November 29, 2000, Richard Bernstein, review of *On a Dark Night I Left My Silent House.*

New York Times Book Review, May 21, 1972; September 15, 1974; April 27, 1975; July 31, 1977; June 18, 1978; July 22, 1984; August 4, 1985; July 17, 1986; August 7, 1988; June 17, 1990, p. 8; August 21, 1994, p. 10; April 6, 1997, p. 16; October 25, 1998, Lee Siegel, review of *My Year in the No-Man's-Bay;* December 17, 2000, Kai Maristed, review of *On a Dark Night I Left My Silent House,* p. 15.

Publishers Weekly, September 12, 1977; October 30, 2000, review of *On a Dark Night I Left My Silent House,* p. 45.

Review of Contemporary Fiction, summer, 2001, Michael Pinker, review of *On a Dark Night I Left My House,* p. 163.

Süddeutsche Zeitung, May 14, 1999, interview with Handke.

Text und Kritik, no. 24, 1969 (Handke issue).

Time, May 9, 1988.

Times (London, England), May 15, 1972; November 13, 1973; December 9, 1973; April 3, 1980; July 25, 1985; August 4, 1988; July 8, 1989.

Times Literary Supplement, April 21, 1972; December 1, 1972; April 18, 1980; July 17, 1981; November 15, 1985; October 3, 1986; October 5, 1990; May 24, 1991; April 26, 1996, p. 29; April 26, 1996, Edward Timms, review of *Eine winterliche Reise zu den Flüssen Donau, Save, Morawa und Drina;* December 22, 2000, Keith Miller, review of *On a Dark Night I Left My Silent House.*

Tribune Books (Chicago, IL), July 3, 1988.

Wall Street Journal, June 3, 1999, John Reed, "Theater: In the Line of Balkan Fire," p. A24.

Washington Post Book World, July 28, 1985.

World Literature Today, spring, 1987, p. 284; spring, 1991, p. 301; autumn, 1992, p. 716; summer, 1993, p. 604; summer, 1995, p. 572; summer, 1997, p. 584; winter, 1997, p. 147; summer, 1999, review of *Am Felsfenster Morgens,* p. 523; autumn, 1999, review of *Die Fahrt im Einbaum,* p. 728; winter, 2001, Scott Abbott, review of *Unter Tränen fragend,* p. 78; April-June, 2003, Erich Wolfgang Skwara, review of *Der Bildverlust, oder Durch die Sierra de Gredos,* p. 77.

ONLINE

World Socialist Web Site, http://www.wsws.org/ (August 11, 1999), Bernd Reinhardt, "The Austrian Writer Peter Handke, European Public Opinion, and the War in Yugoslavia."*

*   *   *

HIAASEN, Carl 1953-

PERSONAL: Born March 12, 1953, in Fort Lauderdale, FL; son of K. Odel (a lawyer) and Patricia (Moran) Hiaasen; married Constance Lyford (a registered nurse and attorney), November 12, 1970 (divorced, 1996); married, 1999; wife's name, Fenia; children: (first marriage) Scott Andrew; (second marriage) Quinn. *Education:* Attended Emory University, 1970-72; University of Florida, B.S., 1974.

ADDRESSES: Office—Miami Herald, 1 Herald Plaza, Miami, FL 33101. *Agent*—Esther Newberg, International Creative Management, 40 West 57th St., New York, NY 10019.

CAREER: Writer. *Cocoa Today,* Cocoa, FL, reporter, 1974-76; *Miami Herald,* Miami, FL, reporter, 1976—, columnist, 1985—. Professor at Barry College, 1978-79.

MEMBER: Authors Guild, Authors League of America.

Carl Hiaasen

AWARDS, HONORS: National Headliners Award, distinguished service medallion from Sigma Delta Chi, public service first-place award from Florida Society of Newspaper Editors, Clarion Award, Women in Communications, Heywood Broun Award, Newspaper Guild, and finalist for Pulitzer Prize in public-service reporting, all 1980, all for newspaper series about dangerous doctors; Green Eyeshade Award from Sigma Delta Chi, first-place award for in-depth reporting, Florida Society of Newspaper Editors, grand prize for investigative reporting, Investigative Reporters and Editors, and finalist for Pulitzer Prize in special local reporting, all 1981, all for newspaper series on drug-smuggling industry in Key West; Silver Gavel Award, American Bar Association, 1982; Newbery honor book, American Library Association, 2003, for *Hoot;* Damon Runyon Award, 2003-2004.

WRITINGS:

NOVELS

(With William D. Montalbano) *Powder Burn,* Atheneum (New York, NY), 1981.

(With William D. Montalbano) *Trap Line,* Atheneum (New York, NY), 1982.
(With William D. Montalbano) *A Death in China,* Atheneum (New York, NY), 1984.
Tourist Season, Putnam (New York, NY), 1986.
Double Whammy, Putnam (New York, NY), 1987.
Skin Tight, Putnam (New York, NY), 1989.
Native Tongue, Knopf (New York, NY), 1991.
Strip Tease, Knopf (New York, NY), 1993.
Stormy Weather, Knopf (New York, NY), 1995.
Naked Came the Manatee, Putnam (New York, NY), 1996.
Lucky You, Knopf (New York, NY), 1997.
Sick Puppy, Knopf (New York, NY), 2000.
Basket Case, Knopf (New York, NY), 2002.
Hoot, Knopf (New York, NY), 2002.
Skinny Dip, Knopf (New York, NY), 2004.

OTHER

Team Rodent: How Disney Devours the World (nonfiction), Ballantine (New York, NY), 1998.
Kick Ass: Selected Columns of Carl Hiaasen, University Press of Florida (Gainesville, FL), 1999.
Paradise Screwed: Selected Columns of Carl Hiaasen, Putnam (New York, NY), 2001.

Also contributor to magazines and newspapers, including *Rolling Stone, Penthouse, Us, Playboy,* and *Esquire.*

ADAPTATIONS: Strip Tease was adapted as a motion picture, written and directed by Andrew Bergman, starring Demi Moore and Armand Assante, Castle Rock Entertainment, 1996.

SIDELIGHTS: As an award-winning investigative reporter for the *Miami Herald,* Carl Hiaasen has written about dangerous doctors, drug smuggling, and other serious crimes. His fictional works reflect his exposure to—and outrage over—Florida's social ills. A native of South Florida, Hiaasen has turned his righteous indignation into humorous satire in which heroes and villains alike exhibit farcical quirks and an attachment to creative forms of violence. The good guys are often eco-terrorists seeking to preserve the ever-dwindling plots of undeveloped land; the bad guys wallow in greed as they pursue the rape of the state. According to Joe Queenan in the *New York Times Book Review,*

Hiaasen "has made a persuasive case that the most barbaric, ignorant and just plain awful people living in this country today reside, nay flourish, in the state of Florida." Desmond Ryan cited Hiaasen in the *Philadelphia Inquirer* for "his customary pungency, wit and flair," adding that the novelist "has a way of leaving the reprobates and sleazebags that infest the land of the hanging chad flattened like roadkill."

The son of an attorney, Hiaasen grew up with dual interests. He wanted to be a writer, but he also enjoyed the outdoors and especially savored Florida's unspoiled wilderness areas. He graduated from the University of Florida in 1974, and by 1976 had earned a position with the *Miami Herald* as a reporter. He soon became a member of the *Herald*'s investigative team, and he continues to write two columns a week that take aim at corruption in every level of government and business. Hiaasen began his fiction-writing career with coauthor William D. Montalbano and then struck out on his own with novels that "turn . . . journalistic experience to fictional advantage," in the words of *New York Times Book Review* contributor Herbert Mitgang. As Polly Paddock put it in the *Charlotte Observer,* "Underneath all Hiaasen's hijinks, there is the righteous indignation that marks both his journalistic and novelistic work. Hiaasen hates hypocrisy, pretension, corporate greed, political corruption and the rape of the environment. He won't let us forget that."

Tourist Season, a tongue-in-cheek account of terrorists who bully Miami tourists in order to depress the tourism industry, received considerable acclaim. *Chicago Tribune Book World* columnist Alice Cromie called the thriller "one of the most exciting novels of the season." Tony Hillerman noted in the *New York Times Book Review* that *Tourist Season* "is full of . . . quick, efficient, understated little sketches of the sort of subtle truth that leaves you grinning. In fact, Mr. Hiaasen leaves you grinning a lot." Regarding the book, Hiaasen once commented that "for inspiration, all I had to do was read the daily newspaper. Crime in Miami is so bizarre that no novelist's inventions could surpass true life."

In *Double Whammy* Hiaasen "comes up with a suitably manic plot, this time involving skullduggery on the bass-fishing circuit," said Kevin Moore in the *Chicago Tribune Book World.* R. J. Decker, a news photographer turned private eye, tangles with a host of bizarre characters, including a former governor of

Florida who lives on roadkill and a murderer with the head of a pit bull attached to his arm. "The writing style is macabre-funny," noted Walter Walker in the *New York Times Book Review,* "and it delivers the plot's myriad twists and turns with breathtaking speed."

Greedy plastic surgeons, sensationalistic television personalities, and money-grubbing lawyers are the targets of *Skin Tight,* another fast-paced mix of satire and thriller. The hero, Mick Stranahan, a former Florida state investigator, is threatened by an old feud with a corrupt plastic surgeon suspected of murder. In self-defense, Stranahan keeps a trained barracuda under his stilt house. In one incident the barracuda eats the hand of a hit man trying to murder Stranahan, but the hit man gets a weed trimmer as a prosthesis—and then comes after Stranahan again. In the *New York Times Book Review,* Katherine Dunn observed that while the author's tone in *Skin Tight* holds no warmth towards its subjects (unlike *Tourist Season*) it is still fascinating and impressive. She added, "No one has ever designed funnier, more terrifying bad guys, or concocted odder ways of doing away with them."

Hiaasen's next novel, *Native Tongue,* garnered similar praise. The story is "a skillful, timely satire—a weird, wild, comic caper of ecological guerrilla warfare that bites as often as it laughs," wrote Richard Martins in the *Chicago Tribune Book World.* In the book, the fragile ecology of the Florida Keys is exploited and damaged by theme-park developers and environmental activists alike. According to Jack Viertel, writing in the *Los Angeles Times Book Review,* Hiaasen "might be termed a South Florida hybrid of Jonathan Swift, Randy Newman, and Elmore Leonard. . . . His novels are shot through with a kind of real passion that lurks beneath the manic prose—an urgent affection for his subject." Viertel concluded, "The ultimate enemy is always the same: overdevelopment of the last remaining wilderness in the state."

Strip Tease features a genuine heroine, Erin Grant, who resorts to nude dancing so that she can continue to finance the fight for custody of her daughter. Grant's ex-husband, the wheelchair-stealing Darrell, is one of the novel's many villains; others include a state congressman beholden to Florida's powerful sugar-growers. Writing in the *Times Literary Supplement,* Karl Miller remarked, "Hiaasen is against graft, exploitation, and the destruction of the environment. This is an ecologically green black comedy, in which men are scum and it is 'women's work,' according to Erin, to destroy them." In 1996 the novel was released as a motion picture starring Demi Moore.

In *Stormy Weather* Hiaasen uses the aftermath of a devastating hurricane to once again skewer the greedy and corrupt in South Florida. Characters include Edie Marsh, a con woman who has tried in vain to blackmail the Kennedys but who recognizes a new opportunity for enrichment when the hurricane blows through; an advertising executive who ends his honeymoon at Disneyland to venture to Miami to videotape the storm's damage; and a recurring Hiaasen bit player, the one-eyed former governor of Florida who now lives in the swamp, sustaining himself with roadkill. Chicago *Tribune Books* reviewer Gary Dretzka noted, "Hiaasen writes with the authority of a documentary filmmaker. . . . He displays no mercy for anyone perceived as being responsible for defiling his home environment." Calling *Stormy Weather* "caustic and comic," *Time* critic John Skow explained the author's use of villains in his literary formula: "turn over a rock and watch in glee and honest admiration as those little rascals squirm in the light."

An eco-terrorist with an anger-management problem serves as the hero in *Sick Puppy.* After seeking revenge on a litterbug, Twilly Spree discovers that the target of his revenge is also a big-time lobbyist involved in expediting the illegal sale of an untouched barrier island. Twilly kidnaps the man's dog and wife in the hope of using them as leverage to save the island. In the meantime, the lobbyist enlists the help of an unscrupulous developer and his sadistic sidekick to put an end to Twilly. A *Publishers Weekly* reviewer deemed the book "a devilishly funny caper" in which Hiaasen "shows himself to be a comic writer at the peak of his powers." Bill Ott observed in *Booklist* that "Hiaasen's brand of apocalyptic surrealism is nothing if not distinctive."

The publication of *Basket Case* marked a departure for Hiaasen. The novel is narrated in the first person by a principled journalist named Jack Tagger, and among the villains is the newspaper industry itself. Still, characteristic Hiaasen humor reigns. Tagger, an obituary writer, investigates the suspicious death of a former rock star, the lead singer of Jimmy and the Slut Puppies. Jimmy's silly lyrics are offered for the reader's perusal alongside Tagger's obsession with

death and with the decline of serious reportage in newspapers. Ott in *Booklist* applauded Hiaasen for venturing beyond "his unique brand of apocalyptic surrealism" to produce "a rip-roaringly entertaining tale." *Orlando Sentinel* reviewer William McKeen declared that *Basket Case* "is what loyal readers have come to expect from the guy—an intelligent, funny, deeply moral book about the decline of Western Civilization." McKeen was particularly delighted with Tagger, declaring him "probably one of Hiaasen's most endearing fictional characters." In the *Fort Worth Star-Telegram,* Jeff Guinn concluded that *Basket Case* "proves two things about . . . Hiaasen: He was brave enough to venture beyond the sarcastic humor/ecological themes that characterized his first eight novels, and he is a huge writing talent whose finest fiction may be yet to come."

In *Hoot* Hiaasen keep his characters dedicated to a higher cause, but this time Hiaasen's audience includes younger readers as he focuses on protagonists who are children. "My stepson, nephews and nieces are always bugging me about reading one of my books," the author was quoted as saying in *Book.* "Obviously, some of the language and adult situations went out the window, but I created the same sensibilities in my kid characters that my adult ones walk around with." *Hoot* tells the story of Roy Eberhardt, a middle-school student who moves into Coconut Cove with his family and tries to adjust to life in South Florida. Before long, he is dealing with a bully, a mysterious boy called Mullet Fingers, and a protest to stop a construction project that threatens the habitat of owls. Writing in the *School Library Journal,* Miranda Doyle found the novel "Entertaining but ultimately not very memorable," while a *Publishers Weekly* contributor predicted that "Characteristically quirky characters and comic twists will surely gain the author new fans." Bill Ott, writing in *Booklist,* praised Hiaasen for letting "his inner kid run rampant" and added that the book "is full of offbeat humor, buffoonish yet charming supporting characters, and genuinely touching scene of children enjoying the wildness of nature."

For his novel *Skinny Dip,* Hiaasen once again writes for adults as he tells the tale of Chaz Perrone, an incompetent and greedy marine scientist who is helping a tycoon to illegally dump fertilizer into the Everglades. Perrone attempts to kill his wife, Joey, after she finds out about his illegal doings. But Joey survives and with the help of former cop Mick Stranahan begins to haunt and taunt her husband, in a comic romp that has its roots in the current events of the Sunshine State.

In addition to novels, Hiaasen has also published several volumes of his collected columns, as well as *Team Rodent: How Disney Devours the World,* a scathing critique of the Walt Disney Corporation. *Atlanta Journal-Constitution* writer Mike Williams observed that in his nonfiction, "Hiaasen wastes no time. He sets his tone to rapid-fire acerbic, squeezes off a few rounds to clear his muzzle, then goes on full automatic, like Rambo taking on the world." In the *Sarasota Herald Tribune* David Grimes remarked that "Reading a collection of Carl Hiaasen's newspaper columns reveals a frightening truth about his loopy novels: They're not that big an exaggeration." *Southern Cultures* reviewer David Zucchino maintained that when "Hiaasen opens fire . . . he is pitiless. He savages the men and institutions he believes are turning his beloved Miami and South Florida into a crass, violent, drug-soaked strip mall." A *Publishers Weekly* critic felt that Hiaasen "writes with an old-time columnist's sense of righteous rage and an utterly current and biting wit."

As to the aims Hiaasen holds for his fiction, the author once told *People* magazine: "All I ever ask of my main characters is that their hearts are in the right place, that when they step over the law it's for a higher cause." Discussing why he became an author, Hiassen told a contributor to the *Writer,* that he "enjoyed writing and getting a reaction" when he was very young. He added: "I think it's some sort of extension of being a class clown—that if you could write something and make somebody laugh, it was a good gig to have. I think there was an element of psychotherapy—it was a legal outlet for some of the ideas I was wanting to express as a kid."

BIOGRAPHICAL AND CRITICAL SOURCES:

PERIODICALS

Atlanta Journal-Constitution, June 14, 1998, Mike Williams, "Hiaasen Tackles 'Rodent' That Ate Florida," p. L11; January 2, 2000, Phil Kloer, "Hiaasen's 'Sick' Tale a Fun Ride," p. K12.

Book, September-October, 2002, "Kidding Around: Youth-Oriented Books by Adult Authors," p. 66.

Booklist, November 1, 1999, Bill Ott, review of *Sick Puppy,* p. 483; May 1, 2001, Bill Ott, "Hiaasen's People," p. 1704; September 15, 2001, David Pitt, review of *Paradise Screwed: Selected Columns of Carl Hiaasen,* p. 184; November 1, 2001, Bill Ott, review of *Basket Case,* p. 444; October 15, 2002, Bill Ott, review of *Hoot,* p. 405.

Charlotte Observer, January 16, 2002, Polly Paddock, review of *Basket Case.*

Chicago Tribune, January 23, 2002, Patrick T. Reardon, review of *Basket Case.*

Chicago Tribune Book World, March 16, 1986; January 31, 1988; September 10, 1989.

Detroit Free Press, May 4, 1986.

Entertainment Weekly, January 18, 2002, Bruce Fretts, "Sunny Delight," p. 72.

Fort Worth Star-Telegram, January 9, 2002, Jeff Guinn, review of *Basket Case.*

Gentleman's Quarterly, June, 1996, p. 92.

Globe and Mail (Toronto, Ontario, Canada), April 26, 1986.

Houston Chronicle, January 16, 2000, Jim Barlow, "Carl Hiaasen: The Kinky Friedman of Thriller Writers," p. 17.

Library Journal, June 15, 1981; March 15, 1986.

Los Angeles Times Book Review, April 29, 1984; October 13, 1991.

Maclean's, October 16, 1995, p. 79; January 17, 2002, Paula Friedman, review of *Basket Case,* p. 2.

New York Times, June 14, 1998, Deborah Stead, review of *Team Rodent: How Disney Devours the World,* p. B9; January 6, 2000, Christopher Lehmann-Haupt, "Lots of Bad-Natured Floridians and One Good-Natured Dog," p. B10; January 3, 2002, Janet Maslin, "An Obit Writer's Renewed Zest for Life," p. B13.

New York Times Book Review, January 10, 1982; February 13, 1983; June 24, 1984; March 16, 1986; March 6, 1988; October 15, 1989; September 3, 1995, p. 15; January 9, 2000, Joe Queenan, "Everything Is Rotten in the State of Florida," p. 10; March 25, 2001, Scott Veale, review of *Sick Puppy,* p. 28.

Orlando Sentinel, September 20, 1981; January 16, 2002, William McKeen, review of *Basket Case.*

People, May 15, 2000, Christina Cheakalos, "Hurricane Hiaasen," p. 139.

Philadelphia Inquirer, January 16, 2002, Desmond Ryan, review of *Basket Case.*

Playboy, October, 1995, p. 34.

Publishers Weekly, August 16, 1993; July 10, 1995, p. 44; October 25, 1999, review of *Kick Ass: Se-*

lected Columns of Carl Hiaasen, p. 61; November 8, 1999, review of *Sick Puppy*, p. 49; November 12, 2001, review of *Basket Case*, p. 36; June 24, 2002, review of *Hoot*, p. 58.

Sarasota Herald Tribune, September 2, 2001, David Grimes, "More Florida Bad Guys in Carl Hiaasen Collection," p. E5.

School Library Journal, Miranda Doyle, review of *Hoot*, p. 188.

Southern Cultures, fall, 2000, David Zucchino, review of *Kick Ass*, p. 73.

Time, August 14, 1995, John Skow, review of *Stormy Weather*, p. 70.

Times Literary Supplement, November 5, 1993, p. 12; March 29, 1996, p. 14.

Tribune Books (Chicago, IL), September 1, 1991; July 10, 1994, p. 8; August 13, 1995, p. 5.

Vanity Fair, August, 1993.

Variety, July 13, 1998, Andrew Paxman, review of *Team Rodent*, p. 6.

Washington Post Book World, May 6, 1984; April 6, 1986.

Writer, June, 2003, "Carl Hiaasen (How I Write)," p. 66.

ONLINE

BookPage, http://www.bookpage.com/ (January 27, 2002), Jay Lee MacDonald, "Carl Hiaasen Takes a Bite out of Crimes against the Environment."

Carl Hiaasen's Home Page, http://www.carlhiaasen.com (April 7, 2004).

*   *   *

HINTON, S(usan) E(loise) 1950-

PERSONAL: Born 1950, in Tulsa, OK; married David E. Inhofe (in mail order business), September, 1970; children: Nicholas David. *Education:* University of Tulsa, B.S., 1970.

ADDRESSES: Home—Tulsa, OK. *Agent*—c/o Author Mail, Tor Books, 175 Fifth Ave., New York, NY 10010. *E-mail*—sehinton@sehinton.com.

CAREER: Writer. Consultant on film adaptations of her novels; minor acting roles in some film adaptations of her novels.

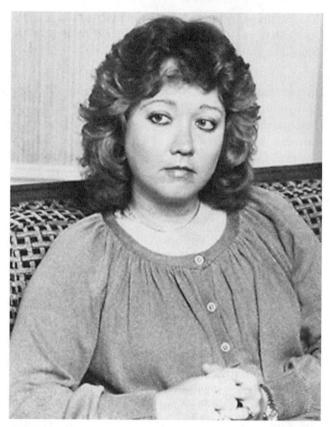

S. E. Hinton

AWARDS, HONORS: New York Herald Tribune best teenage books citation, 1967, *Chicago Tribune Book World* Spring Book Festival Honor Book, 1967, *Media & Methods* Maxi Award, American Library Association (ALA) Best Young Adult Books citation, both 1975, and Massachusetts Children's Book Award, 1979, all for *The Outsiders;* ALA Best Books for Young Adults citation, 1971, *Chicago Tribune Book World* Spring Book Festival Award Honor Book, 1971, and Massachusetts Children's Book Award, 1978, all for *That Was Then, This Is Now;* ALA Best Books for Young Adults citation, 1975, *School Library Journal* Best Books of the Year citation, 1975, and Land of Enchantment Book Award, New Mexico Library Association, 1982, all for *Rumble Fish;* ALA Best Books for Young Adults citation, 1979, *School Library Journal* Best Books of the Year citation, 1979, New York Public Library Books for the Teen-Age citation, 1980, American Book Award nomination for children's paperback, 1981, Sue Hefly Award Honor Book, Louisiana Association of School Libraries, 1982, California Young Reader Medal nomination, California Reading Association, 1982, and Sue Hefly Award, 1983, all for *Tex;* Golden Archer Award, 1983; Recipient of first

ALA Young Adult Services Division/*School Library Journal* Margaret A. Edwards Award, 1988, for body of work.

WRITINGS:

YOUNG ADULT NOVELS

The Outsiders, Viking (New York, NY), 1967.
That Was Then, This Is Now, illustrated by Hal Siegel, Viking (New York, NY), 1971.
Rumble Fish (also see below), Delacorte (New York, NY), 1975.
Tex, Delacorte (New York, NY), 1979.
Taming the Star Runner, Delacorte (New York, NY), 1988.

OTHER

(With Francis Ford Coppola) *Rumble Fish* (screenplay; adapted from her novel), Universal, 1983.
Big David, Little David (for children), illustrated by Alan Daniel, Doubleday (New York, NY), 1995.
The Puppy Sister (for children), illustrated by Jacqueline Rogers, Delacorte (New York, NY), 1995.
Hawkes Harbor (for adults), Tor (New York, NY), 2004.

ADAPTATIONS: Film adaptations of Hinton's novels include *Tex,* starring Matt Dillon, Walt Disney Productions, 1982; *The Outsiders,* starring C. Thomas Howell and Matt Dillon, Warner Bros., 1983; and *That Was Then, This Is Now,* starring Emilio Estevez and Craig Sheffer, Paramount, 1985. *The Outsiders* was adapted as a television series by Fox-TV, 1990. Current Affairs and Mark Twain Media adapted *The Outsiders* and *That Was Then, This Is Now* as filmstrips with cassettes, both 1978. *Rumble Fish* was adapted as a record and cassette, Viking, 1977.

SIDELIGHTS: Ponyboy. Greasers vs. Socs. For millions of fans around the world, these few words will instantly call up the world of *The Outsiders,* S. E. Hinton's classic novel about teen gangs and the troubled process of fitting in. Since publication of this first novel in 1967, "the world of young adult writing

and publishing [has] never [been] the same," according to Jay Daly in the critical study, *Presenting S. E. Hinton.* Daly went on to note that "*The Outsiders* has become the most successful, and the most emulated, young adult book of all time." Ironically, this quiet revolution in book writing and publishing was wrought by a seventeen-year-old girl, who by all rights should have been one of the intended readers of the novel, not its author.

Hinton is credited with revolutionizing the young adult genre by portraying teenagers realistically rather than formulaically and by creating characters, settings, and dialogue that are representative of teenage life in America. *The Outsiders* was the first in her short but impressive list of books to feature troubled but sensitive male adolescents as protagonists. Hinton's subjects include social-class rivalry, poverty, alcoholism, drug addiction, and the cruelty teenagers often inflict on each other and on themselves. Film rights to all five of her novels have been acquired, and four have been adapted as major motion pictures.

Hinton was a high school sophomore at Tulsa's Will Rogers High School when she began writing *The Outsiders.* At the time she had not the slightest dream in the world that her manuscript would be published, let alone that it would sell millions of copies worldwide, spawn a motion picture, and start a trend in publishing toward gritty realism for younger readers. At the time, young Susie was simply working out private concerns. Firstly, she was reacting to divisions apparent in her own high school, and secondly, she was filling a void in subject matter that she herself wanted to read. At the time when Hinton began writing, young adult titles were mostly pure as corn and sweetly innocent; tales in which the major problem was which dress to wear to the prom or whether such-and-such a boy would be the date. "Into this sterile chiffon-and-orchids environment then came *The Outsiders,*" observed Daly. "Nobody worries about the prom in *The Outsiders;* they're more concerned with just staying alive till June."

If Hinton turned the world of publishing upside down with her youthful title, its publication did the same for her life. As word of mouth slowly made the book a classic (it now has eight million copies in print), Hinton was attempting to develop a normal life, studying education at the University of Tulsa, marrying, and having a family. Writing block settled in and it was four years before her second title, *That Was Then, This Is Now,* came out, another edgy story of teen angst. Two further books were published in four-year intervals: *Rumble Fish* in 1975, and *Tex* in 1979. Then nearly a decade passed before publication of her fifth YA title, *Taming the Star Runner.* Since that time, Hinton has published two titles for younger readers. Small in output, Hinton has nonetheless made a major impact on children's literature, a fact confirmed by the 1988 presentation to her of the first annual Margaret A. Edwards Award for career achievement.

Hinton was born in 1948, in Tulsa, Oklahoma, but little more is known about her early years, as Hinton herself is a very private person. Indeed, confusion reins around aspects of her life, such as her year of birth as well as her inspiration for beginning to write. What is known is that she grew up a voluntary tomboy in love with horses. That passion has not diminished over the years, and Hinton is still an avid horsewoman. She was able to use her horse lore in the novel, *Taming the Star Runner.* Hinton's tomboy status also brought her closer to male friends than female. She identified more with active males than with the passive role females of the day were encouraged to project.

A self-confessed outsider as a youngster, Hinton did not belong to any one clique in school, but was friends with a wide variety of types. Along with horses Hinton also developed an early love of reading. Her first writing efforts dealt with horses, and her stories were generally told from a boy's point of view. By the time she reached high school, she was ready to tackle a larger subject, namely the rivalry between two groups in the school, the "greasers" and the affluent "socs" (short for "socials"). "I felt the greasers were getting knocked when they didn't deserve it," Hinton told an interviewer for *Seventeen* shortly after publication of her novel. "The custom for instance, of driving by a shabby boy and screaming 'Greaser!' at him always made me boil. But it was the cold-blooded beating of a friend of mine that gave me the idea of writing a book."

Hinton began the writing in her sophomore year, during the time her father, Grady P. Hinton, was diagnosed with a brain tumor. As Daly put it, "It is not something

she talks about, but one gets the impression that his hospitalization, and the inevitable, unavoidable conclusion that his illness promised, were factors in her withdrawing into herself." While her mother spent more and more time at the hospital, Hinton spent more time in her room or at the dining room table working on her novel. "Susie was very close to her father," Hinton's mother told Yvonne Litchfield of *Tulsa Daily World,* "and I noticed that the sicker he became the harder she worked." Hinton's father died in her junior year, about the time she completed her book.

Hinton worked through four drafts of her story before she was happy with it, but still she gave no thought to publication until the mother of one of her school friends—a professional children's writer—took a look at the manuscript. This reader immediately saw commercial possibilities for the book and urged Hinton to get in touch with her own New York agent. The Oklahoma teenager did just that, and the rest is publishing history.

Hinton's novel was, as Hinton myth has it, accepted for publication the night of her high school graduation, and it appeared in bookstores the spring of her freshman year at college at the University of Tulsa. As the book was written from the male perspective, Hinton's publisher, Viking, prompted her to adapt the more genderless author name of S. E. Hinton. Such a publication was an enormous gamble for a prestigious New York house, but Hinton's book was no overnight success. Slowly and by word of mouth sales grew and continued growing. Letters started arriving at the Hinton household from teenagers all over the country confessing that they never imagined somebody else felt like they did, that they were solaced by the fact that others felt like outsiders just as they did. It was soon apparent that Hinton had touched a raw nerve in American culture.

Hinton's novel deals with a matter of days in the lives of a small group of Tulsa teenagers, loosely modeled after Hinton's own classmates. The book begins and ends with the same lines: "When I stepped out into the bright sunlight from the darkness of the movie house, I had only two things on my mind: Paul Newman and a ride home." In fact the entire book is a composition that the narrator, Ponyboy Curtis, must complete for English class. Trailed home from the movie by a group of Socs (pronounced "soshes" for Socials), Ponyboy is jumped by these rivals, and is saved by his older brothers, Darry and Sodapop, along with other members of his gang, the greasers. These others include the tough guy, Dallas Winston, and the joker who carries a switchblade, Two-Bit Matthews.

Later that night, Ponyboy, Dallas, and another gang member, Johnny, sneak into the drive-in and meet up with two Socs girls, Cherry and Marcia. Confronted after the movie by more Socs, led by Bob Sheldon, their most dangerous fighter, Cherry avoids an altercation by leaving with the Socs. Ruminating about their situation in a vacant lot, Ponyboy and Johnny fall asleep and by the time Ponyboy gets home, he has a run-in with Darry, who has been waiting up for him. Orphaned, the three brothers take care of each other. But Ponyboy has had enough, and decides to run away. Heading off with Johnny, they get only as far as the park before Sheldon and the Socs meet up with them again. In the ensuing fight, Johnny kills Sheldon with a knife.

Heading out is not merely optional now, but vital. Dallas tells the duo of a church hideout in a nearby town, and for the next five days they hole up, reading *Gone with the Wind,* talking about the Robert Frost poem, "Nothing Gold Can Stay," appreciating sunsets and dawns, and munching on baloney sandwiches. When Dally, or Dallas, comes to visit, Johnny says he's through with running; he's going to turn himself in. On the way home, they go by the church and see that it is burning. Perhaps this is a result of the cigarettes they left inside, but whatever the cause they know that children are trapped inside. Without thinking, both Ponyboy and Johnny rush inside to save them. Though they rescue the children, Johnny is badly hurt when a timber falls on his back. Ponyboy and Dallas are also both badly burned.

Cast in the uncommon role of hero, Ponyboy goes to visit Johnny in critical condition at the hospital. Later that evening there is a big rumble between rival gangs, and even the injured Dallas shows up. Victorious, the greasers are jubilant, and Ponyboy and Dallas rush to the hospital to tell Johnny, only to discover him near death. With his dying words, Johnny tells Ponyboy to "Stay gold," referring to the Frost poem about youth and lost innocence. Johnny's death pushes the edgy Dallas over the line. He robs a grocery store and goes down in a hail of police bullets, an unloaded gun in his hands, his death a rather blindly foolish martyrdom.

Suffering from a concussion incurred at the big rumble, Ponyboy collapses, confined to bed for days. He gets

it in his head that he killed Sheldon, not Johnny, and is set to confess at the hearing about the death, but he is acquitted before he has a chance to confess. He remains numb inside, until he discovers another exhortation from Johnny to stay gold, this time in a note left in their copy of *Gone with the Wind.* This breaks through to him and he picks up his pen to start his term paper, writing the first lines of the novel once again.

Critical reception of this publishing phenomenon was mostly laudatory; those with reservations mostly found the book erred on the side of over-sentimentality and cliched writing. "Can sincerity overcome cliches?" asked Thomas Fleming in *New York Times Book Review.* Fleming answered his own question mostly in the positing: "In this book by a now 17-year-old author, it almost does the trick. By almost any standard, Miss Hinton's performance is impressive." Fleming's view was reflected by other reviewers, both then and now. Writing in *Horn Book,* Jane Manthorne called Hinton's work a "remarkable novel . . . a moving, credible view of the outsiders from inside." Lillian N. Gerhardt, reviewing the novel in *School Library Journal,* drew attention to the rare fact in juvenile novels of "confronting the class hostilities which have intensified since the Depression." Gerhardt noted that "Ponyboy . . . tells how it looks and feels from the wrong side of the tracks." Reviewing the book in *Atlantic Monthly,* Nat Hentoff lamented the sometimes "factitious" plot, but declared that Hinton, "with an astute ear and a lively sense of the restless rhythms of the young, also explores the tenacious loyalties on both sides of the class divide." Hentoff concluded that the book was so popular among the young "because it stimulates their own feelings and questionings about class and differing life-styles." A reviewer for *Times Literary Supplement* cut to the chase when noting that it was largely irrelevant whether adult reviewers found the novel dull, contrived, over-sentimentalized, too violent, or just plain implausible. "Young readers will waive literary discrimination about a book of this kind and adopt Ponyboy as a kind of folk hero for both his exploits and his dialogue," the reviewer concluded.

In the event, this critic was dead on. Once word of mouth was established regarding the youth and gender of the writer of *The Outsiders,* sales continued to grow and grow. It was apparent that Hinton and Viking had struck an entirely untapped readership; young kids aching for their stories to be told from their point of view with their voice. Little matter that Hinton's supposed stark realism was really "mythic" as the critic Michael Malone pointed out in an extended piece on the author in *Nation.* "Far from strikingly realistic in literary form," Malone remarked, "[Hinton's] novels are romances, mythologizing the tragic beauty of violent youth." Malone and others have rightly pointed out that the vast majority of teenagers personally experience nothing close to the violence of Hinton's characters, nor do they suffer the vacuum of parental supervision of her Peter Pan-like cast of orphans and near orphans who must look after themselves or watch out that alcoholic, abusive parents do not do them harm.

Never mind, either, the fact of Hinton's sometimes "mawkish and ornate" prose, according to Malone, who noted that Ponyboy "fling[s] adjectives and archaic phrases ('Hence his name,' 'Heaven forbid') around like Barbara Cartland." Ponyboy, through whose eyes the action is viewed, describes characters with an elevated language that is often inappropriate to his spoken thought; he is also prone to quoting Frost. But never mind any of this; Ponyboy and his cast of friends and foes alike are romantic representations, not the viscerally realistic depictions they are usually labeled. Gene Lyons, writing in *Newsweek,* stated, "The appeal of Hinton's novels is obvious. . . . The narrator-hero of each is a tough-tender 14-to 16-year-old loner making his perilous way through a violent, caste-ridden world almost depopulated of grownups. 'It's a kid's fantasy not to have adults around,' says Hinton. While recklessness generally gets punished, her books are never moralistic—all manner of parental rules are broken with impunity."

Royalties from *The Outsiders* helped to finance Hinton's education at the University of Tulsa where she studied education and where she met her husband, David Inhofe. But for several years Hinton suffered from writer's block so severe that, as she told Carol Wallace in *Daily News,* she "couldn't even write a letter." In an interview with Linda Plemons in *University of Tulsa Annual,* Hinton confessed that "I couldn't write. I taught myself to type in the sixth grade, and I couldn't even type or use my typewriter to write a letter. Things were pretty bad because I also went to college and started reading good writers and I thought, 'Oh, no.' I read *The Outsiders* again when I was 20, and I thought it was the worst piece of trash I'd ever seen. I magnified all its faults."

Finally, after she decided that teaching was not for her, and with encouragement from Inhofe, Hinton sat

down to write a second novel. Setting herself the goal of two pages a day, Hinton had, after a few months, a rough draft of the novel, *That Was Then, This Is Now.* Once again Hinton sets her action in the same Tulsa-like surroundings, and focuses on an orphan, Mark, who has lived with the narrator, Bryon, and Bryon's mother since his own parents killed each other in a fight. It is now over a year since the ending of *The Outsiders,* and the old gang and social rivalries are not as clear-cut as they once were. The days of hippies are at hand; drugs are part of the teen landscape. One of the characters, M&M, is a proto-hippy whose LSD overdose tips the balances between Bryon and Mark. No angel himself, Bryon turns in his foster brother for supplying M&M with drugs. There is gang violence aplenty, teens on the prowl and on their own— Ponyboy Curtis even makes an appearance. Overall the book is more disciplined than Hinton's first title, but as Daly and other critics pointed out, "it lacks something." For Daly, it was the inspirational "spark" missing that kept it from breathing true life as had *The Outsiders.*

Other reviewers, however, found Hinton's second novel a moving and heartfelt cry from yet another teenager in pain. For Michael Cart, writing in *New York Times Book Review,* Bryon's struggles with his future and with those he loves form the core of the book. "The phrase, 'if only' is perhaps the most bittersweet in the language," Cart noted, "and Miss Hinton uses it skillfully to underline her theme: growth can be a dangerous process." Though Cart had problems with Bryon's ultimate "life-denying self-pity," turning against his love and life, he concluded that Hinton created "a mature, disciplined novel, which excites a response in the reader. Whatever its faults, her book will be hard to forget." Reviewing the novel in *Library Journal,* Brooke Anson remarked that the book was an "excellent, insightful mustering of the pressures on some teen-agers today, offering no slick solutions but not without hope, either." *Horn Book*'s Sheryl B. Andrews found that this "disturbing" and "sometimes ugly" book "will speak directly to a large number of teen-agers and does have a place in the understanding of today's cultural problems." Selected a Best Books for Young Adults in 1971, *That Was Then, This Is Now* confirmed Hinton as more than a one-book author. Another four years passed between publication of *That Was Then, This Is Now* and Hinton's third novel, *Rumble Fish.* Hinton's narrator, Rusty-James, is another classic sensitive outsider type, who begins his narrative with the blunt declaration: "I was hanging out at Benny's, playing pool, when I heard Biff Wilcox was looking to kill me." Rusty-James's older brother, Motorcycle Boy, something of a Dallas Winston clone, meets a violent death in the novel, echoes of Dallas's demise in *The Outsiders.* And like Hinton's other novels, *Rumble Fish* takes place in compressed time, focusing on incidents which change the life of the narrator forever. Dubbed Hinton's "most ambitious" novel by Geoff Fox and George Walsh, writing in *St. James Guide to Young Adult Writers,* the novel deals with Rusty-James's attempts to make some meaning of life after the passing of the gang conflicts that made his brother such a hero. Now, however, Motorcycle Boy is disenchanted, without hope, and virtually commits suicide, gunned down breaking into a pet store. By the end of the novel Rusty-James is left on his own, having lost his brother, his reputation, and his girl, and is without direction. As Jane Abramson noted in *School Library Journal,* "it is Rusty-James, emotionally burnt out at 14, who is the ultimate victim." Abramson concluded that the "[s]tylistically superb" *Rumble Fish* "packs a punch that will leave readers of any age reeling."

Some reviewers, such as Anita Silvey in *Horn Book,* found the novel unsatisfying and Hinton's further writing potential "unpromising." However, *Rumble Fish* did have admirers both in the United States and abroad. A *Publishers Weekly* contributor declared that "Ms. Hinton is a brilliant novelist," and Margery Fisher, writing in *Growing Point,* commented that "once more is the American urban scene in a book as uncompromising in its view of life as it is disciplined." While others complained of too blatant symbolism in the form of Motorcycle Boy and the fighting fish that give the book its title, Fisher concluded that "Of the three striking books by this young author, *Rumble Fish* seems the most carefully structured and the most probing." Exploring themes from aloneness to biological necessity, *Rumble Fish* tackles large questions in a small package. As Daly concluded about this third novel, "In the end we respond to *Rumble Fish* in a much deeper way than we do to *That Was Then, This Is Now.* It's an emotional, almost a physical response, as opposed to the more rational, intellectual reaction that the other book prompted." Daly went on to note that despite its defects in too-obvious symbolism, it "works as a novel. . . . And there is a name usually given to this kind of success. It is called art."

Hinton herself noted that she had been reading a lot about color symbolism and mythology when writing *Rumble Fish,* and that such concerns crept into the writing of the novel, especially in the character of Motorcycle Boy, the alienated, colorblind gang member looking for meaning. Hinton begins with character, as she has often noted in interviews, but in *Production Notes* for *Rumble Fish,* the screenplay of which she co-wrote with Francis Ford Coppola, she remarked that the novel "was a hard book to write because Rusty-James is a simple person, yet the Motorcycle Boy is the most complex character I've ever created. And Rusty-James sees him one way, which is not right, and I had to make that clear. . . . It's about over-identifying with something which you can never understand, which is what Rusty-James is doing. The Motorcycle Boy can't identify with anything."

The standard four years passed again before publication of Hinton's fourth title, *Tex,* which was, according to Daly, "Hinton's most successful effort" to date. Once again the reader is on familiar ground with near-orphan protagonists, and troubled youths. With *Tex,* however, Hinton opts for a more sensitive and perhaps less troubled narrator than before. Tex McCormick is, as Hinton noted in Delacorte Press's notes from the author, "perhaps the most childlike character I've ever done, but the one who makes the biggest strides toward maturity. I have to admit he's a favorite child." Of course this was several years before the birth of Hinton's own son, Nick.

Another fourteen-year-old lacking parental supervision, Tex has his older brother Mason to look after him while their father is on the rodeo circuit. A story of relationships, Hinton's fourth title focuses on the two teenagers at a time when Mason has had to sell off the family horses to pay bills, as no money has come from their father. This includes Tex's own horse, Negrito. Straining already strained relations between the brothers, this loss of a favored animal sets the plot in motion. Tex tries to run off and find the animal. Neither his friend Johnny nor Johnny's sister Jamie (the romantic attachment) is able to talk Tex out of it, but Mason drags him home in the pickup. Johnny and Tex are forever getting in trouble and things get rougher between Mason and Tex by the time the two brothers are kidnapped by a hitchhiker (Mark from *That Was Then, This Is Now,* who has busted out of jail). Tex's presence of mind saves them, but gets Mark, the hitchhiker, killed by the police. Notoriety at this brings the father home, but disappointment follows when he fails to track down Negrito as he promised. More trouble—in company with Johnny and then with a former friend of Mason's who now deals drugs—lands Tex in the hospital with a bullet wound. He learns that his real father was another rodeo rider, gets a visit from Johnny and Jamie, and once recovered and reconciled with Mason, convinces his older brother that he should go on to college as he's wanted to. Tex tells him he's lined up a job working with horses and can take care of himself.

"Hinton's style has matured since she exploded onto the YA scene in 1967," noted Marilyn Kaye in a *School Library Journal* review of *Tex.* Kaye felt that Hinton's "raw energy . . . has not been tamed—its been cultivated." The outcome, said Kaye, "is a fine, solidly constructed, and well-paced story."*Growing Point*'s Fisher once again had high praise for Hinton, concluding that "In this new book Susan Hinton has achieved that illusion of reality which any fiction writer aspires to and which few ever completely achieve."

Hinton's re-created reality was strong enough to lure Hollywood. Disney productions bought the rights to *Tex,* filming a faithful adaptation of the novel with young Matt Dillon in the lead role, and introducing actors Meg Tilly and Emilio Estevez. Shot in Tulsa, the movie production used Hinton as an advisor, introducing Dillon to her own horse, Toyota, which played the role of Negrito, and teaching the young actor how to ride. It was the beginning of a long and continuing friendship between Hinton and Dillon, who played in three of the four adaptations of her novels. The movie also started a trend of introducing young actors on their way up in her movies.

Next to get a film treatment was *The Outsiders,* though not from Disney this time but from Francis Ford Coppola of *Godfather* fame. Somewhat operatic in its effect, the movie cast Dillon as Dallas Winston, and also starred such future luminaries as Patrick Swayze, Rob Lowe, Tom Cruise, and Estevez. Coppola also filmed *Rumble Fish,* shooting it in black and white to resonate with Motorcycle Boy's color blindness. Once again Dillon starred, with Micky Rourke as Motorcycle Boy. Dennis Hopper, Tom Waits, and Nicolas Cage rounded out the cast. The script was co-written by Hinton and Coppola. In both the Coppola adaptations, Hinton played bit parts as well as worked closely as an advisor during production. However, with the fourth movie adaptation, from a screenplay by Estevez and starring him, Hinton remained on the sidelines. Thus, within a few short years—from 1982 to 1985—all of Hinton's novels were turned into movies and her popularity was at an all-time high, with movie sales driving up book sales. Hinton had the added plus in that her experience with movies was a very positive one. "I really have had a wonderful time and made some very good friends," Hinton told Dave Smith of *Los Angeles Times* regarding her work with Coppola. "Like a lot of authors, I'd heard the horror stories about how they buy the property and then want the author to disappear and not meddle around worrying about what they're doing to the book. But that didn't happen at all. They invited me in right from the start, and I helped with the screenplays."

Throughout the early 1980s, then, Hinton was busy with movie adaptations and with her son, born in 1983. It was not until 1988 that she brought out another novel, *Taming the Star Runner.* Earlier that year Hinton became the first recipient of the Young Adult Services Division/*School Library Journal* Author Achievement Award, otherwise known as the Margaret A. Edwards Award, for career achievement in YA literature. It had been nine years since publication of *Tex;* it was thus fitting that she would have a new title out after receiving such an award. Those first four books had a rough sort of unity to them: a portrayal of the difficult process of sorting through problems of alienation and belonging, with a kind of synthesis if not solution presented by the ending of *Tex.*

Taming the Star Runner, while dealing with some of the old themes, sets off in new directions. Hinton moves from first-to third-person narration in the story of fifteen-year-old Travis Harris who is sent off to his uncle's Oklahoma ranch in lieu of juvenile hall. He has nearly killed his stepfather with a fireplace poker, an attack not unprovoked by the abusive stepfather. What follows is the classic city boy-come-to-the-country motif. Unwillingly, Travis learns hard lessons on the ranch, but the change from urban to rural is not a Technicolor idyll. Travis arrives in the middle of his uncle's divorce, and the man is distant from him. He takes to hanging out at a barn on the property which is rented to Casey Kincaid, three years older than Travis and a horse trainer. She is in the process of taming the eponymous stallion, Star Runner. It is the relationship that grows between this unlikely pair that forms the heart of the book. Another major element—a tip of the hat to Hinton's own history—is the acceptance by a New York publisher of a book that young Travis has written. But there are no easy solutions: the stepfather refuses to give permission for publication, as he comes off less than noble in the pages of the manuscript. Finally Travis's mother stands up to the stepfather and signs permission for him. He has grown closer to Casey, as well as his uncle, but there are no completely happy endings for Hinton, either. Star Runner is killed in an electrical storm and Travis and his uncle are forced to move off the ranch to town, but he is now a published author and has made a real friend in Casey.

Reviews of the novel were largely positive. Nancy Vasilakis commented in *Horn Book* that it "has been generally agreed that no one can speak to the adolescent psyche the way S. E. Hinton can," and now with her fifth novel, Vasilakis felt that the author "hasn't lost her touch." In a lengthy critique in *New York Times Book Review*, Patty Campbell noted that "Hinton has produced another story of a tough young Galahad in black T-shirt and leather jacket. The pattern is familiar, but her genius lies in that she has been able to give each of the five protagonists she has drawn from this mythic model a unique voice and a unique story." Campbell also commented on the "drive and the wry sweetness and authenticity" of the authorial voice, concluding that "S. E. Hinton continues to grow in strength as a young adult novelist." A *Kirkus Reviews* contributor also found much to praise in the novel, remarking that "Hinton continues to grow more reflective in her books, but her great understanding, not of what teen-agers are but of what they can hope to be, is undiminished." Daly, in his critical study, *Presenting S. E. Hinton,* called this fifth novel "Hinton's most mature and accomplished work."

Since publication of *Taming the Star Runner,* Hinton's work has traveled light miles away from her cast of outsiders and bad boys. The year 1995 saw publication of two Hinton titles, both for younger readers. *Big David, Little David* is a picture book based on a joke she and her husband played on their son Nick when the boy was entering kindergarten. In the book, a boy named Nick wonders if a classmate who resembles his father and has the same name could possibly be the same person as his father. Another title inspired by her son is *The Puppy Sister,* about a sibling rivalry between a puppy and an only child, a situation complicated when the puppy slowly changes into a human sister.

Hinton has focused on family in recent years, and on her hobby of horseback riding. As she told James Sullivan in *Book,* "People think I've been sitting here in an ivory tower with minions or something. But I've been wandering around the Safeway wondering what to cook for dinner like everybody else." With her son in college, she has returned to writing. Hinton admitted to Sullivan, "For my writing to be any good, I have to be emotionally committed to it; for a long time, I was just emotionally committed to being a mother. I didn't have anything left over." Hinton published her first novel for adults, a horror/adventure story titled *Hawkes Harbor,* in 2004.

Hinton's books have over ten million copies in print; four of her five YA titles have been filmed; and Hinton still receives bushels of mail from enthusiastic fans for all her books, but especially for *The Outsiders,* now over three decades old, but with a message that continues to speak across the generations. As she told Smith in *Los Angeles Times,* "I understand kids and I really like them. And I have a very good memory. I remember exactly what it was like to be a teenager that nobody listened to or paid attention to or wanted around."

BIOGRAPHICAL AND CRITICAL SOURCES:

BOOKS

Characters in Young Adult Literature, Gale (Detroit, MI), 1997.
Children's Literature Review, Gale (Detroit, MI), Volume 3, 1978, Volume 23, 1991.
Concise Dictionary of American Literary Biography Supplement: Modern Writers, 1900-1998, Gale (Detroit, MI), 1998.
Contemporary Literary Criticism, Volume 30, Gale (Detroit, MI), 1984.
Contemporary Popular Writers, St. James Press (Detroit, MI), 1997.
Daly, Jay, *Presenting S. E. Hinton,* Twayne (Boston, MA), 1987.
Encyclopedia of World Biography, 2nd edition, Gale (Detroit, MI), 1998.
Hinton, S. E., *The Outsiders,* Viking (New York, NY), 1967.
Hinton, S. E., *Rumble Fish Production Notes,* No Weather Films, 1983.
Karolides, Nicholas J., Lee Burress, and John M. Kean, editors, *Censored Books: Critical Viewpoints,* Scarecrow Press (Metuchen, NJ), 1993.
Literature and Its Times, Volume 5, Gale (Detroit, MI), 1997.

Major Authors and Illustrators for Children and Young Adults, 2nd edition, Gale (Detroit, MI), 2002.

Novels for Students, Gale (Detroit, MI), Volume 9, 2000, Volume 15, 2002, Volume 16, 2002.

St. James Guide to Young Adult Writers, St. James Press (Detroit, MI), 1999.

Stanek, Lou Willett, *A Teacher's Guide to the Paperback Editions of the Novels of S. E. Hinton,* Dell (New York, NY), 1980.

Writers for Young Adults, Charles Scribner's Sons (New York, NY), 1997.

PERIODICALS

American Film, April, 1983.

Atlantic Monthly, December, 1967, Nat Hentoff, review of *The Outsiders.*

Book, July-August, 2003, James Sullivan, "Where Are They Now?," pp. 34-41.

Booklist, April 1, 1994, p. 1463; October 15, 1994, p. 413; January 15, 1995, p. 936; June 1, 1995, p. 1760.

Bulletin of the Center for Children's Books, February, 1995, p. 200; November, 1995, p. 92.

Daily News, September 26, 1982, Carol Wallace, "In Praise of Teenage Outcasts."

English Journal, September, 1989, p. 86.

Growing Point, May, 1976, Margery Fisher, review of *Rumble Fish,* p. 2894; May, 1980, Margery Fisher, review of *Tex,* pp. 3686-87.

Horn Book, August, 1967, Jane Manthorne, review of *The Outsiders,* p. 475; July-August, 1971, Sheryl B. Andrews, review of *That Was Then, This Is Now,* p. 338; November-December, 1975, Anita Silvey, review of *Rumble Fish,* p. 601; January-February, 1989, Nancy Vasilakis, review of *Taming the Star Runner,* pp. 78-79.

Kirkus Reviews, August 15, 1988, review of *Taming the Star Runner,* p. 1241.

Library Journal, June 15, 1971, Brooke Anson, review of *That Was Then, This Is Now,* p. 2138.

Los Angeles Times, July 15, 1982, Dave Smith, "Hinton, What Boys Are Made Of."

Nation, March 8, 1986, Michael Malone, "Tough Puppies," pp. 276-78, 280.

Newsweek, October 11, 1982, Gene Lyons, "On Tulsa's Mean Streets," pp. 105-106.

New York Times Book Review, May 7, 1967, Thomas Fleming, review of *The Outsiders,* sec. 2, pp. 10-12; August 27, 1967, pp. 26-29; August 8, 1971, Michael Cart, review of *That Was Then, This Is Now,* p. 8; April 2, 1989, Patty Campbell, review of *Taming the Star Runner,* p. 26; November 19, 1995, Susanna Rodell, review of *The Puppy Sister,* p. 37; November 16, 1997, p. 26.

Publishers Weekly, July 28, 1975, review of *Rumble Fish,* p. 122; December 12, 1994, p. 62; July 17, 1995, p. 230; July 28, 1997, p. 77.

Quill & Quire, April, 1995, p. 37.

School Library Journal, May 15, 1967, Lillian N. Gerhardt, review of *The Outsiders,* pp. 2028-29; October, 1975, Jane Abramson, review of *Rumble Fish,* p. 106; November, 1979, Marilyn Kaye, review of *Tex,* p. 88; December, 1993, p. 70; April, 1995, p. 102; October, 1995, p. 104; May, 1996, p. 76.

Seventeen, October, 1967, "Face to Face with a Teen-Age Novelist."

Signal, May, 1980, pp. 120-22.

Times Educational Supplement, March 10, 1989, Scott Bradfield, review of *Taming the Star Runner,* p. B14.

Times Literary Supplement, October 30, 1970, review of *The Outsiders.*

Tulsa Daily World, April 7, 1967, Yvonne Litchfield, "Her Book to Be Published Soon, But Tulsa Teen-Ager Keeps Cool," p. 20.

University of Tulsa Annual, 1983-84, Linda Plemons, "Author Laureate of Adolescent Fiction," p. 62.

Washington Post Book World, February 12, 1989.

ONLINE

S. E. Hinton Web site, http://www.sehinton.com (April 15, 2004).

Wired for Books Web site, http://wiredforbooks.org/sehinton/ (April 15, 2004), Don Swaim, "Audio Interview with S. E. Hinton."

OTHER

"S. E. Hinton: On Writing and *Tex,*" publicity release from Delacorte Press, winter, 1979/spring, 1980.*

I

IRVING, John (Winslow) 1942-

PERSONAL: Born March 2, 1942, in Exeter, NH; son of Colin F.N. (a teacher) and Frances (Winslow) Irving; married Shyla Leary, August 20, 1964 (divorced, 1981); married Janet Turnbull, June 6, 1987; children: (first marriage) Colin, Brendan, (second marriage) Everett. *Education:* University of New Hampshire, B.A. (cum laude), 1965; University of Iowa, M.F.A., 1967; additional study at University of Pittsburgh, 1961-62, and University of Vienna, 1963-64.

ADDRESSES: Home—Dorset, VT and Toronto, Ontario, Canada. *Agent*—c/o Author Mail, Random House, 201 East 50th St., New York, NY 10022.

CAREER: Novelist. Windham College, Putney, VT, assistant professor of English, 1967-69, 1970-72; University of Iowa, Iowa City, writer-in-residence, 1972-75; Mount Holyoke College, South Hadley, MA, assistant professor of English, 1975-78; Brandeis University, Waltham, MA, assistant professor of English, 1978-79. Teacher and reader at Bread Loaf Writers Conference, 1976. Phillips Exeter Academy, assistant wrestling coach, 1964-65; Northfield Mt. Hermon School, assistant wrestling coach, 1981-83; Fessenden School, assistant wrestling coach, 1984- 86; Vermont Academy, head wrestling coach, 1987-89.

AWARDS, HONORS: Rockefeller Foundation grant, 1971-72; National Endowment for the Arts fellowship, 1974-75; Guggenheim fellow, 1976-77; *The World according to Garp* was nominated for a National Book Award in 1979 and won an American Book Award in 1980; named one of ten "Good Guys" honored for

John Irving

contributions furthering advancement of women, National Women's Political Caucus, 1988, for *The Cider House Rules;* Academy Award for screenplay based on material previously produced or published, 1999, for *The Cider House Rules.*

WRITINGS:

Setting Free the Bears (also see below), Random House (New York, NY), 1969.

269

WRITINGS:

Setting Free the Bears (also see below), Random House (New York, NY), 1969.

The Water-Method Man (also see below), Random House (New York, NY), 1972.

The 158-Pound Marriage (also see below), Random House (New York, NY), 1974.

The World according to Garp, Dutton (New York, NY), 1978.

Three by Irving (contains *Setting Free the Bears, The Water-Method Man,* and *The 158-Pound Marriage*), Random House (New York, NY), 1980.

The Hotel New Hampshire, Dutton (New York), 1981.

The Cider House Rules, Morrow (New York, NY), 1985.

A Prayer for Owen Meany, Morrow (New York, NY), 1989.

Son of the Circus, Random House (New York, NY), 1994.

Trying to Save Piggy Sneed, Arcade (New York, NY), 1996.

The Imaginary Girlfriend: A Memoir (autobiography), Random House (New York, NY), 1996.

A Widow for One Year, Random House (New York, NY), 1998.

The Cider House Rules: A Screenplay (produced by Miramax, 1999), Hyperion (New York, NY), 1999.

My Movie Business: A Memoir, Random House (New York, NY), 1999.

The Fourth Hand, Random House (New York, NY), 2001.

Also contributor of short stories to *Esquire, New York Times Book Review, Playboy,* and other magazines; contributor of introduction to *Leah, New Hampshire: The Collected Stories of Thomas Williams,* Graywolf Press, 1993. Irving's manuscripts are collected at Phillips Exeter Academy in New Hampshire.

ADAPTATIONS: The World according to Garp was released by Warner Bros./Pan Arts in 1982 and starred Robin Williams, Glenn Close, and Mary Beth Hurt, and featured cameo performances by Irving and his sons; *The Pension Grillparzer,* based on portions of *The World according to Garp,* was adapted for the stage by director Mollie Bryce and produced in Hollyood, CA, 2004. *The Hotel New Hampshire* was released by Orion Pictures in 1984 and starred Rob Lowe, Jodie Foster, and Beau Bridges; *The Cider House Rules* was adapted for the stage by Peter Parnell and produced in Seattle, WA, 1996; *Simon Birch,* based on Irving's *A Prayer for Owen Meany,* was released by Buena Vista Pictures in 1998; *The Door in the Floor,* based on Irving's *A Widow for One Year,* was released by Focus Features in 2004. Irving's novels have been adapted as audiobooks by Random Audio.

WORK IN PROGRESS: A screenplay version of *The Fourth Hand,* for Miramax.

SIDELIGHTS: Novelist John Irving is praised as a storyteller with a fertile imagination and a penchant for meshing the comic and the tragic. As *Saturday Review* critic Scot Haller explained, "Fashioning wildly inventive, delightfully intricate narratives out of his sense of humor, sense of dread and sense of duty, Irving blends the madcap, the macabre, and the mundane into sprawling, spiraling comedies of life." Irving is perhaps best known for his critically acclaimed bestseller *The World according to Garp,* which sold more than three million copies in hardback and paperback following its 1978 publication. The novel achieved a cult status—complete with T-shirts proclaiming "I Believe in Garp"—and received serious critical attention, the two combining to propel the novel's author "into the front rank of America's young novelists," according to *Time* critic R. Z. Sheppard.

Though a contemporary novelist, Irving's concerns are traditional, a characteristic some critics have cited as distinguishing Irving's work from that of other contemporary fiction writers. *Dictionary of Literary Biography* contributor Hugh M. Ruppersburg, for example, wrote that "The concerns of Irving's novels are inherently contemporary. Yet often they bear little similarity to other recent fiction, for their author is more interested in affirming certain conventional values—art and the family, for instance—than in condemning the status quo or heralding the arrival of a new age. . . . What is needed, [Irving] seems to suggest, is a fusion of the compassion and common sense of the old with the egalitarian openmindedness of the new." Irving himself likens his fictional values and narrative technique to those of nineteenth-century writers. "I occasionally feel like a dinosaur in my own time because my fictional values are terribly old-fashioned," he stated in *Los Angeles Times.* "They go right back to the deliberately sentimental intentions of the 19th-century novelist: Create a character in whom the reader will make a substantial emotional investment and then visit upon that character an unbearable amount of pain." Like those nineteenth-century novelists, Irving also believes that he is responsible for entertaining the reader. "I think, to some degree, entertainment is the responsibility of literature," Irving told Haller. "I really am looking upon the novel as an art form that was at its best when it was offered as a popular form. By which I probably mean the 19th century."

Irving's nineteenth-century values are reflected in *The World according to Garp,* a work he described in *Washington Post Book World* as "an artfully disguised soap opera." "The difference is that I write well," Irving added, "that I construct a book with the art of construction in mind, that I use words intentionally and carefully. I mean to make you laugh, to make you cry; those are soap-opera intentions, all the way." A lengthy family saga, the novel focuses on nurse Jenny Fields, her illegitimate son, novelist T. S. Garp, and Garp's wife and two sons. Described as a "disquieting" work by *New Republic* contributor Terrence Des Pres, *The World according to Garp* explicitly explores the violent side of contemporary life. Episodes involving rape, assassination, mutilation, and suicide abound, but these horrific scenes are always infused with comedy. As Irving noted in *Los Angeles Times,* "No matter how gray the subject matter or orientation of any novel I write, it's still going to be a comic novel."

"A true romantic hero," according to *Village Voice* critic Eliot Fremont-Smith, Garp is obsessed with the perilousness of life and wants nothing more than to keep the world safe for his family and friends. Ironically then, Garp is the one who ultimately inflicts irreversible harm on his children, illustrating Irving's point that "the most protective and unconditionally loving parents can inflict the most appalling wounds on their children," explained Pearl K. Bell in *Commentary.* While Garp is obsessed with protecting his family and friends, his mother's obsession involves promoting her status as a "sexual suspect"—a woman who refuses to share either her life or her body with a man. Through her best-selling autobiography *A Sexual Suspect,* Jenny becomes a feminist leader. Her home evolves into a haven for a group of radical feminists, The Ellen James Society, whose members have cut out their tongues as a show of support for a young girl who was raped and similarly mutilated by her attackers. Both Garp and Jenny eventually are assassinated—she by an outraged anti-feminist convinced that Jenny's influence ruined his marriage and Garp by an Ellen Jamesian convinced he is an exploiter of women because of a novel he wrote about rape. Discussing these characters in a *Publishers Weekly* inter-

view with Barbara A. Bannon, Irving remarked, "It mattered very fiercely to me that [Garp and Jenny] were people who would test your love of them by being the extremists they were. I always knew that as mother and son they would make the world angry at them."

Critics have noted that *The World according to Garp* demonstrates a timely sensitivity to women—an acknowledgment by Irving of the growing women's liberation movement of the late twentieth century—because it deals sympathetically with issues such as rape, feminism, and sexual roles. *Nation* contributor Michael Malone wrote, "With anger, chagrin and laughter, Irving anatomizes the inadequacies and injustices of traditional sex roles. . . . The force behind a memorable gallery of women characters—foremost among them, Garp's famous feminist mother and his English professor wife—is not empathy but deep frustrated sympathy." A similar opinion was expressed by *Ms.* contributor Lindsy Van Gelder, who admitted admiration for Irving's ability to explore "feminist issues from rape to sexual identity to Movement stardom . . . minus any Hey-I'm-a-man-but-I-really understand self-conscious fanfare." Irving explained in *Los Angeles Times,* however, that his "interest in women as a novelist is really very simple. . . . I see every evidence that women are more often victims than men. As a novelist I'm more interested in victims than in winners." In fact, Irving flatly disagrees with critics who describe *The World according to Garp* in sociological or political terms. He stated in an interview with Larry McCaffery: "Obviously now when people write about *Garp* and say that it's 'about' feminism and assassination and the violence of the sixties, they're ignoring the fact that I lived half of the sixties in another country. I don't know anything about the violence of the sixties; it's meaningless to me. I'm not a sociological writer, nor should I be considered a social realist in any way."

Despite its fairytale-like qualities, Irving's *The Hotel New Hampshire* explores adult issues like incest, terrorism, suicide, freakish deaths, and gang rape, all infused with the novelist's trademark macabre humor. A family saga in the tradition of *The World according to Garp, The Hotel New Hampshire* spans nearly four generations of the troubled Berry family. Headed by Win, a charming but irresponsible dreamer who is ultimately a failure at innkeeping, and Mary, who dies in the early stages of the novel, the Berry family includes five children: Franny, Frank, Egg, Lilly, and John, the narrator. While Egg perishes along with his mother, the remaining children are left to struggle through childhood and adolescence. Irving reflected on the Berry family in *New York: The Hotel New Hampshire* "takes a large number of people and says in every family we have a dreamer, a hero, a late bloomer, one who makes it very big, one who doesn't make it at all, one who never grows up, one who is the shit detector, the guide to practicality, and often you don't know who these people will be, watching them in their earlier years."

The Berrys, along with an array of subsidiary characters—human and animal—eventually inhabit three hotels: one in New Hampshire, one in Vienna, and one in Maine. According to Irving, the hotels are symbols for the passage from infancy to maturity. "The first hotel is the only real hotel in the story," stated Irving in *New York.* "It is childhood. The one in Vienna is a dark, foreign place, that phase called adolescence, when you begin leaving the house and finding out how frightening the world is. . . . The last one is no hotel at all. . . . It is a place to get well again, which is a process that has been going on throughout the novel."

Following such a phenomenally successful work, *The Hotel New Hampshire* naturally invited comparisons to its predecessor. "There is no question in my mind it's better than *The World According to Garp,*" Irving maintained in *New York.* "It certainly is every bit as big a book, and it means much more. It's a more ambitious novel symbolically but with a different point of view, deliberately narrower." Irving nevertheless anticipated that critics would reject the novel. As he stated in *Chicago Tribune Book World:* "There will be people gunning for me—they'll call the book lazy, or worse—sentimental. But getting bad press is better than no press. It's better to be hated than to be ignored—even children know that."

In fact, critics' opinions largely fulfilled Irving's dismal prediction. *Chicago Tribune Book World* contributor Judith Rossner, for example, noted, "I found an emptiness at the core of *The Hotel New Hampshire* that might relate to the author's having used up his old angers and familiar symbols without having found new reasons for his rage and different bodies to make us see it." *Saturday Review* critic Scot Haller wrote that *The Hotel New Hampshire* "could not be mistaken

for the work of any other writer, but unfortunately, it cannot be mistaken for Irving's best novel, either. It lacks the urgency of *Setting Free the Bears,* the bittersweet wit of *The 158-Pound Marriage,* the sly set-ups of *Garp.* The haphazardness that afflicts these characters' lives has seeped into the storytelling, too." *Time* critic R. Z. Sheppard offered the view that, unlike Garp's story, "John Berry's story is not resolved in violent, dramatic action, but in a quiet balancing of sorrow and hope. It is a difficult act, and it is not faultless. The dazzling characterizations and sense of American place in the first part of the novel tend to get scuffed in transit to Europe. There are tics and indulgences. But the book is redeemed by the healing properties of its conclusion. Like a burlesque *Tempest, Hotel New Hampshire* puts the ordinary world behind, evokes a richly allusive fantasy and returns to reality refreshed and strengthened."

Originally intended to be a saga of orphanage life in early twentieth-century Maine, Irving's sixth novel, *The Cider House Rules,* instead became a statement on abortion. The issue of abortion arose during Irving's research for the novel, when he "discovered that abortion was an integral part of the life of an orphanage hospital at that time," as he later explained in *Los Angeles Times.* "This is in part a didactic novel, and in part a polemic," he added. "I'm not ashamed of that. . . . But I remain uncomfortable at the marriage between politics and fiction. I still maintain that the politics of abortion came to this book organically, came to it cleanly."

Evoking the works of Victorian novelists such as Charles Dickens and Charlotte Brontë, Irving's *The Cider House Rules* is set in an orphanage in dreary St. Cloud, Maine, where the gentle, ether-addicted Dr. Larch and his saintly nurses preside lovingly over their orphans. Larch also provides illegal but safe abortions, and although he is painfully aware of the bleak existence many of the orphans endure, he does not encourage expectant mothers to abort. As he puts it, "I help them have what they want. An orphan or an abortion." One unadopted orphan in particular, Homer Wells, becomes Larch's spiritual son and protege. Larch schools Homer in birth and abortion procedures in the hope that Homer will one day succeed him at the orphanage. When Homer comes to believe that the fetus has a soul, however, he refuses to assist with abortions. A conflict ensues, and Homer seeks refuge at Ocean View apple orchard, located on the coast of Maine.

The book's title refers to the list of rules posted in Ocean View's cider house regarding migrant workers' behavior. Several critics acknowledged the significance of rules, both overt and covert, in the lives of the characters. Toronto *Globe and Mail* contributor Joy Fielding, for example, commented that *The Cider House Rules* "is all about rules; the rules we make and break; the rules we ignore; the rules we post for all to see; the invisible rules we create for ourselves to help us get through life; the absurdity of some of these rules and the hypocrisy of others, specifically our rules regarding abortion." Similarly, *Los Angeles Times* critic Elaine Kendall wrote that "Much is made of the literal Cider House Rules, a typed sheet posted in the migrant workers dormitory, clearly and politely spelling out the behavior expected by the owners of the orchard. Sensible and fair as these rules are, they're made to be broken, interpreted individually or ignored entirely, heavily symbolic of the social and moral codes Irving is exploring." *New York Times* reviewer Christopher Lehmann-Haupt similarly noted that Dr. Larch follows his own rules and that "the point—which is driven home with the sledgehammer effect that John Irving usually uses—is that there are always multiple sets of rules for a given society. Heroism lies in discovering the right ones, whether they are posted on the wall or carved with scalpels, and committing yourself to follow them no matter what."

Despite the multiplicity of rules and moral codes explored by Irving, critics tend to focus on abortion as the crucial issue of *The Cider House Rules*. They have expressed different opinions, however, concerning Irving's position on the abortion issue. *Time* critic Paul Gray commented that *The Cider House Rules* "is essentially about abortions and women's right to have them," and Susan Brownmiller described the work in *Chicago Tribune* as "a heartfelt, sometimes moving tract in support of abortion rights." Kendall, on the other hand, maintained that, "Though Dr. Larch's philosophy justifying his divided practice is exquisitely and closely reasoned, the abortion episodes are graphic and gruesome, as if Irving were simultaneously courting both pro-choice and right-to-life factions." *New York Times Book Review* contributor Benjamin DeMott offered this view: "The knowledge and sympathy directing Mr. Irving's exploration of the [abortion] issue are exceptional. Pertinent history, the specifics of surgical procedure, the irrecusable sorrow of guilt and humiliation, the needs and rights of children—their weight is palpable in these pages."

Remarking in a *Time* interview that he has been "moved and impressed by people with a great deal of religious faith," Irving explained to Michael Anderson in *New York Times Book Review* that "Jesus has always struck me as a perfect victim and a perfect hero." What impresses the novelist most is that Christ is aware of his own destiny: "That is truly a heroic burden to carry," he told Phyllis Robinson in *Book-of-the-Month Club News*. In his novel *A Prayer for Owen Meany*, which examines the good and evil—especially the capacity of each to be mistaken for the other—Irving's Christ-like hero knows his destiny, including the date and circumstances of his death. Small in size but large in spirit, Owen Meany has a distinctive but ineffable voice caused by a fixed larynx, and throughout the novel, Irving renders Owen's speech in upper case—suggested to him by the red letters in which Jesus's utterances appear in the New Testament. Believing that nothing in his life is accidental or purposeless, Owen professes himself an instrument of God, and his sacrifices result in the gradual conversion of his best friend, and the book's narrator, Johnny Wheelwright. "No one has ever done Christ in the way John Irving does Him in *A Prayer for Owen Meany*," maintained Stephen King in his review of the novel for *Washington Post Book World*.

In a *Time* review, Sheppard pointed out that "anyone familiar with Irving's mastery of narrative technique, his dark humor and moral resolve also knows his fiction is cute like a fox." Sheppard suggested that, despite its theological underpinnings, *A Prayer for Owen Meany* "scarcely disguise[s] his indignation about the ways of the world," and actually represents "a fable of political predestination." Although finding the book flawed in terms of its structure and development, Robert Olen Butler suggested in Chicago *Tribune Books* that it nevertheless contains "some of the elements that made *The World According to Garp* so attractive to the critics and the bestseller audience alike: flamboyant, even bizarre, characters; unlikely and arresting plot twists; a consciousness of contemporary culture; and the assertion that a larger mechanism is at work in the universe."

More bizarre characters and situations await readers of Irving's *A Son of the Circus*. Dr. Farrokkh Daruwalla is an Indian-born orthopedist who lives in Canada but makes periodic trips to India to work at a children's hospital, conduct genetic research on circus dwarfs, and write second-rate screenplays. As packed with characters and motifs that have come to be seen as characteristically Irving, *A Son of the Circus*, nervetheless disappointed some reviewers. "The quirkiness with which the author customarily endows privileged characters is . . . scarce here," observed Webster Johnson in *Times Literary Supplement*. "In fact, Daruwalla and the rest incline towards the lacklustre; any colour derives chiefly from the compound incidents which entangle them." Bharati Mukherjee wrote in *Washington Post Book World* that the novel is Irving's "most daring and most vibrant. And though it is also his least satisfying, it has a heroic cheekiness. . . . But its very energy and outrageousness make it compete with rather than complement the tragic story of people. . . . Irving India-surfs himself into exhaustion until the subcontinent becomes, for the reader as well as for one of his characters, neither symbol nor place but a blur of alarming images."

Ruth Cole is the protagonist of *A Widow for One Year*, a novel that explores the nature of fiction writing through several of its characters. When the novel opens on Long Island in 1958, four-year-old Ruth witnesses the dissolution of her parents' marriage, which has suffered under the strain of the tragic death of the couple's teenage sons in a car accident before Ruth was born. Each of her parents drowns their pain in different ways; her father with women and alcohol, and her mother by turning their suburban home into a shrine for her dead sons. After Ruth's mother has an affair with her husband's teen-aged assistant, she abandons both her husband and daughter. Eddie O'Hare, the object of Ruth's mother's affections, looks back on the affair years later, writes a novel about the romance, and becomes part of Ruth's literary circle.

The second two sections of the book take place in the 1990s, where tragedy continues to follow Ruth. Now an adult, she finds her father in bed with her best friend, a betrayal that ultimately results in her father's suicide and a spiteful sexual encounter for Ruth that turns violent. She also becomes a famous author, loses her husband, writes a novel called *A Widow for One Year*, and becomes embroiled in the seamy side of Amsterdam during a book tour held where a serial killer is on the loose. Despite its complex plot, *A Widow for One Year* is, at its core, an exploration of writers and writing. The prominence of writers in the story, Michiko Kakutani explained in *New York Times*, is "to make some points about the ordering impulses of art and the imaginative transactions made by artists in grappling with the real world."

A Widow for One Year met with generally favorable reviews. Although Candia McWilliam described the

novel in her *New Statesman* review as a book "in which too many women, alas, behave like men," she complimented Irving's "themes of bereavement and creativity, of love between young men and older women, of widowhood and human hope reborn." Kakutani noted that, while the novel is full of unbelievable coincidences and characters that border on caricature, Ruth is a "complex, conflicted woman" and Irving's "authoritative narrative steamrolls over the contrivances, implausibilities and antic excesses . . . to create an engaging and often affecting fable, a fairy tale that manages to be old-fashioned and modern all at once." William H. Pritchard, writing in *New York Times Book Review*, called *A Widow for One Year* one of Irving's best, commenting that "the writing is very much of the surface, strongly, sometimes even cruelly, outlined, unfriendly to ambiguity and vacillation, secure in its brisk dispositions of people and place."

In *The Fourth Hand* Irving's farcical tendencies are again at play. While a television reporter is on assignment covering a circus in India, his hand is eaten by a lion, the tragedy recorded on live television. The victim, Patrick Wallingford, is a handsome man, prone to affairs with women, who had cruised through life on his charm. Now he is known as the Lion Guy and, instead of attracting attractive women, he becomes a magnet for more offbeat characters. A recently widowed Green Bay, Wisconsin, woman, after her husband is killed in a freak accident, wants Patrick to have her husband's hand. In return, however, she requests visitation rights with the hand and the opportunity to be impregnated by Patrick. A deal is struck, and the anorexic and excrement-obsessed Dr. Zajac of Boston announces that he will perform the world's first hand transplant. Irving uses the character of Patrick to parody the empty world of television news broadcasting and the media's unending fascination with gruesome destruction. In the end, however, Irving turns the story into a tale of love's powers of redemption.

Recognizing Irving's trademark idiosyncratic characters and unlikely scenarios, along with his frequent themes of family and morality, several critics opined that *The Fourth Hand* treads ground that is too familiar. Paul Gray wrote in *Time* that the novel "offers the same mix of the macabre and the moral that Irving's army of admirers has come to expect" but maintained that the vapid Patrick cannot hold readers' interest. "Faced with a virtual cipher at the center of his tale, Irving works energetically to create distractions around the edges," Gray explained. Other critics had more appreciation for the novel's storyline. "Irving's worlds are ludicrous in the most appealing way and expertly sentimental at the same time," wrote Doug McClemont in *Library Journal*, "and his approachable language can be both musical and magical." Bonnie Schiedel, writing in *Chatelaine*, called *The Fourth Hand* "downright weird. . . . but also funny and bracingly original," while Caroline Moore in *Spectator* summarized the symbolism inherent in the novel's title: "It is the phantom 'fourth hand' of the imagination which . . . can bridge the gap between voyeurism and compassion, sensationalism and empathy."

Trying to Save Piggy Sneed collects Irving's non-novel works: memoirs, short stories, and homage pieces. "The Imaginary Girlfriend" details Irving's career as an amateur wrestler and coach and touches on his development as a writer, while other essays present homage to authors Günther Grass and Charles Dickens. The fiction section includes "Pension Grillparzer"—which originally appeared in *The World according to Garp*—and five other short stories. In *New York Times Book Review*, Sven Birkerts stated that *Trying to Save Piggy Sneed* "shows how one of our most widely read novelists fares in what he might consider a triathlon of lesser events. What we find, in this order, are disappointment, confirmations and surprises."

Because of their visual imagery and action, many of Irving's novels have been adapted for film, sometimes on the basis of the novelist's own screenplay. Irving's quest to adapt *The Cider House Rules* for film is the subject of *My Movie Business*, which was published in tandem with the film's release in 1999. The book also covers adaptations from Irving's other novels—from scripts that he did not write—and his experience writing his first screenplay for *Setting Free the Bears*. Along the way, he elaborates on his pro-choice stance, the history of abortion in the United States, and his grandfather's career as an obstetrician.

As Irving explains in his book, in some ways, the story of *The Cider House Rules* encompasses all facets of the Hollywood movie industry. The film was thirteen years in the making. The script went through numerous revisions and directors came and went before Lasse Hallstrom signed on and the film was made. Along the way, Irving had to confront some harsh realities, notably trimming his first draft from nine

hours down to a more theater-friendly two. This severe editorial surgery required leaving out many characters and subplots, but the novelist's efforts paid off when he won an Academy Award for best screenplay. "Irving comes off as a testy collaborator with a decidedly anemic view of the screenwriting process," Jonathan Bing maintained in *Variety*. However, Benjamin Svetkey wrote in *Entertainment Weekly* that *My Movie Business* contains "sweetly personal moments" and would well-serve readers looking for "a charming, sublimely written technical primer" on the movie industry.

Although he is not a prolific novelist, Irving remains highly popular with the reading public, as well as with moviegoers through his increasing activity as a screenwriter. Afforded the opportunity due to his stature within American letters, he regularly and publicly debates the nature and worth of novelists and their works, and in doing so, "he brings a gladiatorial spirit to the literary arena," wrote a critic for *Maclean's*. Long a proponent of character and plot driven fiction, Irving has been compared to such luminaries as Dickens and Henry James, both of whom had a similar preoccupation with the moral choices and failings of their characters. *Maclean's* writer concluded that, "in a postmodern world, Irving remains stubbornly unfashionable—a writer of sprawling yarns knotted with subplots." Making a similar comparison, Caroline Moore noted that "the greatest popular artists—from Dickens to Chaplin—are circus-lovers and showmen, with an unabashed streak of sentimentality and sensationalism. . . . Irving at his best, combining the grotesque, tragic and warm-hearted, has something of their quality."

BIOGRAPHICAL AND CRITICAL SOURCES:

BOOKS

Campbell, Josie P., *John Irving: A Critical Companion*, Greenwood Press (New York, NY), 1998.

Contemporary Literary Criticism, Gale (Detroit, MI), Volume 13, 1980, Volume 23, 1983, Volume 38, 1986, Volume 112, 1999.

Contemporary Novelists, 7th edition, St. James Press (Detroit, MI), 2001.

Contemporary Popular Writers, St. James Press (Detroit, MI), 1997.

Dictionary of Literary Biography, Volume 6: *American Novelists since World War II, Second Series,* Gale (Detroit, MI), 1980.

Dictionary of Literary Biography Yearbook: 1982, Gale (Detroit, MI), 1983.

Encyclopedia of World Literature in the Twentieth Century, St. James Press (Detroit, MI), 1999.

Harter, Carol C., *John Irving,* Twayne (New York, NY), 1986.

Irving, John, *The Cider House Rules,* Morrow (New York, NY), 1985.

Modern American Literature, 5th edition, St. James Press (Detroit, MI), 1999.

Reilly, Edward C., *Understanding John Irving,* University of South Carolina Press (Columbia, SC), 1993.

Runyon, Randolph, *Fowles/Irving/Barthes: Canonical Variations on an Apocryphal Theme,* Ohio State University Press (Columbus, OH), 1981.

PERIODICALS

America, December 31, 1994, p. 27.

Book, July-August, 2001, interview with Irving.

Book-of-the-Month Club News, April, 1989.

Chatelaine, August, 2001, Bonnie Schiedel, review of *The Fourth Hand,* p. 12.

Chicago Tribune, May 12, 1985.

Chicago Tribune Book World, May 11, 1980; September 13, 1981.

Christian Century, October 7, 1981, pp. 986-88; September 27, 1995, p. 905; July 2, 1997, p. 615; December 23, 1998, Christopher Bush, review of *A Widow for One Year,* p. 1253.

Commentary, September, 1978; June, 1982, pp. 59-63.

Contemporary Literature, winter, 1982, pp. 1-18.

Critique, number 1, 1981, pp. 82-96.

Detroit News, August 30, 1981.

Entertainment Weekly, October 22, 1999, Benjamin Svetkey, review of *My Movie Business,* p. 79.

Esquire, September, 1981.

Globe and Mail (Toronto, Ontario, Canada), March 10, 1984; July 6, 1985.

Library Journal, June 1, 2001, Doug McClemont, review of *The Fourth Hand,* p. 216; October 1, 2001, p. 161.

Los Angeles Times, September 16, 1982; March 20, 1983; June 4, 1985; July 10, 1985.

Maclean's, June 11, 1979, pp. 4-6; April 3, 1989, p. 63; September 5, 1994, p. 54; April 15, 1996, p. 61; July 23, 2001, "Iron John: Stepping into the Lion's Den with John Irving," p. 40.

Modern Fiction Studies, summer, 1981, pp. 284-286.

Ms., July, 1979.

Nation, June 10, 1978.

New Republic, April 29, 1978; September 23, 1981; May 22, 1989, p. 36.

New Statesman, September 23, 1994, p. 40; May 22, 1998, Candia McWilliam, review of *A Widow for One Year,* p. 55.

Newsweek, April 17, 1978; September 21, 1981.

New York, August 17, 1981, pp. 29-32; March 20, 1989, p. 82; August 29, 1994, p. 113.

New Yorker, May 8, 1978; October 12, 1981; July 8, 1985.

New York Review of Books, July 20, 1989, p. 30.

New York Times, April 13, 1978; August 31, 1981; May 20, 1985; January 30, 1996, p. C15; May 1, 1998, Michiko Kakutani, "Randomness, Luck, and Fate, but Whew, No Bears," p. 51.

New York Times Book Review, April 23, 1978, pp. 26-27; May 21, 1978; May 26, 1985; March 12, 1989; September 4, 1994, pp. 1, 22; February 4, 1996, p. 9; March 23, 1997; May 24, 1998, William H. Pritchard, "No Ideas! It's a Novel!," p. 7.

Observer (London, England), August 8, 1994, p. 20.

People, December 25, 1978; November 14, 1994, p. 29; July 30, 2001, p. 95.

Prairie Schooner, fall, 1978.

Publishers Weekly, April 24, 1978; July 4, 1994, p. 51; January 16, 1995, p. 31; December 18, 1995, p. 40; February 26, 1996, p. 24; September 7, 1998, a review of *A Widow for One Year,* p. 32; September 3, 2001, review of *The Fourth Hand,* p. 30.

Quill & Quire, March, 1996, p. 65.

Rolling Stone, December 13, 1979, pp. 68-75.

Saturday Review, May 13, 1978; September, 1981, pp. 30-32; May, 1989, p. 65.

Spectator, June 22, 1985; July 21, 2001, Caroline Moore, review of *The Fourth Hand,* p. 36.

Time, April 24, 1978; August 31, 1981, pp. 46-51; June 3, 1985; April 3, 1989, p. 80; July 16, 2001, Paul Gray, "The Sound of One Hand Clapping: John Irving's New Novel Proves Disappointing," p. 72.

Times (London), June 20, 1985.

Times Literary Supplement, October 20, 1978; June 21, 1985; April 9, 1993, p. 21; September 2, 1994, p. 11; March 22, 1996, p. 30.

Tribune Books (Chicago), March 19, 1989.

Variety, March 6, 2000, Jonathan Bing, review of *My Movie Business,* p. 52.

Village Voice, May 22, 1978.

Washington Post, August 25, 1981.

Washington Post Book World, April 30, 1978; May 19, 1985; March 5, 1989; September 4, 1994, p. 5; January 21, 1996, p. 4.

Writer, January, 2002, Dorman T. Schindler, "In High Gear: John Irving Is Writing More than Ever and Loving It," p. 28.

OTHER

Irving according to Irving (film), Landmark Media (Falls Church, VA), 2001.*

*   *   *

ISHERWOOD, Christopher (William Bradshaw) 1904-1986

PERSONAL: Born August 26, 1904, in High Lane, Cheshire, England; immigrated to the United States, 1939, naturalized citizen, 1946; died of cancer, January 4, 1986, in Santa Monica, CA; son of Francis Edward (a military officer) and Kathleen (Machell-Smith) Isherwood; longtime companion of Don Bachardy (an artist). *Education:* Attended Repton School, 1919-22, and Corpus Christi College, Cambridge, 1924-25; King's College, University of London, medical student, 1928-29. *Politics:* Democrat. *Religion:* Vedantist. *Hobbies and other interests:* "I was a born film fan."

CAREER: Writer, 1926-86. Worked as a secretary to French violinist Andre Mangeot and his Music Society String Quartet, London, England, 1926-27; private tutor in London, 1926-27; went to Berlin, Germany, in 1929 to visit W. H. Auden, and stayed, on and off, for four years; taught English in Berlin, 1930-33; traveled throughout Europe, 1933-37; did film script work for Gaumont-British; went to China with Auden, 1938; dialogue writer for Metro-Goldwyn-Mayer, Hollywood, CA, 1940; worked with American Friends Service Committee, Haverford, PA, in a hostel for Central European refugees, 1941-42; resident student of Vedanta Society of Southern California, Hollywood, and coeditor with Swami Prabhavananda of the society's magazine, *Vedanta and the West,* 1943-45; traveled in South America, 1947-48; guest professor at Los Angeles State College (now California State University, Los Angeles) and at University of California, Santa Barbara, 1959-62; Regents Professor at University of California Los Angeles, 1965, and University of California, Riverside, 1966. *Exhibitions:* Huntington Library mounted an exhibition on Isherwood entitled "A Writer and His World," in 2004.

AWARDS, HONORS: Brandeis University creative arts award, 1974-75; PEN Body of Work Award, 1983; Common Wealth Award for distinguished service in literature, 1984.

WRITINGS:

NOVELS

All the Conspirators, Jonathan Cape (London, England), 1928, new edition, 1957, New Directions (New York, NY), 1958.

The Memorial: Portrait of a Family, Hogarth (London, England), 1932, New Directions (New York, NY), 1946.

The Last of Mr. Norris (also see below), William Morrow (New York, NY), 1935, published as *Mr. Norris Changes Trains,* Hogarth (London, England), 1935.

Sally Bowles (also see below), Hogarth (London, England), 1937.

Goodbye to Berlin (also see below), Random House (New York, NY), 1939.

Prater Violet, Random House (New York, NY), 1945.

The Berlin Stories (contains *The Last of Mr. Norris, Sally Bowles,* and *Goodbye to Berlin*), J. Laughlin (New York, NY), 1946, published as *The Berlin of Sally Bowles,* Hogarth (London, England), 1975.

The World in the Evening, Random House (New York, NY), 1954.

Down There on a Visit, Simon & Schuster (New York, NY), 1962.

A Single Man, Simon & Schuster (New York, NY), 1964.

A Meeting by the River (also see below), Simon & Schuster (New York, NY), 1967.

PLAYS

(With W. H. Auden) *The Dog beneath the Skin; or, Where Is Francis?* (three-act; produced in London, 1936; revised version produced in London, 1937), Random House (New York, NY), 1935.

(With W. H. Auden) *The Ascent of F6* (produced in London, 1937; produced in New York, 1939), Random House (New York, NY), 1937, 2nd edition, Faber & Faber (London, England), 1957.

(With W. H. Auden) *A Melodrama in Three Acts: On the Frontier* (produced in Cambridge, England, 1938; produced in London, 1939), Faber & Faber (London, England), 1938, published as *On the Frontier: A Melodrama in Three Acts,* Random House (New York, NY), 1939.

The Adventures of the Black Girl in Her Search for God (based on a George Bernard Shaw novella), produced in Los Angeles at Mark Taper Forum, March, 1969.

(With Don Bachardy) *A Meeting by the River* (based on Isherwood's novel), produced in Los Angeles at Mark Taper Forum, 1972, produced on Broadway at the Palace Theatre, March, 1979.

(With W. H. Auden) *Plays and Other Dramatic Writings, 1928-1938,* Faber & Faber (London, England), 1989.

SCREENPLAYS

(Author of scenario and dialogue with Margaret Kennedy) *Little Friend,* Gaumont-British, 1934.

(Contributor) *A Woman's Face,* Metro-Goldwyn-Mayer (Los Angeles, CA), 1941.

(With Robert Thoeren) *Rage in Heaven* (based on novel by James Hilton), Metro-Goldwyn-Mayer (Los Angeles, CA), 1941.

(Contributor) *Forever and a Day,* RKO (Los Angeles, CA), 1943.

(With Ladislas Fodor) *The Great Sinner,* Loew's, 1949.

Diane, Metro-Goldwyn-Mayer (Los Angeles, CA), 1955.

(With Terry Southern) *The Loved One* (based on the novel by Evelyn Waugh), Filmways, 1965.

(With Don Magner and Tony Richardson) *The Sailor from Gibraltar* (based on the novel by Marguerite Duras), Woodfall, 1967.

The Legend of Silent Night (television special; adapted from a story by Paul Gallico), broadcast by American Broadcasting Company (ABC-TV), 1969.

(With Don Bachardy) *Frankenstein: The True Story* (based on the novel by Mary Shelley; produced, 1972), Avon (New York, NY), 1973.

(With Aldous Huxley) *Jacob's Hands,* St. Martin's Press (New York, NY), 1998.

Also author of dialogue for other films. Also author, with Lesser Samuels, of original story for *Adventure in Baltimore,* RKO, 1949. Also author of scripts for television.

TRANSLATOR

Bertolt Brecht, *Penny for the Poor,* Hale (London, England), 1937, Hillman Curl (New York, NY), 1938, published as *Threepenny Novel,* Grove Press (New York, NY) 1956.

(With Swami Prabhavananda) *Bhagavad-Gita: The Song of God,* Rodd (Los Angeles, CA), 1944, published as *The Song of God: Bhagavad-Gita,* Harper & Row (New York, NY), 1951, 3rd edition, Vedanta Press (Los Angeles, CA), 1965.

(And editor, with Swami Prabhavananda) Shankara, *Crest-Jewel of Discrimination,* Vedanta Press (Los Angeles, CA), 1947.

(With Swami Prabhavananda and Frederick Manchester) *Upanishads: Breath of the Eternal,* Vedanta Press (Los Angeles, CA), 1947.

Charles Baudelaire, *Intimate Journals,* Rodd, 1947.

(And editor, with Swami Prabhavananda) *How to Know God: The Yoga Aphorisms of Patanjali,* Harper & Row (New York, NY), 1953.

OTHER

Lions and Shadows: An Education in the Twenties (autobiography), Hogarth (London, England), 1938, New Directions (New York, NY), 1947.

(With W. H. Auden) *Journey to a War,* Random House (New York, NY), 1939.

(Editor) *Vedanta for the Western World,* Rodd, 1945, published as *Vedanta and the West,* Harper & Row (New York, NY), 1951.

The Condor and the Cows: A South American Travel Diary, Random House (New York, NY), 1949.

(Editor) *Vedanta for Modern Man,* Harper & Row (New York, NY), 1951.

(Editor) *Great English Short Stories,* Dell (New York, NY), 1957.

An Approach to Vedanta, Vedanta Press (Los Angeles, CA), 1963.

Ramakrishna and His Disciples (biography), Simon & Schuster (New York, NY), 1965.

Exhumations: Stories, Articles, Verses, Simon & Schuster (New York, NY), 1966.

Essentials of Vedanta, Vedanta Press (Los Angeles, CA), 1969.

Kathleen and Frank (autobiography), Simon & Schuster (New York, NY), 1971.

Christopher and His Kind, 1929-1939 (autobiography), Farrar, Straus, & Giroux (New York, NY), 1976.

An Isherwood Selection, edited by Geoffrey Halson, Longman (London, England), 1979.

My Guru and His Disciple, Farrar, Straus, & Giroux (New York, NY), 1980.

(With Sylvain Mangeot) *People One Ought to Know* (poems), Doubleday (New York, NY), 1982.

October (autobiographical record of one month in Isherwood's life; with illustrations by Don Bachardy), limited edition, Twelvetrees Press (Los Angeles, CA), 1983.

(With Swami Gambhirananda) *History of the Ramakrishna Math and Mission,* Vedanta Press (Los Angeles, CA), 1983.

The Wishing Tree: Christopher Isherwood on Mystical Religion, edited by Robert Adjemian, Vedanta Press (Los Angeles, CA), 1987.

Where Joy Resides: A Christopher Isherwood Reader, edited by Don Bachardy and James P. White, Farrar, Straus, & Giroux (New York, NY), 1991.

(With Edward Upward) *The Mortmere Stories,* with images by Graham Crowley, Enitharmon Press (London, England), 1994.

Diaries, Volume One: 1939-1960, edited by Katherine Bucknell, Methuen (London, England), 1997.

The Repton Letters, edited by George Ramsden, Stone Trough Books (Settrington, York, England), 1997.

Lost Years: A Memoir, 1945-1951, edited by Katherine Bucknell, Harper & Row (New York, NY), 2000.

Contributor to books, including *The Complete Works of W. H. Auden,* Volume 1: *Plays and Other Dramatic Writings, 1928-1938,* 1990; and *The Faber Book of Gay Short Fiction,* 1991. Contributor to periodicals, including *Harper's Bazaar* and *Vogue.*

ADAPTATIONS: The Berlin Stories was adapted by John Van Druten as a play titled *I Am a Camera,* produced on Broadway in 1951, and published by Random House in 1952. *I Am a Camera* and *The Berlin Stories* were adapted by Joe Masteroff, John Kander, and Fred Ebb as the Broadway musical *Cabaret,* first produced in November, 1966. The screenplay for the movie version of *Cabaret,* written by Jay Presson Allen, was based on Isherwood's *The Berlin Stories,* and the film, directed by Bob Fosse and starring Liza Minnelli and Joel Grey, was released by Allied Artists in 1972.

SIDELIGHTS: Christopher Isherwood's career as a novelist, playwright, diarist, and teacher extended from the late 1920s through his death in 1986. During that era a sea change occurred in the acceptance of homosexuality in Western culture, and Isherwood is widely recognized as having made significant contributions to this trend. Best known for his *Berlin Stories,* from which the plays *I Am a Camera* and *Cabaret* were both adapted, Isherwood chronicled not only his own life but his minute observations of other people, places, and times as recorded in his letters and diaries. In *The Gay and Lesbian Review Worldwide,* Sara S. Hodson called Isherwood "indisputably one of the twentieth century's most important authors in English . . . one of the first self-consciously gay writers to be read extensively by a wider audience." Lewis Gannett in the *Gay and Lesbian Review* noted that Isherwood was an author who came to realize, "significant for both literature and the gay liberation movement, that his identity as a homosexual was inseparable from his identity as a writer. . . . He was living at ground zero of an emerging gay consciousness and was observing it closely."

According to Francis King in his study *Christopher Isherwood,* the British-born, Americanized Isherwood was a "suppose-if" writer. "For such novelists," King explained, "the process of creation begins with something that they themselves have either experienced or observed at close quarters. Taking this foundation of reality, they then proceed to build on it imaginatively by a series of 'suppose-ifs'. . . . When Isherwood has stayed closest to reality, . . . he has been at his best."

During a career spanning a host of genres, Isherwood transformed his life into an often bitingly comic fiction, using what David Daiches called "quietly savage dead-pan observation." He was, according to Frank Kermode, "farcical about desperate matters . . . almost as if what mattered was their intrinsic comic value." Isherwood's unique view of the comic in art, a theory of "High Camp," is explained by a character in *The World in the Evening:* "True High Camp always has an underlying seriousness. You can't camp about something you don't take seriously. You're not making fun of it; you're making fun out of it. You're expressing what's basically serious to you in terms of fun and artifice and elegance. Baroque art is largely camp about religion. The Ballet is camp about love. . . . It's terribly hard to define. You have to meditate on it and feel it intuitively, like Lao-Tze's *Tao.*"

"I believe in being a serious comic writer," Isherwood once said. "To me, everything is described in those terms. Not in the terms of the unredeemably tragic view of life, but at the same time, not in terms of screwballism. Nor in terms of saying, 'Oh, it's all lovely in the garden.' I think the full horror of life must be depicted, but in the end there should be a comedy which is beyond both comedy and tragedy. The thing Gerald Heard calls 'metacomedy'. . . . All I aspire to is to have something of this touch of 'metacomedy.' To give some description of life as it is lived now, and of what it has been like for me, personally, to have been alive."

While still at college in England, Isherwood began to write stories to his friend Edward Upward. The two young men created an entire imaginary village named Mortmere and set stories in this village. Most of their stories were horrific; titles included "The Horror in the Tower," "The Leviathan of the Urinals," and "The Railway Accident." As Upward recounted in the *Spectator,* Isherwood "would write a story and put it on the table in my sitting-room late at night when I was asleep in my bedroom and I would read it with delight at breakfast, and a morning or two later he would find a story by me on his table." In this way, the two budding writers encouraged and critiqued each other's work. In his later writing, Isherwood used much the same technique as he had in his "Mortmere" stories, often exaggerating real-life situations into a kind of comic fantasy.

Isherwood had great success with his Berlin books, *The Last of Mr. Norris* and *Goodbye to Berlin* (collected as *The Berlin Stories*), in which he fictionalized his stay in the pre-Nazi Berlin of the late 1920s and early 1930s. During this time, Isherwood lived with his German lover, Heinz, who was eventually arrested for his homosexuality, imprisoned, and then forced to join the German army. For his part, Isherwood correctly predicted that Nazi Germany would prove hostile to him, and he left before World War II began. In *The Last of Mr. Norris,* Isherwood's narrator is a William Bradshaw (Isherwood's two middle names), while in *Goodbye to Berlin* the narrator is named Christopher Isherwood. This matter-of-fact blend of fact and fiction reflected the naive, honest style Isherwood was seeking in these stories. In both books he uses the phrase "I am a camera" to indicate what he feels his role as narrator should be: a simple recording device.

Through passive, unengaged narrators, Isherwood successfully portrays the decadence of Weimar Germany in startling detail. As Claude J. Summers wrote in the

Dictionary of Literary Biography: British Novelists, 1930-1959, "Isherwood evokes a mythic city of sexual and political excitement only to acknowledge the artificiality of myth in the harsh reality of loneliness and despair." Many reviewers praised Isherwood's unobtrusive writing style which, like the camera Isherwood claimed to be, allowed the reader to see what his narrator saw. "Isherwood's prose," Edmund Wilson noted in the *New Republic,* "is a perfect medium for his purpose. . . . The sentences all get you somewhere almost without your noticing that you are reading them; the similes always have point without ever obtruding themselves before the object. You seem to look right through Isherwood and to see what he sees." Similarly, David Garnett wrote in *New Statesman and Nation* that "the extraordinary effect of life which [Isherwood] achieves is due almost entirely to his power of expressing exactly his observations. Every detail seems true because each is the result of a sharp verbal focus in his mind."

Isherwood's comic touch is evident in *Mr. Norris Changes Trains,* which features the criminal adventures of Arthur Norris, an aging con man who befriends the naive William Bradshaw. Although morally bankrupt, Norris is irresistible to everyone he meets. Summers called him "among the most seductive comic figures in modern literature" and "both lovable and dangerous." B. R. Redman in the *Saturday Review of Literature* observed: "Astonishingly enough, one cannot dislike Arthur Norris. . . . Norris is soft and appealing. No, one does not dislike him. But it is possible, even easy to dislike the shadowy character of William Bradshaw. He is the repellent factor in the novel." Writing in *Books,* Terence Holliday found that "by touches so subtle as to be almost imperceptible in themselves, the delighted reader is made aware that there is rising before him that rarest phenomenon of the novelist's art—solid three-dimensional human character." As Michael de-la-Noy remarked in *Books and Bookmen,* "It was [Isherwood's] humor that very quickly raised his work above the level of mere confessional autobiography, that stamped it with a genius for comic characterisation in the mould of Evelyn Waugh."

Graham Greene, in an article for the *Dictionary of Literary Biography Yearbook: 1986,* described *The Last of Mr. Norris* as "a permanent landmark in the literature of our time." Summers called *Goodbye to Berlin* an "extraordinary achievement," later adding that it is "a book of haunting loneliness" and "a masterful study of an inhibited young man." Julian Symons concluded in the *Sunday Times* that the Berlin stories "remain, and they capture a time, a place, and the people of a disintegrating society in a moving and masterly way. They are a unique achievement." Isherwood's Berlin stories were so popular that they were adapted first as the play *I Am a Camera,* then as the musical *Cabaret,* and finally as the film *Cabaret.* The stage and film versions of the story won a total of seven Tony Awards, a Grammy Award, and eight Academy Awards.

In later works, Isherwood continued to write about his own life in both fiction and nonfiction. James Atlas in the *New York Times* noted that Isherwood "devoted himself to chronicling his life more or less as it happens." A number of his many literary friends are featured as characters in these books. The poet Stephen Spender appears in Isherwood's *Lions and Shadows* as the character Stephen Savage. (Writing of the book in 1986, Spender claimed: "I have the feeling that Stephen Savage is more like the young Stephen Spender than I myself ever was.") Other *Lions and Shadows* characters were modeled after W. H. Auden and Edward Upward, while novelist Virginia Woolf appears in Isherwood's *The World in the Evening.* W. Somerset Maugham, in his novel *The Razor's Edge,* reversed this process, modeling the character of Larry after Isherwood, although Isherwood always denied the resemblance.

In the novel *A Single Man,* a study of a middle-aged homosexual in grief over the death of his longtime companion, Isherwood dealt with key concerns of his life, including spirituality and same-sex love. Set within the confines of a single day, the novel creates a portrait of George, the main character, going about the routine of his life in the face of tragedy. "Beautifully written in a style that alternates between poetic intensity and gentle irony, the book is a technical tour de force in which every nuance is perfectly controlled," Summers enthused. David Daiches in the *New York Times Book Review* found the novel to be "a sad, sly report on the predicament of the human animal," while Elizabeth Hardwick, writing in the *New York Review of Books,* called *A Single Man* "a sad book, with a biological melancholy running through it, a sense of relentless reduction, daily diminishment." Summers, however, saw the novel as culminating "in George's renewed commitment to life and in spiritual

illumination." De-la-Noy judged *A Single Man* to be "not just [Isherwood's] masterpiece but one of the most remarkable novels of the twentieth century," and Summers considered it "among the most undervalued novels of our time."

In such nonfiction works as *Kathleen and Frank,* a remembrance of his parents, and *Christopher and His Kind,* an autobiography in which he first admitted his homosexuality, Isherwood wrote about his life in a novelistic fashion, detailing his childhood, his many years as a Hollywood screenwriter, and such matters as his affair with poet W. H. Auden, and his embrace of the Eastern philosophy of Swami Prabhavananda, a teacher of Vedanta. *Kathleen and Frank* combines Isherwood's mother's diaries with his own running commentary and remembrances. The biography begins with his parents' first meeting in the 1890s and proceeds until 1939, when Isherwood left England for America. The book ends with Isherwood's evaluation of his parents' impact upon his own personal development. Joseph Catinella in the *Saturday Review* praised Isherwood for his "novelist's eye for dramatic movement and detail" which produced "a splendid biography." W. H. Auden, writing in the *New York Review of Books,* claimed: "I cannot imagine any reader, whatever his social background and interests, not being enthralled by it."

In *Christopher and His Kind,* Isherwood describes his activities during the 1930s, looking back at that time and himself with a wry humor. Much new information about his life, previously unrevealed, is unveiled in the book, particularly Isherwood's sexual orientation and his various love relationships. "Invigorated and humanized by his commitment to gay liberation, the book is marred only by his tendency to devalue—in the interest of fact—some of his most brilliant fictional techniques in the Berlin stories," Summers commented. A *New Yorker* critic found the memoir to be written with "delicacy and wit," while Peter Stansky in the *New York Times Book Review* called the work "indispensable for admirers of this truly masterly writer." Lewis Gannett called *Christopher and His Kind* "in my opinion the finest gay autobiography ever written."

In addition to his work as a writer, Isherwood was known as a proponent of Hindu religious teachings, and this in turn informed his writing. His interest in Eastern philosophy began in 1939 when he first arrived in Los Angeles and met Swami Prabhavananda, a Hindu teacher. Prabhavananda's teachings emphasized a serene indifference to the things of the world, as well as a benevolent acceptance of homosexuality. From 1943 to 1945, Isherwood served as coeditor of the Hindu magazine *Vedanta and the West,* the official journal of Prabhavananda's Vedanta Society of Southern California. He also translated the *Bhagavad Gita,* a classic of the Hindu religion, while such books as *My Guru and His Disciple* and *An Approach to Vedanta* presented his own religious beliefs. Summers observed that all of Isherwood's later novels "illustrate the Vedantic belief that happiness lies in escape from the ego and in discovery of the *atman,* the impersonal God within man." Isherwood also became known as an outspoken advocate of homosexual rights, giving speeches and writing articles on the subject. His own relationship with painter Don Bachardy lasted from 1954 until Isherwood's death in 1986. John Boorman remarked in *American Film* that "of all the couples I got to know when I first started visiting Los Angeles more than twenty years ago, Christopher Isherwood and Don Bachardy had the only 'marriage' that survived."

Speaking at a forum in 1974, Isherwood declared that the goal of the gay rights movement should be "to be recognized as entirely natural and not to be questioned at all." British poet Stephen Spender declared in the *Observer* that Isherwood's involvement in gay rights "led to his becoming a kind of hero of the Gay community." After all, noted Felice Picano in the *Lambda Book Report,* Isherwood "accomplished nothing less than a complete coming out, decades before Stonewall, and years before such a thing was being done, or even wise to do."

Virtually all of Isherwood's writing, both fiction and nonfiction, was autobiographical in some way. His ability to create entertaining and meaningful work from the raw facts of his life experience—always rendered in a charming and insightful prose style—was what critics considered his unique talent, and the aspect of his writing that attracted the most praise from critics. King explained that the world Isherwood created was "a solipsistic circle: he himself [at] its centre, his perceptions its radii, his consciousness its circumference. What makes this world, admittedly confined, fascinating to the reader is the tone of voice—humane, totally truthful, ironic, benevolent— that its creator employ[ed] to describe it. It [was] chiefly this unique tone of voice that [gave] Isherwood

his distinction as one of the most entertaining and likeable of novelists at work in the English language." Isherwood's unique tone also comes through in his travel writing, according to Thomas Dukes, a contributor to the *Dictionary of Literary Biography: British Travel Writers, 1910-1939.* "Like his best novels it includes astute, unsentimental observations about people and places situated in a particular time," the essayist observed. *Journey to a War,* which chronicles a visit to China in 1938, while the Sino-Japanese war raged and World War II was about to begin, and *The Condor and the Cows: A South American Travel Diary,* written in the late 1940s, "are valuable historical documents and illustrate Isherwood's talent for making his point through the meaningful anecdote," added Dukes. De-la-Noy described Isherwood as "a writer of genius, a brilliant entertainer and one of the finest prose stylists of his generation." According to Summers, Isherwood "is increasingly recognized as one of the twentieth century's most insightful observers of the human condition."

The entries in *Diaries, Volume One: 1939-1960* cover the period from Isherwood's departure for America on January 19, 1939, with Auden until his fifty-sixth birthday, and they reflect the important matters in his life at the time, including his strict adherence to the Swami's teachings during the war years and his not entirely successful quest to lead a spiritually pure life; his personal relationships, including his longtime partnership with Bachardy and his busy social life in Hollywood; and his work. Alfred Corn wrote in the *Nation* that Isherwood's record is "intimate and compulsively readable," although not comprehensive: "You can see that sometimes Isherwood avoids writing when things have taken an embarrassing turn." *Times Literary Supplement* contributor Zachary Leader found that the tenor of the entries changed after Isherwood met Bachardy: "There are more jokes, though also more anxieties about health, appearance, fame. Bad habits quickly assert themselves, particularly a penchant for rage and resentment. . . . When the diaries ponder writing problems, the tone is the same for film or fiction: level, practical, realistic about audiences and their needs." *Time* reviewer Pico Iyer voiced a similar sentiment, noting that in the latter half of the book "more and more of his entries dwindle into local gossip and silly worries about his boyfriend and his weight." Corn, however, thought "the story of how [Isherwood and Bachardy] managed to overcome enormous differences—in age, nationality, experience and vocation—is touching." Also touching, but "a little exasperating," Corn commented, are the entries on Isherwood's religious pursuits: "Isherwood seems to be the only person not in on the secret that he wasn't cut out for seclusion and abstinence." Iyer concluded that "even at his weakest, he earns our trust with his entirely human cries of 'God, make me pure—but not just yet!'" Leader summed up the diaries by saying, "though not every entry is riveting, there is much here to ponder and praise, in the writing as well as in the life."

Bachardy, along with James P. White, anthologized selections from Isherwood's major works (including *Prater Violet* and the entirety of *A Single Man*) and essays for *Where Joy Resides: A Christopher Isherwood Reader.* In the *New Statesman & Society,* Robert Carver characterized the collection as "A Last Lover's anthology" subject to distortion, noting "what we get in this volume is very much the reconstructed American Gay Lib Vedanta Christopher." However, a *Washington Post Book World* critic praised the anthology, saying, "As always with Isherwood, the novels are a blend of autobiography and fiction, the writing is pellucid, and the artistry of the kind that conceals a high degree of art."

As the twentieth century closed, more Isherwood works were published: *Jacob's Hands,* an unproduced screenplay by Isherwood and Aldous Huxley that was discovered by actress Sharon Stone; and *Lost Years: A Memoir, 1945-1951,* Isherwood's reconstruction of events during a period when he did not maintain his customary detailed diaries. According to David Thomson, critiquing the latter volume for the *New York Times Book Review,* this was a time when, for Isherwood, "the stamina or self-awareness necessary for a journal dissolved in drink and promiscuity." Isherwood began putting together a retrospective of these years in the 1970s, and although he did not finish it, the book still provides important insights, in the opinion of some critics. Isherwood writes about himself in the third person, a device that "allows for greater analysis and intimacy" than one might find in a typical first-person memoir, commented Robert Plunket in the *Advocate.* Isherwood is also candid about his bouts of excessive drinking and his active sex life; he also details his practice of Hinduism, his work as a screenwriter, and his friendships with many figures in the arts, including Bertolt Brecht, E. M. Forster, Marlon Brando, and Georgia O'Keeffe. To Thomson, these mentions amount to mere name-dropping, and he was

unimpressed with the book as a whole: "These are dazzlingly empty years more than they are lost ones. Their record here will do nothing for Isherwood and posterity." A *Publishers Weekly* critic, however, wrote of the book, "While it lacks the artfulness of the memoirs Isherwood chose to publish, it will nevertheless find grateful readers among those who care about his work." Plunket offered higher praise still, calling *Lost Years* "a book that anyone with even a passing interest in Isherwood or gay social history shouldn't miss."

In 2004, the Huntington Library mounted an exhibition called "Christopher Isherwood: A Writer and His World." The exhibition drew upon Isherwood's papers collected at the Huntington, as well as supplemental material provided by Don Bachardy and other sources, including the Margaret Herrick Library of the Academy of Motion Picture Arts and Sciences.

BIOGRAPHICAL AND CRITICAL SOURCES:

BOOKS

Berg, James, and Chris Freeman, editors, *Conversations with Christopher Isherwood,* University Press of Mississippi (Jackson, MS), 2001.
Berg, James, and Chris Freeman, editors, *The Isherwood Century: Essays on the Life and Work of Christopher Isherwood,* University of Wisconsin Press (Madison, WI), 2000.
Contemporary Literary Criticism, Gale (Detroit, MI), Volume 1, 1973, Volume 9, 1978, Volume 11, 1979, Volume 14, 1980, Volume 44, 1987.
Dictionary of Literary Biography, Gale (Detroit, MI), Volume 15: *British Novelists, 1930-1959,* 1983, Volume 95: *British Travel Writers, 1910-1939,* 1998.
Dictionary of Literary Biography Yearbook: 1986, Gale (Detroit, MI), 1987.
Ferres, Kay, *Christopher Isherwood: A World in Evening,* Borgo (San Bernardino, CA), 1994.
Finney, Brian, *Christopher Isherwood: A Critical Biography,* Oxford University Press (New York, NY), 1979.
Fryer, Jonathan, *Isherwood: A Biography of Christopher Isherwood,* New English Library (London, England), 1977, Doubleday (New York, NY), 1978.
Funk, Robert W., *Christopher Isherwood: A Reference Guide,* G. K. Hall (Boston, MA), 1979.

Heilbrun, Carolyn G., *Christopher Isherwood,* Columbia University Press (New York, NY), 1970.

Hynes, Samuel L., *The Auden Generation: Literature and Politics in England in the 1930s,* Bodley Head (London, England), 1976.

Isherwood, Christopher, *Christopher and His Kind,* Farrar, Straus & Giroux (New York, NY), 1976.

Isherwood, Christopher, *Diaries, Volume One: 1939-1960,* edited by Katherine Bucknell, Methuen (London, England), 1997.

Isherwood, Christopher, *Lost Years: A Memoir, 1945-1951,* edited by Katherine Bucknell, Harper & Row (New York, NY), 2000.

Isherwood, Christopher, *The World in the Evening,* Random House (New York, NY), 1954.

Izzo, David Garrett, *Christopher Isherwood: His Era, His Gang, and the Legacy of the Truly Strong Man,* University of South Carolina Press (Columbia, SC), 2001.

Kermode, Frank, *Puzzles and Epiphanies,* Chilmark (Washington, DC), 1962.

King, Francis, *Christopher Isherwood,* Longman (London, England), 1976.

Lehmann, John, *Christopher Isherwood: A Personal Memoir,* Holt (New York, NY), 1988.

Newquist, Roy, *Conversations,* Rand McNally (Chicago, IL), 1967.

Page, Norman, *Auden and Isherwood,* St. Martin's Press (New York, NY), 1997.

Parker, Peter, *Isherwood: A Life,* Picador (London, England), 2004.

Phelps, Gilbert, editor, *Living Writers,* Transatlantic (Albuquerque, NM), 1947.

Westby, Selmer, and Clayton M. Brown, *Christopher Isherwood: A Bibliography, 1923-1967,* California State College (Los Angeles, CA), 1968.

Wilde, Alan, *Christopher Isherwood,* Twayne (Boston, MA), 1971.

PERIODICALS

Advocate, March 12, 1991; March 4, 1997, review of *Diaries, Volume One,* p. 57; September 12, 2000, Robert Plunket, review of *Lost Years,* p. 63.

American Film, October, 1986, John Boorman, "Stranger in Paradise," pp. 53-57.

Antaeus, spring-summer, 1974, Daniel Halpern, "A Conversation with Christopher Isherwood," pp. 366-388.

Ariel: A Review of International English Literature, 1972.

Booklist, September 15, 2000, Brad Hooper, review of *Lost Years,* p. 203.

Books and Bookmen, March, 1986.

California Quarterly, winter-spring, 1977, Jeffrey Bailey, "Interview: Christopher Isherwood," pp. 87-96.

Contemporary Literature, winter, 1972, David P. Thomas, "Goodbye to Berlin: Refocusing Isherwood's Camera," pp. 44-52; autumn, 1975, Alan Wilde, "Language and Surface: Isherwood and the Thirties," pp. 478-491.

Critical Inquiry, March, 1975.

Encounter, August, 1954, Angus Wilson, "The New and Old Isherwood," pp. 62-68; November, 1962.

Gay and Lesbian Review, May, 2001, Lewis Gannett, "Time Regained," p. 35.

Gay and Lesbian Review Worldwide, July-August, 2004, Sara S. Hodson, "An Isherwood Treasure Trail," p. 22.

Journal of Modern Literature, February, 1976.

Lambda Book Report, January, 2001, Felice Picano, "Filling in the Blanks," p. 14.

London Magazine, June, 1961, Stanley Poss, "A Conversation on Tape," pp. 41-58; July, 1965, John Whitehead, "Isherwood at Sixty," pp. 90-100; April, 1968, Charles Higham, "Isherwood on Hollywood," pp. 31-38.

London Review of Books, January 26, 1995, review of *The Mortmere Stories,* p. 19; January 2, 1997, review of *Diaries, Volume One,* p. 32.

Los Angeles Times Book Review, May 5, 1991, p. 14; February 2, 1997, review of *Diaries, Volume One,* p. 6.

Modern Fiction Studies, winter, 1970.

Nation, February 10, 1997, Alfred Corn, review of *Diaries, Volume One,* p. 27.

New Republic, May 17, 1939; February 26, 1990.

New Review, August, 1975, Brian Finney, "Christopher Isherwood—A Profile," pp. 17-24.

New Statesman, October 3, 1986.

New Statesman and Nation, March 11, 1939.

New Statesman & Society, August 25, 1989; January 12, 1990.

New Yorker, December 27, 1976.

New York Review of Books, August 20, 1964; January 27, 1972, W. H. Auden, "The Diary of a Diary," pp. 19-20; February 20, 1997, review of *Diaries, Volume One,* p. 11.

New York Times, March 19, 1939; August 2, 1979; August 27, 1980.

New York Times Book Review, August 30, 1964; March 25, 1973; November 28, 1976; January 5, 1997, John Sturrock, "My Life Will Be What I Make of It," p. 6; March 28, 1999, p. 28; September 17, 2000, David Thomson, "Out of Film."

Observer, January 4, 1990, p. 45; November 10, 1996, review of *Diaries, Volume One,* p. 15.

Paris Review, spring, 1974, W. I. Scobie, "Art of Fiction: Interview," pp. 138-182.

Perspectives on Contemporary Literature, May, 1977.

Publishers Weekly, October 20, 1989; September 6, 1991; November 11, 1996, review of *Diaries, Volume One,* p. 63; July 27, 1998, review of *Jacob's Hands,* p. 53; August 21, 2000, review of *Lost Years,* p. 58.

Saturday Review, January 22, 1972.

Saturday Review of Literature, May 11, 1935.

Shenandoah, spring, 1965, George Wickes, "An Interview with Christopher Isherwood," pp. 22-52.

Sight and Sound, spring, 1986.

Spectator, March 1, 1935; March 3, 1939; January 18, 1986.

Time, January 13, 1997, Pico Iyer, review of *Diaries, Volume One,* p. 74.

Times Literary Supplement, September 10, 1964; November 3, 1995, p. 22; January 10, 1997, Zachary Leader, review of *Diaries, Volume One,* p. 5; May 15, 1998, p. 31.

Twentieth-Century Literature, October, 1976, Carolyn G. Heilbrun, "Christopher Isherwood: An Interview," pp. 253-263.

Washington Post Book World, April 28, 1991.

Washington Times, September 6, 1998, "'Microbiography' of Two Men, One City," p. 6.

Yale Review, autumn, 1989.

ONLINE

Isherwood Century, http://www.theisherwood century. org/ (August 25, 2004), essays and information about Isherwood.

Isherwood Foundation, http://www.isherwood foundation.org/ (August 25, 2004), foundation in honor of Isherwood.

OBITUARIES:

PERIODICALS

AB Bookman's Weekly, January 6, 1986.

Chicago Tribune, January 7, 1986.

Daily Variety, January 6, 1986.

Kenosha News, January 6, 1986.

Los Angeles Times, January 6, 1986.

Newsweek, January 20, 1986.

New York Times, January 6, 1986.

Observer, January 12, 1986.

Publishers Weekly, January 17, 1986.

Sunday Times (London), January 12, 1986.

Time, January 20, 1986.

Washington Post, January 6, 1986.*

*   *   *

ISHIGURO, Kazuo 1954-

PERSONAL: Born November 8, 1954, in Nagasaki, Japan; resident of Great Britain since 1960; son of Shizuo (a scientist) and Shizuko (a homemaker; maiden name, Michida) Ishiguro; married Lorna Anne MacDougall, May 9, 1986. *Education:* University of Kent, B.A. (with honors), 1978; University of East Anglia, M.A. (creative writing), 1980. *Hobbies and other interests:* Music, guitar, piano, cinema.

ADDRESSES: Office—c/o Author Mail, Faber and Faber, 3 Queen Square, London WC1N 3AU, England.

CAREER: Grouse beater for Queen Mother at Balmoral Castle, Aberdeen, Scotland, 1973; Renfrew Social Works Department, Renfrew, Scotland, community worker, 1976; West London Cyrenians Ltd., London, England, residential social worker, 1979-81; writer, 1982—.

AWARDS, HONORS: Winifred Holtby Award, Royal Society of Literature, 1983, for *A Pale View of Hills;* Whitbread Book of the Year Award, 1986, for *An Artist of the Floating World;* Booker Prize, 1989, for *The Remains of the Day;* Premio Scanno (Italy), 1995; Order of the British Empire for services to literature, 1995; honorary Litt.D., University of Kent, 1990, and University of East Anglia, 1995; *When We Were Orphans* shortlisted for Booker Prize, 2000.

WRITINGS:

A Pale View of Hills, Putnam (New York, NY), 1982.

An Artist of the Floating World, Putnam (New York, NY), 1986.

Kazuo Ishiguro

The Remains of the Day, Knopf (New York, NY), 1989.

The Unconsoled, Knopf (New York, NY), 1995.

When We Were Orphans, Knopf (New York, NY), 2001.

Never Let Me Go, Knopf (New York, NY), 2005.

Also contributor to *Introduction 7: Stories by New Writers,* Faber (London, England), 1981. Author of television film scripts, including *A Profile of Arthur J. Mason,* 1984, and *The Gourmet,* 1986. Contributor to literary journals, including *London Review of Books, Firebird, Bananas,* and *Harpers and Queen.*

ADAPTATIONS: The Remains of the Day was adapted into a feature film starring Anthony Hopkins and Emma Thompson by Merchant Ivory Productions, 1993. Ishiguro's unproduced screenplay *The Saddest Music in the World* was adapted by Guy Maddin and George Toles in 2004.

SIDELIGHTS: After his first three novels, Japanese-born Kazuo Ishiguro emerged as one of the foremost British writers of his generation. Ishiguro's novels commonly deal with issues of memory, self-deception, and codes of etiquette, leading his characters to a re-evaluation or realization about the relative success or failure of their lives. His capture of the prestigious Booker Prize for his third novel, *The Remains of the Day,* confirmed the critical acclaim his work received. His fifth novel, *When We Were Orphans,* was also widely praised, and was shortlisted for the Booker Prize in 2000.

Ishiguro's highly acclaimed first novel, *A Pale View of Hills,* is narrated by Etsuko, a middle-aged Japanese woman living in England. The suicide of Etsuko's daughter, Keiko, awakens somber memories of the summer in the 1950s in war-ravaged Nagasaki when the child was born. Etsuko's thoughts and dreams turn particularly to Sachiko, a war widow whose unfortunate relationship with an American lover traumatizes her already troubled daughter, Mariko. Etsuko, too, will eventually embrace the West, and leave her Japanese husband to marry an English journalist. "Etsuko's memories, though they focus on her neighbor's sorrows and follies, clearly refer to herself as well," wrote Edith Milton in *New York Times Book Review.* "The lives of the two women run parallel, and Etsuko, like Sachiko, has raised a deeply disturbed daughter; like her, she has turned away from the strangling role of traditional Japanese housewife toward the West, where she has discovered freedom of a sort, but also an odd lack of depth, commitment, and continuity." Surrounded that summer by a new order that has shattered ancient ways, the two women choose the Western path of self-interest, compromising—to varying degrees—their delicate daughters. "In Etsuko's present life as much as in her past, she is circled by a chain of death which has its beginning in the war," suggested *New Statesman* reviewer James Campbell.

Reviewing *A Pale View of Hills* in *Spectator,* Francis King found the novel "typically Japanese in its compression, its reticence, and in its exclusion of all details not absolutely essential to its theme." While some reviewers agreed with *Times Literary Supplement* writer Paul Bailey that "at certain points I could have done with something as crude as a fact," others felt that Ishiguro's delicate layering of themes and images grants the narrative great evocative power. *A Pale View of Hills* "is a beautiful and dense novel, gliding from level to level of consciousness," remarked Jonathan Spence in *New Society.* "Ishiguro develops [his themes] with remarkable insight and skill," concurred Rosemary Roberts in *Los Angeles Times Book Review.* "They are described in controlled prose that more often hints than explains or tells. The effect evokes mystery and an aura of menace." King deemed the novel "a memorable and moving work, its elements of past and present, of Japan and England held together by a shimmering, all but invisible net of images linked to each other by filaments at once tenuous and immensely strong."

While *A Pale View of Hills* depicts the incineration of a culture and the disjointed lives of the displaced, Ishiguro's novel is not without optimism. Critics saw in the war survivors' tenacious struggle to resurrect some sort of life, however alien, great hope and human courage. "Sachiko and Etsuko become minor figures in a greater pattern of betrayal, infanticide and survival played out against the background of Nagasaki, itself the absolute emblem of our genius for destruction," Milton continued. "In this book, where what is stated is often less important than what is left unsaid, those blanked-out days around the bomb's explosion become the paradigm of modern life. They are the ultimate qualities which the novel celebrates: the brilliance of our negative invention, and our infinite talent for living beyond annihilation as if we had forgotten it." Reiterated Roberts: "There is nobility in determination to press on with life even against daunting odds. Ishiguro has brilliantly captured this phoenixlike spirit; high praise to him."

In *An Artist of the Floating World* Ishiguro again explores Japan in transition. Set in a provincial Japanese town during 1949 and 1950, the story revolves around Masuji Ono, a painter who worked as an official artist and propagandist for the imperialist regime that propelled Japan into World War II. Knowing that his former ideals were errant does little to help Ono adjust to the bewildering Westernization that is going on all around him; nor does it quell his longings for the past, with its fervent patriotism, professional triumphs, and deep comradeship. "Ishiguro's insights . . . are finely balanced," wrote Anne Chisholm in *Times Literary Supplement.* "He shows how the old Japanese virtues of veneration for the Sensei (the teacher), or loyalty to the group, could be distorted and exploited; he allows deep reservations to surface about the wholesale Americanization of Japan in the aftermath of humiliation and defeat. Without asking us to condone Ono's or Japan's terrible mistakes, he suggests with sympathy some reasons why the mistakes were made."

Admiring how "Ishiguro unravels the old man's thoughts and feelings with exceptional delicacy," Chisholm determined that the story "is not only pleasurable to read but instructive, without being in the least didactic." "The old man's longings for his past become a universal lament for lost worlds," added the critic, who judged *An Artist of the Floating World* a "fine new novel."

In the opinion of Christopher Hitchens in *Nation,* Ishiguro's first two novels share a form in their "unmediated retrospective monologue." Hitchens cited their similar themes as well: "Each narrator has lived according to strict codes of etiquette and order; the ethos of actively and passively 'knowing one's place,' and adhering to protocol and precedent." Those same forms and themes shape the third novel, *The Remains of the Day,* which presents the narrative of Stevens, English butler to Lord Darlington of Darlington Hall. After more than thirty years of faithful service to the Lord, Stevens now finds himself in the employ of Mr. Farraday, a congenial American who has purchased the estate and keeps Stevens on as part of the colorful trappings. Farraday urges Stevens to take a motoring holiday through Cornwall. Concurrently, Stevens has received a letter from Miss Kenton (now Mrs. Benn), the exemplary housekeeper who had left Darlington Hall some twenty years before. Mrs. Benn's letter hints at unhappiness in her marriage and suggests a willingness to return to service at Darlington. Short of staff in the downsized estate, the ever-dutiful Stevens justifies his absence with the utilitarian purpose of hiring the former housekeeper.

As the journey proceeds and Stevens rambles about in Farraday's old Ford—taking eight days to go about one hundred miles—he reflects upon the people he meets, the countryside and, tellingly and ironically, his own life. At one point, Stevens proclaims the English landscape the most satisfying in the world precisely because of its lack of obvious drama or spectacle. This fondness to dampen the dramatic and spectacular and to fit in easily does, in fact, control his life. It is the reason he so thoroughly inhabits his role as butler. As he returns to the same memories again and again, the fog of self-deception lifts. One motoring mishap after another—a flat tire, overheated radiator—affords him the time and perspective he has never had. Meeting the ordinary people who actually suffered during the war, Stevens has difficulty admitting to his long service at Darlington. He begins to doubt the Lord's—and his own—judgment. The quiet tragedies of revelation continue as Stevens comes to realize what the perceptive reader has known all along: his proposed rendezvous with Mrs. Benn has more than a utilitarian purpose. She represents, in fact, his last chance to seize happiness in life.

Reviewing *The Remains of the Day* for the London *Observer,* Salman Rushdie noted: "Just below the understatement of the novel's surface is a turbulence as immense as it is slow." Drawing readers into its subtle complexities, the novel met with a highly favorable critical response. Galen Strawson, for example, praised the novel in *Times Literary Supplement,* writing that *The Remains of the Day* "is as strong as it is delicate, a very finely nuanced and at times humorous study of repression. . . . It is a strikingly original book, and beautifully made. . . . Stevens' . . . language creates a context which allows Kazuo Ishiguro to put a massive charge of pathos into a single unremarkable phrase." In *Chicago Tribune,* Joseph Coates described the novel as "an ineffably sad and beautiful piece of work—a tragedy in the form of a comedy of manners." He continued: "Rarely has the device of an unreliable narrator worked such character revelation as it does here." Mark Kamine cited Ishiguro's technique in *New Leader:* "Usually the butler's feelings are hidden in painfully correct periphrasis, or refracted in dialogue spoken by other characters. . . . Few writers dare to say so little of what they mean as Ishiguro."

While many reviews of *The Remains of the Day* were favorable, this was not universally so. Writing for *New Statesman & Society,* Geoff Dyer wondered "if the whole idea of irony as a *narrative strategy* hasn't lost its usefulness." Dyer worried that Stevens's voice had been "*coaxed* in the interests of the larger ironic scheme of the novel." Comparing the novelist to Henry James, however, Hermione Lee defended Ishiguro's style in *New Republic:* "To accuse Ishiguro of costive, elegant minimalism is to miss the deep sadness, the boundless melancholy that opens out, like the 'deserts of vast eternity' his characters are reluctantly contemplating, under the immaculate surface."

Winning the Booker Prize for *The Remains of the Day* allowed Ishiguro "to break through the veil of expectations and constraints that both his success, and his readers' stubborn determination to take him absolutely literally, imposed," and "to try something wild and

frightening that would prevent him from ever being taken as a realist again," according to Pico Iyer in a *Times Literary Supplement* review. Iyer noted that Ishiguro achieves this goal in his fourth novel, *The Unconsoled* "Even though every sentence and theme is recognizably [Ishiguro's]," noted Iyer, "he has written a book that passes on the bewilderment it seeks to portray."

The Unconsoled, much longer than Ishiguro's previous novels, details the journey of Ryder, a famous pianist, who finds himself in an unfamiliar town for a concert he does not remember arranging. Similar to the themes of his earlier books, Ishiguro again deals with codes of etiquette and order. "The book is in large part about assumptions and presumptions, about being put out and put upon—and about putting on a face of obliging acquiescence," stated Iyer. In one scene a hotel manager selfishly intent on making the pianist as comfortable as possible compels Ryder to change rooms, which in the end is an imposition rather than a kindness. *The Unconsoled* unfolds for the reader "a whole society that wonders if it has missed the point and missed the boat, and comes to see that perhaps, at some critical juncture, it was too timid, too accommodating, too dutiful to stand up for its real needs," added Iyer. He concluded: "*The Unconsoled* is a humane and grieving book, as well as one of the strangest novels in memory."

Indeed, *The Unconsoled* puzzled and irritated many reviewers. *Maclean's* contributor Guy Lawson noted that the book is built around "a clever idea: that music, no matter how unmelodic, represents a search for meaning in a confusing, contingent world," but complained that "Ishiguro . . . has written a book so plotless, so oblique, so difficult to read that the idea is lost in maddening digression after maddening digression." Several critics stressed the differences between *The Unconsoled* and Ishiguro's previous novels. *Commonweal's* Linda Simon speculated, "It may have been Ishiguro's aim to subvert the conventions of the novel as a way of underscoring his theme [of the difficulty of communication and connection], but the result is a book lacking the grace and precision that we have come to expect from a writer who, so amply in the past, has proved his intelligence, insight, and talents." A *Newsweek* reviewer added, "It's as if he got sick of reading about how compact his prose is—how he's the poet laureate of the unspoken and unexpressed—and suddenly retaliated with this dense snowstorm of words." In *New York Times,* Michiko Kakutani began by commenting on one of the similarities between *The Unconsoled* and *The Remains of the Day:* "Ryder and Stevens are actually mirror images of each other. Both are unreliable narrators whose fragmented, elliptical reminiscences will gradually expose their self-delusions. Both are willful professionals who hide behind the mask of their vocations. And both are cold, pragmatic men who have cut themselves off from reality and emotional commitment." Kakutani continued, "The biggest difference between the two men, it turns out, concerns the novels they star in. Where *The Remains of the Day* was a narrative tour de force attesting to Mr. Ishiguro's virtuosic control of the language, tone and character, *The Unconsoled* remains an awkward if admirably ambitious experiment weighed down by its own schematic structure."

The Unconsoled had its champions, though. In *New York Times Book Review,* Louis Menaud asserted that, "By the standards of *The Remains of the Day, The Unconsoled* can seem oblique, underpowered and, because of its length, slightly pretentious; but by the standards of *The Unconsoled, The Remains of the Day* is predictable and heavy-handed. If no one had ever heard of Kazuo Ishiguro, if he had never published a word before, it would have been much easier to see how singular the vision behind *The Unconsoled* really is." *Nation* commentator Charlotte Innes, noting that some critics found the book chaotic, contended that "far from being 'chaotic,' *The Unconsoled* is as tightly plotted as anything Ishiguro has written." She added, "*The Unconsoled* conveys the same bleak message as the rest of Ishiguro's much-praised work. Our self-deceptions are intolerable. Denial is a hedge against madness. . . . But his emphasis on the tremendous relief to be drawn from the complementary comforts of kindness and art suggest something more ambivalent here. . . . Music has no moral force. But the feeling it projects, like the lifegiving exuberance of Ishiguro's prose, is unmistakable."

When We Were Orphans offers a "fusion of Ishiguro's talents and techniques," including "the muffled misery and cool, clear prose" of *The Remains of the Day* and the "surreal paranoia" of *The Unconsoled,* according to *Time International* reviewer Elinor Shields. The novel begins in 1930, with its narrator, English detective Christopher Banks still haunted by the central mystery of his own life: the unexplained disappearance of his parents from their home in Shanghai when he was a child. His investigation finally takes him to Shanghai in the late 1930s, when the city is under attack from Japan. While chronicling Banks's pursuit of the truth behind his parents' vanishing, the story also gives us his remembrances of his youth in Shanghai, his education at prestigious British schools, and his rise to a position of prominence in detective work. The novel is at once a mystery, a work of historical fiction, and "a Freudian fairy tale about a painful transition to adulthood," Shields explained.

"The novel has its quiet successes," opined James Francken in a review of *When We Were Orphans* for *London Review of Books.* "The hand-me-down conventions of detective fiction are shown to be too neat. . . . And there are delicate comic details." But, the critic cautioned, "*When We Were Orphans* doesn't work as a detective novel. Banks's stilted narrative relies on the mystery of the unaccountable and the fear of the unexplained, but the danger never really becomes threatening: there is very little evil in the novel and not even much nastiness." Furthermore, he complained, Banks is "starchy" and "predictable." An *Economist* critic cited the novel's "story-telling strengths," but also commented on its inadequate characterization and "monotonous" dialogue. "The strongest impression is of nostalgia-soaked pastiche," the critic observed, a mix of "a novel of manners with a particular kind of detective novel." Shields, however, praised the work's "moments of unnerving suspense" and praised it as "a rich, satisfying read, clear yet complex." In *Publishers Weekly* a critic noted of *When We Were Orphans* that Ishiguro's novel "triumphs with the seductiveness of his prose and his ability to invigorate shadowy events with sinister implications."

In a profile by Susan Chira for *New York Times Book Review,* Ishiguro stated: "What I'm interested in is not the actual fact that my characters have done things they later regret. . . . I'm interested in how they come to terms with it." Ishiguro continued: "On the one hand there is a need for honesty, on the other hand a need to deceive themselves—to preserve a sense of dignity, some sort of self-respect. What I want to suggest is that some sort of dignity and self-respect does come from that sort of honesty."

BIOGRAPHICAL AND CRITICAL SOURCES:

BOOKS

Contemporary Literary Criticism, Volume 27, Gale (Detroit, MI), 1984.

Shaffer, Brian W., *Understanding Kazuo Ishiguro,* University of South Carolina Press (Columbia, SC), 1997.

PERIODICALS

Antioch Review, summer, 2001, Rosemary Hartigan, review of *When We Were Orphans,* p. 637.

Book, September, 2000, Helen M. Jerome, "An Artist of the World," p. 40.

Booklist, July, 2000, Brad Hooper, review of *When We Were Orphans,* p. 1974; April 1, 2001, Karen Harris, review of *When We Were Orphans,* p. 1490.

Chicago Tribune, October 1, 1989, p. 5.

Clio, spring, 2001, Cynthia F. Wong, interview with Ishiguro, p. 309.

Commonweal, March 22, 1996, Linda Simon, review of *The Unconsoled,* p. 25.

Comparative Literature, fall, 2001, Bruce Robbins, "Very Busy Just Now: Globalization and Harriedness in Ishiguro's 'The Unconsoled,'" p. 426.

Economist, May 6, 1995, p. 85; April 15, 2000, "New Novels," p. 12.

Encounter, June-July, 1982.

Harper's, October, 1995, p. 71; February, 1996, p. 30.

Library Journal, August, 2000, Barbara Hoffert, review of *When We Were Orphans,* p. 157.

London Review of Books, April 13, 2000, James Francken, "Something Fishy," p. 37.

Los Angeles Times, June 20, 1986.

Los Angeles Times Book Review, August 8, 1982; October 1, 1989; April 1, 1990; October 14, 1990.

Maclean's, May 22, 1995, Guy Lawson, review of *The Unconsoled,* p. 70.

Modern Fiction Studies, fall, 2002, John J. Su, "Refiguring National Character: The Remains of the British Estate Novel," p. 552.

Nation, June 11, 1990, p. 81; November 6, 1995, Charlotte Innes, review of *The Unconsoled,* p. 546.

New Leader, November 13, 1989, pp. 21-22; September, 2000, Tova Reich, review of *When We Were Orphans,* p. 42.

New Republic, January 22, 1990; November 6, 1995, p. 42.

New Society, May 13, 1982.

New Statesman, February 19, 1982; April 3, 2000, Phil Whittaker, "Return of the Native."

New Statesman & Society, May 26, 1989.

Newsweek, October 2, 1995, review of *The Unconsoled,* p. 92.

New Yorker, April 19, 1982; October 23, 1995, p. 90; September 11, 2000, Joan Acocella, review of *When We Were Orphans,* p. 95.

New York Review of Books, December 21, 1995, p. 17.

New York Times, October 17, 1995, Michiko Kakutani, "Books of the Times."

New York Times Book Review, May 9, 1982; June 8, 1986; October 8, 1989; October 15, 1995, Louis Menand, "Anxious in Dreamland," p. 7.

Observer (London, England), May 21, 1989, p. 53.

Publishers Weekly, July 3, 1995, review of *The Unconsoled,* p. 48; September 18, 1995, p. 105; July 10, 2000, review of *When We Were Orphans,* p. 41.

Sewanee Review, summer, 2001, Ben Howard, "A Civil Tongue: The Voice of Kazuo Ishiguro," p. 398.

Spectator, February 27, 1982.

Time, October 2, 1995, Paul Gray, review of *The Unconsoled,* p. 82.

Time International, April 24, 2000, Elinor Shields, "The End of Innocence," p. 65.

Times (London, England), February 18, 1982; February 28, 1983.

Times Literary Supplement, February 19, 1982; February 14, 1986; May 19, 1989; April 28, 1995.

World Literature Today, summer, 2000, Brian W. Shaffer, review of *When We Were Orphans,* p. 595.

Writer, May, 2001, Lewis Burke Frumkes, "Kazuo Ishiguro," p. 24.

Yale Review, April, 2001, Diana Postlethwaite, review of *When We Were Orphans,* p. 159.

ONLINE

January Magazine, http://www.januarymagazine.com/ (April 20, 2004), Linda Richards, interview with Ishiguro.*

J-K

JENSEN, Muriel 1945-

PERSONAL: Born January 1, 1945, in New Bedford, MA; daughter of Michael and Jeannette (Bourgeois) Pacheco; married Ronald Lee Jensen, August 10, 1968; children: Michael, Patrick, Kathleen. *Ethnicity:* "French Canadian." *Education:* Graduate of public schools in Downey, CA.

ADDRESSES: Home—659 15th St., Astoria, OR 97103. *E-mail*—romance@pacifier.com.

CAREER: Writer.

MEMBER: Romance Writers of America.

WRITINGS:

ROMANCE NOVELS

Lovers Never Lose, Harlequin American Romance (Buffalo, NY), 1985.

Fantasies and Memories, Harlequin American Romance (Buffalo, NY), 1987.

Love and Lavender, Harlequin American Romance (Buffalo, NY), 1987.

The Mallory Touch, Harlequin American Romance (Buffalo, NY), 1987.

The Duck Shack Agreement, Harlequin American Romance (Buffalo, NY), 1988.

Carol Christmas, Harlequin American Romance (Buffalo, NY), 1989.

Side by Side, Harlequin American Romance (Buffalo, NY), 1989.

A Wild Iris, Harlequin American Romance (Buffalo, NY), 1990.

Everything, Harlequin American Romance (Buffalo, NY), 1990.

Trust a Hero, Harlequin Superromance (Buffalo, NY), 1990.

Bridge to Yesterday, Harlequin Superromance (Buffalo, NY), 1991.

Fantasies and Memories, Silhouette (Buffalo, NY), 1991.

The Miracle, Harlequin American Romance (Buffalo, NY), 1991.

Racing with the Moon, Harlequin American Romance (Buffalo, NY), 1991.

In Good Time, Harlequin Superromance (Buffalo, NY), 1992.

Middle of the Rainbow, Harlequin American Romance (Buffalo, NY), 1992.

Milky Way, Harlequin (Buffalo, NY), 1992.

Strings, Silhouette (Buffalo, NY), 1992.

Valentine Hearts and Flowers, Harlequin American Romance (Buffalo, NY), 1992.

The Unexpected Groom, Harlequin American Romance (Buffalo, NY), 1993.

Candy Kisses, Harlequin American Romance (Buffalo, NY), 1994.

Make-Believe Mom, Harlequin American Romance (Buffalo, NY), 1994.

Trust, Harlequin Historicals (Buffalo, NY), 1994.

Night Prince, Harlequin American Romance (Buffalo, NY), 1994.

The Wedding Gamble, Harlequin American Romance (Buffalo, NY), 1994.

A Bride for Adam, Harlequin Historicals (Buffalo, NY), 1995.

The Courtship of Dusty's Daddy, Harlequin American Romance (Buffalo, NY), 1995.

Make Way for Mommy, Harlequin American Romance (Buffalo, NY), 1995.

Merry Christmas, Mommy, Harlequin American Romance (Buffalo, NY), 1995.

Mommy on Board, Harlequin American Romance (Buffalo, NY), 1995.

The Comeback Mom, Harlequin, 1996.

Husband in a Hurry, Harlequin Superromance (Buffalo, NY), 1996.

Christmas in the Country, Harlequin American Romance (Buffalo, NY), 1997.

The Fraudulent Fiancee, Harlequin Superromance (Buffalo, NY), 1997.

The Heart of the Matter, Harlequin Yours Truly (Buffalo, NY), 1997.

Kids & Co., Harlequin American Romance (Buffalo, NY), 1997.

Hot Pursuit (Hometown Reunion), Harlequin (Buffalo, NY), 1997.

The Little Matchmaker, Harlequin Superromance (Buffalo, NY), 1997.

The Prince, the Lady and the Tower, Harlequin American Romance (Buffalo, NY), 1997.

Undercover Mom, Harlequin (Buffalo, NY), 1997.

One and One Makes Three, Harlequin (Buffalo, NY), 1998.

Gout de Passion, Harlequin (Buffalo, NY), 1998.

Daddy by Design, Harlequin (Buffalo, NY), 1998.

Daddy by Destiny, Harlequin (Buffalo, NY), 1998.

Gift-Wrapped Dad/Christmas Is for Kids, Harlequin (Buffalo, NY), 1998.

His Bodyguard, Harlequin (Buffalo, NY), 1999.

Countdown to Baby, Harlequin (Buffalo, NY), 1999.

The Third Wise Man, Harlequin (Buffalo, NY), 1999.

Four Reasons for Fatherhood, Harlequin (Buffalo, NY), 2000.

Father Fever, Harlequin (Buffalo, NY), 2000.

Bride by Surprise, Harlequin (Buffalo, NY), 2000.

Father Formula, Harlequin (Buffalo, NY), 2001.

Billion Dollar Bride, Harlequin (Buffalo, NY), 2001.

Father Found, Harlequin (Buffalo, NY), 2001.

(With Judith Arnold and Bobby Hutchinson) *All Summer Long,* Harlequin (Buffalo, NY), 2001.

Daddy to Be Determined, Harlequin (Buffalo, NY), 2001.

(With Stella Cameron) *Shadows/Daddy in Demand,* Harlequin (Buffalo, NY), 2001.

Mommy and Me, Harlequin (Buffalo, NY) 2001.

(With Jasmine Cresswell) *Marriage on the Run/The Little Matchmaker,* Harlequin (Buffalo, NY), 2002.

Man with a Message, Harlequin Superromance (Buffalo, NY), 2002.

Man with a Mission, Harlequin Superromance (Buffalo, NY), 2002.

Daddy by Default: Who's the Daddy, Silhouette (Buffalo, NY), 2003.

Reinventing Julia, Harlequin (Buffalo, NY) 2003.

(With Kristine Rolofson and Kristin Gabriel) *Date with Destiny,* Harlequin (Buffalo, NY), 2003.

For the Love of Mike!, Harlequin (Buffalo, NY), 2003.

Jackpot Baby, Harlequin American Romance (Buffalo, NY), 2003.

That Summer in Maine, Harlequin (Buffalo, NY), 2003.

Man in a Million, Harlequin Superromance (Buffalo, NY), 2003.

(With Anne Stuart and Cherry Addir) *Date with a Devil: Better the Devil You Know,* Harlequin (Buffalo, NY), 2004.

The Man She Married, Harlequin Superromance (Buffalo, NY), 2004.

His Baby, Harlequin American Romance (Buffalo, NY), 2004.

Contributor to the volumes *Little Matchmakers,* Harlequin (Buffalo, NY), 1994; *My Valentine,* Harlequin (Buffalo, NY), 1994; *This Time . . . Marriage,* Harlequin (Buffalo, NY), 1996; *How to Marry a Millionaire,* Harlequin (Buffalo, NY), 1997; and *Love by Chocolate,* Jove (New York, NY), 1997.

SIDELIGHTS: Muriel Jensen's prolific output consists of over seventy titles in the romance genre. A review of *Merry Christmas, Mommy,* by a *Library Journal* contributor, noted Jensen's ability to create a "warm, satisfying romance." The review also praised her use of secondary characters in creating dimension. Rickey Mallory of *Painted Rock,* commenting in a review of *The Fraudulent Fiancee,* stated that Jensen "gets points" for her writing while comparing the book to "several popular movies" because of the book's "mix-ups, misfortunes, and near misses."

BIOGRAPHICAL AND CRITICAL SOURCES:

PERIODICALS

Library Journal, November 15, 1995, review of *Merry Christmas, Mommy,* p. 62.

ONLINE

Painted Rock, http://www.paintedrock.com/ (August, 1997), Rickey Mallory, review of *The Fraudulent Fiancee.*

* * *

JOHNSON, Elizabeth A. 1941-

PERSONAL: Born December 6, 1941, in Brooklyn, NY. *Ethnicity:* "Caucasian." *Education:* Brentwood College, B.A., 1964; Manhattan College, M.A., 1970; Catholic University of America, Ph.D., 1981.

ADDRESSES: Office—Department of Theology, Fordham University, Bronx, NY 10458. *E-mail*—ejohnson@fordham.edu.

CAREER: Theologian, Roman Catholic nun. Catholic University of America, Washington, DC, professor of theology, 1981-91; Fordham University, Bronx, NY, distinguished professor of theology, 1991—.

MEMBER: Catholic Theological Society of America (president, 1996-97), American Academy of Religion, College Theology Society, American Theological Society.

AWARDS, HONORS: Grawemeyer Award in Religion, University of Louisville, and Crossroad Women's Studies Award, both 1992, for *She Who Is: The Mystery of God in Feminist Theological Discourse;* annual award, *U.S. Catholic,* 1994; Excellence in the Study of Religion Award, American Academy of Religion, 1999, for *Friends of God and Prophets: A Feminist Theological Reading of the Communion of Saints;* University Medal, Siena Heights University, 1999; Sacred Universe Award, SpiritEarth, 1999; Loyola Mellon Award in the Humanities, Loyola University—Chicago, 2000; Elizabeth Seton Medal, Mount St. Joseph College, 2000; honorary doctorates from St. Mary's College, 1992, Maryknoll School of Theology, 1994, Chicago Theological Union, 1997, Siena College, 1998, Le Moyne College, 1999, St. Joseph College—New York, 2001, and Manhattan College, 2002.

WRITINGS:

Consider Jesus: Waves of Renewal in Christology, Crossroad Publishing (New York, NY), 1990.

She Who Is: The Mystery of God in Feminist Theological Discourse, Crossroad Publishing (New York, NY), 1992.
Women, Earth, and Creator Spirit, Paulist Press (Ramsey, NJ), 1993.
(With Susan Rakoczy) *Who Do You Say That I Am? Introducing Contemporary Christology,* Cluster Publications (Pietermaritzburg, South Africa), 1997.
Friends of God and Prophets: A Feminist Theological Reading of the Communion of Saints, Continuum (New York, NY), 1998.
(Editor and contributor) *The Church Women Want: Catholic Women in Dialogue,* Crossroad Publishing (New York, NY), 2002.
Truly Our Sister: A Theology of Mary in the Communion of Saints, Continuum (New York, NY), 2003.

Contributor to books and to scholarly journals and religious magazines, including *Theological Studies, Journal of Ecumenical Studies, Horizons: Journal of the College Theology Society,* and *Concilium: International Journal of Theology.*

Johnson's books have been translated into German, Portuguese, Spanish, Italian, French, and Korean.

SIDELIGHTS: Feminist theologian Elizabeth A. Johnson was the first woman to receive a Ph.D. in theology from the Catholic University of America, and she served on that school's faculty for ten years before going on to Fordham University. Johnson is the author of a number of volumes, including her groundbreaking *She Who Is: The Mystery of God in Feminist Theological Discourse.* In a review for *Christian Century,* Amy Plantinga Pauw wrote that Johnson "is conversant with the full spectrum of contemporary feminism and Christian thought, but it is her knowledge of the breadth of Roman Catholic tradition that is most striking. . . . In constructing her feminist discourse, she draws on distinctively Catholic resources, ranging from the Sophia traditions in Sirach and the Book of Wisdom to the transcendental and liberation themes of twentieth-century Catholicism." *She Who Is* won several awards and was translated into a number of languages. Like her first book, *Consider Jesus: Waves of Renewal in Christology, She Who Is* has been incorporated into courses at both Catholic schools and secular universities, including Harvard and Columbia.

Christian Century's Monica K. Hellwig reviewed *Friends of God and Prophets: A Feminist Theological Reading of the Communion of Saints,* commenting that Johnson, "considers the Catholic doctrine of the communion of saints from a feminist perspective, and discovers that, though this doctrine has played a large role in liturgy, creedal affirmations, devotional practices, and Christian art, it has received little theological attention. She finds this an advantage, since it enables her to analyze the practice of saint-making and saint-reverencing without having to wrestle with entrenched theological interpretations."

Johnson notes that nearly all canonized saints are male, and many of them are of an elevated social class. She also notes that of the few saints who were female, only a small number were married. There is also an absence of references to strong independent women in the liturgical reading of stories from the bible.

Robert P. Imbelli reviewed the volume in *Commonweal,* writing that "whether or not the reality of the communion sanctorum has been so neglected in theology as to merit her description of it as 'a sleeping symbol,' there is no doubt but that its creative reappropriation is desirable, indeed imperative in a culture often marked more by fragmentation and disconnection than communion. *Friends of God and Prophets* is just such a faith-filled and critical reappropriation that seeks to disclose the symbol's 'liberating meaning for today.'" Imbelli continued, noting that Johnson "aims to amplify the symbol's scope, extending it in ways that are explicitly egalitarian, ecumenical, and even ecological. . . . Feminist insights and scholarship help propel this expansion toward greater inclusivity and equality."

Johnson addressed nearly 4,000 Catholics who attended the November 3-5, 2000, meeting of the annual Call to Action convention in Milwaukee, Wisconsin. She said in part that women have been "denied equality with men in access to sacred ties, places, actions, and even identity. . . . Women have been consistently robbed of our full dignity as friends of God and prophets" because of "theories like Augustine's, who claimed a man taken alone was fully in the image of God, but a woman was fully in the image of God only when taken together with man who is her head; or philosophies like Aquinas's which argued that women are misbegotten males with weak minds and defective wills." Johnson went on to describe women of all races

and cultures, performing the tasks that make life possible, women who are victimized and women who are strong and defiant. "All," Johnson said, "are friends of God and prophets through the grace of Holy Wisdom."

In reviewing *Truly Our Sister: A Theology of Mary in the Communion of Saints,* Sally Cunneen wrote in the *National Catholic Reporter* that Johnson "is up front about her aim: to 'articulate a theology of Mary that will promote the flourishing of women and thereby all the relationships and communities of which they are a part.' This includes the church, of course, and makes the book necessary reading for men as for women."

Johnson concentrates on Mary's humanity and the reality of her life. She notes that although Mary has been idealized through the ages by male interpreters, this may have done more harm than good. As Johnson writes, Mary was of the artisan or peasant class and did not have the benefit of either status or education. Hers was a life of toil. Johnson also touches on Mary's virgin status and writes that "divine and human fatherhood are not necessarily mutually exclusive." Cunneen wrote that Johnson "observes fruitfully that the Immaculate Conception is really about the presence of grace, not the absence of sin."

Nancy Hawkins commented in *America* that "probably no other figure in Christianity is more misunderstood, misconstrued, and misinterpreted than Mary. At the same time, she is deeply revered. The numerous layers of historical nuancing make it difficult to find the true Miriam of Nazareth, a Jewess who lived in Roman-occupied Galilee during the first century. It is Johnson's quest to free this Jewish woman from the various projections and misconceptions placed upon her over the centuries."

Johnson is editor of *The Church Women Want: Catholic Women in Dialogue,* a collection of essays from the women who participated in a series of lectures refereed by Margaret O'Brien Steinfels, former editor of *Commonweal.* William Cleary wrote in the *National Catholic Reporter* that Johnson's contribution, "Imaging God, Embodying Christ: Women As a Sign of the Times," "is stunning." Cleary said, "I suspect that women who no longer take the church seriously do so because it does not take them seriously. In that survey of women's opinions collected by Marcy Kaptur in preparation for her powerful chapter—and printed in the book after her speech—someone named Mary Lee Gladieux says it best: 'The Catholic Church needs to do what it won't do—recognize women as full and equal partners with men—and anything else is not worth discussing.'"

BIOGRAPHICAL AND CRITICAL SOURCES:

PERIODICALS

America, June 9, 2003, Nancy Hawkins, review of *Truly Our Sister: A Theology of Mary in the Communion of Saints,* p. 22.

Christian Century, November 17, 1993, Amy Plantinga Pauw, review of *She Who Is: The Mystery of God in Feminist Theological Discourse,* p. 1159; January 20, 1999, Monica K. Hellwig, review of *Friends of God and Prophets: A Feminist Theological Reading of the Communion of Saints,* p. 61.

Commonweal, October 23, 1998, Robert P. Imbelli, review of *Friends of God and Prophets,* p. 24.

Library Journal, June 1, 2003, David I. Fulton, review of *Truly Our Sister,* p. 128.

National Catholic Reporter, October 16, 1998, Pamela Schaeffer, review of *Friends of God and Prophets,* p. 32; November 17, 2000, Tom Roberts, "Theologian Calls for Recognition of Holiness in Women," p. 7; May 23, 2003, Sally Cunneen, review of *Truly Our Sister,* p. 22; December 26, 2003, William Cleary, review of *The Church Women Want: Catholic Women in Dialogue,* p. 18.

Theological Studies, June, 1999, Michael J. Himes, review of *Friends of God and Prophets,* p. 377; March, 2004, Anthony J. Tambasco, review of *Truly Our Sister,* p. 198.

U.S. Catholic, April, 2002, review of *She Who Is,* p. 36.

*   *   *

JOHNSON, Marguerite Annie
    See ANGELOU, Maya

*   *   *

JONES, LeRoi
    See BARAKA, Amiri

KINCAID, Jamaica 1949-

PERSONAL: Born Elaine Potter Richardson, May 25, 1949, in St. Johns, Antigua; daughter of a carpenter/cabinet maker and Annie Richardson; married Allen Shawn (a composer and professor); children: Annie Shawn, Harold. *Education:* Studied photography at New School for Social Research (now New School University); attended Franconia College. *Religion:* Jewish.

ADDRESSES: Home—P.O. Box 822, North Bennington, VT 05257.

CAREER: Writer. *New Yorker,* New York, NY, staff writer, 1976-95. Visiting professor, Harvard University, Cambridge, MA.

AWARDS, HONORS: Morton Dauwen Zabel Award, American Academy and Institute of Arts and Letters, 1983, for *At the Bottom of the River;* honorary degrees from Williams College and Long Island College, both 1991, and Colgate University, Amherst College, and Bard College; Lila Wallace-*Reader's Digest* Fund annual writer's award, 1992; National Book Critics Circle Award finalist for fiction, PEN Faulkner Award finalist, and *Boston Book Review* Fisk Fiction Prize, all 1997, all for *The Autobiography of My Mother;* National Book Award nomination, 1997, for *My Brother.*

WRITINGS:

At the Bottom of the River (short stories), Farrar, Straus (New York, NY), 1983.
Annie John (novel), Farrar, Straus (New York, NY), 1985.
Annie, Gwen, Lilly, Pam, and Tulip ("Artists and Writers" series), lithographs by Eric Fischl, Library Fellows of the Whitney Museum of American Art (New York, NY), 1986.
A Small Place (essays), Farrar, Straus (New York, NY), 1988.
Lucy (novel), Farrar, Straus (New York, NY), 1990.
The Autobiography of My Mother (novel), Farrar, Straus (New York, NY), 1995.
My Brother, Farrar, Straus (New York, NY), 1997.

Jamaica Kincaid

(Author of introduction) *Generations of Women: In Their Own Words,* photographs by Mariana Cook, Chronicle Books (San Francisco, CA), 1998.

(Editor and author of introduction) *My Favorite Plant: Writers and Gardeners on the Plants They Love,* Farrar, Straus (New York, NY), 1998.

Poetics of Place (essay), photographs by Lynn Geesaman, Umbrage (New York, NY), 1998.

My Garden (Book) (essay), Farrar, Straus (New York, NY), 1999.

Talk Stories (essays), Farrar, Straus (New York, NY), 2000.

Mr. Potter, Farrar, Straus (New York, NY), 2002.

Contributor to books, including *Snapshots: Twentieth-Century Mother-Daughter Fiction,* D. Godine (Boston, MA), 2000; and *Whispers from the Cotton Tree Root: Caribbean Fabulist Fiction,* Invisible Cities Press (Montpelier, VT), 2000. Contributor to periodicals, including *New Yorker* and *Architectural Digest.* Recordings include *Jamaica Kincaid Interview with Kay Bonetti,* American Audio Prose Library (Columbia, MO), 1991; *Jamaica Kincaid Reads Annie John (The Red Girl Section), At the Bottom of the River (Girl*

and My Mother Sections), and Lucy, American Audio Prose Library, 1991; and *Jamaica Kincaid Reading Her Short Story At the Bottom of the River,* Library of Congress Archive of Recorded Poetry and Literature, 1995.

SIDELIGHTS: Jamaica Kincaid gained wide acclaim with her first two works, *At the Bottom of the River* and *Annie John.* In these and other books about life on the Caribbean island of Antigua, where she was born, Kincaid employs a highly poetic literary style celebrated for its rhythms, imagery, characterization, and elliptic narration. As Ike Onwordi wrote in *Times Literary Supplement:* "Kincaid uses language that is poetic without affectation. She has a deft eye for salient detail while avoiding heavy symbolism and diverting exotica. The result captures powerfully the essence of vulnerability."

In an interview with Leslie Garis for *New York Times Magazine,* Kincaid noted of her island childhood, "Everyone thought I had a way with words, but it came out as a sharp tongue. No one expected anything from me at all. Had I just sunk in the cracks it would not have been noted. I would have been lucky to be a secretary somewhere." When she was seventeen years of age, Kincaid, whose given name was Elaine Potter Richardson, left the rural island to become an *au pair* in New York City. By the time she returned to Antigua almost twenty years later, she had become a successful writer for *New Yorker* magazine under her chosen name.

In her first collection of stories, *At the Bottom of the River,* Kincaid shows an imposing capacity for detailing life's mundane aspects. This characteristic of her writing is readily evident in the oft-cited tale "Girl," which consists almost entirely of a mother's orders to her daughter: "Wash the white clothes on Monday and put them on the stone heap; wash the color clothes on Tuesday and put them on the clothesline to dry; don't walk barehead in the hot sun; cook pumpkin fritters in very hot sweet oil . . . ; on Sundays try to walk like a lady, and not like the slued you are so bent on becoming." Anne Tyler, in a review for *New Republic,* declared that this passage provides "the clearest idea of the book's general tone; for Jamaica Kincaid scrutinizes various particles of our world so closely and so solemnly that they begin to take on a nearly mystical importance." "The Letter from Home," also from *At the Bottom of the River,* serves as further illustration of Kincaid's style of repetition and her penchant for the mundane. In this tale a character recounts her daily chores in such a manner that the story resembles an incantation: "I milked the cows, I churned the butter, I stored the cheese, I baked the bread, I brewed the tea," Kincaid begins. In *Ms.,* Suzanne Freeman cited this tale as evidence that Kincaid's style is "akin to hymn-singing or maybe even chanting." Freeman added that Kincaid's "singsong style" produces "images that are as sweet and mysterious as the secrets that children whisper in your ear."

With the publication of *At the Bottom of the River* Kincaid was hailed as an important new voice in American fiction. Edith Milton wrote in *New York Times Book Review* that Kincaid's tales "have all the force of illumination, and even prophetic power." David Leavitt noted in *Village Voice* that the author's stories move "with grace and ease from the mundane to the enormous," and added that "Kincaid's particular skill lies in her ability to articulate the internal workings of a potent imagination without sacrificing the rich details of the external world on which that imagination thrives." Doris Grumbach expressed similar praise in her review for *Washington Post Book World* by declaring that the world of Kincaid's narrators "hovers between fantasy and reality." Kincaid's prose "results not so much in stories as in states of consciousness," Grumbach noted, adding that the author's style, particularly its emphasis on repetition, intensifies "the feelings of poetic jubilation Kincaid has . . . for all life."

This exuberance for life is also evident in Kincaid's second book, *Annie John,* which contains interrelated stories about a girl's maturation in Antigua. In *Annie John* the title character evolves from a young girl to an aspiring nurse and from innocent to realist: she experiences her first menstruation, buries a friend, gradually establishes a life independent of her mother, and overcomes a serious illness. She is ultimately torn by her pursuit of a career outside her life in Antigua, and Kincaid renders that feeling so incisively that, as Elaine Kendall noted in her review for *Los Angeles Times,* "you can almost believe Kincaid invented ambivalence." Critically acclaimed as a coming-of-age novel, *Annie John* was praised by a number of reviewers for expressing qualities of growing up that transcend geographical locations. Noting the book's vivid "recollections of childhood," Paula Bonnell remarked

in *Boston Herald* that *Annie John* "conveys the mysterious power and intensity of childhood attachments to mother, father and friends, and the adolescent beginnings of separation from them." Susan Kenney, writing in *New York Times Book Review,* noted Annie John's ambivalence about leaving behind her life in Antigua and declared that such ambivalence is "an inevitable and unavoidable result of growing up." Kenney concluded that Kincaid's story is "so touching and familiar . . . so inevitable [that] it could be happening to any of us, anywhere, any time, any place. And that's exactly the book's strength, its wisdom, and its truth."

Kincaid's novel *Lucy* is a first-person narrative in which the nineteen-year-old title character not only expresses feelings of rage, but struggles with separation from her homeland and especially her mother. Lucy is a young woman from Antigua who comes to an unnamed American city to work as an *au pair.* She is employed by a wealthy, white couple, Mariah and Lewis, to take care of their four young daughters. In *Washington Post Book World,* Susanna Moore commented: "Lucy is unworldly. She has never seen snow or been in an elevator. . . . Written in the first person, [the novel] is Lucy's story of the year of her journey—away from her mother, away from home, away from the island and into the world." Richard Eder mused in *Los Angeles Times Book Review* that Lucy's "anger . . . is an instrument of discovery, not destruction. It is lucid and cool, but by no means unsparing." The novel ends with Lucy writing in a journal given to her by Mariah, the woman for whom she works, and weeping over the very first line: "'I wish I could love someone so much that I would die from it.' And then as I looked at this sentence a great wave of shame came over me and I wept and wept so much that the tears fell on the page and caused all the words to become one great blur."

In a discussion of *Lucy,* Derek Walcott commented in *New York Times Magazine* about Kincaid's identification with issues that thread through all people's lives: "That relationship of mother and daughter—today she loves her mother, tomorrow she hates her, then she admires her—that is so true to life, without any artificiality, that it describes parental and filial love in a way that has never been done before. [Kincaid's] work is so full of spiritual contradictions clarified that it's extremely profound and courageous." Thulani Davis, writing in *New York Times Book Review,* called Kincaid "a marvelous writer whose descriptions are richly detailed; her sentences turn and surprise even in the bare context she has created, in which there are few colors, sights or smells and the moments of intimacy and confrontation take place in the wings, or just after the door closes. . . . Lucy is a delicate, careful observer, but her rage prevents her from reveling in the deliciousness of a moment. At her happiest, she simply says, 'Life isn't so bad after all.'"

The Autobiography of My Mother follows Kincaid's two previous fictional efforts in its West Indies setting and vivid, poetic prose. The book's narrator, Xuela, is an elderly woman who recounts her difficult life, beginning with the death of her mother at Xuela's birth. In what reviewers have termed a chilling, unsparing tone, Xuela describes her childhood abuse at the hands of a stepmother; the corruption of her father, a policeman; and her decision to abort her unborn child after she realizes the baby is intended for its father and his barren wife. At the end of the novel, the narrator calls her account a story of the mother she never knew, of her unborn baby, and of "the voices that should have come out of me, the faces I never allowed to form, the eyes I never allowed to see me," as quoted by Dale Peck in *London Review of Books.*

As with the author's earlier works, *The Autobiography of My Mother* received significant critical praise, especially for Kincaid's lyrical writing style. "Kincaid has written a truly ugly meditation on life in some of the most beautiful prose we are likely to find in contemporary fiction," averred Cathleen Schine in *New York Times Book Review. Maclean's* reviewer Diane Turbide concurred, noting, "Kincaid employs an almost incantatory tone, using repetition and unusual syntax to give the book a hypnotic rhythm." Several reviewers commented that the author's striking prose is not matched by the novel's thematic development. Schine noted, "There is . . . something dull and unconvincing about Xuela's anguish." According to Peck, "The prose is lovely . . . and . . . distinctly, beautifully American, yet the sentiments expressed by the words themselves are trite, falsely universalising, and often just muddled." In contrast, *Time* reviewer John Skow stated of *The Autobiography of My Mother:* "The reward here, as always with Kincaid's work, is the reading of her clear, bitter prose."

Comparing Kincaid's work to that of Toni Morrison and Wole Soyinka, Henry Louis Gates, Jr., told Emily Listfield in *Harper's Bazaar* that "There is a self-contained world which they [each] explore with great detail. Not to chart the existence of that world, but to show that human emotions manifest themselves everywhere." Gates cited as an important contribution by Kincaid that "she never feels the necessity of claiming the existence of a black world or a female sensibility. She assumes them both. I think it's a distinct departure that she's making, and I think that more and more black American writers will assume their world the way that she does. So that we can get beyond the large theme of racism and get to the deeper themes of how black people love and cry and live and die. Which, after all, is what art is all about."

In *Mr. Potter* Kincaid spins a story about an illiterate chauffer who fathers numerous children with various women and abandons them all. The idea is based on Kincaid's own profligate father, showing the author once again blurring the lines between truth and fiction in her novels. As Donna Seaman noted in *Booklist,* "Kincaid cares little about the distinction between fiction and nonfiction since all of her incantatory yet thorny works are insistently self-referential." In an interview with Kim McLarin for *Black Issues Book Review,* Kincaid said the idea came to her while she was thinking about her mother. "The more I thought of her life," Kincaid told McLarin, "and how it was that I grew up without knowing this person that she loathed and who was my father, the more I wanted to write this book. Here was a person she absolutely detested. She never introduced me to him and he never had any interest in me. Although when I became a well-known [author], he came to visit me. When he found me not interested in the idea of his being my dad, he actually disinherited me. It's in his will."

A native Antiguan of African descent, the fictional Mr. Potter leads a predictable and unimaginative life. The book's narrator is one of his many illegitimate children, but Potter has no emotional connection to her and little attachment to anything else in his life. The narrator perseveres, however, in conjuring a connection with her past by bringing her father's life into some type of focus. A *Publishers Weekly* contributor noted that, "As in her previous books, Kincaid has exquisite control over her narrator's deep-seated rage, which drives the story but never overpowers it and is tempered by a clear-eyed sympathy." Lyle D. Rosdahl, writing in *Library Journal,* called *Mr. Potter* "vivid and affecting reading." In a review for *Book,* Paul Evans called the novel "astonishing and baffling, infuriating and gorgeous." Rosdahl also noted that the main character is almost entirely unsympathetic but added that Kincaid manages "to summon up in us a genuine pathos for the man and, more so, his daughter. The author does this with word torrents that build and crest, plunging us mercilessly into the emptiness of Potter's life."

With her memoir *My Brother,* Kincaid recounts the last years of life of her brother, Devon Drew, who died of AIDS in January of 1996 at the age of thirty-three. Kincaid left the island of Antigua when her brother was age three; when she returns they are strangers to each other, and she only learns of his bisexuality after his death. Kincaid reveals that during the period in which she bought medication for him, her brother was still engaging in unprotected sex. The reader also learns that her brother was a drug addict and that he had served time in prison for his involvement in a murder. While *My Brother* provides a portrait of the author's sibling, it also explores Kincaid's own reactions to her brother's life and death. The book also returns to ground made familiar in Kincaid's novels, offering another look at Antigua, which the author describes in *My Brother* as homophobic, and revisiting her problematic relationship with her mother.

As with the author's previous works, reviewers pointed to her distinctive writing style. Anna Quindlen in *New York Times Book Review* noted that Kincaid's "endless incantatory sentences [are] a contrast to the simple words and images—a tower built of small bricks." Even though she pointed out that "the unadorned, often flat style of Kincaid's prose can occasionally feel perfunctory," Quindlen argued that "its great advantage is that within the simple setting the observations glow." Regarding the memoir's narrative structure, Gay Wachman in *Nation* maintained that "the lucid, assertive, deceptively simple voice takes its time in fleshing out the figures of the memoir, both in their present and in the past, circling around Devon and the multiple meanings of his life, illness and death." Referring to "the measured and limpid simplicity of her prose," Deborah E. McDowell in *Women's Review of Books* linked *My Brother* to earlier works by the author in declaring that "despite the grimness of her work, few writers have made the aesthetics of death and darkness more luminous than has Jamaica Kincaid."

In addition to her autobiographical fiction and nonfiction, Kincaid has produced several books on gardening. As the editor and author of introduction of *My Favor-*ite *Plant: Writers and Gardeners on the Plants They Love,* she creates an "enchanting. . . . fascinating compilation," according to *Booklist* contributor Brad Hooper. *My Favorite Plant* contains "thirty-five brief essays and poems" and is, judged a *Publishers Weekly* critic, "often beautiful, though some of its parts are not as radiant as others, and a few have yet to blossom."

Published in 1999, *My Garden (Book)* consists of a "personable and brightly descriptive, if somewhat rambling, book-length essay" that "shuttles constantly and with ease between the practical, technical difficulties of gardening and . . . larger meanings," observed a writer for *Publishers Weekly.* Alice Joyce, writing in *Booklist,* added that "Kincaid's views extend beyond the musings found in your usual garden journal." The author pairs "smart-mouth observations" with "intriguing autobiographical tidbits." Noting that Kincaid's "personality pervades the writing" in *My Garden (Book),* Daniel Starr remarked in *Library Journal* that the author "may be crank, but she is always entertaining." Kincaid reveals "her love-hate relationship with gardening" in this "robust hybrid of memoir and gardener's journal," stated Megan Harlan in an *Entertainment Weekly* assessment of *My Garden (Book).*

Kincaid's *Talk Stories* collects several "Talk of the Town" essays she wrote for the New Yorker from 1978 to 1983. The pieces were written before she became a well-known writer, and only one of them had her by-line when published in the magazine. Nancy P. Shires, writing in *Library Journal,* noted, "The hallmarks of her style are seen developing here: the close observation of the mundane, use of repetition, lyrical and rhythmic qualities, elliptical narration, and ambivalence, experimentation, and humor." The "Talk of the Town" pieces cover a wide range of topics, befitting the diverse city that it focuses on, from New York City's West Indian-American Day carnival to the haunts of the rich and famous. A *Publishers Weekly* contributor called the book "an astounding display of early literary skill and youthful daring," while Donna Seaman, writing in *Booklist,* called the volume "Great fun to read" and "a literary feast of dishes both salty and sweet, bracing and voluptuous."

BIOGRAPHICAL AND CRITICAL SOURCES:

BOOKS

Black Literature Criticism, Volume 2, Gale (Detroit, MI), 1991.

Bloom, Harold, editor, *Jamaica Kincaid,* Chelsea House (Philadelphia, PA), 1998.

Contemporary Literary Criticism, Gale (Detroit, MI), Volume 43, 1987, Volume 68, 1991.

Cudjoe, Selwyn R., editor, *Caribbean Women Writers: Essays from the First International Conference,* Callaloo (Wellesley, MA), 1990.

Ferguson, Moira, *Jamaica Kincaid: Where the Land Meets the Body,* University Press of Virginia (Charlottesville, VA), 1994.

Kincaid, Jamaica, *At the Bottom of the River,* Farrar, Straus (New York, NY), 1983.

Kincaid, Jamaica, *Lucy,* Farrar, Straus (New York, NY), 1990.

Kincaid, Jamaica, *The Autobiography of My Mother,* Farrar, Straus (New York, NY), 1995.

Simmons, Diane, *Jamaica Kincaid,* Macmillan (New York, NY), 1994.

PERIODICALS

Advertising Age, February 12, 1996, p. 19.

Advocate, December 9, 1997, p. 82.

American Visions, April, 1991, p. 36.

Atlantic, May, 1985, p. 104.

Black Issues Book Review, March, 2001, Robert Fleming, review of *Talk Stories,* p. 67; July-August, 2002, Kim McLarin, review of *Mr. Potter,* p. 34.

Book, May-June, 2002, Paul Evans, review of *Mr. Potter,* p. 72.

Booklist, November 1, 1995, p. 449; December 1, 1995, p. 587; January 1, 1996, p. 868; September 1, 1997, p. 5; August, 1998, p. 1946; May 1, 1999, p. 1571; September 15, 1999, p. 210; November 15, 2000, Donna Seaman, review of *Talk Stories,* p. 586; March 1, 2002, Donna Seaman, review of *Mr. Potter,* p. 1052.

Boston Herald, March 31, 1985, Paula Bonnell, review of *Annie John.*

Christian Science Monitor, April 5, 1985.

CLA Journal, March, 2000, K. B. Conal Byrne, "Under English, Obeah English: Jamaica Kincaid's New Language," pp. 276-277.

Commonweal, November 4, 1988, p. 602.

Emerge, March, 1996, p. 60; November, 1997, p. 100.

Entertainment Weekly, February 9, 1996, p. 49; January 17, 1997, p. 59; November 7, 1997, p. 80; December 3, 1999, p. 94.

Essence, May, 1991, p. 86; March, 1996, p. 98; May, 2001, "First Person Singular" (interview), p. 108.

Harper's Bazaar, October, 1990, p. 82; January, 1996, p. 66; April, 1996, p. 28.

Hudson Review, autumn, 1996, p. 483.

Interview, October, 1997, p. 94.

Library Journal, April 1, 1985, p. 158; January, 1986, p. 48; July, 1988, p. 88; December 1, 1989, p. 118; November 1, 1990, p. 125; February 15, 1995, p. 196; October 15, 1995, p. 61; January, 1996, p. 142; June 15, 1996, p. 105; October 1, 1997, p. 94; January 1998, p. 164; October 1, 1999, p. 125; October 15, 2000, Nancy P. Shires, review of *Talk Stories,* p. 70; April 1, 2002, Lyle D. Rosdahl, review of *Mr. Potter,* p. 140.

Listener, January 10, 1985.

London Review of Books, February 6, 1997, Dale Peck, review of *The Autobiography of My Mother,* p. 25.

Los Angeles Times, April 25, 1985, Elaine Kendall, review of *Annie John.*

Los Angeles Times Book Review, October 21, 1990.

Maclean's, May 20, 1985, p. 61; April 8, 1996, p. 72.

Mother Jones, September-October, 1997, p. 28.

Ms., January, 1984, p. 15; April, 1985, p. 14; January-February 1986, p. 90.

Nation, June 15, 1985, p. 748; February 18, 1991, p. 207; February 5, 1996, p. 23; November 3, 1997, p. 43.

Natural History, May, 1999, p. 16.

New Republic, December 31, 1983, Anne Tyler, review of *At the Bottom of the River.*

New Statesman, September 7, 1984, p. 33; September 20, 1985, p. 30; October 11, 1996, p. 45.

New Statesman & Society, October 7, 1988, p. 40.

Newsweek, October 1, 1990, p. 68; January, 1996, p. 62.

New York, January 22, 1996, p. 52.

New Yorker, December 17, 1990, p. 122.

New York Times Book Review, January 15, 1984, p. 22; April 7, 1985, p. 6; May 25, 1986, p. 24; December 7, 1986, p. 82; July 10, 1988, p. 19; October 28, 1990, p. 11; December 2, 1990, p. 16; February 4, 1996, p. 5; October 19, 1997, p. 7; December 5, 1999, p. 10; May 12, 2002, Sophie Harrison, review of *Mr. Potter,* p. 7.

New York Times Magazine, October 7, 1990, p. 42.

People, September 26, 1988, p. 37; November 5, 1990, p. 40; February 19, 1996, p. 27; October 20, 1997, p. 46; December 15, 1997, p. 109; January 24, 2000, p. 41; June 24, 2002, review of *Mr. Potter,* p. 394.

Publishers Weekly, October 14, 1983, p. 45; February 15, 1985, p. 86; August 17, 1990, p. 50; October 2, 1995, p. 67; October 9, 1995, p. 75; January 1,

1996, p. 54; April 1, 1996, p. 38; August 4, 1997, p. 53; August 31, 1998, p. 57; December 6, 1999, p. 67; December 13, 1999, p. 46; January 15, 2001, review of *Talk Stories,* p. 61; March 11, 2002, review of *Mr. Potter,* p. 49.

Saturday Review, June, 1985, p. 68.

School Library Journal, September, 1985, p. 154.

Time, February 5, 1996, p. 71; November 10, 1997, p. 108.

Times Literary Supplement, November 29, 1985; September 20, 1996, p. 22.

Village Voice, January 17, 1984.

Virginia Quarterly Review, summer, 1985.

Vogue, December, 1983, p. 62.

Voice Literary Supplement, April, 1985; February, 1996, p. 11.

Washington Post, April 2, 1985.

Washington Post Book World, October 7, 1990, Doris Grumbach, review of *At the Bottom of the River.*

Women's Review of Books, January, 1998, Deborah E. McDowell, review of *My Brother,* p. 1.

World Literature Today, autumn, 1985.

ONLINE

Salon.com, http://www.salon.com/ (April 9, 2004), Dwight Garner, interview with Kincaid.*

*   *   *

KINGSOLVER, Barbara 1955-

PERSONAL: Born April 8, 1955, in Annapolis, MD; daughter of Wendell R. (a physician) and Virginia (a homemaker; maiden name, Henry) Kingsolver; married Joseph Hoffmann (a chemist), April 15, 1985 (divorced); married Steven Hopp; children: (first marriage) Camille; (second marriage) Lily. *Education:* DePauw University, B.A. (magna cum laude), 1977; University of Arizona, M.S., 1981, and additional graduate study. *Politics:* "Human rights activist." *Religion:* "Pantheist." *Hobbies and other interests:* Music, hiking, gardening, parenthood.

ADDRESSES: Agent—Frances Goldin, 57 East Eleventh St., New York, NY 10003.

CAREER: University of Arizona, Tucson, research assistant in department of physiology, 1977-79, technical writer in office of arid lands studies, 1981-85; freelance journalist, 1985-87; writer, 1987—.

Barbara Kingsolver

MEMBER: Amnesty International, National Writers Union, National TV Turnoff, Environmental Defense, PEN West, Phi Beta Kappa, Heifer International, Green Empowerment.

AWARDS, HONORS: Feature-writing award, Arizona Press Club, 1986; American Library Association awards, 1988, for *The Bean Trees,* and 1990, for *Homeland;* citation of accomplishment from United Nations National Council of Women, 1989; PEN fiction prize and Edward Abbey Ecofiction Award, both 1991, both for *Animal Dreams;* Woodrow Wilson Foundation/Lila Wallace fellow, 1992-93; D.Litt., DePauw University, 1994; Book Sense Book of the Year Award, 2000, for *The Poisonwood Bible;* National Humanities Medal, 2000.

WRITINGS:

The Bean Trees (novel), HarperCollins (New York, NY), 1988.

Homeland and Other Stories (includes "Homeland," "Islands on the Moon," "Quality Time," "Covered

Bridges," "Rose-Johnny," and "Why I Am a Danger to the Public"), HarperCollins (New York, NY), 1989.

Holding the Line: Women in the Great Arizona Mine Strike of 1983 (nonfiction), ILR Press (Ithaca, NY), 1989, with new introduction, 1996.

Animal Dreams (novel), HarperCollins (New York, NY), 1990.

Another America/Otra America (poetry), Seal Press (Seal Beach, CA), 1992, 2nd expanded edition, 1998.

Pigs in Heaven (novel) HarperCollins (New York, NY), 1993.

High Tide in Tucson: Essays from Now or Never, HarperCollins (New York, NY), 1995.

The Poisonwood Bible: A Novel, HarperFlamingo (New York, NY), 1998.

(Author of foreword) Joseph Barbato and Lisa Weinerman Horak, editors, *Off the Beaten Path: Stories Place,* Nature Conservancy (Arlington, VA), 1998.

Prodigal Summer, HarperCollins (New York, NY), 2000.

(Editor, with Katrina Kenison, and author of introduction) *The Best American Short Stories, 2001,* Houghton Mifflin (Boston, MA), 2001.

Small Wonder (essays), illustrated by Paul Mirocha, HarperCollins (New York, NY), 2002.

Last Stand: America's Virgin Lands (nonfiction), photographs by Annie Griffiths Belt, National Geographic Society (Washington, DC), 2002.

(Author of foreword) Norman Wirzhar, editor, *The Essential Agrarian Reader,* University Press of Kentucky (Lexington, KY), 2003.

Contributor to anthologies, including *New Stories from the South: The Year's Best, 1988,* edited by S. Ravenel, Algonquin Books (Chapel Hill, NC), 1988; *New Writers of the Purple Sage: An Anthology of Recent Western Writing,* edited by Russell Martin, Penguin (New York, NY), 1992; *The Single Mother's Companion: Essays and Stories by Women,* edited by Marsha R. Leslie, Seal Press (Seattle, WA), 1994; *Mid-life Confidential: The Rock Bottom Remainders,* edited by Dave Marsh, Viking (New York, NY), 1994; *Journeys,* edited by PEN-Faulkner Foundation, Quill & Bush (Rockville, MD), 1994; *Heart of the Land: Essays on Last Great Places,* edited by Joseph Barbato, Pantheon (New York, NY), 1994; *I've Always Meant to Tell You: Letters to Our Mothers,* edited by Constance Warlow, Pocket Books (New York, NY), 1997; and *Intimate Nature: The Bond between Women and Animals,* edited by Linda Hogan, D. Metzger, and B. Peterson, Ballantine (New York, NY), 1998. Contributor of fiction, nonfiction, and poetry to numerous periodicals, including *Calyx, Cosmopolitan, Heresies, Mademoiselle, McCall's, New Mexico Humanities Review, Redbook, Sojourner, Tucson Weekly, Virginia Quarterly Review, Progressive,* and *Smithsonian.* Reviewer for *New York Times Book Review* and *Los Angeles Times Book Review.*

ADAPTATIONS: Most of Kingsolver's novels have been adapted as audiobooks.

SIDELIGHTS: Best-selling author Barbara Kingsolver infuses her writings with a strong sense of family, relationships, and community. Kingsolver draws her characters from middle America—the shop owners, the unemployed, the displaced, the homeless, the mothers and children struggling to survive—and depicts how, by banding together, these seemingly forgotten people can thrive. As a firm believer in human dignity and worth, Kingsolver fills her works with themes of inspiration, love, strength, and endurance. Many critics have applauded her tenderness toward her characters and praise her insight into human nature, political repression, and ecological imperatives. In *New York Times,* Janet Maslin cited Kingsolver for her "sweet, ennobling enthusiasm for every natural phenomenon" as well as for an "overarching wisdom and passion."

Kingsolver's first novel, *The Bean Trees,* was published to an enthusiastic critical reception in 1988. The novel focuses on the relationships among a group of women and is narrated by Taylor Greer, a young, strong-willed Kentucky woman who leaves her homeland in search of a better life. During her westward travel, Taylor unexpectedly becomes the caretaker of a withdrawn two-year-old Cherokee girl named Turtle. Eventually the two settle in Arizona, where they find "an odd but dedicated 'family' in Tucson," the author once explained. Included in this clan are Lou Ann Ruiz, a dejected mother whose husband has just left her, and Mattie, a warmhearted widow who runs the Jesus Is Lord Used Tires company. According to the author, "a new comprehension of responsibility" motivates Taylor to help Mattie shelter refugees from politically turbulent Central America.

Critics responded enthusiastically to *The Bean Trees,* noting the novel's sensitivity, humor, and lyricism. *The Bean Trees* "is as richly connected as a fine poem, but reads like realism," commented Jack Butler in *New York Times Book Review.* "From the very first page, Kingsolver's characters tug at the heart and soul," Karen FitzGerald noted in *Ms.* that "It is the growing strength of their relationships . . . that gives the novel its energy and appeal." And Margaret Randall in *Women's Review of Books* called *The Bean Trees* "a story propelled by a marvelous ear, a fast-moving humor and the powerful undercurrent of human struggle."

Favorable critical reviews also attended Kingsolver's next work, *Homeland and Other Stories.* Comprised of twelve short stories, *Homeland* relates stirring tales of individuals—mainly women—who struggle to find homes for themselves. Reviewers especially praised the title story, which reveals an aged Indian woman's disillusionment when she sees that her beloved Cherokee homeland has been transformed into a tourist trap. Another tale, "Islands on the Moon," shows how a mother and daughter—both single and pregnant—reconcile after years of estrangement. Among the distinctive characters that fill the remaining stories in the collection are a reformed thief striving for an honest living, a resilient union activist, a middle-class wife engaging in a secret affair, and a poor girl who befriends an outcast. Critics applauded Kingsolver's poetic language, her realistic portrayals of human nature, and her genuinely engaging tales. "Of the twelve stories in this first collection," remarked Russell Banks in *New York Times Book Review,* "all are interesting and most are extraordinarily fine." *Chicago Tribune* reviewer Bill Mahin called Kingsolver "an extraordinary storyteller."

While completing *Homeland and Other Stories* Kingsolver also completed *Holding the Line: Women in the Great Arizona Mine Strike of 1983,* a nonfiction book tracing the role of women during the Phelps Dodge Copper Company labor conflict. A year later, she returned to fiction with *Animal Dreams,* a novel that follows the growth of Codi Noline, an insecure woman who returns to her agricultural hometown of Grace, Arizona, after a fourteen-year absence. Characters' personal conflicts coupled with political struggles form the core of the novel. Codi finds her native community less than ideal: she faces grief, bigotry, disease, and environmental pollution and, through letters from her activist sister, learns of the political brutalities of Central America. Critics called the novel compassionate, humorous, and inspiring and praised Kingsolver's abil-

ity to mix commentary on political, social, racial, and personal turmoil. "*Animal Dreams* belongs to a new fiction of relationship, aesthetically rich and of great political and spiritual significance and power," wrote Ursula K. Le Guin in *Washington Post Book World.* "This is a sweet book, full of bitter pain; a beautiful weaving of the light and the dark." *Animal Dreams* is "a complex, passionate, bravely challenging book," maintained Melissa Pritchard in Chicago's *Tribune Books,* the critic going on to call Kingsolver "a writer of rare ambition and unequivocal talent."

In 1993 Kingsolver published *Pigs in Heaven,* a sequel to *The Bean Trees* that takes place three years after Taylor illegally adopts Turtle. In a strange turn of events, Turtle sees a man fall into the spillway of the Hoover Dam during a family vacation. Because of Turtle's insistence, Taylor sees to it that the man is rescued. The two become local heroes and are invited to appear on *Oprah Winfrey Show.* This newfound fame turns out to have unexpected consequences, however, as Cherokee lawyer Annawake Fourkiller sees the show and decides to investigate Taylor's adoption of Turtle. Threatened with losing her daughter, Taylor flees Arizona, beginning a difficult journey of economic struggle and emotional turbulence. Eventually, Taylor's mother Alice joins the pair in their flight, bringing her own wry perspective on life and undergoing her own personal journey.

Travis Silcox, writing in *Belles Lettres,* noted that, "despite its action, the novel suffers from a midpoint flatness." However, he praised Kingsolver's talent for characterization, adding that her "supporting characters enrich the story." Reviewer Wendy Smith likewise commended the novel, concluding in *Washington Post Book World* that "like all of Kingsolver's fiction, *Pigs in Heaven* fulfills the longings of the head and the heart with an inimitable blend of challenging ideas, vibrant characters and prose that sings. . . . It seems there's nothing she can't do." Karen Karbo averred in *New York Times Book Review* that Kingsolver's grip on the material she is writing is both skillful and satisfying: "As the novel progresses, she somehow manages to maintain her political views without sacrificing the complexity of her characters' predicaments." Karbo concluded that Kingsolver is "possessed of an extravagantly gifted narrative voice, she blends a fierce and abiding moral vision with benevolent, concise humor. Her medicine is meant for the head, the heart and the soul—and it goes down dangerously, blissfully, easily."

While Kingsolver's early novels are typically intimate domestic dramas, 1998's *The Poisonwood Bible* is something quite different: a penetrating exploration of one American family's troubled sojourn in Africa. The novel's sweeping scope and its portrayal of African politics during the cold war marked a thematic departure for the author. It also proved to be a bestseller. In the wake of Kingsolver's success with *The Poisonwood Bible, Nation* contributor John Leonard heralded the writer as "at last our very own [Doris] Lessing and our very own [Nadine] Gordimer, and she is, as one of her characters said of another in an earlier novel, 'beautiful beyond the speed of light.'"

With *The Poisonwood Bible,* Kingsolver established a prominent place in American letters. The epic tale introduces the Price family—father Nathan, an evangelical missionary, his wife Orleanna, and their four daughters. The story begins as the family arrives in the Congo—now Zaire—as missionaries, and events are related from the point of view of Orleanna and the four young girls. Quickly it becomes apparent that Nathan Price is a violent fanatic whose mispronunciation of the local language only serves to alienate the African villagers. The Price women struggle against starvation, sickness, and predatory ants while Nathan sinks further and further into zealous madness. His bumbling serves to indict American behavior in Africa in a microcosm, but Kingsolver also explores the violent American intervention in Congolese affairs during the Eisenhower era and the role that intervention played in destabilizing an emerging nation. According to Verlyn Klinkenborg in *New York Times Book Review, The Poisonwood Bible* is "a story about the loss of one faith and the discovery of another. . . . Ultimately a novel of character, a narrative shaped by keen-eyed women contemplating themselves and one another and a village whose familiarity it takes a tragedy to discover."

Kingsolver animates *The Poisonwood Bible* with recollections of time she herself spent in the Belgian Congo, several years later than the 1963 setting of her novel. To quote Michiko Kakutani in *New York Times,* the "powerful . . . book is actually an old-fashioned nineteenth-century novel, a Hawthornian tale of sin and redemption and the 'dark necessity' of history." Kakutani added that the tale grapples with "social injustice, with the intersection of public events with private concerns and the competing claims of community and individual will." In *Nation,* Leonard likewise called *The Poisonwood Bible* "a magnificent fiction and a ferocious bill of indictment. . . . As in the keyed chords of a Baroque sonata, movements of the personal, the political, the historical and even the biological contrast and correspond. As in a Bach cantata, the choral stanza, the recitatives and the da capo arias harmonize. And a magical-realist forest sings itself to live forever."

Though the majority of reviewers applauded Kingsolver for her work in *The Poisonwood Bible,* there were a few dissenters. *Christianity Today* correspondent Tim Stafford maintained that Kingsolver "offers a cartoonish story of idiot missionaries and shady CIA operatives destroying the delicate fabric of the Congo, like bulldozers scraping their way through the forest jungle." Critics who were not won over by the novel were rare, however. More reflective of the majority view, a *Publishers Weekly* critic described the book as "a compelling family saga, a sobering picture of the horrors of fanatic fundamentalism and an insightful view of an exploited country." In *Booklist,* Donna Seaman commended *The Poisonwood Bible* as an "extraordinarily dramatic and forthright novel. . . a measureless saga of hubris and deliverance." A *Time* reviewer felt that the author's female characters "carry a story that moves through its first half like a river in flood." And in *Progressive,* Ruth Conniff praised Kingsolver for "writing a moving book that makes [political] ideas both personal and timely. Kingsolver is a terrific fiction writer."

Prodigal Summer is similar to Kingsolver's earlier novels in its sense of place and its more intimate scope. Three story lines gradually converge as residents of southern Appalachia respond in various ways to the wealth of nature surrounding them. According to Jennifer Schuessler in *New York Times Book Review,* readers of *Animal Dreams* and *The Bean Trees* "will find themselves back on familiar, well-cleared ground of plucky heroines, liberal politics and vivid descriptions of the natural world."

The three segments of *Prodigal Summer* introduce Deanna Wolfe, a wildlife biologist who seeks to protect a clan of coyotes from a poacher who eventually becomes her lover. Another segment is devoted to the predicament of Lusa Maluf Landowski Widener, a Palestinian-Jewish hybrid housewife who must stake a claim to her piece of Appalachia after her husband dies. The final segment introduces a pair of feuding neighbors, traditional farmer Garnett Walker and his organic opponent Nannie Rawley, whose search for common ground ends in unstated affection for one another. Gradually the three separate plots weave together toward an ending that affirms the power of nature. Maslin, in her *New York Times* review of *Prodigal Summer,* deemed the work "an improbably appealing book with the feeling of a nice stay inside a terrarium." A *Publishers Weekly* reviewer also felt that readers would respond "to the sympathy with which [Kingsolver] reflects the difficult lives of people struggling on the hard edge of poverty." Michael Tyrell, writing in *Us,* suggested that, despite some passages that read like "overzealous lectures on ecology," *Prodigal Summer* excels in its "spirited, captivating heroine."

Kingsolver's 1992 book *Another America/Otra America* proved to be somewhat of a departure. Composed of original poetry, it also includes Spanish translations of her poems within the same volume. Reviewer Lorraine Elena Roses, commenting in *Women's Review of Books* on the presence of the translations, stated that "it's clear from the outset that Kingsolver feels a deep connection to the Spanish-speaking lands that begin before the Rio Grande and stretch all the way to the windswept limits of Tierra del Fuego." Kingsolver's poems explore her feelings about Latino human rights activists, Latin American victimization, and North American prejudices. *School Library Journal* contributor Deanna Kuhn called the book a "powerful collection." While praising Kingsolver's technical skill, Roses questioned whether "lyrical poetry [can] bear the weight of politics," but concluded that Kingsolver's poems "will appeal primarily to those who seek to commemorate and mark political occasions."

In *High Tide in Tucson,* published in 1995, Kingsolver offers opinions on a myriad of topics, from motherhood to the effect of the Gulf War. A *Kirkus Reviews* critic, while finding fault with the author's "hit-or-miss musings" and "smarmy self-reflections," commended Kingsolver's facility with nature writing. A second essay collection, *Small Wonder,* collects twenty-three essays on a variety of topics. While many essays were published previously, the book includes three written in collaboration with Kingsolver's husband, Steven Hopp. Subject matter ranges from the Columbine High School, Colorado, shootings to television, the homeless, and the difficulties of writing about sex. Judith Bromberg pointed out in *National Catholic Reporter* that *Small Wonder* came about after Kingsolver was asked to respond to the September 11, 2001 terrorist attack on the United States. She wrote five responsive essays in one month, all of which are included in this collection. Bromberg noted that, whether written before or after September 11, the essays "reflect [the event's] enormous reality and either draw meaning from it or attempt to lend some clarity to it." Piers Moore Ede commented in *Earth Island Journal* that Kingsolver's essays serve as "compelling, provocative . . . meditations" on how the event changed the world, and commended the author for having the courage to suggest that the attacks were perhaps a political protest against the "American Way."

Kingsolver has described herself as "a writer of the working class" who views her art as a daily job. "My idea of a pre-writing ritual is getting the kids on the bus and sitting down," she said in a *Book Page* online interview. Elsewhere in the same interview she outlined her goals as an author. "I'm extremely interested in cultural difference, in social and political history, and the sparks that fly when people with different ways of looking at the world come together and need to reconcile or move through or celebrate those differences," she said. "All that precisely describes everything I've ever written."

As an extension of her belief in literary fiction as a force for social change, Kingsolver has established and funded the Bellwether Prize. Awarded biennially, the prize consists of a $25,000 cash payment and guaranteed publication for a novel manuscript by an author who has not previously been widely published. The goal of the Bellwether Prize is to promote writing, reading, and publication of literary fiction that addresses issues of social justice and the impact of culture and politics on human relationships.

BIOGRAPHICAL AND CRITICAL SOURCES:

BOOKS

Contemporary Literary Criticism, Volume 55, Gale (Detroit, MI), 1989.

PERIODICALS

African Business, March, 1999, Christy Nevin, review of *The Poisonwood Bible,* p. 56.
Belles Lettres, fall, 1993, Travis Silcox, review of *Pigs in Heaven,* pp. 4, 42.

Bloomsbury Review, November-December, 1990.

Booklist, February 15, 1992, p. 1083; August, 1998, Donna Seaman, review of *The Poisonwood Bible,* p. 1922.

Chicago Tribune, May 18, 1988; June 23, 1989; July 11, 1993, p. 3.

Christianity Today, January 11, 1999, Tim Stafford, review of *The Poisonwood Bible,* p. 88.

Cosmopolitan, March, 1988.

Courier Journal (Louisville, KY), April 24, 1988.

Earth Island Journal, winter, 2002, Piers Moore Ede, review of *Small Wonder,* p. 45.

English Journal, January, 1994.

Entertainment Weekly, November 5, 1999, Rebecca Ascher-Walsh, "Kingsolver for a Day," p. 75.

Kirkus Reviews, August 1, 1995, p. 1080.

Los Angeles Times, April 3, 1988; April 24, 1988.

Los Angeles Times Book Review, July 16, 1989, September 9, 1990; July 4, 1993, pp. 2, 8.

Ms., April, 1988, Karen Fitzgerald, review of *The Bean Trees.*

Nation, January 11, 1999, John Leonard, review of *The Poisonwood Bible,* p. 28.

National Catholic Reporter, March 19, 1999, Judith Bromberg, review of *The Poisonwood Bible,* p. 13; Judith Bromberg, review of *Small Wonders,* p. 30.

New Republic, March 22, 1999, Lee Siegel, "Sweet and Low: The Poisonwood Bible," p. 30.

New Statesman, December 10, 1993.

Newsweek, July 12, 1993.

New Yorker, April 4, 1988.

New York Times, October 16, 1998, Michiko Kakutani, "No Ice Cream Cones in a Heart of Darkness;" November 2, 2000, Janet Maslin, "Three Story Lines United by the Fecundity of Nature."

New York Times Book Review, April 10, 1988, p. 15; June 5, 1988; June 11, 1989; January 7, 1990; September 2, 1990; June 27, 1993, p. 59; October 15, 1995, p. 21; October 18, 1998, Verlyn Klinkenborg, "Going Native;" November 5, 2000, Jennifer Schuessler, "Men, Women and Coyotes."

Progressive, February, 1996, p. 33; December, 1998, Ruth Conniff, review of *The Poisonwood Bible,* p. 39.

Publishers Weekly, August 31, 1990, p. 46; January 27, 1992, p. 93; August 7, 1995, p. 449; August 10, 1998, review of *The Poisonwood Bible,* p. 366; October 2, 2000, review of *Prodigal Summer,* p. 57.

San Francisco Chronicle, March 6, 1988.

School Library Journal, August, 1992, p. 192; November, 1993; February, 1996, p. 134.

Time, September 24, 1990; November 9, 1998, review of *The Poisonwood Bible,* p. 113.

Tribune Books (Chicago, IL), August 26, 1990, Melissa Pritchard, review of *Animal Dreams.*

Us, October 30, 2000, Michael Tyrell, review of *Prodigal Summer,* p. 49.

USA Today, October 11, 1990.

Utne Reader, July-August, 1993.

Washington Post Book World, September 2, 1990; June 13, 1995, p. 3; October 8, 1995, p. 13.

Women's Review of Books, May, 1988, Margaret Randall, review of *The Bean Trees;* July, 1992, Lorraine Elena Roses, review of *Another America/ Otra America,* p. 42.

ONLINE

Barbara Kingsolver Home Page, http://www.king solver.com (April 12, 2004).

Book Page, http://www.bookpage.com/ (April 12, 2004), Ellen Kanner, "Barbara Kingsolver Turns to Her Past to Understand the Present" (interview).

KYLit Web site, http://www.english.eku.edu/services/ kylit/ (December 5, 1994), George Brosi, "Barbara Kingsolver."

NewsHour Online, http://www.pbs.org/newshour/ (November 24, 1995), David Gergen, interview with Kingsolver.

Salon.com, http://www.salon.com/ (December 16, 1995), "Lit Chat with Barbara Kingsolver."

L

LEONARD, Elmore (John Jr.) 1925-

PERSONAL: Born October 11, 1925, in New Orleans, LA; son of Elmore John (an automotive executive) and Flora Amelia (Rive) Leonard; married Beverly Cline, July 30, 1949 (divorced, May 24, 1977); married Joan Shepard, September 15, 1979 (died, January 13, 1993); married Christine Kent, August 19, 1993; children: (first marriage) Jane Jones, Peter, Christopher, William, Katherine Dudley. *Education:* University of Detroit, Ph.B., 1950. *Religion:* Roman Catholic.

ADDRESSES: Agent—Michael Siegel, Michael Siegel & Associates, 11532 Thurston Circle, Los Angeles, CA 90049.

CAREER: Writer, 1967—. Campbell-Ewald Advertising Agency, Detroit, MI, copywriter, 1950-61; freelance copywriter and author of educational and industrial films, 1961-63; head of Elmore Leonard Advertising Company, 1963-66. Producer of film *Tishomingo Blues,* 2002. *Military service:* U.S. Naval Reserve, 1943-46.

MEMBER: Writers Guild of America West, Authors League of America, Authors Guild.

AWARDS, HONORS: Hombre named one of the twenty-five best western novels of all time by Western Writers of America, 1977; Edgar Allan Poe Award, Mystery Writers of America, 1984, for *LaBrava;* Michigan Foundation of the Arts Award, 1985; Hammett Prize, International Association of Crime Writers,

Elmore Leonard

1991, for *Maximum Bob;* Mystery Writers of America Grand Master Award, 1992; Honorary Ph.D., Florida Atlantic University, 1996, University of Detroit Mercy, 1997, and University of Michigan, 2000.

WRITINGS:

WESTERNS

The Bounty Hunters (also see below), Houghton (Boston, MA), 1953.

The Law at Randado (also see below), Houghton (Boston, MA), 1955.

Escape from Five Shadows (also see below), Houghton (Boston, MA), 1956.

Last Stand at Saber River (also see below), Dell (New York, NY), 1957, published as *Lawless River,* R. Hale (London, England), 1959, published as *Stand on the Saber,* Corgi (London, England), 1960.

Hombre (also see below), Ballantine (New York, NY), 1961.

Valdez Is Coming (also see below), Gold Medal (New York, NY), 1970.

Forty Lashes less One (also see below), Bantam (New York, NY), 1972.

Gunsights (also see below), Bantam (New York, NY), 1979.

The Tonto Woman and Other Western Stories, Delacorte (New York, NY), 1998.

Elmore Leonard's Western Roundup #1 (contains *The Bounty Hunters, Forty Lashes less One,* and *Gunsights*), Delta (New York, NY), 1998.

Elmore Leonard's Western Roundup #2 (contains *Escape from Five Shadows, Last Stand at Saber River,* and *The Law at Randado*), Delta (New York, NY), 1998.

Elmore Leonard's Western Roundup #3 (contains *Valdez Is Coming* and *Hombre*), Delta (New York, NY), 1999.

CRIME NOVELS

The Big Bounce, Gold Medal (New York, NY), 1969, revised edition, Armchair Detective, 1989.

The Moonshine War (also see below), Doubleday (New York, NY), 1969.

Mr. Majestyk (also see below), Dell (New York, NY), 1974.

Fifty-two Pickup (also see below), Delacorte (New York, NY), 1974.

Swag (also see below), Delacorte (New York, NY), 1976, published as *Ryan's Rules,* Dell (New York, NY), 1976.

Unknown Man, No. 89, Delacorte (New York, NY), 1977.

The Hunted (also see below), Dell (New York, NY), 1977.

The Switch, Bantam (New York, NY), 1978.

City Primeval: High Noon in Detroit (also see below), Arbor House (New York, NY), 1980.

Gold Coast (also see below), Bantam (New York, NY), 1980, revised edition, 1985.

Split Images (also see below), Arbor House (New York, NY), 1981.

Cat Chaser (also see below), Arbor House (New York, NY), 1982.

Stick (also see below), Arbor House (New York, NY), 1983.

LaBrava (also see below), Arbor House (New York, NY), 1983.

Glitz, Arbor House (New York, NY), 1985.

Bandits, Arbor House (New York, NY), 1987.

Touch, Arbor House (New York, NY), 1987.

Freaky Deaky, Morrow (New York, NY), 1988.

Killshot, Morrow (New York, NY), 1989.

Get Shorty, Delacorte (New York, NY), 1990.

Maximum Bob, Delacorte (New York, NY), 1991.

Rum Punch, Delacorte (New York, NY), 1992.

Pronto, Delacorte (New York, NY), 1993.

Riding the Rap, Delacorte (New York, NY), 1995.

Out of Sight, Delacorte (New York, NY), 1996.

Cuba Libre, Delacorte (New York, NY), 1998.

Be Cool (sequel to *Get Shorty*), Delacorte (New York, NY), 1999.

Pagan Babies, Delacorte (New York, NY), 2000.

Tishomingo Blues, Morrow (New York, NY), 2002.

Mr. Paradise, Morrow (New York, NY), 2004.

A Coyote's in the House, Morrow (New York, NY), 2004.

OMNIBUS VOLUMES

Elmore Leonard's Dutch Treat (contains *The Hunted, Swag,* and *Mr. Majestyk*), introduction by George F. Will, Arbor House (New York, NY), 1985.

Elmore Leonard's Double Dutch Treat (contains *City Primeval: High Noon in Detroit, The Moonshine War,* and *Gold Coast*), introduction by Bob Greene, Arbor House (New York, NY), 1986.

Three Complete Novels (contains *LaBrava, Cat Chaser,* and *Split Images*), Wings Books (New York, NY), 1992.

SCREENPLAYS

The Moonshine War (based on Leonard's novel of the same title), Metro-Goldwyn-Mayer, 1970.

Joe Kidd, Universal, 1972.

Mr. Majestyk (based on Leonard's novel of the same title), United Artists, 1974.

High Noon, Part 2: The Return of Will Kane, Columbia Broadcasting System, 1980.

(With Joseph C. Stinson) *Stick* (based on Leonard's novel of the same title), Universal, 1985.

(With John Steppling) *52 Pick-Up* (based on Leonard's novel of the same title), Cannon Group, 1986.

(With Fred Walton) *The Rosary Murders* (based on the novel by William X. Kienzle), New Line Cinema, 1987.

Desperado, National Broadcasting Corporation, 1988.

(With Joe Borrelli) *Cat Chaser* (based on Leonard's novel of the same title), Viacom, 1989.

(With Quentin Tarantino) *Jackie Brown* (based on Leonard's novel *Rum Punch*), Miramax, 1997.

Also author of filmscripts for Encyclopædia Britannica Films, including *Settlement of the Mississippi Valley, Boy of Spain, Frontier Boy,* and *Julius Caesar,* and of a recruiting film for the Franciscans.

OTHER

When the Women Come out to Dance (short fiction), William Morrow (New York, NY), 2002.

Contributor to books, including *The Courage to Change: Personal Conversations about Alcoholism,* edited by Dennis Wholey, Houghton (Boston, MA), 1984. Contributor of stories and novelettes to *Dime Western, Argosy, Saturday Evening Post, Zane Grey's Western Magazine,* and other publications.

ADAPTATIONS: The novelette *3:10 to Yuma* was filmed by Columbia Pictures, 1957; the story "The Tall T" was filmed by Columbia, 1957; *Hombre* was filmed by Twentieth Century-Fox, 1967; *The Big Bounce* was filmed by Warner Bros., 1969, and 2004; *Valdez Is Coming* was filmed by United Artists, 1970; *Glitz* was filmed for television by NBC; *Get Shorty* was filmed by MGM/UA, 1995; *Touch* was filmed by Lumiere, 1996; *Out of Sight,* directed by Steven Soder-bergh, screenplay by Scott Frank, was filmed by Universal, 1998; *Tishomingo Blues* was adapted for film in 2002; *Karen Sisco* (based on characters from *Out of Sight*) was developed for television by ABC, 2003; screen rights to the novella *Tenkiller* were purchased by Paramount, 2002; *Be Cool* was planned for a film by MGM, 2005. Many of Leonard's novels have been adapted as audiobooks, including *Mr. Paradise,* Harper Audio, 2004.

SIDELIGHTS: Elmore Leonard had been hailed as one of the top crime novelists of the late twentieth century, carrying on the tradition of the early pulp novelists into the next century. With dozens of bestselling crime novels to his credit, Leonard has earned acclaim for imbuing his thrillers with dark humor, moral ambivalence, and a unique prose style that reflects the anxious realities of modern life. Dubbing the novelist the "mastermind behind darkly comic bestellers" like *Get Shorty, Glitz,* and *Out of Sight,* Rob Brookman maintained in a *Book* critique that Leonard combines "whip-smart prose with a seemingly inexhaustible cast of sleazeballs, scam artists and out-and-out psychopaths." While noting that Leonard began his career as a noir writer, Bill Ott explained the author's evolution, writing in *Booklist* that "Happily-ever-aftering, unimaginable in real noir, remains a tempting if hard-won possibility in Leonard's world." Leonard's novels, according to Ott, characteristically offer readers "a violent, hard-boiled, streetwise brand of romantic comedy, usually starring a hero and heroine who . . . find their way out of an outlandish mess."

In the early 1980s Leonard began to receive the kind of attention from reviewers befitting an author whom Richard Herzfelder in *Chicago Tribune* called "a writer of thrillers whose vision goes deeper than thrill." While the plots of Leonard's books remain inherently action-packed and suspenseful, he also earns praise, to quote *Washington Post Book World* critic Jonathan Yardley, "for accomplishments rather more substantial than that of keeping the reader on tenterhooks." These accomplishments, which Yardley described as raising "the hard-boiled suspense novel beyond the limits of genre and into social commentary," led critics previously inclined to pigeonhole Leonard as a crime or mystery novelist to dispense with such labels in their assessments of his work. In the process, several critics have chosen to mention Leonard's name alongside those of other writers whose literary works transcend their genre, among them Ross Macdonald and Dashiell

Hammett. "Leonard is one of our finest humorists, especially when he is not trying to be funny," explained Bruce DeSilva in *New York Times Book Review.* "We laugh because we recognize people we know and sometimes, though it can be hard to admit, something of ourselves in the flawed, very real people of his hard-boiled crime novels."

Leonard began his career in the early 1950s as a writer of western stories for magazines. His first sale was the novelette *Apache Agent* to *Argosy* magazine for $90. He eventually turned his hand to novels in the genre, publishing five of them while pursuing a career as an advertising copywriter for a firm in Detroit. Copywriter was not an occupation much to Leonard's liking. "He says matter-of-factly that he hated the work," noted Bill Dunn in a *Publishers Weekly* interview, "but it allowed him precious time and a steady paycheck to experiment with fiction, which he did in the early morning before going off to work." Leonard told Dunn: "Sometimes I would write a little fiction at work, too. I would write in my desk drawer and close the drawer if somebody came in."

By the early 1960s the western genre had already peaked in popularity, and Leonard found that the market for his fiction had dried up. For several years he wrote no fiction at all, devoting his time to freelance copywriting, primarily for Hurst gear shifters, a popular feature in hot rod cars. He also wrote industrial films for Detroit-area companies and educational films for Encyclopædia Britannica at a thousand dollars apiece. Finally in 1965, when his agent sold the film rights to his last western novel, *Hombre,* for ten thousand dollars, Leonard had the financial leeway to write fiction again. This time he focused on the mystery-suspense genre. As he told Gay Rubin of *Detroiter:* "I began writing westerns because there was a market for them. Now of course there is an interest in police stories . . . suspense, mystery, crime."

Despite the shift in genre, Leonard's fiction has remained in many ways the same. In both his western and crime fiction there is an overriding interest in seeing that justice is done, as well as the world-weary recognition that justice is a very ambiguous concept. Leonard's prose, lean and hard, has consistently been of the same high quality. And his gunfighters and urban detectives approach their work with the same glib, wisecracking attitude. Writing in *Esquire,* Mike Lupica claimed that despite their apparent diversity, all of

Leonard's main characters are essentially the same, but "with a different name and a different job. . . . They have all been beat on by life, they all can drop a cool, wise-guy line on you, they are all tough, don't try to push them around."

Leonard's first crime novel, *The Big Bounce,* was rejected by some eighty-four publishers and film producers before being published as a paperback original by Gold Medal. Unsure about his switch to crime writing because of the trouble he had selling the book, Leonard turned again to westerns, publishing two more novels in the genre. But when the film rights to *The Big Bounce* were sold for $50,000, Leonard abandoned the western genre almost completely, penning only an occasional short story here and there. Since making that decision, all of his subsequent novels have enjoyed both hardcover and paperback editions and have been sold to Hollywood; in fact, *The Big Bounce* was reproduced by original purchaser Warner Brothers in 2004. In *Film Comment,* Patrick McGilligan wrote: "Now there are as many Leonard stories being filmed in Hollywood as there were options left. . . . On the cusp of the millennium, after nearly fifty years in the field, Leonard finds himself the modernist crime writer of choice for all the hip young filmmakers."

The typical Leonard novel, Michael Kernan explained in *Washington Post,* is distinguished by "guns, a killing or two or three, fights and chases and sex. Tight, clean prose, ear-perfect, whip-smart dialogue. And, just beneath the surface, an acute sense of the ridiculous." Leonard has said on several occasions that he has been less influenced by other crime writers than by such writers as Ernest Hemingway, John Steinbeck, and John O'Hara. Their lean, unadorned writing style and ability to remain in the background of their stories appealed to Leonard. As he told Charles Champlin of *Los Angeles Times:* "I became a stylist by intentionally avoiding style. When I go back and edit and something sounds like *writing,* I rewrite it. I rewrite constantly, four pages in the basket for every one that survives." The result impressed Ken Tucker of *Village Voice,* who called Leonard "the finest thriller writer alive primarily because he does his best to efface style."

Many of Leonard's crime novels feature lower-class, somewhat desperate characters hoping to make fast money with a big heist or quick scam. They "fall into crime," according to Tucker, "because it's an easier way to make money than that tedious nine-to-five." George Stade, in *New York Times Book Review,* called Leonard's villains "treacherous and tricky, smart enough to outsmart themselves, driven, audacious and outrageous, capable of anything, paranoid—cunning and casually vicious—and rousing fun." Dick Roraback, in *Los Angeles Times Book Review,* claimed that "it is the mark of the author's craft that his characters do not seem to be created, 'written.' They simply are there, stalking, posturing, playing, loving, scheming, and we watch and listen and are fascinated. And appalled, yes, or approving, but always absorbed. They never let us off the hook."

Although he had been writing critically acclaimed crime novels for a decade, and his work was being adapted for the screen, Leonard had only a small cadre of fans until the early 1980s, when his novels began to attract the attention of a larger audience. With the novel *Stick* in 1982, Leonard suddenly found he had risen to the status of bestselling writer. One sign of this sudden success can be seen in the agreeable change in Leonard's finances that year. The paperback rights for *Split Images* earned him $7,000 in 1981; the rights for *Stick,* a year later, earned $50,000. Then, in 1983, *LaBrava* won an Edgar Allan Poe Award from the Mystery Writers of America as the best novel of the year. Leonard's next novel, *Glitz,* hit the bestseller lists in 1985.

Leonard's popularity continued to increase throughout the 1990s. In *Get Shorty* he drew on his years of experience as a screenwriter to create an intricate story full of inside jokes about the seamy underbelly of Hollywood. The protagonist is Chili Palmer, a Miami loan shark who travels to California in pursuit of a man. He is also being pursued, and in the course of the action, he becomes entangled with a third-rate producer, a washed-up actress, and several cocaine dealers. Writing in *Los Angeles Times Book Review,* Champlin applauded the accuracy of Leonard's portrait of the movie business, calling it "less angry than *Day of the Locust* but not less devastating in its tour of the industry's soiled follies and the gaminess beneath the grandeurs." Even more sweeping praise came from Whitney Balliett in *New Yorker,* who declared that, "Book by book . . . the tireless and ingenious genre novelist Elmore Leonard is painting an intimate, precise, funny, frightening, and irresistible mural of the American underworld. . . . Leonard treats [his characters] with the understanding and the detailed attention

that Jane Austen gives her Darcys and Emma Woodhouses."

The publication of *Maximum Bob* in 1991 spurred reviewers on to even greater superlatives. Praising Leonard as "the greatest living writer of crime fiction," Barry Gifford announced in *New York Times Book Review* that with *Maximum Bob* "Leonard confirms . . . his right to a prominent place in the American *noir* writers' hall of fame. . . . Nobody I've ever read sets up pace, mood and sound better." The title character is a Florida judge whose nickname comes from his fondness for the electric chair. Having tired of his wife, who believes she is possessed by the spirit of a girl eaten by an alligator one hundred and thirty years before, the judge attempts to drive her out of his life so that he can pursue another woman. Thus begins the story, described by Robert Carver in *New Statesman & Society* as "a murder chase in reverse, where the killing hasn't yet happened, so you keep trying to guess both victim and perpetrator." Carver asserted that "this is a brilliant, funny, hugely enjoyable black comedy." Clifford Irving remarked in *Los Angeles Times Book Review* on the profound aspects of the humor found in *Maximum Bob,* stating that Leonard, "like any true comic, has a melancholy view of the world and its primitive denizens. Without moralizing, he is telling us—no, he is showing us—how rotten life is in the heartland of the USA. In *Maximum Bob,* more than ever, he is the great delineator of the macho redneck, the professional thug, the semi-mindless street-wise slob who kills and maims and rapes because it's part of the American mystique of violence and seems like fun. . . . Leonard's prose, in its way, is as good as anything being written in this country."

Laudatory remarks continued with the publication of *Rum Punch* in 1992. The novel inspired Ann Arensberg to write in *New York Times Book Review:* "I didn't know it was possible to be as good as Elmore Leonard. . . . Outpacing the classic hard-boiled novel, leaving the British detective novel in the dust, Elmore Leonard has compressed *Rum Punch* into almost pure drama, as close to playwriting as novel writing can get (and get away with)." *Washington Post Book World* contributor Michael Dirda called the book "as unputdownable as anyone could wish," as well as "a novel about growing old, about the way that time changes us, about the old dream of starting over again and its cost."

Discussing Leonard's 1993 offering, *Pronto,* Teresa Carpenter lamented the fact that "somewhere along the line, it became fashionable to discuss Elmore Leonard in terms formerly reserved for the likes of [French novelist Gustave] Flaubert." The critic readily admitted in *New York Times Book Review* that Leonard's books often "make insightful observations on contemporary culture" and "contain sharply drawn portraits of characters on the fringe of society." Other reviewers also continued to find much more than simple fun in Leonard's books. "Leonard is a literary genius," Martin Amis stated simply in his *New York Times Book Review* assessment of *Riding the Rap,* adding that the novelist "possesses gifts—of ear and eye, of timing and phrasing—that even the most indolent and snobbish masters of the mainstream must vigorously covet."

Out of Sight further cemented Leonard's reputation. The novel captures the "street, the savor and savvy, slyness and swagger of the talk that's talked on street corners and in bars, at taped-off crime scenes and in prison yards," wrote Annie Gottlieb in *Nation.* In *Out of Sight,* twenty-nine-year-old U.S. Marshall Karen Sisco—clothed in a $3,500 Chanel suit—runs into escaping convict Jack Foley. Jack reminds Karen of Harry Dean Stanton in the movie *Repo Man:* as she explains both men appear to be "real guys who seemed tired of who they were, but couldn't do anything about it." As Karen and Jack get together, cop and criminal, romance ensues in a quirky, convoluted plot that involves Foley's hit on the house of an ex-junk bond trader who supposedly has millions hidden inside. Writing for *New York Times Book Review,* Christopher Lehmann-Haupt called *Out of Sight* "an absorbing story full of offbeat characters, funny incidents, vivid locales, [and] dialogue that jumps off the page."

In *Cuba Libre* Leonard reaches for a broader audience than those he attracted with his crime novels and westerns, by combining elements of both genres. Set in Cuba around the time of the Spanish-American War, *Cuba Libre* combines adventure, history, and romance with the requisite nefarious goings-on. In a move worthy of one of his novels, Leonard arranged to have *Cuba Libre* published on the one hundredth anniversary of the sinking of the U.S.S. *Maine.* In *Cuba Libre,* Ben Tyler is a cowboy of the bank-robbing kind; in his vigilantism, he only robs banks that contain the money of people who owe him money. When he grows tired of robbing banks, Tyler joins his friend Charlie

Burke in a scheme to export horses to Cuba. They arrive in Havana just as the Spanish-American War breaks out, and suddenly these petty thieves are embroiled in the larger conflict. A *Kirkus Reviews* critic noted that the "three-cornered conflict"—the heroes and the sugar baron whose price they must meet, the U.S. government and Spain, and the American capitalists's interests in Cuba—"is nothing more than a classic Leonard scam writ large," with the small scam dovetailing smoothly into the larger "scams" of the political powers. Lehmann-Haupt, in *New York Times,* found the novel "unusually rich in period atmosphere," primarily because Leonard is "as always, so uncannily at home with the slang and terminology of the times." Also writing in *New York Times Book Review,* Pico Iyer criticized the lack of character development in the novel: "With so much plot . . . there is almost no room for character or emotion." Lehmann-Haupt stressed, however, that the novel is a political satire, though "Leonard is too good a story teller to let . . . political views shape his characters."

Be Cool is a sequel to *Get Shorty* and once again features dubious Hollywood mogul Chili Palmer. Always in search for film plots, Chili decides to help a struggling young singer make it in the music industry, just to see whether or not her story would make a good movie. In short order, Chili discovers that he has run afoul of the girl's previous manager, the Russian mafia, and a gang of rap artists. To quote Anthony Wilson-Smith in *Maclean's,* "The world that Leonard sketches has remained unchanged—a place where moral ambiguity abounds, and sudden, shocking violence is never more than a flick of the page away. *Be Cool,* like *Get Shorty,* skewers the pretensions of the entertainment industry." A *Publishers Weekly* reviewer noted that Chili "remains a compulsively appealing character, . . . retaining his immaculate cool in lethal situations," while in *Booklist* David Pitt suggested that the novel "reaches a level of comic surrealism that its predecessor only approached." And Lehmann-Haupt, in his *New York Times* review, commended *Be Cool* as "thoroughly entertaining," adding that while the "plot wrinkles involve a very inside knowledge of the music industry," "Leonard seems to have mastered it."

In the opening scenes of *Pagan Babies,* the central character, Terry Dunn, contemplates a ruthless massacre that occurred before his eyes while he said his first Mass in a small church in Rwanda. Five years have passed since the massacre of his congregation, and Dunn has done little in that time except drink whiskey. When the opportunity arises to seek revenge on the murderers, however, Dunn shows his true colors: he is a petty criminal who fled America to avoid arrest for tax fraud, and he has no problem doing some murdering of his own. This tact necessitates Dunn's rapid return to his hometown of Detroit, where, with the help of an ex-convict comedienne, he concocts new and more audacious scams. An *Economist* reviewer deemed *Pagan Babies* "one of Mr. Leonard's funniest books, with a typically colourful cast of oddballs." De Silva likewise commended the novel for its "fast pace, crackling dialogue and dark ironies." In *New York Times Book Review,* Janet Maslin wrote: "The pieces of this crime tale begin falling into place so handily that Mr. Leonard might as well have hung a 'Virtuoso at Work' shingle on his door."

Noting that Leonard "is the only A-list crime fiction writer who doesn't rely on a series hero," *Booklist* critic Bill Ott nonetheless praised the author for providing another in a long line of fascinating if slightly hardened protagonists in *Tishomingo Blues.* The novel finds high-diver Dennis Lenahan working at a Mississippi resort when he spots a murder from atop his eighty-foot ladder. Immediately conspicuous to the murderer, Dennis wants to mind his own business, but he soon finds himself caught up in a sea of events that involve not only the murderer and his status as witness: Civil War reenactors, an aggressive newscaster, and the murderer's seductive and all-too-willing wife. "As usual, Leonard's characters walk onto the page as real as sunlight as shadow," praised a *Publishers Weekly* reviewer, adding that in *Tishomingo Blues* "the dialogue is dead-on, the loopy story line strewn with the unexpected." Calling the novel "as full of pitch-perfect patter, bare-knuckle verbal sparring and whiplash one-liners as anything he has written," an *Economist* contributor noted that "the real pleasure of *Tishomingo Blues* is its diverse voices"; in *New Yorker* a contributor begged to differ, writing that Leonard's "hurtling plot twists keep coming, right up to the perfect rip of a finish."

In an online interview for the *Mr. Showbiz* Web site, Leonard said that his literary tastes and aspirations were laid down in childhood when he read the Book-of-the-Month Club offerings his mother bought. "I read a lot of them," he said. "I was intimidated by most of the novels because I thought that they were just too big and heavy, and had too many words in

them. I still feel that way about most novels—that they have way too many words in them." The author who has said that he always tries "to leave out the boring parts" in his work is a disciplined practitioner of his craft. He writes every day of the week, longhand, sitting at a desk in the corner of his living room. "The satisfaction is in doing it," he told the *Mr. Showbiz* interviewer. "I'm not writing for notoriety; I'm writing to satisfy myself."

BIOGRAPHICAL AND CRITICAL SOURCES:

BOOKS

Contemporary Literary Criticism, Gale (Detroit, MI), Volume 28, 1984, Volume 34, 1985, Volume 71, 1992.
Dictionary of Literary Biography, Volume 173, *American Novelists since World War II,* Gale (Detroit, MI), 1996.
Geherin, David, *Elmore Leonard,* Continuum (New York, NY), 1989.

PERIODICALS

American Film, December, 1984.
Armchair Detective, winter, 1986; spring, 1986; winter, 1989.
Atlantic, June, 1998, Francis X. Rocca, review of *Cuba Libre,* p. 111.
Book, March-April, 2002, Rob Brookman, interview with Leonard, p. 28.
Booklist, November 1, 1998, David Pitt, review of *Be Cool,* p. 452; December 1, 2001, Bill Ott, review of *Tishomingo Blues,* p. 604; November 1, 2002, Keir Graff, review of *When the Women Come out to Dance,* p. 452; November 15, 2003, Bill Ott, review of *Mr. Paradise,* p. 548.
Boston Globe, July 30, 1992, p. 80; November 14, 1993, p. 7.
Chicago Tribune, February 4, 1981; April 8, 1983; December 8, 1983; February 7, 1985.
Christian Science Monitor, November 4, 1983; March 12, 1997.
Commentary, May, 1985, pp. 64, 66-67.
Detroiter, June, 1974, Gay Rubin, interview with Leonard.
Detroit News, February 23, 1982; October 23, 1983.

Economist (US), June 19, 1999, review of *Be Cool*, p. 4; October 14, 2000, "New Thrillers-Hit Men," p. 106; February 23, 2002, reveiw of *Tishomingo Blues*.

Entertainment Weekly, September 22, 2000, Bruce Fretts, review of *Pagan Babies,* p. 68; January 9, 2004, Rebecca Ascher-Walsh, review of *Mr. Paradise,* p. 84.

Esquire, April, 1987, pp. 169-74.

Film Comment, March-April, 1998, Patrick McGilligan, "Get Dutch," p. 43.

Globe and Mail (Toronto, Ontario, Canada), December 14, 1985.

Kirkus Reviews, November 15, 1997, p. 1665; November 15, 2001, review of *Tishomingo Blues,* p. 1571; October 15, 2002, review of *When the Women Come out to Dance,* p. 1497; November 1, 2003, review of *Mr. Paradise,* p. 1290.

Knight-Ridder/Tribune News Service, September 20, 2000, Chauncey Mabe, review of *Pagan Babies,* p. K2148; September 27, 2000, Marta Salij, "Elmore Leonard Reaches beyond Familiar Setting," p. K3888; October 4, 2000, Marta Salij, "Elmore Leonard: A Mob Mentality," p. K7276.

Library Journal, January, 2002, Karen Anderson, review of *Tishomingo Blues,* p. 153.

Los Angeles Times, June 28, 1984; May 4, 1988; January 26, 1998.

Los Angeles Times Book Review, February 27, 1983; December 4, 1983; January 13, 1985; August 30, 1987, pp. 2, 8; April 23, 1989, p. 14; July 29, 1990, p. 9; August 4, 1991, pp. 2, 9; October 24, 1994, p. 8; May 14, 1995, p. 1.

Maclean's, January 19, 1987; March 16, 1998, Brian Bethune, review of *Cuba Libre,* p. 63; March 29, 1999, Anthony Wilson-Smith, "The Master of Crime: Elmore Leonard's 35th Novel Shows Him at the Top of His Form," p. 70.

Nation, December 4, 1995, Annie Gottlieb, review of *Out of Sight,* p. 724.

New Republic, November 13, 1995, p. 32; January 26, 1998.

New Statesman & Society, October 11, 1991; November 13, 1992.

Newsweek, March 22, 1982; July 11, 1983; November 14, 1983; April 22, 1985, pp. 62-64, 67.

New Yorker, September 3, 1990, pp. 106-7; October 23, 1995, p. 96; September 30, 1996; January 12, 1998; January 26, 1998; February 11, 2002, review of *Tishomingo Blues,* p. 86.

New York Times, June 11, 1982; April 28, 1983; October 7, 1983; October 29, 1983; April 26, 1985; May 2, 1988; July 25, 1991, p. C18; September 23, 1993, p. C18; May 11, 1995; August 15, 1996; February 15, 1996; January 18, 1997; June 7, 1997; February 14, 1997; December 24, 1997; January 22, 1998, Christopher Lehmann-Haupt, "Viva la Genre! Elmore Leonard Visits Old Havana;" February 11, 1999, Christopher Lehmann-Haupt, "Get Musical: Chili Palmer's Latest Movie Idea;" September 7, 2000, Janet Maslin, "'New Elmore Leonard?' 'Yeah. You Know. Punks.'"

New York Times Book Review, May 22, 1977; September 5, 1982; March 6, 1983; December 27, 1983; February 10, 1985, p. 7; January 4, 1987, p. 7; July 29, 1990, pp. 1, 28; July 28, 1991, p. 8; August 16, 1992, p. 13; October 17, 1993, p. 39; May 14, 1995, p. 7; September 8, 1996; January 22, 1998; February 8, 1998; September 20, 1998, Charles Salzberg, review of *The Tonto Woman,* p. 24; February 21, 1999, Kinky Friedman, "The Palmer Method," p. 10; September 17, 2000, Bruce DeSilva, "Turned Collar."

New York Times Magazine, November 16, 1997.

People, January 26, 2004, Steve Dougherty, review of *Mr. Paradise,* p. 43.

Publishers Weekly, February 25, 1983; June 15, 1990, p. 55; June 10, 1996, p. 84; November 16, 1998, review of *Be Cool,* p. 52; December 10, 2001, review of *Tishomingo Blues,* p. 48; January 21, 2002, interview with Leonard, p. 52; February 3, 2003, review of *Tishomingo Blues* (audio version), p. 24; November 24, 2003, review of *Mr. Paradise,* p. 42; April 5, 2004, review of *Mr. Paradise* (audio version), p. 22.

Sun-Sentinel (South Florida), September 20, 2000, Chauncey Mabe, review of *Pagan Babies.*

Time, May 28, 1984, pp. 84, 86; February 24, 1997; August 18, 1997; January 12, 1998.

Times Literary Supplement, December 5, 1986, p. 1370; November 30, 1990, p. 1287; September 27, 1991, p. 24; October 30, 1992, p. 21; November 5, 1993, p. 20.

Tribune Books (Chicago, IL), April 10, 1983; October 30, 1983; April 9, 1989, pp. 1, 4; May 21, 1995, p. 5.

TV Guide, August 1, 1998, Lawrence Grobel, "Get Elmore!," p. 23.

Village Voice, February 23, 1982, Ken Tucker.

Wall Street Journal, January 29, 1998.

Washington Post, October 6, 1980; February 6, 1985.

Washington Post Book World, February 7, 1982; July 4, 1982; February 20, 1983; November 13, 1983; December 28, 1986, p. 3; August 23, 1987, pp. 1-2; May 1, 1988; July 14, 1991, pp. 1-2; July 19, 1992, p. 2.

ONLINE

Elmore Leonard Home Page, http://www.elmore
    leonard.com (April 25, 2004).
Mr. Showbiz, http://mrshowbiz.go.com/ (October 19,
    2000), Rick Schultz, interview with Leonard.
Random House Web site, http://www.randomhouse.
    com/ (October 19, 2000), biographical information
    and reviews.
Salon.com, http://www.salon.com/people/ (September
    28, 1999), Sean Elder, interview with Leonard.*

* * *

LUCAS, Henry C(ameron), Jr. 1944-

PERSONAL: Born September 4, 1944, in Omaha, NE;
son of Henry Cameron (an advertising executive) and
Lois (a teacher; maiden name, Himes) Lucas; married
Ellen Kuhbach (a teacher of French), June 8, 1968;
children: Scott Cameron, Jonathan Gerdes. *Ethnicity:*
"White." *Education:* Yale University, B.S. (magna
cum laude), 1966; Massachusetts Institute of Technology, M.S., 1968, Ph.D., 1970. *Hobbies and other interests:* Jogging, cycling, sailing, travel.

ADDRESSES: Home—871 Coachway, Annapolis, MD
21401. *Office*—Center for Electronic Markets and Enterprises, Robert H. Smith School of Business, University of Maryland—College Park, College Park, MD
20742.

CAREER: Arthur D. Little, Inc., Cambridge, MA, consultant on information systems, 1966-70; Stanford University, Stanford, CA, assistant professor of computer
and information system, 1970-74; New York University, New York, NY, associate professor, 1974-78, professor of computer applications and information systems, 1978-88, research professor, 1988-98, professor
at Leonard N. Stern School of Business, 1998-2000,
department chair, 1978-84, University of Maryland—
College Park, Robert H. Smith professor of Information Systems, 2000-, codirector of Center for Electronic Markets and Enterprises, 2001—. INSEAD,
Fontainebleau, France, visiting professor, 1985; Bell
Communications Research, Morristown, NJ, visiting
researcher, 1991; Nanyang Technological University,
Shaw Foundation Professor, 1997-98. Member of
board of directors, AVX Corp., 2000-02, and Kencast,
2000—; INFORMS, member.

MEMBER: Association for Computing Machinery, Institute of Management Sciences, Institute of Electrical
and Electronics Engineers, Association of Information
Systems (fellow; vice president for publications, 1995-
98), Phi Beta Kappa, Tau Beta Pi.

AWARDS, HONORS: Award for Excellence in teaching, Schools of Business, 1982; Westside Alumni Hall
of Fame Award, 1991.

WRITINGS:

*Computer-Based Information Systems in Organiza-
    tions,* Science Research Associates (Palo Alto,
    CA), 1973.
Toward Creative Systems Design (monograph), Colum-
    bia University Press (New York, NY), 1974.
Why Information Systems Fail (monograph), Columbia
    University Press (New York, NY), 1975.
The Implementation of Computer-Based Models
    (monograph), National Association of Accountants
    (New York, NY), 1976.
*The Analysis, Design, and Implementation of Informa-
    tion Systems,* McGraw-Hill (New York, NY),
    1976, 4th edition, 1992.
(With C. F. Gibson) *Casebook for Management Infor-
    mation Systems,* McGraw-Hill (New York, NY),
    1976, 3rd edition, 1985.
Information Systems Concepts for Management,
    McGraw-Hill (New York, NY), 1978, 7th edition
    published as *Information Technology for Manage-
    ment,* 2000.
(Editor, with F. Land, T. J. Lincoln, and K. Supper)
    The Information Systems Environment, North-
    Holland (Amsterdam, Netherlands), 1980.
*Implementation: The Key to Successful Information
    Systems* (monograph), Columbia University Press
    (New York, NY), 1981.
*Coping with Computers: A Manager's Guide to Con-
    trolling Information Processing,* Free Press (New
    York, NY), 1982.
Introduction to Computers and Information Systems,
    Macmillan (New York, NY), 1987.
Managing Information Services, Macmillan (New
    York, NY), 1989.
(Editor, with R. Schwartz) *The Challenge of Informa-
    tion Technology for Securities Markets: Liquidity,
    Volatility and Global Trading,* Dow Jones-Irwin
    (Homewood, IL), 1989.

(With R. Schultz and M. Ginzberg) *Information Systems Implementation: Testing a Structural Model* (monograph), Ablex Publishing (Norwood, NJ), 1990.

The T-Form Organization: Using Technology to Design Organizations for the 21st Century, Jossey-Bass (San Francisco, CA), 1996.

Information Technology and the Productivity Paradox: Assessing the Value of Investing in IT, Oxford University Press (New York, NY), 1999.

Strategies for Electronic Commerce and the Internet, MIT Press (Cambridge, MA), 2002.

Contributor to books, including *Efficient versus Effective Computing,* edited by F. Gruenberger, Prentice-Hall (Englewood Cliffs, NJ), 1973; *Implementing Operations Research/Management Science: Research Findings and Implications,* edited by R. Schultz and D. Slevin, Elsevier Science (New York, NY), 1975; *The Economics of Information Processing,* Volume 2, edited by R. Goldberg and H. Lorin, Wiley (New York, NY), 1982; *The Handbook of Industrial Engineering,* edited by G. Salvendi, Wiley (New York, NY), 1982; and *Understanding and Managing Strategies Change,* edited by H. Ansoff, A. Bosman, and P. Storms, North-Holland (Amsterdam, Netherlands), 1982. Contributor to information systems and management journals. Editor in chief, *Communications of AIS,* 1998-2002, and *Systems, Objectives, Solutions;* editor, *Industrial Management* (now *Sloan Management Review*), 1967-68, and *Performance Evaluation Review,* 1972-73; associate editor, *MIS Quarterly,* 1978-83, *Management Science,* 1985-87, *ACM Transactions on Office Information Systems,* 1985-87, and *Information and Management;* member of editorial board, *Sloan Management Review,* 1980-91.

SIDELIGHTS: Henry C. Lucas, Jr. once told *CA:* "The powerful combination of computers and networks makes it possible to design radically new organizations, a topic I explore in *The T-Form Organization: Using Technology to Design Organizations for the 21st Century.*"

BIOGRAPHICAL AND CRITICAL SOURCES:

PERIODICALS

Academy of Management Review, October, 2002, Jay B. Barney, review of *Strategies for Electronic Commerce and the Internet,* p. 628.

Interfaces, March-April, 2000, Benjamin Lev, review of *Information Technology and the Productivity Paradox: Assessing the Value of Investing in IT,* p. 117.

Library Journal, December, 2001, Bellinda Wise, review of *Strategies for Electronic Commerce and the Internet,* p. 140.

Wisconsin Lawyer, November, 2002, Gail Miles, review of *Strategies for Electronic Commerce and the Internet,* p. 31.

*　*　*

LYNCH, B. Suarez
See BORGES, Jorge Luis

M

MANN, (Paul) Thomas 1875-1955
(Paul Thomas Mann)

PERSONAL: Born June 6, 1875, in Lübeck, Germany; voluntary exile in Switzerland, 1933; German citizenship revoked, 1936; naturalized Czech citizen, 1936; immigrated to United States, 1938; naturalized American citizen, 1944; immigrated to Switzerland, 1952; died of phlebitis, August 12, 1955, in Zurich, Switzerland; buried August 16, 1955, in Kilchberg, Switzerland; son of Thomas Johann Heinrich (a government official and owner of a trading firm) and Julia (da Silva-Bruhns) Mann; married Katja Pringsheim, February 11, 1905; children: Erika, Klaus, Golo, Monika, Elisabeth, Michael. *Education:* Attended Technische Hochschule (Munich) during 1890s.

CAREER: Writer and lecturer. South German Fire Insurance Co., Munich, Germany, apprentice, 1894-95; *Simplizissimus* (periodical), Munich, reader and copyreader, 1898-1900; Princeton University, Princeton, NJ, lecturer in the humanities, 1938-c. 1940; Library of Congress, Washington, DC, consultant in Germanic literature, 1942-44. Member of Munich Censorship Council, 1912-13; German correspondent for *Dial* during 1920s; author and presenter of radio talks for British Broadcasting Corporation (BBC). *Military service:* Royal Bavarian Infantry, 1900.

MEMBER: Prussian Academy of Arts (founding member of literary section, 1926), Union of German Writers (honorary chair, 1949), Bavarian Academy of Fine Arts (honorary chair, 1949), German Academy of Arts (honorary member), Schiller Society (East Germany; honorary member), German Academy of Language and Poetry (West Germany; honorary member), Gerhart Hauptmann Society (honorary member), Society of Those Persecuted by the Nazi Regime (honorary member), Accademia Lincei (Italy), Authors' League of America, American Academy of Arts and Letters, Phi Beta Kappa.

AWARDS, HONORS: Bauernfeld Prize, 1904; Nobel Prize in literature, 1929; Herder Prize for exiled writers from Czechoslovakia, 1937; Cardinal Newman Award, 1938; Goethe Prize from city of Frankfurt, West Germany, 1949; Goethe Prize from East Germany, 1949; Medal of Service from American Academy of Arts and Letters, 1949; Feltrinelli Prize from Accademia Nazionale dei Lincei (Italy), 1952; Officer's Cross of the French Legion of Honor, 1952; honorary citizen of Lübeck, West Germany, 1955; Cross of Orange-Nassau from the Netherlands, 1955; Order of Merit in the Sciences and Arts from West Germany, 1955. Honorary doctorates from numerous colleges and universities, including Bonn, 1919 (withdrawn, 1936, restored, 1947), Harvard, 1935, Columbia, 1938, Rutgers, 1939, Dubuque, 1939, California at Berkeley, 1941, Hebrew Union (Cincinnati, OH), 1945, Oxford, 1949, Lund, 1949, Cambridge, 1953, Friedrich Schiller (East Germany), 1955, and Technische Hochschule (Zurich, Switzerland), 1955.

WRITINGS:

NOVELS

Buddenbrooks: Verfall einer Familie, S. Fischer (Berlin, Germany), 1901, translation by H. T. Lowe-Porter published as *Buddenbrooks: The Decline of a Family,* Alfred A. Knopf (New York, NY), 1924, new translation by John E. Woods published as *Buddenbrooks: The Decline of a Family,* 1993.

Königliche Hoheil, S. Fischer (Berlin, Germany), 1909, translation by A. Cecil Curtis published as *Royal Highness: A Novel of German Court-Life,* Alfred A. Knopf (New York, NY), 1916, new edition, Vintage (New York, NY), 1983.

Bekenntnisse des Hochstaplers Felix Krull: Buch der Kindheit, first fragmentary version, subtitled *Buch der Kindheit,* Rikola (Vienna, Austria), 1922, enlarged edition, Querido (Amsterdam, The Netherlands), 1937, novel-length version, subtitled *Der Memoiren erster Teil,* S. Fischer (Berlin, Germany), 1954; translation of final enlargement by Denver Lindley published as *Confessions of Felix Krull, Confidence Man: The Early Years,* Alfred A. Knopf (New York, NY), 1955, published as *Confessions of Felix Krull, Confidence Man: Memoirs, Part I,* Secker & Warburg (London, England), 1955.

Der Zauberberg: Roman, S. Fischer (Berlin, Germany), 1924, translation by H. T. Lowe-Porter published as *The Magic Mountain,* Alfred A. Knopf (New York, NY), reprinted, 1995.

Die Geschichten Jaakobs (first in the "Joseph and His Brothers" series of novels; also see below), S. Fischer (Berlin, Germany), 1933, translation by H. T. Lowe-Porter published as *Joseph and His Brothers,* Alfred A. Knopf (New York, NY), 1934, published as *The Tales of Jacob,* Martin Secker (London, England), 1934.

Der junge Joseph (second in the "Joseph and His Brothers" series of novels; also see below), S. Fischer (Berlin, Germany), 1934, translation by H. T. Lowe-Porter published as *Young Joseph: Joseph and His Brothers II,* Alfred A. Knopf (New York, NY), 1935.

Joseph in Ägypten (third in the "Joseph and His Brothers" series of novels; also see below), Bermann-Fischer (Vienna, Austria), 1936, translation by H. T. Lowe-Porter published as *Joseph in Egypt: Joseph and His Brothers III,* Alfred A. Knopf (New York, NY), 1938.

Lotte in Weimar, Bermann-Fischer (Stockholm, Sweden), 1939, translation by H. T. Lowe-Porter published as *The Beloved Returns,* Alfred A. Knopf (New York, NY), 1940, reprinted, Vintage, 1983, translation published under original title, Secker & Warburg (London, England), 1940.

Die vertauschten Köpfe: Eine indische Legende, Bermann-Fischer (Stockholm, Sweden), 1940,

translation by H. T. Lowe-Porter published as *The Transposed Heads: A Legend of India,* Alfred A. Knopf (New York, NY), 1941.

Joseph der Ernährer (fourth in the "Joseph and His Brothers" series of novels; also see below), Bermann-Fischer (Stockholm, Sweden), 1943, translation by H. T. Lowe-Porter published as *Joseph the Provider: Joseph and His Brothers IV* (Book-of-the-Month Club selection), Alfred A. Knopf (New York, NY), 1944.

Doktor Faustus: Das Leben des deutschen Tonsetzers Adrian Leverkühn, erzählt von einem Freunde, Bermann-Fischer (Stockholm, Sweden), 1947, translation by H. T. Lowe-Porter published as *Doctor Faustus: The Life of the German Composer Adrian Leverkuehn, As Told by a Friend* (Book-of-the-Month Club selection), Alfred A. Knopf (New York, NY), 1948, reprinted, Random House (New York, NY), 1971, new translation by John E. Woods published as *Doctor Faustus,* Alfred A. Knopf (New York, NY), 1997.

(And author of introduction) *Joseph and His Brothers* (complete series of novels; contains *The Tales of Jacob, Young Joseph, Joseph in Egypt,* and *Joseph the Provider*), translation by H. T. Lowe-Porter, Alfred A. Knopf (New York, NY), 1948, reprinted, 1983.

Der Erwählte: Roman, S. Fischer (Frankfurt, Germany), 1951, translation by H. T. Lowe-Porter published as *The Holy Sinner* (Book-of-the-Month Club selection), Alfred A. Knopf, 1951.

SHORT FICTION

Der kleine Herr Friedemann und andere Novellen (contains "Der kleine Herr Friedemann," "Der Tod," "Der Wille zumGlück," "Enttaeuschung," "Der Bajazzo," "Tobias Mindernickel"; also see below), S. Fischer (Berlin, Germany), 1898, title story translated by Herman George Scheffauer as "Little Herr Friedemann" in *Children and Fools,* Alfred A. Knopf (New York, NY), 1928.

Tristan: Sechs Novellen (contains "Der Weg zum Friedhof," "Tristan," "Der Kleiderschrank," "Luischen," "Gladius Dei," "Tonio Kröger"), S. Fischer (Berlin, Germany), 1903, title story translated by Kenneth Burke in *Death in Venice* (also see below), Alfred A. Knopf (New York, NY), 1925; "Tonio Kröger" translated by B. Q. Morgan in *The German Classics of the 19th and 20th Centuries,* Volume 19, German Publications Society (New York, NY), 1914.

Fiorenza (three-act play; first performed in Frankfurt, Germany, at Schauspielhaus, May 11, 1907), S. Fischer (Berlin, Germany), 1906, translation published in *Stories of Three Decades* (also see below).

Bilse und ich, Bonsels (Munich, Germany), 1906.

Der kleine Herr Friedemann und andere Novellen (includes "Die Hungernden," and "Das Eisenbahnunglück"), S. Fischer (Berlin, Germany), 1909.

Der Tod in Venedig (novella; also see below), Hyperionverlag Hans von Weber (Munich, Germany), 1912, translation by H. T. Lowe-Porter published as *Death in Venice,* Alfred A. Knopf (New York, NY), 1928, reprinted as *Death in Venice: A New Translation, Backgrounds and Contexts, Criticism,* with translation by Clayton Koelb, W. W. Norton (New York, NY), 1994.

Das Wunderkind (contains "Das Wunderkind," "Schwere Stunde," "Beim Propheten," "Ein Glück," "Wie Jappe und Do Escobar sich pruegelten"), S. Fischer (Berlin, Germany), 1914, title story translated by Herman George Scheffauer as "The Infant Prodigy," in *Children and Fools,* Alfred A. Knopf (New York, NY), 1928.

Herr und Hund [and] *Gesang vom Kindchen: Zwei Idyllen* (novella and narrative poem, respectively), S. Fischer (Berlin, Germany), 1919, translation of the former by Herman George Scheffauer published as *Bashan and I,* Henry Holt (New York, NY), 1923, and as *A Man and His Dog,* Alfred A. Knopf (New York, NY), 1930.

Wälsungenblut (novella), Phantasus (Munich, Germany), 1921, translation published as "Blood of the Walsungs" in *Stories of Three Decades* (also see below).

Novellen, two volumes, S. Fischer (Berlin, Germany), 1922.

Death in Venice and Other Stories (contains *Death in Venice,* "Tristan," "Tonio Kröger"), translation by Kenneth Burke, Alfred A. Knopf (New York, NY), 1925, translation by H. T. Lowe-Porter, Martin Secker (London, England), 1928.

Unordnung und frühes Leid (novella; title means "Disorder and Early Sorrow"), S. Fischer (Berlin, Germany), 1926, translation by Herman George Scheffauer published as *Early Sorrow,* Martin Secker (London, England), 1929, Alfred A. Knopf (New York, NY), 1930, translation by H. T. Lowe-Porter published as *Early Sorrow* [and] *Mario and the Magician,* Martin Secker (London, England), 1934, published as "Disorder and Early Sorrow" in *Stories of Three Decades* (also see below).

Children and Fools (contains "Disorder and Early Sorrow," "How Jappe Fought Do Escobar," "The Infant Prodigy," "Tobias Mindernickel," "The Path to the Cemetery," "At the Prophet's," "Little Louise," and "Little Herr Friedemann"), translation by Herman George Scheffauer, Alfred A. Knopf (New York, NY), 1928.

Mario und die Zauberer: Ein Tragisches Reiseerlebnis (novella), S. Fischer (Berlin, Germany), 1930, translation by H. T. Lowe-Porter published as *Mario and the Magician,* Martin Secker (London, England), 1930, Alfred A. Knopf (New York, NY), 1931.

Tonio Kröger, edited with introduction, notes, and vocabulary by John Alexander Kelly, F. S. Crofts, 1931, edited by Elizabeth M. Wilkinson, 2nd edition, Basil Blackwell (London, England), 1968.

(And author of introduction) *Stories of Three Decades* (contains "Little Herr Friedemann," "Disillusionment," "The Dilettante," "Tobias Mindernickel," "Little Lizzy," "The Wardrobe," "The Way to the Churchyard," "Tonio Kröger," "Tristan," "The Hungry," "The Infant Prodigy," "Gladius Dei," "Fiorenza," "A Gleam," "At the Prophet's," "A Weary Hour," "The Blood of the Walsungs," "Railway Accident," "The Fight between Jappe and Do Escobar," "Felix Krull," *Death in Venice, A Man and His Dog,* "Disorder and Early Sorrow," and "Mario and the Magician"), translation by H. T. Lowe-Porter, Alfred A. Knopf (New York, NY), 1936.

Das Gesetz: Erzählung (novella), Pazifische Presse (Los Angeles, CA), 1944, translation by H. T. Lowe-Porter published as *The Tables of the Law,* Alfred A. Knopf (New York, NY), 1945.

Die Betrogene: Erzählung (novella), S. Fischer (Frankfurt, Germany), 1953, translation by Willard R. Trask published as *The Black Swan,* Alfred A. Knopf (New York, NY), 1954, new edition, Harcourt Brace (New York, NY), 1980.

Die Begegnung: Erzählung (novella), Vereinigung Oltner Bücherfreunde (Olten, Germany), 1953.

Das Eisenbahnunglück: Novellen, Piper (Munich, Germany), 1955.

Erzählungen (collection; includes "Vision," "Gefallen," "Geraecht," and "Anekdote"), S. Fischer (Frankfurt, Germany), 1957.

Stories of a Lifetime, two volumes, Secker & Warburg (London, England), 1961, selected edition published as *Little Herr Friedemann and Other Stories,* Penguin (New York, NY), 1972.

Death in Venice, and Seven Other Stories (contains *Death in Venice,* "Tonio Kröger," "Mario and the

Magician," "Disorder and Early Sorrow," *A Man and His Dog,* "The Blood of the Walsungs," "Tristan," and *Felix Krull*), translation by H. T. Lowe-Porter, Vintage (New York, NY), 1964, reprinted, 1989.

Death in Venice and Other Stories, translation by David Luke, Bantam Books (New York, NY), 1988.

Death in Venice and Other Tales, translation by Joachim Neugroschel, Viking (New York, NY), 1998.

Death in Venice: Complete, Authoritative Text with Biographical and Historical Contexts, Critical History, and Essays from Five Contemporary Critical Perspectives, edited by Naomi Ritter, Bedford Books (Boston, MA), 1998.

Death in Venice, Tony Kröger, and Other Writings, edited by Frederick A. Lubich, Continuum (New York, NY), 1999.

Short fiction represented in numerous other collections and anthologies.

NONFICTION

Friedrich und die grosse Koalition (essays; title means "Frederick the Great and the Grand Coalition"), S. Fischer (Berlin, Germany), 1915.

Betrachtungen eines Unpolitischen (essay), S. Fischer (Berlin, Germany), 1918, translation by William D. Morris published as *Reflections of a Nonpolitical Man,* Ungar (New York, NY), 1983.

Rede und Antwort: Gesammelte Abhandlungen und kleine Aufsätze (essays), S. Fischer (Berlin, Germany), 1922.

Goethe und Tolstoi: Vortrag (essay), Verlag "Die Kuppel" (Aachen, Germany), 1923, translation published as "Goethe and Tolstoi" in *Three Essays* and *Essays of Three Decades* (also see below), revised German edition published as *Goethe und Tolstoi: Zum Problem der Humanität,* Bermann-Fischer (Vienna, Austria), 1932.

Von Deutscher Republik (speech), S. Fischer (Berlin, Germany), 1923, translation by H. T. Lowe-Porter published as "The German Republic" in *Order of the Day* (also see below).

Okkulte Erlebnisse (essay), Alf Häger (Berlin, Germany), 1924, translation published as "An Experience in the Occult" in *Three Essays* (also see below).

Bemühungen: Neue Folge der Gesammelten Abhandlungen und kleinen Aufsätze (essays), S. Fischer (Berlin, Germany), 1925.

Pariser Rechenschaft, S. Fischer (Berlin, Germany), 1926.

Lübeck als geistige Lebensform (speech), Otto Quitzow (Lübeck, Switzerland), 1926, translation by Richard and Clara Winston published as *Lübeck As a Way of Life and Thought in "Buddenbrooks,"* Alfred A. Knopf (New York, NY), 1964.

Ausgewählte Prosa, edited by J. van Dam, Wolters (The Hague, The Netherlands), 1927.

Zwei Festreden, Reclam (Leipzig, Switzerland), 1928.

Hundert Jahre Reclam: Festrede, Reclam (Leipzig, Switzerland), 1928.

Three Essays (includes "An Experience in the Occult" and "Goethe and Tolstoi"), translation by H. T. Lowe-Porter, Alfred A. Knopf (New York, NY), 1929.

Sieben Aufsätze, S. Fischer (Berlin, Germany), 1929.

Die Forderung des Tages: Reden und Aufsätze aus den Jahren 1925-1929 (speeches and essays), S. Fischer (Berlin, Germany), 1930.

Lebensabriss, first published in *Die Neue Rundschau,* July 7, 1930, translation by H. T. Lowe-Porter published as *A Sketch of My Life,* Harrison (Paris, France), 1930, Alfred A. Knopf (New York, NY), 1960.

Deutsche Ansprache: Ein Appell an die Vernunft, S. Fischer (Berlin, Germany), 1930.

Goethe als Repräsentant des bürgerlichen Zeitalters (speech), Bermann-Fischer (Vienna, Austria), 1932, translation published as "Goethe As Representative of the Bourgeois Age" in *Essays of Three Decades* (also see below).

Past Masters and Other Papers (essays), translation by H. T. Lowe-Porter, Alfred A. Knopf (New York, NY), 1933.

Goethes Laufbahn als Schriftsteller: Vortrag, Oldenbourg (Munich, Germany), 1933.

Leiden und Grösse der Meister: Neue Aufsaetze (essays), S. Fischer (Berlin, Germany), 1935.

Freud und die Zukunft: Vortrag (essay), Bermann-Fischer (Vienna, Austria), 1936, translation published as "Freud and the Future" in *Freud, Goethe, Wagner* (also see below).

Freud, Goethe, Wagner (essays), translation by H. T. Lowe-Porter and Rita Matthias-Reil, Alfred A. Knopf (New York, NY), 1937.

Vom künftigen Sieg der Demokratie (speech), Europa Verlag Oprecht (Zurich, Switzerland), 1938, translation by Agnes E. Meyer published as *The Com-*

ing *Victory of Democracy,* Alfed A. Knopf (New York, NY), 1938.

Achtung, Europa! Aufsätze zur Zeit (essays), Bermann-Fischer (Stockholm, Sweden), 1938.

Schopenhauer (essay), Bermann-Fischer (Stockholm, Sweden), 1938, translation by H. T. Lowe-Porter published as introduction to *The Living Thoughts of Schopenhauer* (also see below).

Dieser Friede, Bermann-Fischer (Stockholm, Sweden), 1938, translation by H. T. Lowe-Porter published as *This Peace,* Alfred A. Knopf (New York, NY), 1938.

Einführung in den Zauberg für Studenten der Universität Princeton, Bermann-Fischer (Stockholm, Sweden), 1939.

Das Problem der Freiheit, Bermann-Fischer (Stockholm, Sweden), translation published as *The Problem of Freedom,* Rutgers University Press (New Brunswick, NJ), 1939.

Dieser Krieg: Aufsatz, Bermann-Fischer (Stockholm, Sweden), 1940, translation by Eric Sutton published as *This War,* Alfred A. Knopf (New York, NY), 1940.

War and Democracy, Friends of the Colleges at Claremont (Los Angeles, CA), 1940.

Order of the Day: Political Essays and Speeches of Two Decades, translation by Agnes E. Meyer, Eric Sutton, and H. T. Lowe-Porter, Alfred A. Knopf (New York, NY), 1942.

Deutsche Hörer! 25 Radiosendungen nach Deutschland (speeches), Bermann-Fischer (Stockholm, Sweden), 1942, translation published as *Listen Germany! 25 Radio Messages to the German People over the B.B.C.,* Alfred A. Knopf, 1943 (New York, NY), enlarged edition published as *Deutsche Hoerer! 55 Radiosendungen nach Deutschland,* Bermann-Fischer (Stockholm, Sweden), 1945.

The War and the Future, Library of Congress (Washington, DC), 1944.

Adel des Geistes: 17 Versuche zum Problem der Humanität (essays), Bermann-Fischer (Stockholm, Sweden), 1945, translation by H. T. Lowe-Porter published as *Essays of Three Decades,* Alfred A. Knopf (New York, NY), 1947, enlarged edition published as *Adel des Geistes: Zwanzig Versuche zum Problem der Humanität,* Aufbau (Berlin, Germany), 1955.

Leiden an Deutschland: Tagebuchblätter aus den Jahren 1933 und 1934 (diaries), Rosenburg Press (New York, NY), 1946.

(With Frank Thiess and Walter von Molo) *Ein Streitgespräch über die äussere und innere Emigration,*

Durckschriften-Vertriebs-dienst (Dortmund, Germany), 1946.

Deutschland und die Deutschen: Vortrag, Bermann-Fischer (Stockholm, Sweden), 1947.

Nietzsches Philosophie im Lichte unserer Erfahrung (essay), Suhrkamp/S. Fischer (Berlin, Germany), 1948, translation published as "Nietzsche's Philosophy in Light of Recent History," in *Last Essays* (also see below).

Neue Studien (essays), Bermann-Fischer (Stockholm, Sweden), 1948.

Die Entstehung des Doktor Faustus: Roman eines Romans, Bermann-Fischer/Querido (Amsterdam, The Netherlands), 1949, translation by Richard and Clara Winston published as *The Story of a Novel: The Genesis of "Doctor Faustus,"* Alfred A. Knopf (New York, NY), 1961, published as *The Genesis of a Novel,* Secker (London, England), 1961.

Goethe und die Demokratie, Oprecht (Zurich, Switzerland), 1949.

Der Kuenstler und die Gesellschaft (speech), Wilhelm Frick (Vienna, Austria), 1953.

Ansprache im Goethe-Jahr 1949, Suhrkamp (Frankfurt, Germany), 1949.

Goethe/Wetzlar/Werther, Rosenkilde og Bagger (Copenhagen, Switzerland), 1950.

Michelangelo in seinen Dichtungen, Quos Ego Verlag (Cellerina, Germany), 1950.

Mein Zeit: 1875-1950: Vortrag, S. Fischer (Frankfurt, Germany), 1950.

Lob der Vergänglichkeit, S. Fischer (Frankfurt, Germany), 1952.

Gerhart Hauptmann: Rede, gehalten am 9. November 1952 im Rhamen der Frankfurter Gerhart-Hauptmann-Woche (speech), C. Bertelsmann (Gütersloh, Germany), 1953.

Der Künstler und die Gesellschaft: Vortrag, Frick (Vienna, Austria), 1953.

Altes und Neues: Kleine Prosa aus Fünf Jahrzehnten (collected short prose pieces), S. Fischer (Frankfurt, Germany), 1953.

Versuch über Schiller: Seinem Andenken zum 150. Todestag in Liebe gewidmet (essay), S. Fischer, 1955, translation published as "On Schiller" in *Last Essays* (also see below).

Ansprache im Schiller-Jahr 1955, Aufbau (Berlin, Germany), 1955.

Nachlese: Prosa, 1951-1955 (collection), S. Fischer (Frankfurt, Germany), 1956.

Meerfahrt mit Don Quijote, Insel (Wiesbaden, Germany), 1956.

Leiden und Groesse der Meister (essays; not same as earlier collection with same title), S. Fischer, 1956.

Sorge um Deutschland: Sechs Essays, S. Fischer (Frankfurt, Germany), 1957.

Last Essays, translation by Richard and Clara Winston and Tania and James Stern, Alfred A. Knopf (New York, NY), 1958.

Addresses Delivered at the Library of Congress, 1942-1949 (includes "Germany and the Germans"), U.S. Library of Congress, 1963.

Wagner und unsere Zeit: Aufsaetze, Betrachtungen, Briefe (collected writings on Richard Wagner), edited by daughter, Erika Mann, S. Fischer (Frankfurt, Germany), 1963, translation by Allan Blunden published as *Pro and Contra Wagner,* introduction by Erich Heller, University of Chicago Press (Chicago, IL), 1985.

Thomas Mann's "Goethe and Tolstoy": Notes and Sources, edited by Clayton Koelb, translated by Clayton Koelb and Alcyone Scott, University of Alabama Press (University, AL), 1984.

Theodor Storm: Essay, edited by Hermann Kuzke and Stefan Stachorski, S. Fischer (Frankfurt, Germany), 1996.

OMNIBUS VOLUMES

Gesammelte Werke in zehn Bänden, ten volumes, S. Fischer (Berlin, Germany), 1925.

Die erzählenden Schriften, three volumes, S. Fischer (Berlin, Germany), 1928.

Stockholmer Gesamtausgabe der Werke, twelve volumes, Bermann-Fischer (Stockholm, Sweden), 1938-56.

Gesammelte Werke in zwölf Bänden, twelve volumes, Aufbau (Berlin, Germany), 1955.

Das erzählerische Werk: Taschenbuchausgabe in zwölf Bänden, twelve volumes, S. Fischer (Frankfurt, Germany), 1957.

Gesammelte Werke in dreizehn Bändern, thirteen volumes, S. Fischer (Frankfurt, Germany), 1960-74.

Das essayistische Werk, edited by Hans Bürgin, eight volumes, S. Fischer (Frankfurt, Germany), 1968.

Notizen: Zu Felix Krull, Königliche Hoheit, Versuch über das Theater, Maja, Geist und Kultur, Ein Elender, Betrachtungen eines Unpolitischen, Doktor Faustus un anderen Werken, edited by Hans Wysling, Winter (Heidelberg, Germany), 1973.

Romane und Erzählungen, ten volumes, Aufbau (Berlin, Germany), 1974-75.

Thomas Mann: Tagebücher 1918-1921; 1933-1934; 1935-1936; 1937-1939; 1940-1943; 1944-1946, edited by Peter de Mendelssohn, six volumes, S. Fischer (Frankfurt, Germany), 1977, partial translation by Richard, Clara, and Krishna Winston published as *Thomas Mann Diaries, 1918-1939,* Abrams (New York, NY), 1982.

Gesammelte Werke in Einzelbänden, edited by Peter de Mendelssohn, fourteen volumes, S. Fischer (Frankfurt, Germany), 1980.

Notizbücher: Edition in zwei Bänden, edited by Hans Wysling and Yvonne Schmidlin, S. Fischer (Frankfurt, Germany), 1991-92.

Thomas Mann: Tagebücher 1944-1.4.1946, 28.5.1946-31.12.1948, 1949-1950, 1951-1952, 1953-1955, five volumes, edited by Inge Jens, S. Fischer (Frankfurt, Germany), 1986-95.

Essays, six volumes, edited by Hermann Kurzke and Stefan Stachorski, S. Fischer (Frankfurt, Germany), 1993-97.

Also author of introduction for numerous books, including Theodor Fontane, *Ausgewaehlte Werke,* Reclam (Leipzig, Switzerland), 1929; Martin Niemoeller, *"God Is My Fuehrer": Being the Last 28 Sermons,* Philosophical Library and Alliance Book, 1941; *The Short Novels of Dostoevsky,* Dial Press (New York, NY), 1945; *Klaus Mann zum Gedaechtnis,* Querido (Amsterdam, The Netherlands), 1950; and Heinrich von Kleist, *Die Erzaehlungen,* S. Fischer (Frankfurt, Germany), 1956. Contributor of articles and reviews to numerous periodicals.

PERSONAL PAPERS; LETTERS, EXCEPT AS INDICATED

Zeit und Werk: Tagebücher, Reden, und Schriften zum Zeitgeschehen (collected diaries, speeches, and letters), Aufbau (Berlin), 1956.

Briefe an Paul Amann, 1915-1952, edited by Herbert Waegner, Schmidt-Römhild, 1959, translation by Richard and Clara Winston published as *Letters to Paul Amann,* Wesleyan University Press (Middletown, CT), 1960.

(With Karl Kerényi) *Gespraech in Briefen,* edited by Kerényi, Rhein-Verlag (Zurich, Switzerland), 1960, translation by Alexander Gelley published as *Mythology and Humanism: The Correspondence of Thomas Mann and Karl Kerényi,* Cornell University Press (Ithaca, NY), 1975.

Thomas Mann an Ernst Bertram: Briefe aus den Jahren 1910-1955, edited by Inge Jens, Neske (Pfulligen, Germany), 1960.

Briefe, 1899-1955, edited by Erika Mann, three volumes, S. Fischer (Frankfurt, Germany), 1961-65.

(With Robert Faesi) *Briefwechsel,* edited by Faesi, Atlantis, 1962.

Letters of Thomas Mann, 1889-1955, translation by Richard and Clara Winston, two volumes, Alfred A. Knopf (New York, NY), 1970.

(With brother, Heinrich Mann) *Briefwechsel, 1900-1949,* edited by Ulrich Dietzel, Aufbau (Berlin, Germany), 1965, 3rd edition, enlarged, 1975, translation by Don Reneau published as *Letters of Heinrich and Thomas Mann, 1900-1949,* edited by Hans Wysling, with additional translations by Richard and Clara Winston, University of California Press (Berkeley, CA), 1998.

(With Heinrich Mann) *Briefwechsel, 1900-1949,* edited by Hans Wysling, S. Fischer (Frankfurt, Germany), 1968, enlarged edition, 1984.

(With Hermann Hesse) *Briefwechsel,* edited by Anni Carlsson, S. Fischer (Frankfurt, Germany), 1968, enlarged by Volker Michels, 1975, translation by Ralph Manheim published as *The Hesse-Mann Letters: The Correspondence of Hermann Hesse and Thomas Mann, 1910-1955,* Harper & Row (New York, NY), 1975.

Thomas Mann und Hans Friedrich Blunck: Briefwechsel und Aufzeichnungen, edited by Walter Blunck, Troll-Verlag, c. 1969.

(With Erich Kahler) *Briefwechsel im Exil,* edited by Hans Wysling, Thomas Mann Gesellschaft, 1970, translation by Richard and Clara Winston published as *An Exceptional Friendship: The Correspondence of Thomas Mann and Erich Kahler,* Cornell University Press (Ithaca, NY), 1975.

Briefwechsel mit seinem Verleger Gottfried Bermann Fischer, 1932-1955 (correspondence with his publisher, Gottfried Bermann Fischer), edited by Peter de Mendelssohn, S. Fischer (Frankfurt, Germany), 1973.

Briefe an Otto Grautoff, 1894-1901, und Ida Boy-Ed, 1903-1928, edited by Peter de Mendelssohn, S. Fischer (Frankfurt, Germany), 1975.

Thomas Mann, edited by Hans Wysling, Heimeran, 1975.

Die Briefe Thomas Manns (extracts and indexes), edited by Yvonne Schmidlin, Hans Buergin, and Hans-Otto Mayer, five volumes, S. Fischer (Frankfurt, Germany), 1976-87.

(With Alfred Neumann) *Briefwechsel,* edited by Peter de Mendelssohn, Schneider (Darmstadt, Germany), 1977.

Briefwechsel mit Autoren, edited by Hans Wysling, S. Fischer (Frankfurt, Germany), 1988.

Thomas Mann: On Myself and Other Princeton Lectures, edited by James N. Bade, P. Lang (New York, NY), 1996.

(With David Lloyd) *Culture and the State,* Routledge (New York, NY), 1997.

Fragile Republik: Thomas Mann und Nachkriegsdeutschland, S. Fischer (Frankfurt, Germany), 1999.

Collegheft, 1894-1895, V. Klostermann (Frankfurt, Germany), 2001.

OTHER

(Editor) E. von Mendelssohn, *Nacht und Tag* (novel), Verlag der Weissen Buecher, 1914.

(Editor and author of introduction) *The Living Thoughts of Schopenhauer,* Longmans, Green (London, England), 1939.

(Editor and author of introduction) *The Permanent Goethe,* Dial Press (New York, NY), 1948.

Coeditor of the book series *Romane der Welt,* for Knaur, beginning in 1927. Coeditor of periodicals, including (under name Paul Thomas Mann) *Der Frühlingssturm: Monatsschrift fuer Kunst, Litteratur, und Philosophie,*1893, and *Mass und Wert: Zweimonatsschrift für freie deutsche Kultur,*beginning in 1937. Member of advisory committee of *Forum Deutscher Dichter,* for Bermann-Fischer, Allert de Lange (Amsterdam), and Querido, 1938-39.

ADAPTATIONS: Buddenbrooks was adapted for German films of the same title, 1923 and 1959, and for a German television series of the same title, 1982; *Tonio Kröger* was adapted by Erika Mann and Ennio Flajano for the French/German film of the same title, 1968; *Death in Venice* was adapted by Luchino Visconti and Niccolo Badalucco for a film of the same title, Warner, 1971; *Disorder and Early Sorrow* was adapted by Franz Seitz for the film *Disorder and Early Torment,* Jugendfilm, 1977; *The Transposed Heads* was adapted for musical dramas of the same title by Peggy Glanville-Hicks, and by Julie Taymor and Sidney Goldfarb, 1984-86; *The Confessions of Felix Krull, Confidence Man* was adapted by Robert Thoeren and Erika Mann for the film *The Confessions of Felix Krull,* Filmaufbau, 1957, and for a German television series, 1981.

SIDELIGHTS: Thomas Mann, winner of the 1929 Nobel Prize in literature, is considered one of the foremost German novelists of the twentieth century. Admirers have often ranked him, in the words of Alfred Kazin in *Contemporaries,* as "the creative peer . . . of great experimental novelists like [Marcel] Proust and [James] Joyce." Mann is renowned as a novelist of ideas, though commentators generally agree that he expounded no single philosophy and that his ideas changed over time. His accomplishment, admirers suggest, was to use fiction to conduct a lifelong exploration of philosophical issues, ranging from the role of a creative individual in society to the nature of Western culture. He wrote at a time when Europe was experiencing massive and shocking changes: new technology challenged traditional values and ways of life; mass social movements gained unprecedented importance; and Germany erupted with the horrors of Nazism. Reflecting in his work the doubts and fears of his era, Mann held the attention of millions of readers throughout the world.

"At bottom I am aware that my books are not written for Prague and New York, but for Germans," wrote Mann as he neared his sixtieth birthday, quoted by Richard and Clara Winston in *Letters of Thomas Mann, 1889-1955.* "The rest of the world has always been merely an 'extra.'" Though Mann gained a progressively broader understanding of the world outside Germany throughout his life, his work remained steeped in a German tradition that, observers believe, has made him difficult for many English-speaking readers to fully appreciate. Mann was born in 1875 in Lübeck, a German port on the Baltic Sea that was in economic decline throughout the nineteenth century. His diligent and well-respected father was forced to grapple with Lübeck's failing economy, both as head of the family trading firm and as an officer in the city government. The elder Mann chided sons Thomas and Heinrich for their lack of interest in commerce, for he hoped to groom them as his successors in the family business. Mann's mother, of mixed German and Brazilian parentage, seemed exotic by contrast with her business-oriented husband. Highly interested in music, she encouraged her sons' growing interest in the arts. To Mann, his parents embodied a common German view of European culture: a Germanic North, emotionally aloof but dutiful and productive, versus a Latin South, passionate and artistic but potentially irresponsible. In 1891, when Mann was sixteen, his father died at an untimely age, and the trading firm was liquidated. The family relocated to Munich, widely regarded at the time as the leading city of German culture. Thomas and Heinrich soon became professional writers.

Nevertheless, as many biographers suggest, Mann often expressed a businessman's suspicion of the artist's role, fearing that self-expression could lapse into empty self-indulgence. As an established writer he paid tribute to the restraining influence of his father and hometown, most notably in the 1926 speech *Lübeck als geistige Lebensform* ("Lübeck As a Spiritual Concept of Life"). Heinrich and Thomas owed much to their mother's "blithe southern disposition," Mann said, quoted by the Winstons. But "our father endowed us with 'the serious conduct of life'. . . the ethical note that so strikingly coincides with the bourgeois temper." Mann's ideal bourgeois was not the grasping capitalist disdained by Marxism, but rather the German burgher of preindustrial times. The lives of such merchants, wrote biographer R. Hinton Thomas, "signified an ideal humanism—freedom without licence, spirituality without extravagant subjectivism, practicality without philistinism."

When Mann prepared to become a writer in his teens and early twenties, he became acquainted with a wide variety of artists and thinkers. As biographer Henry Hatfield observed, his inspiration often came from beyond the world of fiction writing. While a teenager Mann became infatuated with the music of Richard Wagner, whose operas were known for their complexity, passion, and epic vision; but soon, Mann's love of Wagner became tinged with skepticism. As T. E. Apter explained in *Thomas Mann: The Devil's Avocate,* Wagner's strong appeal to the emotions "can appear as a disturbing attack" on rationality and social responsibility. In the opera *Tristan und Isolde,* for instance, the composer pointedly mixes such powerful and contradictory feelings as the yearning for love and the fascination with death. R. Hinton Thomas observed that "the evil power of music," which could draw its listeners towards "escape from the restraints and commitments of practical existence," became "a major theme of Mann's work."

After discovering Wagner, Mann delved into the works of nineteenth-century German philosophers Arthur Schopenhauer and Friedrich Nietzsche. Both philosophers rejected the truths by which most Europeans, including Mann's burgher class, had directed their lives—that good would be rewarded and evil punished because the world was a rational place, presided over by a benevolent God or by human reason. Schopenhauer believed that life was fundamentally irrational, for all living things were driven by the force of will—an inborn, mindless striving that could never be satisfied. Human reason was only a tool created by this striving force in order to attain its desires, he maintained, and all people were condemned to unhappiness as their individual wills conflicted with each other. Though pessimistic about the human condition, Schopenhauer found limited consolation in the effort to transcend one's own will, either through charity to others, through art, or, possibly, by losing one's sense of self after death.

Nietzsche took Schopenhauer's premises to more audacious conclusions. He detected a clear purpose in the human force of will, which he labeled the "will to power." According to Nietzsche, every human being is driven to dominate their surroundings, including other people; much of human unhappiness comes from misdirecting this natural drive. Accordingly, he blasted Christianity for advocating guilt and submissiveness, finding its followers self-tortured and too weak to meet the demands of life. He also became dubious of Schopenhauer, whose subdued pessimism seemed as unhealthy as Christianity. Aware that modern science was undermining religious faith in the West, Nietzsche feared that disillusioned believers would lapse into nihilism, choosing death and destruction on the grounds that life had lost its purpose. Thus he advocated a new, more confident human being—the superman or overman—who would find a sense of purpose in the innate force of will.

Commentators suggest that Mann's diverse influences—from dutiful burghers to the flamboyant Nietzsche—do not form a unified philosophy, or even a succession of philosophies. For many of Mann's admirers, his ability to pursue several different modes of thought at once is key to his appeal. As Hatfield explained in *Modern German Literature:* "Mann's gift—or curse—of seeing both sides of almost everything and everyone was perhaps his most characteristic talent. It often made him irritating and unsatisfactory as a thinker, and particularly as a political essayist. But in the realm of fiction this 'dual perspective' on man gave his vision a stereoptic quality, and his characters a third dimension. His people are good *and* evil, perceptive *and* blind; they are extraordinarily real. . . . Their very inconsistencies keep them alive and fascinating." Mann's double vision extends to his narrative style, which is well known for its irony. His narrators tend to remain aloof, undercutting characters with bemused skepticism. (Often, reviewers lament, the irony is conveyed by subtleties of the German language that are difficult to reproduce in translation.)

In *Rede und Antwort*, quoted by R. Hinton Thomas, Mann celebrated "the poetic charms and possibilities which arise out of doubt, out of faith called into question." The author asked: "What is poetry if not irony?"

Mann's early writing career was marked by sudden successes. At nineteen he was apprenticed to a Munich insurance firm, where he eluded work in order to write his first short story. Its publication gained him an appreciative letter from Richard Dehmel, a prominent poet of the day. The short story made Mann determined to write professionally, so he quit his job after a few months in order to audit a broad range of courses at Munich's university. A few more short stories quickly led to Mann's first book—*Der kleine Herr Friedemann* ("Little Herr Friedemann"), a collection published by the distinguished literary firm of Samuel Fischer. By the time *Friedemann* was published, Mann was in Italy with his brother, Heinrich, who was a great admirer of Italian culture. Thomas showed little interest in his surroundings, however: he was writing a novel about his German merchant ancestors, whom he thinly disguised as the Buddenbrook family. *Buddenbrooks* was a work with few precursors in German literature. It was patterned on the naturalistic novels of Western Europe and Scandinavia, which used lavish detail to create the portrait of an individual, a family, or a society. Many Lübeckers were soon filled with shock and outrage, for Mann had surveyed his hometown with unsettling detachment, as betrayed by his book's subtitle—*Verfall einer Familie* ("Decline of a Family").

Buddenbrooks opens with a celebration, as Johann Buddenbrook, elderly head of a prosperous trading firm, entertains guests at his new mansion. Hatfield called him "a type of the eighteenth century as popularly conceived—rationalistic, optimistic, skeptical, and of uncomplicated, single-minded energy." Johann soon dies, having virtually disinherited one son who married below the proper station. A dutiful and religious son, Jean, gains control of the family business. In the name of duty Jean persuades his tempestuous daughter, Tony, to boost the family finances through a loveless marriage, but the husband turns out to be a bankrupt swindler. As Tony careens through a succession of unhappy marriages, control of the firm falls to her brother, Tom, a talented and honorable man slowly overwhelmed by his responsibilities. Tom draws solace from the writings of a pessimistic philosopher, reading that after death he will lose his individual identity (Mann later suggested that the philosopher was Schopenhauer). Tom dies while still in middle age, and his son, Hanno, represents the final generation of Buddenbrooks. Hanno, an artistic and sensitive child, fond of Wagner and devoid of willpower, dies at the age of fifteen. Financial success comes to other families, whose crass attitudes, critics suggest, signify the triumph of grasping modern capitalists over the more humane burghers of German tradition.

Buddenbrooks was massive, even by nineteenth-century standards. Fischer, fearful he could not sell a costly two-volume novel, unsuccessfully pressured Mann to condense the book. The first edition sold slowly, but when Fischer reissued the work in a single volume it became wildly popular, and Mann was suddenly celebrated throughout Germany. "Mann has given evidence of a capacity and ability that cannot be ignored," declared poet Rainer Maria Rilke. In a 1902 review, later quoted in Hatfield's *Thomas Mann: A Collection of Critical Essays,* Rilke hailed Mann as both "chronicler" and "poet," a master of detail and of vivid characterization. He praised the "particular subtlety" Mann uses to show how progressive self-absorption speeds the family's decline. Other German-speaking contemporaries praised Mann's skill and chided his wordiness, thus expressing opinions that would follow the author throughout his career. American reviewers had comparable reactions when *Buddenbrooks* appeared in English in the 1920s. "There is a beauty of decay as well as of growth, a charm of fading colors . . . as well as of the dawn," wrote Robert Morss Lovett in the *New Republic.* "Of this beauty and this eloquence Thomas Mann is master."

Despite the popular success of *Buddenbrooks,* Mann never wrote such a highly realistic work again. Admirers stress that he continued to show a flair for realistic detail, including subtle insights into human psychology. Nevertheless, in analyzing most of Mann's fiction, commentators tend to view the characters as representations of ideas. In his study of Mann, Hatfield attempted to reconcile the contrasting views of Mann as philosopher and storyteller. Hatfield advised: "Whatever Mann's importance as a thinker—and many of his critics seem to discuss the 'philosophy' of his stories with a certain pontifical overseriousness—the works can best be read as literature; the artistic *how* is at least as interesting as the ideological *what.* With Mann one cannot afford to neglect either."

Commentators suggest that *Buddenbrooks,* for all its meticulous realism, is based on a philosophical issue: can successive generations of a family become so emotionally sensitive, so preoccupied with personal concerns, that they become unable to survive the vicissitudes of life? In Mann's other early fiction, typically novellas and short stories, he applied such a question to his own situation as a fledgling writer, showing the conflict between life and art. The tone of these stories is often cold and pessimistic: as Hatfield observed, "'life' and its healthy representatives are dull or brutal or both; but the antagonists to 'life,' the isolated and introspective protagonists, are sick, psychologically maladjusted, and frequently grotesque." "Der kleine Herr Friedemann" was the title story of Mann's first book. Friedemann is a hunchback who avoids human society in favor of literature and music. At a performance of Wagner, Friedemann observes a socialite with fascination; the two begin a tentative friendship, but he is soon rejected and attempts suicide. The title character of "Tobias Mindernickel" is a lonely misfit who is taunted by children as he walks the streets. He enjoys comforting his dog when it is weak, but when the dog becomes willful, Mindernickel kills it and weeps over the corpse. Soon after Mann's first short stories appeared, he spent about two years on the editorial staff of *Simplizissimus*—a Munich periodical noted for its strong satire.

In "Tonio Kröger," published shortly after *Buddenbrooks,* Mann made an explicit effort to resolve the controversy between art and life. Son of a North German merchant with a foreign-born wife, Tonio Kröger invites comparison to Mann; his Italian-German name underscores his divided sympathies. As a child Kröger realizes that he is too morbidly introspective to share the simple joys of his handsome, blond, outgoing schoolmates. He matures into a talented writer, but as he circulates among contrasting social settings—the middle class and the artists, northern and southern Europe—he continues to agonize about his relationship to other people. A girlfriend diagnoses him as a "lost burgher" and an artist "with a bad conscience." Finally, Kröger finds a sense of purpose by accepting his ambiguous position in society. "It is precisely [Kröger's] frustrated love for the Nordic-normal-bourgeois which gives him the inner tension that makes him creative," wrote Hatfield. "He will stand between [the art world and the middle class], a sympathetic if ironic mediator."

During the next several years Mann suffered a series of professional setbacks. *Fiorenza,* his only play, was judged too slow-moving for the stage; *Königliche Ho-heit* ("Royal Highness"), a novel based on his happy marriage, was found disappointingly shallow. He soon became stalled on his next novel, a projected multivolume saga titled *Bekenntnisse des Hochstaplers Felix Krull* ("Confessions of Felix Krull, Confidence Man"). Lamenting his inability to write, Mann took his wife on a vacation to Venice. In the decaying Italian port, which largely survived by displaying its Renaissance art treasures to tourists, he met a series of exotic characters who gave him inspiration for a short story. Conceived as a diversion suitable for *Simplizissimus, Der Tod in Venedig* ("Death in Venice") became known as one of the world's finest examples of short fiction.

Death in Venice begins in Munich, as the renowned writer Gustav Aschenbach struggles against the exhaustion of his creativity. Aschenbach is about fifty years old, unmarried, highly disciplined and repressed; he writes tales of spiritual struggle that reassert conservative values. Walking by a cemetery, Aschenbach is startled by an odd-looking traveler standing at the door of a crypt; the writer suddenly decides to leave Munich and refresh himself with a trip to southern Europe. The ominous stranger seems to appear twice more as Aschenbach travels to Venice: once as a decrepit homosexual whose face is rouged in a futile effort to look younger; again as a menacing gondolier who apparently operates without a license. In the city Aschenbach spots an adolescent Polish boy named Tadzio whom he finds strikingly beautiful; he begins following the boy and his family throughout Venice. The writer is alternately frightened and elated by his growing passion for Tadzio, and in a nightmare he joins animals and humans at an orgy in honor of a "stranger god." One day Aschenbach smells the sweet odor of disinfectant on the city's air, denoting an outbreak of cholera; however, he does nothing to save himself or the boy's family. Instead he asks a barber to rouge his face and redden his lips, then eats over-ripe strawberries that are apparently contaminated with the fatal disease. On the beach a few days later Aschenbach shouts to intervene when other boys beat Tadzio, and the boy then stands alone by the sea, returning the writer's gaze. Aschenbach rises from his beach chair, then collapses from illness. "By nightfall," the tale concludes, "a shocked and respectful world learned of his decease." Unsettling and evocative, *Death in Venice* has been treated by commentators as a major work despite its modest length. Many reviewers have praised the carefully controlled tone of Mann's prose. Devoid of either harsh judgment or

sympathy, the narration echoes the degeneration of Aschenbach's personality: the style is austere at the opening, then grows overwrought as the writer sinks into irrationality. Recurrent words and images create an oppressive, deathly atmosphere; reviewers liken the effect to repeated musical themes in Wagner's operas. The word "sweet," for instance, acquires a menacing tone as Mann uses it to describe the smell of overgrown plants, rotting fruit, and disinfectant. The recurring figure of a sinister stranger recalls the imagery of ancient myths, in which men are confronted by the figure of death. Mann, wrote Cyril Connolly in *The Condemned Playground,* has given Aschenbach's demise the impact of an ancient tragedy; the story, he wrote, "has the frozen completeness of a work of art."

Death in Venice has prompted a vast array of interpretations. Some critics have suggested that the work is based on Mann's own homosexual fantasies; by contrast, Mann suggests in his correspondence that the story was often viewed as an attack on homosexuality. D. H. Lawrence, who tried to portray the joys of sexuality in his works, blasted Mann's "sick vision": Lawrence did not object to the story's plot, which he considered largely symbolic, but to Mann's apparent inability to portray human sexuality in terms that were not repulsive. T. E. Apter, noting the story's focus on "death, passion and the debilitating effects of beauty," averred that Mann was repudiating the emotional excess he found in Wagner's work. Martin Swales, in *Thomas Mann: A Study,* pointed out that Aschenbach's widespread popularity as a writer makes him "the spokesman of a generation"; thus Aschenbach's swing between emotional extremes—from strident repression to unthinking frenzy—seems an ominous diagnosis of European society on the eve of World War I. Europe, relatively peaceful and productive for a century, greeted the war in 1914 with what Swales calls "waves of collective enthusiasm."

But as biographers suggest, Mann's perceptiveness as a writer of fiction did not always carry over into his personal life. For example, the year that the rather daring *Death in Venice* was published, Mann paradoxically joined the Munich Censorship Council; he soon withdrew after heated criticism from other writers. After World War I began, Heinrich became a pioneering advocate of peace, praising the more democratic society of Germany's opponent, France. But Thomas cast aside his fiction to write words of encouragement for the German war effort; in such missives, he echoed the nationalist position that Germany was an emerging power, entitled to take an aggressive stand against overbearing countries such as France and England. The Mann brothers began a painful political quarrel that, as many biographers observed, mirrored German society's debate about its future. In the closing years of the war Thomas summarized his view of Germany in a book that remains the most controversial part of his literary legacy—*Betrachtungen eines Unpolitischen* ("Reflections of a Nonpolitical Man"). Drawing a sharp contrast between Germany and France, the book suggests that French democracy, a product of intellectual theories rather than long-term experience with human nature, is by nature didactic and intolerant; whereas Germany's less political, more inward-looking culture is better attuned to the realities of human experience, including society's need for a well-established hierarchy. "To transform Germany into a middle-class democracy," summarized Carolly Erickson in the *Los Angeles Times Book Review,* "would reduce her rich spiritual complexity to something 'dull, shallow, stupid and un-German.'"

In light of Germany's subsequent plunge into Nazism, Mann's nationalist rhetoric seems at best naive; at worst, willfully blind. After World War I, *Reflections* was embraced by German ultraconservatives as a political tract, and for years thereafter Mann faced charges that he had encouraged incipient fascism. Mann's defenders, stressing the confused, tormented nature of the work, echo the view that Mann himself provided several years later in *Lebensabriss* ("A Sketch of My Life"). *Reflections,* Mann suggested, was an inner dialogue, the struggle of a burgherly German conservative to adjust to the changes sweeping Europe in the early twentieth century. For the rest of his life Mann was steadfast in his views about the fundamental differences between Germany and Western Europe, but he concluded that rational democracy was the salvation of the West and that Germany's culture had spurred the country's downfall.

In 1918 Germany surrendered and replaced its imperial government with a Western-style democracy—events that seem to have left Mann temporarily baffled. He asked that *Reflections* be viewed as a novel, and penned a lengthy poem, *Gesang vom Kindchen*) about the birth of his youngest daughter. But by the 1920s Mann showed renewed interest in social issues, for he had begun what admirers call his education in democracy. He shocked conservatives with the speech

Von Deutscher Republik ("The German Republic"), backing the new democratic government and attempting, somewhat awkwardly, to link democracy to German tradition. "My ideas have perhaps altered—not my intention," Mann declared in a preface to the printed work, quoted by Hamilton. "Thoughts are always—however sophistic this may sound—only a means to an end, a tool in the service of an intention." Mann declared that his main concern was "exactly the same as in *Reflectio ns:*namely that of German humanity." The Mann brothers were reconciled in the 1920s, and Heinrich praised his brother's growth from a mere "observer" to a man "involved with his people." The fruit of Thomas Mann's new social consciousness—according to his brother and many literary critics—is his 1924 novel, *Der Zauberberg* ("The Magic Mountain"). Considered a landmark of world literature, *The Magic Mountain* depicts the conflicting cultural and political trends that sundered the Mann brothers and vexed all Europe in the opening decades of the twentieth century.

Set in the years preceding World War I, *The Magic Mountain* takes place on a Swiss mountaintop in a tuberculosis sanatorium. Mann had visited such a place in 1912, when his wife was recovering from the disease. Mann's fictional sanatorium serves as a symbolic gathering place for the nations of Europe, for its patients include wealthy patrons from throughout the continent. As guests undergo the prescribed "rest cure," they lose their sense of the passing of time, for they are removed from the struggles of ordinary existence and turn to pastimes that range from games to endless philosophical discussions. The staff systematically insulates the patients from their most pressing concern—death—by affecting a cheerful attitude and surreptitiously removing the bodies of the dead. The book opens as Hans Castorp, a newly graduated engineer, arrives to visit his sick cousin. When doctors find a trace of tuberculosis in Hans, he agrees to stay at the sanatorium for a few weeks; instead, he becomes captivated by the hospital's unworldly atmosphere and remains for seven years. As an open-minded, somewhat directionless young man, Hans becomes the central character in Mann's revival of the *Bildungsroman,* or "novel of education"—a classic German genre in which thoughtful role models aid a naive youth to become a productive member of society.

But unlike the typical hero of a novel of education, Hans never finds a trustworthy mentor. Instead, he learns moderation by confronting extremists—patients or doctors whose doctrinaire approaches to life are undercut by their self-contradictory personalities. Naptha, named for a flammable liquid, relishes strong emotions. An Eastern European Jew who saw his father crucified in a pogrom, he nonetheless became a Christian and joined the Jesuits, a religious order known for its zealous defense of Catholic doctrine. Now he praises communism as well as Catholicism, for both, he contends, are admirably authoritarian; to reform society, he advocates "anointed Terror." Naptha's opposite is the Italian Settembrini, a humanist whose strong faith in reason, which initially appeals to Hans, proves to be laced with intellectual arrogance. Settembrini relishes the destruction of his enemies much as Naptha does, but he cannot consciously accept the validity of human emotion. Trivializing insanity, Settembrini claims to have cured a madman by giving him a "rational" stare; he also dismisses Hans's pangs of love for a woman patient, prompting Hans to denounce him. Finally Settembrini and Naptha stage a duel that is considered Mann's satire on intellectual excess. Settembrini fires his gun in the air; Naptha, unable to comprehend such a gesture, shoots himself in the head. Hans also seeks out patients who are more comfortable with their physical nature, but his mentors once again prove to be flawed. Claudia Chauchat, a languorous Russian woman, thrills Hans with sexual flirtation but prefers the company of Mynheer Peeperkorn, a charismatic Dutch plantation owner who dominates and frightens her. Peeperkorn, though aggressive and inarticulate, draws the admiration of Hans and many others for his impassioned love of life. As the Dutchman approaches old age, however, he surrenders to despair, and shortly after arriving at the sanatorium he commits suicide. Hans's lessons in the need for moderation end abruptly, for as the book ends he is drafted into the German Army to serve in World War I. Mann last shows him facing enemy fire on a battlefield. Many reviewers surmise that he is killed.

As biographer Hamilton wrote, "*The Magic Mountain* restored [Mann] to his rightful standing: the master novelist of his age." The book received widespread attention in Germany and throughout the Western world, garnering praise from such notables as French novelist André Gide and American literary critic Joseph Wood Krutch. When the novel first appeared, Krutch proclaimed it comparable in stature to Proust's *Remembrance of Things Past*. Mann, wrote Krutch in the *Nation*, had told "the whole story of the modern mind," creating a unique work about the interaction between ideas and individual character. Commentators have reiterated such views for decades. *The Magic Mountain* "is Thomas Mann's most complex creation," wrote T. J. Reed in *Thomas Mann: The Uses of Tradition*, "the summa of his life, thought, and technical achievement to the age of fifty." Reed called the work "spiritual autobiography . . . intricate allegory . . . historical novel, an analysis of Man and a declaration of principle for practical humanism." Five years after *The Magic Mountain* was published, the author received the Nobel Prize in literature.

Mann, biographers believe, hoped that postwar Germany would choose the course of sensible moderation embodied by Hans Castorp. Instead the nation became politically polarized, and when spokesmen of the increasingly fascist right branded Mann a traitor to their cause, he responded by endorsing socialism. While the Nazi Party consolidated its control of Germany after the 1933 elections, Mann and his wife were out of the country. To the author's dismay, he received warnings from his eldest daughter that it was unsafe to return, in part, presumably, because Mann's wife was Jewish. At first Mann avoided an open break with the Nazis, apparently hoping, along with the Jewish president of his publishing house, that prominent moderates could outlast the regime and encourage opposition. As a result Mann's work escaped the first wave of Nazi censorship campaigns, but he was compromised in the eyes of antifascist groups and came to view his forbearance as a mistake. In 1936 Mann issued a series of increasingly strong statements against the Nazi regime, and before the end of the year his German citizenship had been revoked. The University of Bonn promptly withdrew its honorary doctorate, and Mann replied with a blistering open letter that was read throughout the world. If the Nazis held sway, Mann warned, quoted by Hamilton, the German people would become "an instrument of war . . . driven by a blind and fanatical ignorance." He declared: "Woe to the people which . . . seeks its way out through the abomination of war, hatred of God and man! Such a people will be lost. It will be so vanquished that it will never rise again." For the rest of the Nazi era, Mann was widely known for both his attacks on wayward Germany and his praise of democracy. Combined with his Nobel Prize-winning status, such activities made him—perhaps against his wishes—a leading representative of German progressives in the eyes of the public. After receiving a warm welcome on lecture tours of the United States, Mann took up residence there and became an American citizen in 1944.

In contrast to his speeches, Mann's reaction to Nazism in his fiction was at first indirect. His new series of biblical novels about the ancient history of the Jews, for instance, became a refutation of the Nazis' racist mythmaking. The novels focus on the story of Joseph, whose great-grandfather Abraham had initiated the special relationship between the Jews and God. Known collectively as *Joseph und Seine Brüder* ("Joseph and His Brothers"), the series includes four books: *Die Geschichten Jaakobs* ("The Tales of Jacob"), *Der junge Joseph* ("Young Joseph"), *Joseph in Aegypten* ("Joseph in Egypt"), and *Joseph der Ernaehrer* ("Joseph the Provider"). Joseph, supremely talented, confident in his abilities and in God's providence, is for R. J. Hollingdale a benevolent variation on Nietzsche's overman and the leading character in a "cheerful myth." Joseph survives his own egotism, the envy of his brothers, betrayal into slavery, and false imprisonment to become the savior of his Egyptian masters in time of famine. Mann's narrative, lightly irreverent, is a blend of mythology and psychology. The author wished, in Hatfield's words, "to reveal basic human archetypes as they occur in the myths of the gods, in legend, and in history"; to this end the characters often resemble each other or famous persons from history and fiction. At the same time, as Mann himself suggested, he wanted to show the emergence of individuality; accordingly, the characters acquire subtle motivations missing from the short biblical account. The series of "Joseph" novels drew regular praise from reviewers in the United States. "The whole," wrote J. F. Fullington in the *Atlantic Monthly,* "constitutes a work which in encyclopedic scholarship, imaginative power, and magnitude of conception can hardly be approached by any other literary product of our time." But Hatfield observed that the books have also been accused of slow pacing, repetition, and pedantry; such problems could be symptoms, he observed, of "that decrease in intensity often characteristic of aging writers."

Upon completing the "Joseph" books, Mann began a novel he both dreaded and felt compelled to write—an explicit indictment of German culture and its role in fomenting the Nazi regime. Heinrich, one of Germany's first social satirists, had long viewed his native culture as if he were an outsider, but Thomas tended to identify strongly with German tradition: To indict German culture was to indict his own nature. Mann discussed his situation in the 1945 speech "Germany and the Germans," which he delivered at the U.S. Library of Congress just weeks after the fall of

the Nazi regime. Here he rejected his public image as the representative of a "good Germany" that stood apart from the Nazis. There is only a single Germany, Hamilton quoted him, "which has turned its best by devilry into bad." Mann concluded: "It is . . . impossible for a German-born mind to disown the evil, guilt-laden Germany. . . . I have it also in me; I have experienced it in my own body."

To portray Germany's descent into evil, Mann revived the old German legend of Faust, a learned man who sold his soul to the devil in exchange for knowledge and supernatural power. Titling his work *Doktor Faustus* ("Doctor Faustus"), he made his lead character Adrian Leverkühn, a fictional German composer who lives from 1885 to 1940. Adrian spends his childhood on a farm and in a small town, then studies religion at a university where his teachers show a morbid interest in the nature of evil. Soon he opts for a career in music, which remained for Mann a symbol of irrationality, as the author suggested in "Germany and the Germans." As a composer Adrian discovers a problem familiar to creative artists in the sophisticated twentieth century: he believes he has arrived on the world scene too late, and that all the original, expressive works of art have already been made. The complaint also recalls the German nationalist doctrines that Mann had once endorsed; Adrian's cry for an artistic "breakthrough" resembles Nazi rhetoric about overcoming Anglo-French domination. Using the technique he developed in the "Joseph" saga, Mann makes Adrian the embodiment of a menacing human archetype: the arrogant, overreaching German. Adrian's life particularly resembles that of Nietzsche, whose works Nazi propagandists falsely claimed as precursors of their own ideas about a master Germanic race. In his youth Adrian contracts syphilis in a brothel, as Nietzsche is alleged to have done, and thereafter his life is a similar mixture of daring creativity and growing madness. The composer becomes convinced that in Italy he conversed with the devil about music and traded his soul for the chance to write great new compositions. He soon becomes renowned as the inventor of twelve-tone music, a system that abjures the harmonies familiar to Western listeners (and that was actually the brainchild of Mann's fellow expatriate, Arnold Schönberg). In 1930, as the Nazis rise to power, Adrian summons friends and reviewers to his home to introduce his new symphony, "The Lamentation of Doctor Faustus." Before playing parts of the work on his piano, Adrian gives a long, tormented speech that amounts to a confession of his pact with Satan. But his speech is so disordered, the language so archaic, that his auditors assume he is demented. They respond with a mixture of shock and mere embarrassment. As with Nietzsche, Adrian suddenly collapses in insanity and spends the last ten years of his life being tended by his mother. *Doctor Faustus* is narrated by Adrian's friend Serenus Zeitblom, a well-intentioned, burgherly German who is slow to comprehend the evil nature of the composer's genius. Zeitblom writes his reminiscences during the war years from 1943 to 1945, as Germany is driven to defeat. By the end of his account, Zeitblom is conscious of the parallel fates of his friend and his country.

Mann spoke of *Doctor Faustus* as one of the most important and daring works of his career, calling it his "wildest" novel, as biographer Ignace Feuerlicht noted. But even commentators who respected the author's effort often found the book flawed. Mann's characteristic weaknesses—a love of length and complexity, a preoccupation with philosophy—seemed, for many commentators, to have defeated his intention. "This book is a monster: one cannot love it," wrote Hollingdale, citing such problems. Nonetheless, he called the novel "a 'great' book, an enduring book . . . full of faults and yet worth ten thousand petty 'successes.'" "Among [Mann's] longer works," wrote Hatfield, *The Magic Mountain* "is formally more successful, and conveys a far greater sense of intellectual excitement," but *Doctor Faustus* is still much more than "an ambitious failure." Hatfield called the work an "end product"—a writer's final summation of his artistic vision. As with the "vast late works" of other authors, Hatfield averred, the novel is "only partially successful" but contains "an enormous variety of riches."

Mann lived for a decade after World War II, and as a man of high public stature he was the object of both admiration and outrage. He received many prestigious awards throughout Europe, but he was blasted as a fraud by German writers who had lived under Hitler and were compromised by Nazism. At first reluctant to visit Germany at all, he finally insisted on touring the communist eastern half as well as the noncommunist west. Suddenly the man once denounced as a conservative ideologue was branded by the American right as a communist dupe, and he moved from the United States to Switzerland, expressing concern that America might be headed for fascism. Mann's last major work, begun a half-century earlier, was the completed first volume of *Felix Krull*. The novel is of special interest

to admirers of Mann as a burlesque of many ideas that appear in the rest of his writing. The title character, a confidence man, combines the moral blindness of Adrian Leverkühn with the cheerful self-confidence of Joseph. For Felix Krull—who is seen as a mocking self-portrait of the author—fraud is both an art and a philosophy of life.

After Mann died in 1955, he was sometimes recalled as a friend of democracy and humanism—ignoring, perhaps, the complex and ambiguous nature of his work. "I once saw Thomas Mann plain," declared Alfred Kazin, contending that Mann used a "conservative social self" to mask "a mind so complex that his real opinions were always elusive." Hollingdale depicted Mann in Nietzschean terms, as the child of a Western civilization that had become unable to believe in God or anything else. In a world without values, Mann's novels were long because there was, in the critic's words, "no principle of selection." Mann preached no ideology because none was credible; irony was his "self-defence against the meaningless." For a world that *really has no values,* Hollingdale observed, Mann's "fictional world is a *true* mirror." He summarized Mann with a proverb: "As the mirror replied to the monster: 'There is nothing wrong with me, it is *you* who are distorted.'"

BIOGRAPHICAL AND CRITICAL SOURCES:

BOOKS

Apter, T. E., *Thomas Mann: The Devil's Advocate,* New York University Press (New York, NY), 1979.

Bauer, Arnold, *Thomas Mann,* translation by Alexander and Elizabeth Henderson, Ungar (New York, NY), 1971.

Beddow, Michael, *Thomas Mann, Doctor Faustus,* Cambridge University Press (New York, NY), 1994.

Bloom, Harold, editor, *Thomas Mann: Modern Critical Views,* Chelsea House (New York, NY), 1986.

Bloom, Harold, editor, *Thomas Mann's "The Magic Mountain,"* Chelsea House (New York, NY), 1986.

Brennan, Joseph Gerard, *Thomas Mann's World,* Russell & Russell, 1962.

Bürgin, Hans, *Das Werk Thomas Manns: Eine Bibliographie,* S. Fischer (Frankfurt, Germany), 1959.

Bürgin, Hans, and Hans-Otto Mayer, *Thomas Mann: A Chronicle of His Life,* translation by Eugene Dobson, University of Alabama Press (University, AL), 1969.

Cather, Willa, *Not under Forty,* Alfred A. Knopf (New York, NY), 1936.

Connolly, Cyril, *The Condemned Playground: Essays, 1927-1944,* Macmillan (New York, NY), 1946.

De Mendelssohn, Peter, *Der Zauberer: Das Leben des deutschen Schriftstellers Thomas Mann,* S. Fischer (Frankfurt, Germany), 1975.

Dictionary of Literary Biography, Volume 66: *German Fiction Writers, 1885-1913,* Gale (Detroit, MI), 1988.

Domandi, Agnes Koerner, *Modern German Literature: A Library of Literary Criticism,* Ungar (New York, NY), 1972.

Dowden, Stephen D., editor, *A Companion to Thomas Mann's "Magic Mountain,"* Camden House (Columbia, SC), 1998.

Fetzer, John F., *Changing Perceptions of Thomas Mann's "Doctor Faustus": Criticism, 1947-1992,* Camden House (Columbia, SC), 1996.

Feuerlicht, Ignace, *Thomas Mann,* Twayne (Boston, MA), 1968.

Gray, Ronald, *The German Tradition in Literature, 1871-1945,* Cambridge University Press (Cambridge, England), 1965.

Hamilton, Nigel, *The Brothers Mann: The Lives of Heinrich and Thomas Mann, 1871-1950 and 1875-1955,* Yale University Press (New Haven, CT), 1979.

Hatfield, Henry, *Thomas Mann,* New Directions (New York, NY), 1951, revised edition, 1962.

Hatfield, Henry, editor, *Thomas Mann: A Collection of Critical Essays,* Prentice-Hall (Englewood Cliffs, NJ), 1964.

Hatfield, Henry, *From the Magic Mountain: Thomas Mann's Later Masterpieces,* Cornell University Press (Ithaca, NY), 1979.

Hayman, Ronald, *Thomas Mann: A Biography,* Scribner (New York, NY), 1995.

Heilbut, Anthony, *Thomas Mann: Eros and Literature,* Alfred A. Knopf (New York, NY), 1996.

Heller, Erich, *Thomas Mann: The Ironic German,* Regnery/Gateway (New York, NY), 1979.

Hirschbach, Frank Donald, *The Arrow and the Lyre: A Study of Love in the Works of Thomas Mann,* Nijhoff (The Hague, The Netherlands), 1955.

Hollingdale, R. J., *Thomas Mann: A Critical Study,* Bucknell University Press (Lewisburg, PA), 1971.

Kaufmann, Fritz, *Thomas Mann: The World As Will and Representation,* Beacon Press (Boston, MA), 1957.

Kazin, Alfred, *Contemporaries,* Little, Brown (Boston, MA), 1962.

Lawrence, D. H., *Phoenix: The Posthumous Papers of D. H. Lawrence,* edited by Edward D. McDonald, Viking Penguin (New York, NY), 1936.

Mann, Erika, and Klaus Mann, *Escape to Life,* Houghton Mifflin (Boston, MA), 1939.

Mann, Erika, *The Last Years of Thomas Mann,* Farrar, Straus & Cudahy (New York, NY), 1958.

Mann, Katja, *Unwritten Memories,* Alfred A. Knopf (New York, NY), 1975.

Mann, Klaus, *The Turning-Point: Thirty-Five Years in This Century,* S. Fischer (Frankfurt, Germany), 1943.

Mann, Thomas, *A Sketch of My Life,* Alfred A. Knopf (New York, NY), 1960.

Mann, Thomas, *The Story of a Novel: The Genesis of "Doctor Faustus,"* Alfred A. Knopf (New York, NY), 1961.

Mann, Thomas, *Letters of Thomas Mann, 1889-1955,* edited by Richard and Clara Winston, Vintage (New York, NY), 1975.

Mann, Thomas, *On Myself and Other Princeton Lectures,* P. Lang (New York, NY), 1996.

Minden, Michael, *Thomas Mann,* Longman (London, England), 1996.

Neider, Charles, editor, *The Stature of Thomas Mann,* New Directions (New York, NY), 1948.

Nicholls, R. A., *Nietzsche in the Early Works of Thomas Mann,* University of California Press (Berkeley, CA), 1955.

Prater, Donald A., *Thomas Mann: A Life,* Oxford University Press (New York, NY), 1995.

Reed, T. J., *Death in Venice: Making and Unmaking a Master,* Macmillan International (New York, NY), 1994.

Reed, T. J., *Thomas Mann: The Uses of Tradition,* Oxford University Press (New York, NY), 1974, reprinted, 1996.

Ridley, Hugh, *The Problematic Bourgeois: Twentieth-Century Criticism on Thomas Mann's "Buddenbrooks" and "The Magic Mountain,"* Camden House (Columbia, SC), 1994.

Sax, Baria, *Thomas Mann's "Death in Venice,"* Research and Education Association (Piscataway, NJ), 1997.

Scaff, Susan, *History, Myth, and Music: Thomas Mann's Timely Fiction,* Camden House (Columbia, SC), 1997.

Schneider, Ursula W., *Ars Amandi: The Erotic of Extremes in Thomas Mann and Marguerite Duras,* P. Lang (New York, NY), 1995.

Short Story Criticism, Volume 5, Gale (Detroit, MI), 1990.

Stern, J. P., *Thomas Mann,* Columbia University Press (New York, NY), 1967.

Stock, Irvin, *Ironic Out of Love: The Novels of Thomas Mann,* McFarland (New York, NY), 1994.

Swales, Martin, *Thomas Mann: A Study,* Heinemann (London, England), 1980.

Swensen, Alan J., *Gods, Angels, and Narrators: A Metaphysics of Narrative in Thomas Mann's "Joseph und seine Brüder,"* P. Lang (New York, NY), 1994.

Thomas, R. Hinton, *Thomas Mann: The Mediation of Art,* Oxford University Press (Oxford, England), 1963.

Treitel, Ilona, *The Dangers of Interpretation: Art and Artists in Henry James and Thomas Mann,* Garland Press (New York, NY), 1996.

Twentieth-Century Literary Criticism, Gale (Detroit, MI), Volume 2, 1979, Volume 8, 1982, Volume 14, 1984, Volume 21, 1986, Volume 35, 1990, Volume 44, 1992.

Von Gronicka, Andre, *Thomas Mann: Profile and Perspectives,* Random House (New York, NY), 1970.

Weigand, Hermann J., *"Der Zauberberg": A Study,* Appleton-Century (New York, NY), 1933.

Winston, Richard, *Thomas Mann: The Making of an Artist,* Alfred A. Knopf (New York, NY), 1981.

Wysling, Hans, *Correspondence, 1900-1949,* University of California Press, (Berkeley, CA), 1997.

PERIODICALS

American Mercury, October, 1951.

American Scholar, summer, 1957; winter, 1993.

Atlantic Monthly, September, 1944; June, 1975.

Dial, May, 1925, July, 1928.

Germanic Review, February, 1960.

Kenyon Review, winter, 1950.

Los Angeles Times Book Review, May 22, 1983.

Modern Fiction Studies, summer, 1965.

Modern Language Review, April, 1995, p. 526.

Musical Quarterly, winter 1991.

Nation, April 16, 1924; March 25, 1925; December 9, 1925; April 21, 1926; June 8, 1927; December 4, 1929; November 22, 1933; July 13, 1934; May 22, 1935; July 8, 1944; June 11, 1955; September 3, 1955; October 1, 1955.

New Republic, April 9, 1924; July 6, 1927; June 26, 1935; December 7, 1942; November 1, 1948; October 3, 1955.

New Statesman, November 7, 1936; November 5, 1955.

Newsweek, March 8, 1971.

New Yorker, August 31, 1940; July 22, 1944; October 30, 1948.

New York Times Book Review, November 4, 1923; February 17, 1924; February 22, 1925; May 8, 1927; December 8, 1929; July 12, 1931; December 10, 1933; July 10, 1934; April 28, 1935; June 7, 1936; August 8, 1937; June 15, 1947; October 31, 1948; August 8, 1965; February 22, 1971; July 20, 1975; May 15, 1983; April 18, 1992; October 22, 1995, p. 37.

Opera News, March 31, 1990.

Partisan Review, spring, 1956.

Saturday Review, June 27, 1925; July 16, 1927; May 19, 1928; November 11, 1933; June 9, 1934; June 6, 1936; July 31, 1937; October 30, 1948; June 10, 1950; June 4, 1955; September 17, 1955; December, 1981.

Sewanee Review, fall, 1929; summer, 1933.

South Atlantic Quarterly, July, 1937.

Time, July 3, 1944; February 12, 1951.

Times Literary Supplement, August 9, 1923; October 2, 1924; July 7, 1927; June 14, 1934; February 25, 1983; August 5, 1983; March 1, 1996, p. 14.

Washington Monthly, November, 1994, p. 58.

World Literature Today, winter, 1995, p. 134.

Yale Review, winter 1987.*

*   *   *

MATOTT, Justin 1961-
(Gabriel Peters)

PERSONAL: Born August 14, 1961, in Fort Collins, CO; son of Glenn E. (a professor) and Julia M. (a professor; maiden name, Nickel) Matott; married June 22, 1985; wife's name Andrea M. (a doctor); children: J. J., Ethan. *Education:* Earned B.A. *Religion:* Christian. *Hobbies and other interests:* Skiing, jogging, water sports, reading, gardening, brewing.

ADDRESSES: Agent—c/o Author Mail, Clove Publications, Inc., 60 Falcon Hills, Highlands Ranch, CO 80126. *E-mail*—randomwrtr@aol.com.

CAREER: Clove Publications, Inc., Highlands Ranch, CO, owner. Sales and marketing consultant in business reengineering.

WRITINGS:

My Garden Visits (nonfiction), illustrated by Victoria Kwasinski, Clove Publications (Littleton, CO), 1996.

A Harvest of Reflections: Wisdom for the Soul through the Seasons, illustrated by Deborah Chabrian, Ballantine (New York, NY), 1998.

Ol' Lady Grizelda (juvenile), illustrated by John Woods, Jr., Clove Publications (Littleton, CO), 1998.

Drinking Fountain Joe, illustrated by David Schiedt, Clove Publications (Littleton, CO), 2000.

Independence Days: Still Just Boys, and Other Stories, Brewers Publications (Boulder, CO), 2000.

When Did I Meet You, Grandma?, illustrated by Laurie McAdam, Clove Publications (Littleton, CO), 2000.

When Did I Meet You, Grandpa?, illustrated by Laurie McAdam, Clove Publications (Littleton, CO), 2000.

Oliver Kringle, illustrated by Laurie McAdam, Nickel & Beckley Press, 2002.

Also author of *There's a Fly on My Toast!,* illustrated by John Woods, Jr., Nickel & Beckley Press. Contributor to periodicals, including *Rocky Mountain News.* Some writings appear under the pseudonym Gabriel Peters.

SIDELIGHTS: Justin Matott once told *CA:* "I began to write as a cathartic release from an occupation that was not creatively challenging. As daily writing became my practice, I depended on it as any other sustenance. Writing is simply something I must do. Writing allows one to dabble in the darker, lighter, funny, serious side of one's mind. It allows expression in many genres, whether for publication or private practice. Few other activities offer the same.

"An early influence was Truman Capote. His ability to cross over from nonfiction to fiction was intriguing. Dickens was another influence. One of my most relevant influences was my father, an unpublished novelist who created worlds and characters from experience and imagination. As a child I hoped to do the same someday.

"I do not outline much. I allow the work to flow freely with no editorial interruption during the process. Then I go back to tighten and improve upon what I've written. I write every day with few exceptions. I bounce from nonfiction to fiction to children's work, depending on what is most creative. At most times I have ten projects going.

"Inspiration often comes from thin air. Sometimes I follow it to little end; sometimes an inkling of an idea while jogging will consume me until completion. I have a four-foot stack of these printed inspirations. Whether they are ever published or not, they've improved my writing."

*   *   *

MILLHAUSER, Steven (Lewis) 1943-

PERSONAL: Born August 3, 1943, in New York, NY; married Cathy Allis, 1984; children: one son, one daughter. *Education:* Columbia College, B.A., 1965; graduate study at Brown University, 1968-71, 1976-77.

ADDRESSES: Home—235 Caroline St., Saratoga Springs, NY 12866. *Office*—Skidmore College, English Department, Palamountain Hall 307, 815 North Broadway, Saratoga Springs, NY 12866. *E-mail*—smillhau@skidmore.edu.

CAREER: Writer and educator. Williams College, visiting associate professor of English, 1986-88; Skidmore College, Saratoga Springs, NY, associate professor, 1988-92, professor of English, 1992—.

AWARDS, HONORS: Prix Médicis Étranger (France), 1975, for *Edwin Mullhouse: The Life and Death of an American Writer, 1943-1954, by Jeffrey Cartwright;* American Academy/Institute of Arts and Letters award for literature, 1987; World Fantasy award, 1990; Lannan literary award for fiction, 1994; Pulitzer Prize for fiction, 1997, for *Martin Dressler: The Tale of an American Dreamer.*

WRITINGS:

NOVELS

Edwin Mullhouse: The Life and Death of an American Writer, 1943-1954, by Jeffrey Cartwright, Alfred A. Knopf (New York, NY), 1972.

Steven Millhauser

Portrait of a Romantic, Alfred A. Knopf (New York, NY), 1977.

From the Realm of Morpheus, William Morrow (New York, NY), 1986.

Martin Dressler: The Tale of an American Dreamer, Crown Publishers (New York, NY), 1996.

SHORT FICTION

In the Penny Arcade (stories and novella), Alfred A. Knopf (New York, NY), 1986.

The Barnum Museum (stories), Poseidon Press (New York, NY), 1990.

Little Kingdoms (three novellas), Poseidon Press (New York, NY), 1993.

The Knife Thrower and Other Stories, Crown Publishers (New York, NY), 1998.

Enchanted Night: A Novella, Crown Publishers (New York, NY), 1999.

The King in the Tree: Three Novellas, Alfred A. Knopf (New York, NY), 2003.

Contributor of short stories to periodicals, including *New Yorker, Tin House, Grand Street, Harper's,* and *Antaeus.* Contributor of story "A Visit" to CD *The New Yorker out Loud,* 1998.

ADAPTATIONS: Martin Dressler was released in an audio version by Guidall, 1997; *Enchanted Night* was released in audio versions by Dove Audio, 1999.

SIDELIGHTS: Pulitzer prize-winner Steven Millhauser, hailed by many critics as one of America's finest novelists, made his first entry onto the literary scene with *Edwin Mullhouse: The Life and Death of an American Writer, 1943-54, by Jeffrey Cartwright.* It is the fictitious biography of an eleven-year-old novelist as penned by the novelist's twelve-year-old companion. The young novelist, Edwin Mullhouse, completed only one work, the masterpiece *Cartoons,* prior to his untimely death at age eleven. His biographer records Mullhouse's interest in baseball cards and novelty-shop gifts while unwittingly revealing his own obsessions with Mullhouse and *Cartoons.* As the biographer's self-created rivalry with the late Mullhouse develops, *Edwin Mullhouse* evolves into both a parody of literary biographies and a sardonic portrait of the artist.

Published in 1972, *Edwin Mullhouse* was acclaimed by many reviewers. William Hjortsberg, writing in *New York Times Book Review,* called Millhauser's work "a rare and carefully evoked novel, . . . [that] displays an enviable amount of craft, the harsh discipline that carves through the scar tissue of personality painfully developed during the process known as 'growing up.'" J. D. O'Hara, reviewing the work for *Washington Post Book World,* noted that Millhauser's "characters, like J. D. Salinger's in one way . . . are absurdly precocious children, but their story is for adults." A *New Republic* reviewer was equally impressed with Millhauser's work, calling it "a mature, skillful, intelligent and often very funny novel."

Millhauser continues his depiction of childhood in his second novel, *Portrait of a Romantic.* Arthur Grumm, the twenty-nine-year-old protagonist, gives an account of his life between the ages of twelve and fifteen. He sees himself as a sickly, bored only child who says that "by some accident the children in my neighborhood were older than I and so excluded me from their dusty games." Grumm reveals himself as a vaguely suicidal adolescent divided by the polarized beliefs of his two friends, William Mainwaring, an avowed realist whom Grumm refers to as "my double," and Philip Schoolcraft, an equally vehement romantic referred to by Grumm as "my triple." Schoolcraft introduces Grumm to the romantic life, typified by decay, contemplation, and despair—they pass time pondering Poe and playing Russian roulette. Grumm later forms suicide pacts with the pathetic Eleanor Schumann and eventually with the disillusioned Mainwaring. The bizarre events caused by Grumm's suicide pacts provide an offbeat context for his own internal conflict between realism and romanticism and his weighing of the harsh repercussions inherent in submitting to either attitude.

According to John Calvin Batchelor of *Village Voice,* Millhauser, in his attempts to capture completely every detail, writes "with sometimes suffocating amount of sights and sound." *Times Literary Supplement* critic William Boyd noted that too much effort is lavished on "pages of relentlessly detailed description." Nevertheless, *Portrait of a Romantic* stands as a "remarkable book" by a very talented writer, according to George Stade in *New York Times Book Review.* Stade added: "Once you reread the book the particulars begin to look different. The foreshadowings become luminous with afterglow. What first seemed merely realistic . . . becomes symbolic. What seemed mere fantasy . . . becomes the workings of an iron psychological necessity." William Kennedy, who reviewed the novel for *Washington Post Book World,* also responded with respect and praise, declaring that Millhauser's "achievement is of a high order."

Carl Hausman, the young narrator of Millhauser's 1986 novel *From the Realm of Morpheus,* is watching a baseball game. He chases a foul ball and finds an opening to the underworld, which he immediately investigates, and readers are plunged, *Alice in Wonderland*-style, into the world of Morpheus, the God of Sleep. In what John Crowley in *New York Times Book Review* dubbed "a book, wholly odd yet purposefully unoriginal," Millhauser takes readers on a literary tour that parodies a variety of genres and where characters from history, literature, and legend converse and philosophize in a series of disconnected episodes. While Rob Latham, in the *St. James Guide to Fantasy Writers,* contended that this experiment in mock epic writing falls short of its intended goal, *Washington Post Book World* contributor Michael Dirda praised *From the Realms of Morpheus* as "beautifully composed" and "utterly entrancing."

Millhauser's Pulitzer Prize-winning *Martin Dressler: The Tale of an American Dreamer* tells the story of a quintessential Gilded-Age American entrepreneur, his dreams, and his disappointments. The title character works his way up from his father's cigar shop through a dreamy series of promotions, schemes, and machinations to become the owner and proprietor of a Manhattan hotel, The Grand Cosmo, that is "a leap beyond the hotel" in its fantastical atmosphere and consumerist excess. Janet Burroway, writing for *New York Times Book Review,* described the novel as "a fable and phantasmagoria of the sources of our century," calling Martin "not a parody but a paradigm of the bootstrap capitalist." Critics cited the novel for its imaginative and piercing glimpse into the American psyche and the American dream; *Martin Dressler* explores not only Dressler's business success, but also his personal failures and ultimate unhappiness. A *Booklist* reviewer observed that Millhauser "brings descriptive delicacy to this chronicle of Martin's 'falling upwards' and the forces behind the fall." A *Kirkus Reviews* critic described the novel as "a chronicle of obsession, self-indulgence, and, in a curious way, moral growth, expertly poised between realistic narrative and allegorical fable."

In addition to longer works, Millhauser has also authored many short stories and novellas, most of which have been included in published collections. A writer for *Contemporary Literary Criticism Yearbook 1997* commented that the author "writes of the world of the imagination. The subject of his stories is frequently the artist and the dreamer, the illusionist who creates words to satisfy the needs of others for fantasy. Millhauser's artistic motivation is summarized in a line of his short story, 'Eisenheim the Illusionist' from the collection *The Barnum Museum:* 'Stories, like conjuring tricks, are invented because history is inadequate to our dreams.'"

In his first collection of short stories, *In the Penny Arcade,* Millhauser continues his pursuit of "fiction as a mysterious, magical, enlightening experience" according to Robert Dunn in *New York Times Book Review.* The book is divided into three sections, the first containing the novella *August Eschenburg,* a long story about a German boy who is possessed by the desire to create mechanical devices that approximate life. Creating lifelike models for store windows and for an automaton theater, he dreams about infusing these automatons with life. But when a rival exploits this craft for pornographic purposes, August returns to his home and dreams his dreams in solitude.

The second section of *In the Penny Arcade,* comprised of three stories about real-life characters, contrasts to the artificial-life stories of sections one and three. These stories are more delicate; they are subtle, revealing the "fragility of moods in which nothing much actually happens," according to Al J. Sperone in *Village Voice Literary Supplement.* Similarly Irving Malin, in *Review of Contemporary Fiction* contended, "These stories vary in length and setting and time, [and] they must be read as variations on a theme—the 'perfection' of art. . . . They surprise us because they are less interested in plot, character, and philosophy than in magic, dream, and metaphor." Among the three stories in the final section is the title story, in which a young boy returns to an arcade he has idealized in his mind, seeing it in all its seediness. Robert Dunn noted in *New York Times Book Review* that Millhauser "creates for us this splendid arcade. And he asks us also to be vigilant as we venture with him into the common corners of our ragged world, where the marvelous glows and the true meanings breathe life."

The Barnum Museum collects stories that seek a reconciliation between the worlds of illusion and reality. In "The Sepia Postcard," the narrator buys an old post card and finds that as he examines it more closely the figures on it come alive. In "Rain," a man walks out of a theater and into a storm. As he walks on, he washes away as if he were a watercolor painting. Taken as a whole, this collection addresses the broader issue of imagination, according to Jay Cantor in a review for *New York Times Book Review.* The critic wrote that Millhauser "imagines the imagination as a junk shop with a warren of rooms, one chamber linked to another without any reason except the bewildering reason of the heart." This junk shop is the Barnum Museum, which is "named for the patron saint of charming bunco," P. T. Barnum. Many of the ten stories in the collection engage the reader in what Catherine Maclay in *World and I* dubbed "a playful examination of the imaginary and the real . . . [and the attempt to find] a reconciliation of these opposites." In blurring the lines between these two, Millhauser's postmodern stories help us "find a way to maintain a bridge" between them, according to Maclay.

His third short-story collection, *The Knife Thrower and Other Stories,* showcases Millhauser's "rich, sly sense of humor" and a characteristic "tone of whimsy"

that "conceals disturbing subversive energies" noted Patrick McGrath in the *New York Times Book Review.* In the dozen stories included in this collection the author proves himself to be "American literature's mordantly funny and unfailingly elegant bard of the uncanny," according to a *Publishers Weekly* reviewer, who added that the collection addresses two themes: When does the "pursuit of transcendent pleasure degrade rather than exalt?" and can the pursuit of pleasure be sated "without our becoming jaded or corrupt?" In the tales "Flying Carpets" and "Clair de Lune" he addresses these questions in stories imbued with a fairy tale quality that recalls childhood. "The Sisterhood of Night" and "Balloon Flight, 1870," about a hot-air balloonist during the Franco-Prussian war, in contrast, "suggest new avenues of thought in Millhauser's fiction," according to McGrath. In the title story, according to *Washington Post Book World* reviewer A. S. Byatt, the author "steps beyond the bounds of the comfortable" in describing a virtuoso knife thrower in whose public performances are couched private fantasies. Praising "Paradise Park," Byatt added that the strength of this story lies in "Millhauser's ability to weave detail into detail, the lovingly real and possible into the extravagantly impossible." Commenting on the collection in *Boston Globe,* Margot Livesey concluded that Millhauser's characters are intent upon escape. "Sometimes they go too far . . . ," the critic added, "but in their struggles between the real and surreal, the effable and the ineffable, art and life, these characters and their creator illuminate our struggles to live our daily lives and still keep something larger in mind."

Millhauser's first collection of novellas, *Little Kingdoms,* includes *The Little World of J. Franklin Payne, The Princess, the Dwarf, and the Dungeon,* and *Catalogue of the Exhibition: The Art of Edmund Moorash 1810-1846.* Each of these works continues their author's exploration of the theme of the relationship between the life of the world and the life of imagination, according to Michael Dirda in *Washington Post Book World.* Dirda added that these three stories as grouped "subtly question each other about imagination and its power." In the first, J. Franklin Payne, a newspaper cartoonist, becomes obsessed with the making of an animated cartoon film. In doing so, Nicholas Delbanco, writing for *Chicago Tribune* noted that he "invents his own reality—not so much in compensation for artistic disappointment as in an effort to improve upon the diurnal world. What seems vivid to him is his own imagination; reality looks dull." In his fixation on the cartoons he is creating, we are reminded of August Eschenburg's fixation on mechanical figures.

The Princess, the Dwarf, and the Dungeon plays with the conventions of the fairy tale genre: a late-medieval time setting, castles, dungeons, evil, dwarves, jealous princes, and virtuous maidens. Frederick Tuten noted in *New York Times Book Review* that "embedded in this story is the narrator's meditation on the art of his time, paintings so lifelike as to cause a dog to lick the portrait of his master." Millhauser's blurring of the lines between reality and imagination is a continuation of the same techniques in his *Barnum Museum* stories. *Catalogue of the Exhibition: The Art of Edmund Moorash 1810-1846* is perhaps the most clever. In a writing style Daniel Green described in *Georgia Review* as "typically energetic," the story is presented as an extended commentary on an exhibition of paintings by the fictional painter Edmund Moorash. Through a close reading of the explanations of the paintings, however, readers see the world of the painter complete with intimations of incest, devil worship, romance, and betrayal. There are four characters in the tale: Moorash, his sister Elizabeth, his friend William Pinney, and William's sister, Sophia. However, as Dirda pointed out, "passion's cross-currents disturb friendship's pallid surface." The result is that these four end up as figures as tragic as the subjects of the paintings at the exhibition. This novella is a work of art about art works and the theme of imagination and reality and the lines between them. Elizabeth keeps a diary in which she writes, "Edmund wants to dissolve forms and reconstruct them so as to release their energy. Art as alchemy." Delbanco noted in *Chicago Tribune* that this is "the credo of the whole" story. But it very well fits as the credo of all Millhauser's works.

Donna Seaman, in her review of Millhauser's 1999 work *Enchanted Night: A Novella* for *Booklist,* noted that the author "has been drifting into fantasy . . . and now he weaves pure magic in this dreamy tale of one fateful summer night." *Enchanted Night,* which is comprised of seventy-four short prose sections with chapters sometimes only one page long, conjures up toys and a mannequin coming to life, an unsuccessful author and his unsuccessful relationship with the mother of a childhood friend, teenage girls breaking into a house leaving cryptic notes, a lonely drunk stumbling home, and a girl waiting for a lover who may be real or may be fantasy.

The three-novella collection published as *The King in the Tree* focuses on the consequences of forbidden amours. In *An Adventure of Don Juan,* based on Gabriel Tellez's sixteenth-century writings about the legendary Spanish lover, the thirty-year-old Don Juan finds his plans to seduce two sisters frustrated when he inadvertently falls in love with one of them. According to *World and I* contributor Edward Hower, Millhauser's protagonist "experiences the sort of conflict shared by many of this author's characters: how to reconcile the sometimes seductive demands of the outer world with the longings that spring from the inner recesses of the soul." The title story also focuses on obsession, retelling the medieval legend of Tristan and Ysolt while also adding psychological depth. As Michael Dirda noted in his *Washington Post Book World* review, in Millhauser's version "all loyalties, strongly felt and believed in—loyalty to one's sovereign, to the marriage vows, to honor, friendship and ones' very self—are ripped apart by the remorseless claims of passionate love." The short novella *Revenge* takes the form of a monologue as a widow gives a tour of her home—and her own life—to a prospective home buyer who, the reader soon discovers, is actually a former rival for the narrator's late husband's affections.

Praising *The King in the Tree* as "rich in verbal dexterity, ambitious romantic imagery, and fascinating insights into the darker regions of the human heart," Hower commented that Millhauser's construction of a "world of artifice" serves to distill from his characters' lives "the most intense emotional expression and meaning." In *Los Angeles Times* Jeff Turrentine cited Millhauser's "Gothicism" as well as his love for the nineteenth century that permeates the collection. *The King in the Tree* "is a moving, melancholy book about the unlovely toll exacted by love on those it has abandoned," added Turrentine. A *Kirkus Reviews* writer maintained that "some of the best writing of Millhauser's increasingly brilliant career appears in this collection."

Millhauser's fiction remains widely heralded for its perceptive exploration of the problems and pleasures of youth, and the author continues to be lauded for both his stylistic virtuosity and his capacity to evoke the undercurrents of ordinary life. As Dirda commented in *Washington Post Book World:* "So enchanting is his prose, so delicate his touch, that one surrenders to his plangent word-music as one does to the wistful piano pieces of Ravel and Chopin. Reading Millhauser, there are times when you simply lay the book aside and say to yourself, 'I had not known that sentences could be so simple and so beautiful.'"

BIOGRAPHICAL AND CRITICAL SOURCES:

BOOKS

Contemporary Literary Criticism, Gale (Detroit, MI), Volume 21, 1982, Volume 54, 1989, Volume 109, 1999.
Contemporary Novelists, 6th edition, St. James Press (Detroit, MI), 1996.
St. James Guide to Fantasy Writers, St. James Press (Detroit, MI), 1996.

PERIODICALS

Booklist, April 1, 1996, review of *Martin Dressler: The Tale of an American Dreamer;* September 15, 1999, Donna Seaman, review of *Enchanted Night: A Novella,* p. 233.
Boston Globe, May 17, 1998, Margot Livesey, review of *The Knife Thrower and Other Stories,* p. D1; March 9, 2003, David Rollow, review of *The King in the Tree.*
Chicago Tribune, October 3, 1993, Nicholas Delbanco, review of *Little Kingdoms,* p. 5.
Entertainment Weekly, May 17, 1996, p. 55; April 10, 1998, review of *Little Kingdoms,* p. 61.
Georgia Review, winter, 1995, Daniel Green, review of *Little Kingdoms,* pp. 960-967.
Kirkus Reviews, March 1, 1996, review of *Martin Dressler;* December 15, 2002, review of *The King in the Tree.*
Los Angeles Times Book Review, October 31, 1999, review of *Enchanted Night,* p. 29; March 16, 2003, Jeff Turrentine, review of *The King in the Tree.*
Nation, September 17, 1977, pp. 250-252; May 6, 1996, p. 68; May 25, 1998, Benjamin Kunkel, review of *The Knife Thrower and Other Stories,* p. 33.
New Republic, September 16, 1972, review of *Edwin Mullhouse: The Life and Death of an American Writer, 1943-1954, by Jeffrey Cartwright.*
New York Times Book Review, September 17, 1972, p. 2; October 2, 1977, pp. 13, 30; January 19, 1986, p. 9; October 12, 1986, Robert Dunn, review of *In the Penny Arcade,* p. 9; June 24, 1990, Jay Cantor, review of *The Barnum Museum,* p. 16;

October 3, 1993, p. 9, p. 11; May 12, 1996, p. 8; May 10, 1998, Patrick McGrath, review of *The Knife Thrower and Other Stories,* p. 11; November 14, 1999, Tobin Harshaw, review of *Enchanted Night,* p. 109; March 9, 2003, Laura Miller, review of *The King in the Tree,* p. 1.
Publishers Weekly, August 8, 1986; March 23, 1998, review of *The Knife Thrower and Other Stories,* p. 78; January 20, 2003, review of *The King in the Tree,* p. 55.
Review of Contemporary Fiction, summer, 1986, Irving Malin, review of *In the Penny Arcade,* pp. 146-147; summer, 2000, Brian Evenson, review of *Enchanted Night,* p. 180.
Saturday Review, September 30, 1972; October 1, 1977, p. 28.
Spectator, March 7, 1998, review of *Martin Dressler: The Tale of an American Dreamer,* p. 32.
Time, June 10, 1996, p. 67.
Times Literary Supplement, July 28, 1978, William Boyd, review of *Portrait of a Romantic;* April 3, 1998, review of *Martin Dressler,* p. 23.
Village Voice, March 6, 1978, John Calvin Batchelor, review of *Portrait of a Romantic,* pp. 70-73.
Village Voice Literary Supplement, February, 1986, Al. J. Sperone, review of *In the Penny Arcade,* pp. 3-4.
Wall Street Journal, April 24, 1996, p. A12.
Washington Post Book World, September 24, 1972, p. 8; October 9, 1977, p. E5; September 21, 1986, pp. 1, 14; September 5, 1993, p. 5, p. 14; April 28, 1996, p. 3; June 14, 1998, A. S. Byatt, review of *The Knife Thrower and Other Stories,* pp. 1, 10; February 9, 2003, Michael Dirda, review of *The King in the Tree,* p. 1.
World and I, December, 1990, review of *The Barnum Museum,* pp. 406-410; October 1998, review of *The Knife Thrower and Other Stories,* p. 280; June, 2003, Edward Hower, review of *The King in the Tree,* p. 230.
World Literature Today, winter, 1999, review of *The Knife Thrower and Other Stories,* p. 148.

*   *   *

MILTNER, Robert F. 1949-

PERSONAL: Born February 25, 1949, in Cleveland, OH; son of Eugene (in sales) and Jeanne (a homemaker; maiden name, Higgins) Miltner; married Linda Smith, 1975 (divorced, 1996); married Mari Artzner

Wolf (a fiber artist), 1996 (divorced, 2002); children: Alison Elizabeth, Ross Patrick. *Education:* Xavier University, B.A., 1971; John Carroll University, M.Ed., 1987; Kent State University, Ph.D., 1998. *Politics:* Liberal Democrat. *Hobbies and other interests:* Book collecting.

ADDRESSES: *Home*—P.O. Box 20251, Canton, OH 44710-0251. *Office*—Department of English, Stark Campus, Kent State University, 6000 Frank Rd. NW, Canton, OH 44720. *E-mail*—rmiltner@stark.kent.edu.

CAREER: English teacher at private religious high schools in Denver, CO, 1975-77, and Parma, OH (also department head), 1977-87; Kent State University, Stark Campus, Canton, OH, instructor, 1987-95, coordinator for developmental education, 1987-93, director of Writing Center, 1990-92, 1995-97, assistant professor of English, 1998—. Walsh University, instructor, 1993-94.

MEMBER: Associated Writing Programs, American Association of University Professors, Poets and Writers League of Greater Cleveland.

AWARDS, HONORS: Wick Poetry Chapbook Award, 1994, for *Against the Simple;* New Words Award, 2001.

WRITINGS:

POETRY

The Seamless Serial Hour, Pudding House (Johnstown, OH), 1993.
Against the Simple, Kent State University Press (Kent, OH), 1995.
On the Off Ramp, Implosion Press (Stow, OH), 1996.
Ghost of a Chance, Zygote/Idlewild Press (Cleveland, OH), 2001.

Four Crows on a Phone Line, Spare Change Press (Massillon, OH), 2002.
A Box of Light (prose poetry), Pudding House (Johnstown, OH), 2002.

Also author of curriculum materials. Contributor to periodicals, including *New York Quarterly, English Journal, Chiron Review, Ohioana Quarterly, Mid-American Review,* and *Birmingham Poetry Review.*

WORK IN PROGRESS: *Jealous Light,* "microfictions," for Second Story Press (Salem, OH); two poetry collections, *The Diameter of Amazement* and *Northcoast, Ohio.*

SIDELIGHTS: Robert F. Miltner told *CA:* "I write because it helps me to learn what I need to know in order to grow and survive as a human. I also write because, as a teacher of literature and writing, it is important that I practice what I teach, and that I teach what I practice. I write because writing—all the arts, actually—are the last refuge of individualism, the last authentic activities left in America.

"In a sense I am a regionalist, for I believe that a writer who is both local and national avoids the excesses of provincialism and cosmopolitanism. Our thoughts, feelings, intuitions, and our writing reflect our geography, and our writing communities are foremost local and regional. Ohio, in particular, has both a rich literary heritage and a lively contemporary scene.

"Primarily I work in poetry, though I also write short fiction. My growing interest is in prose poetry, that delightful mongrel of literature which barks at the edge of acceptability. Prose poetry allows for the unsayable, in a concentrated form, and it disrupts the reader's expectations of the text. In particular, the 'stanzagraph,' a hybrid of the stanza and the paragraph, creates juxtapositions, contrasts, and leaps in the narrative which highlight the poetic elements embedded in the prose."

O

O'BRIEN, (William) Tim(othy) 1946-

PERSONAL: Born October 1, 1946, in Austin, MN; son of William T. (an insurance salesman) and Ava E. (a teacher; maiden name, Schultz) O'Brien; married, 1973; wife's name, Ann (a magazine production manager). *Education:* Macalester College, B.A. (summa cum laude), 1968; graduate study at Harvard University.

ADDRESSES: Home—Boxford, MA. *Agent*—Lynn Nesbit, International Creative Management, 40 West 57th St., New York, NY 10019.

CAREER: Novelist. *Washington Post,* Washington, DC, national affairs reporter, 1973-74; Breadloaf Writer's Conference, Ripton, VT, teacher. *Military service:* U.S. Army, 1968-70, served in Vietnam; became sergeant; received Purple Heart.

MEMBER: Phi Beta Kappa.

AWARDS, HONORS: O. Henry Memorial Awards, 1976 and 1978, for chapters of *Going after Cacciato;* National Book Award, 1979, for *Going after Cacciato;* Vietnam Veterans of America award, 1987; Heartland Prize, *Chicago Tribune,* 1990, for *The Things They Carried;* has also received awards from National Endowment for the Arts, Massachusetts Arts and Humanities Foundation, and Bread Loaf Writers' Conference; *New York Times Notable Book* designation, American Library Association Notable Book designation, and James Fenimore Cooper Prize for Historical Fiction, all 1995, all for *In the Lake of the Woods.*

Tim O' Brien

WRITINGS:

If I Die in a Combat Zone, Box Me up and Ship Me Home (anecdotes), Delacorte (New York, NY), 1973.
Northern Lights (novel), Delacorte (New York, NY), 1975.

Going after Cacciato (novel), Delacorte (New York, NY), 1978.

The Nuclear Age, Press-22, 1981, Knopf (New York, NY), 1985.

The Things They Carried: A Work of Fiction, Houghton Mifflin (Boston, MA), 1990.

In the Lake of the Woods, Houghton Mifflin (Boston, MA), 1994.

Twinkle, Twinkle, Western Pub. Co. (Racine, WI), 1994.

Tomcat in Love, Broadway Books (New York, NY), 1998.

July, July, Houghton Mifflin (Boston, MA), 2002.

Contributor to magazines, including *Playboy, Esquire,* and *Redbook.*

ADAPTATIONS: July, July was adapted as an audiobook, Houghton Mifflin Audio, 2003.

SIDELIGHTS: Award-winning author Tim O'Brien is perhaps best known for his fictional, yet gripping, portrayals of the Vietnam conflict, especially of its people. Based on his own combat exposure, O'Brien delves into the American psyche and the human experience as he writes not only of what actually happened, but also the emotional and psychological impact of the war. In highly praised novels such as *The Things They Carried, Going after Cacciato,* and *In the Lake of the Woods,* he explores the war and its aftershocks from many vantage points, some intimate and some more distant. "But to label O'Brien a Vietnam author seems limiting, even simplistic," *Library Journal* contributor Mirela Roncevic maintained, "for his work has incessantly challenged his storytelling skills, demonstrating his ability to write both lucidly and succinctly while exploring the arcane relationship between fact and fiction, reality and imagination."

Drafted immediately following his graduation from Macalester College in 1968, O'Brien served two years with the U.S. infantry. In a *Publishers Weekly* interview with Michael Coffey, O'Brien explained his motivation in writing about the war as his need to write with "passion," and commented that to write "good" stories "requires a sense of passion, and my passion as a human being and as a writer intersect in Vietnam, not in the physical stuff but in the issues of Vietnam—of courage, rectitude, enlightenment, holiness, trying to do the right thing in the world."

"Writing fiction is a solitary endeavor," explained O'Brien in an essay quoted in the *Dictionary of Literary Biography Documentary Series.* He elaborated: "You shape your own universe. You practice all the time, then practice some more. You pay attention to craft. You aim for tension and suspense, a sense of drama, displaying in concrete terms the actions and reactions of human beings contesting problems of the heart. You try to make art. You strive for wholeness, seeking continuity and flow, each element performing both as cause and effect, always hoping to create, or to re-create, the great illusions of life."

"It's kind of a semantic game: lying versus truth-telling," described O'Brien, discussing his attitude towards writing in an interview with Ronald Baughman in *Dictionary of Literary Biography Documentary Series.* "But I think it's an important game that writers and readers and anyone interested in art in general should be fully aware of. One doesn't lie for the sake of lying; one does not invent merely for the sake of inventing. One does it for a particular purpose and that purpose always is to arrive at some kind of spiritual truth that one can't discover simply by recording the world-as-it-is. We're inventing and using imagination for sublime reasons—to get at the essence of things, not merely the surface."

O'Brien's first novel, *If I Die in a Combat Zone, Box Me up and Ship Me Home,* is an anecdotal account of an infantryman's year in Vietnam. A semi-fictionalized recounting of his own experiences, O'Brien's book tells the tale of a college educated young man who is drafted, trained for war, and shipped overseas to fight the Vietcong. He relates the story "with as much attention to his own feelings and states of mind as to the details of battle," declared a reviewer in *Times Literary Supplement.* An "interesting and highly readable book," remarked a critic in *New Republic.* Joseph McLellan, writing in *Washington Post Book World,* called *If I Die in a Combat Zone* "powerfully written," and *New York Times Book Review* contributor Annie Gottlieb ended her review with similar praise: "O'Brien writes—without either pomposity or embarrassment—with the care and eloquence of someone for whom communication is still a vital and serious possibility, not a narcissistic vestige. It is a beautiful, painful book, arousing pity and fear for the daily realities of modern disaster."

Northern Lights, O'Brien's next book, creates a progression in the Vietnam tale: the story of the Vietnam soldier coming home to his family. Harvey Perry is the "hero," the soldier who fought for his country, lost an eye in battle, and seems to be all that his father wanted. Paul Perry, on the other hand, is the stay-at-home brother, the "failure" of the family who is married and employed as a farm agent in the family's hometown of Sawmill Landing, Minnesota. *Northern Lights* is about the two brothers' relationship, and the changes that occur during a long and difficult cross-country ski trip. Paul emerges as the real hero after Harvey, upset over the abrupt end of a romance and physically ill, proves to be less adept at survival than his cunning brother. It is Paul who rescues Harvey, much to the surprise of everyone, including himself.

Northern Lights received mixed reviews, with several critics commenting on O'Brien's style. Duncan Fallowell, writing in *Spectator,* called *Northern Lights* "indigestible, as if [the author] is having a crack at raising the great American novel fifty years after it sank." Alasdair Maclean, writing in *Times Literary Supplement,* expressed a similar view, claiming "O'Brien's ambition outreaches his gifts." *New York Times Book Review* contributor John Deck, however, concluded that O'Brien "tells the story modestly and neatly . . . [in] a crafted work of serious intent with themes at least as old as the Old Testament—they still work."

O'Brien takes a new approach to his Vietnam theme in *Going after Cacciato,* winner of the National Book Award in 1979. The chapters read like short stories; several were published seperately before the book's compilation, with two tales winning O. Henry awards. *Cacciato* records the dream journey of Paul Berlin, a U.S. infantryman in Vietnam, and alternates this with the "dreamlike" actualities of war. The story begins in reality when a fellow platoon member, Cacciato—which means "the pursued" in Italian—decides to leave South East Asia and walk to Paris. He never makes it, being found near the Laotian border by a search party that includes Berlin. Berlin later wonders during guard duty one night, what if Cacciato was never found and the group had to track him all the way to Paris? Here Berlin's imagination roams free as fantasies of travel, beautiful women, and, ultimately, Paris, alternate with memories of battle, death, and war. "The fantasy journey is an unworkable idea that nearly sinks the book," claimed a reviewer in *Newsweek.* And Mary Hope, writing in *Spectator,* labeled *Going after Cacciato* a "strained effort." Other critics issued more positive reviews, praising the writing style and the author's abilities. "O'Brien's writing is crisp, authentic and grimly ironic," declared Richard Freedman in *New York Times Book Review. Washington Post Book World* contributor Robert Wilson also commented on the dream elements, calling them "out of place, hard to reconcile with the evocative realism of the rest of the narrative," but closed by writing that "O'Brien knows the soldier as well as anybody, and is able to make us know him in the unique way that the best fiction can."

In *The Nuclear Age,* O'Brien shifts his focus to a civilian's perspective. William Cowling, a Vietnam era anti-war radical, terrorist, and draft dodger, is the protagonist who traded in his radicalism for profits in uranium speculation in the 1990s. A product of the "nuclear age," his childhood fear of nuclear annihilation, a concern rampant during the 1950s, has turned into paranoia in his adulthood. The story opens in 1995, with Cowling digging a bomb shelter in his backyard, but most of the story is told through flashbacks illustrating his childhood and radical young adult years. Eventually, Cowling must accept that the bombs exist and learn to ignore them, ultimately choosing the love of his family over his paranoia. "O'Brien never makes William's hysteria real or convincing," judged Michiko Kakutani in *New York Times.* Richard Lipez, writing in *Washington Post Book World,* called *The Nuclear Age* an "imperfect but very lively novel," an opinion shared by several other reviewers. Lipez praised the "marvelous character" of Cowling, but noted that the impact of O'Brien's "main message" about the craziness of the nuclear age gets lost in the radical actions of another era. *Times Literary Supplement* contributor David Montrose also noted several flaws in the novel, including the characterization of Cowling's friends, but wrote in his conclusion: *The Nuclear Age* "is notable for the lean clarity of O'Brien's prose and the finesse with which, as ever, he evokes states of mind."

O'Brien returns to the subject of Vietnam and the soldier's viewpoint with *The Things They Carried,* a fictional memoir filled with interconnected stories about the conflict and the people involved. The volume is narrated by a character named "Tim O'Brien," whom the author states is not himself, although there are many similarities. One tale records the visit an All-American girl made to her boyfriend in South East Asia, where she eventually becomes so caught up in the war that she wanders off into combat wearing a necklace of human tongues. Another relates the death of a friend whose misstep while playing catch with hand grenades causes him to be blown up by a land mine. The title, *The Things They Carried,* refers to the things a soldier takes into combat with him: not necessarily all physical items, like weapons, but also intangibles such as fear, exhaustion, and memories. Many reviewers praised O'Brien's work, with *New York Times Book Review* contributor Robert R. Harris proclaiming it "a stunning performance. The overall effect of these original tales is devastating." "O'Brien convinces us that such incredible stories are faithful to the reality of Vietnam," declared Julian Loose in *Times Literary Supplement.* Kakutani praised O'Brien's prose, describing it as a style "that combines the sharp, unsentimental rhythms of Hemingway with gentler, more lyrical descriptions . . . [giving] the reader a shockingly visceral sense of what it felt like to tramp through a booby-trapped jungle," and concluded, "With *The Things They Carried,* Mr. O'Brien has written a vital, important book—a book that matters not only to the reader interested in Vietnam, but to anyone interested in the craft of writing as well."

July, July focuses on a group of Darton Hall College students who return to their alma mater for their thirtieth class reunion in July of 1999. In what a *Publishers Weekly* contributor described as "more a group of interwoven short stories or character studies than a traditional novel," O'Brien reveals the disillusionment of a group of middle-agers who look back on their radical, idealistic, free-wheeling, and politically active youth and feel disillusioned with the course of their lives. Describing the characters of *July, July* as "divorced, drunk," and "drifting," *New Statesman* contributor James Hopkin explained that their "reunion reveals old flames, old wounds, and new crises," and noted that O'Brien "shows us how their disenchantment has turned to apathy and political lassitude," a lassitude the author extends to "the nation's body politic." While noting that the novel moves O'Brien away from his characteristic focus on Vietnam, in this tale of disillusioned baby boomers the Vietnam war "hovers in the background like some unfinished business from the past, testing the powers of memory," noted Mirela Roncevic in *Library Journal.*

While the *Publishers Weekly* contributor called *July, July* a "comic tale" in which "sympathy, camaraderie, solidarity and love run deeply throughout," other crit-

ics disagreed. John Mort, in a *Booklist* review, maintained that O'Brien's characters, while engaging in "witty" conversation, are fifty-something narcissists lacking a "social conscience," "seem shallow," and "their youthful contempt for any sort of spirituality has not aged well." Hopkin, praising the author's style as "breathless, bitter and designed to give you the jitters," noted that at the novel's core is a "sense of a Middle America gone ideologically idle and paranoid." In contrast, a *Kirkus Reviews* contributor found the novel to be sensitive to its character's strengths and human weaknesses, noting that, "though its parts are of unequal interest and excellence, *July, July* powerfully dramatizes the long, lingering aftermath of what had seemed to those who grew up during it, a veritable year of wonders." For O'Brien's part, he told *Atlantic Unbound* interviewer Josh Karp that the novel represents the sense of unmet expectations that every adult of a certain age must deal with. "I think every generation knows betrayal and loss," the author noted. "No generation is exempt from that. When I wrote the book, I wasn't thinking of Baby Boomers. I was thinking about human beings . . . and to me they could have been part of any generation. I mean, my father's generation—granted they won World War II—but they thought the world would be changed forever, and it wasn't. They know what disappointment and loss is. So, I really thought of it as a more ubiquitous theme that everybody could identify with."

"What can you teach people, just for having been in a war?," O'Brien pondered in response to a question by Larry McCaffery in a *Chicago Review* interview. "By 'teach,' I mean provide insight, philosophy. The mere fact of having witnessed violence and death doesn't make a person a teacher. Insight and wisdom are required, and that means reading and hard thought. I didn't intend *If I Die* to stand as a profound statement, and it's not. Teaching is one thing, and telling stories is another. Instead I wanted to use stories to alert readers to the complexity and ambiguity of a set of moral issues—but without preaching a moral lesson."

BIOGRAPHICAL AND CRITICAL SOURCES:

BOOKS

Contemporary Literary Criticism, Gale (Detroit, MI), Volume 7, 1977, Volume 19, 1981, Volume 40, 1986.
Dictionary of Literary Biography Documentary Series, Volume 9, Gale (Detroit, MI), 1991.

Dictionary of Literary Biography Yearbook: 1980, Gale (Detroit, MI), 1981.

Herzog, T. C., *Tim O'Brien,* Prentice Hall (London, England), 1997.

Kaplan, Steven, *Understanding Tim O'Brien,* University of South Carolina, 1995.

PERIODICALS

America, September 1, 1973; November 17, 1973.
Antioch Review, spring, 1978.
Atlantic, May, 1973; November, 1994, p. 146.
Book, September-October, 2002, Stephanie Foote, review of *July, July,* p. 76.
Booklist, September 1, 2002, John Mort, review of *July, July,* p. 7.
Books and Bookmen, December, 1973.
Chicago Review, number 2, 1982, pp. 129-149.
Chicago Tribune, April 27, 1990; August 23, 1990.
Chicago Tribune Book World, October 6, 1985, p. 39.
Christian Century, May 24, 1995, p. 567.
Christian Science Monitor, March 9, 1978.
College Literature, spring, 2002, Marilyn Wesley, "Truth and Fiction in Tim O'Brien's *If I Die in a Combat Zone* and *The Things They Carried,*" pp. 1-18.
Commonweal, December 5, 1975.
Critique, fall, 1999, Jack Slay Jr., "A Rumor of War," p. 79.
English Journal, January, 1994, p. 82.
Explicator, spring, 2003, Robin Blyn, review of *The Things They Carried,* pp. 109-191.
Guardian, October 20, 1973.
Harper's, March, 1978; August, 1999, Vince Passaro, review of *The Things They Carried,* p. 80.
Kirkus Reviews, July 15, 2002, review of *July, July,* p. 985.
Library Journal, December 18, 1977; September 1, 1998, Marc A. Kloszewski, review of *Tomcat in Love,* p. 216; May 15, 2001, Nancy Pearl, review of *In the Lake of the Woods,* p. 192; July, 2002, Mirela Roncevic, review of *July, July,* pp. 122-123.
Listener, April 1, 1976.
Los Angeles Times, March 22, 1979; March 11, 1990.
Los Angeles Times Book Review, November 3, 1985, p. 16; April 1, 1990, p. 3.
Massachusetts Review, winter, 2002, Pamela Smiley, "The Role of the Ideal (Female) Reader in Tim O'Brien's *The Things They Carried:* Why Should Real Women Play?," pp. 602-613.

Nation, January 29, 1977; March 25, 1978.
New Republic, May 12, 1973, p. 30; February 7, 1976.
New Statesman, January 4, 1974; May 10, 1999, Phil Whitaker, review of *Tomcat in Love,* p. 45; November 11, 2002, James Hopkin, review of *July, July,* p. 40.
Newsweek, February 20, 1978; April 2, 1990, p. 56; October 24, 1994, p. 77.
New Yorker, July 16, 1973; March 27, 1978; October 24, 1994, p. 111.
New York Review of Books, November 13, 1975.
New York Times, February 12, 1978; March 19, 1979; April 24, 1979; September 28, 1985; April 4, 1987; August 4, 1987; March 6, 1990; April 3, 1990.
New York Times Book Review, July 1, 1973, pp. 10, 12; December 2, 1973; October 12, 1975, p. 42; February 12, 1978, pp. 1, 22; November 3, 1985, p. 16; November 17, 1985, p. 7; August 16, 1987, p. 28; March 11, 1990, p. 8; October 9, 1994, pp. 1, 33.
Progressive, December, 1994, p. 40.
Publishers Weekly, August 9, 1985, p. 65; December 15, 1989, p. 35; January 26, 1990, p. 404; February 16, 1990, pp. 60-61; July 11, 1994, p. 61; July 13, 1998, review of *Tomcat in Love,* p. 61; January 6, 2003, review of *July, July,* p. 20.
Saturday Review, February 18, 1978; May 13, 1978.
Spectator, April 3, 1976, p. 22; November 25, 1978, p. 23.
Time, October 24, 1994, p. 74.
Times Literary Supplement, October 19, 1973, p. 1269; April 23, 1976, p. 498; March 28, 1986, p. 342; June 29, 1990, p. 708.
Tribune Books (Chicago, IL), March 11, 1990, p. 5.
Twentieth-Century Literature, spring, 2000, John H. Timmerman, "Tim O'Brien and the Art of the True War Story," p. 100.
Virginia Quarterly Review, summer, 1978; winter, 2003, review of *July, July,* p. 23.
Washington Post, July 31, 1987; April 23, 1990.
Washington Post Book World, May 27, 1973; June 3, 1973, p. 14; June 30, 1974, p. 4; February 19, 1978, p. E4; October 13, 1985, p. 9; April 7, 1991, p. 12.
Whole Earth Review, fall, 1995, p. 58.

ONLINE

Atlantic Unbound, http://www.theatlantic.com/ (October 30, 2002), Josh Karp, interview with O'Brien.
Tim O'Brien Home Page, http://www.illyria.com/tobhp (April 7, 2004).*

ONDAATJE, (Philip) Michael 1943-

PERSONAL: Born September 12, 1943, in Colombo, Ceylon (now Sri Lanka); immigrated to Canada, 1962; son of Philip Mervyn and Enid Doris (Gratiaen) Ondaatje; married Betty Kimbark, 1963 (marriage ended); married Kim Jones (separated); children: Quintin, Griffin. *Education:* Attended St. Thomas College, Colombo, Ceylon, and Dulwich College, London; attended Bishop's University, Lennoxville, Quebec, Canada, 1962-64; University of Toronto, B.A., 1965; Queen's University, Kingston, Ontario, Canada, M.A., 1967. *Hobbies and other interests:* Hound breeding, hog breeding.

ADDRESSES: Office—Department of English, Glendon College, York University, 2275 Bayview Ave., Toronto, Ontario M4N 3M6, Canada. *Agent*—c/o Ellen Levine, 15 East 26th St., Suite 1801, New York, NY 10010.

CAREER: University of Western Ontario, London, Ontario, Canada, instructor, 1967-71; Glendon College, York University, Toronto, Ontario, Department of English faculty, beginning 1970, currently professor; Coach House Press, Toronto, Ontario, editor, 1970-94; *Mongrel Broadsides,* editor; *Brick* (literary journal), editor. Visiting professor, University of Hawaii at Honolulu, 1979, and Brown University, 1990. Director of films, including *Sons of Captain Poetry,* 1970, *Carry on Crime and Punishment,* 1972, *Royal Canadian Hounds,* 1973, *The Clinton Special,* 1974, and *Inventor of Dragland Hog Feeder,* 1975.

AWARDS, HONORS: Ralph Gustafson award, 1965; Epstein award, 1966; E. J. Pratt Medal, 1966; President's Medal, University of Western Ontario, 1967; Canada Council grant, 1968, 1977; Canadian Governor General's Award for Literature, 1971, for *The Collected Poems of Billy the Kid,* 1980, for *There's a Trick with a Knife I'm Learning to Do,* 1992, for *The English Patient,* 2000, for *Anil's Ghost;* Books in Canada First Novel Award, 1977, for *Coming through Slaughter;* Canadian Governor General's Award for Poetry, 1979; Canada-Australia Prize, 1980; Toronto Book Award, 1988; Booker Prize, British Book Trust, 1992, for *The English Patient;* Literary Lion Award, New York Public Library, 1993; Giller Prize, and Prix Medicis, both 2000, and *Irish Times* Literature Prize shortlist, 2001, all for *Anil's Ghost;* American Cinema Editors' Robert Wise Award, 2003, for *The Conversations: Walter Murch and the Art of Editing Film.*

Michael Ondaatje

WRITINGS:

POETRY

The Dainty Monsters, Coach House Press (Toronto, Ontario, Canada), 1967.

The Man with Seven Toes, Coach House Press (Toronto, Ontario, Canada), 1969.

The Collected Works of Billy the Kid: Left-handed Poems (also see below), Anansi (Toronto, Ontario, Canada), 1970, Berkley (New York, NY), 1975.

Rat Jelly, Coach House Press (Toronto, Ontario, Canada), 1973.

Elimination Dance, Nairn Coldstream (Ilderton, Ontario, Canada), 1978, revised edition, Brick, 1980.

There's a Trick with a Knife I'm Learning to Do: Poems, 1963-1978, W. W. Norton (New York, NY), 1979, published as *Rat Jelly, and Other Poems, 1963-1978,* Marion Boyars (London, England), 1980.

Secular Love, Coach House Press (Toronto, Ontario, Canada), 1984, W. W. Norton (New York, NY), 1985.

All along the Mazinaw: Two Poems (broadside), Woodland Pattern (Milwaukee, WI), 1986.

Two Poems, Woodland Pattern (Milwaukee, WI), 1986.

The Cinnamon Peeler: Selected Poems, Pan (London, England), 1989, Knopf (New York, NY), 1991.

Handwriting, McClelland & Stewart (Toronto, Ontario, Canada), 1998, Knopf (New York, NY), 1999.

NOVELS

Coming through Slaughter (also see below), Anansi (Toronto, Ontario, Canada), 1976, W. W. Norton (New York, NY), 1977.

In the Skin of a Lion (also see below), Knopf (New York, NY), 1987.

The English Patient, Knopf (New York, NY), 1992.

Anil's Ghost, Knopf (New York, NY), 2000.

EDITOR

The Broken Ark (animal verse), illustrated by Tony Urquhart, Oberon (Ottawa, Ontario, Canada), 1971, revised as *A Book of Beasts,* 1979.

Personal Fictions: Stories by Munro, Wiebe, Thomas, and Blaise, Oxford University Press (Toronto, Ontario, Canada), 1977.

The Long Poem Anthology, Coach House (Toronto, Ontario, Canada), 1979.

(With Russell Banks and David Young) *Brushes with Greatness: An Anthology of Chance Encounters with Greatness,* Coach House (Toronto, Ontario, Canada), 1989.

(With Linda Spalding) *The Brick Anthology,* illustrated by David Bolduc, Coach House Press (Toronto, Ontario, Canada), 1989.

From Ink Lake: An Anthology of Canadian Short Stories, Viking (New York, NY), 1990.

The Faber Book of Contemporary Canadian Short Stories, Faber (London, England), 1990.

(With others) *Lost Classics,* Knopf Canada (Toronto, Ontario, Canada), 2000, Anchor (New York, NY), 2001.

(And author of introduction) Mavis Gallant, *Paris Stories,* New York Review Books (New York, NY), 2002.

OTHER

Leonard Cohen (literary criticism), McClelland & Stewart (Toronto, Ontario, Canada), 1970.

The Collected Works of Billy the Kid (play; based on his poetry), produced in Stratford, Ontario, 1973; produced in New York, NY, 1974; produced in London, England, 1984.

Claude Glass (literary criticism), Coach House Press (Toronto, Ontario, Canada), 1979.

Coming through Slaughter (based on his novel), first produced in Toronto, Ontario, Canada, 1980.

Tin Roof, Island (British Columbia, Canada), 1982.

Running in the Family (memoir), W. W. Norton (New York, NY), 1982.

In the Skin of a Lion (based on his novel), Knopf (New York, NY), 1987.

(With B. P. Nichol and George Bowering) *An H in the Heart: A Reader,* McClelland & Stewart (Toronto, Ontario, Canada), 1994.

(Author of introduction) Anthony Minghella, adaptor, *The English Patient: A Screenplay,* Hyperion Miramax (New York, NY), 1996.

The Conversations: Walter Murch and the Art of Editing Film, Knopf (New York, NY), 2002.

Ondaatje's manuscripts are included in the National Archives, Ottawa, Canada, and the Metropolitan Toronto Library.

ADAPTATIONS: The English Patient was adapted as a motion picture, written and directed by Anthony Minghella, produced by Miramax, 1996; *Anil's Ghost* was adapted as an audiobook read by Alan Cummings, Random House AudioBooks, 2000.

SIDELIGHTS: Canadian poet and novelist Michael Ondaatje dissolves the lines between prose and poetry through the breadth of his works in both genres. "Moving in and out of imagined landscape, portrait and documentary, anecdote or legend, Ondaatje writes for the eye and the ear simultaneously," noted Diane Wakoski in *Contemporary Poets.* Whether reshaping recollections of friends and family from his childhood in old Ceylon in *Running in the Family,* or retelling an American myth in *The Collected Works of Billy the Kid,* Ondaatje "focuses on the internal lives of his multigenerational characters and exhibits a fascination with extraordinary personality types," as observed by a *Contemporary Literary Criticism* essayist, utilizing a writing style that is "whimsical and imaginative . . . marked by vivid detail . . . startling juxtapositions, and a preoccupation with intense experiences." In addition to writing novels, plays, and poetry collections,

Ondaatje has edited several books, including *The Faber Book of Contemporary Canadian Short Stories,* praised as a "landmark" by reviewer Christine Bold in *Times Literary Supplement* for its representation of "Canadian voices accented by native, black, French, Caribbean, Indian, Japanese and Anglo-Saxon origins."

Ondaatje's poetry is seen by critics as continually changing, evolving as the author experiments with the shape and sound of words. Although his poetic forms may differ, his works focus on the myths that root deep in common cultural experience. As a poet, he recreates their intellectual expression in depicting the affinity between the art of legend and the world at large. "He cares more about the relationship between art and nature than any other poet since the Romantics," stated Liz Rosenberg in *New York Times Book Review,* "and more than most contemporary poets care about any ideas at all." Some of Ondaatje's verse has approached the fragmentary, as in *Secular Love,* a collection of poems he published in 1985.

New York Times Book Review contributor Adam Kirsch found the poems in *Handwriting* to be "richly sensual images, which are drawn largely from the history, mythology, and landscape of India and China." "*Handwriting* takes one to Ondaatje's Sri Lankan past," wrote Sen Sudeep in *World Literature Today,* "a past that is very much present in his life, one that informs and colors his broader palette, scope, and vision. The fact that he can present Sri Lanka realistically and unexotically lends a believable and even magical edge to his text. His observations are sharp and wry, but at the same time considered, wise, and pragmatic."

Reviewing *Handwriting* in *Poetry,* Henry Taylor wrote that Ondaatje's verses "have sometimes struck me as labored in their seriousness—easier to admire than to like. This new book, in fact, is a deep pleasure to read most of the time, once one has become accustomed to its fragmentary style. This style is singularly appropriate to the themes and subjects of the book, which arise from mixed heritage and the loss of cultural identity." *Library Journal* reviewer Barbara Hoffert called Ondaatje's poetry "deeply evocative and suffused—but never overburdened—with sensuous imagery."

"Concerned always to focus on the human, the private, and the 'real' over the theoretical and the ideological," in his novels and short fiction "Ondaatje examines the internal workings of characters who struggle against and burst through that which renders people passive," noted Diane Watson in *Contemporary Novelists,* "and which renders human experience programmatic and static." The novel *In the Skin of a Lion* focuses on a man raised in rural Canada who, at the age of twenty-one, comes to the growing city of Toronto and lives among the immigrants inhabiting its working-class neighborhoods. Physical actions and inner challenges define Ondaatje's characters as individuals, creators within their own lives, and give both purpose to their existence and redemption to their inner reality. In this work a historical epoch is seen as the struggle of the individual to break free of the confines of his culture rather than simply a collection of social and political goals. As Michael Hulse described *In the Skin of a Lion* in *Times Literary Supplement,* it "maps high society and the sub culture of the underprivileged in Toronto in the 1920s and 1930s. . . . But it is also . . . about communication, about men 'utterly alone' who are waiting (in Ondaatje's terms) to break through a chrysalis."

In *Coming through Slaughter,* a novel well-grounded in the history of early-twentieth-century New Orleans, Ondaatje creates a possible life of the late jazz musician Buddy Bolden, remembered as a brilliant cornetist whose performances were never recorded due to a tragic mental collapse at an early age. Mixing interviews with those who remember Bolden, historical fact, and his richly imagined conception of the musician's inner thoughts on his way to madness, Ondaatje fashions what Watson termed a "fractured narrative . . . [tracing] the personal anarchy of . . . Bolden and the perspectives on him of those who knew him best."

Perhaps Ontaadje's most well-known novel, *The English Patient* tells the story of a Canadian nurse who stays behind in the bombed remains of a villa near the World War II battlefields of northern Italy to tend to an English soldier who has been severely burned. After the couple are joined by two other soldiers, relationships form that parallel, as Cressida Connolly noted in *Spectator,* "those of a small and faded Eden." Ranking the author among such contemporary novelists as Ian McEwan and Martin Amis, Connolly praised the poetic quality of Ondaatje's fiction. "The writing is so heady that you have to keep putting the book down between passages so as not to reel from the sheer force and beauty of it," the reviewer exclaimed, adding that "when I finished the book I felt as dazed as if I'd just awoken from a powerful dream."

Anil's Ghost is a novel set in the present that documents the nearly twenty-year Sri Lankan conflict that began in the 1980s and resulted in the deaths and disappearances of nearly twenty thousand. Anil is a native of Sri Lanka who studied medicine abroad, specializing in forensic pathology, and she has come home as part of a mission to examine the remains of victims to determine possible war crimes. Anil is assisted by Sarath, a government-selected archaeologist, and together they find four skeletons they name Tinker, Tailor, Soldier, and Sailor, the last of which Anil feels will provide the evidence they are seeking. "This narrow examination broadens to involve the wider conflict as Sri Lanka's history and present achieve a simultaneous, terrible maturity," wrote Rebecca J. Davies in *Lancet*. "The earth is oily with wasted blood. Severed heads sit atop stakes. Drivers are crucified on the roadside. Bodies succumb to frail fractures sustained in their dive from helicopters. Even babies and three-year-olds are not immune to the bullets. And yet amid this bloody chaos Ondaatje painstakingly captures the normality of interrupted lives."

New York Times Book Review contributor Janet Maslin compared *Anil's Ghost* to *The English Patient*, writing that it "is a novel more in name than in essence. . . . Ondaatje brings an oblique poetic sensibility to unraveling the mysteries at work here. Layers peel away from both Anil and Sarath, with a past full of ghosts for each of them and assorted vignettes and memories scattered across the book's fertile landscape." Maslin went on to say that "the book's real strengths lie in its profound sense of outrage, the shimmering intensity of its descriptive language and the mysterious beauty of its geography, with so many discrete passages that present the artificer in Mr. Ondaatje so well." *America*'s John Breslin noted that the novel "ends with three pages of acknowledgments to dozens of doctors, lawyers, civil rights workers, Asian scholars, and fellow poets, plus a bibliography that would make any researcher proud. A lot of homework and legwork have gone into this novel."

In addition to poetry and fiction, Ondaatje's interest in filmmaking, fueled perhaps by his involvement in the film adaptation of his novel *The English Patient*, inspired the nonfiction work *The Conversations: Walter Murch and the Art of Film Editing*. Highly praised by reviewers, *The Conversations* examines Murch's life and career as a three-time Oscar winner and collaborator with noted directors Francis Ford Coppola and George Lucas in Zoetrope studios. The creative process is also discussed, as writer and film editor talk about the task of revealing hidden themes and patterns in existing creative works. As Ondaatje noted in an interview with a *Maclean's* contributor, editing—whether of film or one's written work, is "the only place where you're on your own. Where you can be one person and govern it. The only time you control making a movie is in the editing stage." In *Booklist* Carlos Orellana praised *The Conversations* for permitting "readers a peek behind the curtain to reveal a man as mysterious as his art," while in *Publishers Weekly* a reviewer noted: "Through [Murch's] . . . eyes, and Ondaatje's remarkably insightful questions and comments, readers see how intricate the process is, and understand Murch when he says, 'The editor is the only one who has time to deal with the whole jigsaw. The director simply doesn't.'"

Born in Sri Lanka and living in England as a young teen, Ondaatje immigrated to Canada at age eighteen, determined to make a mark as a poet, and gradually moved to fiction. *Running in the Family*, a heartfelt memoir honoring his family and his heritage, blends together family stories with poems, photographs, and personal anecdotes. As his family history follows a path leading from the genteel innocence of the Ceylonese privileged class as the sun set on the British Empire to the harsh glare of the modern age, so Ondaatje's narrative seeks the inner character of his father, a man of whom the author writes, "My loss was that I never spoke to him as an adult." As Anton Mueller in the *Washington Post Book World* wrote, "In reality, this is a mythology exaggerated and edited by the survivors. Seduced by the wealth and luxury of its imaginative reality, Ondaatje enters the myth without disturbing it. With a prose style equal to the voluptuousness of his subject and a sense of humor never too far away, *Running in the Family* is sheer reading pleasure."

BIOGRAPHICAL AND CRITICAL SOURCES:

BOOKS

Contemporary Literary Criticism, Gale (Detroit, MI), Volume 14, 1980; Volume 29, 1984; Volume 51, 1989; Volume 76, 1993.

Contemporary Novelists, fifth edition, St. James (Detroit, MI), 1991, pp. 710-711.

Contemporary Poets, fifth edition, St. James (Detroit, MI), 1991, pp. 724-725.

Cooke, John, *The Influence of Painting on Five Canadian Writers: Alice Munro, Hugh Hood, Timothy Findley, Margaret Atwood, and Michael Ondaatje,* Edwin Mellen (Lewiston, NY), 1996.

Dictionary of Literary Biography, Volume 60: *Canadian Writers since 1960, Second Series,* Gale (Detroit, MI), 1987.

Jewinski, Ed, *Michael Ondaatje: Express Yourself Beautifully,* ECW Press, 1994.

Ondaatje, Michael, *Running in the Family* (memoir), W. W. Norton (New York, NY), 1982.

Siemerling, Winfried, *Discoveries of the Other: Alterity in the Work of Leonard Cohn, Hubert Aquin, Michael Ondaatje, and Nicole Brossard,* University of Toronto (Toronto, Ontario, Canada), 1994.

Solecki, Sam, editor, *Spider Blues: Essays on Michael Ondaatje,* Vehicule Press, 1985.

PERIODICALS

America, February 19, 2001, John Breslin, "War on Several Fronts," p. 25.

American Book Review, March, 1999, review of *The Cinnamon Peeler,* p. 23.

Ariel, April, 1997, Josef Pesch, "Post-Apocalyptic War Histories: Michael Ondaatje's *The English Patient,*" p. 117.

Biography, spring, 2000, S. Leigh Matthews, "'The Bright Bone of a Dream': Drama, Performativity, Ritual, and Community in Michael Ondaatje's *Running in the Family,*" p. 352.

Booklist, March 1, 1999, Donna Seaman, review of *Handwriting,* p. 1145; March 15, 2000, Bonnie Smothers, review of *Anil's Ghost,* p. 1294; September 15, 2002, Carlos Orellana, review of *The Conversations: Walter Murch and the Art of Editing Film,* p. 192.

Canadian Forum, January-February, 1993, p. 39.

Canadian Literature, spring, 2002, Douglas Barbour, "Writing through Terror," pp. 187-188.

Christian Science Monitor, May 4, 2000, "An Island Paradise in the Flames of Terror," p. 17.

Economist, June 17, 2000, review of *Anil's Ghost,* p. 14.

English Studies, May, 1996, p. 266.

Essays on Canadian Writing, summer, 1994, pp. 1, 11, 27, 204, 238, 250; fall, 1995, p. 236; winter, 1995, p. 116; spring, 1999, review of *The English Patient,* p. 236; spring, 2002.

Harper's, February, 2003, John Gregory Dunne, review of *The Conversations,* p. 69.

History and Theory, December, 2002, p. 43.

Hudson Review, spring, 2001, Alan Davis, review of *Anil's Ghost,* p. 142.

Journal of Canadian Studies, summer, 2001, Dennis Duffy, "Furnishing the Pictures: Arthur S. Goss, Michael Ondaatje, and the Imag(in)ing of Toronto," p. 106.

Journal of Modern Literature, summer, 2000, William H. New, review of *Anil's Ghost,* p. 565.

Lancet, January 20, 2001, Rebecca J. Davies, "A Tale of the Sri Lankan Civil War," p. 241.

Library Journal, April 15, 1999, Barbara Hoffert, review of *Handwriting,* p. 100; May 15, 2000, Barbara Hoffert, review of *Anil's Ghost,* p. 126; June 1, 2001, Ron Ratliff, review of *Lost Classics,* p. 160.

Los Angeles Times, May 21, 2000, Jonathan Levi, review of *Anil's Ghost,* p. C1.

Maclean's, April 10, 2000, John Bemrose, "Horror in Paradise: Michael Ondaatje Sifts through Sri Lanka's Strife," p. 78; December 18, 2000, p. 66; September 9, 2002, interview with Ondaatje, p. 40.

Modern Language Review, January, 1997, p. 149.

Mosaic, September, 1999, Douglas Malcolm, "Solos and Chorus: Michael Ondaatje's Jazz Politics/ Poetics," p. 131.

Nation, January 4, 1993, p. 22; June 19, 2000, Tom LeClair, "The Sri Lankan Patients," p. 31.

National Catholic Reporter, November 19, 1993, p. 30.

New Criterion, May, 2000, Brooke Allen, "Meditations, Good & Bad," p. 63.

New Leader, May, 2000, Tova Reich, review of *Anil's Ghost,* p. 37.

New Republic, March 15, 1993, p. 38.

New Statesman & Society, March 19, 1999, Lavinia Greenlaw, review of *Handwriting,* p. 48.

New Yorker, May 15, 2000, John Updike, review of *Anil's Ghost,* p. 91.

New York Review of Books, January 14, 1993, p. 22; November 2, 2000, John Bayley, review of *Anil's Ghost,* p. 44.

New York Times Book Review, April 24, 1977; December 22, 1985, pp. 22-23; April 11, 1999, Adam Kirsch, "Erotic, Exotic," p. 24; May 11, 2000, Janet Maslin, "Unearthing the Tragedies of Civil War in Sri Lanka"; May 14, 2000, Richard Eder, "A House Divided."

Poetry, May, 2000, Henry Taylor, review of *Handwriting,* p. 96.

Prairie Schooner, spring, 2001, Constance Merritt, review of *Handwriting,* p. 182.

Publishers Weekly, February 22, 1999, review of *Handwriting,* p. 88; March 20, 2000, review of *Anil's Ghost,* p. 70; July 3, 2000, review of *Anil's Ghost,* p. 24; August 12, 2002, review of *The Conversations,* p. 290.

Saturday Night, July, 1968; June, 1997, Valerie Feldner, review of *The English Patient,* p. 12.

School Library Journal, September, 2000, Pam Johnson, review of *Anil's Ghost,* p. 258.

Spectator, September 5, 1992, Cressida Connolly, review of *The English Patient,* p. 32; April 29, 2000, John de Falbe, review of *Anil's Ghost,* p. 29.

Studies in Canadian Literature, 2001 (annual), pp. 71-90.

Time, May 1, 2000, Paul Gray, "Nailed Palms and the Eyes of Gods: Michael Ondaatje's *Anil's Ghost* Is a Stark Successor to *The English Patient,*" p. 75.

Times Higher Education Supplement, Roger Crittenden, review of *The Conversations,* p. 27.

Times Literary Supplement, September 4, 1987, p. 948; November 3, 1989, p. 1217; October 19, 1990, p. 1130; September 22, 1992, p. 23; February 5, 1999, Michael O'Neill, review of *Handwriting,* p. 33.

University of Toronto Quarterly, spring, 2001, p. 633; fall, 2001, p. 889.

Virginia Quarterly Review, summer, 1999, review of *Handwriting,* p. 102.

Vogue, May, 2000, John Powers, review of *Anil's Ghost,* p. 201.

Wall Street Journal, April 2, 1999, review of *Handwriting,* p. 6; May 12, 2000, Elizabeth Bukowski, review of *Anil's Ghost,* p. W8.

Washington Post Book World, January 2, 1983, pp. 9, 13; November 1, 1987, p. 4.

World Literature Today, spring, 1999, Sen Sudeep, review of *Handwriting,* p. 333.

ONLINE

BookPage, http://www.bookpage.com/ (October 1, 2001), Ellen Kanner, "New Discoveries from the Author of *The English Patient*" (interview).*

*   *   *

OXENBURY, Helen 1938-

PERSONAL: Born June 2, 1938, in Suffolk, England; daughter of Thomas Bernard (an architect) and Muriel (Taylor) Oxenbury; married John Burningham (an author and illustrator), August 15, 1964; children: Lucy, William Benedict, Emily. *Education:* Attended Ipswich School of Art and Central School of Arts and Crafts, London.

ADDRESSES: Home—5 East Heath Rd., Hampstead, London NW3 1BN, England. *Agent*—Elaine Greene, Ltd., 37 Goldhawk Rd., London W12 8QQ, England.

CAREER: Writer and illustrator of children's books. Stage designer in Colchester, England, 1960, and Tel-Aviv, Israel, 1961; television designer in London, England, 1963.

AWARDS, HONORS: Kate Greenaway Award, British Library Association (BLA), 1969, for *The Quangle-Wangle's Hat;* Baby Book Award, Sainsbury's, 1999, for *Tickle, Tickle;* Kurt Maschler Award, 1999, and Kate Greenaway Award, BLA, 2000, both for *Alice's Adventures in Wonderland;* Boston Globe-Horn Book Picture Book Award, 2003, for *Big Momma Makes the World.*

WRITINGS:

SELF-ILLUSTRATED

Numbers of Things, Heinemann (London, England), 1967, F. Watts (New York, NY), 1968, published as *Helen Oxenbury's Numbers of Things,* Delacorte (New York, NY), 1983.

Helen Oxenbury's ABC of Things, Heinemann (London, England), 1971, published as *ABC of Things,* F. Watts (New York, NY), 1972.

Pig Tale, Morrow (New York, NY), 1973.

The Queen and Rosie Randall (from an idea by Jill Buttfield-Campbell), Heinemann (London, England), 1978, Morrow (New York, NY), 1979.

729 Curious Creatures, Harper (New York, NY), 1980, published as *Curious Creatures,* HarperCollins (New York, NY), 1985.

729 Animal Allsorts, Methuen (London, England), 1980, published as *729 Merry Mix-ups,* Harper (New York, NY), 1980, published as *Merry Mix-ups,* HarperCollins (New York, NY), 1985.

729 Puzzle People, Harper (New York, NY), 1980, published as *Puzzle People,* HarperCollins (New York, NY), 1985.

Bill and Stanley, Benn (London, England), 1981.

Dressing, Simon & Schuster (New York, NY), 1981.

Family, Simon & Schuster (New York, NY), 1981.

Friends, Simon & Schuster (New York, NY), 1981.

Playing, Simon & Schuster (New York, NY), 1981.

Working, Simon & Schuster (New York, NY), 1981.

Holidays, Walker Books (London, England), 1982.

Bedtime, Walker Books (London, England), 1982.

Shopping, Walker Books (London, England), 1982, published as *Shopping Trip,* Dial Books for Young Readers (New York, NY), 1982.

Mother's Helper, Dial Books for Young Readers (New York, NY), 1982.

Good Night, Good Morning, Dial Books for Young Readers (New York, NY), 1982.

Beach Day, Dial Books for Young Readers (New York, NY), 1982.

The Birthday Party, Dial Books for Young Readers (New York, NY), 1983.

The Drive, Walker Books (London, England), 1983, published as *The Car Trip,* Dial Books for Young Readers (New York, NY), 1983.

The Checkup, Dial Books for Young Readers (New York, NY), 1983.

The Dancing Class, Dial Books for Young Readers (New York, NY), 1983.

Eating Out, Dial Books for Young Readers (New York, NY), 1983.

Playschool, Walker Books (London, England), 1983, published as *First Day of School,* Dial Books for Young Readers (New York, NY), 1983.

Gran and Granpa, Walker Books (London, England), 1984, published as *Grandma and Grandpa,* Dial Books for Young Readers (New York, NY), 1984.

The Visitor, Walker Books (London, England), 1984, published as *The Important Visitor,* Dial Books for Young Readers (New York, NY), 1984.

Our Dog, Dial Books for Young Readers (New York, NY), 1984.

(Reteller) *The Helen Oxenbury Nursery Story Book,* Knopf (New York, NY), 1985, excerpts published as *Favorite Nursery Stories* and *First Nursery Stories,* Macmillan (New York, NY), 1994.

I Can, Walker Books (London, England), 1985, Random House (New York, NY), 1986.

I Hear, Walker Books (London, England), 1985, Random House (New York, NY), 1986.

I See, Walker Books (London, England), 1985, Random House (New York, NY), 1986.

I Touch, Walker Books (London, England), 1985, Random House (New York, NY), 1986.

Baby's First Book and Doll, Simon & Schuster (New York, NY), 1986.

All Fall Down, Aladdin Books (New York, NY), 1987.

Say Goodnight, Aladdin Books (New York, NY), 1987.

Tickle, Tickle, Aladdin Books (New York, NY), 1987.

Clap Hands, Aladdin Books (New York, NY), 1987.

Monkey See, Monkey Do, Dial Books for Young Readers (New York, NY), 1991.

It's My Birthday, Candlewick Press (Cambridge, MA), 1994.

Helen Oxenbury's Big Baby Book, Candlewick Press (Cambridge, MA), 2003.

"TOM AND PIPPO" SERIES; SELF-ILLUSTRATED

Tom and Pippo Go for a Walk, Aladdin Books (New York, NY), 1988.

Tom and Pippo Make a Mess, Aladdin Books (New York, NY), 1988.

Tom and Pippo Read a Story, Aladdin Books (New York, NY), 1988.

Tom and Pippo and the Washing Machine, Aladdin Books (New York, NY), 1988.

Tom and Pippo Go Shopping, Walker Books (London, England), 1988, Aladdin Books (New York, NY), 1989.

Tom and Pippo See the Moon, Walker Books (London, England), 1988, Aladdin Books (New York, NY), 1989.

Tom and Pippo's Day, Walker Books (London, England), 1988, Aladdin Books (New York, NY), 1989.

Tom and Pippo in the Garden, Walker Books (London, England), 1988, Aladdin Books (New York, NY), 1989.

Tom and Pippo in the Snow, Aladdin Books (New York, NY), 1989.

Tom and Pippo Make a Friend, Aladdin Books (New York, NY), 1989.

Pippo Gets Lost, Aladdin Books (New York, NY), 1989.

Tom and Pippo and the Dog, Aladdin Books (New York, NY), 1989.

Tom and Pippo on the Beach, Walker Books (London, England), 1992, Candlewick Press (Cambridge, MA), 1993.

Tom and Pippo and the Bicycle, Candlewick Press (Cambridge, MA), 1993.

Tom and Pippo and Tom's Boots, Campbell (London, England), 1999.

Tom and Pippo at the Doctor, Campbell (London, England), 1999.

Tom and Pippo at the Seaside, Campbell (London, England), 1999.

ILLUSTRATOR

Alexei Tolstoy, *The Great Big Enormous Turnip,* translated by E. Scimanskaya, F. Watts (New York, NY), 1968.

Edward Lear, *The Quangle-Wangle's Hat,* Heinemann (London, England), 1969, F. Watts (New York, NY), 1970.

Manghanita Kempadoo, *Letters of Thanks,* Simon & Schuster (New York, NY), 1969.

Margaret Mahy, *The Dragon of an Ordinary Family,* F. Watts (New York, NY), 1969.

Lewis Carroll, *The Hunting of the Snark,* F. Watts (New York, NY), 1970.

Ivor Cutler, *Meal One,* F. Watts (New York, NY), 1971.

Brian Anderson, compiler, *Cakes and Custard,* Heinemann (London, England), 1974, Morrow (New York, NY), 1975, revised abridged version with new illustrations published as *The Helen Oxenbury Nursery Rhyme Book,* Heinemann (London, England), 1986, Morrow (New York, NY), 1987.

Ivor Cutler, *Balooky Klujypop,* Heinemann (London, England), 1975, published as *Elephant Girl,* Morrow (New York, NY), 1976.

Ivor Cutler, *The Animal House,* Heinemann (London, England), 1976, Morrow (New York, NY), 1977.

Fay Maschler, *A Child's Book of Manners,* J. Cape (London, England), 1978, Atheneum (New York, NY), 1979.

Jill Bennett, selector, *Tiny Tim: Verses for Children,* Heinemann (London, England), 1981, Delacorte (New York, NY), 1982.

Michael Rosen, *We're Going on a Bear Hunt,* Macmillan (New York, NY), 1989.

Martin Waddell, *Farmer Duck,* Walker Books (London, England), 1991, Candlewick Press (Cambridge, MA), 1992.

Eugene Trivizas, *The Three Little Wolves and the Big Bad Pig,* Margaret K. McElderry Books (New York, NY), 1993.

Trish Cooke, *So Much,* Walker Books (London, England), 1994, Candlewick Press (Cambridge, MA), 1995.

Lewis Carroll, *Alice's Adventures in Wonderland,* Candlewick Press (Cambridge, MA), 1999.

Harriet Lerner and Susan Goldhor, *Franny B. Kranny, There's a Bird in Your Hair!,* HarperCollins (New York, NY), 2000, Walker Books (London, England), 2001.

Phyllis Root, *Big Momma Makes the World,* Walker Books (London, England), Candlewick Press (Cambridge, MA), 2002.

Ruth Krauss, *The Growing Story,* HarperCollins (New York, NY), 2004.

SIDELIGHTS: "Helen Oxenbury is the book world's foremost authority on the antics (and anatomy) of small people," Tim Wynne-Jones wrote in the *Toronto Globe and Mail.* Oxenbury was one of the first writers to design "board books," the small, durable, thick-paged creations intended especially for toddlers. In stories such as *Friends, The Car Trip,* and those in the "Tom and Pippo" series, Oxenbury shows babies, toddlers, and preschool-age children discovering new things and learning about life. Her uncomplicated and humorous illustrations have as much to tell her "readers" as her words do. As a result, "there is not a wrinkle of pudgy flesh nor bulge of diaper she has not lovingly portrayed in her bright, watercolor survey of early childhood," Wynne-Jones added.

Oxenbury did not plan on becoming an illustrator when she was young. Instead, she found a talent for designing and painting scenery for plays. She began working in local theaters as a teenager, and chose to attend a college where she could study set design. At school, she met her future husband, John Burningham, who was interested in illustration and graphic design. She later followed him to Israel, where she worked as a scenery designer. After the couple returned to England, Burningham published his first book, the award-winning children's story *Borka,* and Oxenbury continued working in the theater. Shortly after the couple married in 1964, they had their first two children. Oxenbury left her career as a designer to care for them. "In those days it was jolly difficult to do two things, and we didn't have money for nannies," Oxenbury explained to Michele Field of *Publishers Weekly.* "I wanted something to do at home, and having watched John do children's books, I thought that was possible."

Two of Oxenbury's first projects were illustrations for books by Lewis Carroll, the author of *Alice in Wonderland,* and Edward Lear, known for his fanciful, colorful poems. In choosing to illustrate these works, Oxenbury found the books' humor most appealing. As she revealed in a *Junior Bookshelf* article, it was "the marvellous mixture of weird people in dreamlike situations surprising one by doing and saying quite ordinary and down-to-earth things one minute, and absurd, out-rageous things the next" that made up her mind to take the jobs. She captured this contradictory feeling in Edward Lear's *The Quangle-Wangle's Hat* with pic-tures of strange creatures and the magical hat of many ribbons, loops, and bows. As Crispin Fisher noted in *Children and Literature,* "Her landscape is wide and magical, neither inviting nor repelling, but inexpli-cable—surely right for a Lear setting."

Oxenbury's first solo project was *Numbers of Things,* a picture book which uses familiar objects and animals to introduce young children to counting. Oxenbury covers single numbers from one to ten, then twenty through fifty by tens. The amusing pictures, "with their twenty balloons and fifty ladybirds, will help the child to comprehend the difference in quantity between these numbers," a *Junior Bookshelf* reviewer said. "But a fiddle-dee-dee on its instructional aspect!," a *Publishers Weekly* reviewer advised. "A hurrah instead for the fun of it all!" With its humorous yet simple ap-proach and "shape, originality, and use of colour," Jean Russell commented in *Books for Your Children, Numbers of Things* "immediately established [Oxen-bury] as a major children's book artist."

Just like *Numbers of Things,* Oxenbury's follow-up *ABC of Things* has "pictures that are imaginative and humorous as well as handsome," creating "a far better than average ABC book," Zena Sutherland said in the *Bulletin of the Center for Children's Books.* Each letter is joined with several pictures that match it and can serve to spur the imagination. "The most incongruous associations are made in a perfectly matter-of-fact way," wrote a *Times Literary Supplement* reviewer, "setting the mind off in pursuit of the stories that must lie behind them."

Oxenbury began developing sturdy books for toddlers when her youngest child, Emily, was sick. "We were up half the night with her," the author told Field in *Publishers Weekly,* "and we had to think of things to show her to keep her mind off [her illness]." To make a book more appealing to such a young "reader," Ox-enbury simplified her drawing style and focused on stories of babies and toddlers. She modified her layout so that a page with words would be paired with a larger, wordless, illustration. Finally, the books were to be made in smaller, square shapes that would be easier for little hands to manage. And the book's thicker pages would stand up to the chewing and abuse that any toddler's toy must survive.

Oxenbury's first series of board books, including *Dressing, Family, Friends, Playing,* and *Working,* are "perfectly in tune with the interests of the teething population, and at the same time executed with wit and the artistic awareness that at this age less is more," Betsy Hearne wrote in *Booklist.* "The pictures them-selves are simple," Robert Wilson similarly noted in *Washington Post Book World,* "yet everywhere in the drawings there is subtle humor," as well as "a keen-ness of observation on the artist's part, a familiarity with the ways of the baby." And with their "masterful" portrayals of young children, especially the "delight-fully lump-faced baby," Oxenbury's books are "cer-tainly the series most likely to appeal to adults," Lucy Micklethwait concluded in the *Times Literary Supplement.*

Other collections have followed the baby as it grows into new abilities and activities. One series shows a toddler going to the beach, going shopping with mother, and helping out at home. The books are "fun, but more than that," Sutherland said in a review of *Shopping Trip* for *Bulletin of the Center for Children's Books;* they are also "geared to the toddler's interests and experiences."

Later series show children doing many things for the first time, such as going to a birthday party, visiting the doctor, going to school, and eating in a restaurant. Each episode usually involves some sort of mishap; in *The Dancing Class,* for example, a little girl trips and causes a pileup of students. "Comedy is always central to Oxenbury's vignettes," observed Denise M. Wilms in *Booklist,* and both kids and adults are targets in "these affectionate mirror views of their own foibles." In addition, Oxenbury "not only knows how children move but also how they think," Mary M. Burns of *Horn Book* said, for her easy writing style resembles "the matter-of-fact reportorial style used by young children." As always, her "clever and colorful" il-lustrations contribute to "the subtle humor" of the story, Amanda J. Williams noted in a *School Library Journal* review of *Our Dog.*

Although she is writing and drawing for a very young audience, Oxenbury tries not to underestimate their ability to understand things. "I believe children to be very canny people who immediately sense if adults talk, write, or illustrate down to them, hence the un-popularity of self-conscious, child-like drawings that appear in some children's books," the author wrote in

Junior Bookshelf. "The illustrator is misguidedly thinking the child will be able to identify more easily with drawings similar to his own, while probably he is disgusted that adults cannot do better." Oxenbury's own drawings are uncluttered rather than simple, and include many humorous details that adults, as well as children, can enjoy.

In *The Helen Oxenbury Nursery Story Book,* for instance, "her drawings really do add another dimension to each tale, and answer some of the questions that spring to a child's mind," Marcus Crouch commented in *Junior Bookshelf.* In this collection, the author retells, with her own illustrations, favorite stories such as "The Three Pigs," "Little Red Riding Hood," and eight others. "A collection of simple folk tales may not be unique," Ethel L. Heins wrote in *Horn Book,* "but an extraordinarily attractive one for early independent reading surely is." A major part of the book's charm lies in its pictures, "which give [the stories] a special, strongly personal and essentially youthful feeling," Margery Fisher commented in *Growing Point.* "At every turning of the page, an illustration delights the eye," Heins added. Throughout the book "the artwork exudes vigor, movement," as well as a lively humor "that manages to be both naive and sly."

In the late 1980s, Oxenbury introduced the recurring characters of Tom and Pippo in a series of picture books. Tom is a young boy with a constant companion in his stuffed monkey, Pippo. Oxenbury's pictures again display her simple yet revealing style; even Pippo's face is "worth watching, whether he is frowning as he is stuffed into the washing machine or reaching down longingly from the clothesline towards Tom's outstretched arm," a *Publishers Weekly* critic remarked. The volumes also exhibit the broadly appealing humor that is the author's trademark. "Oxenbury understands her audience; young people as well as adults will find pleasure in repeated readings of these unassuming gems, and no one will be able to resist the facial expressions and postures of the long-suffering Pippo," Ellen Fader wrote in *Horn Book.*

Returning to the works of Lewis Carroll, Oxenbury took on the challenge of illustrating a new edition of *Alice's Adventures in Wonderland.* Her vision of Carroll's classic's up-side-down land, described by *Booklist* contributor Michael Cart as "a soft, beautiful, springtime world," garnered her the prestigious Kate Greenaway Award for illustration. Oxenbury updates

the setting, which "makes it even more appealing and accessible to modern readers," thought *Christian Science Monitor*'s Karen Carden. Instead of the traditional Alice, with her fancy Victorian dress and well-arranged ring-curls, Oxenbury's heroine wears a denim jumper and sneakers. Oxenbury also softened some of the scarier aspects of Carroll's tale; "the villains here are more stoogelike than menacing," wrote a *Publishers Weekly* reviewer. As a *Horn Book* contributor explained it, "Oxenbury delineates the story's humor with a gentle hand"; her "illustrations have a sweetness of tone and an amiable spirit."

Oxenbury also illustrated Harriet Lerner and Susan Goldhor's *Franny B. Kranny, There's a Bird in Your Hair!,* a humorous story about a free-spirited girl with equally free-spirited, frizzy hair in a family of strait-laced, well-coifed women. "Oxenbury's spirited illustrations . . . give loads of personality to the characters," noted a *Horn Book* reviewer. Oxenbury accomplishes this through telling details, such as Franny's mother's perfect, elaborate hairdo and her flawless manicure, and Mr. Kranny's reading glasses, which "give him a perennially perplexed look," Ann Cook wrote in *School Library Journal.* Reviewing *Franny B. Kranny* in *Booklist,* Gillian Engberg found the title "breezy fun for story hours, with plenty of discussion opportunities."

Oxenbury turned in another award-winning performance with her illustrations for *Big Momma Makes the World,* written by Phyllis Root. Root retells the traditional Creation story from Genesis, but with the twist that the male God is replaced by Big Momma, who does things a bit differently. "Oxenbury's luminous, oversized acrylics perfectly capture the strong, no-nonsense personality of this barefoot creator," thought *School Library Journal* reviewer Laurie von Mehren. Oxenbury's paintings also "aptly convey the tone of each day's production," a reviewer noted in *Kirkus Reviews.* Her palette changes as the creation progresses, from shades of black before the sun is made to an ever-increasing display of color as golden light and multi-colored birds, fish, flowers, and animals appear. Writing in *Horn Book,* Johanna Rudge Long found "the illustrations . . . superb, surprising the eye with their joyous variety," while *Booklist*'s Ilene Cooper called *Big Momma* "an exciting, new version of one of the world's oldest stories."

Although the field of board books is now very popular, "old reliable Helen Oxenbury remains a standard against which to judge new entries," Sandra Martin wrote in the Toronto *Globe and Mail.* A reviewer for the *Bulletin of the Center for Children's Books* likewise found that Oxenbury is "still one of the best in terms of maintaining simple concepts, lively art, and action generated from objects." "All Helen's pictures have a vibrant wit and delicacy which is so vital in stimulating the imaginative child," Russell explained in *Books for Your Children.* "In Oxenbury's case, familiarity breeds not contempt, but admiration," Carolyn Phelan remarked in *Booklist.* "Using everyday concepts, simple drawings, and minimal color, she gives a child's view of ordinary things, creating books that are fresh, original, and appealing to both parents and children."

Despite her success with board books, Oxenbury continues to expand her accomplishments in another area. "I don't want to be pigeonholed," the illustrator told Field in *Publishers Weekly.* "It's that which I want to avoid more than anything else." Her main desire, she continued, is to fill the need for quality children's books that stand out among the crowd. "There are millions and millions of mediocre children's books. I hope we're not part of that."

BIOGRAPHICAL AND CRITICAL SOURCES:

BOOKS

Carpenter, Humphrey, and Mari Prichard, *The Oxford Companion to Children's Literature,* Oxford University Press (Oxford, England), 1984.
Children's Literature Review, Gale (Detroit, MI), Volume 22, 1991, Volume 70, 2001.
Haviland, Virginia, editor, *Children and Literature: Views and Reviews,* Scott, Foresman (Glenview, IL), 1973.
Kingman, Lee, Grace Allen Hogarth, and Harriet Quimby, compilers, *Illustrators of Children's Books, 1967-1976,* Horn Book (Boston, MA), 1978.
Martin, Douglas, *The Telling Line: Essays on Fifteen Contemporary Book Illustrators,* Julia McRae Books (London, England), 1989.
Moss, Elaine, *Children's Books of the Year: 1974,* Hamish Hamilton (London, England), 1975.
St. James Guide to Children's Writers, 5th edition, St. James Press (Detroit, MI), 1999.
Silvey, Anita, editor, *Children's Books and Their Creators,* Houghton Mifflin (Boston, MA), 1995.

Sutherland, Zena, and May Hill Arbuthnot, *Children and Books,* 7th edition, Scott, Foresman (Glenview, IL), 1986.
Ward, Martha E., *Authors of Books for Young People,* 3rd edition, Scarecrow Press (Metuchen, NJ), 1990.
Ward, Martha E., and Dorothy A. Marquardt, *Illustrators of Books for Young People,* 2nd edition, Scarecrow Press (Metuchen, NJ), 1975.

PERIODICALS

Booklist, May 1, 1981, Betsy Hearne, review of *Dressing* and others, p. 1198; May 15, 1983, Betsy Hearne, review of *Beach Day* and others, p. 1258; September 1, 1983, Denise M. Wilms, review of *The Car Trip, The Checkup,* and *First Day of School,* p. 89; June 1, 1986, Carolyn Phelan, review of *I Can* and others, pp. 1462-1463; April 1, 1992, Ilene Cooper, review of *Farmer Duck,* p. 1449; June 1, 1993, Carolyn Phelan, review of *Tom and Pippo on the Beach,* pp. 1859-1860; September 1, 1993, review of *The Three Little Wolves and the Big Bad Pig,* p. 59; March 1, 1995, Ilene Cooper, review of *So Much,* p. 1240; November 15, 1995, Hazel Rochman, review of *The Candlewick Book of Bedtime Stories,* p. 563A; January 1, 2000, Michael Cart, review of *Alice's Adventures in Wonderland,* p. 922; June 1, 2001, Gillian Engberg, review of *Franny B. Kranny, There's a Bird in Your Hair!,* p. 1891; January 1, 2003, Ilene Cooper, review of *Big Momma Makes the World,* p. 881.
Books for Your Children, autumn, 1978, Jean Russell, "Cover Artist: Helen Oxenbury," p. 3.
Bulletin of the Center for Children's Books, February, 1973, Zena Sutherland, review of *Helen Oxenbury's ABC of Things,* p. 96; April, 1982, Zena Sutherland, review of *Shopping Trip,* pp. 155-156; June, 1986, review of *I Can* and others, p. 193.
Christian Science Monitor, November 10, 1989, Heather Vogel Frederick, review of *We're Going on a Bear Hunt,* p. 12; December 9, 1999, Karen Carden, review of *Alice's Adventures in Wonderland,* p. 18.
Entertainment Weekly, June 26, 1992, Michele Landsberg, review of *Farmer Duck,* p. 124; April 30, 1993, Michele Landsberg, review of *Tom and Pippo on the Beach,* p. 69.

Globe and Mail (Toronto, Ontario, Canada), March 16, 1985, Sandra Martin, "By the Boards: Words to Chew On"; April 30, 1988, Tim Wynne-Jones, "A Start to the Page-Turning Experience."

Growing Point, January, 1986, Margery Fisher, review of *The Helen Oxenbury Nursery Story Book,* p. 4548.

Horn Book, February, 1976; April, 1982, review of *Tiny Tim: Verses for Children,* p. 176; June 20, 1983, review of *Eating Out, The Dancing Class,* and *The Birthday Party,* p. 294; November-December, 1984, Mary M. Burns, review of *Grandma and Grandpa, The Important Visitor,* and *Our Dog,* p. 752; January-February, 1986, Ethel L. Heins, review of *The Helen Oxenbury Nursery Story Book,* p. 65; September-October, 1986, Margaret A. Bush, review of *I Can, I Hear, I See,* and *I Touch,* pp. 578-579; January-February, 1989, Ethel L. Heins, review of *Tom and Pippo and the Washing Machine, Tom and Pippo Go for a Walk, Tom and Pippo Make a Mess,* and *Tom and Pippo Read a Story,* p. 56; May-June, 1989, Ellen Fader, review of *Tom and Pippo Go Shopping* and others, pp. 361-362; November-December, 1989, Elizabeth S. Watson, review of *We're Going on a Bear Hunt,* pp. 764-765; September-October, 1992, Ann A. Flowers, review of *Farmer Duck,* p. 606; July-August, 1993, Martha V. Parravano, review of *Tom and Pippo on the Beach,* p. 449; January-February, 1995, Hanna B. Zeiger, review of *Tom and Pippo and the Bicycle,* pp. 51-52; March-April, 1995, Martha V. Parravano, review of *It's My Birthday,* pp. 186-187; January, 2000, review of *Alice's Adventures in Wonderland,* p. 72; July, 2001, review of *Franny B. Kranny, There's a Bird in Your Hair!,* p. 441; March-April, 2003, Joanna Rudge Long, review of *Big Momma Makes the World,* pp. 205-207; January-February, 2004, Phyllis Root and Helen Oxenbury, transcript of *Boston Globe-Horn Book* award acceptance speech, p. 17.

Independent (London, England), October 1, 1999, Judith Judd, "*Tickle, Tickle* Beats Off *Peek-a-Boo,*" p. 7.

Instructor and Teacher, September, 1982, Allan Yeager, review of *Tiny Tim,* p. 20.

Junior Bookshelf, April, 1968, review of *Numbers of Things,* p. 97; August, 1970, Helen Oxenbury, "Drawing for Children," pp. 199-201; October, 1985, Marcus Crouch, review of *The Helen Oxenbury Nursery Story Book,* p. 220.

Kirkus Reviews, January 1, 1989; January 15, 2003, review of *Big Momma Makes the World,* p. 146.

New York Times Book Review, November 16, 1975; March 29, 1981, George A. Woods, review of *Working, Playing, Friends, Family,* and *Dressing,* p. 38; October 9, 1983, Selma G. Lanes, review of *ABC of Things,* p. 38; January 27, 1985, review of *Grandma and Grandpa,* p. 29; November 14, 1993, Linda Phillips Ashour, review of *The Three Little Wolves and the Big Bad Pig,* p. 56; November 21, 1999, Rebecca Pepper Sinkler, review of *Alice's Adventures in Wonderland,* p. 40; May 20, 2001, Jane Margolies, review of *Franny B. Kranny, There's a Bird in Your Hair!,* p. S29; December 22, 2002, Sandy MacDonald, review of *Big Momma Makes the World,* p. 18.

Parenting, April, 1992, Leonard S. Marcus, review of *Farmer Duck,* p. 30; June-July, 1992, Leonard S. Marcus, review of *Beach Day,* p. 29.

Publishers Weekly, April 8, 1968, review of *Numbers of Things,* p. 51; January 22, 1982, review of *Tiny Tim,* p. 65; March 12, 1982, review of *Good Night, Good Morning,* p. 84; March 27, 1982, review of *Working,* p. 51; May 7, 1982, review of *Tiny Tim,* p. 79; March 18, 1983, review of *The Birthday Party,* p. 71; November 11, 1983, review of *Helen Oxenbury's ABC of Things,* p. 48; November 2, 1984, review of *The Important Visitor,* pp. 77-78; April 25, 1986, review of *I Can, I Hear, I See,* and *I Touch,* p. 75; June 26, 1987, review of *Say Goodnight, All Fall Down, Clap Hands,* and *Tickle, Tickle,* p. 69; July 24, 1987, Michele Field, "PW Interviews: John Burningham and Helen Oxenbury," pp. 168-169; July 29, 1988, review of *Tom and Pippo and the Washing Machine, Tom and Pippo Go for a Walk, Tom and Pippo Make a Mess,* and *Tom and Pippo Read a Story,* p. 230; June 30, 1989, review of *We're Going on a Bear Hunt,* p. 104; January 20, 1992, review of *Farmer Duck,* p. 64; June 28, 1993, review of *The Three Little Wolves and the Big Bad Pig,* p. 77; June 20, 1994, review of *It's My Birthday,* p. 104; November 14, 1994, review of *So Much,* pp. 66-67; November 1, 1999, review of *Alice's Adventures in Wonderland,* p. 84; January 3, 2000, Julia Eccleshare, "Emil-Maschler Award," p. 34; May 21, 2001, review of *Franny B. Kranny, There's a Bird in Your Hair!,* p. 107; November 25, 2002, review of *Big Momma Makes the World,* p. 66; August 11, 2003, review of *Farmer Duck,* p. 281.

School Library Journal, March, 1981, Patricia Homer, review of *Merry Mix-Ups, 729 Puzzle People* and *729 Curious Creatures,* p. 135; October, 1981, Joan W. Blos, review of *Working, Playing, Friends,*

Family, and *Dressing,* p. 133; August, 1982, Ellen Fader, review of *Beach Day, Mother's Helper, Shopping Trip,* and *Monkey See, Monkey Do,* p. 104; March, 1983, Marge Loch-Wouters, review of *Beach Day, Dressing, Family, Friends, Good Night, Good Morning, Mother's Helper, Monkey See, Monkey Do, Playing,* and *Shopping Trip,* p. 121; October, 1983, Dana Whitney Pinizzotto, review of *The Checkup,* p. 152; January, 1984, review of *The First Day of School* and *The Car Trip,* p. 67; February, 1985, Amanda J. Williams, review of *Grandma and Grandpa, The Important Visitor,* and *Our Dog,* p. 68; December, 1985, review of *The Helen Oxenbury Nursery Story Book,* pp. 79-80; August, 1986, Jacqueline Elsner, review of *I Can, I Hear, I See,* and *I Touch,* p. 86; September, 1987, Nancy Kewish, review of *All Fall Down, Clap Hands, Say Goodnight,* and *Tickle, Tickle,* pp. 167-168; April, 1989, Sharron McElmeel, review of *Tom and Pippo and the Washing Machine, Tom and Pippo Go for a Walk, Tom and Pippo Make a Mess,* and *Tom and Pippo Read a Story,* pp. 88-89; January, 1990; May, 1992, Trev Jones, review of *Farmer Duck,* p. 94; August, 1993, Jeanne Marie Clancy, review of *Tom and Pippo on the Beach,* p. 149; December, 1993, Karen James, review of *The Three Little Wolves and the Big Bad Pig,* p. 95; November, 1994, Elaine Lesh Morgan, review of *It's My Birthday,* p. 87; January, 1995, Lisa S. Murphy, review of *Tom and Pippo and the Bicycle,* p. 91, and Anna DeWind, review of *So Much,* p. 83; August, 1995, Rose Zertuche Trevino, review of *The Three Little Wolves and the Big Bad Pig,* p. 167; January, 2000, Heide Piehler, review of *Alice's Adventures in Wonderland,* p. 93; June, 2001, Ann Cook, review of *Franny B. Kranny, There's a Bird in Your Hair!,* p. 122; March, 2003, Laurie von Mehren, review of *Big Momma Makes the World,* p. 206.

Seattle Times (Seattle, WA), April 17, 1999, Kari Wergeland, "Big Draw for Kids: Illustrator Helen Oxenbury's Board Books Have Clear, Simple Images—And Often Speak to Both Children and Adults," p. D1.

Times Educational Supplement, September 8, 1989, William Feaver, review of *We're Going on a Bear Hunt,* p. 32; April 14, 1995, Susan Thomas, "Life Drawing," pp. 17-18.

Times Literary Supplement, December 3, 1971, "Good Enough to Keep," pp. 1514-1515; November 23, 1973; July 24, 1981, Lucy Micklethwait, "The Indestructible Word," p. 840; November 20, 1981.

Washington Post Book World, March 8, 1981, Robert Wilson, "Please Don't Eat the Pages," pp. 10-11; March 14, 1982.

ONLINE

Youth Library Review, http://www.cilip.org.uk/ (spring, 2001), "Helen Oxenbury: What It's Like Winning the Kate Greenaway Award."

P

PETERS, Gabriel
See MATOTT, Justin

*   *   *

PIERS, Robert
See PIERS, Anthony

*   *   *

PLIMPTON, George (Ames) 1927-2003

George Plimpton

PERSONAL: Born March 18, 1927, in New York, NY; died September 25, 2003, in New York, NY; son of Francis T. P. (a lawyer and former U.S. deputy representative to the United Nations) and Pauline (Ames) Plimpton; married Freddy Medora Espy (a photography studio assistant), March 28, 1968 (divorced, 1988); married Sarah Whitehead Dudley, 1991; children: (first marriage) Medora Ames, Taylor Ames, (second marriage) Olivia Hartley, Laura Dudley. *Education:* Harvard University, A.B., 1948; King's College, Cambridge, B.A., 1952, M.A., 1954. *Politics:* Democrat.

CAREER: Writer and editor. Editor of Harvard *Lampoon,* c. 1948-50; *Paris Review,* principal editor, beginning 1953, publisher, with Doubleday & Co., of Paris Review Editions (books), beginning 1965. *Horizon,* associate editor, 1959-61; *Sports Illustrated,* contributing editor, beginning 1967; *Harper's,* associate editor, beginning 1972; *Food and Wine,* contributing editor, 1978; *Realities,* member of editorial advisory board, 1978. American Literature Anthology program, director, beginning 1967; National Foundation on the Arts and Humanities, chief editor of annual anthology of work from literary magazines; adviser on John F. Kennedy Oral History Project. Instructor at Barnard College, 1956-58; associate fellow, Trumbull College, Yale, 1967. Occasional actor in films; journalistic par-

359

ticipant in sporting and musical events. Honorary commissioner of New York City fireworks, beginning 1973. Trustee, National Art Museum of Sport, beginning 1967, WNET-TV, beginning 1973, Police Athletic League, beginning 1976, African Wildlife Leadership Foundation, beginning 1980, and Guild Hall, East Hampton, beginning 1980. *Military service:* U.S. Army, 1945-48; became second lieutenant.

MEMBER: PEN, Pyrotechnics Guild International, American Pyrotechniques Association, NFL Alumni Association, Mayflower Descendants Society; clubs include Century Association, Racquet and Tennis, Brook, Dutch Treat, Coffee House, Devon Yacht, Travelers (Paris), Explorers.

AWARDS, HONORS: Distinguished achievement award, University of Southern California, 1967; Mark Twain Award, International Platform Association, 1982; inducted into Ordre des Arts et des Lettres (France), 1994; honorary degrees include Franklin Pierce College, 1968, Hobart Smith College, 1978, Stonehill College, 1982, University of Southern California, 1986, and Pine Manor College, 1988; named chevalier, French Legion of Honor, 2002; inducted into American Academy of Arts and Letters, 2002.

WRITINGS:

EDITOR

Writers at Work: The Paris Review Interviews, Viking (New York, NY), Volume 1, 1957, Volume 2, 1963, Volume 3, 1967, Volume 4, 1976, Volume 5, 1981, Volume 6, 1984, Volume 7, 1986, Volume 8, 1988, Volume 9, 1992.

(With Peter Ardery) *The American Literary Anthology,* number 1, Farrar, Straus (New York, NY), 1968, number 2, Random House (New York, NY), 1969, number 3, Viking (New York, NY), 1970.

(With Jean Stein) *American Journey: The Times of Robert Kennedy* (interviews), Harcourt (New York, NY), 1970.

Jean Stein, *Edie: An American Biography,* Knopf (New York, NY), 1982, published as *Edie: American Girl,* Grove Press (New York, NY), 1994.

(With Christopher Hemphill) Diana Vreeland, *D.V.,* Random House (New York, NY), 1984.

Fireworks: A History and Celebration, Doubleday (Garden City, NY), 1984.

Poets at Work: The Paris Review Interviews, Viking (New York, NY), 1989.

Women Writers at Work, Viking (New York, NY), 1989.

The Writer's Chapbook: A Compendium of Fact, Opinion, Wit, and Advice from the Twentieth-Century's Preeminent Writers, Viking (New York, NY), 1989.

The Best of Bad Hemingway: Choice Entries from the Harry's Bar & American Grill Imitation Hemingway Competition, Harcourt (San Diego, CA), Volume 1, 1989, Volume 2, 1991.

The Paris Review Anthology, Norton (New York, NY), 1990.

Playwrights at Work, Modern Library (New York, NY), 2000.

Home Run, Harcourt (San Diego, CA), 2001.

As Told at the Explorers Club: More than Fifty Gripping Tales of Adventure, Lyons Press (Guilford, CT), 2003.

Latin American Writers at Work/ The Paris Review, introduction by Derek Walcott, Modern Library (New York, NY), 2003.

SPORTS WRITING

Out of My League (baseball anecdotes), Harper (New York, NY), 1961.

Paper Lion (football anecdotes), Harper (New York, NY), 1966.

The Bogey Man (golf anecdotes), Harper (New York, NY), 1968.

(Editor and author of introduction) Pierre Etchebaster, *Pierre's Book: The Game of Court Tennis,* Barre Publishers (Barre, MA), 1971.

(With Alex Karras and John Gordy) *Mad Ducks and Bears: Football Revisited* (football anecdotes), Random House (New York, NY), 1973.

One for the Record: The Inside Story of Hank Aaron's Chase for the Home Run Record, Harper (New York, NY), 1974.

Shadow Box (boxing anecdotes), Putnam (New York, NY), 1977.

One More July: A Football Dialogue with Bill Curry, Harper (New York, NY), 1977.

Sports!, photographs by Neil Leifer, H. N. Abrams (New York, NY), 1978.

A Sports Bestiary (cartoons), illustrated by Arnold Roth, McGraw-Hill (New York, NY), 1982.

Open Net (hockey anecdotes), Norton (New York, NY), 1985.

The Curious Case of Sidd Finch (baseball novel), Macmillan (New York, NY), 1987, reprinted, Four Walls Eight Windows (New York, NY), 2004

The X Factor, Whittle Direct (Knoxville, TN), 1990, revised edition, Norton (New York, NY), 1995.

The Best of Plimpton, Atlantic Monthly Press (New York, NY), 1990.

The Official Olympics Triplecast Viewer's Guide, Barcelona commemorative edition, Pindar, 1992.

The Norton Book of Sports, Norton (New York, NY), 1992.

George Plimpton on Sports, Lyons Press (Guilford, CT), 2003.

OTHER

The Rabbit's Umbrella (juvenile), Viking (New York, NY), 1955.

(With William Kronick) *Plimpton! Shoot-out at Rio Lobo* (script), American Broadcasting Company (ABC-TV), 1970.

Plimpton! The Man on the Flying Trapeze (script), ABC-TV, 1970.

(With William Kronick) *Plimpton! Did You Hear the One About . . . ?* (script), ABC-TV, 1971.

(With William Kronick) *Plimpton! The Great Quarterback Sneak* (script), ABC-TV, 1971.

(With William Kronick) *Plimpton! Adventure in Africa* (script), ABC-TV, 1972.

(Author of introduction) Bill Plympton, *Medium Rare: Cartoons,* Holt (New York, NY), 1978.

(Author of introduction) *Oakes Ames: Jottings of a Harvard Botanist, 1874-1950,* edited by Pauline Ames Plimpton, Harvard University Press (Cambridge, MA), 1980.

(With Jean Kennedy Smith) *Chronicles of Courage: Very Special Artists* (interviews), Random House (New York, NY), 1993.

Truman Capote: In Which Various Friends, Enemies, Acquaintances, and Detractors Recall His Turbulent Career, Doubleday (Garden City, NY), 1997.

Pet Peeves; or, Whatever Happened to Doctor Rawff?, Atlantic Monthly Press (New York, NY), 2000.

A & E Biographies: Ernest Shackleton, DK Publishing (New York, NY), 2003.

The Man in the Flying Lawn Chair: And Other Excursions and Adventures, Random House (New York, NY), 2004.

Contributor to books, including Bernard Oldsey, editor, *Ernest Hemingway: The Papers of a Writer,* Garland (New York, NY), 1981; and *The Great Life: A Man's Guide to Sports, Skills, Fitness, and Serious Fun,* 2000; author of foreword for *The Art of the Bookplate,* by James P. Keenan, Barnes & Noble Books (New York, NY), 2003; contributor of articles to *Time* and other magazines.

ADAPTATIONS: Paper Lion, the story of Plimpton's experiences as a short-term member of the Detroit Lions football team, was filmed by United Artists in 1968. Alan Alda portrayed Plimpton, but the author himself also had a role—he played William Ford.

SIDELIGHTS: "Although throughout his long career George Plimpton devoted considerable energy to literary pursuits of the highest caliber, including editing the prestigious *Paris Review,* he became widely known to the public at large for writing about his failed attempts in sports and other endeavors far beyond his capabilities. Among literary journalists George Plimpton is so unusual that he marches not just to a different drummer but more nearly to a different orchestra," declared Sam G. Riley in *Dictionary of Literary Biography.* Authorities called Plimpton a "professional amateur," for, although writing is his primary occupation, he also pitched in a post-season All-Star game in Yankee Stadium; held the position of last-string rookie quarterback for the Detroit Lions in 1963; golfed in several Pro-Am tournaments; briefly appeared in a basketball game for the Boston Celtics; boxed with former light heavyweight champion Archie Moore; and served as a goalie for the Boston Bruins hockey team in 1977 and the Edmonton Oilers in 1985. He also fought in a bullfight staged by Ernest Hemingway in 1954, and worked as a trapeze artist, liontamer, and clown for the Clyde Beatty-Cole Brothers Circus.

Among his less-strenuous activities, Plimpton developed a stand-up comedy routine and performed it in Las Vegas. He served as a percussionist with the New York Philharmonic and as a guest conductor of the Cincinnati Symphony. He was in several films, including *Rio Lobo, Beyond the Law, Reds,* and *Good Will Hunting.* On television Plimpton hosted specials and appeared in several commercials.

In his writings, Plimpton lost his "professional amateur" status and worked to high standards as a consummate professional. "Plimpton's career as a literary journalist largely has been founded upon the appeal of contrast," mused Riley. "First, there is the internal element of contrast: on one hand, the serious editor of belles lettres, on the other, the purveyor of entertaining journalistic nonfiction and televised specials. Foremost is the contrast that he himself presents vis-a-vis the people he has competed against in his myriad adventures: the tweedy, genteel literary figure at play on the turf of rougher, more hardbitten types, the bon vivant amid serious athletes, and the amateur generalist head to head with professional specialists." Reviewers consider *Paper Lion,* Plimpton's book about his football adventures with the Detroit Lions, a classic of sports writing. It "is the best book written about pro football—maybe about any sport—because he captured with absolute fidelity how the average fan might feel given the opportunity to try out for a professional football team," explained Hal Higdon in *Saturday Review.* As Plimpton recalled many years later in an interview with *Time,* "the story I got was one I couldn't have, if I had not marched onto the field and tried my best. In my big game, as the quarterback, you will remember that I lost 32 yards in four plays. Very humiliating."

The book attracted sports fans not only through its innovative concept—a writer actually taking the field with a professional team—but also through the author's command over language. "Practically everybody loves George's stuff because George writes with an affection for his fellow man, has a rare eye for the bizarre, and a nice sense of his own ineptitude," declared Trent Frayne in the Toronto *Globe and Mail.* Ernest Hemingway once said, according to Frayne, "'Plimpton is the dark side of the moon of Walter Mitty.'"

Many writers have echoed Hemingway's statement. However, although Plimpton's adventures superficially resemble those of James Thurber's famous fictional character, there are many differences between the two. "In his participatory journalism [Plimpton] has been described wrongly as a Walter Mitty, and he is nothing of the sort. This is no daydreaming nebbish," declared Joe Flaherty in *New York Times Book Review.* Plimpton's adventures are tangible rather than imaginary. Yet, while Mitty in his dreams is a fantastic success at everything he undertakes, Plimpton's efforts

almost invariably result in failure and humiliation. "Plimpton has stock in setting himself up as a naif . . . many of us are familiar with his gangling, tweedy demeanor and Oxford accent. He plays the 'fancy pants' to our outhouse Americana," Flaherty asserted. "Plimpton doesn't want to be known as an athlete," explained Cal Reynard in *Arizona Daily Star.* "He figures his role in sports is that of the spectator, but he wants to get closer to the game than the stands."

After more than twenty years of writing nonfiction about sports, Plimpton published his first sports novel, *The Curious Case of Sidd Finch,* in 1987. Plimpton based the story on a *Sports Illustrated* article he had written for the 1985 April Fools Day issue about a former Harvard man-cum-Buddhist-monk, Siddhartha "Sidd" Finch, who can pitch a baseball faster than any other pitcher in the history of the game—about 150 miles per hour. Plimpton, in his article, claimed that Finch was about to sign with the New York Mets and speculated about the impact an unhittable pitcher would have on the game of baseball. *The Curious Case of Sidd Finch* expands on the article, telling how Finch, after much self-doubt, is persuaded to play for the Mets and, on his return to Shea Stadium, pitches what former major league pitcher Jim Brosnan, writing in *Washington Post Book World,* called "THE perfect game;" he strikes out the entire batting lineup of the St. Louis Cardinals in perfect order.

Reviewers have commented on *The Curious Case of Sidd Finch* with mixed feelings. Although Brosnan found the novel "sort of like a shaggy-dog tale that once was a crisp one-liner," he continued, "*The Curious Case of Sidd Finch* is not the rollicking farce I'd hoped for, but it's worth a reading." Lee Green, writing in *Los Angeles Times Book Review,* called the book a "wonderfully wry and whimsical debut novel," while National League president and *New York Times Book Review* contributor A. Bartlett Giamatti stated that "Plimpton's control is masterly," and added that baseball "culture is splendidly rendered with an experienced insider's knowledge, and the whole saga of Finch's brief, astonishing passage through big-league baseball is at once a parody of every player's as-told-to biography, a satire on professional sports, an extended (and intriguing) meditation on our national pastime and a touching variant on the novel of education as Sidd learns of the world."

Although his sports writing remains his best-known work, Plimpton also wrote on a wide range of other subjects. His own upper-class roots provided him with a number of unique social connections, including a close relationship with the Kennedy family. He was a Harvard classmate of Robert Kennedy's, and was walking directly in front of the senator when he was assassinated in 1968. In *American Journey: The Times of Robert F. Kennedy* he edits 347 interviews that form a picture of Robert Kennedy's life and the procession of his funeral train from New York to Washington.

Plimpton's own interest centered on the small literary magazine he edited from 1953 until his death in 2003. As James Warren explained in *Chicago Tribune,* "It's the *Paris Review,* not the chronicles of his own sporting foibles . . . that constitutes the soul—and takes up much of the time—of Plimpton's life." *Paris Review,* unlike many other literary magazines, focuses on creative writing rather than criticism. Many famous American writers—including Jack Kerouac, Philip Roth, Richard Ford, T. Coraghessan Boyle, and V. S. Naipaul—published first efforts or complete works within its pages.

Plimpton's interviews with writers about the craft of writing were a major attraction of the journal. It was the *Paris Review,* explained Nona Balakian in *New York Times,* that first "developed a new kind of extended and articulate interview that combined the Boswellian aim with an exploration of the ideas of major contemporary writers on the art of fiction and poetry." "The thing that makes these interviews different from most interviews," wrote Mark Harris in Chicago's *Tribune Books,* "is that they go on long enough to get somewhere. If they do not arrive at the point I dreamily hoped for—creativity totally clarified with a supplementary manual on How To Write—they supply very good instruction nevertheless." The result, Balakian concluded, is "a heightened awareness of a writer's overall purpose and meaning."

Poets at Work and *Women Writers at Work,* both edited by Plimpton, consist of interviews that originally appeared in *Paris Review. Poets at Work* includes conversations with T. S. Eliot, Marianne Moore, Anne Sexton, Allen Ginsberg, William Carlos Williams, James Dickey, and others. Poet Donald Hall described the interviews in his introduction to the volume as "literary history as gossip." *Women Writers at Work* joins the interviews with Marianne Moore and Anne Sexton with those of Dorothy Parker, Rebecca West, Isak Dinesen, and ten other noted twentieth-century women

writers. Summarizing the significance of both volumes, *Listener* contributor Peter Parker wrote that "these interviews are a permanent and invaluable record of the working practices, opinions and observations of those who have reflected our century in their poetry and prose." In 2000, another volume in the series, *Playwrights at Work,* appeared, collecting interviews conducted by Plimpton and others dating back to a 1956 talk with Thornton Wilder. Among the dozen or so other pieces are discussions with August Wilson, Wendy Wasserstein, and two with Arthur Miller. "There's an authentic edginess throughout this instructive and salutary book that makes it a reminder of the variety, the vulnerability, and the awful strictness of the playwright's art," remarked John Stokes in a *Times Literary Supplement* review of the volume.

The Writer's Chapbook belongs to the same series, bringing together additional interviews from *Paris Review* under the editorial supervision of Plimpton. The emphasis here is on subject matter—plot, character, writer's bloc, etc.—rather than an individual author, and the resulting compendium of miscellany offers insight into the writing profession through intimate and often offhanded conversations with established literary figures such as T. S. Eliot, W. H. Auden, and Ezra Pound. According to *New York Times Book Review* contributor David Kirby, "There is little fact and less advice in the 'Chapbook,' its subtitle notwithstanding, but there are plenty of opinions, most of them rather negative: poetry readings are nightmares, politics and writing don't mix, professors and critics (the terms are interchangeable) don't know what they are talking about."

The Paris Review Anthology, also edited by Plimpton, features selections from the journal since its establishment. "The overall tone of *The Paris Review* is high spirited, even mischievous," wrote Kirby. The volume includes the quintessential *Paris Review* story "Night Flight to Stockholm" by Dallas Wiebe, which describes how an aspiring writer eventually wins the Noble Prize in literature by sending dismembered parts of his body along with submissions to major literary journals. Kirby concluded that *The Paris Review Anthology* "is historically important as well, since it reminds readers how a new era in letters began."

Plimpton returned to sports and the competitive spirit with *The X Factor: A Quest for Excellence,* his investigation into the attributes possessed by winners. After narrowly losing a game of horseshoes to President-elect George Bush, Plimpton set out to uncover the universal secret of success through conversations with various sports legends, coaches, and top executives. "Suffice to say that where Mr. Plimpton draws upon his X factor is in his prose style, in his unfailing ability to find the perfectly funny word or phrase," wrote Christopher Lehmann-Haupt in *New York Times.* "What also never lets him down is his capacity to get the most unlikely people to take part in his offbeat fantasies." In the end, Plimpton managed to get a rematch with President Bush.

In 1997 Plimpton assembled a literary memoir, *Truman Capote: In Which Various Friends, Enemies, Acquaintances, and Detractors Recall His Turbulent Career.* American writer Capote, who during his career had earned several well-placed enemies in the world of literature and high society for his barely disguised caricatures of them in a short story titled "The Côte Basque," died in 1984. "I knew him myself," Plimpton once noted to a *Time* interviewer in discussing the controversial writer. "He lived down the street in Sagaponack, Long Island. A good friend for awhile, though he felt toward the end of his life that I had made fun of him in a story I wrote ['The Snows of Studio Fifty-four'] which was a parody of Ernest Hemingway's 'The Snows of Kilimanjaro.'"

With *The Norton Book of Sports* Plimpton provides an eclectic collection of stories by both sport writers and literary figures, including Mark Twain, Thomas Wolfe, James Joyce, and Robert Bly. Chicago *Tribune Books* contributor Robert Olen Butler wrote, "Plimpton has assembled this collection of commentary, fiction, reminiscence, poetry and journalism wonderfully well, filling us with that impression of sports which is always hard to explain, that behind the seeming triviality of these games there resides something profound." A 2000 collection, *Home Run,* brought together Plimpton's choices for an anthology of baseball writing, but one with a more specific focus: the ultimate, but occasional thrill of the home run. He contributes the first essay himself, on the first recorded statistical occurrence of it in baseball history, when Ross Barnes hit one during a Chicago White Stockings game in 1876. Contributors include John Updike, Don DeLillo, and Bernard Malamud. "Plimpton's selection of pieces is very astute," noted *Library Journal* reviewer John Maxymuk.

The Best of Plimpton brings together examples of the author's writings over a period of thirty-five years.

"While his contemporaries were off writing about war, sex and assorted other social upheavals, Plimpton was writing humorously and indelibly about taking poet Marianne Moore to the World Series, playing the triangle with the New York Philharmonic, boxing heavyweight Archie Moore," wrote Malcolm Jones Jr. in *Newsweek.* "Plimpton's subject is passion, whether he finds it in the major leagues, in a man who catches grapes in his mouth or in a bespectacled boy playing football."

"Plimpton has enjoyed a career unlike that of any other literary figure—journalist, author, editor, or otherwise," concluded Riley. "His varied accomplishments render his career hard to sum up, but a quotation he himself used in *The Norton Book of Sports* from poet Donald Hall . . . says it fairly well: 'Half my poet friends think I am insane to waste my time writing about sports and to loiter in the company of professional athletes. The other half would murder to be in my place.'" Still, he once commented in his *Time* interview, "all sports are predicated on error," and his experiences as a novice were not as crucial to the outcome of the game than one might believe. His month as a percussionist in the New York Philharmonic, in comparison, was far more traumatic. "In music, you cannot make a mistake. And the fear of doing this, particularly since I can't read music, was frightening to put it mildly. Evening after evening of pure terror in London, Ontario, playing an instrument called the bells. I destroyed Gustav Mahler's 'Fourth Symphony' by mishitting an instrument called the sleigh bells. I dream about that from time to time, and wake up covered with sweat."

Following Plimpton's death in September of 2003, *Paris Review* created the Plimpton Prize in honor of its long-time editor. The prize recognizes the best piece of writing by a newcomer. Plimpton's dedication to *Paris Review* also continued after his death when, as reported by JoAnne Viviano in *America's Intelligence Wire,* he stated in his will, "it is my wish and hope that the space in my apartment . . . which is currently made available rent free to the *Paris Review* shall continue to be made available without charge for so long as reasonably possible." In an obituary in *New Yorker,* David Remnick described Plimpton as "a serious man of serious accomplishments who just happened to have more fun than a van full of jugglers and clowns. He was game for anything and made a comic art of his Walter Mitty dreams and inevitable failures."

BIOGRAPHICAL AND CRITICAL SOURCES:

BOOKS

Anderson, Elliott, and Mary Kinzie, editors, *The Little Magazine in America: A Modern Documentary History,* Pushcart Press (New York, NY), 1978.

Authors in the News, Volume 1, Gale (Detroit, MI), 1976.

Contemporary Literary Criticism, Volume 36, Gale (Detroit, MI), 1986.

Dictionary of Literary Biography, Volume 185: *American Literary Journalists, 1945-1995, First Series,* Gale (Detroit, MI), 1997.

Plimpton, George, *Poets at Work: The Paris Review Interviews,* introduction by Donald Hall, Viking (New York, NY), 1989.

Talese, Gay, *The Overreachers,* Harper (New York, NY), 1965.

PERIODICALS

America, February 20, 1993, p. 2.

Antioch Review, winter, 1990, p. 121.

Arizona Daily Star, March 24, 1974, Cal Reynard.

Belles Lettres, summer, 1990, p. 47.

Bloomsbury Review, March-April, 1990, p. 7.

Book, July, 2001, Chris Barsanti, review of *Home Run,* p. 74.

Booklist, September 15, 1989, p. 136; October 1, 1990, p. 248; May 1, 2000, Ray Olson, review of *Playwrights at Work,* p. 1640; November 15, 2003, Gilbert Taylor, review of *As Told at the Explorers Club: More than Fifty Gripping Tales of Adventure,* p. 566.

Book Week, October 23, 1966.

Chicago Tribune, December 22, 1986; June 15-June 16, 1987.

Christian Science Monitor, December 5, 1968.

Commentary, October, 1967.

Commonweal, September 14, 1990, p. 523.

Detroit News, March 16, 1986.

Editor & Publisher, April 20, 1985, pp. 7-8.

Esquire, January, 1976, pp. 115-17, 142, 144, 146; November, 1985, p. 243.

Gentleman's Quarterly, October, 1989, pp. 183, 186.

Globe and Mail (Toronto. Ontario, Canada), July 7, 1984; February 8, 1986; June 14, 1986.

Harper's, June, 2000, "A Writer's Gift," p. 51; December, 2003, Lewis H. Lapham, "Pilgrim's Progress" p. 11.

Harper's Bazaar, November, 1973, pp. 103, 134-35, 142.

Kliatt, September, 1989, p. 25.

Library Journal, November 1, 1989, p. 91; March 1, 1990, p. 94; April 1, 1992, p. 124; March 1, 1995, p. 79; May 15, 2001, John Maxymuk, review of *Home Run,* p. 130; March 15, 2003, Anna Youssefi, review of *Latin American Writers at Work: The Paris Review,* p. 85; November 15, 2003, Alison Hopkins, review of *As Told at the Explorers Club: More than Fifty Gripping Tales of Adventure,* p. 88.

Listener, October 26, 1989, Peter Barker, review of *Poets at Work* and *Women Writers at Work,* p. 33.

Los Angeles Times, July 22, 1982; March 20, 1987.

Los Angeles Times Book Review, September 30, 1984; June 21, 1987.

Midwest Quarterly, spring, 1989, pp. 372-386.

Milwaukee Journal, November 12, 1974.

Nation, June 10, 1991, pp. 762-63.

Newsweek, January 14, 1991, Malcom Jones, Jr., review of *The Best of Plimpton,* p. 52.

New Yorker, November 12, 1966; June 27, 1994, p. 44.

New York Herald Tribune, April 23, 1961.

New York Review of Books, February 23, 1967; February 7, 1974.

New York Times, November 12, 1973; July 29, 1977; November 16, 1977; March 28, 1981; June 14, 1984; November 14, 1985; July 30, 1987; March 6, 1995, Christopher Lehmann-Haupt, review of *The X Factor: A Quest for Excellence,* p. B2, C16.

New York Times Book Review, April 23, 1961; November 10, 1968; January 6, 1974; July 31, 1977; November 6, 1977; June 17, 1984; September 23, 1984; November 24, 1985; July 5, 1987; March 4, 1990, David Kirby, review of *The Writer's Chapbook,* p. 11; July 2, 1995, p. 11.

Observer, June 23, 1991.

Playboy, December, 1990, p. 29; April, 1995, p. 34.

Publishers Weekly, October 2, 2000, review of *The Great Life,* p. 79; April 30, 2001, "Baseball's Been Good to Them," p. 67; February 3, 2003, review of *Latin American Writers at Work,* p. 66.

Saturday Review, December 10, 1966, Hal Higdon, review of *Paper Lion;* August 14, 1971.

Spectator, October 14, 1978.

Sports Illustrated, September 13, 1965, p. 4; August 3, 1992, p. 6; December 22, 2003, "A Feast of Classic Plimpton: Brilliant—and Beautiful—Reissues by a Writer Who Couldn't Just Watch," p. 23.

Time, April 7, 1967, p. 40; December 19, 1977; September 10, 1984; December 8, 1986; April 13, 1987, pp. 9-11; June 8, 1987.

Times Literary Supplement, December 1, 1978; January 21, 1983; December 21, 1984; August 2, 1985; September 5, 1986; March 20, 1987; September 29, 2000, John Stokes, "Raffishness Rampant," p. 21.

Tribune Books (Chicago, IL), May 3, 1981; September 2, 1984; October 14, 1984; November 24, 1985; July 5, 1987; June 14, 1992, p. 6; December 6, 1992, p. 13.

Village Voice, June 11, 1991, p. 30.

Wall Street Journal, August 28, 1984.

Washington Post, January 7, 1986.

Washington Post Book World, May 27, 1984; September 2, 1984; June 21, 1987; July 9, 1989; October 21, 1990; March 12, 1995.

Writers Digest, June, 1974, pp. 17-18.

ONLINE

America's Intelligence Wire, October 21, 2003, JoAnne Viviano "Late Founder of Paris Review Leaves Will Specifying Home for His Literary Journal."

OBITUARIES:

PERIODICALS

Economist (US), October 11, 2003 p. 86.
Nation, October 20, 2003, p. 7.
Newsweek, October 6, 2003, p. 8.
New Yorker, October 6, 2003, p. 46.
New York Times, September 27, 2003, p. A13.
People, October 13, 2003, p. 93.
Sporting News, October 6, 2003, p. 8.
Sports Illustrated, October 6, 2003, p. 40.
Time, October 6, 2003, p. 25.

ONLINE

MSNBC.com, http://www.msnbc.com/ (September 26, 2003).*

POLLACK, William S(helley)

PERSONAL: Male.

ADDRESSES: Home—115 Mill St., Belmont, MA 02478. *E-mail*—polpad@tiac.net; www.williampollack.com.

CAREER: Author and psychologist. Harvard Medical School, Department of Psychiatry, Boston, MA, assistant clinical professor of psychology; McLean Hospital, Center for Men, Belmont, MA, director.

WRITINGS:

(With R. William Betcher) *In a Time of Fallen Heroes: The Re-creation of Masculinity,* Atheneum (New York, NY), 1993.

(Editor with Ronald F. Levant, and contributor) *A New Psychology of Men,* Basic Books (New York, NY), 1995.

Real Boys: Rescuing Our Sons from the Myths of Boyhood, Random House (New York, NY), 1998.

(Editor, with Ronald F. Levant) *New Psychotherapy for Men,* J. Wiley (New York, NY), 1998.

(With Todd Shuster) *Real Boys' Voices,* Random House (New York, NY), 2000.

(With Kathleen Cushman) *Real Boys Workbook: The Definitive Guide to Understanding and Interacting with Boys of All Ages,* Villard (New York, NY), 2001.

SIDELIGHTS: Psychologist William S. Pollack is director of the Center for Men at McLean Hospital and a faculty member at Harvard Medical School. He writes about the role of men in post-feminist America and argues that the cultural view of boys as stoic, testosterone-driven tough guys forces them to stifle their natural feelings of confusion, sadness, and fear and damages their emotional health. Drawing on his clinical findings, as well as on an ongoing Harvard research project, Pollack asserts that boys and men are being given harmful messages from society about the meaning of masculinity, and then become depressed, suicidal, or violent as a result of the power of their repressed emotions. In his books, Pollack describes the problems of today's boys and men, offers practical advice for recovering from society's damaging mes-

William S. Pollack

sages, and submits first-person narratives, journals, poems, and essays from boys and young men who have found Pollack's insights helpful.

In the 1993 book *In a Time of Fallen Heroes: The Recreation of Masculinity,* Pollack and coauthor R. William Betcher say that men should reclaim their masculinity; they use quotes from the Bible and classical myths and legends to illustrate a new persona of masculinity. The authors examine issues in a man's life such as sex, play, fathering, and authority in an attempt to encourage men to reassess their definition of masculinity. H. Robert Malinowsky in *Library Journal* stated that the book's central idea asserts the need for men "to redefine their masculine role in order to make their lives better." A *Publishers Weekly* critic praised the book for being "forcefully argued but never dogmatic."

Pollack and coeditor Ronald F. Levant further examine the dilemma of modern men in the book *A New Psychology of Men.* In a review in *The Journal of the American Medical Association,* David D. Gilmore and James H. Kocsis called this book "a multiauthored synopsis of the current state of profeminist academic men's studies, primarily from a psychological perspective." They described the chapter contributed by Pollack as "an effort to update psychoanalytic theories of human development taking feminist and new male psychology into account. It is among the more in-depth and balanced in the book."

In his book titled *Real Boys: Rescuing Our Sons from the Myths of Boyhood,* Pollack investigates the way boys are raised and offers practical solutions to counter the damage that is sometimes done in childhood. Pollack feels the trouble stems from the complicated relationships boys have with their mothers. Pollack believes that mothers are wrongly encouraged to push their sons away from them too early. Society reinforces the belief that boys should not cling to their mothers but separate willingly. Pollack states that this belief system starts when boys enter kindergarten and soon learn that crying, sadness, and separation anxiety label them as sissies. Pollack feels that boys lose their emotive abilities when shamed into denying their sense of loss. As a result they suffer a loss of creativity and an inability to express emotions other than anger, and they are handicapped by a code of conduct that Pollack terms "gender-straightjacketing." His advice to stay connected and engage in action-oriented activity to open lines of communication has been well received. Peggy Kaye of the *New York Times Book Review* remarked, "Pollack's tone is calm and considered. . . . Throughout *Real Boys,* Pollack gives parents suggestions for helping their sons, and his counsel is almost always sound." Shari Roan, writing in the *Los Angeles Times,* concluded that Pollack "bases his theories on decades of clinical work with boys and helps parents understand how they can break the masculine molds that stereotype boys and thwart their growth. Highly recommended for anyone raising a son."

Some reviewers recognized the increasing number of books about the psychology of boys and men as a welcome antidote or complement to the wealth of books on the development of girls and women that has been published since the 1970s. Of the books written about boys, Pollack's *Real Boys* and *Real Boys' Voices* are considered to be among the most measured, sensible, and grounded in good science. Richard A. Hawley, writing in the *New England Journal of Medicine,* wrote, "*Real Boys* is a thoughtful step in clearing the ideological air. Perhaps with an equally acute and generous *Real Girls,* we might set about addressing the needs of children from an appropriately respectful and loving perspective."

In *Real Boys' Voices,* Pollack reiterates the core insights of *Real Boys,* emphasizing that a failure to recognize and responsibly handle the emotional upheavals of growing up a boy in modern America has led to a wealth of social problems, including a rise in diagnoses of attention deficit disorder and an increase in violent outbreaks in schools, such as the incident at Columbine High School in Colorado in 1999. A chapter is devoted to survivors of the Columbine incident, many of whom expressed sympathy for the repressed rage felt by the young killers who acted out so violently. Pollack also concludes with advice for parents and teachers on creating an environment in which boys feel safe to express all of their feelings. "This insightful and powerful work should be required reading for anyone who works with or lives with boys," contended Susanne Bardelson in *School Library Journal.* Likewise, Sandra Isaacson, writing in *Library Journal,* remarked that for parents, teachers, and grandparents, *Real Boys' Voices* "is essential reading." And in *Booklist* Vanessa Bush dubbed this "an important, comprehensive report 'from the trenches' on the emotional state of American boys."

BIOGRAPHICAL AND CRITICAL SOURCES:

PERIODICALS

American Journal of Psychiatry, November, 1999, Samuel Slipp, review of *New Psychotherapy for Men,* p. 1830.

Booklist, May 1, 1993, p. 1549; May 15, 1998, p. 1562; May 15, 2000, Vanessa Bush, review of *Real Boys' Voices,* p. 1698.

Christian Science Monitor, August 1, 2000, "Boy Talk in Full Throttle," p. 13.

Early Childhood Education Journal, fall, 1999, review of *Real Boys: Rescuing Our Sons from the Myths of Boyhood,* p. 41.

Equity and Excellence in Education, April, 2000, David Sadker, "A Reader's Guide to the Boy Book Bonanza," p. 102.

Journal of the American Medical Association, March 27, 1996, David D. Gilmore and James H. Kocsis, review of *A New Psychology of Men,* p. 952.

Library Journal, June 1, 1993, H. Robert Malinowsky, review of *In a Time of Fallen Heroes: The Recreation of Masculinity,* pp. 160, 168; June 5, 2000, Sandra Isaacson, review of *Real Boys' Voices,* p. 102.

Los Angeles Times, February 1, 1999, Shari Roan, review of *Real Boys,* p. 1.

Ms., October, 1999, review of *Real Boys,* p. 91.

New England Journal of Medicine, January 7, 1999, Richard A. Hawley, review of *Real Boys.*

New Yorker, May 17, 1999, review of *Real Boys,* p. 18; July 10, 2000, Nicholas Lemann, review of *Real Boys' Voices,* p. 79.

New York Times Book Review, September 13, 1998, Peggy Kaye, review of *Real Boys,* p. 28; June 25, 2000, Robert Coles, review of *Real Boys' Voices,* p. 20.

Publishers Weekly, May 17, 1993, review of *In a Time of Fallen Heroes,* pp. 56-57; June 8, 1998, p. 56; June 5, 2000, review of *Real Boys' Voices,* p. 81.

Readings: A Journal of Reviews and Commentary in Mental Health, March, 1999, review of *New Psychotherapy for Men,* p. 23.

Ruminator Review, fall, 2001, Brigitte Frase, "Boys versus Girls?," pp. 16-17.

School Library Journal, October, 2000, Susanne Bardelson, review of *Real Boys' Voices,* p. 197.

SciTech Book News, March, 1999, review of *New Psychotherapy for Men,* p. 94.

Time, July 20, 1998, pp. 46-47.

Virginia Quarterly Review, winter, 1999, review of *Real Boys,* p.27.

Washington Post, November 27, 2000, Kay S. Hymowitz, "Of Growing Concern," p. C03.

ONLINE

ABC News, http://abcnews.go.com/ (November 17, 2001), "Mom-Only Parenting: A Chat with Dr. William Pollack, Author of *Real Boys.*"

Dr. William Pollack Web Site, http://www.william pollack.com (December 18, 2001).*

R

RAMPLING, Anne
   See RICE, Anne

*   *   *

RICE, Anne 1941-
   (A. N. Roquelaure, Anne Rampling)

PERSONAL: Born Howard Allen O'Brien, October 4, 1941, in New Orleans, LA; name changed, c. 1947; daughter of Howard (a postal worker, novelist, and sculptor) and Katherine (Allen) O'Brien; married Stan Rice (a poet and painter), October 14, 1961 (died, December, 2002); children: Michele (deceased), Christopher. *Education:* Attended Texas Woman's University, 1959-60; San Francisco State College (now University), B.A., 1964, M.A., 1971; graduate study at University of California at Berkeley, 1969-70. *Hobbies and other interests:* Traveling, ancient Greek history, archaeology, social history since the beginning of recorded time, old movies on television, attending boxing matches.

ADDRESSES: Agent—Jacklyn Nesbit Associates, 598 Madison Ave., New York, NY 10022.

CAREER: Writer. worked variously as a waitress, cook, theater usherette, and insurance claims examiner. Appeared on television series *Ellen,* 1996.

MEMBER: Authors Guild, Authors League of America.

AWARDS, HONORS: Joseph Henry Jackson Award honorable mention, 1970.

Anne Rice

WRITINGS:

NOVELS

The Feast of All Saints, Simon & Schuster (New York, NY), 1980.
Cry to Heaven, Knopf (New York, NY), 1982.

369

The Mummy: or, Ramses the Damned, Ballantine (New York, NY), 1989.
Servant of the Bones, Knopf (New York, NY), 1996.
Violin, Knopf (New York, NY), 1997.

"VAMPIRE CHRONICLES" SERIES

Interview with the Vampire (also see below), Knopf (New York, NY), 1976.
The Vampire Lestat (also see below), Ballantine (New York, NY), 1985.
The Queen of the Damned (also see below), Knopf (New York, NY), 1988.
Vampire Chronicles (contains *Interview with the Vampire, The Vampire Lestat,* and *The Queen of the Damned*), Ballantine (New York, NY), 1989.
The Tale of the Body Thief, Knopf (New York, NY), 1992.
Memnoch the Devil, Knopf (New York, NY), 1995.
The Vampire Armand, Knopf (New York, NY), 1998.
Pandora: New Tales of the Vampires, Random House (New York, NY), 1998.
Vittorio the Vampire, Knopf (New York, NY), 1999.
Merrick, Knopf (New York, NY), 2000.
Blood and Gold, Knopf (New York, NY), 2001.
Blackwood Farm, Knopf (New York, NY), 2002.
Blood Canticle, Knopf (New York, NY), 2003.

"WITCHING HOUR" TRILOGY

The Witching Hour, Knopf (New York, NY), 1990.
Lasher, Knopf (New York, NY), 1993.
Taltos, Knopf (New York, NY), 1994.

EROTIC NOVELS; UNDER PSEUDONYM A. N. ROQUELAURE

The Claiming of Sleeping Beauty, Dutton (New York, NY), 1983.
Beauty's Punishment, Dutton (New York, NY), 1984.
Beauty's Release: The Continued Erotic Adventures of Sleeping Beauty, Dutton (New York, NY), 1985.
The Sleeping Beauty Novels (contains *The Claiming of Sleeping Beauty, Beauty's Punishment,* and *Beauty's Release: The Continued Erotic Adventures of Sleeping Beauty*), New American Library (New York, NY), 1991.

NOVELS; UNDER PSEUDONYM ANNE RAMPLING

Exit to Eden, Arbor House (New York, NY), 1985.
Belinda, Arbor House (New York, NY), 1986.

OTHER

Interview with the Vampire (screenplay; adapted from the novel of the same title), Geffen Pictures, 1994.
(Author of introduction) Alice Borchardt, *Devoted,* Dutton (New York, NY), 1995.
(Author of foreword) Franz Kafka, *The Metamorphosis, In the Penal Colony, and Other Stories,* Schocken (New York, NY), 1995.
(Author of introduction) Kelly Klein, *Underworld,* Knopf (New York, NY), 1995.
(Author of introduction) Alice Borchardt, *Beguiled,* Dutton (New York, NY), 1997.
The Anne Rice Reader, edited by Katherine Ramsland, Ballantine (New York, NY), 1997.

ADAPTATIONS: Exit to Eden was adapted for film by Deborah Amelon and Bob Brunner, directed by Garry Marshall, starring Dana Delaney and Dan Ackroyd, 1994; *Queen of the Damned* was adapted for film by Scott Abbott and Michael Petroni, directed by Michael Rymer, starring Stuart Townsend, 2001. *The Vampire Lestat* was adapted as a graphic novel by Faye Perozich, Ballantine, 1991; *The Tale of the Body Thief* was adapted as a graphic novel. *Feast of All Saints* was adapted as a television miniseries, Showtime/ABC, 2001. Elton John and Bernie Taupin adapted Rice's "Vampire Chronicles" novels as the stage musical *The Vampire Lestat,* to be produced on Broadway, 2005. Rice's novels have been adapted as audiobooks.

SIDELIGHTS: Considered one of the leading practitioners of Gothic writing in the twentieth century, popular novelist Anne Rice has built her career, according to *New York Times Book Review* critic Daniel Mendelsohn, by sticking to "the Big Themes: good versus evil, mortality and immortality." Indeed, these themes have provided Rice with such prolific material that, as Bob Summer observed in *Publishers Weekly,* "She needs two pseudonyms—Anne Rampling and A. N. Roquelaure—to distinguish the disparate voices in her books, [which have] won both critical acclaim and a readership of cult proportions." Under her own name, Rice crafts novels about the bizarre and the supernatural; under the Rampling pseudonym, she writes contemporary and mainstream fiction; and under the Roquelaure *nom de plume* she spins sadomasochistic fantasies. Rice has pointed out that each name represents a part of her divided self. As she told *New York Times* interviewer Stewart Kellerman, she is "a divided person with different voices, like an actor playing different roles." Discussing this subject with Sarah Booth Conroy in a *Washington Post* interview, Rice said, "I think sometimes that if I had had perhaps a few more genes, or whatever, I would have been truly mad, a multiple personality whose selves didn't recognize each other."

Rice has characterized her early childhood as happy but unconventional. However, at the age of fourteen Rice lost her mother to alcoholism, and soon afterwards the family relocated to Texas. She married her high school sweetheart, poet Stan Rice, at age twenty; "I fell completely in love with Stan, and I'm still completely in love with him," declared Rice in a *New York Times* interview; tragically, after over four decades of marriage, Rice died of cancer in 2002. A year after they were married the Rices moved from Texas to San Francisco, where Rice gave birth to daughter Michele. It was there that she had a prophetic dream: "I dreamed my daughter, Michele, was dying—that there was something wrong with her blood," she recalled in her *People* interview. Several months later, Michele was diagnosed with a rare form of leukemia and died shortly before her sixth birthday. "Two years later, her image was reincarnated as the child vampire Claudia in [*Interview with the Vampire*], Anne's first published work," wrote Gerri Hirshey in *Rolling Stone*. *Interview with the Vampire* "was written out of grief, the author says, in five weeks of 'white-hot, access-the-subconscious' sessions between 10:00 p.m. and dawn," added Hirshey.

As its title indicates, *Interview with the Vampire* recounts the events of one evening in which Louis, the vampire of the title, tells a young reporter his life story. The novel, which Rice actually began in the late 1960s as a short story, developed into something much larger. "I got to the point where the vampire began describing his brother's death, and the whole thing just exploded! Suddenly, in the guise of Louis, a fantasy figure, I was able to touch the reality that was mine," explained Rice in a *Publishers Weekly* interview. "Through Louis' eyes, everything became accessible."

It is Rice's unusual and sympathetic treatment of vampires, according to critics, that gives her "Vampire Chronicles" their particular appeal. "Rice brings a fresh and powerful imagination to the staples of vampire lore; she makes well-worn coffins and crucifixes tell new tales that compose a chillingly original myth," observed Nina Auerbach in *New York Times Book Review*. "Because Rice identifies with the vampire instead of the victim (reversing the usual focus), the horror for the reader springs from the realization of the monster within the self," wrote Ferraro. "Moreover, Rice's vampires are loquacious philosophers who spend much of eternity debating the nature of good and evil. Trapped in immortality, they suffer human regret. They are lonely, prisoners of circumstance, compulsive sinners, full of self-loathing and doubt." All that separates the vampires from humans and makes them outsiders is their hunt for human blood and their indestructible bodies. With flawless, alabaster skin, colorful glinting eyes, and hair that shimmers and seems to take on a life of its own, they were described by H. J. Kirchhoff in a Toronto *Globe and Mail* review as "romantic figures, superhumanly strong and fast, brilliant and subtle of thought and flamboyant of manner."

The status of vampire as outsider, Mendelsohn argued, allows Rice to explore deep human themes like the meaning of suffering and death from the unique viewpoint of "alien characters in . . . exotic milieus" who nevertheless exhibit an "underlying troubled humanity." *Interview with the Vampire*, wrote Mendelsohn, is a success precisely because its main character is aesthetically refined and sensitive, "a nice Byronic departure from your garden-variety Nosferatu with his unkempt nails and bad table manners."

Walter Kendrick praised the scope of *Interview with the Vampire* in *Voice Literary Supplement*, writing that "it would have been a notable tour de force even if its characters had been human." Kendrick also suggested, however, that "Rice's most effective accomplishment . . . was to link up sex and fear again." Several critics made much the same point. Conroy maintained that "not since Mary Shelley's *Frankenstein* and Louisa May Alcott's penny dreadful novelettes has a woman written so strongly about death and sex." Similarly, in a *New York Times Book Review* article, Leo Braudy observed that "Rice exploits all the sexual elements in [vampire myths] with a firm self-consciousness of their meaning." The sensuous description of Louis' first kill is an example: "I knelt beside the bent, struggling man and, clamping both my hands on his shoulders, I went into his neck. My teeth had only just begun to change, and I had to tear his flesh, not puncture it; but once the wound was made, the blood flowed. . . . The sucking mesmerized me, the warm struggling of the man was soothing to the tension of my hands; and there came the beating of the drum again, which was the drumbeat of his heart."

Rice frankly acknowledges her novel's erotic content. "No matter what I write," she told *Lambda Book Report* writer Melinda L. Shelton, "my characters always turn out to be bisexual. It just happens, and I'm very happy with it—I think it's what I see as an ideal." Noting that *The Tale of the Body,* which centers on a homoerotic relationship between Lestat and David Talbot, topped bestseller lists for weeks, Rice observed, "when you talk about desire, and you talk about liberation, you're basically talking about universal things."

Despite the critical and popular success of *Interview with the Vampire,* Rice did not immediately produce a sequel, instead turning her attention to writing mainstream fiction and erotica. When *The Vampire Lestat* appeared nearly ten years later, both fans and critics welcomed Rice's return to her vampire characters. In this second novel of the "Vampire Chronicles," Lestat, creator of Louis in *Interview with the Vampire,* awakens from a sleep of many years to find himself in the 1980s. A rock band practicing in a house nearby rouses him, and a few days later, he is dressed in leather and roaring around on a big black Harley Davidson motorcycle.

The Vampire Lestat is structured as an autobiography written as part of the marketing campaign to launch Lestat's new rock and roll career. It takes the reader through "a history of vampirism, from its beginnings in ancient Egypt, through its manifestations in Roman Gaul, Renaissance Italy, pre-Revolutionary Paris and *belle epoque* New Orleans, and a further discussion of the philosophical, ethical and theological implications of vampirism," wrote Kirchhoff, adding that "Rice is a beautiful writer. Her prose glitters and every character in Lestat's dark odyssey is unique." Although *New York Times* contributor Michiko Kakutani maintained that Rice recounts her history "in lugubrious, cliche-ridden sentences that repeat every idea and sentiment a couple or more times," Auerbach found *The Vampire*

Lestat to be "ornate and pungently witty," and deemed that "in the classic tradition of Gothic fiction, it teases and tantalizes us into accepting its kaleidoscopic world. Even when they annoy us or tell us more than we want to know, its undead characters are utterly alive."

The Queen of the Damned, which also contains background details about vampire history and lore, drew more muted critical response. Kendrick found the novel "verbose, sluggish, and boring," and written as if "Rice didn't believe her fantasies anymore." However, Kakutani appreciated its "well-developed sense of fun," and Laurence Coven, in a *Los Angeles Times Book Review* article, deemed the book "an exhilarating blend of philosophic questing and pure, wondrous adventure."

The Tale of the Body Thief continues the "Vampire Chronicles," and find Lestat so weary of his immortality that he attempts suicide. He fails, but is soon approached by a mortal who offers to exchange bodies for a few days. Eager for even a taste of mortality, Lestat agrees, only to have his partner in this transaction vanish with his immortal body. Sarah Smith, in *Washington Post Book World,* lauded the book's "whiplash speed," "page-turner plot," "beautifully realized atmosphere," and "real storytelling intelligence." The passages in which Lestat, confined to the night for two centuries, once again experiences daylight are "Rice at her best, looking through the outsider's eyes with all the outsider's alienated power," Smith added. Writing in *Chicago Tribune,* Dan Greenberg termed Rice's description of the body exchange "brilliant," and went on to say that "Lestat's reactions to pulling on a mortal body like a suit of ill-fitting clothes and suddenly having to re-learn vulgar, unvampirelike bodily functions—urinating, eating, defecating, making love—are downright dazzling."

In 1995's *Memnoch the Devil* Lestat, accustomed to being the hunter, finds he is now the prey, his pursuer none other than Satan, who tries to enlist Lestat to become his assistant. Lestat refuses, but accepts the Devil's offer for a tour of heaven, hell, and purgatory. After seeing all this, his guide tells him that he will have another chance to accept the job offer. "With the stage thus set, the book transmogrifies into a modern *Paradise Lost,* The Universe according to Rice," explained Kevin Allman in a review of *Memnoch the Devil* for *Washington Post Book World.* "Many, many pages . . . are devoted to her personal cosmology and angelology," Allman added, "to her versions of creation, evolution and the Crucifixion. It's a tour that's interesting at times and poky at others."

Several reviewers complained that *Memnoch the Devil* contains too much talk, and that Rice perhaps took on more than she could handle with this novel. A *Publishers Weekly* reviewer found that Rice's attempts to answer meaning-of-life questions overshadows her narrative, and felt that "God and the Devil . . . too often end up sounding like arguing philosophy majors." For Michael McLeod in *Chicago Tribune*, *Memnoch the Devil* proves a disappointing conclusion to the "Vampire Chronicles." He noted that while the book deals with the mysteries of life, death, and eternity more "dramatically and directly" than any other installment in Rice's series, "the proportions of the author's writing are so epic that her dark hero gets lost among them." "If Rice really is retiring her flagship vampire," McLeod added, ". . . it's puzzling she made him play out his last scene as Satan's sidekick." Allman concluded with a more positive assessment of *Memnoch the Devil*, stating that "Rice has penned an ambitious close to this long-running series, as well as a classy exit for a classic horror character."

The Vampire Armand, the sixth installment in her "Vampire Chronicles," returns to a character first introduced in *Interview with the Vampire*. Armand, a boy in sixteenth-century Italy, is kidnapped and sold as a slave, ending up in the Venetian palace of Marius, a vampire who teaches the boy history and art. Once Marius makes Armand into a vampire, the pair concentrate on hunting down "evil" people, which draws the anger of a Satanic vampire cult intent on making Armand its own. Though some reviewers suggested that *The Vampire Armand* is less powerful than the earlier books in the series, others welcomed the novel warmly. Michael Porter, in *New York Times Book Review,* found it an "absorbing account of another all-too-human ghoul" who is struggling to be a Christian, while a contributor to *Publishers Weekly* praised the novel's "exquisite details of erotic romps and political intrigues" as well as its "lavishly poetic" treatment of Armand's religious crisis.

The "Vampire Chronicles" continue with *Merrick,* a biracial female vampire who has voodoo powers. The action moves from New Orleans to the Central American rainforest, and Rice reunites readers with Lestat and several other characters from past novels. More so than other novels in the series, *Merrick* features strong female characters. "As time passes, I am writing more and more with women characters," Rice noted to Julia Kamysz Lane in *Book*. "It's becoming easier to write about my femininity. But anytime I write a book with a strong woman protagonist, I run a risk because people simply treat women protagonists differently than men. They tend to insult and trivialize female characters in fiction. . . . If *Interview with the Vampire* had been about a male and a female, and Louis had really been a woman, people would have dismissed it out of hand as a cheap romance."

Merrick drew a mixed response from critics. Janet Maslin in *New York Times Book Review* suggested that Rice's powers "have served her mightily, so mightily that the stories now grow weary," but acknowledged that carelessly written passages or recycled plot elements would not bother Rice's legion of fans at all. *Library Journal* reviewer Ann Kim commented that *Merrick* "lacks the resonance and vivid passion of [Rice's] earlier writings," and *Booklist* reviewer Ray Olson expressed a similar opinion. A contributor to *Publishers Weekly,* however, found that Rice's "imaginative talents for atmosphere and suspense" enhance the novel with "riveting" detail.

Although the "Vampire Chronicles" earned increasingly lackluster reviews from critics, the series retained its fan following, and Rice continued to produce further installments. In *Blood and Gold* she profiles Marius, the creature who gave Lestat immortality and also loved the vampire Pandora, herself the subject of another installment in the series. Called "intriguing yet rushed" by a *Publishers Weekly* contributor, *Blood and Gold* follows Marius from his birth in imperial Rome and his transformation into a vampire at the hands of Druids. Readers follow Marius through the millennium, as he acts as the protector of Those Who Must Be Kept. *Blood Canticle* once again finds Lestat center stage, as narrator of his reaction to meeting the devil and his search for redemption. In *Publishers Weekly* a reviewer noted that in *Blood Canticle,* "Writing as if her blood-inked quill were afire, Rice seems truly possessed by her Brat Prince of darkness as she races through the story," and added that *Blood Canticle* might well serve as a closing novel of the series.

The erotic overtones featured in the "Vampire Chronicles" are given full range in books Rice has published under the pseudonym A. N. Roquelaure. *The Claiming of Sleeping Beauty, Beauty's Punishment,* and *Beauty's Release: The Continued Erotic Adventures of Sleeping Beauty* are loosely based on the story of Sleeping Beauty and are described as sadomasochistic pornography by some critics. "A. N. Roquelaure is an S&M pornographer with a shocking penchant for leather collars. . . . and other kinky bijoux," stated Hirshey. Conroy asserted, however, that "despite the content, all is presented with something of the breathless, innocent, gingham-ruffled voice of fairy tales." Rice addresses the critical assessment of these works as pornographic in a *People* interview: "I wrote about the fantasy that interested me personally and that I couldn't find in bookstores. I wanted to create a Disneyland of S&M. Most porno is written by hacks. I meant it to be erotic and nothing else—to turn people on. Sex is good. Nothing about sex is evil or to be ashamed of." Moreover, in a *Lear's* interview, Rice maintained, "They're of high quality. . . . and I'm very proud that I wrote them."

Writing under the pseudonym Anne Rampling, Rice has written two conventional novels, *Exit to Eden* and *Belinda,* which combine erotica and romance. Carolyn See contended in *Los Angeles Times* that "Rampling attempts a fascinating middle ground" between the "straight erotica" of Roquelaure, and the "semi-serious literature" of Rice. *Exit to Eden* tells the story of Lisa Kelly, a gorgeous young woman in skimpy lace and high leather boots who exudes sexuality. Raised by an Irish-Catholic family that abhors the idea of sex, Kelly discovers at an early age that she is obsessed by sadomasochism. This obsession, combined with her executive skills, leads her to an island on the Caribbean where she opens the Club—a resort "which is something between a luxury hotel and an S-M brothel," said See. The second half of the novel relates Kelly's exit with friend Elliott from a lifestyle they once perceived as Edenic. They settle in New Orleans and start dating, proving that "one man and one woman can make a happy life together and be transformed by love, the most seductive fantasy of all," wrote See, adding that Rice "makes a lovely case here. Let's take what we've learned of sex and bring it back into the real world, she suggests. It's time, isn't it?"

Belinda is divided into three parts, the first describing the life of Jeremy Walker, a famous author and illustrator of children's books, who lives alone in an old house. Not only is he desperately lonely, but he is also cut off from his sexuality until Belinda comes along. She is a fifteen-year-old runaway who smokes, drinks, and is willing to partake in every erotic fantasy Jeremy concocts. Although Belinda urges him not to search for clues to her past, he does, so she runs away. The second part of the novel describes Belinda's childhood and her relationship with her mother. The final part of the book follows Jeremy's search for Belinda and includes several happy endings—"True love triumphs," claimed See in her *Los Angeles Times* review of *Belinda.* "Sex is as nice as champagne and friendship, Rampling earnestly instructs us. Value it! Don't be puritanical morons *all* your life."

Rice uses her large antebellum mansion in New Orleans as the setting for her "Witching Hour" trilogy opener, *The Witching Hour.* The mansion in the novel belongs to the Mayfair family and its generations of witches. Rowan, the thirteenth witch, has extrasensory powers and must defend herself from Lasher, the personification of evil. Leading Ferraro through a tour of her home, Rice described the scenes that took place in each of the rooms: "'There's the fireplace where Rowan and Lasher sat on Christmas morning,' she says matter-of-factly, a smile tugging at her lips. . . . Up a flight of stairs, to Rice's office, where she ignores the messy desk and points dramatically to an ornate bed—'where Deirdre died,' she says, of another of the book's characters."

"What is unnerving about all this is not that Rice switches back and forth between her fictional and factual worlds, but that they seem to coexist, with equal intensity. It is as if she has somehow brought about the haunting of her own house," wrote Ferraro. Patrick McGrath, indicated in *New York Times Book Review* that "despite its tireless narrative energy, despite its relentless inventiveness, the book is bloated, grown to elephantine proportions because more is included than is needed." But Susan Isaacs, in a *Washington Post Book World* review, opined that "Rice offers more than just a story; she creates myth. In *The Witching Hour,* she presents a rich, complicated universe that operates by both natural and supernatural law, and she does so with . . . consummate skill."

The "Witching Hour" trilogy also includes the novels *Lasher* and *Taltos;* Rice would later meld the series with her popular "Vampire Chronicles" in the novels *Merrick, Blackwood Farm* and *Blood Canticle.* In *Lasher* the title character, whose presence in spirit was key to *The Witching Hour,* assumes human form as the son of Rowan Mayfair and seeks a woman with whom he can reproduce. *Taltos* centers on a kindly immortal giant named Ashlar who becomes involved with the Mayfair clan.

Numerous reviewers of both books viewed that the large cast of characters and baroque plotlines are weaknesses, and found the series as a whole to be less compelling than the "Vampire Chronicles." "You might . . . need a scorecard to keep all the Mayfair witches separate," wrote Dick Adler in his Chicago *Tribune Books* review of *Lasher.* While Paul West, critiquing *Lasher* for *New York Times Book Review,* wrote that Rice narrates her story "in plodding prose, but she does tell it as if it interested her," Elizabeth Hand in *Washington Post Book World* found much to praise in Rice's "Witching Hour" series. With *Lasher,* Hand explained, Rice "concocts a heady and potent salmagundi of contemporary witchcraft, Caribbean voodoo, aristocratic decadence and good old-fashioned Celtic paganism, and makes what should be an unpalatable mess as wickedly irresistible as a Halloween stash of Baby Ruths." Even though its characters are supernatural, *Lasher* is actually "an old-fashioned family saga," Hand added. "Rice's Mayfairs are as gorgeous and doomed and steeped in the South as Scarlett O'Hara."

During the early 1980s Rice published two historical novels that Conroy considered "of great depth, research and enchantment." In *The Feast of All Saints* she writes about free people of color, those mulattoes who numbered about 18,000 and lived in nineteenth-century Louisiana. The novel centers around the Ferronaire family, focusing on golden-colored Marcel and his sister Marie, who could pass for white. Living in the midst of the antebellum South, they are never really a part of it, and the novel examines this discrimination and the choices each character must make because of it. Penelope Mesic, in a *Chicago Tribune Book World* review, considered *The Feast of All Saints* "an honest book, a gifted book, the substantial execution of a known design," and *Los Angeles Times Book Review* contributor Valerie Miner suggested that "this new book is rare, combining a 'real story,' a profound theme and exquisite literary grace."

Cry to Heaven, another historical novel, enters the world of the Italian castrati, famous male sopranos who were castrated as boys so their voices would re-

main high. Tonio Treschi, the hero, is a Venetian heir whose brother has him abducted, castrated, and exiled from his home. The rest of the novel relates the pursuit of the goals that obsess him—to become one of the best singers in Europe, and to take his revenge on his brother. Alice Hoffman described *Cry to Heaven* in *New York Times Book Review* as "bold and erotic, laced with luxury, sexual tension, [and] music," and added that "here passion is all, desires are overwhelming, gender is blurred." Hoffman concluded that *Cry to Heaven* "is a novel dazzling in its darkness, and there are times when Rice seems like nothing less than a magician: It is a pure and uncanny talent that can give a voice to monsters and angels both."

Rice returned to historical fiction with *Servant of the Bones,* which Mendelsohn dubbed a "supernatural melodrama," and *Violin,* a gothic romance involving a Stradivarius violin. As in *Memnoch the Devil,* Rice packs much information and philosophizing into *Servant of the Bones.* The book centers on the dark angel Azriel, whose history stretches back to ancient Babylon and later brings him into contact with two powerful teachers during the Middle Ages. After sleeping for six centuries, Azriel awakens in the late twentieth century to become embroiled in a plot to stop billionaire Gregory Bilkin from destroying the Third World with a powerful virus. Mendelsohn, admitting that the novel attempts to say interesting things about complex themes, complained that "Rice's reach has seriously exceeded her grasp." The critic argued that, in contrast to her approach in earlier books, Rice presents metaphysical conflicts too literally here; the reviewer missed the richness of atmosphere and detail, the "writing" that he believed made her earlier books so notable. Though similar criticism greeted *Violin,* which *New York Times Book Review* contributor Bill Hayes found "tedious," Rice's popularity remained as high as ever—especially when she turned her attention once again to the subject of vampires.

Rice's "Vampire Chronicles" series created a legion of devoted fans who snapped up each new book and thronged The Anne Rice Collection, the author's New Orleans retail shop that sold everything from clothing and fragrances to dolls based on her fictional characters. Citing her admiration for another bestselling author, Charles Dickens, Rice explained to Lane: "I've discovered that, over time, it is not an insult to be called a popular writer. It's a wonderful compliment, really. If people only read my books for entertainment, if they only read them to take their minds off their troubles, that's fine." While Rice's popularity has showed no sign of waning, following the death of her husband in 2002 the author announced that she was done with vampires. As she explained in *Book,* even before her husband passed away "I had made the decision that I wanted to move away from the witches and vampires altogether. I wanted to write something completely different. I no longer really wanted to write about people who were damned or who were condemned . . . . and I think [*Blood Canticle*] is about that—being the end of the road, the last of the chronicles."

BIOGRAPHICAL AND CRITICAL SOURCES:

BOOKS

Authors and Artists for Young Adults, Volume 9, Gale (Detroit, MI), 1992.

Badley, Linda, *Writing Horror and the Body: The Fiction of Stephen King, Clive Barker, and Anne Rice,* Greenwood Press (Westport, CT), 1996.

Beahm, George, editor, *The Unauthorized Anne Rice Companion,* Andrews and McMeel (New York, NY), 1996.

Charlton, James, editor, *Fighting Words: Writers Lambast Other Writers—From Aristotle to Anne Rice,* Algonquin Books of Chapel Hill (Chapel Hill, NC), 1994.

Contemporary Literary Criticism, Volume 41, Gale (Detroit, MI), 1987.

Dickinson, Joy, *Haunted City: An Unauthorized Guide to the Magical, Magnificent New Orleans of Anne Rice,* Carol Publishing Group (Secaucus, NJ), 1995.

Hoppenstand, Gary, and Ray B. Browne, editors, *The Gothic World of Anne Rice,* Bowling Green Popular Press, 1996.

Marcus, Jana, *In the Shadow of the Vampire: Reflections from the World of Anne Rice,* Thunder's Mouth Press (New York, NY), 1997.

Ramsland, Katherine M., *Prism of the Night: A Biography of Anne Rice,* Dutton (New York, NY), 1991.

Ramsland, Katherine M., *The Vampire Companion: The Official Guide to Anne Rice's The Vampire Chronicles,* Ballantine (New York, NY), 1993.

Ramsland, Katherine M., *The Witches' Companion: The Official Guide to Anne Rice's Lives of the Mayfair Witches,* Ballantine (New York, NY), 1994.

Ramsland, Katherine M., *The Anne Rice Trivia Book,* Ballantine (New York, NY), 1994.

Ramsland, Katherine M., *The Roquelaure Reader: A Companion to Anne Rice's Erotica,* Plume (New York, NY), 1996.

Ramsland, Katherine M., editor, *The Anne Rice Reader: Writers Explore the Universe of Anne Rice,* Ballantine (New York, NY), 1997.

Rice, Anne, *Interview with the Vampire,* Knopf (New York, NY), 1976.

Riley, Michael, *Conversations with Anne Rice,* Ballantine (New York, NY), 1996.

Roberts, Bette B., *Anne Rice,* Twayne (New York, NY), 1994.

Smith, Jennifer, *Anne Rice: A Critical Companion,* Greenwood Press (New York, NY), 1996.

PERIODICALS

Atlanta Constitution, November 11, 1994, p. P5; July 31, 1995, p. B1.

Atlanta Journal and Constitution, October 4, 1992, p. N8; January 27, 1993, p. A3; June 27, 1993, p. A3; October 3, 1993, p. N10.

Book, September, 2000, p. 32; November-December, 2002, Chris Barsanti, review of *Blackwood Farm,* p. 84; November-December, 2003, Steve Wilson, review of *Blood Canticle,* p. 76, and interview, p. 13.

Booklist, May 15, 1996, p. 1547; July, 2000, p. 1975; August, 2001, Kristine Huntley, review of *Blood and Gold,* p. 2051; August, 2002, Kristine Huntley, review of *Blackwood Farm,* p. 1887; September 1, 2003, Kristine Huntley, review of *Blood Canticle,* p. 7.

Boston Globe, September 30, 1994, p. 64.

Chicago Tribune, October 15, 1993, section 1, p. 22; October 26, 1993, section 5, pp. 1, 2; March 5, 1995, section 12, p. 1; August 31, 1995, section 5, p. 2.

Chicago Tribune Book World, January 27, 1980; February 10, 1980.

Christian Science Monitor, November 14, 1994, p. 13.

Entertainment Weekly, March 19, 1999, p. 98; October 31, 2003, Alynda Wheat, review of *Blood Canticle,* p. 77.

Globe and Mail (Toronto, Ontario, Canada), March 15, 1986; November 5, 1988.

Kirkus Reviews, August 15, 1990; August 1, 2003, review of *Blood Canticle,* p. 989.

Lambda Book Report, October, 2000, Melinda L. Shelton, interview with Rice, p. 6.

Lear's, October, 1989, interview with Rice.

Library Journal, September 1, 1999, p. 254; September 1, 2000, p. 252; October 1, 2001, Patricia Altner, review of *Blood and Gold,* p. 143; September 1, 2003, Patricia Altner, review of *Blood Canticle,* p. 210; October 15, 2003, Kristen L. Smith, review of *Blackwood Farm,* p. 113.

Locus, September, 1992, pp. 17, 19; October, 1993, p. 25.

Los Angeles Times, August 18, 1988; August 15, 1993; September 21, 1994, p. F1; November 28, 1994, p. B7.

Los Angeles Times Book Review, February 3, 1980; December 19, 1982; July 1, 1985; October 27, 1986; November 6, 1988; October 25, 1992, pp. 1, 9; August 15, 1993, p. 10; October 31, 1993, p. 3.

MacLean's, November 16, 1992, p. 68.

National Review, September 3, 1976.

New Republic, May 8, 1976, pp. 29-30.

Newsweek, November 5, 1990.

New York Times, September 8, 1982; September 9, 1982, p. C25; October 19, 1985, p. 16; October 15, 1988; November 7, 1988; October 28, 1993, pp. C15, C20; November 11, 1994, p. A51.

New York Times Book Review, March 2, 1976; May 2, 1976, pp. 7, 14; February 17, 1980, p. 17; October 10, 1980; October 10, 1982, p. 14; October 27, 1985, p. 15; November 27, 1988; June 11, 1989; November 4, 1990; October 24, 1993, p. 38; December 4, 1994, p. 82; July 23, 1995, p.14; August 11, 1996; October 19, 1997; April 19, 1998; December 20. 1998; March 28, 1999, p. 18; October 26, 2000

New York Times Magazine, October 14, 1990.

People, December 5, 1988; November 16, 1998, p. 47; January 11, 1999, p. 113; April 5, 1999, p. 51; December 22, 2003, p. 101.

Publishers Weekly, October 28, 1988; February 10, 1989; November 3, 1989; June 5, 1995, p. 51; August 24, 1998, p. 45; October 26, 1998, p. 19; January 11, 1999, p. 53; August 13, 2000, p. 324; October 2, 2000, p. 45; September 24, 2001, review of *Blood and Gold,* p. 74; September 2, 2002, review of *Blackwood Farm,* p. 52; October 6, 2003, review of *Blood Canticle,* p. 66.

Rolling Stone, November 20, 1986; July 13, 1995, p. 92.

Saturday Review, February 2, 1980, p. 37.

Spectator, December 3, 1994, pp. 56-57.

Success, October 2000, p. 96.

Time, September 9, 1989.

Tribune Books (Chicago, IL), October 27, 1988; May 28, 1989; November 11, 1990; October 18, 1992, p. 3; October 17, 1993, p. 3; October 9, 1994, p. 5.

Variety, August 21, 2000, p. 33.

Voice Literary Supplement, June, 1982; November, 1987; November, 1988.

Wall Street Journal, June 17, 1976, p. 14.

Washington Post, November 6, 1988; October 30, 1992, p. B1.

Washington Post Book World, January 27, 1980, p. 6; October 3, 1982, pp. 7, 9; December 1, 1985, pp. 1, 7; October 26, 1986; November 6, 1988; June 18, 1989; February 11, 1990; October 28, 1990; October 30, 1992, p. 1; October 4, 1993, pp. 4-5; October 10, 1993, p. 4; October 9, 1994, p. 4; January 15, 1995, p. 4; August 6, 1995, p. 2.

ONLINE

Official Anne Rice Home Page, http://www.annerice.com (April 23, 2004).*

*   *   *

ROLLYSON, Carl
See ROLLYSON, Carl E(dmund), Jr.

*   *   *

ROLLYSON, Carl E(dmund), Jr. 1948-
(Carl Rollyson, Carl Sokolnicki Rollyson)

PERSONAL: Born March 2, 1948, in Miami, FL; son of Carl Emerson (a bartender) and Emily (a sales clerk; maiden name, Sokolik) Rollyson; married Charlotte Hollander, May 17, 1969 (divorced, September, 1981); married Lisa Olson Paddock (an attorney and author), November 4, 1981; children: (first marriage) Amelia. *Ethnicity:* "Caucasian." *Education:* Michigan State University, B.A., 1969; University of Toronto, M.A., 1970, Ph.D., 1975. *Hobbies and other interests:* Biking, gardening.

ADDRESSES: Home—Cape May County, NJ. *Office*—Bernard M. Baruch College of the City University of New York, 17 Lexington Ave., New York, NY 10010;

fax: 212-387-1785. *Agent*—Elizabeth Frost-Knappman, New England Publishing Associates Inc., Box 5, Chester, CT 06412.

CAREER: English teacher in Rosemont, PA, 1973-76; Wayne State University, Detroit, MI, assistant professor, 1976-82, associate professor, 1982-87, professor of humanities, 1987, coordinator of humanities division, 1982-83, coordinator of Capstone program, 1984-85, acting assistant dean of graduate school, 1985-87, adjunct associate professor of English, 1986-87; Bernard M. Baruch College of the City University of New York, New York, NY, associate dean of School of Liberal Arts and Sciences, 1987-88, professor of art, 1988-95, professor of English, 1995—, associate provost, 1988-90, acting dean of education, 1989-90. University of Gdansk, Fulbright fellow, 1979-80. Amnesty International, death penalty coordinator, 1986; consultant to North Central Associates.

MEMBER: Authors Guild, Authors League of America, Phi Beta Kappa, Tau Sigma, Phi Kappa Phi, Phi Eta Phi.

AWARDS, HONORS: Woodrow Wilson fellow, 1972-73; faculty research award, Wayne State University, 1979; grants from American Philosophical Society, 1986-87, American Council of Learned Societies, 1988-89, and National Endowment for the Humanities, 1995.

WRITINGS:

Uses of the Past in the Novels of William Faulkner, UMI Research Press (Ann Arbor, MI), 1984, reprinted, International Scholars Publications (San Francisco, CA), 1998.

Marilyn Monroe: A Life of the Actress, UMI Research Press (Ann Arbor, MI), 1986.

(Under name Carl Rollyson) *Lillian Hellman: Her Legend and Her Legacy,* St. Martin's Press (New York, NY), 1988.

(Under name Carl Rollyson) *Nothing Ever Happens to the Brave: The Story of Martha Gellhorn,* St. Martin's Press (New York, NY), 1990, revised edition published as *Beautiful Exile: The Life of Martha Gellhorn,* Aurum Press (London, England), 2001.

(Under name Carl Rollyson) *The Lives of Norman Mailer: A Biography,* Paragon House (New York, NY), 1991.

(Under name Carl Rollyson) *Biography: An Annotated Bibliography,* Salem Press (Pasadena, CA), 1992.

(Under name Carl Rollyson) *Pablo Piccaso,* Rourke Publications (Vero Beach, FL), 1993.

(Under name Carl Rollyson) *Rebecca West: A Life,* Scribner (New York, NY), 1996.

(Under name Carl Sokolnicki Rollyson; with wife, Lisa Olson Paddock) *A Student's Guide to Polish American Genealogy,* Oryx Press (Phoenix, AZ), 1996.

(Under name Carl Sokolnicki Rollyson; with Lisa Olson Paddock) *A Student's Guide to Scandinavian American Genealogy,* Oryx Press (Phoenix, AZ), 1996.

(Under name Carl Rollyson) *The Literary Legacy of Rebecca West,* University Press of America (Lanham, MD), 1997.

(Coauthor) *Where America Stands,* Wiley (New York, NY), 1997.

(Under name Carl Rollyson; with Lisa Olson Paddock) *Herman Melville A to Z: The Essential Reference to his Life and Work,* Facts on File (New York, NY), 2000.

(Under name Carl Rollyson; with Lisa Olson Paddock) *Susan Sontag: The Making of an Icon,* Norton (New York, NY), 2000.

(Under name Carl Rollyson) *Reading Susan Sontag: A Critical Introduction to Her Work,* Ivan R. Dee (Chicago, IL), 2001.

Encyclopedia of American Literature, Volume 3: *The Modern and Post-modern Period,* Facts on File (New York, NY), 2002.

(Under name Carl Rollyson; with Lisa Olson Paddock) *The Brontës A to Z: The Essential Reference to Their Lives and Work,* Facts on File (New York, NY), 2003.

To Be a Woman: The Life of Jill Craigie, Aurum Press (London, England), 2003.

Contributor of more than 500 articles, reviews, and film critiques to periodicals, including *New Criterion, Virginia Quarterly Review, Chicago Review, Literature and History, Baltimore Sun, Detroit Free Press,* and *Wilson Quarterly.*

EDITOR

(Under name Carl Rollyson) *Teenage Refugees from Eastern Europe Speak Out,* Rosen Publishing Group (New York, NY), 1997.

(Under name Carl Rollyson; with Frank N. Magill) *Critical Survey of Long Fiction,* eight volumes, Salem Press (Pasadena, CA), 2nd edition, 2000.

Notable American Novelists, three volumes, Salem Press (Pasadena, CA), 2000.

(Under name Carl Rollyson) *Notable British Novelists,* three volumes, Salem Press (Pasadena, CA), 2001.

(Under name Carl Rollyson; with Frank N. Magill) *A Critical Survey of Drama,* eight volumes, Salem Press (Pasadena, CA), 2nd edition, 2003.

SIDELIGHTS: Carl E. Rollyson, Jr. once told *CA:* "Running into James Mason in the Tower of London was my first encounter with a big public name. Already attracted to a life of the theater at the age of thirteen, I was in London in 1963 as part of a touring company of Shakespearean actors. In college, teaching became an extension of acting and writing a way of scripting my life. Most of my biographies focus on women with theatrical personalities who have created a mythology out of their lives. Writing about Marilyn Monroe, Lillian Hellman, Martha Gellhorn, and Rebecca West [Rollyson later added the names of Susan Sontag and Jill Craigie] has allowed me to explore my fascination with the theater, film, literature, and politics.

"When a good part of my research is complete, I begin to write a draft. I write in three-hour spurts, revising the previous day's work and then going on to new material. On a good day, I write a 1,000-1,500 words, usually not less than 500. I write no matter if I am inspired or depressed. The act of writing is a joy—even when I have to revise heavily what seemed like such good work the day or week before. Mornings are the best, when anything seems possible, before the world has gotten to me. Afternoons are for reading, bike riding, and working on my new house."

BIOGRAPHICAL AND CRITICAL SOURCES:

PERIODICALS

History Now, February, 2003, "Confessions of a Serial Biographer" (interview).

Mississippi Quarterly, summer, 2001, David Johnson, review of *Uses of the Past in the Novels of William Faulkner,* p. 412.

Newsday, May 24, 1988.

New York Times Book Review, May 8, 1988.

ROLLYSON, Carl Sokolnicki
   See ROLLYSON, Carl E(dmund), Jr.)

*   *   *

ROQUELAURE, A. N.
   See RICE, Anne

*   *   *

RUSHDIE, (Ahmed) Salman 1947-

PERSONAL: Born June 19, 1947, in Bombay, Maharashtra, India; son of Anis Ahmed (in business) and Negin (Butt) Rushdie; married Clarissa Luard (in publishing), May 22, 1976 (divorced, 1987); married Marianne Wiggins (an author), 1988 (divorced, 1990); married Elizabeth West, 1997 (divorced, 2004); married Padma Lakshmi, 2004. children: (first marriage) Zafar (son); (second marriage) Milan (daughter). *Education:* King's College, Cambridge, M.A. (history; with honors), 1968.

ADDRESSES: Office—c/o Deborah Rogers Ltd., 49 Blenheim Crescent, London W11, England. *Agent*—Wylie Agency Ltd., 36 Parkside, London SW1X 7JR, England.

CAREER: Writer. Fringe Theatre, London, England, actor, 1968-69; freelance advertising copywriter, 1970-73, 1976-80; writer, 1975—. Executive member of Camden Committee for Community Relations, 1976-83; member of advisory board, Institute of Contemporary Arts, beginning 1985; member of British Film Institute Production Board, beginning 1986. Honorary visiting professor of humanities, Massachusetts Institute of Technology, 1993.

MEMBER: International PEN, Royal Society of Literature (fellow; president, 2004—), Society of Authors, National Book League (member of executive committee), International Parliament of Writers (chair).

AWARDS, HONORS: Booker McConnell Prize for fiction, and English-speaking Union Literary Award, both 1981, and James Tait Black Memorial Prize, 1982, all for *Midnight's Children;* British Arts Council bursary

Salman Rushdie

award, 1981; Prix du Meilleur Livre Etranger, 1984, for *Shame;* Whitbread Prize, and Booker McConnell Prize shortlist, 1988, for *The Satanic Verses,* and 1995, for *The Moor's Last Sigh;* British Book Award for author of the year, *Publishing News,* 1995.

WRITINGS:

NOVELS

Grimus, Gollancz (London, England), 1975, Modern Library (New York, NY), 2003.
Midnight's Children, Knopf (New York, NY), 1981.
Shame, Knopf (New York, NY), 1983.
The Satanic Verses, Viking (New York, NY), 1988.
The Moor's Last Sigh, J. Cape (London, England), 1995, Knopf (New York, NY), 1996.
The Ground beneath Her Feet, Holt (New York, NY), 1999.
Fury, Random House (New York, NY) 2001.

OTHER

The Jaguar Smile: A Nicaraguan Journey, Viking (New York, NY), 1987.

Haroun and the Sea of Stories (juvenile), Granta Books (London, England), 1990.
Imaginary Homelands: The Collected Essays, Viking (London, England), 1991, published as *Imaginary Homelands: Essays and Criticism, 1981-1991,* Viking (New York, NY), 1992.
The Wizard of Oz: BFI Film Classics, Indiana University Press (Bloomington, IN), 1992.
Soldiers Three & In Black & White, Viking Penguin (London, England), 1993.
The Rushdie Letters: Freedom to Speak, Freedom to Write, edited by Steve MacDonogh, University of Nebraska Press (Lincoln, NE), 1993.
East, West (short stories), Pantheon Books (New York, NY), 1994.
(Editor with Elizabeth West) *Mirrorwork: Fifty Years of Indian Writing, 1947-1997,* Holt (New York, NY), 1997.
Conversations with Salman Rushdie, edited by Michael Reder, University Press of Mississippi (Jackson, MS), 2000.
(Adapter, with Simon Reade and Tim Supple) *Salman Rushdie's Midnight's Children* (play; produced in London, England, 2004), Modern Library (New York, NY), 2003.
Step across This Line: Collected Nonfiction 1992-2002, Random House (New York, NY), 2003.

Also author of television screenplays *The Painter and the Pest,* 1985, and *The Riddle of Midnight,* 1988; author of screen adaptation of "The Firebird's Nest." Contributor to *Granta Thirty-nine: The Body,* Viking Penguin, 1992; contributor to magazines and newspapers, including *Atlantic, Granta,* London *Times, London Review of Books, New Statesman,* and *New York Times.*

ADAPTATIONS: The Ground beneath Her Feet was adapted for film by Gemini Films. Several of Rushdie's novels have been adapted as audio recordings.

SIDELIGHTS: While Indian-born British author Salman Rushdie began his writing career quietly, he has become one of the twentieth century's most well-known writers, not only for the ire he attracted from Islamic fundamentalists after publication of his *Satanic Verses,* but also for his thought-provoking examinations of a changing sociopolitical world landscape. Rushdie's first published novel, *Grimus,* which tells of a Native American who receives the gift of immortality and begins an odyssey to find life's meaning, initially attracted attention among science-fiction readers. Discovering the novel, Mel Tilden called the book "engrossing and often wonderful" in a *Times Literary Supplement* review. Tilden determined the book to be "science of the word," recognizing at the same time that it "is one of those novels some people will say is too good to be science fiction, even though it contains other universes, dimensional doorways, alien creatures and more than one madman." Though critics variously called the work a fable, fantasy, political satire, or magical realism, most agreed with David Wilson's assessment in *Times Literary Supplement* that *Grimus* is "an ambitious, strikingly confident first novel" and that Rushdie was an author to watch. Rushdie's subsequent career has proven Wilson correct.

Rushdie turns to India, his birthplace, for the subject of his second book. An allegory, *Midnight's Children* chronicles the history of modern India throughout the lives of 1,001 children born within the country's first hour of independence from Great Britain on August 15, 1947. Saleem Sinai, the novel's protagonist and narrator, is one of two males born at the precise moment of India's independence—the stroke of midnight—in a Bombay nursing home. Moonfaced, stained with birthmarks, and possessed of a "huge cucumber of a nose," Sinai becomes by a twist of fate "the chosen child of midnight." He later explains to the reader that a nurse, in "her own revolutionary act," switched the newborn infants. The illegitimate son of a Hindu street singer's wife and a departing British colonist was given to a prosperous Muslim couple and raised as Saleem Sinai. His midnight twin, called Shiva, was given to the impoverished Hindu street singer who, first cuckolded and then widowed by childbirth, was left to raise a son on the streets of Bombay. Thus, in accordance with class privilege unrightfully bestowed, Sinai's birth was heralded by fireworks and celebrated in newspapers; a congratulatory letter from Jawaharlal Nehru portended his future. "You are the newest bearer of the ancient face of India which is also eternally young," wrote the prime minister. "We shall be watching over your life with the closest attention; it will be, in a sense, the mirror of our own."

Midnight's Children begins more than thirty years after the simultaneous births of Sinai and independent India. Awaiting death in the corner of a Bombay pickle factory where he is employed, Sinai—prematurely aged,

impotent, and mutilated by a personal history that parallels that of his country—tells his life story to Padma, an illiterate working girl who loves and tends him. All of midnight's children, Sinai discloses, possess magical gifts, including prophecy and wizardy.

Sinai and the rest of midnight's children "incorporate the stupendous Indian past, with its pantheon, its epics, and its wealth of folklore," summarized *New York Times* critic Robert Towers, "while at the same time playing a role in the tumultuous Indian present." "The plot of this novel is complicated enough, and flexible enough, to smuggle Saleem into every major event in the subcontinent's past thirty years," wrote Clark Blaise in *New York Times Book Review.* "It is . . . a novel of India's growing up; from its special, gifted infancy to its very ordinary, drained adulthood. It is a record of betrayal and corruption, the loss of ideals, culminating with 'the Widow's' Emergency rule." Although *Midnight's Children* "spans the recent history, both told and untold, of both India and Pakistan as well as the birth of Bangladesh," commented Anita Desai in *Washington Post Book World,* "one hesitates to call the novel 'historical' for Rushdie believes . . . that while individual history does not make sense unless seen against its national background, neither does national history make sense unless seen in the form of individual lives and histories."

Midnight's Children was almost unanimously well received and won England's most exalted literary award, the Booker McConnell Prize for fiction, in 1981. The novel also elicited favorable comparisons to Laurence Sterne's *Tristram Shandy,* Gabriel García Marquéz's *One Hundred Years of Solitude,* Günter Grass's *The Tin Drum,* Saul Bellow's *The Adventures of Augie March,* Louis-Ferdinand Celine's *Death on the Installment Plan,* and V. S. Naipaul's *India: A Wounded Civilization.* And yet, opined Blaise, "It would be a disservice to Salman Rushdie's very original genius to dwell on literary analogues and ancestors. This is a book to accept on its own terms, and an author to welcome into world company."

In 2003, Rushdie collaborated with Simon Reade and Tim Supple to adapt *Midnight's Children* for the New York and London stage. Writing in *Back Stage,* Simi Horwitz describes the three-plus hours play as "a frenetic work punctuated by video projections—including fantasy sequences and historical film clips-and brightly flashing lights." In a review of the London staging of the play, Matt Wolf of *Variety* commented, "Within minutes a narrative is set in motion that weds the personal to the political, the past to the present, and some surprisingly crude stagecraft to a use of video and film that after a while makes one wonder whether Rushdie's source novel wouldn't have been better off as the BBC miniseries he has long wanted it to be."

Like *Midnight's Children*, Rushdie's third book, *Shame*, blends history, myth, politics, and fantasy in a novel that is both serious and comic. *Shame* explores such issues as the uses and abuses of power and the relationship between shame and violence. The idea for the novel, reported interviewer Ronald Hayman in *Books and Bookmen*, grew out of Rushdie's interest in the Pakistani concept of *sharam*. An Urdu word, *sharam* conveys a hybrid of sentiments, including embarrassment, modesty, and the sense of having an ordained place in the world. It speaks to a long tradition of honor that permits, and at times even insists upon, seemingly unconscionable acts. In developing this concept, Rushdie told Hayman, he began "seeing shame in places where I hadn't originally seen it." He explained: "I'd be thinking about Pakistani politics; and I'd find there were elements there that I could use. I had a feeling of stumbling on something quite central to the codes by which we live." Rushdie elaborated in a *New York Times Book Review* interview with Michael T. Kaufman: "There are two axes—honor and shame, which is the conventional axis, the one along which the culture moves, and this other axis of shame and shamelessness, which deals with morality and the lack of morality. *Shame* is at the hub of both axes."

Rushdie develops his theme of shame and violence in a plot so complex and densely populated with characters that, as Towers commented in *New York Times,* "it is probably easier to play croquet (as in 'Alice in Wonderland') with flamingos as mallets and hedgehogs as balls than to give a coherent plot summary of *Shame*." The novel's story line spans three generations and centers on the families of two men—Raza Hyder, a celebrated general, and Iskander Harappa, a millionaire playboy. Their life-and-death struggle, played out against the political backdrop of their country, is based on late twentieth-century Pakistani history. The two characters themselves are based on real-life Pakistani President Zia ul-Haq and former Prime Minister Zulfikar Ali Bhutto, who was deposed by Zia in 1977 and later executed.

Sufiya Zinobia, the novel's heroine, is the embodiment of both shame and violence. Her shame is born with her and is evidenced by her crimson blush. Later, as she absorbs the unfelt shame of others, Sufiya's blushes take on such intensity that they boil her bath water and burn the lips of those who kiss her. Eventually the heat of her shame incubates violence, turning Sufiya into a monster capable of wrenching the heads off of grown men. As the incarnation of an entire nation's shame, wrote Una Chaudhuri, "Sufiya Zinobia is the utterly convincing and terrifying product of a culture lost in falsehood and corruption."

The novel's marginal hero is Sufiya Zinobia's husband, Omar Khayyam Shakil. Introduced at length at the beginning of the book, he disappears for long periods of time thereafter. "I am a peripheral man," he admits shamelessly; "other people have been the principal actors in my life story." The son of an unknown father and one of three sisters, all claiming to be his mother, Shakil was "scorned by the townspeople for his shameful origins," observed Margo Jefferson in *Voice Literary Supplement,* and "he developed a defensive shamelessness." Omar Khayyam Shakil feels himself "a fellow who is not even the hero of his own life; a man born and raised in the condition of being out of things."

Rushdie's choice of a "not-quite hero" for a "not-quite country" addresses an issue that Chaudhuri felt to be central to the book's theme. "Peripherality," she postulated, "is the essence of this land's deepest psychology and the novel's true hero: Shame. It is the doom of those who cannot exist except as reflections of other's perceptions, of those who are unable to credit the notion of individual moral autonomy." *New York Times* critic Christopher Lehmann-Haupt concluded that "the tragedy of *Shame* lies both in the evasion of historical destiny and in embracing that destiny too violently."

Following *Shame* and the publication of *The Jaguar Smile: A Nicaraguan Journey,* a nonfiction account of the political and social conditions Rushdie observed during his 1986 trip to Nicaragua, the author published the novel that made his name known even to nonreaders. *The Satanic Verses* outraged Muslims around the world who were infuriated by what they believed to be insults to their religion. The book was banned in a dozen countries and caused demonstrations and riots in India, Pakistan, and South Africa, during which a number of people were killed or injured. Charging

Rushdie with blasphemy, Iranian leader Ayatollah Ruhollah Khomeini proclaimed that the author and his publisher should be executed; multi-million dollar bounties were offered to anyone who could carry out this decree. This *fatwa,* or death sentence, was reaffirmed by the Iranian government as late as 1993; three people involved with the book's publication were subsequently attacked and one, Rushdie's Japanese translator, was fatally injured.

Religious objections to *The Satanic Verses* stems from sections of the book that concern a religion resembling Islam and whose prophet is named Mahound—a derisive epithet for Mohammed. Offense was taken to scenes in which a scribe named Salman alters the prophet's dictation, thus bringing into question the validity of the Koran, the holy book of Islam. In addition, many Muslims claim that Rushdie repeatedly makes irreverent use of sacred names throughout the book. London *Observer* contributor Blake Morrison explained that to many Muslims Rushdie "has transgressed by treating the Holy Word as myth . . . not truth; by treating the Prophet as a fallible human rather than as a deity; and above all by bringing a skeptical, playful, punning intelligence to bear on a religion which, in these fundamentalist times, is not prepared to entertain doubts or jokes about itself."

For his part, Rushdie has argued that *The Satanic Verses* are not meant to be an attack on the Islamic religion, but that it has been interpreted as such by what he called in *Observer* "the contemporary Thought Police" of Islam who have erected taboos in which one "may not discuss Muhammed as if he were human, with human virtues and weaknesses. One may not discuss the growth of Islam as a historical phenomenon, as an ideology born out of its time." Rushdie explained that in Islam Muhammed, unlike Jesus in the Christian religion, "is not granted divine status, but the text is." A number of critics pointed out that the whole controversy could have been avoided if Rushdie's detractors took into consideration that all of the objectionable scenes take place in the character Gibreel Farishta's dreams, and are part of his insanity-inspired delusions. "It must be added," remarked *Time* critic Paul Gray, "that few of those outraged by *The Satanic Verses* have ever seen it, much less opened it."

The Satanic Verses is a complex narrative that tells several stories within a story in a manner that has been compared to *A Thousand and One Nights.* The central story concerns two men who miraculously survive a terrorist attack on an Air India flight. Gibreel Farishta, a famous Indian actor, acquires a halo; Saladin Chamcha, whose occupation involves providing voices for radio and television programs, metamorphoses into a satyr-like creature. Gibreel becomes deluded into thinking he is the archangel Gabriel, and much of the novel is preoccupied with a number of his dreams, which take on the form of "enigmatic and engrossing" parables, according to *Times Literary Supplement* contributor Robert Irwin. Each story, including the controversial tale concerning Mahound, comments on "the theme of religion and its inexorable, unwelcome and dubious demands." The novel concludes with a confrontation between Gibreel and Saladin, but at this point the distinction between which character is good and which evil has been blurred beyond distinction. Michael Wood remarked in *New Republic* that *The Satanic Verses* gives the reader the feeling that the writer is "trying to fill out a Big Book. But the pervading intelligence of the novel is so acute, the distress it explores so thoroughly understood, that the dullness doesn't settle, can't keep away the urgent questions and images that beset it. This is Rushdie's most bewildered book, but it is also his most thoughtful."

After being forced into hiding to escape the ire of Islamic fundamentalists, Rushdie penned a fairy tale for children that appeared in the United States early in 1991. *Haroun and the Sea of Stories,* conceived by the author as a bedtime story for his son, is a fanciful tale with an important underlying message for adults. A talented storyteller, Rashid receives his gift from the Sea of Stories located on a moon called Kahina. When a water genie's error disconnects Rashid's invisible water faucet, the storyteller loses his abilities. His son Haroun, however, resolves to help his father and journeys to Kahina to meet Walrus, ruler of Gup and controller of the Sea of Stories. Haroun arrives to find the people of Gup at war with Chub and its wicked ruler, Khattam-Shud. Khattam-Shud is poisoning the sea with his factory-ship in an effort to destroy all stories because within each story is a world that he cannot control. After many adventures, Haroun and his allies from Gup destroy Khattam-Shud, saving the Sea of Stories and restoring Rashid's storytelling powers.

Underlying the fantastical plot of *Haroun and the Sea of Stories* is a clear message against the stifling of artistic freedom by figures like Khomeini, whom several reviewers pointed out to be represented by

Khattam-Shud. But the Khomeinis of the world are not the only problem; Rushdie's book also tells how the Walrus hordes sunlight for the Sea of Stories by stopping the moon's rotation, thus unwittingly giving Khattam-Shud his power because the evil ruler thrives on darkness. "If a Khomeini can come to power," explained Richard Eder in *Los Angeles Times Book Review,* "it is in part because the West has arrogated sunlight to itself, and left much of the globe bereft of it. Rushdie defies the Ayatolloah's curse. It is he, not his persecutor, who is the true defender of the Third World."

In 1995, six years after Khomeini ordered Rushdie's death, the writer published a collection of short fiction titled *East, West.* Composed of nine short stories divided into three sections—"East," set in India; "West," set in Europe; and "East-West," set in England—the book's central theme is what the author described to *Newsweek* interviewer Sarah Crichton as "cultural movement and mongrelization and hybridity," a reflection, in fact, of Rushdie's own background. Rushdie's "heritage was derived from the polyglot tumult of multi-ethnic, post-colonial India," Shashi Tharoor explained in *Washington Post Book World.* "His style combined a formal English education with the cadences of the Indian oral story-telling tradition. . . . He brought a larger world—a teeming, myth-infused, gaudy, exuberant, many-hued and restless world—past the immigration inspectors of English literature. And he enriched this new homeland with breathtaking, risk-ridden, imaginative prose of rare beauty and originality." Each story contains characters embodying diverse cultures who interact on a variety of social and emotional planes. Most of them are "a pleasure to read," wrote John Bemrose in *Maclean's.* "Like his great master, Charles Dickens, Rushdie goes in for encyclopedic comedy, with rich people and beggars rubbing shoulders across his pages. His language has something of Dickens's energetic verbosity, while his characters like to wear, for the most part, the gaudy clothes of caricature." Bemrose noted that while most of Rushdie's novels are long, sprawling works, "the stories in *East, West* have the careful precision of ivory miniatures. And all of them, beneath their infectiously playful surfaces, ponder the imponderables of human fate."

Rushdie's name was back on bestseller lists in 1995 with *The Moor's Last Sigh.* A novel that offers a satirical view of the politics of India; its publication seemed almost to mirror that of *The Satanic Verses.* Containing an undisguised parody of powerful Hindu fundamentalist leader Bal Thackeray and making gentle fun of India's first prime minister, Nehru—a stuffed dog bears the leader's first name, Jawaharlal—*The Moor's Last Sigh* was quickly yanked from bookstore shelves in India's capital city and subjected to an embargo by the Indian government.

Narrated by Moraes "the Moor" Zogoiby, *The Moor's Last Sigh* is framed by a dilemma reminiscent of that of the storyteller Scheherazade. The Moor's deranged captor, who was an acquaintance of Moraes's late, famous mother, demands to know the woman's family history. The Moor extends his life by cushioning his tale with a thousand incidental facts—some true, some imagined—and follows the thread of narrative from ancestor and Portuguese explorer Vasco da Gama through the rise and fall of a Portuguese trade dynasty, the meeting of his parents in the 1950s, childhood memories of his flamboyant artist mother, Aurora, and his own exile from India. As a *Publishers Weekly* reviewer noted, the novel hints at a dark fate for India: "The society Rushdie portrays so powerfully is rife with corruption; pluralism is dying and a dangerous separatism is on the rise, encouraging hatred and despair."

Although many critics have interpreted everything Rushdie wrote following the imposition of the fatwa as a cloaked reference to the author's unfortunate personal dilemma, Paul Gray maintained in *Time* that *The Moor's Last Sigh* "is much too teeming and turbulent, too crammed with history and dreams, to fit into any imaginable category, except that of the magically comic and sad. . . . The true subject of *The Moor's Last Sigh* is language in all its uninhibited and unpredictable power to go reality one better and rescue humans from the fate of suffering in silence." Rushdie remained ambivalent on the place of the novel within his own body of work, telling Maya Jaggi in *New Statesman* that *The Moor's Last Sigh* is a "completion of what I began in *Midnight's Children, Shame,* and *The Satanic Verses*—the story of myself, where I came from, a story of origins and memory. But it's also a public project that forms an arc, my response to an age in history that began in 1947 [when India formed a democratic socialist state]. That cycle of novels is now complete."

Rushdie's novel *The Ground beneath Her Feet* is a modern-day retelling of the Orpheus myth, with the hero and heroine cast as rock stars. Ormus Cama, a pop star reminiscent of Elvis Presley and John Lennon, seeks to bring back to life the divine Vina Apsara, a celebrity icon on par with Madonna and Princess Diana, who is swallowed up by an earthquake on Valentine's Day, 1989. Their tragic love story is narrated by the power couple's close friend, the photographer Rai Merchant, who has long been obsessed with Vina himself. Ormus' grief leads him to seek out Vina's slavish fans who painstakingly emulate the star. He latches on to one—Mira Celano—who accompanies him on his "Into the Underworld" tour in search of Vina. Many of the themes prominent in Rushdie's earlier novels appear in *The Ground beneath Her Feet* as well. The book "addresses the themes of exile, metamorphosis and flux," wrote Michiko Kakutani in *New York Times,* "and like those earlier books it examines such issues through the prism of multiple dichotomies: between home and rootlessness, love and death, East and West, reason and the irrational."

Complicated and many-layered, the book brought criticism from some reviewers, including Michael Gorra in *Times Literary Supplement.* "There is too much toomuchness" Gorra noted, with "so many characters, so many incidents—and in all that prosy batter something gets lost." Specifically, wrote James Gardner in *National Review,* the novel's main characters are not "compelling." "He makes the fatal mistake of being too impressed by their rock-star glamour," he continued, "and despite the arbitrary complexities that he attributes to them, he never succeeds in animating them with the emotional vitality that has so memorably enlivened his characters in the past." Other critics appreciated Rushdie's intended message. The author's theme, said a reviewer in *Economist,* "is that the ground beneath our feet is always shifting. Modern culture is in a permanent state of fragmentation. . . . Reality exists on many planes." Sven Birkerts, writing in *Esquire,* compared Rushdie's storytelling abilities to those of Ovid and Scheherazade. "Rushdie roves the world like one in mad pursuit of tale and theme," Birkerts wrote, and *The Ground beneath Her Feet* "tells a grand story—a kind of ur-story—of the age of rock 'n' roll, but in the process spins around it half a hundred veils of myth and hidden meaning." Troy Patterson praised the novel in *Entertainment Weekly* as being "about the power of song itself," noting that "the Ulysses-like name-dropping also evokes memories of dreams dreamt and heroes adored."

Fury at first appears to be more straightforward than many of Rushdie's previous novels. The book follows

Malik Solanka, the Indian-born, Cambridge-educated philosopher and creator of the pop-culture phenomenon of the "Little Brain," a philosophically minded doll who becomes the star of a successful television show. Malik succumbs to a serious midlife crisis, hastily leaves his wife and child in London, and attempts to begin anew as an academic at a Manhattan university. Malik is uncomfortable with modern society and is subject to fits of rage, which increasingly come to dominate his life. In Malik's quest for renewal he becomes involved with two women, the second of which, the beautiful Neela, forces Malik into an epiphany of sorts as the narrative veers into the magic realism for which Rushdie has come to be known. Complicating matters is Malik's resemblance to a Panama hat-wearing serial killer, who is murdering young women from the city's society elite. Millennial paranoia, the Internet, American consumerism, and civil war in a small third world country are all elements of Rushdie's canvas in *Fury.*

Some critics took issue with Rushdie's portrayal of American society in *Fury.* By date-stamping the book with names like Monica Lewinsky, Tommy Hilfiger, and Courtney Love, "*Fury* is immediately obsolete," maintained James Wood in *New Republic.* A reviewer for *Economist* said that "Rushdie is usually too effervescent a writer to be pompous, but here he is drawn into making overwrought and grandiose pronouncements on the state of America." Michiko Kakutani in *New York Times* claimed that Rushdie's portrayal of New York "fails not only because it's based on a false observation—the city in 2000 was reeling more from a surfeit of greed and complacency than from free-floating anxiety and anger—but also because Solanka never seems intimately connected to the events he is witnessing in America." Other critics commended Rushdie's scathing view of American society. As Malik attempts to conquer his fury, his story becomes "a fantastic, humorous, and gravely serious tale about the torments of love," wrote Brad Hooper in *Booklist,* "but, even more than that, the abrasions on the soul inflicted by today's cellphone society." Barbara Hoffert of *Library Journal* likewise commended the novel for its evocation of a frantic, skin-deep society: *Fury* "veers precariously through our obsessive times, capturing every nuance exactly."

Other critics focused on different aspects of the novel. Paul Evans, reviewing *Fury* in *Book,* praised Rushdie's fiction as "a metaphysical thriller and a sci-fi-tinged fantasy, a treatise on gender politics and a farce about academia." Evans further concentrated on the idea that to transcend his anger, "Malik must endure the demise of his old self in order to live anew." A reviewer for *Publishers Weekly* wrote that Rushdie "catches roiling undercurrents of incivility and inchoate anger" in "prose crackling with irony." In regards to the book's language, which other critics have compared to that of Vladimir Nabokov, *Publishers Weekly* reviewer said that "his relatively narrow focus results in a crisper narrative; there are fewer puns and a deeper emotional involvement with his characters."

In addition to fiction, Rushdie has published several essay collections. *Imaginary Homelands: Essays and Criticism, 1981-1991* is a selection of essays and other short journalistic pieces. Some of the essays, such as "One Thousand Days in a Balloon," which Rushdie presented at an unannounced appearance at Columbia University in 1991, and "Why I Have Embraced Islam," an explanation of his commitment to the religion whose popular leaders violently reject and continue to persecute him, were written after he was forced into hiding. Others, dating from before the *fatwa,* picture a writer gradually forming his own concepts of what constitutes truth and beauty in literature. These works, *Commonweal* contributor Paul Elie elaborated, "serve as a reminder that once upon a time"—before the wrath of fundamentalist Islam fell upon on the author's head—"he was just another middling British writer, holding forth on this and that with more intelligence and enthusiasm than was required of him."

In 2003 a new collection of Rushdie's nonfiction writings was published as *Step across This Line: Collected Nonfiction, 1992-2002.* Donald Morrison, writing in *Time International,* commented that in this book Rushdie shows himself to be a "thoughtful and feisty essayist." *Booklist* contributor Donna Seaman praised the works included, noting that the author "has written stirring and significant essays about his harrowing, often surreal life."

In September of 1998, the fatwa against Rushdie was lifted by the Iranian government, though certain fundamentalist Muslim groups, claiming that a fatwa cannot be lifted, increased the reward for killing him to $2.8 million. In addition, in 2004 an Iranian extremist Islamic group calling itself the General Staff for the Glorification of Martyrs of the Islamic World offered another 100,000 dollar reward for Rushdie. As a result,

the author continued to keep security tight, although he frequently travels between his homes in London, New York, and India, gives interviews and makes public appearances. In 1999 he even joined the rock group U2 on stage to perform the song "The Ground beneath Her Feet," which was inspired by Rushdie's book. A short time later, Rushdie was finally granted a visa to return to India; he was quoted in *Time* as saying that lifting of this restriction "feels like another step back into the light."

Journalist Christopher Hitchens hypothesized in *Progressive* that "if it were not for the threat of murder, and the fact that this murder has been solicited by a religious leadership, I believe that Salman Rushdie might now be the Nobel Laureate in literature. . . . He has raised a body of fiction that explores the world of the post-colonial multi-ethnic and the multi-identity exile or emigrant. He has done so, moreover . . . by making experiments in language that recall those of [James] Joyce." "All of his works," continued Hitchens, "are designed to show that there is no mastery of language unless it is conceded that language is master."

BIOGRAPHICAL AND CRITICAL SOURCES:

BOOKS

Goonetilleke, D. C. R. A., *Salman Rushdie,* St. Martin's Press (New York, NY), 1998.

Gorra, Michael Edward, *After Empire: Scott, Naipaul, Rushdie,* University of Chicago Press (Chicago, IL), 1997.

Kuortti, Joel, *Place of the Sacred: The Rhetoric of the Satanic Verses Affair,* P. Lang (New York, NY), 1997.

Kuortti, Joel, *The Salman Rushdie Bibliography: A Bibliography of Salman Rushdie's Work and Rushdie Criticism,* P. Lang (New York, NY), 1997.

Kuortti, Joel, *Fictions to Live in: Narration as an Argument for Fiction in Salman Rushdie's Novels,* P. Lang (New York, NY), 1998.

Rushdie, Salman, *Midnight's Children,* Knopf (New York, NY), 1981.

Rushdie, Salman, *Shame,* Knopf (New York, NY), 1983.

PERIODICALS

Atlanta Journal Constitution, January 21, 1996, Alan Ryan, review of *The Moor's Last Sigh,* p. L11.

Atlantic Monthly, February, 1996, Phoebe-Lou Adams, review of *The Moor's Last Sigh,* p. 114.

Back Stage, April 4, 2003, Simi Horwitz, review of *Midnight's Children* (play), p. 3.

Biography, summer, 2003, Ruchir Joshi, review of *Step across This Line: Collected Nonfiction, 1992-2002,* p. 554.

Book, September, 2001, Paul Evans, review of *Fury,* p. 67.

Booklist, November 1, 1995, Brad Hooper, review of *The Moor's Last Sigh,* p. 435; June 1, 2001, Brad Hooper, review of *Fury,* p. 1798; September 15, 2002, Donna Seaman, review of of *Step across This Line,* p. 194.

Books and Bookmen, September, 1983, Ronald Hayman.

Boston Globe, January 14, 1996, Gail Caldwell, "For Love of Mother," p. B43.

Chicago Tribune, February 17, 1989; September 24, 1990.

Chicago Tribune Book World, March 15, 1981; April 26, 1981; January 22, 1984; January 22, 1995, p. 3; January 14, 1996, Beverly Fields, "Salman Rushdie Returns," pp. 1, 4; January 28, 1996, John Blades, "An Interview with Salman Rushdie," p. 3.

Christian Century, October 14, 1998, "Rushdie Hails End of 'Terrorist Threat,'" p. 931.

Christian Science Monitor, March 2, 1989; January 26, 1995, p. B1, B4; February 7, 1996, Merle Rubin, "Extravagant, Madcap Vision of an Indian Clan," p. 13.

Commonweal, September 25, 1981; December 4, 1981; November 4, 1983, Una Chaudhuri, review of *Shame,* p. 590; December 4, 1992; February 9, 1996, Sara Maitland, "The Author Is Too Much with Us," pp. 22-23.

Economist, October 3, 1998, "The Lifting of an Unliftable Fatwa: Iran," p. 49; May 15, 1999, "Boys' Toys," p. 12; August 25, 2001, "Signifying Nothing."

Encounter, February, 1982.

Entertainment Weekly, April 16, 1999, Troy Patterson, "What a Rushdie! The Majestic New Novel from the Author of *The Satanic Verses,* Salman Rushdie, Takes on Sex, Drugs, and Rock & Roll. And Don't Be Surprised if You Hear Some of the Lyrics in a U2 Song," p. 52.

Esquire, May 1, 1999, Sven Birkerts, "Sex, Drugs, and That Other Thing," p. 60.

Harper's, February, 1998, "The Pen Is Crueler than the Sword," p. 18.

Illustrated London News, October, 1988.

India Today, September 15, 1988; October 31, 1988; March 15, 1989.

Interview, May, 1999, Deborah Treisman, "Salman Rushdie's Rock 'n' Roll," p. 122.

Library Journal, August, 2001, Barbara Hoffert, review of *Fury,* p. 166; October 15, 2002, Shelly Cox, review of *Step across This Line,* p. 73.

London Review of Books, September 29, 1988; July 9, 1992, p. 17; September 7, 1995, Michael Wood, "Shenanigans," pp. 3, 5.

Los Angeles Times Book Review, August 26, 1979; December 25, 1983; November 11, 1990; January 7, 1996, Richard Eder, "English as a Wicked Weapon," pp. 3, 13.

Maclean's, March 6, 1995, p. 86; October 9, 1995, John Bemrose, "Tower of Babble," p. 85; May 24, 1999, Anthony Wilson-Smith, "The Revival of Salman Rushdie: While Still Wary, the Author Is Gradually Emerging from the Shadow of a Death Sentence," p. 54.

Mother Jones, April-May, 1990.

Nation, January 1, 1996, Jessica Hagedorn, "They Came for the Hot Stuff," pp. 25-27; December 22, 1997, Christopher Hitchens, "Satanic Curses," p. 8.

National Review, December 31, 1995, James Bowman, "Absolutely Fabulist," pp. 46-7; May 17, 1999, James Gardner, "Rock and Rushdie," p. 61.

New Republic, May 23, 1981; March 6, 1989; March 13, 1989; December 10, 1990; March 18, 1996, James Wood, "Salaam Bombay," pp. 38-41; April 26, 1999, James Wood, "Lost in the Punhouse," p. 94; September 24, 2001, James Wood, "The Nobu Novel," p. 32.

New Statesman, May 1, 1981; September 23, 1994, p. 40; September 8, 1995, Maya Jaggi, "The Last Laugh," pp. 20-21; September 8, 1995, Aamer Hussein, "City of Mongrel Joy," pp. 39-40.

New Statesman & Society, September 30, 1988; March 29, 1991; May 29, 1992, pp. 39-40.

Newsweek, April 20, 1981; February 12, 1990, December 9, 1991, p. 79; February 6, 1995, Sarah Crichton, review of *East, West,* pp. 59-60; January 8, 1996, "The Prisoner in the Tower," p. 70.

New Yorker, July 27, 1981; January 9, 1984.

New York Review of Books, September 24, 1981; March 2, 1989; March 21, 1996, J. M. Coetzee, "Palimpsest Regained," pp. 13-16.

New York Times, April 23, 1981, Robert Towers, review of *Midnight's Children;* November 2, 1983; January 27, 1989; February 13, 1989; February 15, 1989; February 16, 1989; February 17, 1989; February 18, 1989; February 20, 1989; February 21, 1989; February 22, 1989; February 23, 1989;

February 24, 1989; February 25, 1989; March 1, 1989; March 28, 1991, p. 26; December 2, 1995, John F. Burns, "Another Rushdie Novel, Another Bitter Epilogue;" December 28, 1995, Michiko Kakutani, "Rushdie on India: Serious, Crammed yet Light," pp. C13, C20; January 14, 1996, Norman Rush, "Doomed in Bombay," p. 7; January 17, 1996, Nina Barnton, "Sentenced to Death but Recalled to Life," pp. C1-2; April 13, 1999, Michiko Kakutani, "Turning Rock-and-Roll into Quakes;" August 31, 2001, Michiko Kakutani, "A Dollmaker and His Demons in the Big City."

New York Times Book Review, April 19, 1981, Clark Blaise, review of *Midnight's Children,* p. 1; March 28, 1982; November 13, 1983, Michael T. Kaufman, "Author from Three Countries" (interview), p. 3; January 29, 1989; November 11, 1990; June 2, 1991, p. 15; January 15, 1995, pp. 1, 16-17; January 14, 1996, p. 7; April 18, 1999, Charles McGrath, "Rushdie Unplugged."

Observer (London, England), February 9, 1975; July 19, 1981; September 25, 1988; January 22, 1989; February 19, 1989; November 11, 1990, p. 1.

Progressive, October, 1997, Christopher Hitchens, "Salman Rushdie: 'Even This Colossal Threat Did Not Work. Life Goes On,'" p. 34.

Publishers Weekly, November 11, 1983; January 30, 1995, Sybil Steinberg, "A Talk with Salman Rushdie: Six Years into the Fatwa," pp. 80-82; October 2, 1995, review of *The Moor's Last Sigh,* p. 52; July 16, 2001, a review of *Fury,* p. 166.

Quill and Quire, April, 1996, Nancy Wigston, review of *The Moor's Last Sigh,* p. 25.

Saturday Review, March, 1981.

Spectator, June 13, 1981.

Time, February 13, 1989; February 27, 1989; September 11, 1995; January 15, 1996, Paul Gray, "Rushdie: Caught on the Fly," p. 70, "Writing to Save His Life," pp. 70-71; February 22, 1999, Maseeh Rahman, "Homecoming to What? Rushdie's Planned Return to India Is of Symbolic Value to Him but an Opportunity for Vengeance to Many," p. 241; April 26, 1999, Paul Gray, "Ganja Growing in the Tin: Salman Rushdie Reimagines Orpheus as a Modern Rock Star, and Almost Brings It Off," p. 99.

Time International, December 23, 2002, Donal Morrison, review of *Step across This Line,* p. 63.

Times (London, England), October 5, 1995.

Times Literary Supplement, February 21, 1975; May 15, 1981; September 9, 1983; September 30, 1988; September 28, 1990; April 9, 1999, Michael Gorra, "It's Only Rock and Roll but I Like It," p. 25.

Variety, February 10, 2003, Matt Wolf, review of *Midnight's Children* (play), p. 43.

Vogue, November, 1983.

Voice Literary Supplement, November, 1983, Margo Jefferson, review of *Shame.*

Washington Post, January 18, 1989; February 15, 1989; February 17, 1989; February 18, 1989; January 20, 1996, Linton Weeks, "Salman Rushdie, out and About," p. C1.

Washington Post Book World, March 15, 1981; November 20, 1983; January 29, 1989; January 8, 1995, pp. 1, 11; January 7, 1996, Michael Dirda, "Where the Wonders Never Cease," pp. 1-2.

World Literature Today, winter, 1982.

ONLINE

BBC Web site, http://www.bbc.co.uk/ (March 12, 2002).*

S

SEVERANCE, John B(ridwell) 1935-

PERSONAL: Born July 24, 1935, in New York, NY; son of Frank A. F. (a lawyer) and Frances V. Severance; married Gwenith Heuss (marriage ended); married Sylvia Frezzolini, March 16, 1984; children: (first marriage) Rebecca E., Abigail F. *Ethnicity:* "Caucasian." *Education:* Harvard University, B.A., 1958; Wesleyan University, Middletown, CT, M.A.L.S., 1969. *Politics:* Independent.

ADDRESSES: Home and office—6 George St., Westerly, RI 02891.

CAREER: Harper & Row Publishers, Inc., New York, NY, sales representative, 1958-61; schoolteacher in South Kent, CT, 1961-69, Wallingford, CT, 1969-84, and New York, NY, 1986-87; Kent Place School, Summit, NJ, teacher and department head, 1987-91.

MEMBER: Authors Guild, Authors League of America.

WRITINGS:

FOR YOUNG ADULTS

Winston Churchill: Soldier, Statesman, Artist, Clarion Books (New York, NY), 1996.
Grandhi, Great Soul, Clarion Books (New York, NY), 1997.
Thomas Jefferson: Architect of Independence, Clarion Books (New York, NY), 1998.

Einstein: Visionary Scientist, Clarion Books (New York, NY), 1999.
Skyscrapers: How America Grew Up, Holiday House (New York, NY), 2000.
Braving the Fire (novel), Clarion Books (New York, NY), 2002.

WORK IN PROGRESS: A historical novel set in the mid-nineteenth-century United States.

SIDELIGHTS: John B. Severance once told *CA:* "Somewhere in my high school years I discovered that I enjoyed the process of writing, whether it was an expository essay for history or a creative piece for English class. After several decades in education, I still enjoy ordering words, whether it's a free-wheeling letter to a friend or the laborious constructing and reconstructing of sentences in a chapter of a book in progress. To me, all writing seems fundamentally creative.

"I enjoy writing not because it comes easily to me (it doesn't), but I take pleasure in concentrating on phrasing and rephrasing until the juxtaposition of words is as clear and balanced as I can make it. It matters little if the day's output is ten pages or one paragraph. The feeling of accomplishment is the same.

"My current professional efforts are in the field of young adult biographies. My intention is to show that leaders who appear super-human in the pages of history were, in fact, very much like the rest of us. They became great only when they made the effort to reach beyond their ordinary human weaknesses.

"I am busily picking away at projects in nonfiction, but if that vein ever gives out, I would happily try fiction. Language is the raw material awaiting the hand of the wordsmith."

BIOGRAPHICAL AND CRITICAL SOURCES:

PERIODICALS

Booklist, June 1, 2000, Carolyn Phelan, review of *Skyscrapers: How America Grew Up,* p. 1879; December 15, 2000, Gillian Engberg, review of *Skyscrapers,* p. 810; October 1, 2002, Hazel Rochman, review of *Braving the Fire,* p. 313.

Horn Book, September, 2000, review of *Skyscrapers,* p. 600.

Kirkus Reviews, August 1, 2002, review of *Braving the Fire,* p. 1142.

New York Times Book Review, December 17, 2000, Simon Rodberg, review of *Skyscrapers,* p. 31.

School Library Journal, July, 2000, Mary Ann Carcich, review of *Skyscrapers,* p. 122; November, 2002, Elizabeth M. Reardon, review of *Braving the Fire,* p. 176.

Stone Soup, September, 2000, Casey Pelletier, review of *Einstein: Visionary Scientist,* p. 20.

*   *   *

SHIELDS, Carol 1935-2003

PERSONAL: Born June 2, 1935, in Oak Park, IL; died from complications from breast cancer, July 16, 2003, in Victoria, British Columbia, Canada; daughter of Robert E. and Inez (Selgren) Warner; married Donald Hugh Shields (a professor), July 20, 1957; children: John, Anne, Catherine, Margaret, Sara. *Education:* Hanover College, B.A., 1957; University of Ottawa, M.A., 1975.

CAREER: Canadian Slavonic Papers, Ottawa, Ontario, editorial assistant, 1972-74; writer, 1974-2003; University of Manitoba, professor, 1980-2000; Chancellor University of Winnipeg, 1996-2000.

MEMBER: Writers' Union of Canada, Writers Guild of Manitoba, PEN, Jane Austen Society, Royal Society of Canada.

Carol Shields

AWARDS, HONORS: Winner of young writers' contest sponsored by Canadian Broadcasting Corp. (CBC), 1965; Canada Council grants, 1972, 1974, 1976; fiction prize from Canadian Authors Association, 1976, for *Small Ceremonies;* CBC Prize for Drama, 1983; National Magazine Award, 1984, 1985; Arthur Ellis Award, 1988; Marian Engel Award, 1990; Governor General's Award for English-language fiction, National Book Critics Circle Award for fiction, 1994, and Pulitzer Prize for fiction, 1995, all for *The Stone Diaries;* Orange Prize, 1998, for *Larry's Party;* Guggenheim fellow, 1999; Chevalier de l'Ordre des Arts et des Lettres (France), 2000; shortlisted for Booker Prize and James Tait Black Memorial Prize for fiction, both 2002, and Orange Prize for fiction nomination, 2003, all for *Unless;* Charles Taylor Prize for literary nonfiction, 2002, for *Jane Austen;* named Author of the Year, Book Expo Canada, 2003. Honorary doctorates from University of Ottawa, 1995; Hanover College, 1996; University of Winnipeg, 1996; Queen's University, 1996; University of British Columbia, 1997; Concordia University, 1997; University of Toronto, 1998; University of Western Ontario, 1998; Carleton University, 2000; Mount St. Vincent University, 2000; and Wilfrid Laurier University, 2000.

WRITINGS:

Others (poetry), Borealis Press (Ottawa, Ontario, Canada), 1972.

Intersect (poetry), Borealis Press (Ottawa, Ontario, Canada), 1974.

Susanna Moodie: Voice and Vision (criticism), Borealis Press (Ottawa, Ontario, Canada), 1976.

Small Ceremonies (novel), McGraw-Hill (New York, NY), 1976, reprinted, Penguin (New York, NY), 1996.

The Box Garden (novel), McGraw-Hill (New York, NY), 1977, reprinted, Penguin (New York, NY), 1996.

Happenstance (novel; also see below), McGraw-Hill (New York, NY), 1980.

A Fairly Conventional Woman (novel; also see below), Macmillan (Toronto, Ontario, Canada), 1982.

Various Miracles (short stories), Stoddart (Don Mills, Canada), 1985, Penguin (New York, NY), 1989.

Swann: A Mystery (novel), General, 1987, Viking (New York, NY), 1989.

The Orange Fish (short stories), Random House (Toronto, Ontario, Canada), 1989, Viking (New York, NY), 1990.

Departures and Arrivals, Blizzard (Winnipeg, Ontario, Canada), 1990.

(With Blanche Howard) *A Celibate Season* (novel), Coteau (Regina, Canada), 1991, Penguin (New York, NY), 1999.

The Republic of Love (novel), Viking (New York, NY), 1992.

Coming to Canada (poetry), Carleton University Press (Ottawa, Canada), 1992.

Happenstance (contains the novels *Happenstance* and *A Fairly Conventional Woman*), Random House (Toronto, Ontario, Canada), 1993, Viking, 1994.

The Stone Diaries (novel), Random House (Toronto, Ontario, Canada), 1993, Viking (New York, NY), 1994.

Thirteen Hands (drama), Blizzard (Winnipeg, Ontario, Canada), 1993.

(With Catherine Shields) *Fashion, Power, Guilt, and the Charity of Families,* Blizzard (Winnipeg, Ontario, Canada), 1995.

Mary Swann, Fourth Estate (London, England), 1996.

Larry's Party (novel), Viking (New York, NY), 1997.

(With David Williamson) *Anniversary* (play), Blizzard (Winnipeg, Ontario, Canada), 1998.

(Editor) *Scribner's Best of the Fiction Workshops 1998,* Scribner, 1998.

Dressing up for the Carnival (short stories), Viking (New York, NY), 2000.

Jane Austen (biography), Viking (New York, NY), 2001.

(Editor with Marjorie Anderson) *Dropped Threads: What We Aren't Told,* Vintage Canada (Toronto, Ontario, Canada), 2001.

Unless (novel), Fourth Estate (New York, NY), 2002.

(Editor with Marjorie Anderson) *Dropped Threads 2: More of What We Aren't Told,* Vintage Canada (Toronto, Ontario, Canada), 2003.

Author of *The View,* 1982, *Women Waiting,* 1983, and *Face Off,* 1987.

Shields's works have been translated into other languages, including Swedish, Italian, French, Chinese, Norwegian, German, Spanish, Danish, Korean, Japanese, and Polish.

ADAPTATIONS: Swann: A Mystery was adapted for a film starring Miranda Richardson, 1996; several of Shields's novels were adapted as audiobooks.

SIDELIGHTS: "The extraordinariness of ordinary people was Carol's forte," novelist Margaret Atwood noted in an *Entertainment Weekly* remembrance of Pulitzer Prize-winning author Carol Shields. Shields, who died of cancer in 2003, is best remembered for her 1993 novel *The Stone Diaries,* as well as for her highly acclaimed biography of English writer Jane Austen. Praising Shields for her "intellectual daring" and "unambiguous prose," *New Statesman* contributor Rachel Cusk noted that "reading Shields is like talking to a good friend, someone reassuring and wise who, out of modesty or sympathy, keeps her own heart a secret."

Shields was born in Oak Park, Illinois, the youngest of three children. Her mother was a former teacher, and her father managed a candy factory. After graduating from Hanover College, she met Donald Shields while they both studied in England. They married and moved to Vancouver a year later. She began writing while raising her family, and in 1965 submitted a poem to a young writers' competition, which she won.

When her husband landed a job at the University of Ottawa, Shields began to work toward a Master of Arts degree. Urged by professors who recognized her talent, she put together her first book of poems, which was published in 1972. Four years later she was offered an editing position with a small journal, *Canadian Slavonic Papers.* As Shields once said, "it was a jobette, really. I worked in a spare room upstairs. I became the Mother who Typed." Shields's first book, *Small Ceremonies,* was written, in part, from research she did for her thesis on Susanna Moodie. With its publication, she began her long and distinguished writing and teaching career.

Critics have sometimes divided Shields's career as a writer into two distinct phases. Her first four novels—*Small Ceremonies, The Box Garden, Happenstance,* and *A Fairly Conventional Woman*—are portrayals of everyday life, where her protagonists struggle to define themselves and make human connections in their close relationships. Kathy O'Shaughnessy wrote in *Observer* that *Small Ceremonies* "is a novel of ideas: about privacy, knowledge of others, about how we perceive each other, and are perceived by others," while *London Review of Books* writer Peter Campbell, in a review of *Happenstance,* stated that "Shields writes well about decent people, and her resolutions are shrewder than those in the self-help books."

The next phase of Shields's career is marked by risk taking. With her first short-story collection, 1985's *Various Miracles,* she began to experiment more with form by using a variety of voices, while continuing to portray ordinary people in everyday situations. *Books* contributor Andrea Mynard asserted that Shields's "robust realism is typical of the growing sorority of Canadian writers, including Margaret Atwood and Alice Munro, who have been gaining a strong reputation. . . . In her accessibly simple and lucid style, Carol intelligently grasps the minutiae of everyday life and illuminates the quirks of human nature. Her observations of contemporary dilemmas are brilliant."

In her 1987 novel *Swann: A Mystery* Shields continues her experimentation by using four distinct voices to tell the story. In this novel she also develops the theme that will be used in her subsequent work: the mysterious nature of art and creation. *Swann,* noted Danny Karlin in *London Review of Books,* "is a clever book, self-conscious about literature, fashionably preoccupied with questions of deconstruction, of the 'textuality' of identity, of the powers and powerlessness of language. This impression is confirmed by its

confident and playful manipulation of different narrative modes." Some critics, however, castigated what they considered the author's simple characterizations. *New York Times Book Review* writer Josh Robins noted that "the characters remain too one-dimensional, often to the point of caricature, to support sporadic attempts at psychological portraiture." The book, which first brought Shields to the attention of U.S. publishers, was later adapted as a film.

Shields took another risk by attempting the genre of the romance novel in 1992's *The Republic of Love,* but made the form her own by making her main characters wade through the coldness and problems of the twentieth century before reaching the happy ending. "Shields has created a sophisticated [romance] story," stated *Books in Canada* contributor Rita Donovan. "And the 'happy ending,' so traditional to the romance novel, is here refurbished, updated, and— most happily—earned."

Shields's early novels, while popular with readers, were not taken seriously by critics. Some have argued that in the early part of her career Shields was underestimated as a stylist and her works were dismissed as being naturalistic. Critics generally praised Shields when she began experimenting more with form. Some of her risks were originally considered failures, as in the case of the last section of *Swann,* in which she attempts to bring all four voices together in a screenplay form. More recent critical appraisal of her works has found more appreciation for such experimentation.

The Stone Diaries is the fictional biography of Daisy Goodwill Flett, whose life spans eight decades and includes time spent in both Canada and the United States. Written in both the first and third person, the story begins with her birth in 1905 in rural Manitoba, Canada. Daisy's mother, extremely obese and unaware that she is pregnant, dies moments later. Unable to care for his daughter, the infant's father, Cuyler Goodwill, convinces his neighbor Clarentine Flett to raise the child. Soon afterward, Clarentine leaves her husband and, taking Daisy with her, travels to Winnipeg, where she moves in with her son, Barker. Cuyler later takes Daisy to Bloomington, Indiana, where he has become a highly successful stonecarver. There, Daisy marries a wealthy young man who dies during their honeymoon. In 1936 she marries Barker, who has become renowned for his agricultural research, and resettles in Canada. In her role as wife and mother, Daisy appears quiet and content, but after her husband dies, she takes over a gardening column for *Ottawa Recorder,* writing as Mrs. Greenthumb. Her joy—she finds the work incredibly meaningful and fulfilling—is short-lived however, as the editor decides to give the column to a staff writer, despite Daisy's protests. She eventually recovers from the disappointment and lives the remainder of her life in Sarasota, Florida, where she amuses herself playing bridge.

Critical reaction to *The Stone Diaries,* which won Canada's Governor General's Award, the National Book Critics Circle Award, and the Pulitzer Prize, and was also short-listed for the Booker Prize, was overwhelmingly favorable. Commentators have praised Shields for exploring such universal problems as loneliness and lost opportunities and for demonstrating that all lives are significant and important no matter how banal and confined they appear. Others have lauded the novel as a brilliant examination of the divergence between one's inner and outer self, and of the relations between fiction, biography, and autobiography. As Allyson F. McGill wrote in *Belles Lettres,* "Shields and Daisy challenge us to review our lives, to try and see life honestly, even while 'their' act of authorship only reveals how impossible it is to see and speak objective truth." A *Canadian Forum* reviewer noted that "Shields demonstrates there are no small lives, no lives out of which significance does not shine. She makes us aware that banality, ultimately, is in the eye of the beholder."

Shields's follow-up to *The Stone Diaries* was a second award-winning novel, *Larry's Party,* published in 1997. Shields structures this novel thematically; each chapter covers a different area of Larry's life: his marriages and relationships, his friends, and his children. However, readers also follow Larry as he grows from an awkward adolescent to a somewhat settled, typical middle-aged white male. The "party" is one given by Larry and his girlfriend in honor of his forty-seventh birthday, and which is attended by both of his former wives. *Time* reviewer Paul Gray wrote that Shields "captures an unremarkable man in a remarkable light."

What is not typical about Larry is his job. After working as a floral designer for twenty years, he develops an interest in, and becomes an expert at, building elaborate mazes out of shrubbery. According to

Michiko Kakutani in *New York Times,* these mazes "become a metaphor for the path his own life has taken, full of twists and turns and digressions. They also become a metaphor for Ms. Shields's own looping narrative, a narrative that repeatedly folds back on itself to gradually disclose more and more details about Larry's past." Commentators have remarked that in *Larry's Party* Shields portrays Everyman, much as she portrayed Everywoman in *The Stone Diaries.* Verlyn Klinkenborg, in reviewing *Larry's Party* for *New York Times Book Review,* said of Shields that "the mood in which she writes is that of the final act of *A Midsummer Night's Dream*—a mood of complicity and withdrawal, affection and mockery. Like Larry, and like God, she sees the perfect sense that mazes make 'when you look down on them from above.'"

Shields began to attract an international following in the early 1990s, particularly after the American publication of *The Stone Diaries.* Many of her early novels were published for the first time in the United States and England to much popular and critical acclaim. *A Celibate Season,* written with Blanche Howard and originally published in 1991, is the story of Jocelyn "Jock" and Charles "Chas" Selby, a couple married for twenty years, who are separated when Jock takes a temporary government job. They make the decision not to communicate by telephone, but rather keep in touch with letters, in which they talk about their lives, children, and marriage. Shields wrote the letters from Chas, and Howard those from Jock. A *Publishers Weekly* reviewer called the authors "skillful writers, and the epistolary form adds dimension to their thoughtful novel of love, marriage, and forgiveness."

In *Unless,* Shields's final novel, writer Reta Winter should be excited about the response to her first novel; instead she is preoccupied over the reticence of her oldest daughter, Nora. Nora, seemingly withdrawing from life, also withdraws from college, leaving Reta frustrated and looking for reasons, and answers, to Nora's seeming pain. Although a writer, she is voiceless, writing letters she doesn't send, having empty conversations with casual friends, and succumbing to the demands of editors to silence the women's voice in her second novel, a work-in-progress, in favor of a more assertive male presence. "Pain is never far: it's the book's frozen, icy core," Lev Grossman wrote of the novel in *Time,* "and the most vivid moments in *Unless* demonstrate the oblique, unexpected angles at which agony can enter our lives—as when Reta impulsively scrawls MY HEART IS BROKEN in the ladies' room of a bar." *New Statesman* contributor Cusk described *Unless* as "a formidable meditation on reality: it takes the vessel of fiction in its hands and hurls it to the floor." Praising the novel, Cusk added that the novel "speaks without pretension about its strange and singular subject: the relationship between women and culture, the nature of artistic endeavour, and the hostility of female truth to representations of itself."

Dressing up for the Carnival is a collection of twenty-two stories, many of them previously published. "And yet," wrote Paul Gray in *Time,* "the result is not as random or eclectic as might be anticipated. Shields . . . displays in all her writing, long or short, a consistently whimsical ruefulness toward her characters and the dilemmas they face, some of which, in this collection, are engagingly bizarre." In the title story, eleven people choose clothing and accessories to take them through the day. *Maclean's* reviewer John Bemrose wrote that Shields "also specializes in a kind of breezy essay-story—call it Borges-lite—that wittily investigates such topics as keys, inventors, and the cooking habits of an imaginary kingdom. These pieces are heavily theme-driven." In "Dying for Love," three women, who are individually contemplating suicide over love gone wrong, decide that life is worth living. In "Windows" two artists cover their windows to keep daylight from entering when the government institutes a window tax.

"Many of the stories are light and breezy but not unsatisfying," said a *Publishers Weekly* contributor of *Dressing up for the Carnival,* "because the characters are winning even in their mostly cameo-like appearances." *Time International* reviewer Francine Prose wrote that for the couple in "Mirrors," for example, "the decision not to put mirrors in their summer cottage becomes a metaphor for the shifting balance between partnership and solitude, contentment and dissatisfaction, intimacy and concealment." Prose noted that Shields "does a fine job of gauging and charting the subtle but volatile chemistry of domestic happiness, and of depicting the inner lives of her characters."

Prior to her death, Shields also collaborated with fellow editor Marjorie Anderson on *Dropped Threads: What We Aren't Told,* as well as a continuation volume,

each containing over thirty essays by noted Canadian women writers. Inspirational in tone, the collections serve to "celebrate . . . the strength of the female spirit in the face of public and private challenges," explained *Catholic New Times* contributor Colleen Crawley. As Shields noted in her afterword to *Dropped Threads 2; More of What We Aren't Told:* "Frequently we discover that what we believe to be singular is, in fact, universally experienced. No wonder Holocaust survivors seek each other out. No wonder those who have lost a child turn to others who have endured the same loss. We need these conversations desperately." *Dropped Threads 2* was published shortly after Shields's death in July of 2003, following the author's five-year battle with cancer.

BIOGRAPHICAL AND CRITICAL SOURCES:

BOOKS

Contemporary Literary Criticism, Gale (Detroit, MI), Volume 91, 1996, Volume 113, 1999.
Shields, Carol, and Marjorie Anderson, editors, *Dropped Threads 2: More of What We Aren't Told,* Vintage Canada (Toronto, Ontario, Canada), 2003.

PERIODICALS

Belles Lettres, spring, 1991, p. 56; summer, 1992, p. 20; fall, 1994, pp. 32, 34.
Book, May-June, 2002, Beth Kephart, review of *Unless,* p. 76.
Booklist, July, 1997, Donna Seaman, review of *Larry's Party,* p. 1777; April 15, 2000, Donna Seaman, review of *Dressing up for the Carnival,* p. 1525; January 1, 2003, p. 793.
Books in Canada, October, 1979, pp. 29-30; May, 1981, pp. 31-32; November, 1982, pp. 18-19; October, 1985, pp. 16-17; October, 1987, pp. 15-16; May, 1989, p. 32; January-February, 1991, pp. 30-31; April, 1992, p. 40; February, 1993, pp. 51-52; September, 1993, pp. 34-35; October, 1993, pp. 32-33.
Books in Review, summer, 1989, pp. 158-60.
Books Magazine, November-December, 1994, p. 12.
Canadian Forum, July, 1975, pp. 36-38; November, 1993, pp. 44-45; January-February, 1994, pp. 44-45; January, 1996, Christine Hamelin, "Coming to Canada," p. 46; November, 1997, Merna Summers, review of *Larry's Party,* p. 38.
Canadian Literature, summer, 1989, pp. 158-60; autumn, 1991, pp. 149-50; spring, 1995.

Catholic New Times September 7, 2003, Colleen Crawley, review of *Dropped Threads 2*, p. 18.

Chatelaine, April, 1996, Leslie Hughes, "The Shields Diaries," p. 110; May, 2003, Bonnie Schiedel, review of *Dropped Threads 2*, p. 36.

Christian Science Monitor, December 7, 1990, pp. 10-11.

Critique, spring, 2003, p. 313.

Detroit Free Press, September 7, 1997.

Entertainment Weekly, September 19, 1997, Vanessa V. Friedman, review of *Larry's Party*, p. 78; May 31, 2002, Karen Valby, "No Tears" (interview), p. 70.

Kirkus Reviews, May 1, 1976, p. 559; March 15, 2000, review of *Dressing up for the Carnival*, p. 328.

Library Journal, August, 1997, Ann Irvine, review of *Larry's Party*, p. 135; June 15, 1998, Jo Carr, review of *Larry's Party*, p. 122.

London Review of Books, September 27, 1990, pp. 20-21; March 21, 1991, p. 20; May 28, 1992, p. 22; September 9, 1993, p. 19.

Los Angeles Times Book Review, August 20, 1989, p. 2; April 17, 1994, pp. 3, 7.

Maclean's, October 11, 1993, p. 74; September 29, 1997, Diane Turbide, "The Masculine Maze: Carol Shields Gets Inside the Head of the Ordinary Guy," p. 82; March 20, 2000, John Bemrose, "Enriching a Fictional Universe: In Her New Collection of Short Stories, Carol Shields Proves Adept at Finding Wonder in the Unremarkable," p. 66.

Ms., January-February, 1996, Sandy M. Fernandez, reviews of *Small Ceremonies* and *The Box Garden,* p. 90.

New Statesman, August 20, 1993, p. 40; April 29, 2002, Rachel Cusk, review of *Unless,* p. 47.

Newsweek, October 6, 1997, Laura Shapiro, review of *Larry's Party*, p. 76.

New York, March 7, 1994.

New Yorker, May 20, 2002, review of *Unless,* p. 113.

New York Review of Books, June 29, 2000, Joyce Carol Oates, review of *Dressing up for the Carnival,* p. 38.

New York Times, July 17, 1989, p. C15; May 10, 1995.

New York Times Book Review, August 6, 1989, p. 11; August 12, 1990, p. 28; March 1, 1992, pp. 14, 16; March 14, 1992; March 27, 1994, pp. 3, 14; January 7, 1996, Claire Messud, "Why So Gloomy?," p. 12; August 26, 1997, Michiko Kakutani, "Br'er Rabbit, Ordinary in Nearly Every Way;" September 7, 1997, Verlyn Klinkenborg, "A Maze Makes Sense from Above," p. 7; June 20, 1999, Michael Porter, review of *A Celibate Season,* p. 16; June 11, 2000, David Willis Mc-Cullough, "Itemize This."

Observer (London, England), February 19, 1995, Kathy O'Shaughnessy, p. 19.

People, October 6, 1997, Paula Chin, review of *Larry's Party,* p. 43.

Performing Arts & Entertainment in Canada, winter, 1998, Karen Bell, "Carol Shields: All These Years Later, Still Digging," p. 4.

Publishers Weekly, February 28, 1994; August 11, 1997, review of *Larry's Party,* p. 383; April 26, 1999, review of *A Celibate Season,* p. 55; February 28, 2000, review of *Dressing up for the Carnival,* p. 56.

Quill and Quire, January, 1981, p. 24; September, 1982, p. 59; August, 1985, p. 46; May, 1989, p. 20; August, 1993, p. 31.

Scrivener, spring, 1995.

Spectator, March 21, 1992, pp. 35-36; September 24, 1994, p. 41; May 4, 2002, p. 39.

Time, September 29, 1997, Paul Gray, review of *Larry's Party,* p. 92; May 29, 2000, Paul Gray, review of *Dressing up for the Carnival,* p. 82; May 27, 2002, Lev Grossman, "Turning over the Last Page," p. 61.

Time International, February 28, 2000, Francine Prose, "Acts of Redemption: Carol Shields' Book of Stories Brings a Master's Eye to the Transfiguring Aspects of the Everyday," p. 52.

Times (London, England), January 23, 2000, Hilary Mantel, "Full of Domestic Surprises," p. 44.

Times Literary Supplement, August 27, 1993, p. 22; February 17, 1995.

West Coast Review, winter, 1988, pp. 38-56, pp. 57-66.

Women's Review of Books, May, 1994, p. 20.

World Literature Today, October-December, 2003, W. M. Hagen, review of *Unless,* p. 95.

Writer, July, 1998, Carol Shields, "Framing the Structure of a Novel," p. 3.

OBITUARIES:

PERIODICALS

Bookseller, July 25, 2003, p. 11.

Entertainment Weekly, December 26, 2003, p. 103.

Newsweek, July 28, 2003, p. 14.

Prairie Fire, autumn, 2003, p. 4.*

SMOTHERS, Ethel Footman 1944-

PERSONAL: Born April 5, 1944, in Camilla, GA; daughter of Ira Lee (a fruit picker) and Ethel (a maid; maiden name, Jackson) Footman; married Ernest Lee Smothers (a shipping clerk), July 15, 1964; children: Delsey, Darla, Dana, Dion. *Education:* Grand Rapids Community College, A.A., 1981. *Politics:* Democrat. *Religion:* Seventh Day Adventist.

ADDRESSES: Home—441 Adams St. SE, Grand Rapids, MI 49507.

CAREER: Amway Corp., Ada, MI, telephone order clerk, 1980-85, service specialist, 1985-92; author and speaker, 1992—.

AWARDS, HONORS: Junior Library Guild selection, for *The Hard-Times Jar.*

WRITINGS:

Down in the Piney Woods, Knopf (New York, NY), 1991.
Moriah's Pond, Knopf (New York, NY), 1994.
Auntee Edna, illustrated by Wil Clay, Eerdmans (Grand Rapids, MI), 2001.
The Hard-Times Jar, illustrated by John Holyfield, Farrar, Straus & Giroux (New York, NY), 2003.

Contributor of short fiction to *Storyworks.*

SIDELIGHTS: In her stories, author Ethel Footman Smothers chronicles some of the lives of African Americans who lived when Smothers was a child in the 1950s. Her first two novels, *Down in the Piney Woods* and its sequel *Moriah's Pond,* are about Annie Rye, the ten-year-old daughter of a sharecropper in rural Georgia. During the course of the first novel, Annie must confront not only the racism of a neighboring white sharecropper, but her own feelings of resentment and hostility when her three older half-sisters move in with her family. A reviewer for *Publishers Weekly* stated, "This zesty first novel is chock-a-block with fresh, authentic language," and Hazel Rochman, writing in *Booklist,* added, "The pleasure is in the rhythm of the narrative voice, in the sense of place, and in the characters."

After *Moriah's Pond,* Smothers turned to picture books. "I've always loved picture books," Smothers told *Grand Rapids Press* reviewer Ann Byle. "I fell in love with the illustrations when I would take my own children to the library." Her first book for younger children, *Auntee Edna,* is about a girl who dreads being forced to visit her elderly aunt but ends up enjoying the old-fashioned activities that the two share, including spinning button toys, baking, and using strips of paper bags to curl their hair. It is "a fresh tribute to the beneficial bonding of young and old," declared *School Library Journal*'s Jody McCoy.

The Hard-Times Jar is the largely autobiographical tale of a story-loving girl from a poor family of migrant workers who longs for a book to call her own. Eight-year-old Emma Jean Turner is sent to school in Pennsylvania one fall while her parents pick apples. She is scared by the prospect of going to an otherwise all-white school but enthralled by the school's library full of "real" books. Until now, Emma has only had makeshift books that she created herself by writing stories on paper bags and holding them together with safety pins. Although she knows that it is wrong, Emma cannot help taking some of the library books home with her one weekend. Her mother forces her to return the books and apologize, yet she also gives Emma some coins out of the family's hard-times jar to buy a book of her own. "The story provides a convincing portrayal of Emma's firm grounding within a loving family," Carolyn Phelan wrote in *Booklist.* Describing the story as "inspirational," *School Library Journal* critic Susan Pine thought *The Hard-Times Jar*'s "text flows smoothly, and it clearly describes Emma's enthusiasm and fears."

Smothers once commented: "*Down in the Piney Woods* is drawn from childhood memories and imagination. And when I decided to tell my story, I felt that Piney Woods rhythm in my head, with the black English and short, choppy sentences. That's the language of my childhood, and of my people. That uniqueness—that real flavor of our ancestry—must be preserved, or our children—all children—will be deprived of a rare richness that never can be recaptured. You see, it's not just black history. It's American history."

BIOGRAPHICAL AND CRITICAL SOURCES:

PERIODICALS

Booklist, December 15, 1991, Hazel Rochman, review of *Down in the Piney Woods;* January 15, 1995,

Hazel Rochman, review of *Moriah's Pond,* p. 930; August, 2003, Carolyn Phelan, review of *The Hard-Times Jar,* p. 1995.

Grand Rapids Press (Grand Rapids, MI), April 5, 2001, Morgan Jarema, "Local Author Helps Young Writers Brainstorm," p. 2; July 1, 2001, Ann Byle, "'Stale' Visit with Old Aunt Becomes Rare Treat for Young Girl," p. J6; August 12, 2003, Ann Byle, "Smother's Book Teaches about Family, Hard Times," p. B4.

Kirkus Reviews, July 1, 2003, review of *The Hard-Times Jar,* p. 915.

Publishers Weekly, November 29, 1991, review of *Down in the Piney Woods,* pp. 52-53; January 23, 1995, review of *Moriah's Pond,* pp. 70-71; July 28, 2003, review of *The Hard-Times Jar,* p. 94.

Roanoke Times (Roanoke, VA), August 12, 2001, Mary Ann Johnson, review of *Auntee Edna,* p. 6.

School Library Journal, January, 1992, Katherine Bruner, review of *Down in the Piney Woods,* p. 116; February, 1995, Ellen Fader, review of *Moriah's Pond,* p. 100; August, 2001, Jody Mc-Coy, review of *Auntee Edna,* p. 162; October, 2003, Susan Pine, review of *The Hard-Times Jar,* p. 138.

*   *   *

STANCYKOWNA
 See SZYMBORSKA, Wislawa

*   *   *

SUAREZ LYNCH, B.
 See BORGES, Jorge Luis

*   *   *

SZYMBORSKA, Wislawa 1923-
 (Stancykowna, a pseudonym)

PERSONAL: Born July 2, 1923, in Prowent-Bnin, Poland; married (husband deceased). *Education:* Attended Jagellonian University, 1945-48.

ADDRESSES: Home—Ul. Krolewska 82/89, 30-079, Cracow, Poland.

Wislawa Szmborska

CAREER: Poet and critic; Poetry editor and columnist, *Zycie literackie* (literary weekly magazine), 1953-81.

MEMBER: Polish Writers' Association (member of general board, 1978-83).

AWARDS, HONORS: Cracow literary prize, 1954; Gold Cross of Merit, 1955; Ministry of Culture prize, 1963; Knight's Cross, Order of Polonia Resituta, 1974; Goethe Prize, 1991; Herder Prize, 1995; Polish PEN Club prize, 1996; Nobel Prize for Literature, Swedish Academy, 1996.

WRITINGS:

POETRY

Dlatego zyjemy (title means "That's Why We Are Alive"), [Warsaw, Poland], 1952.
Pytania zadawane sobie (title means "Questions Put to Myself"), [Warsaw, Poland], 1954.

Wolanie do Yeti (title means "Calling out to Yeti"), [Warsaw, Poland], 1957.

Sol (title means "Salt"), Panstwowy Instytut Wydawniczy (Warsaw, Poland), 1962.

Wiersze wybrane (collection), Panstwowy Instytut Wydawniczy (Warsaw, Poland), 1964, reprinted 2000.

Sto pociech (title means "A Hundred Joys"), Panstwowy Instytut Wydawniczy (Warsaw, Poland), 1967.

Poezje wybrane (title means "Selected Poems"), Ludowa Spoldzielnia Wydawnicza (Warsaw, Poland), 1967.

Poezje (title means "Poems"), Przedmowa Jerzego Kwiatkowskiego (Warsaw, Poland), 1970.

Wybor poezje (collection), Czytelnik (Warsaw, Poland), 1970.

Wszelki wypadek (title means "There but for the Grace"), Czytelnik (Warsaw, Poland), 1972.

Wybor wierszy (collection), Panstwowy Instytut Wydawniczy (Warsaw, Poland), 1973.

Tarsjusz i inne wiersze (title means "Tarsius and Other Poems"), Krajowa Agencja Wydawnicza (Warsaw, Poland), 1976.

Wielka liczba (title means "A Great Number"), Czytelnik (Warsaw, Poland), 1976.

Sounds, Feelings, Thoughts: Seventy Poems, translated by Magnus J. Krynski and Robert A. Maguire, Princeton University Press (Princeton, NJ), 1981.

Poezje wybrane (II), (title means "Selected Poems II"), Ludowa Spoldzielnia Wydawnicza (Warsaw, Poland), 1983.

Ludzie na moscie, Czytelnik (Warsaw, Poland), 1986, translation by Adam Czerniawski published as *People on a Bridge: Poems,* Forest (Boston, MA), 1990.

Poezje = Poems (bilingual edition), translated by Krynski and Maguire, Wydawnictwo Literackie (Cracow, Poland), 1989.

Wieczor autorski: wiersze (title means "Authors' Evening: Poems"), Anagram (Warsaw, Poland), 1992.

Koniec i poczatek (title means "The End and the Beginning"), Wydawnictwo Literackie (Cracow, Poland), 1993.

View with a Grain of Sand: Selected Poems, translated by Stanislaw Baranczak and Clare Cavanagh, Harcourt (New York, NY), 1995.

Widok z ziarnkiem piasku: 102 Wiersze, Wydawnictwo Literacki (Cracow, Poland), 1996.

Nothing Twice: Selected Poems, selected and translated by Stanislaw Baranczak and Clare Cavanagh, Wydawnictwo Literackie (Cracow, Poland), 1997.

Hundert Gedichte, Hundert Freuden, Wydawnictwo Literackie (Cracow, Poland), 1997.

O asmierci bez przesady = de la mort sans exagerer, Wydawnictwo Literackie (Cracow, Poland), 1997.

Nulla e in regalo, Wydawnictwo Literackie (Cracow, Poland), 1998.

Poems, New and Collected, 1957-1997, translated from the Polish by Stanislaw Baranczak and Clare Cavanagh, Harcourt Brace (New York, NY), 1998.

Nic darowane = Keyn shum masoneh = Nothing's a gift = Nichts ist geschenkt = Me'um lo nitan bematanah, Amerykansko-Polsko-Izraelska Fundacja Shalom (Warsaw, Poland), 1999.

Poczta literacka, czyli, Jak zostac (lub nie zostac) pisarzem, Wydawnictwo Literackie (Cracow, Poland), 2000.

Miracle Fair: Selected Poems, Norton (New York, NY), 2001.

Nowe lektury nadobowiazkowe: 1997-2002, Wydawnictwo Literackie (Cracow, Poland), 2002.

Nonrequired Reading: Prose Pieces, Harcourt (New York, NY), 2002.

Chwila (title means "Moment"), Wydawnictwo Literackie (Cracow, Poland), 2002, published in bilingual edition as *Chwila/Moment,* translations by Clare Cavanagh and Stanislaw Baranczak, 2003.

Wierze, BOSZ (Olszanica, Poland), 2003.

Rymowanki dla duzych dzieci: z wyklejankami autorki, Wydawnictwo Literackie (Cracow, Poland), 2003.

OTHER

Lektury nadobowiazkowe (collected book reviews; title means "Non-Compulsory Reading"), Wydawnictwo Literackie (Cracow, Poland), 1973.

Zycie na poczekaniu: Lekcja literatury z Jerzym Kwiatowskim i Marianem Stala, Wydawnictwo Literackie (Cracow, Poland), 1996.

Contributor to anthologies, including *Polish Writing Today,* Penguin (New York, NY), 1967; *The New Polish Poetry,* University of Pittsburgh Press (Pittsburgh, PA), 1978; and *Anthologie de la poesie polonaise: 1400-1980,* revised edition, Age d'homme, 1981. Also contributor, under pseudonym Stancykowna, to *Arka* (underground publication) and *Kultura* (exile magazine; published in Paris).

SIDELIGHTS: Polish author Wislawa Szymborska was thrust into the international spotlight in 1996 after receiving the Nobel Prize for Literature. Although she is one of her country's most popular female writers and is valued as a national treasure, Szymborska remains little known to English-speaking readers, although by the late twentieth century several of her books—including her poetry—were available in English translation, among them; *People on a Bridge, View with a Grain of Sand,* and *Nonrequired Reading: Prose Pieces.* The reclusive and private Szymborska was cited by the Swedish Academy for "poetry that with ironic precision allows the historical and biological context to come to light in fragments of human reality." Her poetry, described by *Los Angeles Times* critic Dean E. Murphy, is "seductively simple verse . . . [which has] captured the wit and wisdom of everyday life" in Poland during much of the twentieth century.

Explaining Szymborska's work, translator Stanislaw Baranczak noted in *New York Times Book Review:* "The typical lyrical situation on which a Szymborska poem is founded is the confrontation between the directly stated or implied opinion on an issue and the question that raises doubt about its validity. The opinion not only reflects some widely shared belief or is representative of some widespread mind-set," Baranczak added, "but also, as a rule, has a certain doctrinaire ring to it: the philosophy behind it is usually speculative, anti-empirical, prone to hasty generalizations, collectivist, dogmatic and intolerant."

Szymborska received critical acclaim for the first collection of her work to appear in English translation, *Sounds, Feelings, Thoughts: Seventy Poems.* "Of the poetic voices to come out of Poland after 1945 Wislawa Szymborska's is probably the most elusive as well as the most distinctive," wrote Jaroslaw Anders in *New York Review of Books.* Anders commented: "*Sounds, Feelings, Thoughts* contains poems from [Szymborska's] five books written since 1957, comprising more or less half of what the poet herself considers her canon. Its publication is of interest not only because of Szymborska's importance as a poet, but also because her work demonstrates that the diversity of poetic modes in Poland is much greater than is usually perceived." Alice-Catherine Carls, in a review of *Sounds, Feelings, Thoughts* in *Library Journal,* called the work "one of those rare books which put one in a state of 'grace,'" while Robert Hudzik, also in *Library Journal,* maintained that the collection "reveals a poet of startling originality and deep sympathy."

The 1995 collection *Views with a Grain of Sand: Selected Poems* was also praised by many critics who

lauded Szymborska's directness and distinctive voice. Stephen Dobyns in *Washington Post Book World* praised both the humor of Szymborska's work as well as the translation by Baranczak and Clare Cavanagh. Edward Hirsch in a *New York Review of Books* review concurred, arguing that the volume reveals "the full force of [Szymborska's] fierce and unexpected wit." Louis McKee, in a *Library Journal* review, also praised the "wonderfully wicked" wit of Szymborska. Dobyns concluded: "The poems are surprising, funny and deeply moving. Szymborska is a world-class poet, and this book will go far to make her known in the United States."

Publication of *Poems New and Collected, 1957-1997* inspired further critical acclaim. "It may seem superfluous to praise a Nobel Laureate in literature, but Szymborska is a splendid writer richly deserving of her recent renown," affirmed Graham Christian in *Library Journal.* Noting the poet's "unflinching examination of torture and other wrongs inflicted by repressive regimes," Christian went on to say that Szymborska's verse contains "the exhilarating power of a kind of serious laughter." Despite the poems' frequently grim subject matter, "Syzmborska's tough naturalism does allow rays of light to penetrate its bleak landscapes, leaving lasting, sustaining impressions," declared a reviewer for *Publishers Weekly.*

Szymborska's 2002 collection, *Nonrequired Reading: Prose Pieces,* is a collection of short book reviews she wrote while working as a columnist. Nancy R. Ives in *Library Journal* stated, "The skillful simplicity and lyric quality of these essays make them distinctive. With her poet's gift for compression, Szymborska captures large concepts and brilliantly reduces them to pithy, two-page essays." A reviewer for *Publishers Weekly* forecasted, "While the conceit of a commonplace book of reader responses may be a little quirky," reviews would assist the general reader in understanding and appreciating Szymborska's works. "This may very well be the season's sleeper hit among literati," the reviewer added, "particularly among non-regular readers of poetry who nevertheless recognize Szymborska's name."

Many commentators have remarked on the deceptively simple quality of Syzmborska's work. In simple language, she speaks of ordinary things, only to reveal extraordinary truths. In a *Publishers Weekly* article about the poet, Joanna Trzeciak praised "the wit and clarity of Szymborska's turns of phrase. Under her pen, simple language becomes striking. Ever the gentle subversive, she stubbornly refuses to see anything in the world as ordinary. The result is a poetry of elegance and irony, full of surprising turns." And Denise Wiloch, a contributor to *Contemporary Women Poets,* pointed out that "the seemingly casual musings she captures in her poems are deceptive and full of irony. Her work reverberates long after it is read."

Syzmborska "knows philosophy, literature, and history, but mostly she knows common human experience," concludes *Booklist* writer Ray Olson. "Her work is ultimately wisdom literature, written in a first person that expresses a universal humanity that American poets—lockstep individualists all—haven't dared essay since early in this century. She is like Brecht without hatred, Sandburg without socialist posturing, Dickinson without hermetism, Whitman without illusory optimism: a great poet."

Szymborska's works have been translated into Arabic, Hebrew, Japanese, Chinese, and other languages.

BIOGRAPHICAL AND CRITICAL SOURCES:

BOOKS

Balbus, Stanislaw, *Swiat ze wszystkich stron swiata: O Wislawie Szymborski,* Wydawnictwo Literackie (Cracow, Poland), 1996.
Baranczak, Stanislaw, *Breathing under Water and Other East European Essays,* Harvard University Press (Cambridge, MA), 1990.
Contemporary Women Poets, St. James Press (Detroit, MI), 1998.
Levine, Madeline, *Contemporary Polish Poetry: 1925-1975,* Twayne (Boston, MA), 1981.

PERIODICALS

Booklist, April 15, 1998, Ray Olson, review of *Poems New and Collected, 1957-1997;* March 15, 1999, Ray Olson, review of *Poems New and Collected 1957-1997,* p. 1276.

Choice, January, 1992, review of *People on a Bridge,* p. 752.
Humanities Review, spring, 1982, p. 141.
Library Journal, September 1, 1981, p. 1636; July, 1995, p. 85; April 1, 1998, Graham Christian, review of *Poems New and Collected, 1957-1997,* p. 92; November 1, 2002, Nancy R. Ives, review of *Nonrequired Reading: Prose Pieces,* p. 91.
Los Angeles Times, October 4, 1996; October 13, 1996.
Maclean's, October 14, 1996, p. 11.
New Republic, January 1, 1996, p. 36; December 30, 1996, p. 27.
New Yorker, December 14, 1992, p. 94; March 1, 1993, p. 86.
New York Review of Books, October 21, 1982, p. 47; November 14, 1996, p. 17; October 21, 1993, p. 42; April 18, 1996, p. 35; October 8, 1998, p. 37.
New York Times, October 4, 1996, p. C13.
New York Times Book Review, October 27, 1996, Stanislaw Baraczak, "The Reluctant Poet," p. 51.
New York Times Magazine, December 1, 1996, p. 46.
Observer (London, England), August 18, 1991, p. 51.
People, May 5, 1997, review of *View with a Grain of Sand,* p. 41.
Publishers Weekly, April 7, 1997, Joanna Trzeciak, "Wislawa Szymborska: The Enchantment of Everyday Objects," p. 68; March 30, 1998, review of *Poems New and Collected, 1957-1997,* p. 77; September 23, 2002, review of *Nonrequired Reading,* p. 69.
Time, October 14, 1996, p. 33.
Times Literary Supplement, September 17, 1999, Clair Wills, "How Real Is Reality?," p. 25.
U.S. News and World Report, October 14, 1996, p. 32.
Wall Street Journal, October 4, 1996.
Washington Post Book World, July 30, 1995, p. 8.
World Literature Today, spring, 1982, p. 368; winter, 1992, Bogdana Carpenter, review of *People on a Bridge,* pp. 163-164; winter, 1997; summer, 1991, Alice-Catherine Carls, review of *Poezje = Poems,* p. 519.*

T

THEROUX, Paul (Edward) 1941-

PERSONAL: Surname rhymes with "skiddoo"; born April 10, 1941, in Medford, MA; son of Albert Eugene (a salesman) and Anne (Dittami) Theroux; married Anne Castle (a broadcaster), December 4, 1967 (divorced, 1993); married Sheila Donnely, November 18, 1995; children (first marriage): Marcel Raymond, Louis Sebastian. *Education:* Attended University of Maine, 1959-60; University of Massachusetts, B.A., 1963; Syracuse University, further study, 1963. *Hobbies and other interests:* Rowing.

ADDRESSES: Home—35 Elsynge Rd., London SW18 2HR, England. *Office*—c/o Author Mail, Hamish Hamilton Ltd, 27 Wrights Lane, London W8 5TZ, England.

CAREER: Soche Hill College, Limbe, Malawi, lecturer in English, 1963-65; Makerere University, Kampala, Uganda, lecturer in English, 1965-68; University of Singapore, lecturer in English, 1968-71; professional writer, 1971—. Visiting lecturer, University of Virginia, 1972-73. Has given numerous lectures on literature in the United States and abroad.

MEMBER: American Academy and Institute of Arts and Letters, Royal Geography Society, Royal Society of Literature.

AWARDS, HONORS: Robert Hamlet one-act play award, 1960; *Playboy* Editorial Award, 1971, 1976; *New York Times Book Review* Editors' Choice citation,

Paul Theroux

1975, for *The Great Railway Bazaar: By Train through Asia;* American Academy and Institute of Arts and Letters award for literature, 1977; Whitbread Prize for Best Novel, 1978, for *Picture Palace;* American Book Award nominations, 1981, for *The Old Patagonian Express: By Train through the Americas,* and 1983, for *The Mosquito Coast;* James Tait Black Memorial Prize for Best Novel, 1981, for *The Mosquito Coast;* Thomas Cook Travel Book Prize, 1989. Honorary degrees from Trinity College and Tufts University, both in 1980, and University of Massachusetts—Amherst, 1988.

WRITINGS:

NOVELS

Waldo, Houghton (Boston, MA), 1967.

Fong and the Indians, Houghton (Boston, MA), 1968.

Girls at Play, Houghton (Boston, MA), 1969.

Murder in Mount Holly, Alan Ross, 1969.

Jungle Lovers, Houghton (Boston, MA), 1971.

Saint Jack (also see below), Houghton (Boston, MA), 1973, reprinted, Penguin Books (New York, NY) 1997.

The Black House, Houghton (Boston, MA), 1974.

The Family Arsenal, Houghton (Boston, MA), 1976.

Picture Palace, Houghton (Boston, MA), 1978, reprinted, Penguin Books (New York, NY), 1999.

(With Peter Bogdanovich and Howard Sackler) *Saint Jack* (screenplay; based on Theroux's novel), New World/Shoals Creek/Playboy/Copa de Oro, 1979.

The Mosquito Coast, with woodcuts by David Frampton, Houghton (Boston, MA), 1982.

Doctor Slaughter (also see below), Hamish Hamilton (London, England), 1984.

Half Moon Street: Two Short Novels (contains *Doctor Slaughter* and *Doctor DeMarr*), Houghton (Boston, MA), 1984.

O-Zone, Putnam (New York, NY), 1986.

My Secret History, Putnam (New York, NY), 1989.

Doctor DeMarr (also see above), illustrations by Marshall Arisman, Hutchinson (London, England), 1990.

Chicago Loop, Random House (New York, NY), 1991.

Millroy the Magician, Random House (New York, NY), 1994.

My Other Life, Houghton (Boston, MA), 1996.

On the Edge of the Great Rift: Three Novels of Africa (contains *Fong and the Indians, Girls at Play,* and *Jungle Lovers*) Penguin (London, England), 1996.

Kowloon Tong, Houghton (Boston, MA), 1997.

The Collected Short Novels, Penguin Books (London, England), 1999.

SHORT STORIES

Sinning with Annie and Other Stories, Houghton (Boston, MA), 1972.

The Consul's File, Houghton (Boston, MA), 1977.

World's End and Other Stories, Houghton (Boston, MA), 1980.

The London Embassy, Houghton (Boston, MA), 1982.

The Collected Stories, Viking Press (New York, NY), 1997.

Hotel Honolulu, Houghton (Boston, MA), 2001.

The Stranger at the Palazzo d'Oro and Other Stories, Houghton (Boston, MA), 2004.

NONFICTION

V. S. Naipaul: An Introduction to His Works, Deutsch (London, England), 1972.

The Great Railway Bazaar: By Train through Asia, Houghton (Boston, MA), 1975.

The Old Patagonian Express: By Train through the Americas, Houghton (Boston, MA), 1979, reprinted, 1997.

Sailing through China, illustrated by Patrick Procktor, Houghton (Boston, MA), 1984, published as *Down the Yangtze,* Penguin Books (London, England), 1995.

The Kingdom by the Sea: A Journey around Great Britain, Houghton (Boston, MA), 1985.

(With Steve McCurry) *The Imperial Way: By Rail from Peshawar to Chittagong,* Houghton (Boston, MA), 1985.

Sunrise with Seamonsters: Travels and Discoveries 1964-1984, Houghton (Boston, MA), 1985.

(With Bruce Chatwin) *Patagonia Revisited,* illustrated by Kyffin Williams, Houghton (Boston, MA), 1986.

Riding the Iron Rooster: By Train through China, Putnam (New York, NY), 1989.

To the Ends of the Earth: The Selected Travels of Paul Theroux, Random House, (New York, NY), 1990.

Travelling the World: The Illustrated Travels of Paul Theroux, Random House (New York, NY), 1990.

The Happy Isles of Oceania: Paddling the Pacific, Fawcett (New York, NY), 1992.

The Pillars of Hercules: A Grand Tour of the Mediterranean, Putnam (New York, NY), 1995.

Sir Vidia's Shadow: A Friendship across Five Continents, Houghton (Boston, MA), 1998, with a new afterword by the author, 2000.

Fresh Air Fiend: Travel Writings, 1985-2000, Houghton (Boston, MA), 2000.

Nurse Wolf and Doctor Sacks, Short Books (London, England), 2001.

Dark Star Safari: Overland from Cairo to Cape Town, Houghton (Boston, MA), 2003.

Vineyard Days, Vineyard Nights, photographs by Nancy Ellison, Stewart, Tabori & Chang (New York, NY), 2004.

OTHER

A Christmas Card (for juveniles) illustrated by John Lawrence, Houghton (Boston, MA), 1978.

London Snow: A Christmas Story (for juveniles) illustrated by John Lawrence, Houghton (Boston, MA), 1979.

The White Man's Burden: A Play in Two Acts, Hamish Hamilton (London, England), 1987.

ADAPTATIONS: The Mosquito Coast was adapted for film by Paul Schrader, directed by Peter Weir, and starred Harrison Ford, Warner Bros., 1986; *Doctor Slaughter* was adapted for film by Edward Behr and Bob Swain as *Half Moon Street,* directed by Swain, starring Sigourney Weaver and Michael Caine, RKO/Fox, 1986; *London Embassy* was adapted as a British television mini-series by T. R. Bowen and Ian Kennedy Martin, directed by David Giles III, and Ronald Wilson, 1987; *Chinese Box* is a screenplay adaptation by Jean-Claude Carriere and Larry Gross of a story by Gross, Wayne Wang, and Theroux, directed by Wang, starring Jeremy Irons, WW/Trimark, 1997.

SIDELIGHTS: In a career spanning the last four decades of the twentieth century, author Paul Theroux has established a reputation as one of modern literature's most respected chroniclers of the expatriate experience. His novels find themes in the anomalies of post-imperial life, and are set such exotic locales as Malawi, Singapore, and Honduras, as well as in the economic and social decay besetting Great Britain in the late twentieth century. As Samuel Coale noted in *Critique:* "Drastic change indeed stalks the world of [Theroux's] fiction, that precisely rendered realm where cultures clash and characters encounter each other as society's pawns in a larger pattern." An American citizen who lives in London most of the year, Theroux has gained equal renown for his nonfiction travel books, some of which feature continent-crossing railway journeys of months' duration. By traveling, suggested *New Yorker* contributor Susan Lardner, "Theroux has tested a belief in the continuing strangeness of the world, and discovered openings for

melodrama and romantic gestures that other writers have given up for lost." Helen Dudar wrote in *Chicago Tribune Book World* that Theroux has become "our foremost fictional specialist in the outsized outsider, the ravenous wanderer who sees or knows or wants more than most of us allow ourselves to hope for."

Theroux's family background and upbringing in the "prim suburbs of Boston" hardly seem adequate preparation for his adult role as an award-winning novelist, essayist, and world traveler. He was born in Medford, Massachusetts, in 1941, to working-class parents who had, he related in *New York Times,* "no place, no influence, no money nor power." They did, however, have numerous children. In his essay collection *Sunrise with Seamonsters: Travels and Discoveries 1964-1984,* Theroux writes: "It was part of my luck to have been born in a populous family of nine unexampled wits." Included in this roster of six siblings are two elder brothers—Eugene, a Washington, D.C.-based lawyer and expert in Sino-American trade, and Alexander, a novelist whose critical reception has rivaled Paul's. *New York Times* contributor James Atlas characterized the three oldest Theroux brothers as "collective tutors in the acquisition of culture" who "shared their various talents among themselves and passed them down to their younger brothers."

As a sophomore at the University of Massachusetts, Theroux declared himself to be a pacifist and insisted on receiving an exemption from the then-mandatory R.O.T.C. program. Though "neither a brilliant nor inspired student," according to Atlas, Theroux called further attention to himself in 1962 by being arrested for leading an antiwar demonstration—"when demonstrations were rare and actually bothered people," Theroux noted in *Sunrise with Seamonsters.* Upon graduation from the University of Massachusetts in 1963, Theroux joined the Peace Corps, an organization he describes as "a sort of Howard Johnson's on the main drag to maturity." He was sent to Limbe, Malawi, in South Central Africa to teach English.

For a time Theroux supplemented his Peace Corps stipend by writing articles for *Christian Science Monitor* and several African periodicals. In the course of his stay in Malawi, he found himself on friendly terms with a group of political leaders who eventually fell from favor with the unstable Hastings Banda regime. This association, as well as a duplicitous use of some of Theroux's articles by the German equivalent of the

C.I.A., led to Theroux's deportation from Malawi in 1965, under the charge of spying. Several years later, Theroux described the incident in an essay that was reprinted in *Sunrise with Seamonsters.* "My readiness to say yes to favors may suggest a simplicity of mind, a fatal gullibility," he wrote, "but I was bored, and the daily annoyance of living in a dictatorship, which is like suffering an unhappy family in a locked house, had softened my temper to the point where anything different, lunch with a stranger, the request for an article, the challenge of a difficult task, changed that day and revived my mind." Theroux was expelled from the Peace Corps and fined for "six months' unsatisfactory service," but no further government action ensued based on the events in Malawi.

Immediately following his expulsion from the Peace Corps, Theroux returned to Africa, where he became a lecturer in English at Makerere University in Kampala, Uganda. He remained in Uganda until 1968, when he and his wife, Anne Castle, were attacked during a political demonstration against the policies of white-controlled Rhodesia. The violent end to his stay in Uganda notwithstanding, Theroux found much-needed intellectual stimulation at the university, as well as the time to work on his writing. In 1966 author V. S. Naipaul visited Makerere University and struck up an amiable but exacting working relationship with the young writer. Theroux recalls the period in *Sunrise with Seamonsters:* "It was like private tuition—as if, at this crucial time in my life, . . . he had come all the way to Africa to remind me of what writing really was and to make me aware of what a difficult path I was setting out on. . . . With me he was a generous, rational teacher." It was Naipaul, Theroux said, who suggested that he write fiction about Africa, with attention to the comic and the tragic aspects of life there. Theroux, in turn, published a critical appraisal of Naipaul's work, titled *V. S. Naipaul: An Introduction to His Works,* in 1972, and more recently penned *Sir Vidia's Shadow: A Friendship across Five Continents.*

Waldo, Theroux's first novel, was published in 1967, while the author was still living in Uganda. Timothy J. Evans noted in *Dictionary of Literary Biography* that the work "deals with the theme of a man trying to find or create order in his life" and that the book is the first expression of themes Theroux has continued to use. "Order is not discovered by the characters" in *Waldo,* Evans remarked, "and it is not imposed by the writer on the novel." Evans related that critical reaction to

Waldo falls in extremes of praise and disparagement but that the book's quality falls rather midpoint between the two poles. "The novel does have a point," Evans concluded, "and it has some humorous, satiric passages which make it worth reading, but it is very episodic, with vignettes of uneven quality." A *Times Literary Supplement* reviewer offered a similar assessment: "Most of the time, *Waldo* seems to wander along, quite amiably and quite readably, but without much sense of direction."

In 1968 Theroux left Uganda and took a teaching position at the University of Singapore. While there he published three novels set in Africa: *Fong and the Indians, Girls at Play,* and *Jungle Lovers.* As a group, these novels explore the frustrating and potentially tragic difficulties of social interaction in postcolonial Africa. In *New York Review of Books* Robert Towers wrote of Theroux: "Unafraid of ethnic generalizations, he spares no one—African, Englishman, Chinaman, Indian, American—in his wildly absurd confrontations between the old and the new exploiters and the poor bastards caught in the middle; recklessly he juxtaposes the crumbling institutions of colonialism with some of the more bizarre outgrowths of the Third World." In *Fong and the Indians,* for instance, Theroux describes the misadventures of a Chinese Catholic grocer in an imaginary African state. According to *Saturday Review* contributor Constance Wagner, the novel depicts "Africans, Asians, whites, cheating, despising, mistrusting one another. . . . With a smile Theroux lays bare the myopic self-serving not of Africa but of man. . . . Laugh as you will, you realize in the end that this short novel contains more of sanity and truth than a dozen fat morality plays on ugly Americanism."

Critics have found elements of satire and hopelessness in Theroux's novels about Africa. A *Times Literary Supplement* reviewer stated of *Jungle Lovers* that "Increasingly a more wryly observed Africa emerges from the condescension or primitivism of expatriate fiction. . . . [Theroux's] fable, with roots in satiric caricature and documentary terror, uses the linguistic complexity to underscore the wavering relationships between lingering British, Africans, and the two American protagonists." Writing in *Spectator,* Auberon Waugh called *Jungle Lovers* "the most vivid account of the sheer hopelessness of independent Black Africa" and "a serious and excellent novel, welcome above all for its refreshing pessimism." Evans suggested that a "repeated assertion of empathy for the blacks does not convincingly cover an attitude of paternalism" on the author's part in *Jungle Lovers.* Evans nevertheless added that in the book, "The British and American settlers are also viewed with ridicule, and Theroux seems content to leave the Americans' plans for change open to question." The destructive implications of one particularly naive American's plans for change form the violent climax of *Girls at Play,* a work one *Times Literary Supplement* critic characterized as "unremittingly depressing." *New Yorker*'s Lardner felt that Theroux's novels set in Africa reveal him to be "a connoisseur of the conflict of ideals and illusions with things as they turn out to be." Irony, she concluded, "is his natural style."

While teaching in Singapore, Theroux was made to promise that he would not write any fiction about that island. The informal constraint was removed when he relocated in London, and he published *Saint Jack,* a novel set in Singapore. *Atlantic* reviewer Edward Weeks called the work "a highly professional, often amusing, withering account of prostitution in the once glamorous East." A low-key first person narrative by a middle-aged, expatriate American pimp, *Saint Jack* received substantial praise from critics. "There has never been any question about the quality of Theroux's prose or the bite of his satire," wrote Jonathan Yardley in *Washington Post Book World.* "In *Saint Jack,* more than in any of his previous fiction, the sardonic is balanced with compassion, and in Jack Flowers we are given a character whose yearnings touch upon our own." Evans thought the protagonist "could never change, because he represents life in Singapore. . . . Jack may dream of an ideal existence and wish that he could write the novel which would depict it, but he cannot. . . . Life will be a treadmill for him." Though Weeks suggested that under the surface humor "one is aware of the author's scorn for this disheveled, corrupt memento of colonialism," other reviewers cited Theroux for a sympathetic portrayal of a quixotic hero. "Jack Flowers is funny, endearing, outrageous, poignant, noble—and utterly believable," commented Yardley. "He is Paul Theroux's finest accomplishment." In 1979 Peter Bogdanovich directed the movie version of *Saint Jack,* based on a screenplay Theroux helped to write.

Theroux's commercial and critical success was still to a certain extent dependent upon his British readership when he published *The Black House* in 1974. The novel, a gothic tale with psychological dimensions set in a rural part of England, has garnered mixed reviews. *New York Times Book Review* contributor Michael Mewshaw felt that while "it is a tribute to [Theroux's] integrity and ambition that he is not content to keep repeating himself," *The Black House* is "an abrupt departure from the comic vision of his earlier work" and "does a serious disservice to his talent." Claire Tomalin offered a contrasting viewpoint in *New Statesman.* "The book is about a man panicked by doubts about just where he and other creatures do belong," Tomalin wrote. "The degree of skill with which Theroux handles these various themes, and the level of mastery of his writing, have produced a novel of unusual scope and promise still more for the future."

The Mosquito Coast, a novel published in 1982, is among Theroux's best-known works of fiction. Told from the point of view of a thirteen-year-old narrator, the story explores a family's exodus from Massachusetts to the jungles of Honduras under the domination of a manic and eccentric father. *Times Literary Supplement* contributor Valentine Cunningham termed the father, Allie Fox, "a truly amazing and unforgettable figure, an American titan whose actions unlock the essences of oppressive Americanism, revealing evils we're to take as intrinsic to the rationality and mechanization that helped make his country what it is." Towers likewise cited the theme of "Yankee-ingenuity-gone-berserk" in his piece for *New York Review of Books,* adding that Theroux handles the concept "with commendable skill." Towers explained, "Though Allie Fox is an archetypal character whose career follows an emblematic line," "Theroux has avoided the sterility of much quasi-allegorical writing by endowing his main character with a lively and dense specificity." Jonathan Raban, meanwhile, commented in *Saturday Review* that "in Allie Fox, Theroux has created his first epic hero. If one can imagine an American tradition that takes in Benjamin Franklin, Captain Ahab, Huey Long, and the Reverend Jim Jones, then Allie Fox is its latest, most complete incarnation."

The Mosquito Coast garnered an American Book Award nomination along with favorable reviews. Raban termed the work "not just [Theroux's] finest novel so far. It is—in a characteristically hooded way—a novelist's act of self-definition, a midterm appraisal of his own resources. It is a wonderful book, with so many levels to it that it feels bottomless." Some critics, though, were not so impressed. *Los Angeles Times Book Review* contributor Edward M. White remarked that *The Mosquito Coast* is "an abstract and witty book, embodying Theroux's usual themes about the conflict of cultures. The abstraction is particularly damaging, here, however, where it becomes authorial manipulation of characters and plotting in the interests of theoretical design." In *Chicago Tribune Book World,* William Logan voiced the opinion that because Theroux "cannot create a human referent for his characters, the narrative is labored and overlong, the irony clumsy, and the end congested with symbolism." In his *New York Times Book Review* article, Thomas R. Edwards offered an opposite view. "Theroux's book . . . is, characteristically, a fine entertainment, a gripping adventure story, a remarkable comic portrait of minds and cultures at cross-purposes. But under its unintimidating surface, . . . 'The Mosquito Coast' shows a cosmopolitan expatriate novelist pondering his imaginative sources as an American writer, and the relation of those sources to the world as it now seems to be. This excellent story . . . is also an impressively serious act of imagination."

Theroux extended his ruminations on America fifty years into the future in his next work, the lengthy *O-Zone*. The novel, observed Yardley in the *Washington Post Book World,* "is on several counts a striking departure for its author. . . . It is his first genuinely 'American' novel . . . and it deals more directly with questions of American national identity and character than any of his other books, either fiction or nonfiction." The O-Zone of the title is a vast area located in the U.S. heartland that is evacuated after a supposedly disastrous nuclear accident, The inhabitants of an overpopulated and overpoliced New York City, the O-Zone represents both the terror of the unknown and a potential escape from a dreadful reality. The O-Zone, noted Yardley, "is a foreign place within a nation that has become foreign to itself." Eight New Yorkers travel to the O-Zone and are surprised to find themselves in a paradise that allows them to reclaim their common humanity. Their leader is a fifteen-year-old math whiz named Fizzy who, in the words of *New York Times Book Review* contributor Susan Fromberg Schaeffer, is "the kind of man who can lead humanity out of the double wilderness of emotional alienation and dehumanizing science to achieve, in himself, a desperately needed symbiosis between the two."

Some reviewers saw Theroux's next effort, *My Secret History,* as an account of the author's own life, for the story of Andre Parent bears close resemblance to that of his creator. Parent was born in Massachusetts, travels to Africa, marries a British woman, lives in London, and writes popular travel books. He is also a deeply troubled man leading a double life, and certain critics found in Parent's troubles clues to understanding Paul Theroux, despite Theroux's warning in a prefatory note: "Although some of the events and places depicted in the novel bear a similarity to those in my own life, the characters all strolled out of my imagination." The book, commented Yardley in *Washington Post Book World,* "is the story of a man so haunted by guilt and so driven by sexual greed that he is capable only in rare moments of seeing women as anything except agents for the appeasement of his lust." Thus Parent's secret history consists of hidden sexual pleasures and lies and it is not surprising when that history blows up in the character's face, shaking his surface life to its very core. Parent survives the clash of his public and his secret life largely because his wife allows him to transcend it. Thus, related *New York Times Book Review* contributor Wendy Lesser, *My Secret History* becomes a book "about the permanence of marriage in the face of mistrust and infidelity; it's about the wisdom of women and the foolishness of men; and it's about mature love as the necessary and sometimes successful antidote to youthful selfishness."

Theroux followed *My Secret History* with *My Other Life* in 1996. "This is a life I could have lived had things been different," the author noted in prefacing the work, a disclaimer similar to that which appeared in Theroux's previous novel. Characterizing the work as a collection of short stories rather than a novel, Piers Paul Read observed in *Spectator* that "the Theroux of this fiction, if not the real-life Theroux, clearly dislikes his life in London. . . . in [some] stories there are . . . stinging comments on English life, accurate enough when it comes to the literary world but verging on the absurd when it comes, for example, to the royal family. A bitchiness creeps in." In the London *Observer* Kate Kellaway speculated, "Perhaps Theroux's travel writing habits affect his attitude here," "He makes a grand tour of himself observantly but uncritically as if looking through a train window." Much of the book revolves around its protagonist questioning what his life would have been like had it been of the traditional sort—at one point he visits the former husband of an ex-lover, "because whoever he might be he was the man I would have become." Noting particularly the author's "rendering of women as two-dimensional objects" and his "sourness about ex-wives," Rhoda Koenig commented in *Wall Street Journal* that "Theroux offhandedly tells us that things changed after he began spending so much time away writing his travel books. But isn't the real cause whatever it was that took him away?"

Parker Jagoda, the main character in Theroux's disturbing novel *Chicago Loop,* finds his own "other" life encroaching on his public life, but here the results are disastrous. Jagoda is a wealthy and fastidious Chicago businessman who lives with his beautiful wife in a ritzy North Shore neighborhood. He has begun placing personal ads in the Chicago newspapers, and when a pathetic blonde named Sharon responds, Jagoda leads her back to her apartment and brutally kills her, all the while telling himself that she has made him do it. Although Jagoda tries to suppress memories of the murder, the event keeps bubbling up in his consciousness and he decides that the only way to atone for his deed is to reenter Sharon's world—as Sharon. Thus begins an odyssey in which the successful urban professional dresses like the woman he has killed, seeks out situations where he will be sexually abused, and eventually commits a spectacularly appropriate suicide.

Theroux's 1994 novel *Millroy the Magician* also deals with a dual life, but one with overtones far less dark. The satiric tale revolves around narrator Jilly Farina, a fourteen-year-old girl who runs away from an abusive alcoholic father and becomes enthralled by Millroy, a carnival magician who serves as the book's hero. Millroy eventually becomes widely hailed on supermarket tabloids and talk shows for his skills as an evangelist of the American diet; he stars on a children's television show and begins opening up a chain of restaurants run by his dietary converts and featuring his own biblically sanctioned recipes. Jilly, disguised as Millroy's son, Alex, handles the business side of Millroy's career. Noting that the book depends on the technique of magic realism for its believability, Chicago *Tribune Books* critic Nicholas Delbanco thought that the development of the relationship between Jilly and Millroy "is never credible and takes too long. We feel as if we're getting every detail of Millroy's meteoric rise and fall, overhearing every conversation and meeting every visitor to trailer or diner or television studio or hut." Also feeling that the novel loses its effect as a parable due to the same matter-of-factness, Sven Birkets wrote in *Washington Post Book World,* "The thing about Millroy and his narration through Jilly's eyes is that we are never, not even at the last, sure whether

there is genuine goodness in him or whether he is but another power-seeker awed by his own self-myth." Calling the book an "unusual, often funny, dark satire of America's obsession with trim bodies and religious television," *New York Times Book Review* critic Charles Johnson added that *Millroy the Magician* "may strike some readers as maddeningly predictable and aswim in stereotypes of Middle America, gay people, troubled children and people of color. . . . One can only hope that . . . those who reach the end of Mr. Theroux's three-ring circus of a novel see its final act as worth the price of admission."

Kowloon Tong is a timely political thriller in the Graham Greene vein: "Bunt" Mullard and his mother Betty, British expatriates in Hong Kong, live in a world of teas, horse races, and Macao casinos, until the impending takeover by the People's Republic of China throws them into a world of dangerous intrigue. A Chinese gangster is determined to gain control of their textile factory, and he won't take no for an answer. Theroux wryly observes that Hong Kong, originally taken from the Chinese by military force, is on the way to being taken back in a similarly brutal way. Thomas Kenneally, writing in *New York Times,* found Bunt's character excessively passive, but noted that "Theroux's astringent misanthropy and narrative momentum are powerful propellants." In *New York Times Book Review,* Richard Bernstein, deemed *Kowloon Tong* not one of Theroux's more ambitious works, "but one that is recognizably his, full of faulty, off-kilter characters and furnished with a graphic sense of place."

In *Sunrise with Seamonsters* Theroux writes: "Travel is a creative act—not simply loafing and inviting your soul, but feeding the imagination, accounting for each fresh wonder, memorizing and moving on. The discoveries the traveler makes in broad daylight—the curious problems of the eye he solves—resemble those that thrill and sustain a novelist in his solitude." Boarding a train at Victoria Station in London after dropping off his manuscript for *The Black House* with his publisher, Theroux then set off on a four-month odyssey through Asia, the Far East, and the former Soviet Union, eventually returning to his point of departure with "four thick notebooks" on his lap. The edited notebooks became *The Great Railway Bazaar: By Train through Asia.*

Though travel accounts are not generally known for their commercial appeal, *The Great Railway Bazaar* was an enormous success. In *Publishers Weekly,* John F. Baker called Theroux's accomplishment an "amazing first." As Baker explained, the author "made his way onto the best seller list . . . with nothing more than a travel book, . . . thereby becoming probably the first writer since Mark Twain whose travels made a more than fleeting impression in booksellers' accounts." The work also garnered critical praise. *Washington Post Book World* contributor David Roberts thought the account "represents travel writing at its very best—almost the best, one is tempted to say, that it can attain. Paul Theroux . . . here transforms what was clearly a long, ultimately tedious journey by train . . . into a singularly entertaining book." "Though it is a travel book and not a novel," Towers commented, *The Great Railway Bazaar* "incorporates many of the qualities of Theroux's fiction: it is funny, sardonic, wonderfully sensuous and evocative in its descriptions, casually horrifying in its impact."

The success of *The Great Railway Bazaar,* combined with an admitted wanderlust, led Theroux to pen several more travel memoirs. Best known among these are *The Old Patagonian Express: By Train through the Americas, The Kingdom by the Sea: A Journey around Great Britain,* and *The Pillars of Hercules: A Grand Tour of the Mediterranean.* Employing the same elements of rail travel, walking excursion, and personal rumination, these works explore Central and South America and the coastline regions of the British Isles, respectively, although none enjoyed the critical reception that attended publication of *The Great Railway Bazaar.* Some reviewers found the works scornful and repetitive; as Patrick Breslin noted of *The Old Patagonian Express* in *Washington Post Book World,* "Theroux so loses himself in the mechanics of how he got to Patagonia, and the people who irritated him along the way, that there is little room in the book for anything else. And since not very much out of the ordinary happened to him, one's interest flags." In *New York Times,* John Leonard commented that Theroux's traveling style "tends to be contentious; at the drop of an offhand remark in a bar or a dining car, he will opinionize." Leonard added, however, that "One forgives him because one tends to agree with his opinions."

The Pillars of Hercules is Theroux's account of his journey through the Mediterranean realm. Calling the book "a marketing department's dream," Graham Coster added in *London Review of Books* that the book

is "designed with travel-brochure simplicity and accessibility" in mind. *Washington Post Book World* reviewer John Ash questioned many of Theroux's references to location—"Clearly, he travels intuitively, disdaining maps and guidebooks. . . . I'm a little surprised he made it home"—and felt that the author was arrogant and contemptuous toward his location. Regarding Theroux's dismissal of Greece—"The whole of Greece seemed to me to be a cut-price theme park of broken marble, a place where you were harangued in a high-minded way about Ancient Greek culture, while some swarthy little person picked your pocket"—Ash responded, "Theroux is famous for his curmudgeonly verve, but this is not that. It is fatuous and ugly." Stephen Greenblatt, however, wrote in *New York Times Book Review* that the many brief exchanges between Theroux and the people he meets on his journey "disclose a redeeming quality that lies behind Mr. Theroux's grumpiness and cynicism and helps to account for his improvisational energy: he is driven by an intense, insatiable curiosity."

Theroux has continued to produce fiction and travel chronicles into the twenty-first century. *The Stranger at the Palazzo d'Oro and Other Stories* is a collection of tales about sexual desire and its sometimes dangerous complications: One story deals with a Boston boy abused by a Roman Catholic priest, another with interracial love in South Africa. Theroux, "one of our foremost chroniclers of the expatriate experience," in the words of *Library Journal* contributor David W. Henderson, "once again proves his adeptness at exploring otherness." Theroux, noted Rebecca Donner in *People,* handles "the complexities of matters of the heart with subtlety and grace." In the nonfiction work *Dark Star Safari: Overland from Cairo to Cape Town* Theroux revisits some of the African locales where he served with the Peace Corps, gets into arguments with Christian missionaries, and observes the political and social problems that affect much of Africa. "His cogent insights are well integrated," reported a *Publishers Weekly* reviewer, adding that "as a travel guide, Theroux can both rankle and beguile," but overall he has produced a "marvelous report."

Theroux has long labored outside of the realm of academia, and he has occasionally expressed mild contempt for university creative-writing programs and patronage in the form of fellowships, endowments, and grants. Succinctly stating his position in *Sunrise with Seamonsters,* he commented: "The writer doesn't want a patron half so badly as he wants a paying public." The takeover of creative writing by the universities in the United States has, he said, "changed the profession out of all recognition. It has made it narrower, more rarified, more neurotic; it has altered the way literature is taught and it has diminished our pleasure in reading." Theroux's own writing, highly successful commercially, has not gained a great deal of attention within the academic community. As Theroux told *Publishers Weekly,* however, "No serious writer writes for money alone, but it's equally a mistake to think that if your writing makes money you're not serious." He remains greatly concerned, he admitted in a *Chicago Tribune Book World* interview, that his writing should continue to entertain readers. "My fear is that I'll be boring," he said. "You never actually run out of ideas, but you might run out of ideas that are intelligent, amusing, original. I don't want to be a bore. I would rather open a beauty parlor—I swear."

BIOGRAPHICAL AND CRITICAL SOURCES:

BOOKS

Coale, Samuel, *Paul Theroux,* Twayne (New York, NY), 1987.
Contemporary Literary Criticism, Gale (Detroit, MI), Volume 5, 1976, Volume 8, 1978, Volume 11, 1979, Volume 15, 1980, Volume 28, 1984, Volume 46, 1988.
Dictionary of Literary Biography, Gale (Detroit, MI), Volume 2: *American Novelists since World War II, First Series,* 1978, Volume 218: *American Short-Story Writers Since World War II, Second Series,* 1999.

PERIODICALS

Antioch Review, winter, 1977.
Atlantic, October, 1973; April, 1976; October, 1983.
Booklist, July 19, 1997.
Chicago Tribune Book World, September 16, 1979; February 21, 1982; August 15, 1982; March 27, 1983; November 13, 1983; June 30, 1985; February 9, 1986.
Critique, March, 1981.
Detroit News, June 4, 1978; September 9, 1979; November 13, 1983; February 16, 1986.

Economist, July 23, 1988, p. 77; October 24, 1992, p. 102; November 20, 1993, p. 111.
Esquire, December, 1971; April, 1983.
Globe and Mail (Toronto, Ontario, Canada), October 19, 1985.
Kirkus Reviews, April 1, 1997.
Library Journal, March 1, 1994, p. 138; March 15, 1995, p. 102; April 1, 1995, p. 142; September 15, 1995, p. 85; February 1, 1996, p. 90; December, 2003, David W. Henderson, review of *The Stranger at the Palazzo d'Oro and Other Stories,* p. 170.
London Review of Books, February 8, 1996, Graham Coster, review of *The Pillars of Hercules: A Grand Tour of the Mediterranean,* p. 18.
Los Angeles Times, November 13, 1983; October 25, 1984; September 26, 1986.
Los Angeles Times Book Review, October 7, 1979; September 21, 1980; April 18, 1982; March 13, 1983; September 21, 1986.
Maclean's, August 15, 1988, p. 50; August 14, 1989, p. 55.
National Review, June 29, 1971; November 10, 1972; June 2, 1989, p. 58.
New Republic, November 29, 1969; September 25, 1976; November 27, 1976; September 22, 1979; February 24, 1982; April 11, 1983; July 17, 1989, p. 40; March 2, 1992, p. 29.
New Statesman, June 11, 1971; October 4, 1974; October 17, 1975; March 26, 1976; September 1, 1978; October 24, 1980.
New Statesman & Society, September 16, 1988, p. 40; June 30, 1989, p. 33; April 6, 1990, p. 38; November 6, 1992, p. 49; October 8, 1993, p. 38.
Newsweek, September 24, 1973; November 11, 1974; September 8, 1975; June 19, 1976; August 15, 1977; September 10, 1979; March 1, 1982; April 25, 1983; October 24, 1983; October 22, 1984; August 12, 1985.
New York, February 28, 1994, p. 127.
New Yorker, November 11, 1967; November 8, 1969; December 29, 1975; January 7, 1985; February 16, 1987, p. 108; August 10, 1992, p. 80; March 14, 1994, p. 92; June 26, 1995, p. 144.
New York Review of Books, September 23, 1971; September 30, 1976; November 10, 1977; August 17, 1978; April 15, 1982; June 2, 1983.
New York Times, May 29, 1971; July 22, 1976; August 23, 1977; April 30, 1978; May 31, 1978; April 27, 1979; August 28, 1979; February 11, 1982; February 28, 1983; October 13, 1983; October 1, 1984;

June 5, 1985; September 15, 1996; September 23, 1996, p. B2; June 8, 1997.

New York Times Book Review, November 3, 1968; September 28, 1969; August 8, 1971; November 5, 1972; September 9, 1973; September 8, 1974; August 24, 1975; December 28, 1975; July 11, 1976; August 21, 1977; June 18, 1978; July 22, 1979; August 26, 1979; August 24, 1980; February 14, 1982; March 20, 1983; October 23, 1983; April 22, 1984; October 28, 1984; June 2, 1985; November 10, 1985; September 14, 1986; May 10, 1987, p. 34; July 19, 1988, p. 17; June 4, 1989, p. 1; March 17, 1991, p. 7; December 1, 1991, p. 20; June 14, 1992, p. 7; December 6, 1992, p. 52; March 6, 1994, p. 9; November 5, 1995, p. 11; June, 1997.

Observer (London, England), June 30, 1996, p. 15.

People, February 9, 2004, Rebecca Donner, review of *The Stranger at the Palazzo d'Oro and Other Stories,* p. 44.

Publishers Weekly, July 26, 1976; June 24, 1996, p. 43; January 6, 2003, review of *Dark Star Safari: Overland from Cairo to Cape Town,* p. 49.

Saturday Review, September 28, 1968; July 24, 1976; September 3, 1977; July 8, 1978, October 27, 1979; February, 1982; November-December, 1983.

Spectator, June 12, 1971; October 12, 1974; March 15, 1975; October 18, 1975; March 27, 1976; June 4, 1977; September 16, 1978; October 17, 1981; June 30, 1984; June 29, 1985; July 6, 1996, p. 32.

Time, August 23, 1968; August 25, 1975; August 2, 1976; September 5, 1977; June 5, 1978; February 22, 1982; October 31, 1983; July 1, 1985; May 16, 1988, p. 95; May 22, 1989, p. 112; March 25, 1991, p. 71; June 15, 1992, p. 73; March 7, 1994, p. 69; November 6, 1995, p. 83.

Times Literary Supplement, April 11, 1968; June 12, 1969; June 25, 1971; November 17, 1972; April 27, 1973; October 4, 1974; March 14, 1975; March 26, 1976; June 3, 1977; October 31, 1980; November 21, 1980; October 16, 1981; October 8, 1982; October 28, 1983; June 8, 1984; August 2, 1985; October 31, 1986; July 5, 1996.

Tribune Books (Chicago, IL), March 27, 1994, Nicholas Delbanco, review of *Millroy the Magician,* p. 4.

Wall Street Journal, September 13, 1996, Rhoda Koenig, p. A10.

Washington Post Book World, September 14, 1973; September 15, 1974; September 7, 1975; May 30, 1976; July 11, 1976; August 21, 1977; June 25, 1978; September 2, 1979; August 17, 1980; March

6, 1983; October 16, 1983; December 9, 1984; July 7, 1985; February 27, 1994, p. 2; October 8, 1995, p. 5.

Yale Review, spring, 1979.*

*   *   *

THOMAS, Paul
    See MANN, (Paul) Thomas

*   *   *

THOMPSON, Hunter S(tockton) 1937(?)-
    (Raoul Duke)

PERSONAL: Born July 18, 1937 (some sources say 1939), in Louisville, KY; son of Jack R. (an insurance agent) and Virginia (Ray) Thompson; married Sandra Dawn, May 19, 1963 (divorced); married Anita Beymuk, April 24, 2003; children: Juan. *Education:* Studied journalism at Columbia University. *Politics:* "Anarchist." *Hobbies and other interests:* Collecting guns.

ADDRESSES: Home—Owl Farm, Woody Creek, CO 81656.

CAREER: Writer and journalist. Began as a sports writer in Florida; *Time,* Caribbean correspondent, 1959; *New York Herald Tribune,* Caribbean correspondent, 1959-60; *National Observer,* South American correspondent, 1961-63; *Nation,* West Coast correspondent, 1964-66; *Ramparts,* columnist, 1967-68; *Scanlan's Monthly,* columnist, 1969-70; *Rolling Stone,* national affairs editor, 1970-84; *High Times,* global affairs correspondent, 1977-82; *San Francisco Examiner,* media critic, 1985-90; *Smart,* editor-at-large, 1988—. Freelance political analyst for various European magazines, 1988—. Candidate for sheriff of Pitkin County, CO, 1968; member, sheriff's advisory committee, Pitkin County, 1976-81; executive director, Woody Creek Rod and Gun Club. *Military service:* U.S. Air Force, 1956-58; journalist for base magazine.

MEMBER: Overseas Press Club (executive director), National Press Club, American Civil Liberties Union, Fourth Amendment Foundation (founder), National

Hunter S. Thompson

Rifle Association (executive director), U.S. Naval Institute (executive director), Air Force Association (executive director), National Organization for the Reform of Marijuana Laws (NORML; member of national advisory board, 1976—), Hong Kong Foreign Correspondents Club, Kona Coast Marlin Fisherman's Association, Vincent Black Shadow Society, Key West Mako Club.

WRITINGS:

Hell's Angels: A Strange and Terrible Saga, Random House (New York, NY), 1966, reprinted, Modern Library (New York, NY), 1999.

Fear and Loathing in Las Vegas: A Savage Journey to the Heart of the American Dream, illustrated by Ralph Steadman, Random House (New York, NY), 1972, published with an introduction by P. J. O'Rourke as *Fear and Loathing in Las Vegas and Other American Stories,* Modern Library (New York, NY), 1996.

Fear and Loathing on the Campaign Trail '72, illustrated by Ralph Steadman, Straight Arrow Books (San Francisco, CA), 1973.

The Great Shark Hunt: Strange Tales from a Strange Time; Gonzo Papers, Volume One, Summit Books (New York, NY), 1979.

(With Ralph Steadman) *The Curse of Lono,* Bantam (New York, NY), 1983.

Generation of Swine: Tales of Shame and Degradation in the '80s; Gonzo Papers, Volume Two, Summit Books (New York, NY), 1988.

(Author of introduction) Ralph Steadman, *America,* Fantagraphics Books (Seattle, WA), 1989.

Songs of the Doomed: More Notes on the Death of the American Dream; Gonzo Papers, Volume Three, Summit Books (New York, NY), 1990.

Silk Road: Thirty-three Years in the Passing Lane, Simon & Schuster (New York, NY), 1990.

Untitled Novel, David McKay (New York, NY), 1992.

Better than Sex: Confessions of a Political Junkie; Gonzo Papers, Volume Four, Random House (New York, NY), 1993.

The Proud Highway: The Saga of a Desperate Southern Gentleman, 1955-1967, edited by Douglas Brinkley, foreword by William J. Kennedy, Villard (New York, NY), 1997.

(Author of introduction) Ralph Steadman, *Gonzo: The Art,* Harcourt (New York, NY), 1998.

The Rum Diary: The Long Lost Novel, Simon & Schuster (New York, NY), 1998.

Screwjack and Other Stories, Simon & Schuster (New York, NY), 2000.

Fear and Loathing in America: Brutal Odyssey of an Outlaw Journalist, 1968-1976 (correspondence), Simon & Schuster (New York, NY), 2000.

The Kingdom of Fear: Loathsome Secrets of a Star-crossed Child in the Final Days of the American Century, Simon & Schuster (New York, NY), 2003.

Hey Rube, Simon & Schuster (New York, NY), 2004.

Author of the novel *Prince Jellyfish,* 1960. Contributor to *Russell Chatham,* by Etel Adnan, Winn Books, 1984. Contributor of articles and essays, sometimes under pseudonym Raoul Duke, to *Esquire, London Observer, New York Times Magazine, Reporter, Harper's,* and other publications.

ADAPTATIONS: The motion picture *Where the Buffalo Roam* is based on the life and writings of Thompson, written by John Kaye, directed by Art Linson, starring Bill Murray as Thompson, Universal, 1980; *Fear and Loathing in Las Vegas* was adapted as a motion picture, written by Terry Gilliam with Tony Garisoni, Tod Davies, and Alex Cox, directed by Gilliam, starring Johnny Depp and Benicio del Toro, Universal, 1998. An audio version of *Fear and Loathing in Las Vegas* was released by Margaritaville Records, 1996 and features music by Todd Snider and voices of Harry Dean Stanton and Jim Jarmusch. *The Rum Diary* is being made into a motion picture starring Johnny Depp and Benicio del Toro.

SIDELIGHTS: Hunter S. Thompson ranks among the first and foremost practitioners of New Journalism, a genre that evolved in the 1960s to reflect the particular mood of those times. Thompson, who has called his brand of reportage "Gonzo Journalism," was perhaps the most visible and most vituperative of the New Journalism correspondents, a group whose ranks included Tom Wolfe and Gay Talese, among others. As national affairs editor for *Rolling Stone* and author of such widely read books as *Hell's Angels: A Strange and Terrible Saga, Fear and Loathing in Las Vegas,* and *Fear and Loathing on the Campaign Trail '72,* Thompson recorded both the disillusionment and the delirium of a volatile era. According to Morris Dickstein in *Gates of Eden: American Culture in the Sixties,* Thompson "paraded one of the few original prose styles of recent years," a style that indulged in insult and stream-of-invective to an unparalleled degree. He pioneered a new approach to reporting, allowing the story of covering an event to become the central story itself, while never disguising the fact that he was "a half-cranked geek journalist caught in the center of the action," to quote Jerome Klinkowitz in *The Life of Fiction.*

Thompson was considered a seasoned journalist while still in his twenties. His early journalism was conventional, but as the tenor of the nation began to change (and as his own experiments with drugs increased), he embraced the nascent New Journalism style. *New York Times Book Review* contributor Crawford Woods explained that New Journalism's roots lay in "the particular sense of the 1960s that a new voice was demanded by the way people's public and private lives were coming together in a sensual panic stew, with murder its meat and potatoes, grass and acid its spice. How to tell the story of a time when all fiction was science fiction, all facts lies? The New Journalism was born." It was a style that "put the pseudo-objective soporifics of the broadsheets to shame by applying to journalism the techniques of the realistic novel," explained Richard Vigilante in *National Review,* adding, "But, at the same time, it required a romance with reality that undermined the ideologues' lust for self-deceit. For all the literary liberties of the most famous New Journalists, their stories, when done right, were more true than traditional journalism."

Riding and drinking with the Hell's Angels motorcycle gang, taking massive quantities of hallucinogenic drugs, and careening to assignments on little food and less sleep, Thompson became the "professional wildman" of the New Journalists, to quote *Village Voice* contributor Vivian Gornick. He also became a nationally known figure whose work "in particular caused currents of envy in the world of the straight journalists, who coveted his freedom from restraint," according to an *Atlantic* essayist. "He became a cult figure," Peter O. Whitmer wrote in *Saturday Review,* "the outlaw who could drink excessively, drug indulgently, shout abusively, *and* write insightfully."

In *Critique,* John Hellmann wrote: "By conceiving his journalism as a form of fiction, Thompson has been able to shape actual events into meaningful works of literary art." Thompson's "Gonzo Journalism" narratives are first-person accounts in which the author appears as a persona, sometimes Raoul Duke, but more commonly Dr. Hunter S. Thompson, a specialist variously in divinity, pharmaceuticals, or reporting.

To research *Hell's Angels: A Strange and Terrible Saga,* Thompson's 1966 account of the infamous California motorcycle gang, the young author rode with the Angels for almost a year, recording their road rallies, their home lives, and their sexual adventures. The book strives to present the gang objectively while exposing the fact that its brutal reputation was primarily the creation of the scandal-mongering media. *New Republic* contributor Richard M. Elman observed that in *Hell's Angels* Thompson has "managed to correct many popular misconceptions about [the Angels], and in the process, provided his readers with a tendentious but informative participant-observer study of those who are doomed to lose." In *Nation,* Elmer Bendiner likewise noted that throughout the book, "Thompson's point of view remains eminently sane and honest. He does not weep for the Angels or romanticize them or glorify them. Neither does he despise them. Instead, he views them as creatures of an irresponsible society, given their image by an irresponsible press, embodying the nation's puerile fantasy life. He sees the menace not so much in the Hell's Angels themselves, as in the poverty of spirit and perennial adolescence that spawned them." *Hell's Angels* garnered a mixture of critical reactions. *Atlantic* correspondent Oscar Handlin contended that Thompson's "lurid narrative, despite its sympathy for his subjects, reveals the threat they pose." William Hogan in *Saturday Review* called the work "a jarring piece of contemporary Californiana, as well as an examination of a weird branch of present-day show business." According to Elman, Thompson's "fascinating invocation to, evocation *of,* and reportage *about* the Hell's Angels . . . is certainly the most informative, thorough, and vividly written account of this phenomenon yet to appear."

Fear and Loathing in Las Vegas is an all-out display of Gonzo Journalism that remains Thompson's best-known work. As Hellmann described the book in *Fables of Fact: The New Journalism as New Fiction, Fear and Loathing in Las Vegas* "is, in barest outline, the author's purported autobiographical confession of his failure to fulfill the magazine's assignment to 'cover' two events in Las Vegas, the Fourth Annual 'Mint 400' motorcycle desert race and the National Conference of District Attorneys Seminar on Narcotics and Dangerous Drugs. It is more exactly the author's (or 'Raoul Duke's') tale of his hallucinations and adventures. . . . The book is, then, even in its most general subject and presentation, either a report of an actual experience which was largely fantasy or an actual fantasy which is disguised as report."

In the guise of Raoul Duke, Thompson relates a series of episodic adventures revolving around drug use and *carte blanche* access to Las Vegas's finest hotels, accompanied by a three-hundred-pound Samoan attorney named Dr. Gonzo (based on Thompson's friend Oscar Zeta Acosta), who "serves as a parody of noble savage 'sidekicks' from Chingachgook to Tonto," according to Hellmann. *National Observer* contributor Michael Putney called the book "a trip, literally and figuratively, all the way to bad craziness and back again. It is also the most brilliant piece of writing about the dope subculture since Tom Wolfe's *Electric Kool-Aid Acid Test* and, at the same time, an acid, wrenchingly funny portrait of straight America's most celebrated and mean-spirited pleasure-dome, Las Vegas."

Thompson continues to explore "the politics of unreason" in *Fear and Loathing on the Campaign Trail '72,* a collection of articles that first appeared in *Rolling Stone* magazine. *Nation* correspondent Steven

d'Arazien called the work "a New Journalism account of the 1972 presidential campaign from before New Hampshire to Miami and beyond. . . . It will be regarded as a classic in the genre." As national affairs editor for *Rolling Stone,* Thompson traveled with the press corps that followed candidate George McGovern; according to Dickstein he "recorded the nuts and bolts of a presidential campaign with all the contempt and incredulity that other reporters must feel but censor out." According to Jules Witcover in *Progressive* magazine, the book, though "heavily personalized writing-on-the-run, riddled here and there by the clear eye of hindsight, does convey an honest picture of a political writer picking his way through all the hoopla, propaganda, tedium, and exhaustion of a campaign." Critics' opinions of the book depended on their assessment of Thompson's reporting style. *Columbia Journalism Review* essayist Wayne C. Booth characterized the work as "an inflated footnote on how Thompson used the campaign to achieve a 'very special kind of High.'" He concluded, "Cleverness, energy and brashness cannot, finally, make up for ignorance and lack of critical training." On the other hand, *Saturday Review* contributor Joseph Kanon found *Fear and Loathing on the Campaign Trail '72* to contain "the best political reporting in some time," and concluded that the book "manages to give politics, after years of televised lobotomy, some flesh." *New York Times* columnist Christopher Lehmann-Haupt admitted that while Thompson "doesn't exactly see America as Grandma Moses depicted it, or the way they painted it for us in civics class, he does in his own mad way betray a profound democratic concern for the polity. And in its own mad way, it's damned refreshing."

Thompson's subsequent books, *The Great Shark Hunt: Strange Tales from a Strange Time*—in which many of his essays on Watergate are collected—*The Curse of Lono, Generation of Swine: Tales of Shame and Degradation in the '80s,* and *Songs of the Doomed: More Notes on the Death of the American Dream,* have continued to mine his vein of personal, high-energy reporting. *Los Angeles Times Book Review* correspondent Peter S. Greenburg noted that *The Great Shark Hunt* "is not so much an attack on America as it is a frightfully perceptive autopsy of our culture. . . . Thompson is the master of the cosmic metaphor and combines this talent with all the subtlety of a run at someone's jugular with a red-hot rail spike." In *The Curse of Lono* Thompson recounts his antics during a visit to Hawaii with his longtime friend and illustrator, Ralph Steadman. Once again the author demonstrates his "very nearly unrelieved distemper," an attribute William F. Buckley, Jr., described as "the Sign of Thompson" in *New York Times Book Review. Washington Post Book World* reviewer Michael Dirda claimed of the work, "No one writes like Hunter Thompson, though many have tried, and *The Curse of Lono* dispenses pages rabid with his hilarious, frenzied rantings, gusts of '60s madness for the stuffy '80s."

In 1990 Thompson became the subject of media attention when a woman—described variously as an actress, a reporter, and an ex-pornographic film producer—accused him of sexual assault, claiming Thompson had grabbed her when she refused his invitation to join him in his hot tub. Local police conducted an eleven-hour search of Thompson's home, uncovering small quantities of marijuana, cocaine, and LSD, a number of Valium-like pills, an antique Gatling gun, and four sticks of dynamite. Thompson was charged with five felonies and three misdemeanors and faced up to fifty years in prison if found guilty on all counts. Soon, however, the case against Thompson began to erode and, after a preliminary hearing, the charges were dismissed. A number of people suggested that the entire case had simply been an attempt to rid the exclusive Aspen community of someone many of its newer residents considered a nuisance.

These events and others are described in *Songs of the Doomed: More Notes on the Death of the American Dream.* A *Washington Post Book World* contributor suspected that at times, "'Dr.' Thompson has, after years of pursuing the complete derangement of his senses, finally made the journey to real madness, to a place where the parameters of truth and fantasy have blended into each other, and the result of this loss of perspective is often more disconcerting than it is enlightening."

More of Thompson's political writings are collected in *Better than Sex: Confessions of a Political Junkie,* which includes his thoughts on George Bush's presidency and Bill Clinton's campaign and first years in office. While the collection was not rated as highly as Thompson's earlier political ruminations, Thomas Gaughan maintained in *Booklist* that *Better than Sex* "quite shrewdly" asserts that "Bush is so guilty he makes Nixon look innocent . . . and Clinton is a swine, but he's our swine." In contrast, L. S. Klepp of *Entertainment Weekly* felt that the book "reads as if Thompson had emptied the contents of several files

and wastebaskets into a large envelope addressed to his indulgent publisher and let it go at that."

Thompson's early years in journalism are documented in *The Proud Highway: Saga of a Desperate Southern Gentleman.* A compilation of some three hundred letters—just a fraction of his output—to friends and editors, famous writers, and anyone else to whom he wanted to express his opinion, the book reflects Thompson's early thirst for fame and penchant for bombast, according to reviewers. With an eye toward creating a literary persona, Thompson sent thousands of letters in his early years, asking Lyndon Johnson, for example, to appoint him governor of American Samoa, and imploring novelist William Faulkner—whom he had never met—to send him weekly checks. "Like all great wits, from Oscar Wilde to Gore Vidal," wrote Pico Iyer in *Time,* "Thompson saw that a pose was more compelling than a personality, not least because it was more consistent." Iyer concluded that "the pleasure of these letters is that they have all the rude vitality of the man who was not yet a myth."

According to David Gates in *Newsweek, The Proud Highway* illustrates several things about Thompson: "First, though Thompson casts himself as a wild man, he's also a precisionist. Second, he has ungodly energy: these letters are just the warm-up and spillover from his fiction, journalistic pieces and his first book. . . . Third, funny as he is, he's dead serious about his art and his reputation: he made carbons of all these letters. Just in case." Other reviewers duly praised the volume as well. "By turns exasperating and entertaining," wrote a reviewer for *Publishers Weekly,* the book "is also a devastating portrait of the writer as an incorrigible outsider." And Bonnie Smothers in *Booklist* wrote that "letters like Hunter's are a reminder of what a letter can be—our own personal literature that is, indeed, a testament to our life and times."

In 1999 Thompson published his first novel, *The Rum Diary,* written while he was a neophyte reporter in the Caribbean at the dawn of the 1960s. True to the style he developed in his journalism, the novel is mostly autobiographical, recounting the adventures of a young journalist, Paul Kemp, who writes for a Puerto Rican newspaper and lives dangerously, swilling alcohol and pugnaciously tempting fate. The novel received mixed reviews. Vanessa V. Friedman, writing in *Entertainment Weekly,* called it "little more than a fervent first novel by a young man in thrall to both Hemingway and Kerouac." In contrast, Mike Benediktsson, in *Library Journal*, appreciated "the narrative's tight, urgent prose" that "exposes the twisted roots of Thompson's gonzo journalism." Similarly, a *Publishers Weekly* reviewer acknowledged that the novel lays the groundwork for Thompson's later style, but that "the best parts of the book are its occasional, almost grudging, acknowledgments of natural beauty."

Originally published in a limited edition in 1991, Thompson's *Screwjack and Other Stories* was released by Simon & Schuster in 2000. The book contains three stories that "offer the sustained flashes of the brilliance that characterized Thompson's early classics," according to one *Publishers Weekly* contributor. Stories such as "Death of a Poet" contain a mixture of violence, sex, and drugs set in the late 1960s. A *Publishers Weekly* critic considered this a "slight" addition to the author's ouevre, but still worth a look from loyal Thompson fans. The year 2000 also saw the publication of a collection of Thompson's letters titled *Fear and Loathing in America: Brutal Odyssey of an Outlaw Journalist, 1968-1976*. Many of the missives in this book are addressed to publishers and concern books he was working on at the time; critics found them interesting for Thompson's observations of famous politicians, authors, and other renowned figures, such as President Jimmy Carter and Tom Wolfe. "What may surprise readers," commented a *Publishers Weekly* reviewer, "is the sweetness of much of the writing." However, the critic added, "Thompson's strong suit is still invective, of which he remains the unsurpassed master."

In 2003 Thompson's memoir, titled *The Kingdom of Fear: Loathsome Secrets of a Star-crossed Child in the Final Days of the American Century,* was published. A *Publishers Weekly* contributor called the book "an autobiography that is typically unorthodox in style but still revealing previously unknown facts about its subject." The memoir covers everything from Thompson's first brush with the law in 1946 to his run in with Clarence Thomas before he was elected to the Supreme Court to his latest take on the American political scene. "The book makes a strong case for Thompson as both a social prophet (his day-after analysis of the 9/11 tragedy proves particularly prescient) and a patriot," wrote a reviewer in *Book*. Ulrich Baer, writing in *Library Journal*, called Thompson's writing "lazy" but also noted, "There are some canny observa-

tions on the difference between outlaws and lawbreakers, insights into the corruption of politics by politicians' lust for power, and instructive pieces on voter rebellion." *Booklist* contributor Ray Olsen commented that "Thompson remains, in this hodgepodge of pieces spanning most of his life . . . a larger-than-life middle-American humorist whose only peers are Mark Twain and William Burroughs."

Although Thompson's style and his personality have led to conflicting opinions about his writing, more critics have praised Thompson than disparaged him. As Jerome Klinkowitz wrote, "For all of the charges against him, Hunter S. Thompson is an amazingly insightful writer. His 'journalism' is not in the least irresponsible. On the contrary, in each of his books he's pointed out the lies and gross distortions of conventional journalism. . . . Moreover, his books are richly intelligent." According to Gornick, Thompson's talent "lies in his ability to describe his own manic plunge into drink, drugs, and madness through a use of controlled exaggeration that is truly marvelous." John Leonard expressed a similar opinion in *New York Times*. Thompson "became, in the late 1960's, our point guard, our official crazy, patrolling the edge," Leonard wrote. "He reported back that the paranoids were right, and they were. The cool inwardness . . . the hugging of the self to keep from cracking up, is not for him. He inhabits his nerve endings; they are on the outside, like the skin of a baby. . . . He is also, as if this needs to be said, hilarious."

BIOGRAPHICAL AND CRITICAL SOURCES:

BOOKS

Adnan, Etel, *Russell Chatham*, Clark City Press (Livingston, MT), 1987.

Carroll, E. Jean, *Hunter: The Strange and Savage Life of Hunter S. Thompson,* Dutton (New York, NY), 1993.

Contemporary Literary Criticism, Gale (Detroit, MI), Volume 9, 1978, Volume 17, 1981, Volume 40, 1986, Volume 104, 1998.

Contemporary Popular Writers, St. James Press (Detroit, MI), 1997.

Dickstein, Morris, *Gates of Eden: American Culture in the Sixties,* Basic Books (New York, NY), 1977.

Dictionary of Literary Biography, Volume 185: *American Literary Journalists, 1945-1995, First Series,* Gale (Detroit, MI), 1998.

Hellman, John, *Fables of Fact: The New Journalism as New Fiction,* University of Illinois Press (Urbana, IL), 1981.

Klinkowitz, Jerome, *The Life of Fiction,* University of Illinois Press (Urbana, IL), 1977.

McKeen, William, *Hunter S. Thompson,* Twayne (Boston, MA), 1991.

Vonnegut, Kurt, Jr., *Wampeters Foma & Granfalloons,* Delacorte (New York, NY), 1974.

Whitmer, Peter O., *When the Going Gets Weird: The Twisted Life and Times of Hunter S. Thompson: A Very Unauthorized Biography,* Hyperion (New York, NY), 1993.

PERIODICALS

American Spectator, December, 1990, p. 42.

Atlantic, February, 1967, Oscar Handlin, review of *Hell's Angels*; July, 1973.

Book, March-April 2003, review of *Kingdom of Fear: Loathsome Secrets of a Star-crossed Child in the Final Days of the American Century,* p. 80.

Booklist, October 1, 1994, Thomas Gaughan, review of *Better than Sex: Confessions of a Political Junkie,* p. 187; April 15, 1997, Bonnie Smothers, review of *The Proud Highway,* p. 1364; December 15, 2002, Ray Olson, review of *Kingdom of Fear,* p. 706.

Columbia Journalism Review, November-December, 1973, Wayne C. Booth, review of *Fear and Loathing on the Campaign Trail '72*; September-October, 1979; March, 2001, James Boylan, review of *Fear and Loathing in America: The Brutal Odyssey of an Outlaw Journalist, 1968-1976,* p. 70.

Commonweal, April 7, 1967.

Critique, Volume 21, number 1, 1979, John Hellman.

Detroit News, August 26, 1979; November 27, 1983.

Entertainment Weekly, September 9, 1994, L. S. Klepp, review of *Better than Sex,* p. 73; October 16, 1998, Vanessa V. Friedman, review of *The Rum Diary,* p. 82; January 12, 2001, Glenn Gaslin, "Fear and Loathing on the Net: Hunter Thompson Goes Cyber," p. 87; March 23, 2001, Rebecca Ascher-Walsh, "Real World: News from Hollywood," p. 74.

Esquire, April, 1991, p. 152; February, 1993, p. 61.

Harper's, July, 1973.

Kirkus Reviews, June 15, 2004, review of *Hey Rube,* p. 572.

Library Journal, October 15, 1998, Mike Benediktsson, review of *The Rum Diary,* p. 101; February 15, 1999, Theresa Connors, review of *The Rum Diary,* p. 38; November 1, 2000, Michael Rogers, review of *Screwjack and Other Stories,* p. 143; February 1, 2003, Ulrich Baer, review of *Kingdom of Fear,* p. 99.

London Magazine, June-July, 1973.

Los Angeles Times Book Review, August 12, 1979, Peter S. Greenburgy, review of *The Great Shark Hunt: Strange Tales from a Strange Time.*

Nation, April 3, 1967; August 13, 1973; October 13, 1979; June 4, 1990, p. 765.

National Observer, August 5, 1972, Michael Putney, review of *Fear and Loathing in Las Vegas.*

National Review, September 16, 1988, p. 52.

New Leader, November 28, 1988, p. 21.

New Republic, February 25, 1967; October 14, 1972; October 13, 1973; August 25, 1979; January 7, 1991, p. 38.

New Statesman, November 11, 1988, p. 33.

Newsweek, March 6, 1987; May 19, 1997, David Gates, review of *The Proud Highway,* p. 85.

New York, September 26, 1994, p. 102.

New Yorker, March 4, 1967.

New York Review of Books, October 4, 1973.

New York Times, February 23, 1967; June 22, 1972; May 18, 1973; August 10, 1979.

New York Times Book Review, January 29, 1967; March 5, 1967; July 23, 1972; July 15, 1973; December 2, 1973; August 5, 1979; October 14, 1979; January 15, 1984; August 14, 1988, p. 17; November 25, 1990, pp. 7-8; October 23, 1994, p. 18; February 23, 2003, Jack Shafer, review of *Kingdom of Fear,* p. 5.

People, February 10, 2003, review of *Kingdom of Fear,* p. 49.

Progressive, July, 1973, Jules Witcover, review of *Fear and Loathing on the Campaign Trail '72.*

Publishers Weekly, April 21, 1997, review of *The Proud Highway,* p. 49; September 21, 1998, review of *The Rum Diary,* p. 71; October 23, 2000, review of *Screwjack,* p. 38; October 30, 2000, review of *Fear and Loathing in America,* p. 54; January 13, 2003, review of *Kingdom of Fear,* p. 51; January 13, 2003, Lynn Andrian, interview with Thompson, p. 53.

Rolling Stone, June 28, 1990, pp. 64-68; July 12, 1990, pp. 21-22; May 30, 1991, pp. 38-39; January 23, 1992, pp. 22-32; June 16, 1994, pp. 42-44.

Saturday Night, March, 1991, pp. 62-63.

Saturday Review, February 18, 1967, William Hogan, review of *Hell's Angels*; April 21, 1973, Joseph Kanon, review of *Fear and Loathing on the Campaign Trail '72.*

Time, June 16, 1997, Pico Iyer, review of *The Proud Highway,* p. 80.

Times (London, England), May 12, 1982.

Times Literary Supplement, January 11, 1968; November 3, 1972.

Village Voice, November 19, 1979, Vivian Gornick.

Washington Monthly, April, 1981.

Washington Post Book World, August 19, 1979, review of *The Great Shark Hunt*; December 18, 1983, review of *Songs of the Doomed: More Notes on the Death of the American Dream.*

ONLINE

The Great Thompson Hunt, http://www.gonzo.org (April 2, 2002).*

*   *   *

TOMLINSON, Theresa 1946-

PERSONAL: Born August 14, 1946, in Crawley, Sussex, England; daughter of Alan (a vicar) and Joan (a teacher) Johnston; married Alan Tomlinson (an architect), 1967; children: Rosie, Joe, Sam. *Ethnicity:* "White." *Education:* Attended Hull College of Education. *Politics:* Socialist. *Religion:* "Agnostic."

ADDRESSES: Home—65 Hastings Rd., Sheffield, South Yorkshire S7 2GT, England. *Agent*—Caroline Walsh, David Higham Associates, 5-8 Lower John Street, Golden Square, London W1R 4HA, England. *E-mail*—tomterry@blueyonder.co.uk.

CAREER: Author, 1987—.

MEMBER: National Association of Writers in Education, Society of Authors.

WRITINGS:

The Flither Pickers, photographs by Frank Meadow Sutcliffe, Littlewood Press, 1987.

The Water Cat, Julia MacRae Books (London, England), 1988.

Summer Witches, Macmillan (New York, NY), 1989.

Riding the Waves, Julia MacRae Books (London, England), 1990, Macmillan (New York, NY), 1993.

The Rope Carrier, Julia MacRae Books (London, England), 1991.

The Forestwife, Julia MacRae Books (London, England), 1993, Orchard Books (New York, NY), 1995.

The Herring Girls, photographs by Frank Meadow Sutcliffe, Julia MacRae Books (London, England), 1994.

The Cellar Lad, Julia MacRae Books (London, England), 1995.

Haunted House Blues, Walker Books (New York, NY), 1996.

Dancing through the Shadows, Julia MacRae Books (London, England), 1997, DK Ink (New York, NY), 1997.

Meet Me by the Steelmen, Walker Books (New York, NY), 1997.

Little Stowaway, Julia MacRae Books (London, England), 1997.

Child of the May (second book in "Forestwife" trilogy), Orchard Books (New York, NY), 1998.

Ironstone Valley, A. & C. Black (London, England), 1998.

The Path of the She-Wolf (third book in "Forestwife" trilogy), Red Fox, 2000.

Night of the Red Devil, Walker Books (New York, NY), 2000.

Voyage of the Silver Bream, A. & C. Black (London, England), 2001.

Beneath Burning Mountain, Red Fox, 2001.

The Moon Riders, Corgi (London, England), 2003.

Scavenger Boy, Walker Books (New York, NY), 2003.

The Errand Lass, Walker Books (New York, NY), 2003.

Blitz Baby, Orchard Books (New York, NY), 2003.

WORK IN PROGRESS: The Voyage of the Snake Lady, a sequel to *The Mood Riders.*

SIDELIGHTS: "I love writing about people who had a hard life, but worked together and found ways to survive," Theresa Tomlinson once told *CA.* "Resilience is what I admire most in human beings. I think that it is important to find exciting ways of passing a sense of history onto our children. A knowledge of the resilience of ordinary people who have lived before us can inspire modern children, and help them with their own struggles and decisions." Reviewing *The Cellar Lad,* one of Tomlinson's novels for young readers, Marcus Crouch of *Junior Bookshelf* noted that "Theresa Tomlinson has made the fictional interpretation of the English industrial revolution her own." Tomlinson's novels, many of which are set in her native Yorkshire, are regional only in location, while their themes cross borders and continents. Daily courage in the face of hardship is a major Tomlinson motif, yet her books, as many reviewers have noted, are not heavily polemical. They are character-driven and involve the reader in both historical and contemporary situations, generally featuring strong female protagonists. From the angst of a frustrated surfer to the exploits of Maid Marian in the forests of Sherwood, Tomlinson's novels engage young readers on several levels and generally end with an upbeat message delivered not with a sledgehammer but with a smile.

Tomlinson was raised in North Yorkshire and as a child had a strong desire to be a ballet dancer. She had no inclination to become a writer, but her parents read to her and encouraged a love of books in the young girl. "I started making little picture books for my own children when they were small," Tomlinson commented. "As the children got older, the stories got longer and I found that I enjoyed it very much." Tomlinson started her literary career writing stories inspired by the local history of North Yorkshire. "My grandparents used to tell me about the fisherwomen who arrived on the train early in the morning and stories about storms, shipwrecks, and daring lifeboat rescues."

Writing what she knew, Tomlinson first published a novel of the hard life of the wives of Yorkshire fishermen at the turn of the twentieth century. These women endured all sorts of weather to gather shellfish bait, or flithers, for their husbands. *The Flither Pickers* tells the story of the daughter of one such family, Lisa, who has the opportunity to break away from this harsh life by pursuing an education. But Lisa is torn between loyalty to her family and her desire to become a writer. Like all Tomlinson's books, this one was thoroughly researched; it also uses period photographs by Frank Meadow Sutcliffe to illustrate the text.

Tomlinson's next book also employed the setting of Yorkshire, but this time a bit later in history. Set in 1953, *The Water Cat* takes place in a steel-working town and involves a brother and sister who take in a stray cat. This animal turns out to be anything but a garden variety cat; in fact it is a shape-changer, a mer-

man whose access to the sea has been cut off by the steel plant. The children vow to help the merman get back to his rightful home in the ocean. In a *Growing Point* review, Margery Fisher noted that in "plain prose which is circumstantial enough to deny disbelief the author describes the practical contrivances by which Jane and Tom manage to carry the merman/cat past the metal barrier, helped by seagulls and pigeons which put up a diversion."

Further books dealing with social and economic history include *The Rope Carrier, The Herring Girls,* and *The Cellar Lad.* The forgotten craft of rope-making is examined in the first of these, set in a village of such workers who live in the underground cottages vicinity of Sheffield, England. Minnie Dakin is born in this cave and chances are that she will die in it as well, just as generations of rope workers have before her. But when her sister Netty marries and soon thereafter falls ill, Minnie is called from the cave to help. Soon, however, she wonders if life is much better amid the growing metal industries of Sheffield.

In *The Herring Girls,* Tomlinson once again used photographs by Sutcliffe to illustrate the lives of young nineteenth-century women who cleaned fish during the herring season. Thirteen-year-old Dory is among them, forced into the trade in order to save her family from the poor house. More social history was served up in *The Cellar Lad,* a novel dealing with attempts at getting the right to vote for all men and unionization for workers in the steel industry in Sheffield. Young Ben Sterndale and his family are caught up in these fights.

Tomlinson has also written books with contemporary settings and themes, dealing with issues ranging from intergenerational relationships to fighting cancer. In *Summer Witches,* she takes on the misconceptions concerning powerful women. Two young friends, Sarah and Susanna, decide to clean out an old World War II air-raid shelter uncovered in Sarah's back yard and use it as a clubhouse. In doing so, they discover evidence of earlier inhabitants of the shelter, two older women who live nearby—Lily and Rose. They have thought of Lily as something of a witch, for she is unable to speak and has wisdom of healing plants. Eventually the two young girls come to learn that Lily, far from being a witch, has a sad secret involving the shelter and a tragic incident from fifty years ago.

Steven Engelfried, writing in *School Library Journal,* described Tomlinson's *Riding the Waves* as a "strong novel about the surprising relationship that evolves between a boy and an elderly woman." Set in a small English coastal town, the novel deals with the dreams of Matt, who desperately wants to be part of a group of surfers. Such membership is elusive until Matt is forced to visit an old family friend, Florrie, for a class project. A bond is slowly formed between the two when Matt, an adoptee, learns that Florrie was long ago forced to give up her out-of-wedlock child. When Matt accompanies Florrie to the beach one day, their relationship is cemented: expecting to be embarrassed by the old woman, Matt is instead introduced to the surfer group who have a soft spot in their hearts for Florrie from the days when she ran a chip shop. Deborah Abbott noted in *Booklist* that this "startlingly refreshing story about an intergenerational friendship" was "well-paced" and had "an upbeat and satisfying ending."

Tomlinson's own struggle with breast cancer inspired her novel *Dancing through the Shadows.* "When faced with a long period of treatment," Tomlinson commented, "I felt that it would be beneficial to try to keep writing, so I decided to use what was happening to me as the theme for a novel. I wrote as though I was the young daughter of a woman going through the experience. Once I'd decided to do this, I found that I felt much better. When I went to the hospital, suddenly I was a researcher, rather than a patient. It was very therapeutic. The story is quite upbeat and also suggests ways of giving help." In the novel, Ellen's mother has breast cancer, and Ellen, along with the rest of the family, is trying to be supportive. Soon Ellen begins to find some solace at an abandoned spring which her teacher discovers near the school, one that was probably once sacred and had healing powers. Restoring the natural spring to a semblance of its former pristine condition parallels the chemotherapy Ellen's mother is receiving, until both are finally restored to health. "Gracefully avoiding didacticism, Tomlinson . . . makes regular reference to the many sources of healing," noted a writer for *Kirkus Reviews.* "Readers will be borne along by the lively pace and the first-person, dialogue-heavy style." A contributor to *Publishers Weekly* observed that themes of "courage, survival and rebirth are explored in this story of a teenager coping with her mother's illness," concluding that "Tomlinson addresses painful truths about the progression of cancer and at the same time celebrates the resilience of body and spirit."

Personal experience also inspired a trilogy focusing on Marian of Sherwood Forest. Tomlinson recalled: "As a child I loved Robin Hood stories, but felt a little

frustrated that Marian, the only woman that a girl could identify with, was usually locked up in a castle and needing to be rescued. I wanted to imagine Marian rushing through the forest like the men, having adventures and doing the rescuing herself." To satisfy this need for an exciting story, Tomlinson wrote *The Forestwife,* telling the story of Mary de Holt, who runs away from an arranged marriage at age fifteen. Taking to the forest with her nurse, Agnes, the pair try to find the local wise woman, the Forestwife, whom some think of as a witch. But the woman has died, and Agnes takes her role, renaming her young charge Marian, and taking her on as assistant.

Adventures there are in plenty, involving people on the run and a group of defrocked, renegade nuns. Agnes's son, Robert, is a local outlaw whom Marian initially dislikes, but soon grows to love as he becomes Robin Hood. Yet when Agnes dies, Marian's plans for marrying Robin come to an end, for she must now become the new Forestwife, enlisting the many women of the forest into a band to fight injustice. Reviewing the novel in the *Bulletin of the Center for Children's Books,* Deborah Stevenson called it "an atmospheric read about a durable heroine." In a starred review, *Booklist*'s Ilene Cooper called *The Forestwife* a "rich, vibrant tale with an afterword that describes how various legends are braided into the story." Tomlinson followed up this initial Marian tale with two others, *Child of the May* and *The Path of the She-Wolf.*

Whether writing of the medieval forest, the plight of workers in the industrializing nineteenth century, or about contemporary teenagers facing their own modern challenges, Tomlinson fuels her stories with the theme of resiliency. In her dozen-plus novels for young readers, she reveals not only history but the ordinary men and women who created it.

More recently Tomlinton told *CA:* "In recent years I've found that the detailed local history themes that I have so much enjoyed writing are little in demand. I've struggled to find something that I want to write about, that will also be popular on the shelves of bookshops and libraries. *The Moon Riders* was my eventual solution: a mix of mythology, adventure, and a touch of magic."

BIOGRAPHICAL AND CRITICAL SOURCES:

PERIODICALS

Booklist, May 1, 1993, Deborah Abbott, review of *Riding the Waves,* p. 1593; March 1, 1995, Ilene

Cooper, review of *The Forestwife,* p. 1241; November 1, 1997, Michael Cart, review of *Dancing through the Shadows,* p. 463; October 15, 1998, Ilene Cooper, review of *Child of the May,* p. 413; November 15, 1998, Hazel Rochman, review of *Little Stowaway,* p. 600; April 1, 2000, Ilene Cooper, review of *The Forestwife,* p. 1479.

Book Report, September-October, 1995, Kathryn Whetstone, review of *The Forestwife,* p. 42; November-December, 1997, Judith Beavers, review of *Dancing through the Shadows,* p. 43.

Books for Keeps, May, 1992, pp. 20-21; September, 1992, p. 11; July, 1993, p. 32; May, 1996, p. 13.

Bulletin of the Center for Children's Books, May, 1991, p. 229; March, 1995, Deborah Stevenson, review of *The Forestwife,* pp. 252-253.

Growing Point, June, 1989, Margery Fisher, review of *The Water Cat,* p. 5089; January, 1991, p. 5450; January, 1992, pp. 5641-5642.

Horn Book, May-June, 1991, Martha V. Parravano, review of *Summer Witches,* p. 332; November, 1998, Anne Deifendeifer St. John, review of *Child of the May,* p. 742.

Junior Bookshelf, August, 1989, p. 181; December, 1990, p. 302; June, 1991, p. 123; December, 1991, p. 269; June, 1995, Marcus Crouch, review of *The Cellar Lad,* pp. 110-111; June, 1996, p. 126; October, 1996, p. 195.

Kirkus Reviews, April 15, 1991, p. 540; September 15, 1997, review of *Dancing through the Shadows,* p. 1464; October 1, 1998, p. 1465.

Publishers Weekly, May 10, 1993, review of *Riding the Waves,* p. 72; February 13, 1995, review of *The Forestwife,* p. 79; November 3, 1997, review of *Dancing through the Shadows,* p. 86.

School Librarian, February, 1991, p. 33; February, 1992, p. 33; August, 1995, Linda Saunders, review of *The Cellar Lad,* p. 119.

School Library Journal, May, 1991, Virginia Golodetz, review of *Summer Witches,* p. 95; May, 1993, Steven Engelfried, review of *Riding the Waves,* p. 110; March, 1995, Susan L. Rogers, review of *The Forestwife,* p. 225; November, 1997, Rosalyn Pierini, review of *Dancing through the Shadows,* p. 124; November 1, 1998, Cheri Estes, review of *Child of the May,* p. 131.

Times Educational Supplement, November 11, 1988, p. 52; December 7, 1990, Sandra Kemp, review of *The Flither Pickers,* p. 30; November 8, 1991, Gillian Avery, review of *The Rope Carrier,* p. 38; November 11, 1994, Gillian Cross, review of *The Herring Girls,* p. R3; August 11, 1995, p. 17.

Voice of Youth Advocates, June, 1995, p. 100.

U

UPDIKE, John (Hoyer) 1932-

PERSONAL: Born March 18, 1932, in Shillington, PA; son of Wesley Russell (a teacher) and Linda Grace (an author; maiden name, Hoyer) Updike; married Mary Entwistle Pennington, June 26, 1953 (divorced, 1977); married Martha Ruggles Bernhard, September 30, 1977; children: (first marriage) Elizabeth Pennington, David Hoyer, Michael John, Miranda Margaret; (second marriage) three stepchildren. *Education:* Harvard University, A.B. (summa cum laude), 1954; attended Ruskin School of Drawing and Fine Art, Oxford, 1954-55. *Politics:* Democrat. *Religion:* Christian.

ADDRESSES: Home—Beverly Farms, MA. *Agent*—c/o Author Mail, Alfred A. Knopf, 201 East 50th St., New York, NY 10022.

CAREER: Novelist, critic, short story writer, poet, essayist, and dramatist. *New Yorker* magazine, reporter, 1955-57. Visited USSR as part of a cultural exchange program of the U.S. Department of State, 1964.

MEMBER: American Academy and Institute of Arts and Letters (secretary, chancellor), American Academy of Arts and Sciences.

AWARDS, HONORS: Guggenheim fellowship in poetry, 1959; American Academy and National Institute of Arts and Letters Richard and Hilda Rosenthal Foundation Award, 1960, for *The Poorhouse Fair;* National Book Award in fiction, 1964, and Prix Medicis Etranger (France), 1966, both for *The Centaur;* O. Henry Award for fiction, 1966, for short story, "The

John Updike

Bulgarian Poetess;" Fulbright fellow in Africa, 1972; American Book Award nomination, 1980, for *Too Far to Go: The Maples Stories;* Edward MacDowell Medal for Literature, MacDowell Colony, 1981; Pulitzer Prize for fiction, 1981, and National Book award for fiction, 1982, both for *Rabbit Is Rich;* National Book Critics Circle award for criticism, 1984, for *Hugging the Shore: Essays and Criticism;* Medal of Honor for Literature, National Arts Club (New York, NY), 1984; National Book Critics Circle award in fiction nomination, 1986, for *Roger's Version;* PEN/Malamud Memorial Prize, PEN/Faulkner Award Foundation, 1988, for "excellence in short story writing;" National Medal of Arts, 1989; National Book Critics Award and Pulitzer Prize, both 1990, and Howells medal, American Academy of Arts and Letters, 1995, all for *Rabbit at Rest;* Premio Scanno, 1991; named Commandeur de l'Ordre des Arts et des Lettres, 1995; Ambassador Book Award, English-speaking Union, 1996, for *In the Beauty of the Lilies;* Campion Award, *America* magazine, 1997; Harvard Arts First Medal, 1997; National Book Foundation Medal for distinguished contribution to American letters, 1998; Los Angeles Public Library literary award, 1999; Caldecott Medal, 2000, for *A Child's Calendar,* illustrated by Trina Schart Hyman; PEN/Faulkner Award for Fiction, 2004, for *The Early Stories: 1953-1975;* recipient of numerous honorary doctoral degrees, including Ursinsus College, 1962, Moravian College, 1967, Lafayette College, 1974, Albright College, 1982, and Harvard University, 1992.

WRITINGS:

NOVELS

The Poorhouse Fair (also see below), Knopf (New York, NY), 1959, with an introduction by Updike, Ballantine (New York, NY), 2004.

Rabbit, Run (also see below), Knopf (New York, NY), 1960.

The Centaur, Knopf (New York, NY), 1963.

Of the Farm, Knopf (New York, NY), 1965, reprinted, Ballantine (New York, NY), 2004.

The Poorhouse Fair [and] *Rabbit, Run,* Modern Library (New York, NY), 1965.

Couples, Knopf (New York, NY), 1968.

The Indian, Blue Cloud Abbey (Marvin, SD), 1971.

Rabbit Redux (also see below), Knopf (New York, NY), 1971.

A Month of Sundays, Knopf (New York, NY), 1975.

Marry Me: A Romance, Knopf (New York, NY), 1976.

The Coup, Knopf, (New York, NY) 1978.

Rabbit Is Rich (also see below), Knopf (New York, NY), 1981.

Rabbit Is Rich/Rabbit Redux/Rabbit, Run (also see below), Quality Paperback Book Club, 1981.

The Witches of Eastwick, Knopf (New York, NY), 1984.

Roger's Version, Knopf (New York, NY), 1986.

S., Knopf (New York, NY), 1988.

Rabbit at Rest, Knopf (New York, NY), 1990.

Memories of the Ford Administration, Knopf (New York, NY), 1992.

Brazil, Knopf (New York, NY), 1994.

Rabbit Angstrom: The Four Novels (contains *Rabbit Is Rich, Rabbit Redux, Rabbit, Run,* and *Rabbit at Rest*), Knopf/Everymans (New York, NY), 1995, published as *The Rabbit Novels,* Ballantine (New York, NY), 2003.

In the Beauty of the Lilies, Knopf (New York, NY), 1996.

Toward the End of Time, Knopf (New York, NY), 1997.

Gertrude and Claudius, Knopf (New York, NY), 2000.

Seek My Face, Knopf (New York, NY), 2002.

Villages, Knopf (New York, NY), 2004.

POETRY

The Carpentered Hen and Other Tame Creatures (also see below), Harper (New York, NY), 1958, published as *Hoping for a Hoopoe,* Gollancz (London, England), 1959.

Telephone Poles and Other Poems (also see below), Knopf (New York, NY), 1963.

Verse: The Carpentered Hen and Other Tame Creatures/Telephone Poles and Other Poems, Fawcett (New York, NY), 1965.

The Angels (poem; limited edition), King and Queen Press (Pensacola, FL), 1968.

Bath after Sailing (poem; limited edition), Pendulum Press (Monroe, CT), 1968.

Midpoint and Other Poems, Knopf (New York, NY), 1969.

Seventy Poems, Penguin (New York, NY), 1972.

Six Poems (limited edition), Oliphant Press, 1973.

Cunts (poem; limited edition), Frank Hallman, 1974.

Tossing and Turning, Knopf (New York, NY), 1977.

Sixteen Sonnets (limited edition), Halty Ferguson (Cambridge, MA), 1979.

Five Poems (limited edition), Bits Press (Cleveland, OH), 1980.

Spring Trio (limited edition), Palaemon Press (Winston-Salem, NC), 1982.

Jester's Dozen (limited edition), Lord John (Northridge, CA), 1984.

Facing Nature: Poems, Knopf (New York, NY), 1985.

Collected Poems: 1953-1993, Knopf (New York, NY), 1993.

Americana and Other Poems, Knopf (New York, NY), 2001.

SHORT STORIES

The Same Door, Knopf (New York, NY), 1959.

Pigeon Feathers and Other Stories, Knopf (New York, NY), 1962.

Olinger Stories: A Selection, Vintage (New York, NY), 1964.

The Music School, Knopf (New York, NY), 1966.

Bech: A Book, Knopf (New York, NY), 1970.

Museums and Women and Other Stories, Knopf (New York, NY), 1972.

Warm Wine: An Idyll, Albondocani Press (New York, NY), 1973.

Couples: A Short Story, Halty Ferguson (Cambridge, MA), 1976.

From the Journal of a Leper, Lord John (Northridge, CA), 1978.

Too Far to Go: The Maples Stories, Fawcett (New York, NY), 1979.

Three Illuminations in the Life of an American Author (short story), Targ (New York, NY), 1979.

Problems and Other Stories, Knopf (New York, NY), 1979.

Your Lover Just Called: Stories of Joan and Richard Maple, Penguin Books (New York, NY), 1980.

The Chaste Planet, Metacom (Worcester, MA), 1980.

People One Knows: Interviews with Insufficiently Famous Americans, Lord John (Northridge, CA), 1980.

Invasion of the Book Envelopes, Ewert (Concord, MA), 1981.

Bech Is Back, Knopf (New York, NY), 1982.

The Beloved (short story), Lord John (Northridge, CA), 1982.

Confessions of a Wild Bore, Tamazunchale Press, 1984.

More Stately Mansions, Nouveau Press (Jackson, MS), 1987.

Trust Me: Short Stories, Knopf (New York, NY), 1987.

The Afterlife and Other Stories, Knopf (New York, NY), 1994.

Bech at Bay: A Quasi-Novel, Knopf (New York, NY), 1998.

A & P, Harcourt (Fort Worth, TX), 1998.

Licks of Love: Short Stories and a Sequel, "Rabbit Remembered," Knopf (New York, NY), 2000.

The Complete Henry Bech: Twenty Stories, with an introduction by Malcolm Bradbury, Knopf (New York, NY), 2001.

The Early Stories: 1953-1975, Knopf (New York, NY), 2004.

ESSAYS

Assorted Prose, Knopf (New York, NY), 1965.

On Meeting Authors, Wickford (Newburyport, MA), 1968.

A Good Place, Aloe (Atlanta, GA), 1973.

Picked-up Pieces, Knopf (New York, NY), 1975.

Hub Fans Bid Kid Adieu, Lord John (Northridge, CA), 1977.

Talk from the Fifties,, Lord John (Northridge, CA), 1979.

Ego and Art in Walt Whitman, Targ (New York, NY), 1980.

Hawthorne's Creed, Targ (New York, NY), 1981.

Hugging the Shore: Essays and Criticism, Knopf (New York, NY), 1983.

Emersonianism, Bits Press, 1984.

Just Looking: Essays on Art, Knopf (New York, NY), 1989.

Odd Jobs: Essays and Criticism, Knopf (New York, NY), 1991.

Concerts at Castle Hill (music criticism), Lord John (Northridge, CA), 1993.

Golf Dreams: Writings on Golf, Knopf (New York, NY), 1996.

More Matter: Essays and Criticism, Knopf (New York, NY), 1999.

OTHER

(Adapter with Warren Chappell) *The Magic Flute* (juvenile fiction; adapted from libretto of same title by Wolfgang Amadeus Mozart), Knopf (New York, NY), 1962.

(Adapter with Chappell) *The Ring* (juvenile fiction; adapted from libretto by Richard Wagner), Knopf (New York, NY), 1964.

A Child's Calendar (juvenile poetry), Knopf (New York, NY), 1965, new edition with illustrations by Trina Schart Hyman, Holiday House (New York, NY), 1999.

Three Texts from Early Ipswich (historical pageant; produced in Ipswich, MA, 1968), Seventeenth Century Day Committee of the Town of Ipswich, 1968.

(Adapter) *Bottom's Dream* (juvenile fiction; adapted from William Shakespeare's play *A Midsummer Night's Dream*), Knopf (New York, NY), 1969.

(Editor) David Levine, *Pens and Needles: Literary Caricatures,* Gambit (Ipswich, MA), 1970.

A Good Place: Being a Personal Account of Ipswich, Massachusetts, Aloe Editions (New York, NY), 1973.

Buchanan Dying (play; produced in Lancaster, MA, 1976), Knopf (New York, NY), 1974.

(Author of introduction) Henry Green, *Loving, Living, Party Going,* Penguin Books, 1978.

(Author of introduction) Bruno Schulz, *Sanatorium under the Sign of the Hourglass,* Penguin Books, 1979.

(Author of afterword) Edmund Wilson, *Memoirs of Hecate County,* Nonpareil (Boston, MA), 1980.

(Editor with Shannon Ravenel and author of introduction) *The Best American Short Stories: 1984,* Houghton (Boston, MA), 1984.

Self-Consciousness: Memoirs, Knopf (New York, NY), 1989.

The Alligators (children's fiction), Creative Education (Mankato, IL), 1990.

(With Mary Steichen Calderone and Edward Steichen) *The First Picture Book: Everyday Things for Babies,* Fotofolio/Whitney Museum of American Art, 1991.

(Author of introduction) *The Art of Mickey Mouse,* edited by Craig Yoe and Janet Morra-Yoe, Hyperion (New York, NY), 1991.

(Author of introduction) *Heroes and Anti-Heroes,* Random House (New York, NY), 1991.

(Author of introduction) Henry Green, *Surviving,* Viking (New York, NY), 1993.

A Helpful Alphabet of Friendly Objects (juvenile poetry; photographs by David Updike), Knopf (New York, NY), 1994.

(Author of introduction) Edith Wharton, *The Age of Innocence,* Ballantine (New York, NY), 1996.

(Author of introduction) Herman Melville, *The Complete Shorter Fiction,* Knopf (New York, NY), 1997.

(Author of introduction) Jill Krementz, *The Writer's Desk,* Random House (New York, NY), 1997.

(Editor) *A Century of Arts and Letters: The History of the National Institute of Arts and Letters as Told, Decade by Decade, by Eleven Members,* Columbia University Press (New York, NY), 1998.

(Editor with Katrina Kenison, also selector and author of introduction) *The Best American Short Stories*

of the Century, Houghton (Boston, MA), 1999, expanded edition, 2000.

(Author of introduction) Max Beerbohm, *Seven Men,* New York Review Books (New York, NY), 2000.

(Editor) Karl Schapiro, *Selected Poems,* Library of America (New York, NY), 2003.

Also author with Günther Schuller of words and music for *The Fisherman and His Wife,* performed in Boston, MA, 1970. "Talk of the Town" reporter, *New Yorker,* 1955-57. Contributor to books, including Martin Levin, editor, *Five Boyhoods,* Doubleday (New York, NY), 1962; contributor of translations to Jorge Luis Borges, *Selected Poems: 1923-1967,* edited by Norman Thomas di Giovanni, Delacorte (New York, NY), 1972. Contributor of short stories, book reviews, and poems to *New Yorker* and other periodicals.

Updike's papers are housed in the Houghton Library, Harvard University.

ADAPTATIONS: Couples was purchased by United Artists in 1969; *Rabbit, Run* was filmed by Warner Bros. in 1970; *Bech: A Book* was adapted as the play *Bech Takes Pot Luck,* produced in New York, NY, 1970; *The Music School* was broadcast by Public Broadcasting System, 1976; *Two Far to Go* was made into a television movie by National Broadcasting Co. in March, 1979, later revised and released for theater distribution by Sea Cliff Productions, 1982; director George Miller's movie *The Witches of Eastwick,* 1987, was loosely based on Updike's novel of the same title; "The Christian Roommates," a short story, was made into a ninety-minute movie for television.

SIDELIGHTS: John Updike "has earned an . . . imposing stance on the literary landscape," wrote *Los Angeles Times* contributor Katherine Stephen, "earning virtually every American literary award, repeated bestsellerdom and the near-royal status of the American author-celebrity." Hailed by critics and readers as one of the great American novelists of his generation, Updike has been hailed as a premiere chronicler of middle America in all its mundane glory. "A reader would be hard pressed to name a contemporary author other than John Updike who is more in tune with the way most Americans live," wrote Donald J. Greiner in a *Dictionary of Literary Biography* essay. "Man, wife, home, children, job—these . . . concerns have rested at the heart of his art since he published his first book . . . and they have continued to help him dissect, lovingly and clearly, the daily routine of middle America in small town and suburb."

Most critics familiar with Updike have strong opinions about the author's work. As Joseph Kanon explained in *Saturday Review:* "The debate . . . has long since divided itself into two pretty firmly entrenched camps: those who admire the work consider him one of the keepers of the language; those who don't say he writes beautifully about nothing very much." Updike acknowledges this charge but believes the complaint lacks validity. "There is a great deal to be said about almost anything," he explained to Jane Howard in a *Life* magazine interview. "Everything can be as interesting as every other thing. An old milk carton is worth a rose. . . . The idea of a hero is aristocratic. Now either nobody is a hero or everyone is. I vote for everyone. My subject is the American Protestant small town middle class. I like middles. It is in middles that extremes clash, where ambiguity restlessly rules."

Debate about the effectiveness of Updike's writing began in 1957 with publication of *The Poorhouse Fair*, his first novel. As Curt Suplee noted in his *Washington Post* profile of the author: "Updike's fiction is not overburdened by action, and his spare story lines are embellished with a lush and elegantly wrought style that some readers find majestic (John Barth calls him the Andrew Wyeth of American writers) and others intolerable. Norman Podhoretz described his prose in 'The Poorhouse Fair' as 'overly lyrical, bloated like a child who has eaten too much candy.'" Other critics differed: *New York Times* reviewer Donald Barr called *The Poorhouse Fair* "a work of art," and *Chicago Sunday Tribune*'s Fanny Butcher cited the work for "the author's brilliant use of words and . . . subtle observations."

"There is one point on which his critics all agree," observed Rachael C. Burchard in *John Updike: Yea Sayings.* "His style is superb. His work is worth reading if for no reason other than to enjoy the piquant phrase, the lyric vision, the fluent rhetoric." In a cover story on Updike, *Time* magazine's Paul Gray claimed: "No one else using the English language over the past two and a half decades has written so well in so many ways as he." A reviewer for *Books Abroad* noted that "Critics continually comment on the technical virtuosity of Updike," while in *John Updike* Suzanne Henning Uphaus declared: "In the midst of diversity there

are certain elements common to all of Updike's writing. Most important, there is Updike's remarkable mastery of language."

Other commentators fail to see Updike's work in such a favorable light. For example, in her *Partisan Review* commentary on *Couples* Elizabeth Dalton asserted: "In its delicacy and fullness Updike's style seems to register a flow of fragments almost perfectly toned. And yet, after pages and pages of his minutely detailed impressions, the accumulated effect is one of waste." John W. Aldridge wrote in *Time to Murder and Create: The Contemporary Novel in Crisis* that the novelist "has none of the attributes we conventionally associate with major literary talent. He does not have an interesting mind. He does not possess remarkable narrative gifts or a distinguished style. He does not create dynamic or colorful or deeply meaningful characters. . . . In fact, one of the problems he poses for the critic is that he engages the imagination so little that one has real difficulty remembering his work long enough to think clearly about it." Updike "has difficulty in reining in his superfluous facility with words," Edward Hoagland complained in *New York Times Book Review.* "He is too fluent."

Many of the most disparaging reviews of Updike's work have come from critics who object not only to his writing style, but also to the author's subject matter. Commenting on the frenzy of criticism from reviewers that met the 1968 publication of *Couples,* Updike's explicit look at sexual freedom in a small New England town, Robert Detweiler noted in *John Updike:* "As frequently happens, the furor accompanying the depiction of sexual amorality increased the difficulty of judging the novel's artistic quality. Most of the reviews appeared to be impulsive reactions to the subject matter rather than measured assessments." In the case of this novel, negative critical response did little to tone down public enthusiasm for the work; it was on *Publishers Weekly* bestseller list for thirty-six weeks.

Couples was not the first Updike novel to deal with the sexual habits of middle-class America or to receive disapproving reviews from commentators upset by the author's frank language. "Looking back," wrote Eliot Fremont-Smith in *Village Voice,* "it must have been the sexuality that so upset the respectable critics of *Rabbit, Run* in 1960. Their consternation had to do with what seemed a great divide between John

Updike's exquisite command of prose . . . and the apparent no-good vulgar nothing he expended it on." *Rabbit, Run* is the first installment in Updike's continuing saga of Harry "Rabbit" Angstrom that has expanded to include *Rabbit Redux,* the highly celebrated *Rabbit Is Rich,* and *Rabbit at Rest.* Published at ten-year intervals, the novels follow the life of "Rabbit" as he tries to leave his marriage, discovers his wife has been unfaithful, finds himself laid off from his blue-collar job, and as he confronts middle-age, ill health, and death. Greiner noted that in the Rabbit tetralogy, Updike "takes a common American experience—the graduation from high school of a star athlete who has no life to lead once the applause diminishes and the headlines fade—and turns it into a subtle expose of the frailty of the American dream. . . . It is now clear that he has written a saga of middle-class America in the second half of the twentieth century."

Both celebrated and vilified for its sexual focus and its deeply ambivalent central character, the "Rabbit" tetralogy has garnered a number of significant awards. The third volume in the series, *Rabbit Is Rich,* received the Pulitzer Prize, and the National Book Award. The final volume also earned a Pulitzer and a National Book Critics Award. Anthony Quinton in a London *Times* review argued that the "Rabbit novels are John Updike's best since they give the fullest scope to his remarkable gifts as observer and describer. What they amount to is a social and, so to speak, emotional history of the United States over the last twenty years or more, the period of Rabbit's and his creator's conscious life." Greiner wrote: "Like James Fenimore Cooper's Leatherstocking, Hawthorne's Hester, and Mark Twain's Huck, Harry is one of the immortal characters who first absorb and then define a national culture. . . . Personal limitation mirrors national malaise." Greiner concludes: "It is sad to think of death setting its snare for Rabbit Angstrom because, after four decades and four long novels, he has joined the pantheon of American literary heroes. Yet a glimpse of final defeat is the price to be paid for membership in that exclusive club." All four of Updike's Rabbit novels are published together as *The Rabbit Novels,* released in 2003.

In *John Updike and the Three Great Secret Things* George Hunt suggested that sex, religion, and art "characterize the predominant subject matter, thematic concerns, and central questions found throughout [Updike's] adult fiction." According to Greiner, Updike

criticism has shifted since the 1960s from a consideration of the novelist's style to a focus on his themes and how they interrelate. "Later commentators," Greiner asserted, "are concerned with his intellectually rigorous union of theology and fiction and with his suggestion that sex is a kind of emerging religion in the suburban enclaves of the middle class."

Exploring the interrelatedness of sex and religion in Updike's fiction, Jean Strouse observed in a *Newsweek* review, "Readers and critics have accused Updike of being obsessed with sex. Maybe—but I think he is using Harry Angstrom and Piet Hanema in 'Couples,' and Richard Maple in 'Too Far to Go,' to explore that modern search for 'something behind all this . . . that wants me to find it.' Melville—and many others—may have announced the demise of God, but nobody has managed to excise the desire for something beyond death and daily life, a desire that has in the 20th century shifted its focus from God to sex." *New York Times* reviewer Michiko Kakutani offered a similar explanation of the development of what she called Updike's "favorite preoccupations:" "His heroes, over the years, have all suffered from 'the tension and guilt of being human.' Torn between vestigial spiritual yearnings and the new imperatives of self-fulfillment, they hunger for salvation even as they submit to the importunate demands of the flesh."

Updike's 1992 novel, *Memories of the Ford Administration,* centers around a history professor, Alf Clayton, and his contribution to an historical journal concerning the Ford administration. Alf ruminates upon his past and discovers, as Charles Johnson in *New York Times Book Review* noted, he "can only remember two things—his knot of extramarital affairs and his never-completed opus on the life of President James Buchanan." As Richard Eder commented in *Los Angeles Times Book Review,* "Alf's struggles with his formless life and time are intercut with his stabs at portraying Buchanan's hapless struggles with his." Nicholas von Hoffman in a Chicago *Tribune Books* review found the layered plots of *Memories* something "only a writer of great technical accomplishment can bring off. . . . While one of the plots pulls us through the sex, the dissolving marital unions, the saturnalian nights of the Ford years, another works its sinuous way into the past and finds an American male unrecognizable to us moderns." Bruce Bawer in *Washington Post Book World* compared *Memories of the Ford Administration* to Updike's *Rabbit at Rest,* arguing that there "is the same sad sense of life winding down, of the aging eagle stretching his wings; the same fixation on orgasms and grace." Bawer concluded that despite the juxtaposition of Alf and Buchanan offering at times "a touching sense of the isolation and helplessness of the human condition," at other times it "seems sheer contrivance." Hoffman, however, concluded that Updike "has the ability to evoke the micro-epochs that fascinate us." Despite differing appraisals, most critics agree that, as Johnson commented, *Memories* is "quintessential Updike, an exploration of a modern American terrain of desire, guilt and moral ambiguity that he has made distinctly his own."

Breaking with this familiar terrain in 1994, the prolific Updike published his sixteenth novel, *Brazil.* As Tom Shone explained in *Times Literary Supplement, Brazil's* genre, magic realism, makes for "the most bizarrely uncharacteristic novel Updike has yet written." *Brazil* is the story of two lovers: the poor, black Tristao, and the well-to-do white Isabel living in Rio de Janeiro. The plot, as Caroline Moore summarized it in *Spectator,* is uninhibited: "Isabel invited Tristao to deflower her at their first encounter; they steal from her uncle and flee on the proceeds to a hotel. . . . They are pursued, recaptured, re-elope, and undergo severe yet picaresque sufferings in the wilds of western Brazil, including starvation and slavery." Both Isabel and Tristao "survive a transformation of identity," as Alexander Theroux commented in Chicago's *Tribune Books,* "for at one crucial point in the novel there takes place an astonishing role reversal in which she turns black, he white—a piece of fantasy born as much of the ongoing requirements of Updike's parable as of the young lovers' passion."

Brazil received mixed reviews from many critics. Michael Dirda in a *Washington Post Book World* review found aspects of *Brazil* "that irritate, like the nips of tropical insects," but argues that these are "compensated for by the novel's zesty readability." Michiko Kakutani argued in *New York Times* that though "there are occasional passages [in *Brazil*] that sparkle with Mr. Updike's patented gift for the lyrical metaphor, his descriptions of Tristao and Isabel's adventures often feel forced and contrived." Rhoda Koenig gave *Brazil* a similarly mixed review in *New York:* "The main characters themselves are not credible, with their mythic passions, expressed in diction more formal and flowery than would ever issue from a boy of the slums and a girl from the world of pam-

pered inanity." Koenig concluded, however, that Updike's *Brazil* "is a novel of endless and astonishing fertility," and is "the most absorbing and unsettling novel, apart from the Rabbit books, that [Updike] has written in some time." Barbara Kingsolver in a review of *Brazil* for *New York Times Book Review* found that Updike's "prose is measured, layered, insightful, smooth, as addictive a verbal drug as exists on the modern market. For every tiresome appearance of Tristao's yam, there is also an image or observation that seems, against all odds, to mark the arrival of something new in the English language."

Updike returns to more familiar thematic territory in 1996's *In the Beauty of the Lilies,* a four-generation saga of the spiritual emptiness of modern American life. The novel begins, as Julian Barnes of *New York Times Book Review* noted, with "a sly misdirection. D. W. Griffith is filming 'A Call to Arms' . . . in the spring of 1910. Mary Pickford, short of sleep and over-costumed for a hot day, faints." Updike then introduces the Reverend Clarence Arthur Wilmot, and never returns to Griffith and Pickford. The novel follows Clarence's loss of faith, his switch from clergyman to encyclopedia salesman, his death, and then follows his family three further generations. When film is mentioned again in the text, Barnes argues, the connection is made by the reader: "religion and the movies: two great illusionary forces, two worlds in which the primal image is of darkness conquered by light." Sybil S. Steinberg in a *Publishers Weekly* interview with Updike paraphrased: "The four generations that *Lilies* depicts . . . are meant to allude to the biblical line from Abraham to Isaac to Joseph and his brothers." Updike told Steinberg that his Sunday school education left him "haunted by that particular [biblical] saga, and the notion that we are members of our ancestors. I wanted to give an American version of that sense." Barnes concluded that *Lilies* is "a novel of accumulated wisdom, with . . . Updike in full control of his subtle, crafty and incessantly observing art." Steinberg also noted Updike's control, finding that his "gift for exact, metaphorical observation binds matters of the soul to the ephemera of daily life."

Toward the End of Time is unlike typical Updike fare in that it is set in the future. The setting is the year 2020 after a war between the United States and China that has toppled the government and turned the Great Plains into "a radioactive dustbowl and left the management of local affairs to thugs who demand protection money," summarized a *Publishers Weekly* critic. Updike's protagonist, Ben Turnbull, has kept a journal depicting a year in his life. In his journal, Ben reveals his "basic Updikean traits" similar to other Updike characters, including his "importunate sexual urges combined with vague spiritual yearnings, an inclination toward melancholy introspection and a love of golf," noted Michiko Kakutani in *New York Times Book Review*. But, argued Kakutani, Turnbull is less like Rabbit Angstrom and more a "narcissistic and dirty minded old man." "As Ben confronts the looming certainty that time is running out for him and the universe, the narrative sweeps to a bittersweet conclusion," found a critic for *Publishers Weekly*.

Critics of *Toward the End of Time* were typically mixed in their assessment. Kakutani asked: "How could this veteran novelist, who just year published the magisterial and masterly *In the Beauty of the Lilies,* follow that dazzling performance with this callous and perfunctory book? . . . Updike's usual sympathy for—and insight into—his characters gives way to cartoonish caricature, while his fascination with the intricacies of marriage, adultery and male-female relations devolves into the clumsy string-pulling of a chauvinistic puppeteer." James Wood, reviewing the novel for *New Republic,* commented that "too much of this novel advances into serenity when it should retreat into anguish, and too much of it finds what already exists rather than creates what does not." Woods criticized "the novel's reliance on a narrative that is already familiar to us," noting that this "sucks interest away from its fictionalized telling;" still, the critic did have praise for the "gorgeousness in the book" and its "fine words."

Updike's *Gertrude and Claudius* is a fictional exploration of the lives of Hamlet's parents and the relationship between Hamlet's mother and uncle. "Updike has appropriated the old Scandinavian legend about a prince who avenges his father's murder," wrote Ron Charles in *Christian Science Monitor.* "But in this version, Updike wonders if Hamlet's mom and dad were such bad parents after all." In the work, Updike creates the fictional lives of Gertrude, King Hamlet (her first husband), and Claudius, the king's brother who, as in Shakespeare's famous play, murders Claudius and soon after marries Gertrude. "This is a new perspective," found Adam Begley in *People,* citing Updike's plot about "a middle-aged queen falling for her husband's darkly mysterious younger brother."

Critics were again mixed. "Ultimately . . . one wonders what Updike hoped to achieve by deflating this Danish colossus into a soap opera befitting an age in which half of all marriages end in divorce," opined Norah Vincent in her appraisal of *Gertrude and Claudius* for *National Review.* "Turning Hamlet into a spoiled suburban brat may be amusing, but in the end it's a bit like portraying Macbeth as a hen-pecked Walter Mitty. . . . For all its pleasures, *Gertrude and Claudius* can't help being a disappointment to those who still find dignity and meaning in the tragic view of life." "Most likely, Updike's just having fun," countered Rex Roberts in *Insight on the News.* "*Gertrude and Claudius* allowed him to indulge his considerable talents, to writ a bit of Shakespearean rag. . . . Readers will enjoy *Gertrude and Claudius* best by giving themselves over to the book's playful spirit." Richard Eder in *New York Times Book Review* was even more laudatory: "Just as Shakespeare used older chronicles to construct his anguished balance between imagination and action, Updike has used Shakespeare to write a free-standing, pleasurable and wonderfully dexterous novel about three figures in complex interplay with their public state, their private longings and one another."

Like his novels, Updike's short stories and poetry also illustrate his command of language and his deep affection for everyday life in all its banality. "Read as a whole, [Updike's] short-story volumes offer a social commentary on American domesticity since midcentury, and, while the prose is always lyrical and the observations always sharp, a tone of sadness—wistfulness—prevails," wrote Greiner in *Dictionary of Literary Biography.* Reviewing *The Afterlife and Other Stories,* Peter Kemp in the London *Sunday Times* found nearly the entire volume of stories "masterpieces of stead delineation, in which psychological and emotional nuance are traced with as much lucid finesse as the wealth of visual detail." Noting that poetry is not Updike's "primary medium," Mark Ford in *Times Literary Supplement* nonetheless found that Updike's verse "evokes with the clarity and precision of his fiction the contours of particular moments and places." Greiner maintained that the "happy union of lyrical prose and intellectual probing that is the highlight of [Updike's] fiction shows itself everywhere in his nonfiction."

Particularly praised by critics has been the author's collected work *The Early Stories: 1953-1975,* which won the PEN/Faulkner award in 2003. As Scott

Shibuya Brown commented in *Atlantic,* reading through this 864-page volume "is a testament to many things, not least Updike's prodigious work habits (reputedly three pages a day, six days a week)." Beginning with 1953's "Ace in the Hole" and extending to his more experimental work, such as "Love Song, for a Moog Synthesizer," the 103-story collection demonstrates the author's "masterful ability to find beauty in the mundane and foreshadows the emotional complexity of his later novels," according to *Entertainment Weekly* reviewer Michelle Kung. Updike's work "is as prolific and valuable and given to experimentation as it was in those early years," noted Kyle Minor in appraising *The Early Stories* for *Antioch Review,* Minor adding that this comprehensive collection of Updike's formative short fiction "can be considered a good gift to the emerging writer" due to the author's skills as a stylist.

Updike is also a prolific author of prose nonfiction, including "book reviews, essays, addresses, comic feuilletons and random, autobiographical jottings," according to Michiko Kakutani in a review of *More Matter: Essays and Criticism* for *New York Times Book Review.* His other collections include *Hugging the Shore, Odd Jobs,* and the 1996 collection *Golf Dreams.* "In his strongest pieces," wrote Kakutani, "Updike's awesome pictorial powers of description combine with a rigorous, searching intelligence to produce essays of enormous tactile power and conviction. . . . His best pieces manage both to edify and to beguile."

Updike's skill in portraying the anxieties and frustrations of middle-America is considered the outstanding feature of his works. "He is our unchallenged master at evoking the heroic void of ordinary life," Suplee maintained, "where small braveries contend in vain against the nagging entropy of things, where the fear of death drips from a faulty faucet and supermarket daydreams turn to God. With heart-clutching clarity, he transmutes the stubborn banality of middle-class existence into tableaux that shiver with the hint of spiritual meaning." According to Kakutani, Updike's work "has not only lyrically defined the joys and sorrows of the American middle class, but also gives—as he once wrote of another author—'the happy impression of an oeuvre, of a continuous task carried forward variously, of a solid personality, of a plenitude of gifts explored, knowingly.'" A *Publishers Weekly* reviewer maintained that "one looks forward to the changing perspective (though not changing themes) that each decade brings to this masterful writer's work."

BIOGRAPHICAL AND CRITICAL SOURCES:

BOOKS

Aldridge, John W., *Time to Murder and Create: The Contemporary Novel in Crisis,* McKay (New York, NY), 1966.

Baker, Nicholas, *U and I: A True Story,* Vintage (New York, NY), 1995.

Bloom, Harold, editor, *John Updike: Modern Critical Views,* Chelsea House (New York, NY), 1987.

Boswell, Marshall, *John Updike's Rabbit Tetralogy: Mastered Irony In Motion,* University of Missouri Press (Columbia, MO), 2000.

Broer, Lawrence R., editor, *Rabbit Tales: Poetry and Politics in John Updike's Rabbit Novels,* University of Alabama Press (Tuscaloosa, AL), 1998.

Burchard, Rachael C., *John Updike: Yea Sayings,* Southern Illinois University Press (Carbondale, IL), 1971.

Concise Dictionary of American Literary Biography: Broadening Views, 1968-1988, Gale (Detroit, MI), 1989.

Contemporary Authors Bibliographical Series, Volume 1, Gale (Detroit, MI), 1986.

Contemporary Literary Criticism, Gale (Detroit, MI), Volume 1, 1973, Volume 2, 1974, Volume 3, 1975, Volume 5, 1976, Volume 7, 1977, Volume 9, 1978, Volume 13, 1980, Volume 15, 1980, Volume 23, 1983, Volume 34, 1985, Volume 43, 1987, Volume 70, 1991.

De Bellis, Jack, *John Updike: A Bibliography, 1967-1993,* foreword by Updike, Greenwood Press (Westport, CT), 1994.

De Bellis, Jack, editor, *The Critical Response to John Updike's "Rabbit" Angstrom Saga,* Praeger (Westport, CT), 2004.

Detweiler, Robert, *John Updike,* Twayne (Boston, MA), 1972, revised edition, 1984.

Dictionary of Literary Biography, Gale (Detroit, MI), Volume 2: *American Novelists since World War II,* 1978, Volume 5: *American Poets since World War II,* 1980, Volume 143: *American Novelists since World War II, Third Series,* 1994.

Dictionary of Literary Biography Documentary Series, Volume 3, Gale (Detroit, MI), 1983.

Dictionary of Literary Biography Yearbook, Gale (Detroit, MI), *1980,* 1981, *1982,* 1983.

Greiner, Donald J., *John Updike's Novels,* Ohio University Press (Athens, OH), 1984.

Greiner, Donald J., *Adultery in the American Novel: Updike, James, Hawthorne,* University of South Carolina Press (Columbia, SC), 1985.

Hunt, George, *John Updike and the Three Great Secret Things,* Eerdmans (Grand Rapids, MI), 1980.

Kamm, Antony, *Biographical Companion to Literature in English,* Scarecrow Press (Metuchen, NJ), 1997.

Luscher, Robert M., *John Updike: A Study of the Short Fiction,* Twayne (New York, NY), 1993.

Miller, D. Quentin, *John Updike and the Cold War: Drawing the Iron Curtain,* University of Missouri Press (Columbia, MO), 2001.

Neary, John, *Something and Nothingness: The Fiction of John Updike and John Fowles,* Southern Illinois University Press (Carbondale, IL), 1992.

Newman, Judie, *John Updike,* St. Martin's Press (New York, NY), 1988.

Plath, James, editor, *Conversations with John Updike,* University Press of Mississippi (Jackson, MS), 1994.

Ristoff, Dilvo I., *John Updike's Rabbit at Rest: Appropriating History,* P. Lang (New York, NY), 1998.

Schiff, James A., *Updike's Version: Rewriting the Scarlet Letter,* University of Missouri Press (Columbia, MO), 1992.

Schiff, James A., *John Updike Revisited,* Twayne (New York, NY), 1998.

Short Story Criticism, Volume 13, Gale (Detroit, MI), 1993.

Singh, Sukhbir, *The Survivor in Contemporary American Fiction: Saul Bellow, Bernard Malamud, John Updike, Kurt Vonnegut, Jr.,* B. R. Publishing (Delhi, India), 1991.

Tallent, Elizabeth, *Married Men and Magic Tricks: John Updike's Erotic Heroes,* Creative Arts (Berkeley, CA), 1981.

Thorburn, David, and Howard Eiland, editors, *John Updike: A Collection of Critical Essays,* G. K. Hall (Boston, MA), 1982.

Trachtenberg, Stanley, editor, *New Essays on Rabbit, Run,* Cambridge University Press (Cambridge, England), 1993.

Updike, John, *Self-Consciousness: Memoirs,* Knopf (New York, NY), 1989.

Uphaus, Suzanne Henning, *John Updike,* Ungar (New York, NY), 1980.

Yerkes, James, editor, *John Updike and Religion: The Sense of the Sacred and the Motions of Grace,* Eerdmans (Grand Rapids, MI), 1999.

PERIODICALS

America, November 30, 1996, Daniel T. Wackerman, review of *Golf Dreams,* p. 5; October 4, 1997, George W. Hunt, "Of Many Things," p. 2; January 17, 1998, James J. Miracky, review of *Toward the End of Time,* p. 25; March 27, 1999, Diane Fortuna, review of *Bech at Bay,* p. 22.

Antioch Review, spring, 2004, Kyle Minor, review of *The Early Stories: 1953-1975,* p. 367.

Atlantic, December, 2002, review of *Seek My Face,* p. 147; November, 2003, Scott Shibuya Brown, review of *The Early Stories,* p. 160.

Book, November-December, 2000, D.T. Max, "Noticers in Chief: John Updike and Rabbit," p. 33; November-December, 2003, James Schiff, review of *The Early Stories,* p. 84.

Booklist, August, 1997, Brad Hooper, review of *Toward the End of Time,* p. 1849; August, 1998, Brad Hooper, review of *Bech at Bay,* p. 1925; September 1, 1999, Carolyn Phelan, review of *A Child's Calendar,* p. 130; September 1, 1999, Brad Hooper, review of *More Matter,* p. 58; January 1, 2000, Brad Hooper, review of *Gertrude and Claudius,* p. 835; June 1, 2002, Candace Smith, review of *A Childhood in the U.S.A.,* p. 1746; August, 2002, Brad Hooper, review of *Seek My Face,* p. 1888; January 1, 2003, review of *Seek My Face,* p. 793.

Books Abroad, winter, 1967.

Books and Culture, January-February, 2004, p. 32.

Chicago Sunday Tribune, January 11, 1959, Fanny Butcher, review of *The Poorhouse Fair.*

Christian Century, July 17, 1996, p. 730; November 19, 1997, James Yerkes, review of *Toward the End of Time,* p. 1079; November 17, 1999, James Yerkes, review of *More Matter,* p. 1132; February 23, 2000, James Yerkes, review of *Gertrude and Claudius,* p. 220.

Christian Science Monitor, February 14, 1994; February 3, 2000, Ron Charles, review of *Gertrude and Claudius,* p. 21.

Commentary, January, 1999, John Gross, review of *Bech at Bay,* p. 63.

Entertainment Weekly, October 17, 1997, L. S. Klepp, review of *Toward the End of Time,* p. 66; November 6, 1998, review of *Bech at Bay,* p. 82; November 7, 2003, Michelle Kung, review of *The Early Stories,* p. 76.

Insight on the News, November 8, 1999, Rex Roberts, review of *More Matter,* p. 28; March 13, 2000, Rex Roberts, review of *Gertrude and Claudius,* p. 26.

Kenyon Review, spring, 1992.

Kirkus Reviews, September 1, 1994, p. 1162.

Library Journal, September 15, 1997, Edward B. St. John, review of *Toward the End of Time,* p. 103; February 15, 1999, Michael Rogers, "The Gospel of the Book: LJ Talks to John Updike," p. 114; February 15, 2000, David W. Henderson, review of *Gertrude and Claudius,* p. 200; November 15, 2002, Barbara Hoffert, review of *Seek My Face,* p. 104.

Life, November 4, 1966.

London Review of Books, March 11, 1993, p. 9.

Los Angeles Times, January 4, 1987, Katherin Stephen.

Los Angeles Times Book Review, November 1, 1992, p. 3.

Modern Fiction Studies, spring, 1974 (devoted to Updike); autumn, 1975; spring, 1991 (devoted to Updike).

Nation, November 3, 1997, Tom LeClair, review of *Toward the End of Time,* p. 62.

National Review, March 20, 2000, Norah Vincent, review of *Gertrude and Claudius,* p. 57.

New Criterion, November, 1998, Brooke Allen, review of *Bech at Bay,* p. 60.

New Republic, May 27, 1996, James Wood, review of *In the Beauty of the Lilies,* p. 29.; November 17, 1997, Robert Boyers, review of *Toward the End of Time,* p. 38; October 11, 1999, James Wood, review of *More Matter,* p. 41; February 21, 2000, Stephen Greenblatt, review of *Gertrude and Claudius,* p. 32.

Newsweek, November 15, 1971; September 28, 1981; October 18, 1982; October 13, 1997, Jeff Giles, review of *Toward the End of Time,* p. 78.

New York, January 31, 1994, p. 62.

New Yorker, December 1, 2003, Louis Menand, review of *The Early Stories,* p. 104.

New York Review of Books, April 11, 1968; August 8, 1974; April 3, 1975; November 19, 1981; November 18, 1982; November 24, 1983; June 14, 1984; December 4, 1986; February 29, 1996, p. 4.

New York Times, January 11, 1959; October 7, 1982; August 27, 1986; January 25, 1994, p. C19; March 27, 2003, John Russell, review of *Seek My Face,* p. 37.

New York Times Book Review, March 18, 1962; April 7, 1963; April 7, 1968; June 21, 1970; November 14, 1971; September 27, 1981; October 17, 1982; September 18, 1983; May 13, 1984; August 31, 1986; April 26, 1987; November 1, 1992, p. 11; February 6, 1994, p. 1; January 28, 1996, p. 9; September 19, 1996, Christopher Lehmann-Haupt, review of *Golf Dreams;* November 10, 1996, David Owen, review of *Golf Dreams,* p. 57; September 30, 1997, Michiko Kakutani, review of *Toward the End of Time;* October 13, 1998, Michiko Kakutani, review of *Bech at Bay;* September 21, 1999, Michiko Kakutani, review of *More Matter;* February 27, 2000, Richard Eder, review of *Gertrude and Claudius,* p. 9.

New York Times Sunday Magazine, December 10, 1978.

Partisan Review, winter, 1969, Elizabeth Dalton, review of *Couples.*

People, September 23, 1996, Alex Tresniowski, review of *Golf Dreams,* p. 29; December 1, 1997, David Lehman, review of *Toward the End of Time,* p. 56; April 10, 2000, Adam Begley, review of *Gertrude and Claudius,* p. 49.

Publishers Weekly, September 5, 1994, p. 88; January 8, 1996; p. 47; July 29, 1996, review of *Golf Dreams,* p. 79; August 4, 1997, review of *Toward the End of Time,* p. 62; July 20, 1998, review of *Bech at Bay,* p. 204; August 30, 1999, review of *A Child's Calendar,* p. 82; August 30, 1999, review of *More Matter,* p. 66; January 3, 2000, review of *Gertrude and Claudius,* p. 57; September 9, 2002, review of *Seek My Face,* p. 39.

Saturday Review, March 17, 1962; September 30, 1972.

Sewanee Review, spring, 2002, Sanford Pinsker, "Why Updike's Fiction Continues to Matter," p. 332.

Southern Review, spring, 2002, James Schiff, interview with Updike, p. 420.

Spectator, April 9, 1994, Caroline Moore, review of *Brazil,* p. 25.

Sports Illustrated, September 9, 1996, Michael Bamberger, review of *Golf Dreams,* p. 12.

Theology Today, January, 2003, John McTavish, "Myth, Gospel, and John Updike's *Centaur,*" pp. 596-606.

Time, April 26, 1968; October 18, 1982; August 25, 1986; November 18, 2002, Richard Lacayo, review of *Seek My Face,* p. 134.

Times (London, England), January 14, 1982; February 5, 1995.

Times Literary Supplement, January 15, 1982; January 20, 1984; September 28, 1984; October 24, 1986; February 25, 1994, p. 21; April 1, 1994, p. 21.

Tribune Books (Chicago, IL), September 30, 1990, p. 4; November 1, 1992, p. 9; January 30, 1994, p. 9.

Twentieth Century Literature, April, 1966; July, 1967; October, 1971; winter, 1978.

Village Voice, September 30, 1981, Eliot Fremont-Smith.

Washington Post, September 27, 1981; April 26, 1982.

Washington Post Book World, November 1, 1992, p. 9; February 13, 1994, p. 14; February 4, 1996, p. 10.

World Literature Today, winter, 1994, p. 128; October-December, 2003, Daniel Garrett, review of *Seek My Face,* p. 96.

ONLINE

New York Times Online, http://www.nytimes.com/ (May 2, 2004) "Life and Times: John Updike."

Salon.com, http://www.salon.com/ (May 4, 2004), Dwight Garner, interview with Updike.*

OTHER

John Updike: In His Own Words (video recording), Films for the Humanities and Sciences, 1997.

W

WALLACE, David Foster 1962-

PERSONAL: Born February 21, 1962, in Ithaca, NY; son of James Donald (a teacher) and Sally (a teacher; maiden name, Foster) Wallace. *Education:* Amherst College, A.B. (summa cum laude), 1985; University of Arizona, M.F.A., 1987; graduate study at Harvard University. *Politics:* "Independent." *Hobbies and other interests:* Tennis.

ADDRESSES: Office—Department of English, Pomona College, 333 North College Way, Claremont, CA 91711. *Agent*—Frederick Hill Associates, 1842 Union St., San Francisco, CA 94123.

CAREER: Writer. Illinois State University, Bloomington-Normal, associate professor of English, 1993-2002; Pomona College, Claremont, CA, Roy Edward Disney Professor in Creative Writing, 2002—. Judge of 1997 O. Henry Awards, 1997.

AWARDS, HONORS: Whiting Writers' Award, Mrs. Giles Whiting Foundation, 1987; Yaddo residency fellowship, 1987, 1989; John Traine Humor Prize, *Paris Review,* 1988, for "Little Expressionless Animals;" National Endowment for the Arts fellowship, 1989; Illinois Arts Council Award for Nonfiction, 1989, for "Fictional Futures and the Conspicuously Young;" Quality Paperback Book Club's New Voices Award in Fiction, 1991, for *Girl with Curious Hair;* Pulitzer Prize nomination in nonfiction, 1991, for *Signifying Rappers;* National Magazine Award finalist, 1995, for "Ticket to the Fair," and 1997, for "David Lynch Keeps His Head;" Lannan Foundation Award for

David Foster Wallace

Literature, 1996, 2000; MacArthur Foundation fellowship, 1997-2002; named Outstanding University Researcher, Illinois State University, 1998, 1999.

WRITINGS:

The Broom of the System, Viking (New York, NY), 1987.

Girl with Curious Hair (short stories and novellas; includes "Little Expressionless Animals," "My Appearance," "Westward the Course of Empire Takes Its Way," "Lyndon," "John Billy," and "Everything Is Green"), Penguin (New York, NY), 1988.

(With Mark Costello) *Signifying Rappers: Rap and Race in the Urban Present* (nonfiction), Ecco Press (New York, NY), 1990.

Infinite Jest, Little, Brown (Boston, MA), 1996.

A Supposedly Fun Thing I'll Never Do Again: Essays and Arguments, Little, Brown (Boston, MA), 1997.

Brief Interviews with Hideous Men, Little, Brown (Boston, MA), 1999.

Up Simba! (e-book), i.Publish.com, 2000.

Everything and More: A Compact History of Infinity, Atlas Book (New York, NY), 2003.

Oblivion, Little, Brown (New York, NY), 2004.

Contributor of short fiction and nonfiction to numerous periodicals, including *Contemporary Fiction, Harper's,* and *New Yorker.* Short fiction included in anthologies, including *Best American Sportswriting 1997,* Houghton Mifflin, 1997. Contributing editor, *Harper's,* 1995.

SIDELIGHTS: Hailed as the "Generation-X"'s answer to John Barth, John Irving, Thomas Pynchon, and Don Delillo, American writer David Foster Wallace is an author whose talent leaves critics groping for the proper artistic comparison. Filmmaker David Lynch, and even comic David Letterman have all been invoked as readers tackle the sardonic humor and complicated style that have led Wallace to be cited as the late twentieth-century's first avant-garde literary hero. Wallace, according to Frank Bruni in his *New York Times Magazine* profile, "is to literature what Robin Williams or perhaps Jim Carrey is to live comedy: a creator so maniacally energetic and amused with himself that he often follows his riffs out into the stratosphere, where he orbits all alone."

In his debut novel, *The Broom of the System,* Wallace uses a variety of writing techniques and points of view to create a bizarre, stylized world which, despite its strangeness, resonates with contemporary American images. Set in Cleveland on the edge of the state-constructed Great Ohio Desert—also known as G.O. D.—the novel follows Lenore Beadsman's search for her ninety-two-year-old great-grandmother, also named

Lenore Beadsman, who has disappeared from her nursing home. In attempting to find her childhood mentor, the younger Lenore encounters a bewildering assemblage of characters with names such as Rick Vigorous, Biff Diggerence, Candy Mandible, and Sigurd Foamwhistle. It is significant that the elder Lenore was a student of language philosopher Ludwig Wittgenstein, since *The Broom of the System* has been viewed as an elaborate exploration of the relationship between language and reality. Wallace orchestrates Lenore's coming of age through the use of innovative plotting and language. The character's search for her great-grandmother then becomes the search for her own identity.

Critics have praised the skill and creativity evident in Wallace's experimental *bildungsroman.* Rudy Rucker, writing in *Washington Post Book World,* judged *The Broom of the System* to be a "wonderful book" and compared Wallace in particular to novelist Thomas Pynchon. Despite finding the novel to be "unwieldy" and "uneven" in parts, *New York Times* reviewer Michiko Kakutani commended Wallace's "rich reserves of ambition and imagination" and was impressed by his "wealth of talents." *New York Times Book Review* critic Caryn James liked the novel's "exuberance" and maintained that *The Broom of the System* "succeeds as a manic, human, flawed extravaganza."

In Wallace's second work, a collection of short stories titled *Girl with Curious Hair,* the author employs a mix of facts, fiction, and his own distinctive use of language to make observations about American culture. "Little Expressionless Animals," one of several stories that deals with American television, reveals a plan by the producers of the game show *Jeopardy!* to oust a long-time champion because of their sensitivity to her continuing lesbian love affair. The difference between appearance and reality is the subject of "My Appearance," the story of an actress's tranquilizer-induced nervous ramblings while she is waiting to do a guest appearance on the David Letterman show. In the title story, "Girl with Curious Hair," a young, Ivy League-trained corporate lawyer reveals the roots of his sadistic sexual impulses when he reflects on a Keith Jarrett concert he once attended with a group of violent punk rockers.

To reviewers, Wallace's imagination and energy are enticing. Wallace "proves himself a dynamic writer of extraordinary talent," asserted Jenifer Levin in *New*

York Times Book Review, commenting that the writer "succeeds in restoring grandeur to modern fiction." Writing in Chicago's *Tribune Books,* Douglas Seibold commended Wallace's "irrepressible narrative energy and invention" claiming that, "as good a writer as he is now, he is getting better."

The buildup given to Wallace through his first books served as an appetizer to the hype that surrounded his 1996 novel, *Infinite Jest*—a work that, in the words of *Chicago Tribune* writer Bruce Allen, might well "confirm the hopes of those who called Wallace a genius and, to a lesser extent, the fears of those who think he's just an overeducated wiseacre with a lively prose style." The book is massive—over 1,000 pages—and the publicity upon its release was no less so. On the heels of wide-scale publicity, *Infinite Jest* became *de rigueur* as a book that literary fans bought and displayed, but would not—or could not—spend much time reading, according to reviewers. Some of the reason lies in the volume's heft and some in Wallace's dense prose style, peppered for the occasion with numerous pharmacological references that are partly responsible for the novel's 900 footnotes.

Infinite Jest is set in the not-too-distant future, in a date unspecified except as "the Year of the Depend Adult Undergarment," corporate sponsors having taken over the calendar. The United States is now part of the Organization of North American Nations—read ONAN—and has sold off New England to Canada to be used as a toxic waste dump. Legless Quebeçoise separatists have taken to terrorism in protest; what is more, President Limbaugh has just been assassinated. The book's title refers to a lethal movie—a film so entertaining that those who see it may be doomed to die of pleasure.

Into this fray steps the Incandenza brothers: tennis ace Hal, football punter Orin, and the less-gifted Mario. The boys have endured a tough childhood—their father "having committed suicide by hacking open a hole in a microwave door, sealing it around his head with duct tape and making like a bag of Orville Redenbacher," as *Nation* reviewer Rick Perlstein noted. The brother's adventures in this bizarre society fuel the novel's thick and overlapping storylines. Readers looking for a traditional linear ending, however, are in for a surprise: Those who manage to "stay with the novel until the pages thin will come to realize that Wallace has no intention of revealing whether *les Assassins des*

Fauteuils Rollents succeed or fail in their quest," Perlstein continued. "Nor whether . . . Orin will master his awful desires . . . or whether Hal Incandenza will sacrifice himself to the Oedipal grail. Readers will turn the last page, in other words, without learning anything they need to know to secure narrative succor."

For the most part, critical reaction to *Infinite Jest* mixed admiration with consternation. "There is generous intelligence and authentic passion on every page, even the overwritten ones in which the author seems to have had a fit of graphomania," noted *Time's* R. Z. Sheppard. Paul West, writing in *Washington Post Book World,* came prepared for Pynchon but came away with the opinion that "there is nothing epic or infinite about [the novel], although much that's repetitious or long." As West saw it, "the slow incessant advance of Wallace's prose is winningly physical, solid and even, more personable actually than the crowd of goons, ditzes, inverts, junkies, fatheads and doodlers he populates his novel with."

Indeed, noted Kakutani, "the whole novel often seems like an excuse for [Wallace] to simply show off his remarkable skills as a writer and empty the contents of his restless mind." Kakutani's *New York Times* review went on to laud "some frighteningly vivid accounts of what it feels like to be a drug addict, what it feels like to detox and what it feels like to suffer a panic attack." In the crowd of ideas and characters, the critic concluded, "Somewhere in the mess, . . . are the outlines of a splendid novel, but as it stands the book feels like one of those unfinished Michelangelo sculptures: you can see a godly creature trying to fight its way out, but it's stuck there, half excavated, unable to break completely free."

Kakutani had more encouraging words for Wallace's 1997 release, *A Supposedly Fun Thing I'll Never Do Again: Essays and Arguments.* This nonfiction collection "is animated by [the author's] wonderfully exuberant prose, a zingy, elastic gift for metaphor and imaginative sleight of hand, combined with a taste for amphetaminelike stream-of-consciousness riffs." *Supposedly Fun Thing* covers Wallace's observations on cultural themes, such as the influence television has on new fiction. It also contains recollections of the author's childhood in the Midwest, thoughts on tennis—Wallace was a highly ranked player in his youth—and even a tour of the Illinois State Fair. While finding some aspects of the collection flawed, Kakutani ultimately praised *A Supposedly Fun Thing I'll Never Do Again* as a work that "not only reconfirms Mr. Wallace's stature as one of his generation's preeminent talents, but it also attests to his virtuosity, an aptitude for the essay, profile and travelogue, equal to the gifts he has already begun to demonstrate in the realm of fiction."

Inspired by the author's interest in mathematic systems, Wallace's 2003 work, *Everything and More: A Compact History of Infinity,* focuses on nineteenth-century German mathematician Georg F. L. P. Cantor, a man who pioneered set theory in between stays at mental hospitals. Dubbing his work a "piece of pop technical writing," Wallace explores the theoretical history of the concept of infinity, from its roots in ancient paradoxes through its interpretation by scientists such as Galileo, as well as Plato and hosts of other philosophers, to today's theoretical mathematics. While *New Yorker* contributor Jim Holt noted that, with its author's limited mathematical understanding but contagious enthusiasm for his subject, *Everything and More* "is sometimes as dense as a math textbook, though rather more chaotic," is effective as a "purely literary experience." In *Library Journal,* Christopher Tinney praised the book as "classic DFW: engaging, self-conscious, playful, and often breathless," while John Green cited *Everything and More* as "a brilliant antidote both to boring math textbooks and to pop-culture math books that emphasize the discoverer over the discovery." Noting Wallace's characteristic "discursive style," a *Publishers Weekly* contributor praised the volume "as weird and wonderful as you'd expect," adding that, "had he not pursued a career in literary fiction, it's not difficult to imagine Wallace as a historian of science, producing quirky and challenging volumes . . . every few years." Praising *Everything and More* as "inspiring," Troy Patterson added in *Entertainment Weekly* that Wallace's "straightforward engagement with ultimate abstractions and unambiguous truths offers a heady pleasure distinct from that of fiction."

Wallace's first short-story collection in five years, *Oblivion,* "fashions complex tales rife with shrewd metaphysical inquiries, eviscerating social critiques, and twisted humor," according to Donna Seaman in *Booklist.* Charles Matthes for the *Knight Ridder/ Tribune News Service* shared a similar sentiment, but also felt the stories were "soulless" and maintained

that the "verbal tics and tricks soon grow tedious." However, Joel Stein from *Time* described the eight tales contained in the book as "breathtakingly smart."

BIOGRAPHICAL AND CRITICAL SOURCES:

BOOKS

Boswell, Marshall, *Understanding David Foster Wallace,* University of South Carolina Press (Columbia, SC), 2003.

Burn, Stephen, *David Foster Wallace's Infinite Jest: A Reader's Guide,* Continuum (New York, NY), 2003.

Contemporary Literary Criticism, Gale (Detroit, MI), Volume 50, 1988, Volume 114, 1999.

PERIODICALS

American Scholar, winter, 2004, Allen Paulos, review of *Everything and More: A Compact History of Infinity,* p. 147.

Asia Africa Intelligence Wire, June 27, 2004, Brad Quinn, review of *Oblivion.*

Booklist, October 15, 2003, John Green, review of *Everything and More: A Compact History of Infinity,* p. 366; May 15, 2004, Donna Seaman, review of *Oblivion,* p. 1600.

Boston Globe, October 26, 2003, Caleb Crain, interview with Wallace.

Chicago Tribune, March 24, 1996, Bruce Allen, review of *Infinite Jest.*

Comparative Literature Studies, summer, 2001, Timothy Jacobs, "American Touchstone," p. 215.

Critique, fall, 2001, p. 3.

Entertainment Weekly, October 10, 2003, Troy Patterson, review of *Everything and More,* p. 127; June 18, 2004, review of *Oblivion,* p. 89.

Kirkus Reviews, May 1, 2004, review of *Oblivion,* p. 422.

Knight Ridder/Tribune News Service, June 16, 2004, Charles Matthews, review of *Oblivion,* p. K3330.

Library Journal, November 1, 2003, Christopher Tinney, review of *Everything and More,* p. 120.

Los Angeles Times, February 11, 1996; March 18, 1996.

Los Angeles Times Book Review, February 1, 1987.

Nation, March 4, 1996, Rick Perlstein, review of *Infinite Jest.*

New Yorker, November 3, 2003, Jim Holt, review of *Everything and More,* p. 84.

New York Review of Books, February 10, 2000.

New York Times, December 27, 1986; February 13, 1996; February 4, 1997.

New York Times Book Review, March 1, 1987; November 5, 1989; March 3, 1996.

New York Times Magazine, March 24, 1996, Frank Bruni, "The Grunge American Novel," p. 38.

Publishers Weekly, October 13, 2003, review of *Everything and More,* p. 71.

Science News, December 6, 2003, review of *Everything and More,* p. 367.

Time, February 19, 1996; October 30, 2000, p. 94; June 7, 2004, Joel Stein, review of *Oblivion,* p. 123.

Tribune Books (Chicago, IL), January 21, 1990, Douglas Seibold, review of *Girl with Curious Hair.*

Washington Post Book World, January 11, 1987; August 6, 1989; March 24, 1996.

Wilson Quarterly, winter, 2004, Charles Seife, review of *Everything and More,* p. 124.

Wired, October, 2003, Bruce Schecter, review of *Everything and More,* p. 76.

ONLINE

David Foster Wallace Unoffical Web site, http://www.davidfosterwallace.com (November 19, 2003).

Salon.com, http://www.salon.com/ (April 24, 2004), interview with Wallace.*

Edmund White

*   *   *

WALLEY, Byron
  See CARD, Orson Scott

*   *   *

WHITE, Edmund (Valentine III) 1940-

PERSONAL: Born January 13, 1940, in Cincinnati, OH; son of Edmund Valentine II (an engineer) and Delilah (a psychologist; maiden name, Teddlie) White. *Education:* University of Michigan, B.A., 1962.

ADDRESSES: Office—Princeton University, Department of Creative Writing, 185 Nassau St., Princeton, NJ 08544. *Agent*—Amanda Urban, ICM, 40 West 57th St., New York, NY 10019. *E-mail*—ewhite@mail.princeton.edu.

CAREER: Time, Inc., Book Division, New York, NY, staff writer, 1962-70; *Saturday Review,* New York, NY, senior editor, 1972-73; Johns Hopkins University, Baltimore, MD, assistant professor of writing seminars, 1977-79; Columbia University School of the Arts, New York, NY, adjunct professor of creative writing, 1981-83; New York Institute for the Humanities, executive director, 1982-83; Brown University, Providence, RI, professor of English, 1990-92; Princeton University, Princeton, NJ, professor in creative writing, 1998—. Instructor in creative writing at Yale University, New Haven, CT, New York University, New York, NY, and George Mason University, Fairfax, VA. Member of jury, Booker Prize, 1989.

MEMBER: American Academy of Arts and Letters (member of awards committee, 1999-2000), American Academy of Arts and Sciences.

AWARDS, HONORS: Hopwood Awards, University of Michigan, 1961 and 1962, for fiction and drama; Ingram Merrill grants, 1973 and 1978; Guggenheim fellow, 1983; American Academy and Institute of Arts and Letters award for fiction, 1983; citation for appeal and value to youth from Enoch Pratt Free Library's Young Adult Advisory Board, 1988, for *The Beautiful Room Is Empty;* chevalier, Ordre des Arts et Lettres (France), 1993; National Book Critics Circle award for biography, 1994, for *Genet: A Biography;* honorary doctorate, State University of New York at Oneonta, 2000, Deauville Festival prize (France), 2000; Ferro-Grumley Award, Publishing Triangle, 2003, for *The Married Man.*

WRITINGS:

NOVELS

Forgetting Elena, Random House (New York, NY), 1973.

Nocturnes for the King of Naples, St. Martin's Press (New York, NY), 1978.

A Boy's Own Story, Dutton (New York, NY), 1982, with new introduction by White, 1994.

Caracole, Dutton (New York, NY), 1985.

The Beautiful Room Is Empty, Knopf (New York, NY), 1988.

The Farewell Symphony, Knopf (New York, NY), 1997.

The Married Man, Knopf (New York, NY), 2000.

Fanny: A Fiction, Ecco/HarperCollins (New York, NY), 2003.

OTHER

Blue Boy in Black (play), produced Off-Broadway, 1963.

(With Peter Wood) *When Zeppelins Flew,* Time-Life (Alexandria, VA), 1969.

(With Dale Browne) *The First Men,* Time-Life (Alexandria, VA), 1973.

(With Charles Silverstein) *The Joy of Gay Sex: An Intimate Guide for Gay Men to the Pleasures of a Gay Lifestyle,* Crown (New York, NY), 1977.

States of Desire: Travels in Gay America, Dutton (New York, NY), 1980.

(With others) *Aphrodisiac* (short stories), Chatto & Windus (London, England), 1984.

(With Adam Mars-Jones) *The Darker Proof: Stories from a Crisis,* New American Library/Plume (New York, NY), 1988.

(Editor) *The Faber Book of Gay Short Fiction,* Faber & Faber (Winchester, MA), 1991.

(Compiler) *The Selected Writings of Jean Genet,* Ecco Press (New York, NY), 1993.

Genet: A Biography, Knopf (New York, NY), 1993.

The Burning Library: Essays, edited by David Bergman, Knopf (New York, NY), 1994.

Skinned Alive: Stories, Knopf (New York, NY), 1995.

Our Paris: Sketches from Memory, Knopf (New York, NY), 1995.

Marcel Proust ("Penguin Lives" series), Viking (New York, NY), 1999.

The Flaneur: A Stroll through the Paradoxes of Paris ("The Writer and the City" series), Bloomsbury (New York, NY), 2001.

(Editor) *Loss within Loss: Artists in the Age of AIDS,* University of Wisconsin Press (Madison, WI), 2001.

Arts and Letters, Cleis Press (San Francisco), 2004.

Also author of *Argument for Myth.* Contributor to anthologies, including *The Fabric of Memory: Ewa Kuryluk: Cloth Works, 1978-1987,* Northwestern University Press, 1987. Contributor of articles and reviews to *New York Times,* London *Observer, Los Angeles Times, Architectural Digest, Artforum International, Home and Garden, Mother Jones, New York Times Book Review, Savvy Woman, Southwest Review,* and other periodicals. Editor, *Saturday Review* and *Horizon;* contributing editor, *Vogue.*

SIDELIGHTS: American author Edmund White has produced highly acclaimed novels, insightful nonfiction on gay society, and semi-autobiographical novels that combine the best features of fiction and nonfiction. Known as a "gay writer," White also belongs among those writers whose literary reputations transcend simplistic labels. William Goldstein explained in *Publishers Weekly,* "To call Edmund White merely a gay writer is to oversimplify his work and his intentions. Although that two-word label . . . aptly sums up White's status, the first word no doubt helps obscure the fact that the second applies just as fittingly." White's studies of the gay lifestyle and changing attitudes about homosexuality in America, including the impact of AIDS on the gay community, are considered important contributions to late twentieth-century social history. Though male homosexuality is the subject of his nonfiction, White offers insights into human behavior in general, according to reviewers. *Nation* contributor Carter Wilson commented, "White is to be envied not only for his productivity . . . but because he is a gifted writer who has staked himself a distinguished claim in the rocky territory called desire."

Critics praised White's first novel, *Forgetting Elena,* for its satiric and insightful look at social interaction as well as for its elegant prose. A first-person narrative of an amnesia victim struggling to determine his identity and the identities of those around him, *Forgetting Elena* exposes the subtle entrapments of social hierarchy and etiquette. White told *Library Journal* that the novel's premise illustrates the "sinister" aspects of life in an artistically obsessed society. In such a culture, he explained, "Every word and gesture would . . . convey a symbolic meaning. Ordinary morality would be obscured or forgotten. People would seek the beautiful and not the good—and, perhaps, cut free from the ethics, the beautiful would turn out to be merely pretty." Setting the novel's action at a fictitious resort reminiscent of New York's Fire Island, White creates, in the words of *Nation* contributor Simon Karlinsky, "a semiology of snobbery, its complete sign system." Karlinsky stated that "what might at first seem to be merely a witty parody of a particular subculture's foibles and vagaries actually turns out to be something far more serious and profound. . . . He has produced a parable about the nature of social interaction that transcends any given period and applies to the human predicament at large."

Most critics consider *Forgetting Elena* a highly accomplished first novel. Karlinsky called the work "an astounding piece of writing—profound, totally convincing and memorable." Alan Friedman likewise praised the book in *New York Times Book Review,* though not without qualifications. Friedman wrote, "There is something so unfailingly petty about the narrator's apprehensions . . . and something so oppressive about his preoccupations . . . that it is often difficult to be receptive to the book's genuine wonders." Friedman nevertheless concluded that this "tale of a sleuth who strives to detect the mystery of the self" is "an astonishing first novel, obsessively fussy, yet uncannily beautiful."

Nocturnes for the King of Naples, White's second novel, won acclaim for its discerning treatment of human values and relationships. As John Yohalem ex-plained in *New York Times Book Review, Nocturnes* "is a series of apostrophes to a nameless, evidently famous dead lover, a man who awakened the much younger, also nameless narrator . . . to the possibility of sexual friendship. It was an experience that the narrator feels he did not justly appreciate," Yohalem continued, "and that he has long and passionately—and fruitlessly—sought to replace on his own terms." David Shields wrote in *Chicago Tribune,* "Because of the speaker's final realization of the impossibility of ever finding a ground for satisfaction, a home, this book is more than a chronicle of sorrow and regret. It becomes, rather, a true elegy in which sorrow and self-knowledge combine and transform into a higher form of insight. This higher insight is the artistic intuition of the mortality of human things and ways."

While Doris Grumbach suggested in *Washington Post Book World* that White "will seem to the careful reader to be the poet of the burgeoning homosexual literature," she also noted, "The music of White's prose is seductive. It is of course possible that a tone-deaf, a melody-indifferent reader might turn his back on White's homo-erotic narrative." However, she added, White's prose in *Nocturnes* promises satisfaction to "the lover of good fictional writing who is open to this most subtle exploration of the many ways of love, desertion, loss, and regret."

Caracole goes back to an earlier century and retrieves a more elaborate fictional form. Christopher Lehmann-Haupt observed in *New York Times* that White has "certainly conceived a nineteenth century plot steeped in the conventions of romanticism" when he writes of two country lovers forcibly separated who turn to sexual escapades in a large city. The resulting story is a "puzzling melange of comic opera and sleek sensuality," added the reviewer. *New York Times Book Review* contributor David R. Slavitt described *Caracole* as "a grand fantasy. . . . Shrewdness and self-awareness ooze from every intricate sentence, every linguistic arabesque and hothouse epigram." Slavitt concluded that *Caracole* "is, provokingly, a challenge to taste, which is likely to vary from one reader to another or even from moment to moment in the same reader."

White's novel *The Married Man,* called his "most readable novel" by David Bergman in *Review of Contemporary Fiction,* is about the relationship between Austin, an American writer living in Paris, and Julien, a younger married architect Austin meets in a gym and with whom he forges an alliance. The pair travel together and eventually return to Providence, Rhode Island where Austin is to teach a class. Austin is HIV positive, but healthy, and Julien promises to care for him until the end, but it is Julien who wastes away from AIDS, whereupon Austin discovers that Julien's life had been one of secrets and lies. "What is most interesting, however," wrote Alice Truax in *New York Times Book Review,* "is not the revelations themselves but how little the facts really matter: if Julien deceived Austin, Austin also collaborated in his deception. After all, it was that subtle blend of shared illusions and private realities that had nourished the marriage and made it possible—and White seems to be suggesting, perhaps the same can be said of most marriages." Like Julien in the book, White's own lover, Frenchman Hubert Sorin, died in Morocco of AIDS at age thirty-three. *The Married Man* is loosely based on White's years with Sorin.

In *Fanny: A Fiction* White presents what *People* reviewer Bella Stander dubbed a "witty and richly imagined" fictional biography of early nineteenth-century Scottish-born protofeminist Frances "Fanny" Wright. Purportedly authored by Frances "Fanny" Trollope— mother to more famous author Anthony Trollope—the novel is written in a style that mimics Trollope's perfunctory, sometimes harsh, and often unknowingly humorous prose. In the novel, Wright has founded Nashoba, a utopian colony of freed slaves located in Tennessee, and it is here she invites her struggling writer friend, in the hopes that the visit will provide literary inspiration for her *Domestic Manners of the Americans.* At the core of the book is middle-aged Fanny, whom Wright describes as "a funny little snaggle-toothed old woman with ratty hair," along with three of her six children and a French artist, joins Wright on the trip to America, a trip that sets the stage for the rest of the novel. As *New Statesman* contributor Carmen Callil described it, Wright "sails first class, while the Trollope family suffers amid the vomit and creaking of steerage. Nothing improves on arrival; Fanny Trollope's adventures lead her to be disappointed with—and even to hate—America, a place where men pass the day spitting at walls, where utopians and democrats pontificate about about God and indulge in an 'acrobatic Christianity,' which includes demonic treatment of their slaves." Although Callil noted that White's inclusion of a "plethora of historical detail" can sometimes be overwhelming, *Fanny* "captures with an amusing cattiness both Trollope's sharpness of tongue and Wright's self-delusion," noted

Penelope Mesic in her *Book* review, while in *Publishers Weekly* a reviewer noted that "Trollope's struggle to maintain her own little bit of interior civilization is a joy to witness."

White's concern about AIDS has left its mark on his writing, particularly his short fiction, collected in *The Darker Proof* and *Skinned Alive: Stories.* Among the eight tales in the latter collection, several feature "gay love and loss in the shadow of AIDS" as a central motif, commented Maxine Chernoff in Chicago's *Tribune Books.* In "Running on Empty," a man returns to his hometown in Texas after traveling in Europe and confronts his worsening illness. "Palace Days" offers a love triangle in which one character is dying of AIDS while another, though healthy, is coping with the recent discovery that he is HIV-positive. And in "An Oracle," a man grieving for his dead lover falls in love with a young man while traveling in Greece.

"What Edmund White conjures here is a serious, sustained look at how AIDS measures and shapes the meaning of our existence," commented *Los Angeles Times Book Review* contributor Michael Bronski. While noting that the stories dealing with AIDS are "rarely somber," *New York Times Book Review* commentator Morris Dickstein wrote that "in the best stories . . . the author sometimes gives way to a sadness that reverberates more deeply than in anything else he has written." "White is never ponderous but vastly compassionate, and has the grace to be humorous in his compassion," remarked Alberto Manguel in the London *Observer.* James Woods, reviewing *Skinned Alive* for *London Review of Books,* commended "the scattered gorgeousness" in White's writing and concluded that the collection "shows us that for all his confusions, White has lost none of his artistry." As Chernoff observed, White's "subject is the human condition, no matter our sexual practices, and our final estrangement from each other, despite our efforts to hold on."

White's nonfiction on gay life in America is considered by many to be as compelling as his fiction. *The Joy of Gay Sex: An Intimate Guide for Gay Men to the Pleasures of a Gay Lifestyle,* published in the late 1970s, attempted to make the topic less mysterious for curious heterosexuals and to provide useful information for gay men. In 1980 White published *States of Desire: Travels in Gay America.* A documentary on segments of homosexual life in fifteen major American cities,

States of Desire contains interviews, autobiographical reminiscences, and accounts of cultural and entertainment centers for gays. According to Ned Rorem in *Washington Post Book World, States of Desire* "poses as a documentary . . . on our national gay bourgeoisie. Actually it's an artist's selective vision . . . of human comportment which is and is not his own, mulled over, distilled, then spilled onto the page with a melancholy joy."

The Joy of Gay Sex and *States of Desire* qualified White as one of the first prominent spokespersons for gay men in America. He knew that publishing these works would engage him in politics to some extent. He explained in a *Paris Review* interview, "It was a political act for me to sign *The Joy of Gay Sex* at the time. The publisher could not have cared less, but for me it was a big act of coming out. Charles Silverstein, my co-author, and I were both aware that we would be addressing a lot of people and so in that sense we were spokesmen. We always pictured our ideal reader as someone who thought he was the only homosexual in the world. *States of Desire* was an attempt to see the varieties of gay experience and also to suggest the enormous range of gay life to straight and gay people—to show that gays aren't just hairdressers, they're also petroleum engineers and ranchers and short-order cooks."

Since the 1980s White has continued his role as a social historian on the homosexual experience in America. He writes with particular authority about the gay liberation movement because he has been an active participant in it since the Stonewall riot in New York City in 1969. Police had raided the discotheque and the gay men fought back in what is now seen as the official beginning of the campaign for homosexual rights. "The riot itself I considered a rather silly event at the time," he recalled in his *Paris Review* interview; "it seemed more Dada than Bastille, a kind of romp. But I participated in that and then was active from the very beginning in gay liberation. We had these gatherings which were patterned after women's and ultimately, I think, Maoist consciousness-raising sessions. Whether or not our sessions accomplished anything for society, they were certainly useful to all of us as a tool for changing ourselves." Before that time, he explained, gay men tended to think of themselves as primarily heterosexual except for certain sexual habits—"but we weren't homosexuals as people. Even the notion of a homosexual culture would have seemed comical or ridiculous to us, certainly horrifying."

White believes that gay writers should recognize the historical significance of the AIDS epidemic in the context of the larger culture in which they live. In *Rolling Stone* he noted: "No American phenomenon has been as compelling since the Vietnam War, which itself involved most of the same themes. Although obviously a greater tragedy, the war nevertheless took place on a different continent and invited a more familiar political analysis. We knew how to protest the war. In the rancorous debates over AIDS, all the issues are fuzzy and the moral imperatives all questions."

White maintains that while the tragedy of AIDS has caused the gay liberation movement some daunting setbacks, it has not been the only factor in the movement's mixed success. He explained in *Mother Jones:* "Gay liberation grew out of the progressive spirit of the 1960s—a strange and exhilarating blend of socialism, feminism and the human potential movement. Accordingly, what gay leaders in the late 1960s were anticipating was the emergence of the androgyne [a kind of person neither specifically masculine nor feminine], but what they got was the super-butch stud [a muscle-bound type whose homosexuality is a heightened form of masculine aggression]; what they expected was a communal hippie freedom from possessions, but what has developed is the acme of capitalist consumerism. Gays . . . consume expensive vacations, membership in gyms and discos, cars, elegant furnishings, clothes, haircuts, theater tickets and records. . . . Unfortunately, today this rampant and ubiquitous consumerism not only characterizes gay spending habits but also infects attitudes toward sexuality: gays rate each other quantitatively according to age, physical dimensions and income; and all too many gays consume and dispose of each other, as though the act of possession brought about instant obsolescence." White pointed out that finding a solution to this problem, as it is for the AIDS epidemic, is important not only for gays, but for all Americans.

Many of the essays in which White explores the intersection of homosexuality, culture, and AIDS are collected in *The Burning Library: Essays.* Consisting of forty pieces, many of them previously published, the collection chronicles White's literary and personal odyssey from the pre-Stonewall period to the sexually liberating 1970s and into the devastation wrought by AIDS in the 1980s and 1990s. Noting the "unparalleled stylistic elegance deployed" in these essays, *Observer* reviewer Jonathan Keates characterized White as being "armed with [a] . . . deep moral awareness and the . . . ability to charm the socks off the reader even while retailing unpalatable truths." Writing in *Los Angeles Times,* Chris Goodrich called *The Burning Library* "strikingly traditional, a writer's attempt to fathom his own identity and that of the subculture in which he works and lives."

Times Literary Supplement contributor Neil Powell claimed that the more personal essays in *The Burning Library* are stronger than those in which White discusses other writers and their works. Commented Powell, "White's admirable capacity for sympathetic understanding not only inhibits his critical judgment but actually weakens the case being argued." Goodrich, focusing on the more personal essays, noted that White's "reflections on AIDS are uncommonly thoughtful." Keates concurred, writing that White's "own HIV-positive status might have fueled him with accusatory hysteria and recrimination. Instead . . . he has challenged mortality with these noble fragments."

In addition to his social commentary, White has also made his mark as a biographer, and his interest and familiarity with French culture are evident in both *Genet: A Biography* and *Marcel Proust.* White spent seven years researching and writing the biography of acclaimed writer Jean Genet, interviewing those who knew Genet and examining Genet's literary output. He chronicles the writer's early hardships—being abandoned by his parents and becoming a ward of the state—his adolescent initiation into stealing, which became a lifelong addiction, his first burst of literary creativity during the 1940s, which resulted in five novels and secured his fame, and his turbulent personal life, marked by his homosexuality and his apparent brutish ways towards friends and lovers alike. Noting Genet's legendary habit of falsifying the events of his life, *New York Review of Books* reviewer Tony Judt commended White for attempting "to unravel the threads that Genet so assiduously knotted and crossed in his various writings and interviews."

Critical reaction to *Genet* was mostly positive, with several reviewers calling the biography a definitive work. Writing in Chicago's *Tribune Books,* Thomas McGonigle said that "White has written a wonderfully readable account of a thoroughly repulsive individual," adding that the author "brings to bear on the life of Genet a grand literary sensibility." Similarly, *Los Angeles Times Book Review* contributor Daniel Harris called

the work "an extraordinarily lucid biography" and noted, "White delights in ferreting out Genet's most compromising secrets." Some reviewers criticized White for focusing too heavily on Genet's homosexuality as a means of interpreting his life and literary output. Judt, for instance, stated that occasionally White falls "victim to his own anachronistic concern with sexual preference as a key to aesthetic appreciation." Writing in *New York Times Book Review,* Isabelle de Courtivron concurred, noting that "at times White comes perilously close to reducing his subject's complex works to an overinterpretation in light of" Genet's homosexuality. Nevertheless, added the critic, White's work "is so meticulously researched and detailed, his understanding and illumination of the works is so rich, that the book ultimately succeeds in resisting the nagging temptation of reductionism." *New York Times Book Review* contributor Margo Jefferson concluded by saying that White "presents the life meticulously, reads Genet's work intelligently and writes beautifully." Reflecting the positive critical opinion of the book, *Genet* was awarded the National Book Critics Circle award for biography in 1994.

White's biography of French writer Marcel Proust is one of the first in the "Penguin Lives" series that *New York Times Book Review* contributor Peter Ackroyd said "bear[s] testimony to the fact that biographical narratives can aspire to art rather than to history." Ackroyd described the volume as issuing "from imagination and intuition as much as from scholarship and research." Ackroyd continued, "White explores the pathology of a man who was passionate and yet oblique, rhetorical and secretive; sentimental and yet clearsighted, innocent and depraved—a great writer condemned as a flaneur and a gossip who wrote a masterpiece. It requires the skill and intuition of an imaginative artist to make these aspects cohere within a single and living portrait."

In addition to his accomplished fiction and nonfiction, White has produced several semi-autobiographical works that bring together the best features of both kinds of writing, beginning with *A Boy's Own Story,* a first-person narrative of a homosexual boy's adolescence during the 1950s. As a *Harper's* reviewer described it, *A Boy's Own Story* "is a poignant combination of the two genres . . . written with the flourish of a master stylist." The main conflict in this psychological novel is the narrator's battle against negative judgments from society and from within. Emotional turmoil related to homosexuality, though prominent in the novel, is only one difficulty among many related to coming of age, *Harper's* reviewer observed. *A Boy's Own Story* "is an endearing portrait of a child's longing to be charming, popular, powerful, and loved, and of his struggles with adults . . . told with . . . sensitivity and elegance."

More than one reviewer has called *A Boy's Own Story* a "classic" work. Comparing White to James Baldwin, Herman Wouk, and Mary McCarthy, Thomas M. Disch wrote in *Washington Post Book World* that the novel "represents the strongest bid to date by a gay writer to do for his minority experience what the writers above did for theirs—offer it as a representative, all-American instance." *New York Times Book Review* contributor Catharine R. Stimpson found the book "as artful as [White's] earlier novels but more explicit and grounded in detail, far less fanciful and elusive. . . . Balancing the banal and the savage, the funny and the lovely, he achieves a wonderfully poised fiction." *Voice Literary Supplement* columnist Eliot Fremont-Smith concluded, "*A Boy's Own Story* seems intended to be liberating, as well as touching and clever and smart. It is something else as well: unsettling to the willing heart. This makes it a problem, with no happy solution guaranteed, which defines what's wrong with the book. But also what's right, what intrigues." Lehmann-Haupt called the work "superior fiction," adding: "Somehow . . . White does succeed in almost simultaneously elevating and demeaning his self-history. And these extremes of epiphany and emptiness are what is most universal about this haunting Bildungsroman."

In *The Beautiful Room Is Empty*, the sequel to *A Boy's Own Story*, the narrator alternately revels in his homosexuality and rejects himself for it. Psychoanalysis and increasing surrender to sensual activity escalate the young man's battle for self-acceptance. Though his sexuality troubles him, the excitement and audacity of his experiences with gay men in public restrooms seems a needed respite from the blandness of his suburban life. While recreating these scenes, White evokes both humor and terror. The gay characters easily upstage the others in the book with their outspoken opinions, witty banter, and daring sexual exploits, while "White takes us through [the narrator's] unsentimental education like an indulgent pal, making graceful introductions, filling in with pungent details, saving his harshest judgments for himself," Vince Aletti wrote in *Voice Literary Supplement*. Sometimes the adolescent

makes bold moves—as when he shouts "Gay is good!" in a Greenwich Village demonstration. At other times, he acts out his self-loathing, as when he seduces his music teacher and betrays him to the authorities. By depicting both kinds of behavior, the narrator helps White to evoke "the cautious emergence of a gay consciousness" taking place in the surrounding culture, Aletti said.

Some readers did not see how one could come away from *The Beautiful Room Is Empty* with a good feeling about homosexuality. In answer to these critics, White explained in a *Village Voice* interview that his role is not that of a propagandist, but that of a historian. He said, "I like to describe the way people actually are. Some rather young people don't see the historical point of *The Beautiful Room Is Empty*. . . . I was trying to point out that people were even more oppressed [in the 1960s] than they are today." Addressing the topic again in a *Publishers Weekly* interview, the author said, "I feel it wouldn't be true to the experience of the characters if I showed them gliding blissfully through, when it was obviously a painful thing coming out in a period before gay liberation." A *Time* reviewer concluded, "In the era of AIDS, White's novel is a fiercely remembered plea not to push gays back into the closet."

The title of White's *The Farewell Symphony,* is taken from a Haydn symphony that ends with the orchestra leaving the stage, until only the violin remains. Another autobiographical work, it follows his life from the 1970s to the 1990s, from New York to his expatriation, first in Rome, then in Paris. It also follows his success as a writer, and his friends, including those he has lost to AIDS. Kent D. Wolf wrote in *Review of Contemporary Fiction* of the first time period covered by the book, saying, "White's apparent nonstop sexfest . . . seems to defy logic; at one point the narrator does some math and figures he had over 3,000 partners between 1962 and 1982. . . . Putting all calculators . . . aside, amidst all this kissing is plenty of telling." The narrator writes of his growing success as a writer, of his father's death, and his sister's coming to terms with her lesbianism. A *Publishers Weekly* reviewer felt the book is best enjoyed "for its luminous snapshots of New York, Paris, and Rome, and of the vital parade of men—dowdy, forbiddingly gorgeous, sylph-like, ephebic, closeted, defiantly and militantly out that crowd its pages." *Booklist* contributor Whitney Scott called White "an older, maturer talent reflecting on the sweeping power of friendship, caring, and love in all its aspects."

Discussing the role of writer, White believes that originality is the creative writer's foremost concern. As he explained to interviewer Larry McCaffery in *Alive and Writing: Interviews:* "There are two ways of looking at literature. One is to feel that there is one great Platonic novel in the sky that we're all striving toward. I find that view to be very deadening, finally, and certainly it's a terrible view for a teacher or a critic to hold. The other view is that each person has a chance to write his or her own book in his or her own voice; maturing as an artist occurs when you find your own voice, when you write something that *only you* could have written. That's the view I have."

In a *Paris Review* interview White described the two impulses—toward fiction and nonfiction—between which he balances his writing, saying, "Writers can use literature as a mirror held up to the world, or they can use writing as a consolation for life (in the sense that literature is preferable to reality). I prefer the second approach, although clearly there has to be a blend of both. If the writing is pure fantasy it doesn't connect to any of our real feelings. But if it's grim realism, that doesn't seem like much of a gift. I think literature should be a gift to the reader, and that gift is in idealization. I don't mean it should be a whitewashing of problems, but something ideally energetic. Ordinary life is *blah,* whereas literature at its best is bristling with energy."

At a time when books by gay writers are not as widely read as he hopes they will be, White, who once had a novel rejected by twenty-two different publishers, admits to being thrilled by the recognition his writing has received. "I know I'll always be doing this," he told *Publishers Weekly,* "and I know that I'll never make a living from my writing; but that's fine. It's enough to be published. . . . I don't have very exalted notions of what a writer's life should be like." Concurrent with his career as an author, White has taught creative writing at several East Coast universities, including Johns Hopkins, Columbia, and Yale. His reviews and profiles appear frequently in *Vogue* and other magazines. He also writes travel articles, and, from his home in Paris, reports on contemporary trends in art and politics, and French social history.

BIOGRAPHICAL AND CRITICAL SOURCES:

BOOKS

Barber, Stephen, *Edmund White: The Burning World,* St. Martin's Press (New York, NY), 1999.
Contemporary Literary Criticism, Gale (Detroit, MI), Volume 27, 1984, Volume 110, 1999.
Dictionary of Literary Biography, Volume 227: *American Novelists Since World War II, Sixth Series,* Gale (Detroit, MI), 2000.
Gay and Lesbian Biography, St. James Press (Detroit, MI), 1997.
McCaffery, Larry, *Alive and Writing: Interviews,* University Press of Illinois (Champaign, IL), 1987.

PERIODICALS

Advocate, October 5, 1993; September 16, 1997, Sarah Schulman, "The White Party" (interview), p. 61; January 20, 1998, review of *The Farewell Symphony,* p. 102; March 2, 1999, Robert Plunket, review of *Marcel Proust,* p. 65; June 20, 2000, David Bahr, "French Lessons," p. 137, Robert Plunket, review of *The Married Man,* p. 138; April 10, 2001, David Bahr, review of *Loss within Loss: Artists in the Age of AIDS,* p. 66.
American Prospect, May 7, 2001, David L. Kirp, review of *Loss within Loss,* p. 51.
Artforum, January, 1987.
Bloomsbury Review, January, 1998, review of *The Farewell Symphony,* p. 20.
Book, November-December, 2003, Penelope Mesic, review of *Fanny: A Fiction,* p. 86.
Booklist, October 1, 1994; June 1, 1995, p. 732; November 1, 1995, p. 453; September 15, 1997, Whitney Scott, review of *The Farewell Symphony,* p. 211; December 1, 1998, Bryce Christensen, review of *Marcel Proust,* p. 646; May 1, 2000, Donna Seaman, review of *The Married Man,* p. 1654; February 15, 2001, Whitney Scott, review of *Loss within Loss,* p. 1105, Brad Hooper, review of *The Flaneur: A Stroll through the Paradoxes of Paris,* p. 1113; September 15, 2003, Michael Spinella, review of *Fanny,* p. 212.
Chicago Tribune, December 10, 1978; April 6, 1980; February 14, 1994; December 1, 1998, review of *Marcel Proust,* p. 646.

Entertainment Weekly, October 10, 2003, John Freeman, review of *Fanny,* p. 127.

Gay & Lesbian Review, fall, 2000, Christopher Hennessy, "'I See My Life as a Novel as I'm Leading It'" (interview), p. 26, Martha E. Stone, "Sketches from Memory," p. 53; winter, 2000, Nick Radel, "Travels of Young Edmund," p. 48; May, 2001, Karl Woelz, "Epitaph to a Genre," p. 43; September, 2001, p. 43; July-August, 2003, Chris Freeman, interview with White, p. 10.

Harper's, March, 1979; October, 1982; May, 1987.

Journal of European Studies, July, 2003, p. 161.

Kirkus Reviews, October 15, 1998, review of *Marcel Proust,* p. 1522; January 1, 2002, review of *The Flaneur,* p. 44.

Lambda Book Report, June, 2000, Robert Gluck, "The Whole Man in Love," p. 15; March, 2001, Jameson Currier, "The Price We Paid," p. 14.

Library Journal, February 15, 1973; October 1, 1994, p. 82; June 15, 1995, p. 95; November 15, 1995, p. 92; February 1, 1996, p. 75; September 15, 1997, Eric Bryant, review of *The Farewell Symphony,* p. 104; January, 1999, Diane G. Premo, review of *Marcel Proust,* p. 98; May 15, 2000, Brian Kenney, review of *The Married Man,* p. 127; February 15, 2001, Ravi Shenoy, review of *The Flaneur,* p. 190; March 15, 2001, Krista Ivy, review of *Loss within Loss,* p. 83.

Life, fall, 1989, Edmund White, "Residence on Earth: Living with AIDS in the '80s."

London Review of Books, April 17, 1986; March 3, 1988; June 10, 1993, p. 3; August 24, 1995, p. 12.

Los Angeles Times, January 12, 1994, p. C7; September 19, 1997, Charlotte Innes, "He's a Pillar to Some, a Source of Strife for Others" (interview), p. 1.

Los Angeles Times Book Review, May 4, 1980; April 3, 1982; November 21, 1993, p. 1; July 16, 1995, p. 4; December 14, 1997, Michael Frank, review of *The Farewell Symphony,* p. 5; January 22, 1999, Michael Frank, review of *Marcel Proust,* p. 6.

Mother Jones, June, 1983.

Nation, January 5, 1974; March 1, 1980; November 13, 1982; November 16, 1985; April 9, 1988; January 3, 1994; August 28, 1995, p. 214; October 20, 1997, Alfred Corn, review of *The Farewell Symphony,* p. 35.

New Republic, February 21, 1994; July 12, 1999, Andre Aciman, "Inversions," p. 35.

New Statesman, March 14, 1986; January 29, 1988; June 17, 1994, p. 38; February 26, 1999, Charlotte Raven, review of *Marcel Proust,* p. 53; September 1, 2003, Carmen Callil, review of *Fanny,* p. 37.

New Yorker, February 8, 1999, review of *Marcel Proust,* p. 80.

New York Review of Books, October 21, 1993, p. 15; March 18, 1999, Roger Shattuck, review of *Marcel Proust,* p. 10; August 10, 2000, John Banville, review of *The Married Man,* p. 42.

New York Times, January 21, 1980; December 17, 1982; September 8, 1985; March 17, 1988; December 8, 1993, p. C23.

New York Times Book Review, March 25, 1973; December 10, 1978; February 3, 1980; October 10, 1982; September 15, 1985; March 20, 1988; November 7, 1993; October 23, 1994, p. 18; July 23, 1995, p. 6; December 3, 1995, p. 50; September 14, 1997, Christopher Benfey, review of *The Farewell Symphony,* p. 11; November 1, 1998, review of *The Farewell Symphony,* p. 36; January 10, 1999, Peter Ackroyd, "Biography: The Short Form," p. 4; July 2, 2000, Alice Truax, "An Ideal Husband," p. 5; April 8, 2001, Angeline Goreau, "A Walker in the Cité," p. 7.

Observer (London, England), March 16, 1986; December 14, 1986; January 24, 1988; November 13, 1988; June 20, 1993; June 19, 1994; June 14, 1995; July 12, 1998, review of *The Farewell Symphony,* p. 18; February 28, 1999, Robert McCrum, "Books: Home to Proust," p. 11; August 8, 1999, Stephen Barber, "Arts: Edmund White Went to a Bath House for Sex, and Found a Whole New World—of Art, Love and Loss," p. 5; February 4, 2001, Peter Conrad, review of *The Flaneur,* p. 16.

Paris Review, fall, 1988 (interview).

People, November 3, 2003, Bella Stander, review of *Fanny,* p. 54.

Publishers Weekly, September 24, 1982 (interview); March 21, 1994, p. 8; April 17, 2000, review of *The Married Man,* p. 48; January 8, 2001, review of *The Flaneur,* p. 54; February 5, 2001, review of *Loss within Loss,* p. 82; August 11, 2003, review of *Fanny,* p. 37.

Review of Contemporary Fiction, fall, 1996, "Edmund White Speaks with Edmund White;" spring, 1998, Kent D. Wolf, review of *The Farewell Symphony,* p. 224; spring, 2001, David Bergman, review of *The Married Man,* p. 187; fall, 2003, David Bergman, review of *Fanny,* p. 127.

Rolling Stone, December 19, 1985.

Spectator, March 5, 1988; May 10, 1997, Alain de Botton, review of *The Farewell Symphony,* p. 35; March 20, 1999, Jonathan Keates, review of *Mar-*

cel Proust, p. 69; February 24, 2001, Euan Cameron, review of *The Flaneur,* p. 36.

Time, April 11, 1988; July 30, 1990; December 27, 1993.

Times Literary Supplement, September 5, 1980; August 19, 1983; January 22, 1988; July 1, 1994, p. 13; March 17, 1995, p. 20; May 2, 1997, Nicholas Jenkins, review of *The Farewell Symphony,* p. 23; May 21, 1999, review of *Marcel Proust,* p. 8; March 17, 2000, Sylvia Brownrigg, review of *The Married Man,* p. 21; April 6, 2001, John Stokes, review of *The Flaneur,* p. 31.

Tribune Books (Chicago, IL), October 24, 1993, p. 3; August 13, 1995, p. 4.

Village Voice, January 28, 1980; June 28, 1988 (interview).

Vogue, February, 1984; November, 1984; May, 1985; January, 1986; July, 1986; July, 1987.

Voice Literary Supplement, December, 1982; April, 1988; June, 1988; March, 2001, Richard Klein, "Wander, Lust."

Washington Post Book World, November 12, 1978; December 10, 1978; January 27, 1980; October 17, 1982; October 6, 1985; April 3, 1988; February 28, 1999, Greg Varner, "Passionate Lives," p. 4; June 11, 2000, Michael Dirda, "In Health and in Sickness," p. 1.

ONLINE

Beatrice, http://www.beatrice.com/ (April 24, 2004), Ron Hogan, "Beatrice Interview: Edmund White."

Edmund White Home Page, http://www.edmundwhite.com (May 3, 2004).

Gay.com, http://www.gay.com/ (October 1, 2001), "Edmund White Discusses *The Married Man,* Life, and Love."

PlanetOut, http://www.planetout.com/ (October 1, 2001), Lawrence Chua, "Interview with Edmund White."

Thebestofmen.com, http://thebestofmen.com/ (October 21, 2001), "Fiction."*